Boyle & Birds' Company Law

8th Edition

Boyle & Birds'
Company Law

8th Edition
2011

Editors

John Birds LLM, FRSA
Emeritus Professor in the School of Law, University of
Manchester and Honorary Professor in the School of Law,
University of Sheffield

Bryan Clark BA, LLM, PhD
Reader in Law, University of Strathclyde

Iain MacNeil LLB, PhD
Alexander Stone Professor of Commercial Law, University of
Glasgow

Gerard McCormack BCL, LLM, PhD
Professor of International Business Law, University of Leeds

Christian Twigg-Flesner LLB, PCHE, PhD
Reader in Law, University of Hull

Charlotte Villiers LLM, Solicitor
Professor of Company Law, University of Bristol

Consultant Editor

A. J. Boyle LLM, SJD, Barrister
Emeritus Professor of Law, Queen Mary, University of London

JORDANS

Published by
Jordan Publishing Limited
21 St Thomas Street
Bristol BS1 6JS

British Library Cataloguing-in-Publication Data
A catalogue record for this book is available from the British Library.

ISBN 978 1 84661 287 9

Typeset by Letterpart Ltd, Reigate, Surrey

Printed in Great Britain by CPI Antony Rowe Ltd, Chippenham and Eastbourne

PREFACE TO THE 8TH EDITION

With the publication of this edition, we seek to keep the work up to date by incorporating significant case-law developments over the past two years, as well as, for example, covering the UK Corporate Governance Code 2010 and recent developments at the European level. We have also been able fully to incorporate the implementation of the Shareholders' Rights Directive.

As we said in the prefaces to the last two editions, time will tell whether or not the Companies Act 2006 will prove to be all that has been claimed for it in terms of deregulation and simplification. The sheer volume of statutory company law to some extent militates against that view, as does the fact that it has already been amended in some quite significant ways. Although a review for government of the Act in 2010 seemed to indicate a general level of satisfaction, it is notable that the Department for Business, Innovation and Skills is working on various possible further reforms. In particular it is expected that there will soon be formal proposals to modernise and simplify the current system for the registration of charges, there is to be a review of whether a new corporate form for single person businesses could reduce costs for small entrepreneurs and consideration is being given to a range of options to simplify accounting and audit requirements, especially for small and medium enterprises.

It is hoped that this book continues to be a reliable and fairly comprehensive guide to this difficult subject.

Responsibilities for this edition have been as follows: John Birds (chapters 4, 9, 12, 13, 15, 16 and 17 and overall editorial responsibility), Tony Boyle (chapters 1, 3 and 18), Bryan Clark (chapters 7 and 8), Iain MacNeil (chapters 19 and 20), Gerard McCormack (chapter 21), Christian Twigg-Flesner (chapters 2, 5, 6 and 10) and Charlotte Villiers (chapters 11 and 14).

John Birds

August 2011

CONTENTS

TABLE OF CASES

References are to paragraph numbers.

TABLE OF STATUTES

References are to paragraph numbers.

TABLE OF STATUTORY INSTRUMENTS

References are to paragraph numbers.

CHAPTER 1

THE DEVELOPMENT OF THE REGISTERED COMPANY

1.1 INTRODUCTION

This chapter is concerned with issues that have a general bearing on the various specific aspects of company law examined in the chapters that follow. It also seeks to explain in a concise way how the body of legislation[1] and case-law that today governs the affairs of registered companies first developed and came to take its present form. There are two other issues with an important bearing on company law as a whole. These are the impact of European Union company law on the relatively recent history of company legislation in Britain, which is considered in Chapter 2, and the key concept of corporate personality as developed by the courts, considered in Chapter 3. This chapter concludes with a brief discussion of the relevance of 'law and economics' theory for company law.

1.2 HISTORICAL BACKGROUND

The first topic is the development of modern company law. The account given here is in no sense a history of company law as a whole – too large an undertaking for our purpose. Instead, it is intended to show how the unincorporated joint-stock company of the early nineteenth century was transformed by the legislation of the 1840s and 1850s into a registered company of recognisably modern shape. For an understanding of the earlier history of company law, which had its origins in the sixteenth and seventeenth centuries, the readers are referred elsewhere.[2] There they will find an account of how the scandal and financial collapse produced in the early eighteenth century by the 'South Sea Bubble', and the resulting

---

[1]   Ie principally the Companies Act 2006, although as will be seen, some parts of the earlier legislation have survived the passing of this Act.

[2]   For a lively and stimulating summary of this earlier period, see P Davies, *Gower's Principles of Modern Company Law* (Sweet & Maxwell, 6th edn, 1997) Ch 2. See further: CA Cooke, *Corporation, Trust and Company* (Manchester, 1950); AB Dubois, *The English Business Company After the Bubble Act, 1720–1800* (New York, 1938); BC Hunt, *The Development of the Business Corporation in England, 1800–1867* (Harvard Economic Studies, 1936). See Jean J du Plessis 'Corporate Law and Coporate Governance Lessons from the Past' (2009) 30 Company Lawyer 71.

Bubble Act of 1720,[3] not only put down an illicit trade in the charters of incorporated companies but also placed an already flourishing number of unincorporated joint-stock companies under a cloud of official disapproval for over a century. Until the repeal of the Bubble Act in 1825,[4] such companies had a shadowy legal existence. The more favourable legal opinion of them was that, so long as their shares were not freely transferable, they were not liable to prosecution under the Bubble Act. Even after the Act's repeal, the only hope for those forming a corporate business enterprise (however economically important and substantial its operations) was to form a 'statutory company' by means of a private Act of Parliament. This gave the obvious advantage of legal personality with the attendant privilege of limited liability. Only in the case of very major undertakings (such as the canal and railway companies and other early utilities) which needed to raise large amounts of capital from the public would the delay, trouble and very great expense entailed by the private bill procedure be justified. By this period the modern practice of refusing to grant a Royal Charter of Incorporation to those engaged in trade or commerce was becoming established.[5] It may be noted that, although the common law protected the members of trading corporations from liability, it was common for provisions in their charters to allow the corporation to make 'leviations' on members to pay its debts. The courts of equity permitted creditors direct action against the members.

1.3   THE INCORPORATION OF JOINT-STOCK COMPANIES BY REGISTRATION

At common law, despite the repeal of the Bubble Act in 1825, there remained some doubt about the legality of unincorporated joint-stock companies with freely transferable shares. These doubts had been fostered by Lord Eldon, who succeeded in inserting in the repealing Act a provision that their position at common law (with the taint of possible illegality) should be as it was before the Bubble Act was repealed. In the boom of the 1830s there was, nevertheless, a proliferation of unincorporated joint-stock companies, which in turn produced a growing demand for their legal regulation. In particular, there was a need to clarify their right to sue and be sued. There was also a growing demand for limited liability as a protection for shareholders who invested in them. In the case of formal written contracts, this was often obtained by express terms in those contracts, but this was obviously not possible in the case of the everyday informal contracts of a growing number of industrial and commercial companies. It has been seen that incorporation by charter was now deemed unsuitable for industrial and commercial companies, and a private Act of Parliament was prohibitively expensive.

---

[3]   6 Geo I, c 18.

[4]   6 Geo IV, c 91.

[5]   As to types of business organisation other than the registered company, see **1.5**.

1.3.1 Legislative control

The Trading Companies Act 1834 and the Chartered Company Act 1837 made a half-hearted attempt to deal with the problems of joint-stock companies, but the first was very restrictively applied by the Board of Trade and the second had little more success. Without conferring incorporation, these Acts made available some of the incidents of that status (eg the right to sue and be sued) and even (in the 1837 Act) limited liability to those seeking and obtaining the appropriate letters patent.

Especially during the cyclical slumps that followed economic booms in the nineteenth century, fraudulent promotion and other abuses were frequently revealed. This led to the appointment of a Committee of Parliament (which was eventually chaired by Gladstone when he became President of the Board of Trade). Gladstone undoubtedly had a strong influence on the eventual report.[6] This seminal report resulted in what is still referred to as 'Gladstone's Act' – the Joint Stock Companies Act 1844.[7]

It is this piece of legislation that laid the foundation of the modern registered company; but modern company law still owes very much to those principles of partnership and trust law that the courts had already developed to cope with the unincorporated joint-stock company. However, 'Gladstone's Act' set company law on what is still its modern course by conferring ready access to incorporation by a process of registration.[8] It set up the office of Registrar of Companies who had not only to supervise the original registration, but had to keep up-to-date information about each company's constitution, directors and annual returns and make it available on 'public file'. At this stage the company's constitution was expressed in a 'deed of settlement', essentially the same document used by unincorporated joint-stock companies. It had broadly the same function as the modern articles of association, but in its original form was a trust deed which provided, *inter alia*, for the trustees in whom the assets of the old-style unincorporated joint-stock company might be vested.

The new Act applied henceforth to all joint-stock companies with more than 25 members or which allowed shares to be transferred without the consent of all the members. Thus began the divorce of partnership law from company law and the origin of the legislative practice that used to limit the size of membership in a 'private partnership', although the limit of 20 partners has since been abolished.[9] Existing unincorporated

---

6   1844 BPP Vol VII.
7   This Act did not apply to Scotland where the more liberal Scots common law applied until the Joint Stock Companies Act of 1856.
8   There was a system of 'provisional registration' prior to the filing of the appropriate deed of settlement. Only after a full registration was the company incorporated.
9   With effect from 20 December 2002; see 24 Co Law 113–114. See further *Gore-Browne*

joint-stock companies could gain the privileges conferred by the Act if they altered their existing deeds of settlement and registered in compliance with the Act's provisions.[10]

1.3.2   Limited liability

Limited liability was not conferred by Gladstone's Act. This was still a hotly debated issue in 1844 both in respect of 'private partnerships' and joint-stock companies. Thus the new type of registered company was like a modern unlimited company. There were some hesitations in the legislature's policy on winding up these new registered companies. The earliest winding-up Acts applied the ordinary bankruptcy law to companies while producing a conflict of jurisdiction between the bankruptcy courts and the Court of Chancery. By 1857, this confusion was resolved by conferring sole jurisdiction on the Chancery.[11] At the same time, certain principles of bankruptcy law were carried over to a new corporate setting.

The question of conferring limited liability on the new registered companies (and also upon certain forms of partnerships) was a strongly debated issue in the mid-nineteenth century in Parliament, in officially appointed committees, and in the press and the business community.[12] While there was a strong movement for introducing a form of 'limited partnership' (based on the French model of the *société en commandite*), this had to wait in limbo for eventual enactment in the Limited Partnerships Act 1907, by which time it proved to be of little practical utility.[13] Instead, in the mid-nineteenth century, the Government chose to confer limited liability only upon registered companies[14] – or more exactly upon those registered companies which opted to register in compliance with the requirements for a company limited by shares (then, as today, the vast majority).

As at first introduced (in the Limited Liability Act 1855), there were a number of important safeguards attached to the concession of limited liability. Some of these have a contemporary ring in that they have been reintroduced in modern legislation. Thus there were requirements of at least 25 members as well as specified amounts in respect of issued and paid-up capital. The word 'limited' had to be added at the end of the

---

on Companies (Jordans, 45th edn, loose-leaf) at 4 [17]. As to the practical choice to be made between the small private limited company and the limited liability partnership, see **3.3**.

[10]   Those that did not do so still had to file certain information.

[11]   See the Joint Stock Companies Act 1856 and the Companies Winding Up (Amendment) Act 1857.

[12]   For an account of the 'struggle for limited liability' see Davies, *op cit*, at pp 40–44.

[13]   The more flexible form of the registered company was by then readily available to small private companies. This gave the advantage of limited liability for all members and much else besides.

[14]   Banking and insurance companies were at first excluded.

company's name everywhere it was displayed as an awful warning of the new risks faced by creditors. There were also safeguards to maintain the capital raised against the hazard of improperly paid dividends or unjustified loans to directors. The company had to have auditors approved by the Board of Trade. However, within a very short time, what has been termed the first 'modern Companies Act' – the Joint Stock Companies Act 1856 – consolidated and reformed earlier legislation. It abolished the old system of registering deeds of settlement and introduced the twin constitutional documents – the memorandum of association and the articles of association. Rather less happily, this Act removed most of the safeguards for limited liability in the 1855 Act. In somewhat different form, most of these safeguards have been reintroduced into company law in the legislation of recent years.[15]

Undoubtedly, the grant of the benefit of limited liability helped to make possible the growth of the large modern company that today dominates the private sector of the economy. At an earlier period in the nineteenth century, those enterprises which had need to raise share and loan capital on a grand scale (notably the railway companies) had enjoyed limited liability as statutory companies created by Act of Parliament.[16] The conferment of the same privilege on the registered company made it available to entrepreneurs and investors in industry and commerce generally.

It can be argued that in the case of the old unincorporated joint-stock company, with large numbers of shareholders whose liability was unlimited, this was not (for procedural and practical reasons) of great use in satisfying the claim of the unpaid creditors. Nevertheless the absence of limited liability was undoubtedly a major deterrent to investors in large-scale enterprises under the management of others. This does not of course silence the past and present critics of the unrestricted availability of limited liability for every small private company (or indeed for the subsidiaries in groups of companies). Where such companies are seriously (and deliberately) under-capitalised, the possibilities of abuse are self-evident.[17]

---

[15] See Chapters 8 and 14.

[16] The Companies Clauses Consolidation Act 1845 standardised the procedure in respect of statutory companies which were still used for new railways or utilities. This Act allowed the standard provisions normally included in private bills seeking to incorporate companies to be incorporated by reference. A separate Act in 1845 (8 and 9 Vict c 17) dealt with Scottish statutory companies.

[17] For a valuable review, with references to the earlier literature, see Freedman 'Limited liability: large company theory and small firms' (2000) 63 MLR 317.

1.4 DEVELOPMENTS IN THE LATE NINETEENTH AND TWENTIETH CENTURIES

During the remainder of the nineteenth century the legislature made only minor changes in company law, but the courts were responsible for the development of a number of important principles. As regards legislation, a general pattern began in 1862 of reforming legislation followed by a consolidating Act. The Companies Act 1862 was the first Act of that name. This process continued at regular intervals (1908 and 1929) until the Companies Act 1948. The courts were faced with the task of evolving a number of new principles to fill out the statutory structure. In many areas, they could elaborate upon an existing body of partnership, trust and agency law already evolved to meet the needs of the old unincorporated joint-stock companies.[18] Alternatively they might draw wide inferences from hints dropped by the legislature. Thus, from a somewhat slender statutory foundation, a substantial body of new judge-made principle might be created. Two obvious examples are the *ultra vires* doctrine[19] and the principles governing the raising and maintenance of share capital.[20] In other areas of company law, new concepts owed their origin to commercial practice and the skills of conveyancing counsel. These in due course received the scrutiny and approval of the courts.[21]

In the twentieth century and into the twenty-first century, two issues continued to preoccupy those who write official reports on company law reform and shape the consequent legislation. These issues are the need to increase the disclosure requirements in the Companies Act and the related question of how far to exempt private companies from the accounting and other publicity requirements that apply to public companies. While the expense and administrative burden of disclosure has continued to grow, the question of how to handle the small private company has produced different answers at different times.

As regards publicity in respect of company accounts, this started with an annual balance sheet and then moved to a profit and loss account, to consolidated accounts for groups of companies and certain information as to 'associated companies'.[22] Today it includes further refinements such as information as to turnover and details about methods of valuation of assets, as well as requiring the accounts to be based either on a historical cost basis or, alternatively, on 'alternative accounting rules'. The general effect of these is to allow certain assets to be included in the accounts on the basis of their market value or their current costs. A wide range of

---

[18] See, eg, directors' duties (Chapters 16 and 17), minority shareholders' actions (Chapter 18).
[19] See Chapter 5.
[20] See Chapter 8.
[21] Eg preference shares (see Chapter 8), debentures and floating charges (see Chapter 10).
[22] See Chapter 14.

other information must also be given about the company's activities, relating to its members and to its share and loan capital. An area of particular growth in respect of disclosure requirements in recent years relates to directors and their various interests in their company (or group of companies) such as interests in its shares, material contracts with it, loans made to them, etc. All this information is usually disclosed on an annual basis via publicly filed annual returns (or the accounts, or the directors' report). Much of this information (in addition to being made available at the Companies Registry) must be made available on a more immediate basis by means of registers kept at the company's own registered office.[23]

A good deal of the information that must thus be disclosed is (and was) inappropriate in the case of those private companies whose small numbers of shareholders had the remedy in their own hands, and where outside investors (or lenders) could bargain for themselves. Only unsecured trade creditors need the disclosure of such accounting and other information as was appropriate to their needs. Although the private company as a distinct species with certain privileges of its own dates back to the Companies Act 1908, it was not until the Companies Act 1948 that the legislature decided that the burden of the accounting obligations imposed on most companies should not apply to small family or 'closely held' companies. These were termed 'exempt private companies'[24] and were exempt from the necessity to file public accounts (and were given certain other special privileges).[25] The pendulum of policy swung the other way in the Companies Act 1967 which abolished the exempt private company, thus visiting most of the accounting and auditing requirements (increased by that Act) on private limited companies of any size.[26] In the Companies Act 1981 the policy of the 1948 Act was reverted to in some measure. In line with the requirements of the EC Fourth Company Law Directive (on company accounts), new categories of 'medium' and 'small' companies were created with publicity and accounting requirements appropriately scaled down.

Despite these changes, the general burden of disclosure (both at the Companies Registry and at each company's own registered office) has been the target of considerable criticism both in the business community and in those learned professions concerned with company administration, as well as by some academic writers.[27] The clear lines of segregation between public and private companies first laid down in the Companies

---

[23] As to the registered office, see **5.8**.

[24] See Sch 7 to the 1948 Act as to the complex conditions that had to be met to retain exempt status.

[25] Loans could be made to directors, and the company's auditors did not need professional qualifications.

[26] Unlimited companies provided an escape hatch for those dismayed by the new burden imposed as well as the risk of exposure to competitors.

[27] See Sealy, 'The Disclosure Philosophy and Company Law Reform' (1981) 2 Co Law 51.

Act 1980[28] had already made it possible for the legislature to place a lesser burden on the private company (or at any rate medium or small private companies). However, while limited liability remains overwhelmingly the norm for private companies, and while they are in most instances seriously under-capitalised for the risks involved, there must be a limit on how far the burden of disclosure can be lifted. There has not been much reduction on the burden placed on public companies either by Parliament or by the UK Listing Authority.[29]

1.5   OTHER TYPES OF CORPORATE BUSINESS ORGANISATION

The brief historical account given in this chapter has concerned the development of the registered company, since that is the subject of this book. Over the same period of time there also evolved a number of different types of association based not upon the principle of investment for profit by proprietors but on quite distinct principles of co-operation or mutual self-help. In this the archetype was originally the unincorporated friendly society. In the course of the nineteenth century, bodies and associations concerned with specialised activities of this kind came to be regulated by their own special legislation. This usually conferred corporate personality as well as limited liability. One feature common to this type of legislation is that the body for which it was intended might not register under the Companies Acts. This is true of co-operative societies, working men's clubs and other friendly societies. It also applied to trade unions, trustee savings banks and building societies.[30] In the case of trustee savings banks legislation brought their business activities within the sphere of company law. The 'privatisation' of trustee savings banks converted them into public companies offering their shares to the public as well as existing investors.[31] The building societies legislation made it possible for them to convert themselves into public limited companies.[32] Many of the larger building societies have converted into public limited companies under this legislation. A new form of business association, which is a hybrid of partnership and company law, suitable for privately owned profit-making businesses, was created by the Limited Liability Partnerships Act 2000.[33]

---

[28] See **4.2**.

[29] As to the requirements under the *Listing Rules* as to continuous disclosure, see Chapter 14. The UK Listing Authority is now the Financial Services Authority; see Chapter 18. See Companies Act 2006, Part 15, Chapter 8 (Public Companies: laying of accounts and reports before general meetings) and Chapter 9 (Quoted Companies: Members' approved of directors' remuneration report).

[30] As to the legislation applicable, see *Gore-Browne on Companies* (Jordans, 45th edn, looseleaf) at 4 [20].

[31] Savings Bank Act 1985.

[32] Building Societies Act 1986, as amended by the Building Societies Act 1997.

[33] See further **3.3.1**.

Another modern form of business enterprise is the 'community interest company' (CIC).[34] The CIC is a new, flexible and easily registered corporate vehicle for businesses whose profits and assets are to be used for the benefit of the community. Bodies wishing to become CICs must pass a community interest test and produce an annual report to show that they have contributed to community interest aims. A new independent regulator oversees CICs, with wide powers including the power to approve registration, to appoint, suspend or remove directors, to make orders concerning their property, to set a dividend cap and to apply to wind them up.

1.6 THE COMPANIES ACTS: CONSOLIDATION AND RECONSOLIDATION IN THE 1980S

The unwieldy mass of legislation in the Companies Acts 1948–1983 was consolidated into the Companies Act 1985. Even at a technical level, it can be argued that neither the timing nor the scope of the 1985 consolidating legislation was entirely happily chosen. While this legislation was going through Parliament, the Bill that became the Insolvency Act 1985 was also being enacted. This process entailed amendment of substantial parts of the Companies Act 1985 in respect of the winding up of insolvent companies. Scarcely were these two Acts of 1985 on the statute book when a change of policy was made. This produced a reconsolidation of the parts of the Companies Act 1985 concerning the winding up of *solvent* companies with the recent legislation on insolvency. This produced the Insolvency Act 1986. At the same time the Department of Trade and Industry decided to reconsolidate the legislation on the disqualification of directors.[35] In this same period, the provisions in the Companies Act 1985 relating to public issues, insider dealing and the compulsory acquisition of shares, were substantially changed by the Financial Services Act 1986.[36] This Act broke much new ground by introducing a long overdue system of 'securities regulation'. It was itself expanded by the Financial Services and Markets Act 2000.

Following the consolidating legislation of 1985 there was one major legislative development regarding company law in the strict sense. The Companies Act 1989 contained a mélange of significant legislative innovation and a great number of technical reforms. It implemented the EC Seventh and Eighth Directives on group accounts and the appointment of auditors.[37] It also contains a new regime for private companies.[38] This allowed more scope for avoiding the formality of

---

[34] The Companies (Audit, Investigation and Community Enterprise) Act 2004, Part 2.
[35] The Company Directors Disqualification Act 1986.
[36] This Act has been substantially amended and extended by the Financial Services and Markets Act 2000.
[37] See Chapter 14.
[38] See Chapter 13.

company meetings by means of written resolutions or by the adoption of a more generalised 'elective regime'. In addition to these major changes, the 1989 Act contained a great number of significant reforms of the Companies Act 1985.[39]

There was much to be said in favour of the companies legislation of 1985. In terms of its simplicity and lucidity of style and the ordered clarity of the arrangement of subject matter in the principal Act, it represented a considerable achievement for the draftsman and those who instructed him. Nevertheless, even the most dazzling skills of draftsmanship (in the case of a consolidating Act) cannot cure the substantive defects in the state of existing legislation to be consolidated. The cogent criticism made of the unconsolidated Companies Acts 1948–1983 by, among others, Professor LS Sealy[40] went beyond matters of legislative style and arrangement. The general thrust of this criticism is that our company legislation (whether carried forward from the past or the subject of recent reform) is over-technical and over-'sanctioned'. It was not directed to enabling businesses large and small to be run honestly and efficiently in the real commercial world. It was law created by civil servants and company lawyers who have had insufficient regard for the real needs of the industrial and commercial world. Our legislation made very out-of-date assumptions about how private companies are formed, how public companies develop and about the realities of shareholders' meetings and resolutions as a genuine way of expressing shareholders' consent or effectively restraining directors and others who manage companies. While increasingly influenced by the rigid, elaborate and often inappropriate example of the European Union harmonisation programme, our legislation has ignored the more radical and simplifying reforms that have been successfully adopted in the Commonwealth and the United States.

There is much force in Professor Sealy's detailed critique of the then existing company legislation which was deployed to support this more general thesis, and indeed the Companies Act 2006 responds in part to such criticisms, as will be seen below. It is inevitable, however, that not everyone will agree that the general policy of those reforming company law (especially in regard to large public companies) should be how best to meet the institutional needs of businessmen. The real political and social world will inevitably demand that company law reflect a more complex, if sometimes competing, range of interests. In that sense, it is entirely understandable that the DTI, what is now the Business Department, regard company law (like labour law) as too politically sensitive to be left without close supervision to the Law Commission or to any other 'neutral' reforming body. The political priorities will inevitably change with the colour of the government in power. Thus, both in the UK and in

---

[39]   See in particular Part III 'Investigations and Powers to Obtain Information' and Part VII 'Financial Markets and Insolvency'.

[40]   See *Company Law and Commercial Reality* (Sweet & Maxwell, 1984), especially Ch 4.

the European Union, company law remains more than a matter of commercial law. This latter body of law may be well described as 'the totality of the law's response to the needs and practices of the mercantile community. This then is the essence of commercial law – the accommodation of principles, rules, practices and documents fashioned by the world of business: the facilitation, rather than the obstruction, of commercial development'.[41]

Company law, as part of a different body of law – the law of institutions – must inevitably have a different character from that governing the law of commercial transactions. It will retain this character, even when freed from the burden of history and the 'Chancery mentality'.

1.7   THE COMPANIES ACT 2006

After a long period of gestation by the Company Law Review Steering Group (CLRSG) and the Department of Trade and Industry,[42] the Company Law Reform Bill began its parliamentary progress in the autumn of 2005 and became the Companies Act 2006 a year later. In the course of this progress (as the change in title indicates) its scope was broadened from a piece of reforming legislation so as to include the codification of existing legislation (ie where this was unaffected by the reforms). It is now the longest Act of Parliament in history with 1,300 sections. Insolvency legislation remains (as under the earlier legislation) beyond the scope of the new Act. Likewise the law relating to company investigations by the Department of Trade and Industry, though amended, has not been consolidated into the 2006 Act, nor have the provisions regarding CICs.

The CLRSG was originally set up by the Department of Trade and Industry in March 1998 with the following terms of reference:[43]

> '(i) To consider how core company law can be modernised in order to provide a simple, efficient and cost-effective framework for carrying out business activity which:
> (a)   permits the maximum amount of freedom and flexibility to those organising and directing the enterprise;

---

[41]   RM Goode *Commercial Law* (Penguin, 1982) p 984, cited by Professor LS Sealy in *Company Law and Commercial Reality, op cit*, at p 81.

[42]   See *Modern Company Law for a Competitive Economy*, Final Report (DTI, 2001) and *Modernising Company Law*, Cm 5553-1, July 2002. Note that the Department of Trade and Industry is now the Department for Business, Enterprise and Regulatory Reform (DBERR).

[43]   For general reviews of the reform process, see, eg, Birds and Parkinson 'Company Law' in D Hayton (ed) *Law's Future* (Hart, 2000); Birds 'Reforming United Kingdom Company Law in a European Context: a Long and Winding Road' chapter 2 in SM Bartman (ed) *European Company Law in Accelerated Progress* (Kluwer, 2006).

    (b)   at the same time protects, through regulation where necessary, the interests of those involved with the enterprise, including shareholders, creditors and employees; and

    (c)   is drafted in clear, concise and unambiguous language which can be readily understood by those involved in business enterprise.

(ii) To consider whether company law, partnership law, and other legislation which establishes a legal form of business activity together provide an adequate choice of legal vehicle for business at all levels.

(iii) To consider the proper relationship between company law and non-statutory standards of corporate behaviour.

(iv) To review the extent to which foreign companies operating in Great Britain should be regulated under British company law.

(v) To make recommendations accordingly.'[44]

The CLRSG brought together over 200 interested parties in an effort to forge a consensus. In the 3 years of its deliberations, it produced four principal documents under the general title of *Modern Company Law for a Competitive Economy.*

These were the *Strategic Framework* (February 1999), *Developing the Framework* (March 2000), *Completing the Structure* (November 2000), and the *Final Report* (July 2001).[45] There were other related documents under the same general title of *Modern Company Law for a Competitive Economy.*[46]

Despite the lapse of time between these reports and the introduction of the Bill that became the 2006 Act, which was partly occupied by two Government White Papers,[47] two of these matters, company charges and capital maintenance, have only been partially tackled. Company charges were the subject of extensive further consultation, including two reports from the Law Commissions.[48] Capital maintenance, at least for public companies, is subject to the Second European Company Law Directive,[49] which is still being reconsidered at a European level. Powers to amend these areas by statutory instrument have been taken.[50]

---

[44]   Appendix A to the CLRSG Final Report, July 2001.

[45]   Respectively, URN 99/654, 00/656, 00/1335 and 01/942.

[46]   See also *Company General Meetings and Shareholder Communications* (October 1999), *Reforming Company Law Concerning Overseas Companies* (October 1999), *Capital Maintenance: Other Issues* (June 2000), *Registration of Charges* (October 2000). See respectively URN 99/1144, 99/1145, 99/1146. 00/880 and 00/1213.

[47]   *Modernising Company Law*, CM 5553-I and 5333-II (2002); *Company Law Reform*, Cm 6456 (2005).

[48]   *Report on Registration of Rights in Security by Companies*, Scot Law Com No 197 (September 2004) and *Company Security Interests*, Law Com No 296 (August 2005).

[49]   1977/91/EEC.

[50]   Companies Act 2006, ss 657, 737 and 894. As to capital maintenance, see Chapter 7, at **7.11** below.

Even those parts of the CLRSG's reports on which there was relative unanimity were subject to further scrutiny and amendment. In its passage through Parliament, 1,800 amendments were accepted, very many connected with the late consolidation.

Notable examples of areas of significant reform in the 2006 Act are the law on directors' duties,[51] and that on shareholders' derivative claims,[52] the reduction of capital,[53] and the law on company resolutions and meetings.[54] The first two of these were among the ones that caused the greatest debate in Parliament.

Among the general recommendations of the CLRSG was one that the primary companies legislation be redrafted in order to leave much of the detail to secondary legislation, so that it could be easily amended and by a delegated company law review body. In the original Bill, the Government adopted the first of these recommendations, but proposed sweeping delegated legislation powers for the Department of Trade and Industry rather than a specific body. Controversy about the width of this power led to the relevant part of the Bill being dropped, but nonetheless the Act does contain many provisions that confer power to amend and repeal its provisions by regulation or order.

Reflecting the aims behind the establishment of the Company Law Review, the 2005 White Paper stated the purpose of the reform to be the following, aims that were restated in the parliamentary debates:

- to enhance shareholder engagement and a long-term investment culture;

- to ensure better regulation and a 'Think Small First' approach;

- to make it easier to set up and run a company; and

- to provide flexibility for the future.

We have seen that the last of these aims was substantially removed during the course of the Bill. Only time will tell whether the other aims will be achieved. While it cannot be doubted that the drafting of the Act represents a considerable improvement on earlier versions, it is still, and perhaps inevitably, a highly complex piece of legislation, which will be made even more so by the secondary legislation that has followed it. There is no hint of a response to points made earlier in this chapter about the possible abuse of the corporate form and limited liability, which remains a matter for insolvency legislation; indeed the thrust of the second and third

---

[51] See Chapters 16 and 17.
[52] See Chapter 18, Part 1.
[53] See Chapter 10.
[54] See Chapter 13.

aims, and the change in focus from provisions aimed at public companies with small company exceptions to small company provisions with public company additions, is very much against this. It also remains to be seen whether enhanced shareholder engagement and a longer-term investment culture will in practice be achieved. Overall it is not thought that the 2006 Act is in any sense revolutionary and that even the controversial codification of directors' duties, which is considered in Chapter 16, is unlikely to have any great effect in practice. Some of the economic and political assumptions that shaped the CLRSG proposals may need to be re-assessed as a result of the changes in the economic climate brought about by the 'credit crunch' of 2008–09.

A key question, certainly so far as the objective of simplification is concerned, is the application of the 2006 Act to companies already existing before it comes fully into effect. This will depend on the transitional provisions that are to be made. Among other things, these are likely to provide for the following:[55]

- Consequent on the removal of the importance of the memorandum of association, as described in Chapter 4, that most existing provisions in memoranda become part of existing companies' articles.

- The removal of authorised capital, given the abolition of that as a requirement.

- The removal of requirements that the articles of private companies authorise various alterations in share capital.

- The removal of the articles that require a private company to have a secretary and to hold annual general meetings, given that the Act abolishes these requirements.

1.8   THE IMPACT OF LAW AND ECONOMICS THEORY

Some attention may here be given briefly to the work of the law and economics theorists. This theory has been applied to many branches of law, including tort, contract and, above all, commercial law. This intellectual movement has been very influential in the United States[56] but

---

[55]   The detail is and will continue to be available on the DBERR's website, where general progress regarding the implementation of the Act can be found; see www.berr.gov.uk/bbf/co-act-2006/index.html.

[56]   See RA Posner *Economic Analysis of Law* (Boston, Little Brown & Co, 1992); FL Easterbrook and DR Fischel *The Economic Structure of Corporate Law* (Cambridge, MA, Harvard University Press, 1991).

also has a number of adherents in Britain.[57] It will be seen that law and economics theorists have provided a distinct analysis of company law as viewed from the perspective of this type of economic theory. Inevitably, this 'movement' has its critics among other corporate theorists, including economists.[58] Some critics object to the theory as 'anti-regulatory bias', but its adherents reject this charge. They maintain that the aim of their work is to encourage a better quality of legislative intervention based on sound economic theory.[59]

It is not appropriate in a book which does not claim to be influenced by law and economics theory to engage in detailed discussion of the assumptions made and the concepts employed by this theory,[60] except insofar as they have a particular bearing upon company law. One key idea advanced by this type of economic analysis is to stress the contractual basis of company law. In economic terms the company is analysed as a 'network of contracts'. This essentially means that all the relationships within any particular company are best described in terms of a network of explicit or implicit bargains. This way of characterising the company is obviously at odds with the legal conception of the company[61] which centres upon the legal personality of the registered company. Nevertheless, it is argued that, from an economic standpoint, thinking about the company as a nexus of contracts is an illuminating analytical exercise. The key participants – shareholders, directors and employees – can be said to become involved with their company on a voluntary basis, and to continue to interact on the basis of reciprocal expectations and behaviour. A linked theory is that of the 'role of the firm'.[62] Here again, the term 'firm' does not have its usual legal meaning. Theorising about the economic utility of the 'firm' applies to enterprises which may adopt various legal forms (eg a partnership, a private or public limited company, or even a sole proprietorship with a number of employees). In the light of such economic 'realism', it has been observed that 'company legislation has had, in and of itself, only a modest impact on the bargaining dynamics which account for the nature and form of business enterprises. Thus, analytically an incorporated company is, like other types of firms, fundamentally a nexus of contracts'.[63]

---

[57] Eg A Ogus *Regulation, Legal Reforms and Economic Theory* (Oxford University Press, 1994); B Cheffins *Company Law: Theory Structure and Operation* (Oxford, Clarendon Press, 1997).

[58] See generally J McCahery, S Picciotto and C Scott (eds) *Changing Structures and Dynamics of Regulation* (Oxford, Clarendon Press, 1993). See further: Goodhart 'Economics and law – too much one way traffic' (1997) 60 MLR 1.

[59] See Cheffins, *op cit*, at p 7.

[60] See generally Cheffins, *op cit*, Ch 1: 'Economics and the Study of Company Law' for an excellent introduction to the subject.

[61] See the historical section of this chapter (above) and Chapter 3 as to the concept of legal personality and the consequences of incorporation.

[62] See RH Coase *The Firm, the Market and the Law* (University of Chicago Press, 1988).

[63] Cheffins, *op cit*, at p 41.

Another theory applied by law and economics theory to the company (or any substantial enterprise) is that of 'agency costs'. Here yet again, the term 'agency' (or the correlative 'principal') is not used in a legal sense. The theory of 'agency costs' is designed to deal with inevitable conflicts of interest between the various participants in a business enterprise. From an economic perspective, an agency relationship arises when one participant depends on another for business activity. This obviously applies to the trust that shareholders must place in company directors or officers who manage the assets and undertake the business activity of their company. This delegation by the 'principal' of the power to manage to the 'agent' raises the problem of 'agency costs'. This means the costs of monitoring the performance of the management to prevent an 'agent' putting his own interests above those of his 'principal'. Here again, a bargaining process should establish legal arrangements that will seek to reduce agency 'costs' both in terms of the costs of continuing monitoring and the costs caused by misbehaviour or incompetent management.

In Britain, law and economics theorising about company law has received a mixed reception. Some scholars argue strongly for its application in order to understand the impact of company law upon business enterprises so as to maximise their economic welfare.[64] It has been adopted in a Law Commission Consultative Paper concerned with reforming the law of directors' duties.[65]

Other scholars, however, find serious shortcomings in the 'nexus of contracts' analysis of the company and indeed in the whole approach of the law and economics school. They question the neo-liberal economic assumptions on which this theory rests. It can be argued that it is particularly inappropriate when applied to the legal regulation of public listed companies. Its application may compound the weakness and ineffectuality of the present system of company law in restraining corporate abuses in such companies.[66]

---

[64] Cheffins, *op cit*. For a more qualified appraisal, see Deakin and Hughes 'Economics and company law reform: a fruitful partnership?' (1999) 20 Co Law (Special Issue) 212. See also Riley 'Contracting out of company law: section 459 of the Companies Act 1989 and the role of the court' (1992) 55 MLR 782. See further Maugham and Copp 'Company law reform and economic methodology revisited' (2000) 21 Co Law 14; Copp 'Company law and alternative dispute resolution: an economic analysis' (2002) 23 Co Law 361.

[65] See *Company Directors: Regulating Conflicts of Interests and formulating a Statement of Duties*, A Joint Consultative Paper of the English and Scottish Law Commission, Law Com No 153 (1998). See Part III by Deakin and Hughes 'Economic Considerations'. See also the Law Commission's final report: 1B in Law Com No 261 (Cm 4436, 1999).

[66] See Sugarman, 'Is Company Law founded on contract or public regulation? The Law Commission's Paper on Company Directors' (1999) 20 Co Law (Special Issue) at 178–183; Dine 'Fiduciary Duties as default rules, European influences and the need for caution in the use of economic analysis' (1999) 20 Co Law (Special Issue) 190, at 193–195.

The neo-liberal assumptions that lie behind the 'law and economics' theory are today much more open to question as a consequence of the failure of 'market forces' to prevent the economic collapse of 2008–09.

The stimulating and continuing debate these arguments have produced may be further pursued in the literature referred to in the footnotes. Any more detailed assessment clearly lies beyond the scope of an introductory chapter to a company law text.

Other corporate scholars have advanced alternative theoretical approaches to company law which stress many non-economic dimensions in formulating a more comprehensive conceptualisation of company law and corporate reality.[67]

1.9   THE MARKET FOR CORPORATE CONTROL

In the case of listed public companies, the role of 'market economics' must be taken seriously at an everyday and severely practical level. Here there is not only a market for the company's goods or services but also an active market for its listed securities. Where all (or at least a controlling majority) of the company's voting shares are issued to the investing public at large,[68] it is clearly possible for control of the company to pass a result of a successful takeover bid.[69] Even where this does not occur, the discipline of market will operate through the rise or fall of the company's share price to reward or punish successful or unsuccessful performance by the management. This may prove much more significant as a sanction against incompetence or carelessness than any legal remedy.

The idea of the market for corporate control had gained increasing attention since the early 1980s. It obviously reflects the neo-liberal ideology which has prevailed in a period when the concept of 'markets' and 'market forces' has been at the centre of most political as well as economic discussion. The undoubted pragmatic basis for this concept is to be found in the regularly occurring battle for control of large public companies by means of contested takeover bids. The conditions that make this possible in Britain (perhaps alone among the member states of the European Union) require at least a majority of the voting equity shares in the target company to be widely distributed among institutional

---

[67]   See especially JE Parkinson *Corporate Power and Responsibility, Issues in the Theory of Company Law* (Oxford, Clarendon Press, 1994). This study is especially concerned with directors' duties and the issue of corporate governance. It is further considered in Chapter 11. See also the classical study of the separation of ownership and control in large corporations: AA Berle and GR Means *The Modern Corporation and Private Property* (New York 1932, rev edn 1967). See a recent assessment of this classic work by Ireland, '"Back to the future", Adolf Berle, the Law Commission and Directors' Duties' (1999) 20 Co Law (Special Issue) 203.

[68]   As to public issues, see Chapter 19.

[69]   As to the regulation of takeover bids by the City Code on Takeovers and Mergers, see Chapter 20.

investors as well as individual shareholders. Institutional investors (such as pension funds, insurance companies and unit trusts) are 'key players' in the takeover market. Their role is an essential one not only in deciding the success or failure of a takeover bid (or rival bids) but in generating such bids in the first place.

There is a significant connection between an active takeover market and the efficient and honest management of large public companies. It has long been argued that in such Stock Exchange listed companies, with very widely distributed shareholding, pressure from institutional investors performs a vital function in disciplining incompetent or corrupt boards of directors. It is the threat or actuality of a takeover bid which brings the main shareholders' voting power to bear.[70]

Until relatively recently, the whole question of corporate governance was largely unregulated by company law or indeed by City self-regulation. The corporate governance issue describes the practices and committee structures by which boards of directors conduct their affairs and seek to monitor senior management so as to make them accountable to the board. Such questions were seen as being an internal matter for each listed public company and not one for the law maker or City regulator. As a matter of basic political policy the Government throughout the 1980s and much of the 1990s regarded the way boards of directors functioned as part of 'the prerogative of management to manage'. It was contended that the market for corporate control would provide the necessary corrective to any corporate abuses that might occur.

In more recent years, the harsh experience of corporate fraud and company failure, extending to well-known public companies, reduced confidence in the market for corporate control to cope on its own with this problem. The system of self-regulation of corporate governance, by what became the 'Combined Code', is examined elsewhere in this book.[71] In the present century the development of 'shareholder activism', mostly by institutional investors, has sought to challenge, sometimes successfully, incompetent senior executives in public listed companies as well as similar executives who have been excessively rewarded despite their obvious lack of success in managing their companies.

The serious shortcomings in financial regulation revealed by the banking collapse of 2008–09 will require a major revision in the way the boards of banking companies operate and will also require a more effective role for the Financial Services Authority.

---

[70] For a variety of reasons, including board control of the proxy-voting machinery, most general meetings are dominated by the board. This includes the procedure to elect and re-elect directors.

[71] See Chapter 11.

1.9.1 Venture capital and private equity

In recent years the development of 'private equity' companies has provided a new way of acquiring and funding large public companies. There are two kinds of private equity funding. The older version of private equity, known as 'venture capital', involves outside investment in small 'start-up' companies. The other form is more contentious and operates on a much larger scale. The aim is to target large businesses (usually Stock Exchange listed public companies) that may have been badly run, under-valued and in need of more aggressive management. Private equity buys the shares in such companies with money raised from wealthy individuals and financial institutions (such as pension funds), supported by substantial bank loans which are then secured on the target company's assets. 'Private equity' has flourished in Britain partly because the public companies acquired can then claim tax relief on the interest payments on the bank loans raised as part of such 'financial leverage'. The interest payments can be set against profits earned by the company. This sharply reduces the company's liability to corporation tax.

As has been seen, the most 'high-profile' acquisitions involving private equity concern public companies so that they cease to be listed on the Stock Exchange. The aim is to restructure the business by loading the target company with debt secured on its assets. This is linked to changing the managers and cutting costs by reducing the work force and disposing of some of the company's assets. All this should produce returns by way of dividends and management fees over a period of a few years. This in turn should enable a profitable exit to be made either by floating the company again once more on the stock market or by 'selling it on' to another public company or group.

In contrast, the role of 'venture capital' in funding small private companies is necessarily more benign. The option of slashing costs by reducing the number of employees and disposing of assets is non-existent. Instead the emphasis is on the opportunity presented by a new business opportunity in a start-up company.

The private equity method of acquiring and funding public companies has many critics (especially among the trade unions) who point to the job losses as well as the reduction in job security and pension rights for those employees who are not dismissed. There is also a lack of the disclosure requirements imposed both by the Stock Exchange rules and by company law on public listed companies. Even leading figures in the private equity 'industry' have called for more openness in operation of the private equity system. However, there are strong arguments advanced in favour of the system not only by significant figures in the private equity world and in the City of London generally, but also by Government ministers and Treasury civil servants. They point to the industrial growth and employment opportunities created by that growth. The sheer financial success of private equity controlled companies make it likely that the system will long survive but with more regulations as to transparency. The devastation of many private equity funds as a result of the 'credit crunch' and their role in the banking crises of 2008–09 is bound to lead to a careful consideration of how they should be regulated both nationally and internationally.

CHAPTER 2

THE EUROPEAN COMMUNITY AND COMPANY LAW

2.1 INTRODUCTION

A little over a decade ago, an editorial[1] in *The Company Lawyer* criticised the treatment of European company law by academic scholarship in the UK, noting that beyond an 'obligatory introductory section', few references are made to European Union (EU) material. It is true that company law is perceived largely as a matter for domestic law and that the influence of the EU on domestic company law is often treated too superficially. This is despite the fact that several of the central provisions of the Companies Act 2006 are based on EU directives, or affected by the existence of corresponding EU rules. Although it is strictly speaking correct that English lawyers apply the provisions of the Companies Act, they should not ignore the relevance of corresponding EU directives and, crucially, judgments by the European Court of Justice (ECJ).[2] Although this chapter divorces the treatment of EU matters from the corresponding domestic provisions, it does so to raise awareness of the areas which have been affected by EU law. The EU has pursued a wide-ranging programme of harmonisation, and is considering proposals for further harmonising measures. In addition, the provisions of the EU Treaty on the freedom of establishment of companies have given rise to several important judgments by the ECJ, shedding new light on the scope of those provisions. Finally, after many years of negotiation, member states agreed on a 'European Company Statute' in 2001, which came into force in October 2004. A proposal for a 'European Private Company Statute' was presented in 2008, but has, as yet, not managed to secure political agreement.[3] The EU has therefore made a far-reaching contribution to the development of company law. The purpose of this chapter is to chart these developments, in particular the still-evolving case-law on the freedom of establishment of companies, and the European Company Statute. The harmonisation programme will be presented in outline only,

---

[1] Adenas 'European Company Law Reform and the United Kingdom' (2000) 21 Co Law 36.

[2] Seminally, see *Marleasing v La Comercial Internacional de Alimentación SA (Case C-106/89)* [1990] ECR I-4135.

[3] The Competitiveness Council did not agree unanimously to a compromise text presented to its meeting on 30 May 2011. As the legal basis is Article 352 TFEU (ex Article 308 EC), unanimity is required for a measure to be adopted.

and appropriate reference to the relevant directives will be made when dealing with the corresponding areas of domestic law.[4]

In May 2003, the European Commission outlined its plans to modernise EU Company Law over a period of five years or so,[5] and many relevant measures have now been adopted. This process has involved the modernisation of existing directives[6] as well as the adoption, or further steps towards this, of several measures that have been in the pipeline for some time. Many such amendments reflect the availability of electronic means of publication as an alternative to paper-based documents. The Commission has plans to legislate to give all listed companies the choice between the one-tier and two-tier board system, as well as to enhance the responsibilities of board members by developing harmonised wrongful trading and disclosure rules. In addition, in order to improve corporate governance, several recommendations have been adopted, dealing with fostering an appropriate regime for the remuneration of directors of listed companies[7] and non-executive directors.[8] Most recently, the Commission established a 'Reflection Group on the Future of European Company Law' to consider remaining problems with EU Company Law and possible solutions. The Group's report was published in April 2011.[9] In addition, the Commission also published a *Green Paper on the EU Corporate Governance Framework*,[10] which consideres three broad issues: (i) the board of directors and expertise to be provided by non-executive directors; (ii) how to deal with passive shareholders; and (iii) how to apply the 'comply or explain' approach which is central to the EU's corporate governance framework. Space precludes a discussion of all of these developments; they will be referred to in the relevant chapters in this book as appropriate.

---

[4]　For a detailed, if now dated, account of the various directives, see V Edwards *EC Company Law* (Oxford, Oxford University Press, 1999).

[5]　*Modernising Company Law and Enhancing Corporate Governance in the European Union – A Plan to Move Forward* COM (2003) 284 final, 21 May 2003 and *Reinforcing the Statutory Audit* (2003) OJ C236/2. *Modernising Company Law* is based on the High Level Group Report *A Modern Regulatory Framework for Company Law in Europe* (November 2002).

[6]　Noted below where appropriate.

[7]　(2004) OJ L385/55.

[8]　(2005) OJ L52/51.

[9]　Available at:
http://ec.europa.eu/internal_market/company/docs/modern/reflectiongroup_report_en.pdf [last accessed 25 July 2011].

[10]　COM (2011) 164 final. The consultation period closed at the end of July 2011.

2.2 FUNDAMENTAL FREEDOMS: THE FREE MOVEMENT OF COMPANIES

2.2.1　A fundamental problem

One of the fundamental objectives of the EU is to enable the free movement of persons around the Single Market. This includes the right for nationals of a member state to establish themselves in another member state. The main provision in this respect is Art 49 TFEU (ex Art 43 EC),[11] which provides as follows:

> 'Restrictions on freedom of establishment of nationals of a Member State in the territory of another Member State shall be prohibited. Such prohibition shall also apply to restrictions on the setting-up of agencies, branches or subsidiaries by nationals of any Member State established in the territory of any Member State.'

This right is extended to companies by Art 54 TFEU (ex Art48 EC):

> 'Companies formed in accordance with the law of a Member State and having their registered office, central administration or principal place of business within the Community shall be treated in the same way as natural persons who are nationals of Member States.'

Companies which are formed in one of the member states are therefore, in principle, entitled to move around the internal market in the same way as individuals. This may be done in two ways: either by setting up a *primary* establishment in another member state by moving the company's registered office there; or merely by opening a *secondary* establishment through the setting up of an agency, branch or a subsidiary formed under the laws of the host member state. Although this may sound straightforward enough at first sight, it has, in fact, hitherto been very difficult for companies to exercise their right of primary establishment in the Community. A fundamental problem is that a company formed and registered in a particular member state will only be deemed to have legal capacity and be recognised as a separate legal entity in accordance with the laws of that state. Should a company wish to move its registered office to another member state, it would have to be wound up in the state of origin and be re-registered as a new company in accordance with the requirements of the host member state. An attempt was made in 1968 by the then six member states[12] to enable companies to move freely around the Community by providing for the mutual recognition of companies with a Convention on the Mutual Recognition of Companies.[13] The

---

[11]　Following the ratification of the Treaty of Lisbon, the EC Treaty is now known as the 'Treaty on the Functioning of the European Union', or 'TFEU'.

[12]　Belgium, France, Germany, Italy, Luxembourg and the Netherlands.

[13]　Prior to the Treaty of Lisbon, Article 293 EC provided a legal basis for member states to negotiate to secure the mutual recognition of companies and the retention of their legal personality in the event of a transfer of their seat from one member state to another.

Netherlands ultimately chose not to ratify the Convention and it never entered into force. In the wake of the adoption of the Statute on a European Company,[14] the European Commission was to present a proposal for a Fourteenth Directive on the cross-border transfer of a company's registered office, but ultimately chose not to do so.[15]

Faced with such difficulties, companies wishing to take advantage of the freedom of establishment have the option of setting up a branch in another member state, or of incorporating a subsidiary company in another member state to do business there (secondary establishment). Indeed, an entrepreneur who intends to set up a company might even be tempted to incorporate in a member state which has a relatively liberal regime, and then, by taking advantage of the right to create a secondary establishment, to conduct most or all of his business in another member state. A significant difficulty in this context is that the member states do not follow the same principle of private international law for determining the law applicable to a company (*lex societas*). Broadly speaking, it is possible to divide member states on the basis of two different, and irreconcilable, theories, the 'incorporation' doctrine (used in Denmark, Finland, Ireland, the Netherlands, Sweden and the UK), and the real seat doctrine (or *siège réel*) (all other member states).[16] In essence, the real seat doctrine specifies that the law applicable to a company is determined with reference to the location of its head office, its central management or even its centre of activity.[17] A consequence of this is that the company's registered office must be located in the same jurisdiction as the head office. For example, a company which has its head office in Germany (a 'real seat' jurisdiction) would be treated as subject to German law by that legal system. Consequently, if the head office of a company registered in the UK is moved to Germany, the German courts, applying German law, would refuse to recognise its existence unless the company was re-registered as a German company.

In contrast, the 'incorporation' doctrine uses the registered office as the relevant criterion. Consequently, the company will be governed by the law of its country of incorporation. Thus, its legal personality would, for example, depend on the position as it obtains it in the jurisdiction where its registered office is based, even if its head office was based in another member state.

---

[14] Discussed below at **2.5**.

[15] See below at **2.3.9**.

[16] See Wymeersch 'The Transfer of the Company's Seat in European Company Law' (2003) 40 CML Rev 661–695 for a more detailed exposition of these theories. This does not include the new member states which joined after May 2004.

[17] Sometimes defined as 'the location where the internal management decisions are transformed into day-to-day activities of a company'. See Roth 'From *Centros* to *Überseering*: free movement of companies, private international law and Community law' (2003) 52 ICLQ 177, at 181.

2.2.2 The jurisprudence of the ECJ

The compatibility of the real seat doctrine with the principle of freedom of establishment guaranteed by the EC Treaty has been tested in a number of recent cases. Some of these cases involved companies which were incorporated, but did not trade, in the UK.

In the so-called *Daily Mail* case,[18] a company incorporated under English law wished to transfer its central management to the Netherlands. The primary motive behind this decision was to avoid capital gains tax on the sale of shares.[19] Consent from the Treasury was required before the move could go ahead. Although it was willing to grant such consent, the Treasury required that the sale of shares had to be effected *before* the move. The company argued that this was contrary to Art 49 TFEU (ex Art 43 EC). The ECJ held that because of the divergent rules on the transfer of the registered office or head office between the member states, legislation was required to resolve the problem. There was no right under Art 49 TFEU (ex Art 43 EC) to move the head office of a company to another member state whilst retaining legal status as a company in the original member state. Consequently, the home member state was entitled to impose conditions on a company wishing to exercise its free movement rights.

The position in the host member state was addressed for the first time in the famous *Centros* decision.[20] A private limited company had been registered in the UK, but it never traded there. It had been formed for the sole purpose of setting up a branch of the company in Denmark to trade there, without having to comply with the Danish minimum capital requirements. These are stricter than in the UK, applying also to private companies.[21] The Danish registrar refused to register the branch because, in his view, rather than being a branch of a company from another member state, it seemed to be a company with its principal establishment in Denmark. As it had not complied with the minimum capital rules, he refused to register the company, although it was conceded that if Centros had traded in the UK, registration of the branch would not have been refused. The question before the ECJ was therefore whether Centros was entitled to rely on Art 49 TFEU (ex Art 43 EC), or whether the Danish registrar was justified in his refusal to register the branch. The ECJ was unequivocal in its decision, holding that the refusal to register the branch

---

[18] *R v HM Treasury and Commissioners of Inland Revenue, ex parte Daily Mail and General Trust plc (Case C-81/87)* [1988] ECR 5483.

[19] The sum that would have been payable in the UK amounted to some £13m, whereas following the move to the Netherlands, tax would only have been payable on any increase in the shares' value since the date of the move.

[20] *Centros Ltd v Ehrvervs og Selskabsstyrelsen (Case C-212/97)* [1999] ECR I-1459, [2000] 2 WLR 1048, [1999] BCC 983.

[21] The Second EC Directive requires a minimum capital requirement only for public companies, but many member states have extended this requirement to private companies, as well. See **2.3.2**, below.

was a breach of EU law and could not be justified in the interest of protecting creditors or preventing fraud, especially in light of existing EU rules on accounting. The deliberate choice of a member state with more lenient requirements for incorporation and subsequent use of the right of secondary establishment was simply an exercise of rights inherent in the notion of freedom of establishment. This in itself would not be an abuse of the right of establishment, even though it had the effect of circumventing requirements in the home member state. Not trading in the member state where the company was incorporated and only trading through a branch was not in itself enough to constitute abuse.[22] This decision gave rise to a significant amount of debate among commentators,[23] and many felt that *Centros* marked the beginning of the end of the 'real seat' doctrine.[24] In *Centros*, the company's registered office was located in the UK whereas its activities were carried on in Denmark. In accepting that this was perfectly lawful under EU law, the ECJ appeared to hold that, as a matter of EU law, the registered office, which was not in the same member state where the company mainly operated, was the law applicable to the company. This, of course, would be in direct conflict with the real seat principle, which, on the facts of *Centros*, would have applied Danish law to the company.

In *Überseering*,[25] the ECJ was given the opportunity to clarify its rulings in *Daily Mail* and *Centros*. In this case, a Dutch company (ÜBV) had acquired land in Germany and contracted with NCC, a German company, for renovation work. This work was not carried out to ÜBV's satisfaction and it tried to sue NCC in the German courts. The shares in ÜBV had been acquired by German shareholders and it seemed to the German court that the company had transferred its real seat to Germany. In German law, a company's legal capacity is determined on the basis of its real seat. As ÜBV had not reincorporated in Germany after the acquisition of its shares by German shareholders, the court refused to recognise the company's legal capacity. The German Federal Supreme Court was concerned about the compatibility of this ruling with Art 49 TFEU (ex Art 43 EC). It referred two questions to the ECJ for a preliminary ruling:

---

[22] Cf *Segers v Bestuur van de Bedrifsvereniging voor Bank en Verzekeringswezen (Case C-79/85)* [1986] ECR 2375.

[23] See eg, Micheler 'The Impact of the *Centros* case on Europe's Company laws' (2000) 21 Co Law 179.

[24] One aspect of *Centros* (and *Segers*) is open to doubt: the ECJ assumed that Centros Ltd was established in the UK and sought to exercise its right to set up a secondary establishment in Denmark. However, ECJ jurisprudence appears to determine 'establishment' on the basis of both physical presence *and* the exercise of an economic activity. Centros Ltd was not economically active, however, and it may therefore be questioned whether it was really established in the UK: see Xanthaki '*Centros*: Is this really the end for the theory of the siège réel?' (2001) 22 Co Law 2, at 7.

[25] *Überseering BV v Nordic Construction Company Baumanagement GmbH (Case C-208/00)* [2002] ECR I-9919.

(1)   If a company validly incorporated in A moves its actual centre of administration to B, and rules in B would prevent the company from having legal capacity, can B maintain its rules in light of Art 43 EC (now Art 49 TFEU)?

(2)   If so, does Art 43 EC (now Art 49 TFEU) require that the legal capacity of a company should be determined according to the law of the state where the company is incorporated?

The ECJ first distinguished *Daily Mail* because that case concerned restrictions imposed by the home member state.[26] In the present case, it held that ÜBV could rely on Art 49 TFEU (ex Art 43 EC), because it was validly incorporated in the Netherlands and had its registered office there. It was of little significance that its shares had been acquired by German shareholders because this had no effect on ÜBV's legal status under Dutch law. On that basis, the refusal of the host member state (B) to recognise the legal capacity of a company formed in accordance with the law in its home member state (A) on the ground that the company has moved its centre of administration was in principle incompatible with Art 49 TFEU (ex Art 43 EC). However, it could be justifiable if it was applied without discrimination, required by overriding requirements relating to the general interest, and was proportionate to the objectives pursued. The ECJ accepted that requirements relating to the protection of the interests of creditors, minority shareholders, employees or taxation authorities may justify restrictions on the freedom of establishment, but this did not extend to denying altogether legal capacity to a company and therefore its capacity to bring legal proceedings. Thus, moving the actual centre of management cannot result in loss of legal capacity in the host member state. In relation to the second question, the ECJ held that where a company has its registered office in member state A and exercises its right to freedom of establishment in member state B, Arts 49 and 54 TFEU (ex 43 and 48 EC) require that B must recognise the legal capacity which the company enjoys under the law of its state of incorporation.[27]

This was followed by *Chamber of Commerce Amsterdam v Inspire Art Ltd*,[28] involving a challenge to the legality of a Dutch law on 'formally foreign companies' (FFC law). This law applies to companies incorporated in a member state other than the Netherlands which predominantly or exclusively operate in the Netherlands. These must be entered in the commercial register as a 'formally foreign company' and comply with detailed disclosure obligations. The law further imposes

---

[26]   This has been criticised by Roth 'From *Centros* to *Überseering*: free movement of companies, private international law and Community law' (2003) 52 ICLQ 177.

[27]   The ruling in this case does not mean that company can move its *registered* office to another member state and demand recognition under Art 49 TFEU (ex Art 43). For this, legislation is required and a proposal for a Fourteenth Directive on the transfer of the registered seat is expected soon.

[28]   *Chamber of Commerce Amsterdam v Inspire Art Ltd (Case C-167/01)* [2003] ECR I-10155.

minimum capital requirements and sanctions for non-compliance. Inspire Art Ltd (IAL) was a company incorporated in England, but it operated exclusively in the Netherlands through a branch in Amsterdam. The Amsterdam Chamber of Commerce demanded that IAL comply with the Dutch law. The Dutch court held that the FFC law applied, but requested a ruling from the ECJ on its compatibility with EU law. The ECJ first held that to the extent that the FFC law reflected the requirements of the relevant company law directives as they applied to IAL, the Dutch law was compatible, provided that the penalties for non-compliance were the same as for Dutch companies. Many of the disclosure provisions implemented the requirements of the Eleventh Directive[29] and were therefore not a problem. However, several disclosure requirements in the FFC law, such as recording in the commercial register that the branch is an FFC and providing an auditor's certificate of compliance with minimum capital requirements, went beyond the Eleventh Directive. As the Eleventh Directive was exhaustive, no further requirements could be imposed. The minimum capital requirement fell outside any relevant directive[30] and therefore had to be tested against the relevant Treaty provisions. The ECJ confirmed its holding in *Centros* and *Überseering* that it is immaterial that a company was formed in one member state solely for the purpose of establishment in a second member state where its main or entire business is conducted. In the absence of fraud, its reasons for doing so are irrelevant; in fact, incorporating in a particular member state solely for the purpose of benefiting from more favourable legislation is fully compatible with the Treaty. Imposing the Dutch minimum capital requirement on branches in such circumstances was contrary to the freedom of establishment, although it might be justifiable. On the facts of *Inspire Art*, this was not possible because IAL was clearly held out as an English company, and, more significantly, it had not been improper for IAL to have recourse to the freedom of establishment in trying to avoid the stricter incorporation rules of Dutch law.

A fresh attempt to revisit the *Daily Mail* approach was *CARTESIO*.[31] Here, an Hungarian 'company'[32] wanted to move its head office/real seat to Italy whilst remaining registered under and subject to Hungarian law, but this was not permitted. The company sought to challenge the relevant Hungarian legislation, but the ECJ held that national legislation which does not allow a company to transfer its real seat to another Member State whilst retaining its status as a company governed by the law of the state of incorporation was acceptable under Art 49 TFEU (ex Art 43 EC).

---

[29]   See below at **2.3.7.**

[30]   As noted in the context of *Centros*, EC law only imposes a minimum capital requirement on public companies.

[31]   C-210/06 *Re CARTESIO Oktakó és Szolgáltó bt* [2009] BCC 232.

[32]   Cartesio was a limited partnership, rather than a company, without separate legal personality (see S Rammeloo 'The 14th EC Company Law Directive on the Cross-border Transfer of the Registered Office' (2008) 15 Maastricht Journal of European and Comparative Law 359-94, at 368-9). However, the ECJ proceeded on the assumption that this was a question of *company* law.

This case confirms that questions of capacity are therefore decided under the law of the state of incorporation, and that state can specify the conditions that need to be fulfilled in order for a company to be regarded as such under their law. The ECJ expressed this in terms of a Member State's right 'to define the connecting factor required of a company if it is to be regarded as incorporated under the law of that Member State',[33] and the requirements for a company subsequently to retain that status. So Cartesio's plan to move its head office to Italy whilst remaining an Hungarian company could be thwarted by Hungarian law without infringing the Treaty, because Hungary could require that the head office remain within Hungary if Cartesio wished to remain a Hungarian company. Moreover, the ECJ also noted that it would not be acceptable for a Member State to require a company that seeks to convert from one country to another to be wound up or liquidated in the first Member State – such restrictions on the possibility of conversion *would* violate Art 49 TFEU (ex 43 EC).[34] However, as Cartesio wished to remain an Hungarian company, it was permissible for Hungary to refuse to register the transfer of Cartesio's head office to Italy.

2.2.3   The impact of the ECJ's case-law

In the wake of these cases, it is perhaps not surprising that commentators have suggested that the 'real seat' doctrine has to all intents and purposes been abolished by the ECJ, although opinions on this diverge. Some clearly think that post-*Überseering*, the incorporation theory is fully accepted.[35] However, that case was concerned with a rather narrow question regarding the legal recognition of a company fully recognised in its home member state. Although this ruling has a distinct flavour of incorporation theory, it seems difficult to extrapolate a general preference for either the 'real seat' or the 'incorporation' principle from it. Rather, one can explain all these cases in terms of the 'home-country control' principle, ie it is for the country of a company's incorporation to determine various issues (a matter implicitly confirmed in *Cartesio*). It was observed (following *Centros*) that just as the TFEU itself does not prefer one of the two principles, referring instead to three alternative criteria in Art 49 TFEU (ex Art 43 EC),[36] so it would be surprising if the ECJ's jurisprudence were to be a departure from these basic alternatives.[37] Indeed, it is likely that the ECJ would have come to a different decision in *Centros*, had the company been incorporated in Austria and tried to

---

[33]   Para 110.

[34]   Para 112.

[35]   See, eg, Ebers 'Company Law in Member States against the Background of Legal Harmonisation and Competition between legal systems' [2003] ERPL 509, at 511.

[36]   These are (1) registered office, (2) central administration or (3) principal place of business in the Community. The third factor is relevant for companies incorporated outside the EC.

[37]   Xanthaki '*Centros*: Is this really the end for the theory of the siège réel?' (2001) 22 Co Law 2.

establish a branch in Germany.[38] *Überseering* does refer to the country of incorporation for determining the fundamental question of legal capacity, but this does not mean that the incorporation principle should apply to determining all other company law matters.[39] A crucial issue here is the extent to which a host country can impose its rules on a company which is incorporated elsewhere, but active primarily or exclusively in the host member state. Following *Inspire Art*, it seems that a company would only have to comply with the requirements of its home state (state of registration), unless requirements of the host member state are justified in public interest. It remains to be seen which rules could be justified on this basis – one possibility might be rules on worker participation imposed by the host member state on companies which have their registered office in its territory.[40] What does seem clear is that this is a question which will occupy academic commentators for some time to come, and may ultimately only be settled if the EU adopts legislation to allow companies to move freely around the EU.[41]

The ECJ has, however, given general support to the existence of a 'market' for incorporation.[42] Because of the variations in the domestic company law systems, member states could be competing for 'incorporation' business. Indeed, the various recent ECJ cases suggest that there is demand for 'easy incorporation' regimes and that the UK is fairly popular. This raises the suggestion that the UK could even become the EU's Delaware.[43] However, although the Treaty rules grant companies the right to incorporate in any member state, a significant degree of competition between legal systems could undermine the whole idea of the internal market. To some extent, this is mitigated by the *Cartesio* ruling, which upheld a national law requiring a company's head office to remain in the jurisdiction of incorporation, thereby precluding a rush of companies to incorporate in a country with a light regulatory regime and operate entirely in another country. Also, the company law harmonisation programme has levelled the European playing field by increasingly dealing with those matters which would otherwise make incorporation elsewhere attractive – although it does not rule this out altogether. The absence of a minimum capital requirement in the UK has proven to be a significant element – but if plans to modernise the Second Directive include an

---

[38] Ibid, p 7.

[39] Thoma 'The *Überseering* ruling: a tale of serendipity' [2003] ERPL 545. Note that UK law applies a 'real seat' criterion in the context of taxation, despite being an 'incorporation' jurisdiction.

[40] Roth, 'From *Centros* to *Überseering*: free movement of companies, private international law and Community law' (2003) 52 ICLQ 177.

[41] Adenas, 'Free Movement of Companies' (2003) 119 LQR 221, at 226; Roth (2003) 52 ICLQ 177; Wymeersch (2003) 40 CML Rev 661.

[42] See further B Cheffins *Company Law – Theory, Structure and Operation* (Oxford University Press, 1997) Ch 9.

[43] Although it has been observed that the 'Delaware' effect involves public listed companies, whereas the *Centros* effect is more likely to be relevant to small private companies: Micheler 'The Impact of the *Centros* case on Europe's Company laws' (2000) 21 Co Law 179, at 182.

extension of the minimum capital requirement to private companies, then this may dampen the enthusiasm of those from other member states to incorporate in the UK and then utilise their rights under the Treaty.

2.2.4 Further developments regarding the freedom of establishment of companies

In *SEVIC Systems AG*,[44] the ECJ was asked to examine the compatibility of a German law on the registration of mergers, with the freedom of establishment. The case involved a merger of a company established in Luxembourg with SEVIC, a German company. The relevant German law only applied to mergers (and other transformations) of companies established in Germany. Consequently, the application to register the merger was refused by the German courts. The ECJ held that this restriction was incompatible with Arts 49 and 54 TFEU (ex Arts 43 and 48), and the blanket refusal to register a cross-border merger was not capable of objective justification. It had been argued by the Dutch and German Governments that, in the absence of a harmonising directive on cross-border mergers,[45] there was no infringement, but the ECJ rejected this, noting that such harmonisation could not be a precondition to the freedom of establishment. Consequently, national legislation which makes cross-border mergers impossible, as was the case here, was incompatible with the freedom of establishment.

2.3 THE HARMONISATION PROGRAMME: COMPANY LAW DIRECTIVES

The legal basis for the harmonisation programme in the field of company law is Art 50 TFEU (ex Art 44 EC). Harmonisation has proceeded by way of directives, requiring that domestic law is adjusted to comply fully with the requirements of a directive without having to follow the exact wording of each measure.[46] Most of the harmonisation directives have been incorporated into the Companies Act 2006.

It is possible to identify four distinct 'generations' of directives:[47] the first generation (the First and Second Directives) is heavily influenced by the German drafting style and these are therefore very detailed.[48] The second generation (covering the Third, Fourth, Sixth, Seventh and Eighth Directives) is still fairly precisely worded, but there is greater flexibility, thereby allowing for some diversity between the domestic laws and some

---

[44] [2005] ECR I-10805.

[45] A directive on this has since been adopted: see **2.3.4** below.

[46] For a discussion of harmonisation generally, see J Steiner and L Woods, *EU Law* (Oxford University Press, 10th edn, 2009) Ch 16.

[47] C Villiers *European Company Law – Towards Democracy?* (Aldershot, Ashgate, 1998) p 28.

[48] Although some of the substantive provisions are based on other jurisdictions, including UK law, e g in respect of some of the capital maintenance rules.

discretion regarding their implementation. The third generation (Eleventh and Twelfth Directives[49]) follows the so-called 'new approach' to harmonisation, specifying only the essential requirements to be met rather than the detail of how these are to be met. Finally, there may be a fourth generation of 'framework' directives, such as the recently adopted Thirteenth Directive, as well as the proposed Fourteenth Directive on the transfer of the seat.

The purpose of this part is to chart the harmonisation programme in outline, rather than to engage in a detailed discussion of the various directives. Later chapters make reference to specific provisions of these directives where appropriate. A general overview helps to illustrate the significance of the EU's harmonisation programme on the development of domestic company law.

2.3.1   First Company Law Directive

The First Directive[50] is concerned with three basic issues: disclosure, validity of obligations entered into by a company and nullity of companies. It requires that companies disclose details of their constitutions, including subsequent amendments, company officers, the subscribed capital and their profit and loss accounts. Moreover, all company documents must include basic details, including the company's registration number. All member states must have a central register of companies. The Directive was amended[51] to provide for the creation of an electronic register and disclosure of information by electronic means from January 2007. The national *Gazette* may be kept in electronic form or replaced altogether with an electronic system that will fulfil the same purpose.

With regard to the validity of obligations entered into by a company, and with an eye on the legal basis for the Directive, there are a number of provisions designed to protect outsiders where particular transactions would not ordinarily bind the company. Thus, in the case of pre-incorporation contracts, it is provided that a person purporting to act for a non-incorporated company may be personally liable to a third party. Moreover, an outsider contracting with a company will be protected in instances where the company has exceeded its capacity (*ultra vires*) or

---

[49]   The 12th Directive was replaced by Directive 2009/102/EC because it had been amended on several occasions since its adoption. This was simply a consolidation exercise.

[50]   Directive 68/151/EEC on co-ordination of safeguards which, for the protection of the interests of members and others, are required by Member States of companies within the meaning of the second paragraph of Article [48] of the Treaty, with a view to making such safeguards equivalent throughout the Community (1968) OJ L65/8; English Special Edition 1968 (I), p 41.

[51]   By Directive 2003/58/EC amending Council Directive 68/151/EEC, as regards disclosure requirements in respect of certain types of companies (2003) OJ L221/13.

where the relevant organ in the company has exceeded its authority. Finally, the Directive specifies the circumstances when a member state may declare a company a nullity.[52]

As part of the European Commission's drive to reduce administrative burdens on companies, a proposal for facilitating disclosure of information through a central electronic platform at no additional cost to companies was presented in 2008.[53]

2.3.2 Second Company Law Directive

The Second Directive[54] applies to public companies only and has had a significant impact on domestic rules on capital maintenance.[55] It pursues two broad objectives: first, it imposes further disclosure requirements on public companies in addition to those already contained in the First Directive, and secondly, it lays down numerous rules on capital maintenance.

As far as the additional disclosure requirements are concerned, it is required that information is provided about the type and name of company, its objects and the amount of subscribed and authorised share capital. More detailed disclosure of information on the documents lodged with the Registrar of Companies is also required.

The Directive requires that all public companies have a minimum subscribed share capital of at least €25,000.[56] There are then several detailed provisions to ensure that the integrity of share capital is preserved. Thus, share capital must be represented in assets capable of economic assessment. Shares may not to be issued at a discount and must be paid up by a minimum of 25%. There is a prohibition against distributions out of capital, and it is further provided that any amount distributed to shareholders must not exceed the company's net profits. Public companies are permitted to increase or reduce their share capital, but any such changes must be approved by the shareholders. Furthermore, there are rules on pre-emption rights of existing shareholders.

---

[52] This provision has no relevance to UK law.

[53] COM (2008) 194 final. The European Parliament completed its first reading in November 2008, but at the time of writing, the Council had yet to deal with the first reading of the proposal.

[54] Directive 77/91/EEC on co-ordination of safeguards which, for the protection of the interests of members and others, are required by Member States of companies within the meaning of the second paragraph of Article [48] of the Treaty, in respect of the formation of public limited liability companies and the maintenance and alteration of their capital, with a view to making such safeguards equivalent (1977) OJ L26/1.

[55] It was amended once in 1992 by Directive 92/101/EEC (1992) OJ L 47/64, inserting a new Art 24a.

[56] This is about £18,000; note that the minimum capital requirement specified for UK public companies is £50,000.

As originally adopted, the Directive included a general prohibition against the company providing financial assistance for the acquisition of its own shares, and there are rules on the purchase by a company of its own shares. However, the provisions of this Directive, which are very detailed and technical, have been criticised for being overly complex.[57] The Commission therefore announced[58] that it would implement legislation to simplify the Directive as a short-term priority, and an amending directive was adopted in September 2006,[59] with the changes in force in April 2008. The main changes introduced mean that it will now become possible for a company to purchase its own shares and to provide financial assistance to the acquisition of its shares within the limits of distributable profits (reserves). Furthermore, where shares are provided in return for a non-cash asset, the mandatory expert valuation may be dispensed with where there is other clear evidence regarding this valuation. However, shareholders remain entitled to request an expert valuation. Finally, in circumstances where a company reduces its capital, existing creditors are entitled to get security in respect of claims which have not yet fallen due.

The Commission had also considered the introduction of shares without a par value, and to allow public companies to ignore pre-emption rights where shares are issued at the market price, but these were not carried forward into the amending directive. Furthermore, the minimum capital requirement has been retained as a deterrent factor. In the longer term, the Commission will consider whether the capital maintenance system could be replaced with an alternative regime based on a new solvency test before company funds may be used for certain purposes, but this is not expected for some time yet.

2.3.3 Third and Sixth Directives: mergers and divisions of public companies

The Third Directive[60] deals with mergers of public limited companies. It requires that member states put procedures into place to facilitate such mergers within their territories.[61] The Directive deals with two types of merger: the first is a merger by acquisition, whereby one of the merging companies will receive all the assets and assume the obligations and liabilities of the other companies. The second is a merger by the formation of a new company, to which all the assets and liabilities of the merging companies will be transferred. In either case, the management bodies of

---

[57] Indeed, the DTI noted that this stood in the way of simplifying the capital maintenance regime for public companies as part of the 'modernising company law' project.

[58] See COM (2003) 284 final (EU Action Plan on modernising company law), pp 17–18.

[59] Directive 2006/68/EC (2006) OJ L264/32.

[60] Directive 78/855/EEC concerning mergers of public limited liability companies (1978) OJ L295/36.

[61] Note that this Directive does not deal with cross-border mergers. On such mergers, see Directive 2005/56/EC (2005) OJ L310/1.

participating companies must draw up terms of proposed merger and provide information on the effect of proposed merger on shareholdings. Furthermore, it must account for any benefits to the management team resulting from the merger. A report by the management and an independent expert report evaluating the proposed merger must be approved by a minimum two-thirds majority of the shareholders in general meeting. Once a merger has been completed details must be publicised in the *Gazette*. The Directive seeks to provide protection for shareholders as well as others affected by the merger (such as employees, creditors or debenture holders). Generally, the management boards must provide detailed information. The Sixth Directive[62] provides for similar rules where a public limited company separates into divisions. Both directives apply to domestic transactions only, but the recently adopted Tenth Directive on cross-border mergers of public limited companies now deals with mergers across national borders (see below). This directive allows the shareholders of the companies concerned to dispense with the requirement of the independent expert's report if all agree to do so, and the Third and Sixth Directives have been amended accordingly.[63] A proposal to modify reporting and publicity requirements to encompass electronic means, including internet sites, was presented in 2008,[64] and adopted as Directive 2009/109/EC,[65] with changes to national law due to have been brought into force by 30 June 2011.

2.3.4 Tenth Directive: cross-border mergers

Following the adoption of the European Company Statute (see **2.5**), which provides as one method for the formation of a European Company the cross-border merger of two or more public companies, the European Commission presented a fresh proposal for a Tenth Directive on cross-border mergers of companies with share capital in November 2003,[66] which became law in October 2005 and had to be implemented by December 2007.[67] The Tenth Directive follows the same basic scheme as is contained in the Third Directive, but specifies which national authority is to be involved in scrutinising the legality of the proposed merger and, more significantly, provides that cross-border mergers which follow the procedure in the Directive could not be declared null and void. Also, if all

---

[62] Directive 82/891/EEC concerning the division of public limited liability companies (1982) OJ L378/47.

[63] Directive 2007/63/EC (2007) OJ L300/47.

[64] COM (2008) 576.

[65] Directive 2009/109/EC of the European Parliament and of the Council of 16 September 2009 amending Council Directives 77/91/EEC, 78/855/EEC and 82/891/EEC, and Directive 2005/56/EC as regards reporting and documentation requirements in the case of mergers and divisions (2009) OJ L 259/14.

[66] Proposal for a Directive of the European Parliament and Council on cross-border mergers of companies with share capital COM (2003) 703 final, 18 November 2003. For background to earlier proposals, see V Edwards *EC Company Law* (Oxford University Press, 1999) pp 391–393.

[67] Directive 2005/56/EC on cross-border mergers of limited liability companies (2005) OJ L310/1.

the shareholders of the companies concerned agree that the independent expert's report is not needed, it need not be prepared. As far as employee participation is concerned, the Directive seeks to ensure continuity of established participation and expressly refers to the relevant provisions regarding employee participation in the European Company (see **2.5.11**). A proposal to modify reporting and publicity requirements to encompass electronic means, including internet sites, was presented in 2008.[68]

2.3.5   Fourth, Seventh and Eighth Directives: accounting and audit

The Fourth Directive[69] is also known as the Accounts Directive. It sets out the requirements for accounts to be drawn up and submitted to a central registry. The aim of this Directive is to achieve comparability and equivalence of financial information throughout the EU. The Directive provides for a choice of different accounts formats. It also requires that accounts are audited and that the publication of accounts and the auditor's report is duly authorised. The Directive applies to all business forms and not merely to public companies, although it contains a number of exemptions for certain small and medium-sized enterprises. The Seventh Directive[70] extends this to corporate groups. It requires that a parent company, in addition to its annual accounts, also prepares consolidated accounts for the corporate group which it heads. As part of the ongoing modernisation process, both Directives were recently amended to provide for the collective responsibility of board members for drawing-up and publishing annual accounts, to require the disclosure of material transactions with related parties and off-balance-sheet arrangements, and to require the inclusion of a corporate governance statement in the annual accounts.[71] Moreover, there have been further amendments to simplify the financial reporting burden on small and medium-sized enterprises, and to clarify the relationship of the consolidation rules with international reporting standards.[72]

Both Directives are supplemented by the Eighth Directive on the statutory audit of annual accounts and consolidated accounts. Originally

---

[68]   COM (2008) 576. The European Parliament's first reading was completed on 31 March 2009. The Council's first reading was pending at the time of writing.

[69]   Directive 78/660/EEC on the annual accounts of certain types of companies (1978) OJ L222/11. This has been amended several times, eg, by Directive 2003/38/EC on the annual accounts of certain types of companies as regards amounts expressed in euro (2003) OJ L120/22, and Directive 2003/51/EC on the annual and consolidated accounts of certain types of companies (2003) OJ L178/16.

[70]   Directive 83/349/EEC on consolidated accounts (1983) OJ L193/1.

[71]   Directive 2006/46/EC amending Council Directives 78/660/EEC, 83/349/EEC and 91/674/EEC (2006) OJ L224/1.

[72]   Directive 2009/49/EC of the European Parliament and of the Council of 18 June 2009 amending Council Directives 78/660/EEC and 83/349/EEC as regards certain disclosure requirements for medium-sized companies and the obligation to draw up consolidated accounts (2009) OJ L164/42.

adopted in 1984,[73] a replacement Directive was adopted in 2006,[74] based on a proposal by the Commission which marked the culmination of a review process which began in 1996.[75] The Directive specifies the conditions for the approval of auditors. These requirements relate to the competence and independence of auditors and the Directive pursues as its overall objective that accounting of company accounts is carried out with integrity and independence. Auditors must have undertaken university-level study of theoretical and practical aspects and have passed an examination of professional competence (or demonstrate long-term practical experience). Each member state has to maintain a public register of statutory auditors. The new version of the Eighth Directive modernises the existing rules on auditors, and introduces new rules on auditor independence and quality assurance. It also requires the establishment of an audit committee for all 'public interest entities' (essentially, public companies, banks and insurance companies). The new rules came into force at the end of June 2008.

2.3.6 Thirteenth Directive: Takeovers

A controversial directive is the Thirteenth Directive on takeover bids, agreement on which was reached in late 2003.[76] It establishes the general principles which all the member states are required to apply when dealing with takeover bids, contains rules for establishing the domestic supervisory authority that will deal with the bid, and lays down rules on shareholder protection and mandatory offers, as well as detailed disclosure obligations. A controversial aspect of the Directive is that it permits defensive measures only with prior authorisation of the general meeting and modifies voting rights in that context, but the Directive permits member states to opt out of these provisions. Perhaps unsurprisingly, the Commission, whose proposal[77] was significantly modified, expressed disappointment with this Directive. In a report on the implementation of the Directive,[78] the Commission notes that the impact of the Directive as adopted may be to undermine, rather than promote, the market for corporate control, and expresses surprise at the number of member states acting in a 'seemingly protectionist way'.

---

[73] Directive 84/253/EEC on the approval of persons responsible for carrying out the statutory audits of accounting documents (1984) OJ L126/20.

[74] Directive 2006/43/EC on statutory audits of annual accounts and consolidated accounts (2006) OJ L157/87.

[75] *Proposal for a Directive on statutory audit of annual accounts and consolidated accounts and amending Council Directives 78/660/EEC and 84/349/EEC*, COM (2004) 177 final, March 2004.

[76] Directive 2004/25/EC on takeover bids (2004) OJ L142/12.

[77] (2003) OJ C45/1.

[78] Commission Staff Working Document *Report on the implementation of the Directive on Takeover Bids*, COM (2007) 268, 21 February 2007.

2.3.7 Eleventh and Twelfth Directive: branches and single-member companies

The Eleventh Directive[79] applies to branches (rather than subsidiaries) of companies registered in another member state. In essence, it extends the requirements of the First, Fourth, Seventh and Eighth Directives to such branches. Moreover, the details of such branches must be disclosed to outsiders. A host Member State can require that certain documents are translated into that state's official language and that the translation is certified. A recent proposal by the European Commission would provide that such translations/certifications can be undertaken by any officially recognised translator.[80]

Finally, Directive 2009/102/EC (formerly known as the 'Twelfth Directive'[81]) requires all member states to permit the creation of single-member private limited companies. The Directive harmonises the principle but leaves the detail to the member states. In essence, it permits single-member companies and requires that this status must be disclosed. A sole member is deemed to have the powers of the general meeting, but is still required to keep records of all decisions.

2.3.8 Cross-border exercise of shareholder rights

In order to facilitate the exercise of voting rights by shareholders (in listed companies) in a cross-border context, a Directive on the exercise of certain rights of shareholders in listed companies was adopted in 2007.[82] The Directive requires the equal treatment of all shareholders entitled to participate and vote in general meeting. Specified information has to be provided at least 21 days before a meeting is held. Moreover, shareholders are entitled to table items for discussion or for adoption by resolution. In addition, there are rules regarding participation and voting in general meeting, including the use of electronic means to facilitate this; the right to ask questions; proxy voting; and voting by correspondence. The date for implementation of the Directive was 3 August 2009.

In addition, the Commission has been consulting on adopting further measures, such as a recommendation, to complement the Directive on the

---

[79] Directive 89/666/EEC concerning disclosure requirements in respect of branches opened in a Member State by certain types of company governed by the law of another State (1989) OJ L395/36.

[80] COM (2008) 194 final.

[81] Directive 89/667/EEC on single-member private limited-liability companies (1989) OJ L395/40. This was repealed by Directive 2009/102/EC the area of company law on single-member private limited liability companies (2009) OJ L258/20, which is a re-enactment of the earlier directive consolidated with later amendments.

[82] Directive 2007/36/EC on the exercise of certain rights of shareholders in listed companies (2007) OJ L184/17.

exercise of voting rights.[83] This might address issues such as the language of meeting documents; depositary receipts and the exercise of voting rights; stock lending; the position of intermediaries; and management companies of investment schemes. Although a recommendation regarding these matters was tentatively scheduled for late 2007, nothing has appeared as yet.

2.3.9 Abandoned Fourteenth Directive

In 2004, the Commission undertook an initial consultation regarding plans for a draft Fourteenth Directive[84] which suggested that the Fourteenth Directive would provide a framework for the transfer of a company's registered office from one member state to another, which would ensure that a company would continue to exist, rather than require it to be wound up and re-incorporated in the host member state. Following such a transfer, a company would be removed from the register in its home member state on registration in the host member state, having amended its constitution to comply with host state requirements. It would, in essence, have followed the same procedure that applies to the transfer of the registered office of a European company (see **2.5.6**), although it would not contain any rules regarding the location of the company's head office. In light of an impact assessment which noted the insufficient experience regarding the operation of the Tenth Directive and pending litigation before the ECJ, it was concluded in December 2007 that there was insufficient need for European action, and no legislative proposals will be made for the time being.[85]

2.3.10 Other Abandoned proposals (Fifth and Ninth Directives)

Despite the relative success of the harmonisation programme, there are some areas where discussions for EU action stalled at a very early stage. Thus, the proposal for a Fifth Directive on the structure of public limited companies and the powers of its organs (including directors' duties and shareholders' remedies) never really got off the ground and had been largely abandoned by 1997. In its Action Plan, the Commission confirmed that this proposal would not be pursued any further. A similar fate has befallen the Ninth Directive on groups of companies. This would have introduced parent liability for subsidiaries, as well as further disclosure obligations. This initiative never progressed beyond internal draft documents and had been abandoned by 1984. Nevertheless, these Directives are still referred to by their respective numbers.

---

83 *Fostering an appropriate regime for shareholders' rights* – Third Consultation Document (MARKT/30.04.2007).
84 *Company Law: Commission consults on the cross-border transfer of companies' registered offices* (IP/04/270, 26 February 2004).
85 SEC(2007) 1707, 12 December 2007.

2.4 HARMONISATION OF SECURITIES REGULATION

In addition to the harmonisation programme affecting particular aspects of core company law, the EU has adopted common rules in the field of securities regulation. A first wave of directives was adopted in the late 1970s and early 1980s.[86] A directive on prospectuses followed in 1989,[87] as did a directive on insider dealing.[88] Most were eventually consolidated in Directive 2001/34/EC on the admission of securities to official stock exchange listing and on information to be published on those securities.[89]

These are now being replaced with updated measures to give effect to the EU's ambitious plan to create an internal market for financial services by 2005. Three major directives have already been adopted: the directive on insider dealing has been replaced by Directive 2003/6/EC on Insider Dealing and Market Manipulation.[90] This was the first to be adopted under the new procedure for the regulation of the European securities markets. Essentially, the directives only specify broad principles. Detailed implementing rules are subsequently drafted by the European Commission, which has to consult the European Securities Regulators Committee.[91] Several implementing measures have subsequently been adopted, including: a regulation providing an exemption for buy-back programmes and stabilisation of financial instruments,[92] a directive on the definition and public disclosure of inside information and the definition of market manipulation,[93] a directive on the fair presentation of investment recommendations and the disclosure of conflicts of interest,[94] and a directive on the definition of inside information.[95] More recently, a new Prospectus Directive[96] was adopted which is intended to require the drafting of one prospectus only, even if securities are offered in more than one member state. It will require such prospectuses to be vetted by a competent authority even where the securities concerned will not be listed. A further major development was the adoption of the Investment Services (MiFID) Directive in 2004.[97] Finally, a third directive on transparency

---

[86] Directives on Admissions of securities to listing (79/279/EEC) and Listing particulars (80/390/EEC).

[87] Directive 89/298/EEC.

[88] Directive on insider dealing (89/592/EEC).

[89] (2001) OJ L184/1.

[90] Directive 2003/6/EC on insider dealing and market manipulation (market abuse) (2003) OJ L96/16.

[91] Established by Commission Decision 2001/528/EC (2001) OJ L191/45.

[92] Regulation 2273/2003/EC (2003) OJ L336/33.

[93] Directive 2003/124/EC (2003) OJ L339/70.

[94] Directive 2003/125/EC (2003) OJ L339/73.

[95] Directive 2004/72/EC (2004) OJ L162/70.

[96] Directive 2003/71/EC on the prospectus to be published when securities are offered to the public or admitted to trading (2003) OJ L345/64. See also Commission Regulation 809/2004 of 29 April 2004 on the content and format of prospectuses.

[97] Directive 2004/39/EC on markets in financial instruments (2004) OJ L 145/1, as amended by Directive 2006/31/EC.

requirements for securities issuers was adopted in 2004,[98] with an implementing directive adopted in March 2007.[99] These are important developments, but it is beyond the scope of the present chapter to discuss these measures in any detail. Appropriate reference will be made in subsequent chapters in this book.

2.5 THE EUROPEAN COMPANY STATUTE[100]

2.5.1 Background

Perhaps one of the most significant contributions in recent years has been the adoption, after a long gestation period, of the European Company Statute.[101] The idea for this particular measure pre-dates establishment of the EU.[102] In 1970, the European Commission presented its first proposal, but negotiations had stalled by 1982. The idea was revived in 1985 when the Commission proposed the two-pronged approach of a Regulation together with a separate directive on worker participation. The latter issue had been one of the main obstacles in previous negotiations, partly due to the conflicting views of the German and UK Governments. Negotiations progressed slowly, but in 2001, the European Company Statute and a directive on worker participation were adopted. The Regulation came into force on 8 October 2004. The purpose of this part is to provide an overview of the general framework of the European Company Statute (ECS),[103] and to note the salient features of its implementation into UK law. For a review of the operation of the ECS across the EU, the reader should consult the European Commission's *Report on the Application of Council Regulation 2157/2001 on the Statute for a European Company*.[104]

---

[98] Directive 2004/109/EC on the harmonisation of transparency requirements in relation to information about issuers whose securities are admitted to trading on a regulated market (2004) OJ L390/38.

[99] Commission Directive 2007/14/EC (2007) OJ L69/27.

[100] This chapter will not consider the European Economic Interest Grouping (see, eg, C Villiers *European Company Law – Towards Democracy?* (Aldershot, Ashgate, 1998) pp 156–158), nor the Regulation on a European Co-operative Society.

[101] Regulation 2157/2001 of 8 October 2001 on the Statute for a European Company (2001) OJ L294/1. See, eg, Ebert 'The European Company on the level playing field of the Community' (2003) 24 Co Law 259.

[102] See Edwards 'The European company – essential tool or eviscerated dream?' (2003) 40 CHL Rev 442. See also C Villiers *European Company Law – Towards Democracy?* (Aldershot, Ashgate, 1998) pp 58–59 and V Edwards *EC Company Law* (Oxford University Press, 1999) pp 399–404.

[103] See further C da Costa and A de Meester Bilreiro *The European Company Statute* (The Hague, Kluwer, 2003).

[104] COM (2010) 676 final.

2.5.2 Implementation into domestic law

Although the Regulation is, by definition, directly applicable,[105] there are several provisions which give member states the option whether to give legal effect to these, and consequently implementing measures need to be adopted by the member states. In addition, the rules on employee involvement are contained in a directive which requires separate implementation in any event. Finally, in order to accommodate the new type of company within the existing legal framework of domestic company law, it is necessary to make some adjustments to this. The Government set out its position on the options given in the ECS and the proposed implementing measures in a consultation document in October 2003.[106] Final implementing measures, the European Public Limited-Liability Company Regulations 2004 (EPLLCR),[107] came into force in October 2004.

The EPLLCR implement both the Directive on Employee involvement (in Part 3 of the EPLLCR) and various aspects of the ECS, especially the various regulatory options given to the member states in the Directive (in Part 4 of the EPLLCR). In addition, Part 2 of the EPLLCR provides for the registration, and generally only specifies which form has to be used for which method of formation. The corresponding provisions of the Companies Act on registration, including registration numbers, etc also apply to the registration of a European Company in the UK.[108]

2.5.3 Scope

Article 1 ECS provides that it will be possible to set up a new form of public limited liability company known as a *Societas Europeae* (SE) which will have legal personality.[109] It must also include the letters 'SE' in its name,[110] and in future, these letters will be reserved for European companies.[111] However, as there is no central Registrar of Companies for the European Union, an SE will have to be registered in one particular member state, ie the state where the SE's registered office is to be located.[112] Registration is subject to compliance with the rules on employee involvement.[113] The rules on registration and disclosure in force

---

[105] See Art 288 TFEU (ex Art 249 EC).
[106] *Implementation of the European Company Statute: The European Public Limited-Liability Company Regulations 2004 – A Consultative Document* (DTI, October 2003).
[107] SI 2004/2326.
[108] Regulation 14 EPLLCR.
[109] Article 1(3) ECS.
[110] Article 11(1) ECS.
[111] Article 11(2) ECS. However, if the abbreviation 'SE' already appears in the names of companies or other business entities, no change in name will be required by the ECS: Art 11(3).
[112] Article 12(1) ECS.
[113] Article 12(2)–(4) ECS; see **2.5.11**, below.

in the member states in accordance with the First Directive[114] also apply to SEs.[115] Notice of the registration of an SE will be published in the *Official Journal.*[116]

Each SE will have statutes, which is the term used in the ECS for the instrument of incorporation and, if contained in a separate document, the statutes.[117] For a UK lawyer, therefore, the statutes comprise the SE's constitution.

2.5.4 Interaction between ECS and domestic law

The ECS requires considerable interaction between the ECS and domestic measures. Article 9 ECS specifies the sources for the rules which will govern the formation and operation of an SE. The starting point is the ECS itself,[118] followed by provisions in the SE's statutes,[119] but only to the extent that the ECS authorises this. Where the ECS does not regulate a matter at all, or only partially, the relevant provisions are member state rules which implement EU measures relating specifically to SEs, followed by the member state rules applicable to public companies where the SE has its registered office and, finally, the SE's statutes in the same way as the constitution of a public company would apply under the rules of the relevant member state.[120] If the SE carries on a business activity for which there are specific national provisions, then these apply in full to the SE.[121] In any other respect, an SE should be treated like any other public limited company in the state where it has its registered office.[122] The extent to which domestic law has a role to play in the regulation of SEs is open to the criticism that this approach largely undermines the objective pursued by the ECS, namely the creation of a pan-European business entity which is not restricted by domestic rules. The ECS contains very little of substance as far as the operation of an SE is concerned, and domestic law will be the main determinant in this regard. Although there has been some approximation of the rules applicable to public companies through the harmonisation programme,[123] there will be areas where there is variation.[124] Consequently, rather than creating one SE, there will, in fact, potentially be as many as 25 different types of SEs.[125] The Commission is

---

[114] 68/151/EEC. See **2.3.1**.
[115] Article 13 ECS.
[116] Article 14 ECS.
[117] Article 6 ECS.
[118] Article 9(1)(a) ECS.
[119] Article 9(1)(b) ECS.
[120] Article 9(1)(c) ECS.
[121] Article 9(3) ECS.
[122] Article 10 ECS.
[123] This has been outlined above at **2.3**.
[124] Now that the draft Fifth Directive has been consigned to the scrap heap, the regulation of directors' duties and shareholder remedies will remain a matter for domestic law.
[125] Ebers 'Company Law in Member States against the Background of Legal

required to report on the operation of the ECS five years after its entry into force (ie by 8 October 2009),[126] which may provide evidence of the severity of this problem.

2.5.5 Share capital

The SE will have a share capital and the liability of a shareholder will be limited to the amount he has subscribed.[127] The capital of an SE must be expressed in euros,[128] and there is a minimum share capital requirement of €120,000,[129] except where the domestic law of the country where the SE is registered requires a higher amount for public companies carrying on particular activities.[130] As far as the rules on capital maintenance and variation, and rules on shares, bonds and similar securities are concerned, the provisions applicable to public companies in the member state where the SE is registered will apply.[131]

2.5.6 Registered and head offices

The registered office and the head office must be located within the same member state.[132] This seems to be a nod in the direction of those member states which adhere to the 'real seat' doctrine.[133] It has been argued[134] that in light of the developing case-law in the context of the freedom of establishment, the compatibility of this provision with the Treaty is in doubt. However, the ECJ has not (yet) explicitly declared the real seat doctrine incompatible with the Treaty, and it seems unlikely, therefore, that this provision is problematic. The Commission is required to consider whether the separation of head office and registered office should be enabled when it reports on the ECS in 2009.[135]

If an SE fails to comply with this requirement, the member state where the SE's registered office is based must take appropriate measures to oblige the SE either to move its head office back to the member state where its registered office is based, or to transfer its registered office in

---

Harmonisation and Competition between legal systems' [2003] ERPL 509, at 515 and Enriques 'Silence is golden: the European Company as a catalyst for company law arbitrage' (2004) 4 JCLS 77.

[126] Article 69 ECS.

[127] Article 1(2) ECS.

[128] Article 4(1) ECS.

[129] Article 4(2) ECS.

[130] Article 4(3) ECS.

[131] Note that the bulk of the capital maintenance and variation rules is provided by the Second Directive (above at **2.3.2**).

[132] Article 7. Member states may require that both offices are based in the same location, but the UK has not exercised this option.

[133] See **2.2**, above.

[134] Ebers 'Company Law in Member States against the Background of Legal Harmonisation and Competition between legal systems' [2003] ERPL 509, at 514.

[135] See Article 69(a).

accordance with the procedure laid down in Art 8.[136] This procedure seeks to ensure that a company may move its registered office to another member state (effectively change its nationality) without having to wind up the SE in its home member state or create a new SE in the host state.[137] However, an SE may not move its registered office if it is subject to proceedings for winding up, liquidation, insolvency, or similar proceedings.[138] The management of the SE must draw up a 'transfer proposal' which has to be publicised,[139] as well as a report explaining and justifying the transfer and its implications for shareholders, creditors and employees.[140] There are then a number of steps to be followed to ensure that all the relevant procedures have been followed before the competent authority[141] in the home member state issues a certificate which confirms that all necessary steps for the transfer have been taken.[142] The transfer of the SE takes effect once it has been registered in the new member state, of which the registry where it was previously registered must be notified.[143] The SE is then deleted from its old register, but until that has happened, third parties may continue to use the old registered office, unless they are aware of the new registered office.[144]

2.5.7 Formation

The bulk of the ECS deals with the procedures for creating an SE. Article 2 ECS specifies the methods by which an SE may be formed, and Title II (Arts 15–37 ECS) lays down the relevant detailed procedures. It must be emphasised that there the ECS does not permit the incorporation of an SE *ab initio*. Furthermore, a general rule is that the companies involved in the creation of an SE must have both their registered and head offices in the Community (but not, it seems, in the same member state).[145]

The formation procedures are now considered in turn. The starting point is that an SE should be formed in accordance with the rules applicable to the formation of public companies in the relevant member state, subject

---

[136] Implemented in reg 73 EPLLCR.

[137] Article 8(1) ECS.

[138] Article 8(15) ECS.

[139] In the *Official Journal* in accordance with Art 13, as well as in line with any applicable domestic requirements: Art 8(2) ECS. In the UK, the SE has to notify its shareholders and creditors in writing of the right to examine the transfer proposal, as well as include on every invoice or order that it intends to transfer to its registered office: reg 56 EPLLCR.

[140] Article 8(3) ECS.

[141] In the UK for this purpose, the Secretary of State: reg 75(a) EPLLCR.

[142] Article 8(8) ECS.

[143] Article 8(10)–(12) ECS.

[144] Article 8(13) ECS.

[145] Although note Art 2(5) ECS, which permits a member state to allow a company to participate in the creation of an SE where its head office is based outside the Community, provided that its registered office is in that member state and the company has a 'real and continuous link' with a (but not 'that'!) member state's economy. The UK has exercised this option: reg 55 EPLLCR.

to any specific rules laid down in the ECS.[146] As already noted, the SE must be registered in the member state where its registered office will be based, and it will acquire legal personality from the date of registration.[147] Interestingly, the ECS contains a provision on 'pre-incorporation' contracts based on Art 7 of the First Company Law Directive,[148] according to which the persons (legal or natural) who performed acts in the SE's name before its registration will be jointly and severally liable for these, unless there is an agreement to the contrary.[149] This is subject to the proviso that the SE does not 'assume the obligations arising out of such acts after its registration',[150] a provision which sits rather uneasily with the UK's approach to pre-incorporation contracts.[151]

2.5.7.1 Merger of two public companies

An SE may be formed if two or more public limited companies from at least two different member states decide to merge.[152] This merger may be carried out in accordance with the procedures for mergers laid down in the Third Company Law Directive[153] and therefore take the form of either a merger by acquisition or a merger by the formation of a new company. However, the ECS imposes several additional requirements. Thus, the management of the merging companies must prepare draft terms of merger which must include numerous details about the SE to be formed, including procedures for employee involvement.[154] Information about the merger must also be published in the national *Gazette* of the relevant member states.[155] Whereas Art 10 of the Third Directive requires a separate experts' report on each of the merging companies, examining the draft terms of merger and reporting to the shareholders, Art 22 ECS allows for the preparation of a single report covering all of the merging companies.

The legality of the merger, as well as the protection of creditors and debenture holders,[156] is subject to the domestic rules applicable to each of the merging companies.[157] Matters relating specifically to the formation of the SE are subject to the rules applicable in the member state where the

---

[146] Article 15(1) ECS.
[147] Article 16(1) ECS.
[148] See **2.3.1**.
[149] Article 16(2) ECS.
[150] Article 16(2) ECS.
[151] See, eg, Twigg-Flesner 'Full Circle: Purported Agent's Right of Enforcement Under s 36C of the Companies Act 1985' (2001) 22 Co Law 274–278.
[152] Article 2(1) ECS and Title II, Section 2.
[153] Directive 78/855/EEC concerning mergers of public limited companies (1978) OJ L295/36. The Directive is limited to domestic mergers, but note the new Tenth Directive. See **2.3.4**.
[154] Article 20 ECS.
[155] Article 21 ECS.
[156] Article 24 ECS.
[157] Article 25 ECS.

SE will have its registered office.[158] A failure to comply with these rules could lead to the winding up of the SE.[159]

The merger itself takes place and the SE is formed on the date when the SE is registered.[160] If the merger is one by acquisition, all assets and liabilities of the companies being acquired are transferred to the acquiring company,[161] and the shareholders of the companies being acquired become shareholders in the acquiring company.[162] The acquiring company then becomes the SE and the acquired companies cease to exist.[163] However, if the merger is one between a parent company and a subsidiary, some of the rules on disclosure, the expert's report and the exchange of shares in the acquired company for those in the acquiring company do not apply.[164]

If the merger is one by formation of a new company, all assets and liabilities of the merging companies are transferred to the new SE, the shareholders of the merging companies become shareholders in the SE and the merging companies cease to exist.[165] In either case, this is subject to any relevant domestic rules protecting third parties with regard to the transfers of assets, rights and obligations by the merging companies.[166]

This procedure is noteworthy for two reasons: first, it is an instance where the ECS, which is designed to operate in a cross-border context, utilises provisions which are based on existing measures which are applicable only in a domestic context. Secondly, the fact that it has been possible to create a procedure for cross-border mergers in the context of SEs appears to have made it possible to pursue a directive on cross-border mergers of public companies.[167]

2.5.7.2 *Formation of holding company as SE*

The second route for the formation of an SE is available both to public and private limited companies.[168] Two or more companies may come together to form a holding SE, provided that at least two are governed by the law of a different member state[169] or have had, for at least 2 years, a subsidiary or branch in another member state.[170] Once again, the

---

[158] Article 26 ECS.
[159] Article 30 ECS.
[160] Article 27(1) ECS.
[161] Article 29(1)(a) ECS.
[162] Article 29(1)(b) ECS.
[163] Article 29(1)(c) and (d) ECS.
[164] Article 31 ECS.
[165] Article 29(2) ECS.
[166] Article 29(3) ECS.
[167] The Tenth Directive has now been adopted. See **2.3.4**.
[168] Article 2(2) ECS.
[169] Article 2(2)(a) ECS.
[170] Article 2(2)(b) ECS.

management of the relevant companies must produce draft terms for the formation of the holding SE, providing similar information as in the case of formation by merger[171] as well as the proportion of the shares in each of the companies which the shareholders must contribute to the formation of the holding SE.[172] There are requirements about publicity,[173] and an expert report for the shareholders on the draft terms of formation must also be produced.[174] Those shareholders who have contributed their shares to the formation of the holding SE will receive shares in the SE.[175] Member states are given the option to adopt provisions for the protection of minority shareholders opposed to the formation of a holding SE, creditors, and employees.[176]

2.5.7.3   Creation of subsidiary SE

All companies within the definition of Art 54 TFEU[177] and other legal bodies may form a subsidiary company that will take the shape of an SE, provided that at least two of these are governed by the law of a different member state[178] or have had, for at least 2 years, a subsidiary or branch in another member state.[179] The only further provision in the ECS is Art 36, which makes this subject to the rules applicable to the formation of a subsidiary in the form of a public limited company under domestic law.

An SE will be able to create subsidiaries which may also take the form of an SE, including wholly owned subsidiaries. Where the subsidiary is also an SE, but wholly owned by its parent SE, there may be a conflict with national rules requiring at least two shareholders for public companies,[180] but Art 3(2) requires that this rule is disapplied in this context and that the provision implementing the Twelfth Directive on single-member *private* companies[181] apply *mutatis mutandis*. This is therefore another instance where existing rules are utilised in the context of the ECS.

2.5.7.4   Conversion of existing public company into an SE

Finally, a single public limited company may be converted into an SE provided that it has had a subsidiary incorporated in another member

---

[171]   In particular, details required by Art 20(1)(a)–(c) and (f)–(i).
[172]   Article 32(2) ECS.
[173]   Article 32(3) ECS.
[174]   Article 32(4) ECS.
[175]   Article 33(4) ECS.
[176]   Article 34. The UK has not adopted any specific provisions over and above those that would already apply.
[177]   Set out above at **2.2.1.**
[178]   Article 2(3)(a) ECS.
[179]   Article 2(3)(b) ECS.
[180]   In the Companies Act 1985, s 1(1) was such a restriction, but s 7(1) of the Companies Act 2006 now states that a single person can form a company.
[181]   Directive 89/667/EEC (1989) OJ L395/40, now Directive 2009/102/EC. See above at **2.3.7.**

state for at least 2 years.[182] There are the usual requirements for the drawing up of draft terms of conversion,[183] as well as the experts' report.[184] The conversion must be approved by the general meeting, following the procedure in domestic law which implements Art 7 of the Third Directive.[185] This requires a majority of at least two-thirds, although member states may permit a simple majority where at least half of the subscribed capital is represented.[186] Once all the procedural steps have been taken, the conversion takes effect. The conversion will neither result in the winding up of the company that has been converted, nor in the creation of a new legal entity.[187] It is therefore essentially a change of status of the company concerned, and the new SE is not permitted to move to another member state at the same time as the conversion takes place.[188]

2.5.8 Structure

Title III ECS specifies how the running of an SE should be organised. An SE must consist of a general meeting of shareholders, and either a supervisory and management organ or an administrative organ ('the SE organs').[189] There is therefore a choice between the 'one-tier' and 'two-tier' system.[190] Irrespective of which system is adopted, membership of SE organs is limited to a maximum of 6 years, although reappointments are possible.[191] Insofar as this is not against the relevant domestic law where the SE's registered office is based, a company may be a member of the SE's organs, although that company must designate a natural person to act on its behalf.[192] No one may be a member of the SE organs (or act as representative) if they are disqualified from being a member of the corresponding organ in a public company in the state where the SE's registered office is located, either by law or as the result of disqualification proceedings.[193] The SE's statutes must specify any transactions which require either authorisation from the supervisory organ in the two-tier system or an express decision by the administrative

---

[182] Article 2(4) ECS.
[183] Article 37(4) ECS.
[184] Article 37(6) ECS.
[185] Article 37(7) ECS.
[186] For the UK's position, see Companies Act 2006, ss 895–904 [CA 1985, ss 425–427A]. A three-quarters majority would be required.
[187] Article 37(2) ECS.
[188] Article 37(3) ECS.
[189] Article 38 ECS.
[190] Note that Art 39(5) ECS provides that member states which do not have rules for a two-tier system in relation to domestic public companies, such as the UK, may adopt specific rules in relation to SEs. Such rules would go beyond the provisions in the ECS requiring the possibility to incorporate an SE with a two-tier system. However, the UK has not adopted specific rules.
[191] Article 46 ECS.
[192] Article 47(1) ECS.
[193] Article 47(2) ECS.

organ in the one-tier system.[194] The default quorum rules for meetings of the SE's organs are that half of the members are to be present, and decisions to be carried by half of those present.[195] Finally, members of SE organs are subject to a duty of confidentiality,[196] as well as the same duties that would be required of directors in public limited companies in the member state where the SE's registered office is located.[197]

Under the two-tier system, the management organ is appointed and removed by the supervisory organ and responsible for managing the SE.[198] Membership of the management organ precludes membership of the supervisory organ, and vice versa.[199] The number of members should be determined by the SE's statutes, although member states may fix a minimum or a maximum number.[200] The supervisory organ is responsible for supervising the management board and is appointed by the general meeting.[201] It may also elect a chairman. The management organ must report to the supervisory organ at least once every 3 months about the SE's performance.[202]

Where the SE uses the one-tier system, it has full responsibility for managing the SE.[203] If employee participation is regulated in accordance with the rules of Companion Directive 2001/86/EC,[204] there must be a minimum of three members.[205] The members of the administrative organ are appointed by the general meeting. The organ must elect a chairman, subject to the requirement that if half of the members of the organ are appointed by employees, the chairman must be a shareholder representative.[206] The administrative organ must meet at least once every 3 months.[207]

The general meeting of the SE will have responsibility for certain matters by virtue of the ECS or companion Directive 2001/86/EC, as well as under the law applicable to public limited companies in the member state

---

[194] Article 48(1) ECS. Member states may provide that the supervisory board can make additional categories of transactions subject to authorisation. The UK has not made use of this provision.

[195] Article 50 ECS.

[196] Article 49 ECS.

[197] Article 51 ECS.

[198] Article 39(1) and (2) ECS. Member states are given the option to make the appointment of managing director(s) mandatory. The UK has not made use of this option.

[199] Article 39(3) ECS.

[200] Article 39(4) ECS. The UK requires a minimum of at least two members for the management organ of an SE (reg 61 EPLLCR), reflecting the requirement in the Companies Act 2006, s 154(2) [CA 1985, s 282], that public companies must have at least two directors.

[201] Article 40 ECS.

[202] Article 41 ECS.

[203] Article 43(1) ECS.

[204] Discussed below at **2.5.11.**

[205] Article 43(2) ECS.

[206] Article 45 ECS.

[207] Article 44 ECS.

where the SE is registered.[208] Generally, the rules and procedures for convening a general meeting are left for the relevant domestic rules on public companies,[209] although the ECS requires that a meeting be held at least once each calendar year and within 6 months of the end of the SE's financial year.[210] Furthermore, one or more shareholders holding at least 10% of the SE's subscribed capital may request the SE to convene a meeting, and, if this is not done within 2 months, a court or competent administrative authority[211] may order that the meeting be convened or allow the shareholders themselves to do so.[212] The general meeting has the power to amend the SE's statutes by a majority of no less than two-thirds[213] of the votes cast.[214] Furthermore, where decisions by the general meeting affect the rights of a particular class of shares, a separate vote of the affected class must be held.[215]

2.5.9 Accounting

Article 61 ECS provides that an SE is subject to the rules on the preparation of annual and consolidated accounts which apply to public limited companies in the member state where its registered office is situated.[216] Credit and financial institutions will be subject to the domestic law provisions implementing Directive 2000/12/EC relating to the taking up and pursuit of the business of credit institutions,[217] and insurance companies will be subject to the rules in Directive 91/674/EEC[218] on annual and consolidated accounts of insurance undertakings.[219]

2.5.10 Winding up, liquidation, insolvency and cessation of payments

As far as winding up, liquidation, insolvency, cessation of payments and similar matters are concerned, an SE will be governed by the rules applicable to public companies in the member state where its registered

---

[208] Article 52 ECS.
[209] Article 53 ECS.
[210] Article 54(1) ECS. If the SE carries on a type of business for which domestic law requires more frequent meetings, then the domestic rules apply.
[211] The Secretary of State is the competent authority: reg 75(a) EPLLCR.
[212] Article 55 ECS. This procedure differs somewhat from the requisitioning procedure in the Companies Act 2006, ss 303–305 [CA 1985, s 368]. See **13.7.2.**
[213] In the UK, this would be three-quarters (75%), in line with domestic provisions.
[214] Article 59 ECS.
[215] Article 60 ECS.
[216] These will be based on the Fourth and Seventh Directives.
[217] (2000) OJ L126/1.
[218] (1991) OJ L374/7.
[219] Article 62 ECS.

office is based.[220] Where such procedures are initiated, this must be published in the *Official Journal*, as well as in accordance with the relevant domestic rules.[221]

The ECS also provides for the conversion of an SE into a public limited liability company governed by the law of the member state where the SE has its registered office, although no such conversion will be permitted within two years from registration as an SE, or before two sets of annual accounts have been approved.[222] Management must prepare draft terms of conversions and a report justifying the proposal to convert the SE into a domestic public company,[223] and an expert's report certifying that the company's assets are at least equivalent to its capital must be drawn up.[224] There then has to be a vote of the general meeting to approve the conversion.[225] Significantly, the conversion will not result in the winding up of the SE, nor in the creation of a new public company following the conversion.[226]

2.5.11   Employee involvement

As noted previously, the ECS regulation is supplemented by Directive 2001/86/EC on the involvement of employees in the SE.[227] This has been implemented in Part 3 of the EPLLCR. Its objective is to govern the involvement of employees in the affairs of an SE.[228]

As soon as the decision is taken to form an SE, by whichever route, a special negotiating body representing the employees of the participating companies must be set up in accordance with the procedure laid down in Art 3 (implemented via regs 16–26 and 29–31 EPLLCR).[229] The purpose of this negotiating body is to come to an agreement on the arrangements for the involvement of employees within the SE.[230] Although parties are free to determine their arrangements, the Directive requires that the agreement covers, among other things, the composition of the body representing employees, its resources, the frequency of meetings, and the implementation of any consultation procedures that may be established. Member states are required to lay down standard rules which regulate the involvement of employees in an SE, and these need to satisfy the

---

[220] Article 63 ECS.
[221] Article 65 ECS.
[222] Article 66(1) ECS.
[223] Article 66(3) ECS.
[224] Article 66(5) ECS.
[225] Article 66(6) ECS.
[226] Article 66(2) ECS.
[227] Directive 2001/86/EC supplementing the Statute for a European Company with regard to the involvement of employees (2001) OJ L294/22.
[228] Article 1(1) of the Directive.
[229] For present purposes, it is unnecessary to discuss the exact procedure in detail.
[230] Article 4(1) of the Directive, implemented in regs 27–28 EPLLCR.

provisions specified in the Annex to the Directive.[231] The negotiating body may agree to adopt these rules expressly, or they may come into effect by default if negotiations have not been concluded within the time-limit specified in Art 5.[232] Once an agreement has been adopted and a body of employee representatives has been established, the representative body and the competent organ in the SE are required to work together in a spirit of co-operation.[233]

2.6 TOWARDS A EUROPEAN PRIVATE COMPANY

After some debate, the European Commission proposed a Statute for a European Private Company ('SPE') in 2008.[234] This forms part of the Commission's action package towards a 'Small Business Act for Europe' and is intended to make it easier for SMEs to operate throughout the internal market. In many ways, the proposal for the SPE follows the lead set by the ECS. The proposal deals with the nature of an SPE, its formation (in which respect there are no restrictions, and in contrast to the ECS, an SPE can be set up from scratch), shares and shareholding, capital requirements (a minimum capital of €1) and distributions, internal organisation (with a large degree of freedom given to SPE shareholders), employee participation (as required under the national law in the country of incorporation), transfer of the registered office, and restructuring, dissolution and nullity. At the time of writing, there was some uncertainty as to when the Statute for the SPE would be adopted, following the failure to reach unanimous support of a compromise text presented in May 2011.

2.7 CONCLUSIONS

This chapter has revealed the extent to which company law, and the law relating to public companies in particular, is governed by measures based on European directives and regulations. The extensive harmonisation programme of both core company law and the rules on investor protection, adopted to facilitate the completion of the internal market, has left its mark on domestic company law legislation. Furthermore, as the internal market becomes more attractive for companies, the right to move freely and become established in another member state has become more significant, as evidenced in the string of ECJ cases on this matter. Despite its impact, European company law has not displaced domestic

---

[231] Article 7(1) of the Directive (reg 32 EPLLCR).

[232] Article 7(1) (reg 32 EPLLCR). The time-limits in Art 5 are 6 months after establishing the negotiating body, subject to an extension by a further 6 months if the negotiating parties so agree.

[233] Article 9 of the Directive (reg 27 EPLLCR).

[234] COM (2008) 396 final. This proposal is based on Art 308 EC, which requires only that the European Parliament is 'consulted'. It completed its first reading in March 2009. The Council had been unable to agree on a final text (which requires unanimity) when it considered the proposal most recently in May 2011. The future of the proposal remains unclear at the time of writing.

initiatives; indeed, the ECS is based on a principle of mutuality, leaving significant aspects of the operation of this new type of business vehicle to the relevant laws of the member state where the SE is registered.

It is hoped that this chapter will assist the reader in placing domestic company law, discussed in the remainder of this book, in the relevant European context.

CHAPTER 3

LEGAL PERSONALITY: ITS CONSEQUENCES AND LIMITATIONS

3.1 INTRODUCTION

The general issue broached in this chapter is that of the basic principle of corporate personality. The separate[1] personality of the company is an inevitable consequence for a company (or any other body) upon which the privileged status of incorporation has been conferred. This is a judicially created doctrine but the courts have nevertheless shown themselves prepared, when moved by sufficiently strong policy considerations, to depart from this fundamental principle. This process is usually termed 'lifting the veil of incorporation'. The difficulty is to discover by what principle or principles the courts are guided in determining whether to adhere to the safe rule of respecting the separate legal persona of the company or whether to 'lift the veil'. It will be seen that this is an area in which the legislature has intervened on an *ad hoc* basis, especially in the case of 'groups' of holding and subsidiary companies.

Particular attention will also be given to the problem posed, in the case of 'groups', by the separate legal personality of each company in the group. Legislation has created a statutory regime to govern the relationship between member companies in a group for certain statutory purposes. In more general terms, it is necessary to look to case-law for guidance. Here, separate legal personality is usually respected.

Another aspect of legal personality dealt with in this chapter concerns how far the state of mind of directors or senior managers can be attributed to a company for the purpose of making that company criminally or civilly liable.

3.2 THE CONSEQUENCES OF INCORPORATION

Lord Justice Lindley gave this definition of the old unincorporated joint stock company: 'I understand by a company – an unincorporated company – some association of members, the shares of which are transferable. As distinguished from a partnership, I know of nothing else

---

[1] Ie separate from that of the company's directors, shareholders, employees, creditors, etc.

except the transferability of shares.'[2] But with regard to an *incorporated* company there are other important distinctions: eg that, while in an ordinary partnership each partner is personally responsible for all the debts contracted by the firm, in an incorporated company the members have no individual liability to its creditors for debts owing by the company and their personal liability is satisfied if they pay the calls properly made upon them by the company or its liquidator. These calls may be limited in amount or unlimited, accordingly as the company is limited or unlimited, but they are enforceable only by the company or its liquidator. In most limited companies the shares will have been fully paid at the time of allotment. The company, moreover, is a distinct legal personality,[3] and can own and deal with property, sue and be sued in its own name,[4] and contract on its own behalf. The members are not personally entitled to the benefits or liable for the burdens arising thereby: their rights are confined to receiving from the company their share of the profits or, after a winding-up, of the surplus assets, and their liabilities to paying the amounts due from them to the company. The creditors of a limited company accordingly know that they cannot, as in the case of an ordinary partnership, look to the whole property of the individual members to pay them, but are restricted to the property of the company, including such further amounts (if any) as the members are liable to pay in respect of shares held by them in the capital, and in the case of companies limited by guarantee the sums payable in accordance with the guarantee contained in the memorandum of association.

An incorporated company is a 'person' within the meaning of the Interpretation Act 1978, unless the contrary intention appears.[5] A company cannot, however, be convicted under a section which inflicts only imprisonment as the penalty.[6] It can be fined for contempt of court, although it cannot be attached.[7] Any judgment or order against a company wilfully disobeyed may, by leave of the court or a judge, be

---

[2]   *R v Registrar of Joint Stock Companies* [1891] 2 QB 598, at 610.

[3]   Where a partnership of eight persons transferred their property to a company in exchange for shares in the same proportions as their interests in the partnership, this was held to be a sale to a distinct person: 'We have two parties, one party consisting of several individuals, and the other party consisting of a corporation.' per Lindley LJ: *John Foster & Sons v Commissioners of Inland Revenue* [1894] 1 QB 516, at 528.

[4]   A limited company can maintain an action for defamation: *South Hetton Coal Co v North Eastern News Association* [1894] 1 QB 133; *D & L Caterers & Jackson v D'Ajou* [1945] KB 364. A company cannot appear in person, but must be represented in proceedings: *Tritonia Ltd v Equity and Law Life Assurance Soc* [1943] AC 584 (HL) (except in the county courts: *Kinnell & Co v Harding* [1918] 1 KB 405 (CA)). Further, a company cannot be subpoenaed to give evidence: *Penn-Texas Corp v Murat Anstalt* [1964] 1 QB 40 (CA). But see CPR, r 39.6, which allows a company to be represented at trial by an employee if authorised by the company to appear and if the court gives permission.

[5]   See s 5 and Sch 1. This applies to Acts passed in or after 1889: Sch 2, para 4(1)(a).

[6]   *Hawke v E Hulton & Co* [1909] 2 KB 93. The criminal liability of companies is discussed further at **3.7**.

[7]   *R v JG Hammond & Co* [1914] 2 KB 866. As to the liability of a director for a contempt by his company, see *Biba Ltd v Stratford Investments* [1972] 3 WLR 390.

enforced by sequestration against the property of the company, or by attachment against its directors or other officers, or by writ of sequestration against their property.[8] A company may be convicted of offences where the punishment is a fine.[9] A company may be 'a respectable and responsible person' within the meaning of those words in a licence to assign leasehold property.[10] A commercial company can make a complaint under the Broadcasting Act 1996 to the Broadcasting Standards Commission in respect of 'fairness' and 'unwarranted infringement of fairness'.[11]

3.3   THE ADVANTAGES OF INCORPORATION

It is conventional in a textbook on company law to say something about the advantages of incorporation. This involves essentially a comparison of the limited company and the partnership. Most of the more obvious advantages of the corporate form (limited liability, the vesting of the business assets in the company, suing and being sued in the company's name, perpetual succession and transferable shares) have already been indicated earlier.[12] Other advantages (such as the ability to create a floating charge over its assets or to make a public issue of its securities) will become apparent in later chapters.[13] There are also disadvantages in using the corporate form (especially in the case of the limited company). As compared with a partnership there is a much greater degree of formality (as well as publicity and expense) attendant not only upon the formation of a limited company[14] but also required throughout its life.[15] Furthermore, the rules about directors' and shareholders' meetings (as well as resolutions and voting) are likely to be observed more in the breach than honoured in the observance in the case of the really small private company. The flexible rules about the internal conduct of partnerships are more realistic and appropriate for the small business. The advantage to partners in being able readily to withdraw their capital from a partnership is now to some extent available even in the case of limited companies. The Companies Act 2006 allows private companies considerable freedom to purchase or to redeem issued share capital.[16] It should also be noted that the modern partnership has many of the practical advantages of a corporate body. It can sue and be sued in its

---

[8]   CPR, Sch 1, and see: *Benabo v William Jay & Partners* [1941] Ch 52; *Phonographic Performance v Amusement Caterers (Peckham) Ltd* [1964] Ch 195. This does not apply in Scotland.

[9]   *Pharmaceutical Society v London and Provincial Supply Association* (1880) 5 App Cas 857, at 869; *Chuter v Freeth & Pocock Ltd* [1911] 2 KB 832.

[10]   *Ideal Film Renting Co v Nielsen* [1921] 1 Ch 575; *Willmott v London Road Car Co* [1910] 2 Ch 525. See also *In re Greater London Property Ltd's Lease* [1959] 1 WLR 503.

[11]   *R v Broadcasting Standards Commission, ex parte BBC* [2000] 3 All ER 989 (CA).

[12]   See **3.2**.

[13]   See Chapters 10 and 19.

[14]   See Chapter 4.

[15]   See Chapter 14.

[16]   See Part 18, Chapter 5. See Chapter 13.

own name. With a properly drafted agreement, it can 'survive' over long periods of time despite the death or retirement of individual partners.[17] The former limit of 20 partners has now been abolished.

Ultimately, the question of choice as between the company or partnership form will depend upon the impact of taxation. In the case of companies, corporation tax (and capital gains tax) apply. Income tax will apply to the salaries of directors and in respect of the dividends distributed to shareholders.[18] Partners are subject to income tax and capital gains tax on their trading profits. In the case of the small business the advice given by professional advisers will take into consideration the level of trading income of the business and the number of participants in the business, as well as their separate sources of earned or investment income. Obviously the larger the scale of any business enterprise the more likely it is that there will be tax advantages in the corporate form. At a certain level this will become essential.

3.3.1 Limited liability partnerships

A new hybrid form of business organisation was created by the Limited Liability Partnerships Act 2000.[19] In brief, the essential features of a limited liability partnership (LLP) registered under the Act, which are drawn from existing partnership and company law, are as follows. An LLP is a body corporate with a separate legal personality and unlimited capacity, that is it can do anything a natural person can do. The liability of individual members is limited in accordance with their stake in the LLP. It must be registered with the Registrar of Companies, with information including its name, registered office and a list of its members. It must file an annual report and accounts. It will be taxed as a partnership. Certain features of company law in respect of creditor protection and winding-up apply to an LLP.[20]

LLPs do offer an alternative to limited companies and in some circumstances have tax advantages. However, their most significant drawback is the lack of the sort of default provisions found in the

---

[17] It does not of course enjoy limited liability, and the partners' separate estates are at risk to creditors during the continuance of the partnership – not just on winding-up as in the case of an unlimited company. It has been seen that the Limited Partnerships Act 1907 has been little used. The small private company is of much more utility. As to the Limited Liability Partnership Act 2000, see **3.3.1** below.

[18] See further *Gore-Browne on Companies* (Jordans, 45th edn, loose-leaf), Chaps 47 and 48.

[19] Although originally intended to be restricted to regulated professional partnerships, in its enacted form it is available to any two or more persons carrying on a trade or profession. A proper analysis of the Act's provisions is beyond the scope of a textbook on registered companies. See J Whittacker, J Machell and C Ives *The Law of Limited Liability Partnerships* (Jordans, 2004).

[20] Notably the provisions on fraudulent and wrongful trading and the provisions relating to the disqualification of directors.

legislation applying to companies and partnerships.[21] In the case of an LLP this is left to the formation documentation to be drafted prior to its registration.

3.4 THE PRINCIPLE OF CORPORATE PERSONALITY

The separate personality of a company and its entity as distinct from its shareholders was established by the House of Lords in *Salomon v Salomon & Co*,[22] where it was held that however large the proportion of the shares and debentures owned by one man, even if the other shares were held in trust for him, the company's acts were not his acts, nor were its liabilities his liabilities; nor is it otherwise if he has sole control of its affairs as governing director.[23] It is important to note that the House of Lords found no evidence whatever of fraud or deliberate abuse of the corporate form. Indeed, Salomon did his best to rescue his company by cancelling the debentures he took and reissuing them to an outside creditor who provided fresh loan capital. The *Salomon* decision gave express recognition to what were even then called 'one man' companies. The modern practice of having undercapitalised private companies (with the founding shareholders as creditors in their own company) stems from this case. This is certainly a use of the corporate form not contemplated when limited liability was made generally available.

The principle of the *Salomon* case,[24] that a company is a legal entity distinct from its members, is strictly applied by the courts whenever it is sought to attribute the rights or liabilities of a company to its shareholders, or regard the property of a company as belonging in law or equity to the shareholders. Thus the fact that one shareholder controls all or virtually all the shares in a company is not a sufficient reason for ignoring the legal personality of the company.[25] Further, a company cannot be characterised as an agent of its shareholders unless there is clear evidence to show that the company was in fact acting as an agent in a particular transaction or series of transactions.[26] Likewise, the property of a company in no sense belongs to its members.[27] The company is not a

---

[21] Eg the Table A model set of articles that can be adopted when registering a limited company.

[22] [1897] AC 22.

[23] *Inland Revenue Commissioners v Sansom* [1921] 2 KB 492. See also *Re Hydrodam (Corby) (in Liquidation)* [1994] BCC 161. The fact that a body corporate was director of a company did not necessarily mean that that body corporate's directors were therefore directors of the company.

[24] [1897] AC 22. See *FJ Neale (Glasgow) Ltd v Vickery* 1974 SLT 88 for an application of the *Salomon* principle.

[25] See, eg, *Tunstall v Steigmann* [1962] 2 QB 593 (CA); *Lee v Lee's Air Farming Ltd* [1961] AC 12 (PC).

[26] *Ebbw Vale UDC v South Wales Traffic Area Licensing Authority* [1951] 2 KB 366 (CA); *Pegler v Graven* [1952] 2 QB 69 (CA).

[27] *Bank voor Handel en Scheepvaart NV v Slatford* [1953] 1 QB 248. See further *Coleg Elidyr (Caerphill Communities Wales) Ltd v Koeller* [2005] 2 BCLC 379, at 401.

trustee of its property for its shareholders even where the directors have been appointed trustees of some or all of the shares in a company.[28] A shareholder does not have an insurable interest in the assets or business of the company.[29]

3.4.1   Corporate personality and directors' liability

As a matter of general principle, corporate personality will prevent directors from being held liable in respect of company obligations. In *Williams v Natural Life Health Foods,*[30] the House of Lords, overruling the Court of Appeal,[31] carefully restricted the circumstances in which a director of a company would be personally liable to plaintiffs for loss which they suffered as a result of negligent advice given them by the company. First, there had to be an assumption of responsibility. This assumption had to be determined objectively. The primary focus had to be on exchanges (including statements and conduct) between the director and the plaintiffs. Secondly, the test of reliance on the assumption was not simply one of reliance in fact but whether the plaintiffs could reasonably rely on the assumption of responsibility.

The action in *Williams* was originally brought primarily against the company on the basis of the 'extended *Hedley Byrne* principle' established by the House of Lords in *Henderson v Merrett Syndicates Ltd.*[32] This decision settled that the assumption of responsibility principle enunciated in *Hedley Byrne* is not confined to statements but may apply to any assumption of responsibility for the provision of services.[33] In *Williams* the company, after judgment for financial loss had been obtained against it, became insolvent and was wound up. The proceedings were continued instead against the defendant director when the judgment against the company remained unsatisfied.

In analysing the 'triangular' relationship between the plaintiff, the company and the director, Lord Steyn observed that:[34]

> 'the *internal* arrangements between a director and his company cannot be the foundation of a director's personal liability in tort. The inquiry must be whether the director, or anybody on his behalf conveyed directly or indirectly to the [plaintiffs] that the director assumed personal responsibility towards [them].'

---

[28]   *Butt v Kelsen* [1952] Ch 197 (CA).
[29]   *Macaura v Northern Assurance Co* [1925] AC 619 (HL (Ir)).
[30]   [1998] 1 WLR 830.
[31]   [1997] 1 BCLC 131. See the judgment of Hirst LJ at 152, where a more flexible approach to imposing tort liability on a director was taken.
[32]   [1995] 2 AC 145.
[33]   See Lord Steyn, [1998] 1 WLR 830, at 834–837. The other members of the court concurred in Lord Steyn's judgment.
[34]   Ibid, at 695.

Lord Steyn emphasised the relevance of the basic concept of corporate personality in differentiating between the tort liability of a company and its director. He observed that 'in the context of directors of companies the general principle must not 'set at nought' the protection of limited liability'.[35] The essential issue is that of corporate personality:[36]

> 'What matters is not that liability of the shareholders of a company is limited but that a company is a separate entity, distinct from its directors, servants or other agents. The trader who incorporates a company to which he transfers his business creates a legal person on whose behalf he may afterwards act as director. For present purposes, his position is the same as if he had sold his business to another individual and agreed to act on his behalf. Thus the issue in this case is not peculiar to companies. Whether the principal is a company or a natural person, someone acting on his behalf may incur personal liability in tort as well as imposing vicarious or attributed liability upon his principal. But in order to establish personal liability under the principle of *Hedley Byrne*, which requires the existence of a special relationship between plaintiff and tortfeasor, it is not sufficient that there should have been a special relationship with the principal. There must have been an assumption of responsibility such as to create a special relationship with the director or employee himself.'

The House of Lords concluded that in the circumstances of *Williams* no such duty existed.[37]

In later Court of Appeal cases the reasoning in *Williams* has been carefully followed to determine whether there has been a personal assumption of liability. Liability in respect of negligent misrepresentation may arise where private negotiations between the parties support this inference.[38] A director (and controlling shareholder) can be held liable as a joint tortfeasor with the company in an action for infringement of copyright.[39] Chadwick LJ stressed, however, that a director will not be held liable 'if he does no more than carry out his constitutional role in the governance of the company – that is to say, by voting at board meetings. That, I think, is what policy requires if a proper recognition is to be given to the company as a separate legal person.' He said that for liability to arise, it had to be shown either that the director committed the breach of copyright personally or that he procured or induced such breach by the company or 'that in some other way he and [the company] joined together in concerted action to secure that those acts were done'.[40]

---

[35] Lord Steyn refers to the judgment of Waite LJ in the Court of Appeal. See [1997] 1 BCLC 131, at 154 and Cook P in *Trevor Ivory Ltd v Anderson* [1992] NZLR 517, at 524.

[36] [1998] 1 WLR 830, at 835.

[37] Ibid, at 838.

[38] *Partco Group Ltd v Wragg* [2002] EWCA Civ 594, [2002] 2 BCLC 323.

[39] *MCA Records Inc v Charly Records Ltd* [2003] 1 BCLC 93.

[40] Ibid, at 116. See also *Konnikliske Philips v Princo Digital Disc GmBH* [2004] BCLC 50 at 53–54.

The House of Lords has refused to extend the reasoning of its own decision in *Williams* to liability for fraudulent misstatements by a director. Here, while the company becomes vicariously liable on ordinary principles, the director committing the tort of deceit remains personally liable.[41]

3.4.2 Controlling shareholders and the corporate veil

A controlling shareholder may also be an employee for the purpose of claiming rights under the Employment Rights Act 1996. Whether or not an employee/employer relationship exists will be determined by having regard to all relevant facts. Having a controlling shareholding will certainly be a significant fact and in some cases may be decisive of the issue. This is a different question from whether there is a controlling shareholder.[42]

3.5 LIFTING THE VEIL OF INCORPORATION

Notwithstanding the principle of *Salomon's* case[43] there are certain situations where the courts have shown themselves willing to 'lift the veil of incorporation', that is to ignore or set aside the separate legal personality of a company. It is not possible to formulate any single principle as the basis for these decisions, nor are all the decisions, as to when the separate legal entity of the company must be respected or when it may be disregarded, entirely consistent with one another.[44]

It is well established that the courts will not allow the corporate form to be used for the purposes of fraud,[45] or as a device to evade a contractual or other legal obligation. Thus in *Gilford Motor Co v Horne*[46] the respondent had contracted with the appellant company not to solicit its customers when he left its employment. On ceasing employment, Horne formed a company to carry on a competing business and this company started to solicit Gilford Motor Co's customers. The court granted an injunction to enforce the covenant not to solicit against both Horne and the company he had formed as a cloak for his activities. In *Jones v*

---

[41] *Standard Chartered Bank v Pakistan National Shipping Corp* [2002] UKHL 43, [2003] 1 AC 959. Compare the agency power of directors to bind their company contractually: see **6.19** to **6.33**, below.

[42] *Secretary of State for Trade and Industry v Bottrill* [1999] BCC 177 (CA). See *Ringway Roadmarking v Adbruf Ltd* [1998] 2 BCLC 625 as to a clause in a contract entitling parties to terminate if a 'controlling shareholder in a party' passed to new ownership. The transfer of such control within a group of companies was not 'new ownership'.

[43] [1897] AC 22.

[44] See, eg, *Wurzel v Houghton Main Home Service Ltd* [1937] 1 KB 380 and *Trebanog Working Men's Club and Institute Ltd v Macdonald* [1940] 1 KB 576.

[45] *Re Darby* [1911] 1 KB 95. See also *Wallersteiner v Moir (No 1)* [1974] 1 WLR 991 (CA), at 1013.

[46] [1933] Ch 935 (CA).

Lipman[47] the defendant had entered into a contract to sell his house. He sought to escape his obligation to complete by conveying the property to a company in which he and a nominee of his controlled all the shares and were the directors. Russell J, in granting a decree of specific performance, described the company as 'the creature of the first defendant, a device and a sham, a mask which he holds before his face in an attempt to avoid recognition by the eye of equity'.[48]

In some cases, the courts have found on the particular evidence before them that a holding company was in fact carrying on a business through the agency of its subsidiary company. It is important to note that the mere fact that one company is the subsidiary of another, even a 'wholly owned' subsidiary, is not by itself sufficient to make the subsidiary an agent of its holding company.[49] The activities of the subsidiary must be so closely controlled and directed by the parent company that the latter can be regarded as merely an agent conducting the parent company's business.[50]

For certain purposes, the courts, while respecting the separate legal personality of a company, have treated the conduct or characteristics of its directors, managers or members as attributable to the company itself. This attribution does not in the true sense involve 'lifting the veil of incorporation'. For example, where the courts have had to determine the residence of a company, they look not to the place of registration but to the way the company is actually managed in order to find where the centre or centres of management are in fact located.[51] The cases examined in **3.6** and **3.7**, on the attribution of *mens rea* to a company for the purposes of criminal or civil liability, are another illustration of the same principle. Another example is *Re Greater London Property Ltd's Lease*[52] where a subsidiary company was held a responsible assignee of a lease despite the landlord's contention that it was not financially viable without the support of its holding company. Danckwerts J refused to disregard the real economic link between the holding and subsidiary company. Again,

---

[47] [1962] 1 WLR 832. See also *H & H Elliott Ltd v Pierson* [1948] Ch 852.

[48] [1962] 1 WLR 832, at 836. See also *Re FG (Films) Ltd* [1953] 1 WLR 483 and *Merchandise Transport Ltd v BTC* [1962] 2 QB 173. See further *International Investment Co v Adhams* [1998] BCC 134.

[49] *Kodak Ltd v Clark* [1903] 1 KB 505 (CA); *Gramophone & Typewriters Ltd v Stanley* [1908] 2 KB 89 (CA); *IRC v Sansom* [1921] 2 KB 492 (CA).

[50] See the judgment of Atkinson J, in *Smith Stone and Knight Ltd v Birmingham Corporation* [1939] 4 All ER 116 and the cases there cited. See also *Firestone Tyre and Rubber Co v Llewellin* [1957] 1 WLR 464 (HL). As to lifting the veil in the case of groups of companies, see **3.8**.

[51] See, eg, *De Beers Consolidated Mining Ltd v Howe* [1906] AC 455 (HL) and *Unit Construction Co Ltd v Bullock* [1960] AC 351 (HL). See further *Wood v Holden (Inspector of Taxes)* [2006] 2 BCLC 210 (CA).

[52] [1959] 1 WLR 503. A similarly realistic approach can be found in other cases concerning remedies for minority shareholders (eg *SCWS v Meyer* [1959] AC 324, and *Ebrahimi v Westbourne Galleries Ltd* [1973] 3 AC 360 (HL)) and with the construction of the objects clause of the memorandum (*Charterbridge Corporation Ltd v Lloyds Bank Ltd* [1970] Ch 62).

this is not a true case of 'lifting the veil of incorporation'. In *The Abbey, Malvern Wells Ltd v Ministry of Local Government and Planning*,[53] a limited company was formed to run a school for the profit of its shareholders. Later it was converted into a non-profit-making body by vesting its shares in charitable trustees and altering its articles to provide that it would be run by the trustees. Danckwerts J held that the company could claim charitable status so as to exempt it from paying a development charge under the Town and Country Planning Act 1947. This decision is not inconsistent with the generally established rule that a company is not a trustee for its members. In determining whether for a particular statutory purpose it had charitable status, Danckwerts J realistically attributed the characteristics of its shareholders as trustees of a charitable trust to the company itself.

Where fraud or deliberate breach of trust can be shown, the courts show a willingness to set aside the corporate form even where this involves a network of interlocking foreign and English companies. The plaintiff companies in *Re a Company Ltd*[54] were in liquidation and had brought an action against the defendant alleging deceit and breach of trust. The defendant, in the knowledge that the plaintiff companies were insolvent, had disposed of his personal assets so that they were held by a network of interlocking foreign and English companies and trusts so that his true beneficial interests were concealed. This was intended to prevent the plaintiffs from recovering those assets in an action against the defendant alleging fraud and breach of trust. The court granted injunctions[55] restraining the defendant from disposing of shares in the foreign companies, or interests under trusts or shares in English or foreign companies entitled to those assets. The injunction also restrained the defendant from procuring the disposition of English assets by the trusts or the companies. The Court of Appeal upheld the grant of these injunctions explicitly on the basis that in the circumstances the court should pierce the corporate veil in order to achieve justice. The only qualification was that the relief granted was restricted to those companies and trusts over which the defendant exercised substantial or effective control.[56] Once again, fraudulent[57] abuse opened doors that would otherwise be kept firmly closed in the absence of that factor. It is clear that the rather loose language in this case, referring to the court using 'its powers to pierce the corporate veil if it is necessary to achieve justice irrespective of the legal efficacy of the company under consideration',[58] must be understood strictly in the context of fraudulent abuse. Later

---

[53] [1951] Ch 728. See also the Court of Appeal's interpretation of the term 'establish a place of business' in s 409 of the Companies Act 1985 in *Re Oriel Ltd* [1985] BCLC 343.

[54] [1985] BCLC 333 (CA).

[55] It also granted discovery by interrogatories of an unusually extensive nature.

[56] *Re a Company Ltd* [1985] BCLC 333, at 337. See also *Gencor ACP v Dalby* [2000] 2 BCLC 734 at 744.

[57] The Court of Appeal regarded the decision as a straightforward application of *Wallersteiner v Moir* [1974] 1 WLR 991.

[58] [1985] BCLC 333, at 337–338, per Cumming-Bruce LJ.

Court of Appeal decisions make it clear that it is not sufficient that the company has been involved in some impropriety *not* linked to the use of the company structure to avoid or conceal that liability.[59]

The question of how far the courts are prepared to lift the veil in groups of companies is considered separately below[60] in its own context. It will be seen that distinctive, if not wholly dissimilar principles have been evolved where groups of companies are concerned.

Parliament is not of course bound by the principle laid down by the House of Lords in *Salomon*.[61] For varying reasons of policy the legislature can, for example, impose personal liability for the company's obligations in shareholders or directors in particular circumstances. This achieves the same result as judicial veil-lifting but requires no doctrinal justification by the courts. See, for example, the statutory treatment of group of companies at **3.8** below.

3.6 THE CRIMINAL LIABILITIES OF COMPANIES

The proof of *mens rea* on the part of the accused is an essential element in most serious criminal offences. Since a company, or any other corporate body, is a legal abstraction without a real mind of its own, the courts at one time were unwilling to convict a company of an offence involving proof of mental state, whether of intention, malice or dishonesty. At this period, it was only possible to charge a company with criminal offences of strict liability. In a number of cases the courts were prepared to allow a company to be prosecuted for offences committed by its employees where the statutes creating the offence could properly be construed as imposing vicarious liability upon the company as employer.[62]

In order to hold a company liable for crimes involving proof of *mens rea*, the courts have had to develop a new principle of corporate liability which is sometimes referred to as the *alter ego* doctrine. This allows the law to attribute the mental state of those who in fact control and determine the management to the company itself as being its 'directing mind and will'. The criminal intentions of a company's ordinary servants and agents will not suffice for this purpose, since the company is not being called to answer simply on the principle of *respondeat superior*.

The question of whether the mental state of the directors or other officers, collectively or individually, can be attributed to the company as

---

59 See *Adams v Cape Industries plc* [1990] Ch 443 and *Ord v Bellhaven Pubs Ltd* [1998] 2 BCLC 447, as applied in *Trustor AB v Smallbone* [2001] 2 BCLC 437. See further *Kensington International Ltd v Republic of Congo* [2006] 2 BCLC 296, at 343–345.

60 See **3.8**.

61 [1897] AC 22.

62 *Pearks, Gunston & Tee Ltd v Ward* [1902] 2 KB 1; *Chuter v Freeth & Pocock Ltd* [1911] 2 KB 832; *Moussell Bros Ltd v L & NW Rly* [1917] 2 KB 836.

its own act must 'depend on the nature of the charge, the relative position of the officer or agent and other relevant facts and circumstances of the case'.[63] This test applies both as to whether there is evidence to go to the jury on the issue and as to how the jury should satisfy themselves that *mens rea* on the part of the company has been proved.[64] On this basis, companies have been convicted of crimes involving dishonesty whether created by statute[65] or by common law.[66] Conduct after the occurrence of irregularities may supply grounds for inferring that persons in control of a company (and consequently the company itself) had knowledge or means of knowledge at the time of the irregularities.[67]

The court will investigate as a question of fact how the management of the company has in reality been conducted so as to determine who is the responsible officer in the area of activity in which the offence occurred. The 'directing mind and will' of the company need not, in an appropriate case, be in the exalted position of the board of directors or the managing director. Thus in *Moore v Bresler Ltd*,[68] a company was convicted of an offence requiring proof of an intention to deceive where those responsible were its secretary and a branch manager.[69]

> 'It is not every "responsible agent" or "high executive" or "manager of the housing department" or "agent acting on behalf of a company" who can by his actions make the company criminally responsible. It is necessary to establish whether the natural person or persons in question have the status and authority which in law makes their acts in the matter under consideration the acts of the company, so that the natural person is to be treated as the company itself. It is often a difficult question to decide whether or not the person concerned is in a sufficiently responsible position to involve the company in liability for the acts in question according to the law as laid down by the authorities.'[70]

---

[63] *R v ICR Haulage* [1944] KB 551, at 559 (CCA).

[64] [1944] KB 551, at 559. A similar principle has yet to be accepted by the Scottish courts. See *Dean v John Menzies (Holdings) Ltd* [1981] SLT 50 and Alan Paterson (1982) 3 Co Law 30.

[65] *DPP v Kent & Sussex Contractors Ltd* [1944] KB 146 (Div Ct).

[66] *R v ICR Haulage* [1944] KB 551.

[67] *Knowles Transport v Russell* [1975] RTR 87 (Div Ct).

[68] [1944] 2 All ER 515 (Div Ct). Cf *Tesco Supermarkets Ltd v Nattrass* [1972] AC 153 (HL): here it was held that a shop manager, one of several hundred employed by the company, could not be regarded as an organ of the company.

[69] However, where a statute creates an offence which distinguishes between the 'actual offender' and 'an employer or principal', the company cannot be convicted as 'actual offender': *Melias Ltd v Preston* [1957] 2 QB 380 (Div Ct). Further, on a charge of conspiracy it was held that a company could not conspire with its sole director who was the directing mind of the company: *R v McDonnell* [1966] 1 QB 233. Cf *R v Robert Millar (Contractors) Ltd* [1970] 2 QB 54 (CA), *Richmond-upon-Thames LBC v Pinn & Wheeler* [1989] RTR 354 (company cannot be convicted of driving a lorry without a permit). Certain offences (eg bigamy and sexual offences) cannot be committed by a company as an artificial person.

[70] *R v Andrews Weatherfoil Ltd* [1972] 1 WLR 118, at 124, per Eveleigh J. See also *R v Rozeik* [1996] 1 BCLC 380 at 385-386 CA (Criminal Division).

Where both the shareholders and directors (in a small private company) consented to various payments of money from the company's bank account for their private use, the Court of Appeal held[71] that such consent did not of itself create a defence to a charge of theft. The Court found that on the evidence the various ingredients of a charge of theft under the Theft Act 1968 could still be satisfied, and the issue of the dishonesty of the payments of the company's money to the defendants might be left to a jury to decide. The Court of Appeal distinguished cases where the consent of shareholders, unanimously given, was held to bar a civil action for breach of fiduciary duty or for negligence.[72] Where fraud upon the company is alleged in a civil action (or a criminal offence is charged whether under the Theft Act or on the basis of conspiracy) the unanimous consent of shareholders will not bar such criminal proceedings.[73] The purpose of the *alter ego* principle is, in the appropriate circumstances, to impose criminal (or sometimes civil) liability on the company for the acts of those who are regarded in law as its 'deciding mind and will'.[74] Its purpose is not to give such persons a defence for their own wrongdoing at the company's expense.

3.7   CORPORATE MANSLAUGHTER

The common law of manslaughter when applied to the prosecution of companies and other corporate bodies proved unsatisfactory in that it was almost impossible to secure a conviction. After much delay and the failure of earlier attempts to legislative, the Corporate Manslaughter and Corporate Homicide Act 2007[75] provides a new solution to this problem. The 2007 Act replaces the common law of manslaughter where a corporate body is prosecuted. The Act provides:[76]

> 'An organisation is guilty of an offence ... if the way its activities are managed or organised:
> (a)   causes a person's death; and
> (b)   amounts to a gross breach of a relevant duty care owed by the organisation to the deceased ...'.

It must be shown[77] 'that the way in which its activities are managed or organised by senior management is a substantial element in the breach' and 'the conduct ... falls far below what can reasonably be expected of the

---

71   *Attorney-General's Reference (No 2 of 1983)* [1984] 2 QB 456.
72   The Court of Appeal distinguished *Salomon v Salomon & Co Ltd* [1897] AC 22 and *Multinational Gas and Petrochemical Co v Multinational Gas and Petrochemical Services Ltd* [1983] 2 All ER 653.
73   *Belmont Finance Ltd v Williams (No 1)* [1979] Ch 256; *R v McDonnell* [1966] 1 QB 233.
74   On this basis the Court of Appeal distinguished *Tesco Supermarkets v Nattrass* [1972] AC 153.
75   The Act came into force in April 2008.
76   Section 1(1).
77   Section 1(1), (3) and (4)(b).

organisation in the circumstances'. The Act does not require proof of guilt by any particular individual, and individuals cannot be found guilty of ancillary offences

3.8 APPLICATION TO CIVIL LAW

The alter ego principle has been employed by the courts where in civil proceedings it is necessary to attribute a particular mental state to a company. In most civil actions against companies this question does not arise, since the company may be affixed with liability on some other basis. Thus in tort the ordinary principles of vicarious liability will as a rule determine the matter, and contractual liability will depend on that special adaptation of the principles of agency known to company lawyers as the 'rule in *Turquand's Case*',[78] as well as s 40 of the Companies Act 2006.

Nevertheless in some cases it is necessary to attribute an intention or actual default to the company. Thus under s 502 of the Merchant Shipping Act 1894 the owner of a vessel has a defence which allows him to exempt himself from liability for injury which is caused without 'his actual default or privity'. But what, as will usually be the case, if the owner is a company? In the leading case of *Lennard's Carrying Company v Asiatic Petroleum Ltd*,[79] the House of Lords held that the default of Lennard, as the managing director and 'directing mind and will' of his company, could be attributed to it so as to deprive it of the defence which s 502 provided. Viscount Haldane's judgments articulated the *alter ego* doctrine peculiar to company law as one quite distinct from the ordinary principles of agency or vicarious liability.

In a justly celebrated passage he observes that:[80]

> '... a corporation is an abstraction. It has no mind of its own any more than a body of its own; its active and directing will must consequently be sought in the person of somebody who for some purposes may be called an agent, but who is really the directing mind and will of the corporation, the very ego and centre of the personality of the corporation.'

As in criminal law, the *alter ego* of a company may, depending on the circumstances of the case, be found at a lower level in the managerial hierarchy than that of the board of directors or the managing director. Thus in *The Lady Gwendolen*[81] the marine superintendent, to whom the assistant managing director and the traffic manager had surrendered 'all the relevant powers of control'[82] over the operation of its ships, was held to be a directing mind for this purpose.

---

[78] (1856) 5 E & B 248. See **6.25**.
[79] [1915] AC 705 (HL).
[80] [1915] AC 705, at 713.
[81] [1965] P 294 (CA).
[82] Ibid, at 355, per Winn LJ. The company sought to limit its liability under s 503 of the

The principle enunciated by Lord Haldane and the significance of the phrase 'directing mind and will' have been scrutinised by the Privy Council in *Meridian Global Funds Management Asia Ltd v Securities Commission*.[83] The judgment of the Board (on an appeal from New Zealand) was delivered by Lord Hoffmann who emphasised that the court must fashion a special rule of attribution for the particular substantive rule.[84]

> 'This is always a matter of interpretation: given that it was intended to apply to a company, how was it intended to apply? Whose act (or knowledge or state of mind) was *for this purpose* intended to count as the act etc of the company? One finds the answer to this question by applying the usual canons of interpretation, taking into account the language of the rule (if it is a statute) and its context and policy.'[85]

Lord Hoffmann, while making it clear that this was the principle applied by Lord Haldane in *Lennard's Case*, warns against the literal application of the phrase 'directing mind and will'. Lord Haldane is not to be taken as 'expounding a general metaphysic of companies'.[86] Lord Hoffmann specifically rejected the 'anthropomorphism' of Denning LJ in *HL Bolton (Engineering) Co Ltd v TJ Graham & Sons Ltd*.[87] It is not possible to make a generalisation about companies 'as such'. Such anthropomorphism 'by the very power of the image distracts attention from the purpose for which Lord Haldane said he was using the notion of directing mind and will, namely to apply the attribution rule derived from section 502 [of the Merchant Shipping Act 1984][88] to the particular defendant in the case'.

In *Meridian Global* the appeal concerned the interpretation of s 20 of the New Zealand Securities Amendment Act 1988. This required every person who became a substantial security holder[89] of a public company listed on the New Zealand Stock Exchange to give notice of his interest in the company to the Stock Exchange. He had to do this as soon as he

---

Merchant Shipping Act 1894 on the basis that a collision occurred without 'actual fault or privity' on the part of the owners. The Court of Appeal held that the company was not entitled to do so. In *Registrar of Restrictive Trading Agreements v WH Smith and Sons Ltd* [1969] 1 WLR 1460 (CA), a branch manager of a company was held not to be a 'manager' or 'officer' for the purposes of s 15(3) of the Restrictive Trade Practices Act 1956 (power to interrogate on oath). See also *Tesco Supermarkets v Nattrass* [1972] AC 153.

[83] [1995] 3 WLR 413. Applied in *Lebon v Acqua Salt Ltd* [2009] 1 BCLC 549 at 556 (PC).
[84] Where on other more conventional principles liability can be attributed to a company (eg vicarious liability or agency), there will be no need to seek a 'directing mind and will': see *Deutsche Genossenschaftsbank v Burnhope* [1995] BCC 488 (CA); see further Lord Hoffmann in *Meridian Global Funds* [1995] 1 WLR 413, at 419.
[85] [1995] 1 WLR 413, at 419. See further *Z Bank v DTI* [1994] 1 Lloyd's Rep 656 in respect of contempt by a corporation in respect of a *Mareva* injunction.
[86] [1995] 1 WLR 413, at 421.
[87] [1957] 1 QB 159, at 172 where Denning LJ likens a company to a human body.
[88] [1995] 3 WLR 413, at 421.
[89] Defined as holding a relevant interest in 5% or more of the voting shares.

knew, or ought to have known, that he was a substantial security holder in the company. Where another company became a substantial security holder, the knowledge of two senior investment managers was sufficient to attribute that knowledge to their company for the purposes of s 20 since they acquired the securities with the authority of the company. It would defeat the policy of the Act to require the board of directors or someone else in senior management to know.[90]

The same principle, identifying the state of mind of the senior management with that of the company itself, has been employed to determine whether a company intended to occupy premises for its own business under the Landlord and Tenant Act 1954,[91] and to decide whether an inducement to breach of contract operates upon the company itself (as opposed to its servants) to persuade it to break its contract.[92]

The directing mind and will doctrine, which attributes the mind and will of a natural person to the company, was applied by the Court of Appeal in *El Ajou v Dollar Landholdings plc*.[93] Nourse LJ held that, in order to apply the doctrine, it was necessary to identify the person who had actual management and control in relation to the relevant act. The fact that the person so identified in this case was a non-executive nominee director with ostensibly no authority to undertake business decisions is not relevant to the application of the directing mind and will doctrine. The important point was that this director made all the arrangements for receiving and dispersing the moneys and signed all the documents causing the company to become involved in a fraud. In these circumstances this director's state of mind and, in particular, the fact that he knew that the company had received assets representing the proceeds of the fraud, should be attributed to the company as he represented its directing mind

---

[90] Lord Hoffmann contrasted two decisions of the House of Lords interpreting different statutory provisions. In *Tesco Supermarkets Ltd v Nattrass* [1972] AC 153, the failure of a shop manager to comply with s 11(2) of the Trade Descriptions Act 1968 did not prevent the company pleading a defence, under s 24(1) of the Act, that it took 'all reasonable precautions and exercised due diligence'. In contrast, in *Re Supply of Ready Mixed Concrete, Director General of Fair Trading v Pioneer Concrete (UK) Ltd* [1995] 1 AC 456, the House of Lords held that the actions of the company's employees constituted the carrying on of business by the company for the purposes of the Restrictive Trade Practices Act 1976. Thus, when local managers of a company concluded allocation agreements, they were fully competent to make the agreement on behalf of the company and see that it was carried out. The company could not escape liability under the 1976 Act by pleading that a prohibition at senior management level was ignored by certain employees. Here there was no statutory defence based on all reasonable preventative measures being taken. Further, liability for contempt of court for disobedience of a court order did not require any direct intention on the part of the company. The House of Lords in *Ready Mixed Concrete* overruled the Court of Appeal decision in *Director of Fair Trading v Smiths Concrete Ltd* [1992] QB 213.

[91] Landlord and Tenant Act 1954, s 30(1)(g). *Bolton (Engineering) Co Ltd v Graham & Sons* [1957] 1 QB 159. The 1954 Act does not apply in Scotland.

[92] *DC Thompson & Co v Deakin* [1952] Ch 646 (CA).

[93] [1994] 1 BCLC 464 (CA). Applied in *Lebon v Acqua Salt Ltd* [2009] 1 BCLC 549 at 557 (PC).

and will in relation to these acts. Thus, a victim of the fraud was able to enforce a constructive trust against the company on the basis that it had knowingly received the proceeds of the fraud.

In *Stone & Rolls Ltd v Moore Stephens*[94] a fraud was perpetrated by a company whose directing mind and will was its sole shareholder. He was held solely responsible for its actions. The House of Lords held that the fraud was to be attributed to the company and, therefore, any claim by the company against its auditors for not detecting the fraud was barred by the *ex turpi causa non oritur actio* principle.[95]

3.9   GROUPS OF COMPANIES

It is a commonplace of commercial life today that businesses are conducted not only in the form of a single private or public company, but also in the form of a group of companies consisting of a holding company (which may often be a listed public company) and a number of usually wholly owned subsidiaries and possibly sub-subsidiaries. Nowadays the group form may be employed at quite a small level of private business for tax or other reasons. As with larger groups of companies, different branches of the business or different properties will be located in each subsidiary.[96]

3.9.1   The group relationship in the Companies Act 2006

The Companies Act 2006 contains two separate definitions applicable to groups of companies.[97] For general purposes there is a definition of 'holding' and 'subsidiary' company whenever these terms are used throughout the Act.[98] There is a separate definition of the term 'parent and subsidiary undertaking' used for the purpose of 'group accounts'.

As to the statutory definition of 'holding and subsidiary company' the Act provides two alternative tests:

(1)   the holding company holds a majority of voting shares in the subsidiary; and

(2)   the holding company is a member of the subsidiary and has the right to appoint or remove a majority of the board of directors.[99]

---

[94]   [2009] 2 BCLC 563.
[95]   See Lord Phillips at 583–594.
[96]   See further T Hadden, *The Control of Corporate Groups* (IALS, 1983).
[97]   See, eg, directors' duties (see Part 10, s 192), and financial assistance for the purchase of own shares (see Part 18, s 679).
[98]   See Part 38: Companies: Interpretation.
[99]   See s 1159(1)(a) and (b).

As to (1) this includes the holding company being a member of the subsidiary and controlling 'alone, pursuant to agreement with other members, a majority of voting rights in it'.[100] The requirement of being 'a member' would be satisfied by holding a single share or (in companies without a share capital) by being a single member. This provides an obvious way to sidestep the definition of holding and subsidiary even though there is effective control of the board or of a majority of voting rights. Sub-subsidiaries which meet the same criteria in relation to a subsidiary are to be treated as subsidiaries of the holding company.[101] The term 'company' in s 1159 includes 'any body corporate'.[102] Section 1159 refers to Sch 6 to the Act to explain in detail 'expressions used in this section and otherwise supplementing this section'. *Inter alia*, Sch 6 excludes certain types of right attached to shares in determining whether a putative holding company holds a majority of voting rights. This exclusion refers to 'rights exercisable only in certain circumstances', rights 'held by one person on behalf of another',[103] and rights attached to shares held by way of security.[104]

In the specific case of group accounts the terms employed to designate a group relationship differ from that of 'parent and subsidiary company' used generally in the Act. Instead the correlative terms are 'parent and subsidiary undertaking'[105] as interpreted by s 1162 of and Sch 7 to the Companies Act 2006. Section 1162 begins by repeating the same criteria as are used in s 1159 (ie holding a majority of voting shares and the right to remove a majority of the board). But it also includes a wider criterion of a more judgmental and subjective nature. This is the 'right to exercise a dominant influence over the undertaking by virtue of provisions in the undertaking's articles or by virtue of a control contract'.[106]

Section 1161 gives the meaning of 'undertaking' (in relation to both parent and subsidiary undertakings) as comprising a body corporate or a partnership as well as 'an unincorporated association carrying on a trade or business, with or without a view to profit'.[107]

3.10   THE TREATMENT OF GROUPS BY THE COURTS

In *DHN Food Distributors Ltd v Tower Hamlets LBC*,[108] the Court of Appeal was prepared to go some way towards recognising the economic

---

[100] See s 1159(1)(c).

[101] As to the definition of a 'wholly owned subsidiary' see s 1159(2).

[102] Section 1159(4).

[103] Ie rights held by a person in a fiduciary capacity or by a person as a nominee for another (Sch 6, paras 5 and 6).

[104] Schedule 6, para 7. See *Enviroco Ltd v Farstad Supply A/S* [2010] 1 BCLC 477 (CA).

[105] See s 404 of the Companies Act 2006.

[106] Section 1162(2). For the interpretation of 'the right to exercise dominant influence' and 'control contract' see Sch 7, para 4.

[107] Section 1161(1).

[108] [1976] 1 WLR 852. See especially the judgment of Lord Denning at 860, citing LCB

entity of a tightly controlled group of companies so as to ignore (or set aside for a particular statutory purpose) the separate legal entities of the companies within the group. This allowed a holding company to claim compensation for compulsory acquisition of premises owned by its wholly owned subsidiary but in which the holding company carried on its business. If the holding company had been treated as a bare licensee of the premises owned by its subsidiary it would not have been entitled to compensation for disturbance to its business. However, though the Court of Appeal was agreed as to the result, the degree of domination of the subsidiary by the holding company, or of unity in the enterprise conducted formally by them, is nowhere stated with precision. It is difficult to predict with any certainty when the separate legal personality of the companies within a group will be set aside by the courts. It will be seen that the courts will not ignore the limited liability of a subsidiary so as to allow the creditor of an insolvent subsidiary to seek redress from the holding company.

The decision of the House of Lords in *Woolfson v Strathclyde Regional Council*[109] threw some doubt on the soundness of the Court of Appeal's decision in *DHN v Tower Hamlets*. Lord Frazer observed that he had 'some doubt whether in this respect the Court of Appeal properly applied the principle that it is appropriate to pierce the corporate veil only where special circumstances exist indicating that it is a mere façade concealing the true facts'.[110] The *DHN* decision was not overruled but was distinguished on the basis that there the company that owned the land was the wholly owned subsidiary of the company that carried on the business. The latter was in complete control of the situation as respects anything that might affect its business. In *Woolfson*, by contrast, the company that carried on the business had 'no sort of control whatever over the owners of the land'. The owners were the appellant and a company in which he held two-thirds of the shares. Further, Woolfson was not shown to be beneficially entitled to his wife's single share but owned all the shares in the company that carried on the business. A legitimate response is that this seems a thin basis for distinguishing the case, and it would seem to reflect a different judicial philosophy relating to lifting the veil of incorporation in the case of groups of companies.[111] In

---

Gower *Principles of Modern Company Law* (Sweet & Maxwell, 3rd edn, 1969) at p 216. Somewhat surprisingly, the decision in *Smith, Stone and Knight Ltd v Birmingham Corporation* [1939] 4 All ER 116 was not relied upon. See also the judgment of Lord Denning in *Littlewoods Mail Order Stores Ltd v CIR* [1969] 1 WLR 1241.

[109] *1978 SLT 159*, at 161.

[110] Lord Frazer further observes that the decisions of the House of Lords in *Harold Holdsworth & Co v Caddies* [1955] 1 WLR 352 and *Scottish Co-op v Meyer* [1959] AC 324, which were relied upon by Goff LJ (and by Denning MR as regards *Meyer*) 'do not with respect appear to me to be concerned with that principle'.

[111] A clearer basis for distinguishing the Court of Appeal's decision was found in the reasoning of Goff LJ and Shaw LJ in respect of the land held by the subsidiary, on the basis of an irrevocable licence or a resulting trust.

DHN v Tower Hamlets LBC[112] (and in other cases where a holding company and its subsidiary has been treated as 'an enterprise entity'),[113] the court has been persuaded to do so at the insistence of the holding company and consequently for its benefit. Where a stranger to the group wishes to lift the veil, the courts continue to show the greatest reluctance to do so. Thus in *Multinational Gas v Multinational Services*,[114] the Court of Appeal refused to allow the liquidator of an insolvent subsidiary to serve a writ out of jurisdiction on three international oil companies which had set up their jointly owned subsidiary. They were held to have a good defence in law for any claim of negligence based on the permitted misconduct of the directors of the subsidiary appointed by them. As shareholders they could consent to negligent conduct and owed no duties to any third parties (such as the creditors whose interests the liquidator represented).

In *Lonrho Ltd v Shell Petroleum Ltd*,[115] the House of Lords rejected an attempt to compel a joint holding company to use its powers to compel a foreign subsidiary and its sub-subsidiaries to release documents in their possession to comply with an order for discovery of documents in the context of litigation against the holding company. It was held that there was no obligation to use the voting powers available to change the articles of the subsidiary or otherwise to override the discretion of its board of directors. In both the *Multinational* and *Lonrho* cases, it was clear that other policy factors were present which influenced the court in refusing to extend its jurisdiction, or make available a procedural remedy, against an overseas subsidiary or a foreign multinational company. However, these decisions give scant support to the more optimistic views that the courts were more prepared to lift the veil in the case of groups of companies.[116]

3.10.1 *Adams v Cape Industries plc*

In its landmark decision in *Adams v Cape Industries plc*,[117] the Court of Appeal took the opportunity to attempt to bring some order to the rather confused body of case-law relating to the question of lifting the veil where groups of companies are concerned. The case was concerned with the enforcement in an English court of judgments obtained in a United States

---

[112] [1970] 1 WLR 852.

[113] See, eg, *Prenn v Simmonds* [1971] 1 WLR 1381 (HL) and *Harold Holdsworth & Co v Caddies* [1955] 1 WLR 352 (HL); *Bird & Co v Thomas Cook & Sons Ltd* [1937] 2 All ER 227. See *The Roberta* (1937) 58 Lloyd's Rep 159.

[114] [1983] 3 WLR 493.

[115] [1980] 1 WLR 627 (HL).

[116] Some decisions in the field of labour law have been even more hostile to such an approach, and have been prepared to follow the *Salomon* principle to the most artificial extreme. Here policy arguments in favour of the rigorous application of industrial relations legislation may have prevailed. See *Dimbleby v NUJ* [1984] 1 WLR 427 (HL) and *National Dock Labour Board v Pinn Wheeler Ltd* [1989] BCLC 647.

[117] [1990] Ch 433.

court. One aspect[118] of the question of the exercise of foreign jurisdiction involved the alleged presence of various subsidiaries[119] of Cape Industries in the United States. The respondent and its subsidiaries operated an asbestos mining business in South Africa, selling this product in various parts of the world including the United States. The judgments obtained in a federal court in Texas were concerned with the liability in tort for asbestos-related injuries. Counsel for the appellant raised three arguments as a basis for asserting that, through its subsidiaries, Cape was present in the United States. The Court of Appeal structured its new and more restrictive approach to lifting the veil around these three possible arguments for the 'presence' of Cape Industries in the United States.

(1) The single economic unit argument

This concept of the group as a single economic entity found no support as an independent basis on which the corporate veil might be lifted. It could not justify any departure from the normal rule that 'each company in a group of companies ... is a separate legal entity possessed of separate legal rights and liabilities'.[120] The considerable number of cases where the court has been prepared to ignore the distinction in law between a group of companies on the basis that 'justice so demands' or if 'the business realities' require it were all explained by Slade LJ as being turning 'on the wording of particular statutes or contracts'.[121] While this may be a very satisfactory explanation of some of these cases which explicitly turn on the liberal interpretation of an agreement in *re mercatoria*,[122] or on the construction of the wording of a particular statutory provision,[123] it cannot satisfactorily explain all of them. It certainly gives a strained interpretation to *DHN Food Distributors Ltd v Tower Hamlets LBC*.[124] Whatever doubts were cast upon the Court of Appeal's decision in this case by the House of Lords in *Woolfson v Strathclyde Regional Council*,[125] its authority cannot be wholly dismissed. In particular, the judgment of Lord Denning MR clearly expounds a doctrine about the corporate group as an economic entity which is very different from that of Slade LJ in *Cape Industries*. The Court of Appeal in *Cape Industries* recognised that the rigid doctrine now espoused by the English courts differs markedly from that of the European Court of Justice[126] where a group of

---

[118] The Court of Appeal also considered whether the defendants had consented to a foreign court exercising jurisdiction over them.

[119] In the discussion below of the Court of Appeal's judgment two of these subsidiaries are referred to (as in the judgment itself) as AMC and CPC.

[120] [1990] Ch 433, at 532 citing Roskill LJ in *The Albazero* [1977] AC 774, at 807.

[121] [1990] Ch 433, at 530, *Revlon Inc v Cripps Lee Ltd* [1980] FSR 85, at 105. See [1990] Ch 433, at 534–535.

[122] Eg *Harold Holdsworth & Co (Wakerfield) Ltd v Caddies* [1955] 1 WLR 352, at 367. See [1990] Ch 433, at 537.

[123] *Scottish Co-operative Wholesale Soc Ltd v Meyer* [1959] AC 324, at 342. See [1990] Ch 433, at 537.

[124] [1976] 1 WLR 852, at 860 and 861. See [1990] Ch 433, at 533–534.

[125] 1978 SLT 159. See [1990] Ch 433, at 536.

[126] See the discussion of *Istitutu Chemioterapico Italiano SPA v The Commission* [1974]

companies may be treated as a single economic entity. Clearly, English courts applying EU law to groups of companies must follow the lead of the European Court of Justice.

(2) Piercing the corporate veil

The Court of Appeal in *Cape Industries* accepted that there is 'one well recognised exception to the rule prohibiting the piercing of the "corporate veil"'. This referred to Lord Keith's well-known observations in *Woolfson v Strathclyde Regional Council*[127] that it is appropriate to pierce the corporate veil only where special circumstances exist indicating that it is a mere facade concealing the true facts. Slade LJ in *Cape Industries*[128] cited *Jones v Lipman*[129] as illustrating this principle.[130] As applied to the case itself, the 'facade' principle was applicable to 'AMC' which was not only a wholly owned subsidiary of Cape but had been used by Cape and its subsidiaries as a corporate name on their invoices.[131] This, however, did not help the appellants since the court found that AMC was not in fact carrying on business in the United States. Another company, CPC, was incorporated and carrying on business in the United States but was held not to be a facade. It was an independent corporation which was carrying on its own business in the United States and not that of Cape or its subsidiaries. Significantly, its shares were wholly owned by its chief executive even if it had been set up at the behest of, and with funding from, Cape.[132]

At a more general level, the Court of Appeal stressed that it is legitimate to use a corporate structure 'to ensure that legal liability (if any) in respect of particular future activity of the group ... will fall on another member of the group rather than the defendant company. Whether or not this is desirable, the right to use a corporate structure in this manner is inherent in our corporate law'.[133] The Court of Appeal stressed that the *motive* with which a subsidiary was formed (or an existing subsidiary used) is crucial. Slade LJ stressed that the arrangements involving CPC were not shown to involve actual or potential illegality, nor were they intended to deprive anyone of their existing rights.[134]

ECR 223 in *Cape Industries* [1990] Ch 433, at 535. See further *SAR Schotte GmbH v Parfums Rothschild SARL* [1992] BCLC 235. See further *Gore-Browne on Companies* (Jordans, 45th edn, loose-leaf) at 789D

[127] 1978 SLT 159, at 161.

[128] [1990] Ch 433, at 542–543.

[129] [1962] 1 WLR 832.

[130] Slade LJ found little help in other authorities in terms of reasoned principle. Even the dicta of Lord Denning MR in *Wallersteiner v Moir* [1974] 1 WLR 991, at 1013 and in *Littlewoods Mail Order Stores Ltd v Inland Revenue Commissioners* [1969] 1 WLR 1241, at 1254 were not supported by other members of the Court of Appeal.

[131] [1990] Ch 543.

[132] Ibid, at 543–544.

[133] Ibid, at 544.

[134] Ibid.

(3) The agency argument

The Court of Appeal in *Cape Industries* was careful to confine the possibility that a subsidiary might be treated as the agent of its holding company to situations where such an inference was factually justified. It was made clear that, in the absence of an express agreement,[135] it will be difficult to establish such a relationship.[136] The fact that CPC acted as agent for Cape in particular transactions was not sufficient to establish that Cape was present in the United States through its agent.[137]

In later cases, the guidelines laid down in *Adams* have been followed. Unless dishonesty or clear abuse of the corporate form can be shown, the courts will refrain from piercing the veil of incorporation.[138]

3.10.2   The problem of insolvent subsidiaries

One area where the tendency of Parliament to put the obligations of a company on to a group basis has stopped short, is that of the liability of a holding company for the debts of its insolvent subsidiary. Here neither the legislature nor the courts are willing to depart from the strict corporate entity principle and its attendant privilege of limited liability.[139] The fact that all or a majority of the shares in a company are owned by a holding company makes no difference to the ordinary rule that the shareholders in a limited company are not liable for its debts beyond the amount paid up (or to be paid up) on the shares held by them. In the case of the holding/subsidiary relationship, this of course ignores the common reality that the subsidiary may be very thinly capitalised or indeed grossly undercapitalised. Moreover, the subsidiary may be capitalised by a loan repayable on demand which may also be secured on the assets of the subsidiary. This may make the holding company the principal creditor in the insolvent winding-up of its subsidiary and, moreover, a creditor with priority over the ordinary trade creditors. As the House of Lords decided in *Salomon v Salomon & Co*,[140] this will not, in the absence of fraud (or the statutory offences of fraudulent or wrongful trading), be a ground for lifting the veil. This is equally true of the relationship between a holding company and a subsidiary company.

For some years, the unenviable position of creditors in subsidiary companies has become a matter of concern.[141] In the case of banks and

---

[135] See, eg, *Southern v Watson* [1940] 3 All ER 439 (CA).

[136] [1990] Ch 543, at 545–549.

[137] Ibid, at 548–549.

[138] See *Ord v Bellhaven Pubs Ltd* [1998] 2 BCLC 447 (CA) and *Trustor AB v Smallbone* [2001] 2 BCLC 437. See further *Kensington International Ltd v Republic of Congo* [2006] 2 BCLC 296, at 343–345.

[139] Unless fraudulent or wrongful trading can be shown. See **15.17**.

[140] [1987] AC 22.

[141] See the Cork Report, Chapter 51, paragraphs 1922–1929 and Templeman LJ in *Re Southard & Co* [1979] 1 WLR 1198.

other lending institutions, the lender can be relied upon to make the appropriate contractual arrangements (eg lending directly to the holding company, or obtaining a guarantee for a loan to the subsidiary). In the case of an economically powerful creditor (eg an energy supplier or an oil company), the holding company may hesitate before evading its moral obligation and relying upon its strict legal rights, since it may still need to obtain credit for itself or for its other subsidiaries. However, the lot of small trade creditors which have supplied goods or services to an insolvent subsidiary remains an unhappy one. In the German Federal Republic, the 'law of integration'[142] has imposed, in the appropriate conditions, the responsibility of the group for the obligations for subsidiaries. Likewise, the EC Ninth Draft Directive proposed a reform in the company law of the other member states on broadly the same lines.

The Cork Committee,[143] while recognising the deeply unsatisfactory nature of the present law, was also impressed by the difficulties in framing satisfactory proposals to make holding companies liable for the debts of insolvent subsidiaries.[144] These difficulties relate to questions both of legal definition and of policy.[145] The Committee also felt that a fundamental change would have to be made not only in the law governing the winding-up of insolvent companies but also in many aspects of company law in general (eg the duties of directors in holding companies could no longer relate primarily to that company).[146] The Committee therefore shied away from so fundamental a change in company law:[147]

> 'The matter is of such importance and such gravity that there should be the widest possible review of the different considerations, with a view to the introduction of reforming legislation in the near future. We would wish to see such a review undertaken as a matter of urgency.'

The question of group liability was explored by the Company Law Review Steering Group (CLRSG). In *Completing the Structure*,[148] it proposed an

---

[142] See H Würdinger *German Company Law* (Oyez Publishing, 1975), Ch 2, at pp 138–140. There is also a lesser degree of group liability where, though the conditions of 'integration' do not apply, there is nevertheless a 'control contract': ibid, pp 148–149. See further F Wooldridge *Groups of Companies: The Law and Practice in Britain, France and Germany* (IALS, 1981); K Hopt (ed) *Groups of Companies in European Laws*, vol II (Berlin, New York, Walter de Gruyter, 1982).

[143] *Insolvency Law and Practice, Report of the Review Committee* (Cmnd 8558) 1982. See as to the EC Ninth Draft Directive, ibid, para 1936.

[144] It reviewed various possibilities which varied in the range of severity from the viewpoint of the holding company, ibid, paras 1934 and 1947–1949.

[145] The Committee was particularly concerned with the problems of: 'partly owned' subsidiaries (para 1942); *de facto* control; the danger of discouraging entrepreneurial activity through the creation of subsidiaries (para 1940); the added complexity of winding-up groups of companies (para 1943); the impact of any change in the practice of buying and selling subsidiaries (para 1944); and the application to foreign subsidiaries or a foreign holding company of any change in the law (para 1945).

[146] Ibid, para 1951.

[147] Ibid, para 1952.

[148] Chapter 10.

'elective regime for groups'. At the option of the parent company, such an elective regime could be adopted in respect of wholly owned subsidiaries in the group. This would have enabled the subsidiaries thus elected to escape the obligation to prepare, have audited and file individual company accounts. In return for this 'reduction of administrative burdens', the parent would have to guarantee the liabilities, both in contract and tort, of the elective subsidiaries.[149] It is apparent that this proposal was not concerned to address the problems of small unsecured creditors and involuntary tort creditors of insolvent subsidiaries. It was designed to achieve a saving in administrative costs for the group. In its Final Report,[150] the CLRSG abandoned the whole idea on the basis that the savings would not justify the loss of information in respect of substantial groups. The injustice caused in particular to involuntary tort creditors remains to be addressed.

---

[149] The elective subsidiaries would not give reciprocal guarantees to the parent or to other subsidiaries.

[150] Volume 1 at 8.23–8.28; see Boyle 'The Company Law Review and "group reform"' (2002) 23 Co Law 35.

CHAPTER 4

REGISTRATION, FORMATION AND PROMOTION OF COMPANIES

4.1 INTRODUCTION

This chapter describes the different types of company that can exist and the mechanisms which are provided for their registration and, occasionally, re-registration. Although the vast bulk of registered companies are companies limited by shares, the legislation makes provision also for unlimited and guarantee companies. The nature of these is briefly explained later in this chapter.[1] It is appropriate also to consider the law which applies to those people, known as promoters, who are actually engaged in the business of forming a company, and, briefly, the law which applies to foreign companies doing business in Britain. The chapter concludes with an examination of the provisions regarding company names.

Historically, the registered company form was made available for enterprises wishing to involve a large or at least reasonable number of investors. However, as has been seen in Chapter 1, it was also adopted by small concerns, even where there was only one person really involved, a move that was sanctioned by the House of Lords in *Salomon v Salomon & Co*.[2] At the time of this decision, the law made no distinctions between different types of registered company; that happened in 1909 when the concept of the private company, as something distinct from the basic form, the public company, was introduced. Under the law then, the private company was a special category meeting particular requirements (e g as to the number of members). All companies not registered as private fell into the residual category of public company. In order to implement the provisions of the EC's Second Directive on Company Law,[3] a new way of classifying public and private limited companies was introduced by the Companies Act 1980. Many of the more onerous requirements first imposed by this Act (which stem from the Directive)[4] apply only to public companies. To prevent evasion of these requirements it was necessary to introduce a more rigid and watertight dividing line between public and

---

[1]   A further registered business association is the European Economic Interest Grouping.
[2]   [1987] AC 22; see **3.4**.
[3]   77/91/EEC (1977) OJ L26/1.
[4]   As to these, see Chapter 7.

private companies.[5] Under this modern system of classification, which better reflects the reality of company registration, all proposed companies must be registered as private unless they are specifically registered as public companies and meet the special requirements of such. The most important of these are a minimum capitalisation for public companies and an addition to their name (public limited company) indicating a public company's special status.

The Companies Act 2006 maintained this approach and, indeed, introduced further measures, in particular downgrading the importance of the memorandum of association that every proposed company must present for registration and abolishing the previous requirement that all companies limited by shares had to have an authorised capital on registration. It is also drafted in a way that by and large deals with the law applying to private companies before that applying to public companies.

4.2　THE CLASSIFICATION OF PRIVATE AND PUBLIC COMPANIES

Section 4 of the Companies Act 2006[6] defines a 'private company' as any company that is not a public company and a 'public company' as a company limited by shares (or limited by guarantee and having a share capital)[7] whose certificate of incorporation states that it is a public company and in relation to which the requirements of the Act or the former Companies Acts as to registration or re-registration as a public company have been complied with. Section 4(4) points to the two major differences between private and public companies in Part 20. For present purposes,[8] the key difference is the minimum capital requirement for public companies. By s 761, a public company must not do business or exercise borrowing powers unless the registrar has issued it with a trading certificate, and this can be done only if the nominal value of the company's allotted share capital[9] is not less than the authorised minimum, defined in s 763 as £50,000 or the prescribed euro equivalent.[10] The euro equivalent is €65,000.[11] The requirement must be met in one of the

---

5　This applies to the original registration of public and private companies and also to the re-registration of a private company as a public company or vice versa.

6　[CA 1985, s 1].

7　Guarantee companies with a share capital have not been able to be formed as such since 22 December 1980 (in Great Britain) or 1 July 1983 (in Northern Ireland) but those existing prior to 1980 could re-register as public; see s 4(3).

8　The other key difference is the prohibition on private companies offering their securities to the public, which is considered in Chapter 19.

9　As to the meaning of this, see **7.1**.

10　Or as altered under s 764. As to the minimum capital requirement, see further **4.7**.

11　The Companies (Authorised Minimum) Regulations 2008, SI 2008/729.

currencies only, and no account can be taken of share capital denominated in any other currency.[12]

Both types of company can now be formed with only one member.[13] Section 58[14] requires that the name of a public company must end with the words 'public limited company',[15] which can be abbreviated to 'plc'.[16] The name of a private limited company must end with 'limited' or 'Ltd',[17] unless it is exempted as described below,[18] or is a community interest company.[19] The definition of 'private company' in s 4(1) obviously includes all companies limited by shares which, when they are registered, are not specifically registered as public companies. It also includes all companies already registered as private companies under earlier Companies Acts and all unlimited companies or companies limited by guarantee.

Sections 89–111 provide for the various types of company to be re-registered as another type of company. These provisions are described below.

4.3 FORMING A COMPANY

The person or persons forming a company must subscribe their name(s) to a memorandum of association and comply with the requirements of ss 9–13.[20] A company may not be formed for an illegal purpose.[21] The memorandum of association no longer has the importance that it used to have; under the previous law it was the fundamental document that had to be prepared,[22] and it contained key information including the objects of the company. However, now it is simply a memorandum stating that the subscribers wish to form a company and agree to become members of the company[23] and, in the case of a company with a share capital, to take at

---

[12] Section 765. See also s 766 regarding the power to make regulations where shares are denominated in different currencies, etc; see the Companies (Authorised Minimum) Regulations 2008, SI 2008/729.
[13] Section 7(1). Previously this was the case only for a private company.
[14] [CA 1985, s 25].
[15] It is an offence for a 'person' (eg a private company) which is not registered as a public company to carry on any trade, profession or business under a name which includes as its last part the words 'public limited company' or their Welsh equivalent: s 33(1).
[16] In the case of a Welsh company, this may be rendered in Welsh as 'cwmni cyfyngedig cyhoeddus', which may be abbreviated as 'ccc'.
[17] Or the Welsh equivalents, where appropriate, of 'cyfyngedig' or 'cyf'.
[18] See **4.10**.
[19] Section 59.
[20] Section 7(1).
[21] Section 7(2); see below at **4.6**.
[22] The memoranda of companies existing before 1 October 2009, when this Part of the 2006 Act came into force, are treated as provisions of the articles: see s 28 and the Companies Act 2006 (Commencement No 8, Transitional Provisions and Savings) Order 2008, SI 2008/2860, Sch 2, para 7.
[23] See further **12.2.1**.

least one share. In practice, subscribers usually sign for only one share each; but there is no reason why they should not sign for as many shares as they intend to take up and pay for. The memorandum must be in the prescribed form[24] and be authenticated by each subscriber.[25] Some of the contents formerly required to be in the memorandum are now covered by the application for registration and the statements described below.

4.4 THE ARTICLES OF ASSOCIATION

The principal document which must be prepared for registration is the articles of association. Articles must be contained in a single document and divided into paragraphs numbered consecutively.[26] The purpose, contents and drafting of the articles of association are considered further in Chapter 5.

Unlimited companies must register articles, but a company limited by shares or by guarantee need not register articles if the prescribed model articles are to apply.[27] Section 20 provides for the default application of model articles,[28] either if articles are not registered or if they are, insofar as they do not exclude or modify the relevant model articles. Section 19 contains the power to prescribe model articles, which are contained in the Companies (Model Articles) Regulations 2008.[29] They do not follow the time-honoured practice over many years of being known as Table A (for companies limited by shares). They are more appropriately tailored to the needs of the different types of company than the Table that was prescribed under the Companies Act 1985.[30]

4.5 REGISTRATION

Section 9 of the Companies Act 2006 requires that the memorandum of association must be delivered to the registrar[31] together with an application for registration, the documents required by the section and a statement of compliance. Under s 14, if the registrar is satisfied that the requirements of the Act as to registration are complied with, he must register the documents. The application for registration must state:

---

[24] The Companies (Registration) Regulations 2008, SI 2008/3014, Sch 1.
[25] Section 8. Note that there is no bar on all the subscribers to a British company being foreigners: *Re General Company for Promotion of Land Credit* (1870) 5 Ch App 464; as to the significance of this within the European Union, see Chapter 2.
[26] Companies Act 2006, s 18(3).
[27] Section 18(2).
[28] Those prescribed at the date the company is registered: s 20(2).
[29] SI 2008/3229.
[30] This version, and indeed its predecessor under the Companies Act 1948, will continue to apply to many companies registered before 1 October 2009.
[31] This will be the English registrar if the company is to be registered in England and Wales (or Wales), the Scottish registrar if the company is to be Scottish or the Northern Irish registrar if the company is to be registered there.

(1) the company's proposed name;[32]

(2) whether its registered office is to be situated in England and Wales (or Wales), in Scotland or in Northern Ireland;

(3) whether the liability of the members is to be limited and if so whether by shares or guarantee; and

(4) whether the company is to be a private or a public company.[33]

If it is delivered by a person as agent for the subscribers, it must state his name and address.[34] It must contain a statement of the intended address of the company's registered office and a copy of any proposed articles unless one of the default models is being used.[35]

The application in respect of a company with a share capital must contain a statement of capital and initial shareholdings.[36] The detail is prescribed by s 10 and this is a new requirement. Previously the memorandum would state the amount of the company's initial authorised share capital, but the concept of authorised capital was abolished by the 2006 Act and that requirement has been replaced by a statement of capital that reflects the actual number of shares issued.[37] A statement of capital has to be registered every time there is a change in the amount of issued share capital, as described in chapters 7 and 8. The statement of capital must state:

(1) the total number of shares to be taken on formation by the subscribers to the memorandum;

(2) the aggregate nominal value of those shares;

(3) for each class of shares:

    (a) prescribed particulars of the rights attached to the shares;[38]
    (b) the total number of shares of that class;

---

[32] As to the name, see **4.22**.

[33] Section 9(2).

[34] Section 9(3).

[35] Section 9(5).

[36] Section 9(4)(a).

[37] As regards companies existing before 1 October 2009, which will have had an authorised capital in their memorandum, the Companies Act 2006 (Commencement No 8, Transitional Provisions and Savings) Order 2008, SI 2008/2860, Sch 2, para 42 provides that the provision for this is to be treated as a provision of the articles, but it may be amended or revoked by ordinary resolution.

[38] These are prescribed by the Companies (Shares and Share Capital) Order 2009, SI 2009/388, art 2(3) and are (a) particulars of any voting rights attached to the shares, including rights that arise only in certain circumstances; (b) particulars of any rights attached to the shares, as respects dividends, to participate in a distribution; (c) particulars of any rights attached to the shares, as respects capital, to participate in a

     (c)   the aggregate nominal value of shares of that class; and

(4)   the amount paid up and the amount (if any) unpaid on each shares (whether on account of the nominal value of the shares or by way of premium).[39]

By s 10(3), it must contain information to be prescribed for the purposes of identifying the subscribers and state the above information with respect to each subscriber. This is the name and address of each subscriber.[40]

The application in respect of a company to be limited by guarantee must contain a statement of guarantee.[41] This must contain the prescribed information for the purpose of identifying the subscribers, namely their names and addresses,[42] and state that each member undertakes that, if the company is wound up while he is a member or within one year of his creasing to be a member, he will contribute to the assets of the company an amount not exceeding a specified amount to pay the debts and liabilities of the company contracted before he became a member, the expenses of winding-up and the cost of adjusting the rights of the contributories among themselves.[43]

All applications must contain a statement of the company's proposed officers.[44] This[45] will contain the required particulars of the first director or directors and, in the case of public companies and private companies that choose to have a secretary,[46] of the first secretary or joint secretaries of the company. These particulars are the same as those required under ss 162–166 and ss 277–279, respectively, as described in **15.14**. There must also be a consent to act by each of these persons and they are deemed, on the incorporation of the company, to have been appointed to the office in question.[47]

Section 13 deals with the statement of compliance that the requirements in respect of registration have been complied with, which the registrar may accept as sufficient evidence of compliance.

The other requirement for registration of a company is payment of the appropriate fee.[48]

---

    distribution (including on winding up); and (d) whether the shares are to be redeemed or are liable to be redeemed at the option of the company or the shareholder.

[39]   Section 10(2).

[40]   The Companies (Registration) Regulations 2008, SI 2008/3014, reg 3.

[41]   Section 9(4)(b).

[42]   See note 39.

[43]   Section 11.

[44]   Section 9(4)(c).

[45]   Section 12.

[46]   As to this choice, see **15.16.2**.

[47]   Section 16(6).

[48]   This is governed by regulations made under s 1063 but note that the Companies

4.6 THE CERTIFICATE OF INCORPORATION

Section 15(1) of the Companies Act 2006 requires that on the registration of a company, the registrar shall give a certificate that the company is incorporated. The certificate must state:

(1) the name and registered number of the company;

(2) the date of its incorporation;

(3) whether it is limited or unlimited and, in the case of the former, whether it is limited by shares or by guarantee;

(4) whether it is a private or public company; and

(5) whether the registered office is to be in England and Wales (or Wales), in Scotland or in Northern Ireland.[49]

From the date of incorporation, the subscribers of the memorandum together with such other persons as may from time to time become members of the company are a body corporate by the name stated in the certificate, which is capable of exercising all the functions of an incorporated company, with the status and registered office of the company as stated in the application for registration.[50]

Section 1064[51] requires the registrar to publish in the *Gazette* or in a manner specified under s 1116, which will allow publication via the Internet, notice of the issue by him of any certificate of incorporation of a company. This must state the name and registered number of the company and the date of issue.

Section 15(4) deals with the problem of irregularities in the process of registration. It provides that a certificate shall be conclusive evidence that the requirements of the Act as to registration have been complied with, and that the company is duly registered under the Act. Under predecessors to this provision it has been held that the certificate of incorporation is conclusive evidence that there is a company, and that it is duly incorporated.[52] The certificate is also conclusive evidence that the

---

Act 2006 (Commencement No 8, Transitional Provisions and Savings) Order 2008, SI 2008/2860, Sch 2, para 94 provides that the regulations prescribed under s 708 of the Companies Act 1985 have effect as if made under s 1063. These are the Companies (Fees) Regulations 2004, SI 2004/2621.

[49] Section 15(2). As to the right to require a copy of the certificate, see s 1065. The certificate must be signed by the registrar or authenticated by his official seal. Note that it is possible to obtain registration on the same day as the documents are handed in or to obtain it online.

[50] Section 16(2), (3) and (4).

[51] [CA 1985, s 711].

[52] *Hammond v Prentice Brothers* [1920] 1 Ch 201.

registration and incorporation of the company were fully effected on the day mentioned in the certificate. The date mentioned in the certificate is the first day of the company's existence, and the company is deemed to have been incorporated on the first moment of that day.[53] However, s 15(4) deals only with ministerial acts, and a certificate does not establish the fact that the company is not a trade union and therefore incapable of registration.[54] The registrar will refuse registration if he is of the opinion that any object of the company is illegal, and an appeal from his decision can be brought to the High Court by way of judicial review seeking an order that he be required to register.[55] Where the registrar permits registration, the Attorney-General may be given leave for judicial review where the objects of the company involve entering into contracts which are sexually immoral.[56]

4.7 TRADING CERTIFICATE FOR PUBLIC COMPANIES

As a way of guaranteeing that a newly incorporated public company satisfies the requirement as to its authorised minimum capital described in **4.2**, s 761 of the Companies Act 2006[57] provides an administrative safeguard. A company registered as a public company (other than by virtue of re-registration) may not do business or exercise any borrowing powers unless the registrar issues a trading certificate. The registrar must issue such a certificate if, on an application for it, he is satisfied that the nominal value of the company's allotted share capital is not less than the authorised minimum.[58] This presumably still leaves him the discretion in an appropriate case to inquire further. Shares allotted in pursuance of an employees' share scheme may not be taken into account in determining the nominal value of the company's allotted share capital unless they are paid up at least as to one-quarter of their nominal value and the whole of any premium.[59]

An application for a trading certificate must:[60]

(1)   state that the nominal value of the company's allotted share capital is not less than the authorised minimum;

---

[53]   *Jubilee Cotton Mills v Lewis* [1924] AC 958 (HL).

[54]   *Edinburgh and District Aerated Water Manufacturers' Defence Association v Jenkinson* (1904) 5 F 1159 (Ct of Sess): *British Association of Glass Bottle Manufacturers v Nettlefold* (1911) 27 TLR 527.

[55]   *R v Registrar of Companies, ex parte More* [1941] 2 KB 197 (CA). If the conditions laid down in the Act have been complied with (and the purpose of the company is not illegal) the court will compel the registrar to issue a certificate of incorporation: *R v Registrar of Companies, ex parte Bowen* [1914] 4 KB 1161.

[56]   *R v Registrar of Companies, ex parte Attorney-General* [1991] BCLC 476.

[57]   [CA 1985, s 117].

[58]   Section 761(2).

[59]   Section 761(3).

[60]   Section 762.

(2)   specify the amount, or estimated amount, of the company's preliminary expenses;

(3)   specify any amount or benefit paid or given or intended to be paid or given to any promoter of the company, and the consideration for the payment or benefit; and

(4)   be accompanied by a statement of compliance, which is a statement that the company meets the requirements for the issue of a trading certificate.

The registrar may accept the statement of compliance as sufficient evidence of the matters stated in it.[61]

A trading certificate is 'conclusive evidence that the company is entitled to do business and exercise any borrowing powers'.[62] Where a company does business or exercises borrowing powers in contravention of the section, criminal penalties are imposed on the company and any officer in default.[63] There are, however, two further sanctions. First, the Secretary of State may present a petition to wind up a company on the ground that it is a public company which was registered as such on its original incorporation but that it has not been issued with a certificate under s 761 and more than a year has expired since it was registered.[64] It may be noted that, unlike the criminal penalties, this sanction may be invoked against a company incorporated as public even though it has not otherwise infringed s 761 by doing business, etc. The fact that it has lain dormant for a year would be sufficient. However, such a company (eg where it is unable to raise the authorised minimum capital) could apply to re-register as a private company.[65] An undertaking to do so might persuade the court not to grant a winding-up order.

The second additional sanction concerns transactions entered into by a company in contravention of its provisions.[66] It is important to note that such transactions are expressly declared to be valid. If, however, a company fails to comply with its obligations under such a transaction within 21 days of being called upon to do so (ie by the other party), the directors who were directors at the time the company entered into the transaction become jointly and severally liable to indemnify the other

---

[61]   Section 762(3). The registrar has wide powers under s 1068 to impose requirements as to the form, authentication and manner of delivery of documents delivered to him.

[62]   Section 761(4). In view of the protection given to third parties even where no certificate is issued (see below), this must be intended to protect the company and its officers.

[63]   Section 767(1) and (2).

[64]   Insolvency Act 1986, ss 122(1)(b) and 124(4). This would not seem to exclude others entitled to present a petition under s 124(1) doing so on this ground.

[65]   The predecessor to s 761 expressly so provided and indeed made it mandatory to re-register following a failure to show the required minimum capital. This is not repeated in the 2006 Act provisions, but the option must be there.

[66]   Section 767(3) and (4).

party to the transaction in respect of any loss or damage suffered by him by reason of the failure of the company to comply with those obligations.

4.8 UNLIMITED COMPANIES

So far in this chapter it has mainly been assumed that a company is formed with the liability of its members limited, but it has long been possible to register a company with unlimited liability. However, before the Companies Act 1967 very few companies, other than estate companies, were registered with unlimited liability, and many banking and other companies originally constituted as unlimited companies were re-registered with limited liability. When the 1967 Act relieved unlimited companies from the disclosure requirements in respect of accounts that apply to limited companies (private or public),[67] some encouragement was provided for the registration or re-registration of unlimited companies. The members of an unlimited company are liable in a liquidation to contribute until the whole of the company's debts or obligations (however heavy they may be) are paid, but their primary liability is at an end once they have ceased to be members.[68] An unlimited company must always now be classified as a private company.

Unlimited companies may be registered either with or without a capital divided into shares. The capital (if the company has a capital) may be varied at any time by special resolution without the sanction of the court, and, if the articles allow it, capital may be returned to members, and they may cease to be members on such terms as may be agreed upon.[69]

So far as regards the powers of an unlimited company and of its directors, the conduct of its business and proceedings, the amendment of its articles, and its winding-up, the same considerations apply as in the case of a limited company. The returns required to be made by unlimited companies are the same as those by other companies, although there is a different form for a return of allotments made by an unlimited company with a share capital.[70]

4.9 COMPANIES LIMITED BY GUARANTEE

Companies limited by guarantee are usually formed for the purpose of carrying on business as mutual insurance and trade protection societies, social, athletic and other clubs, and concerns in which it is not intended to

---

[67] Although many private limited companies are now relieved from many of the disclosure requirements; see **1.4** and Chapter 14.

[68] Past members may in certain circumstances escape liability, e g if they have ceased to be members of the company a year or more before the commencement of the winding-up; see s 74 of the Insolvency Act 1986.

[69] *Re Borough Commercial and Building Society* [1894] 2 Ch 242.

[70] See **7.10**.

make a profit. There are two kinds of guarantee company still provided for under the Companies Act 2006:[71] companies limited by guarantee and not having a share capital; and companies limited by guarantee and having a share capital. It is only the first kind that is considered here, since the hybrid variety was in practice rarely used, and, since the Companies Act 1980, it has not been possible to register any more such companies. It should be noted that there is no provision for a company limited by shares to re-register as a company limited by guarantee or vice versa.

The principle on which these companies are constituted can be seen from the statement of guarantee described in s 11, which was considered in **4.5**. The guaranteed amount may be any sum the subscribers to that document think fit – £1 or £1,000, or any other sum, large or small. The amount is not part of the capital of the company, and cannot be mortgaged or charged by debentures.[72]

In the form which is usually adopted the amount of the guarantee of each member remains the same, whatever his pecuniary interest in the company may be, and (beyond that interest) is the utmost extent to which he can be a loser in the event of the company going into liquidation. The guarantee, moreover, is only so much per member, and accordingly, if the number of members is reduced, the aggregate amount guaranteed is also reduced. Thus the security of a creditor is lessened to that extent, unless the articles provide for membership continuing until some other person takes the place of the member then on the register. Section 37 provides that in respect of a guarantee company without a share capital any provision in the articles or in any resolution of the company purporting to give any person a right to participate in the divisible profits of the company otherwise than as a member is void.

There is no longer any special provision regarding the articles of a guarantee company,[73] so that the same considerations will apply as described in **4.4**.

4.9.1 Exemption from using 'limited' as part of the name

Guarantee companies whose business is charitable or similar may be entitled to an exemption from using 'limited' as a part of their name. The exemption has been in existence for some years, but was redrafted somewhat in the 2006 Act. Section 60 does not itself confine the exemption to guarantee companies, but the regulations do so,[74] as described below. Section 61 of the 2006 Act preserves an exemption for

---

[71] See ss 3 and 5.

[72] *Re Pyle Works* (1890) 44 Ch D 544, at 574 and 584; *Re Irish Club Co* [1906] WN 127.

[73] This was s 8(4) of the Companies Act 1985, the predecessor to which was construed liberally in *Gaiman v National Association for Mental Health* [1971] 1 Ch 317.

[74] The Companies and Business Names (Miscellaneous Provisions) Regulations 2009, SI 2009/1085, reg 2.

private companies limited by shares that were exempt on 25 February 1982 (for British companies) or on 30 June 1983 (for Northern Irish companies). With the qualification that this section prohibits the return of share capital, the requirements are broadly the same as the exemption in s 62, as described below.

Section 62 preserves the exemption of guarantee companies conferred by s 30 of the Companies Act 1985 in relation to such companies exempt immediately before the commencement of Part 5 of the 2006 Act.[75] The objects of the company must be the promotion of commerce, art, science, education, religion, charity or any profession and anything incidental or conducive to those objects. In addition the articles must require that its income is applied in promoting its objects, and prohibit the payment of dividends to members. The articles must also require all the assets (which would otherwise be available, on a winding-up, to its members generally) to be transferred on its winding-up either to another body with objects similar to its own, or to another body whose objects are the promotion of charity and anything incidental or conducive to it. A company so exempt may not amend its articles so that it ceases to comply with the conditions for exemption.[76]

From the commencement of the 2006 Act, companies not within the above exemptions are governed by s 60. This provides exemption for a private company that is either (a) a charity or (b) is exempt by regulations made by the Secretary of State. To claim the exemption, a statement must be delivered to the registrar that the company meets the conditions for exemption, which the registrar may accept as sufficient evidence of the matters stated in it. The effect of the regulations is that a guarantee company is subject to exemption on the same basis as under the previous law described above.[77]

In respect of exemptions under any of the above sections, by s 64, if it appears to the Secretary of State that a company has ceased to be entitled to it, he may, in writing, direct the company to change its name (by resolution of the directors) within a specified period so that the name ends with 'limited' or a permitted alternative. Notice of the resolution must be filed with the registrar. A company which has received such a direction may not subsequently change its name so that it does *not* include the word 'limited' or a permitted alternative.[78]

4.10 THE RE-REGISTRATION OF COMPANIES

The Companies Act 2006 provides for a number of ways in which a company may be re-registered, for example from private to public. The

---

[75] That is, 1 October 2009.
[76] Section 63(1).
[77] See footnote 74.
[78] Section 64(7), except on re-registration or conversion to a community interest company.

principal requirements are examined in the following paragraphs. It should be noted that none of the provisions permits a limited company to change to a different form of limited liability (ie a company limited by share capital to one limited by guarantee or vice versa).

4.11 THE RE-REGISTRATION OF PRIVATE COMPANIES AS PUBLIC

Sections 90–96[79] provide for the re-registration of private companies, whether limited or unlimited, as public companies. Section 90 requires the company to pass a special resolution to re-register and then to make an application accompanied by the documents required by s 94 and a statement of compliance.[80] It must also meet certain conditions specified in s 90(2), namely that:

(1) it has a share capital;

(2) it meets the requirements in s 91 as to the nominal value of its allotted share capital;

(3) it meets the requirements in s 92 as regards its nets assets;

(4) it meets the requirements of s 93 relating to shares recently allotted for a non-cash consideration, if relevant; and

(5) it has not previously been re-registered as unlimited.

The detailed requirements as to (2), (3) and (4) are described in **4.11.1**. The company must make such changes in its name and in its articles as are necessary in connection with its becoming a public company. For example, articles restricting the transfer or transmission of shares, or entrenching the position of the existing directors on the board, might have to be changed. This would certainly be necessary where admission of the shares to trading on a recognised investment exchange was contemplated. An unlimited company must make such changes in its articles as are necessary to its becoming a limited company.

Under s 94, the application must contain a statement for the company's proposed name on re-registration and, in the case of a company without a secretary, a statement of the proposed secretary.[81] It must be accompanied by the following documents:

---

[79] [CA 1985, ss 43–47].

[80] This is a statement that the requirements as to re-registration have been complied with, which the registrar may accept as sufficient evidence that the company is entitled to be re-registered: s 94(3) and (4).

[81] This must include the particulars that will have to be included in the register of secretaries under s 277–299 (see **15.16.3**) and a consent to act: s 95.

(1) a copy of the special resolution (unless that has already been filed under s 30);

(2) a copy of the articles as proposed to be amended;

(3) a copy of the balance sheet and other documents in s 92(1); and[82]

(4) a copy of the valuation report required where shares have been issued for non-cash consideration.[83]

4.11.1   Requirements as to share capital, net assets and valuation

As explained above, there are three key requirements that a private company seeking re-registration as a public company must comply with. Section 91(1) provides that, at the time the special resolution required by s 90 is passed, the following requirements as to the company's share capital must be satisfied.[84]

(1) The nominal value of the company's allotted share capital must be not less than the authorised minimum.[85]

(2) Each of the allotted shares must be paid up at least as to one-quarter of the nominal value of that share and the whole of any premium on it.

(3) If any shares in the company or any premium payable on it have been fully or partly paid up by an undertaking given by any person that he or another should do work or perform services for the company or another, the undertaking must have been performed or otherwise discharged.

(4) If shares in the company have been allotted as fully or partly paid up as to their nominal value or any premium payable on them otherwise than in cash and the consideration for the allotment consists of or includes an undertaking to the company (other than one to which (3) above applies), then either:

    (a) that undertaking must have been performed or otherwise discharged; or
    (b) there must be a contract between the company and any person pursuant to which that undertaking must be performed within five years from the time of the special resolution.

---

[82] See **4.13**.
[83] See **4.13**.
[84] There are qualifications in respect of shares allotted before the dates on which the predecessor to this section first came into force: see s 91(2)–(4).
[85] See **4.7**.

The requirements as to net assets are in s 92. These impose a capital maintenance requirement[86] to the effect that the amount of the company's net assets, that is its net worth taking account of the value of its assets and the value of its liabilities, must not be less than the aggregate of its called-up share capital and undistributable reserves. This must have been the case as at the last balance sheet date, which must be no more than 7 months before delivery of the application to re-register, as conformed by the auditor, and nothing must have happened in the interim that has caused the net assets to become worth less than the aggregate of its called-up share capital and undistributable reserves.

A valuation is required by s 93 where shares are allotted by the company between the balance sheet date and the passing of the special resolution as fully or partly paid up as to their nominal value or any premium on them otherwise than in cash. In this event, s 93 applies the general provisions applying to public companies allotting shares for non-cash considera-tion.[87]

4.11.2   The effect of re-registration under s 90

If the registrar is satisfied that a company may be re-registered as a public company, he must do so and issue the company with an altered certificate of incorporation stating that the company is a public company.[88] On the issue of this certificate, the company becomes a public company and the changes in its name and the articles take effect.[89]

4.12   PUBLIC COMPANIES RE-REGISTERING AS PRIVATE

Section 97[90] allows companies registered as public companies to re-register as private companies. This can apply to companies registered on incorporation as public and also to private companies which have re-registered as public.

The procedure for re-registration follows the usual pattern in requiring first a special resolution that the company be re-registered. The name of the company (ending 'public limited company') will of course have to be changed to simply 'limited' and it must make such changes as are necessary in its articles. The application must contain a statement of the company's proposed name on re-registration and be accompanied by a

---

[86]   As to this generally for public companies, see **7.14**.
[87]   See **7.14.3**.
[88]   Section 96(1) and (2).
[89]   Section 96(4). So also does an appointment of a secretary when the company did not, as a private company, have one.
[90]   [CA 1985, s 53].

copy of the resolution and of the articles as proposed to be amended, together with a statement of compliance.[91]

The special resolution may be challenged by dissenting members applying to the court to have the resolution cancelled under s 98. An application may be made to the court within 28 days after the passing of the resolution on behalf of the persons entitled to make it by such one or more of their number as they may appoint for the purpose. The persons entitled to make the application are members who did not consent to or vote in favour of the resolution and who meet any of the following criteria:

(1)   holders of not less in aggregate than 5% in nominal value of the company's issued share capital or any class thereof;

(2)   if the company is not limited by shares, by not less than 5% of the company's members; or

(3)   by not less than 50 of the company's members.

Where such an application is made, the applicants must immediately give notice to the registrar, and on being served with notice of the application, the company itself must immediately notify the registrar.[92] The company must also deliver a copy of the court order to the registrar within 15 days from the making of the order or within such longer time as the court may at any time by order direct.

The court which hears an application to cancel or confirm a resolution is given wide powers. It may make that order on such terms or conditions as it thinks fit. Further, it may, if it thinks fit, adjourn the proceedings in order that an arrangement may be made to the satisfaction of the court for the purchase of the interest of dissentient members. It may give such directions and make such orders as it thinks expedient for facilitating or carrying into effect any such arrangement. The court is given the further power to provide for the company itself to purchase the shares of any member of the company. Where that is ordered, the company's capital will be reduced accordingly. Such an order may make the necessary alterations in the articles that are required in consequence. Quite apart from the power to order the company to purchase dissenters' shares, there is a further power to require the company not to make any, or any specified, amendments to its articles without the leave of the court.

The wide powers which s 98 confers on the court are similar to those conferred on a court hearing a petition by unfairly prejudiced minority shareholders under Part 30 of the Companies Act 2006.[93] It remains to be

---

[91]   Section 100.
[92]   Section 99(1) and (2).
[93]   See Part 2 of Chapter 18.

seen how the courts will exercise these powers in this context, since the ground for giving relief is quite distinct from that of unfair prejudice. Since the complainants under s 98 will, if the resolution is confirmed, be deprived of a market for their shares (e g the company will cease to be a listed company, where that had been the case), it is to be hoped the court will as a rule be prepared to grant some form of relief where it decides not to cancel the resolution. The most obvious solution is that indicated by s 98 – the purchase of the dissenter's shares by or on behalf of the majority shareholders or by the company itself.

4.13 RE-REGISTRATION OF PRIVATE AND PUBLIC LIMITED COMPANIES AS UNLIMITED COMPANIES

Section 102[94] allows the conversion of a private limited company into an unlimited one on application to the registrar for re-registration,[95] provided that:

(1) the unanimous consent of the members[96] has been obtained;

(2) the company has not previously been re-registered as limited; and

(3) the application is accompanied by the documents required by s 103 and a statement of compliance.

The company must make the necessary changes in its name and articles including the appropriate ones if it is to have a share capital. The application will contain a statement of the proposed new name and be accompanied by the prescribed form of assent, authenticated by or on behalf of all the members of the company, and a copy of the articles as proposed to be amended. The statement of compliance must contain a statement by the directors that the persons who have authenticated the form constitute the whole membership of the company and, if any of them have not authenticated the form themselves, that the directors have taken all reasonable steps to satisfy themselves that each person who authenticated it on behalf of a member was lawfully empowered to do so.

The 2006 Act also allows a public company to re-register directly as an unlimited private company.[97] The requirements and conditions are effectively the same as those just discussed in the case of private companies seeking re-registration as unlimited companies, in particular the requirement for unanimous consent of the members. The company must not previously have been re-registered as limited or as unlimited.

---

94 [CA 1985, s 49.]
95 This procedure was first introduced by the Companies Act 1967 to enable private companies to escape the disclosure obligations imposed on them by that Act.
96 This includes, where appropriate, a trustee in bankruptcy of a member or a personal representative of a deceased member.
97 Section 109; this mode of re-registration was new in the 2006 Act.

4.14   RE-REGISTRATION OF UNLIMITED COMPANIES AS PRIVATE LIMITED COMPANIES

The converse procedure for re-registering an unlimited company as a private limited company follows broadly the same pattern. However, instead of the unanimous consent of all the members, s 105[98] requires the passing of a special resolution. This resolution must state whether the liability of members is to be limited by shares or by guarantee.

Section 77 of the Insolvency Act 1986 provides that those who were members at the time of re-registration shall remain liable to contribute if the company is wound up within 3 years of the re-registration, even though they have become past members by the time the winding-up commences. Such past members remain liable to contribute to the company's debts and liabilities incurred before the re-registration as if the company had not been re-registered as limited. Further, where none of the members at the time of the re-registration remain members at the commencement of the liquidation, those who were existing or past members at the time of re-registration are liable to contribute without limit to the debts and liabilities incurred before re-registration. This is notwithstanding the fact that the existing members at the time of winding up have 'satisfied the contribution required to be made by them' under the Companies Act 2006 and the Insolvency Act 1986.

4.15   PROMOTING COMPANIES

It is now appropriate to consider the legal position regarding those who are involved in the formation of a company, conventionally called promoters. The legal principles were developed at a time (the mid to late nineteenth century) when it was common to form what would now be a public limited company to launch a business venture or take over an existing one with money raised from the public. It is now less common for that to happen, as most public companies have been private and are re-registered as public. It is not entirely clear that the people involved in this process of re-registration and public offering are promoters as described below. They may be, although potential liability is perhaps more likely to fall under the provisions regarding prospectuses that are covered in Chapter 19. There will be promoters of private companies, although given that the vast majority of these are formed by a small number of people who are fully informed as to each of their circumstances, it is not that likely that there will in practice be any problems arising from the duties that the law imposes on promoters. The following account should be read in the light of these points

The courts have always refused, rightly, to define what constitutes a 'promoter'. If a rigid definition were given, those who want to avoid the

---

[98]   [CA 1985, s 51].

liabilities of the position would be careful to come very close to the line without crossing it. The best description is that of Bowen LJ:[99]

> 'The term "promoter" is a term not of law but of business, usefully summing up in a single word a number of business operations, familiar to the commercial world, by which a company is generally brought into existence.'

But probably there should be added 'and by which its original capital is provided'. The promotion does not necessarily cease with the registration of the company, for 'a person not a director may be a promoter of a company which is already incorporated but the capital of which has not been taken up'.[100]

In seeking to ascertain who are the promoters of a company, it is useful to ask the following questions.

(1) Who started the idea of forming a company for the purpose in question?

(2) Who decided what was to be included in the articles of association and in the prospectus, or gave the lawyers instructions to prepare them and information upon which they might be prepared?

(3) Who undertook the liability for the costs of preparing those documents, registering the company and making the preliminary agreements?

(4) Who sought out the persons who ultimately became the first directors, and induced them to undertake the office?

(5) Who procured the subscription of the capital?

(6) Who benefited by the formation of the company?

However, none of these questions is decisive. A person may have done one or more of these things, and yet not be a promoter; or a person may have kept in the background and have appeared to do none of these things, and yet be a promoter. Usually, however, persons who have busied themselves in procuring subscriptions or underwriting will find it very hard to escape from being held to be promoters. Further, a person may be a promoter who is acting only as agent for others, or as a director of a promoting syndicate, if he has personally taken an active part in the promotion.[101]

---

[99] *Whaley Bridge Calico Printing Co v Green* (1880) 5 QBD 109.
[100] *Emma Silver Mining Co v Lewis* (1879) 4 CPD 396, at 407.
[101] *Lydney and Wigpool Iron Ore Co v Bird* (1886) 44 Ch D 85, at 94.

Frequently, the vendors of property to a company are the promoters,[102] but if they have done no more than agree to sell, they will not be promoters; nor will the solicitors who, as part of their professional duty, prepared the contracts.[103] However, the courts will look at the substance of a transaction, and vendors or others who are in reality the promoters will not escape liability by the interposition of a nominal vendor or a nominal promoter, who professes to purchase and resell the property or to undertake the financial operations incidental to forming and floating a company.[104]

4.16 DUTIES OF PROMOTERS

The relation of a promoter to the company he is about to form, although not strictly that of a trustee to his beneficiary, or of an agent to his principal, is of the same nature. It follows that he may not secretly make a profit for himself, nor otherwise benefit at the expense of the company. Thus Lindley LJ described the relationship between a promoter and his company as follows:[105]

> 'Although not an agent of the company nor a trustee for it before its formation, the old familiar principles of the law of agency and of trusteeship have been extended, and very properly extended, to meet such cases. It is perfectly well settled that a promoter of a company is accountable to it for all moneys secretly obtained by him from it, just as if the relationship of principal and agent, or of trustee and *cestui que trust*, had really existed between him and the company when the money was so obtained.'

The fiduciary relationship extends, moreover, not only to the company as constituted at the time, but also to future allottees of shares. Thus disclosure of profits made by the promoters must be made not only to the subscribers to the memorandum.

The fiduciary position commences as soon as the promoter begins to act for or promote the company, but not earlier. The fact of acquiring property with the intention of ultimately forming a company that will acquire and develop it does not render the purchaser accountable for the profit he makes on the resale, so long as the company, on coming into existence, is informed that the person selling to the company and the promoter are identical.[106] The same rule applies even though the

---

[102] *Twycross v Grant* (1877) 2 CPD 469; *Gluckstein v Barnes* [1990] AC 240, at 249 (HL).

[103] *Re Great Wheal Polgooth Co Ltd* (1884) 54 LJ Ch 42.

[104] See *Twycross v Grant* (1877) 2 CPD 469; *Bagnall v Carlton* (1877) 6 Ch D 471; *Emma Silver Mining Co v Lewis* (1879) 4 CPD 496; *Erlanger v New Sombrero Phosphate Co* (1878) 3 App Cas 1218 (HL); *Emma Silver Mining Co v Grant* (1879) 11 Ch D 918; *Nant-y-Glo and Blaina Ironworks Co v Grave* (1878) 12 Ch D 748; *Lydney and Wigpool Iron Ore Co v Bird* (1886) 33 Ch D 85.

[105] *Lydney and Wigpool Iron Ore Co v Bird* (1886) 33 Ch D 85, at 94.

[106] *Cavendish Bentinck v Fenn* (1887) 12 App Cas 652 (HL); *Gover's Case* (1875) 1 Ch D

acquisition is only in the form of an option or uncompleted contract,[107] or where the promoter contracted to sell 'the benefit of a lease agreed to be granted', and in fact there was no agreement for the lease, but only negotiations which ultimately resulted in a lease which was assigned to the company.[108] But any profit which the promoter makes after he has begun to promote the company, and the benefit of any contracts into which he enters during the period, *prima facie* belong to the company.[109] It is, however, too much to say that what a promoter acquires after he has commenced the promotion *ipso facto* belongs to the company. The question whether the promoter is in fact acquiring as agent for the intended company or for himself is one of fact; but where the scheme throughout is that he will resell at a profit, the natural inference is that he is not acting as agent for the company, and if there is no concealment of the fact that he is the vendor when he resells the company, the company cannot claim the profit.[110]

If the promoter was not at the time he bought in a fiduciary position, though subsequently and at the time of his resale of the company he is in a fiduciary position and does not disclose his interest, the company is entitled to rescind. If in such a case rescission has become impossible, the company cannot recover from the promoter, as money had and received, the profit he has made, or damages.[111]

However, if an additional secret profit has been made under a separate transaction which it is still open to the company to rescind, or under an ancillary transaction to which it was not a party, such a profit may be recovered.[112] Furthermore, a promoter will be liable in deceit if it can be shown that he has caused loss to the company by making fraudulent statements.[113]

182; *Erlanger v New Sombrero Phosphate Co* (1878) 3 App Cas 1218; *Ladywell Mining Co v Brookes* (1887) 35 Ch D 400. Compare *Burland v Earle* [1902] AC 83 (PC): the case of a director purchasing privately and selling to his company.

[107] *Gover's Case* (1875) 1 Ch D 182, followed in *Ladywell Mining Co v Brookes* (1887) 35 Ch D 400.

[108] *Omnium Electric Palaces v Baines* [1914] 1 Ch 332 (CA).

[109] *Ladywell Mining Co v Brookes* (1887) 35 Ch D 400; *Re Cape Breton Co* (1885) 29 Ch D 795, affirmed sub nom *Cavendish Bentinck v Fenn* (1887) 12 App Cas 652 (HL).

[110] *Omnium Electric Palaces v Baines* [1914] 1 Ch 332 (CA).

[111] *Gover's Case* [1875] 1 Ch D 182; *Re Cape Breton Co* (1885) 29 Ch D 795; *Ladywell Mining Co v Brookes* (1887) 35 Ch D 400; *Re Lady Forrest (Murchison) Gold Mine* [1901] 1 Ch 582; *Burland v Earle* [1902] AC 83; *Re Jacobus Marler Estates v Marler* (1913) 114 LT 640 note; *Cook v Deeks* [1916] AC 554 (PC). But in *Cavendish Bentinck v Fenn* (1887) 12 App Cas 652 (HL) Lord Hershell, at 664, suggested there might be a remedy in damages.

[112] *Gluckstein v Barnes* [1900] AC 240 (HL); *Jubilee Cotton Mills v Lewis* [1924] AC 958 (HL).

[113] *Re Leeds & Hanley Theatre of Varieties* [1902] 2 Ch 809 (CA). Where misstatements are made negligently which induce the company to enter into a contract in reliance on them, there may be liability under s 2(1) of the Misrepresentation Act 1967 (this Act does not apply in Scotland, but the Law Reform (Miscellaneous Provisions) (Scotland) Act 1985, s 10, allows for the award of damages for a negligent misrepresentation). Where the

4.16.1   To whom disclosure must be made

Promoters will not be protected by disclosures made before the public has joined the company unless there is an independent board or body of shareholders to receive and act upon the information, and the directors who participate in the profits must not be counted as independent.[114] Thus mere communication to the subscribers to the memorandum of association who are clerks in the vendor's office is obviously a farce, even though they hold a meeting and are the only members of the company. Equally, disclosure to directors who are mere nominees of the vendors or promoters will not be sufficient.[115] In such a case the information should be given in the prospectus;[116] and even if all the facts are known to all the members of the company at the time the contract is made, but a misleading prospectus is subsequently issued by the promoters to the public inviting them to join the company, the promoters will be liable.[117] If, however, there is no intention of making a public issue of shares, and no such issue is in fact made, the knowledge by all the directors and members of the company of the facts will exonerate the promoters, even where the purchase price has been greatly inflated.[118]

Where a promoter has to account to the company for secret profits, the measure of recovery is the amount of profit made by the promoter,[119] but he is allowed to deduct from the amount all reasonable expenses he has been put to, and is liable only for the net profits made.[120]

4.17   THE REMUNERATION OF PROMOTERS

The traditional way for promoters to obtain their reward was in the form of the profit made on property sold to the company or in some other

---

promoter can establish a reasonable ground for belief, he will have a defence to an action under s 2(1). However, the court under s 2(2) may now award damages in lieu of rescission when this latter remedy would otherwise be available for innocent misrepresentation. Finally, the company may have an action for negligent misstatement at common law within the principle laid down in *Hedley Byrne & Co Ltd v Heller & Partners Ltd* [1964] AC 465 (HL).

[114] *Re Leeds and Hanley Theatre of Varieties* [1902] 2 Ch 809 (CA); *Erlanger v New Sombrero Phosphate Co* (1878) 4 App Cas 1218 (HL); *Re Olympia* [1898] 2 Ch 153, affirmed sub nom *Gluckstein v Barnes* [1900] AC 240 (HL).

[115] *Re Olympia* [1898] Ch 153 affirmed sub nom *Gluckstein v Barnes* [1990] AC 240. Cf *Kaye v Croydon Tramways* [1898] 1 Ch 358 (CA) and *Lagunas Nitrate Co v Lagunas Syndicate* [1899] 2 Ch 392, at 431 (CA).

[116] *Re Leeds and Hanley Theatre of Varieties* [1902] 2 Ch 809 (CA).

[117] *Lagunas Nitrate Co v Lagunas Syndicate* [1899] 2 Ch 392, at 428 (CA).

[118] *Re Ambrose Lake Tin and Copper Mining Co* (1880) 14 Ch D 390; *Re British Seamless Paper Box Co* (1881) 17 Ch D 467; *Re Innes & Co* [1904] 2 Ch 254; *Attorney-General for Canada v Standard Trust Co* [1911] AC 498 (PC).

[119] *Re Leeds and Hanley Theatre of Varieties* [1902] 2 Ch 809 (CA).

[120] *Emma Silver Mining Co v Grant* (1879) 11 Ch D 918; *Lydney and Wigpool Iron Ore Co v Bird* (1886) 33 Ch D 85.

ancillary transaction connected with its formation. It has been seen that if proper disclosure is made, such transactions are binding on the company.

Promoters have no right to any remuneration simply because the articles state that the promoters are entitled to a certain sum for their services. This does not of itself create a contract between the promoter and the company.[121] The promoter must prove the existence of a binding contract with the company,[122] and, as will be explained below, a contract purporting to be made with a company before it is formed is not binding upon it. This applies even to a claim for the preliminary expenses connected with the formation, such as registration fees.[123]

4.18   UNDERWRITING COMMISSION

The function at one time performed by the traditional promoter is now carried out in the case of public companies by a city issuing house. The remuneration of such a body will take the form of an underwriting commission and there are a number of statutory provisions governing such commission. Section 553 of the Companies Act 2006[124] allows an underwriting commission of up to 10% of the price at which the shares were issued to be paid if this is authorised by the company's articles and the commission paid or agreed to be paid does not exceed 10% of the price at which the shares are issued or the amount or rate authorised by the articles,[125] whichever is the less. Section 553(3) allows vendors or promoters the power to apply part of the money or shares received from the company in the payment of an underwriting commission which would have been lawful under the section if paid directly by the company.

Section 552[126] prohibits a company, save as authorised by s 553, from applying any of its shares or capital money either directly or indirectly in payment of commission; this applies to private as well as public companies.[127] However, there is no prohibition against paying commission unconditionally *out of profits* and this would seem to be lawful unless contrary to any stipulation in the articles.[128] Section 552 is very wide in its language, s 552(2) extending the prohibition in the following way:

---

[121]   *Re Rotherham Alum and Chemical Co* (1883) 25 Ch D 103 (CA). Moreover the directors may not rely on such a clause authorising payment unless they have made proper inquiry: *Re Englefield Colliery Co* (1878) 8 Ch D 388.

[122]   *Re English & Colonial Produce Co* [1906] 2 Ch 435 (CA).

[123]   *Re National Motor Mail Coach Co* [1908] 2 Ch 515 (CA).

[124]   [CA 1985, s 97].

[125]   If the articles allow a commission at a specified rate. This is not satisfied by a commission consisting of a lump sum: *Booth v New Afrikander Gold Mining Co* [1903] 1 Ch 295 (CA).

[126]   [CA 1985, s 98].

[127]   *Dominion of Canada General Trading & Investment Syndicate v Brigstocke* [1911] 2 KB 648.

[128]   In addition, the share premium account (see **7.15**) can be applied to paying commission.

'... it is immaterial how the shares or money are so applied, whether by being added to the purchase money of property acquired by the company or to the contract price of any work to be executed for the company, or being paid out of the nominal purchase money or contract price, or otherwise.'

Further, the court will look at the substance of the transaction, and will prohibit a pretended purchase and resale which is in fact only a device to cover payment of a commission.[129] However, an agreement giving underwriters an option to subscribe for further shares as consideration for underwriting is not an application of shares in payment of commission within the section and is lawful.[130]

Commission paid in respect of shares[131] must be disclosed in the annual return filed with the registrar.[132]

4.19   PRE-INCORPORATION CONTRACTS

Whether a company is formed to acquire a business, to work a mine, to develop a patent, to undertake financial business, or for any other purpose, those acting on its behalf may have entered into preliminary agreements for the purchase of the property or rights to be acquired, or for securing the services and connection of some manager or expert. In the case of the promotion of a public company, the promoters will want to offer the benefit of such agreements or contracts as an inducement to the public to take shares, and so it becomes necessary that the contracts should be made before the formation of the company, or at least before the general allotment of shares. Accordingly, an agreement or contract is usually prepared.

Where incorporation of the company has not yet been effected, the contract may be expressed to be made between the vendor and the company, the draft being initialled for the purpose of identification, or it may be made between the vendor and a trustee for the intended company and dated and executed. But in the latter case the company is not bound by the contract until it has entered into a direct agreement, after incorporation, to become so, since a company cannot ratify a contract made before it came into existence.[133] However, the company may be able to enforce the contract under the Contracts (Rights of Third Parties) Act 1999.

A contract can be made with a trustee for the company before the company has any existence, in which case the trustee will be personally bound by the contract unless he expressly protects himself from liability

---

[129]   *Booth v New Afrikander Gold Mining Co* [1903] 1 Ch 295 (CA).
[130]   *Hilder v Dexter* [1902] AC 474 (HL).
[131]   And debentures.
[132]   See Chapter 12.
[133]   *Rover International Ltd v Cannon Film Sales Ltd* [1987] BCLC 540.

by including a power to rescind it.[134] It is usual in such a case to provide in the articles that the directors shall adopt the preliminary agreement; but this will not render the company under an obligation unless a distinctly new contract is made by which the company agrees to be bound by the terms of the preliminary agreement.[135] Nor will a resolution of the board of the new company adopting the agreement create a contract between the new company and the vendor.[136] A new contract may, however, sometimes be inferred from the circumstances and the conduct of the parties.[137] But the mere fact that the directors of the company think they are bound by the contract with the trustee, and act accordingly, is not enough, even though large sums of money are expended and work is done in that mistaken belief.[138]

Where the contract is expressed to be made with the company itself, it is usually prepared before the incorporation of the company, and then referred to in the articles as an 'agreement already prepared and intended to be executed', and, for identification, signed or initialled by some of the subscribers to the memorandum or by a solicitor. In this case, the agreement must be executed by the company and this must be done after proper consideration by the directors and not merely *pro forma*; in fact, they must exercise their judgment upon it, and if they are not an independent board the company may repudiate the contract.[139]

A third party prepared to sell or lease property to the company may not be prepared to wait until the company is formed and the contract executed. Here an agreement can be made between the vendor and the promoters on identical terms to the draft contract which it is intended the company will execute. The agreement with the promoters will provide that their liability is to cease once the company is incorporated and the contract with it executed.

Although, therefore, a company is not bound by a contract made in its name before incorporation, where, subsequent to incorporation, it has made payments or rendered services on the basis of an invalid pre-incorporation contract, it may succeed in a claim made in restitution,

---

[134] *Kelner v Baxter* (1866) LR 2 CP 174; *Re Empress Engineering Co* (1880) 16 Ch D 125, at 129 (CA).

[135] *Kelner v Baxter* (1866) LR 2 CP 174; *Scott v Lord Ebury* (1867) LR 2 CP 255.

[136] *Re Olympia* [1898] 2 Ch 153, at 168; *Re Northumberland Avenue Hotel Co* (1866) 33 Ch D 16; *Natal Land Co v Pauline Collier* [1904] AC 120 (PC); *Kelpongs Prospecting Ltd v Schmidt* [1968] AC 810 (PC).

[137] *Re Johannesburg Hotel Co* [1891] 1 Ch 119; *North Sydney Investment Co v Higgins* [1899] AC 263 (PC).

[138] *Re Northumberland Avenue Hotel Co* (1866) 33 Ch D 16; *Howard v Patent Ivory Co* (1888) 38 Ch D 156; *Natal Land Co v Pauline Colliery* [1904] AC 120, at 126 (PC). Nor can the company be bound by an estoppel based on facts occurring before it came into existence: *Rover International Ltd v Cannon Film Sales Ltd* [1987] BCLC 540.

[139] See the discussion of promoters' duties, above.

for money had and received or *quantum meruit*.[140] The same principle would apply against a company that had received payments or enjoyed services.

4.20 THE LIABILITY OF PROMOTERS OR OTHER 'AGENTS' TO THIRD PARTIES

Even though a pre-incorporation contract is not, as such, binding upon the company, there may be a remedy against those who purported to act on behalf of the non-existent company. At common law the position was, however, unclear and unsatisfactory. In *Kelner v Baxter*,[141] promoters who signed an agreement 'on behalf of' a company about to be formed were held to be personally liable on the contract as principals in the place of the non-existent company.[142] By contrast, in *Newborne v Sensolid (GB) Ltd*[143] it was held that, where a contractual document is signed by the company and the 'agent's' signature is added simply to authenticate the signature of the company, then neither the 'agent' nor the company can sue on the contract. It was also stated, *obiter*, that the 'agent' would not be personally liable to be sued on the contract nor would he be liable for breach of warranty of authority as he had not acted in the capacity of an agent.[144] It is difficult to see why a claim for breach of warranty of authority would not lie in such a case.

What is now s 51(1) of the Companies Act 2006[145] made a change in the law as regards the liability of those who purport to act on behalf of the company before it is incorporated. It provides as follows:

'A contract that purports to be made by or on behalf of a company at a time when the company has not been formed has effect, subject to any agreement

---

[140] *Rover International Ltd v Cannon Film Sales Ltd* [1988] BCLC 710 (CA), reversing in this respect [1987] BCLC 540. A claim in contract may now succeed under the Contracts (Rights of Third Parties) Act 1999.

[141] (1866) LR 2 CP 174.

[142] Ie liability was not founded on breach of warranty of authority.

[143] [1954] 1 QB 45 (CA).

[144] This reasoning was applied in the Australian case of *Black v Smallwood* [1966] ALR 744 (Aust HC). In *Cumming v Quartz AG Ltd* [1981] SLT 205, an attempt to rely on the principle of a stipulation in favour of a third party (which may be effective under Scots contract law) rejected because the promoter had signed as an agent and not as a principal. See *MacQueen* [1982] SLT 257.

[145] Section 51 implements a provision of the EC First Directive on Company Law. The current version replaces one first inserted into the Companies Act 1985, as s 36C, by the Companies Act 1989, with some improved wording, to extend its coverage to deeds. See further, Green 'Security of transactions after Phonogram v Lane' (1984) 47 MLR 671. The Court of Appeal has held that in the forerunner to s 51, 'company' means registered company and not a foreign corporation created by its own special statute: *Janred Properties v Ente Nazionale Italiane per il Turismo* (unreported) 14 July 1983; see also *Rover International Ltd v Cannon Film Sales Ltd* [1987] BCLC 540.

to the contrary, as one made with the person purporting to act for the company or as agent for it, and he is personally liable on the contract accordingly.'[146]

This provision does not change the position of the company once it is formed. It is not bound by such contracts and cannot ratify them.

The purpose of s 51(1) would appear to be to remove the subtle distinction between *Kelner v Baxter* and *Newborne v Sensolid (GB) Ltd*. Its effect is that even if the defendant did not contract as agent *or* assume personal liability but (as in *Newborne*) his signature is appended to that of the company's name to authenticate it, he will nevertheless be personally liable. Here there will be a contract which 'purports to be made by the company' which 'has effect as a contract entered into by the person purporting to act for the company'. This interpretation was adopted by the Court of Appeal in *Phonogram Ltd v Lane*,[147] where it was held that 'purports' does not require that there should be a representation that the company is already in existence. The court also held that the section is not confined to the case where the company is already in the course of formation. In this case, no steps had been taken to do so.[148]

It should be noted that where liability is imposed by s 51(1), it is not based on breach of warranty of authority but on the personal liability 'on the contract'. This will be so even where the contract has been made 'by a person as agent for a company'. Although this is not made explicit, the Court of Appeal[149] has clarified the issue and held that the agent is made 'personally liable on the contract' and consequently has a right to enforce it. This construction was based not on the Directive (whose text would not require this) but on the application of common law principles to give meaning to what Parliament has decreed by employing the words 'personally liable on the contract'.[150] This means that in some situations the 'agent' would not succeed (eg if there had been a misrepresentation, or if the identity of the unformed company as, say, an employer, were significant to the third party). Thus the general right to enforce the contract under s 51(1) cannot be allowed to prejudice the third party.[151] Where he is a promoter, he might in some circumstances have to account to the company for the fruits of the contract.[152]

---

[146] By s 51(2), the section applies to the making of a deed (obligation in Scotland) as it applies to the making of a contract.

[147] [1981] 3 WLR 746.

[148] The Court of Appeal rejected an argument which rested on the French text of the First EEC Directive on Company Law. The court observed that under Art 189 (now Art 249) of the EC Treaty a directive is binding insofar as its spirit and intent are concerned. What is now s 51 satisfied this requirement, and its plain meaning should be applied even if it went further than the scope of the Directive.

[149] *Braymist Ltd v Wise Financing Co Ltd* [2002] EWCA Civ 127, [2002] 1 BCLC 415.

[150] See Arden LJ [2002] 1 BCLC 415, at 425–429.

[151] See Arden LJ, ibid, at 428–431, and Judge LJ, at 434–435.

[152] See **4.19**.

The qualifying proviso to s 51(1) – 'subject to any agreement to the contrary' – appears to require, for the application of the section to be excluded, that there should be an express term to that effect in the contract, whether oral or written.[153]

The courts have imposed sensible limits on the protection afforded by s 51(1). So, it has been held that it did not apply to save a contract in the name of a company which had not existed for five years by the registration of a new company, because there was no intention to form the new company when the contract was made.[154] It does not apply to a company awaiting a new certificate of incorporation on a change of name,[155] since that is not a company that 'has not been formed'.[156] Similarly, there is no basis for applying the section to a contract made by a company which has been formed but which is not accurately named.[157]

4.21 OVERSEAS COMPANIES

It is appropriate to include in this chapter a brief examination of the law concerning companies which are not registered in the UK.[158] The law has long recognised the existence of companies incorporated abroad and, as regards those which set up business in some way in the UK, imposes a number of formal requirements.

Part 34 of the Companies Act 2006 applies to such overseas companies.[159] Pursuant to recommendations of the Company Law Review,[160] this Part has simplified the former provisions somewhat, so that the previous parallel arrangements for EEA companies and others have been consolidated into one system, wherever the company is incorporated. However, much of the detail is prescribed in regulations, which may make different provision as regards the registration of particulars depending on the place of incorporation or activities conducted.[161] Under s 1046, there is no longer any distinction between companies which have established a place of business and those which have a branch. There is no definition of

---

[153] See *Phonogram Ltd v Lane*, above. See Green (1984) 47 MLR 671, at 677–82 as to the effect of the parol evidence rule where an oral 'agreement to the contrary' relates to a written contract.

[154] *Cotronic (UK) Ltd v Dezonie, t/a Wendaland Builders Ltd* [1991] BCC 200 (CA).

[155] See **4.6**.

[156] *Oshkosk B'Gosh v Dan Marbel Inc* [1989] BCLC 507 (CA).

[157] *Badgerhill Properties Ltd v Cottrell* [1991] BCLC 805 (CA).

[158] For detail on this and on how the Companies Act applies to unregistered companies and certain other associations, see *Gore-Browne on Companies* (Jordans, 45th edn, loose-leaf) Chap 5. Of course, a UK-registered subsidiary of a foreign company is not an overseas company.

[159] It implements the Eleventh EC Directive (89/666/EC), insofar as it applies to companies within the European Economic Area (EEA).

[160] See *Modern Company Law for a Competitive Economy, Reforming the Law Concerning Oversea Companies*, October 1999.

[161] Companies Act 2006, s 1046; see the Overseas Companies Regulations 2009, SI 2009/1801.

the term 'branch' except by reference to the Eleventh Directive, and reference should be made to relevant decisions of the European Court of Justice.[162] From these it seems that the concept of a branch implies the actual transaction of business to a greater extent than simply that of having a place of business.

The regulations must require registration of the details of anyone in the UK authorised by an overseas company to accept service or that there is no such person,[163] and must allow the non-disclosure of directors' residential addresses on a corresponding basis to that offered to UK company directors.[164] The Secretary of State may make regulations, subject to negative resolution, clarifying with which registrar or registrars an overseas company must register and requiring notification to such registrar(s) when an overseas company no longer has a connection to the UK.[165]

Registered overseas companies can choose to register under their official incorporated name or an alternative UK trading name which will be treated as its corporate name. EEA-incorporated companies have the right to register their official name, subject to the limit on permitted characters, but companies incorporated elsewhere must comply with all the UK restrictions on corporate names other than the use of plc, limited, etc.[166] An alternative trading name may be registered at any time and may thereafter be changed and re-registered (including to the official incorporated name). It is for all UK purposes deemed to be the corporate name and any registered change does not affect legal proceedings already started.[167]

The Act no longer contains detailed requirements regarding the filing of accounts, directors' reports and audit; these are specified in regulations.[168] Regulations can also be made requiring overseas companies conducting business in the UK (not necessarily with a UK branch) to display information in specified locations, in specified documents and communications and to provide specified information on request from those they conduct business with. This must at least include the UK registered name.[169] Registered overseas companies are still required to

---

[162] See especially *Etablissements Somafar SA v Saar-Ferngas AG* [1979] 1 CMLR 490.
[163] Section 1056.
[164] Section 1055; as to such non-disclosure, see **15.14.1**. A change of branch within a UK jurisdiction does not require to be notified, but a change from one UK jurisdiction to another is treated as a closing down and reopening: s 1059.
[165] Sections 1057 and 1058.
[166] Section 1047.
[167] Section 1048.
[168] Sections 1049 and 1050. The Overseas Companies Regulations 2009, SI 2009/1801 contain the detail.
[169] Section 1051.

register some charges over property in the UK, but again the detail is contained in regulations,[170] although these follow the provisions for UK companies.

Generally, the sanctions for failure to comply with these regulations are only fines,[171] but a company that has failed to comply with the display regulations under s 1051 may have any attempt to enforce a contract affected by the failure.[172]

4.22   COMPANY NAMES

An important feature of the registration of a company under successive Companies Acts has been the choice and registration of the company's name. Over the years a number of restrictions on what names can be chosen have developed, in addition to the basic requirement to display 'limited', etc,[173] and these have been tidied up in the Companies Act 2006, which also introduced a new system of company names adjudicators to determine complaints where there are objections to a registered name on the grounds of damage to goodwill or confusion with another person.[174] It should be noted that, although a company must give its official corporate name on various documents and at specified locations, as described in **4.23**, it does not have to use the name as its primary business name. There are controls over the use of business names,[175] which largely follow the provisions on company names, but there is no system of registration for them.

The company names that may not be registered are any:

(1)   the use of which, in the opinion of the Secretary of State, would constitute an offence or be offensive;[176]

(2)   giving an impression of connection to HM Government (in the UK or Northern Ireland), the Scottish administration, local authorities

---

[170]   Section 1052; see the Overseas Companies (Execution of Documents and Registration of Charges) Regulations 2009, SI 2009/1917.
[171]   Section 1054.
[172]   Section 1051(3), under which the civil consequences specified in s 83 (see **4.22.4**) can be applied.
[173]   See **4.2**.
[174]   Note that the registration of names applies not just to companies formed and registered under the Companies Acts, but also to other corporate bodies, including other UK registered and unregistered companies to which provisions of the Companies Acts apply, overseas companies required to register, limited and limited liability partnerships (LLPs), European Economic Interest Groupings (EEIGs), Open-Ended Investment Companies (OEICs) and Industrial and Provident Societies registered in the UK.
[175]   These are now contained in Part 41 of the 2006 Act, but this is not technically part of the 'Companies Acts': see s 2.
[176]   Section 53 [CA 1985, s 26(1)(d) and (e)].

anywhere in the UK and other public authorities specified in regulations made by the Secretary of State, unless prior permission is granted;[177]

(3) including a sensitive word or expression specified by regulations made by the Secretary of State, again unless prior permission is granted;[178]

(4) including words, expressions or other indications (including ones similar to them) which are associated with a particular type of company or organisation and specified by regulations made by the Secretary of State;[179]

(5) including letters, other characters, punctuation, style, etc not permitted by regulations made by the Secretary of State;[180]

(6) that are the same as an existing name on the registrar's index.[181] The Secretary of State may also direct the change of a name for being the same or in his opinion 'too like' another registered name (or one that should have been registered);[182] and

(7) that in the opinion of the Secretary of State 'gives so misleading an indication of the nature of the activities of the business as to be likely to cause harm to the public' and the Secretary of State has directed to be changed.[183]

4.22.1 Directions to change a registered name

The case in **4.22**(7) differs from the others in that it does not prevent initial registration but only applies if the Secretary of State has given a direction in writing to change the name within 6 weeks (or such longer period as he stipulates). The company has three weeks from the direction to appeal to court, which if it upholds the direction will reset a time-limit.[184] It is really a 'sweep-up' clause for when the Secretary of

---

[177] Section 54 [CA 1985, s 26(2)(a)].

[178] Section 55 [CA 1985, ss 26(2)(b) and 29(1)]. The list is specified in the Company and Business Names Regulations 1981, SI 1981/1685, as amended, and includes United Kingdom, its constituent countries (and their adjectives but not abbreviations like UK and GB), references to royalty (including Windsor) and to the medical profession, like dentist, nurse, midwife, chemist, and certain types of bodies, like chamber of commerce, trade or industry, charity, co-operative, friendly society, polytechnic, university, police.

[179] Section 65 [CA 1985, s 26(1)(a)–(bbb)]. See the Companies and Business Names (Miscellaneous Provisions) Regulations 2009, SI 2009/1085.

[180] Section 57. See the Companies and Business Names (Miscellaneous Provisions) Regulations 2009, SI 2009/1085.

[181] Section 66 [CA 1985, s 26(1)(c) and (3)]. The index includes not just UK registered companies, but LLPs, OEICs, EEIGs, overseas companies and other corporate bodies.

[182] Sections 67 and 68 [CA 1985, s 28(2)].

[183] Section 76(1) [CA 1985, s 32(1)].

[184] Section 76(2)–(5) [CA 1985, s 32(2) and (3)].

State cannot use the direction powers under (6). The powers under the latter are more specific and limited to 12 months following registration. The direction, which must be in writing, specifies the period for compliance which may be extended.[185] There is also a power to direct a change of name where misleading information has been given or undertaking or assurances not fulfilled in respect of a name registration, limited to five years following registration.[186] Finally, there is a power to direct a change of name where a company no longer qualifies for an exemption from including 'limited' or 'Ltd' in its name.[187]

4.22.2   Company names adjudicators

In addition to the fact that the registrar should refuse to register the same name as already appears in the register and the Secretary of State may direct a change of name that is the same or similar within 12 months of registration, any person may object at any time to a registered name on the grounds of damage to existing goodwill or causing confusion by applying to a company names adjudicator.[188] The objector does not have to be a company protecting its corporate name – it could be a business protecting its business name – but the grounds of objection are quite narrow – that either the registered name: '(a) is the same as a name associated with the applicant in which he has goodwill [ie reputation of any description apparently anywhere in the world], or (b) is sufficiently similar to such a name that its use in the United Kingdom would be likely to mislead by suggesting a connection between the company and the applicant.'

Although the registered company must be the primary respondent, any members and directors may be joined. There are a number of defences:

(1)   the name was registered before the activities generating the goodwill commenced;

(2)   the company is or was operating under the name, or is proposing to do so, and has already incurred substantial start-up costs;

(3)   the name is available from a company formation business;

(4)   the name was adopted in good faith; or

(5)   the applicant has not been significantly affected.

---

[185] Section 68(1)–(4) [CA 1985, s 28(3) and (4)].
[186] Section 75 [CA 1985, s 28].
[187] Section 64 [CA 1985, s 31(2)–(4) and (6)].
[188] Section 69. As indicated earlier, this was a new provision in the 2006 Act. See ss 70–74, supplemented by the Company Names Adjudicator Rules 2008, SI 2008/1738, for the detail on who the adjudicators will be, their powers, etc.

The first three defences will fail if the main purpose of the registration was to obtain a return from or obstruct the applicant.

4.22.3   Change of name

Traditionally a company changed its name by special resolution, a copy of which has to be filed, but now specific notice must also be given to the registrar and the 2006 Act also now allows for articles to provide for an alternative to a special resolution; in this case the notice must state that such means have been used. If the change is conditional on a later event, that must be stated in the notice and a further notice given when the event occurs before the registrar will act.[189]

The registrar must satisfy himself that the procedures have been followed and the proposed name does not breach any of the limitations described above. The change is only effective on the registrar issuing a new certificate of incorporation, but that does not affect any rights, obligations or legal proceedings (continuing or to be commenced).[190]

A company which is in the process of changing its name and which is awaiting a certificate of incorporation with its new name is *not* a company that has not been formed. Accordingly, there can be no question of the contracts which it enters into at that time being 'pre-incorporation' contracts for which those who act on its behalf could incur personal liability under s 51.[191]

4.22.4   'Phoenix companies'

The Insolvency Act 1986 attempts to stamp out the notorious practice of incorporating 'phoenix companies'. A phoenix company is one which is formed with a name which is the same as, or very similar to, the name of a company which has recently gone into liquidation. The reason for choosing the same, or a very similar, name is usually to try to hide the fact that the earlier company has gone into liquidation from its creditors and thus ensure that the new company can continue to enjoy the goodwill of the old business.[192] Under s 216 of the Insolvency Act 1986, the directors[193] of a company which has gone into insolvent liquidation are

---

[189] Sections 77–79.

[190] Sections 80 and 81.

[191] *Oshkosh B'Gosh Incorporated v Dan Marbel Incorporated Ltd* [1989] BCLC 507, (1988) 4 BCC 795, [1989] 1 CMLR 94. As to s 51, see **4.20**.

[192] But s 216 is not limited in its application to this particular form of abuse: *Thorne v Silverleaf* [1994] BCC 109; *Ricketts v Ad Valorem Factors Ltd* [2003] EWCA Civ 1706, [2004] 1 BCLC 1. See also *First Independent Factors and Finance Ltd v Mountford* [2008] EWHC 835 (Ch), [2008] 2 BCLC 297.

[193] That is, the persons who were directors at the time of liquidation or at any time in the preceding 12 months. Shadow directors are also caught: s 216(1).

prohibited[194] for a period of five years from being involved in another company which has the same name as one by which the old company was known[195] at any time in the period of 12 months preceding its liquidation or a name which is so similar as to suggest some association with the old company. Contravention of this prohibition attracts civil liability and criminal penalties.[196]

Under s 216(3), the court may authorise the continued use of a prohibited name. In considering applications under this provision, the court should have regard only to the purposes for which s 216 was enacted, namely, the danger that the business of the old company has been acquired at an undervalue to the detriment of its creditors and that those creditors may be misled into the belief that there has been no change in the corporate vehicle.[197]

4.23   TRADING DISCLOSURES

Previously the primary legislation[198] specified in what locations and documents a company's name had to be displayed, but the matter is now dealt with in regulations made by the Secretary of State regarding what the Companies Act calls 'trading disclosures'.[199] The requirements are not confined to displaying the corporate name, but also cover a range of other information.

Breach of the disclosure requirements without reasonable excuse is an offence on the part of the company and any officer in default. In addition, the company may not be able to pursue any contractual claim against parties that are able to show that the breach caused them, in turn, to be unable to claim under the contract or caused some other financial loss. A court can allow the claim to continue, but only if it is satisfied that it is just and equitable to do so.[200]

The detailed requirements are contained in the Companies (Trading Disclosure) Regulations 2008.[201] Any display or disclosure of information required by these must be in characters that can be read with the naked eye.[202]

---

[194] Except with the leave of the court or as permitted by the Insolvency Rules 1986 (rr 4.228–4.230): s 216(3).

[195] This includes business names as well as corporate names: s 216(6).

[196] Sections 216(4) and 217. See *Thorne v Silverleaf*, above. The offence under s 216 is a strict liability offence: *R v Cole, Lees & Birch* [1998] BCC 87.

[197] *Penrose v Official Receiver* [1996] 1 BCLC 389.

[198] Section 348 of the Companies Act 1985.

[199] Sections 82–85.

[200] Sections 83 and 84.

[201] SI 2008/495.

[202] Ibid, reg 2.

The first set of requirements relate to the display of the registered name at various locations. A company[203] must display its registered name at its registered office and any inspection place, the latter being any location, other than a company's registered office, at which a company keeps available for inspection any company record that it is required under the Companies Acts to keep available for inspection.[204] In addition it must display its registered name at any other location at which it carries on business, unless that is primarily used for living accommodation.[205] The registered name must be so positioned that it may be easily seen by any visitor to any of the above places and displayed continuously, but where any of those places is shared by six or more companies, each such company is only required to display its registered name for at least 15 continuous seconds at least once in every three minutes.[206]

In addition, a company must disclose its registered name on a range of documents and on its websites.[207] The documents, which may be in hard copy, electronic or any other form[208] are:

(1) its business letters, notices and other official publications;

(2) its bills of exchange, promissory notes, endorsements and order forms;

(3) cheques purporting to be signed by or on behalf of the company;

(4) orders for money, goods or services purporting to be signed by or on behalf of the company;

(5) its bills of parcels, invoices and other demands for payment, receipts and letters of credit;

(6) its applications for licences to carry on a trade or activity; and

(7) all other forms of its business correspondence and documentation.[209]

As well as disclosing its registered name in the ways described above, there are particulars that must be disclosed on a company's business letters and websites.[210] These are:

---

[203] Unless it is dormant.
[204] Ibid, reg 1(2)(c). As to 'company record', see reg 1(2)(b).
[205] Ibid, reg 4.
[206] Ibid, reg 5.
[207] 'Websites' includes any part of a website relating to the company that the company has caused or authorised to appear: reg 1(2)(e).
[208] See reg 1(2)(d).
[209] Ibid, reg 6.
[210] Ibid, reg 7.

(1)   the part of the United Kingdom in which it is registered;

(2)   its registered number;

(3)   the address of its registered office;

(4)   in the case of a limited company exempt from the obligation to use the word 'limited' as part of its registered name,[211] the fact that it is a limited company;

(5)   in the case of a community interest company that is not a public company, the fact that it is a limited company; and

(6)   in the case of an investment company,[212] the fact that it is such a company.

If a company with a share capital discloses the amount of share capital on its business letters, order forms or websites, that disclosure must be to paid up share capital.

The next set of disclosure requirements relate to disclosure of the names of directors. There is no general requirement to disclose these on business letters but, where such a letter includes the name of any director of a company, other than in the text or as a signatory, the letter must disclose the name of every director of that company.[213]

Finally, there is a requirement for a company to disclose information to any person who makes a written request for it.[214] The information that can be so requested is the address of its registered office, any inspection place and the type of company records which are kept at that office or place. The company must send a written response to that person within five working days of the receipt of that request.

---

[211]   See **4.9.1.**
[212]   Within the meaning of s 833.
[213]   Reg 8; as to the meaning of 'name', see reg 8(2).
[214]   Reg 9.

CHAPTER 5

THE COMPANY'S CONSTITUTION

5.1 FROM MEMORANDUM AND ARTICLES TO CONSTITUTION

Prior to the Companies Act 2006, the constitution of every registered company was embodied in both its memorandum of association and articles of association. The memorandum of association of every company had to state its name, the situation of the registered office (ie whether in England and Wales or in Scotland) and its objects,[1] as well as further items where the company is limited either by share capital or by guarantee.

In its first White Paper on reforming company law, the Government proposed that the requirement for a separate memorandum and articles of association would be replaced with the requirement to have a constitution contained in a single document.[2] By the time of the second White Paper, that proposal had been watered down to something closer to the *status quo*, retaining the separate memorandum and articles.[3] The memorandum, however, would become a more basic document, and no longer be a central feature of the company's constitution. This position is now reflected in the provisions of the Companies Act 2006.

Under the Companies Act 2006, most of the information that had to be included in the memorandum under the Companies Act 1985 now has to be given in the company's registration documents.[4] The detail of this has already been discussed in Chapter 4 in the context of formation of a company.

As far as the company's constitution is concerned, the Companies Act 2006 states that the company's constitution includes its articles of association, as well as any resolutions and agreements which affect a company's constitution.[5] The latter are defined in s 29 as:

---

[1]   Companies Act 1985, s 2.
[2]   *Modernising Company Law* (July 2002), paras 2.2–2.5.
[3]   *Company Law Reform* (March 2005) pp 33–36.
[4]   Companies Act 2006, ss 9–13.
[5]   Companies Act 2006, s 17.

(1)   any special resolution;[6]

(2)   resolutions or agreements which were agreed to by all the members
       of a company which, had they not been agreed to by all the
       members, would not have been effective unless adopted as a special
       resolution,[7] or by some other particular majority or in some
       particular manner;[8]

(3)   a resolution or agreement effectively binding all members of a class
       of shareholders, even though this was not agreed to by all those
       members;[9] and

(4)   any other resolution or agreement determined by other legislation.[10]

This seems to be a rather broad understanding of the term 'constitution',
in that many resolutions are treated as part of the constitution. The
intention is to reflect the constitutional importance of many such
documents, although it may be asked whether treating them as part of the
constitution is the best approach.

5.2   THE ARTICLES OF ASSOCIATION

The central part of the constitution is therefore the articles of association.
Every company must have articles of association which contain the rules
for how the company is to be run.[11] The articles of association govern the
internal affairs of the company, and may from time to time be altered by
the members to an almost unlimited extent.

The purpose of this chapter is to examine certain more general questions
about the articles of association. These are:

(1)   the drafting of articles of association and the adoption of model
       articles;

(2)   the power to alter the articles under s 21 and the equitable doctrine
       whereby the court may restrain the exercise of this power; and

(3)   more generally, the status of the constitution, including the articles,
       as a contract of membership as defined by s 33 [CA 1985, s 14].

---

6   Companies Act 2006, s 29(1)(a).
7   Companies Act 2006, s 29(1)(b).
8   Companies Act 2006, s 29(1)(c).
9   Companies Act 2006, s 29(1)(d).
10   Companies Act 2006, s 29(1)(e).
11   Companies Act 2006, s 18(1) [CA 1985, s 7(1)].

5.3 THE CONTENTS OF THE ARTICLES OF ASSOCIATION

The articles of association regulate a great range of matters affecting almost every aspect of company law as it applies to each individual company. Such internal regulations are of course subject to the requirements of the Companies Acts and the general principles of company law laid down by the courts. The following[12] are some of the important matters which are commonly governed by the articles: the status and the powers of management of the board of directors, their appointment and conduct of meetings;[13] decision-making by members, including voting rights, proxies, and meetings;[14] shares and distributions (dividends), including the capitalisation of profits, the transfer and transmission of shares; and the alteration of capital.[15] Detailed provisions in the articles are discussed in their proper context in later chapters, in terms of the relevant model articles specified in Regulations made under s 22 of the Companies Act 2006.[16]

5.4 DRAFTING ARTICLES: ADOPTION OF MODEL ARTICLES

A limited company (whether by shares or guarantee) may adopt the model articles prescribed by the Secretary of State, or draft its own articles. If the model articles do not apply to the company, then it is required to register articles of association.[17] This will be the case with unlimited companies, as well as limited companies in respect of which some or all of the model articles are not to apply. The articles must be contained in a single document and divided into paragraphs numbered consecutively.[18]

As under the previous Acts, the Secretary of State can prescribe model articles by regulation.[19] Prior to the Companies Act 2006, such articles (then known as 'Table A') applied to all companies (public and private) which registered under the 1985 Act. In the case of companies registered under the Companies Acts 1948 and 1980 (of which there are still many), the Table A contained in Sch 1 to the Companies Act 1948 or, depending on the date of incorporation, the 1948 Act Table A as amended by

---

[12] As to companies registered before 1 July 1985, see Table A in Sch 1 to the 1948 Act (as amended). As to companies registered under the 1985 Act, see the Companies (Tables A to F) Regulations 1985, SI 1985/805. For companies registered under the Companies Act 2006, see the Companies (Model Articles) Regulations 2008, SI 2008/3229.

[13] Part 2 of the Model Articles (for companies limited by shares or guarantee).

[14] Part 3 of the Model Articles (for companies limited by shares or guarantee).

[15] Part 4 of the Model Articles (for companies limited by shares only).

[16] See the Companies (Model Articles) Regulations 2008, SI 2008/3229.

[17] Companies Act 2006, s 18(2).

[18] Section 18(3) [CA 1985, s 7(3) with amendments].

[19] Section 19 [cf CA 1985, s 8(1) and the Companies (Tables A to F) Regulations 1985, SI 1985/805].

subsequent companies legislation, applied.[20] A significant change under the 2006 Act is that the Secretary of State can now prescribe different model articles for different types of company,[21] and Regulations containing separate model articles for public companies, private companies limited by shares, and private companies limited by guarantees are in place.[22]

Large companies almost always adopt their own special regulations in which case the articles begin with a provision to the effect that the relevant model articles (or Table A, as it was) are excluded. Where a company is adopting new articles and excluding the model articles, the articles to be excluded are those in force at the date of the company's registration. Other companies, instead of wholly excluding the model articles, may adopt the suitable parts of the model articles applicable to the type of company,[23] with a few special articles containing the desired modifications. In such cases, the articles will commence with a provision to the effect that the regulations contained in the relevant model articles are to apply to the company, save insofar as they are excluded or varied. The model articles, or such portions of it as are adopted, need not be registered.[24]

Every company is required to supply any of its members, on request, with an up-to-date copy of its articles (if any), or other constitutional documents (as per s 29) free of charge.[25]

5.5   DRAFTING ARTICLES: EXAMPLES OF INVALID PROVISIONS

The articles cannot vary rights given by the Companies Act, and must be rejected if inconsistent with the Act or the general law.

Articles cannot deprive a company of the powers which are conferred on it by statute: thus a provision in the articles which purports to make them unalterable is invalid because a company is empowered by s 21 of the Companies Act 2006 [CA 1985, s 9] to alter its articles by special resolution.[26] Note, however, that it is possible to 'entrench' certain

---

[20]   Section 8(3) of the Companies Act 1985 stated that companies registered before the Companies Act 1985 came into operation continued to be governed by the articles which were in force at the time of registration.

[21]   Companies Act 2006, s 19(2).

[22]   Companies (Model Articles) Regulations 2008, SI 2008/3229.

[23]   Companies Act 2006, s 19(3).

[24]   Companies Act 2006, s 18(2).

[25]   Companies Act 2006, s 32(1).

[26]   *Walker v London Tramways Co* (1879) 12 Ch D 705; *Allen v Gold Reefs of West Africa* [1900] 1 Ch 656, at 671; *Southern Foundries (1926) Ltd v Shirlaw* [1940] AC 701, at 739; *Russell v Northern Bank Development Corporation* [1992] 3 All ER 294, [1992] 1 WLR 588, [1992] BCLC 1016, [1992] BCC 578. The power to alter articles and the extent to which (if it all) it can be fettered are discussed further at **5.9**.

provisions in the articles, which means that more than a special resolution is required for their alteration or removal.[27]

Articles cannot free a member from paying in full for his shares, or deprive members of their right to petition for the winding up of the company or to dissent in a reconstruction under what is now s 110 of the Insolvency Act 1986,[28] nor can they validly provide for the transfer of shares without a written instrument of transfer where one would otherwise be required by virtue of s 770(1) [CA 1985, s 183].[29]

5.6 STATEMENT OF COMPANY'S OBJECTS

Prior to the Companies Act 2006, every company was required to include in its memorandum of association a statement of its objects ('the objects clause').[30] This obligation has now been removed in favour of a default position whereby a company's objects are not restricted.[31] However, it remains possible to restrict the objects of a company by including a statement of the company's objects in the articles of association. Such a restriction would not affect the validity of any acts by a company which are in contravention of the statement of objects.[32] Directors, however, are required to act in accordance with the company's constitution,[33] and may be in breach of this obligation if they cause a company to act outside its objects.[34]

5.7 ENTRENCHED PROVISIONS

In the past, it had been possible to include aspects regarding a company's constitution in its memorandum rather than articles to make it more difficult to remove or alter such provisions.[35] This made the law rather complex, with some provisions in the memorandum subject to a different procedure for alteration than those found in the articles.

One of the key changes introduced by the Companies Act 2006 is the possibility to 'entrench' certain provisions of the article, making it more difficult to amend or remove them. This may be appropriate, for example, to give a particular shareholder the right to appoint a director, irrespective of the strength of his shareholding.

---

[27] Companies Act 2006, s 22. See **5.7**.
[28] *Welton v Saffery* [1897] AC 299 (HL); *Re Peveril Gold Mines* [1898] 1 Ch 122 (CA); *Payne v Cork Co* [1900] 1 Ch 308.
[29] *Re Greene* [1949] Ch 333. Listed shares may now be transferred without the use of a written instrument; see **9.3**.
[30] Companies Act 1985, s 2(1)(c).
[31] Companies Act 2006, s 31(1).
[32] Companies Act 2006, s 39(1). See further **6.4**.
[33] Companies Act 2006, s 171(1)(a). See further **16.4**.
[34] See also Companies Act 2006, s 40(5) [CA 1985, s 35A(5)]; see **6.7**.
[35] See Companies Act 1985, s 17.

Whilst articles can normally be amended by special resolution,[36] entrenched provisions will be subject to more restrictive conditions, or a more restrictive procedure.[37] Thus, it may be possible to set a higher majority, or even impose a requirement of unanimity of all shareholders, in order to amend the articles. Alternatively, a longer notice period than required for special resolutions could be imposed, or an alteration could be made subject to the approval of certain shareholders. However, these restrictions can be overridden if all the members of the company agree to an alteration,[38] or by an order by a court or other authority having such power, to amend the articles.[39] Therefore, unanimity among all the members makes it possible to side-step both the conditions and procedures applicable to an alteration of entrenched articles.

Articles may only be entrenched where this is done at the time of formation,[40] or where the articles are amended with the agreement of all the members of the company.[41] With regard to companies formed under earlier Companies Acts, certain provisions contained in the memorandum of association may also be treated as entrenched under the 2006 Act.[42]

If a company's articles contain provisions for entrenchment, whether at formation or as a result of a subsequent amendment, including one made by order, notice of this fact has to be given to the registrar.[43] Notice also has to be given where a provision for entrenchment is removed.[44]

Furthermore, where a company's articles are subject to provisions for entrenchment, or an order which restricts or excludes the company's power to amend its articles, and the company resolves to amend its articles, the company may have to deliver a statement of compliance to the registrar.[45] Such a statement must be provided where the company would be required to send to the registrar a document making or evidencing the amendment,[46] and the statement must certify that the amendment has been made in accordance with the company's articles, or the applicable order.[47]

---

[36] Companies Act 2006, s 21(1); see below at **5.9**.
[37] Companies Act 2006, s 22(1).
[38] Section 22(3)(a).
[39] Section 22(3)(b).
[40] Section 22(2)(a).
[41] Section 22(2)(b).
[42] Section 28(2). See **5.8**.
[43] Companies Act 2006, s 23(1).
[44] Section 23(2).
[45] Companies Act 2006, s 24(2).
[46] Section 24(2)(b).
[47] Section 24(3).

5.8 PROVISIONS OF MEMORANDUM TO BE TREATED AS PROVISIONS OF ARTICLES

As mentioned earlier, the old-style memorandum of association used to contain a number of clauses no longer to be included in the memorandum under the 2006 Act, such as the objects clause.[48] In addition, certain other provisions, such as special class rights attaching to preferred shares might, in the past, have been included in the memorandum so as to make it more difficult to remove them. Although it is no longer possible to include such provisions in the memorandum under the 2006 Act, the introduction of the power to entrench certain provisions in the articles provides a similar mechanism.[49]

Companies formed before the 2006 Act came into force will still have old-style articles and memoranda of association. With regard to provisions contained in a memorandum which can no longer be included there under s 8 of the 2006 Act, s 28 states that such provisions are to be treated as provisions of the articles of association instead.

An old-style memorandum of association might have provided that some provisions could only be altered by following a specific procedure, or not changed at all.[50] Prior to the 2006 Act, this was the route by which certain rules could be entrenched in the company's constitutional documents. In order to preserve this position under s 28, which will treat these provisions of the memorandum as part of the articles, it is provided that the entrenching effect will be maintained.[51]

5.9 ALTERATION OF ARTICLES: S 21

Section 21 of the Companies Act 2006 [CA 1985, s 9] provides that the articles of a company may, subject to certain restrictions applicable to companies which are charities, be altered by special resolution. The company can amend both its own tailor-made articles and the provisions of the relevant model articles which it has adopted. The fact that articles may be altered with the consent of three-quarters of those voting on the resolution (ie the majority required for a special resolution[52]) and unanimity is not required is an illustration of different nature of the statutory contract formed by the articles of association compared to a normal contract.[53] Where all of the members who would have been entitled to attend and vote at a meeting to consider a resolution to change the articles consent informally to an alteration, that is also effective[54] but

---

48   Companies Act 2006, s 8.
49   Companies Act 2006, s 22.
50   Companies Act 1985, s 17(2)(b).
51   Companies Act 2006, s 28(2).
52   Section 283(1) [CA 1985, s 378(2)].
53   *Bratton Seymour v Oxborough* [1992] BCC 471, [1992] BCLC 693.
54   *Cane v Jones* [1981] 1 All ER 533, [1980] 1 WLR 1451.

altering the articles by unanimous consent is likely to be feasible only in the very smallest of companies. Exceptionally, a long period of acquiescence under particular articles may be held to be effective even though they have not been adopted as the articles of the company.[55] Articles may also be altered by statute.[56]

The company has power to adopt any new article which could lawfully have been included in the original articles.[57] However, it is clearly established that no majority of shareholders can by altering the articles retrospectively affect, to the prejudice of non-consenting owners of shares, rights already existing under a contract,[58] nor take away rights already accrued: for example, after a transfer of shares is lodged the company cannot create a right of lien so as to defeat the transfer.[59]

The power to alter articles is subject to any class rights which may be attached to particular shares. Class rights are discussed in Chapter 8.

5.10   EFFECT OF ALTERATION: S 25

As was the case under s 16 of the 1985 Act, no alteration of the articles of association after a person becomes a member can bind him either to take up more shares than he held at the date when the alteration was made, or in any way increase his liability as at that date to contribute to the share capital of, or otherwise to pay money to, the company, unless he agrees in writing, either before or after the alteration is made, to be bound thereby.[60]

5.11   NOTIFICATION OF AMENDMENTS TO REGISTRAR

If amendments are made to the company's articles, then the company must send to the registrar a copy of the amended articles within 15 days of the amendment taking effect (except for provisions of model articles applied by the articles, or applied by default under s 20).[61] Failure to do so is an offence by the company and every officer in default, and may result in a fine.[62]

---

[55] *Ho Tung v Man On Incee Co* [1902] AC 232.
[56] Companies Act 2006, s 34(2) [CA 1985, s 18 with amendments]. In a change from the 1985 Act, notice now only needs to be given for amendments which are other than changes to the general law.
[57] *Sidebottom v Kershaw Leese & Co* [1920] 1 Ch 154.
[58] Per Rigby LJ in *James v Buena Ventura Syndicate* [1896] 1 Ch 456, at 466; per Lord Watson in *Welton v Saffery*, above at 309; per Vaughan Williams LJ in *Allen v Gold Reefs of West Africa*, above at 676.
[59] *McArthur v Gulf Line* 1909 SC 732.
[60] Companies Act 2006, s 25.
[61] Companies Act 2006, s 26(1).
[62] Section 26(3) and (4).

If the registrar becomes aware that a company has altered its articles, but has not notified the registrar as required, then he may issue a notice to the company requiring it to comply within 28 days of the date of the notice.[63] If the company complies during that period, then no criminal proceedings may be brought in respect of the earlier failure to comply.[64] However, if the company does not comply with the notice, then a civil penalty of £200 becomes payable in addition to any liability to criminal proceedings.[65]

The obligation to notify the registrar also applies to resolutions and agreements affecting a company's constitution as defined in s 29 of the Companies Act 2006. A copy of such a resolution or agreement has to be sent to the registrar within 15 days.[66] Failing to do is an offence which can render the company and every officer in default liable to a fine.

5.12   FILING OF AMENDMENTS TO THE ARTICLES: ENACTMENTS AND ORDERS

Section 34 makes provision for the forwarding to the registrar of a copy of any enactment (other than an amendment to the general law) which alters a company's constitution together with a copy of the articles as altered. This also applies to 'special enactments' such as a private Act of Parliament affecting the company. Notice must be given to the registrar within 15 days after the enactment comes into force. Similarly, s 35 provides that where the constitution is altered by a court order (or an order by another authority), a copy of the order, as well as the articles or other constitutional documents (if amended), must be notified to the registrar within 15 days of the alteration taking effect. Failure to comply with these obligations is a criminal offence committed by both the company and every officer in default,[67] and a fine may be imposed.[68] Members of a company have a right to request copies of the articles, including any enactment or order amending them, free of charge.[69]

5.13   REQUIREMENTS AS TO PUBLICITY OF ALTERATION OF ARTICLES

Requirements as to the procedure for effecting an alteration of the articles were introduced by the European Communities Act 1972 and are now contained in ss 34, 1077, 1078 and 1079 of the Companies Act 2006.

---

[63]   Section 27.
[64]   Section 27(3).
[65]   Section 27(4).
[66]   Companies Act 2006, s 30(1).
[67]   Sections 34(5) and 35(3).
[68]   Sections 34(6) and 35(4).
[69]   Companies Act 2006, s 32.

Section 1077(1) of the Companies Act 2006 [CA 1985, s 711 with amendments] requires various documents there described to be published by the registrar in the *Gazette*, or by alternative means to be specified in secondary legislation (to include electronic means).[70] Section 1078(2)(b) includes among this category 'any amendment of the company's articles (including every resolution or agreement required to be embodied in or annexed to copies of the company's articles issued by the company)' and 'the text of the articles as amended'. The registrar is required to state in the *Gazette* notice the name of the company, the description of the document and the date of receipt.[71]

A company which does not furnish the registrar with such information is put under a disability. Section 1079(1) provides that a company shall not be entitled to rely against other persons on the happening of certain 'events' – which include the alteration of the articles of association – if the 'event' had not been officially notified (ie in the *Gazette*) at the material time.

Section 1079(1)(b) then goes on to provide, as a qualification to the requirement of official notification, that 'the company shows that the person concerned knew of the event at the material time'. Since the section is there not for the protection of the company but of outsiders dealing with the company, an outsider who is shown to have actual knowledge of the relevant event cannot insist that the company may not rely on the event because it failed to '*Gazette*' it.[72] Furthermore, it has been held by the Court of Appeal[73] that official notification of an event in the *Gazette* (as required by s 1077(1)) does not give constructive notice of the event in question to all third parties. Its effect is merely to prevent the company relying on a specified event which has not been duly '*Gazetted*'.

The term 'other person' in s 1079(1) would appear to bear the same meaning as 'a person dealing with the company' in s 40 [CA 1985, s 35A].[74]

Section 1079(3) further provides that a company will not be entitled to rely on an event if the material time fell 'on or before the fifteenth day after the date of official notification' (or where the fifteenth day was a non-working day,[75] on or before the next day that was a working day) and it was shown that the person concerned was 'unavoidably prevented from knowing of the event at that time'.

---

[70]	Companies Act 2006, s 1116 gives the Secretary of State the power to specify by regulations alternative means of publishing notices that would otherwise have to be published in the *Gazette*. This will, in particular, include electronic means.

[71]	Companies Act 2006, s 1077(2).

[72]	See Art 3(5) of the First Company Law Directive (see **2.3.1**) and *Official Custodian for Charities v Parway Estates Developments* [1985] Ch 151.

[73]	*Official Custodian for Charities v Parway Estates*, above.

[74]	See the discussion of the latter term at **6.8.1**.

[75]	Defined by s 1173(1) of the Companies Act 2006.

5.14 AGREEMENTS NOT TO ALTER THE ARTICLES AND VOTING AGREEMENTS

It is clear that a company cannot deprive itself of the power to alter its articles by a statement to that effect in its articles of association,[76] but can it agree not to alter (some of) the articles through a separate contract? In principle, there are three possible answers to the question whether, or to what extent, an extrinsic contract by a company not to alter its articles is valid, namely:

(1)   such a contract is entirely ineffective;

(2)   such a contract cannot prevent a company from exercising its statutory power to alter the articles but in that event the company will be in breach of contract and may be liable to pay damages to the other contracting party;

(3)   such a contract is effective and in a suitable case the company can be prevented by injunction from seeking to exercise the statutory power to alter its articles.

Which of these propositions is correct depends essentially on the extent to which the powers conferred by the Companies Act 2006 must be viewed as a mandatory code which cannot be modified, as opposed to a series of standard provisions which a company might ordinarily want to adopt but which it can depart from as it thinks fit. The issue was clarified by the House of Lords in *Russell v Northern Bank Development Corporation*.[77] This case concerned a contract by a company not to alter the nominal capital clause in its memorandum but the principles discussed are equally applicable to contracts not to alter the articles. The House of Lords ruling means that an extrinsic contract by a company not to alter its articles was as obnoxious as a provision to that effect contained in the articles themselves. It is entirely invalid and cannot be enforced even by way of damages.

Despite this unequivocal rejection of the freedom of the company to contract out of its statutory powers, the House of Lords upheld the right of individual shareholders to enter into contracts regarding the exercise of

---

[76]   *Walker v London Tramways Co*, above; *Allen v Gold Reefs of West Africa*, above; *Southern Foundries (1926) Ltd v Shirlaw*, above; *Russell v Northern Bank Development Corporation*, above.

[77]   [1992] 1 BCLC 1016, HL. See further Ferran 'The Decision of the House of Lords in *Russell v Northern Bank Development Corporation Limited*' [1994] CLJ 343. A narrower interpretation of the ratio in *Russell* is suggested by Davenport 'What Did *Russell v Northern Bank Development Corporation Ltd* Decide?' (1993) 109 LQR 553. Other comments on the decision in *Russell* include Riley 'Vetoes and Voting Agreements: Some Problems of Consent and Knowledge' (1993) 44 NILQ 34; Sealy 'Shareholders' Agreements – An Endorsement and a Warning from the House of Lords' [1992] CLJ 437; Shapira 'Voting Agreements and Corporate Statutory Powers' (1993) 109 LQR 210.

their votes.[78] This right is consistent with the well-established principle that a vote attached to a share is a property right to be exercised as its owner thinks fit.[79] Thus, the position now is that a company may not contract not to alter its articles,[80] but its shareholders may agree amongst themselves that they will not vote in favour of a proposal to alter the articles and in a suitable case this shareholders' agreement can be enforced by injunction.[81] This means that it may be possible to achieve the aim of ensuring that articles are entrenched by drafting the agreement in the form of a shareholders' agreement rather than a covenant by the company itself. However, it may not be practicable to enter into a shareholders' agreement which is effective for this purpose where the company has a large number of shareholders: a shareholders' agreement will ensure only that the articles cannot be changed where the parties to it have sufficient voting strength to block the passing of a special resolution, since, as a normal contract, a shareholders' agreement will of course not be binding on non-contracting shareholders. Even where a company has only a few shareholders, the entrenching effect of a shareholders' agreement not to vote in favour of an alteration to the articles may not survive when a new shareholder, who is not party to the agreement, joins the company.[82]

Shareholders' agreements are often encountered in the type of company which is commonly referred to as a 'quasi-partnership' company where, despite the corporate form, the individuals forming the company intend to run their operations on partnership lines. By entering into a shareholders' agreement each individual seeks to protect himself against the principle of majority rule, which is the normal hallmark of corporate decision-making, and to ensure that the bargain which he reached with his 'partners' when they established the business cannot be changed without his consent.

---

[78] Lord Jauncey of Tullichettle, who delivered the Opinion of the House, found support for this conclusion in *Welton v Saffery* [1897] AC 299, at 331.

[79] Leading authorities are *Pender v Lushington* (1877) 6 Ch D 70; *Northern Counties Securities Ltd v Jackson & Steeple Ltd* [1974] 1 WLR 1133; *North-West Transportation Co Ltd v Beatty* (1887) 12 App Cas 589.

[80] In *Cumbrian Newspapers Group Ltd v Cumberland & Westmorland Herald Newspaper & Printing Co Ltd* [1987] Ch 1, Scott J suggested that the power to alter articles belonged to the members rather than to the company, an interpretation which seems rather at odds with the wording of s 21 [CA 1985, s 9; wording altered]: '... a *company* may amend its articles by special resolution' (emphasis added). Scott J thought that a promise by a company not to alter the articles amounted to no more than a promise not to *initiate* the process of alteration.

[81] The possibility of a shareholders' agreement being enforced by injunction was accepted in *Russell*, although the only remedy sought and granted in that case was a declaration.

[82] To bind the new shareholder, the agreement regarding voting rights would have to be in the articles but such a provision in the articles would be regarded as an invalid fetter on the statutory power: *Russell* [1992] 3 All ER, at 167. But this would not preclude the formation of a new shareholders' agreement to which the new shareholder is a party.

It should also be borne in mind that the Companies Act 2006 makes it possible to entrench certain provisions in the articles,[83] and the procedure for altering or removing such provisions can be more restrictive than the special resolution required under s 21(1). Whilst this does not seem to permit the introduction of unalterable provisions, it can make entrenched provisions very difficult to amend or remove, and may therefore achieve the same result as would be pursued by a shareholders' agreement. However, as a provision can only be entrenched at the time of formation or with the agreement of all the members, shareholders' agreements of the kind discussed in this section may still be of use in some companies.

5.15   ACTING ON ALTERED ARTICLES

Although a company cannot contract not to alter its articles, acting on altered articles may amount to a breach of an earlier contractual promise which the company has given. The distinction between the situations is illustrated by *Southern Foundries (1926) Ltd v Shirlaw*,[84] where the company altered its articles to remove directors from office and then used this power to remove Shirlaw, the managing director, from his office. The House of Lords held that this action breached Shirlaw's service contract and ordered the company to pay damages. Lord Porter summarised the approach of the House in the following terms:[85]

> 'The general principle therefore may, I think, be thus stated. A company cannot be precluded from altering its articles thereby giving itself power to act upon the provisions of the altered articles – but so to act may nevertheless be a breach of contract if it is contrary to a stipulation in a contract validly made before the alteration.'

In a suitable case, an injunction might be granted to prevent a company acting on its altered articles in breach of an earlier contract.[86] Although the distinction may be quite fine, this does not infringe the principle that a company cannot fetter its power to alter the articles, because the company is not actually prevented from altering the articles and can rely on the altered articles against everyone apart from parties to the earlier contract in whose favour the court is persuaded to grant the discretionary remedy of an injunction.

The same principle seems to apply where there is a contract between the shareholders not to alter the articles but an alteration is subsequently made. That this may give rise to a claim for damages in the event of

---

[83]   Companies Act 2006, s 22. See **5.7**.

[84]   [1940] AC 701. *Baily v British Equitable Life Assurance Co*, above, is also more concerned with the consequences of acting on altered articles than with a contract not to alter articles.

[85]   [1940] AC 701, at 740–741.

[86]   *Allen v Gold Reefs of West Africa*, at 672, per Lindley LJ, quoted by Lord Wright in *Shirlaw*, at 725. On this point see further Trebilcock 'The Effect of Alterations to Articles of Association' (1967) 31 Con (NS) 95, at 113–116.

breach was supported by *Punt v Symons*.[87] This was subsequently considered in *British Murac Syndicate Ltd v Alperton Rubber Co Ltd*[88] where it was held that a contract not to alter articles was capable of being enforced by way of injunction, *Punt v Symons* being treated as having been implicitly overruled by a later Court of Appeal decision. On closer examination the analysis in *British Murac* is questionable. In the Court of Appeal decision relied upon, *Baily v British Equitable Assurance Co*,[89] the court actually granted a declaration rather than an injunction. Also, this decision was not precisely in point, because the Court of Appeal was mainly concerned with the wider principle (well established by other authorities) that a company cannot by altering its articles justify a breach of an extrinsic contract.

5.16 'BONA FIDE FOR THE BENEFIT OF THE COMPANY AS A WHOLE'

The power conferred by s 21 of the Companies Act 2006 [CA 1985, s 9] to alter the articles by special resolution may not be abused by a majority of shareholders so as to oppress the minority.[90] Even though a special resolution, valid in all respects as to form, has been passed as required by s 21, the minority may have it set aside for 'fraud on a minority'.[91] The courts will intervene where it is established that the majority have *not* acted '*bona fide* in the interests of the company as a whole'. This equitable principle was first clearly stated by Lord Lindley in *Allen v Gold Reefs of West Africa*.[92]

Later cases have sought to elucidate the precise meaning of the phrase '*bona fide* for the benefit of the company as a whole'.[93] It is clear that a heavy burden of proof rests on those seeking to prevent alteration of the

---

[87] [1903] 2 Ch 505 following an unreported case in the Court of Appeal. *Malleson v National Insurance Corp* [1894] 1 Ch 200, in spite of the headnote, is not an authority for this proposition.

[88] [1915] 2 Ch 186.

[89] [1904] 1 Ch 373 (reversed by House of Lords [1906] AC 35 but not on grounds relevant to this point).

[90] The Companies Act 2006 has no effect on the cases decided under the earlier Companies Acts dealing with this matter, and these cases continue to be of relevance.

[91] The principle considered here is only one form of the wider concept of 'fraud on a minority'. See further **18.4.**

[92] [1900] 1 Ch 656, at 671 (CA). A provision in the original articles of association, which might be open to attack if introduced as an alteration, will not be set aside on this basis: *Borland's Trustee v Steel Bros Co Ltd* [1901] 1 Ch 279; *Phillips v Manufacturers' Securities Ltd* (1917) 86 LJ Ch 305 (a power of compulsory acquisition of shares).

[93] These cases are examined thoroughly by Rixon 'Competing Interests and Conflicting Principles: An Examination of the Power of Alteration of Articles of Association' (1986) 49 MLR 446.

articles. It must be shown that the object of the majority in altering the articles is not capable of being for the benefit of the company as a whole.[94]

Some first instance decisions suggest that '*bona fide*' and 'the interests of the company as a whole' are separate requirements so that, regardless of the view of the majority, an alteration can be held to be invalid where, on an objective assessment, the court concludes that it is not in the interests of the company.[95] These cases have not been overruled but the Court of Appeal has strongly criticised the reasoning in the earlier first instance judgments[96] and has repeatedly affirmed that corporate benefit is not an independent ground for intervention: '*bona fides* in the interests of the company' is a single composite standard by which the majority decision is to be judged.[97] The better view is that it is primarily for the majority to decide what is in the interests of the company, since in principle the majority is best qualified to decide this question. It is thus a subjective rather than an objective test.

5.17 A MALICIOUS ALTERATION

If it can be shown that the majority acted maliciously or fraudulently, the alteration will not be allowed to stand because it cannot be said that the majority has acted *bona fide* in the interests of the company.[98] Malice for this purpose is used in the sense of a desire to harm or injure the minority.[99] Even if, on objective grounds, the alteration would be justifiable as being for the benefit of the company, it will be tainted by the bad motive of the majority. In *Sidebottom v Kershaw, Leese & Co*, the articles were altered to allow the company compulsorily to acquire the shares of any member who was in competition with the company's business. The Court of Appeal considered that this alteration in fact benefited the company, but indicated that it would not have stood if the evidence had shown that the alteration was directed at an individual for any malicious motive or with any dishonest intention.[100] In *Shuttleworth v Cox*, the articles were altered to add an additional event which disqualified a director from office. In the circumstances, the Court of

---

[94] *Dafen Tinplate Co v Llanelly Steel Co* [1920] 2 Ch 124, at 137; *Sidebottom v Kershaw, Leese & Co* [1920] 1 Ch 154, at 163(4) and 169 (CA); *Shuttleworth v Cox Bros & Co* [1927] 2 KB 9, at 18, 23 and 27 (CA).

[95] *Brown v British Abrasive Wheel Co* [1919] 1 Ch 290; *Dafen Tinplate Co v Llanelly Steel Co* [1920] 2 Ch 124.

[96] *Sidebottom v Kershaw, Leese & Co Ltd*, above at 172 where Astbury J in *Brown* is said by Warrington LJ to have 'confused himself' by treating *bona fides* and corporate benefit as separate things: see also Lord Sterndale MR at 167. The reasoning in *Dafen* was criticised by the Court of Appeal in *Shuttleworth*, especially at 19, 22 and 27.

[97] See *Sidebottom*, at 163 and 172; *Shuttleworth*, at 18 and 22; and *Greenhalgh v Arderne Cinemas Ltd* [1951] Ch 286, at 291.

[98] *Sidebottom*, above at 163.

[99] *Sidebottom*, above at 161, per Lord Sterndale MR.

[100] At 166, per Lord Sterndale MR and at 172 per Warrington LJ.

Appeal concluded that there was no 'trace of any vindictiveness or bad motive'[101] or of the decision having been taken 'maliciously', or with any desire to spite the plaintiff, or from any motive but that of doing what they thought best 'in the interest of the company';[102] it can be inferred that the alteration would not have stood if there had been such evidence.

Those seeking to prevent an alteration to articles becoming effective may find it difficult to establish positive evidence of malice, especially since, in all but the very smallest of companies, what will be in issue will be the motives of the group of persons who comprise the majority of the shareholders, rather than that of one majority shareholder. An inference may be drawn where an alteration is so oppressive of the minority as to cast suspicions on the honesty of the majority[103] but it is important to note that the mere fact that an alteration is directed at a particular individual and may involve expropriation of that person's shares does not, in itself, constitute sufficient evidence of oppression for such an inference to be drawn.[104] In both *Sidebottom* and *Shuttleworth*, the articles were altered to enable the company to rid itself of a particular individual but in both cases the Court of Appeal considered that in the circumstances the action of the majority was not suspicious: in *Sidebottom* the circumstances surrounding the alteration were that the individual against whom it was directed could exploit the information which came to him as a shareholder for the benefit of his own business and to the detriment of the company, whilst in *Shuttleworth* the individual had already been validly dismissed from his employment as managing director because of his laxity in running the company's affairs. Again, in *Allen v Gold Reefs of West Africa*, the company altered its articles to impose a lien on fully paid shares. The background to the alteration was that one shareholder owed a particularly large debt to the company and the imposition of the lien was one way of giving the company some security for the debt. Although the alteration was thus directed at one particular individual, it was upheld.

The reluctance of the English courts to strike down alterations to articles even where they are directed at particular individuals is to be contrasted with the more interventionist approach of the High Court of Australia in *Gambotto v WCP Ltd*.[105] In *Gambotto*, the company altered its articles so as to include a provision which would give the holder of 90% or more of its shares the right to buy out the minority. The High Court held that a test of proper purchase and fairness, rather than that of acting *bona fide* for the benefit of the company as a whole, governed the question of the validity of the new expropriation article and that the onus lay on those

---

101   At 17, per Bankes LJ.
102   At 21, per Scrutton LJ.
103   *Shuttleworth*, at 18, per Bankes LJ, and at 27, per Atkin LJ; *Rights & Issues Investment Trust Ltd v Stylo Shoes Ltd* [1965] 1 Ch 250.
104   *Sidebottom*, at 173, per Eve J.
105   (1995) 16 ACSR 1, noted Prentice 'Alteration of Articles of Association – Expropriation of Shares' (1996) 112 LQR 194.

supporting expropriation to prove the validity of the article.[106] However, this approach was not endorsed by the Privy Council in *Citco Banking v Pusser's*,[107] with Lord Hoffmann noting that *Gambotto* 'has no support in English authority'.

5.18   AN ALTERATION OUTSIDE THE BOUNDS OF REASONABLENESS

It is not for the court to impose its own view of what is reasonable on the company but if the alteration is such that no reasonable body of persons could consider it for the benefit of the company, it will not be allowed to stand.[108] In *Shuttleworth*, Bankes LJ indicated that an apt analogy is that of the grounds on which an appellate court will quash the verdict of a jury.[109] Bankes LJ also stated an alternative test which could be suitable in some cases: whether the action of the majority is capable of being considered for the benefit of the company.[110]

The absence of any reasonable grounds for deciding that an alteration is for the benefit of the company does not necessarily indicate malice but the alteration can still be set aside because the majority has not considered the matters which it ought to have considered.[111] In this respect, the 'jury' test is slightly wider than the malice test. Nevertheless, as the decisions of the Court of Appeal in *Sidebottom* and *Shuttleworth* indicate, it is still extremely difficult to persuade a court to set aside an alteration on this ground. An example of a claim that might succeed is where the articles are altered to allow the majority an unlimited power to expropriate or acquire compulsorily the shares of the minority and there are no valid commercial reasons, as there were in *Sidebottom* and *Shuttleworth*, to explain that alteration.[112] Another is if the majority alter the articles so as to restrict the dividend that would otherwise be due to the minority.[113]

---

[106] The CLRSG preferred the existing approach; see also *Constable v Executive Connections Ltd and others* [2005] 2 BCLC 638, at [26].

[107] *Citco Banking Corp NV v Pusser's Ltd* [2007] UKPC 13.

[108] *Shuttleworth,* at 18, per Bankes LJ.

[109] Ibid, at 18.

[110] Ibid, at 18–19.

[111] *Shuttleworth,* at 23, per Scrutton LJ. *Estmanco (Kilner House) Ltd v GLC* [1982] 1 All ER 437, at 444, per Megarry V-C: 'Where the majority shareholders genuinely believe that it is in the best interests of the company as a whole ... that is decisive, unless no reasonable shareholder in their position could hold this belief.'

[112] *Dafen Tinplate & Llanelly Steel*, on its facts, could support the proposition in the text because the alteration went further than what was required in the company's interest.

[113] *Dafen*, at 143.

5.19　THE DISCRIMINATION TEST AND THE 'INTERESTS OF THE COMPANY AS A WHOLE'

In *Greenhalgh v Arderne Cinemas Ltd*,[114] Lord Evershed MR formulated another way of testing whether an alteration is *bona fide* in the interests of the company as a whole: an alteration would be liable to be impeached 'if the effect of it were to discriminate between the majority shareholders and the minority shareholders, so as to give the former an advantage of which the latter were deprived'. Taken out of context, this comment may suggest that the circumstances in which the court can invalidate an alteration are judged on objective grounds but passages elsewhere in the judgment of the Master of the Rolls confirm that what is for 'the benefit of the company' is primarily for the majority of the shareholders to decide.[115] Also, the actual decision in *Greenhalgh* indicates that the discrimination test is not satisfied simply because, objectively, the alteration favours the majority over the minority: the articles were altered to allow existing members to sell their shares to outsiders provided they had the sanction of an ordinary resolution of the shareholders in general meeting; if the majority wanted to sell its shares to an outsider it would be assured of obtaining the necessary resolution but the minority would not; this objective discrimination against the minority did not invalidate the alteration. Unfortunately, the decision leaves open what type of discrimination is required for the court to intervene on this ground.[116]

Lord Evershed MR also formulated his test in this way:[117] 'the case may be taken of an individual hypothetical member and it may be asked whether what is proposed is, in the honest opinion of those who voted in favour, for that person's benefit'. The concept of 'an individual hypothetical member' is difficult to grasp and this test has not proved to be easy to apply. In *Clemens v Clemens*,[118] the company had two shareholders and, in purported reliance on the *Greenhalgh* hypothetical member test, Foster J considered whether in voting on a particular resolution the majority shareholder had honestly believed that it would benefit the plaintiff who was the minority shareholder. The representative member chosen by Foster J could hardly be described as hypothetical;[119]

---

[114]　Above, at 291.

[115]　At 291.

[116]　Discrimination as a basis for impeaching an alteration of articles is mentioned by Pennycuick J in *Rights & Issues Investment Trust Ltd v Stylo Shoes Ltd* [1965] 1 Ch 250 but the meaning of 'discrimination' for this purpose is not explained.

[117]　At 291.

[118]　[1976] 2 All ER 268.

[119]　The decision in *Clemens* can also be criticised on other grounds: see Joffe (1977) 40 MLR 71. The resolution in question did not relate to an alteration of the articles and the court's assertion of a general power to review shareholder decisions is questionable. The subjecting of majority power to equitable constraint on the basis of the decision in *Ebrahimi v Westbourne Galleries Ltd* [1973] AC 360 is doubtful because that case concerned a specific discretion conferred by statute in particular circumstances (but note *Pennell v Venida Investments* (1974) which is unreported but is discussed extensively by Burridge (1981) 44 MLR 40). *Clemens* hints at a fiduciary relationship between majority

but how such a member could have been constructed from the circumstances of the dispute defies description since it is difficult to see what common benefit could have transcended the interests of the warring factions. A further criticism of the hypothetical member test is that it seems to require the majority to act altruistically; this does not sit easily with the principle that a vote attached to a share is a property right which can be used as the owner of the share thinks fit. Lord Evershed MR himself acknowledged that persons in the majority did not have to dissociate themselves from their own interests when voting on the resolution to alter the articles.[120]

An important aspect of the decision in *Greenhalgh* is what Lord Evershed MR had to say about the meaning of the phrase 'the company as a whole'. The company is of course an entity distinct and separate from its shareholders and in cases such as *Allen v Gold Reefs, Sidebottom* and *Shuttleworth* it may be sufficient to consider whether the alteration is capable of being in the interests of the company as a commercial entity. However, cases such as *Greenhalgh* involve alterations which affect groups of shareholders differently but which have little or no effect on the company as a commercial entity; accordingly, 'the phrase, "the company as a whole", does not (at any rate in such a case as the present) mean the company as a commercial entity, distinct from the corporators: it means the corporators as a general body'.[121]

In *Peter's American Delicacy Co Ltd v Heath*,[122] the High Court of Australia accepted the need to distinguish alterations to articles which affected the rights *inter se* of shareholders from those which affected the interests of the company as a separate entity.[123] In cases of alterations involving competing shareholders' interests, 'the interests of the company as a whole' was thought to be an inappropriate, if not meaningless, test.[124] Inhuman altruism was not expected of the shareholders in the majority. According to Dixon CJ, provided the resolution to alter the articles involved no oppression, no appropriation of an unjust or reprehensible nature and did not imply any purpose outside the scope of the power, it would be allowed to stand.[125] Latham CJ expressed the test in slightly

---

and minority shareholders but, although this has been accepted in certain American and Commonwealth jurisdictions, it is not yet part of English company law: Sealy 'Equitable and Other Fetters on the Shareholder's Freedom to Vote' in NE Eastham and B Krivy (eds) *The Cambridge Lectures* (1981) at p 80. See also Rider [1978] CLJ 148: Prentice (1976) 92 LQR 502.

[120] At 291.

[121] *Greenhalgh*, at 291, per Lord Evershed MR.

[122] (1939) 61 CLR 457.

[123] At 481, per Latham CJ: at 512–13, per Dixon J.

[124] Per Dixon CJ at 513. Similarly, Latham CJ at 481: 'The benefit of the company cannot be adopted as a criterion which is capable of solving all the problems in this branch of the law ... In cases where the question which arises is simply a question as to the relative rights of different classes of shareholders the problem cannot be solved by regarding merely the benefit of the corporation.' Also Rich J at 495.

[125] At 513.

different language, but to the same effect: a resolution altering articles would be held to be invalid if there was 'fraud or trickery' or 'evidence of oppression' or if the alteration could be 'described as extravagant, so that reasonable men could not regard it as a fair alteration'.[126] In *Gambotto v WCP Ltd*,[127] Mason CJ said that where a change to articles gave rise to a conflict of interests and advantages the general test for judging its validity was whether it was '*ultra vires*, beyond any purpose contemplated by the articles or oppressive as that term is understood in the law relating to corporations'. If, however, the article involved expropriation or shares or other valuable proprietary rights, it would be subject to the stricter test of proper purpose and objective fairness.

The judgments of the High Court of Australia in *Peter's American Delicacy* and *Gambotto* explicitly address the considerations which underlie the court's assertion of a power to review decisions to alter articles of association and the factors which restrict the scope of this power of review. It is a well-established principle of company law that voting rights attached to shares are property rights which shareholders can in general use as they think fit. It would be impossible to investigate the thoughts and motives with which each shareholder casts his votes. However, the court must set some limit on the power of the majority because of, in the words of Dixon J, 'the fear or knowledge that an apparently regular exercise of power may in truth be but a means of securing some personal or particular gain, whether pecuniary or otherwise, which does not fairly arise out of the subjects dealt with by the power and is outside and even inconsistent with the contemplated objects of the power'.[128]

Emphasising misuse of power by the majority[129] as a trigger which allows the court to intervene seems in many ways a much more realistic and workable test than those outlined in *Greenhalgh*. In *Redwood Master Fund Ltd v TD Bank Europe Ltd*,[130] a case concerning an alteration to an agreement for a syndicated loan facility (rather than a company's articles of association) which affected some of the parties, Rimer J reviewed the case-law on the alteration of articles. In that context, he preferred a different test for circumstances where there is 'a clear potential for conflicting interests between the three classes of lenders, an assessment of the validity of a majority decision exclusively by reference to whether or not it is "for the benefit of the lenders as a whole" is ... a misplaced one'.[131] Instead, the concern is with the 'potential for dishonest abuse' of the majority's power, and the focus should be on whether a power was exercised in good faith for the purpose for which it was conferred. This

---

[126] At 491, and see also 482.
[127] (1995) 16 ACSR 1, at 8–9.
[128] *Peter's American Delicacy,* at 511–512.
[129] Or as it may be described in equity: 'fraud on a power' *Estmanco (Kilner House) Ltd v GLC*, above at 445.
[130] [2006] 1 BCLC 149 (case decided in December 2002).
[131] At [105].

approach has been welcomed,[132] although it remains to be seen whether it will find favour with the courts when dealing with a case involving the alteration of a company's articles.[133] It is becoming increasingly unlikely, though, that the courts will have much opportunity in the future to refine further the meaning of the '*bona fide* in the interests of the company' test enunciated in *Allen v Gold Reefs* because a minority which objects to an alteration to the articles can now voice the complaint by petitioning the court under Part 30 of the Companies Act 2006 for relief from unfairly prejudicial conduct. This form of statutory relief is very flexible, both in terms of the conduct which can be regarded as 'unfairly prejudicial' and with regard to the remedies which the court can grant where a claim is made out.[134] The difficult state of the case law was noted in *Constable v Executive Connections Ltd*,[135] a hearing at the interim stage. Judge Christopher Nugee QC, having discussed the case-law, concluded that the law in this area was neither clear nor easy to apply, and that 'this somewhat untidy state of the law seems ... to raise precisely the sort of difficult questions that call for "detailed argument and mature consideration", especially as ... the point is potentially one of some general importance'.[136] But even in this case, it was noted that the statutory remedy now in Part 30 of the Companies Act 2006 provided 'real protection'[137] for minority shareholders. With the Privy Council in *Citco Banking Corp NV v Pusser's Ltd* seemingly not wishing to suggest the need for departure from established authority, it is unlikely that there will be any developments in this area any time soon.

5.20 LEGAL EFFECT OF CONSTITUTION: CONTRACT

Section 33(1) of the Companies Act 2006 states that the provisions of a company's constitution bind the company and its members to the same extent as if there were covenants on the part of the company and each member to observe those provisions. The effect of this[138] is to create an obligation binding alike on the members in their dealings with the company,[139] on the company in its dealings with the members as members,[140] and on the members in their dealings with one another as

---

[132] Payne 'Company Law' [2006] All ER Annual Review, at [4.18].

[133] In *Citco Banking v Pusser's* [2007] UKPC 13, the Privy Council did not consider this approach. It also did not support the *Gumbotto* approach, preferring instead to support the approach established in *Greenhalgh*, *Allen v Gold Reefs* and *Shuttleworth*.

[134] The section is discussed further in Chapter 18.

[135] [2005] 2 BCLC 638.

[136] At [30].

[137] The words of counsel, cited at [27].

[138] For a full discussion of the earlier authorities, see *Hickman v Kent or Romney Marsh Sheep-Breeders' Association* [1915] 1 Ch 881.

[139] *Bradford Banking Co v Henry Briggs & Co* (1886) 12 App Cas 29 (HL); *Wood v Odessa Waterworks Co* (1889) 42 Ch D 636; *Quin & Axtens v Salmon* [1909] AC 442 (HL); *Hickman v Kent or Romney Marsh Sheep-Breeders' Association*, above.

[140] *Oakbank Oil Co v Crum* (1882) 8 App Cas 65 (HL).

members.[141] Thus, where the articles impose a duty on shareholders to purchase the shares of a member who wishes to dispose of them, such as individual right of membership can be directly enforced against the other shareholders without making the company a party.[142] It is not clear how far the rule in *Foss v Harbottle*[143] permits a minority shareholder to enforce any provision in the articles, as part of his contract of membership, where no individual right of membership is concerned.[144] A member may seek to challenge a failure to comply with the articles under Part 30 of the 2006 Act on the grounds that this failure amounts to unfairly prejudicial conduct. However, trivial or technical infringements of the articles are not intended to give rise to petitions under this Part.[145]

The legal effect of the constitution has therefore not changed materially from what it was under s 14 of the Companies Act 1985 and its predecessors, although the wording of s 33 of the 2006 Act has been simplified and amended to reflect the change in the documents comprising a company's constitution. When the Company Law Review (CLR) debated this issue, there was a degree of uncertainty as to whether the constitution, as then proposed, would have retained the contractual character of the articles. In its *Final Report*, the Company Law Review Steering Group (CLRSG) adopted a neutral position, preferring instead to explain to the draftsman of the Companies Bill how the constitution should operate and how this could best be reflected in the drafting. In the end, no major change was introduced, and the position of the constitution as a form of contract remains. However, there is potential for some confusion, because s 33 of the 2006 Act talks about the legal effect of the company's *constitution*, rather than the articles. As noted above, the constitution of the company includes not only its articles, but also certain resolutions and agreements affecting a company's constitution. All of these will have contractual effect by virtue of s 33.

Although s 33 [CA 1985, s 14] uses the language of contract, the s 33 [CA 1985, s 14] contract is of a special kind, as was noted by Steyn LJ in *Bratton Seymour Service Co Ltd v Oxborough*.[146] Distinctive features of the s 33 [CA 1985, s 14] contract include the following:[147]

(1)   it derives its binding force not from a bargain struck between the parties but from the terms of the statute;

---

[141] *Eley v Positive Government Security Life Assurance* (1876) 1 Ex D 88 (CA).

[142] *Rayfield v Hands* [1960] Ch 1.

[143] (1843) 2 Hare 461.

[144] This question is further considered at **18.4**.

[145] *Re Saul D Harrison & Sons plc* [1994] BCC 475.

[146] [1992] BCC 471, [1992] BCLC 693. See also *Shareholder Remedies*, Law Com CP No 142 (1996) paras 2.6–2.14.

[147] [1992] BCC 471, at 475, [1992] BCLC 693, at 698.

(2)   it is binding only insofar as it affects rights and obligations between the company and its members acting in their capacity as members;[148]

(3)   it can be altered by special resolution without the consent of all of the contracting parties;[149]

(4)   it is not defeasible on the grounds of misrepresentation, common law mistake, mistake in equity, undue influence or duress;

(5)   it cannot be rectified on the grounds of mistake.[150]

Although this analysis largely holds under the revised wording of s 33 of the Companies Act 2006, (3) above now needs to be read in the light of the rules permitting the entrenchment of provisions in the articles.[151] Beyond that, however, the case-law and scholarly debate about the nature of the articles of association (now the constitution) continues to be of relevance.

In addition to the special features of the s 33 contract, the principles regarding the implication of terms are different, the courts taking a very restrictive attitude. In *Bratton Seymour*, the Court of Appeal refused to imply a term into articles on the grounds of business efficacy which would have had the effect of imposing on members an obligation to make a financial contribution to certain expenses incurred by the company. The Court of Appeal indicated that terms would not easily be implied into articles from extrinsic circumstances because of the special nature of the contract. Steyn LJ and Sir Christopher Slade emphasised the importance of third parties (in particular potential shareholders) being able to rely on the articles as registered.[152] In *Re Benfield Greig Group plc*,[153] in the context of a share transfer restriction in the articles requiring an independent valuation of the shares concerned, Arden J refused to imply a term giving both parties to the transaction the right to be treated equally because this was not a matter of necessity, irrespective of whether it was a matter of fairness or reasonableness.[154] However, in *Folkes*

---

[148]   This feature is discussed further at **5.21**.

[149]   Discussed at **5.9**.

[150]   *Evans v Chapman* [1902] WN 78; *Scott v Frank F Scott (London) Ltd* [1940] 1 Ch 794.

[151]   Companies Act 2006, s 22; see **5.7**.

[152]   See also *Mutual Life Insurance Co v The Rank Organisation* [1985] BCLC 11 where Goulding J refused to imply pre-emption rights into articles. Limited pre-emption rights are now provided by statute: see **7.3**. *Bratton Seymour* was followed in *Towcester Racecourse Co Ltd v The Racecourse Association Ltd* [2002] EWHC 214 (Ch), [2003] 1 BCLC 260.

[153]   [2000] 2 BCLC 488; decision reversed by the Court of Appeal on different grounds [2001] EWCA Civ 397, [2002] 1 BCLC 65.

[154]   It had been argued that the valuation requirement should be subject to Lord Hoffmann's observations in *O'Neil v Phillips* on the valuation of shares in the context of a s 459 petition (see [1999] 2 BCLC 1, at 17; [1999] 1 WLR 1092, at 1107) and that a term to that effect should be implied.

Group plc v Alexander,[155] Rimer J did add five words to a specific provision in the articles of a listed public company. The articles contained a definition of 'qualifying shares' for the purposes of calculating the shareholding of the Folkes family, which originally included a reference to 'any voting share which is for the time being beneficially owned by or held in trust for a member of the Folkes family ...'. This was amended in 1999 to read 'any voting share which is for the time being beneficially owned by a member of the Folkes Family Company or held in trust for a member of the Folkes family ...'. This seemed to remove shares beneficially owned by the family from the definition, although it created a new category of qualifying shares based on membership of the Folkes Family Company, although there was no such company. The consequence of this was a reduction of the family's voting shares from 40% to 24%. Having concluded that 'an interpretation of [the article] according to the face value of the words is so absurd that something must have gone seriously wrong with its drafting',[156] Rimer J construed the article by supplying the words 'or by a Folkes Family', inserted before 'Company'. Although he regarded this still as an exercise of construction, Rimer J acknowledged that it was 'close to the limits of what is permissible'.[157] This is an unusual case where the court added words to a term primarily to correct what the evidence showed to be a drafting error.[158]

More recently, the Privy Council in *Attorney-General of Belize v Belize Telecom*[159] was prepared to imply a term into the articles of association in circumstances where the holders of a certain class of shares (C shares) were entitled to appoint a director once their shareholding exceeded a set threshold (37.435%). This had happened but subsequently, the shareholding fell below the threshold and the question arose whether a director appointed in this situation could remain in office. Although there was a general article dealing with the retirement of directors, it did not deal with the specific circumstances which had arisen. Lord Hoffmann reviewed the principles on implying terms into a contract, noting that if a document is silent in respect of a certain situation, the assumption is that nothing should happen unless it was clear to a reasonable person that read against the relevant background, something must have been intended to happen to avoid a commercially absurd result. On the facts, it was necessary to imply a term that a director appointed whilst the shareholding of the C shareholder was above the threshold would have to leave office if the shareholding fell below the threshold. However, where

---

[155] [2002] EWHC 51 (Ch), [2002] 2 BCLC 254.
[156] Ibid, at [20].
[157] Ibid, at [22].
[158] See also *Stanham v NTA* (1989) 15 ACLR 87, at 90–91 to support the possibility of implying a term purely from the language of the document itself.
[159] [2009] UKPC 10, [2009] 2 BCLC 148.

the wording of the articles is clear and deals with a situation, then the articles are likely to be read literally and the threshold for 'commercial absurdity' is a high one.[160]

So the general position remains that whilst the articles must be interpreted in a businesslike way, the focus has to be on the articles themselves and not any surrounding circumstances, nor can terms be implied unless this could be done by inference from the other articles – but not by invoking extrinsic evidence.[161]

5.21   OUTSIDERS' RIGHTS AND THE ARTICLES AS A CONTRACT

In accordance with normal contractual principles, those who are not members cannot enforce the provisions of the articles either against the company or its members.[162] A special feature of the s 33 [CA 1985, s 14] contract is that even a member cannot enforce provisions for his benefit in some other capacity than that of member: eg he cannot assert a right to be appointed solicitor, secretary, or director[163] by reason of provisions contained only in the articles.[164] So an article providing for the reference of disputes to arbitration may be enforceable by or against a member in his capacity as such, but not in some other capacity, eg that of director.[165] On the other hand, the shareholder is not bound in his personal capacity. 'The purpose of the ... articles is to define the position of the shareholder as shareholder, not to bind him in his capacity as an individual.'[166]

The wording of s 33 of the 2006 Act does rectify some of the problems associated with the somewhat unclear wording of s 14 of the 1985 Act (and its predecessors, eg s 16 of the 1862 Act and s 20 of the 1948 Act),

---

[160]   *Thompson v Goblin Hill Hotels Ltd* [2011] UKPC 8, [2011] 1 BCLC 587.

[161]   *Dashfield v Davidson* [2009] 1 BCLC 220.

[162]   *Re Rotherham Alum and Chemical Co* (1883) 25 Ch D 103; *Melhado v Porto-Allegre Co* (1874) LR 9 CP 503; *Re Empress Engineering Co* (1881) 16 Ch D 125 (CA); *Re English and Colonial Produce Co* [1906] 2 Ch 435. These cases establish that a clause in the articles requiring the company to pay preliminary charges cannot be enforced unless some other contract has been made. Equally, a contract made with a trustee before the company is formed does not become enforceable merely because the articles purport to adopt the contract: *Re Northumberland Avenue Hotel Co* (1886) 33 Ch D 16 (CA).

[163]   *Eley v Positive Government Security Life Assurance Co*, above; *Browne v La Trinidad* (1888) 37 Ch D 1.

[164]   The Contracts (Rights of Third Parties) Act 1999, which allows a third party to enforce a term in a contract to which he is not party but which seeks to confer a benefit on him, expressly excludes the s 33 [CA 1985, s 14] contract from its application: s 6(2) of the 1999 Act.

[165]   *Hickman v Kent or Romney Marsh Sheep-Breeders' Association* [1915] 1 Ch 881; *Beattie v E and F Beattie* [1938] Ch 708; *London Sack and Bag Co v Dixon* [1943] 2 All ER 763 (CA).

[166]   Per Buckley LJ, *Bisgood v Henderson's Transvaal Estates* [1908] 1 Ch 743, at 759 (CA). See also *Baring-Gould v Sharpington Combined Pick and Shovel Syndicate* [1899] 2 Ch 80 (CA).

which long gave rise to conflicting judicial interpretation. This stemmed in part from the fact that, under s 14 of the 1985 Act, although the memorandum and articles 'shall, when registered, bind the company and the members', this was based on a putative statutory signing and sealing by the members and not by the company. Likewise, the memorandum and articles were deemed to contain 'covenants on the part of each member' (but not the company) to observe their provisions.[167] Until the end of the nineteenth century the courts were divided as to the parties to this statutory contract of association (ie parties in the sense of having rights of action and liabilities thereunder). There were authorities both for and against there being a contract between the members *inter se*,[168] as well as both for and against s 14 creating a contract between the company and its members.[169] The modern law was eventually settled that the contract created by s 14 of the 1985 Act confers rights between the company and its members and between the members *inter se*. This position is affirmed in s 33 of the Companies Act 2006, which clearly states that the constitution is binding on the company and its members 'as if there were covenants on the part of the company and of each member to observe those provisions'.[170]

However, the still conflicting reasoning in the cases considered by Astbury J in *Hickman v Kent or Romney Marsh Sheep-Breeders' Association*[171] induced his attempt to provide a perhaps novel reconciling principle with regard to the scope of the contractual effect of the articles.[172] This has received substantial criticism from some academic commentators.[173] It is argued that Astbury J's decision in *Hickman* conflicts with earlier decisions which do not recognise the principle which he attempted to elicit from them. Moreover, it is said that the *Hickman* principle appears to ignore the wording of what is now s 33(1) of the Companies Act 2006, which creates a contractual obligation in respect of all 'the provisions of

---

[167] The explanation of this omission lies in the conveyancing background to this section. See 44 MLR 526, at 528–529. Under the Companies Act 1844, each shareholder executed an indenture with a trustee for the company. This incorporated or referred to the company's constitution. This requirement was dropped in the Companies Act 1856. The covenant was simply deemed to exist by the statute but no covenant with the company was expressed.

[168] Cf *Eley v Positive Government Security Life Association Co* (1876) LR 1 Ex 88, at 89, with *Welton v Saffery* [1897] AC 299, at 315, per Lord Herschell.

[169] Cf *Johnson v Lyttle's Iron Agency* (1877) 5 Ch D 687, at 693, with *Browne v La Trinidad* (1888) 37 Ch D 1, at 12 and 15.

[170] Companies Act 2006, s 33(1).

[171] Above.

[172] The earlier cases were influenced by other grounds than the *Hickman* principle: eg the old view that members were not parties to the contract (*Baring-Gould v Sharpington Combined Pick and Shovel Syndicate* [1899] 2 Ch 80) or that the article in question was directory rather than mandatory (*Pritchard's Case* (1873) 8 Ch App 956, at 960), or that the plaintiff, as a matter of procedural form, sued not as a member but in some external capacity (eg as a solicitor or promoter): *Eley v Positive Government Security Life Association Co*, above. See (1981) 44 MLR 526, at 531–539.

[173] See Gregory 'The Section 20 Contract' (1981) 44 MLR 526. This amplifies views earlier expressed by Lord Wedderburn: [1957] CLJ 194, at 212–13.

the company's constitution'. The view contended for by these commentators is that an 'outsider', so long as he sues in his capacity as shareholder, can compel the company not to depart from the contract with him under the constitution. This is so even if that results indirectly in the enforcement of 'outsider' rights vested in third parties or in the claimant shareholder. The case-law, which remains in a state of some confusion (not resolved by the limited changes introduced under the 2006 Act), reveals that in some situations the courts have allowed a member, suing as such, to enforce a non-shareholder right conferred by the articles. This has been done to protect shareholder-directors whose rights to hold office, or to participate in management, or to exercise a veto over board decisions or to commence litigation, have been brushed aside in breach of a provision in the articles.[174] However, it is a long step from this to conclude that every shareholder has a right to have all and every one of the articles enforced by declaration or injunction.[175] To do so is to ignore not only the authorities on the *Hickman* principle (which, whatever its questionable provenance, has never been overruled and has been applied by the Court of Appeal).[176] It also overlooks the rule in *Foss v Harbottle*[177] and the related question of the majority shareholders' right to ratify some, but not all, breaches of the articles.[178] The Court of Appeal has, on more than one occasion, indicated that the members' contract of association cannot be used to 'short-circuit' the rule in *Foss v Harbottle*, especially in the case of shareholders' actions to remedy directors' breaches of fiduciary duty to the company.[179] This is clearly of more significance than the confusion of the courts in the late nineteenth century as to the parties to the statutory contract of association.[180] The point is reinforced by Steyn LJ's comments in *Bratton Seymour* which

---

[174] *Imperial Hydropathic Hotel v Hamson* (1882) 23 Ch D 1; *Pulbrook v Richmond Consolidated Mining Co* (1878) 9 Ch D 610; *Quin and Axtens v Salmon* [1909] AC 442; *Hayes v Bristol Plant Hire* [1957] 1 All ER 685; *Breckland Group Holdings Ltd v London and Suffolk Properties Ltd* [1989] BCLC 100, noted Wedderburn (1989) 52 MLR 401. Attempts have been made by commentators to explain, on 'organic' or constitutional grounds, when the courts will allow 'non-shareholder rights' in the articles to be enforced. See Goldberg (1972) 35 MLR 362; Bastin [1977] JBL 17; Prentice (1980) 1 Co Law 179.

[175] It is clear that (claims for arrears of dividend and the like aside) damages will not be awarded for breach of this very special contract. This alone may indicate its special character: a case perhaps of *ibi remedium, ubi jus*.

[176] *Beattie v E and F Beattie Ltd* [1938] Ch 708, at 713–714. See also *London Sack and Bag Co Ltd v Dixon* [1943] 2 All ER 763.

[177] (1843) 2 Hare 461.

[178] See *Grant v UK Switchback Railways* (1889) 40 Ch D 135 (CA).

[179] See *Bamford v Bamford* [1970] Ch 212; *Prudential Assurance v Newman Industries (No 2)* [1982] Ch 204. See a further discussion of these issues at **18.4**.

[180] See further Drury 'The Relative Nature of a Shareholder's Right to Enforce the Company Contract' [1986] CLJ 219. This is an interesting attempt to reconcile the cases on the basis that the courts weigh various factors in the balance in deciding whether to enforce the shareholder's 'relative right'. This is more satisfying than some earlier theories in getting to grips with the institutional reality produced by the shareholder's contract. It still remains open to the criticism levied at earlier theories that it is essentially an *ex post facto* rationalisation.

indicate that it is incorrect to attach too much importance to the 'contractual' nature of the relationship formed by s 33 [CA 1985, s 14] between a company and its members (and between the members *inter se*) since the normal incidents of a contract do not necessarily apply.

The restrictions on a shareholder's ability to bring a personal action to enforce the provisions of the articles of association were considered by the Law Commission in the context of its wide-ranging review of shareholder remedies.[181] The Law Commission concluded that no hardship was being caused by potential difficulties in identifying enforceable personal rights conferred by the articles and accordingly, it declined to recommend reform of s 14 (now s 33 of the 2006 Act). The question of reform of s 14 was also raised by the CLRSG in its general review of company law. In consultation documents,[182] the CLR questioned whether the articles should continue to be treated as a contract, although it decided not to recommend a specific change.[183] Nevertheless, the CLR did recommend that in future, all duties imposed on the members by the constitution should be enforceable by individual shareholders, subject to specific disapplication of this right in relation to particular provisions.[184] As already noted, no significant changes were made under the 2006 Act.

5.22 CONTRACTS INCORPORATING PROVISIONS IN THE ARTICLES

If individuals have been engaged in some capacity without an agreement setting out the terms of employment,[185] the articles may be looked at to see what these terms are. On this footing, the directors may be sued for payment of their qualification shares or sue for the remuneration specified in the articles,[186] although it seems that a director cannot derive a prospective entitlement to remuneration from a contract inferred on this basis.[187] In any other case where a contract is established, but the terms are not specified, the articles may be referred to for the purpose of supplying the terms.[188]

---

[181] *Shareholder Remedies*, Law Com CP No 142 (1996) paras 2.13–2.28 and *Shareholder Remedies,* Law Com No 246 (1997) paras 7.4–7.11.

[182] *Modern Company Law for a Competitive Economy: Company Formation and Capital Maintenance* (1999) and *Developing the Framework* (March 2000) paras 4.72–4.99.

[183] *Completing the Structure* (November 2000) paras 5.68–5.69, where it was proposed that the desired result about the status of the constitution should be explained to the draftsman, leaving him to find the best way of expressing the result in the drafting.

[184] *Completing the Structure* (November 2000) para 5.73; *Final Report* (July 2001), paras 7.34–7.40.

[185] *Boston Deep Sea Fishing and Ice Co v Ansell* (1888) 39 Ch D 339 (CA).

[186] *Re New British Iron Co, ex parte Beckwith* [1898] 1 Ch 324. On the relevance of the articles to directors' service contracts, see **17.3.**

[187] *Re New British Iron Co, ex parte Beckwith* [1898] 1 Ch 324.

[188] *Pritchard's Case* (1873) 8 Ch App 956; *Swabey v Port Darwin Co* (1889) 1 Meg 385 (CA); *Boston Deep Sea Fishing and Ice Co v Ansell* (1888) 39 Ch D 339, at 366 (CA).

5.23 THE CHARACTER OF OBLIGATIONS IN THE CONSTITUTION

All money payable in pursuance of the constitution becomes in England an ordinary contract debt from a member to the company,[189] so that the debt remains enforceable for 6 years before s 5 of the Limitation Act 1980 affords a good defence to proceedings. This is a change from the 1985 Act, which treated this as a specialty debt,[190] which is subject to a longer limitation period of 12 years. Before this change, it had been held that money payable from the company to the members in pursuance of the articles is not a specialty debt so that the relevant limitation period is that which applies to actions based on simple contract, namely 6 years.[191] The change made by the 2006 Act therefore removes the complexity which had arisen, following the recommendations of the CLR.[192]

---

[189] Section 33(2).

[190] Companies Act 1985, s 14(2).

[191] *Re Compania de Electricidad de la Provincia de Buenos Aires Ltd* [1980] 1 Ch 146.

[192] See *Modern Company Law for a Competitive Economy. Company Formation and Capital Maintenance* (Company Law Review Steering Group Consultation Document, 1999) para 2.9, which proposed that debts owing to the company should cease to be specialty debts.

CHAPTER 6

COMPANY CONTRACTS

6.1 INTRODUCTION

This chapter is concerned with the ability of a company to make legally binding contracts and to enter into other transactions with valid effect.[1] In the past this would have involved detailed examination of two quite distinct areas of law, namely the *ultra vires* doctrine and agency principles.

The *ultra vires* doctrine is related to the capacity of the company: in its original and strictest form, the *ultra vires* doctrine meant that no transaction which was beyond the capacity of a company could ever be binding on it.[2] The strictness of the *ultra vires* doctrine was first ameliorated as a consequence of the UK's accession to the European Community because it was incompatible with Community law. The European Communities Act 1972 contained a provision[3] which allowed transactions which were beyond a company's capacity to be enforced against it in certain circumstances; eventually, the relevant provisions became ss 35, 35A, 35B and 322A of the Companies Act 1985. With the Companies Act 2006, the *ultra vires* doctrine has, to all intents and purposes, been abolished. As will be seen, the assumption is that companies have general capacity, and if restrictions are introduced into the company's constitution through a statement of objects,[4] then this will be a limitation on the authority of directors rather than the company itself. In this respect, remnants of the doctrine are still lingering: the *ultra vires* doctrine retains some relevance because the directors will be in breach of duty if they fail to act in accordance with the company's constitution. If the company has a statement of objects, and directors take action which is not covered by these objects, then they will be acting both without authority and in breach of their general duty.[5] Establishing a breach of duty and a lack of authority on this basis may entail the

---

[1]   See generally, A Griffiths *Contracting with Companies* (Oxford, Hart Publishing, 2005).

[2]   It is now generally accepted that the courts will not apply the *ultra vires* doctrine to limit a company's liability in tort or crime: Welch 'The Criminal Liability of Corporations' (1946) 62 LQR 345.

[3]   Section 9.

[4]   See Chapter 5 at **5.6**.

[5]   Companies Act 2006, s 171; see Chapter 16.

application of the relevant principles on *ultra vires*. However, this will only be necessary where a company has included a statement of objects in its articles of association.[6]

As a legal, as opposed to a natural, person a company must act through others,[7] but simply because someone purports to act on a company's behalf does not mean that it is bound: the authority of those who act on behalf of the company to bind it is governed by agency principles together with a special principle of company law known as the *Turquand* rule. Although this aspect is now generally covered by the Act,[8] agency principles remain important in determining when a company is bound by a transaction. Agency principles are derived mainly from case-law but statutory reforms have affected these principles to a certain extent.

It is important to understand the distinction between 'capacity' and 'authority' at the outset. References to 'capacity' normally relate to the ability of the *company* to enter into a particular transaction. If it does not have this ability, the act is *prima facie* '*ultra vires*'. The term '*ultra vires*' used in a strict sense in relation to a registered company meant acts which were outside the scope of the objects of the company set forth in the objects clause of its memorandum.[9]

In contrast, the term 'authority' refers to acts by *individuals* who purport to take a decision on behalf of the company, such as its directors or managers. Their power to take decisions in the company's name is not restricted, and if they exceed this, they are acting 'without authority'.

In company law, the term '*ultra vires*' has sometimes been used to describe acts which are not beyond the *capacity* of the company, but simply beyond the authority of either the board of directors or a simple majority of the shareholders. Such acts may be in breach of the articles of association, but they are not, strictly speaking, beyond the powers of the company. Acts of this type can be ratified and, once properly ratified, they become binding on the company. Another use of the term *ultra vires* in a wider sense is to describe transactions which, although within the scope of the powers of the company, are entered into for an unauthorised purpose.

---

[6] As permitted under s 31 of the Companies Act 2006.

[7] *Meridian Global Funds Management Asia Ltd v Securities Commission* [1995] 2 AC 500 (PC).

[8] Companies Act 2006, s 40 [CA 1985, s 35A].

[9] In the case of statutory companies created by private Acts of Parliament, the Act itself will define the company's objects. This will usually be done in much narrower terms than the objects clause of a modern registered company. The *ultra vires* doctrine does not apply to companies incorporated by Royal Charter. A chartered company which fails to observe restrictions in its charter may find itself subject to proceedings in the nature of *scire facias* for the revocation of its charter: *British South Africa Co v de Beers Mines* [1910] 1 Ch 354. A member may obtain an injunction to restrain the company from acting in a manner inconsistent with its charter: *Rendall v Crystal Palace Co* (1858) 4 K & J 326; *Breay v Royal British Nurses Association* [1897] 2 Ch 272; *Jenkins v Pharmaceutical Society of Great Britain* [1921] 1 Ch 392.

These transactions are not void and can confer rights on a third party who is unaware of the improper purpose.[10] In *Rolled Steel Products (Holdings) Ltd v British Steel Corp*,[11] Slade and Browne-Wilkinson LJJ rightly commented on the potential for confusion caused by the use of the term *'ultra vires'* in these wider senses and suggested that its use should be confined to its strict sense.

An act may also be void on the ground of illegality as being contrary to the provisions of the Companies Acts. A company cannot take power to do something which is contrary to the Companies Acts so that an act which is illegal can also properly be described as being *ultra vires*.[12]

6.2 *ULTRA VIRES*: A BRIEF OVERVIEW

As stated above, the effect of the Companies Act 2006 is to further reduce the relevance of the common law doctrine of *ultra vires*, but it has not disappeared altogether. As s 28 provides that provisions of the old-style memorandum are to be treated as provisions of the articles, most companies will have a statement of objects unless this is removed from the articles. Initially, therefore, most companies will have a (usually very lengthy) statement of objects by virtue of s 28, although many of them may decide to remove these altogether. Those who do not will thereby restrict the authority of their directors. Establishing whether directors have exceeded their authority may therefore involve the application of the common law doctrine. This section therefore provides a general overview of this doctrine.[13]

6.2.1 The doctrine stated and its impact mitigated

At common law (prior to what eventually became s 35 of the Companies Act 1985), a transaction which was *ultra vires* in the strict sense was that it was beyond the company's capacity and could not be ratified even by a unanimous vote of the shareholders.[14]

---

[10] *Rolled Steel Products (Holdings) Ltd v British Steel Corpn* [1982] Ch 478, [1982] 3 All ER 1057, [1982] 3 WLR 715 (Vinelott J). See Birds (1982) 3 Co Law 123.

[11] [1986] Ch 246.

[12] In *Aveling Barford Ltd v Perion Ltd* [1989] BCLC 626, (1989) 5 BCC 677 the term *'ultra vires'* is used in respect of an illegal act. Because such acts are illegal as well as void, third parties will not be entitled to the same consequential relief that is open to a party to a contract that is *ultra vires* but not contrary to the Companies Acts. The rules as to illegal contracts are applied: *South Western Mineral Water Co v Ashmore* [1967] 1 WLR 1110.

[13] This is shorter than in earlier editions of this book. Readers interested in greater detail are advised to consult the fifth, or earlier, edition.

[14] *Ashbury Railway Carriage & Iron Co v Riche* (1875) LR 7 HL 653; *Rolled Steel Products (Holdings) Ltd v British Steel Corpn* [1986] Ch 246, [1985] 3 All ER 52, [1985] 2 WLR 908, [1984] BCLC 466, (1983–1985) 1 BCC 99, at 158.

The *ultra vires* doctrine was created by judges in the nineteenth century but companies soon realised that a way around the restrictions which it imposed was to draft the objects clause as widely as possible. Initially there was judicial hostility to the practice of drafting very wide objects but, with some reluctance, the key clauses which companies wanted to include in their objects were accepted by the courts. Eventually the attitude of the courts shifted and in the more modern cases they have tended to endorse companies' efforts to express their capacity in the widest possible terms.

The *ultra vires* doctrine was never so harshly applied as to make void everything which was not expressly authorised by the memorandum, because the courts accepted that whatever might fairly be regarded as incidental to or consequential upon the objects specified ought not, unless expressly prohibited, to be held to be outside the powers of the company.[15] Nevertheless, it soon became commonplace to insert into the objects clause some general words empowering the company to 'do all such other things as may be deemed to be incidental or conducive to the attainment of the above object or any of them'. Such a clause has been treated as extending the powers of the company[16] but the words will be held only to cover operations of a nature similar to the business previously mentioned, and will not include any wholly fresh business.[17]

As well as including general incidental wording, companies began to include a wide range of objects (in the sense of types of business) and powers in the objects clause. It became the established practice for companies to adopt very long objects clauses which authorised a wide range of activities.[18] The judicial response to this practice was to evolve the main object rule of construction: the main object rule involved identifying the main object of the company and then construing the other objects and the powers specified in the objects clause as being ancillary to that main object.[19] Thus, for example, if the company's objects clause commenced with a paragraph authorising it to acquire rubber and

---

[15]   *Attorney-General v Great Eastern Rly Co* (1880) 5 App Cas 473; *Small v Smith* (1884) 10 App Cas 119; *Deuchar v Gas Light and Coke Co* [1925] AC 691 (HL); *Attorney-General v Smethwick Corporation* [1932] 1 Ch 562.

[16]   *Re Baglan Hall Colliery Co* (1870) 5 Ch App 346; *Simpson v Westminster Palace Hotel Co* (1860) 8 HLC 712; *Taunton v Royal Insurance Co* (1864) 2 H & M 135; *Re Peruvian Railways Co* (1867) LR 2 Ch 617.

[17]   *London Financial Association v Kelk* (1884) 26 Ch D 107.

[18]   The Companies Act 1989 introduced s 3A into the 1985 Act which gave companies the option of using a short-form objects clause to the effect that the object of the company was to carry on business as a general commercial company. However, it failed to have a significant impact in practice, and in light of the changes made by the 2006 Act, no corresponding provision now exists.

[19]   As explained in *Anglo-Overseas Agencies v Green* [1961] 1 QB 1, at 8. For cases considering whether to wind up a company on the grounds that its principal object had failed, see *Re Haven Gold Mining Co* (1882) 20 Ch D 151; *Re German Date Coffee Co* (1882) 20 Ch D 169 (CA); *Re Kitson & Co* [1946] 1 All ER 435; *Re Eastern Telegraph* [1947] 2 All ER 104.

tobacco estates but a subsequent paragraph gave it the power to underwrite shares,[20] under the main object rule of construction, the underwriting power would be viewed as ancillary to, and to be exercisable only for the purposes incidental or accessory to, the acquisition of rubber or tobacco estates.

In order to avoid the operation of the main object rule of construction altogether, companies then started to include wording in their objects clause to the effect that each paragraph of the clause was to be read separately and without limitation by reference to the other clauses. The effect of this wording was considered by the House of Lords in *Cotman v Brougham*.[21] The House held that once a company was registered, its memorandum of association had to be viewed as a valid instrument and the provisions which it contained had to be given effect to accordingly.[22] Therefore, effect had to be given to an independent objects paragraph by treating every object and power specified in the objects clause as independent objects, and not as ancillary to the main object.

This liberal policy of allowing the draftsman of the objects clause to defeat the apparent purpose of the *ultra vires* doctrine was carried a stage further by the Court of Appeal in *Bell Houses Ltd v City Wall Properties Ltd*.[23] In that case, clause 3(c) of the memorandum of association allowed the company to 'carry on any other trade or business whatever which can, *in the opinion of the board of directors*,[24] be advantageously carried on by, in connection with, or ancillary to, any of the above businesses or general businesses of the company'. The appellant company maintained that clause 3(c) allowed them to charge a procuration fee for introducing a source of finance (which they did not wish to use themselves at the time) to another property company, even though there was no express power to do so. The Court of Appeal held that, provided the directors of the plaintiff company honestly formed the view that that particular business could be carried on advantageously in connection with, or as an ancillary to, the company's main business,[25] then the agreement to charge a procuration fee was within the company's powers by virtue of clause 3(c).[26]

---

20 The factual situation is taken from *Cotman v Brougham* [1918] AC 514 (HL).

21 Above. This must be taken to overrule *Stephens v Mysore Reefs (Kangundy) Mining Co* [1902] 1 Ch 745.

22 But the Crown can bring proceedings to quash the registration of a company which is registered with illegal objects: see Chapter 4.

23 [1966] 2 QB 656. For an application of this case in New Zealand, see *American Home Assurance Co v Tjmonis Properties* [1984] NZLR 452 (CA). See also *H & H Logging Co Ltd v Random Services Corp Ltd* (1967) 63 DLR (20) 6 and *HA Stephenson & Sons Ltd v Gillanders, Arbuthnot & Co Ltd* (1931) 45 CLR 476 (Aust HC).

24 Italics supplied.

25 This is an important qualification to the discretion conferred on directors to determine what is within the objects clause of the company. It is clear that the courts would not accept an unqualified discretion which allowed the company to do anything the directors thought fit to decide: *Re Crown Bank* (1890) 44 Ch D 634; *Introductions Ltd v National Provincial Bank* [1970] Ch 199, at 209, per Harman LJ. This should be

The *Bell Houses* decision appeared to indicate a marked shift in the judicial attitude towards the value of the *ultra vires* doctrine. It permitted the draftsman by a simple and flexible drafting device to give the company's management reasonable freedom of manoeuvre in developing and diversifying the company's activities. However, in a later Court of Appeal decision a more rigorous approach was taken.

6.2.2   Reaffirming the doctrine

In *Introductions Ltd v National Provincial Bank Ltd*,[27] a company originally formed for the purpose of offering services and information to overseas visitors to the Festival of Britain was taken over and, under new management, it began pig-breeding as its only business. A bank which had advanced money to finance this business was held unable to recover on the company's liquidation. The bank was fully aware of the purpose of the loan and that the objects for which the company was formed were those set out in its memorandum, of which the bank had a copy. It was contended for the bank that, even if pig-breeding were *ultra vires*,[28] it might rely on a sub-clause (N) of the objects clause that enabled this company 'to borrow or raise money in such manner as it thought fit'. This was linked with a provision (similar to that in *Anglo-Overseas Agencies v Green*) that each sub-clause 'should be construed independently of, and should be in no way linked by, reference to any other sub-clause, and that the objects set out in each sub-clause were independent objects of the company'.

The Court of Appeal made a sharp distinction between *powers* as opposed to *objects* in the memorandum. On the true construction of the sub-clause conferring a general power to borrow, this was a power not an object. Thus the power to borrow had to be used for the legitimate *intra vires* objects of the company. Since the explicit purpose of the loan (pig-breeding) was *ultra vires*, the borrowing itself was *ultra vires*. Despite the final provision declaring all the objects set forth to be independent,

---

contrasted with a more expansive approach (to a less qualified discretion conferred upon the directors) taken by the Australian High Court in *HA Stephenson & Sons Ltd v Gillanders, Arbuthnot & Co Ltd* (1931) 45 CLR 476 (Aust HC). See the judgment of Dixon J at 490–491.

[26]   The decision in *Bell Houses Ltd* also rested on the alternative ground that, apart from the subjective discretion conferred on the directors, the obtaining of the procuration fee was, as a matter of objective construction, reasonably incidental to certain specific objects of the company: see [1966] 2 QB 656, at 680 (Danckwerts LJ) and 692–693 (Salmon LJ).

[27]   [1970] Ch 199 (CA).

[28]   Buckley J had held that pig-breeding was *ultra vires* the company and this point was not contested on appeal: [1968] 2 All ER 1221.

the power to borrow on sub-clause (N) was not on its wording capable of being a wholly independent object. As a power it was necessarily ancillary to the objects of the company.[29]

Attempts have been made to exclude the distinction drawn in *Introductions* between objects and powers by explicitly providing that no such distinction is to be made, but the effect of this wording has not been tested in the courts. In any event, in retrospect it can be seen that *Introductions* was a high point of judicial antipathy to the practice of drafting very broad objects clauses. Since then, two important cases decided by the Court of Appeal have greatly reduced the significance of the distinction between objects and powers.[30]

In *Re Horsley & Weight Ltd*,[31] the objects clause of a company which carried on the business of shopfitters authorised it 'to grant pensions to employees and ex-employees and directors and ex-directors'. There was also an independent objects clause. The Court of Appeal held that the granting of pensions was capable of subsisting as a substantive object rather than as an ancillary power and that, having regard to the independent objects clause, it was to be so construed in this case. The Court of Appeal thus confirmed the existence of a distinction between objects and powers but, by classifying a provision as an object when it might easily have been regarded as a power, sidestepped the need to consider whether a power had been exercised otherwise than in pursuit of the objects, and the consequences in that event.

6.2.3   Restating the law: *Rolled Steel*

Rolled Steel Products (Holdings) Ltd v British Steel Corporation[32] provided an opportunity for a more detailed examination of the distinction between objects and powers and its consequences because, despite an independent objects clause, the relevant provision authorising the giving of guarantees and debentures was classified by the first instance judge, Vinelott J, and by the Court of Appeal as a mere power. This led to the question: given that the power to give guarantees and debentures had been exercised otherwise than in pursuit of the substantive objects of the company, were the guarantee and debenture binding on the company? The Court of Appeal held that they were not, not because they were beyond the company's capacity but because the directors had exceeded the authority and the contracting party was aware of this.

---

29   For a Scottish case following the restrictive approach in *Introductions* see *Thompson v J Barke & Co (Caterers) Ltd* 1975 SLT 67.

30   Note also *Re New Finance and Mortgage Co* [1975] Ch 420 and *Newstead v Frost* [1980] 1 All ER 363, [1980] 1 WLR 135 (HL) where the courts did not adopt a restrictive approach in determining the scope of objects clauses.

31   [1982] Ch 442, [1982] 3 All ER 1045, [1982] 3 WLR 431.

32   Above.

The judgments of Slade and Browne-Wilkinson LJJ contain a valuable restatement of the law relating to the use of a power in the objects clause otherwise than in pursuit of the objects.[33] The learned Lords Justices sought to explain earlier decisions such as *Introductions* so as to reconcile them with their own analysis of the position. When the judgments in some earlier cases are compared closely with those of Slade and Browne-Wilkinson LJJ in *Rolled Steel* it is questionable whether the reconciliation is entirely persuasive[34] but, consistent with legislative developments in this area of the law, the approach in *Rolled Steel* embodies the policy of not penalising innocent outsiders dealing with a company when those who act on the company's behalf fail to observe limits which are imposed by the company's constitution.

The essence of the restatement of the law in *Rolled Steel* is that if an act performed pursuant to an ancillary power stated in the memorandum is of a category which, on a true construction of the company's memorandum, is capable of being performed as reasonably incidental to the attainment or pursuit of its substantive objects, it will not be rendered *ultra vires* by the company merely because in a particular instance its directors, in performing the act in its name, are doing so for purposes other than those set out in its memorandum.

The only limitation put upon the protective shield thus thrown around the use of powers in the memorandum, is that 'due regard must be paid to any express condition attached to, or limitation on, powers contained in a company's memorandum' (eg a power to borrow only up to a specified amount).[35] However, the court will not ordinarily construe a statement in the memorandum that a particular power is 'exercisable for the purpose of the company' (or similar phraseology) as a condition limiting the company's corporate capacity to exercise the power (as opposed to limit on the authority of the directors).[36]

In *Rolled Steel*, it was held that the knowledge of the person dealing with the company was generally irrelevant to the question of *corporate capacity* but that it was significant with regard to matters of *authority*. Slade LJ explained this on the basis that the directors of a company are held out as having ostensible authority to bind the company in any

---

[33] Lawton LJ gave a brief judgment in which he considered the misfeasance aspects of the case (and certain matters arising from the handling of the case by the trial judge) but otherwise he agreed with Slade LJ. Browne-Wilkinson LJ also expressed agreement with Slade LJ.

[34] It is particularly difficult to reconcile *Rolled Steel* with the decision of the House of Lords in *Sinclair v Brougham* [1914] AC 398. Their Lordships were mainly concerned with the consequences of *ultra vires* but accepted that the power to borrow money must be limited to borrowing for the purposes of the company, borrowing for any other purpose being *ultra vires*. This aspect of the decision in *Sinclair v Brougham* is unaffected by the House of Lords' departure from it in *Westdeutsche Landesbank Girozentrale v Islington Borough Council* [1996] AC 669.

[35] Slade LJ at 295 summarising his conclusions.

[36] Ibid.

transaction falling within the express or implied powers in its memorandum.[37] Unless put on notice to the contrary, a person dealing in good faith with a company which is carrying on an *intra vires* business is entitled to assume that the directors are properly exercising these powers for the purposes of the company set out in the memorandum and can therefore hold the company to any transaction of this nature. However, if a person dealing with a company is on notice that the directors are exercising the relevant power for purposes other than the purposes of the company, he cannot rely on the directors' ostensible authority to hold the company to the transaction.[38]

The vigorous restatement of the nature and proper scope of the *ultra vires* doctrine in *Rolled Steel* was welcomed both for its logical character and the evident judicial policy aimed at reducing the scope of possible harm it may cause to innocent third parties. However, the Court of Appeal's decision 'restatement' of what had become a difficult and confused body of case-law, is not free from its own difficulties when related to well-established principles and authorities. The distinction between substantive objects and ancillary powers will, sometimes at least, be difficult to draw, although it must be accepted that not only *Re Introductions*[39] but *Re Horsley & Weight Ltd*[40] and *Rolled Steel v British Steel Corporation*,[41] too, are adamant that this distinction must be made.[42] Moreover, the doctrine enunciated by the Court of Appeal in *Rolled Steel* is not easy to square with the treatment of subordinate powers by Buckley LJ in *Horsley v Weight* or with that of Harman LJ in *Re Introductions*. The contention in *Rolled Steel* that in the latter case Harman LJ was not concerned with *ultra vires* acts beyond the company's corporate capacity (as regards the bank's reliance on the power to borrow) seems open to serious question.

6.2.4   The decline of the *ultra vires* doctrine

When the *ultra vires* doctrine was first developed by the courts in the nineteenth century, it was perceived to be a valuable protection to shareholders and creditors from risky and wasteful ventures by the directors: shareholders and creditors could be assured that their money would not be put to uses beyond those authorised by the company's memorandum. As companies began to draft their way around the restrictions of the doctrine by devising ever more extensive objects, the usefulness of the objects clause as a source of information to shareholders

---

[37]   At 295.

[38]   Section 40 of the Companies Act 2006 enables an outsider to enforce a transaction against the company where the directors were acting without authority, even where the outsider had knowledge of this. See below at **6.7**.

[39]   [1970] Ch 199 (CA).

[40]   [1982] Ch 442 (CA).

[41]   [1986] Ch 246.

[42]   However, it is not beyond argument that it may still be possible to draft a way out of this distinction.

and creditors about the uses to which their money could be put declined. Judicial antipathy to devices such as the independent objects clauses ultimately failed to prevent companies from ensuring, by suitable drafting, that they had capacity to do virtually anything.

At the same time, company law was developing alternative rules to protect shareholders and creditors against dissipation by the directors of the funds made available to the company. Throughout the twentieth century, the rules regarding the funds which could be used to pay dividends or make other distributions to shareholders were progressively tightened.[43] Provisions of the insolvency legislation attacking preferences or transactions at an undervalue also sought to prevent unwarranted disposals of corporate funds.[44] Accounting and reporting obligations imposed on directors by the companies legislation became more onerous thus giving those dealing, or considering dealing, with a company the opportunity to monitor the stewardship of its affairs by consulting its published financial information.[45] Fiduciary duties, as well as specific personal liabilities under the insolvency legislation for wrongful trading, also served as deterrents against abuse of position by directors.

6.3 CORPORATE GIFTS

Historically, the courts used the *ultra vires* doctrine to control the application of corporate funds, particularly gratuitous payments. With the decline of that doctrine, and its eventual disappearance in the wake of the Companies Act 2006, other rules have been put in place to deal with corporate gifts.

In *Re Horsley & Weight Ltd*,[46] the Court of Appeal endorsed the approach taken in *Charterbridge*. Where on its true construction a clause in the memorandum allowed for the payment of pensions as a separate object, and not merely as an ancillary power or object to the main object of the company, the purchase of a pension policy could not be challenged by the liquidator as *ultra vires* the objects of the company. The clause in this case also allowed the making of grants for charitable, benevolent or public purposes or objects. Buckley LJ observed that 'the objects of a company need not be commercial; they can be charitable or philanthropic; indeed, they can be whatever the original incorporators wish, provided that they are legal. Nor is there any reason why a company should not part with its funds gratuitously or for non-commercial reasons if to do so is within its declared objects'.

---

[43] See **6.3**.
[44] See **21.55**.
[45] See Chapter 14.
[46] [1982] 3 All ER 108. See also *Re Halt Garage* (1964) Ltd [1982] 3 All ER 1016, where Oliver J adopted a similar approach. He regarded the test of 'good faith' and 'the benefit of the company' as irrelevant to express powers.

However, whilst a gift or gratuitous payment may not be challenged as *ultra vires* for the reasons stated, it may still be impugned as an unlawful return of capital (eg where a payment is made under the guise of directors' remuneration where the real intention is to make a gift of capital to shareholders)[47] or as a transaction at an undervalue under s 238 of the Insolvency Act 1986.[48] Directors who authorise the making of corporate gifts at a time when, to their knowledge, the company's solvency is in doubt may also be liable for misfeasance under s 212 of the Insolvency Act 1986.[49] An argument based on misfeasance will not succeed where gifts are made with the knowledge and consent of all of the shareholders at their instigation and the company is fully solvent.[50] It has been held that in addition to rules prohibiting the return of capital to members, a company which has no distributable profits cannot make gifts to outsiders except for the advancement of the company's business.[51] The best explanation for this rule would appear to be that the making of such gifts amounts to a fraud on the company's creditors, which is something that the shareholders are powerless to authorise.[52]

Where no express power has been conferred by the memorandum, the extent of the company's implied powers to make gifts must be determined. In the early case of *Attorney-General v Great Eastern Rly*,[53] it was said that whatever could fairly be regarded as incidental to, or consequential upon, the stated objects would be implied.

In this regard, the power had to be exercised for the benefit of the company, but this restriction was not used to determine whether a particular exercise was *ultra vires*, but rather whether the directors had exceeded their authority in exercising that power. In *Charterbridge Corporation v Lloyds Bank*[54] Pennycuick J commented that the 'benefit to the company' test was appropriate in part to the scope of implied powers and in part, and perhaps principally, to the duty of directors.[55] In *Re Halt Garage* Oliver J stated that the test of benefit to the company was, in his view, really only appropriate to the question of the propriety of an

---

[47]   *Re Halt Garage*, above; *Aveling Barford Ltd v Perion Ltd* [1989] BCLC 626; *Barclays Bank plc v British and Commonwealth Holdings plc* [1995] BCC 19, *affirmed* [1996] 1 All ER 381 (indirect return of capital). See **6.3**.

[48]   The company must have gone into liquidation or an administrator must have been appointed. The conditions which must be satisfied for s 238 to apply are discussed in Chapter 21. Note also s 423 of the Insolvency Act 1986 (transactions defrauding creditors).

[49]   *Re Horsley & Weight*, above.

[50]   *Brady v Brady* [1989] AC 755, at 776.

[51]   *Barclays Bank plc v British and Commonwealth Holdings plc*, above.

[52]   *ANZ Executors & Trustee Co Ltd v Qintex Australia Ltd* (1990) 8 ACLC 980; *Plain Ltd v Kilney & Royal Trust Co* (1931) 1 DLR 468; *Re George Newman & Co* [1985] 1 Ch 674.

[53]   (1875) LR 7 HL 653. Note also *Hutton v West Cork Railway co* (1883) 23 Ch D 654, at 671 per Bowen LJ.

[54]   [1970] Ch 62. Pennycuick J's reasoning in *Charterbridge* was followed in *Thomson v J Barke & Co (Caterers) Ltd* 1975 SLT 67, at 70–71.

[55]   At 71.

exercise of a power.[56] Pennycuick J in *Charterbridge* and Oliver J in *Re Halt Garage* had the same view of the *bona fides* test: that it was relevant to the fiduciary duties of the directors and did not affect the construction of the company's implied powers.[57]

Neither *Charterbridge* nor *Re Halt Garage* required the court to rule on the scope of a company's implied powers and the comments on implied powers were therefore strictly *obiter*. This was also the position in *Rolled Steel* where the actual decision of the Court of Appeal related to the company's express power in its memorandum to give guarantees.

Three types of corporate gifts require special mention. These are pensions to former employees and their dependants, redundancy payments, and charitable or political donations.

6.3.1   Pensions

Historically, where the paying of pensions was an independent object of the company, pensions paid under that power in the company's memorandum could not be *ultra vires*.[58] Where the memorandum authorised the paying of pensions but, as a matter of construction, that provision was only a power and not a substantive object, provided that power was capable of being used in a manner which was reasonably incidental to the attainment or pursuit of its substantive objects, its use in particular cases would not be *ultra vires* although the directors may be liable for breach of their fiduciary duties if they have abused the power.[59] The power to pay pensions could be viewed as being capable of being exercised reasonably incidentally to the company's business on the grounds that it is conducive to business to seek to retain the workforce by being seen to be a generous employer.[60]

Where there was no express power in the memorandum to pay pensions, the test was whether this can be implied as being reasonably incidental to the company's business.[61] In an ordinary trading company that test would normally be satisfied; thus Plowman J in *Re W & M Roith Ltd*[62] was 'disposed to agree' with counsel 'that a widow's pension is reasonably incidental to carrying on a company's business'. In *Roith*, a pension granted under an express power in the memorandum was held to be *ultra vires* by application of the *Re Lee, Behrens* tests; in view of *Re Horsley &*

---

[56]   At 1034.
[57]   *Charterbridge,* at 71; *Re Halt Garage,* at 1034.
[58]   *Re Horsley & Weight*, above.
[59]   *Rolled Steel*, above.
[60]   Similar arguments could be used to justify the provision of sporting and social welfare facilities.
[61]   *Henderson v Bank of Australasia* (1888) 49 Ch D 170; *Normandy v Ind Coope & Co Ltd* [1908] 1 Ch 84, 104; *Cyclists' Touring Club v Hopkinson* [1910] 1 Ch 179.
[62]   [1967] 1 WLR 432, at 437.

Weight and *Rolled Steel, Roith* may now be better regarded as an instance where the directors abused the corporate powers in breach of their fiduciary duties.

6.3.2 Charitable or political donations

The Companies Act 1985 required that charitable and political donations which exceed £200 in any financial year had to be disclosed in the directors' report.[63] This provision did not of itself validate gifts, being concerned simply with disclosure. Where a political or charitable gift was covered by an express provision in the memorandum, *Re Horsley & Weight Ltd*[64] made it clear that like any other gift it is not open to challenge on grounds of lack of capacity. Where there was no express power, the question of the company's capacity to make charitable donations depended on whether this is reasonably incidental to the company's business. For most practical purposes, the *ultra vires* rule had faded away as a mechanism for controlling the funding of political parties or the making of charitable gifts by companies. Directors remain subject to fiduciary duties and they must make decisions about the use of company money in accordance with the duty to act in the interests of the company.[65]

In recent years, there has been concern from some institutional investors and from government about the accountability of directors to shareholders with regard to these matters and the perception has grown that fiduciary duties and disclosure requirements may not be sufficient to prevent directors from choosing to use company money to support causes that reflect their own personal interests rather than those of the company. A recommendation from the Committee on Standards in Public Life, chaired by Lord Neill, that any company wishing to make a donation to a political party should have the prior authority of its shareholders[66] has been accepted by the Government. The Political Parties, Elections and Referendums Act 2000 inserted a new Part XA into the Companies Act 1985 to give effect to this proposal, and this is now found in Part 14 of the Companies Act 2006.[67] In essence, political donations and other political expenditure require the approval by the shareholders of a company before donations are made.[68] Such approval is not, however, required for a particular transaction, but rather sanctions political donations and expenditure up to a specified amount for a period of up to

---

[63] See the Companies Act 1985, Sch 7, para 3. New secondary legislation to be made under s 416(4) of the Companies Act 2006 on the content of directors' reports had not yet been published at the time of writing.

[64] [1982] 3 All ER 1045.

[65] See Chapter 16.

[66] Cm 4057–I *The Funding of Political Parties in the United Kingdom* (October 1998), recommendation 34. The Government's views are set out in *Political Donations by Companies* (URN 99/757) (Consultative Document, March 1999).

[67] These provisions are only summarised briefly here.

[68] Companies Act 2006, s 366.

4 years ('approval resolutions'). Directors are liable to repay to the company any donations made in breach of these provisions,[69] and may also have to pay compensation for any loss or damage suffered by the company as a result.

6.3.3   Redundancy payments

In *Parke v Daily News*,[70] it was held that gratuitous redundancy payments paid to former employees were *ultra vires* since they were motivated by a desire to treat the employees generously, and were not made to benefit the company (which was to cease to be an employer in the newspaper industry). The categorisation of these payments as '*ultra vires*' the powers of the company might now be reassessed because of the reliance placed by Plowman J on the discredited *Lee, Behrens* tests.[71] In any event, two statutory innovations originally made by the Companies Act 1980 would mean that a different decision would now be made where employees are affected. Where the company is a going concern, s 172(1) of the Companies Act 2006 provides that the 'a director of a company must act in the way he considers, in good faith, would be most likely to promote the success of the company for the benefit of its members as a whole, and in doing so have regard (amongst other matters) to— ... (b) the interests of the company's employees ...'.[72] Further, s 247(1) states that the powers of the directors of a company include a power to make provision 'for the benefit of persons employed or formerly employed by the company or any of its subsidiaries in connection with cessation or transfer to any person of the whole or part of the undertaking of that company or that subsidiary'.

The power conferred by s 247 may be exercised notwithstanding the general duty of directors to promote the success of the company.[73] Prior to the 2006 Act, the effect of this provision was to extend the capacity of the company and to free it from a restriction that the *ultra vires* doctrine might otherwise impose on such voluntary (ie non-statutory) redundancy or retirement payments.[74] Under the 2006 Act, this power is one given to the directors, and authorisation for its exercise is required. Section 247(4) provides that the power it confers may only be sanctioned by a resolution of the company or a resolution of the directors. However, a sanction by a resolution of the directors has to be authorised by the company's articles,[75] and where the articles make no provision for this, a sanction of the company will be required. In a change from the position under s 719 of the 1985 Act, a directors' resolution cannot be used in respect of a

---

[69]   Companies Act 2006, s 369.
[70]   [1962] Ch 927.
[71]   *Re Lee, Behrens & Co* [1932] 2 Ch 46, Eve J.
[72]   See **16.5**.
[73]   Section 247(2). See also s 187 of the Insolvency Act 1986.
[74]   See Companies Act 2006, s 247.
[75]   Section 247(5)(a).

payment to be made to the directors, former directors or shadow directors;[76] for this, a resolution by the company is required. The articles may impose additional requirements for the exercise of this power, and these also need to be complied with.[77] On the winding up of a solvent company (whether by the court or a voluntary winding-up), the liquidator may make any payments which the company decided to make before commencement of the winding-up. Provision is also made for the liquidator to exercise this power himself if the company's liabilities have been fully satisfied and provision made for the costs of winding up. He must also obtain the authorisation of the shareholders by a resolution.[78] In the case of payments made before commencement of winding-up, these must be made out of the profits of the company available for dividend.[79] In the case of payments made after the commencement of winding-up, these must be made out of the assets of the company which are available to its members on its winding-up.[80]

6.4 CORPORATE CAPACITY – THE CURRENT LAW: S 39 OF THE COMPANIES ACT 2006

The preceding sections have sought to provide an overview of the law pertaining to the doctrine of *ultra vires*. Under the 2006 Act, companies are no longer required to state the objects of a company, and where nothing is said in the company's constitution, a company will have unlimited capacity. However, it seems that even where there is a statement of objects in the constitution (articles), this will only serve to restrict the authority of the board of directors to act, rather than imposing any limitations on the capacity of the company itself. The assumption is that questions of capacity have now become largely redundant, and s 39(1) of the Companies Act 2006 provides that 'the validity of an act done by a company shall not be called into question on the ground of lack of capacity by reason of anything in the company's constitution'.[81] The effect of s 39(1) is to prevent that a lack of capacity could be raised as a defence to any contractual claim brought against a company, and also to ensure that such a lack cannot be pleaded against a company by the other party. In other words, s 39(1) is two-way in its effect, operating to protect both the company and those who deal with it from the consequences of a lack of capacity.

---

[76] Section 247(5)(b).

[77] Section 247(6).

[78] See s 187 of the Insolvency Act 1986. This may be an ordinary resolution or one by more than a simple majority if the company's constitution so requires. A resolution of the directors will not suffice.

[79] Section 247(7)(b). See **7.21** on how to determine funds available for dividend.

[80] Section 187(3) of the Insolvency Act 1986.

[81] There are special rules in relation to charitable companies: ss 39(2) and 42 of the 2006 Act.

The surprising aspect of this provision is that it is almost identical to its predecessor, s 35(1) of the Companies Act 1985 (save for the substitution of 'constitution' for 'memorandum' in the 2006 Act). That provision related to a context in which the memorandum of association still limited the capacity of the company. If the effect of the new law is to give a company unlimited capacity and merely impose restrictions on the authority of the directors,[82] then it seems strange that the wording found in the 1985 Act has been retained in the 2006 Act.[83] It would have seemed much more logical to include a provision which specifies that the capacity of a company is unlimited, but that the company's constitution may limit the authority of the board of directors to act through a statement of objects.

For s 39 to apply, the act in question must have been done by a company. When is an act done by a company for these purposes? In contractual matters, English company law has not adopted an organic theory whereby the acts of the board and of the general meeting are treated automatically as acts of the company.[84] Whether a company is bound by a transaction or other act which purports to be done on its behalf is normally determined by reference to agency principles, as modified by the *Turquand* rule and by s 40 of the Companies Act 2006 which is discussed later in this chapter.[85] Nothing in s 39(1) appears to displace or override these principles and, although this is not spelt out, it would therefore seem that they should determine what is an 'act of the company' for this purpose: so interpreted, s 39(1) ensures that an act done on behalf of a company which would otherwise be enforceable against it does not cease to be so simply because it is not authorised by the company's constitution.[86] Prior to the 2006 Act, this had some relevance, but, if, as discussed above, the post-2006 position is indeed that any restrictions in the company's constitution only affect the authority of the directors, then this aspect of s 39(1) has become superfluous, because s 40, dealing with restrictions on the power of directors to bind the company, would already have this effect.

The current position is rather unsatisfactory. Section 39(1) makes little sense in the context of the new framework on corporate capacity and the company's constitution. It is regrettable that the language of the sections predecessor was retained and that a clearer provision was not adopted. It

---

[82] See *Explanatory Notes to the Companies Act 2006*, para 123.

[83] Furthermore, the remaining aspects of s 35 of the 1985 Act have not been retained – see *Explanatory Notes*, para 123.

[84] See e g *Rolled Steel*, at 295, per Slade LJ and at 304, per Browne-Wilkinson LJ.

[85] See **6.7-6.12.**

[86] This interpretation of the phrase 'act of the company' in the context of s 35 of the 1985 Act is explored further in Ferran 'The Reform of the Law on Corporate Capacity and Directors' and Officers' Authority' (1992) 13 Co Law 124. See also Poole 'Abolition of the Ultra Vires Doctrine and Agency Problems' (1991) 12 Co Law 43.

remains to be seen if this will have a significant impact in practice, however – there has been no case in recent years where s 35 of the 1985 Act was in issue.

6.5   JUST AND EQUITABLE WINDING-UP

Shareholders who object to a company undertaking a new type of activity when its original business is abandoned may have a form of relief open now that invoking the *ultra vires* doctrine appears to be no longer available. They may petition the court under s 122(1)(g) of the Insolvency Act 1986 for a compulsory winding-up order on the ground that it is just and equitable to do so. One basis on which the court will make a just and equitable winding-up order is that the substratum of the company, the main object for which it was incorporated, has ceased to exist.[87] However, now that a company is no longer required to have a statement of objects at all (and even where it has such a statement, it has no impact on its capacity), it may be rather difficult to conclude that a company's substratum no longer exists. Section 122 of the Insolvency Act 1986 was not amended by the Companies Act 2006.

6.6   AUTHORITY TO BIND THE COMPANY

Where the company possesses undoubted contractual capacity in respect of a particular contract, there still remains the question whether those who purported to make a contract on the company's behalf had the authority to do so. The authority to bind the company must be conferred either directly by the articles of association or by delegation under a power contained in them. Almost invariably, the general power to manage the company will be conferred upon the board of directors[88] and the board itself will usually have a power to delegate its power to manage the company's affairs (eg to one or more managing directors[89]). On some important matters, the approval of the general meeting may be required

Any want of authority can be cured by ratification by a resolution of the shareholders in general meeting by ordinary resolution.[90] Where a contract is neither originally binding upon the company nor subsequently ratified, the third party may be entitled to recover on a restitutionary basis if the company has received money or goods have been supplied or services have been rendered.

---

[87]   For detailed treatment of the grounds on which a court will make a just and equitable order, see **18.14**, where the cases on the disappearance of the substratum of a company are examined.

[88]   Article 3 of the model articles for all types of companies. See the Companies (Model Articles) Regulations 2008, SI 2008/3229.

[89]   Eg art 5.

[90]   *Grant v United Kingdom Switchback Railway Co* (1889) 40 Ch D 135 (CA); *Phosphate of Lime Co v Green* (1871) LR 7 CP 43; *Campbell's Case* (1873) 9 Ch App 1.

A director or other lesser agent who lacks the authority to bind the company that he claims, may be liable for breach of warranty of authority. Where a wilful or reckless misrepresentation on the part of the directors can be established, an action for deceit might be brought.[91]

A contract for which there is no actual authority (express or implied) may nevertheless become binding on the company under a number of principles. The directors or other officers of a company have no actual authority to bind the company in matters falling outside the constitutional limits imposed by its memorandum and articles. However, by virtue of s 40 of the Companies Act 2006 [CA 1985, s 35A], transactions authorised by the directors which are outside the constitutional limits can usually be enforced against the company.[92] Under the doctrine of ostensible (or apparent) authority, a person who has no actual authority to act on the company's behalf may be able to bind the company if he has been held out by someone with appropriate authority as a duly authorised agent of the company. The doctrine of ostensible authority is part of the general law of agency and it applies irrespective of whether the principal is a company or a natural person. A special modification of the doctrine known as the 'rule in *Turquand's* case' applies only in relation to corporate principals.

6.7   THE PROTECTION OF PERSONS DEALING WITH THE COMPANY IN GOOD FAITH: S 40

It is through s 40 of the Companies Act 2006 [CA 1985, s 35A] (and the surrounding sections) that the UK seeks to comply with its obligation to implement Art 9 of the First Company Law Directive.[93] Article 9 seeks to protect third parties in transactions with a company from 'limitations upon the powers of the competent organs imposed by the Charter or by a decision of the competent organs'. Such limitations 'may never be invoked against third parties even if they have been published'. The First Directive was adopted before the UK joined the European Community and its language is unfamiliar because, in contractual matters, English law traditionally has not regarded the board and the general meeting as 'organs' of a company. Possibly because of differences in established terminology, Art 9 was badly implemented by s 9 of the European Communities Act 1972 (which, on consolidation of the companies legislation, became s 35 of the Companies Act 1985).[94] The UK's second attempt to implement the Directive became s 35A (and surrounding

---

91   Or an action for negligent misstatement under *Hedley Byrne & Co v Heller Partners* [1964] AC 465.

92   See **6.7**.

93   Directive 68/151/EEC (1968) OJ L65/8. See **2.3.1**. As to the European Community's programme of company law directives generally, see **2.3**.

94   Commentaries on the implementation of Art 9 by the European Communities Act 1972 include: Prentice (1973) 89 LQR 518; Farrar and Powles (1973) 36 MLR 270; Sealy and Collier [1973] CLJ 1; Wyatt (1978) 94 LQR 182.

sections) of the 1985 Act. That section met many of the criticisms which were levelled at its predecessor but some points of uncertainty or difficulty remained. Although a proposal for further reform to this and related sections was made in *Modernising Company Law* (2002), the Companies Act 2006 re-enacts s 35A with only one amendment in s 40.

Section 40(1) [CA 1985, s 35A(1)] provides that:

> 'In favour of a person dealing with a company in good faith, the power of the directors to bind the company, or to authorise others to do so, is deemed to be free of any limitation under the company's constitution.'

The main change is that s 40 refers to the 'power of the directors', whereas its predecessor applied to the powers of the *board* of directors. It seemed to envisage that actions taken by the company could be related back to the board, which caused some difficulties in *Smith v Henniker-Major & Co*.[95] in circumstances where the board was inquorate (discussed further below). However, whilst this change might remove that difficulty, it raises fresh questions. Most significantly, s 40 refers to 'the director*s*', ie the plural form, but under s 6(c) of the Interpretation Act 1978, 'unless contrary intention appears ... words in the plural include the singular'. This means that s 40 now applies even where a single director has acted beyond the limitations imposed on his powers under the company's constitution. There is nothing in s 40 which would evidence contrary intention; indeed, if the term 'directors' only covered the plural, then deleting the words 'board of' would make little difference, as it would still require collective action by the directors.

The extension of the scope of s 40 to acts by single directors is significant, and could have the effect of rendering the common law principles of agency (see **6.15–6.21**, below) all but redundant in the context of corporate directors. However, in practice, it would be uncommon for the authority of individual directors or officers to be limited by the company's constitution; such limitations are more usually imposed in the contracts of employment of the relevant individuals. These contractual limitations fall outside the scope of s 40 and their effect on outsiders is governed by agency principles and the rule in *Turquand's* case.

There is one possible instance where the constitution might impose a restriction: according to art 7 of the model articles for all companies, any decision taken by the directors must be a collective decision. Therefore, any decision not taken by the directors collectively (as a board!) would not be a proper decision at all (in those companies which apply model art 7). The question arises, therefore, whether art 7 is a limitation on the powers of the directors to bind the company which is overcome by s 40, thus

---

[95] [2002] 2 BCLC 655.

allowing individual directors to bind the company without proper authorisation or a decision taken at a board meeting (see the discussion further below).

The current position, then, is that if a person negotiates a contract with the company and it subsequently emerges that the authority of the directors (or of a single director) to conclude that contract was in fact limited by the company's constitution, that person can nevertheless hold the company to the contract provided he is in 'good faith'. The limitation on the directors' authority may stem from a statement of objects in the company's articles, where it is beyond the directors' powers to enter into contracts of that type. Limitations may also be imposed by other provisions in the company's articles. Thus s 40 applies where the directors exceed a limit imposed by the articles on its power to manage the company's affairs. By virtue of s 40(3) [CA 1985, s 35A(3)], limitations under the company's constitution also include limitations deriving from a resolution of the company or a meeting of any class of shareholders, or from any agreement between the members of the company or any class of shareholders.

It is usually not practicable for the directors, whether acting as a board or on individual delegation, to play a significant role in the day-to-day contracts which are entered into in the ordinary course of the company's business, especially where this is a large company with many employees and customers. These contracts are normally the responsibility of other corporate officers.

This is taken into account in s 40 [CA 1985, s 35A] because, as well as protecting outsiders who deal with directors directly, it also deems the power of the directors to authorise others to bind the company to be free of any limitations under the company's constitution. But for s 40, if the directors (or possibly even an individual director – see the discussion above) purport to delegate, say to a managing director, in breach of limitations on its powers to delegate in the company's constitution, the managing director cannot be said to have authority to bind the company. Although, in a factual sense, the managing director may have been held out by the directors as having authority, the principle of ostensible authority does not apply because the directors have no authority under the company's constitution to make the representation.[96] In favour of an outsider, s 40 deems the directors to have that authority.

As noted, the predecessor to s 40 (s 35A Companies Act 1985) applied to limitations on the powers of the *board*. One difficult question in this context had been whether the requirements regarding the constitution of the board, such as quorum requirements, fell within the section. This was debated during the passage of the Companies Act 1989 through

---

[96]   See further **6.19**.

Parliament.[97] The view of the government spokesperson was that articles specifying the quorum for board meetings, voting rights at board meetings and the like were to be regarded as provisions which defined the board rather than limitations on the powers of the board.[98] This issue was considered in *Smith v Henniker-Major & Co.*[99] In that case, a director had attempted to assign to himself the company's right of action against a firm of solicitors by passing a resolution at an inquorate board meeting. He subsequently sought to rely on s 35A to defeat a challenge to the validity of the assignment. At first instance,[100] Rimer J held that s 35A did not apply to an inquorate board, because that section referred to the 'powers of the board of directors', which can only be exercised if directors act as a board. An inquorate board is not a board at all and therefore has no powers, and consequently cannot exceed these.[101] If the quorum requirement were a limitation within s 35A, which would then effectively override this requirement, no useful effect would be served by having a quorum requirement in the articles. The Court of Appeal differed on this issue, undoubtedly influenced by the unusual facts of the case. Walker LJ disagreed with Rimer J and thought that s 35A could apply to an inquorate board, provided that the 'irreducible minimum'[102] of a 'genuine decision taken by a person or persons who can on substantial grounds claim to be to board of directors acting as such'[103] had been attained. On the facts, therefore, the director could benefit from s 35A, although the company could have recourse to what was s 322A of the 1985 Act (now, with amendments, s 41 of the 2006 Act) to avoid the transaction (see **6.10**). Carnwath LJ, whilst accepting that a purposive interpretation of s 35A might admit its application to a decision by an inquorate board, took the view that this case, the facts of which he regarded as 'exceptional' was inappropriate for laying down a general rule. Instead, he held that because the director was also the company's chairman and therefore under a duty to ensure that the constitution was properly applied, he could not rely on s 35A 'to turn his own decision, which had no validity of any kind under the company's constitution, into a decision of "the board"'.[104] Schiemann LJ expressed no view on the quorum point at all, preferring instead to hold that a director who is responsible for exceeding any limitations in the company's constitution cannot benefit from the section.[105] The reasoning of Carnwath and

---

[97] In the context of enacting s 40's predecessor, s 35A of the Companies Act 1985.

[98] *Hansard*, HL Debs, cols 685–687 (7 November 1989).

[99] [2002] EWCA Civ 762, [2002] 2 BCLC 655.

[100] [2002] BCC 544.

[101] The views are reproduced at [32] in Walker LJ's judgment in the Court of Appeal. See also Howell (2002) 23 Co Law 96.

[102] Although the headnote to the report of the case at [2002] 2 BCLC 655 suggests that Robert Walker LJ's 'irreducible minimum' forms part of the *ratio* (with Carnwath LJ dissenting), this does not correspond with what Carnwath and Schiemann LJJ actually say in their judgments.

[103] [2002] 2 BCLC 655, at [41].

[104] [2002] 2 BCLC 655, at [110].

[105] Ibid, at [128].

Schiemann LJJ is rather unsatisfactory for not giving clear guidance on the question whether s 35A applied to a decision by an inquorate board.[106]

In any event, it is well established in English company law that the rule in *Turquand's* case protects outsiders against internal irregularities of which they are unaware. The fact of a board being improperly constituted is an internal irregularity and an outsider would not usually be aware of it in his dealings with the company. Accordingly, even if s 40 does not apply in this situation, the outsider could still be protected under the older *Turquand* rule.[107] Rimer J adopted this reasoning at first instance, and also held that the director in question could not benefit from *Turquand* because he was, or ought to have been, aware of the quorum requirement. The final outcome, ie that the director could not overcome the consequences of the inquorate board, are the same whether one adopts Rimer J's reasoning or the rather more strained reasoning favoured by Carnwath and Schiemann LJJ, although Rimer J's approach is preferable for its clarity.[108]

Now that s 40 of the 2006 Act has omitted the words 'board of', the difficulties posed by a decision of an inquorate board for the applicability of s 35A of the 1985 Act are no longer of relevance. As noted above, new difficulties have emerged. The section now appears to cover the actions of an individual director as well as several directors acting together, whether at a properly convened board or not. So it is no longer necessary to define some sort of threshold ('irreducible minimum') for the board. However, it may be that the problem has simply been shifted to a new aspect: the person with whom the third party is dealing has to be a director, or a person authorised by a director. If a person has not been properly appointed to the position of director, then it may be necessary to employ a variation of the 'irreducible minimum' test and establish whether an individual could claim to be a director. Whether this will ever become a practical issue remains to be seen. Moreover, model art 7 requires that decisions are taken collectively, and it is not clear if that obligation is a 'limitation' on the power of the directors for the purposes of s 40. Whilst a quorum requirement might be a pre-condition to the existence of a board, a collective forum is not a pre-condition to the existence of a director, and so the case for regarding art 7 as a limitation on the powers of directors to bind the company is stronger. The case in favour of treating art 7 as such a limitation is reinforced by considering the question

---

[106] See also Howell (2003) 24 Co Law 264.

[107] Note that the protection afforded by the *Turquand* rule is more limited than that given by s 40. Section 40 protects persons who are in good faith, and good faith is not incompatible with knowledge that a limitation under the constitution has been breached: **6.8.2**. However, an outsider who knows of an internal irregularity or who is put on inquiry cannot rely on the rule in *Turquand's* case: **6.13**.

[108] See Walters (2002) 23 Co Law 325. Note that other conditions regarding board meetings, such as specific notice requirements, could probably be overridden by s40 if the meeting itself is quorate: cf *Ford v Polymer Vision Ltd* [2009] 2 BCLC 160.

whether a decision taken by a director individually without authority and outside the collective decision-making process can be regarded as an action by the director at all. It still must be a decision by a director because a properly appointed director will be a director irrespective of whether he is in a correctly convened meeting or not. Therefore, it will still be a decision by a director, albeit one taken outside the appropriate forum in breach of art 7 and therefore a decision which lacks authority. If only one thing seems clear, it is that the amendment to s 40 that has resulted in the deletion of the words 'board of' has created as many problems as it may have solved.

6.8 A PERSON DEALING WITH A COMPANY IN GOOD FAITH

A person deals with a company if he is a party to any transaction or other act to which the company is a party.[109] The reference to 'any other act' makes clear that the protection of the section extends beyond purely commercial matters and includes charitable gifts and other gratuitous distributions of assets.[110]

6.8.1 'Person dealing with a company'

The use of the term 'person' might suggest a potentially very wide scope of s 40, and could, in principle, enable directors and shareholders to rely on this section where there has been a transaction beyond the authority of the board. In two separate cases, the Court of Appeal has had the opportunity to consider the application of the section to directors and shareholders respectively, and reached two rather different conclusions.

The question of whether directors could invoke s 40 [CA 1985, s 35A] was considered in *Smith v Henniker-Major & Co*,[111] where the court was not unanimous in its approach. Walker LJ took the view that a director could be a person dealing with the company for the purposes of s 40, because he had the right to avoid the transaction under s 41 [CA 1985, s 322A]. Walker LJ argued that there was a hierarchy between the two sections, with s 40 a 'first filter', and s 41 [CA 1985, s 322A] as a 'second filter'[112] in respect of transactions which involve a director or a connected person. Section 40 could 'play its card', but s 41 could '[trump] it to the extent that a director or associate is involved'.[113] Carnwath LJ agreed that the

---

[109] Section 40(2)(a).
[110] Under the predecessor section, this point was doubtful: in *Re Halt Garage* [1982] 3 All ER 1016, above at 1039–1040, Oliver J took the view, without deciding the point, that s 9 of the European Communities Act 1972 only protected those who were in a contractual relationship with the company. See also *International Sales v Marcus*, above at 560.
[111] [2002] 2 BCLC 655, CA.
[112] [2002] 2 BCLC 655, at [48].
[113] [2002] 2 BCLC 655, at [50].

availability of s 40 to directors is implicit in what was s 322A (now s 41 of the 2006 Act),[114] whereas Schiemann LJ had no firm view.[115] The difficulty with this view is that it was not clear in the context of the 1985 Act whether there was a firm link between what was then s 35A and s 322A. In the earlier case of *Re Torvale Group*,[116] a case involving the application of s 322A of the 1985 Act (now s 41) to a transaction with both a director and outsiders, Neuberger J observed that, whilst the outsiders were protected under s 40 [CA 1985, s 35A], but 'one of [the parties to the transaction] would be prevented in principle from relying upon [s 40], namely Mr Lee, who was a director of Torvale ...'.[117] This reflected an alternative view that s 40 [CA 1985, s 35A] applies only to persons other than directors.

The Court of Appeal's decision in *Smith v Henniker-Major* established that s 40 is available to directors of the company. Walker LJ thought that s 40 would always apply where the person dealing with the company was a director, but Carnwath and Schiemann LJJ did not agree entirely with Walker LJ's reasoning, although Carnwath LJ did concur that s 41 [CA 1985, s 322A] was relevant to determining whether a director could be a 'person dealing with the company' within s 40. Both Lords Justices felt that it was necessary to qualify the position adopted by Walker LJ. Carnwath LJ said that the fact that Smith was also the company's chairman and therefore under a duty to ensure that the constitution was properly applied meant that he could not invoke s 40 [CA 1985, s 35A] 'to turn his own decision, which had no validity of any kind under the company's constitution, into a decision of "the board"'.[118] Similarly, Schiemann LJ stated that 'the word "person" is on its face wide enough to include such a director' but also that 'there is no difficulty in excluding from such persons the very directors who overstepped the limitations in the company's constitution'.[119] Of course, in *Smith v Henniker-Major*, the predecessor to s 40 applied, and this related to limitations on the powers of the *board of* directors. However, the underlying principle – that the director(s) responsible for overstepping the limits of their authority cannot benefit from the section – can also be applied in the case of individual directors. The position that has emerged, therefore, is that directors can invoke s 40, except those directors responsible for overstepping their authority.

The position of shareholders is different. Here, it is possible to distinguish transactions affecting shareholders acting in that capacity ('inside'

---

[114] [2002] 2 BCLC 655, at [109].

[115] He did note that whilst s 40 [CA 1985, s 35A] is concerned with the relationship between the company and a third party, s 41 [CA 1985, s 322A] focuses on the relationship between the company and those acting on its behalf, ie its directors (see [2002] 2 BCLC 655, at [120]–[122]).

[116] [1999] 2 BCLC 605.

[117] [1999] 2 BCLC 605.

[118] [2002] 2 BCLC 655, at [110].

[119] [2002] 2 BCLC 655, at [125] and [128].

transactions, such as the issuing of bonus shares), and those where the transaction is between the company and a third party who is also a shareholder (an 'outside' transaction). There is no doubt that shareholders can rely on s 40 for 'outside' transactions, but the situation is different with regard to 'inside' transactions. Although the term 'person dealing with the company' could include shareholders acting in that capacity, there are reasons for not permitting this. To do otherwise would produce the rather strange result that internal procedural irregularities, ie a breach of the s 33 [CA 1985, s 14] contract (the articles), could be cured by invoking s 40.

The question of applying s 40 [CA 1985, s 35A] to 'inside' transactions was dealt with in *EIC Services*.[120] The directors had decided to issue bonus shares but had not obtained the sanction of an ordinary resolution by the shareholders' general meeting. The validity of the bonus issue was therefore in dispute. The shareholders relied on s 40 [CA 1985, s 35A] to avoid the impact of the procedural irregularity, and succeeded at first instance. On appeal, a unanimous court reversed that decision and held that shareholders could not invoke s 40. Gibson LJ examined whether a shareholder can be 'person dealing with the company', and therefore able to rely on s 40.[121] He referred to Art 9 of the First EC Company Law Directive, which uses the term 'third parties', rather than 'person dealing with the company'. Although 'third parties' was not defined in the Directive, its preamble offered some assistance: Recital 6 states that 'whereas it is necessary, in order to ensure certainty in the law as regards relations between the company and third parties, and also between members, to limit the cases in which nullity can arise ...'. The separate reference to 'members' points towards an interpretation that would regard 'members' as being separate from 'third parties' for the purposes of the Directive. Although not stated explicitly, it appears to have influenced Gibson LJ's conclusions when he held that Art 9(2) of the Directive is not available to the members (shareholders) of a company and that, *prima facie*, the same must be true of s 40, which is designed to implement Art 9(2). If Parliament had wanted s 40 to cover shareholders, then a clearer indication (going beyond use of the term 'person') was needed. The result of this case is that shareholders cannot benefit from the protection of s 40 in the context of an 'inside' transaction.

As far as the availability of s 40 is concerned, the current position is that shareholders acting in that capacity cannot rely on the section, whereas directors can, except – if one adopts the approach by the Court of Appeal in *Smith v Henniker-Major* – where they are responsible for entering into a

---

[120] *EIC Services Ltd v Phipps* [2003] 3 All ER 804, ChD; [2004] EWCA Civ 1069 (30 July 2004), CA.

[121] In *Cottrell v King* [2004] EWHC 397 (Ch), it was held that a transfer of shares, which requires the involvement of the company in registering the transfer, is only a transaction between the shareholders concerned. There is no 'dealing with the company', and s 40 cannot apply.

transaction in excess of their own authority. This seems to be an unnecessarily confusing position, and it is regrettable that the opportunity was not taken in the Companies Act 2006 to clarify the law.[122]

6.8.2 'Good faith'

Good faith[123] is presumed so that the burden of proof lies with the person who asserts that the outsider did not deal in good faith.[124] The burden of proof would thus normally fall on the company. Section 40(2)(b)(iii) [CA 1985, s 35A(2)(b)] expressly provides that a person is not to be regarded as acting in bad faith by reason only of his knowing that an act is beyond the powers of the directors under the company's constitution. This provision clarifies some doubts that were created by the wording of the predecessor section but it also gives rise to some new uncertainties. Section 9 of the European Communities Act 1972 protected those who dealt with a company 'in good faith' but gave no guidance as to the meaning of that phrase. In *International Sales v Marcus*,[125] Lawson J judged lack of good faith to be found either in actual knowledge or where 'it can be shown that such a person could not in view of all the circumstances have been unaware'.[126] In *Barclays Bank Ltd v TOSG Trust Fund Ltd*,[127] Nourse J rejected objective standards, stating that in his judgment a person acted in good faith if he acted 'honestly and genuinely in the circumstances of the case'. It is now clear from s 40(2)(b) that even actual knowledge of the constitutional limits does not amount to bad faith. An example of the type of situation where an outsider might be held to be in good faith, notwithstanding its knowledge, is where the outsider is itself a large organisation which is deemed[128] to have technical knowledge of the company's constitutional limitations, because they are known to some of its departments, but the particular individuals within the organisation who are dealing with the company lack the relevant knowledge.[129] Another example is where the outsider reads but fails to understand, or to interpret properly, the company's constitution.

---

[122] Twigg-Flesner 'Sections 35A and 322A revisited: who is a "person dealing with a company"?' (2005) 26 *The Company Lawyer* 195-202.

[123] See also Griffiths 'An Assessment of Sections 35–35B and 322A of the Companies Act 1985 and the protection of third parties dealing with companies' in De Lacy (ed) *The Reform of United Kingdom Company Law* (London, Cavendish Publishing, 2002).

[124] Section 40(2)(b)(ii).

[125] Above.

[126] At 559.

[127] [1984] BCLC 121. Nourse J's judgment was reversed on appeal but not on grounds relevant to this point: [1984] AC 626.

[128] Law Commission *Fiduciary Duties and Regulatory Rules: A Consultation Paper*, Law Com No 124 (HMSO, 1992), section 2.3 considers the ways in which a firm can acquire knowledge.

[129] This example was given by Lord Fraser of Carmyllie during the passage of the Companies Act 1989 through Parliament: *Hansard*, HL Debs, col 683 (7 November 1989).

However, what would now constitute bad faith cannot be stated with any certainty. If, for example, the outsider knows that the directors are acting contrary to constitutional limitations and also that the transaction is part of a scheme by the directors to defraud the company, there could surely be no question of his sheltering behind a protection given only to those who are in good faith. Thus, if the circumstances in which a particular transaction is made should put the outsider on inquiry, but the outsider does not make appropriate inquiries, then such a failure will rebut the presumption of good faith.[130]

Moreover, it is not provided that lack of knowledge of the constitutional limitations automatically equates to good faith, so that it is conceivable (although perhaps unlikely) that there could be circumstances where a person could be held to be in bad faith despite not being positively aware of the constitutional limitations.[131]

6.9   NO DUTY TO ENQUIRE

Section 40(2)(b)(i) of the Companies Act 2006 [CA 1985, s 35B] adds to the burden which falls on a company which is trying to establish that an outsider who dealt with it did so in bad faith. Under this section, a person dealing with a company is not bound to inquire whether the powers of the directors to bind the company or authorise others to do so is limited. Failure to make these inquiries cannot therefore be regarded as evidence of bad faith.

An established judge-made rule states that outsiders dealing with a company are deemed to know the contents of its constitution (as registered documents open to public inspection).[132] The constructive notice rule, as it is known, extends to certain other documents which require registration such as the register of charges[133] and also, it is thought, to special resolutions and other resolutions requiring registration under s 30 [CA 1985, s 380] and the particulars relating to directors which require filing under s 162 [CA 1985, s 288].

6.10   DIRECTORS WHO DEAL WITH THEIR COMPANY

Where the person dealing with the company is a director of the company or of its holding company (or is a person connected with such a director

---

[130] *Wrexham AFC Ltd v Crucialmove Ltd* [2006] EWCA Civ 237, para 47. In this case, the outsider was aware that the director concluding the transaction had a clear conflict of interest.

[131] For a recent example of whether an outsider acted in 'good faith', see *Ford v Polymer Vision Ltd* [2009] 2 BCLC 160, although this is a summary judgment so does not fully discuss all the issues.

[132] *Ernest v Nichols* (1857) 6 HL Cas 401; *Rolled Steel*, above.

[133] *Wilson v Kelland* [1910] 2 Ch 306, at 313, per Eve J.

or a company with which such a director is associated[134]), special rules apply. Where a director, or a connected person or associated company, is a party to a transaction[135] with the company, in connection with which the directors exceed any limitation under the company's constitution, the transaction is voidable at the instance of the company, notwithstanding s 40 [CA 1985, s 35A].[136] Whether or not the transaction is avoided, the director or, as the case may be, the connected person or associated company is liable to account to the company for any gain which he has made directly or indirectly by the transaction, and to indemnify the company for any loss or damage resulting from the transaction.[137] The directors of the company who authorised the transaction are also liable to the company to the same extent.[138] Directors of the holding company, connected persons and associated companies, but not directors of the company itself, have a defence to the personal liability imposed by s 41 [CA 1985, s 322A] if they can show that at the time when the transaction was entered into they did not know that the directors were exceeding their powers.[139]

A transaction which is voidable under s 41 ceases to be voidable in any of the following circumstances:

(1) restitution of any money or other asset which was the subject matter of the transaction is no longer possible;

(2) the company is indemnified for any loss or damage resulting from the transaction;

(3) rights acquired *bona fide* for value and without actual notice of the directors exceeding their powers by a person who is not a party to the transaction would be affected by the avoidance;

(4) the transaction is ratified by the company in general meeting, by ordinary or special resolution or otherwise as the case may require.[140]

---

[134] 'Connected' and 'associated' are defined by s 252. See **17.2.1**.

[135] This includes any act: s 41(7)(a) [CA 1985, s 322A(8)]. A non-contractual payment, such as that which was in issue in *Guinness v Saunders* [1990] 2 AC 663 (HL), is thus within the scope of the section; see **17.2.1**. The remedy afforded by s 40 [CA 1985, s 322A] is in addition to any other claims which the company may have; s 41(1) [CA 1985, s 322A(4)].

[136] In the 2006 Act, a subsection has been added to s 41 [CA 1985, s 322A] which states that s 41 applies with regard to a transaction which depends for its validity on s 40. Although not as unequivocal a clarification as one might hope, it does make it clear that ss 40 and 41 are linked: ss 41(1) and 40(6).

[137] Section 40(3) [CA 1985, s 322A(3)].

[138] Ibid.

[139] Section 41(5) [CA 1985, s 322A(6)].

[140] Section 41(4) [CA 1985, s 322A(5)].

Where the directors exceed limits imposed by the articles, ratification by ordinary resolution suffices.[141]

Section 41(6) [CA 1985, s 322A(7)] addresses the problem of multi-party transactions where some of the parties are protected by s 40 but others are not because they are caught by s 41. In that case, either a party protected by s 40 or the company can apply to the court for an order affirming, severing or setting aside the transaction on such terms as appear to the court to be just. The court has a very wide and unfettered discretion under this section.[142]

6.11 THE 'INTERNAL' ASPECTS OF S 40

Section 40(4) of the Companies Act 2006 [CA 1985, s 35A(4)] provides that s 40(1) does not affect the right of a member of the company to bring proceedings to restrain the doing of an act which is beyond the powers of the directors; but no such proceedings shall lie in respect of an act to be done in fulfilment of a legal obligation arising from a previous act of the company. However, this section merely preserves such right as the member may have to seek to restrain acts beyond the powers of the directors. The extent to which a member has standing to enforce the provisions of the articles depends on the scope of statutory contract formed by s 33 [CA 1985, s 14] and on the rule in *Foss v Harbottle*. Both of these questions are explored elsewhere.[143]

The qualification contained in s 40(4) preserves the binding nature of transactions with outsiders who are protected by s 40 but it means that shareholders can seek only to restrain contemplated transactions or those which are not binding on the company because the other party is not protected by s 40. The practical effect of s 40(4) is likely to be limited because shareholders will rarely discover the directors' plans at a time before a legal obligation has been incurred.

Section 40(5) [CA 1985, s 35A(5)] preserves any liability incurred by the directors, or any other person,[144] by reason of the directors exceeding

---

[141] *Grant v United Kingdom Switchback Railway Co*, above.

[142] *Re Torvale Group Ltd* [1999] 2 BCLC 605.

[143] See **5.20** and **18.2**.

[144] A person dealing with a company may become implicated in the directors' breach of duty and thus incur liability to the company as a constructive trustee. It seems that a person who is in good faith for the purposes of s 40 could nevertheless be held to be a constructive trustee. In *International Sales v Marcus*, Lawson J held that s 9 of the European Communities Act 1972 did not affect constructive trust liability. See also *Coöperatieve Rabobank 'Vecht en Plassengebied' BA v Minderhoud* [1998] 2 BCLC 507 (enforceability as against third parties of acts done by directors in circumstances where there is a conflict of interest with the company fall outside the normative framework of the First Directive).

their powers. Entering into an unauthorised transaction may amount to a breach of the directors' fiduciary duties.[145]

6.12   A FAILED REFORM PROPOSAL

In the first White Paper, *Modernising Company Law*, it was proposed that ss 35A, 35B and 322A of the 1985 Act should be replaced with a single provision, then contained in draft clause 17.[146] This would have deemed the board of directors to have authority to exercise all the powers of the company and authorise others do so irrespective of any limitations in the company's constitution (including resolutions by the company). However, as far as transactions with directors and connected persons are concerned, this rule would not have applied. This would have changed the current position which grants provisional validity to such transactions but makes them voidable, by removing these from the scope of the statutory rule altogether. Furthermore, it would be provided that no reference may be made to the company's constitution when determining questions of ostensible authority, thus aiding the application of the *Turquand* principle insofar as the ostensible authority of the relevant person would not be affected merely by the existence of a provision to the contrary in the constitution. It is unfortunate that this proposal was not enacted in the 2006 Act.

6.13   THE *TURQUAND* RULE: THE INDOOR MANAGEMENT PRINCIPLE

The purpose of the rule first clearly set forth in *Royal British Bank v Turquand*[147] is to provide some measure of protection for those who enter into contracts with the company from the consequences of the complex internal organisation of companies. The essence of the *Turquand* rule is that those dealing with a company are not affected by what is called the 'indoor management' of companies. They are entitled to assume that the internal procedures of a company, both at directors' and shareholders' meetings, have been regularly conducted in the absence of actual notice to the contrary. The Companies Act 2006 gives indirect support to this principle. It provides that where the minutes of shareholders' or directors' meetings are kept as the section requires, there is a presumption, until the contrary is proved, that all meetings have been regularly convened and conducted.[148] However, where it applies, the *Turquand* rule is conclusive and does not simply raise a rebuttable presumption.

It has been held by the Court of Appeal that the rule in *Turquand's* case is not a mere plea of law (which therefore does not have to be pleaded). It is

---

[145]   See Chapter 17.

[146]   See Cm 5553–II.

[147]   (1856), 6 E & B 327 (Exch Ch).

[148]   See ss 249(2) (directors' meetings) and 356(5) (shareholders' meetings) respectively.

a plea of mixed law and fact. It must therefore be pleaded and may not be raised if it has not been pleaded unless the court permits the pleadings to be amended.[149]

The rule in *Turquand's* case ameliorated the severity of the constructive notice rule whereby outsiders were deemed to know the contents of documents registered at the Companies Registry. With the enactment of the wide-ranging protection afforded to those dealing with a company by s 40 of the Companies Act 2006 [CA 1985, s 35A], the importance of the *Turquand* rule has decreased. In many circumstances it overlaps with s 40: for example, if the articles cap the directors' borrowing power by requiring them to seek the approval of the shareholders in general meeting by ordinary resolution for borrowings over a certain amount, the lender can either assume that the ordinary resolution has been obtained, because, under the *Turquand* rule, this is a matter of internal management, or can disregard the need for the resolution because this is a limitation on the directors' power which is overridden by s 40.[150]

The rule in *Turquand's* case cannot be relied upon by an outsider who knows the true position or who is put on inquiry.[151] The very nature of a proposed transaction can be sufficient to put an outsider on inquiry.[152] In circumstances where there is an overlap between s 40 and the rule in *Turquand's* case, s 40 may thus offer greater protection because even actual knowledge of the irregularity does not amount to 'bad faith' putting the person dealing with the company outside the scope of that section.

6.14 'OUTSIDERS'

The *Turquand* rule is designed to protect 'outsiders' dealing with the seemingly authorised agents of the company. If they are unaware of any irregularity, the rule will protect not only complete outsiders, such as creditors, but also the members of the company (at any rate *vis-à-vis* the conduct of board meetings). Even a director in some circumstances may be treated as an outsider. If a director has not acted on behalf of the company in connection with the transaction he seeks to enforce, he may invoke the *Turquand* rule in order to bind the company.[153] Where he has

---

[149] *Rolled Steel Products v British Steel Corporation*, above.

[150] In practice, lenders may insist on seeing a copy of the resolution as a pre-condition of the loan especially if the amounts involved are significant.

[151] *B Liggett (Liverpool) Ltd v Barclays Bank Ltd* [1928] 1 KB 48; *Morris v Kanssen* [1946] AC 459; *Rolled Steel*, above.

[152] *AL Underwood Ltd v Bank of Liverpool and Martins* [1924] 1 KB 775; *Northside Developments Pty Ltd v Registrar-General* (1989–1990) 2 ACSR 161, (1990) 64 ALJR 427, noted [1991] CLJ 47.

[153] *Hely-Hutchinson v Brayhead Ltd* [1968] 1 QB 549, per Roskill J. (The decision was confirmed on other grounds in the Court of Appeal.)

acted on behalf of the company and it is his duty to have knowledge of the true state of affairs, he will not be able to rely on the rule.[154]

Section 41 of the Companies Act 2006 [CA 1985, s 322A] does not draw a distinction between insider and outsider directors. A contract between a director and his company which infringes constitutional limits is voidable irrespective of the director's involvement on behalf of the company. A director cannot rely on the *Turquand* rule in relation to a transaction which is voidable under s 41.[155]

6.15   GENERAL AGENCY PRINCIPLES AND THE *TURQUAND* RULE

Although the *Turquand* rule will protect an outsider in regard to internal procedures at general meetings and board meetings, when it comes to the powers of individual officers and agents of the company the outsider cannot rely solely on the internal management rule. Whether a company is bound by acts which are done on its behalf depends on whether the director, or other individual, who acted for the company had authority to do so.

There are two main types of authority, namely actual authority and ostensible (or apparent) authority. Actual authority is authority which the principal confers, either expressly or impliedly, on the agent. The board of directors of a company has express actual authority to exercise such powers of the company as are vested in it by the company's memorandum and articles; an executive director appointed under a written service contract has express actual authority to bind the company to the extent that this is authorised by his contract. Where the terms on which someone is appointed to an executive position within a company are not spelt out in an express service contract, actual authority to bind the company may nevertheless be implied from the circumstances. Such authority may also be implied where a person is allowed *de facto* to assume a position but is never expressly appointed. In *Hely-Hutchinson v Brayhead Ltd*,[156] the Court of Appeal held that the *de facto* managing director (or chief executive officer (CEO) as persons holding this office are now commonly described in practice) of the company had implied actual authority to bind the company to contracts of guarantee and indemnity.

---

[154] *Morris v Kanssen* [1946] AC 459 (IIL); *Howard v Patent Ivory Co* (1888) 38 Ch D 156. Where the third party is a company, notice will not be binding unless given to an officer in the course of the company's business, or in such circumstances that it was his duty to communicate it to the company. Thus, one of two companies having directors, or a secretary, in common will not by reason of that fact be taken to have notice of the manner in which the acts of the other are carried out: *Re Hampshire Ltd Co* [1896] 2 Ch 743; *Re Marseilles Extension Rly Co* (1871) 7 Ch App 161; *Re Fenwick, Stobart & Co* [1902] 1 Ch 507; *Re David Payne & Co* [1904] 2 Ch 608 (CA).

[155] Nor can he rely on the rule where he knows that a board meeting is improperly constituted and unable to act: *Smith v Henniker-Major*, above.

[156] [1968] 1 QB 549.

The crucial distinction between actual authority and ostensible authority is that actual authority is a relationship between the principal and agent[157] and ostensible authority is the authority of an agent as it *appears* to others.[158] Ostensible authority is created 'by a representation, made by the principal to the contractor, intended to be and in fact acted upon by the contractor, that the agent has authority'.[159] The agent is not a party to the relationship created by the principal's representation and the representation, when acted upon, acts as an estoppel preventing the principal from claiming that it is not bound.[160] Actual authority and ostensible authority can coincide[161] but an important feature of ostensible authority is that it can exist in circumstances where the agent has no actual authority. Thus, if the company restricts the powers of its managing director in some respect, the managing director has no actual authority, whether express or implied, to bind the company in matters covered by the restriction; but an outsider dealing with the managing director who is unaware of the restriction may be able to hold the company to the transaction on the basis of ostensible authority.

Ostensible authority can take one of two forms: either the directors and officers have a 'usual' authority attached to their office, giving a certain scope of authority implied by law; or the company may be estopped from denying that it held out its agent as having authority to act in a particular transaction. If this representation by words or conduct is relied upon by an outsider, who acts to his detriment in entering into the contract, the company will be bound.

The *ultra vires* doctrine and the constructive notice rule (as ameliorated by the *Turquand* rule) have, in their time, complicated the application of the principles of ostensible authority in relation to companies. The complications have largely disappeared either through statutory developments or through judicial reassessment of the scope of the constructive notice rule, but it is important to have their earlier significance in mind when considering some of the relevant authorities.

6.16 USUAL AUTHORITY

Depending on the context in which it is used, the term 'usual authority' can denote a species of implied actual authority or, alternatively, a form

---

[157] The scope of which is to be ascertained by applying ordinary principles of construction: *Freeman & Lockyer v Buckhurst Park Properties (Mangal) Ltd* [1964] 2 QB 480.

[158] *Freeman & Lockyer* [1964] 2 QB 480, at 503, per Diplock LJ; *Hely-Hutchinson v Brayhead* [1968] 1 QB 549, at 583, per Lord Denning MR.

[159] *Freeman & Lockyer* [1964] 2 QB 480, at 503, per Diplock LJ.

[160] Ibid. Also at 498, per Pearson LJ.

[161] *Freeman & Lockyer,* at 502, per Diplock LJ; *Hely-Hutchinson,* at 583, per Lord Denning MR.

of ostensible authority.[162] A person who is appointed to a particular office may be said to have usual authority by which it is meant that he has implied actual authority to do whatever falls within the usual scope of that office.[163] Implied actual authority to do whatever acts are necessarily incidental to the performance of the agency is a form of usual authority.[164]

When a person is appointed to an office, he may also be said to have usual authority, meaning that he has ostensible authority to do whatever falls within the usual scope of the office.[165] In this case, the company will be bound where the agent acts within the scope of his usual authority even though he may exceed specific restrictions which the company has imposed on his actual authority. Appointing someone to an office can be regarded as one form of 'holding out'[166] but it is helpful to distinguish ostensible authority in the form of usual authority from ostensible authority in the form of holding out. This is because where someone has been appointed to a position, there is no doubt that the factual element of holding out has been satisfied and the relevant issue of potential dispute is as to the scope of the usual authority attached to that position.[167]

6.17 DIRECTORS, EXECUTIVE DIRECTORS AND CHAIRMEN

The exact scope of the usual authority of individual directors, chairmen of boards, managing directors and other executive directors and officers of the company differs considerably. In the case of managing directors, most modern articles empower the board to delegate to them wide powers of management (under the general supervision of the board).[168] In consequence, the courts have held that a managing director's usual authority has a wide scope. It extends to the management of the ordinary business of the company.[169] It will be seen that, where no managing director has been appointed despite a power to do so, the courts will readily infer, on the basis of estoppel, that either a chairman of the board or another director, acting *de facto* as chief executive, has been held out by

---

[162] *First Energy UK (Ltd) v Hungarian International Bank Ltd* [1993] BCLC 1409, [1993] BCC 533. In *Armagas Ltd v Mundogas SA* [1986] AC 717 (ostensible) usual authority is described as 'general ostensible authority'.

[163] *Hely-Hutchinson*, above.

[164] *First Energy* [1993] BCLC 1409, at 1418, per Steyn LJ.

[165] Ibid.

[166] *Egyptian International Foreign Trade Co v Soplex Wholesale Supplies Ltd, The Raffaela* [1985] BCLC 404, at 411.

[167] The courts often distinguish between ostensible authority in the form of usual authority and in the form of holding out: see, eg, *Freeman & Lockyer*; *The Raffaella*; *Armagas v Mundogas*; *First Energy*, above.

[168] Articles 3 and 5 of the model articles for all types of company (SI 2008/3229).

[169] *Freeman & Lockyer v Buckhurst Park Properties (Mangal) Ltd* [1964] 2 QB 480 (CA).

the company as managing director.[170] However, the better view is that a chairman, *qua* chairman, has no wider usual authority than a director.[171] Individual directors, as such, have almost no usual authority[172] beyond a power to execute documents to clothe a transaction with formal validity which has already been authorised by the board or the managing director.[173] It has been held that a single director has usual authority to sign cheques or other negotiable instruments on behalf of the company.[174] Where a director has a service agreement which requires him to perform a particular task (eg sales manager[175]) then, like any other management executive, he will possess the usual authority that his function requires.[176] This is a matter of ordinary agency law but, in terms of general powers of management, directors must act collectively, unless the articles give a power to delegate to individual directors.[177] This is subject to s 40 [CA 1985, s 35A] because, where that section applies, the directors are deemed to have power to authorise others to act on behalf of the company free of any limitations under the company's constitution. For this purpose, a 'limitation' should include a matter on which the constitution is silent as well as express restrictions.[178]

The position of company secretary has grown in importance over the years. In the nineteenth century, the company secretary was described as a mere servant[179] but, by the 1970s, it was accepted by the Court of Appeal that the company secretary was the chief administrative officer of the

---

[170] *Freeman & Lockyer v Buckhurst Park Properties Ltd*, above; *Hely-Hutchinson v Brayhead* [1968] 1 QB 549, per Roskill J, affirmed by the Court of Appeal on other grounds.

[171] Some of the earlier cases appear to invest the chairman with a usual authority equivalent to a managing director: *British Thomson-Houston Co v Federated European Bank Ltd* [1932] 2 KB 176 (CA) and *Clay Hill Brick Co v Rawlings* [1938] 4 All ER 100, but the sounder view is that the company is liable because the chairman has been held out as managing director. See *Biggerstaff v Rowatts Wharf Ltd* [1986] 2 Ch 93 (CA); *Hely-Hutchinson v Brayhead Ltd* [1968] 1 QB 549, at 560 (Roskill J) and 586 (Lord Wilberforce in CA).

[172] *Rama Corporation Ltd v Proved Tin & General Investments Ltd* [1952] 2 QB 147; *Houghton & Co v Nothard, Lowe & Wills* [1927] 1 KB 247 (CA) – affirmed on other grounds [1928] AC 1.

[173] The power to execute documents is discussed below.

[174] *Re Land Credit Co of Ireland* (1869) LR 4 Ch 460. See also s 52 of the Companies Act 2006 and *Dey v Pullinger Engineering Co* [1921] 1 KB 77.

[175] Cf *SMC Electronics Ltd v Akhter Computers Ltd and others* [2001] 1 BCLC 433, CA.

[176] But if an executive goes beyond the confines of his routine duties, he will lack authority: *Kreditbank Cassel GmbH v Schenkers* [1927] 1 KB 826 (CA); *British Bank of the Middle East v Sun Life Assurance Co of Canada* [1983] 2 Lloyd's Rep 9 (HL). See *Harmond Properties Ltd v Gajdzis* [1968] 1 WLR 1858 (a director acting as general agent of his company in giving notice to quit).

[177] Articles 3 and 5 of the model articles for all companies. However, even though it is not uncommon for the articles to provide for this, delegation cannot be assumed, ie such an article does not add to a director's 'usual' authority.

[178] See **6.7**.

[179] *Barnett, Hoares & Co v South London Tramways Co* (1887) 18 QBD 815, at 817, approved by Lord Macnaghten in *George Whitchurch Ltd v Cavanagh* [1902] AC 117, at 124 and supported by the decision in *Ruben v Great Fingall Consolidated* [1906] AC 439.

company and that, as such, he had ostensible authority to bind the company in contracts of an administrative nature such as employing staff and hiring cars.[180]

Where three companies were controlled by one individual, who was the major shareholder in and chairman, managing director and the organiser of each of the three companies, it was held that the affairs of these companies were so 'mixed up' that the individual controlling them must be regarded as having actual or ostensible authority to act for any of the companies.[181]

6.18   WHEN AN OUTSIDER CANNOT RELY ON USUAL AUTHORITY

There are a number of general rules which limit the right of an outsider to rely on the usual authority of any agent of the company. As in agency law in general, if the third party has knowledge of a relevant restriction on a particular agent's authority, the company will not be liable.[182] The result will be the same if the circumstances surrounding the transaction are sufficiently suspicious to put the third party on inquiry as to the agent's authority.

Restrictions on an agent's usual authority which are contained in the company's articles give rise to special considerations. The constructive notice rule means that outsiders dealing with a company are deemed to know of such restrictions and therefore cannot rely on an agent's usual authority in respect of any matter within the scope of the restrictions. Where the restrictions are not absolute but require a particular use of power to be authorised by the shareholders in general meeting or by the board, sometimes the internal management may be invoked to mitigate the constructive notice rule and to enable the outsider to hold the company to the transaction. This is possible where the required authorisation takes the form of an ordinary resolution of the shareholders or of a board resolution because these are matters of internal management.[183] It is not possible where the required authorisation takes the form of a special resolution, because an outsider can discover from the Registrar of Companies whether a special

---

[180] *Panorama Developments (Guildford) Ltd v Fidelis Furnishing Fabrics Ltd* [1971] 3 All ER 16. See also *First Energy*, above at 1422. Note, however, that it is no longer necessary for a private company to have a secretary; see **15.16.2**.

[181] *Ford Motor Credit Co v Harmack* (1972) *The Times*, 7 July (CA).

[182] *AL Underwood Ltd v Bank of Liverpool*, above; *Rolled Steel*, above.

[183] *Mahoney v East Holyford Mining Co* (1875) LR 7 HL 869. This was provided that the outsider did not know that the required internal authorisation had not been obtained and there was no ground for suspicion.

resolution has been passed and is therefore fixed with constructive notice of the existence or otherwise of such a resolution.[184]

It should be stressed, however, that, insofar as the usual authority of directors and officers is concerned, an outsider need not have read the articles. The articles can have a negative effect in limiting authority but they need not have been read as a positive basis for the usual authority of a particular agent. Here it is the appearance of authority with which a particular agent is commonly vested that determines the scope of his usual authority.[185]

6.19 THE 'HOLDING OUT' PRINCIPLE

The classic statement of the principles of ostensible authority in the form of holding out as applied to companies is to be found in Diplock LJ's judgment in *Freeman & Lockyer*, where he summarised the conditions which had to be fulfilled for a contractor to be entitled to enforce a contract against a company in the following terms:[186]

(1) a representation that the agent had authority to enter on behalf of the company into a contract of the kind sought to be enforced must be made to the contractor;

(2) such representation must be made by a person or persons who had actual authority to manage the business of the company either generally or in respect of those matters to which the contract relates;

(3) the contractor must be induced by the representation to enter into the contract (ie in fact he must rely on it); and

(4) under the memorandum or articles of association of the company, the company must not be deprived of the capacity to enter into a contract of the kind sought to be enforced or to delegate authority to enter into a contract of that kind to the agent.

Section 40 [CA 1985, s 35A] modifies conditions (2) and (4). The board may make a representation of authority to a contractor which exceeds its

---

[184] *Irvine v Union Bank of Australia* (1877) 2 App Cas 366, at 379. Copies of special resolutions must be filed with the Registrar of Companies: s 380.

[185] *Freeman & Lockyer v Buckhurst Park Properties (Mangal) Ltd* [1964] 2 QB 480, at 496 (Willmer LJ). There was formerly some uncertainty on this point, which this case has dispelled. See the reporter's note appended to *British Thomson-Houston Co v Federated European Bank* [1932] 2 KB 176, and the subsequent history of this note in *Clay Hill Brick Co v Rawlings* [1938] 4 All ER 100 and in *Rama Corporation v Proved Tin & General Investments Ltd* [1952] 2 QB 147.

[186] At 506. Diplock LJ's analysis in *Freeman & Lockyer* has been applied in numerous subsequent cases including *IRC v Ufitec Group Ltd* [1977] 3 All ER 924; *British Bank of the Middle East v Sun Life Assurance of Canada*, above; *Rhodian River Shipping v Halia Maritime* [1984] 1 Lloyd's Rep 373; *The Raffaella*, above.

actual authority under the company's constitution but, by virtue of s 40, the contractor, provided he is in good faith, is entitled to assume that the directors' authority is unlimited. The reference to lack of capacity in (4) can now be disregarded, as the capacity of companies is generally no longer restricted by anything in its constitution.

The elements of holding out and reliance embodied in conditions (1) and (3), as stated by Diplock LJ in *Freeman & Lockyer*, are essentially matters that will be determined by reference to the factual circumstances of each case. It is not essential for the body with actual authority to state expressly that the agent has authority, as the holding out may be inferred from the circumstances.[187] The representation by which the company may be said to have held out the individual as having authority will usually take the form of knowingly permitting a director or officer to assume an authority he does not in fact possess. In a one-off transaction, however, an express holding out may be necessary for an estoppel to arise.[188]

Most of the cases illustrating this form of ostensible authority have concerned directors who were held out as managing directors, even though they had never been appointed to that office.[189] The estoppel principle overcomes the lack of valid appointment and confers on the director the same scope of usual authority as if he were a regularly appointed managing director. In accordance with the second of Diplock LJ's conditions, the representation must have been made by an individual or organ of the company with actual authority to make the appointment. In the case of the appointment of the managing director, most articles confer this power on the board of directors. The board will be estopped by their conduct in knowingly allowing a director either expressly to represent himself as managing director, or by his conduct impliedly to represent that he has the powers of such. In *Freeman & Lockyer v Buckhurst Park Properties*,[190] for example, no managing director had been appointed, despite a power in the articles to do so, in a company formed to purchase and develop certain properties. Two directors allowed the third director, Kapoor, the whole management of the company's business. The Court of Appeal held that the company was estopped from denying that Mr Kapoor was managing director and that it was within the usual authority of such to engage a firm of architects to obtain planning permission for the development of certain properties.

---

[187] See the remarks of Pearson LJ in *Freeman & Lockyer* above at 498 as qualified by his later remarks in *Hely-Hutchinson* above at 593.

[188] *Armagas v Mundogas*, above at 777.

[189] The holding out principle may also extend the scope of the actual authority of an agent of the company: *Mercantile Bank of India v Chartered Bank of India* [1937] 1 All ER 231. (Agents authorised to borrow by power of attorney. A limitation on the amount imposed by the directors did not appear in the power of attorney. A charge granted to secure an amount in excess of the limitation was held to estop the company, since it had held out the agents by the power of attorney as having unlimited power to borrow.)

[190] Above.

6.20   KNOWLEDGE OF THE ARTICLES

As in cases involving usual authority, where liability is founded on the holding out principle, it is *not* essential that the third party should have read the articles. The conduct of the board in acquiescing in the pretensions of a self-styled managing director will bind the company, even though the articles conferring the power to appoint a managing director have not been read. Conversely, the existence of a power to delegate, e g to a managing director, will not of itself raise an estoppel where no managing director has been appointed. The *Turquand* rule cannot be invoked by a person who knows of the contents of the articles to raise an estoppel against the company in circumstances where the articles permitted delegation but there is no evidence of an individual having being held out. The significance of a power to delegate in the articles, if known, is simply that this may help to establish[191] that the company is estopped, but it can scarcely do so alone without more positive evidence that a particular individual was held out as holding an executive position by an organ which had the authority to appoint him.

In *Freeman & Lockyer*, the Court of Appeal was divided on whether the holding out principle could bind the company even where the articles did not specifically provide a power to appoint a managing director.[192] The point may now be covered by s 40 [CA 1985, s 35A] which, irrespective of the actual contents of the articles, allows a person dealing with the company in good faith to assume that the directors have unlimited powers to authorise others to act on the company's behalf.

6.21   'SELF-AUTHORISING' AGENTS

The second of the conditions of ostensible authority outlined by Diplock LJ in *Freeman & Lockyer* is that the agent must be held out by someone who has actual authority in the matter to which the representation relates. It follows from this that an agent should not be able to increase his own power to bind the company by holding himself out as having more authority than he actually has. Likewise, an agent who lacks authority should not be able to bind the company by over-representing someone else's authority. These propositions are supported by the decision of the House of Lords in *British Bank of the Middle East v Sun Life Assurance Co of Canada (UK) Ltd*,[193] where it was held that the general manager of a branch office of an insurance company had no authority to give an undertaking on the company's behalf and had no authority to represent that a more junior employee, a unit manager, had

---

[191] See *Houghton & Co v Nothard, Lowe & Willis Ltd* [1927] 1 KB 246, at 266, per Sargant LJ.

[192] Diplock LJ at 505–506 thought that this was possible but Willmer LJ at 492 and Pearson LJ at 480 thought otherwise.

[193] Above.

the requisite authority.[194] It has, however, been accepted that an agent may have the ostensible authority to make a representation about the authority of another agent to act on behalf of the principal, provided that the second agent's apparent authority could be traced back directly to the principal's actual authority.[195]

A gloss on this is, however, indicated by *The Raffaella*[196] where Browne-Wilkinson LJ said:

> 'It is obviously correct that an agent who has no actual or apparent authority either (a) to enter into a transaction or (b) to make representations as to the transaction cannot hold himself out as having authority to enter into the transaction so as to affect the principal's position. But, suppose a company confers actual or apparent authority on X to make representations and X erroneously represents to a third party that Y has authority to enter into a transaction; why should not such a representation be relied on as part of the holding out of Y by the company? By parity of reasoning, if a company confers actual or apparent authority on A to make representations on the company's behalf but no actual authority on A to enter into the specific transaction, why should a representation made by A as to his authority not be capable of being relied on as one of the acts of holding out?'

This was applied by the Court of Appeal in *First Energy (UK) v Hungarian International Bank*,[197] where it was held that a bank manager who had no authority to make an offer on the bank's behalf had ostensible authority by virtue of his position (ie what has been described in this chapter as a form of usual authority) to communicate that head office approval had been given to the transaction in question. Whether it was possible to draw a distinction between authority to enter into a transaction and authority to represent that it had been approved at a higher level, had been put in some doubt by the decision of the House of Lords in *Armagas v Mundogas*. However, the Court of Appeal distinguished the earlier House of Lords decision on two grounds: first, *Armagas* was not concerned with the ostensible authority of an agent arising from his position but with ostensible authority arising from holding out on specific occasions, and the evidence in that case did not establish that such authority existed; secondly, the House of Lords had not ruled out altogether the possibility of an agent who had no authority to conclude the transaction having authority to communicate decisions, but had merely decided that it would be somewhat rare for that situation to arise.[198]

---

[194] See also *Armagas v Mundogas*, above.
[195] *ING Re (UK) Ltd v R&V Versicherung AG* [2007] 1 BCLC 108, Toulson J.
[196] Above.
[197] Above.
[198] *British Thomson-Houston Co Ltd v Federated European Bank Ltd* [1932] 2 KB 176 can be explained as a case where the agent's authority to conclude transactions was not commensurate with his authority to communicate decisions.

The pragmatic commercial considerations that underlie agency principles, and also the rule in *Turquand's* case, were emphasised by the Court of Appeal in *First Energy*. On the one hand, a contractor who is dealing with an agent acting on behalf of a company cannot know, nor be expected to inquire into, all of the internal approval procedures within the company; on the other hand, merely because someone (who may have no other connection with the company) purports to act for a company should not necessarily mean that the company is bound, since this could facilitate fraud and operate to the detriment of the company's innocent creditors and shareholders. A balance has to be struck which allows a contractor to hold the company to a transaction, without having to go to the (usually impossible) lengths of ensuring that the transaction is approved at board level, in circumstances where the contractor acts reasonably in assuming that appropriate corporate approvals have been obtained. Normally, the contractor will rely on the authority of the agent to conclude the transaction, but the decision of the Court of Appeal in *First Energy* recognises that an agent who lacks the authority to conclude the transaction may, in limited circumstances, bind the company by communicating, within the scope of his authority, that it has been approved at a higher level.[199]

6.22   FORGERY, THE *TURQUAND* RULE AND AGENCY PRINCIPLES

There is authority from the House of Lords for the proposition that a forgery as such is a *nullity* and cannot bind the company.[200] On the other hand, if an organ or official of the company with the authority to bind the company held out the person who committed the forgery as having authority to execute the document in question, the company may be estopped from denying the validity of the forgery. In *Ruben v Great Fingall Consolidated*,[201] a company secretary, without authority to do so, issued a share certificate with the company's seal attached and under his own signature and the forged signatures of two directors. The execution of the share certificate was therefore a nullity, and there was no ground for holding the company estopped from denying this. In other cases, a director or other official has been held to have 'forged' his own signature to a parol agreement.[202] This would seem to be a misuse of the word 'forgery' and such cases should have been decided instead on the basis of

---

[199] For a criticism of the decision, see *Reynolds* (1994) 110 LQR 21. For a recent case which came down on the *Armagas* side of the divide, see *Hudson Bay Apparel Brands LLC v Umbro International Ltd* [2011] 1 BCLC 259.

[200] *Ruben v Great Fingall Consolidated* [1906] AC 439 (HL), at 443, per Lord Loreburn.

[201] [1906] AC 439 (HL); see further *Slingsby v District Bank* [1931] 2 KB 588, at 605, per Wright J (*affirmed* by [1932] 1 KB 544 (CA)).

[202] *Kreditbank Cassel GmbH v Schenkers Ltd* [1927] 1 KB 826; *South London Greyhound Racecourses v Wake* [1931] 1 Ch 496.

lack of authority (whether actual or ostensible).[203] Indeed, it is difficult to see why even forgery, as in *Ruben's* case, must be treated as being governed by a special rule. So far as actual authority is concerned a forgery is clearly a nullity. However, whether or not it binds the company should depend on the general principles. It is clear that under general agency law[204] forgeries are not treated differently from other fraudulent acts which may be binding on the principal if the agent acts within his usual or apparent authority.[205]

6.23 STATUTORY PROVISIONS AFFECTING APPOINTMENTS

Section 161 of the Companies Act 2006 [CA 1985, s 285] appears to give additional protection to an outsider dealing with a director or manager who has been invalidly appointed. This section provides that 'the acts of a director or manager are valid notwithstanding any defect that may afterwards be discovered in his appointment or qualification'. However, the House of Lords in *Morris v Kanssen* gave a very restricted interpretation to this section. Lord Simmonds distinguished 'between (a) an appointment in which there is a defect or, in other words, a defective appointment and (b) no appointment at all'.[206] Thus it will validate a mere slip or procedural defect in the appointment of a director, but it will not cover even an originally valid appointment which has been vacated by reason of a statutory provision requiring qualification shares to be taken up within 2 months.[207] Thus the *Turquand* rule and agency principles will normally give an outsider better protection in dealing with invalidly appointed officers than does s 161.[208]

The publicity that the Companies Act 2006 requires about the identity of directors may, in some circumstances, prevent the company from denying the validity of an appointment of a director or officer. Thus the company is required to keep a register of directors and file a copy of this with the Registrar of Companies.[209] Where names of invalidly appointed directors are publicised, third parties who have read and relied on this information might hold the company liable if the company could be shown to have acquiesced in the registration or display of erroneous information as to the identity of any of the directors. It might then be argued that there was implied actual authority for their appointment even though there had

---

[203] See *Northside Developments Pty Ltd v Registrar-General*, above, where this distinction is drawn.

[204] *Uxbridge Building Society v Pickard* [1939] 2 KB 248 (CA).

[205] *Lloyd v Grace, Smith & Co* [1912] AC 716 (HL).

[206] [1946] AC 459, at 471.

[207] *Morris v Kanssen*, above.

[208] Although s 161 includes members as well as outsiders, it will not protect anyone who knew or ought to have known of the defect: *Re Staffordshire Gas and Coke Co* (1892) 66 LT 413; *Tyne Mutual Steamship Insurance Association v Brown* (1896) 74 LT 283. See also *John v Rees* [1969] 1 WLR 1294, at 1320.

[209] Section 162 [CA 1985, s 288].

been no formal election to the board. Such an argument is more likely to succeed in the case of a private company with a small number of members.

6.24 PUBLICATION IN THE *GAZETTE* OF RETURNS RELATING TO THE REGISTER OF DIRECTORS

Section 1077(1) of the Companies Act 2006 [CA 1985, s 711 with amendments] requires the registrar to publish in the *Gazette* 'any return relating to a company's register of directors, or notification of a change among its directors'. Under s 1079(2) of the 2006 Act, 'a change among the company's directors' is an 'event' on which 'the company shall not be entitled to rely against other persons' if the event has not been officially notified at the material time. See further **5.13**.

6.25 THE FORM OF CONTRACTS BY COMPANIES

A company may make a contract in writing under its common seal and a contract may be made on its behalf by its duly authorised agent.[210] Any formalities required by law in the case of a contract made by an individual also apply, unless a contrary intention appears, to a contract made by or on behalf of a company.[211]

6.26 THE EXECUTION OF COMPANY DOCUMENTS

Certain special rules apply to the execution of documents. Here a distinction has to be drawn between *formal* authority to execute a document and *substantive* authority to enter into the transaction (which is then clothed with formal validity by the execution of the document). Although the substantive validity of a transaction may require a decision by the board of directors or a managing director, the execution of documents will usually be left to lesser officers of the company. So long as the requirements of the articles have been complied with, the outsider will not have to prove that there was actual authority to execute the document. Where a document has to be sealed, most articles provide that this may be done by a director and the secretary, or by two directors. The cases establish that where a document is executed with the signature or signatures that the articles require, its formal validity cannot be contested

---

[210] Section 43 [CA 1985, s 36].
[211] Ibid.

by the company,[212] but where this is not the case the document is not binding on the company[213] unless s 40 of the Companies Act 2006 [CA 1985, s 35A] applies.[214]

Section 44 of the Companies Act 2006 [CA 1985, s 36A] provides that a document is executed by a company by the affixing of its common seal. It is not now obligatory for a company to have a common seal.[215] Whether or not a company has a common seal, a document signed by two authorised signatories (a director and the secretary of the company or two directors of the company), or by a director signing in the presence of a witness who attests the signature, and expressed (in whatever form of words) to be executed by the company has the same effect as if executed under the common seal of the company.[216] It is common practice for the common seal to be affixed to important documents which are not deeds such as share and stock certificates.[217]

6.27   PROTECTION FOR PURCHASERS

Section 44(5) of the Companies Act 2006 [CA 1985, s 36A(6)] provides that in favour of a purchaser[218] a document is deemed to have been duly executed by a company if it purports to be signed by a director and the secretary of the company and, where it makes it clear on its face that it is intended by the person or persons making it to be a deed, to have been delivered upon its being executed. The meaning of 'purports to be signed' is not certain. It would presumably cover any lack of authority on the part of the signing officers but it is open to argument whether it would also encompass forged signatures. If this were the case, s 44(5) would, in effect, repeal *Ruben v Great Fingall*[219] in respect of documents within its scope. The Law Commission has noted the uncertainty on this point but its view is that the presumption[220] does not and should not give protection where the signature of the company's officers has been forged.[221]

---

[212] *County of Gloucester Bank v Rudry Merthyr, etc, Colliery Co* [1895] 1 Ch 629 (CA); *Duck v Tower Galvanizing Co* [1901] 2 KB 314.

[213] *TCB Ltd v Gray* [1987] Ch 458.

[214] Ibid, at 125.

[215] Section 45(1) [CA 1985, s 36A(3)]. Where a company has a common seal, the name of the company must be engraved on it in legible characters: s 45(2) [CA 1985, s 350(1)].

[216] Section 44(2)–(4) [CA 1985, s 36A(4)].

[217] A share certificate is not a deed: *South London Greyhound Racecourses v Wake* [1931] 1 Ch 496, at 503, per Clausen J. See s 768 [CA 1985, s 186] as to the effect of sealing a share certificate. A company which has an official seal may have a securities seal which is a facsimile of its common seal (with the addition of the word 'securities') specifically for use in sealing documents creating and evidencing securities: s 50 [CA 1985, s 40].

[218] For this purpose, a purchaser means a purchaser in good faith for valuable consideration and includes a lessee, mortgagee or other person who, for valuable consideration, acquires an interest in the property.

[219] See **6.17**.

[220] In s 74(1) of the Law of Property Act 1925 as well as in s 44(5).

[221] *The Execution of Deeds and Documents by or on Behalf of Bodies Corporate*, Law Com No 253 (1998) paras 5.34–5.37.

According to the Law Commission, the presumption in s 44(5) should apply where the signatures are genuine but the officers in question lack authority to sign the document, and where the document is attested by persons who are no longer office-holders but notice of their resignation has not yet been filed with the Registrar of Companies or where there was some defect in their appointment.

Section 44(5) is in similar terms to a more limited protection for purchasers provided by s 74 of the Law of Property Act 1925.

CHAPTER 7

SHARE CAPITAL – ALLOTMENT AND MAINTENANCE

7.1 INTRODUCTION

This chapter is concerned with one way in which companies raise capital by means of issuing shares. All companies, of course, need capital and, although in practice share capital is often less important than other sorts of capital, company law has traditionally paid particular attention to share capital in two particular respects. The first matter concerns allotment of shares,[1] where rules exist primarily to protect shareholders. The second matter pertains to the rules which seek to ensure that share capital is properly raised, and then maintained for the benefit of the company's creditors. Although the bulk of the provisions of the Companies Act 1985 dealing with such matters were retained in the Companies Act 2006, the relevant law was reformed in some respects, particularly to strip back unnecessary regulatory complexity for private companies.

7.2 METHODS OF CAPITALISING COMPANIES[2]

The overwhelming majority of private companies are small businesses which have chosen for tax or other reasons to incorporate. They are 'small' both in their capitalisation and in the number of their participators. They frequently take the form of 'one-man companies' or small 'corporate partnerships'. Almost without exception, they will register as a private company limited by shares. The capital of such a company will typically comprise a mixture of loan capital (eg debentures) and share capital. The participators will fix the initial capital at a level appropriate to the activities of the company, but this has no direct relationship with the economic value of the enterprise. The function of share capital in such a company is largely to allocate control rights in the

---

[1]   Note that, as confirmed by the House of Lords (*National Westminster Bank plc v IRC* [1995] 1 AC 119), the terms 'issue' and 'allotment' in relation to shares have different technical meanings. Shares are allotted when there is a contract to take them in accordance with the procedures described later in this chapter; they are issued only when the allottee has been entered in the register of members (as to which, see Chapter 12) to complete the title of the allottee.

[2]   For a detailed account of corporate financing, see Ferran *Company Law and Corporate Finance* (Oxford University Press, 1999) esp Chap 2.

manner agreed by the participators. The function of loan capital is generally to enable the company to acquire (possibly from the participators) the assets required by the company to run its business. Issuing loan capital to the participators allows them to become creditors (possibly secured) in their own business.

This common form of initial capitalisation in the case of small companies has tax advantages for the company. Interest payments are deductible from operating profits for taxation purposes,[3] whereas dividend payments are not. Where all the shareholders/debenture-holders are likely also to be directors, and to be closely involved in working for and running the company, there may be tax advantages in participating in profits in the form of salaries (or other remuneration) rather than in the form of dividends. When it comes to 'ongoing' finance for such companies, this is most likely to take the form of bank borrowings[4] and retaining (instead of distributing) profits earned by the company.[5] Other factors may come into play as further finance is needed. Thus the company may seek 'venture' capital from institutions or individuals prepared to take an 'equity stake' in the company. As the business matures the original 'participators' may need to dispose of their interest in the company. These and other factors may lead to the company issuing a substantial share capital as it continues to grow in size. The ultimate stage of such development may be a public issue of some or all of the company's share capital.[6]

In the case of large public listed companies, share capital obviously has a much more significant role. Nevertheless, in terms of continuing sources of fresh finance, share capital[7] is nowadays less important than loan capital[8] and self-financing by the company itself through retained profits. However, the concept of 'gearing' in the prudent financing of public companies will discourage companies from relying too heavily on loan capital. 'High gearing' means that the ratio of loan capital (as well as preference shares on which there is a fixed return) to equity capital (ordinary shares) is too high[9] in regard to the proportion of the former to the latter. High gearing makes profits more volatile and puts the owners of equity shares at risk in that it may increase the chances of insolvency. The owners of such shares will also suffer in a period of low profits or actual

---

[3]   However, a shareholder/creditor who receives dividend/interest payments remains liable to tax on them.

[4]   And other forms of commercial credit such as industrial hire-purchase and 'factoring' of debts owed to the company.

[5]   This is limited by the tax regime established for 'close' companies. See *Gore-Browne on Companies* (Jordans, 45th edn, loose-leaf) at 47 [37].

[6]   See Chapter 6.

[7]   This is true of both ordinary and preference shares. See the Committee to Review the Functioning of Financial Institutions (the Wilson Committee) (Cmnd 7937, 1980, Table 34 at p 133).

[8]   See Chapter 10. Today this takes the form of bank borrowings over a relatively short term rather than a public issue of debentures over a medium to long-term period.

[9]   What this ratio should be will depend on a number of factors, primarily the cost of (equity or loan) capital and the profitability of the company's business.

losses in the company's (or group's) trading operations. Thus, especially in a time of high interest rates, capital and income repayments in respect of loan capital may absorb much too high a proportion of the company's earnings from its business activities. This may necessitate a fresh issue of equity shares to the existing ordinary shareholders in the form of a rights issue in order to restore an appropriate balance between equity and loan capital.

7.3   ALLOTMENT OF SHARES

The next part of this chapter examines the two forms of statutory protection for shareholders against the traditional power of control of the board of directors over the issue of a company's share capital and is followed by a brief examination of the control under the general duties of directors. Statutory protection was first introduced in 1980 to implement what was required by the Second EC Directive on Company Law.[10] The first form requires the authority of the shareholders for the allotment[11] of shares. Secondly, in the case of issuing equity shares, the Companies Act 2006 confers what are known as 'pre-emptive' rights on holders of existing equity shares in proportion to their holdings of such shares.

There is an evident need to circumscribe the power of the directors of public companies and of larger private companies to issue share capital. They may be tempted to do this to resist external takeover bids, or to entrench themselves when threatened by internal struggles for control of majority voting power at shareholders' meetings. There is also the problem of what is known as dilution following a new issue of shares. 'Vote dilution' means that the existing shareholders will lose their existing voting strength. This process, if carried far enough, may tip the balance of control in a company. 'Earnings dilution' is of most concern to existing equity shareholders.[12] This is so because, following a new issue, the existing and future earnings of the company will be divided among a larger number of shareholders. If the return on new capital does not match that on existing capital, a new issue of shares will cause earnings

---

[10]   See **2.3.2**.

[11]   Their prior authority for the creation of the company's 'authorised' but unissued share capital was always required. This, however, allowed the directors to have a 'bank' of unissued shares at their disposal. The concept of authorised share capital ended when the relevant provisions of CA 2006 took effect: see especially s 542, effective from 1 October 2008. Note, however, that in the case of companies formed under earlier Acts, a provision relating to authorised share capital in its memorandum will continue to have effect (as part of the articles) and may be revoked or amended by the company by ordinary resolution: Companies Act 2006 (Commencement No 8, Transitional Provisions and Savings) Order 2008, SI 2008/2860, Sch 2, para 42.

[12]   It will usually also have the effect of vote dilution but this need not be the case (e g where the fresh issue consists of non-voting equity shares).

per share to fall. This will have obvious implications for the value of those shares on the stock market or their value in a private company.[13]

These statutory provisions arguably provide a somewhat less than satisfactory bulwark against both vote and earnings dilution. Section 549 of the Companies Act 2006, described below, has only limited criminal sanctions for breach, and the pre-emption provisions can be fairly easily disapplied.

7.4   AUTHORITY REQUIRED TO ALLOT SHARES

Section 549(1) of the Companies Act 2006 restricts the power of directors of a company to allot shares in the company or grant rights to subscribe for, or convert any security into, shares in the company unless they are authorised to do so by the company either in general meeting or by virtue of the articles. Moreover, new deregulatory provisions allow private companies with a single class of shares to allot shares in accordance with procedures set out in s 550.[14]

Any authority (given in general meeting or by the articles) may be given for a particular exercise of that power or for its exercise generally.[15] It may be unconditional or subject to conditions. Any authority must state the maximum amount[16] of shares that may be allotted under it and the date on which such authority will expire, which must not be more than the five years from the relevant date applicable.[17] This date, in the case of an authority contained at the time of the original incorporation of the company in the articles, is the date of incorporation. In any other case, it is the date on which the resolution is passed by which the authority required by s 551 is given.[18] Any authority may be renewed by the company in general meeting for further successive periods not exceeding five years. The resolution renewing such authority must state (or restate) the amount of shares which may be allotted or, as the case may be, remains to be allotted under its authority, and the date on which the renewed authority will expire.[19] Even though any authority required by s 551 has expired, the directors may allot shares if they are allotted in

---

[13]   If a share is valued on a price/earnings basis, any increase in the number of shares that is not matched by a similar increase in earnings per share will lead to a fall in the share price and a loss to shareholders.

[14]   Based on CA 1985, s 80(1). By virtue of subsection (2), s 549 does not apply to share allotments made pursuant to employees' shares schemes, nor to subscription rights to, or to convert any securities into shares so allotted. As to the relationship between s 549 and the protecting of class rights, see **8.7.3**.

[15]   Section 551(2) [CA 1985, s 80(3)].

[16]   Where the 'securities' are not shares but rights to subscribe for shares or to convert any security into shares, then the 'maximum amount' of relevant securities means the maximum which may be allocated pursuant to the rights: s 551(6) [CA 1985, s 80(6)].

[17]   Section 551(3) [CA 1985, s 80(4)].

[18]   Section 551(3)(b)(i) and (ii) [CA 1985, s 80(4)].

[19]   Section 551(5) [CA 1985, s 80(5)].

pursuance of an offer or agreement made by the company before the authority expired. However, the authority must have allowed the company to make an offer or agreement which would or might require shares to be allotted after the authority expired.[20]

A company may give, vary, revoke or renew an authority by ordinary resolution even though it alters the articles of the company. However, the requirements of s 30 of the 2006 Act (copies of resolutions or agreements to be forwarded to the registrar) apply to such a resolution.[21] While criminal penalties are provided for any director who knowingly contravenes, or permits or authorises the contravention of, s 549,[22] this will not affect the validity of any allotment of shares.[23]

Section 550 provides that directors of private companies with a single class of shares may, without any further authorisation, allot shares (or grant rights to subscribe for or convert any security into shares). This power may be limited, however, by a provision in the articles.[24] The issue as to whether or not a private company has only one class of shares is important. If not, then the deregulatory regime set out in s 550 will not apply. Although hitherto there was no general statutory definition of 'classes of shares', guidance can be found in s 629 of the 2006 Act in which a single class of shares refers to those shares in which all rights attached thereto are uniform. Clearly, what 'all rights' means in this context is key. Generally, rights attached to shares would include such matters as voting, dividends and return of capital on winding-up. At least in relation to variation thereof, class rights have been interpreted as more expansive than the core issues noted above. In the case of *Cumbrian Newspapers Group Ltd v Cumberland & Westmorland Newspapers and Printing Co Ltd*[25] it was held that rights conferred on a shareholder by the company's constitution amounted to class rights even though they were not attached to any class of shares differentiated in respect of voting, dividend or capital rights. If too liberal an interpretation of 'all rights' is attached to shares in the context of s 550, then much of the de-regulatory thrust of the provisions may be lost.[26]

---

[20] Section 551(7) [CA 1985, s 80(7)].

[21] Section 551(9) [CA 1985, s 80(8)]. The provisions of s 1077 [CA 1985, s 711] (documents to be published by the registrar in the *Gazette*) apply to such a resolution.

[22] Section 549(4) [CA 1985, s 80(9) and Sch 24].

[23] Section 549(6) [CA 1985, s 80(10)].

[24] Misuse of the power may amount to a breach of directors' duty – see *Hogg v Crampton Ltd* [1967] Ch 254 and *Howard Smith Ltd v Ampol Petroleum Ltd* [1974] AC 821.

[25] [1986] 3 WLR 26.

[26] Given the de-regulatory impact of s 550 for private companies, previous de-regulatory provisions in s 80A of the 1985 Act applicable to private companies that had opted into the 'elective regime' have become obsolete and were not re-enacted in the 2006 Act.

7.5 PRE-EMPTION RIGHTS

As already noted, statute has, since 1980, conferred pre-emptive rights on existing equity shareholders when further shares are allotted.[27] This right applies to both public and private companies, but private companies have been able to exclude it by a provision in their memorandum or articles. In keeping with its deregulatory nature, the Companies Act 2006 extends the opt-out provisions for private companies hitherto in place, albeit that many of the relevant 1985 Act provisions (ss 89–94) are restated.

The right conferred by s 561 of the Companies Act 2006[28] may, subject to various qualifications and exemptions to be considered later, be stated as follows. A company proposing to allot any 'equity securities'[29] shall not allot any of those equity securities on any terms to any person, unless it has first made an offer to each person who holds ordinary shares to allot to him, on the same or more favourable terms, a proportion of those securities which is as nearly as practical equal to the proportion in nominal value held by him of the ordinary share capital of the company.[30]

There is a 14-day period during which the pre-emptive rights may be taken up or refused.[31] The offer may not be withdrawn before the end of that period.[32] During this period, the company may not allot any securities subject to the pre-emptive rights conferred by s 561 to any other person, unless the period during which any such offer may be accepted has expired, or the company has received notice of the acceptance or refusal of every offer so made.[33] Shares offered by virtue of s 561(1) may be allotted either to the existing holders of ordinary shares *or* to anyone in whose favour such a person has renounced his right to allotment.[34] Provisions in the Companies Act 2006 bestow power on the Secretary of State to bring forward regulations to vary the 14-day period.[35]

---

[27] It has been common for the articles of private companies to make such provision. The *Listing Rules* confer what amounts to a right of pre-emption upon existing holders of equity shares in listed companies. Such rights do not exist at common law: *Mutual Life Insurance Co v The Rank Organisation* [1985] BCLC 11. The common law in the United States recognised such rights at an early stage. See generally MacNeil 'Shareholders' Pre-Emptive Rights' [2002] JBL 78. See further *Pre-emption Rights: Final Report* 2005 (URN 05/679).

[28] [CA 1985, s 89(1)].

[29] Defined in s 560 as 'ordinary shares in the company' or 'rights to subscribe for, or to convert securities into, ordinary shares in the company'.

[30] Section 561(1)(a) [CA 1985, s 89(1)].

[31] Section 562(5) as amended by the Companies (Share Capital and Acquisition by Company of its Own Shares) Regulations 2009, SI 2009/2022, reg 2.

[32] Section 562(5) [CA 1985, s 90(6)]. The offer may be made in hard copy or in electronic form (s 562(2)).

[33] Section 561(1)(b) [CA 1985, s 89(1)(b)].

[34] Section 561(2) [CA 1985, s 89(4)]. This facilitates the existence of a market in 'nil paid rights' in which a shareholder can sell the right to allotment to a third party.

[35] Section 562(6) and (7). The period may be increased or reduced (but not to below 14 days). The period was recently reduced from 21 to 14 days: see n 31.

Section 561(1) does not apply to an allotment of equity securities if they are to be paid up (or are in fact paid up) wholly or partly otherwise than in cash.[36] Further, it does not apply in relation to the allotment of any equity securities which would, apart from a renunciation or assignment of the right to their allotment, be held under or allotted or transferred pursuant to an employees' share scheme.[37] Finally, s 556(1) does not apply to the allotment of bonus shares.[38]

Subject to these exemptions and the provision described in **7.5.1**, pre-emptive rights are mandatory in the case of public companies. However, the requirements of ss 561 and 562 may be excluded by a provision contained in the articles of a private company. The provisions may be excluded generally in relation to the allotment by the company of equity securities or in relation to allotments of a particular description.[39] Furthermore, a requirement or authority contained in the articles of a private company, if it is inconsistent with the requirements of ss 561 or 562, shall have effect as a provision excluding the pre-emptive rights conferred by s 561.[40] A new provision in the 2006 Act, set out in s 569, stipulates that directors of private companies with only one class of share may be empowered by the articles or by special resolution to allot shares of that class as if the provisions of s 561 did not apply, or applied with such modifications as the directors may determine.[41] Furthermore, s 568 sets out another new provision this time applicable to all companies limited by shares. This provision applies in a case in which s 561 would otherwise apply, where there is a provision in the company's articles prohibiting the company from allotting ordinary shares of a particular class unless it has complied with the condition that it makes such an offer in accordance with the provisions in s 561(1).[42] In that case the terms of the articles will replace the statutory provisions, albeit that the allotment must be made in accordance with s 562 (in respect of communicating the offer), unless, the company being a private one, has excluded such requirements (in accordance with s 567).[43] Civil liability follows breach of this provision. Where there is a contravention of any pre-emption provision in the company's articles, the company and any officer who knowingly authorised or permitted the contravention are jointly and severally liable to compensate any person to whom an offer should have been made for loss or damage sustained.[44]

---

[36] Section 565 [CA 1985, s 89(4)].
[37] Section 566 [CA 1985, s 89(5)]. As to the definition of 'employees' shares scheme', see s 1166.
[38] Section 564.
[39] Section 567(1) and (2) [CA 1985, s 91].
[40] Section 567(3) and (4) [CA 1985, s 91(1) and (2)]. The 'implied' exclusion referred to in the text does not of course extend to provisions in the constitution conferring pre-emptive rights of the kind contemplated by s 561 (2) and (3).
[41] Section 569(1).
[42] Section 568(1) and (2).
[43] Section 568(3).
[44] Section 568(4) and (5).

The above section follows the language of general liability imposed upon companies and their officers for breach of ss 561 and 562. In this sense, s 563 provides a civil, but not a criminal, sanction for a contravention of ss 561 and 562. Again the company, and every officer of the company who knowingly authorised or permitted the contravention, are jointly and severally liable to compensate any person to whom an offer should have been made[45] for any loss, damage, costs or expenses which that person has sustained or incurred by reason of that contravention.[46] However, no such proceedings may be commenced after the expiration of 2 years from the delivery to the Registrar of Companies of the return of allotments in question.[47] Section 563 does not appear to invalidate any allotment not complying with shareholders' pre-emptive rights.[48] They are simply left to the civil remedy provided by the subsection. It has been left to the courts to determine the measure and scope of loss or damage that may be recovered. It is not clear whether the loss of 'control' of a company would be compensable over and above the market price for shares of that class.

7.5.1   When authority under s 551 overrides pre-emptive rights

Previous provisions in this respect set out in the Companies Act 1985 were largely repeated in the 2006 Act. Section 570[49] attempts to reconcile the provisions of s 551 with those of s 561. It does this by providing for the disapplication of s 561 in certain circumstances. Section 570(1) provides that where directors of a company are *generally* authorised for the purposes of s 551, they may be given power by the articles or by special resolution to allot equity securities pursuant to their s 551 authority as if s 561 did not apply to the allotment. Alternatively, s 561 may apply to the allotment with such modifications as the directors may determine. Where the directors are not generally authorised for the purposes of s 551, s 561 can be disapplied or modified in respect of an allotment by special resolution.[50]

The power conferred by s 570 (and any special resolution under s 571) will cease to have effect when the authority to which it relates is revoked or would, if not renewed, expire. However, if the authority required by s 551 is renewed, the power conferred by ss 570 or 571 may also be renewed (for a period not longer than that for which the authority is renewed) by a special resolution of the company.[51]

---

[45] Ie an offer under s 561(1).

[46] Section 563(2) [CA 1985, s 92(1)].

[47] Where equity securities other than shares are granted it is 2 years from the date of the grant: s 563(3) [CA 1985, s 92(2)]. The same provisions apply to civil liability incurred under s 568.

[48] This is probably so in the case of an allotment to a large number of shareholders, but an allotment in a small company where the (hitherto) 21-day period was not allowed was declared invalid in *Re Thundercrest Ltd* [1994] BCC 857.

[49] [CA 1985, s 95].

[50] Section 571(1) [CA 1985, s 95(2)].

[51] Sections 570(3) and 571(3) [CA 1985, s 95(3)].

As in the case of an authority for the purposes of s 551, the directors may allot equity securities in pursuance of an offer or agreement previously made by the company even though the power or resolution required by ss 570 or 571 has expired at the time of the allotment. However, the power or resolution must have enabled the company to make an offer or agreement which would or might require equity securities to be allotted after it expired.[52]

A special resolution conferring the power given by s 571(1) (which applies where the directors are authorised for the purposes of s 551 generally and *otherwise*) may not be proposed unless it is recommended by the directors.[53] In addition, there must be circulated with the notice of the meeting at which the resolution is proposed, to the members entitled to have that notice, a written statement by the directors. This must set out:

(1) their reasons for making the recommendation;

(2) the amount to be paid to the company in respect of the equity securities to be allotted; and

(3) the directors' justification of that amount.[54]

7.6 OTHER CONTROLS ON ALLOTMENTS

The statutory controls on allotments articulated above have their limitation. The remedies for breach are limited and do not appear to include avoidance of an allotment even for a breach of the pre-emption provisions. Where the directors of a company are in control of the voting power at general meetings, there will still be the possibility of abuse notwithstanding s 549 of the Companies Act 2006. The observance of statutory pre-emption rights in a private company may amount to an indirect method of squeezing out minority shareholders who lack the means to take up their proportionate share of a new issue.[55] Further, as has been seen, pre-emption rights do not apply to certain types of issue, in particular issues of equity shares not paid for wholly in cash; this leaves a very wide gap in the statutory protection, as it seems that a minor amount of non-cash consideration will suffice. In all of these cases, the only possible remedies for abuse will be for breach of directors' duties in respect of an allotment and/or for breach of controlling shareholders' duties, perhaps by way of a petition for unfair prejudice under s 994 of

---

[52] Sections 570(4) and 517(4) [CA 1985, s 95(4)].

[53] Section 571(4). Special resolutions required by s 571 must be also *Gazetted* under s 711.

[54] Section 571(6) and (7) [CA 1985, s 95(5)]. A criminal sanction is imposed in respect of misleading, false, or deceptive matters in the statement: s 572 [CA 1985, s 95(6)].

[55] See the unreported decision in *Pennell v Venida Investments*, 25 July 1974, discussed in *Burridge* (1981) 44 MLR 40.

the Companies Act 2006.[56] The latter is considered elsewhere,[57] but it is appropriate to look briefly here at the law regarding directors' duties in this area.[58]

In deciding upon the making of allotments, the directors 'must dispose of their company's shares on the best terms obtainable, and must not allot them to themselves or their friends at a lower price in order to obtain a personal benefit. They must act *bona fide* for the interests of the company'.[59] But this does not mean that when the market price is at a premium, shares cannot be issued at par. In *Hilder v Dexter*, Lord Davey observed that he was not aware 'of any law which obliges a company to issue its shares above par because they are saleable at a premium in the market. It depends on the circumstances of each case whether it will be prudent or even possible to do so, and it is a question for the directors to decide'.[60] When the shares command a premium, the directors must not allot them at par to members of their own body or their friends, for they should either offer them equally to all the shareholders or obtain the benefit of the premium for the company.[61] However, an allotment to the directors sanctioned by a general meeting of the company has been held to be unimpeachable notwithstanding that the directors held the majority of the shares and voted in favour of the allotments of the shares to themselves.[62] Directors, moreover, must not allot shares to themselves or their friends for the purpose of obtaining the control of the voting power in the company. If they do so, the court will declare the allotment invalid and rectify the register, and in the meantime will restrain the allottees from voting in respect of the shares thus allotted.[63] Directors may, however, purchase shares from existing members to increase their voting power.[64] But they must not, when allotting shares to themselves or their friends, make the terms or time of payment more favourable to themselves than to the general body of members or to the public unless the latter are expressly informed of the arrangement.[65] Any profit the directors make out of shares improperly allotted to themselves will belong to the

---

[56] [CA 1985, s 459].

[57] See **18.4** for the common-law controls on majority shareholders' voting, and **18.10** *et seq* for s 994.

[58] The general duties of directors were codified in the Companies Act 2006, albeit that cases determined under the common law will continue to be of relevance in interpreting the new statutory provisions. For directors' duties in general, see Chapter 16.

[59] Per Swinfen Eady J, *Percival v Wright* [1902] 2 Ch 421, at 425.

[60] [1902] AC 474, at 480 (HL).

[61] *York and North Midland Railway Co v Hudson* (1853) 16 Beav 485; *Parker v McKenna* (1874) 10 Ch App 96; *Shaw v Holland* [1900] 2 Ch 305 (CA).

[62] *Ving v Robertson and Woodcock* (1912) 56 SJ 412. Such conduct may now be actionable under the statutory derivative claim, however: see Chapter 18.

[63] *Fraser v Whalley* (1864) 2 H & M 10; *Punt v Symons & Co* [1903] 2 Ch 506; *Piercy v Mills Co* [1920] 1 Ch 77; *Hogg v Cramphorn* [1967] Ch 254; *Bamford v Bamford* [1969] 2 WLR 1107 (CA). See further, **16.4**.

[64] *North-West Transportation Co v Beatty* (1887) 12 App Cas 589 (PC).

[65] *Alexander v Automatic Telephone Co* [1900] 2 Ch 56 (CA).

company, or if they have retained the shares they will be liable for the difference between the nominal value and the market value at the time of allotment.[66]

7.7 THE CONTRACT OF ALLOTMENT

The contract to take shares is generally made by application and allotment, and for this purpose in public issues, a form of application for shares is usually issued with the prospectus, to be filled up by the applicant and left at the office of the company or with its bankers, accompanied by a deposit of a specified amount for each share applied for.[67]

7.8 LETTERS OF ALLOTMENT

Public companies do not, in making an allotment in response to an application, immediately issue a share certificate to the allottee. Instead, the allottee receives a letter of allotment which will be replaced by the share certificate (or its equivalent[68]) only when the full issue price has been paid.[69] The position of the allottee,[70] before his name is entered on the register of members and a share certificate is issued to him, is that he is a shareholder and enjoys the rights and is subject to the liabilities of such. However, he is not yet a member of the company and, unless the articles otherwise provide, he cannot exercise a membership right such as the right to vote or attend meetings.[71] However, as a shareholder, he is entitled to any dividends declared and must pay any calls that are made.[72] If the company is wound up he may be made a contributory if the contract of subscription is still enforceable against him.[73]

The Companies Act 2006 gives an allottee of shares the right to apply to the court to have his name entered on to the register[74] and to have a share certificate issued to him if the company fails to do so within 2 months of

---

[66] *Shaw v Holland* [1900] 2 Ch 305 (CA).

[67] However, a letter or even a verbal application for shares is perfectly valid: *Cookney's Case* (1859) 3 De G & J 170; *Bloxam's Case* (1864) 4 De GJ & S 447.

[68] When shares have been dematerialised certificates are replaced by electronic records of ownership. See **9.3.3**.

[69] As to share certificates, see **9.10**.

[70] Subscribers to the memorandum are members from the time of subscription: see **12.2**.

[71] See s 284, which confers the right on 'every member ... of one vote in respect of each share' in the case of companies 'originally having a share capital' insofar as the articles make no other provision.

[72] See *McEuen v West London Wharves & Warehouses Co* (1871) 6 Ch App 655, at 661–662.

[73] See *Re Direct Birmingham, Oxford, etc, Rly Co, ex parte Capper* (1851) 20 LJ Ch 148, at 151; *Re Pennant and Craigwen Mining Co, Fenn's Case* (1852) 1 Sm & G 26; and the definition of contributories in s 79 of the Insolvency Act 1986.

[74] Section 125(1) [CA 1985, s 359(1)].

allotment.[75] The company also has the right to register a subscriber if he (or his renouncee) does not apply for registration.[76] It should be noted that none of the above references to share certificates will apply if, as is normally the case for listed companies, the shares in question are 'dematerialised'.[77]

Nowadays a letter of allotment issued by a public company will always have attached to it a blank letter of renunciation and a registration application form. The former allows the original allottee to renounce his right to allotment in favour of whoever completes the appropriate registration application form.[78] However, the allottee may not wish to renounce and will then himself complete his registration application form and submit the letter of allotment to the company. Alternatively, the allottee may wish to renounce some shares in his allotment and retain others. He will do this by executing the letters of renunciation in respect of those shares he wishes to renounce and submitting the letter of allotment to the company. The company will then issue 'split letters of allotment' to the allottee and the renouncee.

It should be noted that where a public issue is made by way of 'offer for sale'[79] by an issuing house, the allotment is made by the issuing house and not the company. The applicant is sent in response to his application a 'letter of acceptance' (instead of an allotment letter). Until the allottee (or his renouncee) has his name entered on the register of members, his contract of subscription is with the issuing house, which may sue him if he is in default.

The usual practice in the case of allotments of shares by private companies is to dispense with the letter of allotment and, on allotment, to proceed at once to the issue of a share certificate and entry of the allottee's name on the register of members.[80] Sometimes public companies issue 'renounceable share certificates'. Within the period provided the renouncee may send it to the company to be entered on the register of members. An ordinary share certificate will then be sent to him. If the

---

[75]   Section 769 [CA 1985, s 185(1)].

[76]   *McEuen v West London Wharves and Warehouses Co* (1871) 6 Ch App 655.

[77]   See generally **9.3.3**. Regulation 38 of the Uncertificated Securities Regulations 2001, SI 2001/3755 (as amended) prohibits the issue of a share certificate in respect of dematerialised (uncertificated) shares.

[78]   The directors cannot refuse to accept a renouncee by relying on the article entitling them to refuse transfer because this does not amount to a transfer: *Re Pool Shipping Co* [1920] 1 Ch 251. An article might be so drawn as to allow the directors to refuse to register the renouncee, but this is not usually done.

[79]   See **19.8**.

[80]   Since shares in private companies are not as a rule freely transferable, there is no reason to issue renounceable allotment letters.

original allottee decides not to renounce, he may retain the original share certificate as permanent evidence of title by cancelling or destroying the attached letters of renunciation.[81]

7.9   RESTRICTIONS ON ALLOTMENT OF SHARES BY PUBLIC COMPANIES

There are two restrictions on the power of public companies to make a valid allotment of shares. First, s 578 of the Companies Act 2006[82] imposes a restriction on the allotment of any share capital of a public company. Such an allotment may not be made unless either that capital is subscribed in full, or the offer states that, even if the capital is not subscribed for in full, the amount of that capital subscribed for may be allotted in any event or in the event of the conditions specified in the offer being satisfied. Where such conditions are imposed, no allotment must be made unless those conditions are satisfied. The 'offer' document will, in the normal case of a public company offering shares to the public, be listing particulars or a prospectus subject to the requirements described in Chapter 19.

Section 578(2) and (3) provides for the consequences of allotting shares in breach of s 578(1). Thus all money must be repaid to applicants within 40 days after the making of the offer. Personal liability is imposed on directors if this money is not repaid within 48 days of the first making of the offer. The director has the defence open to him of proving that this was not due to any misconduct or negligence on his part. Such an allotment will also be voidable at the instance of the applicant under s 579.[83] Section 578 applies in the case of shares offered as wholly or partly payable otherwise than in cash as well as to shares offered for subscription in cash.[84]

The second restriction is that a public company may not allot a share except as paid up at least as to one-quarter of the nominal value of the share and any premium on it.[85] Where a public company allots a share in contravention of this provision, the share will be treated as if one-quarter of its nominal value together with the whole of any premium had been received. However, the allottee shall be liable to pay the company the minimum amount which, in respect of the share, should have been received less the value of any consideration actually supplied in payment (up to any extent) of the share and any premium on it; and the interest at

---

[81]   The reason for this practice is to save unnecessary expense, but it will only be used where the shares are to be paid in full at the time of allotment or in the case of a capitalisation issue.

[82]   [CA 1985, s 84].

[83]   [CA 1985, s 85].

[84]   Section 578(4).

[85]   Section 586(1) [CA 1985, s 101(1)]. This section does not apply to shares allotted in pursuance of an employees' share scheme: s 586(2).

the appropriate rate on the amount so payable.[86] This liability will not apply in relation to an allotment of a bonus share unless the allottee knew or ought to have known that the share was allotted in contravention of s 586.[87]

7.10   RETURN AND REGISTRATION OF ALLOTMENTS

By virtue of s 555,[88] whenever a company limited by shares or limited by guarantee and having a share capital makes any allotment of its shares, either upon public subscription or otherwise, it must within one month thereafter lodge with the registrar for registration a return of the allotments, which must contain certain 'prescribed information' and be accompanied by a statement of capital.[89] The statement of capital must state in respect of the company's share capital at the date to which the return is made up: the total number of shares in the company and their aggregate nominal value; for each class of shares, prescribed particulars of rights attached to those shares, total number of shares in that class and their aggregate nominal value; and the amount paid up and amount unpaid (if any) on each share (whether on account of the nominal value of the shares or by way of premium).[90]

The court may grant relief and extend the time for delivery of the document if the omission was accidental or due to inadvertence or if it is just and equitable to grant relief.[91]

Section 554 of the Companies Act 2006 sets out the requirement that all companies must register allotments of shares as soon as practicable and in any event within 2 months of the date of allotment, except where it has issued a share warrant in respect of the shares. Contravention is again a criminal offence.[92]

7.11   MAINTENANCE OF CAPITAL

As we have seen earlier in this chapter, although the raising of finance by the issue of shares is often the least important method, company law has always paid special attention to share capital and has developed sophisticated rules relating to what is called 'the raising and maintenance

---

[86] Section 586(3). As to the liability of subsequent holders, see s 605 [CA 1985, s 112]; see **7.14**.

[87] Section 586(4).

[88] [CA 1985, s 88].

[89] Section 555(3).

[90] Section 553(4). Fines may be imposed for default on an officer of the company 'knowingly a party to the default' – s 557(1). This means knowing of the default at the time, not subsequently: *Beck v Solicitor to Board of Trade* (1932) *The Times*, 23 April; see *Gore-Browne on Companies* (Jordans, 45th edn, loose-leaf) at 22 [12].

[91] Section 557(3) [CA 1985, s 88(5)].

[92] Section 554(3) and (4).

of capital'. It should be noted that the term 'capital' here means only capital in the narrow sense of money raised by the issue of shares and the assets (eg land, plant and machinery) acquired with that money. It bears no necessary relationship to the more normal use of that word in economic jargon, which is simply the net worth of a business, the amount by which the value of its assets exceeds its liabilities. The purpose of the legal rules is primarily to protect the creditors of a company limited by shares, whose existence is of course quite independent of any individual members of it, so that the creditors can be sure that there is something they can look to for payment of their debts. The fact that share capital may play a very small role in a company's financing means that these rules often have less significance than their volume and complexity would otherwise suggest.

The artificiality of these rules is compounded by the fact that there is no minimum share capital for private companies. Of course, public companies must have such a minimum,[93] but the figure of £50,000 – unchanged in the 2006 Act – is paltry indeed compared to the actual worth of the vast majority of public companies. Despite these points, detailed attention must be paid to the law relating to the raising and maintenance of capital. The regime was initially developed by the courts and the general principle established by the cases may be stated as requiring that a company with a share capital is bound to obtain a proper consideration for the shares that it issues and to refrain from handing back any or all of the fund so acquired to its members except by a lawful distribution of profits or a lawful reduction of capital. Although much of the detail is now consolidated and modified by statute, recent case-law has illustrated its vitality: denying the validity of 'unearned' remuneration awarded to a director who was also a shareholder;[94] striking down a sale of company A's assets to B, a company controlled by A's sole substantial shareholder, at a gross undervalue;[95] holding unlawful an agreement which sought to impose a liability to make a gratuitous payment at a future date when it was likely that the company would have no distributable profits;[96] and holding that the sale of a company's assets at undervalue to its shareholder in circumstances in which the director concerned subjectively believed that the transaction was at fair value did not amount to an unlawful distribution of capital.[97]

The statutory provisions are now largely contained in Parts 17, 18 and 23 of the Companies Act 2006. The comparable 1985 Act provisions represented a consolidation of part of the Companies Act 1980 which

---

[93] Section 763.

[94] *Re Halt Garage (1964) Ltd* [1982] 3 All ER 1045; see also *Re George Newman & Co* [1895] 1 Ch 974, at 686 and the discussion of corporate gifts at **6.3**.

[95] *Aveling Barford Ltd v Perion Ltd* (1989) 5 BCC 677.

[96] *Barclays Bank plc v British & Commonwealth Holdings plc* [1996] 1 BCLC 1 (CA).

[97] *Progress Property Company Limited v Moorgarth Group Limited* [2010] UKSC 55.

implemented the Second EC Directive,[98] the measure which necessitated the statutory enactment of the rules. Some of the Directive's provisions – and hence those of the 1985 Act – appeared to be rather pointless in practice.[99] Some simplification of the rules occurred in the aftermath of the Companies Act 2006, albeit that the reform was not perhaps as radical as might have been envisaged. The issues surrounding the nature and rights of shares themselves and the ways in which a company may reorganise its capital structure are considered in the next chapter.

7.12   PRICE OF ALLOTTED SHARES

The principle of maintenance of capital requires that as a general rule the total consideration received by a company in return for each share allotted by it must not be less than the nominal amount, or 'par value', of the share; that is, shares must not be allotted at a discount.[100] The basis of the rule is that a company should not overstate the size of its share capital, which is the money paid to it in return for shares. This rule applies whether the shares are issued fully paid or partly paid in the first instance.[101] It was, however, relaxed by the Companies Act 2006 in one specific instance, namely where commission or brokerage is paid under s 553.[102] Except in this case, where shares are allotted at a discount, the allottee is liable to pay the company the amount of the discount and interest thereon at the appropriate rate.[103] A subsequent holder of the shares is jointly and severally liable with the allottee unless he is a purchaser for value without actual notice of the issue at a discount at the time of the purchase or he derived title, directly or indirectly, from such a purchaser.[104] Sections 580 and 588 impose this liability upon an actual allottee and the subsequent holders described. It seems, therefore, that a mere contract to issue or allot shares at a discount is void and unenforceable under previous authority.[105]

Any liability to pay the amount of a discount may be enforced in a winding-up for the benefit of creditors or other shareholders,[106] as the case may be, but the mere fact that some members received their shares at a discount does not entitle other members holding shares properly issued

---

[98]   (1977) OJ L26/1.

[99]   See Ferran 'Creditors' Interests and "Core" Company Law' (1999) 20 Co Law 314; Armour 'Share Capital and Credit Protection: Efficient Rules for a Modern Company Law' (2000) 63 MLR 355.

[100] Section 580 [CA 1985, s 100] confirming *Ooregum Gold Mining Co of India v Roper* [1892] AC 125 (HL).

[101] As to the minimum price payable on allotment of a public company's shares under s 586, see **7.9**. As to the minimum capital requirements for public companies, see **4.2**.

[102] [CA 1985, s 97].

[103] Section 580(2) [CA 1985, s 100(2)]. The appropriate rate for interest is 5% per annum or such other sum as is specified by statutory instrument: s 592 [CA 1985, s 107].

[104] Section 588 [CA 1985, s 112(1)].

[105] *Re Almada & Tirito Co* (1888) 38 Ch D 415 (CA).

[106] *Welton v Saffery* [1897] AC 299 (HL).

to bring a winding-up petition.[107] As an alternative to these remedies, the company may make the directors who were responsible for the shares issue liable to pay the amount of the discount as damages for breach of duty.[108]

The rule that a proper consideration must be obtained for issued shares is applicable in a wide range of situations which clearly survive the statutory confirmation of the principle. For example, the issue of £1 debentures at a discount with a provision that they may be exchanged for fully paid £1 shares immediately or at any time before a fixed date is unlawful, as the shares would be issued at a discount.[109] A company cannot issue 200 £1 shares in satisfaction of a debt of £100,[110] nor can it allot 200 £1 shares for 50p each in consideration of the allottee making a loan of £100 to the company.[111]

The rule does not go so far as to require that shares must be paid for in cash. That payment in money's worth is sufficient is confirmed in respect of both nominal value and premium by s 582.[112] Furthermore, s 583 provides that payment in cash includes the following: cash in foreign currency; cheques received by the company which the directors have no reason for suspecting will not be paid; the release of a liability of the company for a liquidated sum;[113] and an undertaking to pay cash to the company at a future date.[114] However, apart from these cases, the Companies Act 2006 provides important qualifications in respect of the payment for shares in public companies by non-cash consideration. Thus, this question must be considered separately in respect of private and public companies respectively.

7.13 ALLOTMENTS OF SHARES FOR NON-CASH CONSIDERATION BY PRIVATE COMPANIES

As far as private companies are concerned, any valuable consideration *prima facie* suffices – for example, an agreement to render services, as by becoming manager for five years.[115]

However, a company cannot by a contract make that which is not a good consideration in law a valid payment for shares – for example, past

---

[107] *Re Pioneers of Mashonaland Syndicate* [1893] 1 Ch 731.

[108] *Hirsche v Sims* [1894] AC 654.

[109] *Mosley v Koffyfontein Mines Ltd (No 1)* [1904] 2 Ch 108 (CA).

[110] *Re Wragg Ltd* [1897] 1 Ch 796, 831 (CA).

[111] *Re James Pitkin & Co Ltd* [1916] WN 112.

[112] [CA 1985, s 99(1)]. 'Money's worth' is expressly stated to include goodwill and know-how.

[113] This does not cover the case where a price for property is stated to be satisfied by an allotment of shares: *Re Bradford Investments plc (No 2)* [1991] BCLC 688.

[114] [CA 1985, s 378].

[115] *Re Theatrical Trust Ltd, Chapman's Case* [1895] 1 Ch 771.

services for which the company was not liable to pay.[116] But if the consideration is in kind, the court will not inquire whether it was really of a value equal to the nominal amount of shares issued, unless the consideration was illusory or had an obvious money value showing that a discount had been allowed.[117] Thus, a private company can agree to purchase property and pay for services at any price it thinks proper, and may make the payment in shares, provided that it does so honestly and not disingenuously, and has not been so imposed as to be entitled to repudiate the bargain.[118] The bargain must, however, represent a real valuation of the property transferred as an equivalent for the shares issued. Thus, if the directors have not considered at all whether the property and the shares are of equivalent value, the issue is bad.[119]

7.14 ALLOTMENTS OF SHARES FOR NON-CASH CONSIDERATION BY PUBLIC COMPANIES

In accordance with the requirements of the Second EC Directive on Company Law, the Companies Act 2006 contained detailed provisions governing the payment for shares allotted by public companies otherwise than in cash. The 2006 Act provisions substantially repeated those previously set out in the 1985 Act.[120]

In one case, payment other than in cash is totally prohibited. This is where shares are taken by a subscriber to the memorandum by virtue of an undertaking by him in the memorandum; the nominal value and any premium on the shares must be paid up in cash.[121]

In the other cases described below, the Act imposes various sanctions for breach.[122] Criminal liability to pay a fine may be imposed on the company and on every officer in default.[123] The recipient of the shares is immediately liable to pay in cash[124] the difference between any cash actually paid and the nominal value of, plus any premium payable on, the shares. A subsequent holder of the shares is jointly and severally liable

---

[116] *Re Eddystone Marine Insurance Co* [1893] 3 Ch 9 (CA). In Scotland, past consideration may be good: *Park Business Interiors Ltd v Park* [1990] BCC 914.

[117] *Re Wragg Ltd* [1897] 1 Ch 796.

[118] Ibid.

[119] *Tintin Exploration Syndicate Ltd v Sandys* (1947) 177 LT 412.

[120] As to what is payment in cash, see s 583, discussed in **7.12**. The payment of, or an undertaking to pay, cash to any person other than the company is non-cash consideration.

[121] Section 584 [CA 1985, s 106].

[122] Note that where the consideration is an undertaking caught by the provisions described in **7.14.1** and **7.14.2**, the company can still enforce the undertaking: s 591 [CA 1985, s 115(1)].

[123] Section 590 [CA 1985, s 114].

[124] See *Re Bradford Investments plc* [1990] BCC 740, where it was held that, as a result, until cash is paid or the recipient of the shares is relieved from liability, under standard articles (see, now art 41 of the Model Articles for public companies) the recipient will be disenfranchised in respect of the shares.

with an original recipient, unless he is a purchaser for value from him without actual notice[125] of the contravention at the time of purchase, or unless he derived title, directly or indirectly, from such a purchaser.[126] The court can grant relief from civil liability in accordance with the conditions laid down in s 589.[127] Among other things,[128] these conditions impose a requirement to have regard to the principle of capital maintenance and to whether or not the company has benefited from the transaction which was in breach of the statute. It has been held that very good reasons will be required before the court can accept that it is just and equitable to exempt an applicant from liability, notwithstanding that the company has not received sufficient value,[129] but relief is more than likely to be given if the company has in fact received good value for shares, notwithstanding a failure to observe the valuation requirements described in **7.14.3**.[130]

7.14.1 Prohibited non-cash consideration

One form of non-cash consideration is prohibited by s 585(1).[131] This is consideration which consists of an undertaking to do work or perform services for the company or any other person, whether in respect of payment of the nominal value of shares or any premium payable on them.

7.14.2 Future non-cash consideration

By s 587,[132] it is prohibited for a public company to allot shares as fully or partly paid up, whether as to their nominal value or in respect of any premium payable on them, other than for cash, if the consideration for the allotment is or includes an undertaking which is to be or may be performed more than five years after the allotment.[133]

---

[125] This means actual notice of the facts constituting the breach; ignorance of the statutory requirements is no defence: *System Control plc v Munro Corporate plc* [1990] BCLC 659.

[126] Section 588 (1) and (2) [CA 1985, s 112(1) and (3)].

[127] [CA 1985, s 113].

[128] The list of matters in s 589 to which the court should have regard is not exhaustive: *Re Bradford Investments plc (No 2)* [1991] BCLC 688 (determined in relation to the equivalent s 113 of CA 1985).

[129] *Re Bradford Investments plc (No 2)*, above.

[130] *Re Ossory Estates plc* [1988] BCLC 213.

[131] [CA 1985, s 99(2)].

[132] [CA 1985, s 102].

[133] Section 587(1). Any variation of a contract to allot shares, or an ancillary contract relating to payment in respect of those shares, which originally complies with subsection (1), which purports to vary its terms so that the subsection would have been broken had the variation been in the original contract, is void; and this applies to the variation by a public company of the terms of such a contract entered into before it was re-registered as a public company (s 587(3)).

7.14.3   Valuation of non-cash consideration

In those cases where it is permissible for a public company to allot shares for a non-cash consideration, ie in cases other than those just described, s 593 imposes a general requirement of valuation of the consideration.[134]

For the allotment to be valid, a report on the value of the consideration must have been made to the company within the 6 months preceding the allotment, and a copy of the report sent to the proposed allottee. The requirement does not apply, however, to the following:

(1)   a bonus or capitalisation issue of shares (s 593(2));

(2)   allotments in connection with takeovers and mergers falling within the terms of s 594;

(3)   allotments in connection with a proposed merger within the terms of s 595.

The provisions of ss 1150–1153 (general provisions as to independent valuation and report) apply to the valuation and report required by s 593.[135] These provisions need to be read in tandem with s 596 to build up a full picture of the valuation and report requirements in this context.[136] The valuation and report must be made by an independent person qualified at the time of the report to be appointed or to continue to be auditor of the company, whom the Act refers to as the valuer.[137] However, he may arrange for or accept a valuation of the consideration or part of it made by another person, eg a surveyor, where it appears to him to be reasonable for it to be made by that person and where that person appears to him to have the requisite knowledge and experience and is not an officer or employee[138] of the company or its subsidiary or holding company or of another subsidiary of the company's holding company or a partner or employee of such an officer or servant. Where the consideration or part thereof is valued by someone other than the valuer himself, the latter's report must state that fact and shall also state the former's name and relevant knowledge and experience and describe the extent of the consideration valued by the other person, the valuation method deployed and date of valuation.[139]

---

[134] [CA 1985, s 103]. This applies whether the shares are fully or partly paid up and the requirement also applies when an allotment of shares is mixed with other consideration given by the company in exchange for non-cash consideration. Here the valuer must also value the other consideration to determine what proportion of the consideration provided by the allottee is attributable to the shares.

[135] Section 596(1).

[136] [CA 1985, s 108].

[137] Section 1150(1) [CA 1985, s 108(1)]. This can clearly be the company's own auditor. As to who is qualified to be an auditor, see **14.28.3**.

[138] Other than an auditor; see s 1150 (3) [CA 1985, s 108(3)].

[139] Section 1151(4).

The valuer's report must state:

(1) the nominal value of the shares to be wholly or partly paid for by the consideration in question;

(2) the amount of any premium payable on the shares;

(3) the description of the consideration and of that part of it which he himself has valued, the method used to value it and the date of the valuation; and

(4) the extent to which the nominal value of the shares and any premium are to be treated as paid up on allotment by the consideration and in cash.[140]

Where the valuation was made by a delegate, the report must also state this fact. The name of the delegate and the knowledge and experience he had to carry out the valuation must also be given. The report must describe so much of the consideration as was valued by the delegate, the method used to value it and the date of valuation.[141]

In addition, the report must contain, or be accompanied by a note containing, statements to the following effect:

(1) in the case of a valuation made by a delegate, that it appeared to the valuer reasonable to arrange for it to be so made or to accept a valuation so made;

(2) that the method of valuation was reasonable in all circumstances;

(3) that it appears to the valuer that there has been no material change in the value of the consideration in question since the valuation; and

(4) that on the basis of the valuation, the value of the consideration, together with any cash by which the nominal value of the shares or any premium payable on them is to be paid up, is not less than so much of the aggregate of the nominal value and the premium as is treated as paid up by the consideration and any such cash.[142]

Any person making a valuation or report under s 593 is by s 1153 given the right to require from the officers of the company such information and explanation as he thinks necessary.[143]

---

[140] Section 596(2) [CA 1985, s 108(4)].

[141] Section 1150(4) [CA 1985, s108(5)].

[142] Section 596(3) [CA 1985, s 108(6)].

[143] It is an offence for an officer to mislead the valuer: s 1153(2) and (3).

A copy of any report must be delivered to the Registrar of Companies for registration at the same time as the return of the allotment of the shares concerned is made under s 555.[144]

By way of comment, it may be thought that the provisions described in this section were a complex overreaction to a not very real problem, given that the shares of many public companies are or will be traded on The Stock Exchange or dealt in under the auspices of some other body recognised under the Financial Services and Markets Act 2000, the rules of which should ensure the full disclosure of all relevant information. Like some other measures emanating from the Second Directive, they have complicated company law without any apparent benefit thereto and it is a pity that these considerations were not in the minds of those negotiating or implementing the Directive. The relevant provisions were largely retained in the 2006 Act and the fact that there was little dilution of these unnecessary complexities in the company law reform process may be seen as an opportunity missed.[145]

7.14.4   Non-cash assets acquired from subscribers and others

Sections 598–604 deal with certain agreements which may be entered into by public companies which, although they are not necessarily confined to allotments of shares, will often be so concerned and which it is convenient to describe here.[146] The sections impose valuation, report and public filing requirements similar to those just described,[147] where a public company enters into an agreement with an appropriate person for the transfer by him to the company or another person of one or more non-cash assets[148] equal to one-tenth or more of the company's issued share capital within what is described as the 'initial period'.

Where a company is formed as a public company, the appropriate person is any subscriber to its memorandum and the initial period is 2 years from the issue of the company's trading certificate.[149] Where a joint-stock company is registered as a public company, or a private company is re-registered as a public company, the appropriate person is any member of the company at the time of registration or re-registration and the initial period is 2 years from the date of registration or re-registration.

These sections are open to even more criticism than the related ones on valuation discussed above. Their purpose is presumably the prevention of

---

[144] Section 597(2) [CA 1985, s 111]; see **7.10**.

[145] See, also, Sealy *Company Law and Commercial Reality* (Sweet & Maxwell, 1984) pp 68 and 82.

[146] This is a very brief account of the provisions; for more detail, see *Gore-Browne on Companies* (Jordans, 45th edn, loose-leaf) at 24 [9].

[147] Note that both valuations will be required when a company is allotting shares as all or part of the consideration for the transfer of a non-cash asset to it.

[148] Property or interests in property: s 1163 [CA 1985, s 739].

[149] Under s 761; see **4.7**.

fraud by promoters of public companies, but they can be easily evaded. Public companies are never in practice formed as such and hence the provision as to their subscribers to the memorandum is in effect redundant. When public companies are converted from private companies, the sections apply, as described above, only to members at the time of registration or re-registration; an intending fraudster need only ensure that he does not become a member of a company at the appropriate time.

7.15   ISSUE OF SHARES AT A PREMIUM

It is very common for shares in a company to be issued in return for a consideration greater than the par or nominal value of the shares, whether the company is a public company making a public issue or a private company formed with a £100 share capital which is issued in return for the transfer of property worth much more than £100. The fact that such a premium is obtainable does not of itself impose a duty on the company to demand it.[150] However, if shares are issued at a premium, whether for a cash or non-cash consideration,[151] *prima facie* s 610 of the Companies Act 2006[152] requires the company to transfer a sum equal to the aggregate amount or value of the premiums on those shares to a share premium account which, like issued share capital, must appear on the liabilities side of the balance sheet.[153] In certain cases where shares are issued in return for shares or in other consideration from another company, s 610 does not apply by reason of ss 611–615, which are described below.

Where s 610 does apply, the share premium account is to some extent treated as if it were share capital so that the provisions regarding reduction of capital apply to it and it cannot be used to finance a payment of dividends.[154] However, it may be applied:

(1)   to finance an issue of fully paid bonus shares (though not a partly paid issue nor to finance an issue of debentures);

(2)   in writing off the expenses of, or commission paid on any issue of those shares.[155]

---

[150]   *Hilder v Dexter* [1902] AC 474 (HL). But it may be a breach of duty by the directors who fail to obtain such a premium; see **7.6**.

[151]   *Henry Head & Co Ltd v Ropner Holdings Ltd* [1952] Ch 124; *Shearer v Bercain* [1980] 3 All ER 295.

[152]   [CA 1985, s 130].

[153]   See Chapter 14.

[154]   Although, using the reduction of capital procedure (see Chapter 8), a company may be able to cancel the share premium account and in effect convert it into distributable profits: *Quayle Munro Ltd, Petitioners* [1994] 1 BCLC 410.

[155]   Section 610(2). It may also be used by private companies making a lawful purchase of shares out of capital under the provisions of the 2006 Act; see **7.17**. Following the recommendations of the Company Law Reform Steering Group (CLRSG) (see *Completing the Structure* para 7.8 and *Modernising Company Law* (Cmnd 5553) paras 76

7.15.1 Relief from s 610

In *Shearer v Bercain Ltd*,[156] it was clearly established that the obligation to create a share premium account applied wherever a company in fact acquired assets worth more than the par value of the shares issued, and particularly in the case of a merger of companies by exchange of shares where the shares acquired by the new holding company were worth more than the par value of the shares issued by it.[157] This decision, though logically unimpeachable on the construction of what is now s 610, was felt to cause unnecessary difficulties in certain contexts, and mergers by exchange of shares were frequently effected since the introduction of what is now s 610 (at the time of *Shearer* s 56 of the 1948 Act) on the basis of a different interpretation.[158] As a result, the Companies Act 2006 retained a number of provisions for exemption from the need to establish a share premium account in limited circumstances previously set out in the Companies Act 1985. These are principally mergers by exchanges of equity shares which satisfy the provisions of s 612 and capital reconstructions within a group which satisfy the requirements of s 611.[159]

7.16 ACQUISITION BY A COMPANY OF RIGHTS IN RESPECT OF ITS OWN SHARES

One of the most fundamental common law principles relating to the maintenance of capital was that which made it illegal for a limited company to purchase its own shares.[160] To have allowed otherwise would in many cases have permitted a company unilaterally to reduce the capital fund available for creditors. The prohibition is now in statutory form (Companies Act 2006, s 658(1)) and applies to the acquisition by a company of its own shares by purchase, subscription or otherwise except, *inter alia*, when fully paid shares are acquired other than for valuable consideration.[161] This exception permits, for example, a company acting as trustee to hold its own shares in that capacity, provided that someone else paid for them. An acquisition in breach of s 658 is void and the company and every defaulting officer is liable to a criminal penalty.[162] Section 658 does not apply where a company acquires the whole of the

---

and 77) the share premium account can no longer be used for the writing off of expenses or discount in relation to debentures issued nor in respect of any premium payable on redemption of any debentures.

[156] [1980] 3 All ER 295.

[157] It was also decided that the pre-acquisition profits of the acquired company were to be treated as capital, not profit.

[158] For an account of the debate that *Shearer v Bercain* stimulated, see (1980) 1 Co Law 293.

[159] For detail, see *Gore-Browne on Companies* (Jordans, 45th edn, loose-leaf) at 24 [13]–24 [19A].

[160] *Trevor v Whitworth* (1887) 12 App Cas 409 (HL).

[161] [CA 1985, s 143(1)].

[162] See s 658(2). In *Vision Express (UK) Ltd v Wilson* [1995] 2 BCLC 419, part of a *Tomlin* order under which a company was to purchase all the rights in shares in itself held by the other party was void for infringing the corresponding s 143 of CA 1985.

issued share capital of another company where the sole asset of the latter is a shareholding in the first company.[163]

However, shortly after the introduction of what is now s 658, the 1981 Act made substantial inroads into the prohibition and, as will be seen in the following sections, statute does permit the purchase by a company of its own shares under stringent conditions. There are other exceptions to s 658[164] covering reductions of capital,[165] purchases pursuant to court orders under various sections of the Companies Act 2006, and forfeitures and surrenders of shares for failure to pay calls.[166]

The basic prohibition in s 658 cannot be evaded by the issue of shares to someone acting as nominee for the company or by such a nominee acquiring partly paid shares in the company. In most cases, by s 660,[167] the nominee is deemed to hold the shares on his own account and is liable to pay for them.[168] However, this does not apply where the company does not have any beneficial interest in such shares, for example, because it did not provide or agree to provide any consideration. In addition, if the nominee of a public company acquires shares in the company with financial assistance given to him directly by the company, the shares must be disposed of or cancelled under s 662.[169]

A nominee for a company has always been able to acquire from a member, and hold, already issued fully paid shares in the company – provided that the company provides no consideration.[170] If, however, the company is a public company, the regime of s 662[171] applies and the nominee cannot exercise any voting rights attached to the shares.[172]

7.17 THE REDEMPTION OR PURCHASE OF A COMPANY'S OWN SHARES

The Companies Act 1981 first introduced a number of important provisions that allowed companies to purchase their own shares and, in respect of private companies, permit this to be financed out of capital. Although in part these represented a considerable departure from traditional principles of maintenance of capital, they were to some extent

---

[163] *Acatos & Hutcheson plc v Watson* [1995] BCC 446.
[164] See s 659(2) [CA 1985, s 143(3)].
[165] See **8.13**.
[166] See **8.14**.
[167] [CA 1985, s 144].
[168] See s 661(2) which also provides that if the nominee fails to pay a call, then the subscribers to the memorandum or the directors, as the case may be, are liable to pay it.
[169] [CA 1985, s 146]. See **8.14**.
[170] *Kirby v Wilkins* [1929] 2 Ch 444; *Re Castiglione's Will Trusts* [1958] Ch 549. This course is unnecessary now that s 658, as described above, permits the company itself to hold such shares.
[171] See **8.14**.
[172] Section 662(5).

only an extension of a longstanding provision which allowed companies to issue preference shares which would be redeemable by the company.[173]

There seems little doubt that the idea underlying these provisions was worthwhile, since there is no reason why a purchase of its own shares by a company should necessarily infringe the capital maintenance principle and this is certainly not the case if the consideration is not provided out of capital, and it may be economically advantageous for unwanted capital to be freed in this way. However, it was arguable that the legislature was far too cautious. The Companies Act 1985 provisions were complex and the exercise of the power to redeem or purchase surrounded by restrictive requirements. Some welcome relaxation of the relevant rules, however, resulted in the Companies Act 2006 on the back of proposals made by the CLRSG.

7.17.1　Redeemable shares

By s 684(1), a limited company having a share capital may, subject to the conditions laid down, issue shares which are to be redeemed or are liable to be redeemed at the option of the company or the shareholder. While a private company may limit or exclude the issue of redeemable shares in its articles,[174] a public limited company may only issue redeemable shares if it is authorised to this effect in its articles.[175] No redeemable shares may, however, be issued by a company unless it has at the time issued shares which are not redeemable. The directors of a limited company may determine the terms, conditions and manner of the redemption of shares if they are authorised to do so by either the articles of the company or by resolution of the company.[176] If directors are so authorised, such authorisation must take place before the shares are allotted and the statement of capital required to accompany such shares must set out the terms, conditions and manner of redemption.[177]

The conditions of redemption are as follows.

(1)　Redeemable shares may be redeemed only if they are fully paid.[178]

(2)　Subject to any agreement between the company and the holder of the shares in question, the amount payable on redemption may be paid on a date later than the redemption date, but in the absence of such agreement must be paid for on redemption.[179]

---

[173]　Section 58 of the Companies Act 1948.

[174]　Section 684(2).

[175]　Section 684(3).

[176]　Section 685(1). A resolution in this sense may be an ordinary resolution even if it has the effect that it alters the articles – s 685(2).

[177]　Section 685(3).

[178]　Section 686(1).

[179]　Section 686(2) and (3); *Pena v Dale EWHC 1065 (Ch)*, [2004] 2 BCLC 508, at 107–114 for the default position.

(3) The redeemable shares of public companies may be redeemed only out of distributable profits[180] or out of the proceeds of a fresh issue of shares[181] made for the purposes of the redemption, and except as described below, any premium payable on redemption must be paid out of distributable profits.

Private companies may additionally redeem shares out of capital.[182]

Where redeemable shares were issued at a premium, any premium payable on their redemption may be paid out of the proceeds of a fresh issue of shares made for the purposes of the redemption up to an amount equal to the lesser of: (a) the aggregate of the premiums received by the company on the issue of the shares redeemed; and (b) the current amount of the company's share premium account (including any sum transferred to that account in respect of premiums on the new shares). In such a case, the amount of the company's share premium account must be reduced by a sum corresponding (or by sums in the aggregate corresponding) to the amount of any payment made under this provision out of the proceeds of the issue of the new shares.

Shares redeemed under s 684 must be treated as cancelled on redemption and the amount of the company's issued capital[183] is diminished by the nominal value of the shares.[184] However, capital is maintained either because the proceeds of a fresh issue are used or by the requirement to create a capital redemption reserve.[185] Where in pursuance of the section a company is about to redeem any shares, it has power to issue shares up to the nominal amount of the shares to be redeemed as if those shares had never been issued.

Notice of each redemption accompanied by a statement of capital must be given to the registrar within one month, failing which, the company and every officer in default is liable to a default fine.[186]

7.17.2 Purchase by a company of its own shares

Section 690 gives companies limited by shares, or limited by guarantee and having a share capital, the general power to purchase their own shares, including any redeemable shares, provided that a purchase must not result in there being no member holding other than redeemable shares in the company or shares held as treasury shares. This power may,

---

[180] Section 687(2)(a). That is profits distributable under s 830, as to which, see **7.21** *et seq*. A redemption (or purchase) of shares made when a company does not have distributable profits is invalid: *BDG Roof-Bond Ltd v Douglas and Others* [2000] 1 BCLC 401.

[181] Section 687(2)(b).

[182] Section 687(1). As to private companies, see **7.17.10–7.17.13**.

[183] But not its authorised capital.

[184] Section 688.

[185] As to the capital redemption reserve, see **7.17.9**.

[186] Section 698.

however, be restricted or prohibited by a provision in the company's articles. Purchases of companies' own shares may take place on the same conditions and with the same consequences as the redemption of redeemable shares, as described above.[187]

However, the exercise of a purchase of a company's own shares is governed by strict additional requirements, in terms of the authority which must be obtained for particular purchases, the publicity which must be given and certain other matters. These are described in the following sections. They are not purely procedural and for the benefit of current members, but also exist to protect creditors; there is thus no basis for waiving them.[188]

A purchase by a company of shares that are to be held by the company as treasury shares is subject to additional provisions.[189] Treasury shares are qualifying shares[190] purchased by a company out of distributable profits that are held by the company pending future sale, transfer or cancellation of the shares.[191] The requirement that shares redeemed or purchased by a company be cancelled does not apply to treasury shares.[192] The company must be entered on the register as the owner of treasury shares and therefore cannot hold them through nominees. Dividend and voting rights associated with treasury shares are suspended.[193] Proceeds of the sale of treasury shares are treated as a realised profit to the extent that they are less than or equal to the purchase price, while proceeds above that level must be transferred to the share premium account.[194]

7.17.3   Authority required for off-market purchases

Following its 1985 predecessor, the 2006 Act drew a distinction between what are described as 'off-market purchases' and 'market purchases' of a company's own shares. Off-market purchases are defined as purchases otherwise than on a recognised investment exchange and purchases on a recognised investment exchange but not subject to a marketing arrangement on that exchange.[195] Shares are subject to such a marketing arrangement if either: (a) they are listed under Part VI of the Financial

---

[187] See ss 692 and 693.

[188] See *Re RW Peak (Kings Lynn) Ltd* [1998] 1 BCLC 193, especially at 204–205, where the informal consent of all shareholders was not sufficient to validate an off-market purchase under s 164 of CA 1985 (now s 694) (see below).

[189] Holding shares in treasury provides an additional tool to companies for managing their financing requirements. See further Morse 'The introduction of treasury shares into English law and practice' (2004) JBL 303. Note that the limit on the percentage of shares that can be held in treasury was abolished in 2009.

[190] See s 724 [CA 1985, s 162 (as amended)].

[191] See ss 724, 727 and 729 [CA 1985, s 162 (as amended) and CA 1985, ss 162A and 162D].

[192] Section 706 [CA 1985, s 162(2B) (as amended)].

[193] Section 726 [CA 1985, s162C].

[194] Section 731 [CA 1985, s 162F]. Treatment of proceeds as distributable profits recognises the origin of the purchase funds as distributable profits.

[195] Section 693(2) [CA 1985, s 163(1)].

Services and Markets Act 2000;[196] or (b) the company has been accorded facilities for dealings in those shares to take place on that investment exchange without prior permission for individual transactions from the authority governing that investment exchange and without limit as to the time during which these facilities are to be available. Principally, therefore, purchases by private and non-listed public companies and over-the-counter purchases by listed companies are 'off-market' purchases.

An off-market purchase may be made only if the terms of the contract of purchase are authorised before the company enters into the contract by a special resolution of the company[197] or if the company has previously authorised a contingent purchase contract under s 694(3) (as described in **7.17.4**). The authority can be varied, revoked or from time to time renewed by special resolution. In the case of a public company, the special resolution conferring or renewing authority must specify a date for its expiry which must be within five years[198] of the date of the resolution.

If a member (or his proxy) whose shares are the subject of a proposal to purchase them votes on the special resolution, on a poll or otherwise, his votes must not be counted. Notwithstanding anything in a company's articles, any member of the company (or his proxy) may demand a poll on the question whether any such resolution shall be passed.[199]

No such resolution is effective unless a copy of the proposed contract of purchase, if it is in writing, or a written memorandum of its terms, if it is not in writing, is available for inspection by members of the company both at the registered office of the company for at least 15 days before the date of the meeting at which the resolution is passed, and at the meeting itself.[200] Any memorandum must include the names of any members holding shares to which the contract relates, and any copy of the contract must have annexed to it a written memorandum specifying any such names which do not appear in the contract itself.

A variation of an existing approved contract may be made by the company but only if authorised by special resolution. The same requirements as described above apply to such a special resolution and a copy or memorandum of the original contract (and any previous variations) must be available for inspection as well as a copy or memorandum of the proposed varied contract.

---

[196] See Chapter 19.

[197] Section 694(2) [CA 1985, s 164]. The provisions are modified if authority is conferred by a statutory written resolution (see **13.5**), rather than by special resolution.

[198] Section 694(5) as amended by the Companies (Share Capital and Acquisition by Company of its Own Shares) Regulations 2009, SI 2009/2022, reg 4. The previous limit was 18 months.

[199] Section 695.

[200] The requirement here is modified where the statutory written resolution procedure is used.

No specific or civil penalties are prescribed if the requirements of s 694 are not complied with, but a contract purportedly entered into in pursuance of a resolution which is not effective according to the section is void as a contract to perform an unlawful act, namely an unauthorised purchase by a company of its own shares, and the criminal penalties specified in s 658 will apply.[201] An agreement between the company and a shareholder for the purchase of his shares is not enforceable until it has been sanctioned under s 694,[202] but specific performance of such a contract may be granted subject to such sanction.[203]

7.17.4   Conditional contracts

An alternative procedure in respect of off-market purchases is provided for by s 694(3). This allows the company to enter into a contract not amounting to an actual contract to purchase but under which the company may, subject to any conditions, become entitled or obliged to purchase its own shares, in other words, an option.

The purchase of shares pursuant to such a contract may be made only if the terms of the proposed contract are authorised by special resolution before the company enters into the contract, and the relevant provisions of s 694 (described in **7.17.3**) apply to such a resolution and to variations of existing conditional contracts.

7.17.5   Authority required for market purchase

A market purchase is defined by s 693(4)[204] as a purchase made on a recognised investment exchange other than a purchase on an investment exchange of shares not subject to a marketing arrangement. Most purchases by companies whose shares are listed on a stock market will be market purchases.

Section 701[205] requires such a purchase to have the prior authority of the company in general meeting, that is by ordinary resolution only.[206] The resolution may confer general authority to purchase the company's own shares of any particular class or description, and the authority may be unconditional or conditional. By s 701(3) and (5), the authorising resolution must do three things.

(1)   It must specify the maximum number of shares authorised to be acquired.

---

[201]   *Re RW Peak (Kings Lynn) Ltd* [1998] 1 BCLC 193.
[202]   *Western v Rigblast Holdings Ltd* 1989 GWD 23–950.
[203]   *Vision Express (UK) Ltd v Wilson* [1998] BCC 173.
[204]   [CA 1985, s 163(3)].
[205]   [CA 1985, s 166].
[206]   Listed companies are required by ABI guidelines to adopt a special resolution in these circumstances. See Ferran, footnote 2 at p 167.

(2) It must determine both the maximum and minimum prices which may be paid for those shares either by specifying a particular sum or by providing a basis or formula for calculating the amount of the price in question without reference to any person's discretion or opinion.

(3) It must specify a date within five years[207] on which the authority is to expire. Note though that a purchase can be made outside the time-limit, where the contract was concluded before it and the terms of the authority permitted the company to make a contract which could or might be executed wholly or partly after the authority expires.

Subject to these requirements, any authority may be varied, revoked or renewed from time to time by the company in general meeting.

A printed copy of any resolution conferring, varying, revoking or renewing authority within s 701 must be forwarded to the registrar within 15 days.

7.17.6 Assignments and releases of a company's right to purchase its own shares

The rights acquired by a company under any contract to purchase its own shares, whether a contract for an off-market purchase approved under s 694 or a contract for a market purchase authorised under s 701, cannot be assigned.[208]

If a company proposes to release its rights under a contract for an off-market purchase approved under s 694, the terms of the proposed release agreement must be authorised by special resolution before the company enters into the agreement. In the absence of such a resolution, any such agreement to release rights is void.[209]

7.17.7 Payments other than of the purchase price

Certain payments which may be made by companies in connection with a purchase of their own shares, other than payments of the purchase price for the shares, must be made out of distributable profits.[210] The payments in question are any payments made by a company in consideration of:

---

[207] The previous limit of 18 months was extended to five years by way of the Companies (Share Capital and Acquisition by Company of its Own Shares) Regulations 2009, SI 2009/2022, reg 4.

[208] Section 704 [CA 1985, s 167(1)].

[209] Section 700 [CA 1985, s 167(2)].

[210] Section 705 [CA 1985, s 168]. As to distributable profits, see **7.21.2**.

(1) acquiring any right to purchase its own shares under a contingent purchase contract;

(2) the variation of any contract or contingent purchase contract for an off-market purchase of its own shares;

(3) the release of any of the company's obligations to purchase any of its own shares under any contract for an off-market or market purchase of its own shares.

If any such payment is not made out of distributable profits, a purchase of shares within (1) above and a purchase of shares following a variation within (2) above is unlawful, and a release within (3) above is void.

7.17.8 Publicity for purchases

The requirements that companies deliver a return of purchases of their own shares to the registrar are contained in s 707.[211] It should be noted that private companies taking advantage of the power to purchase out of capital are subject to the additional requirements described in **7.17.10**. Within 28 days of the date of delivery of the shares to the company, it must deliver to the registrar a return in the prescribed form stating with respect to shares of each class purchased the number and nominal value of those shares and the date they were delivered to the company. A single return may cover shares delivered on different dates and under different contracts of purchase. The return sent by a public company must also state the aggregate amount paid by the company for all the shares covered by the return and the maximum and minimum prices paid in respect of shares of each class purchased.

In addition, a statement of capital must be filed with the registrar when shares are cancelled following their purchase.[212]

The company is also bound under s 702 to keep a copy of any contract to purchase its own shares (and any variation of it), or a memorandum of its terms if it was not in writing, at its registered office for the period from the conclusion of the contract to the date 10 years after the date on which the purchase of the shares was completed. Every copy or memorandum must be open to the inspection of any member of the company without charge and, if the company is a public company, to the inspection of any other person without charge. Inspection must be permitted during business hours, subject to such reasonable restrictions as the company in general meeting may impose, but for at least 2 hours in each day.[213]

---

[211] [CA 1985, s 169].

[212] Section 708.

[213] The right of inspection is governed by s 1136 and the Companies (Company Records) Regulations 2008, SI 2008/3006.

Failure to deliver the return, to keep copies or memoranda, or to permit an inspection may be punished by fines on the company and every officer in default, and the court may order immediate inspection of a copy or memorandum where an inspection has been refused.

7.17.9 The capital redemption reserve

Often when a company redeems redeemable shares or purchases its own shares, it will be obliged to transfer a sum to its capital redemption reserve under the provisions of s 733.[214] This reserve, like share capital, appears on the liabilities side of the balance sheet[215] and is treated as capital. It can be reduced only by a proper reduction of capital.[216] However, it can be used to finance an issue to existing members of fully paid bonus shares.[217]

The requirement to transfer to this reserve applies only to the extent that the shares redeemed or purchased are not represented by new shares, that is when their redemption or purchase is financed wholly or partly by the use of distributable profits. So, when profits alone are used, the amount to be transferred is the nominal value of the shares redeemed or purchased. When a combination of profits and the proceeds of a new issue of shares is used, it is the amount, if any, by which the nominal value of the shares redeemed or purchased exceeds the amount of the proceeds of the new issue. Note, however, that by s 733(3), this latter requirement does not apply when a private company makes an authorised payment out of capital to finance a redemption or purchase, as described in the next section; this is because when a company is permitted to use capital, there is obviously no point in having the same capital maintenance requirement.

7.17.10 Private companies redeeming or purchasing shares out of capital

As has been mentioned earlier, s 709[218] permits private limited companies, subject to any restriction or prohibition included in the company articles and the stringent conditions laid down in the Act, to redeem redeemable shares and purchase their own shares out of capital. In effect, the relevant provisions lay down an easier procedure whereby private companies may

---

[214] [CA 1985, s 170].

[215] Details of any redeemable shares must be given in the notes to the accounts: Sch 4, Part 2, para 4(2) of the Small Companies and Groups (Accounts and Directors' Report) Regulations 2008, SI 2008/409; Sch 3, Part 3, para 58(2) of the Large and Medium-sized Companies and Groups (Accounts and Reports) Regulations 2008, SI 2008/410.

[216] See **8.13**.

[217] So far as the company at least is concerned, this really amounts to no more than a juggling around of the items on its balance sheet.

[218] [CA 1985, s 171].

reduce their share capital,[219] as well as making it easier for them, for example, to satisfy the claims of a retiring member or the estate of a deceased member.[220]

The payment which may be made out of capital, described as 'the permissible capital payment for the shares', is such an amount as, taken together with any available profits and the proceeds of a fresh issue of shares made for the purpose of the redemption or purchase, is equal to the price of redemption or purchase. It seems that a company must use its 'available profits', the meaning of which is described below, before it can touch capital. This somewhat restricts the advantages of the section.

Where the permissible capital payment for any shares redeemed or purchased is not combined with the proceeds of a fresh issue, and it is less than the nominal amount of the shares redeemed or purchased, the amount of the difference must be transferred to the capital redemption reserve. If it is greater than the nominal amount of the shares redeemed or purchased, the amount of the difference may be used to reduce the amount of any capital redemption reserve, share premium account or fully paid share capital of the company and any amount representing unrealised profits of the company for the time being standing to the credit of any reserve maintained by the company in accordance with Sch 1, Part 2, para 35 to the Large and Medium-sized Companies and Groups (Accounts and Reports) Regulations 2008 (the revaluation reserve).[221] In any case where the proceeds of a fresh issue of shares are applied in the redemption or purchase of a company's own shares, in addition to a payment out of capital, if the aggregate of the proceeds and payment is less than the nominal amount of the shares, the amount of the difference must be transferred to the capital redemption reserve.[222] If the aggregate is greater, the difference may be used to reduce any capital redemption reserve, share premium account or fully paid share capital of the company, together with any amount in the revaluation reserve, as described above.

For the purpose of redemption or purchase of its own shares by a private company out of capital, s 711 prescribes that available profits are profits available for distribution within the meaning of Part 23 of the 2006 Act[223] but determined in the way laid down in s 712 rather than in accordance with the accounts normally required[224] to determine a company's distributable profits. They must be determined within the period of 3 months before the date of the statutory declaration of the directors

---

[219] As to reduction of capital otherwise, see **8.13** *et seq.*

[220] For a full description of the circumstances where the power may be taken advantage of, see the Green Paper, *The Purchase by a Company of its own Shares,* Cmnd 7944 (1980).

[221] And Sch 1, Part 2, para 35 to the Small Companies and Groups (Accounts and Directors' Report) Regulations 2008, SI 2008/409.

[222] Section 733(3).

[223] As described in **7.21.2–7.21.4**.

[224] See **7.21.1**.

required by s 714[225] by reference to such accounts prepared within that period as are necessary to enable a reasonable judgment to be made of any of the company's profits, losses, assets, liabilities, provisions, share capital and reserves. For the purpose of determining the amount of the permissible capital payment for any shares, the amount of the company's available profits thus determined is to be treated as reduced by the amount of any distributions lawfully made by the company after the date of the relevant accounts and before the date of the statutory declaration.

Payments out of capital under s 709 must comply with certain procedural and publicity requirements as set out below. In addition, there is provision for objecting members or creditors to apply to the court, and liabilities may arise under the terms of s 76 of the Insolvency Act 1986 where a winding-up ensues within one year of payment out of capital. These matters are examined in the following sections.

7.17.11   Procedure and publicity

According to s 713, for a payment out of capital to be effective it must be made in accordance with a number of safeguards variously set out in ss 714–720 and s 723,[226] the chief of which are as follows:

(1)   The directors must make a statement which specifies the permissible capital payment and is otherwise essentially a declaration of existing solvency and that, in the view of the directors, the company will continue to trade and be solvent for one year. In forming this opinion the directors must take into account all the company's liabilities (including contingent or prospective liabilities).

(2)   The auditors of the company must make a report to the directors confirming the permissible capital payment and that they are not aware of anything to indicate that the statement is unreasonable.

(3)   A special resolution must be passed approving the payment out of capital on, or within one week of, the date of the statement, at a general meeting at which the statement and auditors' report are available for inspection and in respect of which resolution the votes of any member holding shares to which it relates cannot be counted [227]

(4)   The payment out of capital can be made only between 5 and 7 weeks after the date of the resolution.

---

[225] See **7.17.11**.

[226] [CA 1985, ss 173–185].

[227] This requirement is appropriately modified when a company uses the statutory written resolution procedure (see **13.5**).

(5)   The company must publish notice in the *Gazette* and either notice in a national newspaper or notice in writing to each of its creditors within one week of the special resolution. The notice must give the details specified in s 719, namely the fact and date of the resolution, the amount of the permissible capital payment, that the directors' statement and auditors' report can be inspected at the company's registered office, and that any creditor can seek to restrain the payment out of capital by applying to the court under s 721. From the date of this notice the declaration and report must be kept at the registered office and be open to inspection by any member or creditor without charge until the end of the fifth week following the special resolution.

(6)   Copies of the statement and auditors' report must be delivered to the registrar by the date of the public notice.

Criminal penalties are specified for directors making a knowingly false statement and for refusals to allow inspections of the statement and report. The latter can also be remedied by court order.

7.17.12   Applications to the court

Within 5 weeks of a special resolution made under s 716, any member of the company other than one who consented to or voted in favour of the resolution and any creditor may apply to the court for the cancellation of the resolution.[228] The court has wide powers.[229] It may adjourn proceedings so that arrangements can be made to purchase the interest of dissentient members or protect creditors. Failing this, it must confirm or cancel the resolution on such terms and conditions as it thinks fit. It has the specific power to provide for the company to purchase the shares of any member, reducing capital in consequence, and to make any necessary alterations in the memorandum and articles.

The Act does not spell out when the court might accede to such an application. It would obviously do so for a serious default in procedure or if available profits had not been fully utilised. However, it is not clear whether, for example, a minority shareholder would succeed if he could show that he was discriminated against because the chance to have his shares bought by the company was denied to him whereas the majority had caused the company to purchase some or all of theirs. Compare, for example, s 633 which gives the court power to disallow a variation of class rights[230] and expressly directs the court to consider fairness. It is thought that s 721 should not be used for such complaints, given the absence of

---

[228]   Section 721 [CA 1985, s 176].
[229]   Section 721(3)–(7) [CA 1985, s 177].
[230]   See **8.7.5**.

any reference to fairness in this provision and given the fact that the minority which has been unfairly treated can use the statutory remedy under s 994.[231]

7.17.13 Liability of past shareholders and directors

Where, in redeeming or purchasing any of its own shares, a company has made a payment out of capital, and it is subsequently wound up, and is insolvent, on winding-up commencing within one year of the payment, liability to contribute to the assets of the company may be imposed under s 76 of the Insolvency Act 1986 upon the person from whom the shares were redeemed or purchased to the extent of the amount of capital he received and the directors of the company who signed the relevant statement who are jointly and severally liable with that person, except a director who shows that he had reasonable grounds for forming the opinion set out in the statement.

7.17.14 Failure of a company to redeem or purchase its own shares

Section 735[232] contains provisions dealing with cases where a company has issued redeemable shares or agreed to purchase any of its own shares, under the provisions described in the preceding sections, and has failed to perform its obligations.

A company cannot be liable in damages for any failure to perform its obligations, but other remedies for a breach of contract are available to the shareholder, provided that the court must not grant an order for specific performance if the company shows that it is unable to meet the cost of redeeming or purchasing the shares in question out of distributable profits. The exclusion of liability for damages refers to claims in respect of a company's breach of duty to redeem or purchase shares; it does not prevent other damages claims, eg for breach of a covenant contained in a financing agreement entered into to facilitate redemption.[233]

Where a company is being wound up and, at the commencement of the winding-up, has failed to meet an obligation to redeem or purchase its own shares which has already accrued, the terms of redemption or purchase may be enforced by the shareholder, provided that, during the period between the due date for redemption or purchase and the date of the commencement of the winding-up, the company could have lawfully made a distribution equal in value to the price at which the shares were to have been redeemed or purchased.

---

[231] See **18.10**.
[232] [CA 1985, s 178].
[233] *Barclays Bank plc v British & Commonwealth Holdings plc* [1996] 1 BCLC 1 (CA).

Any money so owed is deferred to the claims of all creditors and preference shareholders having capital rights ranking in preference to those of the shares redeemed or purchased; but it ranks before the claims of other shareholders.

7.18 FINANCIAL ASSISTANCE BY A COMPANY FOR THE ACQUISITION OF ITS OWN SHARES

Sections 151–154 of the Companies Act 1985, which consolidated the replacement of s 54 of the Companies Act 1948, acted as a reinforcement of the rule that a company may not, except subject to the strict conditions, purchase its own shares. Uncertainty surrounding the exact scope of the repealed s 54[234] led to the introduction in 1981 of what became ss 151–154 of the 1985 Act. The prohibitions in these sections were relaxed in comparison to the 1948 provision in respect of private companies. Many uncertainties surrounding the operation of these provisions, however, continued to cause difficulties in practice. As a result of a recommendation made by the CLRSG,[235] the prohibition on private companies providing financial assistance for the acquisition of its own shares was abolished in the Companies Act 2006.[236]

7.18.1 Prohibitions under s 678

The basic prohibition, which is now applicable only to public companies, subject to the exceptions discussed below, is twofold. First, where a person is acquiring or is proposing to acquire any shares in a public company, it is unlawful for the company or any of its subsidiaries to give financial assistance directly or indirectly for the purpose of that acquisition[237] before or at the same time as the acquisition of the shares takes place.[238] Secondly, where a person has acquired any shares in a company and any liability has been incurred by him or any other person for the purposes of that acquisition, it is unlawful for the company or any of its subsidiaries to give any financial assistance directly or indirectly for the purpose of

---

[234] See in particular the cases of *Belmont Finance Corp Ltd v Williams Furniture Ltd (No 2)* [1980] 1 All ER 393 (CA) and *Armour Hick Northern Ltd v Whitehouse* [1980] 1 WLR 1520, discussed in (1980) 1 Co Law 99 and 145. Section 54 was notorious for often hitting the innocent and failing to deter the guilty; see the Jenkins Report (Cmnd 1749, paras 170–176) for a general review.

[235] Final Report, para 10.6.

[236] Accordingly, the 'whitewash procedure' set out in ss 155-158 of the 1985 Act by which private companies were permitted to provide financial assistance for the acquisition of their shares has been abolished.

[237] The equivalent words in s 54 of the 1948 Act were 'purchase or subscription'. 'Acquisition' is wider since it covers cases where the payment for shares is not in cash. For a recent case involving alleged assistance from a subsidiary see *AMG Global Nominees (Private) Ltd v Africa Resources Ltd* [2008] EWCA Civ 1278.

[238] Section 678(1) [CA 1985, s 151(1)].

reducing or discharging the liability incurred if, at the time the assistance is given, the company in which the shares were acquired is a public company.[239]

The reference above to a person incurring any liability includes the case of a person changing his financial position by making any agreement or arrangement (whether enforceable or unenforceable and whether made on his own account or with any other person) or by any other means.[240]

The reference to a company giving financial assistance to reduce or discharge a liability incurred by a person for the purpose of acquiring shares in the company includes the case where the company gives financial assistance for the purpose of wholly or partly restoring his financial position to what it was before the acquisition took place.[241]

Financial assistance is defined in s 677(1)[242]as meaning any of the following:

(1)   financial assistance given by way of gift;

(2)   financial assistance given by way of guarantee, security or indemnity, other than an indemnity in respect of the indemnifier's own neglect or default, or by way of release or waiver;[243]

(3)   financial assistance given by way of a loan or any other agreement under which any of the obligations of the person giving the assistance are to be fulfilled at a time when, in accordance with the agreement, any obligation of any other party to the agreement remains unfulfilled or by way of the novation or assignment (in Scotland, assignation) of any rights arising under the loan or such other agreement;[244] or

(4)   any other financial assistance given by a company the net assets[245] of which are thereby reduced to a material extent[246] or which has no net assets.

---

[239]   Section 678(3) [CA 1985, s 151(2)]. See *Re Hill and Tyler Ltd* [2004] EWHC 1261, (Ch). Under s 679 a public company which is a subsidiary of a private company cannot give financial assistance, either before or after the acquisition, for an acquisition of shares in its private holding company.

[240]   Section 683(2)(a) [CA 1985, s 152(3)(a)].

[241]   Section 683(2)(b) [CA 1985, s 152(3)(b)].

[242]   [CA 1985, s 152(1)(a)].

[243]   The words 'guarantee' and 'indemnity' bear their ordinary legal meaning: *Barclays Bank plc v British & Commonwealth Holdings plc* [1996] 1 BCLC 1, at 37–40.

[244]   See, eg, the facts in *Coulthard v Neville Russell* [1998] BCC 359.

[245]   In this context 'net assets' means the actual net assets, not necessarily those as stated in the company's accounting records, at the time of the giving of assistance, so that any value received by the company in return for the assistance should be taken into account: *Parlett v Guppys (Bridport) Ltd* [1996] BCC 299.

[246]   'Material extent' is not defined. In *Parlett v Guppys (Bridport) Ltd* [1996] BCC 299,

It is thought that 'assistance' necessarily involves the existence of at least two persons, one giving and one receiving the assistance. So where, for example, a company borrows money and gives security in order to finance a purchase of its own shares, this can hardly be regarded as the giving of financial assistance within s 678. A surrender of tax losses by a subsidiary company to another company within the same group, as part of a wider agreement for the sale of its shares to one of its directors, was held not to amount to the giving of financial assistance where there was no evidence that the surrender reduced the price which the director would otherwise have paid.[247] *Barclays Bank plc v British & Commonwealth Holdings plc*[248] concerned the issue of liability to pay damages for breach of a covenant given under a court-sanctioned scheme of arrangement. The company in question had given the covenant to the plaintiff banks as part of a scheme under which the banks became liable to finance the purchase by another party of shares in the company. This was held not to amount to financial assistance given by the company; while the giving of the covenants may have induced the banks to enter into the commitments that they did, they did not financially assist anybody to acquire shares. In *Parlett v Guppys (Bridport) Ltd*,[249] an agreement to transfer shares in one member of a group of companies was entered into where the consideration was the payment of a salary and pension by all the members of the group. As the agreement could be performed lawfully without breaching s 151 (of the 1985 Act), by the payment being made by members of the group other than the company whose shares were the subject of the agreement, it did not infringe the prohibition against the giving of financial assistance.

An interesting recent case is *MT Realisations v Digital Equipment Ltd*[250] in which a loss-making company, M, owed £8m to another company in its group. H subsequently purchased all of M's shares for £1 and took over the debt for £6.5m. It was argued that when money owed to M was used to finance payment of the debt, this amounted to financial assistance for the purchase of M's shares. The Court of Appeal, upholding the decision at first instance, held, however, that on both legal principles and with regard to the commercial realities of the situation, no financial assistance had been provided by M to H 'for the purpose of' reducing or discharging a liability incurred for the purpose of acquiring shares in M. M was merely paying an outstanding debt, so this did not amount to giving assistance to H.

---

where counsel were disposed to agree that a reduction of 5% or more would have been material, Nourse LJ commented that there can be no rule of thumb and the question is one of degree to be answered on the facts of the particular case.

[247] *Charterhouse Investment Trust Ltd v Tempest Diesels Ltd* [1986] BCLC 1.

[248] [1996] 1 BCLC 1 (CA).

[249] [1996] BCC 299. See also *Grant v Lapid Developments Ltd* [1996] BCC 410.

[250] [2003] ECWA Civ 494, [2003] 2 BCLC 117. For a useful discussion see Hirt 'The scope of prohibited financial assistance after *MT Realisations Ltd (in liquidation) v Digital Equipment Co Ltd*' (2004) 25 *Company Lawyer* 9.

On the other hand, in the leading case of *Brady v Brady*,[251] in order to effect the reorganisation and division of a company, Brady Ltd, between the two principal shareholders (brothers who had fallen out), two new companies (A and B) were created which would ultimately each be owned by one brother and run one side of the previously merged businesses. Company A acquired the share capital of Brady in return for loan stock issued to company B. Subsequently, A was to redeem the loan stock by arranging for Brady to transfer to B one-half of Brady's assets. It was accepted that Brady would give financial assistance by this transfer when A redeemed stock to discharge the liability it had incurred in acquiring the shares in Brady. Payment by a target company of expenses incurred by a bidder prior to making a takeover offer has been held to constitute financial assistance.[252]

Further examples of the sorts of transactions prohibited by s 678 can be found in some of the cases decided on s 54 of the Companies Act 1948: a loan made by a company to finance the borrower's purchase of shares in the company;[253] the case of a purchaser of shares undertaking a liability as part of the consideration which he never discharges or causes the company to discharge;[254] or the purchase by a company of assets at an inflated price to enable the vendor of the assets to buy shares in the company.[255]

The company which is prohibited by s 678 from giving financial assistance must be a company registered in Britain.[256] In addition, the phrase 'a company that is a subsidiary of that company', must be construed as limited to British companies.[257] So the section does not prohibit a foreign subsidiary of an English parent company from giving financial assistance for an acquisition of shares in its parent, nor, it seems, does it prohibit the giving of financial assistance by an English subsidiary to acquire shares in its foreign parent.[258]

A contravention of s 678 attracts severe criminal sanctions,[259] and the transaction itself is void and unenforceable.[260] However, the directors responsible and, possibly, any third parties involved, can be sued for breach of trust[261] to compensate the company for any loss suffered.

---

[251] [1989] AC 755 (HL). The significance of the decision lies in the construction of the purpose exceptions, discussed below. See also *Plant v Steiner* (1989) 5 BCC 352.

[252] Even where the financial assistance is not detrimental to the company – see *Chaston v SWP Group plc* [2002] EWCA Civ 1999, [2003] 1 BCLC 675.

[253] See, eg, *Selangor United Rubber Estates Ltd v Cradock (No 3)* [1968] 1 WLR 1555.

[254] See the 'circular cheque' transaction in *Wallersteiner v Moir (No 1)* [1974] 1 WLR 991.

[255] See *Belmont Finance Corp Ltd v Williams Furniture Ltd*, above.

[256] Section 1158 [CA 1985, s 735].

[257] *Arab Bank plc v Mercantile Holdings Ltd* [1994] 1 BCLC 330.

[258] Ibid.

[259] See s 680 [CA 1985, s 151(3)].

[260] See *Brady v Brady*, above; *Selangor United Rubber Estates Ltd v Cradock*, above; *Re Hill and Tyler Ltd*, above.

[261] *Steen v Law* [1964] AC 287 (PC); *Selangor United Rubber Estates Ltd v Cradock*, above;

7.18.2   Exceptions

It is important that, for financial assistance to be given unlawfully, it is given *for the purpose of* an acquisition or discharge of liability.[262] This requirement is reinforced by s 678(2).[263] Section 678(2) provides that s 678(1) does not prohibit a company from giving any financial assistance if:

(1)   the company's principal purpose in giving it is not to give it for the purpose of an acquisition or the giving of it for that purpose is but an incidental part of some larger purpose of the company; and

(2)   the assistance is given in good faith in the interests of the company.

Section 678(4)[264] contains similar provisions to cover the prohibition in s 678(3). Thus, for example, a transaction under which a company buys from another a chattel or commodity it genuinely wants but with the intention also of putting the vendor in a position to acquire shares in the company is not prohibited provided that the latter purpose is not the principal purpose and the transaction is entered into in good faith in the interests of the company.[265] Whether the purpose exceptions have much more scope is doubtful following the House of Lords' decision in *Brady v Brady*.[266] Here they were said to contemplate two alternative situations. The first envisages a principal and a secondary purpose and was enacted to cover the sort of situation just described. The second situation is where it is not suggested that the financial assistance was intended to achieve any object other than the giving of assistance or the reduction or discharge of indebtedness, but where the result is merely incidental to some larger purpose of the company. Lord Oliver stated that in construing the word 'purpose' in the context of the sections regulating the provision of finance by a company in connection with the purchase of its own shares, there had always to be borne in mind the mischief against which s 151 (of the 1985 Act) was aimed. If this section was not to be deprived of any useful application, it was important to distinguish between a purpose and the reason why a purpose was formed. The reason for a scheme which involved the provision of financial assistance might be

---

Wallersteiner v Moir (No 1), above; *Belmont Finance Corp Ltd v Williams Furniture Ltd (No 2)*, above. On appropriate facts, an alternative cause of action is in the tort of conspiracy: see the *Belmont Finance* case.

[262]   In s 54 of the 1948 Act, it was sufficient in the alternative that assistance was given 'in connection with' an acquisition, and this caught some otherwise legitimate transactions; see *Armour Hick Northern Ltd v Whitehouse*, above.

[263]   [CA 1985, s 153(1)].

[264]   [CA 1985, s 153(2)].

[265]   This phrase is traditionally used to describe the fundamental duties of company directors (see **16.5**) and in this context requires consideration of the interests of creditors: see *Brady v Brady*, above.

[266]   See above. It was correctly pointed out that the section is complex and not altogether easy to construe.

a needed reorganisation or takeover which was regarded as commercially desirable or even necessary, but that could not be regarded as a larger purpose:[267]

> 'The purpose and the only purpose of the financial assistance is and remains that of enabling the shares to be acquired and the financial or commercial advantages flowing from the acquisition, whilst they may form the reason for forming the purpose of providing financial assistance, are a by-product of it rather than an independent purpose of which the assistance can properly be said to be an incident.'

So, in the case itself,[268] the purpose of the financial assistance was to enable the acquisition of shares and the commercial desirability of the reorganisation was not a larger corporate purpose. The scheme was not saved by the then s 153(2) of the 1985 Act.[269] It has to be said that this construction leaves very little room for the operation of the second situation.[270]

Quite apart from the 'purpose' exception, a number of occurrences which are totally outside the general prohibition are listed in s 681 of the Act. These are:

(1) a distribution of a company's assets by way of a dividend lawfully made or a distribution made in the course of the company's winding-up;

(2) the allotment of bonus shares;

(3) any reduction of capital confirmed by order of the court under Chapter 10 of Part 17;[271]

(4) a redemption or purchase of any shares made in accordance with the provisions described above;[272]

(5) anything done in pursuance of an order of the court made under Part 26, that is a court-approved reconstruction;[273]

---

[267] [1989] AC at 780.

[268] The facts are given briefly above.

[269] Although it was open to be saved by the 'whitewash' procedure set out in ss 155–158 of the 1985 Act.

[270] Which partly explains why the prohibition has been abolished in respect of private companies.

[271] See **8.13**.

[272] See **7.17** *et seq.*

[273] See **20.19**.

(6)   anything done under an arrangement made in pursuance of s 110 of the Insolvency Act 1986, that is a reconstruction linked to a voluntary winding-up;[274] and

(7)   anything done under an arrangement made between a company and its creditors which is binding on the creditors by virtue of Part I of the Insolvency Act 1986.[275]

Section 682[276] provides for further 'conditional' exceptions, but advantage can be taken of these only if they do not reduce the company's current worth according to the value of its assets and liabilities in its accounting records or, to the extent that they do reduce it, if the financial assistance is provided out of distributable profits. The first exception here exempts the lending of money in the ordinary course of its business by a company whose ordinary business includes moneylending.[277]

The other three exceptions are all essentially concerned with the acquisition of or dealing in a company's shares by employees and are thus designed to encourage employee shareholding. First, a company can provide financial assistance for the purposes of an employees' share scheme[278] for the acquisition of fully paid shares in the company or its holding company. Secondly, it, or a subsidiary of it, can provide assistance for the purposes of or in connection with anything done by it, or by a company in the same group, to enable or facilitate transactions in its shares between or for the benefit of employees and others.[279] Thirdly, it can make loans to *bona fide* employees, other than directors, with a view to enabling them to acquire fully paid shares in it or its holding company to be held by way of beneficial ownership.

7.19   THE HOLDING BY A SUBSIDIARY OF SHARES IN ITS HOLDING COMPANY

A further statutory reinforcement of the rule that a company may not purchase its own shares is contained in s 136.[280] This section forbids a

---

[274] See **20.13**.

[275] See Chapter 20.

[276] [CA 1985, s 153(4)].

[277] A loan made by a moneylending company for the specific purpose of financing a purchase of its shares is not made 'in the ordinary course of business'; *Steen v Law* [1964] AC 287 (PC); *Fowlie v Slater* (1979) 129 NLJ 465.

[278] An employees' share scheme is defined in s 1166 as a scheme for encouraging or facilitating the holding of shares or debentures in a company by or for the benefit of the *bona fide* employees or former employees of the company, its subsidiary or holding company or a fellow subsidiary, or the wives, husbands, widows, widowers or children or stepchildren under the age of 18 of such employees or former employees.

[279] The 'others' are the same people as are mentioned in s 1166.

[280] [CA 1985, s 23].

body corporate[281] from being a member (or having its nominee as a member) of its holding company, and any allotment or transfer of shares in a company to its subsidiary (or nominee) is void.[282] This would be tantamount to the holding company owning its own shares. The provision is of long standing, although it was revised in 1989, and these days appears somewhat inadequate because it is limited to situations where there is a holding company/subsidiary company relationship. Control of another company may be obtained by a holding of less than 50% of voting shares, for example, by the use of cross and circular holdings,[283] but s 136 will not apply in those cases.[284]

In any event, the section has no application where a subsidiary holds shares in its holding company as personal representative or as trustee, unless the holding company or a subsidiary thereof is beneficially interested[285] under the trust and is not so interested only by way of security for the purpose of a transaction entered into by it in the ordinary course of a business which includes the lending of money.[286]

7.20   SERIOUS LOSS OF CAPITAL BY PUBLIC COMPANIES

Section 656[287] sets out a provision first introduced in the 1980 Act as a result of the Second EC Directive. It provides that where the net assets of a public company are half or less of the amount of the company's called-up share capital, the directors of the company must duly convene a general meeting of the company to consider whether any, and if so, what, measures should be taken to deal with the situation. The meeting must be convened not less than 28 days after the earliest day on which a director learns of the fact, to take place at a date not later than 56 days after that day.[288]

---

[281] This term is defined in s 1174 and comprehends all companies, including foreign companies, except for corporations sole and Scottish firms.

[282] For the definitions of 'holding company' and 'subsidiary company', see s 1159 [CA 1985, ss 736 and 736A].

[283] See the example cited in Gower, *Principles of Modern Company Law* (Sweet & Maxwell, 4th edn, 2001) p 226, footnote 63: company A holds 45% of the voting shares of company B and company B holds 45% of the voting shares of company A. In effect, the directors of both are irremovable and the companies are grouped together, but s 1159 will not apply. See also Pickering at (1965) 81 LQR 248.

[284] The Jenkins Committee thought that it should, but that enacting the appropriate provision would be too difficult: Cmnd 1749, para 153.

[285] Section 138. As to the meaning of 'beneficial interest' see *Gore-Browne on Companies* (Jordans, 45th edn, loose-leaf) at 24 [46].

[286] In addition, it does not apply where shares in the holding company are held by the subsidiary in the ordinary course of its business as an intermediary involved in dealing in securities and satisfying certain other conditions: see s 141 [CA 1985, s 23(3)].

[287] [CA 1985, s 142].

[288] The section does not dispense with the need for proper notices, etc, of any resolution which might be proposed: subsection (6).

Failure to comply with the section renders the director responsible liable to criminal sanctions,[289] but there are no civil consequences, nor does the section provide any specific guidance as to the position, if, following the meeting, the company resolves to do nothing. It is really a rather curious provision which looks like another example of an ill-thought-out implementation of the Second Directive. In fact it may be wondered whether it really does implement Art 17 of the Directive, which requires the meeting 'to consider whether the company should be wound up or any other measures taken' and which thus at least has a more specific point in mind than s 656.

7.21   DIVIDENDS

The next sections of this chapter are concerned with profits and dividends, namely how profit is assessed and how it is distributed or otherwise dealt with. The differing entitlement of different classes of shares to such profits, where appropriate, is considered in the next chapter.

The common law rule, in accordance with the general principle of maintenance of capital, was that dividends could not be paid out of capital,[290] but this rule has now been largely overtaken by statute.[291] The basic rule now is that a distribution, a generic term including a dividend,[292] can only be made out of profits available according to the rules laid down in Part 23 of the Companies Act 2006 and only by reference to properly prepared accounts. The latter point will be examined first.[293]

---

[289]   Section 656 (4) and (5).

[290]   *Re Exchange Banking Co, Flitcroft's Case* (1882) 21 Ch D 519.

[291]   The common-law rule was notoriously out of touch with good commercial and accounting practice; see Yamey (1941) 4 MLR 273. By virtue of s 851, the common law rules restricting distributions continue to apply, except as provided for by the section.

[292]   The full definition in s 829 [CA 1985, s 263(2)] is every description of distribution of a company's assets to members of the company, whether in cash or otherwise, except distribution made by way of: (1) a fully or partly paid issue of bonus shares (see **7.23**); (2) the redemption or purchase of any of the company's own shares under Chapter 3, 4 or 5 of Part 18 (see **7.17** *et seq*); (3) the reduction of share capital by extinguishing or reducing the liability of any partly paid shares or by paying off paid-up share capital (see **8.13** *et seq*); and (4) a distribution of assets to members of the company on its winding-up. It might be argued that the width of this definition means that it covers such distributions as the payment of remuneration to directors of a small company, especially where they are its only members and this is the usual way in which profits are shared. However, in *Macpherson v European Strategic Bureau Ltd* [1999] 2 BCLC 203, it was held that provision made in a severance agreement for the retrospective remuneration of shareholders for the work they had done as executives was not a distribution within the then s 263(2) of the 1985 Act.

[293]   For detailed technical guidance on distributable profits see, ICAEW Technical Release, *Guidance on the Determination of Realised Profits and Losses in the Context of Distributions under the Companies Act 2006* (October, 2010).

7.21.1 The relevant accounts

Section 836[294] requires that companies determine the question of whether a distribution can be made, and its amount, by reference to a list of items in the 'relevant accounts'. The items amount to the basic contents of accounts, ie profits, losses, assets, liabilities, provisions, share capital and reserves.[295] There are three descriptions of relevant accounts; in all cases they must have been properly prepared so as to give a true and fair view,[296] but only the first two descriptions must have been audited.[297] They are:

(1) the last annual accounts, that is the standard accounts prepared annually in accordance with s 423;[298]

(2) initial accounts, that is accounts prepared to allow for a distribution to be made by a recently formed public company, during the company's first accounting reference period or before accounts are laid in respect of that period;[299]

(3) interim accounts, that is accounts prepared by a public company which wishes to declare an interim dividend, as such companies frequently do in the course of the financial year.[300]

Where a company has made a distribution by reference to particular accounts and wishes to make a further distribution by reference to the same accounts, it must take account of the earlier distribution and of certain other payments made, if any, as listed in s 840.[301]

7.21.2 Determination of profits

The Act, consequent upon the need to comply with the Second EC Directive, lays down what can be termed the 'balance sheet surplus method' of determining profits available for distribution.[302] Under this

---

[294] [CA 1985, s 270].
[295] Section 836(1).
[296] As to this classic formula, see **Chapter 14**.
[297] If the audit is qualified and the qualification does not state whether it is material to determining the legality of a distribution, a distribution thus in breach of the statute (as a result of the now s 837(4)) is unlawful: *Precision Dippings Ltd v Precision Dippings Marketing Ltd* [1985] 3 WLR 812 (CA). The same consequence must apply to any breach of the relevant accounts provisions. Certain small companies can dispense with the audit requirement, for this as well as general, purposes, see **14.28**.
[298] See s 837 [CA 1985, s 271].
[299] Section 839 [CA 1985, s 272].
[300] Section 838 [CA 1985, s 273].
[301] [CA 1985, s 274]. These relate to various categories of financial assistance given for the purpose of an acquisition of a company's shares (see **7.18** *et seq*) and various payments in respect of a company's purchase of its own shares (see **7.17** *et seq*).
[302] For a very clear general account, see Renshall (1980) 1 Co Law 194.

approach, a company can distribute what amounts to the net profit on both capital and revenue at the particular time, that is according to the relevant accounts.

Section 830(2)[303] lays down a basic rule of thumb here, but it does not apply to investment companies[304] and is qualified in respect of public companies by s 831.[305] It states that a company's profits available for distribution are its accumulated, realised profits (on both revenue and capital)[306] not previously distributed or capitalised,[307] less its accumulated realised losses (on both revenue and capital) not written off in a proper reduction or reorganisation of capital.[308]

Under s 841(1), realised losses to be taken account of in the calculation include amounts written off or retained for depreciation.[309] Development costs must also *prima facie* be treated as a realised loss.[310]

The inclusion of 'accumulated' is important, making it clear that the current year's position cannot be taken in isolation. As indicated, realised profits include both trading profits and profits on the sale of capital assets,[311] but obviously not unrealised profit arising as a result of a revaluation of assets. An unrealised profit cannot be used to pay up debentures or amounts outstanding on partly paid shares.[312] However, such a profit can sometimes be capitalised,[313] and in certain circumstances can be treated as realised if made on a revaluation of fixed assets and a sum is set aside for depreciation of the assets.[314]

A reform proposed by the CLRSG,[315] which found its way into s 845 of the 2006 Act, seeks to facilitate the intra-group transfer of assets at book value (which may in fact be at undervalue) where the company does have sufficient distributable profits. In such circumstances the transaction could otherwise amount to a distribution thereby requiring the company

---

[303] [CA 1985, s 263(3)].

[304] See *Gore-Browne on Companies* (Jordans, 45th edn, loose-leaf) at 25 [12].

[305] See **7.21.3**.

[306] Section 853(2) [CA 1985, s 280 (3)].

[307] This means used to finance a bonus issue or the purchase or redemption of the company's own shares with a resulting transfer to the capital redemption reserve: s 853(3) [CA 1985, s 280(2)].

[308] The ability to write off losses by a reduction of capital has led to an increased use of the reduction procedure under s 641 since these provisions were first introduced in 1980: see *Re Jupiter House Investments* [1985] 1 WLR 975 and *Re Grosvenor Press plc* [1985] 1 WLR 980, discussed in **8.13.2**.

[309] [CA 1985, s 275(1)]. These are 'provisions'.

[310] But there are exceptions; see s 844 [CA 1985, s 269].

[311] 'Realised' is not defined and its application could cause difficulties in certain cases; see Renshall, *op cit*, p 195.

[312] Section 849 [CA 1985, s 263(4)].

[313] Section 848 [CA 1985, s 278]; see **7.23**.

[314] See s 841(5) [CA 1985, s 275(2)].

[315] See *Capital Maintenance: Other Issues* URN 00/880 (June 2000) paras 24–43.

to have distributable profits sufficient to cover the difference in value.[316] The effect of s 845, however, is that it determines the amount of a distribution consisting of or including, or treated as arising in consequence of, the sale, transfer or other disposition by a company of a non-cash asset where the company has profits available for distribution and the amount of the distribution determined under the section would not contravene the general provisions in Part 23 of the 2006 Act. The amount of the distribution, or relevant part thereof, is calculated by reference to the asset's value as stated in the company's accounts, ie its 'book value'.[317] Thus, if an asset is transferred for a consideration equal to or above its book value, the amount of the distribution is zero, but if transferred for a consideration less than its book value, the amount of the distribution is equal to the shortfall (which will therefore need to be covered by distributable profits). The company may treat any profit that would arise on the proposed disposition of the non-cash asset as increasing its distributable profits.[318] This obviates the potential need for companies to engage in the oft expensive business of asset revaluations prior to making distributions of non-cash assets.

A further reform is effected in s 846,[319] to render that provision consistent with s 845. Where a company makes a distribution of (or including) a non-cash asset, it could previously, if it had revalued assets showing an unrealised profit in the accounts, treat that profit as a realised profit. Under s 846, this also applies where a company makes a distribution arising from the sale, transfer or other disposition by it of a non-cash asset.

7.21.3 Public companies

It is not sufficient that a public company has made a distributable profit under s 830. Section 831[320] imposes an additional capital maintenance requirement, to ensure that the net worth of the company is at least equal to the amount of its capital. A public company can only distribute profit if at the time the amount of its net assets, that is the total excess of assets over liabilities, is not less than the total of its called-up share capital and its undistributable reserves, and only if and to the extent that the distribution does not reduce the amount of the net assets to less than that total. Undistributable reserves are:

(1) the share premium account;

---

[316] See *Aveling Barford Ltd v Perion Ltd* [1989] BCLC 626; *Clydebank Football Club Ltd v Steedman* 2002 SLT 109.

[317] This the amount at which the asset is stated in the relevant accounts or, where it is not valued in those accounts, zero: s 845(4).

[318] Section 845(3).

[319] [CA 1985, s 276].

[320] [CA 1985, s 264].

(2)   the capital redemption reserve;

(3)   the amount by which unrealised uncapitalised profits exceed unrealised losses not written off; and

(4)   any other reserve which the company is prohibited from distributing by statute or its memorandum or articles.

7.21.4   Improperly paid dividends

The Act provides[321] that a member who knows or has reasonable grounds to believe that a distribution or part of it is unlawful[322] is liable to repay it or that part of it,[323] but it does not specify any further consequences of an improper dividend.

It is clear, though, that the additional remedies provided by the common law in respect of a dividend out of capital will apply to a payment illegal under the Act. Thus directors are liable to compensate the company if they know or should know that a distribution is illegal.[324] Any member can restrain a proposed illegal distribution by injunction,[325] but a member who has knowingly received such a distribution cannot bring a derivative action against the directors,[326] and will be liable to account to the company as a constructive trustee.[327] It is not possible for the members to ratify an illegal distribution or absolve directors from their liability in making such a distribution.[328]

Rather curiously, perhaps, a creditor has no *locus standi* to restrain an illegal distribution, unless he has an enforceable security which is thereby put in jeopardy.[329] His only remedy is to seek a winding-up.

---

[321]   Section 847 [CA 1985, s 277].

[322]   Although ignorance of the existence or operation of the relevant sections is not an excuse – see *It's a Wrap (UK) v Gula* [2006] EWCA Civ 554 [2006] BCC 626.

[323]   This remedy does not apply to any unlawful financial assistance given to members in contravention of ss 678 or 679 (see **7.18.1**) or to payments in respect of the redemption or purchase of a company's own shares (see **7.17** *et seq*).

[324]   See, eg, *Flitcroft's Case* (1882) 21 Ch D 519 and *Bairstow and Others v Queens Moat Houses plc* [2000] 1 BCLC 549. Where directors do not know, e g because they rely upon others, the question becomes one as to their liability for negligence, as to which see **16.7**.

[325]   See, eg, *Hoole v Great Western Railway Co* (1867) 3 Ch App 262.

[326]   *Towers v African Tug Co* [1904] 1 Ch 558. As to derivative actions, see **18.5**.

[327]   *Precision Dippings Ltd v Precision Dippings Marketing Ltd* [1985] 3 WLR 812 (CA).

[328]   *Aveling Barford Ltd v Perion* [1989] BCLC 626.

[329]   *Mills v Northern Railway of Buenos Aires* (1870) 5 Ch App 621.

7.22 RESERVES

Directors have power to set aside a proportion of profits, before a dividend is declared, to form a reserve.[330] Whether or not a company chooses to set aside profits in this way depends on its particular circumstances. A reserve generally remains undivided profit and can be used, for example, to pay dividends in bad years. However, it can be capitalised, and thus cease to be profit, as described in the next section.

Reserves in the sense described above must be distinguished from provisions, that is amounts written off or retained to provide, for example, for depreciation or bad debts. It should also be noted that, despite its name and despite the fact that it is often funded from distributable profits, the capital redemption reserve required under s 170[331] is, for most purposes, a capital account.

7.23 CAPITALISATION OF PROFITS

In times of prosperity it is common practice for companies which have large undistributed profits to convert them into capital and distribute fully paid bonus shares representing the increased capital amongst the members in proportion to their right. This requires express sanction in the memorandum or articles.

Under the common-form articles, art 6 of the Model Articles for private companies limited by shares and art 78 of the Model Articles for public companies, the directors may, with the authority of an ordinary resolution, capitalise any undivided profits not required for paying any preferential dividend, whether or not they are available for distribution,[332] or any sum standing to the credit of the share premium account[333] or capital redemption reserve.[334] They may then appropriate the capitalised sum to the members who would have been entitled to it by way of dividend, by issuing fully paid-up bonus shares to them.[335] A bonus issue may be declared void for mistake if it was made on the false premise that there were profits available for capitalisation.[336]

---

[330] This may be expressed in the articles. If no such power is expressed, however, it is implied from the fact that, usually, no dividend can exceed the amount recommended by the directors (see **7.24**).

[331] See **7.17.9** and **7.23**.

[332] Thus including unrealised profits.

[333] See **7.15**.

[334] See **7.17.9**.

[335] If the capitalisation is of distributable profits, it can also be used to fund the issue of fully paid-up debentures and to pay up, wholly or partly, any amount owing on hitherto partly paid-up shares.

[336] *Re Cleveland Trust plc* [1991] BCC 33.

7.24   MODE OF DISTRIBUTION OF PROFITS

Unless the memorandum or articles provide or imply otherwise, a dividend is not payable until it has been declared,[337] and any proceedings to recover it from the company before it has been declared are premature. However, it has been stated that members are entitled to have profits distributed so far as is commercially possible, and that directors who fail to make an appropriate recommendation are exercising their powers for an improper purpose.[338] Once a dividend is properly declared, it is a debt payable to the members. The articles generally state which organ of the company has the power to declare a dividend. Under the Model Articles, art 30(1) for private companies limited by shares and art 70(1) for public companies, this power is vested in the general meeting,[339] subject to the proviso that it may not declare a dividend exceeding the amount recommended by the directors. By virtue of art 30(1) for private companies and art 70(1) for public companies, the directors also have power to pay 'interim dividends', ie dividends on account of the 'final dividend' declared by the general meeting.[340] The general meeting cannot interfere with the directors' exercise of this power.[341] But the power to resolve that a distribution of profits should take some other form than that of a cash dividend is vested by art 34(1) for private companies limited by shares and art 76(1) for public companies in the general meeting by ordinary resolution on the recommendation of directors.

Dividends can only be paid in cash, unless there are words authorising payment by the issue of shares or debentures in the company fully or partly paid up (ie capitalisation), or the distribution among the members of assets (as, for instance, shares in other companies) *in specie*.[342]

If the articles are silent as to the distribution of profit, or declare that it shall be divided among the shareholders 'in proportion to their shares', the division must be made in accordance with, not the amount paid up on the shares, but the nominal amount of the shares, so that a shareholder whose shares are fully paid up gets no more per share than one whose shares are only partly paid up.[343] However, s 581(c)[344] authorises companies, if they so wish, to pay dividends in proportion to the amount paid up on the shares, where a larger amount is paid up on some shares

---

[337] *Bond v Barrow Haematite Steel Co* [1902] 1 Ch 353.

[338] *Re a Company, ex parte Glossop* [1988] BCLC 570, at 577. Habitual abuse may justify a winding-up on the just and equitable ground (see **18.12**) or more likely an unfair prejudice petition: *Re Sam Weller & Sons Ltd* [1989] 3 WLR 923.

[339] It is usually exercised at the company's annual general meeting.

[340] There must be a legitimate profit available according to the rules already set out.

[341] *Scott v Scott* [1943] 1 All ER 582. The directors can, however, rescind their decision before the date for payment: *Lagunas Nitrate Co. v Schneder* (1901) 85 LT 22.

[342] *Wood v Odessa Waterworks Co Ltd* (1889) 42 Ch D 645: see art 34 of the Model Articles for private companies limited by shares and art 76 of the Model Articles for public companies.

[343] *Oakbank Oil Co v Crum* (1882) 8 App Cas 65 (HL).

[344] [CA 1985, s 119(c)].

than others. Unless the articles otherwise provide, dividends and bonuses are payable to those who are registered holders at the time of the declaration.[345]

---

[345] The question of entitlement to dividends upon shares which have been transferred or transmitted is dealt with at **9.5** and **9.15**.

CHAPTER 8

RIGHTS AND LIABILITIES ATTACHED TO SHARES: REORGANISATIONS OF CAPITAL

8.1 SHARES

The ways in which a company may raise capital were described in a general way at the beginning of the previous chapter. It now falls to consider the nature of shares, the rights and liabilities attached to them and different classes thereof, and the ways in which share capital may be recognised.

Looking first at the nature of a share, we find that the Companies Act 2006 describes it as an item of personal property transferable in the manner provided by the company's articles.[1] A share is in fact a chose-in-action (in Scotland, incorporeal moveable property), one of those property interests which do not give the owner the right to possess anything physical. This bare description does not in fact seem to help very much. A more vivid description is provided by the oft-cited *dictum* of Farwell J:[2]

> 'A share is the interest of a shareholder in the company, measured by a sum of money for the purpose of liability in the first place and of interest in the second, but also consisting of a series of mutual covenants entered into by all the shareholders *inter se* in accordance with section [33] of the Companies Act [2006] ... A share is not a sum of money ... but is an interest measured by a sum of money, and made up of various rights contained in the contract.'

This points to a share having a dual nature as both contract and property. It also distinguishes the share from the debenture, the other standard form of security issued by companies, the holder of which, a lender of money to the company,[3] simply has rights against the company and not in it.

---

[1] Section 541 and 544(1) [CA 1985, s 182(1)]; as to transfer, see Chapter 9. A share must also have a fixed nominal value (see **4.11**).
[2] *Borland's Trustee v Steel Bros & Co Ltd* [1901] 1 Ch 279, at 288. As to s 33, see **5.20**.
[3] See Chapter 10.

In practice, however, as regards the securities of at least a public listed company, this distinction is to some extent illusory.[4] What is really important is to distinguish a security which gives real ownership rights in terms of votes at company meetings from one that does not. In practice, only ordinary shares generally confer such rights. The nature of the preference share is described below, as it is still conventional to compare and contrast it with the ordinary share, but it must not be forgotten that in practice it is lumped together with the debenture and the two are collectively referred to as preferred stock or securities. This is because, as well as having no or limited voting rights, the preference share usually shares the characteristic of the debenture of having the right to a prior, but fixed, rate of return.

8.2 CLASSES OF SHARES

As the above introductory remarks have indicated, a company may divide its share capital into different classes, although this would be relatively unusual for a private company. The power to create shares with varying rights is normally contained in the articles,[5] but occasionally it has been found in the memorandum.[6]

Whatever preferences or postponements or other special rights are intended to be created for a class of shares should be clearly expressed in the articles or in the resolution authorising the issue, and also in the prospectus inviting subscriptions for the shares. The mere use of a name such as 'preference shares' or 'preferred ordinary shares' is not enough of itself to indicate what special rights are to be attached to the shares. It is particularly important to express clearly the rights of the various holders in the case of a winding-up.

Historically, if there was any conflict between the memorandum and the articles as to what rights are conferred on a particular class of shareholders, the memorandum prevailed.[7] Where, however, there was an ambiguity in the memorandum, recourse to the articles could be had to resolve such unclarity.[8] As noted above, with provisions in the memorandum now treated as being part of the articles under s 28 of the Companies Act 2006, it is unlikely that those provisions which were

---

[4]   It will normally hold for private companies, since the issue by them of more than one class of share is unusual.

[5]   See art 22(1) of the Model Articles for private companies limited by shares and art 43(1) of the Model Articles for public companies.

[6]   Provisions that prior to the commencement of the Companies Act 2006 were included in a company's memorandum (save for those set out in the 'new style' memorandum in accordance with s 8) are now to be treated as provisions of the articles – s 28 (see Chapter 4) If necessary, a company can generally adopt the power by altering the articles.

[7]   *Re Duncan Gilmour and Co Ltd* [1952] 2 All ER 871; *Guinness v Land Corp of Ireland* (1883) 22 Ch D 349 (CA).

[8]   *Angostura Bitters Ltd v Kerr* [1933] AC 550 (PC).

formally parts of the memorandum would necessarily take precedence over those originally in the articles and that best interpretations will require to be gleaned by courts by all relevant provisions now in the articles as a whole. *Prima facie*, the articles, the resolution authorising the issue and, it is submitted, the share certificates express all the rights of the holders. The prospectus, however, cannot be examined for the purpose of interpreting such rights.[9] This rule as to interpretation does not, however, exclude proof that the prospectus did, in fact, contain part of the contract, or constitute a binding collateral contract.[10]

8.3   ORDINARY SHARES

Except insofar as the articles or terms of issue provide otherwise, an ordinary shareholder is entitled to receive dividends when declared (subject to any priority as to dividend enjoyed by preference shareholders), to have his appropriate proportion of the company's assets after payment of creditors paid or transferred to him on a winding-up (subject again to any priority enjoyed by preference shareholders) and to exercise one vote for each share that he holds at the general meetings of the company.[11] It should be noted that these rights as to dividend and return of capital include a right to participate in any surplus; thus in a winding-up, the holder of a £1 ordinary share is not confined to receiving back his £1 if the value of the assets available for distribution among the ordinary shareholders exceeds the nominal amount of the issued ordinary shares.

These rights of an ordinary shareholder may be, and often are, varied in specific respects by express provision in the articles or terms of issue. A company may, for instance, have two or more classes of ordinary shares, with each class carrying different voting rights, or indeed, with one such class having no voting rights at all.[12]

8.4   PREFERENCE SHARES

Preference shares may give a preferential right as to dividend only, or as to return of capital only, or both as to dividend and to return of capital. In either case the preferential dividend may be cumulative, or it may be payable only out of the profits of each year.

In addition to their fixed preferential rights, preference shares sometimes give further rights to participate in profits or assets. In this case, they may be known as 'participating preference shares'.

---

[9]   *British Equitable Assurance Co Ltd v Baily* [1906] AC 35, at 38–41 (HL).
[10]   *Jacos v Batavia and General Plantations Trust Ltd* [1924] 2 Ch 329 (CA) (which related to an issue of short-term notes).
[11]   See s 284(3) [CA 1985, s 370(6)].
[12]   See **8.6**.

In the last resort, the rights of a preference shareholder as to dividend and capital turn upon the construction of the relevant parts of the articles, or of the terms of issue. The courts have developed certain rules to govern this task of construction, as it is not always an easy one. It is proposed now to examine these rights, first as regards dividend and secondly as regards capital.

8.4.1 Preferential rights

The dividend on a preference share is generally a fixed one: that is, it is expressed in terms of a fixed percentage of the par value of the share.

A fixed preferential dividend is *prima facie* cumulative.[13] That is, arrears in one year must be made up from profits in subsequent years before any ordinary dividends are declared.[14] But this presumption may be rebutted, eg where the dividend is declared to be payable from 'yearly profits'[15] or 'out of the net profits of each year'.[16]

Payment of a preference dividend is dependent on 'distributable profits'[17] being available for that purpose. The holders of preference shares cannot prevent the company setting aside profits earned in any year to make good the losses sustained in previous years or to build up reserves if good faith is observed, even where they are entitled to a cumulative preferential dividend at a fixed rate. Their right to dividend is, in the absence of express bargain to the contrary, subject to the director's right to carry sums to reserve, and as with ordinary dividends, it only accrues when the dividend is declared.[18]

When a winding-up supervenes, the question arises whether the holders of cumulative preference shares have a right to receive the whole or any part of undeclared dividends from surplus assets.[19] There is no rule applicable to all circumstances as the issue turns on the construction of the relevant provision in the articles.[20] If there are no constitutional provisions regarding distribution of assets on winding up, the assets are shared equally between all members, including preference shareholders. This conclusion follows from the presumption that *prima facie* all shareholders rank equally.[21]

---

[13] *Webb v Earle* (1875) LR 20 Eq 556.

[14] However, the payment of such arrears is a dividend for the year in which it was declared, not in respect of the year when no payment was made: *Re Wakley* [1920] 2 Ch 205.

[15] *Adair v Old Bushmills Distillery Co* [1908] WN 24.

[16] *Staples v Eastman Photographic Materials Co* [1896] 2 Ch 303 (CA).

[17] See **7.21.2**.

[18] See **7.24**.

[19] This is sometimes referred to as arrears of dividend. See further *Palmer's Company Law* para 6.114.

[20] See, eg, *Re Walter Symons Ltd* [1934] Ch 308.

[21] *Birch v Cropper* (1889) 14 App Cas 525, at 543 and 546, per Lord Macnaghten.

If the articles declare that the preference shares do confer priority in a winding-up, or that the surplus assets shall be applied first in repaying the preference shares, but do not further deal with the capital, it is in every case a question of construction whether the preferential rights are given by way of priority only or by way of delimitation. Generally speaking, however, such a provision will constitute an exhaustive declaration of the preference shareholders' rights in a winding-up,[22] so as to exclude them from participation in any surplus remaining after repayment of the ordinary capital.[23] Any preference shareholder who wishes to displace the presumption must shoulder the onus of so doing.[24] The fact that his shares carry a right of participation in any surplus profits available for dividend does not displace the presumption; indeed it strengthens it if anything.[25]

Where the preference shareholders do have a right to participate, it extends to all the available assets, including those representing profits which before the winding up of the company could have been distributed as an ordinary dividend,[26] unless a provision in the articles makes it clear that such profits 'belong to' the ordinary shareholders[27] or in some other way reserves them for such holders.

8.5 OTHER CLASSES OF SHARES

There is no limit to the classes of shares which can be created, even within a single company. Founders' shares, often issued to promoters, in respect of which the receipt of a dividend was deferred until after the preference and ordinary shares had been paid a dividend at a specified rate, used to be common but are now rare.[28]

Alternatively, a company may issue shares which, like preference shares, carry the right to a fixed preferential dividend, but, like ordinary shares, carry the right to participate in surplus profits after their own fixed dividend and a fixed dividend attached to the ordinary shares have been paid. Such 'hybrid' shares are sometimes labelled 'participating preference shares' or 'preferred ordinary shares'. Also commonly found in practice are employees' shares, the issue of which has been encouraged by recent

---

22   This question is also especially relevant in a reduction of capital: see **8.13.4**.

23   *Scottish Insurance Corporation Ltd v Wilsons & Clyde Coal Co Ltd* [1949] AC 462 (HL (Sc)); *Re Isle of Thanet Electricity Supply Co Ltd* [1950] Ch 161 (CA); *Re Saltdean Estate Co Ltd* [1968] 1 WLR 1844.

24   *Re Isle of Thanet Electricity Supply Co Ltd*, above.

25   Ibid.

26   *Dimbula Valley (Ceylon) Tea Co Ltd v Laurie* [1961] Ch 353; *Re Saltdean Estate Co Ltd*, above; cf *Scottish Insurance Corp Ltd v Wilsons & Clyde Coal Co Ltd*, above.

27   *Re Bridgewater Navigation Co Ltd* [1891] 2 Ch 317 (CA).

28   As to these and the requirements of the Companies Act in respect of them, see *Gore-Browne on Companies* (Jordans, 45th edn, loose-leaf) at 21 [7].

British governments.[29] Shares of any class may be issued as redeemable under the terms of s 684 of the Companies Act 2006.[30]

8.6 VOTING RIGHTS

The holders of all classes of shares have equal rights of voting[31] unless restrictions are specifically imposed. Nonetheless, a provision in the articles that holders of any class of shares shall not have votes or shall have only limited rights of voting in respect of those shares is good; and resolutions passed by those having votes may be binding even when they affect the interests of all classes.[32] It has been suggested from time to time that voteless shares should be made illegal,[33] but this suggestion has never been implemented, and even listed shares may be voteless provided that they are clearly designated as such.[34] Under art 41 of the Model Articles for public companies, where shares are not fully paid up the holder will not be entitled to vote in respect of them.

Often, by the provisions of the articles, the holders of preference shares are not entitled to receive notice of or to attend or vote at general meetings in respect of their preference shares. It is nonetheless desirable that they should have the right to vote on any resolution involving a variation of their rights or a reduction of capital or a winding-up, and usually cumulative preference shareholders are given voting rights during any period when their dividend is in arrears for longer than a specified period.[35]

Sometimes even the holders of debentures are given votes in pursuance of a provision to that effect in the articles of association, and accordingly have a voice in the management of the company. Such votes could not be counted for the purpose of a special resolution, however, for the Companies Act 2006 provides that such a resolution must be passed by the specified majority of *members* entitled to vote.[36]

---

[29] See further *Gore-Browne on Companies* (Jordans, 45th edn, loose-leaf) at 21 [25].

[30] [CA 1985, s 159]. See **7.17.1**.

[31] See also **13.19**.

[32] *Re Barrow Haematite Steel Co (No 1)* (1888) 39 Ch D 582; *Re Mackenzie & Co Ltd* [1916] 2 Ch 450. This proposition is, however, subject to the specific rules governing variation of class rights, discussed at **8.7** *et seq*.

[33] See, eg, the Note of Dissent in the Report of the Jenkins Committee (Cmnd 1749), p 207.

[34] Albeit that the practice is frowned upon both by the market and Listing authorities.

[35] See, eg, *Re Bradford Investments plc* [1990] BCC 740, where it was held that the preference shareholders' right to vote if their dividend had not been paid for 6 months after the due date was exercisable, whether or not there were profits available to pay the dividend.

[36] See s 283(1) [CA 1985, s 378(1) and (2)], discussed at **13.3**.

An article which vests the primary right to vote at meetings in persons other than the registered shareholders or members is not lawful.[37] Section 286 of the Companies Act 2006 provides that in the case of joint holders of shares, the right to vote is given to the senior who tenders a vote. Seniority for this purpose is determined by the order in which the names stand in the register of members, although the articles may deviate from the statutory position. Under articles in the usual form, a joint holder can give a proxy without the concurrence of the other joint holders.

Every shareholder is entitled to vote in accordance with his own interests, although they may appear to be different from those of the company at large, unless the vote is given to him as a member of a class, in which case he must conform to the interest of the class itself when seeking to exercise the power conferred on him in his capacity of a member of that class,[38] or unless in so doing he infringes the broad principle, discussed elsewhere,[39] that members must exercise their voting power in what they *bona fide* believe to be the interests of the company. Subject to this principle, the general law held that a shareholder could vote in favour of property being purchased from himself even though he was also a director, and the resolution was binding even though passed by the votes of such shareholders.[40] This particular application, though, has now been reversed by s 239(4) of the Companies Act 2006.[41] An agreement by a vendor of shares with the purchaser that until they are transferred he will vote in a particular manner will be enforced by the court by a prohibiting injunction[42] (although it seems the company could not take notice of the fact that a vote was given in breach of such an agreement). In addition, an agreement in a mortgage that the mortgagor should retain the right of voting has in fact been enforced by a mandatory injunction.[43] An agreement made for a money consideration to vote for the advantage of another person in the course of a winding-up is, however, void.[44]

If by transferring his shares into other names or altering the order of the names a member can increase his voting power, he is entitled to do so.[45]

---

[37] *Shears v Phosphate Co-operative Co of Australia Ltd* (1988) 14 ACLR 747.

[38] *Re Holders Investment Trust Ltd* [1971] 1 WLR 583

[39] See **18.4**.

[40] *North-West Transportation Co v Beatty* (1887) 12 App Cas 589 (PC); *Pender v Lushington* (1877) 6 Ch D 70; *Burland v Earle* [1902] AC 82, at 94 (PC); *Dominion Cotton Mills Co Ltd v Amyot* [1912] AC 546 (PC).

[41] See **17.9.1**.

[42] *Greenwell v Porter* [1902] 1 Ch 530. As to the duration of a voting agreement, see *Greenhalgh v Mallard* [1943] 2 All ER 234 (CA).

[43] *Puddephatt v Leith* [1916] 1 Ch 200.

[44] *Elliot v Richardson* (1870) LR 5 CP 744.

[45] *Pender v Lushington*, above; *Moffat v Farquhar* (1878) 7 Ch D 591; *Burns v Siemens Brothers Dynamo Works Ltd* [1919] 1 Ch 225.

8.7 VARIATION AND ABROGATION OF THE CLASS RIGHTS OF SHAREHOLDERS

Special provisions exist in the Companies Act 2006, principally ss 630–634,[46] to protect the 'class rights' of shareholders, so that they cannot simply be varied or altered or, indeed, removed by alteration of the documents in which they are contained, ie the articles or a resolution passed under the authority of the articles. Where a company has only one class of shares, then variation of their rights would in general be effected by such alteration, although even in these circumstances, it seems that rights may be class rights.[47] In general, the relevant law hitherto contained in the Companies Act 1985 was restated with the provisions simplified somewhat in the Companies Act 2006.[48] An important addition to the relevant rules, however, is that the protection afforded under these sections was extended to classes in companies without a share capital.

A number of questions arise, including:

(1) What is a 'class right'?

(2) What constitutes a 'variation' or 'abrogation' of such a right?

(3) What is the appropriate procedure for varying or abrogating class rights?

Further questions will arise once these have been considered.

8.7.1 The concept of a 'class right'

When Parliament enacted the statutory provisions protecting class rights,[49] it chose not to define what it meant by 'class rights' or, to use the statutory phase, 'rights attached to any class of shares', nor even what it meant by 'class'.[50] This was probably because it was thought that there was no difficulty in determining what class rights were – if the shares in a company are divided into different classes according to the criteria set out earlier in this chapter, so that they have differing rights in respect of dividend, capital and voting or any of these, then the rights specifically

---

[46] [CA 1985, ss 125–127].

[47] See **8.7.1**.

[48] To some extent to account for the demise of the traditional memorandum.

[49] (The now) s 630 of the Companies Act 2006 was introduced only in 1980, implementing part of the Second EC Directive. (The now) s 633 of the Companies Act 2006 was first introduced in 1929.

[50] Albeit it is made clear by s 629(2) that rights attached to shares are not to be considered different to those attached to other shares simply by virtue that they do not carry the same rights to dividends in the 12 months immediately following their allotment [CA 1985, s 128(2)].

conferred in contrast to one or more of the other classes are class rights.[51] The rights might be conferred by the articles, the terms of issue or the resolution authorising the issue (as originally framed or subsequently varied).[52] That such rights are class rights was confirmed in the only reported case properly to consider the meaning of the term, namely *Cumbrian Newspapers Group Ltd v Cumberland & Westmorland Herald Newspaper & Printing Co Ltd*,[53] although, as will be seen below, the actual decision in that case went somewhat further. It was also, clearly correctly, decided in that case that a right unrelated to any shareholding cannot by any stretch of imagination be a class right.[54]

In addition to rights conferred specifically on a class, it is thought that the basic rights of all the classes as to dividends, capital and voting should be treated as class rights even when on a particular aspect there happens to be no difference between the various classes. Thus, for example, where preference and ordinary shares are clearly demarcated as regards dividend, but both classes participate *pari passu* in the assets on a winding-up, a resolution giving the preference shareholders the normal position of priority without further participation on a winding-up should be treated as varying a class right of the preference shares. Furthermore, the right to insist upon a variation of rights clause[55] is a class right, not least since s 630(5)[56] provides that any amendment of a variation of rights clause in the articles or the insertion of such a clause into the articles shall be treated as a variation of class rights.

As well as rights of the sort already described which are clearly class rights, articles of association in particular often confer other sorts of rights on shareholders not attached to a conventional 'class' of shares, for example, weighted voting rights in certain circumstances[57] or rights of pre-emption over shares. These will normally be found only in the articles of private companies. In the *Cumbrian Newspapers* case, the question arose as to whether such rights, even when not conferred on a shareholder as a member of a conventional class, could be class rights. Here, the plaintiff was given rights under the defendant company's articles, including a pre-emptive right regarding the transfer of any shares in the

---

[51] *Re John Smith's Tadcaster Brewery Co Ltd* [1953] Ch 308, at 319–320 (CA), per Jenkins LJ.

[52] As in *Re Old Silkstone Collieries Ltd* [1954] Ch 159 (CA).

[53] [1986] 3 WLR 26.

[54] See also *Re Blue Arrow plc* [1987] BCLC 587, at 590 rejecting, in line with the reasoning of Scott J in *Cumbrian Newspapers*, the idea that a right in the articles to be 'president' of the company, unrelated to any shareholding, could be a class right.

[55] This is not contained in the Model Articles because of the existence of s 630, but will still be relevant to companies which have the old style Table A of the 1985 Act, art 4 (see **8.7.2**).

[56] [CA 1985, s 125(7)].

[57] Cf *Bushell v Faith* [1970] AC 1099 (HL), discussed in **15.9**. The right which was the subject of this decision – weighted voting on a resolution to remove a director – was used as an example of a class right in the *Cumbrian Newspapers* case; see [1986] 3 WLR at 37.

defendant and the right to nominate a director to the board of the defendant so long as it held 10% of the issued ordinary shares of the defendant. It was held that rights of this sort were class rights, provided that they were conferred on a shareholder as such,[58] and thus subject to the protection of the then s 125. The learned judge, Scott J, found no basis for this result in the wording of the statute and justified it by what he perceived to be the legislative purpose behind the then s 125, namely the protection of such rights lest they be subject to removal by simple alteration of the articles.

It is submitted, with respect, that this conclusion is open to question.[59] There are other bases for protecting minority shareholders,such as the statutory derivative action[60] and unfair prejudice remedy.[61] The premise of s 125 was to implement part of the Second EC Directive, the purpose of which was the harmonisation of provisions relating to shares and share capital in *public* companies. If the decision is correct and followed, it has wide-ranging implications for rights often conferred by the articles of private companies, as already indicated. In effect, these rights are unalterable save with the consent of the individual shareholder concerned, since that person alone would constitute the class for the purposes of the now s 630 which, as will be seen below, requires the consent of a proportion of the class by itself to a variation of class rights. It is submitted that, if it is thought proper that such rights should be unalterable, this should be provided for in the context of a properly thought-out code for private companies, not by a 'surprisingly wide'[62] construction of a provision which had its origins in a code for public companies.

8.7.2   The meaning of 'varying' or 'abrogating' class rights

It is easy to discern that a class right is being 'varied' or 'abrogated'[63] when the proposed alteration directly conflicts with, and purports to override, the particular provision under which the right arises. Thus a resolution reducing a preferential dividend from 10% to 5% clearly involves the 'variation' of a class right, and a resolution depriving a class of preference shares of a right, guaranteed by a previous special

---

58   This limitation was not framed as narrowly as that which is often said to surround the statutory contract created out of the memorandum and articles by s 33 [CA 1985, s 14]; see **4.18**.

59   See also (1986) 7 Co Law 202; [1986] CLJ 399. Sealy & Worthington *Cases and Materials in Company Law* (Butterworths, 9th edn, 2010) at p 526 refers to the decision as 'surprisingly wide'.

60   See **18.3** *et seq*.

61   See **18.10**.

62   See footnote 59, above.

63   These are the vital words in ss 630, 631, 633 and 644. Further, by virtue of ss 630(6) (variation of class rights in companies with a share capital) and 631(8) (variation of class rights in companies without a share capital), in any provision for the variation of class rights, except where the context requires otherwise, references to variation include references to abrogation.

resolution, to participate in compensation accruing to the shareholders under impending nationalisation legislation, has been held to involve the 'modification or abrogation' of a class right attached to the preference shares.[64]

This is not to say that variation or abrogation of a class right belonging to a particular class cannot arise in some other way, eg through a variation of the literal terms of the class rights of another class, or through some measure not on its face involving class rights at all. It would seem, for example, that a resolution raising the voting power of one class of shares from one vote to ten votes per share alters the class rights, not only of that particular class, but of all other classes carrying voting rights.[65] Equally, it has in general been assumed[66] that a reduction of capital under which the various classes are not treated in accordance with their capital rights on a winding-up involves a variation of class rights. Probably the removal of a modification of rights clause constitutes such a variation also. The articles can extend the meaning of a variation of class rights, for example, by providing that any reduction of capital is deemed to be such.[67]

Despite the examples cited above, the general tendency of the courts has, however, been to rule that the class rights attached to (say) 'class X' of shares have not been 'varied' or 'abrogated', or even 'affected' or 'dealt with',[68] by a resolution which alters the literal terms of the class rights of another, 'class Y', or on its face does not bear upon class rights at all. The following measures have been held not to vary or abrogate the class rights attached in each case to 'class X' and therefore not to fall within the scope of a modification of rights clause:

(1)   an issue of new shares ranking *pari passu* with class X;[69]

---

[64]   *Re Old Silkstone Collieries Ltd* [1954] Ch 169 (CA).

[65]   *Greenhalgh v Arderne Cinemas Ltd* [1946] 1 All ER 512, at 516 (CA); *Lord St David's v Union Castle Mail Steamship Co Ltd* (1934) *The Times*, November 24. But cf the actual decision in the *Greenhalgh* case, referred to in the next paragraph, and cf the approach of the Court of Appeal in *White v Bristol Aeroplane Co Ltd* [1953] Ch 65 (CA) and *Re John Smith's Tadcaster Brewery Co Ltd* [1953] Ch 308 (CA).

[66]   See, eg, *Scottish Insurance Corp Ltd v Wilsons & Clyde Coal Co Ltd* [1949] AC 462 (HL (Sc)); *Re Old Silkstone Collieries Ltd*, above. The adjustment of rights as between different classes of shareholders on a reduction of capital is discussed more fully at **8.13.4**.

[67]   See *Re Northern Engineering Industries plc* [1993] BCC 267. As to reductions of capital and class rights generally, see **8.13.4**.

[68]   These extra terms are sometimes inserted in modification of rights clauses in an attempt to widen their scope, but no decision to date has shown them to have any substantial effect. In *Re Mackenzie & Co Ltd* [1916] 2 Ch 450, they seem to have been ignored, but in *White v Bristol Aeroplane Co Ltd*, above, and *Re John Smith's Tadcaster Brewery Co Ltd*, above, they did come under discussion by the Court of Appeal.

[69]   *Re Schweppes Ltd* [1914] 1 Ch 322 (CA) (a decision under the Companies (Consolidation) Act 1908).

(2)   an issue ranking in priority to class X,[70] there being no extrinsic
       contractual promise to the holders of class X that this would not be
       done;[71]

(3)   an issue of bonus shares (whether ordinary or preference) to the
       holders in class Y (ordinary shares), when it had the effect of greatly
       increasing their voting power as against that of the holders in class X
       (preference shares),[72] or of reducing the amount which would come
       in a liquidation, on a distribution of surplus assets, to the holders in
       class X (preference shares);[73]

(4)   a subdivision of shares in class Y so that the holders in that class
       acquired a greatly increased voting power in comparison to class
       X;[74]

(5)   the cancellation of paid-up capital to an equal extent on both class
       X (preference shares) and class Y (ordinary shares), with the result
       that the fixed preferential dividend payable to class X, though
       unaltered in percentage, was substantially reduced in amount,
       whereas the dividend for class Y remained at large;[75] and

(6)   the alteration of the place of payment (and thus the currency) of
       dividends from England to Australia, causing the fixed preferential
       dividend payable to class X to be of lesser value because the
       Australian pound was worth less than the English pound sterling.[76]

Lord Evershed MR[77] suggested an explanation for such decisions, namely
that it was not the class rights of the complaining class that were varied or
abrogated or affected, but merely the 'enjoyment' of those rights.[78] No
doubt this is a valid theoretical distinction. It is submitted, however, that
more than once minority classes have lost the benefit of their rights,
without any class meeting being held, in circumstances where the relevant
modification of rights clause seems clearly to have been intended to

---

[70]   *Pulbrook v New Civil Service Co-operation* (1878) 26 WR 11; *Underwood v London Music
       Hall Ltd* [1901] 2 Ch 309; *Hodge v James Howell & Co Ltd* [1958] CLY 446 (CA).
[71]   See *Allen v Gold Reefs of West Africa Ltd* [1900] 1 Ch 656, at 673–674 and 679 (CA).
[72]   *White v Bristol Aeroplane Co Ltd*, above; *Re John Smith's Tadcaster Brewery Co Ltd*,
       above.
[73]   *Dimbula Valley (Ceylon) Tea Co Ltd v Laurie* [1961] Ch 353.
[74]   *Greenhalgh v Arderne Cinemas Ltd* [1946] 1 All ER 512 (CA).
[75]   *Re Mackenzie & Co Ltd*, above.
[76]   *Adelaide Electric Supply Co Ltd v Prudential Assurance Co* [1934] AC 122 (HL).
[77]   In *White v Bristol Aeroplane Co Ltd* [1953] Ch 65, at 74 (CA).
[78]   A distinction was drawn in this case between the rights attached to a share within a
       particular class and the relative influence (in terms of voting) of that class within the
       company following a variation. The latter was categorised as 'enjoyment' of rights, as it
       could be varied without any variation in the former (eg as a result of the issue of new
       voting shares of a different class).

supply protection to them.[79] A narrow and literal approach to the concept of 'variation of rights' has in general been the cause of such instances.

8.7.3 Procedure for variation

Once it is clear that a 'class right' is being sought to be 'varied' or 'abrogated', the procedure to be adopted depends upon whether the articles or terms of issue contain an express provision for variation (ie a 'variation of rights clause'). The procedure is largely governed by s 630 (for companies with a share capital) and s 631 (for companies without a share capital).[80]

In respect of companies with a share capital, rights attached to a particular class of the company's shares may only be varied either in accordance with a provision in the company's articles for the variation of those rights, or where no such provision exists in the articles, members of that class consent to the variation in question.[81] Such consent may be given in writing by holders of at least three-quarters of the nominal value of the issued shares of that class (excluding any held as treasury shares) or by a special resolution passed at a separate general meeting of that class of shareholders.[82] Where provision is made in the company's articles for variation of class rights, then such a procedure may deviate from (ie either increase of reduce) the 75% approval required in the default provision.[83] It should be noted that these provisions are without prejudice to any other restriction upon the variation of class rights which may exist.[84] For example, an attempted variation would fail in the face of entrenchment of certain class rights in a company's articles in accordance with s 22.

New provisions were introduced by the Companies Act 2006 in respect of the variation of class rights in companies without a share capital, in particular companies limited by guarantee.[85] Hitherto the question of whether such class rights could be varied would have hinged upon whether there was provision to this effect in the articles or simply whether the articles were to be altered by way of the general statutory procedure.

---

[79] Notably in *Greenhalgh v Arderne Cinemas Ltd*, above, and *Re Mackenzie & Co Ltd*, above.

[80] Albeit that by virtue of s 632, nothing in s 630 or 631 affects the power of the court in the respect of s 98 (application to cancel resolution of a public company to be registered as private), Part 26 (arrangements and reconstructions), or Part 30 (protection of members against unfair prejudice).

[81] Section 630(2).

[82] Section 630(4).

[83] At one stage the Companies Bill 2006 had dispensed with any alternative to the 75% majority route: See cl 644(2) of the Companies Bill, as amended in Standing Committee D and published in July 2006.

[84] Section 630(3).

[85] In s 631.

Subject to necessary terminological variation, s 631 sets out identical provisions to those in s 630 applying to companies with a share capital as described above.

8.7.4   Notice for class meetings and filing requirements

If, under any of the circumstances described, a class meeting is held, whether required by statute or by a variation of rights clause, then the general requirements of Part 13 of the Companies Act 2006 as to the length of notice for calling meetings, general provisions regarding meetings and votes,[86] and circulation of members' resolutions,[87] along with any relevant provisions in the articles must be complied with. In particular, the quorum at any such meeting must be two persons at least holding or representing by proxy one-third of the issued shares of the class concerned or where the company is one without share capital, one-third of the voting rights concerned, except at an adjourned meeting where one person holding shares (or voting rights) of the class is sufficient; any holder of shares of the class concerned present in person or by proxy may demand a poll.[88]

Where rights attached to any shares in a company are varied then within one month of so doing, the company must deliver to the registrar in the prescribed form notice of the variation. Contravention of this section is an offence levied against the company concerned and every officer who is in default.[89] Identical provisions apply to a company without a share capital that varies the class rights of members.[90] Additionally, where a company assigns or changes a name or other designation of a class of shares, within one month of so doing it must deliver to the registrar in the prescribed form notice of the name or designation so assigned. Contravention of this section is again an offence levied against the company concerned and every officer who is in default.[91] Again, identical provisions apply to a company without a share capital that assigns or changes a name or other designation of a class of members.[92] Furthermore, where a company without a share capital creates a new class of members, the company must similarly within one month send to the registrar in the prescribed form notice of particulars of the rights attached to the class.[93]

---

[86]   See **13.7.5** *et seq.*

[87]   See **13.8.2**.

[88]   See ss 334 and 335 [CA 1985, s 125(6)].

[89]   Section 637 [CA 1985, s 128(3)].

[90]   Section 640.

[91]   Section 636 [CA 1985, s 128(4)].

[92]   Section 639.

[93]   Section 638. Where a limited company with a share capital creates a new class of shares, it provides details of the rights attached to the shares in the return of allotments required under CA 2006, s 555. An unlimited company creating a new class of shares will similarly file under CA 2006, s 556.

8.7.5 Protection for minority in class

Where a variation of class rights in a company with a share capital has taken place in accordance with s 630, s 633[94] provides that the holders of not less than 15% of the issued shares of the class affected, if they did not consent to or vote in favour of the variation, may apply to the court to have the variation cancelled (for this purpose any of the company's share capital held as treasury shares is disregarded). The court may, if satisfied that the variation would unfairly prejudice the shareholders of the class represented by the applicant, disallow the variation; if not so satisfied, it must confirm it. Application may be made by such one or more of the shareholders affected as may be appointed by them in writing and must be made within 21 days after the appropriate consent was given or resolution passed.[95] An identical provision (save for any necessary terminological variation) applies in respect of challenges made to the variation of class rights in accordance with s 631 for companies without a share capital.[96]

Sections 633 and 634 do give a measure of protection to minorities within a class of shareholders who consider that their rights have been unjustly overridden by the majoritybut its narrow scope must be noted. Such protection applies only where there is: (a) a variation under s 630 or 631; and (b) a genuine 'variation' or 'abrogation' of a 'class right'. The narrow meaning of these terms has already been described. Further, there is no reported use of the section. On the other hand, there are House of Lords *dicta*[97] to the effect that a minority shareholder within the relevant class has a right at general law to challenge a class resolution on the ground of lack of good faith and that the then s 127[98] was not intended to deprive him of such right. To enforce this general law right, a holding of 15% of shares of the class in question is not necessary.[99]

---

[94] [CA 1985, s 127].

[95] Section 633(4) [CA 1985, s 127(3)]. The court's decision is final (s 633(5) [CA 1985, s 127(4)]) and a copy of any order made must be lodged with the registrar within 15 days of the date thereof (s 635 [CA 1985, s 127(5)]).

[96] Section 634.

[97] *Carruth v Imperial Chemical Industries Ltd* [1937] AC 707, at 756 and 765; see too *British American Nickel Corp v O'Brien* [1927] AC 369 (PC) and *Re Holders Investment Trust Ltd* [1971] 1 WLR 583. The latter case, which is described in **8.13.5** and where the issue arose on a petition to confirm a reduction of capital, is perhaps the best reported example of what might be regarded as 'unfair prejudice' under (the now) ss 633 and 634.

[98] Now ss 633 and 634 of the Companies Act 2006.

[99] The matter could also be litigated on a petition to confirm a reduction of capital (see **8.13**) or by a petition under s 994 [CA 1985, s 459], the general remedy for unfairly prejudiced minority shareholders (see **18.10**).

8.8   LIABILITIES ON SHARES

The fact of becoming a member of a company renders the person liable to contribute to its assets to the extent and in the manner prescribed by the Companies Act 2006, taken along with the general law and the articles of association, as outlined below.

In an unlimited company, the members are liable while the company is a going concern to pay to it the nominal amount of the shares (if any) held by them as and when called up, together with any premium payable on issue, and upon winding up to pay whatever amount is necessary to satisfy the debts of the company and the expenses of liquidation,[100] but as far as possible all the members contribute rateably.

In a company limited by guarantee, the members are liable while the company is a going concern to pay to it the amount payable on the shares (if any) held by them as and when called up, and on a winding-up they are liable for any balance of the amount of their shares unpaid and, in addition, the amount guaranteed by them in the articles or memorandum of association, if required for the purpose of paying the debts of the company and the costs of liquidation, but no more.[101]

In the case of a company limited by shares, each member is liable to pay only the nominal amount of the shares held by him (together with any premium which he may have agreed to pay);[102] and notwithstanding any provision of the articles, no member is bound by any alteration thereof, to which he has not previously or at the time thereof given his assent in writing, which requires him to subscribe for more shares than he then holds or in any way increases his liability to pay money to the company.[103]

In each of the above cases, until a liquidation takes place, the amounts are payable at the times and in the manner prescribed by the articles of association, which almost invariably declare that so much as is not paid on application and/or allotment may be called up by the directors as and when they think fit.[104]

---

[100]   Insolvency Act 1986, s 74(1); and see s 3(4) of the Companies Act 2006 [CA 1985, s 1(2)(c)].

[101]   Ibid, s 74(3); and see s 3(3) of the Companies Act 2006 [CA 1985, s 1(2)(b)].

[102]   Ibid, s 74(2)(d); and see s 3(2) of the Companies Act 2006 [CA 1985, s 1(2)(a)]. In exceptional circumstances the liability of a member or a director may become unlimited: see Chapter 3.

[103]   Section 25 of the Companies Act 2006 [CA 1985, s 16].

[104]   See, eg, art 54 of the Model Articles for public companies, As to calls by a liquidator when a company is being wound up, see **21.52**.

8.9   INITIAL PAYMENTS ON SHARES

Payments on applications for shares and/or allotment are dealt with in connection with the general topics of public issues and allotment of shares.[105] For present purposes it is sufficient to note that, subject to certain specific statutory provisions relating to public companies only,[106] and to any provisions in the articles or any agreement between the company and the member, the mere fact of becoming a member, whether as a subscriber to the memorandum or otherwise, does not of itself impose any obligation on the member to make an immediate payment to the company in respect of his shares.[107] In practice, of course, at least part of the price of the shares will in any event be made payable on application where the process of application is resorted to. Similarly, all, or the balance outstanding, or a part, will be payable on allotment.

8.10   CALLS

A call is the way in which amounts due on shares not fully paid up on application are raised.[108] These amounts can in general be called up by a proper authority at any time, subject to the articles.[109] In the early days of company law, when the holding of partly paid shares for a considerable time was common, calls would be made at regular intervals. This is infrequent, and perhaps unknown, these days, but the articles, as in art 56 of the Model Articles for public companies, usually deem any amount payable in respect of a share on allotment, at any fixed date, or on the occurrence of a specified event in the future to be a call. The result is that, for example, a failure to pay the balance or an instalment due on allotment of shares, a sum having been paid on application, or to pay the balance due at a later specified date or on the occurrence of a specified event, will attract the prospect of the shares being forfeited.[110]

Article 64 of the Model Articles for public companies provides that, subject to the terms of allotment, the directors may from time to time make calls upon the members in respect of any moneys unpaid on their

---

[105] See Chapters 7 and 19.

[106] Especially s 586(1) [CA 1985, s 101], by which shares in a public company must not be allotted to any person unless not less than one-quarter of the nominal value of the shares together with the whole of any premium has been received by the company (see **7.9**).

[107] *Alexander v Automatic Telephone Co* [1900] 2 Ch 56 (CA).

[108] For more detail, see *Gore-Browne on Companies* (Jordans, 45th edn, loose-leaf), 21[18] *et seq*.

[109] A member cannot escape liability unless he shows that he has been wrongly made a member and has used all diligence to have his name removed from the register: see **12.5**.

[110] As to forfeiture, see **8.14**. Note that in the absence of a provision like art 56, payments on application or allotment are not calls (*Croskey v Bank of Wales* (1863) 4 Giff 314) and that in the absence of a provision to the contrary in the articles or in some other agreement, there is no obligation to make any payment on shares subsequent to allotment until a call is made; *Re Russian Spratt's Patent Ltd* [1898] 2 Ch 149 (CA).

shares (whether in respect of nominal value or premium),[111] and requires at least 14 days' notice to be given to the members, who are then liable to pay at the time(s) and place(s) appointed by the directors.

If calls remain unpaid, the members liable should be sued for the amount. In England, a call is an ordinary contract debt,[112] and accordingly can be recovered by action at any time within 12 years of the date of the call.[113] In Scotland, five years is the equivalent period.[114]

The Model Articles for public companies provides that calls in arrears shall bear interest.[115] Any dividends becoming payable upon the shares of defaulting members should be retained by the company, and in addition any rights of lien[116] or refusal to register a transfer of the shares[117] exercised. As a last resort (if the articles give the power) the shares should be forfeited.[118]

8.11   LIENS ON SHARES

Articles[119] generally give a company a lien on the shares of a member for the calls or any debts as are due to the company from such member. The lien can generally be enforced by sale[120] or forfeiture[121] of the shares concerned.[122]

While such liens are generally valid in so far as private companies are concerned,[123] in the case of public companies, s 670 of the Companies Act 2006[124] restricts their right to take liens or other charges on their shares. Section 670(1) provides that a lien or other charge of a public company is void unless permitted by the section. This permits only the following categories of lien or charge:

---

[111] They must act in good faith and not for a collateral purpose. For example, it is prima facie improper to make calls on only some of a class of members: *Galloway v Hallé Concerts Society* [1915] 2 Ch 233. See further, as to directors' duties, Chapter 16.

[112] Section 33(2) and Insolvency Act 1986, s 80.

[113] Limitation Act 1980, s 8.

[114] Prescription and Limitation (Scotland) Act 1973, s 6.

[115] Article 57. At no more than 5% above the Bank of England's base lending rate.

[116] See **8.11**.

[117] See **9.3**.

[118] See **8.14**.

[119] See, eg, arts 52 and 53 of the Model Articles for public companies, in which a lien for calls or other moneys payable on the shares is given in respect of partly paid shares. Under the *Listing Rules*, the articles of a company seeking quotation must not provide for any lien on fully paid shares.

[120] See, eg, art 53 of the Model Articles for public companies.

[121] See **8.14**.

[122] For more detail on liens, see *Gore-Browne on Companies* (Jordans, 45th edn, loose-leaf) at 21 [22] *et seq*.

[123] *Bradford Banking Co Ltd v Henry Briggs & Co Ltd* (1886) 12 App Cas 29 (HL); *Bank of Africa Ltd v Salisbury Gold Mining Co* [1892] AC 281 (PC).

[124] [CA 1985, s 150].

(1) in respect of any public company, a charge on partly paid shares for any amount payable in respect of the shares;

(2) in respect of a public company whose ordinary business includes the lending of money or consists of the provision of credit or the bailment or (in Scotland) hiring of goods under a hire-purchase agreement, or both, a charge on any of its shares, fully or partly paid, which arises in connection with a transaction entered into by the company in the ordinary course of its business;

(3) in respect of a company which is re-registered as a public company, a charge on its own shares in existence immediately before its application for re-registration or registration.

8.12 THE REORGANISATION OF CAPITAL

The Company Law Review recommended a number of changes to the law governing reorganisations of capital which found their way into the Companies Act 2006. Some significant alterations in this sphere of law were made from that which hitherto existed as are noted below. In general, rather than mimicking the approach of the Companies Act 1985 in permitting particular alterations of capital, the starting point of the Companies Act 2006 provisions is that the alteration of capital is generally prohibited except in respect of certain specified conduct.[125] By virtue of s 617 of the Companies Act 2006, a company having a share capital may not alter its share capital except in the following ways:

(1) an increase in capital by the allotment of new shares under Part 17;[126]

(2) a reduction of capital;

(3) a sub-division or consolidation of shares under s 618;

(4) a reconversion of stock into shares under s 620; and

(5) a redenomination of shares (and, if appropriate, a consequential reduction) under ss 622 and 626 of the 2006 Act.[127]

Section 617(5) provides that nothing in the section affects the redemption or purchase of a company's own shares under Part 18,[128] the purchase of

---

[125] Section 617.

[126] These are considered in Chapter 7.

[127] Note also that the concept of authorised share capital was abolished (see **4.5**) and thus procedures in the Companies Act 1985 concerned with increasing the authorised share capital were not carried forward into the Companies Act 2006.

[128] See Chapter 7.

own shares pursuant to a court order,[129] the forfeiture of shares for non-payment of a sum due in respect thereof,[130] the cancellation of shares under s 662, and the powers under Part 26.

8.13   REDUCTION OF CAPITAL

A number of important de-regulatory provisions regarding reduction of capital are included in the Companies Act 2006; chiefly that private companies no longer require the approval of the court for a reduction of capital and neither is it essential that companies are empowered to that effect by their articles, albeit that the articles may prohibit or limit the exercise of this power. The provisions as to reduction of capital are set out in ss 641–653 of the Companies Act 2006.[131]

Under s 641, a private company limited by shares[132] may, by passing a special resolution[133] supported by a 'solvency statement',[134] reduce its share capital 'in any way'.[135] Additionally the same section provides that any limited company may reduce its share capital by way of a special resolution confirmed by the court. Thus for private companies limited by shares they need not reduce their capital via the new route, but rather may seek approval of the court through the traditional pathway.[136]

The words 'in any way' indicate that the power to reduce capital is unlimited, but s 641(4)[137] also sets out special instances, providing expressly that such a company may:

(1)   extinguish or reduce the liability on any of its shares in respect of share capital not paid up; or

---

[129]   By virtue of ss 98, 721(6) and 759 or Part 30.

[130]   This is not governed by statute but the power exists if a company has authority in its articles.

[131]   [CA 1985, ss 135–141].

[132]   An unlimited company may reduce capital at will, without the confirmation of the court being required, as long as there is power in the articles: *Re Borough Commercial and Building Society* [1893] 2 Ch 242.

[133]   The requirement for a special resolution is not usually displaced by the unanimous agreement of all the shareholders: *Re Barry Artist Ltd* [1985] BCLC 283, but a private company can use the statutory written resolution procedure; see **13.5**. The court can correct a trivial error in the resolution: *Re Willaire Systems plc* [1986] BCLC 67.

[134]   In accordance with s 643.

[135]   Although a reduction cannot be made in this way where the result would be that no member holds any shares other than redeemable shares – s 641(2).

[136]   Early research suggests that despite doubts as to its utility, the new route of reduction of capital by way of solvency statement has been well received by companies, primarily on the basis of reduced costs – see Department for Business Innovation and Skills, *Evaluation of the Companies Act 2006* (2010) volume 1, at 177.

[137]   [CA 1985, s 135(2)].

(2)   either with or without extinguishing or reducing liability on any of
      its shares, cancel any paid-up share capital which is lost or
      unrepresented by available assets; or

(3)   either with or without extinguishing or reducing liability on any of
      its shares, pay off any paid-up share capital which is in excess of the
      wants of the company.

A further common use of the power to reduce capital is to reduce the
share premium account. In addition, a company may take power to issue
redeemable shares and to purchase its own shares subject to the
conditions of Part 18 of the Act.[138] The fact that a private company in
certain circumstances may purchase its own shares out of capital provides
for an alternative procedure for reducing capital.[139] The court has power
to make an order for reduction of capital under s 996.[140]

Section 641 deals with the reduction of *share capital*, so that, in cases
under (3) above, a reduction may be confirmed, although the money to
make the payment off is to be borrowed,[141] and even if it is to be
borrowed (eg on the security of debentures) from the very persons whose
shares are to be reduced.[142] The amount by which the share capital is to
be reduced may be satisfied by the distribution of assets in specie even
though the value of those assets may exceed the nominal amount by
which the share capital is reduced.[143]

8.13.1   The solvency statement

By virtue of s 642, the solvency statement required by the new procedure
for private companies cannot be made by directors more than 15 days
before the resolution to reduce the capital of the company is passed and
both the resolution and statement must be lodged with the registrar in
accordance with s 644.[144] A copy of the statement must be made available
to the company's members at the time of the vote to reduce the capital. If
the resolution is proposed as a written resolution, it must be sent or
submitted to every eligible member at or before the time at which the

---

[138]   See **7.17** *et seq.*

[139]   This was hitherto seen as an easier route, but is no longer necessarily the case in view of
        the new procedure for private companies to reduce capital in the Companies Act 2006.
        In fact the requirement for a solvency statement when private companies seek a
        reduction of capital without the court's consent mirrors that required in respect of the
        purchase by a private company of its own shares out of capital.

[140]   [CA 1985, s 461]. See **18.13**.

[141]   *Re Nixon's Navigation Co* [1897] 1 Ch 872.

[142]   *Re Thomas de la Rue & Co Ltd* [1911] 2 Ch 361.

[143]   *Ex parte Westburn Sugar Refineries Ltd* [1951] AC 625 (HL (Sc)).

[144]   Section 642(1).

proposed resolution is served on him.[145] Where it is proposed at a general meeting, a copy must be made available for inspection by members throughout the meeting.[146]

The solvency statement, which must be made by all directors, is an affirmation that each is of the opinion that: (a) in relation to the company's situation at the date of the statement, there is no ground upon which the company could then be found unable to pay or otherwise discharge its debts; and also (b) that if it is intended to commence winding up of the company within 12 months of that date, then the company will be able to pay or otherwise discharge its debts within 12 months of commencement of the winding-up or, in another case, that the company will be able to pay or otherwise discharge its debts in the year immediately following that date.[147] In forming this opinion, directors must take into account all the company's liabilities (including prospective and contingent liabilities).[148] Where the statement is made without reasonable grounds for the opinions set out above, every officer in default commits a criminal offence.[149] It should be noted that the registrar is empowered by s 1068 to impose requirements as to how the statement is to be authenticated by directors although it is clear from s 643 that the statement must state the name of each director and the date upon which it is made.[150]

8.13.2   Matters incidental to a reduction

In the course of reducing its capital with the court's confirmation,[151] it has been held that a company may do things which would otherwise be illegal, such as repurchasing its own shares.[152] A reduction may also be confirmed even though its purpose is one not apparently contemplated by the section provided that it has a discernible purpose. This may occur,for example, where the company has ceased to carry on business and the only aim of the reduction is to distribute the assets,[153] where a holding company wishes to reduce its share premium account in order to eliminate goodwill arising on consolidation of the group's accounts,[154] where a subsidiary company wishes to cancel its share premium account to increase its distributable reserves and produce a tax advantage for its

---

[145] Section 642(2).

[146] Section 642(3). Albeit that under s 642(4) any irregularity in the notice provisions will not lead to the invalidity of the resolution. Any officer in default in this respect commits an offence punishable by a fine, however, under s 644(7).

[147] Section 643(1).

[148] Section 643(2).

[149] Section 643(4) and (5).

[150] Section 643(3).

[151] Under s 645 [CA 1985, s 136].

[152] *British and American Trustee Corp v Couper* [1894] AC 399 (HL); of course it is not now always illegal to do so: see **7.17.2**.

[153] See *Scottish Insurance Co Ltd v Wilsons & Clyde Coal Co Ltd* [1949] AC 462 (HL (Sc)).

[154] *Re Ratners Group plc* (1988) 4 BCC 293; *Re Thorn EMI plc* (1988) 4 BCC 698.

holding company,[155] or where the company wishes to convert ordinary shares into redeemable deferred shares.[156] Insofar as such circumstances are applicable to a private company limited by shares seeking to reduce its capital without the court's consent and thus supported by a solvency statement, it is likely that such instances of reduction will also be allowable in respect of reductions under the new route.

8.13.3   Matters relevant to confirmation by the court

Where a reduction is sought with the approval of the court, once provision has, where relevant, been made for creditors,[157] the court's attitude to confirming a reduction of capital depends on three factors:

(1)   that the reduction is fair and equitable between the different classes of shareholders in the company, where there is more than one class;

(2)   that the proposal affects all shareholders of the same class in a similar manner, unless those treated differently have consented to it; and

(3)   that the causes of the reduction were properly put to shareholders so that they could exercise an informed choice and that the cause is proved by evidence before the court.[158]

8.13.4   Shareholders' class rights

The first two of these factors have traditionally posed the most problems and merit examination here. There is no general rule that a reduction of capital must bear equally upon all the shares of the company, or even

---

[155]   *Re Ransomes plc* [1999] 1 BCLC 775. On appeal ([1999] 2 BCLC 591), the decision was confirmed even though, subsequent to the decision at first instance, the company no longer wished to distribute the reserve so created. The case had become 'very unusual' (at 603).

[156]   *Forth Wines Ltd, Petitioner* [1991] BCC 638.

[157]   As to creditors, see **8.13.6**.

[158]   See the *dictum* of Harman J in *Re Jupiter House Investments (Cambridge) Ltd* [1985] BCLC 222, at 224. This *dictum* actually omits the first factor, but its importance is well established by the cases cited in the next section. See also *Re Ratners Group plc* (1988) 4 BCC 293 and *Re Thorn EMI plc* (1988) 4 BCC 698, requiring that all shareholders be treated 'equitably'. Note that Harman J expressed disapproval of *dicta* to the effect that the public interest, in terms of people who might become shareholders in the future, was a relevant factor (per Lord Macnaghten in *Poole v National Bank of China Ltd* [1907] AC 229, at 239 (HL)); see also *Re Grosvenor Press plc* [1985] BCLC 286, at 290–291. It was clear, previously, that the public interest, if relevant, did not extend to the interests of the community at large: *Ex parte Westburn Sugar Refineries Ltd* [1951] AC 625 (HL). As regards the third factor, although the court has recently forgiven a less than full explanation where the matter was urgent and it was satisfied as to the substantive fairness of the scheme, it was stated that 'no company would be well advised to follow [this] course … if it has any minority shareholders on whose agreement it cannot count': *Re Ransomes plc* [1999] 1 BCLC 775, at 786. See also [1999] 2 BCLC 591, at 599–600 (CA).

upon all the shares in a particular class, and reductions have been confirmed as fair and equitable where only some of the shares in a particular class have been wholly or partly paid off[159] or cancelled.[160] Where, however, different shareholders or classes of shareholders have different rights as to return of capital on a winding-up, there is a *prima facie* rule that a reduction of capital should be framed so as to conform with these rights, unless consent is obtained from the particular shareholders or classes of shareholders whose rights are prejudiced.[161]

The most important instance of this rule is that where there are preference shares having priority as to return of capital (but no rights of further participation in surplus assets) and there are ordinary shares as well, then in a reduction involving a return of capital in excess of the company's wants, the preference shares should be paid off first,[162] whereas in a reduction involving partial or total cancellation of shares on account of losses, it is the ordinary shares that should first be cancelled.[163] Sometimes the preference shareholders in a prosperous company may feel aggrieved at losing a favourable investment through being thus paid off at par in advance of the ordinary shareholders, but this of itself gives them no legal grounds of objection,[164] not even if under the articles they had a right of participation in distribution of surplus profits by way of dividend.[165] It is only when they have clearly defined[166] rights of participation in surplus assets on a winding-up (whether under the articles or terms of issue, or under some special statutory provision),[167] or (perhaps) where there is an independent agreement between them and the company that capital will not be reduced without their consent,[168] that they can raise the objection

---

[159] Eg *British and American Trustee Corporation v Couper*, above; *Re Robert Stephen Holdings Ltd* [1968] 1 WLR 522 (but note that in this case the court suggested that a scheme of arrangement under the then s 425 of the Companies Act 1985 (now s 895 of the Companies Act 2006) would have been a more appropriate procedure, because minority interests would have been better protected thereby).

[160] Eg *Re Gatling Gun Ltd* (1890) 43 Ch D 628; *Re Pinkney & Sons Steamship Co* [1892] 3 Ch 125.

[161] *Bannatyne v Direct Spanish Telegraph Co* (1887) 34 Ch D 287, at 300 (CA).

[162] *Re Chatterley-Whitfield Collieries Ltd* [1948] 2 All ER 593, at 596 (CA), affirmed sub nom *Prudential Assurance Co Ltd v Chatterley-Whitfield Collieries Ltd* [1949] AC 512 (HL); *Re Saltdean Estate Co Ltd* [1969] 1 WLR 1844; *House of Fraser plc v ACGE Investments* [1987] AC 387 (HL); and see *Scottish Insurance Corporation Ltd v Wilsons & Clyde Coal Co Ltd* [1949] AC 462 (HL (Sc)).

[163] *Re Floating Dock Co of St Thomas Ltd* [1895] 1 Ch 691; *Re London and New York Investment Corporation* [1895] 2 Ch 860; *Poole v National Bank of China Ltd* [1907] AC 229 (HL).

[164] *Scottish Insurance Corporation Ltd v Wilsons & Clyde Coal Co Ltd*, above.

[165] *Re Saltdean Estate Co Ltd*, above; *House of Fraser plc v ACGE Investments*, above.

[166] Inchoate rights (eg an expectation of compensation under the Coal Industry Nationalisation Act 1946, s 25) will not suffice: *Scottish Insurance Corp Ltd v Wilson & Clyde Coal Co Ltd*, above; *Prudential Assurance Co Ltd v Chatterley-Whitfield Collieries Ltd* [1949] AC 512 (HL).

[167] Eg where their expectation of compensation under the Coal Industry Nationalisation Act 1946, s 25, has been confirmed by resolution, as in *Re Old Silkstone Collieries Ltd* [1954] Ch 169 (CA).

[168] See ibid.

that their rights are not being strictly observed. This vulnerability of preference shareholders who have no such rights of participation is sometimes overcome in quoted companies by the use of the so-called 'Spens formula', namely a provision in the articles or terms of issue that where preference shares are paid off, the price should be tied to the quoted market value at the time and the preference shareholders should have voting rights on the resolution for reduction. An alternative method of protection is to provide that any reduction of capital is deemed to be a variation of class rights, so that the special procedure described in **8.7.3** must be complied with.[169]

8.13.5 Reduction not in accordance with class rights

In certain cases, the courts were prepared to confirm reductions that did not accord with class rights on a winding-up, even though the consent of the shareholders or classes affected had not been obtained. In such a case, however, the onus lay on the company to prove that the reduction was fair and equitable, and the court would examine its terms and effect with particular care.[170]

Even if the variation procedure has *prima facie* been complied with, the court can still disallow the variation and hence the reduction if the variation was improper. In one case,[171] the court refused to confirm a reduction whereby redeemable preference shares were cancelled and the holders received an equivalent amount of unsecured loan stock, it being conceded by the company that this entailed a modification of the class rights of the preference shareholders. The court found: (a) that the resolution for class consent was ineffectual because the majority had not voted with a view to the interests of the class; and (b) that, having regard to the terms of issue of the loan stock, the reduction had not been shown by the company to be fair and equitable.

Where class consent is obtained (which may be done by dint of a three-quarters majority of that class or in accordance with a provision in the articles providing for the variation concerned under s 630, or under an accompanying scheme of arrangement under s 895),[172] class rights may on a reduction be changed or overridden to a substantial degree. For example, the preference shareholders may agree to surrender their priority as to capital[173] or to forgo arrears of cumulative preferential dividend,[174]

---

[169] *Re Northern Engineering Industries plc* [1993] BCC 267.

[170] *British and American Trustee Corp v Couper* [1894] AC 399, at 406 (HL); *Carruth v Imperial Chemical Industries Ltd* [1937] AC 707, at 744 and 749 (HL); *Re Holders Investment Trust Ltd* [1971] 1 WLR 583.

[171] *Re Holders Investment Trust Ltd*, above.

[172] [CA 1985, s 425]. As to s 895, see **20.17**.

[173] *Re Hyderabad (Deccan) Co Ltd* (1897) 75 LT 23; *Re National Dwellings Society Ltd* (1898) 78 LT 144; *Balmenach Glenlivet Distillery Ltd v Croall* (1907) 8 F 1135.

[174] *Oban and Aultmore Glenlivet Distillery Ltd* (1904) 5 F 1141.

or the voting powers of the respective classes may be altered,[175] or the reduction may be accompanied by other arrangements reconstituting for the future the class rights of the different classes.[176]

8.13.6 Rights of creditors

Under s 645,[177] if a reduction involves any diminution of liability or any repayment of capital, and in any other case if the court so directs, creditors are entitled to object. The court can, however, under s 654(3),[178] dispense with creditors' rights and will generally do so if there is obtained a guarantee of their debts from a bank or if satisfied that the company has cash and liquid assets exceeding the claims of the creditors and the amount of the capital to be returned.

A typical 'other case' where the rights of creditors are relevant is where a company is reducing capital in order to write off a loss, but the loss is not expected to be permanent, for example, because the company has acquired a loss-making business which it is hoped will prove profitable in the future.[179] Here the reduction will be confirmed if the company undertakes to put into a capital fund not available for distribution any money received in respect of the business up to the amount of the reduction.[180]

If the rights of creditors are not dispensed with, s 648[181] requires the court to be satisfied on the hearing of the petition to confirm the reduction with respect to every creditor that either: (a) his consent to the reduction has been obtained; or (b) his debt or claim has been discharged or determined, or has been secured by setting apart and appropriating, in such manner as the court may direct, a sufficient sum.[182]

---

[175] *Re James Colmer Ltd* [1898] 1 Ch 524.

[176] *Re Allsopp & Sons Ltd* (1903) 51 WR 644 (CA); *Re Welsbach Incandescent Gas Light Co Ltd* [1904] 1 Ch 87 (CA).

[177] [CA 1985, s 136].

[178] [CA 1985, s 136(3)].

[179] See *Re Jupiter House Investments (Cambridge) Ltd* [1985] BCLC 222 and *Re Grosvenor Press plc* [1985] BCLC 286, which illustrate that using the reduction procedure in this way can increase the amount of profits available for distribution under s 829 [CA 1985, s 263] (as to which, see **7.21** *et seq.*).

[180] Ibid. These authorities also make it clear that the interests of future creditors are irrelevant.

[181] [CA 1985, s 137]. The Companies (Share Capital and Acquisition by Company of its Own Shares) Regulations 2009, reg 3 provided an amendment to s 646 thus excluding those creditors who cannot show that there is a real likelihood that the reduction would result in the company being unable to pay them at the due time from entitlement to object.. For a recent discussion on this issue in the Outer House of the Court of Session see *Royal Scottish Assurance Petitioners* [2011] CSOH 2, where Lord Glennie viewed that the test for creditors in this regard was stringent.

[182] For more detail as to procedure in respect of creditors, see *Gore-Browne on Companies* (Jordans, 45th edn, loose-leaf) at 64 [18]. Note also the provisions of s 653 [CA 1985, s 140] whereby a creditor ignorant of the reduction and who did not therefore object to

8.13.7 Procedure on a reduction of capital

Detailed consideration of the procedure involved in the presentation of a petition to confirm a reduction of capital is unnecessary here.[183] If the court sanctions the reduction, the order and a statement of capital, approved by the court, showing the particulars of the capital as reduced must be registered with the registrar,[184] and notice of this registration must be published in such manner as the court directs. By virtue of s 649(3), the reduction does not take effect until the registration has been carried out,[185] as recommended by the CLRSG,[186] to enable a reduction forming part of a compromise or arrangement under Part 27 to take effect simultaneously to other aspects of that compromise or arrangement.

The registrar then certifies the registration and the statement of capital.[187] Notice of the registration and statement of capital must be published in a form as the court may direct.[188]

The court can require the company to publish the reasons for the reduction,[189] but rarely does so.

8.14 FORFEITURE AND SURRENDER OF SHARES

A forfeiture or surrender of shares is a reduction of capital and in consequence cannot usually be carried out without either the confirmation of the court or in accordance with the new procedure for private companies limited by shares under s 641. It has, however, been held that without the court's confirmation[190] shares may be forfeited, but only for non-payment of calls and provided it is done under an express power in the articles.[191] In cases where such forfeiture would be permissible, the shares may be validly surrendered.[192] A company's

---

it, may be entitled if the company is wound up insolvent, to receive payment from the shareholders whose shares were reduced up to the amount of the reduction.

[183] See *Gore-Browne on Companies* (Jordans, 45th edn, loose-leaf) 64 [11]–64 [25].

[184] Section 649(1). The statement of capital must be made in accordance with the standard format articulated in s 555(4).

[185] [CA 1985, s 138(2)].

[186] Final Report, para 13.11.

[187] Section 649(5).

[188] Section 649(4) [CA 1985, s 138(3)].

[189] Section 648(3) [CA 1985, s 137(2)].

[190] As was otherwise always required for a reduction of capital under the equivalent Companies Act 1985 provisions.

[191] *Lane's Case* (1862) 1 De GJ & Sm 504; *Kipong v Todd* (1878) 3 CPD 350 (CA). See arts 57–61 of the Model Articles for public companies permitting forfeiture and note the extended meaning of 'call' under art 56; see **8.10**.

[192] *Trevor v Whitworth* (1887) 12 App Cas 409 at 417, 429, 438 (HL); art 62 of the Model Articles for public companies.

articles may be altered so as to introduce a power of forfeiture,[193] subject to the general limitations upon alteration of articles.[194]

Where shares are forfeited in the absence of any such authorisation in the articles, or in a manner falling outside the relevant clause thereof, the forfeiture is invalid and cannot be ratified, even by a majority of shareholders.[195]

By the same token, a surrender of partly paid shares in circumstances not justifying a forfeiture is invalid, because the shareholder is purportedly released from his liability for uncalled capital.[196] A voluntary surrender of fully paid shares in such circumstances may perhaps be valid if it is authorised by the articles and new shares are issued in exchange so as to prevent diminution of the company's capital.[197] A surrender in return for any other form of valuable consideration is clearly invalid as being in substance a purchase by the company of its own shares.[198] On the other hand, a voluntary transfer of fully paid shares to a nominee to hold them as trustee for the benefit of the company is valid. In such a case, the company pays nothing for the shares, and its capital is not reduced.[199]

The procedure specified by the articles for forfeiture must be strictly complied with,[200] and directors must exercise the power for a proper purpose, not, for example, simply to get rid of an obnoxious shareholder.[201]

If a forfeiture is invalid, the invalidity is not cured by lapse of time and the holder remains a member of the company as regards both liabilities and rights.[202]

8.14.1 Reissue of forfeited shares

The company usually has power to reissue forfeited shares (eg under art 60(2)(c) of the Model Articles for public companies)[203] and on such reissue may treat them as paid up to any extent not exceeding the amount

---

[193] *Dawkins v Antrobus* (1881) 17 Ch D 615 (CA).

[194] See **5.9** *et seq.*

[195] *Spackman v Evans* (1868) LR 3 HL 171; *Houldsworth v Evans* (1868) LR 3 HL 263.

[196] *Bellerby v Rowland and Marwood's Steamship Co Ltd* [1902] 2 Ch 14 (CA).

[197] *Re County Palatine Loan & Discount Co Teasdale's case* (1873) 9 Ch App 54.

[198] *Trevor v Whitworth* (1887) 12 App Cas 409, at 438 (HL).

[199] *Kirby v Wilkins* [1929] 2 Ch 444. See further **7.16**. However, as far as public companies are concerned, the consequences of a lawful acquisition by a nominee are the same as those of a forfeiture, by virtue of ss 662–669 [CA 1985, ss146 to 149]. See **8.14.2**.

[200] See, eg, *Johnson v Lyttle's Iron Agency* (1877) 5 Ch D 687.

[201] As to directors' duty to act for the proper purpose, see **16.4**.

[202] *Garden Gully United Quartz Mining Co v McLister* (1875) 1 App Cas 39. However, a shareholder may be precluded from setting aside a forfeiture after acquiescing in it over a long period: *Jones v North Vancouver Land and Improvement Co* [1910] AC 317.

[203] A public company is in effect obliged to reissue them by virtue of s 662 [CA 1985, s 146], described in **8.14.2**.

paid by the former holders. If in exercise of this power it reissues shares irregularly forfeited, it may be liable in damages to the original holder.[204] When forfeited shares have been reissued, the company may make a fresh call upon the new holder in respect of the amount remaining unpaid by the former holder upon which the forfeiture was made.[205]

8.14.2   Treatment of forfeited and surrendered shares in public companies

By s 662(1), shares in public companies[206] which are forfeited or surrendered for failure to pay calls and shares which are subject to the other circumstances described below are subject to a special regime. The other circumstances are:

(1)   where shares in the company are acquired by the company other than in accordance with Part 18 (acquisition by a limited company of its own shares) or a court order under Part 30 (protection of members against unfair prejudice) and it has a beneficial interest[207] in them;

(2)   where the nominee of the company acquires shares in the company from a third person without financial assistance being given directly or indirectly by the company and the company has a beneficial interest in those shares;[208]

(3)   where any person acquires shares in the company with financial assistance given to him directly or indirectly by the company for the purpose of or in connection with the acquisition[209] and the company has a beneficial interest in those shares;

(4)   where shares in the company are surrendered to the company in accordance with s 102C(1)(b) of the Building Societies Act 1986 (cl 53).

---

[204]   *Re New Chile Gold Mining Co* (1890) 45 Ch D 598.

[205]   *New Balkis Eersteling Ltd v Randt Gold Mining Co* [1904] AC 165 (HL), but any payment by the former holder goes to reduce this amount (*Re Randt Gold Mining Co* [1904] 2 Ch 468) and, conversely, any payment by the new holder reduces the debt of the former holder (*Re Bolton* [1930] 2 Ch 48).

[206]   Where a private company is re-registered as a public company (see **4.11**), and shares in it have been forfeited, surrendered or otherwise acquired in circumstances to which s 662 applies, the provisions of the section apply, the relevant period for disposal or cancellation of the shares (see below) commencing with the date of re-registration; s 668 [CA 1985, s 148].

[207]   'Beneficial interest' is subject to the qualifications in Sch 1; see *Gore-Browne on Companies* (Jordans, 45th edn, loose-leaf) at 24 [46]–24 [49] and 26 [16].

[208]   On the acquisition of shares by a nominee, see **7.16**.

[209]   See **7.18**.

If such shares are not disposed of within the relevant period of the date of forfeiture, surrender or acquisition, the company must cancel them and diminish the amount of its share capital by the nominal value of the shares concerned and, where the effect of the cancellation will be to bring the level of the company's allotted share capital below the authorised minimum,[210] apply for re-registration as a private company, stating the effect of the cancellation.[211] The relevant period in all cases except that described in paragraph (3) above is 3 years. In the cases of shares acquired in the circumstances described in paragraph (3), it is one year.[212] In addition, shares forfeited, surrendered or acquired in these circumstances cannot carry voting rights.[213] Failure to comply with either of the requirements mentioned renders the company and every officer in default liable to a fine.[214] Failure to comply with the requirement to apply to be re-registered as a private company within the relevant period means that the company is treated as a private company for the purpose of Chapter 1 of Part 20;[215] ie it is unable to offer its securities to the public, but otherwise it continues to be treated as a public company until it is re-registered.[216]

The cancellation procedure required may be effected by a resolution of the directors of the company without complying with the statutory procedures for a reduction of capital under ss 641–653.[217] If a public company is obliged to register as a private company in accordance with s 666 then the directors may pass a resolution that the company be so re-registered and such a resolution may include changes to both the company's name and articles such as are necessary to effect the re-registration.[218]

Where a public company or its nominee acquires shares or an interest in shares in the company, and those shares or that interest are shown in a balance sheet of the company as an asset, an amount equal to the value of the shares or the interest must be transferred out of profits available for dividend[219] to a reserve fund and is not available for distribution.[220]

---

[210] See **4.2**.
[211] Section 666(2) [CA 1985, s 146(2)].
[212] Section 662(3) [CA 1985, s 146(3)].
[213] Section 662(5) [CA 1985, s 146(4)].
[214] Section 667 [CA 1985, s 149(2)].
[215] See **19.3**.
[216] Section 666 [CA 1985, s 149(1)].
[217] Section 662(4) [CA 1985, s 147(1)]. As to these, see **8.13** *et seq.*
[218] Section 664.
[219] See **7.21.2**.
[220] Section 669(1) [CA 1985, s 148(4)].

8.15 OTHER CAPITAL ALTERATIONS

A limited company having a share capital can under s 671(3)[221] consolidate and divide all or any of its share capital into shares of a larger amount than its existing shares or subdivide its shares into shares of a smaller amount, and reconvert stock into paid-up shares of any denomination. Additionally, a new provision in the 2006 Act explicitly affords the company the right to redenominate any or all of its shares.[222]

Regarding the consolidation or subdivision of shares, unlike the hitherto applicable 1985 Act provisions, power for this purpose need not be set out in the articles (although the articles may exclude or limit the power) and a limited company may proceed in this regard by the passing of an ordinary resolution.[223] It should be noted that such a resolution may allow the company to exercise more than one of the powers conferred on it under the section: for example, the resolution may authorise both a subdivision of one class of the company's shares and a consolidation of another. It may also authorise the company to exercise a power conferred on it under this section on more than one occasion or at a specified time or in specified circumstances.[224] The company has one month within which to give notice to the registrar of the subdivision or consolidation and specify the shares affected. The notice should also be accompanied by a statement of capital in the usual form.[225] If default is made in respect of compliance with the notice provision, then both the company and every officer in default will face a fine.[226]

While companies are no longer empowered to convert fully paid shares into stock,[227] under s 620 existing stock may be reconverted into shares. Again, there no longer exists the need that this power be expressed in the articles and the ordinary resolution required by s 620(2) can confer power to reconvert stock into fully paid shares on more than one occasion; at a specified time; or in specified circumstances.[228] Similar requirements apply in respect of notification to the registrar of re-conversion as to those pertaining to the subdivision or consolidation of a company's shares.[229]

It was hitherto appropriate for a UK company to issue shares with values other than in pounds sterling, although the minimum capital required for

---

[221] [CA 1985, s 121(2)].

[222] Ie convert the fixed nominal value of shares from one currency to another: s 671(4).

[223] Section 618(3).

[224] Section 618(4).

[225] Section 619.

[226] Section 619(4) and (5).

[227] Stock is 'simply a set of shares put together in a bundle': *Morrice v Aylmer* (1875) LR 7 HL 717, at 725, per Lord Hatherley. Conversion of shares into stock has been very rare of late.

[228] Section 620(3).

[229] See s 621.

a public company must originally be in sterling or euros.[230] However, there was previously no procedure for changing currencies except by a cancellation through a reduction of capital followed by the making of a new issue. Under new procedures in s 622 of the Companies Act 2006, subject to any prohibition or limitation in the company's articles,[231] a redenomination of shares may be effected by an ordinary resolution of the members. The conversion under the new provisions must take place at the appropriate 'spot rate' of exchange specified in the resolution. Such a rate must either be the rate prevailing at a date set out in the resolution or determined by taking the average of rates on each consecutive day of a period specified in the resolution (but the day or period must be within the period of 28 days ending on the day before the resolution is passed).[232] The conversion may be conditional upon the meeting of certain conditions set out in the resolution.[233]

As one might expect, the effect of such a redenomination is that it does not affect any rights or obligations under the company's constitution – in particular, rights to dividends, voting rights and shareholders' obligations in relation to amounts unpaid on shares. Again similar notice requirements apropos information tendered to the registrar apply in respect of a redenomination as to re-conversion of stock and the consolidation or subdivision of shares.[234]

Reduction of capital is the final issue that arises in respect of redenomination that warrants discussion. As a redenomination may render shares left in cumbersome fractions in the new currency, a special procedure for reduction of capital in this context is set out in s 626. Any such reduction may not exceed 10% of the nominal value of the company's allotted share capital as it stands in the immediate aftermath of the redenomination and must be approved by a special resolution of the company passed within 3 months of the redenomination resolution. In such circumstances, capital is maintained by the requirement of s 628 that the reduction must be transferred to the new redenomination reserve. While this may be used to pay for a capitalisation of shares by the issue of bonus shares,[235] it is otherwise undistributable.[236] Again similar requirements to give notice to the registrar as to any reduction of capital

---

[230] Albeit that once a trading certificate has been obtained, a public company would be free to redenominate its minimum capital.

[231] Section 622(7).

[232] Section 622(2) and (3).

[233] Section 622(4).

[234] See s 627.

[235] Section 628(2).

[236] Section 628(3).

resulting from redenomination apply as to those in respect of the redenomination itself, re-conversion of stock into shares and consolidation or subdivision of shares.[237]

---

[237] Albeit that the company is bound to give notice to the registrar within 15 days of the resolution to reduce capital instead of the monthly period applying in other contexts – see s 627.

CHAPTER 9

TRANSFER AND TRANSMISSION OF SHARES

9.1   THE TRANSFER OF SHARES

The original allottee of the shares of a company remains personally entitled to the benefits and subject to the obligations of the shares until he has disposed of them either:

(1)   by transfer;

(2)   by death or bankruptcy;

(3)   by forfeiture or surrender; or

(4)   on a reduction of capital or other form of capital reorganisation.

The last two processes have been considered in the previous chapter. The first two, which are commonly referred to as 'the transfer and transmission of shares', will be dealt with in this chapter. In cases of transfer the transferee takes the place of the transferor, and in cases of transmission the estate of the former holder takes his place as regards benefits and liabilities.

It should be noted that, unless the contrary is provided, the term 'transfer' in a company's articles refers only to a transfer of the legal title to shares, that is the registered membership,[1] and not to transfer of an equitable interest.[2] This can have important consequences as regards restrictions on the transfer of shares, as will be discussed in the following sections.

The legal technique by which shares are transferred is novation.[3] Strictly speaking, it is inaccurate to refer to shares being 'transferred' by novation, as the process of novation establishes a new contract (the 'statutory

---

[1]   As to the register of members, see Chapter 12.

[2]   *Theakston v London plc* [1984] BCLC 390. As to the consequences of this, see **9.2.2**; neither an allotment nor the renunciation of an allotment of shares is a transfer of them: *System Control plc v Munro Corporate plc* [1990] BCLC 659, at 662–663.

[3]   Novation is a general principle of contract law: see *Chitty on Contracts* (Sweet & Maxwell, 28th edn, 1999) para 20–086, 1067.

contract' created by s 33 of the Companies Act 2006)[4] as between a
company and a (new) member and as between the new member and
existing members. But the economic effect of novation is similar to
transfer as the old and new contracts are on the same terms.[5] A purchaser
of shares becomes a member by being entered in the company's register of
members[6] and thereby becomes a party to the statutory contract. This
process differs from assignment (the legal technique by which unregistered
securities are transferred) in that novation extinguishes the old and creates
a new contract, whereas an assignee takes legal title from an assignor
subject to equities.[7]

9.2   TRANSFERABILITY OF SHARES

Subject to certain limited restrictions imposed by law,[8] a shareholder has
prima facie the right to transfer his shares when and to whom he pleases.[9]
This freedom to transfer may, however, be significantly curtailed by
provisions in the articles. Restricting provisions are legal;[10] on the other
hand, the transfer of fully paid listed shares must not be restricted by the
articles in any way.[11] In determining the extent of any restriction on
transfer contained in the articles, a strict construction is adopted; that is
to say, the restriction must be set out expressly, or must arise by necessary
implication, and any ambiguous provision is construed in favour of the
shareholder wishing to transfer.[12]

Two common forms of restriction found in the articles of private
companies are: (a) provisions that the board of directors should have a
power, general or limited in scope, to refuse to register transfers as they
should deem fit; and (b) pre-emption clauses, ie provisions that a member
wishing to transfer should first offer his shares to other specified persons,
such as the directors or the other members. These two forms of restriction
will now be discussed in turn, although it must be borne in mind that
many other forms of restriction exist as well.

---

[4]   See **5.20**.

[5]   See generally J Benjamin *Interests in Securities* (Oxford University Press, 2000)
      para 2.04.

[6]   Section 112; see **12.5**. See in respect of dematerialised securities **9.3.3**.

[7]   Although equitable interests in property are not recognised in Scotland, a similar
      distinction can be drawn between novation and assignation as an assignee takes legal
      rights subject to the principle *assignatus utitur jure auctoris.*

[8]   These are briefly discussed at **9.2.4**.

[9]   *Re Smith Knight & Co, Weston's Case* (1868) 4 Ch App 20; *Re Bede Steam Shipping Co*
      [1917] 1 Ch 123, at 132–133 (CA).

[10] Since 1980 there has not been any obligation on private companies (as existed
      previously) to restrict the right of transfer, although restrictions of the sort discussed
      below are still usual.

[11] *Listing Rules*, LR 2.2.4–.2.6. This rule does not prohibit the imposition of purely formal
      requirements as to transfer.

[12] *Re Smith & Fawcett Ltd* [1942] Ch 304, at 306 (CA); *Moodie v W & J Shepherd
      (Bookbinders) Ltd* [1949] 2 All ER 1044 (HL (Sc)).

9.2.1 Power to refuse registration

Any discretionary power vested in the directors to refuse to register transfers of shares is a power that must be exercised in accordance with the core duties of the directors, especially to exercise the power for a proper purpose and to act in good faith in what they consider would be most likely to promote the success of the company.[13] If the transferor can show that the directors have acted wantonly or capriciously or from an improper motive or with a collateral purpose in refusing to register the transfer, the court will order the transfer to be registered.[14] Evidence that the directors were acting upon undertakings given to outsiders would be evidence that their discretion was being improperly exercised,[15] as too would evidence that they had an explicit policy of refusing to allow a particular shareholder to transfer his shares to anyone.[16]

An important change regarding the power of refusal was introduced by the Companies Act 2006. Section 771 requires a company refusing to register a transfer to give reasons for the refusal as soon as practicable, and within a maximum period of 2 months, and such further information about the reason for the refusal as the transferee may reasonably request, although this does not include copies of minutes of directors' meetings. Previously the only requirement was to give notice of refusal and the court would not compel the directors to state their reasons for the rejection,[17] nor would it examine the directors' particular reasons when the power to refuse was limited to specified grounds.[18] These authorities are clearly now redundant and the case-law described below must be read in the light of the fact that the transferee has the statutory rights described.

If the directors, having a general and absolute power of refusal, decide to reject a transfer, the court will not interfere provided the requirements as to good faith and proper purpose are satisfied.[19] But the power will be construed strictly, in the sense that in the absence of clear words it will not be held to authorise the directors to refuse to register the executor of a deceased member on a transmission[20] or, in the case of shares being issued to members with a right to renounce, a person to whom a member

---

[13] See ss 171 and 172, discussed in Chapter 16. The leading authority on the fiduciary principles applicable as now codified in those sections is *Re Smith & Fawcett Ltd* [1942] Ch 304 (CA).

[14] *Ex parte Penney* (1873) 8 Ch App 446; *Re Coalport China Co* [1895] 2 Ch 404 (CA).

[15] *Clark v Workman* [1920] 1 Ir R 107.

[16] *Robinson v Chartered Bank* (1865) LR 1 Eq 32.

[17] *Ex parte Penney* (1873) 8 Ch App 446; *Berry v Tottenham Hotspur Football and Athletic Co Ltd* [1935] Ch 718.

[18] *Re Coalport China Co* [1895] 2 Ch 404 (CA).

[19] *Re Smith & Fawcett Ltd* [1942] Ch 304 (CA); *Charles Forte Investments Ltd v Amanda* [1964] Ch 240 (CA); *Village Cay Marina Ltd v Acland* [1998] 2 BCLC 327 (PC); *Mactra Properties Ltd v Morshead Mansions Ltd* [2008] EWHC 2843 (Ch).

[20] See *Re Bentham Mills Spinning Co* (1879) 11 Ch D 90 (CA).

has duly renounced his right to subscribe.[21] Neither of these transactions involves a 'transfer' strictly so-called.

Where the board's power of refusal is limited to grounds specified in the articles, the refusal must be based on at least one of the specified grounds and the directors may be compelled to identify the particular ground on which their decision to refuse is based.[22] In general, the rule of strict construction applies again. Thus, if the directors' power is expressed to be a right to refuse to register a transfer to a person of whom they do not approve, or whose membership would, in their opinion, be contrary to the interests of the company, their objection must be to something personal to the transferee (for instance, that he cannot pay calls or is a quarrelsome person, or is acting in the interests of a rival business), and if their refusal is on the ground of something which relates only to the transferor (such as that the transfer is made only to increase his voting power), or is on the ground that the directors desire that only members of a particular family should be shareholders, or that there should not be a number of small holdings, this is in excess of the power, and the court will order registration of the transfer.[23]

Unless the articles expressly make the directors' approval of transfers a condition precedent to their registration, a transfer fails only if there is a positive decision by the directors to reject it; thus if the directors are equally divided on the matter, or there is no board at all, the transfer is entitled to registration.[24] The same applies if a decision is not reached within a reasonable time after lodgement of transfer[25] and since s 711 requires that any company refusing to register a transfer must notify the transferee accordingly as soon as practicable and in any event within two months of lodgement, it will normally be safe to say that once the two-month period has elapsed, the transfer can no longer be rejected.[26] However, if a proper decision to refuse to register a transfer is taken, a failure to communicate that decision within the two-month period does not render the transfer void,[27] although the company and any officer in default will be liable to the criminal penalty specified in s 711(4).

---

[21]   *Re Pool Shipping Co Ltd* [1920] 1 Ch 251.
[22]   *Sutherland v British Dominions Land Settlement Corp* [1926] Ch 746.
[23]   These instances are taken from *Moffat v Farquhar* (1878) 7 Ch D 591; *Re Bell Brothers Ltd* (1891) 65 LT 245; *Re Bede Steam Shipping Co* [1917] 1 Ch 123 (CA).
[24]   See three cases on transmission: *Re Hackney Pavilion Ltd* [1924] 1 Ch 276; *Moodie v W & J Shepherd (Bookbinders) Ltd* [1949] 2 All ER 1044 (Sc); *Re New Cedos Engineering Co Ltd* [1994] 1 BCLC 797.
[25]   *Re Joint Discount Co, Shepherd's Case* (1866) 2 Ch App 16.
[26]   *Re Swaledale Cleaners Ltd* [1968] 1 WLR 1710 (CA); *Tett v Phoenix Property and Investment Co Ltd* [1984] BCLC 599; *Re Inverdeck Ltd* [1998] BCC 256. During the 2-month period, the transferee has no rights, even if the company has no directors to exercise the right of refusal: *Re Zinotty Properties Ltd* [1984] 1 WLR 1249.
[27]   *Popely v Planarrive Ltd* [1997] 1 BCLC 8.

9.2.2 Pre-emption clauses

Pre-emption clauses constitute valid restrictions upon the transfer of shares.[28] They are enforceable against individual members by the company[29] and by the persons upon whom the rights of pre-emption are bestowed, at least if they are members of the company.[30] A pre-emption clause will be strictly construed; in particular, the court will be reluctant to hold that such a clause fetters the right of a member to transfer his shares to another member at any price that may be agreed upon between them.[31] On the other hand, the court will be prepared to construe a pre-emption clause with sufficient liberality to prevent its obvious purpose being thwarted.[32] Thus, in *Lyle & Scott Ltd v Scott's Trustees*[33] when a company's articles provided that any member 'desirous of transferring his shares' should serve a 'transfer notice' upon the company, thereby setting in train certain procedures whereby other members could exercise rights of pre-emption, the House of Lords held that a member who in return for a sale price executed a transfer of his shares to a non-member and gave him an irrevocable proxy in respect of the votes thereon was 'desirous of transferring' within the meaning of the article, even though both parties to the sale had sought to evade the article by refraining from requesting registration of the transfer. The member was accordingly directed to serve a 'transfer notice'.

This decision was distinguished in *Safeguard Industrial Investments Ltd v National Westminster Bank Ltd*.[34] Here, subject to certain exceptions, the articles required a 'proposing transferor' to give notice to the company to set in motion a pre-emption procedure. The bank, executor of a deceased member who had bequeathed his shares to two members of the company, was registered as holder of the shares which it would hold for the latter on completion of the administration of the estate. However, at their request, it did not propose to transfer the shares to the two members. It was held that the bank did not fall within the articles. It had no intention of transferring the shares and the word 'transfer' was apt to cover only the transfer of the legal title to the shares, not the transfer of beneficial interests.

---

[28] Altering the articles to remove such a clause may be unfairly prejudicial conduct within Part 30: *Re Kenyon Swansea Ltd* [1987] BCLC 514; see **18.10** *et seq.*

[29] *Borland's Trustee v Steel Brothers & Co Ltd* [1901] 1 Ch 279; *Lyle & Scott Ltd v Scott's Trustees* [1959] AC 763 (HL (Sc)); *Jarvis Motors (Harrow) Ltd v Carabott* [1964] 1 WLR 1101.

[30] Cf *Rayfield v Hands* [1960] Ch 1, where a clause entitling members who wished to sell their shares to require the directors (who were subject to a share qualification) to buy them out at a fair price was held to be enforceable against the directors without the company having to be joined as a party to the proceedings. See further **5.20**.

[31] *Delavenne v Broadhurst* [1931] 1 Ch 234; *Greenhalgh v Mallard* [1943] 2 All ER 234 (CA).

[32] *Lyle & Scott Ltd v Scott's Trustees* [1959] AC 763 (HL(Sc)); and see *Jarvis Motors (Harrow) Ltd v Carabott* [1964] 1 WLR 1101.

[33] Above.

[34] [1982] 1 All ER 449 (CA).

The court left open the question of the effect of an uncompleted agreement to sell shares on the operation of the articles. It may be that, unless the articles are drafted to cover dispositions of equitable interests, nothing short of a declaration of trust or the execution of a transfer and the handing over of an irrevocable proxy, as in the *Lyle & Scott* case, would suffice to bring a member within the terms of standard-form pre-emption provisions such as these.[35]

Where a company's articles provided in essence that shares could not be transferred to any person not already a member of the company if any member was willing to purchase the same, it was held that a term would be implied requiring a member wishing to transfer to take reasonable steps to give notice of his wishes to existing members.[36]

Pre-emption clauses often provide that for the purpose of any sale carried out in accordance therewith the value of the shares should be determined by an accountant, who in performing this task is to act as an expert and not as an arbitrator.[37] An accountant acting under such a clause cannot be compelled to state the basis on which he makes his valuation. If he does not, the valuation is referred to as 'non-speaking' and can be challenged only if not made honestly by the correct person.[38] If the valuer does give reasons (a 'speaking' valuation), his valuation can also be challenged if its basis is significantly erroneous.[39] If the auditor or accountant reaches an incorrect valuation through negligence, he can be sued in damages by the aggrieved party; his function is not sufficiently akin to the judicial to render him immune from such proceedings.[40]

---

[35] See the comments of Vinelott J at first instance, [1980] 3 All ER 849, at 859. The *Safeguard* decision was followed in *Theakston v London Trust plc* [1984] BCLC 390, where a member had taken a transfer of shares (not restricted by the articles) with the aid of a loan, charging the shares to the lender as security. At the chargee's request, he was obliged to set in motion the pre-emption procedure in the company's articles. The loan was interest-free and only repayable if and when the member disposed of the shares. It was held that he was not a 'person proposing to transfer' as there was 'no unequivocal obligation to execute any instrument at all at present' (per Harman J at 401). See also *Re Ringtower Holdings plc* (1989) 5 BCC 82, at 99 and *Re Macro (Ipswich) Ltd* [1994] 2 BCLC 354. In the latter case, there had been declarations of trust and transfer documents completed and Arden J had no difficulty in holding (at 401–403) that the members in questions were 'desiring to sell'.

[36] *Tett v Phoenix Property Co* [1986] BCLC 149 (CA). It was held on the facts that the transferor had failed to give such notice and thus the alleged transfer of his shares was void. However, the 'transferee' who had paid the price held the equitable interest in the shares. See also footnote 39, below.

[37] An alternative method is valuation by reference to the last set of audited accounts; see *Dashfield v Davidson* [2008] EWHC 486 (Ch).

[38] For a recent decision where a non-speaking valuation was unsuccessfully challenged, see *Doughty Hanson & Co Ltd v Roe* [2007] EWHC 2212 (Ch).

[39] See, in particular, *Dean v Prince* [1953] Ch 590, [1954] Ch 409 (CA); *Burgess v Purchase & Sons Ltd* [1983] 2 All ER 4.

[40] *Arenson v Casson, Beckman Rutley & Co* [1977] AC 405 (HL).

If shares are sold in contravention of a pre-emption clause and the purchase price is paid, the purchaser acquires an equitable title to them, so that, for instance, a subsequent charging order purporting to bind them in the hands of the vendor is ineffective.[41] There is, of course, no transfer of the legal title while the vendor remains on the register. However, a person who is entitled under the pre-emption clause to have the shares first offered to him can sue to have the register rectified by insertion of his name as legal holder.[42]

9.2.3 Compulsory transfer

A clause to the effect that in the event of bankruptcy a member should sell his shares to particular persons at a particular price cannot be impeached by the member's trustee in bankruptcy, unless the price stipulated is shown to be less than the fair price which could otherwise be obtained. It is likewise not open to attack on the ground that such a restriction upon ownership is repugnant to the nature of personal property.[43]

A company's articles may furthermore contain a clause to the effect that a member infringing any specified regulation or regulations may be compelled by resolution to sell his shares to other members at a specified price. Any resolution passed in pursuance thereof will be valid and effective provided that it is passed *bona fide* in what the members conceive to be the interests of the company as a whole.[44]

---

[41] *Hawks v McArthur* [1951] 1 All ER 22. Despite dicta to the contrary in *Hunter v Hunter* [1936] AC 222, at 261 (HL), *Hawks v McArthur* was followed in *Tett v Phoenix Property Co* [1984] BCLC 599 by Vinelott J. The point was not argued and was left open by the Court of Appeal ([1986] BCLC 149), where the decision of Vinelott J was overruled on other grounds (see footnote 2, above), but it seems implicit in the Court of Appeal judgment that the purchaser obtains *an* equitable title and this is consistent with the notion that the question of title to property of any sort is relative: cf *Battersby* and *Preston* (1972) 35 MLR 268 arguing in favour of the notion of relative title to goods, but whose argument is applicable, *mutatis mutandis*, to intangible personal property such as shares. See also *Borrowdale* [1988] JBL 307 and *Luxton* [1990] JBL 14. Scots law does not recognise equitable ownership and therefore a transferee has no proprietary right until his name appears on the register.

[42] *Hunter v Hunter*, above. As to rectification of the register, see **12.5.3**.

[43] *Borland's Trustee v Steel Brothers & Co Ltd* [1901] 1 Ch 279. A provision for compulsory transfer without consideration or compensation may be valid in exceptional circumstances: *Money Markets International Stockbrokers Ltd v London Stock Exchange Ltd* [2002] 1 WLR 1150.

[44] See *Phillips v Manufacturers' Securities Co* (1917) 116 LT 290 (CA); *Sidebottom v Kershaw, Leese & Co* [1920] 1 CH 154 (CA); *Gaiman v National Association for Mental Health* [1971] Ch 317. As to the application of the same test in determining whether the introduction or deletion of such a clause by an alteration of the articles is valid, see **5.16**.

9.2.4 Restrictions not arising out of the articles

Where the articles impose no restrictions upon the transfer of shares, the right to transfer fully paid shares is unlimited,[45] except as follows:

(1) the transferee must have capacity to hold the shares;[46]

(2) the principle of maintenance of capital must be observed;[47]

(3) certain important restrictions come into operation once a winding-up has commenced; and

(4) a transfer can be set aside if it was a sham or tainted by illegality.[48]

There is thus nothing objectionable, for instance, in a member transferring some of his shares in order to increase his voting power,[49] and a misdescription of the transferee, even if intentional, gives no ground for setting a transfer aside.[50]

With regard to partly paid shares, the restrictions just mentioned apply, and in addition there are certain grounds upon which a liquidator may in a winding-up set aside transfers made before the commencement thereof.[51]

9.3 THE MODE OF TRANSFER OF SHARES

The formalities of a transfer of shares in an unlisted company are in general regulated by the articles and, when applicable, the Stock Transfer Act 1963. If the articles provide for the issue of share warrants to bearer, the transfer of shares comprised in any warrants that are issued is effected by delivery of the warrant.[52] In all other cases, however, s 770(1) of the Companies Act 2006 provides that a company may not register a transfer unless a 'proper instrument of transfer' has been delivered to it.[53] This phrase means a written instrument 'such as will attract stamp duty under the relevant fiscal legislation'; it does not carry any further implication as

---

[45] Assuming of course that the transferor is the beneficial owner free from any encumbrance.

[46] See **12.5**.

[47] See **7.11**.

[48] *Chase Manhattan Equities Ltd v Goodman* [1991] BCLC 897.

[49] *Re Stranton Iron and Steel Co* (1873) LR 16 Eq 559.

[50] *Re Smith, Knight & Co, Battie's Case* (1870) 39 LJ Ch 391; *Re Financial Insurance Co, Bishop's Case* (1872) 7 Ch App 296n.

[51] As partly paid shares are rare nowadays, no detail is given here; see *Gore-Browne on Companies* (Jordans, 45th edn, loose-leaf) at 23[22].

[52] As to share warrants, see **9.12**.

[53] Note, however, that s 770(2) expressly disclaims any effect on the power of the company to register as shareholder any person to whom the right to any shares in the company has been transmitted by operation of law: see **9.15**.

to the form of the transfer.[54] As a result of s 770(1), an oral transfer is ineffective even if the articles purport to make it effective. Furthermore, a clause in the articles purporting to effect an automatic transfer of shares in stipulated circumstances without any written instrument (eg from a deceased member to his widow as a beneficial holder) is invalid.[55]

Except where partly paid shares are involved, the actual form of the instrument of transfer may be one of those provided by the Stock Transfer Act 1963; as these are relatively short and simple, they are used for the vast majority of transfers of unlisted shares.[56]

The transfer of listed securities is increasingly effected under the CREST system described in **9.3.3**.

9.3.1 The Stock Transfer Act 1963

Under s 1 of the Stock Transfer Act 1963, simplified forms are provided for the transfer of fully paid shares or stock[57] in any company within the meaning of the Companies Act 2006 except an unlimited company or a company limited by guarantee. The section provides for transfer by an instrument in the form set out in Sch 1, called a 'stock transfer', or any form substantially corresponding thereto.[58] This instrument must be executed by the transferor, execution under hand being sufficient, but need not be executed by the transferee. It must contain particulars of the transferor and of the description and number or amount of the shares or stock and, save where the transfer takes place in pursuance of a 'stock exchange transaction',[59] the nature and amount of the consideration and the full name and address of the transferee must be included. Attestation is unnecessary, and, where the transfer is in pursuance of a stock exchange transaction, these particulars of the consideration and of the transferee may be inserted either in the stock transfer or supplied by means of separate instruments in the form set out in Sch 2, called 'broker's transfers', or in any form substantially corresponding thereto. Each of these instruments identifies the stock transfer and the particular shares to which it relates, and specifies the consideration paid for such shares.

Section 1 of the Stock Transfer Act 1963 provides forms which are permissible alternatives to, and not in substitution for, those provided for by the articles. Furthermore, any instrument purporting to be in any form

---

54   *Re Paradise Motor Co Ltd* [1968] 1 WLR 1125, at 1141 (CA); *Nisbet v Shepherd* [1994] 1 BCLC 300 (CA).

55   *Re Greene* [1949] Ch 333.

56   When they are not used, the transfer must accord with the articles, although modern articles are unlikely to impose any particular requirements.

57   The section also covers debentures and other specified forms of security: see s 4(4).

58   The relaxation in favour of 'forms substantially corresponding' is contained in s 3(1).

59   'Stock exchange transaction' is defined by s 4(1), coupled with the Stock Transfer (Recognition of Stock Exchanges) Order 1973, SI 1973/536.

which was common or usual for the transfer of shares before the commencement of the Act, or in any other form authorised or required for that purpose save under s 1 itself, is sufficient to transfer shares falling within s 1, whether or not it is completed in accordance with such form, provided that it complies with the requirements as to execution and contents which apply to a stock transfer.[60]

Section 1 of the Act does not affect any right of the company to refuse to register a transfer on any ground other than the form of the transfer, nor does it affect the existing position as regards execution of documents by companies or other bodies corporate. It does, however, apply notwithstanding anything to the contrary in any enactment or instrument relating to the transfer of shares; thus its provisions cannot be excluded by a company's memorandum or articles.[61] Any enactment or instrument relating to the transfer of fully paid shares such as falls within s 1 applies, *mutatis mutandis*, in relation to stock transfers and broker's transfers authorised by that section.[62]

9.3.2   Procedure on transfer of unlisted shares

Provided that the share certificate currently issued in respect of unlisted shares does not also contain shares which are not being transferred as part of the same transaction, the transferor normally delivers the certificate to the transferee along with the executed transfer, receiving in exchange any consideration that is payable. Where, however, the certificate contains more shares than those being transferred, an alternative procedure is adopted. The transferor lodges the certificate at the company's office and the fact of lodgement is certified by the company's secretary on the margin of the form of transfer.[63] The certified transfer is returned by the company to the transferor, who in due course delivers it to the transferee, receiving the consideration, if any, payable. After lodgement and registration, two new certificates are made out by the company: one in the name of the transferee, for the shares transferred, and the other in the name of the transferor, for the shares retained by him.

After execution and delivery of the form of transfer to the transferee, it must be stamped, and duty paid[64] within 30 days of execution.[65]

---

60   Section 1(3).
61   Section 2(1).
62   Section 2(2). Where both a stock transfer and a broker's transfer are used, any reference in any enactment or instrument to the delivery or lodging of an instrument (or proper instrument) of transfer is to be taken as referring to the delivery or lodging of the stock transfer and the broker's transfer; any such reference to the date of lodgement is to be taken as referring to the date on which the later of the two forms of transfer to be lodged was lodged; and it is the broker's transfer that operates as the conveyance and transfer for stamp duty purposes.
63   As to this, see **9.11**.
64   Generally, a transfer on sale attracts *ad valorem* duty of 0.5%. See further, *Gore-Browne on Companies* (Jordans, 45th edn, loose-leaf) at 48 [9].

Registration of an improperly stamped transfer cannot operate to bring about a legal transfer of the shares into the name of the transferee.

After stamping, the instrument of transfer is delivered to the company, with a request that a new certificate may be prepared and issued to the transferee. Either the transferor[66] or the transferee may be the party who delivers it. Except where the transfer has been certified, the old certificate should accompany the instrument of transfer for the purpose of being cancelled or destroyed, and a new certificate issued in its place. Indeed, the articles may provide that unless the certificate is produced the transfer will not be passed, and a company receiving the purchase money for shares, the certificate for which was, to the knowledge of the directors, in the hands of a stranger, has been held liable to pay over the amount to the holder of the certificate, who was, in fact, a mortgagee of the shares.[67]

Upon receiving a transfer,[68] it is the duty of the secretary, or other appropriate person,[69] to satisfy himself that the instrument is properly executed and bears the requisite stamp, and is correct in other particulars, such as the distinctive numbers (if any) of the shares, and that the transferor is the registered holder of the shares expressed to be transferred. If the secretary or other person is a responsible person, the directors are not personally liable to the transferee if they accept his investigations as sufficient.[70] Before issuing the new certificate to the transferee the secretary may, for the company's protection, send notice of impending registration of the transferee to the transferor.[71] If the transfer is in order, and no objection is received from the reputed transferor, the document should be put before the directors at the next board meeting.

On a transfer being brought before the board, the directors should consider whether or not it should be passed for registration.[72] In addition, if they know that a transfer is made in breach of trust or in fraud of a person having equitable rights, they should not pass the transfer without notifying the person interested,[73] and if they do pass the transfer they

---

[65] Stamp Act 1892, s 15.

[66] See Companies Act 2006, s 772.

[67] *Rainford v James Keith and Blackman Co* [1905] 2 Ch 147 (CA).

[68] The secretary giving a receipt for the transfer is no warranty that the transfer will be accepted for registration: *Longman v Bath Electric Tramways Ltd* [1905] 1 Ch 646 (CA).

[69] As described in **15.16.2**, a private company need not now have a secretary. If it does not, someone else should be charged with dealing with share transfers.

[70] *Dixon v Kennaway & Co* [1900] 1 Ch 833, but note that the position of a director who actually signs the certificate in the transferee's favour was left open.

[71] But the sending of such a notice does not protect the company where the transfer is forged, even if the true owner makes no reply: *Barton v London & North-Western Rly Co* (1890) 24 QBD 77 (CA); *Welch v Bank of England* [1955] Ch 508.

[72] In accordance with the principles discussed in **9.2.1**.

[73] Notification is mandatory when a 'stop notice' has been served on the company: see **9.8.1**.

may come under a personal liability, although the company is protected by s 126 of the Companies Act 2006[74] which forbids notices of trusts being entered in the register.

If the transfer is passed, a certificate in favour of the transferee must be prepared and ready for delivery to him within 2 months, unless the terms of issue of the shares otherwise provide.[75]

9.3.3 Procedure on transfer of listed shares

Increasingly, listed shares and other securities are transferred under the paperless and computerised system known as CREST.[76] Chapter 2 of Part 21 of the Companies Act 2006 provides the foundation for the legal regime. The detailed rules are contained in the Uncertificated Securities Regulations 2001.[77] The section and the regulations provide for title to securities[78] to be evidenced and transferred[79] without a written instrument, a process described as 'dematerialisation'.[80] Provision is made for securities to become dematerialised[81] but there is no requirement for this to occur. Securities can be admitted to the system if the articles of the company permit,[82] or if the directors resolve to join.[83] It remains possible for the ownership and transfer of listed securities to be managed in the traditional manner using certificates.[84] The CREST system is run by what

---

[74] *Société Générale de Paris v Walker* (1885) 14 QBD 424 (CA); (1886) 11 App Cas 20 (HL). As to s 126, see **12.6**.

[75] Section 776; see further **9.10**.

[76] CREST is a recognised clearing house under the Financial Services and Markets Act 2000 and an approved system under the Uncertificated Securities Regulations 2001, SI 2001/3755. It is part of Euroclear, the leading securities settlement organisation in Europe. CREST calculates and collects stamp duty on behalf of HM Revenue and Customs.

[77] SI 2001/3755. These are the rules at the time of writing, made under the provision (s 207 of the Companies Act 1989) replaced by Chapter 2 of Part 21. They may in time be replaced by new regulations made under this Chapter, although the detail is unlikely to alter very much, save that 'dematerialisation' may be extended and even made compulsory in some cases under the powers in the 2006 Act.

[78] Including any legal or equitable interest in securities: s 783(b). The very wide definition of 'securities' (s 783(a)) is shares, debentures, debenture stock, loan stock, bonds, units of a collective investment scheme and other securities of any description.

[79] References within the section to a transfer of title include a transfer by way of security: s 783(c).

[80] See generally Goode 'The Nature and Transfer of Rights in Dematerialised and Immobilised Securities' in F Oditah (ed) *The Future for the Global Securities Market: Legal and Regulatory Aspects* (Oxford, Clarendon Press, 1996).

[81] The form of transfer under which 'certificated' securities become 'dematerialised' (ie held in electronic form by a system member) is prescribed in the Stock Transfer (Addition and Substitution of Forms) Order 1996, SI 1996/1571.

[82] Uncertified Securities Regulations 2001, reg 15; the articles must be consistent with Regulations.

[83] Ibid, reg 16; this is subject to the right of the general meeting to veto the directors' resolution.

[84] There are, however, economic incentives favouring the dematerialisation of listed securities as transaction costs are higher for certificated transfers. Over 80% of the UK

the Regulations call an Operator who requires Treasury approval and is subject to ongoing Treasury supervision.[85]

An Operator is required to maintain an 'Operator register of members' in respect of every company which is a participating issuer.[86] This register is required to show, in respect of each class of participating security, the names and addresses of members who hold uncertificated shares and the number of shares held.[87] A participating issuer is required to maintain an 'issuer register of members' showing the date on which each person was registered as a member, a statement of the certificated shares held by each member and the amount paid or agreed to be paid on those shares. A participating issuer is also required to maintain a 'record of uncertificated shares',[88] which replicates the entries made in the 'Operator register of members'. A participating issuer is not required to comply with s 113 (the obligation to keep a conventional register of members),[89] the rationale presumably being that all the information required to be entered in a conventional register is shown in the registers (above) required by the Regulations.

References in any enactment or instrument to a company's register of members shall, unless the context otherwise requires, be construed in relation to a company which is a participating issuer as referring to the company's issuer register of members and Operator register of members.[90] An entry on both the Operator and issuer register of members has the same legal effect in respect of title to dematerialised shares as does a certificate in respect of certificated shares. In each instance the entry or certificate is *prima facie* evidence (in Scotland sufficient evidence unless the contrary is shown) of legal title to shares.[91]

Transfer of title to uncertificated shares is effected by the Operator, which gives an Operator-instruction,[92] pursuant to which the company must register the transfer on its register of securities; the company must then notify the Operator it has done so by what is called an issuer-instruction. Except in a case where title has been transmitted by operation of law, a company cannot register a transfer of title to uncertificated units of a

---

equity market by value is now dematerialised. As noted above, the 2006 Act allows for regulations to make dematerialisation compulsory (see s 786).

[85] See Part II of and Sch 1 to the Uncertificated Securities Regulations 2001. In principle, it is possible for another operator to compete with CREST by seeking approval as a 'relevant system'.

[86] Regulation 20(3) of and Sch 4, para 4 to the USR 2001.

[87] Only system members can be shown in this register as holders of uncertificated shares. Non-members (such as private investors) must arrange for a system member to hold uncertificated shares as trustee.

[88] Regulation 20(6) of and Sch 4, para 5 to the USR 2001.

[89] See **12.5**.

[90] See eg s 116, providing for the right to inspect the register of members.

[91] Section 768 and reg 24 of the USR 2001.

[92] Regulation 27(7) USR 2001. See Part IV of the Regulations regarding authentication etc of dematerialised instructions.

security unless instructed by an Operator or by court order or in certain other limited situations, and any other purported transfer of title is of no effect.[93] From the time that an Operator-instruction is generated which will require a company to register a transfer of title, until that transfer is registered, the transferee acquires an equitable interest in the requisite number of uncertificated units of the security in question, notwithstanding that the units in question or in which an interest arises may be unascertained.[94] It does not matter that the transferor acquires his equitable interest at the same time as the transferee in a situation, for example, where there is a series of transactions all entered in the system at more or less the same time.[95]

The Regulations contain a number of miscellaneous provisions to ensure, among other things, that holders of uncertificated shares are not prejudiced by not having paper evidence of their holdings. By reg 37, references in any enactment or rule of law to a proper instrument of transfer of securities, or any expression having like meaning, is to be taken to refer to a reference to an Operator-instruction to a participating issuer to register a transfer of title on the relevant register of securities in accordance with the Operator-instruction. Regulation 40 exonerates trustees and personal representatives from any liability for breach of trust or default in dealing with uncertificated securities, unless they are expressly prohibited from so dealing, but also mirrors the general principle of company law[96] in providing that the Operator is not bound or compelled to recognise any express, implied or constructive trust or other interest in respect of uncertificated units of a security, even if he has actual or constructive notice of the said trust or interest.[97] By reg 38, any requirements in an enactment or rule of law which apply in respect of the transfer of securities otherwise than by means of a relevant system shall not prevent an Operator-instruction from requiring a participating issuer to register a transfer of title to uncertificated units of a security. Notwithstanding any enactment, instrument or rule of law, a participating issuer may not issue a certificate in relation to any uncertificated units of a participating security, and a document issued by or on behalf of a participating issuer purportedly evidencing title to an uncertificated unit of a participating security shall not be evidence of title to the unit; in particular s 768 of the Companies Act 2006[98] shall not

---

[93] Ibid, reg 28(6).

[94] Ibid, reg 31.

[95] The CREST system implements the principle of 'delivery versus payment', meaning that transfer of legal title and payment occur simultaneously. In principle this limits the need to refer to equitable interests as a party to a transaction will have either legal title or payment at any point in time during which a transfer is taking place (unlike the position prior to the introduction of CREST).

[96] Companies Act 2006, s 126; see **12.5.1**.

[97] Uncertified Securities Regulations 1995, reg 40(3). Note that s 126 does not apply to Scottish companies and reg 40(3) does not prevent an Operator giving notice of a trust to such a company.

[98] See **9.10**.

apply to any document issued with respect to uncertified shares.[99] Transfers of uncertificated shares are made subject to stamp duty reserve tax, at the rate of 0.5% of the consideration, payable by the purchaser.[100]

9.4 THE POSITION AS BETWEEN TRANSFEROR AND TRANSFEREE

Quite apart from the effect of a proper transfer of shares as between the transferor or transferee and the company, questions may arise as to the legal relationship between the transferor and the transferee, particularly when the transfer is, quite properly, refused registration[101] or the parties choose not to seek registration of the transfer. The answers may vary depending on the nature of the transfer, namely whether it was a sale, a gift or a mortgage. These points are explored in the following sections.

9.5 SALES OF SHARES

A contract for the sale of shares may be oral. If the shares are sold through a stock exchange, the usages of the exchange are incorporated into and form part of the contract;[102] an important effect of this principle is that once a vendor and a purchaser are brought together by the negotiations of their brokers on the exchange, the brokers 'drop out' and in general are not parties to the contract of sale ultimately formed.[103]

If the shares to be sold are not specified by the contract, they may be specified at a later stage by appropriation; in some cases this may not occur until the transfer form is filled in. Once the shares have been specified (whether by the contract, or subsequently) the contract becomes enforceable in most cases[104] by specific performance.[105]

A further effect of the shares being specified is that whilst the vendor remains the holder of the legal title to the shares, and is treated by the

---

[99] As to the special provisions regarding notice of and attending and voting at meetings, see Uncertified Securities Regulations 1995, reg 41. Regulation 42 makes special provision to enable the exercise of the powers of compulsory purchase in what is now Part 23 of the Companies Act 2006, as to these, see **20.23**.

[100] See Part IV of the Finance Act 1986. Stamp duty is a tax on documents and therefore a special regime had to be established for dematerialised securities. The Treasury is authorised to abolish both stamp duty reserve tax and stamp duty on certificated share transfers (see Finance Act 1990, s 110) but has not yet exercised this power.

[101] In accordance with a restriction on transfer of the sort discussed earlier in this chapter.

[102] *Coles v Bristowe* (1868) 4 Ch App 3; *Bowring v Shepherd* (1871) LR 6 QB 309.

[103] *Bowring v Shepherd*, above.

[104] An exception is where a winding-up supervenes, because a transfer would *prima facie* be void under what is now s 127 of the Insolvency Act 1986; *Sullivan v Henderson* [1973] 1 WLR 333.

[105] *Duncuft v Albrecht* (1841) 12 Sim 189; *Grant v Cignan* [1996] 2 BCLC 24.

company as the owner thereof,[106] beneficial ownership passes to the purchaser,[107] even though the sale is in breach of a pre-emption clause in the articles.[108]

Once the beneficial ownership thus passes, a number of consequences ensue. In the absence of express provision in the contract, the purchaser becomes entitled as against the vendor to any dividends subsequently declared in respect of the shares, even if such dividend relates back wholly or partly to a period prior to the passing of beneficial ownership.[109] Dividends declared before the beneficial ownership passes but paid thereafter may, however, be retained by the vendor.[110] In practice, where shares are sold on the Stock Exchange near the time of declaration of a dividend the contract normally provides whether the sale is to be *ex div* or *cum div*. If after the beneficial ownership has passed a call is made or a contribution sought in a winding-up in respect of the shares, the vendor is the person liable to the company,[111] but he is entitled to an indemnity from the purchaser[112] (unless the contract of sale provides otherwise), or indeed against any sub-purchaser who has become beneficially entitled to the shares.[113] As to calls made before the beneficial ownership passes, the vendor has no indemnity, but if he fails to pay, the company may make a fresh call against the purchaser after registration of the transfer.[114]

Voting rights are subject to slightly different principles. The vendor, while he remains the registered holder, is from the company's point of view the person entitled to exercise the voting rights attached to the shares. The purchaser acquires the right to direct how the votes should be cast, not when the beneficial ownership passes to him, but when he has paid the full purchase price for the shares.[115] When the purchaser is in default in paying for the shares, a clause in the contract of sale providing that all rights pass to the purchaser on a specified date before completion will be construed, in the absence of compelling language to the contrary effect, as not depriving the unpaid vendor of his right to vote.[116]

---

[106] See s 126, discussed at **12.5.1**.

[107] *Re National Bank of Wales, Taylor, Phillips and Rickard's case* [1897] 1 Ch 298, at 305–306 (CA); *Wood Preservation Ltd v Prior* [1969] 1 WLR 1077 (CA). As to the passing of beneficial ownership where an option is granted and exercised, see *Hare v Nicoll* [1966] 2 QB 131 (CA).

[108] *Hawks v McArthur* [1951] 1 All ER 22; and see **9.2.2**.

[109] *Black v Homersham* (1879) 4 Ex D 24; *Re Wimbush* [1940] Ch 92. The vendor is, moreover, bound to take steps to collect the dividend so as to be able to pay it over to the purchaser: *Stevenson v Wilson* 1907 SC 445.

[110] *Re Kidner* [1929] 2 Ch 121.

[111] *Ex parte Hennessy* (1849) 2 Mac & C 201.

[112] *Bowring v Shepherd* (1871) LR 6 QB 309; *Re National Bank of Wales, Taylor, Phillips and Rickard's Case* [1897] 1 Ch 298, at 305–306 (CA).

[113] *Spencer v Ashworth, Partington & Co* [1925] 1 KB 589 (CA).

[114] *New Balkis Eersteling v Randt Gold Mining Co* [1904] AC 165 (HL).

[115] *Musselwhite v C H Musselwhite & Son Ltd* [1962] Ch 964; see also *Re Piccadilly Radio plc* [1989] BCLC 683, at 696.

[116] *JRRT (Investments) Ltd v Haycraft* [1993] BCLC 401, applying the principle in

Upon a sale of shares the seller is bound only to execute a proper transfer and deliver it with the share certificate to the purchaser. He does not warrant that the company will accept the transferee,[117] and even if the company wrongfully refuses to register the purchaser he can, it seems, keep the purchase money.[118] He must not, however, do anything to hinder registration; if he does, he may be made liable in damages.[119]

Subject to the terms of the contract, the obligations of the purchaser are to prepare the form of transfer[120] (though often in practice the vendor takes over the task), to execute it (if this is necessary to obtain registration), to pay the purchase price and stamp duty and to lodge the transfer for registration.[121]

Where an unpaid vendor of shares executes a transfer and delivers it to the purchaser along with the share certificate, he has, unless the contract of sale otherwise provides, a lien upon the shares for payment of the purchase price. The company cannot, however, be required to accept notice of the lien, which may therefore be overridden if the shares are transferred to a *bona fide* purchaser for value without notice.[122]

9.6 GIFTS OF SHARES

Where shares are transferred by way of gift, the beneficial ownership does not pass to the donee until the donor has done all within his power to implement registration of the donee as transferee.[123] In the ordinary course, this means executing a transfer in the proper form and delivering it to the donee or to the company along with the relevant certificate, but if further requirements are imposed upon the donor by the articles or by statute these must also be complied with.[124] Until the donor has done all within his power to implement registration, the intended gift is revocable, the donee having no equity to compel the donor to perfect it and no right to ask the court to construe it as a declaration of trust.[125] On the other hand, if the donor has done everything that is required of him, but registration does not occur through some act or omission of one or more third parties (eg a refusal by the board to register the transfer, in exercise

---

    Alghussein Establishment v Eton College [1988] 1 WLR 587 (HL), that it is to be presumed that the parties did not intend that either should enjoy benefits between the contract date and completion arising from their own default.

[117] *Skinner v City of London Marine Corp* (1885) 14 QBD 882 (CA).

[118] *London Founders Association v Clarke* (1888) 20 QBD 576 (CA).

[119] *Hooper v Herts* [1906] 1 Ch 549 (CA).

[120] *Birkett v Cowper-Coles* (1919) 35 TLR 298.

[121] *Re Stranton Iron and Steel Co* (1873) LR 16 Eq 559. The vendor may do this if the contract so permits: s 772.

[122] *Langen & Wind Ltd v Bell* [1972] Ch 85; and see the discussion of priorities at **9.8**.

[123] *Re Rose* [1949] Ch 78; *Re Rose* [1952] Ch 499 (CA); *Re Paradise Motor Co Ltd* [1968] 1 WLR 1125 (CA); *Vandervell v CIR* [1967] 2 AC 291, at 330 (HL).

[124] *Re Fry* [1946] Ch 312.

[125] *Milroy v Lord* (1862) 4 De G F & J 264.

of a power in the articles), the donor is, it seems, treated as a trustee of the shares for the donee.[126] Further, if there is a clear declaration of trust of shares, whether oral or written, and even if expressed as simply a percentage of the donor's holding of shares in a particular company, this is effective to pass the equitable interest in the shares.[127] In addition, the modern view appears to proceed on the rather more liberal basis that 'although equity will not aid a volunteer, it will not strive officiously to defeat a gift'.[128] Thus the execution of a transfer form, in circumstances where there was a plain intention to make an immediate gift of shares, but without delivery of the share certificate has been held to constitute a valid equitable assignment of the shares.[129]

9.7   MORTGAGES OF SHARES

A legal mortgage of shares can be implemented only by registration of a transfer to the mortgagee, though the parties will, of course, agree between themselves that it is a transfer by way of security only. From the point of view of the company the transfer will operate as an out-and-out transfer, so that, if the shares are partly paid, the mortgagee will be personally liable for calls.[130] Equally, anyone inspecting the share register or the share certificate issued to the mortgagee will be induced, if he does not know the true position, to treat the mortgagee as the absolute owner of the shares at law and in equity. The mortgagor may accordingly protect his equity of redemption by serving a 'stop notice' on the company.[131]

An equitable mortgage or charge upon shares can be created simply by deposit of the share certificate as security for the relevant advance.[132] Alternatively, or in addition, the parties may execute and deliver to the mortgagee a transfer in blank. If the mortgagee receives both the share certificate and a transfer in blank, he may exercise his power of sale in the event of default by the mortgagor without having to apply to the court for an order for sale just as a legal mortgagee may do.[133] Furthermore, subject to certain difficulties which arise when the transfer is required by the articles to be by deed,[134] he may at any time convert the mortgage into a

---

[126] *Re Rose* [1952] Ch 499, at 510 (CA), per Evershed MR.

[127] *Hunter v Moss* [1994] 1 WLR 452 (CA); and see *Re Harvard Securities Ltd* [1997] 2 BCLC 369.

[128] *T Choithram International SA v Pagarini* [2001] 1 WLR 1, at 11 (PC), per Lord Browne-Wilkinson.

[129] *Pennington v Waine* [2002] EWCA Civ 227, [2002] 1 WLR 2075 (CA). However, this may be in breach of a pre-emption clause in the company's articles of association and thus the company will be able to resist registration of the donee as legal owner: *Hurst v Crampton Bros (Coopers) Ltd* [2002] EWHC 1375 (Civ).

[130] *Re Land Credit Co of Ireland, Weikersheim's Case* (1873) 8 Ch App 831.

[131] See **9.8.1**. This is not possible in a Scottish company.

[132] *Harrold v Plenty* [1907] 2 Ch 314. In a Scottish company, only registration of the mortgagee by the company will constitute a valid mortgage.

[133] *Stubbs v Slater* [1910] 1 Ch 632 (CA). This is not possible in a Scottish company.

[134] See *Gore-Browne on Companies* (Jordans, 45th edn, loose-leaf) at 23[12].

legal mortgage by filling in his own name as transferee and procuring registration of the transfer.[135] While the mortgage remains equitable only, it is the mortgagee who should consider protecting his interest; this he may do by serving a stop notice.[136]

9.8 PRIORITIES IN ENGLAND

Competing claims to the beneficial entitlement to shares sometimes arise in the context of share transfers in England.[137] Contests may arise between the registered holder of the shares and a claimant asserting a prior or a subsequent equity, or between two equitable claimants.[138]

Generally speaking, the registered holder, as legal owner, will prevail over a prior equitable claimant if he gave valuable consideration for the transfer through which he acquired his legal title[139] unless before the time of giving such consideration he had notice of the prior equity.[140] As against a subsequent equitable claim not created by his own act or with his authority, he will generally prevail, but not if his conduct has been such as to disentitle or estop him from asserting his rights against the person asserting the claim.[141]

As between two equitable claimants, the earlier in point of time prevails,[142] unless his conduct has been such to disentitle or estop him,[143] or, it has been said, the later claimant has acquired 'a present, absolute unconditional right to registration'.[144] It is not clear what this last phrase means, as in a later case a transferee for value who had lodged a transfer for registration was held not to have acquired such a right even though the directors had no power to refuse to register the transfer.[145]

---

[135] *Re Tahiti Cotton Co* (1874) LR 17 Eq 273.

[136] See **9.8.1**.

[137] The problems discussed here do not arise in Scots law, which does not recognise purely equitable interests in property.

[138] It should be noted that particular problems can arise when transfers of shares are executed in blank. These are considered in *Gore-Browne on Companies* (Jordans, 45th edn, loose-leaf) at 23[12].

[139] *Shropshire Union Railways and Canal Co v R* (1875) LR 7 HL 496; *Guy v Waterlow Brothers and Layton Ltd* (1909) 25 TLR 515; *Langen & Wind Ltd v Bell* [1972] Ch 685. Where the articles give a company a 'first and paramount' lien over the shares of any shareholder indebted to it, this will prevail over an equitable charge over those shares given to a third party: *Champagne Perrier-Jouet SA v HH Finch Ltd* [1982] 3 All ER 713.

[140] See *Dodds v Hills* (1865) 2 H & M 424. *Sheffield v London Joint Stock Bank* (1888) 13 App Cas 333 (HL). For a recent example of a transfer without valuable consideration where the legal title was therefore held subject to a prior equity, see *Cottrell v King* [2004] EWHC 397 (Ch).

[141] *Fry v Smellie* [1912] 3 KB 282 (CA).

[142] *Roots v Williamson* (1888) 38 Ch D 485; *Peat v Clayton* [1906] 1 Ch 659.

[143] See *Shropshire Union Railways and Canal Co v R*, above, in which disentitling conduct was said to comprise 'misconduct or fraud or negligence' (at 514).

[144] *Société Générale de Paris v Walker* (1886) 11 App Cas 20 at 29 (HL).

[145] *Ireland v Hart* [1902] 1 Ch 522.

Some authority is available as to the type of conduct that will disentitle or estop a legal or equitable claimant as against a subsequent equitable claimant. The mere fact that the beneficiaries under a trust of shares leave the share certificate in the hands of the trustees does not constitute such conduct,[146] but, according to an Irish case, a first mortgagee who fails to obtain the certificate relating to the mortgaged shares will be 'disentitled' as against a subsequent claimant who has acquired an equitable interest for value from the mortgagor, *bona fide* believing him to have an unencumbered title because he held the certificate.[147]

9.8.1 Notice to the company

In cases involving questions of priority, the mere fact that the company has notice of an equitable claim is not enough of itself to give that claimant priority over other claims of which the company has no notice; in other words, the rule in *Dearle v Hall* has no application.[148] The company is bound by statute not to enter on the register notice of any trust, express, implied or constructive,[149] and this rule is often widened in the articles[150] to take in any equitable interest whatsoever. On receiving notice of an equitable claim, the company may, however, decide against registering a competing transferee,[151] or may even remove such a transferee from the register,[152] in which event this transferee's position may be weaker through being based on equitable rights only.

With the same purpose in mind – that of preventing a competing claimant from strengthening his position by obtaining registration of a transfer – any person claiming a beneficial interest in shares may apply *ex parte*, by summons or motion in the Chancery Division, for an order prohibiting the registration of any transfer of the shares.[153] This will serve to 'freeze' the position while the rights of the competing claimants are worked out.

A final form of protection for equitable claimants is the serving of a 'stop order', a procedure which is regulated by the Civil Procedure Rules.[154] By the terms of these rules, any person who has such an interest may, upon making and filing an affidavit of his interest, and serving an office copy of

---

[146] *Shropshire Union Railways and Canal Co v R*, above.

[147] *Kelly v Munster and Leinster Bank* (1891) 29 LR Ir (Eq) 19.

[148] *Société Générale de Paris v Walker* (1886) 11 App Cas 20 (HL).

[149] Companies Act 2006, s 126. For an instance of the application of a similar provision in Commonwealth legislation, see *Simpson v Molson's Bank* [1895] AC 270 (PC). This rule apparently extends to notice of an unpaid vendor's lien: see *Langen & Wind Ltd v Bell* [1972] Ch 85. In this case, Brightman J may, however, have been thinking of common-form provisions in company articles such as the provision referred to in the next footnote.

[150] See, eg, Table A to the 1985 Act, art 5 and arts 23 and 45, respectively, of the model articles for private and public companies prescribed under the 2006 Act.

[151] See, eg, *Roots v Williamson* (1888) 38 Ch D 485; and see **9.3.2**.

[152] This was done in *Peat v Clayton* [1906] 1 Ch 659.

[153] RSC Order 50, r 15.

[154] Rules 73.11–73.15.

the affidavit and a notice on the company, require it to stop the transfer of or the payment of dividends upon the shares in question. This notice is not enough to give the server priority over a claimant to whom, under the rules just discussed, he ranks subject.[155] However, it prevents the company from registering a transfer of the shares or paying the dividends without giving the server an opportunity of applying to the court to prevent the transfer or payment. But if the person in whose name the shares stand requests the company to transfer or pay, the company must notify the server of the notice, and if he does not within 14 days obtain an order from the court, the company may proceed, despite the notice, to deal with the shares or pay the dividends as requested. This course is, in practice, very little resorted to; but it will be obvious that a very valuable method is provided for checking any anticipated or possible misappropriation of shares by a trustee or person whose title to them is not absolute. If such a notice is served on the company, it must be careful not to register any transfer or pay any dividend without referring to the server of the notice. If it does register a transfer, so as to cause the interest asserted by the server of the notice to be overridden, the directors,[156] and possibly also the company itself, will be liable to him in damages for the loss which he has suffered.

A judgment-creditor who has taken out a charging order in respect of shares does not thereby obtain the right to receive notice of and oppose the impending registration of any transfer presented by the registered holder. He does, however, have a sufficient interest in the shares to provide the basis for a stop notice, and if he proceeds to serve such a notice, he will be protected to the extent described.[157]

9.9 FORGED TRANSFERS

A forged transfer is in law no transfer, and gives the alleged transferee no rights, not even if the company issues to him a certificate stating that he is the holder of the shares which the transfer purports to assign.[158] If the company, acting upon a forged transfer, removes the true owner from the register and substitutes the supposed transferee, it can be compelled to reinstate the true owner and replace or restore his shares.[159] In England, the Limitation Act 1980 only runs against the true owner as from the time

---

[155] *Wilkins v Sibley* (1863) 4 Giff 442, at 446.

[156] *Société Générale de Paris v Walker* (1884) 14 QBD 424, at 453 (CA) (affirmed (1885) 11 App Cas 20 (HL)).

[157] *Adams v Bank of England* (1908) 52 SJ 682.

[158] *Simm v Anglo-American Telegraph Co* (1879) 5 QBD 188 (CA).

[159] *Barton v North Staffordshire Rly Co* (1888) 38 Ch D 458. This applies even if the true owner has been notified of the transfer before its registration but has failed to make any objection to it: see **9.3**.

when his demand for reinstatement to the register is refused.[160] He can claim any intervening dividends from the company, which can in turn claim them from the transferee.[161]

By reason of a general law principle of estoppel discussed in the next section, persons who suffer damage through relying on the share certificate issued pursuant to a forged transfer can in general recover compensation for their loss from the company.[162] But estoppel cannot be invoked by a person who has presented for registration a forged transfer in his favour. Indeed, such a person may instead be required by the company to reimburse it for any damages that it has been compelled to pay out to a third party under the estoppel principle.[163] Thus a transferee taking a forged transfer can claim damages only under the estoppel principle when two conditions are satisfied: (a) that someone other than him presented the transfer for registration; and (b) that he relied on the certificate to his detriment, eg in being 'put to rest' thereby so that he delayed in taking action against the forger until the forger, through becoming bankrupt or for some other reason, ceased to be able to satisfy the transferee's claim against him in respect of the forgery.[164]

The proposition, just stated, that a company can claim reimbursement for any damages it has had to pay out on a forged transfer, from the person who presented the transfer for registration, stems from the wider principle that a person presenting a transfer impliedly warrants that it is genuine and given with due authority. Thus a broker who deposits a forged transfer in good faith is liable to the company for loss it may suffer thereby,[165] and, if a broker represents, whether in good faith or not, that he has authority to act for the supposed transferor when in fact he has not, he is liable to the company upon an implied warranty that he has authority.[166] There is no liability, however, if the broker who instructed the issuer to amend the register did so in reliance on genuine but inaccurate share certificates issued by the issuer or its registrar.[167]

---

[160] *Barton v North Staffordshire Rly Co*, above; *Welch v Bank of England* [1955] Ch 508.

[161] *Foster v Tyne Pontoon and Dry Dock Co* (1893) 63 LJQB 50.

[162] *Re Bahia and San Francisco Rly Co* (1868) LR 3 QB 584; *Dixon v Kennaway & Co* [1900] 1 Ch 833.

[163] *Sheffield Corp v Barclay* [1905] AC 392 (HL); *Welch v Bank of England*, above; *Yeung v Hong Kong and Shanghai Bank* [1981] AC 787 (PC); *Royal Bank of Scotland plc v Sandstone Properties Ltd* [1998] 2 BCLC 429.

[164] *Dixon v Kennaway & Co*, above.

[165] *Sheffield Corp v Barclay*, above; *Yeung v Hong Kong and Shanghai Bank*, above. It may be, though, that this principle should be reviewed in the light of the Civil Liability (Contribution) Act 1978: ibid, at 799–800, but only the House of Lords can do this: *Royal Bank of Scotland plc v Sandstone Properties Ltd*, above.

[166] *Starkey v Bank of England* [1903] AC 114 (HL). This is not affected by the fact that the company or its registrar has issued a duplicate share certificate to the fraudster: *Royal Bank of Scotland plc v Sandstone Properties Ltd* [1998] 2 BCLC 429.

[167] *Cadbury Schweppes plc v Halifax Share Dealing Ltd* [2006] EWHC 1184 (Ch), [2007] 1 BCLC 497.

9.10 SHARE CERTIFICATES

The articles may give to each member a right, free of charge, to a certificate or certificates indicating the share or shares to which he is entitled;[168] indeed, by virtue of s 769(1) of the Companies Act 2006 on an allotment of shares and s 776(1) on a transfer of shares, a member is entitled to a certificate unless this right is expressly excluded by the conditions of issue.[169] The usual practice is to include in one certificate all the shares of the same class held by a member. The articles will also provide as to the form of the certificate. The 1985 Table A, arts 6 and 101, require it to be under the seal of the company, and to be signed by a director and by the secretary or by a second director, unless the directors determine that some other or others shall sign it. In contrast, the model articles prescribed under the 2006 Act are somewhat less prescriptive; for both private[170] and public[171] companies, certificates must have affixed to them the company's common seal[172] or be otherwise executed in accordance with the Companies Acts. Section 44 of the Companies Act 2006 provides for the execution of documents.[173] Even if under seal, the certificate is not a deed,[174] however, and it does not attract stamp duty.

Section 776 requires every company, unless the conditions of issue provide otherwise, to complete and have ready for delivery the certificates of shares within 2 months after lodgement of any transfer of shares.[175] If notice has been served requiring the company to make good any default with respect to the issue of certificates and the default is not made good within 10 days after service of the notice, the court may, on the application of the person entitled to have the certificate delivered to him, order the company and any officer of the company to make good the default within a specified time, and the order may provide that all costs of and incidental to the application shall be borne by the company or by any officer responsible for the default.[176]

A share certificate (as opposed to the share itself which is a chose in action, in Scotland incorporeal moveable property) is a personal chattel (in Scotland corporeal moveable property) and can be the subject of a claim in conversion at the suit of someone who has either possession or

---

[168] This is provided for by Table A to the 1985 Act, art 6, and by art 24 of the model articles for private companies and art 46 of the model articles for public companies.

[169] In the case of 'dematerialised' securities, in respect of which legal title is evidenced by an electronic record, there is no right to a certificate. See **9.3.3** above.

[170] Article 24.

[171] Article 47(2).

[172] Or its 'securities seal' in the case of public companies.

[173] See **6.26**.

[174] *South London Greyhound Racecourses v Wake* [1931] 1 Ch 496; *R v Williams* [1942] AC 541 (PC).

[175] 'Transfer' here means a transfer duly stamped and otherwise valid, and does not include any transfer which the company is for any reason entitled to refuse to register and does not register. The obligation on allotment is covered separately in s 769.

[176] Section 782.

an immediate legal right to possession at the time of conversion. However, someone with merely an equitable title, such as the beneficiary of a trust, has no standing to bring such an action.[177]

9.10.1   Evidence of title

A certificate under the seal of the company is *prima facie* evidence of the title of the person named to the shares;[178] but it does not give the person an indefeasible right to the shares. If it can be shown that the holder obtained the shares from some person who could not give him a title to them, the name of the true owner will be retained upon or restored to the register, and the holder will lose the shares.[179] But if the holder acquired the shares in good faith and for value, relying upon an untrue certificate issued to his predecessor by the company, the company will be estopped from denying his title to the shares which he has been induced to buy or pay for by being shown the certificate.[180] Similarly, if after acquiring the shares in good faith and for value, he makes a contract to resell them in reliance on an untrue certificate issued to him and is then compelled to pay damages to his purchaser or buy other shares in order to fulfill the contract, he may recover his loss from the company.[181] If, however, the certificate is a forgery, the company comes under no liability, even when the forgery was the act of its secretary.[182] Furthermore, if the certificate is in fact correct, stating that a certain person is the registered holder of the shares, the company will not be liable to a purchaser from him by reason of having certified a previous transfer of the shares to another person, even though the company has parted with the certificate to the registered holder after certifying the transfer, thus enabling the registered holder to deal with the shares again. The proximate cause of the loss by the purchaser is taken to be the fraud of the registered holder and not the negligence (if any) of the company, and in any event any duty of the company to ensure that the certificate in such circumstances is sent to the registered holder is owed to the registered holder only, not to third parties such as purchasers.[183]

Another form of estoppel may arise against the company if it issues a certificate which states that the shares comprised in it are fully paid when in fact they are only partly paid or have nothing paid up on them. If the

---

[177] *MCC Proceeds Inc v Lehman Brothers International (Europe)* [1998] 2 BCLC 659 (CA).

[178] Section 768.

[179] See **9.9**.

[180] *Re Bahia and San Francisco Rly Co* (1868) LR 3 QB 584; *Re Ottos Kopje Diamond Mines Ltd* [1893] 1 Ch 618 (CA). This estoppel arises when the holder, having been refused registration or having been removed from the register to make way for the true owner, sues the company for damages for wrongful refusal or wrongful removal.

[181] *Balkis Consolidated Co Ltd v Tomkinson* [1893] AC 396 (HL).

[182] *Ruben v Great Fingall Consolidated* [1906] AC 439 (HL); *South London Greyhound Racecourses Ltd v Wake* [1931] 1 Ch 496; but these cases may not be followed today – see **6.22**.

[183] *Longman v Bath Electric Tramways Ltd* [1905] 1 Ch 646 (CA).

shares come into the hands of a *bona fide* transferee for value who relied upon such a statement in the certificate held by his predecessor and had no knowledge of the true position, the company will be estopped as against him from denying that they are fully paid and thus will be prevented from claiming from him the amount unpaid on the shares or any part thereof.[184]

9.11 CERTIFICATION OF TRANSFERS

The act of certification of a transfer of shares is often a step in the process of transfer; its general nature and purpose have already been described.[185] The position of persons, such as transferees, who act on the faith of a certification by the company, is dealt with in s 775:

'(1) The certification by a company of any instrument of transfer [[186]] of any shares in, or debentures of, the company is taken as a representation by the company to any person acting on the faith of the certification that there have been produced to the company such documents as on their face show a prima facie title to the shares or debentures in the transferor named in the instrument.

(2) The certification is not to be taken as a representation that the transferor has any title to the shares or debentures.'

For the purposes of the section, a transfer is to be deemed to be certified if it bears the words 'certified lodged', or words to this effect.[187]

The section further provides that when any person acts on the faith of a false certification made negligently, the company is under the same liability to him as if the certification had been made fraudulently.[188]

Decisions[189] prior to 1948 established that where an agent of a company had authority to certify transfers but fraudulently did so without the share certificates having been lodged, he was not acting within the scope of his authority and accordingly his act was not the act of the company. These decisions were substantially overruled by what is now s 775(4)(b), which provides that certification is made by a company if: (a) the person issuing the instrument is a person authorised to issue certificated instruments of transfers on the company's behalf; and (b) the certification is signed by a person authorised to certificate transfers on the company's

---

[184] *Burkinshaw v Nicholls* (1878) 3 App Cas 1004 (HL); *Re British Farmers' Pure Linseed Cake Co* (1878) 7 Ch D 533 (CA).

[185] See **9.3.2**.

[186] 'Instrument of transfer' includes a broker's transfer under the Stock Transfer Act 1963; see s 2(2) of that Act.

[187] Section 775(4)(a).

[188] Section 775(3).

[189] *George Whitechurch Ltd v Cavanagh* [1902] AC 117 (HL); *Kleinwort v Associated Automatic Machine Corp* (1934) 50 TLR 244 (HL).

behalf or by an officer or employee either of the company or of a body corporate so authorised. It would seem, however, that the old law still applies where the secretary or other officer fraudulently certifying the transfer had no authority to certify transfers at all.

A certification is treated as signed by a person if it purports to be authenticated by his signature or initials (whether handwritten or not), and it is not shown that the signature or initials was or were placed there neither by himself nor by a person authorised to use the signature or initials for the purpose of certificating transfers on the company's behalf.[190]

9.12   SHARE WARRANTS

Section 779 permits a company limited by shares, if authorised by its articles, to issue with respect to any fully paid shares a 'share warrant', stating that the bearer is entitled to the shares specified in it.[191] It is also clear from the wording of s 122 (considered below) that a company can issue a share directly in bearer form, without it having to be registered first. The effect of the issue of a share warrant is to make the bearer of it absolutely entitled to the shares named in it, and the ownership can accordingly be passed by mere delivery.[192] No person purchasing a share warrant need make any inquiry as to the title of the person who sells it, any more than if he were receiving a banknote, but if the holder has in fact stolen or fraudulently obtained a share warrant, he can, of course, be compelled to surrender it in the same way as a thief would have to give up a banknote.

The company may provide for the payment of dividends by coupons or otherwise.[193] It is usual to do this by coupons attached to the warrant, each stating that the bearer is entitled to the dividend for a certain year or half-year, or to the first, second, or third dividend declared, and in such case the bearer of the coupon, and not of the warrant, is entitled to the dividend.

On the issue of a share warrant a company must enter in its register of members the fact of the issue of the warrant, a statement of the shares included in it, distinguishing each share by its number (if any), and the date of issue of the warrant. If the shares have previously been registered, the register must be amended so that no person is named as the holder of

---

[190]   Section 775(4)(c).
[191]   Table A to the 1985 Act contains no relevant article and traditionally share warrants were not popular in the UK, partly because of former exchange control legislation. However, there is evidence of their increasing use and art 51 of the model articles for public companies provides for them.
[192]   Section 779(2).
[193]   Section 779(3).

the relevant shares.[194] If the warrant is surrendered the date of the surrender must be entered in the register.[195] Subject to the company's articles, the bearer of a share warrant is entitled, on surrendering it for cancellation, to have his name entered as a member in the register of members,[196] in which case the company must, unless the articles provide otherwise, complete and have ready for delivery a share certificate in respect of the shares.[197] The company is responsible for any loss incurred by any person if the name of a bearer of a share warrant is entered in the register without the warrant being surrendered and cancelled.[198]

The bearer of a share warrant may, if the articles of the company so provide, be deemed to be a member of the company, either to the full extent or for any purposes defined in the articles.[199]

9.13   THE TRANSMISSION OF SHARES

A transmission of shares occurs upon the holder dying, becoming a patient under the Mental Health Act 1983, or becoming bankrupt. The persons or person with whom the company must deal in such a case are the executors or administrators of a deceased shareholder, the committee or receiver of a Mental Health Act patient, or the trustee of a bankrupt, all of whom may be described by the words 'the representatives of the former holder'.

9.14   TRUSTEES IN BANKRUPTCY

The title of the trustee in bankruptcy to the shares of the bankrupt is conferred by the Insolvency Act 1986, which vests the property in the shares in him,[200] empowers him to exercise the right of transfer to the same extent as the bankrupt could have done,[201] and authorises him to disclaim the shares.[202] Thus, unless the articles otherwise provide, the trustee can take the shares into his own name, leave them in the name of the bankrupt, transfer them without first taking them into his own name, or disclaim them, but in each case the rights of third parties are left unaffected.[203]

---

[194] Section 122(1).
[195] Section 122(6).
[196] Section 122(4).
[197] Section 780.
[198] Section 122(5).
[199] Section 122(4).
[200] Section 306. The equivalent in Scotland is s 31(1) of the Bankruptcy (Sc) Act 1985.
[201] Section 314 and Sch 5. For Scotland, see s 39 of the Bankruptcy (Sc) Act 1985.
[202] Section 315. As to the trustee's power to disclaim, see *Gore-Browne on Companies* (Jordans, 45th edn, loose-leaf) at 26[17].
[203] See *Re Cannock and Rugeley Colliery Co* (1885) 28 Ch D 363 (CA); *Wise v Lansdell* [1912] 1 Ch 420.

When the trustee takes the shares into his own name he can insist upon a 'clean' certificate; ie he can object to an entry in the register or upon the certificate to the effect that he holds them as trustee or subject to a lien.[204] By taking partly paid shares into his own name, he becomes personally liable for calls on them.

If the trustee elects to leave the shares in the bankrupt's name, the bankrupt can vote upon the shares and give proxies, but he must exercise these powers in accordance with the trustee's directions.[205] He cannot sue the company to enforce his personal rights, but in appropriate cases he probably has the *locus standi* to bring a derivative action to redress a wrong done to the company.[206] The trustee for his part does not have the *locus standi* to present a petition to wind up the company.[207] The bankrupt estate, and not the trustee, is liable for calls on any partly paid shares, and the company can prove for the estimated value of any future calls.[208]

9.15 EXECUTORS AND ADMINISTRATORS

On the death of a shareholder other than a joint holder, even if he bequeaths his shares to a specific legatee, the executor or administrator is the person entitled to the shares so far as the company is concerned, because he has the legal title to them.[209] The title of the executor or administrator is shown by the probate or letters of administration, which must be produced to the company for registration.[210] Thereafter, the executor or administrator is the person with whom the company must deal in all matters relating to the shares. His title cannot be bypassed by an article purporting on the death of the holder to vest the shares in someone else.[211] Equally, the directors cannot reject an executor's claim to be registered as the holder of shares held by the testator, relying upon an article which enables them to refuse transfers, because such an article does not apply to a transmission by operation of law.[212] There must instead be an express power of veto conferred by the articles to justify a refusal to enter the name of an executor on the register of members.[213] The articles may give the directors in such a case the same right to decline registrations

---

[204] *Re W Key & Sons Ltd* [1902] 1 Ch 467.

[205] *Morgan v Gray* [1953] Ch 83.

[206] *Birch v Sullivan* [1957] 1 WLR 1247.

[207] *Re H L Bolton Engineering Co Ltd* [1956] Ch 677. There is nothing to prevent the bankrupt presenting a petition on the trustee's behalf: see *Re K/9 Meat Supplies (Guildford) Ltd* [1966] 1 WLR 1112.

[208] *Re McMahon* [1900] 1 Ch 173.

[209] See *Roberts v Letter 'T' Estates Ltd* [1961] AC 795 (PC). This is normally confirmed in the articles.

[210] See the Companies Act 2006, s 774. In a Scottish estate, confirmation as executor is the equivalent.

[211] *Re Greene* [1949] Ch 333.

[212] *Re Bentham Mills Spinning Co* (1879) 11 Ch D 900 (CA).

[213] *Scott v Frank F Scott (London) Ltd* [1940] Ch 794 (CA).

they would have had in the case of a transfer of the share by the deceased.[214] A provision in the articles that on the death of a member his shares must be offered to the other members at par can be enforced against the executors of a deceased member, and has been construed so as to operate even when there is only one member surviving.[215] Where the articles of a company permitted the transfer of shares to, among others, 'privileged relatives', while allowing the directors to refuse to register other transfers, and incorporated the provisions of the applicable Table A[216] providing for the same position to apply in the case of transmission by death or bankruptcy, it was held that the personal representatives of a deceased member could not be prevented from transferring the shares to his beneficiary who was within the class of privileged relative.[217]

Articles sometimes compel representative holders either to take the shares in their own names, assuming all the responsibilities of a member of the company, or to nominate some other person to take the shares. If such provisions are not in the articles, there is nothing to prevent representative holders from continuing to allow the shares to remain in the name of the deceased shareholder.[218] But in the absence of express provisions in the articles, the representatives are not entitled to have any notice sent to them or to the registered address of the deceased unless such representative holders become members by formal registration.[219] If the company has not been notified of the death of a member, it is entitled to assume that a notice sent to his registered address has been duly received.[220]

While the shares remain in the name of the deceased holder, his estate is *prima facie* entitled to any subsequent benefits deriving from the shares and is liable to pay any subsequent calls.[221] It follows that, if the articles require that new shares must be offered to the members, the estate of a deceased member must not be ignored when a new issue is made.[222] Similarly, in the event of reconstruction under s 110 of the Insolvency Act 1986, an executor or administrator can exercise the statutory right of dissent.[223] He has also the necessary *locus standi* to present a petition to

---

[214] See, eg, the particular articles in issue in *Village Cay Marina Ltd v Acland* [1998] 2 BCLC 327 (PC).

[215] *Jarvis Motors (Harrow) Ltd v Carabott* [1964] 1 WLR 1101.

[216] The relevant Table A articles were articles 30 and 31 of the 1948 Table A; in this respect the 1985 Table A and the model articles prescribed under the 2006 Act have the same effect.

[217] *Re William Steward (Holdings) Ltd* [1994] BCC 284 (CA).

[218] *City of Glasgow Bank in Liquidation, Buchan's Case* (1879) 4 App Cas 549, at 588–589 (HL (Sc)).

[219] See *Allen v Gold Reefs of West Africa Ltd* [1900] 1 Ch 656 (CA), where, however, the point was expressly covered by an article.

[220] *New Zealand Gold Extraction Co (Newbery-Vautin Process) v Peacock* [1894] 1 QB 622 (CA).

[221] *James v Buena Ventura Syndicate Ltd* [1896] 1 Ch 446, at 464–465 (CA).

[222] Ibid.

[223] *Llewellyn v Kasintoe Rubber Estates Ltd* [1914] 2 Ch 670.

wind up the company,[224] or to challenge a resolution for voluntary winding up,[225] or to institute proceedings under Part 30[226] or s 1029,[227] but he is not to be counted in determining whether there is a sufficient quorum at a general meeting unless the articles otherwise provide.[228]

Whether the personal representatives have taken the shares into their own names or not, they can transfer them.[229]

---

[224] See *Re Cuthbert Cooper & Sons Ltd* [1937] Ch 392; *Re Chesterfield Catering Co* [1976] 3 WLR 879.

[225] *Howling's Trustee v Smith* (1905) 7 F 390.

[226] Section 994(2); see **18.10**.

[227] *Re Bayswater Trading Co Ltd* [1970] 1 WLR 343.

[228] *Re J Franklin & Son Ltd* [1937] 4 All ER 43.

[229] Section 773. See further as to the procedure to be adopted on a transmission of shares, *Gore-Browne on Companies* (Jordans, 45th edn, loose-leaf) at 23 [32].

CHAPTER 10

DEBENTURES, CHARGES AND REGISTRATION

10.1   INTRODUCTION

The immediately preceding chapters have been concerned with various aspects of share capital.[1] This chapter is concerned with loan capital raised by companies. Loan capital is a form of corporate finance that is mainly governed by the law of contract, and lenders and borrowers are free to bargain for such contractual terms as are appropriate to their particular circumstances and their assessment of risk. It is inappropriate in a general company law text such as this to delve too far into the detail of the corporate debt financing structures and loan terms that are used in practice (not least because of the dynamic and evolving nature of the debt capital markets),[2] but some general considerations that are relevant to corporate borrowing are briefly outlined. The types of charge that can be issued by companies, and the distinction between fixed and floating charges, are then considered. This in turn leads to an examination of the relative priority of fixed and floating charges *inter se* and in respect of various other interests. This necessarily involves consideration of the system for the registration of charges created by companies.

In earlier editions of this book, there was a detailed discussion of receivership, once the main remedy employed when a debenture is secured by a floating charge. This has largely fallen out of use as a result of major changes made by the Enterprise Act 2002.[3] A key change is that the holder of a 'qualifying floating charge' created after 15 September 2003[4] is prohibited from appointing an administrative receiver.[5] A 'qualifying floating charge' is defined in s 14(2) of a new Sch B1 of the Insolvency Act 1986 as follows:

---

[1]   As to the relationship between equity and loan capital, known as 'gearing', see **7.2**.

[2]   For more detailed treatment, see standard banking law texts such as Cranston *Principles of Banking Law* (Oxford University Press, 1997). Specifically with regard to corporate debt finance, see also *Gore-Browne on Companies* (Jordans, 45th edn, loose-leaf), Ch 50; Ferran *Company Law and Corporate Finance* (Oxford University Press, 1999) Chs 14–16; Pennington *Bank Finance for Companies* (Sweet & Maxwell, 1987).

[3]   For a summary, see Walters (2004) 25 Co Law 1.

[4]   The date is confirmed in the Insolvency Act 1986, s 72A (Appointed Date) Order 2003, SI 2003/2095, reg 2.

[5]   Section 72A of the Insolvency Act 1986.

(a)   it is stated that the floating charge falls within s 14(1) of Sch B1;

(b)   it purports to empower the holder of the charge to appoint an administrator of the company;

(c)   it purports to empower the holder of the charge to make an appointment which would be the appointment of an administrative receiver; or

(d)   it purports to empower the holder of a floating charge in Scotland to appoint a receiver who on appointment would be an administrative receiver.

A person is a holder of a qualifying floating charge where his security arrangements include one or more qualifying floating charges which together cover the whole or substantially the whole of the company's property.[6] This means that a lender holding several forms of security will be caught by the prohibition in s 72A if one of these is a qualifying floating charge. It seems that such a lender could not exercise a right to appoint an administrative receiver based on a floating charge which is not a qualifying charge.

The overall objective pursued by these change is to promote a 'rescue culture', and the main procedure that should now be invoked where a company is in financial difficulties is the administration procedure.[7] This has also been significantly reformed by the Enterprise Act 2002, which replaced the old Part II of the Insolvency Act 1986 with Sch B1 which now contains the administration procedure. An important change here is that the holder of a qualifying floating charge now has the right to appoint an administrator.[8] The administration procedure is examined in detail in Chapter 21.

Administrative receivership is therefore likely to disappear in due course, and so it is no longer discussed here. It will still be available in respect of non-qualifying floating charges, but only if the holder of such a charge is not also the holder of a qualifying floating charge. Moreover, there are some exceptions to the prohibition in s 72A in ss 72B–72G. The recourse open to the holder of a qualifying floating charge is to appoint an administrator under the new administration procedure.[9]

---

[6]   Paragraph 14(3) of Sch B1.

[7]   It has been argued that the new scheme effectively heralds the demise of the floating charge: see Mokal 'The Floating Charge – An Elegy' in Worthington (ed) *Commercial Law and Commercial Practice* (Oxford, Hart, 2003).

[8]   Paragraphs 14–21 of Sch B1 to the Insolvency Act 1986.

[9]   As to the administration procedure under the new Part II of the Insolvency Act 1986 (now contained in a new Sch B1 to that Act), see **21.13**. As to the effect of a voluntary arrangement (whether consequent upon an administration order or not) under Part I of the 1986 Act, see **21.7**.

There are many defects in the existing system for the creation and registration of company charges. One is the complexity of the rules governing the relative priority of the floating charge in relation to fixed charges. Recent case-law has also made the task of distinguishing between fixed and floating charges more difficult. Another problem with the existing system is that some transactions commonly used by companies to obtain credit, such as industrial hire-purchase and leasing agreements, are not considered to involve the creation of a charge and therefore will not appear on the register of charges. Even certain types of undoubted charge (e g over shares in other companies) are not registrable.

Radical proposals for the reform of the law relating to security interests have been made periodically, albeit with no success. Indeed, the most recent proposals made by the Law Commission have not been included in the Companies Act 2006.[10] At the end of the chapter, there is a brief account of the main proposals which have been made previously and an attempt is made to assess why the proposals have not made it onto the statute books.

PART 1: GENERAL CONSIDERATIONS

10.2 BORROWING POWERS

Besides raising capital by means of shares, companies frequently, either at the time of their incorporation or subsequently, raise money by borrowing. This may be done in various ways – by an ordinary unsecured loan, by making bills of exchange or promissory notes, by a mortgage on the property of the company, or by the issue of debentures. In all these cases, it is necessary to see, first, whether the directors have authority to exercise the company's borrowing powers without a resolution of the company or, as is sometimes required, the consent of a class of shareholders; secondly, whether there is any limit on the amount which may be borrowed, and, if so, whether that limit is reached; and, thirdly, whether the company or the directors have power to secure the repayment of the money borrowed by a mortgage or charge on all or any part of the assets of the company. These general questions as to the authority of the directors and officers to bind the company have been examined in an earlier chapter.[11]

If a company has power (express or implied) to borrow, it can create mortgages or charges to secure the repayment of the loan;[12] but if the

---

[10] Law Commission, *Registration of Security Interests: Company Charges and Property other than land*, Law Com CP No 164 (2002).

[11] See Chapter 6.

[12] *Re Patent File Co* (1870) LR 6 Ch App 83; *Australian Auxiliary Steam Clipper Co v Mounsey* (1858) 4 K & J 733; *Byron v Metropolitan Saloon Omnibus Co* (1858) 3 De G & J 123.

power is express, its directors must observe any limitations in the power. Thus, if the constitution contains the necessary authority, the company can charge or mortgage all its property, of whatever nature, including future property, such as book debts not yet due.[13] It may also charge its uncalled capital,[14] although this is, 'strictly speaking, more in the nature of power than of property'.[15] Uncalled capital capable of being charged does not include capital which can only be called up in the event of a winding-up,[16] nor the amount payable under the guarantee in the case of a company limited by guarantee, this not being part of the capital of the company nor at any time under the control of the directors.[17]

10.3   BORROWING ON DEBENTURES

One form of borrowing by a company is on debentures. When the term 'debenture' is used in its familiar commercial sense, it means a series of bonds which evidence the fact that the company is liable to pay the amount specified, with interest, and generally charge the payment of it upon the property of the company. They may be offered to the public by means of a prospectus in the same manner as shares. The procedure governing the application for and allotment of debentures is similar to that in the case of shares; but, as a debenture-holder is a creditor, and not a member of the company, widely different results follow.[18]

Although debentures are well-known instruments in the business world and are the subject of various provisions in the Companies Act 2006, there is no complete legal definition of them. It was said by Chitty J that 'a debenture means a document which either creates a debt or acknowledges it, and any document which fulfils either of these conditions is a debenture'.[19] But this is possibly too wide a definition:[20] for example, a bank statement may be an acknowledgment of a debt, but it would not ordinarily be regarded as a debenture. At any rate, an

---

[13] *Illingworth v Houldsworth* [1904] AC 353 (HL); *Bloomer v Union Coal Co* (1873) 16 Eq 383; cf *Tailby v Official Receiver* (1888) 13 App Cas 523 (HL).

[14] *Newton v Anglo-Australian Investment Co* [1895] AC 244 (PC); *Re Pyle Works (No 1)* (1890) 44 Ch D 534 (CA).

[15] *Bank of South Australia v Abrahams* (1875) LR 6 PC 265, at 271.

[16] *Bartlett v Mayfair Property Co* [1898] 2 Ch 28 (CA).

[17] *Re Pyle Works (No 1)* (1890) 44 Ch D 534, at 574: but capital which can be called up only with the sanction of a special resolution may be charged, and the charge enforced in a winding-up even though no such resolution has been passed: *Newton v Anglo-Australian Investment Co* [1895] AC 244 (PC).

[18] Companies, like individuals and partnerships, may resort to other means of obtaining credit (eg overdrafts on bank accounts, and the issue of negotiable instruments). Companies also obtain finance by means of hire-purchase agreements and commercial leasing arrangements. Such arrangements, however, have no special provision (eg as to registration) made for them in the Companies Act 2006.

[19] *Levy v Abercorris Slate and Slab Co* (1887) 37 Ch D 260. See also *Edmonds v Blaina Furnaces Co* (1887) 36 Ch D 215; *Knightsbridge Estates Trust v Byrne* [1938] Ch 741, at 769 *et seq*; and *R v Findlater* [1939] 1 KB 594 (CCA).

[20] See (per North J) *Topham v Greenside Co* (1888) 37 Ch D 281, at 291.

acknowledgment of indebtedness fulfils the primary qualification of a debenture. It does not matter by what name the company calls the document. Thus an 'income stock certificate' containing such an acknowledgment but no charge has been held to be a debenture, having regard to the terms and conditions under which it was issued.[21] A document, with coupons attached, promising to 'pay the amount of this debenture to A. B. or order', has been held to be liable to duty as a debenture and not as a promissory note.[22] A document may be a debenture even though the debt to which it relates it not quantified at the date of its creation.[23]

Section 738 of the Companies Act 2006 [CA 1985, s 744] states that for the purpose of the Act[24] 'debenture' includes debenture stock, bonds, and any other securities of a company, whether constituting a charge on the assets of the company or not. An ordinary mortgage of freehold land is a debenture within this section.[25]

In *Re SH & Co (Realisations) 1990 Ltd*,[26] Mummery J acknowledged the absence of a precise definition of the term 'debenture' but commented that this rarely seemed to cause problems in practice.

Debentures may be either: (a) a mere promise to pay; or (b) a promise to pay secured by a mortgage or charge. The mortgage or charge may be created by words in the debenture itself, or by a deed to the benefit of which the debenture holders are declared to be entitled or by a combination of these two methods.[27]

Debentures may be payable to the registered holder and those persons to whom he assigns or to bearer, in which latter case they pass by delivery.

10.4 SIGNIFICANCE OF THE TERM 'DEBENTURE'

Various provisions of the Companies Act 2006, the Insolvency Act 1986, the Financial Services and Markets Act 2000 and the Prospectus Regulations 2005[28] relate to debentures. These include the following.

---

[21] *Lemon v Austin Friars Investment Trust* [1926] 1 Ch 1 (CA).

[22] *British India Steam Navigation Co v Commissioners of Inland Revenue* (1881) 7 QBD 165.

[23] *NV Slavenburg's Bank v Intercontinental Natural Resources* [1980] 1 All ER 955, at 976.

[24] And unless the contrary intention appears.

[25] *Knightsbridge Estates Trust v Byrne* [1940] AC 613 (HL).

[26] [1993] BCC 60.

[27] The extent of the company's indebtedness covered by the security given will depend in the proper construction of the debenture itself. It was held in *Re Quest Cae Ltd* [1985] BCLC 266, that even a widely drafted 'all moneys' debenture did not cover unsecured loan stock issued to a third party and subsequently acquired by the debenture holder.

[28] SI 2005/1433.

(1) Section 769(1) of the Companies Act 2006 [CA 1985, s 185(1)] requires debenture certificates to be complete and ready for delivery within 2 months after allotment, unless the conditions of issue provide otherwise.

(2) Section 752 of the Companies Act 2006 [CA 1985, s 194] allows a company that has redeemed debentures to re-issue them or to issue other debentures in their place.[29] The re-issued or replacement debentures enjoy the same priority as if the debentures had never been redeemed.[30] Thus, if the company has created a security that ranks behind the original debentures, the security does not take priority over the re-issued debentures, even though it would rank before an entirely new issue of debentures.[31]

(3) Section 740 of the Companies Act 2006 [CA 1985, s 195] makes a contract with a company to take up and pay for debentures of the company enforceable by an order for specific performance.

(4) If a register of debenture-holders is kept, ss 743 and 744 of the Companies Act 2006 [CA 1985, ss 190 and 191] impose certain obligations regarding the maintenance, inspection and provisions of copies thereof.

(5) Under s 29(2) of the Insolvency Act 1986, a receiver or manager appointed by or on behalf of the holders of debentures (other than a qualifying floating charge)[32] may be an administrative receiver.

(6) The admission of debentures to listing must comply with Part VI of the Financial Services and Markets Act 2000. A public offer of unlisted debentures must be done in accordance with the Prospectus Regulations 2005. The regulation of public offers and listing of securities is considered in Chapter 19.

10.5   MAIN TERMS OF LOANS

The main terms of loans relate to the payment of interest and the repayment of principal.

10.5.1   Principal

The loan agreement fixes the date when, or the circumstances in which, the principal is repayable. A loan may be for a fixed term, or may be

---

[29] This power can be excluded in the articles or by contract, or by a manifestation by the company of its intention to cancel the debentures: s 752(1).

[30] Section 752 (3) [CA 1985, s 194(2)].

[31] *Fitzgerald v Persse* [1908] 1 Ir R 279.

[32] Section 72A of the Insolvency Act 1986.

repayable on demand or on notice. The equitable rule which invalidates restrictions on a mortgagor's[33] right to redeem does not apply to debentures, with the consequence that a debenture may be 'perpetual' or 'irredeemable'.[34] It may be slightly misleading to describe a debenture as 'irredeemable'[35] or 'perpetual' because closer examination of the terms will usually indicate that, although the holder has no right to redeem, the company has an option to redeem in given circumstances.[36]

As well as specifying a final redemption date or period, the terms of the loan agreement may also give the company the power to make early repayment or may provide for the establishment of a sinking fund which the company is obliged to apply in repaying principal from time to time.

10.5.2 Interest

At common law, interest is not payable on a debt except by agreement.[37] The loan agreement must therefore contain a covenant to pay interest, and should provide that if the capital is not paid at the due date, interest shall continue to be payable at the agreed rate. If there is no such provision, although interest may be recovered as damages for non-payment of the principal, it will be allowed only at the 'merchantable rate', or at the rate previously paid, whichever is less.[38] The interest on a loan is a debt, and, although usually expressed to be payable half-yearly, accrues from day to day.[39] It is payable whether or not there are profits. Sometimes, however, interest is declared to be payable only out of profits, in which case the company must apply all available profits for this purpose, and not set aside any part as reserve until the interest is paid in full.[40] Debentures in this form are sometimes called 'income bonds'.

10.6 DEBENTURES ISSUED AT A DISCOUNT

Debentures may be issued at a discount: eg a debenture for £100 may be issued in consideration of £95 advanced to the company, the effect of the

---

[33] For this purpose, this includes a company which has given a floating charge: *Kreglinger v New Patagonia Meat Co* [1914] AC 25 (HL) dispelling doubts expressed in *De Beers Consolidated Mines v British South Africa Co* [1912] AC 52.

[34] Section 739 of the Companies Act 2006 [CA 1985, s 193], *Knightsbridge Estate Trust v Byrne*, above.

[35] 'Irredeemable' may mean, if the context so requires, 'not liable to be called in': *Willey v Joseph Stocks & Co* [1912] 2 Ch 134n.

[36] Stock which is expressed to be 'redeemable at the option of the company' is not repayable on the demand of the holder: *Edinburgh Corporation v British Linen Bank* [1913] AC 133 (HL (Sc)).

[37] *Higgins v Sargent* (1823) 2 B & C 348; *Page v Newman* (1829) 9 B & C 378.

[38] *Price v Great Western Rly* (1847) 16 M & W 244; *Re Roberts* (1880) 14 Ch D 49 (CA); *Mellersh v Brown* (1890) 45 Ch D 225.

[39] Apportionment Act 1870, ss 2 and 5; *Re Rogers' Trusts* (1863) 1 Dr & Sm 338.

[40] *Heslop v Paraguay Central Rly* (1910) 54 SJ 234.

discount being an addition to the interest paid,[41] and commission may be paid to underwriters or others for placing or guaranteeing the taking up of debentures. However, convertible debentures must not be issued at a discount so as to evade the rule against issuing shares at a discount. In *Moseley v Koffyfontein Mines*,[42] debentures issued at a discount entitled the holder to call for the allotment of fully paid up shares in satisfaction of the same nominal amount as the debentures. Since the debentures here were immediately convertible it was obviously a device for issuing shares at a discount. Cozens-Hardy LJ left open the question of whether an option to convert is valid if it is not exercisable until some time after the debentures are issued.[43] Although convertible debentures are frequently issued, there will usually be a premium element in the conversion terms so that a discount will not arise.

PART 2: CHARGES

10.7   FIXED AND FLOATING CHARGES

The charge created by a debenture may be either 'fixed' or 'floating'. When the charge is fixed it is like an ordinary mortgage and affects the title to the property, so that the company can only deal with the property affected, subject to the charge. But where the charge is a 'floating' one the company may in the ordinary course of its business[44] deal with the property covered by the charge, mortgaging it so that the mortgage takes priority over the floating charge, or selling or disposing of it, free from the floating charge, or using it up as the business requires at any time before the charge attaches.[45]

---

[41]   *Re Anglo-Danubian Steam Co* (1875) 20 Eq 339; *Campbell's Case* (1876) 4 Ch D 470; *Webb v Shropshire Rly Co* [1893] 3 Ch 307 (CA).

[42]   [1904] 2 Ch 108 (CA).

[43]   Ibid, at 120.

[44]   *Re Old Bush Mills Distillery Co* [1897] Ir R 488. What is within the 'ordinary course of business' will depend on the circumstances of each case. A specific mortgage to raise money for the purpose of carrying on the business of the company is within the words: *Cox Moore v Peruvian Corp* [1908] 1 Ch 604. Some cases have equated the 'ordinary course of business' to what is permitted by the company's objects clause: *Re HH Vivian & Co Ltd* [1900] 2 Ch 654; *Re Borax Co* [1901] 1 Ch 326, at 342; *Re Automatic Bottle Makers Ltd* [1926] Ch 412, at 421; *Hamilton v Hunter* (1982) 7 ACLR 295. But *intra vires* transactions which would cause a cessation of the company's business may fall outside the ordinary course: *Hubbuck v Helms* (1887) 56 LJ Ch 536. The consequences of acting outside the ordinary course have been discussed more in Australia than in England: *Hamilton v Hunter*, above; *Torzillu Pty Ltd v Brynac Pty* (1983) 8 ACLR 52; see generally Worthington 'Floating Charges – An Alternative Theory' [1994] CLJ 81 at pp 99–102. The absence of relevant English authority suggests that this point rarely causes difficulty in practice.

[45]   *Re Florence Land Co* (1878) 10 Ch D 530 (CA): *Wheatley v Silkstone etc Coal Co* (1885) 29 Ch D 715; *Re Hamilton's Windsor Ironworks* (1879) 12 Ch D 707; *Re Colonial Trusts Corporation* (1879) 15 Ch D 465, at 472; *In re HH Vivian & Co* [1900] 2 Ch 654.

It is common to create the security in such manner that the lands and immovable property of the company are covered by a fixed charge, while the stock-in-trade, chattels, and book debts of the company and its future property are included in a floating charge. In recent years, however, attempts to create fixed charges on present and future book debts have become more common.[46] The debentures usually specify in what events (such as liquidation, default in payment of principal or interest for a stated period, etc) the charge is to be enforceable, and in interpreting these the court will always lean against treating the charge on goods required for the business as being fixed while the business is going on.[47] Where an intention appears that the company should receive and deal with the property charged, it is assumed that only a floating security is intended.[48] A charge, though expressed in words which would otherwise suffice to create a fixed mortgage, will be treated as a floating charge if it appears that it was intended that the company should continue to use the articles charged and turn them over in its business.[49] Similarly, a charge described as 'floating' will, in fact, be a fixed charge if the company cannot use the assets and withdraw them from the scope of the charge.[50]

The test for classifying a charge as 'fixed' or 'floating' requires the court first to construe the relevant document to ascertain the parties' intentions,[51] and then to categorise this on the basis of relevant legal principles, as stated by Lord Millet in *Agnew v Commissioner of Inland Revenue*:[52]

> 'In deciding whether a charge is a fixed charge or a floating charge, the court is engaged in a two-stage process. At the first stage it must construe the instrument of charge and seek to gather the intentions of the parties from the language they have used. But the object at this stage of the process is not to discover whether the parties intended to create a fixed or floating charge. It is to ascertain the nature of the rights and obligations which the parties intended to grant each other in respect of the charged assets. Once these have been ascertained, the court can then embark on the second stage of the

---

46   See **10.9**.

47   *Government Stock Investment Co v Manila Rly* [1897] AC 81 (HL); *Evans v Rival Granite Quarries* [1910] 2 KB 979 (CA).

48   *Illingworth v Houldsworth* [1904] AC 355 (HL); *Re GE Tunbridge Ltd* [1995] 1 BCLC 34; *Agnew v Commissioner of Inland Revenue* [2001] 2 BCLC 188 (PC).

49   *National Provincial Bank v United Electric Theatres* [1916] 1 Ch 132, *United Builders Pty Ltd v Mutual Acceptance Ltd* (1980) 33 ALR 1; *Boambee Bay Resort Ltd (in Liquidation) v Equus Financial Services Ltd* (1991) 6 ACSR 532.

50   *Russell-Cooke Trust Co Ltd v Elliott* [2007] 2 BCLC 637.

51   As does the determination of the extent of the property covered by the charge: *Northern Bank Ltd v Ross* [1991] BCLC 504, [1990] BCC 883 (charge on book debts did not extend to bank account); *Re HiFi Equipment (Cabinets) Ltd* [1998] BCLC 65, (1987) 3 BCC 478 (machines were not 'fixed plant and machinery' and were therefore not caught by a fixed charge (not following *Tudor Heights Ltd v United Dominion Corporation Finance Ltd* [1977] 1 NZLR 532).

52   [2001] 2 BCLC 188. This case is also known as *Re Brumark Investment* (the name in the New Zealand Courts: see [2000] 1 BCLC 353), but will here be referred to as *Agnew*.

process, which is one of categorisation. This is a matter of law. It does not depend on the intention of the parties.'[53]

The principal indicia of a floating charge have been stated by the Court of Appeal as follows: first, if it is a charge upon all of a certain class of assets, present and future; secondly, if the assets charged would in the ordinary course of business be changing from time to time; and, thirdly, if expressly or by necessary implication the company has the power, until some step is taken by the debenture-holders or trustees, of carrying on its business in the ordinary way so far as regards the assets charged.[54]

It is important to bear in mind that these tests are descriptive and that they do not amount to a precise definition of a floating charge.[55] Thus, although there is a *prima facie* rule that the property secured by a floating charge on the company's undertaking includes future property as well as such property as is owned by the company when the charge is created,[56] it has been held that a charge on present property only can be a floating charge.[57] Equally, a charge can be a fixed charge where the property secured includes future, as well as present, property.[58]

Land owned by a company which is not in the business of property trading would not be regarded as a class of asset changing from time to time in the course of the company's business. Nevertheless, in *Welch v Bowmaker (Ireland) Ltd*,[59] the majority of the Irish Supreme Court[60] held that a charge secured on land could be a floating charge.

The essence of a floating charge is embodied in the third of the characteristics outlined in *Re Yorkshire Woolcombers* and relates to control. Millett LJ (as he then was) once said that whether a charge is fixed or floating depends on the freedom of the chargor to deal with the proceeds of the charged assets in the ordinary course of business free

---

[53] Ibid, at [32]. For an example of how this test is applied, see *Re Txu Europe Group plc* [2004] 1 BCLC 519.

[54] *Re Yorkshire Woolcombers' Association* [1903] 2 Ch 284 (CA), affirmed in the House of Lords *sub nom Illingworth v Houldsworth* [1904] AC 355, where it was held that a general charge on book debts, present and future, was a floating charge, although not expressed to be so, and required registration under the Companies Act 1900.

[55] *Re Yorkshire Woolcombers,* at 295, per Romer LJ and 298, per Cozens Hardy LJ; *Re Croftbell Ltd* [1990] BCLC 844, [1990] BCC 781.

[56] *Re Panama, New Zealand and Australia Royal Mail Co* (1870) LR 5 Ch App 318; *Illingworth v Houldsworth* [1904] AC 355; *Re Croftbell Ltd,* above. This rule can assist where there is some doubt about the extent of the security: *Re Alfred Priestman & Co Ltd* [1936] 2 All ER 1340.

[57] *Re Bond Worth Ltd* [1980] 1 Ch 228, at 267; *Re Atlantic Medical Ltd* [1992] BCC 653, at 658 ('it is very unusual indeed that a floating charge would be limited to existing assets of a company'); *Re Cimex Tissues Ltd* [1994] BCC 626, at 637–639.

[58] *Tailby v Official Receiver* (1883) 13 App Cas 583. See further, **10.9**.

[59] [1980] IR 251.

[60] Kenny J dissented precisely because the second characteristic of a floating charge, as outlined in *Yorkshire Woolcombers,* was not present.

from the security,[61] but in a later case he reformulated the correct question as being whether the chargee is in control of the charged assets.[62] In *Agnew*, Lord Millett noted that:[63]

> '[I]n construing a debenture to see whether it creates a fixed or a floating charge, the only intention which is relevant is ... whether the charged assets were intended to be under the control of the company or of the charge holder.'

The 'control test' recognises that some restrictions on the chargor's powers to deal with the charged assets, for instance, limitations on the power to create further charges ranking in priority, may be compatible with a floating charge. The degree of control (or freedom) required to create a fixed (or floating) charge has been discussed extensively in cases concerned with the nature of charge on book debts (discussed at **10.9**).

Precisely because it confers greater control, lenders might be expected to prefer fixed security and to take floating security only on assets where the frequency of turnover makes fixed security impracticable. An inherent risk in a floating charge is that the company will dissipate the subject-matter of the security through imprudent trading, leaving the lender with a security that is virtually worthless. Also, a lender who has taken only floating security, risks finding himself postponed to other creditors of the company who have themselves obtained fixed security or who are afforded a preferential status by the insolvency legislation.[64]

The Insolvency Act 1986 provides a reason why it can be important for a lender to take a floating charge, either on its own or in addition to fixed security.[65] Under the Act, an administrator can be appointed by the court and, following changes made by the Enterprise Act 2002, the holder of a 'qualifying floating charge', to administer the affairs of a company in financial difficulties. Administration is a collective insolvency procedure and no one creditor, or group of creditors, is entitled to control the administrator in the exercise of his powers. The administrator's statutory powers are extensive and include the ability to sell property which is

---

[61]   *Royal Trust Bank v National Westminster Bank plc* [1996] BCC 613, at 616. In *Re ASRS Establishment Ltd* [2000] 1 BCLC 631, Otton LJ advised that this should be approached 'with some caution' (at 643).

[62]   *Re Cosslett (Contractors) Ltd* [1997] BCC 724, at 734. See also *Re Cimex Tissues Ltd* [1994] BCC 626 and cases such as *Re Brightlife Ltd* [1987] 1 Ch 200 and *Re Westmaze Ltd* [1999] BCC 441 (charge on book debts was a floating charge despite restrictions on the chargor's power to assign or factor the debts). For a fixed charge, the chargee must enjoy his power to control the charged assets as chargee and not in some other capacity, such as director of the chargor company: *Re Double S Printers Ltd* [1999] BCC 303.

[63]   [2001] 2 BCLC 188, at [32].

[64]   Although the number of preferential creditors has been greatly reduced by the Enterprise Act 2002.

[65]   On this function of the floating charge, see Mokal 'The Floating Charge – An Elegy' in Worthington (ed) *Commercial Law and Commercial Practice* (Oxford, Hart, 2003).

subject to a charge without the consent of the holder of that security.[66] The significant restriction on the administration procedure is that an administrator may not be appointed where an administrative receiver[67] has been appointed to the company unless the appointor of the administrative receiver consents.[68]

An administrative receiver is defined by s 29(2) of the Insolvency Act 1986 as a receiver or manager of the whole (or substantially the whole) of a company's property, appointed by or on behalf of the holders of any debentures of the company secured by a charge which, as created, was a floating charge, or by such a charge and one or more other securities.[69] However, following the changes made to the Insolvency Act by the Enterprise Act 2002, the holder of a 'qualifying floating charge'[70] created after 15 September 2003[71] may no longer appoint an administrative receiver.

Since the coming into force of the administration procedure contained in the Insolvency Act 1986, there has emerged the concept of the 'lightweight' floating charge.[72] Where a company's assets consist wholly or mainly of property which is not expected to be the subject of rapid turnover, an example being a holding company with assets consisting almost entirely of shares in subsidiaries, the lender can take a fixed charge on the assets without unduly impeding the company's business affairs. This fixed charge will largely satisfy the lender's desire for control, save for the fact that it will not enable the lender to prevent the appointment of an administrator. Prior to 15 September 2003, this need could be met by also taking a floating charge over the company's undertaking. This floating charge may be almost identical in scope to the fixed charge and the detailed covenants which would usually be required from the company if the floating charge stood alone can be dispensed with, thus making the charge 'lightweight'.

---

[66] The administrator requires the consent of the court to sell property which is subject to a fixed charge; the court's consent is not required where the security is a floating charge: s 15(1) and (2).

[67] See Part 3, below. An administrative receiver may now not be appointed by a creditor who holds a 'qualifying floating charge': s 72A of the Insolvency Act 1986, as amended.

[68] Paragraph 39(1) of Sch B1 to the Insolvency Act 1986 (inserted by the Enterprise Act 2002).

[69] Or a person who would be such a receiver or manager but for the appointment of some other person as the receiver of part of the company's property: s 29(2)(b).

[70] Defined in para 14 of Sch B1 to the Insolvency Act 1986.

[71] Section 72A and the Insolvency Act 1986, section 72A (Appointed Date) Order 2003, SI 2003/2095, reg 2.

[72] Oditah 'Lightweight Floating Charges' [1991] JBL 49; Marks and Emmet 'Administrative Receivers: Question of Identity and Double Identity' [1994] JBL 1.

10.8 THE NATURE OF A FLOATING CHARGE

A floating charge is a present charge, not a future one, but it does not specifically affect any item until some event happens which causes it to become fixed.[73] Thus the debenture holder has under his floating charge an immediate equity or charge on the property, but the company can continue to deal with the property charged in the course of its business until the charge attaches as a fixed charge, or, as it is often described, 'crystallises'.

Some of the earlier cases,[74] reasoning by analogy to the fixed charge, explained what was then a novel form of security as being like a specific mortgage plus a licence to the mortgagor to dispose of the company's assets in the ordinary course of business. Buckley LJ[75] repudiated this explanation of the floating charge in favour of the concept of 'a floating mortgage applying to every item comprised in the security, but not specifically affecting any item until some event occurs, or some act on the part of the mortgagee is done, which causes it to crystallize into a fixed security'. This notion of a floating charge, characterising it as a 'present security on a shifting fund of assets',[76] better accords with the detailed rules governing the functioning of the floating charge between the time of its creation and its crystallisation.

The nature of the lender's interest in the company's property created by a floating charge and the related question of the basis of the company's power to continue to deal with the assets are issues which have intrigued commentators and on which there is an extensive amount of literature.[77] Gough argues that a floating charge gives the lender no proprietary interest in the company's property until such time as the charge crystallises into a fixed charge[78] but this view has been disputed by many other writers.[79] The cases are not consistent and whilst the argument that

---

[73] See (per Buckley LJ) *Evans v Rival Granite Quarries* [1910] 2 KB, at 999; *Mercantile Bank of India v Chartered Bank of India & Co* [1937] 1 All ER 231.

[74] Eg *Re Florence Land Co* (1878) 10 ChD 543; *Davey & Co v Williamson* [1898] 2 QB 194, at 200.

[75] *Evans v Rival Granite Quarries* [1910] 2 KB 979, at 999. See also *Biggerstaff v Rowatts Wharf Ltd* [1896] 2 Ch 93, at 105, per Kay LJ.

[76] *Re Cimex Tissues*, above, at 635.

[77] Gough *Company Charges* (LexisNexis Butterworths, 3rd edn, 2007).

[78] A view also asserted by the same author in Ch 9 of Finn (ed) *Equity and Commercial Relationships* (Law Book Company, 1978).

[79] For example: Goode 'It can now be taken as settled that the floating charge creates an immediate interest *in rem*' in *Legal Problems of Credit and Security* (Sweet & Maxwell, 2nd edn, 1988), p 46; Farrar 'World Economic Stagnation Puts the Floating Charge on Trial' (1980) 1 Co Law 83; Ferran 'Floating Charges – the Nature of the Security' [1988] CLJ 213; Worthington 'Floating Charges – An Alternative Theory' [1994] CLJ 81; and Worthington *Proprietary Interests in Commercial Transactions* (Oxford University Press, 1996), Ch 4. See also Pennington 'The Genesis of the Floating Charge' (1960) 23 MLR 630.

a floating charge confers a proprietary interest has support,[80] so too does the alternative view.[81] Although its true nature has proved to be somewhat elusive, this has not prevented the floating charge from becoming an important element of corporate financing. Bearing this in mind, it may be that it is unnecessary to attempt to pinpoint in an absolute sense the proprietary interest created by a floating charge and that a more fruitful line of inquiry is to consider whether in specific contexts, the floating charge gives the lender an interest which, for the purpose in question, is to be regarded as 'proprietary'.[82] In *Re Margart Pty*, the Supreme Court of New South Wales[83] held that a statutory provision[84] which invalidated dispositions of a company's property after the commencement of its liquidation did not apply to dispositions made to a debenture holder who held an uncrystallised floating charge, because, for that purpose, the debenture-holder had a beneficial interest in the property transferred. In *Re Goldcorp Exchange Ltd*[85] Lord Mustill, delivering the judgment of the Judicial Board of the Privy Council, stated that the chargor's freedom to deal with the secured assets prior to crystallisation did not mean that the chargee's right to the assets was circumscribed by an indebtedness of a purely personal nature and held that the floating charge gave its holder a sufficient proprietary interest to defeat a claim by a third party to an estoppel arising from statements made by the company. In *Queens Moat Houses v Capita Trustees*,[86] Lightman J noted that whilst the right of the chargor to deal with the asset charged was inconsistent with a fixed charge where he could do so without reference to the chargee, this was not the case where the chargor has a contractual right to request the chargee to release an asset from the charge.[87]

---

[80]   *Driver v Broad* [1893] 1 QB 744; *Wallace v Evershed* [1899] 1 Ch 891; *Landall Holdings Ltd v Caratti* [1979] WAR 97, at 102–103; *Hamilton v Hunter* (1982) 7 ACLR 295, at 306; *Re Margart Pty Ltd, Hamilton v Westpac Banking Corp* (1984) 9 ACLR 269, at 271–272; *Canadian Imperial Bank of Commerce v Coopers & Lybrand* (1989) 57 DLR (4th) 633; *Wily v St George Partnership Banking Ltd* (1997) 30 ACSR 204.

[81]   *Tricontinental Corp v FCT* (1987) 12 ACLR 421, citing, *inter alia, Evans v Rival Granite Quarries Ltd* [1910] 2 KB 979.

[82]   See *Wily v St George Partnership Banking Ltd* (1997) 30 ACSR 204, at 204, per Sackville J: 'That different views continue to be expressed on such an apparently fundamental question [the juridical nature of the floating charge] reflects the fact that particular cases (like the present) usually turn on more prosaic issues, such as the construction of a statute or the terms of the particular charge.'

[83]   Although an Australian decision, this was followed by Vinelott J in *Re French's Wine Bar Ltd* [1987] BCLC 499 and would seem to represent English law.

[84]   The equivalent provision in the Insolvency Act 1986 is s 127.

[85]   [1994] 3 WLR 199, at 212–213.

[86]   [2005] 2 BCLC 199.

[87]   For an example of how these principles were applied to a clause in a trust agreement between a retailer and a credit-card processing provider, see *Re F2G Realisations Ltd (in liquidation); Gray and another v GTP Group Ltd* [2011] 1 BCLC 313.

10.9   CHARGES ON BOOK DEBTS

The characteristics of fixed and floating charges have received close judicial scrutiny in a line of cases concerned with charges on book debts or other debts or receivables such as rental payments.[88] 'Book debts' are simply debts which, as a matter of accounting practice, would ordinarily be entered in the books of the company.[89] The case-law was recently clarified by the decisions in *Agnew v Commissioners of Inland Revenue*,[90] and *National Westminster Bank v Spectrum plus Ltd; Re Spectrum Plus Ltd*,[91] but to put those decisions in context, it is necessary to review several previous decisions eventually leading to these rulings.

In the landmark decision of *Siebe Gorman & Co Ltd v Barclays Bank Ltd*,[92] the court held that a debenture effectively created a fixed charge on present and future book debts. The significant terms of the debenture obliged the company not to assign or charge its book debts without the lender's consent and required the company to pay the proceeds of book debts into an account held with the lender. Slade J held that the bank effectively had a lien on the proceeds paid into the bank account and could prevent the company from making withdrawals in the course of its business. It was held that the restrictions on the book debts and on their proceeds together gave the lender a degree of control which was inconsistent with the freedom to the company that was the vital characteristic of a floating charge. Despite condemnation from the Review Committee on Insolvency Law and Practice,[93] the decision in

---

[88]   For an explanation of the tendency of banks in recent years to move from a floating charge to a series of fixed charges giving a greater degree of protection, see Robbie and Gill 'Fixed and Floating Charges. A New Look at the Banks' Position' [1981] JBL 95. For further analysis of the cases, see Pennington 'Fixed Charges over Future Assets of a Company' (1985) 6 Co Law 9; McCormack 'Fixed Charges over Future Book Debts' (1987) 8 Co Law 3; Pearce 'Fixed Charges Over Book Debts' [1987] JBL 18.

[89]   *Tailby v Official Receiver; Independent Automatic Sales Ltd v Knowles and Foster* [1962] 1 WLR 974; *Paul & Frank Ltd v Discount Bank (Overseas) Ltd* [1967] Ch 348. However, the credit balance on a company's bank account is not a book debt: *Re Buildlead Ltd (No 2)* [2006] 1 BCLC 9.

[90]   [2001] 2 BCLC 188 (PC). This has subsequently been followed by the House of Lords in *Smith (Administrators of Cosslett (Contractors) Ltd) v Bridgend County Borough Council* [2001] UKHL 58, [2002] 1 BCLC 77.

[91]   [2005] 2 BCLC 269.

[92]   [1979] 2 Lloyd's Rep 142.

[93]   Cmnd 8558 (1982), paras 1584–1586.

Siebe Gorman was not reversed by the 1980s' insolvency legislation and was followed[94] and distinguished,[95] before finally being overruled in *Re Spectrum Plus Ltd.*[96]

In *Re New Bullas Ltd*, the Court of Appeal[97] established that control of the debts *and* of their proceeds is not the prerequisite of a fixed charge on book debts: the charging document can treat the debts and their proceeds as divisible and create a fixed charge on the debts, but only a floating charge on the proceeds of those debts.[98] The debenture in question was expressed to create a fixed charge over debts and provided for their proceeds to be paid into a current account or another designated account. In the absence of directions from the debenture-holder, on payment into the account the proceeds were released from the fixed charge and became subject to a floating charge. Even though the proceeds of the debts could thus cease to fall within the debenture-holder's control as soon as they were paid into the account, the charge on the debts themselves was held to be a fixed charge. This decision attracted much comment[99] and doubts were soon cast over the *New Bullas* concept of the divisibility of debts and their proceeds in the courts.[100] *New Bullas* and subsequent cases[101] left the law on the identifying characteristics of fixed and floating charges on book debts or other receivable in a state of disarray. However, much-needed clarity was restored by the Privy Council decision in

---

[94] *Re Keenan Bros Ltd* [1986] BCLC 242 (Supreme Court (Ireland)); *William Gaskell Group Ltd v Highley* [1993] BCC 200.

[95] *Re Brightlife Ltd* [1987] Ch 200, [1986] 3 All ER 673, [1987] 2 WLR 197, [1986] BCLC 418, (1986) 2 BCC 99, at 359. *Siebe Gorman* was not followed on indistinguishable facts in *Supercool Refrigeration & Air Conditioning Ltd v Hoverd Industries Ltd* [1994] 3 NZLR 300. See further Ferran *Company Law and Corporate Finance* (Oxford University Press, 1999) at pp 517–529.

[96] [2005] 2 BCLC 269.

[97] [1994] BCLC 485, [1994] BCC 36, noted, (1994) 110 LQR 340, [1994] CLJ 225. See also Goode 'Charges over Book Debts: a Missed Opportunity' (1994) 110 LQR 592.

[98] Cf *Waters v Widdows* [1984] VR 503, Victoria, Australia and *Re Holidair Ltd* [1994] ILRM 481 (Ireland, Supreme Court).

[99] See Berg 'Charges Over Book Debts – a Reply' [1995] JBL 433; Worthington 'Fixed Charges over Book Debts and Other Receivables' (1997) 113 LQR 562; Gregory 'Fixed Charges on Book Debts – The Conceptual Light Still Hid From Our Eyes' (1996/97) 3 RALQ 65; Gregory and Walton 'Book Debt Charges – The Saga Goes On' (1999) 115 LQR 14.

[100] *Royal Trust Bank v National Westminster Bank plc* [1996] BCC 613, at 619, per Millett LJ. See also *Oakdale (Richmond) Ltd v National Westminster Bank plc* [1997] 1 BCLC 63, at 75, per Chadwick J.

[101] Such as the *Atlantic* decisions *(Re Atlantic Computer Systems plc* [1992] Ch 505 and *Re Atlantic Medical Ltd* [1992] BCC 653). The Court of Appeal's conclusion in *Computer* that the charge in question was a fixed charge seems to have been strongly influenced by the fact that the subject-matter of the security was a set of present assets and did not extend to future assets. However, it is well established (as was acknowledged by Vinelott J in *Medical*) that that specificity of the charging clause is not determinative of the nature of the charge as fixed or floating. The authorities to this effect were not, however, considered by the Court of Appeal. See further, Bridge (1994) 107 LQR 394; Goode (1994) 110 LQR 340; Berg [1995] JBL 433; Worthington (1997) 113 LQR 562; and Ferran *Company Law and Corporate Finance* (Oxford University Press, 1999) at pp 517–529.

Agnew.[102] In that case, Brumark Investment Ltd had granted a *New Bullas*-style charge in favour of its bank, and, having gone into liquidation, the question arose who would be entitled to the proceeds of the outstanding book debts. The Privy Council had to consider whether a charge over uncollected book debts which the company was free to collect and which allowed it to use the proceeds in the ordinary course of its business was a fixed or a floating charge. The opinion was given by Lord Millett, who undertook an extensive review of the relevant case-law that eventually resulted in the decision in *New Bullas*. His conclusion was that *New Bullas* was 'wrongly decided'[103] for a number of reasons: first, the Court of Appeal in *New Bullas* had taken an approach to construction which was 'fundamentally mistaken'[104] because it focused exclusively on the parties' intentions.[105] Secondly, Nourse LJ's argument that the book debts ceased to be subject to the fixed charge because of what the parties had agreed rather than because the company was free to collect the debts would be 'entirely destructive of the floating charge'.[106] The third, and most crucial, point related to the question whether debts can be separated from their proceeds, a matter crucial to the *New Bullas*-style charge. Lord Millett accepted that property and its proceeds are two different assets, and a book debt could be assigned, as well as realised by collection (when the debt is wholly extinguished).[107] However, the value of a debt, which is a right to receive payment, can only be exploited by exercising that right; separating ownership of debts from that of their proceeds 'makes no commercial sense'.[108] Consequently, in determining whether the charge was fixed or floating, the crucial question was not merely whether the company was free to collect the debts, but whether it could do so for its own benefit. It is not necessary that the company is prevented from realising the debt, as long as the proceeds are not at the company's disposal. A *New Bullas*-style charge left the company free to realise the debt and to replace it with assets not subject to a fixed charge and therefore at the free disposal of the company, and that is why it could not be a fixed charge.

This decision restored much-needed clarity,[109] although it did not resolve all difficulties.[110] In particular, it raised fresh doubts over the decision in

---

[102] Known at first instance in New Zealand as *Re Brumark Investments Ltd* (16 February 1999, unreported), NZHC, noted (1999) 115 LQR 365, which followed *New Bullas*, but the NZ Court of Appeal reversed that decision: [2000] 1 NZLR 223. *Agnew* was an appeal from the NZ CA decision.

[103] Paragraph [50].

[104] Paragraph [32].

[105] See **10.7**, above, for the correct approach.

[106] Paragraph [34].

[107] Paragraph [43].

[108] Paragraph [46].

[109] A similar approach had been adopted by Hart J in *Chalk v Khan* [2000] 2 BCLC 361. In that case, the company did not have a current account with the charge holder, and had therefore been directed to pay any proceeds into an account held at another bank, which it was free to access. See also *Re ASRS Establishment Ltd* [2000] 1 BCLC 631 (CA).

[110] See, eg, *McCormack* (2002) 23 Co Law 84; *Capper* (2003) 24 Co Law 325.

Siebe Gorman, which assumed that where the proceeds of the book debts are paid into a bank account with the lender (a clearing bank), the charge would be a fixed charge. The difficulty with this had always been that the company was free to draw on the account,[111] and several comments by Lord Millett in *Agnew* were thought to be critical of *Siebe Gorman*.[112]

The matter was resolved by a seven-strong House of Lords in *National Westminster Bank v Spectrum Plus Ltd*.[113] This case was a test-case by the Inland Revenue to challenge the *Siebe Gorman* decision.[114] In *Spectrum Plus*, the charge in question followed closely that in issue in *Siebe Gorman*. Thus, an overdraft facility had been secured by a charge, and the company was required to pay receipts from its book debts into that bank account. However, the bank remained free to draw against the overdraft. At first instance, Sir Andrew Morritt V-C reviewed the opinion given in *Agnew* and concluded that because the account into which the proceeds were paid was an ordinary current account on which no restrictions had been imposed and which had been set up to provide working capital for the company, the charge was a floating, and not a fixed, charge.[115] Whilst undoubtedly the correct outcome, it ignored the binding precedent established in *Re New Bullas*, and this was one of the grounds on which Court of Appeal reversed the decision to hold that the charge was a fixed charge.[116]

The second reason given by the Court of Appeal was based on principles of banking law. In essence, when money is paid into a bank account, the money belongs to the bank, and the bank can use it for its purposes, whereas the customer has a contractual right to receive back from the bank an amount equivalent to the sum paid in. So when Spectrum Plus (or the company in *Siebe Gorman*) paid the proceeds of its book debts into the bank account, these became the property of the bank. Payments into an overdrawn bank account reduce the indebtedness to the bank by the amount paid in. If the bank subsequently permits further advances on the overdraft, then that is a loan of new money. Phillips MR therefore concluded that 'a debenture which prohibits a [company] from disposing of book debts before they are collected and requires him to pay them, beneficially, to the [Bank] as and when they are collected properly falls within the definition of a fixed charge, regardless of the extent of his

---

[111] Contrast *Re Keenan Brothers* [1986] BCLC 242, Irish Supreme Court.

[112] At [38], he used the words '... was thought to obtain in *Siebe Gorman* ...', and at [48], it was noted that 'their Lordships would wish to make it clear that it is not enough to provide in the debenture that the account is a blocked account if it is not operated as one in fact'. See also *Capper* (2003) 24 Co Law 325.

[113] [2005] 2 BCLC 269.

[114] Capper (2003) 24 Co Law 325, at 332 notes that as the decision technically 'declares' the law, previous decisions in conflict with it could be unscrambled. In the case of *Siebe Gorman*-style charges, this would be an impossible undertaking.

[115] [2004] EWHC 9 (Ch), [2004] 1 BCLC 335.

[116] [2005] 2 BCLC 30.

contractual rights to draw out sums equivalent to the amounts paid in'.[117] Consequently, the company never had any control of the proceeds. The charge was therefore a fixed charged, and, according to Phillips MR, the decision in *Siebe Gorman* was correct.[118]

The House of Lords overturned the Court of Appeal's decision, and overruled *Siebe Gorman* by holding that the charge in that case was a floating charge.[119] The charge did not impose any restrictions on the company's use of the bank account, including the overdraft facility; however, had the account been blocked, then the charge could have been a fixed charge. The House of Lords disagreed with Phillips MR's analysis, emphasising the need to take into account 'the commercial nature and substance of the arrangement' rather than a 'formalistic analysis of how the bank clearing system works'.[120] The crucial issue was whether any restrictions had been placed on the use the company could make of the credit to the account based on each payment in. As long as the company is able to drawn on the account, irrespective of whether it is in credit or in debit, the charge on the account cannot be a fixed charge. Similarly, if proceeds of book debts remain freely available to a company under the terms of the debenture, it can only be a floating charge, even if restrictions are subsequently imposed on the use of such proceeds.[121]

The decision in *Spectrum Plus* concludes a long and complex line of cases, but it remains to be seen if this is, indeed, the final chapter in the saga of fixed charges on book debts.[122]

10.10 FLOATING CHARGES AND THE BILLS OF SALE ACTS

A debenture of a company formed under the Companies Act 2006 is not within the Bills of Sale Acts 1878 and 1882, and may therefore create a charge on chattels, without being in the form prescribed by or registered under the last-named Act.[123]

As a consequence of the requirements of the Bills of Sale Acts, it is generally thought that it is not practicable for partners (or sole traders) to

---

[117] Paragraph 94.

[118] See Berg 'Charges over book debts: the Spectrum case in the Court of Appeal' [2004] JBL 581; I support this analysis.

[119] The House of Lords also had to consider whether it should have limited the temporal effect of its ruling, but declined to do so in this instance, because this case was not sufficiently exceptional.

[120] Lord Scott, para 116.

[121] *Re Beam Tube Products Ltd* [2007] 2 BCLC 732.

[122] For a detailed analysis, see Berg 'The cuckoo in the nest of corporate insolvency: some aspects of the *Spectrum* case' [2006] JBL 22.

[123] See s 17 of the Bills of Sales Act 1882. *Re Standard Manufacturing Co* [1891] 1 Ch 627 (CA); *Richards v Overseers of Kidderminster* [1896] 2 Ch 212. Registration is, however, necessary under the Companies Act 2006, s 860; see **10.23**.

create an effective floating charge. This inability was made the greater by the 'reputed ownership' provision of the Bankruptcy Act 1914[124] (now repealed), which used to apply in the bankruptcy of partnerships and individuals but not in the liquidation of insolvent companies.[125] The report of the Review Committee on Insolvency Law and Practice[126] proposed the abolition of 'reputed ownership' together with 'appropriate amendments' of the Bills of Sale Acts so as to permit individuals (and partners) to create effective floating charges over their business undertaking.[127] This would not extend to assets not used in the debtor's business, trade or profession. Professor Diamond in his review of security interests in property other than land also proposed that the floating charge form of security should be made available to businesses generally, irrespective of the form in which the business was carried on.[128] There is no indication that repeal or reform of the Bills of Sale Acts is likely to be forthcoming in the immediate future. However, under the Limited Liability Partnerships Act 2000, limited liability partnerships are bodies corporate[129] and have the capacity to grant a floating charge.

10.11   CRYSTALLISATION OF THE FLOATING CHARGE

The charge crystallises or becomes fixed when the chargee takes possession or appoints a receiver on the occurrence of one of the events which under the provision of the charge renders the security enforceable. Moreover, if the company goes into liquidation the charge will crystallise, even though the liquidation is for reconstruction purposes and the provisions of the charge stipulate only that the principal shall become payable on the company going into liquidation otherwise than for the purpose of reconstruction.[130] But while the company continues in business,[131] the charge does not crystallise merely by the happening of the events which entitle the chargee to intervene,[132] for 'unless something has occurred entitling the debenture holders to make such an application' (ie an application to the court for a receiver), 'and the application has in fact been made, or an action brought by them or on their behalf to realise their security, or unless something has happened which entitles the debenture holders to determine their licence to the company to carry on their business, and they have actually done so, the company is entitled to

---

[124] Section 38(c).

[125] See *Gorringe v Invell Rubber Co* (1886) 34 ChD 128.

[126] Cmnd 8558, June 1982.

[127] Ibid, paras 1093 and 1569.

[128] *A Review of Security Interests in Property* (HMSO, 1989) para 16.15.

[129] Section 1(2) of the Limited Liability Partnerships Act 2000.

[130] *Player v Crompton & Co* [1914] 1 Ch 954.

[131] The 'cessation of the company's business' is preferable to 'ceasing to be a going concern' as a description of this crystallising event. *Re Woodroffes (Musical Instruments) Ltd* [1986] Ch 366, [1985] 2 All ER 908, [1985] 3 WLR 543, [1985] BCLC 227.

[132] *Edward Nelson & Co v Faber* [1903] 2 KB 367. The text assumes that the charge does not contain an automatic crystallisation clause. Such clauses are discussed in **10.12**.

do all the things which the licence entitles them to do'.[133] If, therefore, the company assigns a book debt which is covered by the floating charge, it becomes the property of the assignee, and the receiver subsequently appointed cannot obtain priority by giving the debtor notice to pay him after the assignment.[134] Equally, a contractual lien will take priority over a floating charge where it arises from a contract made in the ordinary course of business before crystallisation.

It is established that a floating charge will crystallise in the event of the cessation of business of the chargor company.[135] It is uncertain whether the commencement of administration proceedings or the appointment of an administrator would cause a floating charge to crystallise in the absence of express provision to that effect in the charge.[136] Since 1986, when the administration procedure was first introduced, it has become common for debenture terms to provide expressly for crystallisation in the event of administration.

The crystallisation of a floating charge over the undertaking of the company effects an equitable assignment to the debenture-holders of the company's present assets which are comprised in the security[137] and also, unless excluded by the terms of the charge, of future assets accruing to the company as they arise. In *NW Robbie & Co Ltd v Witney Warehouse Co Ltd*,[138] the majority of the Court of Appeal held that after the appointment of a receiver each future debt to the company became, as it arose, a chose in action belonging to the company subject to an equitable charge in favour of the debenture-holder.

---

[133] *Evans v Rival Granite Quarries* [1910] 2 KB 979 at 986, per Vaughan Williams LJ. At 993, Fletcher Moulton LJ says: 'Mere default on the part of the company does not change the character of the security; the debenture holder must actually intervene.' At 1002, Buckley LJ says: 'No equity arises in a debenture holder whose security is a floating charge from his merely giving notice to seize a particular asset of the company. He must do something to turn his security from a floating into a fixed charge.'

[134] *Re Ind, Coope & Co* [1991] 2 Ch 223.

[135] *Re Woodroffes (Musical Instruments) Ltd* [1986] Ch 366; *Re Brightlife Ltd* [1987] Ch 200; *Bank of Credit and Commerce International SA v BRS Kumar Brothers Ltd* [1994] 1 BCLC 211; *Re The Real Meat Co Ltd* [1996] BCC 254.

[136] In *Re GE Tunbridge Ltd* [1994] BCC 563, the parties conceded that the appointment of an administrator would not cause crystallisation.

[137] *George Barker (Transport) Ltd v Eynon* [1974] 1 All ER 900, [1974] 1 WLR 462, [1974] 1 Lloyd's Rep 65; *Leyland DAF Ltd v Automotive Products Ltd* [1993] BCC 389, at 392; *Re ELS Ltd, Ramsbottom v Luton Borough Council* [1994] 3 WLR 616, [1994] BCLC 743, [1994] BCC 449 (local authority precluded from levying distress on goods for non-payment of rates after charge had crystallised).

[138] [1963] 1 WLR 1324 (CA). The reasoning in *Witney Warehouse* was applied in *Rendell v Doors & Doors Ltd* [1975] 2 NZLR 199. See also *Security Trust v Royal Bank of Canada* [1976] 2 WLR 437 (PC), at 491 in respect of land acquired after a floating charge has crystallised by the appointment of a receiver.

10.11.1   Notices of crystallisation

It has become increasingly common for floating charges to include a
provision whereby the holder is entitled to cause the charge to crystallise
by serving a notice to that effect on the company. In *Re Woodroffes*,
above, the effectiveness of a notice of crystallisation was assumed and in
Re Brightlife, above, Hoffmann J decided the point. Hoffmann J held that
crystallising events were not prescribed by law[139] and were to be
determined by the parties to a charge as a matter of contract;
crystallisation on winding-up, receivership or cessation of business would
be implied into a charge unless expressly excluded but it was open to the
parties to agree upon additional crystallising events. A notice of
crystallisation served in accordance with the terms of the charge would
therefore be effective to cause the crystallisation of a floating charge.

10.12   AUTOMATIC CRYSTALLISATION

Crystallisation on the service of a notice requires positive action by or on
behalf of the chargee. Is it possible to dispense altogether with the need
for positive action and to provide for crystallisation to occur
automatically upon the occurrence of specified events? It is established
that an event which is of such magnitude as to lead to the cessation of the
company's business is an implied automatic crystallising event: in that
situation the *raison d'être* of the floating charge, namely continued
freedom for the chargor company to use the charged assets in the course
of its business, disappears. Greater controversy has in the past surrounded
the possibility of providing for automatic crystallisation upon the
happening of some lesser event which is not necessary incompatible with
continued trading by the company, such as the creation of a second
mortgage or charge without the debenture-holder's consent; but it is now
clear that freedom of contract prevails in this area of the law.

The validity of an automatic crystallisation clause was upheld in New
Zealand in *Re Manurewa Transport Ltd*.[140] The concept of automatic or
'self-generating' crystallisation has also been accepted in Australia,[141]
although it has been rejected in Canada.[142] In England, *dicta* of

---

[139] As suggested by *Edward Nelson & Co Ltd v Faber & Co* [1903] 2 KB 367, at 376.
Hoffmann J explained the statements in the earlier case by saying that the judge (Joyce J)
was simply stating the crystallising events that would be implied unless expressly
excluded by the parties.

[140] [1971] NZLR 909. See McLauchlan [1972] *New Zealand Law Journal* at p 330.

[141] *Stein v Saywell* (1969) 121 CLR 529; *DCT (Vic) v Horsburgh* [1984] VR 773; *Fire
Nymph Products Ltd v The Heating Centre Pty Ltd (in Liquidation)* (1991–1992) 7
ACSR 365. Cf *Re Bismark Australia Ltd* [1981] VC 527. See also Burns 'Automatic
Crystallisation of Company Charges: Contractual Creativity or Confusion' (1992) 290
ABLR 125.

[142] *The Queen in Right of British Columbia v Consolidated Churchill Copper Corporation Ltd*
(1978) 5 WWR 652.

Buckley LJ in *Evans v Rival Granite Quarries Ltd*[143] supported automatic crystallisation, but both Vaughan Williams and Fletcher Moulton LJJ stated in the same case (also *obiter*) that the debenture-holder was required to intervene. The matter finally arose for decision in England in *Re Permanent House (Holdings) Ltd*[144] where, confirming views which he had expressed *obiter* in *Re Brightlife*, above, Hoffmann J held that an automatic crystallisation clause was valid and effective. In *Brightlife*, Hoffmann J preferred the New Zealand authority to the approach taken in Canada and did not feel constrained by earlier English decisions to reach the opposite conclusion. In his view, automatic crystallisation was essentially a matter of explicit contractual provision. The rights and duties which the law might or might not categorise as a floating charge were derived from the agreement of the parties, as supplemented by implied terms, and merely because some terms deviated from what might be regarded as the 'standard' terms of a floating charge did not preclude the charge from being a floating charge. Hoffmann J considered that any policy objections to automatic crystallisation were matters to be settled by an appellate court or by Parliament.

Policy objections to automatic crystallisation clauses include the potential prejudice that they may cause to innocent third parties, who may be unaware (and have no means of knowing) that the charge has crystallised.[145] There is also the uncertainty that could result from a situation where a debenture-holder tacitly waives a crystallisation which has occurred in accordance with an automatic crystallisation clause and allows the company to continue its business.[146]

A particular objection, considered in *Re Brightlife* and *Re Permanent Houses*, above, but now, because of legislative developments, of no more than historical interest, was the effect of automatic crystallisation clauses on the position of preferential creditors. In a receivership or liquidation, preferential debts rank before debts secured by a floating

---

[143] [1910] 2 KB 979.

[144] (1989) 5 BCC 151.

[145] The policy objections have been considered by various commentators and review bodies. The literature includes Farrar 'The Crystallisation of a Floating Charge' (1976) 40 Conv 397; Gough *Company Charges* (Butterworths, 2nd edn, 1996) Chs 11 and 16 and 'The Floating Charge' in Finn (ed) *Equity and Commercial Relationships* (Law Book Company, 1987) at p 239; Boyle 'The Validity of Automatic Crystallisation Clauses' [1979] JBL 231; Dean 'Crystallisation of a Floating Charge' (1982–4) 1–2 *Company and Securities Law Journal* 185; Review Committee on Insolvency Law and Practice (Cmnd 8558, 1982) paras 1577–1580; Goode *Legal Problems of Credit and Security* (Sweet & Maxwell, 2nd edn, 1988) at pp 69–75; Pennington 'Loans to Companies' in Pettet (ed) *Company Law in Change* (Stevens, 1987) at pp 99–107.

[146] McLauchlan [1972] *New Zealand Law Journal* at 330. On 'decrystallisation' see Goode, op cit pp 73–76 and Lightman and Moss *The Law of Receivers of Companies* (Sweet & Maxwell, 2nd edn, 1994) at paras 3.41–3.45. See also Grantham 'Refloating a Floating Charge' [1997] CfiLR 53; Tan 'Automatic Crystallisation, De-Crystallisation and Convertibility of Charges' [1998] CfiLR 41.

charge,[147] but before reforms enacted by the 1980s insolvency legislation, it was held[148] that the preferential status could only be claimed over debts secured by a floating charge which *was floating at the time of the receivership or liquidation.* If a floating charge had crystallised prior to the receivership or liquidation, the preferential debts ranked behind the debt secured by the charge. An automatic crystallisation clause could thus enable the holder of a floating charge to be repaid before the preferential debts. It may be noted that this objection could be levelled not just at automatic crystallisation clauses but also at clauses permitting crystallisation on the service of a notice and at crystallisation upon cessation of business prior to receivership or liquidation. However, automatic crystallisation clauses attracted particular criticism because they were thought to increase significantly the power of creditors lending money on the security of a floating charge to structure the lending to their advantage at the expense of the holders of preferential debts. This objection to automatic crystallisation has disappeared because, for the purposes of the relevant provisions of the Insolvency Act 1986, a floating charge is now defined as a charge which as created was a floating charge.[149] The status of the charge when it is created is all important and it now makes no difference that the charge may have crystallised before receivership or liquidation.

The possible ill effects of such clauses on innocent third parties remain.[150] A potential solution was offered by a provision, never brought into force and repealed by the Companies Act 2006, of the Companies Act 1989,[151] whereby the Secretary of State was to be empowered to make regulations requiring notice of the occurrence of crystallising events to be filed at the companies registry. It was envisaged that the regulations could provide for the crystallisation to be ineffective until notified.

10.13   CRYSTALLISATION AND RIGHTS OF SET-OFF

A right of set-off which accrues to a debtor of the company before crystallisation can be raised against a claim by the receiver against the debtor: in *Rother Iron Works Ltd v Canterbury Precision Engineers Ltd*[152]

---

[147] Sections 40 and 175 of the Insolvency Act 1986. The categories of preferential debts are set out in Sch 6 to the Act, although after the Enterprise Act 2002, there are only a few categories left. Preferential debts are therefore much less significant now than they once were.

[148] *Re Griffin Hotel Co* [1941] Ch 129; *Re Christonette International* [1982] 3 All ER 227; *Re Brightlife,* above; *Re Permanent Houses,* above; *William Gaskell v Highley,* above.

[149] Sections 40 and 251 contain the definition.

[150] Goode, op cit, argues that potential unfairness to third parties disappears if the position is analysed on agency principles. He suggests that automatic crystallisation may terminate the company's actual authority to use the charged assets in the course of its business, but that, until the fact is brought to their attention, outsiders can continue to rely on the company's apparent authority.

[151] Section 100.

[152] [1973] 2 WLR 281 (CA).

Russell LJ distinguished *Robbie v Witney Warehouse Co Ltd*,[153] where the cross-claim was assigned to the debtor after the crystallisation of the charge. Moreover, there the claim made by the receiver arose out of a contract made by the receiver subsequent to his appointment. In *Rother Iron Works* the contract to sell goods, which the receiver was seeking to enforce, had been made before his appointment.[154]

10.14 PRIORITIES AND THE FLOATING CHARGE

The rules as to priority between charges created by a company are basically the same as those governing legal and equitable charges generally. These rules are derived from the cases and they have not been codified in statutory form. The registration requirements of the Companies Act 2006 may affect the operation of the priority rules but it is important to note that they do not supplant those rules. The absence of clear statutory rules governing priority is open to criticism because it leads to uncertainty. The position is different in Scotland where clear statutory rules are laid down as to priority.[155]

As between equitable charges, priority is governed by the order of creation, the charge created first ranking first in order of priority. A legal mortgage will rank before a previous equitable security where the legal interest is acquired by a *bona fide* purchase for value without notice of the earlier interest. The special qualities of the floating charge mean that these general rules are modified in relation to a security of that type. In principle, a floating charge will be postponed to any subsequently created fixed security (legal or equitable) regardless of notice, because the company is permitted to continue to deal with the assets which are the subject-matter of the floating charge and this dealing power includes the power to charge or mortgage them.[156]

As between two floating charges, the first created will prevail since there is no implied authority to create subsequent floating security ranking first. A second floating charge will only have priority if either: (a) the instrument creating the first floating charge gave an express power to create later floating charges ranking first;[157] or (b) the second floating charge is over part only of the company's assets and the court construes the express reservation in the general floating charge of the right to create

---

[153] [1963] 1 WLR 1324 (CA).

[154] See further, as to the legal position of an 'administrative receiver' appointed under a general floating charge, Part 3 of this chapter. The right to appoint an administrative receiver has been removed for floating charges created after 15 September 2003.

[155] Sections 463–464 of the Companies Act 1985 (which remain after the Companies Act 2006). For an example of the application of the statutory ranking provisions see *AIB Finance Ltd v Bank of Scotland* [1994] BCC 184.

[156] *Wheatley v Silkstone and Haigh Moor Coal Co* (1885) 29 ChD 715.

[157] *Re Benjamin Cope & Sons Ltd* [1914] 1 Ch 800.

prior charges as embracing particular types of floating charge.[158] Crystallisation of a second floating charge before a first floating charge should not enable the second charge to move ahead of the first charge, because that result would be inconsistent with the bargain between the company and the holder of the first charge.[159]

To avoid the risk of being postponed to future charges by the creation of fixed mortgages or charges on all or part of the property of the company, it has become common in the case of floating charges to insert a declaration that the company shall not have the power to mortgage the property in priority to or equally with the floating charge created by the debentures. This restriction is not incompatible with the nature of the floating charge.[160] The effect of inserting this restriction, which is sometimes referred to as a negative pledge, into a floating charge is that, if the equities are otherwise equal, it will bind a subsequent equitable fixed chargee even without notice.[161] Equities will not be equal where the debenture-holder allows the company to retain the title deeds to the property which is the subject of the subsequent security.[162] In that event, the holder of the subsequent security will not be bound in the absence of notice of the restriction in the earlier floating charge.[163] The owner of a subsequent legal mortgage will be bound only where he has notice of the restriction.[164] Merely because a lender is aware of the existence of an earlier floating charge does not put the lender on inquiry or fix him with notice of a restriction that may be contained in that charge.[165]

10.15   THE EFFECT OF REGISTRATION ON PRIORITIES

The requirement of registration under s 860(1) of the Companies Act 2006 [CA 1985, s 395] affects the rules as to priorities in two ways. First of all, a charge which is not duly registered[166] within the 21-day period is void and will lose all priority it would otherwise possess.[167] Secondly, registration, besides giving actual notice to those who search the register, has been held to give constructive notice to subsequent

---

[158]   *Re Automatic Bottlemakers Ltd* [1926] Ch 412. The second floating charge must not affect substantially the whole of the company's property: ibid, at 423.

[159]   *Re Benjamin Cope & Sons Ltd*, above; *Re Household Products Co Ltd* (1981) 124 DLR (3d) 325. But note *Griffiths v Yorkshire Bank* [1994] 1 WLR 1427, where a contrary view is taken. The statutory order of priority governing Scottish floating charges does not depend on, nor is it affected by, order of crystallisation.

[160]   *Re Brightlife* [1987] 1 Ch 200, at 209; *Re Cimex Tissues*, at 635.

[161]   *Re Castell & Brown Ltd* [1898] 1 Ch 315.

[162]   As in *Castell & Brown*, above.

[163]   Ibid.

[164]   *English & Scottish Mercantile Investment Co v Brunton* [1892] 2 QB 700, at 707.

[165]   *English & Scottish Mercantile Investment Co v Brunton*, above (where inquiries were in fact made); *Re Valletort Sanitary Steam Laundry Co Ltd* [1903] 2 Ch 654.

[166]   See **10.32** as to the possibility of rectifying the register. But this will not be allowed so as to regain priority.

[167]   Section 874(1) of the Companies Act 2006.

mortgagees or chargees.[168] Thus a registered fixed equitable charge will be protected as against a legal mortgage created after the time of registration of the equitable charge.

It should be noted that, subject to the effect of constructive notice, priority is based on the date of creation, not that of registration, though subsequent registration is necessary if the charge is to be effective.

It was held in *Wilson v Kelland*[169] that registration of a charge gave constructive notice of the charge, but not of the terms contained in the deed creating it. Thus registration of a floating charge will not by itself give constructive notice of the prohibition contained in that charge so as to postpone a subsequent mortgage.[170]

In order to give greater protection to floating charges, the practice has developed, which the registrar has accepted, of including the prohibition in the charging document among the registered particulars of the charge. It is sometimes thought that this will give constructive notice of the prohibition but this is doubtful. The practice has not yet been tested in the courts in England,[171] and it has been rejected in New Zealand and Ireland.[172]

A provision enacted in the Companies Act 1989 was designed to clarify the position with regard to registration and notice. This provision never came into force and was repealed by the Companies Act 2006, but it is nevertheless useful to consider it briefly. Under this provision,[173] a person taking a charge over a company's property was deemed to have notice of any matter requiring registration and disclosed on the registration at the time the charge was created. Otherwise, a person was not to be taken to have notice of any matter by reason of its being disclosed on the register or by reason of his having failed to search the register in the course of making such inquiries as ought reasonably to have been made. Thus, under this provision, a chargee (which would include a mortgagee) was conclusively presumed to have notice of the matters which required

---

[168] *Wilson v Kelland* [1910] 2 Ch 306; *Re Standard Rotary Machine Co* (1906) 95 LT 829.

[169] [1910] 2 Ch 306.

[170] *Re Valletort Laundry* [1903] 2 Ch 654; *Re Standard Rotary Machine Co* (1906) 95 LT 829.

[171] See also the effect of a clause providing for 'automatic crystallisation', discussed at **10.12**. For an argument that constructive notice is not given by including the prohibition among the registered particulars, see Farrar, 38 *Conveyancer* 315 at p 325 *et seq*. The author argues in favour of the different concept of 'inferred notice'. This inference would rest on the common practice but would be open to rebuttal; ibid, p 319. This distinction was made in *Siebe Gorman v Barclays Bank* [1979] 2 Lloyd's Rep 142.

[172] *Dempsey v The Traders Finance Corporation Ltd* [1933] NZLR 1258 (New Zealand); *Welch v Bowmaker (Ireland) Ltd* [1980] IR 251 (Ireland). The problem does not arise in Scotland, because the existence of a clause in a floating charge which prohibits, restricts or regulates the power of the company to grant further securities ranking in priority to or *pari passu* with the floating charge is a registrable particular: ss 885(3)(e) [CA 1985, s 417(3)(e)] of the Companies Act 2006.

[173] Section 103 of the Companies Act 1989.

registration and which were disclosed on the register but a purchaser was conclusively presumed not to have such notice.

The Companies Act 1989 also provided for the matters requiring registration to be prescribed by the Secretary of State in regulations. When that legislation was enacted, it was envisaged that the Secretary would follow existing provisions governing registration of charges under Scots law[174] and make the existence, or otherwise, of restrictions in floating charges a matter requiring registration, and hence bring such restrictions within the ambit of the notice provision.[175]

10.16   FURTHER ADVANCES AND SUBSEQUENT CHARGES

A particular case should be noted. Mortgages and debentures are often created in favour of banks and others to secure a current account. In such a case, if a subsequent mortgage is created on the same property and the bank entitled to the prior security has notice of such subsequent mortgage, it cannot make further advances upon its own security to the prejudice of the later mortgagee. Further, if it continues the current account, payments made by the debtor company will go in reduction of the debt existing at the time of the later mortgage,[176] so that in course of time the bank or lender on current account will become postponed to the later lender, for all subsequent advances will rank after the amount advanced by the later lender.[177] To meet this danger banks usually rule off and close the current account as soon as they learn of the subsequent mortgage, thus retaining their charge for the balance then due on current account.

10.17   PURCHASE MONEY, SECURITY INTERESTS AND FLOATING CHARGES

If property is acquired subject to an existing charge or upon the terms of the purchase price being advanced on the security of the property, these charges will take priority over a floating charge on the company's undertaking or a fixed charge on the company's present and future assets of a description which covers the property so acquired. The implications of acquiring property on a mortgage and the priority position of the

---

[174] Section 885(3)(e) [CA 1985, s 417(3)(e)] of the Companies Act 2006.

[175] Section 103 of the Companies Act 1989 expressly mentioned restrictions in floating charges as one of the matters which the Secretary of State could prescribe as a particular requiring registration.

[176] Under what is known as the rule in *Clayton's Case* (1816) 1 Mer 572: see also next footnote.

[177] *Deeley v Lloyds Bank* [1912] AC 756 (HL); *Hopkinson v Rolt* (1861) 9 HLC 514; *London and County Bank v Ratcliffe* (1881) 6 App Cas 722 (HL); *Bradford Banking Co v Henry Briggs & Co* (1886) 12 App Cas 29 (HL). *Siebe Gorman v Barclays Bank* [1979] 2 Lloyd's Rep 142.

mortgagee as against others with competing interests in the same property were considered by the House of Lords in *Abbey National Building Society v Cann*.[178] This case concerned an individual acquiring residential property with the help of a mortgage, but the reasoning of their Lordships is equally applicable to corporate finance.

The House of Lords held that where a conveyance and a mortgage or charge take place at approximately the same time, in reality the purchaser never acquires more than an equity of redemption.[179] According to Lord Jauncey of Tullichettle:

> 'a purchaser who can only complete a transaction by borrowing money ... cannot in reality even be said to have acquired even for a scintilla temporis the unencumbered freehold or leasehold interest in the land whereby he could grant interests having priority over the mortgage ...'

Thus a pre-existing charge must rank behind a later purchase-money security.

10.18 POSTPONEMENT AND AVOIDANCE OF FLOATING CHARGES BY STATUTE

Certain special provisions affect the priority or validity of floating charges. The position of preferential debts has already been noted: preferential debts[180] which cannot otherwise be met have priority over debts secured by a charge which as created was a floating charge.[181] In *Re GL Saunders Ltd*,[182] it was settled that where the realisation of a fixed charge produced a surplus (after satisfying the claims of the chargee) the surplus was not part of the assets subject to the floating charge. The company was in receivership and the significance of the decision was that it meant that the receiver had no obligation to pay preferential debts from the surplus because that obligation was limited to payment out of

---

[178] [1991] 1 AC 56, [1990] 1 All ER 1085, [1990] 2 WLR 832. Gregory 'Romalpa Clauses as Unregistered Charges – a Fundamental Shift' (1990) 106 LQR 550; McCormack 'Charges and Priorities – The Death of the Scintilla Temporis Doctrine' (1991) 12 Co Law 11; de Lacy [1991] LMCLQ 531; Bennett and Davis 'Fixtures, Purchase Money Security Interests and Dispositions of Interests in Land' (1994) 110 LQR 448. Commentators note some uncertainty regarding the application of the Companies Act registration requirements to purchase money securities. eg [1991] LMCLQ 531, at 535–537, (1994) 110 LQR 448, at 479–483.

[179] Following *Re Connolly Brothers Ltd (No 2)* [1912] 2 Ch 25 and *Security Trust Co v Royal Bank of Canada* [1976] AC 503, [1976] 1 All ER 381, [1976] 2 WLR 437, and overruling the *scintilla temporis* approach favoured in *Church of England Building Society v Piskor* [1954] Ch 553.

[180] These are now limited to contributions to occupational pension schemes, remuneration of employees, and, where relevant, levies on steel and coal production, following amendments by s 251(1) of the Enterprise Act 2002.

[181] Sections 40 and 175 of, and Sch 6 to, the Insolvency Act 1986, as amended by the Enterprise Act 2002.

[182] [1986] BCLC 40.

floating-charge assets. Moreover, s 176A of the Insolvency Act 1986[183] now requires a liquidator, administrator or receiver to set aside a prescribed part[184] of the company's net property for the benefit of the company's unsecured creditors. This part may not be given to the holder of a floating charge. The holder of a floating charge cannot be treated as an unsecured creditor to the extent that the secured assets are insufficient to pay the holder in full, although if there is a surplus after all unsecured debts have been paid, the holder may participate in that surplus.[185] However, this provision does not apply if the company's net value is less than £10,000[186] and the liquidator, administrator or receiver thinks that making a distribution to the unsecured creditors would be disproportionate to the benefits.[187]

In a winding-up, s 245[188] of the Insolvency Act 1986 renders invalid certain floating charges created within 12 months of the winding-up in favour of persons not connected with the company. In the case of 'connected persons' this period is two years. The charge may be valid where value has been given to the company. All charges, fixed as well as floating, may be open to attack under s 239 of the Insolvency Act 1986 on the basis that the transaction has given one of the company's creditors (or a surety or guarantor of its debts) a preference.[189] All these matters are examined at length in the context of the winding up of companies.[190]

10.19 PRIORITY AGREEMENTS

If a fixed charge is expressed to be subject to an earlier floating charge it will rank behind the earlier floating charge even though it would otherwise have taken priority.[191] Also, where there are two (or more) existing securities affecting the same property, the holders of the securities can agree amongst themselves to alter their priority and this does not require the company's consent.[192]

---

[183] Inserted by s 252 of the Enterprise Act 2002.

[184] This is calculated in accordance with reg 3 of the Insolvency Act 1986 (Prescribed Part) Order 2003, SI 2003/2097. If the company's net property is below £10,000, the prescribed part is 50% of the property. Where the company's net property exceeds £10,000, the prescribed part is 50% of the first £10,000 and 20% for the part of the company's property exceeding £10,000 in value. However, the total value of the prescribed part is fixed at £600,000.

[185] *Re Airbase UK; Thorniley v Revenue and Customs Coms* [2008] 1 BCLC 436.

[186] Section 176A(3)(a) of the Insolvency Act 1986 and regulation 2 of the Insolvency Act 1986 (Prescribed Part) Order 2003, SI 2003/2097.

[187] Section 176A(3)(b).

[188] See further **21.55.6**.

[189] Sections 239–241. See **21.55.3**.

[190] See Chapter 21.

[191] *Re Robert Stephenson & Co* [1913] 2 Ch 201 (CA); *Re Camden Brewery Ltd* (1912) 106 LT 598.

[192] *Cheah Theam Swee v Equiticorp Finance Group Ltd* [1992] 1 AC 472, [1991] 4 All ER 989, [1992] BCLC 371, [1992] BCC 98.

A priority agreement between the holders of fixed and floating charges can produce circularity problems concerning preferential debts: this problem arises where, under the insolvency legislation, the preferential debts rank behind debts secured by a fixed charge but before debts secured by a floating charge, whilst under the priority agreement, the debts secured by the floating charge rank before those secured by the fixed charge. How is this conundrum to be resolved?

The question was considered by Chadwick J in *Re Portbase (Clothing) Ltd, Mond v Taylor*.[193] Chadwick J held that the effect of the priority agreement was to postpone the fixed charge to the floating charge. Preferring the approach taken in the Australian case of *Waters v Widdows*,[194] to the *obiter* views of Nourse J in *Re Woodroffes*,[195] he concluded that this postponement meant that the preferential debts ranked before the debt secured by the floating charge and also the debt secured by the fixed charge. If Chadwick J had followed the solution suggested in *Re Woodroffes* (where construction of a priority agreement did not arise for decision),[196] the debt secured by the floating charge would have ranked before the preferential debts to the extent of the fixed-charge security. Chadwick J noted that this solution might apply where the parties, by their agreement, exchanged their rights under their respective securities but that, as a matter of construction, it was not the effect of the agreement in question.

10.20 RETENTION OF TITLE CLAUSES AND FLOATING CHARGES

A receiver appointed on behalf of a debenture-holder has no better title to goods in the company's possession whose ownership lies elsewhere than the company itself. Consequently, the owner of goods which are hired to the company or are the subject of a hire-purchase agreement may recover them from the receiver. The same principle will apply to a 'title retention' clause in a sale of goods contract. Such clauses are known as *Romalpa* clauses from the leading case[197] in which their validity was upheld. They provide that the goods purchased shall remain the property of the seller until the purchase price is paid (as well, sometimes, as money outstanding in other contracts between the buyer and seller). In consequence the unpaid purchaser will be able to recover goods still in the company's possession against the claims of a receiver subsequently appointed under

---

[193] [1993] Ch 388, [1993] 3 All ER 829, [1993] 3 WLR 14, [1993] BCLC 796, [1993] BCC 96.
[194] [1984] VR 503.
[195] [1986] Ch 366. Nourse J adopted the analysis in Goode, *Legal Problems of Credit and Security* (Sweet & Maxwell, 1st edn, 1982), pp 54–55 (see also 2nd edn, 1988, pp 97–98).
[196] The solution adopted by Nourse J was conceded by counsel.
[197] *Aluminium Industrie Vaassen BV v Romalpa Aluminium Ltd* [1976] 1 WLR 676 (CA). The Scottish courts have also recognised title retention clauses: *Armour v Thyssen Edelstahlwerke AG* [1991] 2 AC 339, [1990] 3 All ER 481, [1990] 3 WLR 810, [1991] 1 Lloyd's Rep 395, [1991] BCLC 28, [1990] BC 925.

a floating charge. In *Romalpa*,[198] there was a further provision that if the purchasing company resold any of the contract material it should do so as agent of the seller. It was held on that basis the buyer was accountable to the seller for the proceeds of the sub-sales. As agent a fiduciary duty was owed in respect of these proceeds which could be traced in equity.

Subsequent cases have tended to limit the protection which is afforded by a title retention clause to an unpaid seller who is in competition with the claims of a receiver appointed by a debenture-holder.[199] The simplest type of clause where the seller retains title[200] to the very goods sold (as provided for in the Sale of Goods Act 1979, s 19(1)) until specified debts are paid[201] is effective and it does not create a charge which must be registered so long as the goods supplied are identifiable and in the possession of the buyer.[202] If the goods supplied are subjected to a manufacturing process[203] with other materials, ordinarily a title retention clause does not vest title to the new product in the supplier[204] and, furthermore, does not give a right to trace into the resulting new product.[205] Any rights[206] given by the contract in the newly created

---

[198] Above.

[199] There is a large amount of literature on retention of title clauses, including the following: Goodhart and Jones 'The Infiltration of Equitable Doctrine into English Commercial Law' (1980) 43 MLR 489; McCormack 'Reservation of Title – Past, Present and Future' [1994] Conv 129; and for a recent comprehensive review of this area, see Bradgate '25 years of *Romalpa*' in Davies (ed) *Security Interests in Mobile Equipment* (Aldershot, Ashgate, 2002).

[200] That is, legal title. 'Retention' of equitable ownership has been held to amount to a charge granted by the buyer in favour of the supplier; *Re Bond Worth Ltd* [1980] Ch 228, [1979] 3 All ER 919, [1979] 3 WLR 629; *Stroud Architectural Systems Ltd v John Laing Construction Ltd* [1994] BCC 18.

[201] The title retention clause in *Armour v Thyssen*, above, was an 'all monies' clause; title was retained pending payment of all debts between the parties. On 'all monies' retention of title clauses see further *McCormack* [1991] LMCLQ 154; *Mance* [1992] LMCLQ 35; *McCormack* [1994] Conv 129.

[202] *Clough Mill v Martin* [1984] 3 All ER 982, [1985] 1 WLR 111, [1985] BCLC 64 (CA), noted Goodhart, (1986) 49 MLR 96; *Armour v Thyssen*, above; *Hendy Lennox (Industrial Engines) Ltd v Grahame Puttick Ltd* [1984] 2 All ER 152, [1984] 1 WLR 485; *Re Andrabell Ltd* [1987] 3 All ER 407, at 414.

[203] The extent of the processing to which the goods are subjected may be significant. In *Armour v Thyssen*, some of the goods supplied (steel strips) had been cut but this did not prejudice the claim of the original supplier.

[204] In *Clough Mill v Martin* [1984] 3 All ER 982, at 989–990, 993, Goff and Oliver LJJ thought that in principle it would be possible for parties to agree that title to manufactured goods would vest in the supplier of part of the goods used in the manufacturing process but that, in practice, it was unlikely that they would so agree. Goff LJ at 989 noted problems that would result from the conclusion that an agreement conferred absolute ownership of (or a right to trace in respect of manufactured goods) in a supplier: (1) buyer may have paid for some of the goods supplied; (2) buyer may have supplied part of the materials used in the manufacturing process and will have borne the cost of the manufacturing process; and (3) part of the materials used in the manufacturing process may have been supplied, subject to a title retention clause, by another supplier.

[205] *Borden (UK) Ltd v Scottish Timber Products* [1981] Ch 25, [1979] 3 All ER 961, [1979] 3 WLR 672 (CA); *Re Peachdart Ltd* [1984] Ch 131, [1989] 3 All ER 204, [1983] 3 WLR

product would normally be a charge granted by the buyer to the seller and requiring registration under the Companies Act 2006.[207]

Despite the fact that such a claim was successful in *Romalpa* itself, suppliers' claims to the proceeds of resale of goods supplied on title retention terms (irrespective of whether those goods are processed before resale) have usually failed.[208] The obstacles are that the supplier must establish that there is a fiduciary relationship between himself and the buyer in respect of the proceeds of sale and that he has a beneficial interest in the proceeds of sale otherwise than by way of charge. The courts are reluctant to characterise the relationship between buyer and supplier as fiduciary. Instead, any interest of the supplier in the proceeds which is defeasible upon the payment of specified debts owing from the buyer to the supplier is usually characterised as a charge granted by the buyer to the supplier and, as such, it requires registration under the Companies Act 2006.[209]

10.21 EXECUTION CREDITORS AND FLOATING CHARGES

If the chargee takes steps promptly to enforce its security then its rights under a floating charge to the property comprised in their security take precedence over those obtained by an execution creditor where execution is incomplete. Execution is incomplete for this purpose where even though a sale by the sheriff has been avoided by the payment of money by the chargee, provided the money still remains in his hands;[210] but where money has been paid by the debtor company to the sheriff on the terms that he shall not sell the property seized, the title of the execution creditor to the money prevails as against the receiver.[211] If an execution is put in, or garnishee order obtained, the chargee ought at once to give the sheriff

---

878, [1983] BCLC 225, (1983) 1 BCC 98, at 920; *Specialist Plant Services Ltd v Braithwaite* (1987) 3 BCC 119; and *Ian Chisholm Textiles Ltd v Griffiths* [1994] BCC 96.

[206] In *Borden*, the court found that the seller had no interest whatsoever in the manufactured product.

[207] *Re Peachdart Ltd; Clough Mill: Modelboard Ltd v Outer Box Ltd* [1993] BCLC 623. Note *Hendy Lennox (Industrial Engines) Ltd v Grahame Puttick Ltd* (diesel engines supplied subject to title retention clause incorporated into generators but remained readily identifiable and easily disconnected; title retention effective despite incorporation)

[208] In *Tatung (UK) Ltd v Galex Telesure Ltd* (1989) 5 BCC 325 (noted McCormack [1989] LMCLQ 198; Wheeler (1989) 10 Co Law 188), Phillips J questioned whether *Romalpa* had been correctly decided on the point.

[209] *Re Peachdart Ltd; Re Andrabell Ltd; E Pfeiffer Weinkellerei-Weineinkauf GmbH & Co v Arbuthnot Factors Ltd* [1988] 1 WLR 150, [1998] BCC 608; *Tatung v Galex Leisure Ltd Re Weldtech Equipment Ltd* [1991] BCC 16, [1991] BCLC 393, noted de Lacy (1991) 65 MLR 736; *Compaq Computers Ltd v Abercorn Group Ltd* [1991] BCC 484, noted Hicks (1992) 13 Co Law 217; de Lacy (1992) 13 Co Law 164; *Modelboard v Outer Box*, above.

[210] *Re Opera* [1891] 3 Ch 260 (CA); *Taunton v Sheriff of Warwickshire* [1895] 2 Ch 319 (CA).

[211] *Robinson v Burnell's Vienna Bakery* [1904] 2 KB 624.

notice to withdraw, or to the debtor not to pay the garnishor, and proceed to the appointment of a receiver, for if the security becomes a fixed one before the goods are sold or the debt paid the charge will prevail.[212]

The equities of the holder of the charge entitle him to oust the sheriff after he has seized if the security has crystallised before he has sold,[213] or to deprive the garnishor of his advantage if the crystallisation of the security has taken place before he has collected the money.[214] But if the security is allowed to continue to float, the execution creditor's or garnishor's right will prevail, and a garnishee order *nisi* will be made absolute notwithstanding the opposition of the holder of the charge or a claim made by him on the debtor to pay the money direct to him,[215] for a debenture-holder cannot single out and take a particular debt or piece of property while allowing the company to trade with the rest of its assets.[216]

PART 3: THE REGISTRATION OF CHARGES

10.22 LEGISLATIVE FRAMEWORK

Part 25 of the Companies Act 2006 governs the registration of company charges. Details of most, but not all, charges created by companies must be delivered to the companies registry within 21 days of creation. The Registrar of Companies is required to maintain a register of charges and this is available for public inspection. Failure to deliver the requisite particulars to the companies registry results in the charge becoming void against certain categories of person. There is provision for late filing but this requires an order of the court. Where particulars are duly filed in accordance with the statutory requirements, the priority of the charge depends on the rules already discussed.[217] Priority of company charges is not governed by order of filing at the companies registry.

The system for the registration of company charges is open to criticism. The 21-day period allowed for delivery of particulars means that the register may not give a searcher an accurate picture of the existing registrable charges on a company's property. The fact that not all charges which can be created by companies require registration further detracts from the register as a comprehensive source of information. The company also has to keep its own register of charges at its registered office and this register, which extends to all charges, can be searched to obtain a more complete picture; but a charge is not rendered void if it is not entered on

---

[212] *Davey & Co v Williamson & Sons Ltd* [1898] 2 QB 194, as explained in *Evans v Rival Granite Quarries* [1910] 2 KB 979, at 1000 (CA); *Norton v Yates* [1906] 1 KB 112.

[213] *Re Opera* [1891] 3 Ch 260; *Davey & Co v Williamson & Sons Ltd* [1898] 2 QB 194; *Duck v Tower Galvanising Co* [1901] 2 KB 314.

[214] *Norton v Yates* [1906] 1 KB 112.

[215] *Evans v Rival Granite Quarries* [1910] 2 KB 979 (CA).

[216] *Robson v Smith* [1895] 2 Ch 118; approved by CA [1910] 2 KB at 989 and 998.

[217] See **10.15**.

this register, which means that there is less incentive to ensure its accuracy. The existence of financing arrangements, such as conditional sales and hire-purchase agreements, which are not in law regarded as charges will not be disclosed by either register. A further criticism of the existing system is that it preserves old, complex priority rules. A system of priority is based on date of filing would be far more straightforward than a series of rules which depend on order of creation of competing securities, equality of equities and notice.

A number of wide-ranging and fundamental reform proposals are considered at the end of this chapter, including the most recent push for reform made by the Law Commission.

10.23   CHARGES REQUIRING REGISTRATION

Every limited company must keep a register of charges, and enter therein particulars of all charges specifically affecting property of the company and of all floating charges.[218]

In addition to keeping such a register, ss 860–865 require particulars of certain mortgages and charges[219] created by companies registered in England to be delivered to the registrar within 21 days after the date of their creation if they come within any of the descriptions mentioned below:

(a)   a charge on land or any interest in land, other than a charge for any rent or other periodical sum issuing out of land;

(b)   a charge created or evidenced by an instrument which, if executed by an individual, would require registration as a bill of sale;

(c)   a charge for the purposes of securing any issue of debentures;

(d)   a charge on uncalled share capital of the company;

(e)   a charge on calls made but not paid;

(f)   a charge on book debts of the company;

(g)   a floating charge on the company's property or undertaking;

(h)   a charge on a ship or aircraft, or any share in a ship;

---

[218]   Section 876(1) [CA 1985, s 407], see **10.37**.

[219]   For the purposes of Chapter 1 of Part 25, 'the expression "charge" includes mortgage'; s 861(5) [CA 1985, s 396(4)].

(i)   a charge on goodwill or on any intellectual property.[220]

Anything which creates a charge in equity or law (being of any of the classes above described) therefore requires registration: that is to say, anything which would create a charge as between individuals will suffice. 'When there is a contract for value between the owner of a chose in action and another person which shows that such person is to have the benefit of the chose in action, that constitutes good charge on the chose in action. The form of words is immaterial so long as they show an intention that he is to have such benefit.'[221]

However, if the charge consitutes a 'security financial collateral arrangement' within the meaning of reg 3 of the Financial Collateral Arrangements (No 2) Regulations 2003,[222] then it is exempt from the registration requirements of the Companies Act 2006.[223]

Moreover, an absolute assignment (eg of book debts) is not a charge and will not require registration. Thus in *Lloyds and Scottish Finance Ltd v Cyril Lord Carpets Ltd*,[224] the House of Lords held that assignments to a finance house of credit sale agreements, under a block discounting agreement, were absolute assignments and therefore did not require registration under s 93 of the Northern Ireland Companies Act 1960 (the equivalent of s 860 of the 2006 Act). Factoring arrangements are equally effective and do not require registration.[225] A company may enter into a complex financing arrangement, involving the sale of assets rather than a loan secured on those assets, specifically in order to avoid the need for registration (such arrangement may also fall outside the ambit of covenants in the company's existing loans whereby it has promised not to create any new security). This sale may be accompanied by an option in favour of the company allowing it to recover the assets at a later date so

---

[220] 'Intellectual property' for this purpose is defined by s 861(4) [CA 1985, s 396(3A) as inserted by the Copyright, Designs and Patents Act 1988].

[221] *Gorringe v Irwell India Rubber Works* (1886) 34 ChD 128, at 134, per Cotton LJ (CA). In *National Provincial and Union Bank of England v Charnley* [1924] 1 KB 431 (CA), at 449, 450, Atkin LJ expressed his views as follows: 'I think there can be no doubt that where in a transaction for value both parties evince an intention that property, existing or future, shall be made available as security for the payment of debt, and that the creditor shall have a present right to have it made available, there is a charge, even though the present legal right which is contemplated can only be enforced at some future date, and though the creditor gets no legal rights of property, either absolute or special, or any legal right to possession, but only gets a right to have the security made available by an Order of the Court ... If, on the other hand, the parties do not intend that there should be a present right to have the security made available, but only that there should be a right in the future by agreement, such as a licence to seize the goods, there will be no charge.'

[222] SI 2003/3226, implementing Directive 2002/47/EC on Financial Collateral Arrangements (2002) OJ L168/43.

[223] Regulation 4 of the 2003 Regulations; see *Re F2G Realisations Ltd (in liquidation); Gray and another v GTP Group Ltd* [2011] 1 BCLC 313, paras [41]-[63].

[224] [1992] BCLC 609.

[225] *Re George Inglefield Ltd* [1933] Ch 1.

that, in economic terms, the arrangement may be indistinguishable from a secured loan. In *Welsh Development Agency v Export Finance Co Ltd,*[226] a complex sale of this type was challenged by a debenture-holder as amounting in substance to no more than a secured loan on the assets supposedly sold. The Court of Appeal rejected the claim on its facts but emphasised that the label attached to a financing arrangement is not conclusive and, if it is a sham or the substance of the arrangement does not accord with the label the parties have given it, the arrangement will not be allowed to stand.

Space does not permit even a cursory consideration of the special characteristics of various types of charge listed in s 860(7) [CA 1985, s 396].[227] However, it should be noted that fixed charges over certain types of property are not included in the list in s 860(7).[228] The most important of these omissions is that of any fixed charge over shares held by the company in any other company.[229]

10.24 EFFECT OF FAILING TO REGISTER A CHARGE

Any registrable mortgage or charge not registered within 21 days after the date of its creation is, 'so far as any security on the company's property or undertaking is conferred by the charge', void against the liquidator, the administrator and any creditor of the company,[230] and this is so even though the creditor is a second mortgagee who had notice of the prior unregistered mortgage.[231] Although the section refers only to the 'liquidator or administrator', it also applies to the company in liquidation or administration itself.[232] It is to be noted that the charge is not avoided as against the company *before* liquidation or administration, and a chargee of goods who has seized the goods before liquidation, in pursuance of a licence to seize contained in the charge, is entitled to the benefit of the security as against the liquidator, despite non-registration of the charge.[233] An unregistered registrable charge is not avoided against purchasers. Section 874(3) states that a failure to register does not invalidate the contract or obligation for repayment of the money thereby

---

[226] [1992] BCLC 148, [1992] BCC 270, noted Oditah [1992] JBL 541. See also *Orion Finance Ltd v Crown Financial Management Ltd* [1996] 2 BCLC 78 (assignment of rentals was by way of security rather than sale and repurchase).

[227] See further, *Gore-Browne on Companies* (Jordans, 45th edn, loose-leaf) at 31 [2], where the question of 'dual registration' under other legislation is also considered.

[228] Apart from charges upon shares referred to in the text, other examples are charges upon *non-book* debts and charges upon registered designs.

[229] *Arthur D Little Ltd (in administration) v Ableco Finance LLC* [2002] EWHC 701 (Ch), [2002] 2 BCLC 799.

[230] Section 874 [CA 1985, s 395(1)]. As to the similar provision made for Scotland, see s 889 [CA 1985, s 410(2)].

[231] *Re Monolithic Building Co* [1915] 1 Ch 643 (CA).

[232] *Smith (Administrator of Cosslett (Contractors) Ltd) v Bridgend County Borough Council* [2001] UKHL 58, [2002] 1 BCLC 77.

[233] *Mercantile Bank of India v Chartered Bank of India* [1937] 1 All ER 231. See also *Re Toomer, ex parte Blaiberg* (1883) 23 ChD 254 (CA).

secured, which will accordingly, even if not registered, rank in a liquidation as an unsecured debt; and before liquidation the charge will be enforceable against the company by all the remedies of a mortgagee, although void against an execution creditor of a secured creditor.[234] Section 874(3) [CA 1985, s 395(2)], moreover, makes the money secured become immediately payable when the charge becomes void. It has been held that an unregistered charge is void in a solvent liquidation as well as where the company is wound up insolvent. That interpretation of what is now s 874(1) must be correct as a literal interpretation of the words 'void against any liquidator ..., administrator... or creditor of the company'. It may, however, be doubted that that was the real intention of the draftsman. Where in the course of liquidation it is still unclear (as was here the case) whether the company is or is not insolvent, the validity of a charge will still be of great concern to the secured creditor.[235]

Failure to effect registration of a charge renders the company, and every officer in default, liable to a fine.[236]

10.25 THE PARTICULARS OF A CHARGE TO BE REGISTERED

Under s 869(4) [CA 1985, s 401(1)], the registrar is to keep a register of all charges required to be registered, and to enter the following particulars:

(1) in the case of a charge to the benefit of which the holders of a series of debentures are entitled, the particulars as are specified in s 863(4) [CA 1985, s 397(1)], namely:

    (a) the total amount secured by the whole series;

    (b) the dates of the resolutions authorising the issue of the series and the date of the covering deed, if any, by which the security is created or defined;

    (c) a general description of the property charged; and

    (d) the names of the trustees (if any) for the debenture-holders;

(2) in the case of any other charge:

    (a) if the charge was created by the company, the date of its creation, and if the charge was a charge existing on property acquired by the company, the date of the acquisition of the property;

---

[234] Note that there was some concern about the compatibility of CA 1985, s 395 (now ss 860 and 874 of the 2006 Act) with the Human Rights Act 1998, a matter which is now unlikely to give rise to further worry in light of the House of Lords ruling in *Wilson v First Country Trust Ltd* [2003] UKHL 40, [2003] 3 WLR 568.

[235] *Re Oriel Ltd* [1984] BCLC 241.

[236] Sections 860(4)–(6) [CA 1985, s 399(3)] and 862(4)–(5) [CA 1985, s 400(4)]. See s 878 [CA 1985, s 410] for the equivalent provision in Scotland.

(b)   the amount secured;

(c)   short particulars of the property charged; and

(d)   the names of the persons entitled to the charge.

Any person may inspect such register.[237]

The registration of a series of debentures under this subsection protects all debentures properly issued in the series, and also agreements to issue such debentures, without separate registration, even when such agreements are to be found only in documents which were intended to be debentures, but from a technical defect can only be treated as agreements for debentures.[238]

Section 864(1) [CA 1985, s 397(2)] requires the amount or rate of any underwriting commission paid, or any allowance or discount made on the placing or issue of debentures, to be included in the particulars filed; but omission to do this will not affect the validity of the debentures issued, and the deposit of debentures to secure a debt of the company is not, for the purposes of this subsection, an issue of the debentures at a discount.

10.26   THE 'DATE OF CREATION' FOR PURPOSES OF REGISTRATION

Registration of a mortgage or charge under ss 860(1) and 870(1) [CA 1985, s 395(1)] is required to be effected within 21 days beginning with the day after the date of its creation. The 'date of creation' of a charge may differ from the 'date of issue' of the debenture it secures. The date of creation is the date when the trust deed or agreement creating the charge is executed or entered into.[239] This will be so even though no money is owing when the deed is executed.[240] Where a series of debentures is issued, the charge must be registered within 21 days after the date of issue of the first debenture.[241]

Where, under a power in the debenture trust deed, other property of the company is substituted for the property originally charged, no new registration is required. No new charge requiring registration is thereby created.[242]

The charge created in equity by an agreement to issue debentures, if duly registered, will give an equal protection to the debenture-holder as a

---

[237]   Section 869(7) [CA 1985, s 401(3)].

[238]   *Re Fireproof Doors* [1916] 2 Ch 142.

[239]   *Watson & Co v Spiral Globe Co* [1902] 2 Ch 209; *Re New London & Suburban Bus Co* [1908] 1 Ch 621. Cf *Re Harrogate Estates Ltd* [1903] 1 Ch 495.

[240]   *Esberger & Sons v Capital & Counties Bank* [1913] 2 Ch 366 and see *Transport & General Credit Corporation v Morgan* [1939] Ch 531.

[241]   Section 870(3).

[242]   *Cunard SS Co Ltd v Hopwood* [1908] 2 Ch 564.

complete debenture,[243] and so will a debenture informally issued if the holder had no notice of the informality.[244]

10.27   THE REGISTRATION OBLIGATION

Prescribed particulars of the charge,[245] together with any instrument creating or evidencing the charge, must be delivered to the Registrar of Companies within 21 days after the date of creation of the charge.[246] The duty to fulfil this registration requirement falls on the company but registration may instead be effected by any person who is interested in the charge.[247] It is in the lender's interest to take responsibility for registration, because the security will become void if it is overlooked. Section 860(3) [CA 1985, s 399(2)] allows the lender to recover from the company any fee which has to be paid to the registrar.

The Registrar of Companies is required to check the details of the prescribed particulars which are submitted against the charging document. When the checking process is complete, the registrar registers the charge and issues a certificate of registration.

10.28   THE REGISTRAR'S CERTIFICATE AS CONCLUSIVE EVIDENCE

The registrar must give a certificate of the registration of any mortgage or charge, stating the amount thereby secured, and the certificate will be conclusive evidence that the requirements of the Act as to registration have been complied with.[248] The company must cause a copy of the certificate so given to be endorsed on every debenture or certificate of debenture stock issued, the payment of which is secured by the charge so registered.[249] Where, however, the company has issued debentures or certificates of debenture stock, and further charges are created, to the benefit of which the holders are entitled, it will not be necessary for the company to endorse on the debentures or debenture stock certificates

---

[243] *Simultaneous Colour Printing Syndicate v Foweraker* [1901] 1 KB 771.

[244] *Duck v Tower Galvanising Co* [1901] 2 KB 314, 70 LJKB 625, DC.

[245] Note that a company's registered number, although necessary to complete the application for registration, is not a particular of the charge. Consequently, providing an incorrect number does not amount to a failure to comply with s 860: *Grove v Advantage Healthcare (T10) Ltd* [2000] 1 BCLC 661 (ChD) (A (T10) had granted charge but the application contained the number for A (T9). The companies had swapped names shortly before the relevant transactions took place.)

[246] Companies Act 2006, ss 860(1) and 870(1) [CA 1985, s 395]. Note also s 863 [CA 1985, s 397] which specifies the documents which must accompany particulars relating to a series of debentures.

[247] Section 860(2) [CA 1985, s 399]. If a charge is not registered, the company and its responsible officers are liable to a fine: s 860(4)–(6) [CA 1985, s 399(3)].

[248] Section 869(5) and (6) [CA 1985, s 401(2)]. This certificate will either be signed by the registrar or authenticated by his official seal.

[249] Section 865(1) [CA 1985, s 402(1)].

already issued a certificate of the registration of the charge.[250] Any person who knowingly and wilfully authorises or permits the issue of any debenture or certificate of debenture stock requiring registration without a copy of the registrar's certificate being endorsed thereon incurs liability to a fine.[251]

The certificate of the registrar is conclusive evidence that the requirements of the Act as to registration have been complied with, even if there is an omission in supplying the necessary particulars, eg the date of the resolution authorising the issue of the series,[252] or of some class of property which is to be subject to the charge.[253] The court will refuse to go behind this certificate, and will not inquire whether there has been any irregularity.[254] Thus, where a creditor sent in defective particulars, omitting to state that the instrument conferred a charge over chattels, and the registrar, by mistake or oversight, omitted to mention that charge in the register, his certificate was held to be conclusive that the document creating the charge was properly registered.[255] In the same case, it was also decided that the requirement as to stating in the certificate 'the amount thereby secured' is sufficiently complied with by the words 'all sums now due or to become due'.

If the particulars submitted at the time the charge is registered do not give the true date of creation, and as a result the charge is registered and a certificate is issued by the registrar, the charge will be valid even though more than 21 days have elapsed between the creation and registration of the charge.[256] The decision of the Court of Appeal in *Re CL Nye Ltd*[257] illustrates the degree of protection afforded by s 869(6)(b) [CA 1985, s 401(2)]. A company was granted loan and overdraft facilities by a bank against the security, *inter alia*, of its business premises. All the necessary documents for registration (including an undated charge) were delivered to the bank's solicitor on 28 February 1964. The charge was stamped on 19 March, but thereafter was mislaid in the office of the bank's solicitor, and was not discovered until 19 June 1964. The solicitor thereupon inserted that date as being the date when the charge was created, and lodged for registration on 3 July the prescribed particulars of the charge in accordance with s 860 [CA 1985, s 395(1)]. The Court of Appeal held that, notwithstanding that the date of the charge was incorrectly stated in the particulars delivered to the registrar, once the certificate was granted

---

250   Section 865(2) [CA 1985, s 402(2)].
251   Section 865(3) and(4) [CA 1985, s 402(3) and Sch 24].
252   *Cunard SS Co v Hopwood* [1908] 2 Ch 564.
253   *National Provincial and Union Bank of England v Charnley* [1924] 1 KB 431 (CA); *Re Mechanisations (Eaglescliffe) Ltd* [1966] Ch 20.
254   *Re Yolland, Husson and Birkett* [1908] 1 Ch 152 (CA); *National Provincial and Union Bank of England v Charnley*, above.
255   *National Provincial and Union Bank of England v Charnley*, above; *Re Mechanisations (Eaglescliffe) Ltd*, above.
256   *Re Eric Holmes (Property) Ltd* [1965] Ch 1052.
257   [1971] 1 Ch 442.

s 869(6)(b) [CA 1985, s 401(2)] applied. The certificate was conclusive evidence that all the requirements of the Act as to registration had been complied with. The requirement for delivery of the particulars within 21 days in ss 860(1) and 870(1) [CA 1985, s 395(1)] was not a condition precedent to the registrar's jurisdiction to register a charge or grant a certificate.[258]

In *R v Registrar of Companies, ex parte Central Bank of India*,[259] it was held that judicial review should not be allowed so as to challenge the registrar's decision to register a charge where there were defects in the original registration of a charge in respect of the time allowed. What is now s 869(6)(b) [CA 1985, s 401(2)] did not exclude the jurisdiction of the court. It merely excluded the admission of evidence to challenge the decision of the registrar in the exercise of his statutory duty. Only the Attorney-General could obtain judicial review of the registrar's decision to register a charge because the Crown was not bound by s 869(6)(b).[260]

If inaccurate or incomplete particulars are delivered to the registrar, he is not obliged to register the charge[261] and can return the particulars for correction.[262] Where defective particulars are returned, the obligation to file within 21 days remains unfulfilled and the lender may have to move quickly to ensure that correct particulars are filed within the 21-day period.

10.29 THE TRANSFER OF CHARGES

Where the benefit of a mortgage or charge on land owned by a company is transferred, and the company is a party to the transfer, the practice is to register the transfer as a new charge, but the question of registration does not arise if the company is not a party to the transfer.

The proper means of obtaining a decision of the court as to whether registration is necessary is by proceedings instituted for the purpose.[263]

---

[258] [1971] 1 Ch 442 (applying *National Provincial Bank v Charnley* [1924] 1 KB 431), per Harman LJ (470), Russell LJ (472 and 474) and Megaw LJ (476).

[259] [1986] QB 1114, [1986] 2 WLR 177, [1986] 1 All ER 105 (CA), overruling Mervyn Davies J, in *R v Registrar of Companies, ex parte Esal Commodities* [1985] 2 WLR 447.

[260] Except that the Court of Appeal left open the possibility of a challenge by someone other than the Attorney-General where the certificate disclosed an error on its face, or the challenge was based on fraud or duress.

[261] *Sun Tai Cheung Credits Ltd v AG of Hong Kong* (1987) 3 BCC 357.

[262] The registrar's practice of not accepting defective particulars in satisfaction of the filing obligations was endorsed by Lawton and Slade LJJ in *Central Bank of India*.

[263] *Re Cunard SS Co* [1908] WN 160.

10.30   PROPERTY ACQUIRED SUBJECT TO A CHARGE

Section 862 [CA 1985, s 400] requires companies registered in England which acquire property already subject to a charge to register the charge within 21 days of the completion of the acquisition.[264] Although a penalty is provided for failure to register such charges on the register of charges kept by the registrar, this failure does not render the charge void, as is the case with charges created by the company and not registered under s 860 [CA 1985, s 395].[265] Where property was conveyed to a company, which created a legal mortgage in favour of the vendor for the unpaid balance of the purchase price, it was held that registration had to be effected under what is now s 860 and not under s 862.[266] Some doubt has been cast on this by the decision of the House of Lords in *Abbey National Building Society v Cann*[267] because it is now the case that there is never a moment when the purchaser of a property on a mortgage holds the property free of the security so that it is arguable that the purchaser does not create a charge over its own property for the purposes of s 860.[268]

10.31   REGISTRATION AND PRIORITIES

Registration of a registrable charge 'perfects' the security against others who have competing interests in the same property and prevents the security becoming void. Registration, however, does not determine priority. Thus, the priority of two fixed charges on the same property, both of which are duly registered, is determined by order of creation, not by order of registration. Registration of a charge does give notice of the existence of that charge to subsequent charges, so that where priority depends on notice (eg where a fixed charge is followed by a legal mortgage of the same property), compliance with the registration requirement can be a significant factor in establishing priority.[269]

10.32   RECTIFICATION OF THE REGISTER OF CHARGES[270]

Section 873 of the Companies Act 2006 [CA 1985, s 404] provides that the register of charges may be rectified by supplying any omission or

---

[264] If the property charged is situated outside Great Britain the material date becomes 21 days after the copy of the instrument could in due course of post, if dispatched with due diligence, have been received in the UK: s 870(2) [CA 1985, s 400(3)].

[265] *Capital Finance Co Ltd v Stokes* [1969] 1 Ch 261 (CA).

[266] Ibid. Equivalent provision is made for Scotland by s 880 [CA 1985, s 416].

[267] [1991] 1 AC 56.

[268] The arguments against this view which are put forward in de Lacy [1991] LMCLQ 531 at pp 536–537 are, however, persuasive.

[269] For a general discussion of the rules governing the priority of competing securities, see **10.24**.

[270] McCormack 'Extension of Time for Registration of Company Charges' [1986] JBL 282.

correcting any misstatement,[271] or the time for registration may be extended. Any such rectification or extension must be authorised by the court on the application of the company or any person interested.[272] But this will be allowed only if the court is satisfied that the omission to register a charge within the time required by the 2006 Act, or that the omission or misstatement of any particular with respect to any such charge, or in a memorandum of satisfaction, was accidental, or due to inadvertence or to some other sufficient cause, or is not of a nature to prejudice the position of creditors or shareholders of the company, or that on other grounds it is just and equitable to grant relief: s 873(1) [CA 1985, s 404(1)].[273] In *Igroup Ltd v Ocwen*,[274] a company involved in mortgage lending had submitted details of charges to be registered on the prescribed form, with a reference to a schedule giving customer details. The company became concerned about the disclosure of this information and sought rectification in order to preserve the customers' confidentiality, but Lightman J held that there was no power of rectification under s 873 [CA 1985, s 404] in respect of this matter.

The court may impose terms as the condition of the grant of relief. Where a solicitor had advised that it was not necessary to register, that was held to be 'sufficient cause'.[275]

It is now[276] usual to make the order in the following form: 'That the time for registering the debentures [*or* mortgage] be extended until the day of; and this order is to be without prejudice to the rights of parties acquired during the period between the date of creation of the said (charge) and the date of its actual registration).'[277]

Where a charge was created but not registered within the specified time, and leave to register was subsequently given, the charge was held to be postponed to a duly registered mortgage given before such registration to a director who had full knowledge of the earlier charge at the time he

---

[271] Eg cancelling a notice of satisfaction of a mortgage entered by mistake: *Re C Light & Co* [1917] WN 77. Once a certificate of registration has been given by the registrar, it is, apparently, unnecessary for the secured creditor to take any steps to rectify the register, however defective or even misleading it may be: *National Provincial and Union Bank of England v Charnley* [1924] 1 KB 431 (CA).

[272] Swinfen-Eady J has held that it is not proper to apply for an extension of time as a means of determining whether or not registration is necessary: *Re Cunard SS Co* [1908] WN 160.

[273] *Re Chantry House Developments plc* [1990] BCC 646, [1990] BCLC 813 (relief granted by means of an interlocutory notice of motion).

[274] [2004] 2 BCLC 61.

[275] *Re S Abrahams & Sons Ltd* [1902] 1 Ch 695.

[276] This contains the new form of proviso introduced as a result of *Watson v Duff Morgan & Vermont (Holdings) Ltd* [1974] 1 WLR 450.

[277] *Re The Mendip Press* (1901) 18 TLR 38; *Re Joplin Brewery Co* [1902] 1 Ch 79 as to the original form of the proviso. A more elaborate form is given for the case where there are duly registered debentures in *Re IC Johnson & Co* [1902] 2 Ch 101 (CA).

advanced his money.[278] Where, however, the only directors of a company learnt that the company had failed to fulfil its obligation to register a charge and then registered a charge in their own favour, the order extending time for registration of the earlier charge did not include the normal proviso which would have protected the rights of the directors.[279] The reasoning behind this is that the court will modify the order to exclude the proviso where its inclusion would facilitate an equitable fraud.[280] A chargee who discovers that, by mistake, he is unregistered, should act without delay. He should not deliberately defer action to see which course suits him best.[281]

10.33   EFFECT OF A WINDING-UP

Except in very exceptional circumstances, an order extending the time for registration will not be made once a winding-up has commenced,[282] because a winding-up, whether compulsory or voluntary, is a proceeding for the benefit of the unsecured creditors, so as to establish their right not to be postponed to the holders of debentures subsequently registered.[283] It has been held that where a winding-up is imminent, the court may exercise its discretion to refuse registration out of time.[284] Alternatively, where liquidation appears to be imminent, the court may insert a proviso permitting the company to make an application to discharge the extension order within a specified period after a winding-up becoming effective on or before a specified date.[285]

Where there is no winding-up before the actual registration of the debentures, an order in the usual form does not prevent the debentures, when registered, from taking priority over existing unsecured creditors who have not levied execution or taken some effective step to enforce their debts before the registration of the debentures.[286] Thus it is clearly established that the order only protects creditors who have acquired a

---

278   *Re Monolithic Building Co* [1915] 1 Ch 643 (CA).

279   *Re Fablehill Ltd* [1991] BCLC 830, [1991] BCC 590.

280   *Re Telomatic Ltd, Barclays Bank plc v Cyprus Popular Bank Ltd* [1993] BCC 404.

281   *Victoria Housing v Ashpurton Estates* [1982] 3 All ER 655; *Re Telomatic*, above.

282   *Re S Abrahams & Sons* [1902] 1 Ch 695 (the order was refused on the ground that it would be of no value); *Re Anglo-Oriental Carpet Co* [1903] 1 Ch 914; *Re Mechanisations (Eaglescliffe) Ltd* [1966] Ch 20, at 36–37. *Re Spiral Globe Company* [1902] 1 Ch 396 and *Re RM Arnold & Co Ltd* [1984] BCLC 535 are examples of exceptional cases where an order was granted after the commencement of winding up. In *Re Resinold and Mica Products Ltd* [1982] 3 All ER 677, the Court of Appeal did not accept any qualification to the general rule, but earlier authorities were not cited to the court.

283   *Re Anglo-Oriental Carpet Co* [1903] 1 Ch 914.

284   *Re Ashpurton Estates* [1983] Ch 110.

285   *Re LH Charles & Co Ltd* [1935] WN 15; *Re Braemar Investments Ltd* [1989] Ch 54, (1988) 4 BCC 366, [1988] BCLC 556; *Exeter Trust Ltd v Screenways Ltd* [1991] BCLC 888, [1991] BCC 477; *Barclays Bank plc v Stuart Landon Ltd* [2001] EWCA Civ 140, [2001] 2 BCLC 316.

286   *Re Ehrmann Bros* [1906] 2 Ch 697 (CA); *Re IC Johnson & Co* [1902] 2 Ch 101; cf *Re Cardiff Workmen's Cottage Co* [1906] 2 Ch 627.

security or levied execution on the property which is the subject matter of the charge, and that the court will not insert any terms for the protection of the unsecured creditors of the company.[287]

10.34   MEMORANDUM OF SATISFACTION

When a registered charge is paid or satisfied in whole or in part, a memorandum of satisfaction in the prescribed form, verified by a statutory declaration by a director and the secretary, should be lodged with the registrar. Registration of the satisfaction or partial satisfaction of the debt is optional and may be effected at any time[288] but it is obviously desirable to record the fact that the company's indebtedness has been discharged or reduced. A similar memorandum may be lodged with the registrar where part of the property or undertaking charged has been released from the charge or has ceased to form part of the company's property or undertaking. Section 872 [CA 1985, s 403] requires that the memorandum be recorded by the registrar on his register.

Omissions or misstatements in a memorandum of satisfaction may be rectified by the court under s 873 [CA 1985, s 404], discussed above.

10.35   CHARGES OVER FOREIGN PROPERTY

Section 866(2) of the Companies Act 2006 [CA 1985, s 398(3)] provides that if the mortgage or charge is created within the UK[289] but comprises property outside the UK, the instrument purporting to charge such property must be lodged for registration. Registration must be effected even if further proceedings (eg registration in a foreign country) are necessary to make the charge valid in accordance with the law of the country in which such property is situated. Section 866(1) [CA 1985, s 398(1)] provides that 'in the case of a mortgage or charge created out of the United Kingdom comprising property situated outside the United Kingdom', a copy verified in the prescribed manner, delivered to or received by the registrar, with the proper particulars, within 21 days after the date on which the instrument or copy could in due course of post, if dispatched with due diligence, have been received, will be sufficient to comply with the requirements of the Act. Companies instructing their agents abroad to create a mortgage must therefore be careful also to instruct them to forward a verified copy of the mortgage by the earliest possible post.

---

[287]   *Re MIG Trust* [1933] 1 Ch 542; *Re Kris Cruisers* [1949] Ch 138.

[288]   *Scottish & Newcastle plc Petitioners* [1993] BCC 634 (on the equivalent Scottish provision).

[289]   Ie Great Britain and Northern Ireland. Equivalent provision for Scotland is made by s 411.

When a charge comprises property situate in Scotland or Northern Ireland and registration in the country where the property is situate is necessary to make the charge valid or effectual according to the law of that country, the delivery to and the receipt by the registrar of a copy, verified in the prescribed manner, of the instrument by which the charge is created or evidence, together with a certificate in the prescribed form stating that the charge was presented for registration in Scotland or Northern Ireland, as the case may be, on the date on which it was so presented is, for the purposes of s 395, to have the same effect as the delivery and receipt of the instrument itself.[290]

10.36 CHARGES ON PROPERTY IN BRITAIN CREATED BY AN OVERSEAS COMPANY

The Companies Act 1985 contained a provision in s 409 on extending the registration requirements of that Act to charges on property in England and Wales which were created, and to charges on property in England and Wales which was acquired, by a company (whether a company within the meaning of the Act or not) incorporated outside Great Britain which has an established place of business in England and Wales. This provision has not been restated in the Companies Act 2006. In its report on *Company Security Interests*,[291] the Law Commission noted the difficulties with the current scheme, and suggested improvements as part of its wider proposals to reform the registration system. Whilst the Government has yet to act on the vast majority of the Law Commission's recommendations, it has made some changes to the registration obligation in respect of overseas companies. Section 1052 of the 2006 Act empowers the Secretary of State to introduce regulations regarding the registration of charges over property in the UK by an overseas company which has registered its particulars with the registrar in accordance with s 1046. Thus, unlike the previous requirement, not all overseas companies will be subject to the obligation to register charges on property in Britain; this will only apply if the overseas company has registered its particulars in accordance with regulations made under s 1046. At the time of writing, no regulations had been adopted under either s 1046 or 1052.

10.37 THE COMPANY'S REGISTER OF CHARGES: S 876

In addition to registering with the registrar those charges specified in s 860(7) [CA 1985, s 396], s 876 of the Companies Act 2006 [CA 1985, s 407][292] requires that every limited company must keep at its registered office a register of all charges specifically affecting property of the company and of all floating charges on the undertaking or any property of the company. In this register must be entered a short description of the

---

[290] Section 867(1) [CA 1985, s 398(4)].
[291] Law Com No 296 (August 2005) paras 3.259–3.268.
[292] Equivalent provision is made for Scotland by s 891.

property charged, the amount of the charge and, except in the case of securities to bearer, the names of the persons entitled to such charge. If any property of the company is charged[293] without such entry being made, every officer of the company who knowingly and wilfully authorises or permits the omission is liable to fine.[294]

A person entitled to the benefit of a charge, however, even though a director of the company, does not lose his security by an omission to see that it is entered in the company's register of charges.[295] (It has been seen that he does so if the charge is one that requires registration under s 860 [CA 1985, s 395] and is not registered with the registrar.) The priority of charges is not affected by any imperfection of the register kept by the company.[296] Debentures containing a specific charge on the property of the company must be included in this register, and also those only containing a floating charge.

The company must also keep at its registered office a copy of every instrument creating a charge requiring registration.[297] In the case of a series of uniform debentures, it will suffice to keep a copy of one of such debentures.[298]

Under s 877 [CA 1985, s 408], the register of charges, and copies of all instruments creating charges which are required to be registered with the registrar, must be open to the inspection of any creditor or member of the company without charge, and to any other person on payment of a fee to be prescribed. The right to inspect the register of charges involves a right to take copies of it.[299] Any officer refusing to allow such inspection is liable to a penalty. In the case of such refusal in relation to a company registered in England, the court may by order compel an immediate inspection.[300]

An advantage for a creditor, or prospective creditor, in searching the company's register of charges in addition to the register maintained by the Registrar of Companies is that this may disclose the existence of charges which do not require registration with the registrar. Some idea of the amount of a company's existing secured debt can also be gleaned from its

---

[293] The expression 'charge' includes mortgage: s 861(5).

[294] Section 876(3) and (4).

[295] *Wright v Horton* (1987) 12 App Cas 371 (HL).

[296] *Re General South American Co* (1876) 2 ChD 337 (CA).

[297] Sections 875(1) and 877(2) [CA 1985, s.406(1)]. Equivalent provision is made for Scotland by s 892 [CA 1985, s 423].

[298] Section 875(2) [CA 1985, s 406(2)].

[299] *Nelson v Anglo-American Land, etc Co* [1897] 1 Ch 130. Note that, as these sections do not give the persons inspecting a right to have a copy supplied on payment, the case is different from that of the register of members. See **12.5.2**.

[300] Section 877(7) [CA 1985, s 408(4)].

last annual return, but this is necessarily a historical record of the amount as at the date of the annual return, which may since have become out of date.

10.38   THE REFORM OF THE LAW OF SECURITY OVER PERSONAL PROPERTY

Prior to the Law Commission review, the law of security over personal property had been the subject of two major reviews since the 1970s. The first review was conducted by the Committee on Consumer Credit, chaired by Lord Crowther (the 'Crowther Committee').[301] The Crowther Committee put forward a proposed new framework for the law relating to security over personal property. This framework was largely based on art 9 of the United States Uniform Commercial Code which governs all secured transactions over personal property.[302]

In a White Paper published in 1973,[303] the Government accepted that aspects of the law caused difficulty and announced its intention to institute consultations to determine whether there was a need for a major recasting of the law on new principles and whether the proposed Crowther scheme commanded general support. Apart from a report relating to Scots law[304] and limited reference to the Crowther scheme in the *Report of the Review Committee on Insolvency Law and Practice*,[305] thereafter there were few significant developments with regard to possible reform of personal security law until, in March 1986, the Department of Trade and Industry appointed Professor AL Diamond to undertake a 'review of security over property other than land'. One of his criticisms was that the law was too fragmented and treated transactions which were similar in different ways. An illustration of the fragmentation of the law is the fact that a genuine[306] sale of assets coupled with an option to repurchase which is entered into to enable the company to raise finance, although it may be economically indistinguishable from a loan secured on those assets, does not require registration at the companies registry because it is not, in legal terms, a 'charge'. The non-registrable status of retention of title clauses and hire-purchase agreements also illustrates the point. Professor Diamond's final report, *Review of Security Interests in Property* (HMSO, 1989), was published in 1989.[307]

---

[301]   1971, Cmnd 4596.

[302]   Article 9 also formed the foundation of the Canadian Personal Property Security Act.

[303]   *Reform of the Law on Consumer Credit* (Cmnd 5427).

[304]   Halliday Working Party Report, published by the Scottish Law Commission in March 1986.

[305]   1982, Cmnd 8558.

[306]   *Welsh Development Agency v Export Finance Co Ltd* (CA), above. Cf *Re Curtain Dream plc* [1990] BCLC 925 where a transaction which the parties designated a sale was held to be a registrable charge.

[307]   See also Diamond 'The Reform of the Law of Security Interests' [1989] CLP 231.

Professor Diamond made various criticisms of the statutory regime for the registration of charges. He made specific recommendations regarding company charges which were intended as interim measures pending larger reform proposed in his report.[308] The proposed interim measures included amending the list of registrable charges, streamlining the registration procedure and, in particular, reducing the burden of the Registrar of Companies, making 'negative pledge' restrictions in floating charges registrable, introducing a system of priorities related to the date of registration, eliminating the need to apply to court for an order authorising late registration, and removing anomalies in the law relating to the registration of charges by oversea companies. Some of Professor Diamond's interim measures were included in the Companies Act 1989.[309] Part IV of that Act contained a set of provisions which were designed to replace in their entirety the existing sections of Part XII of the Companies Act 1985, but these were never brought into force and have now been repealed.

The main thrust of Professor Diamond's report was directed at recommending a fundamental overhaul of the law relating to security interests generally. He advocated[310] the introduction of a new simplified law which was similar to the Crowther scheme and which was based on the United States and Canadian models. Under the new law, substance would have precedence over form, and any arrangement, having as its true purpose the transfer or creation of rights over or interests in property other than land, as security for the provision of finance or the performance of any other obligation, would be treated as giving rise to a 'security interest'. Hire-purchase agreements and retention of title clauses, which are not presently registrable, would become security interests under this scheme, as could sales of assets entered into for financing purposes.

The creation of security interests enforceable against third parties would require a degree of formality in the form of a written financing agreement,[311] and as a general rule non-possessory securities interests would be required to be made public by some form of registration or filing.[312] Priority of competing securities would be governed by date of filing, not, as is presently the case, by date of creation and questions of notice.[313] One particular question raised by Professor Diamond at the consultative stage was the treatment of floating charges under a new scheme. In his final report, he recommended[314] the preservation of the

---

[308] *Review of Security Interests in Property*, Part III.
[309] In September 1987 the DTI had heralded the amendments by publishing its own proposals for amendment of the company charges requirements: 'Outline Proposals for Amendment of Sections 395 to 424 Companies Act 1985', noted (1988) 9 Co Law 101 and (1988) 9 Co Law 220.
[310] Chapter 9 of the report sets out the main recommendations.
[311] Chapter 10 of the report.
[312] Chapter 11 of the report.
[313] Ibid.
[314] Chapter 16 of the report.

essence of the floating charge, namely the freedom for the debtor to dispose of the property secured in the ordinary course of business, and the attachment of the charge to after-acquired property falling within the description of the security. Professor Diamond specifically recommended that the floating-charge form of security should be made available to all businesses, whether incorporated or not.

Reaction to Professor Diamond's final proposals was muted[315] and in 1991 the Secretary of State for Trade and Industry indicated that they would not be adopted.[316] The Minister stated that consultations had established that the majority of interested parties were opposed to major reform and that it could not be commercially justified. One argument against reform is that, although it is widely accepted that the current law is complex and lacking in any functional basis, it is a system with which lenders, and their advisers, are familiar and which does allow lenders to achieve the object of obtaining adequate security for their loans. Another is that radical reform initiatives should not be pursued in domestic law in advance of European Union harmonisation measures.[317]

As part of the Review of Company Law which was launched in 1998 and culminated in the *Modernising Company Law* White Paper in 2002, the Law Commission was asked to investigate and review the registration of security interest. A consultation paper setting out the Law Commission's preliminary recommendations was published in 2002,[318] and the final report, *Company Security Interests,* in August 2005. Although the Government had originally announced that the Commission's proposals would be included in a new Companies Bill in the 2002 White Paper *Modernising Company Law,*[319] the Companies Act 2006 has made no significant changes to the existing system.

The Law Commission does not believe that the shortcomings of the existing system could be remedied and it therefore argues that an entirely new system for registration should be adopted.[320] The system favoured by the Law Commission is a 'notice filing system'. This would be an electronic system.[321] The relevant information would be entered into an

---

[315] The Company Law Committee of the Law Society and the Joint Working Party of the Bar and the Law Society on Banking Law were against implementation of the radical reforms: 'Comments on "A Review of Security Interests in Property"' (November 1989, Memorandum No 211).

[316] *Hansard,* HC vol 189, col 482, 24 April 1991.

[317] The memorandum published by the Company Law Committee of the Law Society and the other bodies mentioned in footnote 310, above, cites possible European developments as a reason for not adopting the Diamond reforms at this stage: 'it would be unfortunate if a major change in the law were to be implemented and then followed by another major change to accommodate any EEC requirements', para 8.2.10.

[318] Law Commission, *Registration of Security Interests: Company Charges and Property other than Land,* Consultation Paper 164.

[319] See Cm 5553–I, para 6.20.

[320] Law Commission *Company Security Interests,* Law Com No 296 (August 2005).

[321] Ibid, paras 3.69–3.71.

online form and processed automatically, thereby ensuring that the relevant information appears on the register much more quickly than is the case at present. The form would be known as a 'financing statement', and require only minimum details of the charge, and a general description of the secured property.[322] The responsibility for registration would fall on the person in whose favour the charge is granted, rather than the company, and the consequences of non-registration would remain (ineffectiveness against administrator or liquidator, and loss of priority).[323] The registrar would no longer be responsible for checking the information that has been provided, nor would there be a certificate of registration. Instead, the person registering the charge would have to ensure that the relevant particulars are correct. Furthermore, the current 21-day limit for registration would be removed, and charges would appear on the electronic register as soon as the relevant details have been submitted.[324] Additionally, the scheme proposed by the Law Commission would introduce clear priority rules for competing charges, ie charges taken over the same asset, giving priority according to the date of filing.

However, a proposal made at the consultation stage has not been carried forward to the final report: the Law Commission had suggested that the new system would encompass not only those securities recognised as registrable at present, but also any arrangements which are functionally equivalent ('quasi-securities'),[325] such as hire-purchase and conditional sale agreements and retention of title clauses. Instead, this matter is to be left for consideration in the context of a further project on the transfer of title by non-owners.

---

[322] Ibid, paras 3.97–3.120.
[323] Ibid, para 3.77.
[324] Ibid, paras 3.149–3.155.
[325] Law Commission *Registration of Security Interests: Company Charges and Property other than Land*, Law Com CP No 164, para 7.20.

CHAPTER 11

CORPORATE GOVERNANCE

11.1 INTRODUCTION

This chapter focuses upon the control mechanisms available for ensuring that managers and directors do not abuse their corporate powers and seeks to set the background to the descriptions of the law in the following chapters. Corporate governance is traditionally concerned with how the company is directed and the relationship between the board of directors, management and shareholders.[1] The structure of the company as recognised by company law is central to corporate governance. Corporate governance contributes both to business prosperity and to accountability and requires an appropriate balance to be established for these two important goals. The term 'corporate governance' is laden with a variety of meanings and expectations which give to it significant practical importance. It carries with it recognition of the fact that corporate boards enjoy extensive powers while individual owners and shareholders face a potential struggle to hold those boards to account. Corporate governance is therefore concerned with how companies are structured, controlled and operated to ensure that the long term goals of shareholders and other stakeholders are satisfied. It is about the creation of board cultures appropriate for corporate success and ethical integrity. In the UK, concern about standards of financial reporting and accountability, heightened by a series of major corporate collapses and controversy over directors' pay brought corporate governance to the centre of attention. The global financial crisis raised many corporate governance issues and led to many reviews and changes to the corporate governance system in the UK and abroad. Notably, the Walker Review led to changes in financial regulation and the Financial Reporting Council replaced the Combined Code on Corporate Governance with a new UK Corporate Governance Code in 2010.[2] As discussed later, the question also arises

---

[1]   There is a vast literature on corporate governance. For a comprehensive discussion and extensive bibliography, see e g Chris Mallin, *Corporate Governance*, (3rd edn) (Oxford: OUP, 2009); Goergen, et al (eds) *Corporate Governance and Complexity Theory* (Cheltenham: Edward Elgar, 2010); Solomon, *Corporate Governance and Accountability* (3rd edn) (Chichester: Wiley, 2010).

[2]   HM Treasury, Press Release, 10/09, 9 February 2009, 'Independent review of corporate governance of UK banking industry by Sir David Walker'. See also Financial Reporting Council, UK Corporate Governance Code 2010, available at www.frc.org.

whether or not it should be the proper concern of company law to ensure that interests other than those of the traditional constituents are protected. This question, which alludes to the issue of corporate social responsibility and sustainability, is even more relevant in the context of globalisation.

11.2   CORPORATE STRUCTURE

Traditionally, company directors have been regarded effectively as agents who act on behalf of the company in general meeting.[3] In practice, they have been required to act on behalf of the shareholders collectively. This approach has shaped the legal duties of directors.[4] More recently, the Companies Act 2006 introduced a developed statutory duty for directors to promote the success of the company for the benefit of its members as a whole, and having regard to broader factors than were traditionally considered to correspond to the shareholders' interests. A new 'enlightened shareholder value' approach requires directors to have regard to the long-term consequences of decisions, the interests of the company's employees, the need to foster the company's business relationships, the impact of the company's operations on the community and the environment, the desirability of the company maintaining a reputation for high standards of business conduct and the need to act fairly as between members of the company.[5]

As companies grew in size, the position of directors and managers altered. This corporate demographic change led to a delegation of wide powers to the board of directors with the general meeting unable to interfere in the exercise of those powers. This situation is generally known as the 'separation of ownership and control' following the seminal work of Berle and Means,[6] who described the new position of the shareholder in the 1930s:[7]

> 'The shift of powers from the individual to the controlling management combined with the shift from the interests of the individual to those of the group have so changed the position of the stockholder that the current conception with regard to him must be radically revised. Conceived originally as a quasi-partner, manager and entrepreneur, with definite rights in and to property used in the enterprise and to the profits of that enterprise as they accrued, he has now reached an entirely different status. He has, it is

---

[3]   See Chapter 15. For discussions of the relationship between directors and shareholders historically and today, see, eg, Stokes 'Company Law and Legal Theory' in Twining (ed) *Legal Theory and Common Law* (Blackwell, 1986) at p 155; Ireland 'Property and Contract in Contemporary Corporate Theory' (2003) 23 *Legal Studies* 453. See further, Ferran *Company Law and Corporate Finance* (Oxford University Press, 1999) ch 4.

[4]   See Chapter 16.

[5]   CA 2006, s 172. See further 16.5 and 16.6.1.

[6]   Berle and Means *The Modern Corporation and Private Property* (New Brunswick, Transaction Publishers, 1991, originally published in 1932).

[7]   Ibid, at p 245.

true, a series of legal rights, but these are weakened in varying degree (depending upon the completeness with which the corporation has embodied in its structure the modern devices) by the text of the contract to which the stockholder is bound. His power to participate in management has, in large measure, been lost to him, and has become vested in the "control". He becomes simply a supplier of capital on terms less definite than those customarily given or demanded by bondholders; and the thinking about his position must be qualified by the realisation that he is, in a highly modified sense, not dissimilar in kind from the bondholder or lender of money.'

Berle and Means were describing the corporate environment of the United States in the early twentieth century. A similar pattern occurred in the UK. However, there are two objections that can be raised today against the description of the corporate structure as one that encompasses a separation of ownership and control. First, in small private companies it is often the same people who are the owners and the controllers so that those same individuals have management and shareholder roles. Secondly, in public companies there has been a dramatic growth in the level of institutional investment. This growing dominance of institutional shareholders on both sides of the Atlantic during the 1980s and 1990s and into the twenty-first century[8] means that the shareholders' position might not be as weak as the analysis of Berle and Means would suggest. The most recent statistical breakdown of share ownership in the UK provided by the Office of national Statistics was published in 2008 and was as follows: investors from outside the UK owned 41.5 per cent of shares listed on the London Stock Exchange at the end of 2008, up from 40.0 per cent at end of 2006. Rest of the world investors held £481.1 billion of UK shares, of which investors in Europe held £163.6 billion (34 per cent) whilst investors in North America held £144.3 billion (30 per cent). Holdings by other sectors include insurance companies with £154.9 billion (13.4 per cent) and pension funds with £148.8 billion (12.8 per cent). The combined holdings of these two sectors are at the lowest level, in percentage terms, since 1975. Individuals in the UK held £117.8 billion of shares (10.2 per cent), the lowest proportion recorded in the history of the survey, which began in 1963. Overall, the UK stock market was valued at £1,158.4 billion at the end of 2008, a decrease of almost £700 billion (37.7 per cent) since the previous survey was published for end of 2006 holdings.[9] Arguably, the divide between shareholders and directors continues because shareholders are not cohesively organised to enable them to use their potential collective weight to bring the managers to account. The key decisions are still for the board to take. Moreover, if

---

[8] The Hampel Report notes that approximately 80% of shares in listed UK companies are held by institutions: *The Hampel Report on Corporate Governance* (Gee, 1998) para 5.1. Davies estimates around 60%: Davies *Gower and Davies' Principles of Modern Company Law* (Sweet & Maxwell, 7th edn, 2003) at p 338. The Myners Report suggests that in 1999 the institutional investors held 51.9%: Paul Myners, *Institutional Investment in the UK: A Review* (HM Treasury, April 2001) at p 27.

[9] Office for National Statistics: see http://www.statistics.gov.uk/cci/nugget.asp?id=107.

the roles of the shareholders and directors are not wholly clear then directors may be in a position to pursue their own interests rather than act in the interests of the company or even of the shareholders.

11.3 DEFINING CORPORATE GOVERNANCE

The most authoritative definition of corporate governance in the UK was provided by the Cadbury Committee, which reported on the *Financial Aspects of Corporate Governance* in 1992. The Cadbury Committee's report defined corporate governance as 'the system by which companies are directed and controlled'.[10] The Cadbury Committee explained this definition further in the following manner:

> 'Boards of directors are responsible for the governance of their companies. The shareholders' role in governance is to appoint the directors and the auditors and to satisfy themselves that an appropriate governance structure is in place. The responsibilities of the board include setting the company's strategic aims, providing the leadership to put them into effect, supervising the management of the business and reporting to shareholders on their stewardship. The board's actions are subject to laws, regulations and the shareholders in general meeting.'

This definition was adopted by the Department of Trade and Industry (DTI) in 1998 in the paper that established the Company Law Review.[11] In this relationship, responsibility rests with directors to establish the company's policies and to supervise how the company is managed. The directors are, in turn, accountable to the shareholders. Auditors have a role of acting as a representative for the shareholders collectively by guarding against financial irregularities and aiming for the directors to provide a 'true and fair view' of the company's performance.[12] As the shareholders supply equity capital to the company, they seek maximisation of their financial return from the company so that the general aim of the system of corporate governance may be to maximise the company's profits. Indeed, the Hampel Report on corporate governance, published in 1998, stated that the single overriding objective shared by all listed companies, whatever their size or type of business, is the preservation and the greatest practicable enhancement over time of their shareholders' investment.[13]

---

[10] Cadbury Committee *Report on the Financial Aspects of Corporate Governance* (Gee, 1992), para 2.5. The DTI adopted this definition in its consultation paper *Modern Company Law for a Competitive Economy* (HMSO, March 1998), para 3.5 at p 9. See also Hampel Report *op cit*, para 1.16.

[11] *Modern Company Law for a Competitive Economy*, 1998, para 3.5, at p 9.

[12] As to auditors, see Chapter 14.

[13] Hampel Committee, *Report on Corporate Governance* (Gee, 1998), para 1.16.

11.4 HOW IS THIS SYSTEM TO BE ACHIEVED?

This relationship in which the directors monitor the activities of management and then report to the shareholders rests on the assumption that the shareholders have the ability to exercise their powers in general meeting. This they do by voting on resolutions. In particular, the shareholders have power to appoint or remove the directors from office.[14] Managers are forced to recognise the risk that shareholders will use their voting powers to limit their discretion or indeed to remove them from office. Yet, in large public companies at least, the voting powers of shareholders comprise a limited form of control of management activities. In reality, shareholders are more likely to sell their shares if they are dissatisfied with the manner in which the company is being run. This is generally regarded as shareholders using powers of 'exit' rather than 'voice' to influence the company's management.[15] This response of 'rational apathy' by shareholders occurs because there is little incentive for them to attend and vote at general meetings.[16] Each individual shareholder's vote is unlikely to carry sufficient weight and collective action is difficult when shareholders are dispersed. In addition, existing corporate governance provisions seem to place obstacles in the way of shareholders who question decisions of directors rather than assist them. Indeed, shareholders who seek to challenge directors' actions in the courts[17] face procedural barriers and judicial reluctance to intervene in commercial decisions.[18] This fact brings about a requirement for more effective controls upon management activity. The increased proportion of shares held by institutional investors has given to them a greater significance in corporate governance. However, empirical evidence suggests that rather than exercise their votes, institutional investors prefer to influence the managers through dialogue.[19] They are generally prepared to intervene only to a limited extent, regarding their role primarily as investors rather than as managers.[20] In practice this approach has resulted

---

[14] For powers of appointment, see Draft Model Articles for Private Companies Article 17 and for Public Companies Article 20 and for power to remove see CA 2006, s 168. As to these, see **15.3** and **15.7**.

[15] These terms were introduced by Hirschman in *Exit, Voice and Loyalty: Responses to Decline in Firms, Organizations and States* (Cambridge, MA, Harvard University Press, 1970).

[16] The problems and limitations of shareholders' meetings are described at **13.1**.

[17] All UK company lawyers are familiar with the difficulties caused by *Foss v Harbottle* (1843) 2 Hare 461; see Chapter 18.

[18] See, eg, Lord Greene MR stating in *Re Smith & Fawcett Ltd* [1942] Ch 304, at 306 (CA) that directors are bound to exercise the powers conferred upon them 'bona fide in what they consider – not what a court may consider – is in the interests of the company'.

[19] Holland *Corporate Communications with Institutional Shareholders: Private Disclosures and Financial Reporting* (Edinburgh, Institute of Chartered Accountants of Scotland, 1998). For example, in the United States, the California Public Employees Retirement Scheme (CalPERS) adopts 'intensive dialogue' and 'heightened monitoring' to assert its influence.

[20] Thus for example, the Institutional Shareholders' Committee *Statement of Principles on the Responsibilities of Institutional Shareholders and Agents* (2005) states in its introduction: 'The policies of engagement set out below do not constitute an obligation

in a poor level of shareholder activism. Thus, the 2002 White Paper *Modernising Company Law* noted failure of some institutional investors and fund managers to intervene actively to protect and enhance the value of the investment in cases where companies are being ineffectively, or even dishonestly, managed by their boards.[21] Following the financial crisis the Treasury Select Committee and the Walker Review targeted the institutional shareholders for their failure of vigilance and made clear the need for them to be more actively engaged as is discussed below.

An additional control mechanism arising from the analysis of Berle and Means is that of the so-called market for corporate control,[22] which imposes on managers the threat of displacement. According to this theory, 'inefficient managers, if not responsible to, and subject to displacement by, owners directly, can be removed by stockholders' acceptance of take-over bids induced by poor performance and a consequent reduction in stock value'.[23] This control mechanism operates to the effect that if a company is not managed efficiently this will reduce its share prices. This will present a control opportunity for a 'predator' to acquire the company and replace the managers with a new board. The new board will manage the company more efficiently and maximise the share price. This precedent will encourage managers in other companies to act efficiently in order to avoid being displaced. This ability of the market for corporate control to curtail inefficient or irresponsible managerial behaviour is subject to a number of qualifications. First, the ability of the market to respond speedily to inefficient management is limited. Secondly, a company's managers may be able to defend themselves against takeover threats, eg, by using devices such as 'poison pills'.[24] Thirdly, the market for corporate control could cause managers to be too preoccupied with the company's short-term results. In turn this could lead to various social costs, such as job losses or reduced training opportunities.

A number of legal controls exist which seek to ensure that directors and managers act within their powers and run the company effectively. There is a broad range of directors' duties.[25] The Companies Act 2006 has put into legislative form the fiduciary and common law duties that have

---

to micro-manage the affairs of investee companies, but rather relate to procedures designed to ensure that shareholders derive value from their investments by dealing effectively with concerns over under-performance. Nor do they preclude a decision to sell a holding, where this is the most effective response to such concerns.'

[21] Cm 5553–I, para 2.43 at p 24.

[22] For a detailed discussion of the theory of the market for corporate control see Bradley 'Corporate Control: Markets and Rules' (1990) 53 MLR 170.

[23] See Herman *Corporate Control, Corporate Power* (Cambridge University Press, 1981) at p 10, quoted by Bradley, *op cit*.

[24] Poison pills are tactics used by companies threatened with unwelcome takeover bids to make themselves unattractive to the bidder, e g the target company issues large amounts of shares to the shareholders in order to dilute the shareholding that the hostile acquirer might establish.

[25] For further detail on directors' duties, see Chapters 16 and 17.

regulated the role of directors. These include fiduciary duties aimed at promoting honesty and disclosure, and at combating conflicts of interest. These duties have and continue to impose upon directors a duty to act in good faith to promote the success of the company and not to exercise their powers for any collateral purpose; a duty not to make a secret profit by use of their position; and a duty to avoid a conflict between their duty to the company and their personal interests. Other statutory provisions guard against self-dealing by directors, for example, by obliging directors to disclose their interest in relevant transactions. Criminal and civil sanctions apply against breach of many of these provisions. The Act also lays down financial disclosure provisions and obligations with regard to disclosure of remuneration.[26] Many of these disclosure obligations are supplemented by requirements and standards set by City institutions such as the Financial Reporting Council, the London Stock Exchange and relevant professional bodies such as the Accounting Standards Board and the Institute of Chartered Accountants, and by the Financial Services Authority as UK Listing Authority.[27] The Financial Services Authority is soon to be replaced by the Financial Conduct Authority which will focus on consumer protection and the markets.

Despite the existence of these internal, market and legal controls the concerns about corporate governance have not disappeared. The response in the UK to the inadequacies of these control mechanisms has not been to introduce new statutory provisions. Instead, self-regulation has been encouraged as a supplement to existing legislative provisions. Indeed, back in 1998 it was noted by the Law Commissions of both Scotland and England and Wales that a 'significant interdependency now exists between voluntary codes and formal law'.[28] A number of Committees have been central to the development of corporate governance, their efforts culminating in a Combined Code now operated by the Financial Reporting Council with subsequent revisions in 2006 and 2008. In 2010 this was transformed by the Financial Reporting Council into the UK Corporate Governance Code.[29] The Company Law Review[30] expressed the view that there was no intention to replace the use of best practice, for which the Corporate Governance Code is said to be more suitable, provided best practice is seen to be working.[31]

---

[26] See Chapter 14.

[27] See Chapter 19.

[28] Law Commission *Regulating Conflicts of Interests and Formulating a Statement of Duties: A Joint Consultation Paper*, Law Com No 153 and Law Com Discussion Paper No 105, para 1.21 at p 8.

[29] The UK Corporate Governance Code, June 2010, (FRC) available at www.frc.org.

[30] See generally, **1.7**.

[31] DTI *Modern Company Law for a Competitive Economy* (HMSO, March 1998) para 3.7 at p 9. The 2002 White Paper did not suggest any change to this approach.

11.5   THE CORPORATE GOVERNANCE COMMITTEES

Since the beginning of the 1990s the corporate governance debate has been shaped to a large degree by the work of the Cadbury Committee, the Greenbury Committee, the Hampel Committee and the Turnbull Committee. An understanding of the approach towards corporate governance adopted in the UK requires a brief description of the work of these committees. The collapse of ENRON and other companies in the United States and Western Europe also led to further moves to strengthen the protections afforded by the corporate governance regime. The financial crisis also gave impetus to further reforms to the corporate governance system, many of which have been implemented by and are overseen by the Financial Reporting Council.

11.5.1   The Cadbury Committee

The Cadbury Committee was set up as a private initiative in response to a number of corporate collapses, notably the demise of the Bank of Credit and Commerce International, Polly Peck, a FT-SE 100 company, and the Maxwell empire. The Cadbury Committee regarded the public attention on its work as an opportunity to raise standards of financial reporting and accountability. It sought to ensure that boards would be free to drive their companies forward in a competitive environment but that they would exercise that freedom within an effective framework of accountability. The Committee focused on the control and reporting functions of boards and on the role of auditors. Thus while its remit was limited to the aspects of corporate governance specifically related to financial reporting and accountability, it was hoped that the proposals would contribute positively to the promotion of good corporate governance as a whole.

In its *Report on the Financial Aspects of Corporate Governance*, the Committee concentrated on the tripartite relationship between the board, auditing and the shareholders. The Committee created a Code of Best Practice to be complied with by public listed companies. This Code was based on the principles of openness, integrity and accountability. Briefly, the Code included, *inter alia*, the following provisions: the board should meet regularly, retain full and effective control over the company and monitor the executive management; there should be a clearly accepted division of responsibilities at the head of the company to ensure a balance of power and authority; the board should include non-executive directors of sufficient calibre and number for their views to carry significant weight in the board's decisions; non-executive directors should bring an independent judgement to bear on issues of strategy, performance, resources, and standards of conduct and their fees should reflect the time which they commit to the company; there should be full and clear disclosure of directors' total emoluments and those of the chairman and highest-paid UK director and executive directors' pay should be subject to the recommendations of a remuneration committee; the board should establish an audit committee of at least three non-executive directors; the directors should report that the business is a going concern, with supporting assumptions or qualifications as necessary.

The Committee also recommended that companies should expand their interim reports to include balance sheet information and that interim reports should be reviewed by the auditors; that fees paid to audit firms for non-audit work should be fully disclosed; that the accountancy profession should draw up guidelines on the rotation of audit partners; and that institutional investors should disclose their policies on the use of their voting rights.

11.5.2 The Greenbury Committee

The Greenbury Committee was established on the initiative of the CBI in January 1995 in response to public and shareholder concerns about directors' remuneration. The terms of reference were to identify good practice in determining directors' remuneration and prepare a code of such practice for use by public companies. The Committee focused on similar themes to the Cadbury Committee: accountability, responsibility, full disclosure, alignment of director and shareholder interests, and improved company performance. The Committee published its Report in July 1995.[32]

In brief, the Greenbury Committee recommended:

(1) that directors' remuneration be determined by an independent remuneration committee directly accountable to shareholders and consisting exclusively of non-executive directors;

(2) full disclosure to shareholders of the salaries of named directors, with information covering all aspects of pay, including share options and pension entitlements;

(3) that directors' service contracts with notice periods for longer than one year should be disclosed and the reasons for the longer notice period explained;

(4) that shares should not vest and options should not be exercisable in under 3 years and that directors should be encouraged to hold onto them; and

(5) that gains from executive share options should be taxed as income at the time of the exercise rather than capital gains on disposal.

---

[32] Greenbury Committee *Report on Directors' Remuneration* (Gee, 1995).

The Committee urged performance-based pay and compensation so that poor performance should not be rewarded, and that compensation payments should be paid in instalments so that they can be mitigated if the director obtains new employment or earns money elsewhere.

11.5.3   The Hampel Committee

The Hampel Committee published its final *Report on Corporate Governance* in January 1998, just over 2 years after the Committee was established on the initiation of the Financial Reporting Council. The Hampel Committee built on the recommendations of the Cadbury and Greenbury Committees and had a broader remit, covering the more general aspects of corporate governance. The Report covered corporate governance, principles of corporate governance, the role of directors, directors' remuneration, the role of shareholders and accountability and audit.

In summary, the Committee recommended, *inter alia*:

(1)   that executive and non-executive directors should continue to have the same duties under the law;

(2)   that new directors should receive appropriate training;

(3)   that the majority of non-executive directors should be independent and that to be effective, non-executive directors should make up at least one-third of the membership of the board comprising of people from a wide range of backgrounds;

(4)   that a senior non-executive director should be identified in the annual report to whom concerns could be conveyed;

(5)   that all directors should submit themselves for re-election at least every 3 years;

(6)   that a remuneration committee should be established and made up of independent non-executive directors to develop a policy on remuneration and devise remuneration packages for individual executive directors;

(7)   simplification of disclosure requirements for remuneration;

(8)   that institutional investors should vote the shares under their control but that voting should not necessarily be compulsory;

(9)   that shareholders should be able to vote separately on each substantially separate issue;

(10) that the chairman should provide questioners with written answers to significant questions which cannot be answered on the spot;

(11) that each company should establish an audit committee of at least three non-executive directors; and

(12) that the audit committee should keep under review the overall financial relationship between the company and its auditors.

11.5.4 The Combined Code and the UK Corporate Governance Code

The Combined Code, embracing the work of the Cadbury, Greenbury and Hampel Committees, was initially produced in June 1998. In the wake of the collapse of ENRON in the United States it was revised by the Financial Reporting Council in 2003, incorporating recommendations in the Higgs Review on non-executive directors and the Smith Review on the role of audit committees. In addition, the Turnbull Working Party was established by the Institute of Chartered Accountants in England and Wales to provide guidance to assist listed companies to implement the new requirements in the Combined Code relating to internal control. The purpose of this guidance is to help manage and control risk appropriately rather than to eliminate it. This Working Party published its final report in September 1999.[33] The Financial Reporting Council revised the Turnbull Guidance in 2005 and revised the Combined Code in 2006 following a review of the implementation of the Code in 2005 and subsequent consultation on possible amendments to the Code. Further revisions were made in 2008.

The UK Corporate Governance Code was published in May 2010 and this largely retains the principles of the Combined Code. Like the Combined Code the new Corporate Governance Code contains main and supporting principles and provisions of corporate governance. It focuses on directors, remuneration of directors, accountability and audit and relations with shareholders. The aim of the Code is to allow companies to create and establish their own governance policies in the light of the main and supporting principles. This seeks to offer flexibility for companies in order to take account of their diversity but within a broad framework of requirements. The *Listing Rules* require listed companies to describe their corporate governance in their annual report and accounts from two points of view.[34] First, the company must report on how it applies and adheres to the Code's principles. It is for the companies to define and explain their own governance policies in the light of the principles, including any special circumstances applying to them which have led to a particular approach. It is for their shareholders and others to evaluate this part of

---

[33] *Internal Control: Guidance for Directors on the Combined Code* (ICAEW, 1999). See also *The Combined Code: A Practical Guide* (KPMG and Gee Publishing, October 1999).

[34] See section entitled 'Comply or Explain' within the Code, para 2.

the company's statement. The company must confirm where it complies with the Code's provisions. From the second point of view the company must describe its non-compliance with any of the Code's provisions. The comply or explain approach adopted in the Code is favoured as having been in operation since the Code's beginnings in 1992 and for the flexibility it offers which 'is strongly supported by both companies and shareholders and has been widely admired and imitated internationally.'[35]

Again the shareholders and others must evaluate such explanations. In the same way as its predecessors the Code reflects the Hampel Committee's objective 'to restrict the regulatory burden on companies eg by substituting principles for detail wherever possible'.[36]

The main differences introduced by the 2010 Corporate Governance Code focus on more effective leadership and commitment from directors. Therefore the chairman is encouraged to report personally to shareholders in the annual report how the principles relating to the role and effectiveness of the board have been applied. Non-executive directors are expected to challenge the board and to help develop proposals relating to the company's strategy. The board should have more balanced skills, experience, independence and knowledge. Directors should devote sufficient time to their role to discharge their responsibilities more effectively and FTSE 350 directors should be subject to reelection every year. The Code contains provisions relating to external review of board effectiveness to be conducted every three years. The Code also seeks greater transparency with regard to the company's business model and its approach to risk with explanation in annual reports of a company's long-term business model and strategy for delivering its objectives.

Alongside the Corporate Governance Code and associated requirements many companies have also created their own codes of conduct. Bodies such as the Organisation for Economic Co-operation and Development and the International Labour Organisation have also published codes and guidelines.[37]

The various Committees had in common their preference for a self-regulatory approach to the issue of corporate governance. The adoption of a Code avoids resort to statute and the courts. The obvious point to note is that codes of practice are not legally binding. In *Re Astec (BSR) plc*,[38] it was held that the exercise of a majority shareholder of its legal rights contrary to the Cadbury Code was not capable of giving rise

---

[35] Section, entitled Comply or Explain, para 1.
[36] Hampel Report, *op cit* Annex B, at p 66.
[37] The OECD published its *Principles of Corporate Governance* on 22 June 1999; the text was recently revised in 2004 and can be downloaded from www.oecd.org. See also International Labour Office *Tripartite Declaration of Principles Concerning Multinational Enterprises and Social Responsibility* (November 1977, revised 1991 and 2001), which can be downloaded from www.ilo.org.
[38] [1999] BCC 59.

to a claim for unfair prejudice even though investors might expect compliance with voluntary codes on corporate governance.[39] Furthermore, as was noted by the Law Commissions,[40] the civil and criminal remedies are far less than those available for a breach of a rule of the general law or of some legislative provision.

The principles established in the Combined Code and the new Corporate Governance Code apply to listed companies but unlisted and private companies are also encouraged to adopt the principles recommended.[41] The flexibility offered by self-regulation and the opportunity it provides for speedy action compared with legislative regulation makes it an attractive form of regulation for corporate governance, as was recognised both by the DTI and the Law Commissions. However, the principles for best practice adopted in the self-regulatory codes have also been subjected to considerable criticism.[42] As is stated by Dignam,[43] the codes are 'at the very loose end of any regulatory control system'. The flexibility that they offer may allow directors to abuse the system. A recent survey of FTSE 350 companies shows that whilst more than half of the companies claim full compliance with the Code, only 16% of those companies provide all of the required disclosures to fully support their claim.[44] Heavy reliance is placed upon the disclosure of information and the monitoring of management activity by non-executive directors.

11.5.5 Disclosure

Disclosure of information is required for many activities, the most obvious being in the accounts and the annual report and directors' remuneration.[45] Sealy has noted that this has been an underlying principle

---

[39] Cf *Re BSB Holdings Ltd (No 2)* [1996] 1 BCLC 155 and *Re Macro (Ipswich) Ltd* [1994] 2 BCLC 354.

[40] Law Commissions of Scotland and of England and Wales, *op cit* (September 1998) para 1.44, at p 15.

[41] See also European Federation of Directors' Association, *Corporate Governance Guidance and Principles for Unlisted Companies in Europe* (March 2009) and Institute of Directors, *Corporate Governance Guidance and Principles for Unlisted Companies in the UK* (2009).

[42] For discussion of the Cadbury Report, see Belcher 'Regulation by the Market: The Case of the Cadbury Code and Compliance Statement' (1995) JBL 321; 'Compliance with the Cadbury Code and the Reporting of Corporate Governance' (1996) 17 Co Law 11; for discussion of the Greenbury Report, see Villiers 'Directors' Pay: An Ill Not yet Cured' (1995) *Utilities Law Review* 100; for discussion of the Hampel Report, see Dignam 'A Principled Approach to Self-Regulation? The Report of the Hampel Committee on Corporate Governance' (1998) 19 Co Law 140; Villiers 'Self-Regulatory Corporate Governance: Final Attempt or Last Rites?' (1998) 3 *Scottish Law and Practice Quarterly* 208.

[43] Alan Dignam, 'A Principled Approach To Self-Regulation? The Report Of The Hampel Committee On Corporate Governance' (1998) 19 *Company Lawyer*, 140, at 141.

[44] Grant Thornton, *Evolving with the Code – A changing landscape: are you ready?* (Corporate Governance review, December 2010).

[45] For the detail, see Chapter 14.

of company law in the UK 'ever since companies were accorded the twin privileges of incorporation and limited liability by the legislation of 1844 and 1855'.[46]

The claim that the disclosure philosophy stems from the privilege of limited liability might imply that it is third parties rather than shareholders who should benefit from such disclosure. Indeed, shareholders ought to be responsible for ensuring that information is provided and to bear the costs of that publicity. However, the disclosure obligations, in particular financial disclosure obligations, require directors to furnish the shareholders with this information. Additionally, the corporate governance reports of the 1990s emphasise the role of shareholders as recipients of information by the directors. The Hampel Report, for example, states that the directors are accountable to shareholders. These facts suggest that shareholders are entitled to information that might affect their investment and that, for corporate governance purposes, shareholders are expected to monitor the directors.

In the UK, disclosure activity falls into three categories: legal disclosure obligations, self-regulatory disclosure requirements and voluntary disclosure. Each of these categories of disclosure may cover the same or distinct areas of corporate activity. For example, financial disclosure is covered by legal obligations as well as requirements imposed by the accounting professional bodies, in particular the Accounting Standards Board. Although the 'accounting standards' do not have the force of law they do have a measure of underpinning in the Companies Act 2006 which provides for such standards to be issued by those bodies prescribed by the regulations.[47] Additionally, for listed companies there are detailed financial disclosure requirements under the *Listing Rules*. It may also be possible that companies provide financial details above the legal and self-regulatory demands. On the other hand, there may be areas which are not covered by legal or self-regulatory rules, but which are offered by the company, such as certain aspects of social reporting.[48]

Disclosure is a key aspect of corporate governance but it has a number of limitations. An example of the limitations of disclosure may be provided by a brief examination of directors' remuneration. The Greenbury Report and Code of Best Practice laid down detailed provisions relating to disclosure of directors' remuneration as a step towards ensuring a closer relationship between pay and performance. The Greenbury Report suggested that one of the benefits of disclosure would be that it might encourage remuneration committees to be sensitive to the wider scene. Yet

---

[46] Sealy 'The Disclosure Philosophy and Company Law Reform' (1981) 2 Co Law 51. See also Villiers 'Disclosure Obligations in Company Law: Bringing Communication Theory into the Fold' (2001) 1 JCLS 181 and Villiers *Corporate Reporting and Company Law* (Cambridge University Press, 2006).

[47] Companies Act 2006, s 464. See also Part 15.

[48] See Parkinson 'Disclosure and Corporate Social and Environmental performance: Competitiveness and Enterprise in a Broader Social Frame' (2003) 3 JCLS 3.

the Hampel Report noted that full disclosure had led to an upward pressure on remuneration in a competitive field. In addition, it has been observed by Ernst and Young that the Greenbury Code led to an increase in the length of annual reports, with the result that such reports would be less likely to be read by the shareholders.[49] Importantly, the then Secretary of State for Trade and Industry in a speech[50] noted that disclosure by itself is not a sufficient guarantee of aligning executive pay with company or individual executive performance. Disclosure also requires vigilance by the shareholders. The Secretary of State stressed that accountability can work properly only if there is a framework in place that allows shareholders to exercise their influence effectively over remuneration policy. The eventual outcome is that increasingly stringent and detailed disclosure requirements have developed over time to remedy the problems arising from previous less demanding disclosure rules.[51] These steps indicate clearly that disclosure is only a part of corporate governance and that to be effective it requires a response by those to whom it is aimed. In particular, vigilance is required by non-executive directors and by shareholders, especially the institutional shareholders.

11.5.6 Non-executive directors

The various corporate governance reports and codes have stressed the importance of non-executive directors for corporate governance.[52] They have both strategic and monitoring functions. They may also contribute expertise or act as mentors to relatively inexperienced executives. A survey report published by BDO Binder Hamlyn in 1995 reveals that their monitoring role is perceived generally to be the most important role for non-executives.[53] Recognising the importance of their monitoring role, the Cadbury and Hampel Reports express the need for a majority of non-executive directors to be independent. Both adopt the same definition of independence: that non-executive directors are 'independent of management and free from any business or other relationship which could materially interfere with the exercise of their independent judgment'. Despite these statements, empirical data indicates that the

---

[49] Ernst and Young *Corporate Governance: Greenbury Implementation* (1996).

[50] Speech of Stephen Byers, Secretary of State for Trade and Industry, 19 July 1999.

[51] See now the Directors' Remuneration Report Regulations 2002, SI 2002/1986.

[52] For an overview of the role of non-executive directors, see Ferran *Company Law and Corporate Finance* (Oxford University Press, 1999) at pp 217–223.

[53] BDO Binder Hamlyn *Non-executive Directors – Watchdogs or Advisers?* (City Research Associates, 1994): 85% of those who responded to the survey considered the role of non-executive directors in protecting shareholder interests as either very or fairly important, 80% considered they should be custodians of good corporate governance, and only 13% considered as very or fairly important the role of providing detailed advice and assistance to executive management in the running of the company. Most respondents felt that it was realistic for non-executive directors to shoulder responsibility for ensuring the maintenance of high standards of corporate practice: see especially at p 5 and p 14.

presence of significant numbers of 'insider' non-executives does not seem consistent with independent outsider judgments.[54]

One problem is that companies (especially small companies) may have difficulty in appointing independent non-executive directors. The Hampel Report suggests that non-executive directors could be chosen from a variety of backgrounds beyond political and technical expertise, and with overseas knowledge. However, the report does not state which other backgrounds it envisages for these non-executive directors. The Tyson Report also advocates recruitment of non-executive directors from a more diverse pool of talent.[55] In any event, research by BDO Binder Hamlyn promises little optimism in this regard. That survey revealed that 78% of the respondents considered a top-level management role in another company to be the most relevant career background compared with 21% supporting a merchant banker, 15% supporting a practising accountant, 10% supporting a practising solicitor and 9% supporting a career non-executive director.[56] One problem may be that the skills and qualifications relevant to other careers might not necessarily contribute to successful corporate or commercial performance.

This issue received attention in the Company Law Review as well as in the post-ENRON scrutiny of corporate governance. The Company Law Review acknowledged concerns by respondents about 'the genuineness of the independence of non-executive directors, their real ability to hold management to account, the absence of clear legal support for the Code, the effectiveness of the current disclosure approach and the weight which this approach gives to institutional enforcement'.[57]

The 2002 White Paper *Modernising Company Law* identified the role of non-executive directors as key in corporate governance in respect of accountability and business prosperity. This gave support to the work of Derek Higgs. The Higgs *Review of the role and effectiveness of non-executive directors* was subsequently published in January 2003. The Trade and Industry Select Committee in its Sixth Report welcomed the Higgs Report, stating that its proposals were modest but could contribute to good corporate governance standards without being overly

---

[54]   Cosh and Hughes 'The Changing Anatomy of Corporate Control and the Market for Executives in the United Kingdom' (1997) 24 *Journal of Law and Society* 104–123, at p 111 and 121. See also Brudney 'The Independent Director – Heavenly City or Potemkin Village?' (1982) 95 Harv LR 597; Prodham *Corporate Governance and Long-Term Performance*, Management Research Paper, Templeton College, Oxford, 93/13 (1993); Lowry 'Directorial Self-Dealing: Constructing a Regime of Accountability' (1997) 48 NILQ 211–242, at pp 234–235.

[55]   *The Tyson Report on the Recruitment and Development of Non-Executive Directors* (London Business School, June 2003).

[56]   See footnote 5 at p 337.

[57]   *Completing the Structure* (2000) para 4.47. These concerns were highlighted by Brenda Hannigan in *Company Law* (London, Butterworths, 2003).

prescriptive.[58] Following endorsement by the Committee and the Government the proposals set out in the Higgs Report were incorporated into the revised Combined Code. Primarily these included: challenging and helping to develop proposals on strategy; scrutiny of management's performance in meeting agreed goals and objectives and monitoring the reporting of performance; checking the integrity of financial information and ensuring robust and defensible financial controls and systems of risk management; monitoring remuneration levels and appointing and removing executive directors.[59] Additionally, a senior independent non-executive director should be available to shareholders and in particular to act as an alternative contact with the chairman, chief executive or finance director when the normal channels have failed or are inappropriate.[60] What is not clear is how the non-executive directors will communicate with the shareholders, or more fundamentally, how they will increase accountability to the shareholders.[61]

Following the financial crisis, the Walker Report made a number of recommendations in relation to the role of non-executive directors in banks and other financial institutions. Walker suggested, for example, that non-executive directors should have an awareness of the financial industry and they should be given increased training and support to help them to make an effective contribution, and that they should increase their time commitment on the board. These recommendations were followed by the Financial Reporting Council and incorporated into the Corporate Governance Code. The main principle relating to non-executive directors in the Code is that they should constructively challenge and help develop proposals on strategy.[62] In support of principle B.3 of the Code supporting principle B.3.2 requires non-executives to undertake that they will have sufficient time to meet what is expected of them and main principle B.4 requires all directors to receive induction on joining the board and to update and refresh their skills and knowledge. Further steps were taken by the Financial Reporting Council by commissioning the Institute of Chartered Secretaries and Administrators to develop new guidance that would replace the Higgs Guidance. This advises the non-executive directors to focus on being well informed about the company and its business and to engage with senior and middle managers. They should confirm in their appointment letter that they can give sufficient time required of their role and for induction the Guidance

---

[58] Trade and Industry Select Committee Sixth Report, White Paper, *Modernising Company Law*, HC 439, para 49.

[59] See Higgs Review, Chapter 6 and Combined Code, Section 1A.

[60] See Higgs Review, Chapter 7 and Combined Code Provision A.3.3. It is notable that the role of the senior independent director is essentially a passive one. See Trade and Industry Select Committee Sixth Report, White Paper, *Modernising Company Law*, HC 439, para 44.

[61] Davies, Gower and Davies *Principles of Modern Company Law* (Sweet & Maxwell, 7th edn, London) at p 326.

[62] Principle A.4

recommends that non-executives are partnered with an executive director in order to increase their understanding of the business and significant risk areas for the business.[63]

Non-executive directors continue to face a number of challenges including the problem of talent and succession, as identified above; establishing the appropriate balance between compliance and performance; and growth and globalisation.[64] Ultimately, as Davies suggests, 'executive management is unlikely easily to accept supervision by the non-executives, so that the non-executives may well have a battle on their hands to impose their will where there is a divergence of view'.[65]

11.5.7   The auditors and institutional investors

The role of the auditors and their independence are key issues, as was stated in the various Committee Reports, yet arguably these remain insufficiently clarified. Auditors have a statutory role of providing shareholders with independent and objective assurance on the reliability of the financial statements and of certain other information provided by the company but their role is limited insofar as they do not have an executive role in corporate governance. They may identify only the deficiencies of directors in this regard but they cannot make good those deficiencies. The independence of auditors is an important principle and the Hampel Committee acknowledged that audit firms have strong commercial reasons for maintaining independence but could be tempted to compromise on independence where they depend for a significant proportion of income on a single audit client.[66] The issue of non-audit work that has a strong potential to compromise the independence of auditors came under the spotlight again in the wake of scandals like the collapse of ENRON in the United States.[67]

The Government stated its intention to put in place a package of measures on auditor independence set out in detail in the CGAA Report[68] and the Auditing Practices Board is also to develop necessary standards on auditor independence. In summary the CGAA Report proposed that some non-audit services should not be provided if they would involve the audit firm performing management functions for its client or if it would mean auditing its own work. Auditors should also avoid providing valuations services that would involve a degree of subjectivity. The CGAA

---

[63]   See further ICSA, *Guidance on Board Effectiveness*, (2011).
[64]   See Ernst and Young Survey 'Fifty Under Fifty: Views From Chairs of the Future' (December 2005) available at www.ey.com/uk.
[65]   Davies, above note 60, at p 326.
[66]   For further details on auditors, see Chapter 14 and on independence, see, eg, Macgregor and Villiers 'Independence of Auditors: A Comparison between Spain and the UK' (1998) 3 *European Business Law Review* 318.
[67]   See the discussion in the *Report of the Co-ordinating Group on Audit and Accounting Issues* DTI and Treasury, URN 03/567 (January 2003).
[68]   Ibid.

Report also recommended stronger disclosure provisions relating to non-audit services as well as regular rotation of auditor partners. Many of these recommendations have been put into effect by professional bodies such as the ICAEW.[69] The Companies Act 2006 also contains provisions aimed at increasing auditors' independence. The company must disclose the name of the auditor and of the senior statutory auditor where the auditor is a firm, in audit reports, though confidentiality may be maintained in exceptional cases.[70] More recently the Department of Business, Innovation and Skills, in response to a European Commission Green paper, 'Audit Policy: Lessons from the Crisis',[71] made clear that it does not favour a ban on the provision of non-audit services to audit clients. The Auditing Practice Board has since revised its ethical standards for auditors and the Financial Reporting Council has updated its guidance on Audit Committees, and urges them to set and apply a formal policy specifying types of non-audit services for which use of the external auditor is pre-approved as a matter of policy, for which prior approval must be sought from the audit committee and from which the external auditor is excluded.[72]

The importance of institutional investors lies in the proportion of their shareholdings, in particular in listed companies where they own approximately 80% of the shares. The Corporate Governance Code requires institutional investors to give due weight to all relevant factors drawn to their attention when evaluating companies' governance arrangements and should bear in mind in particular the size and complexity of the company and the nature of the risks and challenges it faces. Another change brought about by the financial crisis was for the Financial Reporting Council to adopt the Institutional Shareholder Committee's *The Responsibilities of Institutional Shareholders and Agents – Statement of Principles*.[73] These were amended and became in 2010 the UK Stewardship Code. This Stewardship code sets out the responsibilities of institutional investors as shareholders and provides them with guidance for meeting those responsibilities. The seven key principles of the code include: institutional investors should publicly disclose their policy on how they will discharge their stewardship responsibilities; they should have a robust policy on managing conflicts of interest in relation to stewardship and this policy should be publicly disclosed; they should monitor their investee companies; they should establish clear guidelines on when and how they will escalate their activities as a method of

---

[69] See for example, *Additional Guidance on the Independence of Auditors* which supplements their *Guide to Professional Ethics*. See also the Guidance in the Combined Code on the Role of the Audit Committee, following recommendations made by the Smith Report *Report to the FRC* (January 2003) *Audit Committee Combined Code Guidance*.

[70] CA 2006, s 505.

[71] European Commission, COM(2010) 561 final, Brussels, 13.10.2010.

[72] See Financial Reporting Council, *Guidance on Audit Committees*, December 2010.

[73] Originally drawn up in 1991 and revised subsequently, the most recent revision being in 2007.

protecting and enhancing shareholder value; they should be willing to act collectively with other investors where appropriate; they should have a clear policy on voting and disclosure of voting activity; they should report periodically on their stewardship and voting activities.[74]

The evidence on institutional shareholder vigilance[75] has been mixed with earlier reports demonstrating a significant level of indifference.[76] However, other reports provide evidence of such investors acting to influence the behaviour of company boards.[77] In practice the low-key approach adopted has resulted in a poor level of shareholder activism. Thus, the 2002 White Paper noted failure of some institutional investors and fund managers to intervene actively to protect and enhance the value of the investment in cases where companies are being ineffectively, or even dishonestly, managed by their boards.[78] The Company Law Review also noted a number of problems connected with the role of institutional investors. Thus, for example, it highlighted concerns about failures in the vote execution process and lack of transparency in the voting system as well as possible conflicts of interest that might inhibit institutional investors in the performance of their governance role.[79]

The Treasury took up the issue of shareholder activism as part of its response to the Myners Report on Institutional Investment in the UK published in 2001. The Government endorsed the proposals of the Company Law Review for improving the effectiveness of the voting process in quoted companies, in particular by a requirement to disclose the results of polls at general meetings on their websites and in annual reports as well as a new right for members to require a scrutiny of any poll.[80] The Government appeared, in the White Paper, to be more reluctant to tackle the conflicts of interests issue through company law and said that it would set out its position fully at a later date.[81]

---

[74] See Financial Reporting Council, *UK Stewardship Code, 2010*. See also National Association of Pension Funds, *UK Stewardship Code: Guidance for Investors*, November 2010.

[75] See generally, Ferran *Company Law and Corporate Finance* (Oxford University Press, 1999) at pp 248–249 and 271–275.

[76] See, eg, Cosh and Hughes 'The Changing Anatomy of Corporate Control and the Market for Executives in the United Kingdom' (1997) 24 *Journal of Law and Society* 104.

[77] See e g Holland, *The Corporate Governance Role of Financial Institutions in their Investee Companies*, Research Report 46 (London, ACCA, 1995).

[78] White Paper *Modernising Company Law* Cm 5553–I, para 2.43 at p 24.

[79] Company Law Review *Modern Company Law for a Competitive Economy: Completing the Structure* paras 4.49–4.62 and *Final Report* Ch 6, paras 6.19–6.40.

[80] White Paper, para 2.45. See 13.14 et seq for the detail of the legal requirements now applicable.

[81] White Paper, paras 2.46–2.47.

The response to the Government's comments by the Trade and Industry Select Committee in the Sixth Report was still less enthusiastic about the role of institutional investors as corporate governance actors:[82]

> 'Ultimately, the primary concern of institutional investors is to maximise the returns on their investments. Whilst this may bring with it some pressure on companies hoping to attract funds from institutional investors to ensure that they have adequate corporate governance systems in place, there is a limit to the extent to which the institutional investors are willing or able to police the probity of the UK's companies.'

The Government, in contrast, said that it believes institutional investors have a key role to play in ensuring the good governance of the companies in which they invest and considers best practice guidelines to be the most efficient way of achieving higher levels of corporate behaviour. The Government added that it would monitor the situation and take action if necessary.[83] The Treasury conducted a review in 2004[84] and concluded that whilst voluntary action had been taken in applying the Myners Principles, progress was lagging in several key areas. Thus the Government proposed to revise the Principles to 'strengthen and amplify what they said in respect of these problem areas'. The National Association of Pension Funds (NAPF) agreed to undertake a further progress review in 2007. This review was launched in January 2007[85] and the final report was to be presented to the Government in autumn 2007. In the light of the evidence and recommendations made by NAPF, the Treasury consulted on the need for policy action on the role of institutional investors. Following the Consultation, the Treasury responded by stating that there would be a smaller number of simplified, higher-level principles and that these principles will be linked to a body of higher quality, more selective and accessible guidance and trustee tools. The Treasury also said that there will be greater industry ownership of the principles, guidance and trustee tools through the establishment of a joint Government-industry Investment Governance Group[86] and that there will be a more robust approach to disclosure and industry debate, within a voluntary 'comply or explain' approach.[87] In the wake of the recent

---

[82] Trade and Industry Select Committee *Sixth Report*, HC 439, para 120, at p 38.

[83] Trade and Industry Select Committee, Thirteenth Report, Government Response, para 23.

[84] *Myners Principles for institutional decision-making: review of progress* (HM Treasury, 2004).

[85] National Association of Pension Funds *Institutional Investment in the UK Six Years On* (22 January 2007) available at www.napf.co.uk.

[86] The Investment Governance Group is an industry led body with its membership comprised of experienced figures directly involved in the governance of investment decision-making. This group has a mandate to tackle the issues identified in the NAPF's proposals and endorsed by the consultation.

[87] HM Treasury *Updating the Myners principles: a response to consultation* (October 2008) available at www.hm-treasury.gov.uk/consult_myners_index.htm.

financial and banking crisis, the Treasury Select Committee exposed numerous weaknesses in monitoring by institutional investors in terms of their corporate governance role.[88]

The Tomorrow's Company research organisation recently published a document entitled *Tomorrow's Owners – Stewardship of Tomorrow's Company*[89] in which institutional investors are identified as universal owners who 'have a natural interest in sustainability because they either receive the benefits of companies managing their external impacts or suffer the negative consequences if they don't'.[90] In addition, with the proliferation of institutional holdings there has been a growth of the corporate governance standards globally, largely promulgated through collective action by institutions[91] such as the OECD with its *Principles of Corporate Governance* 1999, revised 2004, the UN – see its *Global Compact*, launched in 2000, and *Principles for Responsible Investment*, 2006. What is noticeable about these standards is that increasingly they focus on long-term considerations rather than on short-term success, reflecting the long-term investment horizons of the institutional shareholders whose investments are also highly diversified. It is clear that institutional investors have a role to play in corporate governance and, following the recent financial crisis, more will be expected of them. It is uncertain, however, whether they will meet such expectations adequately.[92] Perhaps more optimistically, the Investment Management Association recently reported a high level of adherence to the FRC's Stewardship Code. Their survey findings indicate that over 90% of major institutional investors vote all or the great majority of their shares in UK companies; that nearly two thirds of institutional investors publish their voting records; and almost all investors who responded to the survey had published a statement of adherence to the Code.[93]

11.6 THE NARROW FRAMEWORK OF CORPORATE GOVERNANCE IN THE UK

One limitation on corporate governance in the UK is the arguably narrow perspective that has been adopted. The Hampel Committee, accepting the Cadbury definition of corporate governance, also conceded that it is a restrictive definition that 'excludes many activities involved in managing a

---

[88] Treasury Select Committee 'Banking Crisis – Hedge Funds and Short-Selling', HC 144-iii, 27 January 2009.

[89] *Centre for Tomorrow's Company* (London, October 2008).

[90] Ibid, at 51.

[91] JP Hawley and AT Williams 'Shifting ground: emerging global corporate-governance standards and the rise of fiduciary capitalism' (2005) 37 Environment and Planning 1995, cited in *Tomorrow's Owners – Stewardship of tomorrow's company*, ibid.

[92] For a discussion of the role that institutional investors played in the financial crisis see Villiers 'Has the financial crisis revealed the concept of the 'responsible owner' to be a myth?' in MacNeil and O'Brien (eds) *The Future of Financial Regulation* (Hart, 2010).

[93] Investment Management Association, *Adherence to the FRC's Stewardship Code*, 2011.

company which may nevertheless be vital to the success of the business'.[94] Indeed, it is limited by the fact that it concentrates only on the internal structure of the company. This approach limits the goal of corporate governance to profit maximisation since it prioritises the interests of the shareholders. Thus the Hampel Committee, in its Report, stated that a board's first responsibility is to enhance the prosperity of the business over time.[95]

The marketplace requires companies to attract investment, not only in terms of purchase of shares but also in obtaining credit for the supply of goods and services as well as in terms of purchase of goods and services offered by companies. However, the participants in these aspects, creditors and suppliers, are normally viewed as outside the company and are not therefore in a position to bargain so effectively with regard to positional conflicts with the company or its managers. The UK's corporate governance system, framed by Cadbury's definition that concentrates on the internal processes, does not adequately address these needs.[96] Despite the Hampel Committee's claims that good governance ensures that constituencies (stakeholders) with a relevant interest in the company's business are fully taken into account,[97] the system adopted makes this objective difficult to achieve in practice. The Companies Act 1985 provided a classic example of the problem. Under s 309 of that Act directors were required to take the interests of the employees into account when performing their functions for the company, but since their duties are owed only to the company, the employees were not able to pursue their interests under that provision.[98] The current s 172 of the Companies Act 2006 is broader in its scope but is in practice unlikely to strengthen the position of employees or other stakeholders.[99]

Sheridan and Kendall[100] provide a potentially broader definition of corporate governance that recognises the relationship between the company and the community and goes beyond the notion that profit maximisation is the only relevant objective of the enterprise. They argue that good corporate governance consists of a 'system of structuring, operating and controlling a company' such as to achieve the following:[101]

> '(i)   Fulfil the long-term strategic goal of the owners, which, after survival
>   may consist of building shareholder value or establishing a dominant

---

[94] Hampel Report, at para 1.15.

[95] Ibid, at para 1.1.

[96] For a more detailed argument against this narrow approach see Dine and Villiers, noted above.

[97] Ibid, at para 1.3.

[98] See further below and **16.5** as to s 172 of the 2006 Act that has replaced s 309. See also Villiers 'Section 309 of the Companies Act 1985: Is it Time for a Reappraisal?' in Collins, Davies and Rideout *Legal Regulation of the Employment Relation* (Kluwer, 2000) at p 593.

[99] See below.

[100] *Corporate Governance* (Financial Times and Pitman, 1992).

[101] *Op cit*, pp 27–28.

market share or maintaining a technical lead in a chosen sphere, or something else, but will certainly not be the same for all organisations.

(ii) Consider and care for the interests of employees, past, present and future, which we take to comprise the whole life-cycle including planning future needs, recruitment, training, working environment, severance and retirement procedures, through to looking after pensioners.

(iii) Take account of the needs of the environment and the local community, both in terms of the physical effects of the company's operations on the surroundings and the economic and cultural interaction with the local population.

(iv) Work to maintain excellent relations with both customers and suppliers, in terms of such matters as quality of service provided, considerate ordering and account settlement procedures, etc.

(v) Maintain proper compliance with all the applicable legal and regulatory requirements under which the company is carrying out its activities.'

This approach is much broader than that of the Cadbury Committee and its successors since it addresses the 'external' as well as the 'internal' aspects of corporate activity. It suggests that the shareholders' profit-oriented interest is not the only relevant goal of the company but that other constituent interests are also relevant to the company.[102] Such other constituent interests must influence how that company is run as well as the control structure that seeks to ensure that the company's activities are managed properly. In order for these other groups to have an effective influence, mandatory rules will be required because they have less bargaining power, and market forces alone are unlikely to protect them adequately. Others have argued for a similarly broad approach to the question of corporate governance. John Parkinson's *Corporate Power and Responsibility*[103] is a most important contribution to the debate, informed as it is by detailed knowledge and discussion of current company law rules. The Royal Society of Arts' work on *Tomorrow's Company* is a further important development.[104] Obviously, fundamental changes to the current system and corporate law framework would be necessary to achieve the goals argued for by these contributions to the debate.

---

[102] For interesting arguments challenging the whole basis for the primacy of shareholders, see Ireland 'Corporate Governance, Shareholding and the Company: Towards a Less Degenerate Capitalism' (1996) 23 *Journal of Law and Society* 287; Grantham 'The Doctrinal Basis of the Right of Company Shareholders' [1998] CLJ 554; Ireland 'Company Law and the Myth of Shareholder Ownership' (1999) 62 MLR 32. A major focus of these writers is to dispel the notion that shareholders own the company which, they argue, is the basis for the law as traditionally understood. Perhaps, though, the law is based more on the concept of membership. It does not seem surprising that the traditional view of the law is that prima facie any association must be run primarily in the interests of its members. This is not to say that this is necessarily an appropriate view for today's company law.

[103] Oxford University Press, 1993. See also Parkinson, Gamble and Kelly (eds) *The Political Economy of the Company* (Hart, 2001).

[104] *Tomorrow's Company: The Role of Business in a Changing World* (1995). See also www.tomorrowscompany.com.

A key aspect of these contributions is the stakeholder concept.[105] This represents a view that company law should recognise interests beyond those of the shareholders. Its most critical, although not the only, application is in terms of the fundamental duty of company directors to act *bona fide* 'in the interests of the company'.[106] Among these 'stakeholder' interests might be included employees, creditors and consumers as well as the wider community. The work of the Royal Society of Arts' Centre for *Tomorrow's Company* seems to show that encouraging worker and community links and involvement produces not only a better and more productive operational environment, but in the long term more secure and 'successful' financial performance.

The Consultation Document issued in February 1999[107] discussed the interests which company law should serve, focusing on the actual changes to the law which different approaches would imply. A case was recognised for ensuring that company managers have regard, where appropriate, to the need to ensure productive relationships with a range of interested parties and have regard to the longer term. A distinction was drawn between the 'enlightened shareholder value' approach, which asserts that this can be achieved within present principles, but ensuring that directors pursue shareholders' interests in an enlightened and inclusive way, and the 'pluralist' approach, which asserts that co-operative and productive relationships will be optimised only where directors are permitted (or required) to balance shareholders' interests with those of others committed to the company. The pluralist approach would require changes to company law, especially to the fundamental duties of directors.

The subsequent Consultation Document from the Company Law Review Steering Group gave primary consideration to issues of corporate governance.[108] Following responses to the earlier consultation, the Steering Group provisionally concluded that 'the overall objective should be pluralist in the sense that companies should be run in a way which maximises overall competitiveness and wealth and welfare for all'. However, it continued by stating that 'the means which company law deploys for achieving this objective must take account of the realities and dynamics which operate in practice in the running of commercial enterprise. It should not be done at the expense of turning company directors from business decision makers into moral, political or economic arbiters, but by harnessing focused, comprehensive, competitive business decision making with robust, objective professional standards and

---

[105] See Kelly and Parkinson 'The conceptual foundations of the law: a pluralist approach' [1998] CfiLR 174. Cf Goldenberg 'Shareholders v Stakeholders: The Bogus Argument' (1998) 19 Co Law 34.

[106] Discussed in **16.5**.

[107] *Modern Company Law for a Competitive Economy: The Strategic Framework*, Ch 5.1, 'The scope of company law'.

[108] *Modern Company Law for a Competitive Economy: Developing the Framework*, March 2000, Chs 2–5.

flexible, but pertinent, accountability'.[109] To this end, the final proposal, supported in the White Paper, was for an 'inclusive' statement of directors' duties, which would continue to give primacy ultimately to the interests of shareholders as a whole, together with an 'inclusive' Operating and Financial Review for public and large private companies.

The Company Law Review and the White Paper, *Modernising Company Law*, have effectively endorsed a shareholder-centred approach but with an additional dimension which requires the directors to take account in good faith of all the material factors that might be relevant to the company's success.[110] This 'enlightened shareholder value' approach is intended to take into account the interests of other participants in the company whose interests materially affect the success of the company. In the new Companies Act 2006, s 172 requires a director to act in a way in which he considers would be most likely to promote the success of the company and in doing so have regard to a non-exhaustive list of matters.[111] Additionally the Act requires a director to exercise the care, skill and diligence of a reasonably diligent person with both the knowledge, skill and experience which may reasonably be expected of a director in his or her position; and any additional knowledge, skill and experience which the particular director has.[112]

It could be argued that the new statutory duty offers little to the non-shareholder interest groups. First, the directors are still required to act from a shareholder-centred perspective. Other participant interests remain secondary to the interests of the shareholders. Their interests are recognised but only where they are considered *by the directors* to be relevant to the company's overall success *for the benefits of its members as a whole*. Regard to other interests is purely at the discretion of the directors acting in good faith and they have only to take such interests into account. The directors are not compelled to give priority to such other interests. Again, only the company, via its shareholders, has capacity to enforce the duty thus leaving open to doubt the practical effectiveness of this 'enlightened' approach.[113]

The proposed Operating and Financial Review (OFR) continued this 'enlightened shareholder' stance.[114] The main objective of the proposed

---

[109] Ibid, para 2.21.

[110] See Company Law Review *Developing the Framework* (2000) paras 3.40, 3.45–3.48; *Completing the Structure* (2000) paras 3.13–3.14; *Final Report*, Vol I (2001) Annex C; and also *Modernising Company Law* (2002) Cm 5553–I.

[111] See Chapter 16.

[112] See Chapter 16.

[113] See, eg, Johnston 'After the OFR: Can Shareholder Value Still be Enlightened?' (2006) EBOLR 817. See also Andrew Keay, 'Tackling the Issue of the Corporate Objective: An Analysis of the United Kingdom's 'Enlightened Shareholder Value Approach' (2007) *Sydney Law Review* 23.

[114] See DTI *Draft Regulations on the Operating and Financial Review and Directors' Report, A Consultative Document* (May 2004).

OFR was to provide more qualitative and forward looking reporting, in addition to information that is quantitative, historical or concerns internal company affairs.

The dramatic abolition of the OFR requirements announced by the then Chancellor, Gordon Brown, in November 2005 was greeted with considerable dismay among the financial and business communities. Great amounts of effort by quoted companies had gone into preparations for the OFR which seemed to have been wasted if the OFR was no longer to be required. However, the EU Accounts Modernisation Directive meant that there continued to exist a requirement for all companies, other than small companies, to produce a business review.

The provisions in the Companies Act 2006[115] seek to streamline requirements for narrative reporting so that the requirements for quoted companies will be more closely aligned to those for unquoted companies. Thus, s 417 provides that unless the company is subject to the small companies' regime, the directors' report must contain a business review.[116]

The business review aims to balance the need to provide a narrative, forward-looking account of the company's business with the need to keep regulatory burdens to a minimum. Not only are all small companies exempt from the need to provide a business review, but also, in seeking this balance, the result is that the business review has a decidedly lighter regulatory touch than did the OFR proposals.

The purpose of the business review is stated in s 417 of the Companies Act 2006 to be 'to inform shareholders of the company and help them assess how the directors have performed their duty under s 172 (duty to promote the success of the company)'.[117]

The OFR legislation was to be accompanied by a prescriptive, mandatory Reporting Standard, published by the Accounting Standards Board. When that legislation was repealed, the Reporting Standard was converted to a Reporting Statement of Best Practice that will still provide guidance but which no longer mandates companies to present their business review with specific contents. Section 417(3), (4), (6) and (8) specifies the contents required by all companies required to produce a business review. Section 417(5) provides further prescription for quoted companies and this subsection highlights more obviously the connection with the s 172 duty.

Section 417(3) and (4) state that:

---

[115] Note the insertion of new clauses in the Companies Bill, following extensive consultations: DTI 'New Clauses to Keep Company Law Reform "Light Touch"' (3 May 2006) available at www.dti.gov.uk.

[116] Section 417(1).

[117] Section 417(2).

(3) The business review must contain—

(a)   a fair review of the company's business, and

(b)   a description of the principal risks and uncertainties facing the company.

(4) The review required is a balanced and comprehensive analysis of—

(a)   the development and performance of the company's business during the financial year, and

(b)   the position of the company's business at the end of that year,

consistent with the size and complexity of the business.

Section 417(6) specifies that the review:

'must, to the extent necessary for an understanding of the development, performance or position of the company's business, include—

(a)   analysis using financial key performance indicators, and

(b)   where appropriate, analysis using other key performance indicators, including information relating to environmental matters and employee matters.'

According to the subsection, 'key performance indicators' means factors by reference to which the development, performance or position of the company's business can be measured effectively.

Section 417(8) provides that the review must, where appropriate, include references to, and additional explanations of, amounts included in the company's annual accounts.

These provisions, as with the current business review requirements, underline the importance of financial information – insofar as financial key performance indicators are compulsory and the business review is required, where appropriate, to link itself to and provide further explanation of the annual accounts. The other key performance indicators, including environmental and employee matters need only be included 'where appropriate'. Inclusion of these matters will be for the directors to decide. Moreover, according to s 417(7) 'where a company qualifies as medium-sized in relation to a financial year (see ss 465 to 467), the directors' report for the year need not comply with the requirements of subsection (6) so far as they relate to non-financial information'.

The key performance indicators are essential to the contents of the business review. The Reporting Statement advises provision of a fairly detailed explanation of each KPI so that it can be understood by the members. Such information should include the definition and the method by which it is calculated, its purpose, the source of the underlying data, and where relevant, the assumptions explained, quantification or commentary on future targets, a reconciliation where information from the financial statements has been adjusted for inclusion in the report, the corresponding amount for the previous year, an explanation for any changes to KPIs or the calculation method used, including significant changes in the underlying accounting policies adopted in the financial statements.

The Companies Act 2006 specifies the information to be provided by quoted companies. Section 417(5) provides:

> 'In the case of a quoted company the business review must, to the extent necessary for an understanding of the development, performance or position of the company's business, include—
> (a)　the main trends and factors likely to affect the future development, performance and position of the company's business; and
> (b)　information about—
> > (i)　environmental matters (including the impact of the company's business on the environment),
> > (ii)　the company's employees, and
> > (iii)　social and community issues, including information about any policies of the company in relation to those matters and the effectiveness of those policies; and
> (c)　subject to subsection (11), information about persons with whom the company has contractual or other arrangements which are essential to the business of the company.
>
> If the review does not contain information of each kind mentioned in paragraphs (b)(i), (ii) and (iii) and (c), it must state which of those kinds of information it does not contain.'

Section 417(5) gives to quoted companies more specific direction on the contents to be included in the business review though they only have to provide such details to the extent that they consider is necessary for an understanding of the development, performance or position of the company's business. The information identified is closely linked to the matters that directors must consider in the duty to promote the success of the company in s 172 explained above. None of the specified matters to be included are in fact compulsory but if they are not covered the business review must state that fact. The subsection does not require an explanation why such matters are not covered but arguably the investors might expect an explanation if the business review is to be seen as a credible and worthwhile document. The subsection is arguably rather vague on the points it identifies for coverage and so what is to be included is left very open. So long as the information given can be considered to help in understanding the company's business development, performance or position then the directors may determine for themselves what information is provided. Such matters need only be included if necessary for an understanding of the business. The section gives no hint about what degree of understanding is needed or how directors should decide to what extent such matters are necessary to this understanding of the business.

The directors are given power to decide not to disclose information relating to matters under negotiation, approaching developments or persons with whom the business has a relationship if they consider that disclosure of such information would be seriously prejudicial to the company's interests or to the third person's and the public interests. Thus, according to s 417(10):

> 'Nothing in this section requires the disclosure of information about impending developments or matters in the course of negotiation if the disclosure would, in the opinion of the directors, be seriously prejudicial to the interests of the company.'

Section 417(11) states, in addition:

> 'Nothing in subsection (5)(c) requires the disclosure of information about a person if the disclosure would, in the opinion of the directors, be seriously prejudicial to that person and contrary to the public interest.'

Section 417(11) deals with the opposition expressed by a significant number of business organisations to the requirement to disclose information relating to suppliers. Not only did the Government try to provide reassurance by saying that it was only necessary to disclose information regarding significant relationships that would be likely to influence the performance of the company's business or its value, but also this exemption is designed to maintain safety of persons with whom the company has a relationship. The exemption only applies if it is also in the public interest not to disclose the information; it is not concerned with protecting the company's interests.

During June 2007 Margaret Hodge, the Minister for Industry and the Regions, reported in Parliament that, in response to a consultation on secondary legislation relating to the Companies Act 2006, she would draft a single set of accounting and reporting regulations for all companies other than small companies and that she would retain the disclosure requirements of Sch 7 of the Companies Act 1985 in respect of employment of disabled persons and in respect of employee involvement in company matters. New regulations entitled the Large and Medium-sized Companies and Groups (Accounts and Reports) Regulations 2008, which cover form and content of accounts, directors' report, and directors' remuneration report, came into force in April 2008.[118] Under these Regulations, the directors' report must include details about employment, training and advancement of disabled persons, and on the involvement of employees in the affairs, policy and performance of the company as well as on the company's policy and practice on the payment of creditors.

---

[118] However, the requirement for disclosure in para 4 of Sch 8, relating to consideration of conditions in company and group applies in relation to financial years beginning on or after 6 April 2009.

Initial responses to the business review were lukewarm. The Association of Chartered Certified Accountants, comparing it to the OFR, described the business review as a 'decidedly inferior reporting tool.'[119] Whilst business leaders were more welcoming, praising the Government's attempts to reduce the regulatory burden, environmentalists and other stakeholder representatives expressed disappointment. For example, Friends of the Earth was critical of the fact that the Government would not be re-instating the OFR – the only legislation requiring companies to report clearly on their environmental impacts. Friends of the Earth warned that the business review would fail to remedy companies' worst abuses of the environment both here and overseas:

> 'This is a very disappointing result. The Government is saying that when profits come into conflict with responsible behaviour, companies must put profit first. There is nothing here that will provide justice for the victims of corporate irresponsibility or guarantee high environmental standards for UK companies.'[120]

Whilst Friends of the Earth welcomed new reporting requirements that state companies must provide information on environmental matters including companies' environmental impacts and social and community issues and their policies on this, it considered that the absence of statutory reporting standards, 'meaning companies will be free to decide what information is included in their report', undermined this progress. It is probably fair to conclude that the business review is unlikely to draw a line under the issue of narrative reporting. In the words of Craig Bennett, the Senior Corporate Accountability Campaigner for Friends of the Earth:

> 'This is not the end of the story... Ninety per cent of the public support enforceable rules to ensure companies behave responsibly. This issue is not going to go away.'

One consultant group, Radley Yeldar, conducted a survey of narrative reporting content in 2007 from the FTSE 100. They noted that where reporting was to be commended was in respect to marketplace discussions (still improving), explanation of the business up front, strategic objectives, forward-looking information (on the up) and risk information being moved to the front. Where companies appear to be weak was with respect to: failure to link strategy to measurement, information on risk management, integrated corporate responsibility content, employee information and navigational pointers. The requirements in s 417 may well force companies to address some of those weaker areas of reporting practice.

---

[119] Allen Blewitt, Chief Executive of ACCA, in a letter to the *Financial Times*, 9 May 2006.

[120] Friends of the Earth, archived press release, 'Government drops OFR, and puts profit before environment' 3 May 2006, available at www.foe.co.uk/resource/press_releases/government_drops_ofr_and_p_03052006.html.

The Government indicated that it would monitor implementation of the business review legislation. Margaret Hodge stated that a review would be conducted two years after the Act commences to ensure the business review provisions do 'lead companies to provide meaningful and useful narrative reporting on issues relevant to the particular company'. She added that it 'would be open' to the Government to revert to the issue 'if the law does not work in the way we intend. We have the power in the Bill to add to the contents of the business review'.[121] The Government has a reserve power to amend the disclosure requirements if this appears to be necessary following the review.

The Coalition Government has set in motion a review of the narrative reporting requirements. In August 2010 the Department of Business Innovation and Skills published a consultation on the future of narrative reporting, in which it asked for views on: the value of narrative reporting, the business review and the possible return of the operating and financial review and the content of the directors' remuneration report. It asked whether a reporting standard would help to improve the quality of reporting and whether it would be more beneficial to limit the narrative report to a summary of the strategic issues with separate reports covering more detailed information. This consultation awaits a response from the government. At the international level the International Accounting Standards Board has published an IFRS Practice Statement on management commentary. This aims to provide a non-binding framework for the presentation of narrative reporting to accompany financial statements prepared in accordance with IFRS. The Practice Statement is not an IFRS but it provides a set of common principles with the aim of promoting comparability of management commentaries.

Numerous other issues have come to the fore during the last decade and especially since the financial crisis. These are likely to have a significant influence on the development of corporate governance in the UK. In particular, one potential culprit for the financial crisis was the problem of 'group think' and this has led to discussions about increasing diversity in the boardroom, given that in 2010 only 12.5% of FTSE 100 company directors and 7.8% of FTSE 250 company directors were women. The Coalition Agreement contained a pledge to 'look to promote gender equality on the boards of listed companies'.[122] Since then the Davies Report, published in February 2011, concluded that the informal networks influential in board appointments, the lack of transparency around selection criteria and the way in which executive search firms operate, were together considered to make up a significant barrier to women reaching boards. The Davies Report, stopping short of supporting the introduction of legislative gender quotas, recommended that all FTSE 350 companies should set out the percentage of women they aim to have on their boards and executive committees in 2013 and 2015, and FTSE

---

[121] See Margaret Hodge, Hansard, col 915, 18 October 2006.
[122] *The Coalition: Our Programme for Government*, May 2010, at 18.

100 boards should aim for 25% female representation, and that quoted companies should be required to disclose the proportion of women in senior positions and on the boards as well as the number of women employees in the whole organisation, and that the UK Corporate Governance Code should contain a provision requiring companies to establish a boardroom diversity policy that will be disclosed and progress in achieving the objectives also published annually. The Financial Reporting Council is consulting on how to make the necessary changes to the Code. Given developments in other European countries that have included the introduction of legislative quotas, and sentiments expressed in the European Commission on the slow pace of progress on equality between women and men across Europe this subject is likely to develop and it may well be the case that ultimately the UK will be forced to introduce more forceful measures for achieving greater female representation in company boardrooms.[123]

Another area of corporate governance which is likely to continue to develop is that of executive remuneration. Concern is widespread that there is little evidence of a link between remuneration, performance and shareholder value, and that not only is the independence of remuneration committees open to question but also they are increasingly shifting from longer term incentives to shorter term annual bonuses. An independent high pay commission has been established to conduct an inquiry into high pay and boardroom pay across the public and private sectors.[124] The Department of Business, Innovation and Skills is also due to consult on regulating executive pay, recognizing that regulation in place is not effective in preventing excessive pay or so-called 'rewards for failure'. It is likely that greater transparency will be demanded which reveals comparisons between the highest paid and average pay in companies.

11.7 In contrast to the position in the UK, the 'stakeholder' approach has for a long time influenced corporate governance developments more strongly in other countries, especially in some fellow European Union member states. The Peters Report in the Netherlands[125] opened by stating that 'companies and the enterprise connected therewith play an important role in society' and 'they must seek a good balance between the interests of the providers of risk capital (investors) and the other stakeholders'. In France, the Viénot Report[126] emphasised that the 'interests of the company may be understood as an overriding claim of the company as a separate economic agent, pursuing its own objectives which are distinct

---

[123] See Further C. Villiers 'Achieving Gender Equality in Company Boardrooms: Is it Time for legislative Quotas?' (2010) 30 *Legal Studies* 533, and see also European Commission, *Report on Progress on Equality between Women and Men in 2010: The gender balance in business leadership*, (Brussels, 2011).

[124] See High Pay Commission, *More for Less: what has happened to pay at the top and does it matter?* (Interim Report, May 2011).

[125] *Corporate Governance in the Netherlands: Forty Recommendations* (25 June 1997).

[126] *The Boards of Directors of Listed Companies in France*, Report of the 'Viénot Committee' (July 1995).

from those of shareholders, employees, creditors including the internal revenue authorities, suppliers and customers. It none the less represents the common interest of all these persons which is for the company to remain in business and prosper'. Under German law, a management board is required to run the company in the interests of the company as a whole. Shareholders are regarded as only a part of the differing groups of 'stakeholders'.[127]

The European Commission has highlighted the need for some harmonisation of roles relating to corporate governance.[128] The Commission took steps to ensure improvements in transparency with a requirement for listed companies to provide an annual corporate governance statement as well as introduction of minimum standards relating to the role and responsibilities of directors. In 2005 the European Commission published a Recommendation fostering an appropriate regime for the remuneration of directors of listed companies[129] and in 2005 it published a Recommendation on the role of non-executive or supervisory directors of listed companies and on the committees of the supervisory board.[130] The introduction of the European Company Statute,[131] whilst greatly compromised from its earlier versions, at least introduced the possibility of a variety of board structures across the European Union.

A Directive on Shareholder Rights was adopted in 2007[132] which introduced minimum standards to ensure that shareholders of companies whose shares are traded on a regulated market would have timely access to the relevant information ahead of the general meeting and simple means to vote at a distance, for example by abolishing obstacles to electronic voting and abolishing constraints on the eligibility and appointment of proxy holders.

The Commission published two reports in 2007 on how Member States apply the recommended standards on directors' remuneration and on independent non-executive directors.[133] The Commission found that there was widespread disclosure of remuneration, but some reluctance to involve shareholders fully in the decision over remuneration policy. The

---

[127] German law heavily influenced the draft Fifth EC Directive, with its proposals for compulsory employee representation, but this Directive has now been abandoned; see **2.3.10**.

[128] See, eg, European Commission Communication *Modernising Company Law and Enhancing Corporate Governance in the European Union – A Plan to Move Forward*, Com (2003) 284 final, 21.5.2003.

[129] OJ L385/55, 29.12.2004.

[130] OJ L52/51, 25.2.2005.

[131] See **2.5**.

[132] Directive 2007/36/EC of the European Parliament and of the Council of 11 July 2007 on the exercise of certain rights by shareholders in listed companies. This was due to be implemented by August 2009.

[133] See http://ec.europa.eu/internal_market/company/directors-remun/index_en.htm; http://ec.europa.eu/internal_market/company/independence/index_en.htm.

Commission's 2004 Recommendation on the role of non-executive or supervisory directors and on supervisory board committees[134] aimed at improving shareholders' control over executive management by reinforcing the presence of independent directors on boards and board committees. In its 2007 Report, the Commission found that a majority of Member States comply to a large extent with the recommendations, but some weaknesses remain. For example, in some Member States a former chief executive officer of a company may still become its chairman without any cooling-off period, thereby undermining the independence of non-executive supervision. Some Member States fail to recommend a sufficient number of independent board members in remuneration and audit committees.

In response to the financial crisis, the Commission published a new Recommendation to supplement its earlier Recommendations on directors' remuneration. The new Recommendation set out best practices for the design of an appropriate remuneration policy. It focused on certain aspects of the structure of directors' remuneration and the process of determining directors' remuneration, including shareholder supervision. The aim was for directors' remuneration to be clearly linked to performance and not to reward failure. The Recommendation provides that for the structure of directors' pay there should be a limit (two years maximum of fixed component of directors' pay) on severance pay (golden parachutes) and a ban on severance pay in case of failure. There should be a balance between fixed and variable pay and variable pay linked to predetermined and measurable performance criteria to strengthen the link between performance and pay. There should also be a balance between long- and short-term performance criteria of directors' remuneration, deferment of variable pay, a minimum vesting period for stock options and shares (at least three years) and retention of a proportion of shares until the end of employment. Companies should be allowed 'clawback' opportunities. In determining directors' remuneration, the Recommendation suggests that Member States extend certain disclosure requirements to improve shareholder oversight of remuneration policies and that they ensure that shareholders, in particular institutional investors, attend general meetings where appropriate and make considered use of their votes regarding directors' remuneration. Member States should provide that non-executives do not receive share options as part of their remuneration to avoid conflict of interests. The role and operation of the remuneration committee should also be strengthened through new principles on the composition of remuneration committees; the members of the remuneration committee should be present at the general meeting where the remuneration policy is discussed in order to provide explanations to shareholders; conflicts of interest by remuneration consultants should be avoided.[135]

---

[134] IP/04/1182.

[135] The Commission has also adopted a Recommendation on remuneration policy in the financial services sector (see IP/09/674).

The European Corporate Governance Forum also issued a public statement concerning the main principles that should govern the remuneration of executive directors.[136] The Forum considered that Member States should ensure that these principles are incorporated in national corporate governance codes and suggested that the Commission should issue a recommendation to this end. The Forum also advocated the introduction of a directive to ensure that listed companies disclose their remuneration policy and the pay of individual directors. The Forum highlighted adherence to best practices such as level of variable pay being reasonable in relation to total pay level and that it should be linked to factors that represent real growth of the company and real creation of wealth for the company and its shareholders. The Forum suggested that shares granted to executive directors under long-term incentive plans should vest only after a period during which performance conditions are met and that severance pay for executive directors should be restricted to two years of annual remuneration and should not be paid if the termination is for poor performance.

Work on corporate governance is likely to continue at the European Level and the establishment of the European Corporate Governance Forum in October 2004 has been significant in this context. Notably that Forum gave its formal endorsement to the 'comply or explain' principle as a better alternative to detailed regulation. Indeed, the better regulation principles are the widely favoured approach to company law and corporate governance across Europe as evidenced by the consultation on future priorities for the Action Plan.[137] Nevertheless, if corporate governance is to succeed in its present format (ie comply or explain) and be accepted across the EU as such, there has to be provision for 'shareholder engagement'. In this regard, DG Internal Market and Services commissioned a study on the monitoring and enforcement systems concerning Member States' corporate governance codes. The objectives of the study were to describe the relationship, in each of the Member States, between legislation and 'soft' law (codes) in corporate governance; to examine the existing monitoring and enforcement mechanisms in the Member States as far as corporate governance codes are concerned and to evaluate their effectiveness; to obtain an impression of the companies' perception of the codes; and to evaluate the perception of shareholders as to the quality of companies' disclosure on the application of corporate governance principles and of explanations given where the company declares not to comply, and of their reactions to disclosure perceived as insufficient.

Across Europe, Member States have developed codes and recommenda-tions for best practice in corporate governance.[138] The view of the

---

[136] See http://ec.europa.eu/internal_market/company/ecgforum/index_en.htm.

[137] See *Consultation and public hearing on future priorities for the Action Plan, Report*, at http://ec.europa.eu/internal_market/company/consultation/index_en.htm#060706.

[138] For an index of all such codes see the ecgi website at www.ecgi.org/**codes**/.

Commission and of industry participants is that there is no requirement for the creation of a uniform European corporate governance code since agreement for such a code would be difficult to reach and many of the principles within the various codes are similar anyway. The Commission does encourage greater coordination on the application of these different codes.[139] The European Corporate Governance Forum has also recommended rules for avoiding the potential problem of double application of two codes for companies with cross-border share listing.[140]

In April 2011 the European Commission published a Green paper on the European corporate governance framework in which it seeks views on issues relating to boards of directors, such as diversity, remuneration and time commitments, and with regard to shareholders, such as lack of appropriate shareholder engagement, short-termism of capital markets role of institutional investors, shareholder identification and minority shareholder protection, and on how to apply the comply or explain approach which underpins the corporate governance framework, and in this regard the quality of companies' corporate governance statements is open to question. The European Commission is asking how best to take account of the potential difficulty of applying some corporate governance practices across the range of types and sizes of companies. The Commission also asks if EU action is needed on corporate governance in unlisted companies.[141]

Increased globalisation of markets ensures that corporate governance issues have international significance. In this regard a number of international level institutions have also adopted codes and guidelines outlining corporate governance principles. The OECD Principles of Corporate Governance, established in 1999 and revised in 2004, are of particular relevance since these have inspired the creation of further codes and guidelines by industry participants. For example the International Corporate Governance Network bases its own Guidelines on the OECD's Principles. The United Nations has also been host to the Principles for Responsible Investment introduced in 2006 and signed by institutional investors. With such developments there is also an increasing emphasis on social and environmental impacts. For example the UN Principles for Responsible Investment demonstrate a commitment to sustainable development through the fulfilment by investors of their fiduciary duty. The stated aim is that 'applying the Principles should not only lead to better long-term financial returns but also a closer alignment between the objectives of institutional investors and those of society at large'. The Principles state a belief that environmental, social and governance issues

---

[139] For a discussion see Zornica Zafirova 'A uniform European Corporate Governance Code?' at http://papers.ssrn.com/sol3/papers.cfm?abstract_id=970085.

[140] See 'Statement from the European Corporate Governance Forum on Cross-border issues of Corporate Governance Codes' 24 March 2009, at http://ec.europa.eu/internal_market/company/ecgforum/index_en.htm.

[141] See European Commission, Green Paper, *The EU corporate governance framework*, Brussels, 5.4.2011, COM (2011) 164 final.

(ESG issues) can affect the performance of investment portfolios and that the Principles may better align investors with broader objectives of society. The participating investors commit, on this basis, where consistent with their fiduciary duties, to incorporating such issues into investment analysis and decision-making processes; to be active owners and incorporate ESG issues into their ownership policies and practices; to seek appropriate disclosure on ESG issues by the entities in which they invest; to promote acceptance and implementation of the principles within the investment industry; to work together to enhance their effectiveness in implementing the Principles; and each to report on their activities and progress towards implementing the Principles. More recently, the OECD revised its Guidelines for Multinational Enterprises which contain more detail on combating bribery, bribe solicitation and extortion and incorporate new recommendations on human rights abuse linked to business operations, products or services.[142] The political power of responsiveness to climate change and to poverty provides strong incentives for companies and investors to pursue ESG policies in their corporate and investment strategies.

---

[142] OECD, *Guidelines for Multinational Enterprises: Recommendations for Responsible Business Conduct in a Global Context* (May 2011).

CHAPTER 12

MEMBERSHIP OF A COMPANY

12.1 INTRODUCTION

A number of varied issues arise under the heading of membership of a company, including some which have already been considered in earlier chapters, particularly the effect of the contract of membership under s 33 of the Companies Act 2006[1] and the transfer of shares by members.[2] This chapter is concerned with the general characteristics of membership of a company, with the register of members which every company must maintain, with the obligation to file an annual return and with the disclosure of interests by substantial shareholders holding voting shares in public companies. Part 8 of the Companies Act 2006 restates and makes a number of amendments to the previous law regarding membership of a company, in particular with regard to restrictions on the right to inspect a company's register of members. Part 9 of the 2006 Act also contains important new provisions regarding the rights of beneficial owners of shares. It is, however, appropriate to introduce the chapter with a brief discussion of who in effect owns and/or controls companies; that is, who are the real members. This relates closely to some issues discussed below, not least the disclosure provisions described in **12.8** *et seq*.

It has long been recognised that the control of a company with a widely held shareholding[3] may in fact be obtained by the holding of considerably less than a majority of the company's issued voting shares. As long ago as 1932, Berle and Means[4] found that the ownership of shares in typical large United States corporations was so widely dispersed that no individual or group was in a position to control the corporation; instead management was in control. This was probably not quite so true of British public companies, where at least a substantial proportion were controlled by their owners.[5] In recent years, the crucial factor in the UK has been the level of institutional shareholding, which has risen

---

[1] [CA 1985, s 14.] See **5.20**.
[2] See Chapter 9.
[3] That is, the typical public company. Much of this discussion is irrelevant to the numerically much more common private company.
[4] *The Modern Corporation and Private Property*; see **11.2**.
[5] See Florence *Ownership, Control and Success of Large Companies* (1961) and *The Logic of British and American Industry* (Routledge and Kegan Paul, 3rd edn, 1972).

considerably while the level of individual shareholding has fallen dramatically.[6] Although the levels have fluctuated and currently domestic institutions such as pension funds and insurance companies hold about a quarter of UK shares, their dominance being challenged by newer owners such as hedge funds and sovereign wealth funds, it is still clear that they 'remain the giants of the investment community'.[7] The foreign investors who now own around 50% of UK shares are predominantly institutional shareholders.[8] This complicates the question of control even more. While institutions are likely, at least together, to be in a position to have actual control of a majority of voting power in many large public companies, the fact is that they very rarely appear to use this control openly.[9] Of course their decision will be crucial in a takeover battle and there is no doubt a considerable amount of behind-the-scenes lobbying and discussion, but it is probably safe to say that on the whole the management of large public companies is in *de facto* control.[10]

The law's response to these factors has generally been piecemeal.[11] It could well be argued that the problem of supervising management

---

[6]   The figures are not consistent but what can be said with confidence is that institutional investors are in the majority. The Hampel Report indicated figures as high as 80%: Hampel Committee *Combined Code on Corporate Governance and Report* (London, Gee, 1998) para 5.1, at p 40. Davies estimates around 60%: Davies *Gower and Davies' Principles of Modern Company Law* (Sweet & Maxwell, 7th edn, 2003) at p 338. The Myners Report suggested that in 1999 the institutional investors held 51.9%: Paul Myners *Institutional Investment in the UK: A Review* (HM Treasury, April 2001) at p 27. See also Farrar and Russell (1984) 5 Co Law 107. Note the attempts by the Conservative governments to reverse this trend, particularly in respect of nationalised industries which were 'privatised'.

[7]   Tomorrow's Company, *Tomorrow's Owners – Stewardship of tomorrow's company* (Centre for Tomorrow's Company, London, October 2008) at 49.

[8]   Chris Mallin 'Institutional shareholders: their role in the shaping of corporate governance' (2008) 1 International Journal of Corporate Governance 97 at 98.

[9]   Institutions often prefer to 'vote with their feet', i e sell out rather than interfere. Perhaps this is inevitable given that the principal institutions are pension funds and insurance companies which have duties to their beneficiaries and policyholders. See for information on the role of institutional shareholders: *The Responsibilities of Institutional Shareholders in the UK* (Institutional Shareholders' Committee, 1991, and revised further in 2005 and again in 2007). See also ABI, *Guidelines on Responsible Investment Disclosure*, January 2007, providing guidelines on social responsibility. See further Finch (1992) 55 MLR 179; Stapledon *Institutional Shareholders and Corporate Governance* (Clarendon, 1996); Myners *Developing a Winning Partnership – How Companies and Institutional Investors are Working Together* (DTI, URN 95/551).

[10] See also **13.1**. The law generally recognises this; see **15.15**. For a discussion of behind the scenes lobbying see Holland *Corporate Communications with Institutional Shareholders: Private Disclosures and Financial Reporting* (Edinburgh, Institute of Chartered Accountants of Scotland, 1997).

[11] Attempts can be made to bring together various themes in the case-law regarding control and the duties of institutional investors, but it seems clear that in this country there are still no coherent principles, and it is not certain that there is much likelihood of these being developed, however desirable that might be. There is no doubt, though, that the concept of control could be relevant at common law, especially regarding the former 'fraud on a minority' exception to the rule in *Foss v Harbottle*; see **18.2**. As far as statute is concerned, there are isolated provisions in the Companies Act 2006 which recognise

remains a critical and important one and that present practices leave much to be desired.[12] The role of institutional investors could be regarded as a vital one in this context and it has been discussed earlier at **11.5.7**.

12.2 THE MEMBERS OF A COMPANY

The law defines the members of a company in s 112 of the Companies Act 2006[13] as comprising, first, the subscribers to a company's memorandum, who are deemed to have agreed to become members and on registration must be entered on the register of members, and, secondly, any other person who agrees to become a member of a company and whose name is entered in the register of members. Section 112(1) confirms that subscribers are members even if the company fails to enter their names in the register of members. These two categories must be examined in more detail.

12.2.1 Subscribers to the memorandum

As s 112 provides, a subscriber to the memorandum is a member whether he has otherwise agreed to become so or not, and whether or not his name is entered in the register, and he is bound to take and pay for the number of shares written opposite his name,[14] although if he subsequently applies for and receives an allotment of an equal or greater number of shares this may be treated as a satisfaction of his obligation under the memorandum.[15] The directors have no power to release a subscriber from his obligation to take shares,[16] and he can therefore escape only by taking up and transferring the shares. He will, however, be relieved from liability if the whole of the shares are allotted to other persons, so that no shares are left in respect of which he can be registered.[17] When the liability is thus extinguished, it does not revive on a forfeiture of shares putting shares at the disposal of the directors.[18]

---

that control of a company can be obtained by a holding of less than 50% of voting shares, e g s 254(4) and there are the disclosure provisions in Part 22 described in detail in **12.8** *et seq*. The question of control of a company may also arise in other areas of law, especially in relation to taxation and employment law. Regarding the latter, see especially the discussion by McMullen [1986] *Law Society's Gazette* 2923

[12] See Chapter 11 above; Boyle (1978) 24 ICLQ 487.
[13] [CA 1985, s 22.]
[14] *Re Tyddyn Sheffrey Slate Co* (1869) 20 LT 105; *Drummond's Case* (1869) 4 Ch App 772; *Pell's Case* (1869) 5 Ch App 11. See further, Smith 'Subscribers: their status on incorporation' (1982) 3 Co Law 99 which, after an exhaustive examination of the cases, comes to the same conclusion as that expressed in the text. These cases are now confirmed by s 112(1).
[15] *Gilman's Case* (1886) 31 Ch D 420.
[16] *Re London and Provincial Consolidated Coal Co* (1877) 5 Ch D 525.
[17] *Tuffnell and Ponsonby's Case* (1885) 29 Ch D 421 (CA).
[18] *Mackley's Case* (1875) 1 Ch D 247.

12.2.2 Entry in the register of members

As stated above, the other persons who are members are those who have agreed to take shares *and* whose names are entered in the register. Even if they are not so entered, if there is complete agreement between them and the company, subject to the possibility of that agreement being rescinded by mutual consent,[19] they will not escape liability, for the register can be amended under s 125 while the company is a going concern,[20] or under s 148 of the Insolvency Act 1986 when the company is in liquidation.[21] However, the entry in the register of the name of a person does not make him a member if he never agreed to become one, and his name can be removed in the same way. It is possible for the court to make an order for removing his name retrospectively in order to free him from liability as a contributory, if that name has remained on the register when it should have been removed.[22]

A corporation may be a member if authorised by its constitution to hold shares,[23] but an English partnership should not be entered in the firm name, as the firm is not a 'person', and the names of the individual holders of the shares must be entered in the register.[24] If, however, the firm name is in fact entered with the consent of the partners, they become liable as members.[25] A Scottish firm is a 'person' and may be entered in its firm name.[26]

The simplest and most usual form of agreement to become a member is an application for and an allotment of shares.[27] But an agreement may be made in other ways.[28] For instance, it may be part of the preliminary contract with the vendor that he shall take shares; persons may by underwriting letters bind themselves to take any shares not subscribed for by the public; or there may be contracts to take shares which are not in writing, for a person may agree with the company by word of mouth, or even by conduct, to become a member. An agreement for value to take up shares in a company if called upon is enforceable notwithstanding the

---

19   *Nicol's Case* (1885) 29 Ch D 421, at 444, per Bowen LJ (CA).

20   See **12.5.3**.

21   *Winstone's Case* (1879) 12 Ch D 239; cf *Portal v Emmens* (1877) 1 CPD 664 (CA).

22   *Nation's Case* (1866) 3 Eq 77; cf *Re Sussex Brick Co* [1904] 1 Ch 598 (CA).

23   *Bath's Case* (1878) 8 Ch D 334; *Re Barned's Banking Co, ex parte Contract Corporation* (1867) 3 Ch App 105.

24   A purported transfer to a firm in its firm name may be rejected: *Re Vagliano Anthracite Collieries* [1910] WN 187.

25   *Weikersheim's Case* (1873) 8 Ch App 831.

26   The same will apply to a limited liability partnership.

27   This is dealt with at **7.7**.

28   See s 112(2) and *Re Nuneaton Borough Association Football Club* [1989] BCLC 454, where the Court of Appeal held that the phrase 'agrees to become a member' in (now) s 112(2) is satisfied where someone assents to become a member. It does not require that there be a binding contract between the person and the company. Thus, where a person is entered on the register of members with his consent, he is a member of the company.

death of the person making the contract.[29] 'A formal agreement is not necessary ... If the substance of an agreement is made out the form is not material.'[30] Thus, if a person who has not previously agreed to take shares knows that they have been allotted to him, and afterwards acts as a member of the company (for instance, by attending meetings, giving proxies, or selling or attempting to sell some of the shares), he will be held to have accepted the allotment and to be a member in respect of the shares. Or a person accepting the office of director when the articles make it a condition of his office that he shall take shares from the company may be held to have agreed to become a member.

Where the articles specify a procedure for admission to membership this must be complied with. Where, for example, admission to membership of a company required a decision of the company's council, but where in practice the procedure followed was a virtual automatic admission on an administrative basis of any person who applied for membership, this does not comply with the company's articles.[31]

A statement in the prospectus that directors or others have agreed to take shares will not alone be sufficient to render them liable.[32]

An agreement to take shares may be made through an agent.[33] The authority of the agent must be considered under the ordinary doctrines of principal and agent.

If an agreement to take shares (not arising merely by subscribing to the memorandum) is brought about by misrepresentation, made either by the company or its agents, the member can, before a winding-up, obtain rescission of the contract, repayment of what he has paid, and removal of his name from the register. However, a contract procured by misrepresentation being only voidable and not void, if the company has gone into liquidation and other interests have come into existence, it is too late to set the contract aside, and the person remains a member. If, however, there was in fact no contract to take shares, the supposed member can at any time have his name removed from the register, for he was never really a member.[34]

---

[29] *William Beardmore v Park's Executrix 1927 SLT 143*. See also *Warner Engineering Co v Brennan* (1913) 30 TLR 191, at 196.

[30] Per James LJ in *Risto's Case* (1877) Ch D 782.

[31] *POW Services Ltd v Clare* [1995] 2 BCLC 435.

[32] *Re Moore Bros & Co* [1899] 1 Ch 627; *Todd v Miller* 1910 SC 869.

[33] *Levita's Case* (1870) 5 Ch App, 489; *Fraser's Case* (1871) 24 LT 746; *Barnett's Case* (1864) 4 De GJ & S 416. See further, *Gore-Browne on Companies* (Jordans, 45th edn, loose-leaf) at 10 [4A].

[34] *Oakes v Turquand* (1867) LR 2 HL 325; *Alabaster's Case* (1869) 7 Eq 273.

12.3　THE TERMINATION OF MEMBERSHIP

A person ceases to be a member of a company upon a transfer of his shares being made and the name of the transferee being entered in the register of members,[35] but he remains liable to a limited extent in the event of a liquidation occurring within one year after the transfer. On the death of a shareholder his membership, of course, ceases, but his estate remains entitled to the benefits and subject to the burdens arising from his membership until some other person is entered in the register in respect of his shares. An executor or administrator, however, does not become a member unless he consents to be treated as such and to be entered in the register:[36] subject to the provisions of the articles, he is entitled, if he desires, to have his name entered in the register.[37] A person may also cease to be a member by a surrender or forfeiture of his shares properly made; and in the case of unlimited companies the articles may provide for a person ceasing to be a member in any manner which may be agreed, for in such cases the company has power to reduce its capital without reference to the court.[38] Thus in the case of mutual ship insurance companies, it is often provided that a person is a member only so long as he has ships insured in the company. It would seem, however, that in a company limited by shares a person cannot cease to be a member in any manner which would reduce the capital of the company other than in the ways referred to above. Therefore, as a company cannot purchase its own shares, except in the ways provided by Chapter 1 of Part 18 of the Companies Act 2006,[39] a transfer purporting to be made to the company will not relieve the transferor from liability.[40]

The fully paid shares of a company can be bequeathed or transferred to a nominee of the company.[41] The shares of a company can also be held on trust for it.[42]

The representatives of a deceased or bankrupt member are entitled to receive on behalf of the estate any dividends, bonuses, or benefits attaching to the shares, and are liable to contribute in respect of the estate in their hands and to be put on the list as representative contributories (see s 81 of the Insolvency Act 1986), but are not themselves members

---

[35]　The rights and liabilities of the transferor and transferee of shares, both *inter se* and in relation to the company, are discussed in Chapter 9.

[36]　*Bowling and Welby's Contract* [1895] 1 Ch 663, at 670 (CA).

[37]　*Scott v Frank F Scott (London)* [1940] Ch 794. The executor can (subject to the provisions of the articles of association) insist on being entered as a member in his own right: *Re T H Saunders & Co* [1908] 1 Ch 415.

[38]　See *Re Borough Commercial and Building Society* [1893] 2 Ch 242.

[39]　See **7.16** *et seq.* As to reduction of capital, see **8.14**.

[40]　*Trevor v Whitworth* (1877) 12 App Cas 409 (HL).

[41]　See **7.16**.

[42]　*Re Castiglione's Will Trusts* [1958] Ch 549; *Kirby v Wilkins* [1929] 2 Ch 444.

unless they take the shares into their own names.[43] Until they do this, however, they are not entitled to receive notices from the company,[44] unless the articles expressly so direct.

A shareholder who is bankrupt may continue to use his right to vote at shareholders' meetings while his name remains on the register, but he is obliged to do so in accordance with the instructions of his trustee in bankruptcy.[45] Such a shareholder may also bring a minority shareholders' action.[46]

The company cannot refuse to enter executors in the register or insist on inserting a notice that they hold in a representative capacity unless the articles contain some authority to do so.[47] The company must also enter the names in the order desired by the executors – a matter which often affects the right to vote and receive notices. Moreover, where articles allowed only the person first named upon the register to vote, as such person might be unable to attend meetings, the court, with a view to protecting the voting rights of the joint holders, ordered the company to enter the names in its register so that one name came first in respect of some of the shares and another name came first in respect of other of the shares.[48]

12.4 MINORS AS MEMBERS

The following refers to persons domiciled in England who are 'minors' in English law in reference to their membership of a company. The Scots law in relation to capacity is now contained in the Age of Legal Capacity (Scotland) Act 1991.

A minor[49] may become a member of a company and hold shares either by subscribing to the memorandum of association[50] or by taking a transfer of shares,[51] but the company has power to refuse to accept a minor as a shareholder or transferee of shares,[52] and should always do so in any case

---

43 *James v Buena Ventura Syndicate* [1896] 1 Ch 456 (CA); *New Zealand Gold Extraction Co v Peacock* [1894] 1 QB 622 (CA); cf *Bowling and Welby's Contract* [1895] 1 Ch 633.
44 *Allen v Gold Reefs of West Africa* [1900] 1 Ch 656 (CA).
45 *Morgan v Gray* [1953] Ch 83.
46 *Birch v Sullivan* [1957] 1 WLR 1247.
47 *Re TH Saunders & Co* [1908] 1 Ch 415; *Scott v Frank F Scott (London)* [1940] Ch 794.
48 *Burns v Siemens Brothers Dynamo Works* [1919] 1 Ch 225; see also *Re Hobson, Houghton & Co* [1929] 1 Ch 300.
49 At common law the age of majority was 21. By the Family Law Reform Act 1969, s 1, the age of majority was reduced to 18 as from 1 January 1970. Section 12 of that Act authorises the use of the term 'minor' to describe those not of full age in place of the term 'infant' previously used.
50 *Re Laxon & Co (No 2)* [1892] 3 Ch 555; *Re Nassau Phosphate Co* (1876) 2 Ch D 610.
51 *Lumsden's Case* (1868) 3 Ch App 31.
52 *Symon's Case* (1970) 5 Ch App 298; *Castello's Case* (1869) 8 Eq 504.

where a liability is attached to the shares, for the minor can, on or before attaining his majority, repudiate the shares if they are then burdensome.[53]

12.5   THE REGISTER OF MEMBERS

Every company[54] is required to keep a register of its members and s 113 of the Companies Act 2006[55] prescribes that the following particulars must be entered therein:

(1)   the names and addresses of the members, and in the case of a company having a share capital a statement of the shares held by each member distinguishing each share by its number so long as the share has a number,[56] and, where the company has more than one class of issued shares, by its class, and of the amount paid or agreed to be considered as paid on the shares of each member;[57]

(2)   the date at which each person was entered in the register as a member; and

(3)   the date at which any person ceased to be a member.

In the case of a private company limited by shares or by guarantee, if the number of members falls to one, on that event occurring a statement that the company has only one member (and the date on which this happened) must be entered into the register of members.[58]

Section 113(5) requires that for the purposes of the register, joint holders of a share fall to be treated as a single member with a single address to be shown against their entry, although all their names are to be stated in the register. It is the right of joint holders to determine in what order their names shall be entered, a matter which will under most articles affect the right of attending meetings and voting.[59] An article declaring that only the first named shall be entitled to attend and vote will not be so construed as to prevent shareholders from fairly and reasonably exercising

---

[53]   *Dublin and Wicklowe Rly Co v Black* (1852) 8 Ex 181; *Ebbett's Case* (1870) 5 Ch App 302; *Re Laxon & Co (No 2)* [1892] 3 Ch 555. See further as to the legal position of minors who become members by allotment or transfer, *Gore-Browne on Companies* (Jordans, 45th edn, loose-leaf), 10 [9].

[54]   This does not apply to companies whose shares are traded on CREST (see **9.3.3**), but equivalent information will be maintained in the operator and the issuer registers of members required by the Uncertificated Securities Regulations 2001, SI 2001/3755, reg 20 and Sch 4.

[55]   [CA 1985, s 352.]

[56]   As to when shares have to be numbered, see s 543.

[57]   As to the entries to be made on the register in relation to share warrants, see s 122. See also **9.12**. As to when shares have been converted into stock, see s 113(4).

[58]   Section 123 [CA 1985, s 352A.]

[59]   *Re TH Saunders & Co* [1908] 1 Ch 415; see also s 286 of the Companies Act 2006, replacing old Table A, art 55.

their powers as members of the company. Accordingly, where shares were registered in the joint names of two trustees, and the first-named holder might not be able to attend meetings and the second-named holder could neither vote nor be appointed a proxy for a poll, he court rectified the register and directed the company to have the names of the holders entered as to some of such shares in one order and as to other of such shares in the reverse order.[60]

Under s 121 of the Companies Act 2006, an entry relating to a former member of the company may be removed from the register after the expiration of 10 years from the date on which he ceased to be a member. This section replaced s 352(7) of the CA 1985, under which the time-limit was 20 years, with effect from 6 April 2008.[61] The power conferred by s 121 is exercisable on and after that date, whenever the period of 10 years expired, but a copy of any details that were included in the register immediately before that date and that are removed under the power must be retained by the company until 6 April 2018 or, if earlier, 20 years after the member concerned ceased to be a member.[62] Liability incurred by a company, from the making or the deletion of an entry in the register of members or from a failure to make or delete an entry, is not enforceable more than 10 years after the date on which the entry was made or deleted or, as the case may be, the failure first occurred. This is without prejudice to any lesser period of limitation.[63]This limit applies to causes of action arising on or after 6 April 2008. As regards causes of action arising before that date the limit is 10 years from 6 April 2008 or 20 years from when the cause of action arose, whichever expires first.[64]

By s 114,[65] the register is to be kept at the registered office of the company, or at any other place where the company is registered.

Notice is to be sent to the registrar of the place where the register of members is kept and of any change in that place. Such notice need not, however, be given where the register has, at all times during its existence or since 1 July 1948, been kept at the company's registered office.[66]

---

[60] *Burns v Siemens Brothers Dynamo Works* [1919] 1 Ch 225; see also *Re Hobson, Houghton Co* [1929] 1 Ch 300.

[61] Companies Act 2006 (Commencement No 5, Transitional Provisions and Savings) Order 2007, SI 2007/3495, art 3(1).

[62] Ibid, Sch 4, para 2, as amended by the Companies Act 2006 (Commencement No 6, Savings and Commencement Nos 3 and 5 (Amendment) Order 2008, SI 2008/674, Sch 3, para 6(2).

[63] Companies Act 2006, s 128, replacing, with effect from 6 April 2008, Companies Act 1985, s 352(7), under which the limitation period was 20 years: the Companies Act 2006 (Commencement No 5, Transitional Provisions and Savings) Order 2007, SI 2007/3495, art 3(1).

[64] Companies Act 2006 (Commencement No 5, Transitional Provisions and Savings) Order 2007, SI 2007/3495, Sch 4, para 3.

[65] [CA 1985, s 353.]

[66] As to when an index to the register must be kept, see s 115 [CA 1985, s 354].

There are special provisions in s 129 of the Companies Act 2006[67] relating to 'overseas branch registers'. These allow the keeping in a particular country or territory of a register of members resident in that country or territory by a company with a share capital transacting business there in accordance with its objects.[68]

12.5.1 The register, equitable interests and notice

The register of members is *prima facie* (but not conclusive) evidence of any matters directed or authorised to be inserted therein.[69] By s 126,[70] it is provided that no notice of any trust shall be entered on the register or be receivable by the registrar in the case of companies registered in England, Wales or Northern Ireland,[71] and the company may not enter particulars of a lien it may claim to have on the shares.[72] 'It seems to me extremely important', said Lord Coleridge in the Court of Appeal, 'not to throw any doubt on the principle that companies have nothing whatever to do with the relation between trustees and their *cestuis que trust* in respect of the shares of the company'.[73] But the court will intervene to protect equitable rights by injunction if application is made before a transfer is complete.[74]

The rule does not mean that the company, with knowledge of the rights of other people, can make advances to the registered holder on the security of the shares, ignoring the rights of which it has knowledge, for the company is not relieved from the obligation of giving effect to equitable rights of which it in fact has notice: eg its own lien will not take precedence of charges prior in date of which it has notice at the time of making the advance which gives rise to the lien.[75] Nor can it enforce its

---

[67] [CA 1985, s 362 and Sch 14.]

[68] For more detail, see *Gore-Browne on Companies* (Jordans, 45th edn, loose-leaf) at 10 [11]. The countries and territories in question are any part of Her Majesty's Dominions outside the UK, the Channel Islands and the Isle of Man and any in the list in s 129(6).

[69] Section 127 [CA 1985, s 361].

[70] [CA 1985, s 360.]

[71] *Société Générale v Tramways Union Co* (1884) 14 QBD 424 (CA), affirmed *sub nom Société Générale de Paris v Walker* (1885) 11 App Cas 20 (HL), where it was held that the company is not liable, though the directors may be, for ignoring notices of trust. See also *Simpson v Molson's Bank* [1895] AC 270 (PC). Scottish companies may recognise trusts (although this is excluded for most purposes by the articles).

[72] *Re W Key & Son* [1902] 1 Ch 467. A person who has only a beneficial interest in shares cannot exercise the rights of a member, eg to have proposals included in a circular sent to members prior to a meeting: *Verdun v Toronto-Dominion Bank* (1996) 139 DLR (4th) 415, SC (Can).

[73] *Re Perkins* (1890) 24 QBD 613 (CA). In a case, however, where it was alleged that an irregular disposition of the company's property by the directors had been authorised or approved by all the shareholders, the Privy Council seem to have thought it material to consider whether the shareholders were the beneficial owners of the shares; see *EBM v Dominion Bank* [1937] 3 All ER 555 (PC).

[74] *Binney v Ince Hall Coal Co* (1866) 35 LJ Ch 363.

[75] *Bradford Banking Co v Henry Briggs & Co* (1886) 12 AC 29 (HL); *Rearden v Provincial Bank of Ireland* [1896] 1 Ir R 532 (CA); *Binney v Ince Hall Coal Co* (1866) 35 LJ Ch 363.

own lien against the holder upon shares held by trustees if at the time of making the advance it knew that the shares were held in trust.[76] Where a company had notice of a transfer to trustees for creditors or others, it was held that it was justified in refusing to give effect to a subsequent transfer by the debtor to a purchaser for value.[77] When a company upon receiving a transfer has notice of an adverse claim, it usually gives notice to the claimant that it will register the transfer unless he takes proceedings within a specified time. But a company is not concerned to inquire whether trustees who are registered as shareholders are acting within their powers in dealing with the shares,[78] and can enforce its own rights against the actual holders of shares irrespective of the rights of the persons for whom they are trustees.[79] Nor does priority in giving notice to the company affect the priority of two charges one against another.[80]

If an official of the company, under a mistake, strikes out the name of a member properly registered, this is a nullity and must be disregarded, and if disputes arise as to the propriety of the act the court will, on being satisfied that a mistake was made, order rectification of the register so as to 'restore and retain' the name of the person entitled to the shares.[81]

The register of members gives particulars of the shares as they were originally issued, with the changes from time to time made. A register of transfers which is usually kept, though not specifically required by the Companies Act 2006, gives particulars of the changes which take place in the ownership of shares.

A company not entering in the register the name of a person entitled to be put therein is liable to pay him damages for any loss he may have sustained by its neglect or refusal to do its duty.[82] By s 128(1),[83] any liability incurred by a company from the making or deletion of any entry in its register of members or from a failure to make or delete any such entry, is not enforceable more than 10 years after the date on which the

---

[76] *Mackereth v Wigan Coal and Iron Co* [1916] 2 Ch 293.
[77] *Peat v Clayton* [1906] 1 Ch 659; *Roots v Williamson* (1888) 38 Ch D 485; *Moore v North-Western Bank* [1891] 2 Ch 599.
[78] *Simpson v Molson's Bank* [1895] AC 270 (PC).
[79] *London and Brazilian Bank v Brocklebank* (1892) 21 Ch D 302 (CA). But it would seem that if the company had notice of the trust before the debt to itself was incurred, the doctrine of *Bradford Banking Co v Henry Briggs & Co* (1886) 12 AC 29 would apply, and the company would be postponed.
[80] *Société Générale de Paris v Walker* (1886) 11 AC 20 (HL).
[81] *Re Indo-China Steam Navigation Co* [1917] 2 Ch 100. If the company loses its register, it should apply to the court before compiling a new one: *Re Data Express Ltd* (1987) *The Times*, 27 April.
[82] Section 125(2), replacing s 359(2). See *Re Ottos Kopje Diamond Mines* [1893] 1 Ch 618 (CA); *Tomkinson v Balkis Consolidated Co* [1893] AC 397 (HL).
[83] [CA 1985, s 352(7).]

entry was made or deleted or, in the case of any such failure, the failure first occurred. This provision is 'without prejudice to any lesser period of limitation'.[84]

Section 121[85] allows any entry relating to a *former* member of the company to be removed from the register of members after the expiration of 10 years from the date on which he ceased to be a member.

12.5.2   Inspection and copies of the register

The register of members, and the index (where required to be kept) must be open to the inspection of any member without charge and of any other person on payment of a fee as may be prescribed.[86] Section 116 also specifies that any person is entitled to a copy of the register of members or any part of it on payment of the relevant fee. Under s 116(3) and (4) any person seeking to inspect or to be provided with a copy of the register of members must provide their names and addresses, the purpose for which the information is to be used and similar information relating to a person on whose behalf the information is sought. If the information is to be disclosed to others that must be stated as well as the purpose for which that person will use the information. When a company receives a request under s 116 it must within 5 working days either comply with the request or apply to the court. Section 117 gives to the court powers to direct the company not to comply with a request if the court is satisfied that the inspection or copy is not sought for a proper purpose. The court shall direct the company not to comply and not to comply with any similar requests and may further order that the company's costs on the application be paid in whole or in part by the person who made the request even if he is not party to the application. If the court does not direct the company not to comply with the request, the company must comply with the request immediately upon the court giving its decision or the proceedings being discontinued. The Act does not provide any guidance on what would not be a proper purpose. The Company Law Review Steering Group (CLRSG) did recommend in its *Final Report* that 'use of information in a company's register of members be restricted to purposes relevant to either the holding of interests recorded in the register, or the exercise of rights attached to them, and to other purposes approved by the company'.[87] However, the view of the CLRSG does not provide a definitive guide to the interpretation of what is a 'proper

---

[84]   Section 128(2). Section 128 reduced the time-limit for claims from 20 years to 10 years, following a recommendation in the Company Law Review Steering Group *Final Report* URN 01/943 (July 2001) at para 11.40.

[85]   [CA 1985, s 352(6).]

[86]   Section 116 [CA 1985 ss 356 and 723A and the Companies (Inspection and Copying of Registers, Indices and Documents) Regulations 1991, SI 1991/1998]. The penalties for failing to comply with s 116 are imposed upon the company and 'every officer in default' (s 118).

[87]   CLRSG *Final Report* URN 01/943 (July 2001) at para 11.44.

purpose'.[88] Section 118 gives to the court power to compel an immediate inspection or direct that the copy required be sent to the person requesting it in the event of a refusal or default made otherwise than in accordance with an order of the court.

If a request under s 116 is refused, otherwise than in accordance with an order of the court, the company and every officer who is in default is liable to a fine.[89] The court is given power where inspection is refused or copies of the register are not supplied to order an immediate inspection or direct copies required to be sent to the persons requiring them.[90] As a general rule the court will make a mandatory order to give effect to the right to be supplied with a copy of the register on request, but 'it is not a matter of unqualified right'.[91] It was decided under the provision replaced by s 118(3) that there may be special circumstances that lead the court to refuse to make an order. The scope of the residual discretion to refuse an order may be narrow, but it is not non-existent. Thus this may be the case where it would be pointless to make the order because the request has been complied with after the application under s 118(3) was issued but before it was heard, or where the request was physically impossible to comply with because the register had been destroyed or lost. There are other circumstances where the court can make an order on qualified terms. It can cater both for the applicant's wish to gain access to the register for the purpose of legitimately communicating with members, as well as the company's proper and understandable concerns about the detrimental effects of an unqualified order for the disclosure of the names and addresses of the members.[92] These factors could clearly still be relevant, although it is thought that they are more likely now to be raised when the company makes an application under s 117, as described above.

Section 120 of the Companies Act 2006 introduced a further reform of the law governing inspections of the register. In accordance with a recommendation of the CLRSG,[93] it requires a company to advise anyone exercising their right of inspection or right to demand a copy of the register of the most recent date (if any) on which alterations were made and there were no further alterations to be made and to advise anyone inspecting the index whether there is any alteration to the register not reflected in the index. Failure can lead to a criminal penalty on the company and any officer in default.

---

[88] Further useful but unofficial guidance has been issued by the Institute of Chartered Secretaries and Administrators and is described in Gore-Browne on Companies, 10A[10].

[89] Companies Act 2006, s 118(1) and (2).

[90] Companies Act 2006, s 118(3).

[91] *Armstrong v Sheppard & Short Ltd* [1959] 2 QB 384 at 396. The court is not deprived of its discretion because of the criminal penalties in s 118(2).

[92] *Pelling v Families Need Fathers Ltd* [2002] 1 BCLC 645 at 652–653.

[93] *Final Report*, para 11.43.

The right to inspect ceases upon the commencement of a winding up,[94] and if inspection is required after liquidation, an order of the court must be obtained under s 155 of the Insolvency Act 1986.[95] Such an order entitles the party to inspect and take copies himself. He need not pay the liquidator a fee for having them made.[96]

12.5.3 Rectification of the register

It is of the greatest importance that the register of members should be promptly and accurately entered up, as delay or inaccuracy may lead to an expensive lawsuit. Section 125[97] prescribes that if the name of any person is, without sufficient cause, entered in or omitted from the register of members of any company, or if default is made or unnecessary delay takes place in entering in the register the fact of any person having ceased to be a member, the person aggrieved, or any member of the company, or the company itself, may apply for the order of the court[98] that the register be rectified, and the court may 'either refuse the application or may order rectification of the register and payment by the company of any damages sustained by any party aggrieved'.[99] Such an order must be notified to the registrar.[100] Where the issue is not rectification but damages, the court cannot give damages upon a motion made under s 125, the proper course being for the person aggrieved to bring an action.[101] The court has power to determine any question relating to the title of any party to the application.[102] If no dispute arises as to the rights of the person who seeks to have his name entered in or removed from the register, this section presents no difficulty. But as the inclusion or exclusion of a person's name in or from the register determines his right to the benefit of the shares or his liability to pay calls upon them, a number of cases have arisen under the similar section in the earlier Acts.

The court will interfere and rectify the register, upon a motion made under s 125, where the error is due to the neglect or default of the company, and generally when the question arises between the company and a member or alleged member whether his name is properly included or excluded.[103] The power of the court is discretionary, and regard must

---

94   *Re Kent Coalfields Syndicate* [1898] 1 QB 754, CA.
95   This section in terms applies only to a winding up by or under supervision of the court, but in the case of a voluntary winding up, s 112 of the Insolvency Act 1986 allows an order to be made under s 155 of that Act (per Chitty LJ in *Re Kent Coalfields Syndicate*, above).
96   *Re Arauco Co* [1899] WN 134.
97   [CA 1985, s 359.]
98   'The court' means the court having jurisdiction to wind-up the company (s 744).
99   As to the measure of damages see *Re Ottos Kopje Diamond Mines* [1893] 1 Ch 618.
100 Section 125(4).
101 See *Re Ottos Kopje Diamond Mines* [1893] 1 Ch 618 (CA).
102 Section 125(3).
103 *Ward and Henry's Case* (1867) 2 Ch App 431; *Reese River Silver Mining Co v Smith* (1869) LR 4 HL 64, at 75.

be had to the 'justice of the case'.[104] In a dispute between two individuals as to which ought to be registered as a member of the company, if the matter is a simple one the court will decide it upon a motion under this section, and will make the necessary order for rectifying the register. But if the question is complicated, or if the rights of third parties intervene, the court will not make an order upon a motion, but will allow the party aggrieved to seek his remedy by an action.[105] In a case where the issue is whether there was an enforceable contract for the allotment of shares, the discretion under s 125 is the same as the discretion whether or not to order specific performance of the contract and can therefore be affected by delay on the part of the applicant and prejudice to a third party.[106]

There is authority for the proposition that where a person on the register has a right to rectification and the company recognises that right, the register may be rectified without an application to the court.[107] It has been said, however, that 'the protection of the court's order is in the ordinary case essential to any rectification of the register by the removal of the name of a registered holder of shares'.[108] The company cannot, however, unilaterally alter the register by removing the name of a person who continues to assert his right to be a member.[109]

12.6 SINGLE MEMBER COMPANIES

If a limited company has only one member a statement to this effect must be entered in the company's register.[110]

12.7 THE ANNUAL RETURN

Companies are required to file annual returns with the registrar at least once each year. The provisions governing this requirement, which dates back to early companies legislation, can now be found in Part 24 of the Companies Act 2006 (ss 854–859).

Section 854(1) requires every company to deliver to the registrar successive annual returns, each of which is made up to the company's

---

[104] *Sichell's Case* (1868) LR 3 Ch App, at 122; *Re Dronfield Silkstone Co* (1880) 17 Ch D 76, at 97 (CA); *Trevor v Whitworth* (1888) 12 App Cas 409 (HL), at 440, per Lord Macnaghten.

[105] *Ward and Henry's Case* (1867) 2 Ch App 431; *ex parte Shaw* (1877) 2 QBD 463; *ex parte Sargent* (1874) 17 Eq 273; *Re Greater Britain Products Development Corp* (1924) 40 TLR 488.

[106] *Re Isis Factors plc* [2003] EWHC 1653 (Ch), [2003] 2 BCLC 411.

[107] *Reese River Silver Mining Co* (1869) LR 4 HL 64, at 74; *Re Poole Firebrick Co* (1875) 10 Ch App 157; *First National Reinsurance Co v Greenfield* [1921] 2 KB 260, at 278–280.

[108] *Re Derham and Allen* [1946] Ch 31, at 36. For a further discussion of the procedure under s 125 and the cases decided on application under this section (and its predecessors), see *Gore-Browne on Companies* (Jordans, 45th edn, loose-leaf) at 10A [12].

[109] *Majujaya Holdings Sdn Bhd v Pens-Transteel Sdn Bhd* [1998] MLJ 399, CA (Malaysia).

[110] Section 123.

return date. The return date is defined as the anniversary of the company's incorporation or the anniversary of the date to which the company's last annual return was made if that date is different. Section 854(3) requires the return to contain the information required by ss 855–856 (and s 857 where applicable).[111] The return must be delivered within 28 days from the date on which it is made up.[112]

12.7.1   The contents of the annual return

Section 855 sets out the general required contents of annual returns in respect of every type of registered company.[113] Companies which have a share capital, where further particulars of share capital and shareholders are required, are dealt with by ss 856, 856A and 856B. Section 855 requires the following information about the company:[114]

(a)   the address of the company's registered office;

(b)   the type of company it is and its principal business activities;

(c)   the particulars required by s 855A of:

    (i)   the directors of the company; and
    (ii) in the case of a private company with a secretary or a public company, the secretary or joint secretaries;[115]

(d)   if company records are kept at a place other than its registered office, the address of that place and the records kept there.

Under s 856 a company having a share capital is required to supply in its annual returns a statement of capital and specified particulars about the members of the company. The statement of capital must state with respect to the company's share capital:[116]

'(a) the total number of shares of the company;

(b) the aggregate nominal value of those shares;

(c) for each class of shares—

---

[111] Like many other filing requirements, this can be done online or by email.
[112] Section 854(3)(b).
[113] Section 857 allows the Secretary of State by regulation to amend the contents of the annual return and this power has been used with respect to annual returns made up to 1 October 2011 or a later date by the Companies Act 2006 (Annual Returns) Regulations 2011, SI 2011/1487. Earlier amendments were made by the Companies Act 2006 (Annual Return and Service Addresses) Regulations 2008, SI 2008/3000.
[114] Including the date to which the annual return is made up.
[115] This is the same information that the company must keep in its register of directors and register of secretaries (where the company has a secretary) – see **15.14** and **15.6.3**.
[116] Section 856(2).

(i)   prescribed particulars of the rights attached to the shares;
(ii) the total number of shares of that class; and
(iii) the aggregate nominal value of shares of that class; and

(d) the amount paid up and the amount (if any) unpaid on each share (whether on account of the nominal value of the share or by way of premium).'

The return must state whether any of the company's shares were, at any time during the return period, admitted to trading on a 'relevant market' or on any other market outside the UK.[117] If they were not, s 856A requires the return to contain the name of every person who was a member of the company at any time during the return period and the number of shares of each class held at the the end of the date of the return together with details of transfers of shares during the period. Section 856B requires companies with shares traded on a relevant market also to give details of persons who held at least 5% of the issued shares of any class, but this does not apply to companies subject to the Disclosure and Transparency Rules of the Financial Services Authority. The latter are described in **12.10**.

12.8   DISCLOSURE OF INTERESTS IN VOTING RIGHTS IN PUBLIC COMPANIES

While, as we have seen in **12.5.1**, a company with a share capital is prima facie concerned only with the registered ownership of its shares, there have long been felt to be good reasons why the true beneficial ownership of the shares in public companies should be discoverable.[118] Otherwise, for example, the real identity of persons building up an interest, perhaps with a view to obtaining control by a cheaper means than the making of a takeover bid, may be concealed. Our present concern is with the provisions which require the disclosure of interests in the voting shares of public companies. These provisions are contained in Part 22 of the Companies Act 2006. Part 22 concerns a public company's right to investigate who has an interest in its shares. Part 22 replaces equivalent provisions in Part 6 (ss 212–219) of the Companies Act 1985. The provisions came into force on 20 January 2007, coinciding with the introduction of rules by the Financial Services Authority relating to the Transparency Directive. Those rules replace the obligations about disclosure of shareholdings contained in ss 198–211 of Part 6 of the 1985 Act.

---

[117] This term is defined by reference to Directive 2004/39/EC (see SI 2001/996 as amended) and basically includes the Stock Exchange and equivalent markets in the EEA.
[118] See also the discussion in **12.1**.

12.9   THE COMPANY'S RIGHT TO INVESTIGATE WHO HAS AN INTEREST IN ITS SHARES

Part 22 applies only to a public company's issued shares carrying rights to vote in all circumstances at general meetings of the company, including any shares held as treasury shares.[119] A temporary suspension of voting rights will not affect the application of Part 22.[120]

Section 793 provides that a public company may give notice to any person whom the company knows or has reasonable cause to believe to be interested in the company's shares or to have been so interested at any time during the previous 3 years. The notice may require that person to confirm that fact or to state whether or not they have or have had such an interest. The notice (which can be in electronic form) may request, within a reasonable time (undefined), details of his interest and of any others he shares or has shared the interest with, including details of any concert party agreement to purchase shares. If it is a past interest, it may request, so far as is known, who acquired the interest. Failure to comply with a request is not only an offence punishable by 2 years in prison and/or a fine (subject to a defence that the request was frivolous or vexatious), it also allows the company to seek a court order (interim or final) to freeze the votes and transfer of the shares. The court may attach conditions, particularly to protect any third parties. The Secretary of State may, after consulting the Bank of England, exempt a person from complying with a s 793 notice if satisfied that there are special reasons for doing so.

Restriction orders may also be granted in connection with investigations under s 794, in accordance with ss 797–802. The effect of a restriction order under s 794 is that any transfer of the shares is void, voting rights in respect of such shares are not exerciseable, no further shares may be issued in right of the shares or in pursuance of an offer made to their holder, and no distributions can be made except in liquidation. Attempts to evade these restrictions by the holder, a proxy or where shares are issued, by the company or an officer of the company is an offence punishable by an unlimited fine.[121] The court may relax or remove restrictions or order the sale of restricted shares,[122] although the net proceeds must be paid into court for the benefit of the beneficial holders.[123]

A s 793 notice may be requested by 10% of the voting shares (measured by paid up capital and excluding shares in treasury).[124] The request may be in hard copy form or in electronic form, and it must state that the

---

[119]   Section 792(1).
[120]   Section 792(2).
[121]   Section 798.
[122]   Sections 799 and 800.
[123]   Section 802.
[124]   Section 803.

company is requested to exercise its powers under s 793; specify the manner in which the company is requested to act; give reasonable grounds for the request and it must be authenticated by those making the request. The company must exercise its powers in the manner specified in the requests and failure to comply is a criminal offence on the part of every officer in default, punishable by a fine.[125] Under s 805, after the company has carried out an investigation the company must produce a report of the information which has been received. The report must then be made available at the company's office within 15 business days of completion. If a report is not completed within 3 months a report of that period and each succeeding 3-month period should be made available. Those making the request must be informed of this availability within 3 business days. Reports need only now be retained for 6 years. They must be available at the registered office or any specified alternative that has been notified to the registrar within 14 days for inspection free of charge and copies provided at a prescribed fee. Failure to comply is an offence by the company and every officer in default punishable by up to a level 3 fine and a daily default provision for continuing breach. The court may order inspection and/or copies.

Under s 808 the company is required to keep a register of information received by it in pursuance of a requirement imposed by a s 793 notice. The information must be recorded in a register against the names in chronological order, of the present holder of the relevant shares or if there is no present holder or the present holder is not known, against the name of the person holding the interest, with a name index if necessary, within 3 business days of receipt. This register is to be kept available along with the register of members (usually the registered office, but it may be at a specified alternative) with a free right of inspection and copies for a prescribed fee. The applicant must, in accordance with s 811, provide his name and address, or the name of an individual responsible for making a request on behalf of an organisation, he must state the purpose for which the information is to be used and to whom it may be disclosed including the name and address of an individual or an individual responsible for receiving such information on behalf of an organisation and the purpose for which that person will use the information. Under s 814, knowingly or recklessly making a false or misleading statement or disclosing the information knowing or having reason to suspect its misuse is an offence punishable by up to 2 years in prison and an unlimited fine.

A company may refuse a request if it is not satisfied that the request is made 'for a proper purpose'.[126] The person whose request is refused may apply to the court for a direction.[127] If the court is not satisfied that the request is for a proper purpose, it will direct the company not to comply and, if other similar requests are expected, may direct it not to comply

---

[125] Section 804.
[126] See above **12.5.2** and CA 2006, s 117.
[127] Section 812.

with any such requests. Continued failure to comply without court permission is an offence punishable by up to a level 3 fine with a daily default fine for continuing breach.[128] Entries must be available and not removed for 6 years[129] (even if the company ceases to be a public company) unless a third party's name has been incorrectly given as a holder.[130] If a concert party member claims no longer to be so, the company must satisfy itself that this is the case and record the fact.[131] If the company refuses, the member can seek a court order. Failure to comply again is a criminal offence punishable with up to a level 3 fine with a daily default fine for continuing breach.

The Act provides a very broad definition of an 'interest in shares'[132] and includes rights to subscribe for shares, family and corporate interests, agreements to acquire shares and concert party share acquisition agreements. The wide definition provided by the legislation is designed 'to counter the limitless ingenuity of persons who prefer to conceal their interests behind trusts and corporate entities'.[133]

The Secretary of State may make regulations, subject to affirmative resolution, amending what shares and interests are covered and the notice required.[134]

12.10 NOTIFICATION OF MAJOR SHAREHOLDINGS

Sections 198–202 of the old Part VI of the Companies Act 1985 were replaced by new rules introduced on 20 January 2007 in order to comply with the Transparency Directive.[135] Sections 1266–1268 of the Companies Act 2006 insert new provisions into the Financial Services and Markets Act 2000 designed to enable investors to know who holds and who controls voting rights attached to the company's shares. These provisions

---

[128] Section 813.

[129] Section 816.

[130] Section 817.

[131] Section 818.

[132] Section 820 provides a general definition and states that a reference to an interest in shares includes an interest of any kind whatsoever in the shares, and any restraints or restrictions to which the exercise of any right attached to the interest is or may be subject shall be disregarded: s 820(2). Section 820(4) provides that a person is treated as having an interest in shares if (a) he enters into a contract to acquire them, or (b) not being the registered holder, he is entitled (i) to exercise any right conferred by the holding of the shares, or (ii) to control the exercise of any such right. Under s 820(6) a person is treated as having an interest in shares if he has a right to call for delivery of the shares to himself or to his order, or he has a right to acquire an interest in shares or is under an obligation to take an interest in shares.

[133] See *Re TR Technology Investment Trust plc* [1988] BCLC 256, at 261, cited by House of Lords *Explanatory Notes to the Company Law Reform Bill*, 17 November 2005, HL, Session 2005–2006, para 1127, explanation of then cl 608. See also *Explanatory Note* to the Act by the Department of Trade and Industry, para 1142, 2 January 2007.

[134] Section 828.

[135] 2004/109/EC.

give power to the competent authority – ie the Financial Services Authority (FSA) – to make rules for the purposes of the Transparency Obligations Directive and the competent authority may make rules 'for the purpose of ensuring that voteholder information in respect of voting shares traded on a UK market other than a regulated market is made public or notified to the competent authority'.[136] The new rules have been introduced by the FSA under the Transparency Obligations Directive (Disclosure and Transparency Rules) Instrument 2006[137] which introduces Rule 5 of the Disclosure and Transparency Rules.[138] These apply to all UK companies listed on the main market or on AIM or PLUS.

Generally, a direct or indirect shareholder must notify a company and the FSA if he acquires or disposes of shares carrying voting rights exceeding or falling below 3% or any whole percentage above 3% of the issuer's total voting rights and capital in issue; and if their holdings change to reach, exceed or fall below every 1% above 3% of the issuer's total voting rights and capital in issue. Voting rights must be calculated on the basis of all the shares to which voting rights are attached even if the exercise of such rights is suspended. The number of voting rights to be considered when calculating the percentage of voting rights should be based on the issuer's most recent month-end disclosure, disregarding any treasury shares held by the issuer. Issuers are required[139] to disclose the total number of voting rights and capital for each class of shares which they issue at the end of each month where there has been a change. Shareholders required to notify the FSA must file the information in electronic format. Notifiable interests include direct interests (holdings of shares with voting rights attached); indirect interests (those with access to voting rights); and financial instruments which give the holder the formal entitlement to acquire shares with voting rights attached.

An issuer of shares must, if it acquires or disposes of its 'own shares', make public the percentage of voting rights attributable to those shares, where the acquisition or disposal reaches, exceeds or falls below 5% or 10% of voting rights.[140]

The DTR retains the previous notification thresholds, ie every whole per cent starting at 3% (or 10% for market-makers and certain other interests) and the previous deadlines which are stricter than those in the Transparency Directive, but in both cases this can only be done for

---

[136] Section 89A of FSMA 2000, inserted by s 1266 of CA 2006.
[137] FSA 2006/70.
[138] These were previously known as the Disclosure Rules but were renamed with the introduction of these provisions. See further FSA, *List!* Number 14, December 2006. The rules were finalised when the text of the implementing directive became available (Directive 2007/14 of March 8 [2007] OJ L69/27. See also www.fsa.org.uk.
[139] Under DTR 5.6.1.
[140] DTR 5.5.1R.

companies for which the FSA has responsibility (ie for AIM and Plus Market companies and listed companies for which the UK is the home state).

Some entities, individuals or types of holdings are either fully or partially exempt from the notification requirements. Where a shareholder has a combination of different holdings the conditions for disclosure may vary. Managers of lawfully managed investments; assets of a collective undertaking and open-ended investment companies must only disclose holdings at 5% or above (as opposed to 3%) of the issuer's total voting rights and capital in issue. They must also notify their holdings if they reach, exceed, or fall below a 10% threshold. When their holdings reach 10% the exemption no longer applies. The shareholder/manager must make notifications if their holdings exceed 10% of the total voting rights and capital in issue. Disclosures are required for every 1% increase or decrease above this threshold.

Following the appointment of a fund manager, the beneficial owner (the pension fund trustees) ceases to have a separate notifiable interest and the fund manager acting as an indirect holder of shares (as per DTR 5.2.1(h)) should make a notification if there are changes in the holdings of shares. Even if the client has retained power to give the fund manager instructions in respect of its assets, the client does not have a separate notifiable interest unless and until it exercises that power. It is also likely that the fund manager will only need to disclose when holdings breach 5% and 10% (DTR 5.1.5). Similar situations are also likely to arise for some insurance companies who appoint a fund manager. The lending or borrowing of notifiable interests may not constitute a disposal or acquisition of the voting rights so no notification is necessary. For a stock lender acting under a standard stock-lending agreement a loan of shares will not amount to a disposal. The shares acquired by the borrower should be on-lent or otherwise disposed of by no later than the close of business on the next trading day. In addition the borrower should not declare any intention (and not exercise) the voting rights attached to the shares. Shareholders acquiring for the sole purpose of clearing or settlement within the T+3 settlement cycle do not need to disclose the change in holdings. Custodians or nominees who can only exercise the voting rights attached to such shares under instructions given to them in writing or by electronic means do not have to disclose. Market makers (as defined in DTR 5.1.4R) are exempt from disclosing holdings up to 10% of the issuer's total voting rights and capital in issue. This exemption falls away if they reach, exceed, or fall below the 10% threshold. So market-makers must disclose their total holdings if they change to reach, exceed or fall below every 1% above 10% of the issuer's total voting rights and capital in issue. A market-makers is broadly defined by the Transparency Directive (via cross-reference to the Markets in Financial

Instruments Directive[141]) as 'a person who holds himself out on the financial markets on a continuous basis as being willing to deal on own account by buying and selling financial instruments against his proprietary capital at prices defined by him'. Provided that shares held by credit institutions or investment firms are held on the trading book and their voting rights are not exercised or used to intervene in the management of the issuer then the holdings do not need to be disclosed below 5% of the issuer's total voting rights and capital. At the 5% threshold the exemption of disclosure falls away and credit institutions and investment firms must disclose their total holdings if they change to reach, exceed or fall below every 1% above 5% of the issuer's total voting rights and capital in issue. Provided a collateral taker does not declare any intention to or actually exercise the voting rights attached to shares under a collateral transaction (which involves the outright transfer of securities) they are exempt from major shareholding notification requirements. Where the parent undertaking controls the voting rights of a controlled undertaking at its discretion, the parent undertaking must aggregate its holding with the controlled undertaking's holding. Where a management company exercises its voting rights independently from the parent undertaking (including voting rights attached to the management company's holdings which the parent undertaking has invested in), that parent undertaking is not required to aggregate its holdings with the holdings managed by the management company. Similarly, where an investment firm (authorised under MiFID) exercises its voting rights independently from its parent undertaking (including those voting rights attached to the investment firm's holdings which the parent undertaking has invested in), that parent undertaking is not required to aggregate its holdings with the holdings managed by the management company. A parent of an undertaking whose registered office is in a non-EEA state (or head office within the Community in the case of an investment firm) is exempt from aggregating its holdings (in issuers whose home member state is the UK).

12.11 DISCLOSING USE OF VOTES

Although not part of the Transparency Directive, a closely related and very controversial subject is the disclosure by institutional investors of how they used their votes in general meeting. The CLRSG took the view that such disclosure was desirable as a matter of transparency since institutions are exercising that power in effect on behalf of those investing through them. Indeed, there has been a growing trend of voluntary disclosure. Sections 1277–1280 of the Companies Act 2006 gives to HM Treasury or the Secretary of State power to make regulations, subject to affirmative resolution, to enforce such disclosure by UK:

---

[141] Directive 2004/39/EC of the European Parliament and of the Council of 21 April 2004 on markets in financial instruments amending Council Directives 85/611/EEC and 93/6/EEC and Directive 2000/12/EC of the European Parliament and of the Council and repealing Council Directive 93/22/EEC.

(1)	authorised unit trusts and open-ended investment companies (and other collective investment schemes from designated jurisdictions, like the Channel Islands and Bermuda);

(2)	investment trusts;

(3)	pension schemes; and

(4)	insurers conducting long-term (as against general) insurance.

However, s 1278(2) provides a general power to add other institutions or exclude specific types. The regulations may determine which traded shares count, which may be held through a depositary receipt or a collective investment scheme and what information has to be provided about exercise of votes, instructions to others to exercise the vote or delegation of voting powers. This reserve power is rather vague as to what information must be provided, when and how. This is presumably because of the considerable practical difficulties in implementing such an obligation. As was pointed out in the debates:[142]

> 'First, resolutions are decided by a show of hands and, unless a poll is called, an instruction to vote may not be exercised. Secondly, the voting instructions may well go through a chain – the beneficial owner, the fund manager, the custodian, the custodian's nominee, a registrar and, possibly, a proxy voting service ... Moreover, this provision seems to carry with it several potential disadvantages. First, it may drive firms who are not generally active to vote without giving due consideration to the issues at stake in order to be seen to be doing something ... Secondly, the disclosure of every resolution where voting rights have not been exercised would result in pages and pages of meaningless tables. Furthermore, in the case of an authorized collective investment scheme ... it is the authorized fund manager, rather than the scheme itself, which exercises the voting rights ... In addition, other institutional investors – for example, pension funds, life companies and investment trusts – will often give fund managers discretion to vote on their behalf.'

The Government minister responding said:[143]

> 'If it is decided in due course to proceed to establish a statutory disclosure regime, there would, of course, be full consultation and a cost-benefit analysis to make sure that any final regime was proportionate and properly targeted.'

Failure to provide the information required by any regulations is not a criminal offence but enforceable by any person to whom the information should have been provided or by a specified authority (presumably the FSA).

---

[142]	Lord Hodgson of Astley Abbots, *Hansard*, HL Deb, col G C70 (25 April 2006).
[143]	Lord Sainsbury of Turville, *Hansard*, col G C72 (25 April 2006).

12.12 EXERCISE OF MEMBERS' RIGHTS BY BENEFICIAL OWNERS

Part 9 of the Companies Act 2006 contains important new provisions regarding the rights of persons who hold the beneficial interests in shares, but who are not registered as members. They are based on, but in their final form go further than, recommendations of the CLRSG. The fact that investors increasingly hold their shares through intermediaries (eg when shares in a quoted company are held through the CREST system) means that the intermediaries are registered as members and the beneficiaries have to reply on their arrangements with the intermediaries regarding both the obtaining of information from the company and the giving of instructions as to the exercise of voting rights.

The final form of these provisions differs considerably from those in the original Bill and indeed from amendments made in the House of Lords. The result is something of a compromise between the original proposals, designed to ensure that nothing in the Act hindered companies from making arrangements of the kind described and giving the Secretary of State power to require companies to make such arrangements in the event that a voluntary approach did not work, and members of Parliament who wanted mandatory rights for beneficial owners. The final version maintains the first proposal but also introduces a set of provisions on what are called 'information rights' together with a more specific provision in s 153.

Section 145 provides for the optional and general approach and is applicable to any type of company. Its effect is that, where a company's articles provide that a member can nominate another person or persons as entitled to enjoy or exercise all or any specified rights, the nominee can exercise them notwithstanding anything in the Act. This is designed to ensure that all relevant references in the Act to a 'member' should be read as if the reference was a reference to the nominee. The Act refers to the beneficial owner as 'the nominated person', but this account will use 'nominee' instead.

There are a number of statutory rights to which s 145 applies 'in particular', but clearly the list is not exhaustive and other rights can be specified, nor is it necessary that all the rights are in fact specified in a particular company's articles. The list is as follows:

(1)   the right to be sent proposed written resolutions;

(2)   the right to require the circulation of a written resolution;

(3)   the right to require the directors to call a general meeting;

(4)   the right to notice of general meetings;

(5)   the right to require circulation of a statement;

(6)   the right to appoint a proxy;

(7)   the right to require the circulation of a resolution at the annual general meeting of a public company;

(8)   the right to include matters in the business dealt with at the annual general meeting of a traded company; and

(9)   the right to be sent a copy of the annual accounts and reports.

The only right of a member that cannot be included in such a provision is the right to transfer shares, because s 145(4)(b) provides that the section and any provision in the articles do not affect the requirements for an effective transfer or other disposition of the whole or part of a member's interest in the company. Section 145(4)(a) provides also that the section and any relevant provision do not confer rights enforceable against the company by anyone other than the member, with the result that such provisions do not give beneficiaries directly enforceable rights against the company, only against the member.

12.12.1   Information rights

Sections 146–151 are concerned with information rights, which are quite extensive, but which apply only in respect of a company whose shares are admitted to trading on a regulated market, which does not, among other things, include shares traded on the Alternative Investment Market. A member of such a company who holds shares on behalf of another person may nominate that person to enjoy information rights, although a company need not act on a nomination purporting to relate to only certain of these rights. These rights are:

(1)   the right to receive a copy of all communications that the company sends to its members generally or to any class of its members that includes the person making the nomination – communications sent generally include the company's annual accounts and reports;

(2)   rights to require copies of accounts and reports; and

(3)   the right to require hard copy versions of a document or information provided in another form.

12.12.2   Voting rights

There is a specific provision, s 149, regarding voting rights, which is clearly designed to encourage participation by nominees, although its effectiveness will depend on agreements between them and the registered member of the shares. Where a nominee receives a copy of a notice of a meeting from the company, it must be accompanied by a statement that he may have the right under an agreement between him and the member who nominated him to be appointed, or to have someone else appointed, as a proxy for the meeting or if he has no such right or does not want to exercise it, he may have a right under such an agreement to give instructions to the member as to the exercise of voting rights. In this situation, the statutorily required notice of proxy rights must either be omitted from the copy or stated not to apply to the nominee.

12.12.3 Status of information rights

The Act does not give a nominee direct rights against the company. Rather, as regards information rights and, where applicable, the rights to hard copy communications and information as to possible voting rights, s 150 provides that the member can enforce them against the company as if they were rights conferred by the company's articles. These rights are in addition to the rights of the member himself and do not affect any rights exercisable by virtue of s 145, but failure to give effect to a nominee's rights does not affect the validity of anything done by the company. Any enactment or provision of the company's articles relating to communications with members has a corresponding effect in relation to communications with the nominee, a provision that is particularly directed at the circumstances mentioned in s 150(4), namely determining the date or time at which or the address to which information is to be sent or supplied. So a company that does not receive a nomination in time, or when nomination is suspended, or that does not have a current address, is excused from communicating with a nominee.

12.12.4 Formalities

The nominee has the right to choose the form in which he receives copies of documents or information, but if he wishes to receive it in hard copy, he must, before the nomination is made, request the member to notify the company and provide an address to which the copies may be sent. If the member acts on this request by notifying the company and passing on the address, the nominee has the right to hard copy. However, this is subject to the general provisions on electronic communications by a traded company in Sch 5, Parts 3 and 4. In the absence of notification or the provision of an address, the nominee is taken to have agreed that documents or information may be sent or supplied to him by means of a website, but this 'agreement' may be revoked by the nominee and does not affect his right under s 1145 to require hard copy of a document or information. The result of this appears to be that a nominee has the right to hard copy information, but if that is not exercised in time, he will receive electronic copy generally except that he still has the s 1145 right to have a hard copy of a particular document.

Section 148 deals with the termination or suspension of a nomination, although if that happens in the circumstances described below, the company is not required to act on it and can do so to such extent or for such period as it thinks fit. This is no doubt to cover a situation where a member's holdings in the company and the number of nominees may fluctuate from time to time and the cost of suspension might outweigh the cost of suspending and recommencing rights. Either the member or the nominee may terminate the nomination, and it automatically terminates if either dies or becomes bankrupt or, if a body corporate, is wound up other than for the purposes of a reconstruction. In addition, the company may inquire of a nominee whether he wishes to retain information rights and, if it does not receive a response within 28 days from sending the inquiry, the nomination ceases to have effect at the end of that period. However, a company can make such an inquiry only once in any 12-month period. The provisions on suspension cover the situation where there are more nominees than the member has shares in the company or shares or a particular class, which could arise in respect of shares held on the basis of, for example, an individual savings account; here any nominations by the member are suspended.

12.12.5 Exercise of rights in different ways

As has been already mentioned, often a member will hold shares on behalf of a number of different people. Section 152 provides that the rights attached to the shares and the rights under any enactment that are exercisable by virtue of holding the shares need not all be exercised and need not all be exercised in the same way. If a member does not exercise all his rights or exercises them in different ways, he must inform the company either of the extent to which he is exercising the rights or of the different ways and to what extent they are exercised in each way. The sanction for failure to inform the company is that, in the absence of information to the contrary, the company is entitled to assume that a member is exercising all his rights and doing so in the same way. This would protect the company from any claim by a nominee that a member had not acted in accordance with his instructions.

12.12.6 Special rights

Section 153 confers special rights over and above the information rights previously discussed. They concern various statutory rights, namely:

(1)   s 314 regarding the circulation of statements to members;

(2)   s 338 regarding the right of members of a public company to require the circulation of a resolution at the AGM;

(3)   s 338A regarding the right of members of a traded company to require the inclusion of matters in the business dealt with at the AGM;

(4)   s 342 regarding the power of members of a quoted company to require an independent report on a poll; and

(5)   s 527 regarding the power of members of a quoted company to require the website publication of concerns about the audit.

All these rights are exercisable if, among other things, 100 members act together. Section 153 essentially allows the 100 to include beneficial owners and not just members of the company. It is, however, subject to the conditions specified in s 153(2), as well as the individual requirements of the sections to which it applies.

These conditions are as follows:

(1)   the request must be made by at least 100 persons and authenticated by all of them;

(2)   that as regards non-members, it must be accompanied by a statement:

   (a)   of the full name and address of a person ('the member') who is a member of the company and holds shares on behalf of that person;
   (b)   that the member is holding those shares on behalf of that person in the course of a business;
   (c)   of the number of shares in the company that the member holds on behalf of that person, of the total amount paid up on those shares;
   (d)   that those shares are not held on behalf of anyone else or, if they are, that the other person or persons are not among the other persons making the request;
   (e)   that some or all of those shares confer voting rights that are relevant for the purposes of making a request under the section in question; and
   (f)   that the person has the right to instruct the member how to exercise those rights;

(3)   that as regards members, it must be accompanied by a statement:

   (a)   that he holds shares otherwise than on behalf of another person; or
   (b)   that he holds shares on behalf of one or more other persons but those persons are not among the other persons making the request;

(4)   it must be accompanied by such evidence as the company may reasonably require of the matters in (1) and (2) above;

(5)   the total amount paid up on all the shares held by such members and non-members, divided by the number of persons making the request, must be not less than £100.

CHAPTER 13

SHAREHOLDERS' MEETINGS AND RESOLUTIONS

13.1 INTRODUCTION

This chapter is concerned with what is sometimes called the 'machinery of corporate democracy' – ie the legislation and case-law which regulates the summoning and conduct of meetings (including voting, proxies and quorums). The ordinary business of the company is transacted by the directors. The company exercises its control, and does such acts as are reserved to it, by the votes of a majority at general meetings. 'Whenever a certain number are incorporated, a major part may do any corporate act; so if all are summoned and part appear a major part of those that appear may do a corporate act',[1] but if the articles prescribe a quorum, no less number of members can do business. There is a certain artificiality about the way this machinery works in respect of the modern company, even if it worked well enough in the world of Victorian shareholders and their companies.

In the case of small private companies (by far the most numerous type of company) the formal rules about holding shareholders' meetings (and directors' meetings) used to wear an awkward air of unreality. A handful of 'corporate partners' (ie shareholders/directors) will tend to meet perhaps every day just to run the company's business. In practice, they may have often forgotten the formalities of shareholders' and directors' meetings and have been unsure which corporate 'hat' they were wearing on any particular occasion. To some extent modern company law (in the Companies Act 1985, in Table A and in the case-law) recognised this problem and the Companies Act 2006 has amended those earlier provisions, in Part 13, to take such realities into account. The Act simplifies the law and assumes that private companies will almost entirely conduct their business outside formal meetings by making use of the written resolution procedure, and they are no longer obliged to hold annual general meetings (AGMs) unless they are dismissing a director or auditor before their term of office, in which case a general meeting must be called.[2] Thus s 281(1) provides that a resolution of the members or of a

---

[1]   Per Lord Hardwicke in *Attorney-General v Davy* (1741) 2 Alk 212; see also per Wills J in *Merchants of the Staple v Bank of England* (1887) 21 QB 160.

[2]   CA 2006, s 288(2)(a).

class of members of a private company must be passed (a) as a written resolution in accordance with Chapter 2 of Part 13 or (b) at a meeting of the members (which is then subject to the provisions of Chapter 3). In contrast, by s 281(2), such a resolution of the members of a public company must be passed at a meeting. A further consequence of this section, which had no equivalent in the previous legislation, is that the requirements for both types of company are mandatory and it is no longer possible to pass a written resolution under provision made by the articles.[3] Meetings in private companies can still be instituted by the directors at any time or by members representing 10% of voting shares (5% if it is more than 12 months since the members met). Nevertheless, the Act is drafted on the basis that most decision making by members in private companies will be by written resolution.

In the case of large public companies, the law of meetings, voting, etc, operates in a somewhat unreal context of a different order from that affecting small private companies. Of course, shareholders' meetings will be summoned and conducted, and votes counted, with scrupulous regard for what the law requires. The problem is that such public company meetings are extremely poorly attended (even where every effort is made to encourage good attendance). Although there may be thousands (or hundreds of thousands) of shareholders, research has shown that about one in a thousand bothers to attend.[4] This stems in part from the obvious trouble and time involved in travelling to company meetings, where individual shareholders have a small interest at stake.

The use of what is called the 'proxy voting machinery' by the board of directors ensures that where an issue is contested at a company meeting (and the vote goes beyond a show of hands to a poll),[5] the board is extremely likely to win. This stems from the power of the board to 'solicit proxies' at the company's expense. The evidence of experience is that the vast number of individual shareholders, who do not attend company meetings, either return a proxy vote in favour of the board's proposal (or counter proposal) or remain passive. It is true that the growth of 'institutional shareholders' (pension funds, unit trusts, etc) has in recent decades tended to redress the balance somewhat. However, as was pointed out in **12.1**, it has not always been the usual practice of institutional shareholders to contest issues at company meetings. It is much more

---

[3] To that end, reg 53 in Table A prescribed by the Companies (Tables A to F) Regulations 1985, SI 1985/805, ceased to have effect on 1 October 2007 as regards companies registered on or after that date: the Companies (Tables A to F) (Amendment) Regulations 2007, SI 2007/2541, reg 6.

[4] See Midgley (1974) 114 *Lloyds Bank Review* 24. Even where a company has well-advertised problems and stormy shareholders' meetings, the average attendance only rises to 1%. See further Midgley *Companies and Their Shareholders: The Uneasy Relationship* (The Institute of Chartered Secretaries and Administrators, 1975); Butcher 'Reform of the General Meetings' in Sheikh and Rees (eds) *Corporate Governance and Corporate Control* (Cavendish, 2nd edn, 2000).

[5] See **13.7.10**.

common for a prestigious institution to raise a matter 'behind the scenes' by approaching the chairman of the board (or other senior executive) directly. This may be done either by a number of institutional investors individually, or through various shareholder protection committees to which they belong.[6] This can sometimes be quite successful in rectifying the abuses or inadequacies of management, or in preventing what are thought to be undesirable initiatives by the board.[7]

It must be conceded that the unstated threat behind such pressure by the institutions obviously comes from the proportion of voting shares held by them. This can be used to override the de facto control exercised by the boards of most large public companies. Thus, at the end of the day, the 'machinery of corporate democracy' has a vital role to play but rather through the implied threat it presents than in its actual use.[8] Recognising these realities the law has been amended and includes provisions to increase the use of information technology and electronic communications and importantly there are new provisions that require the disclosure on a website of the results of polls at general and class meetings of quoted companies and an independent report on a poll if a sufficient number of members demand one.

The provisions in Part 13 of the Companies Act 2006, as well as replacing Chapter 4, Part XI of the Companies Act 1985, introduced changes arising from consultations on company general meetings and shareholder communications and recommendations in Chapters 2, 6 and 7 of the Final Report of the Company Law Review as well as the consultations on the White Papers of July 2002 and March 2005. Further changes were made, in order to implement the EU Shareholders' Rights Directive[9] by the Companies (Shareholders' Rights) Regulations 2009.[10] As well as making some general changes, the concept of the 'traded company' was introduced. Section 360C of the 2006 Act defines this as a company any shares of which carry rights to vote at general meetings and are admitted to trading on a regulated market in an EEA state by or with the consent of the company. This can include a private company; in particular it could include a private unlimited company as such a company is not prohibited, by s 755 of the 2006 Act, from offering its shares to the public.

13.2   INFORMAL AGREEMENT

It is well established at common law that if all the shareholders are present at a meeting and unanimously give their assent to a proposal, it does not

---

[6]   See the Wilson Committee, Cmnd 7937, Chapter 19 at paragraphs 909–913. The institutions each have their own investment protection committee as well as the collective body for all types of institution – the institutional shareholders' committee.

[7]   As to the role of institutional investors in corporate governance generally, see **11.5.7**.

[8]   See also the discussion in **12.1**.

[9]   Directive 2007/36/EC.

[10]   SI 2009/1632.

matter that no formal resolution was put to the vote.[11] Likewise, any requirements as to the length of notice for a meeting (or for a resolution thereat), whether imposed by the Companies Act 2006 or by the articles, may be waived by the consent of all the members of a company.[12] It would also appear that, if all the shareholders have given their consent to a proposal, it is not necessary that they should have held a meeting. Although in *Re George Newman Ltd*[13] the Court of Appeal held that 'for the purpose of binding a company in its corporate capacity individual assents given separately are not equivalent to the assent of a meeting',[14] more recent decisions have come to a different conclusion. In two cases the members of a company were held to have informally ratified acts by directors beyond their powers even though no shareholders' meeting had been held. In *Parker and Cooper v Reading*,[15] it was held that all the members had informally ratified a debenture granted by the directors even though no meeting had been held. In *Re Duomatic Ltd*,[16] directors' salaries had been paid without the authority of a shareholders' resolution. It was held by Buckley J that the agreement of the two directors who held all the voting shares, even though they had not constituted themselves as a shareholders' meeting, amounted to an informal ratification of the payment of unauthorised salaries. This decision also establishes that all that is required is the unanimous assent of the shareholders with the right to vote.[17] It is of course only in small private companies that the informal agreement of all the shareholders is likely to occur.[18]

Further, there must be real assent, that is the shareholders must know what it is that they are assenting to.[19] Where a shareholder attended a meeting at a solicitor's office that he thought was merely preparatory to a

---

[11]   *Re Express Engineering Works* [1920] 1 Ch 466 (CA). Here the meeting consisted of directors who were also all the shareholders. See also *Baroness Wenlock v River Dee Company* (1883) 36 ChD 675n, at 681. This has been applied to unanimous agreement to vary a provision in the articles: *Cane v Jones* [1980] 1 WLR 1451, and to a reduction of capital: *Re Barry Artist plc* [1985] BCLC 283 (although only here 'with great reluctance' and with a warning that this procedure would not be accepted in future reductions).

[12]   *Re Oxted Motor Co* [1921] 3 KB 32. There is also provision in s 307(5) and (6) permitting notice to be waived by a 'requisite percentage' in value of the shares carrying a right to vote at the meeting (or if the company has no share capital a 'requisite percentage' of the total voting rights. See **13.6.5**.

[13]   [1895] 1 Ch 674 (CA). A possible explanation of this decision is that it concerned acts beyond the powers of the company.

[14]   Ibid, at 686, per Lord Lindley, who noted, however, that such assents would preclude those who had given them from complaining of what had been sanctioned.

[15]   [1926] Ch 975.

[16]   [1969] 2 Ch 365.

[17]   In *Re Duomatic Ltd* [1969] 2 Ch 365, the company had a share capital of 100 £1 ordinary shares and 80,000 £1 non-voting preference shares. The shareholder who held all the preference shares had not been consulted. But a different conclusion was reached as to disclosure to 'members' for the purposes of s 312. See also *Souter of Stirling (Sports Turf) v The Monument Golf Club Ltd* 1996 GWD 736.

[18]   See *Attorney-General for Canada v Standard Trust Co* [1911] AC 498 (PC); *Re Innes & Co* [1903] 2 Ch 254 (CA). These cases suggest that as a matter of legal principle the rule as to the effect of unanimous consent is confined to such companies. *Sed quaere.*

[19]   *EIC Services Ltd v Phipps* [2004] 2 BCLC 589, paras 120 to 147, applying dicta in

subsequent properly summoned general meeting, it was held by the Court of Appeal that he had not assented to the meeting at the office as a valid and effective general meeting.[20]

In *Cane v Jones*,[21] it was held that by unanimous agreement the members might without passing a special resolution alter the articles so that the chairman should no longer have the casting vote. Such an agreement will be registrable under s 30 of the Companies Act 2006 (previously s 380 of the Companies Act 1985). In *Atlas Europe Ltd v Wright*,[22] the Court of Appeal applied the principle in recognising the approval of a director's service contract under what was then s 319 of the Companies Act 1985 (now s 188 of the Companies Act 2006). The principle will also apply to a requirement of consent of a class of shareholders[23] and in respect of provisions in a shareholders' agreement and will therefore allow unanimous agreement to abrogate procedural requirements therein.[24] However, it cannot be effective to validate something that a general meeting itself cannot do, such as a purported ratification of a director's breach of duty that is not ratifiable even with the consent of all shareholders[25] or an unlawful distribution or return of capital.[26]

Differing views have been expressed as to whether the principle is only effective as regards the agreement of all registered shareholders, because it looks to all members entitled to attend and vote at a general meeting, or whether the agreement of the shareholders with the beneficial interest in the shares suffices. In *Domoney v Godhino*,[27] Lindsay J thought not, relying on a dictum to this effect of Buckley J in *Re Duomatic Ltd*.[28] However, in *Shahar v Tsitekkos*,[29] Mann J expressed the contrary view. These views were expressed in the context of summary judgment applications and both judges regarded the point as not appropriate for determination in this context. More recently, in *Re Tulsesense Ltd*,[30] Newey J, after hearing full argument, was willing to assume, without deciding, that the assent of the beneficial owners of shares would satisfy

---

Herrman v Simon (1990) 4 ACSR 81, CA (NSW). The decision of Neuberger J was reversed on other grounds: [2004] 2 BCLC 589.

20 *Schofield v Schofield* [2011] EWCA Civ 154, [2011] All ER (D) 274 (Feb). The dictum of Newey J referred to in the previous footnote was cited with approval at [32].

21 [1980] 1 WLR 1451.

22 [1999] BCC 163. Cf *Demite Ltd v Protec Health Ltd* [1998] BCC 638, where it was doubted whether the principle applied to approval under s 320, although a different view was taken in *Re Conegrade Ltd* [2002] EWHC 2411, [2003] BPIR 358, ChD.

23 *Re Torvale Group Ltd* [1999] 2 BCLC 605.

24 *Euro Brokers Holdings Ltd v Monecor (London) Ltd* [2003] EWCA Civ 105, [2003] 1 BCLC 506.

25 *Bowthorpe Holdings Ltd v Hills* [2002] EWHC 2331 (Ch), [2003] 1 BCLC 226.

26 *Secretary of State for Business, Innovation and Skills v Doffman* [2010] EWHC 3175 (Ch), [2011] All ER (D) 89 (Dec), citing the decision of Hoffmann J in *Aveling Barford Ltd v Period Ltd* [1989] BCLC 626. See the judgment of Newey J at [37] to [45].

27 [2004] BCLC 15.

28 [1967] 2 Ch 365 at 373.

29 [2004] EWHC 2659 (Ch) at [67].

30 [2010] EWHC 244 (Ch), [2010] 2 BCLC 525 at [42] and [43].

the principle, but held, clearly correctly, that the assent of just one of a number of such owners would not normally do so.

The unanimous consent rule, or *Duomatic* principle, is effectively preserved as an alternative to the written resolution and formal resolution procedures by s 281(4) of the Companies Act 2006, which provides that nothing in Part 13 affects any enactment or rule of law as to: (a) things done otherwise than by passing a resolution; (b) circumstances in which a resolution is or is not treated as having been passed; or (c) cases in which a person is precluded from alleging that a resolution has not been duly passed. This seems particularly important for small private companies. While it may be assumed that the larger and/or well-advised private company will follow the provisions relating to written resolutions, the small quasi-partnership type of private company is less likely in practice to observe any formalities and to conduct its business in a wholly informal way.

13.3   RESOLUTIONS

Section 281 provides that members' resolutions can only be passed in accordance with the provisions in Part 13 of the Companies Act 2006. Part 13, Chapter 1 provides general rules relating to the passing of all resolutions. Section 281 makes clear the distinction between private and public companies with regard to resolutions. Thus, s 281(1) provides that a resolution of the members, or of a class of members, of a private company may be passed either as a written resolution or at a meeting, whereas, s 281(2) makes clear that for a public company, whatever its size, this can be done only at general or class meetings.[31] However, for both private and public companies, the common law principle that the informal assent of all members[32] is equivalent to the passing of a resolution is preserved as a result of the provision in s 281(4) noted above.

A further general and new provision, in s 281(3), provides that where a provision of the Companies Act requires a resolution of a company or of the members (or a class of the members) of a company, without specifying the kind of resolution, what is required is an ordinary resolution unless the articles require a higher majority or unanimity.[33] There are many instances where the legislation simply requires a resolution and to which this subsection will apply. Thus in such cases the default will be an ordinary resolution. When a provision in the Act specifies that an ordinary resolution is required the articles will not be able to specify a higher majority.

---

[31]   Section 281(2).

[32]   The 'unanimous consent' rule: see, e g *Re Duomatic Ltd* [1969] 2 Ch 365.

[33]   This provision was inserted at the final parliamentary stages of the Companies Bill, replacing a number of specific provisions to the same effect.

The Act goes on to restate the provisions regarding resolutions of a company and in doing so makes some new provisions and abolishes the concept of the extraordinary resolution.

Section 282 provides a definition of an ordinary resolution applicable to members generally or to a class of members and applicable as a written resolution or as a resolution passed at a meeting. An ordinary resolution requires a simple majority – ie 50% plus 1 – of the total voting rights of all members or of the class, whether on a written resolution,[34] or a poll.[35] This is required because of the change to the requirements for written resolutions, which no longer need to be agreed unanimously. For a resolution passed on a show of hands, s 282(3) has been amended to implement the EU Shareholders Rights Directive[36] so that a simple majority will be counted from the votes cast by those entitled to vote.[37] Section 282 also makes clear that anything that can be done by ordinary resolution may also be done by special resolution.[38]

Section 283 defines a special resolution, whether of the members generally or of a class of the members, and whether as a written resolution,[39] or by a poll.[40] Class resolutions are covered because of the abolition of the extraordinary resolution.[41] For a resolution passed at a meeting by a show of hands, s 283(4) has been amended to implement the EU Shareholders Rights Directive[42] so that a 75% majority will be counted from the votes cast by those entitled to vote.[43] If a resolution is proposed as a special resolution, there is a requirement to state this, either in the text of the written resolution[44] or in the notice of the meeting.[45] Where a resolution is proposed as a special resolution, it can only be passed as such.[46]

There is no longer a special requirement for 21 days' notice of a special resolution. As to the length of notice for meetings, see **13.6**.

13.4 WRITTEN RESOLUTIONS OF PRIVATE COMPANIES

Provisions to 'deregulate' and simplify private company procedures were first introduced by the Companies Act 1989. Under these, unanimous

---

[34] Section 282(2).
[35] Section 282(4).
[36] Directive 2007/36/EC.
[37] See the Companies (Shareholders' Rights) Regulations 2009, SI 2009/1632, reg 2(1).
[38] Section 282(5).
[39] Section 283(2).
[40] Section 283(5).
[41] See ss 630 and 631, where a special resolution may be required for a variation of class rights; see **8.7**.
[42] Directive 2007/36/EC.
[43] See the Companies (Shareholders' Rights) Regulations 2009, SI 2009/1632, reg 2(2).
[44] Section 283(3)(a).
[45] Section 283(6)(a).
[46] Section 283(3)(b) and (6)(b).

consent could be obtained for a particular proposal without the necessity for a meeting (the written resolution procedure) and such consent could be obtained to disapply a Companies Act requirement for certain types of resolution (the elective resolution procedure). In accordance with the same philosophy, the statutory requirements now contained in Chapter 2 of Part 13 of the Companies Act 2006 have modernised and in part simplified the rules governing written resolutions, as well as completely abolishing the statutory requirement for a private company that is not a traded company[47] to hold an annual general meeting.

A crucial change to the previous position is that a written resolution no longer has to be agreed by all members, but merely by a simple majority or a three-quarters majority, as appropriate, depending on whether it is an ordinary or special resolution.[48] Because of this, Chapter 2 of Part 13 is more extensive than the provisions it replaced.[49] Further, there are, as under the previous legislation, two types of resolution for which the written resolution procedure cannot be used,[50] namely a resolution to remove a director[51] and a resolution to remove an auditor.[52] Even the smallest private company will still be obliged to hold a meeting for either of these purposes, but otherwise the expectation is that private companies will not hold formal general or class meetings. The application of these provisions cannot be excluded by anything in a company's articles.[53]

For the sake of completeness, s 288(4) makes it clear that any references to resolutions in any statutes or statutory instruments passed or made before Chapter 2 comes into force have effect as if they included references to written resolutions and s 288(5) ensures that written resolutions have the same effect as resolutions at meetings, whether general meetings or class meetings.

Section 285A[54] is concerned with voting rights on written resolutions, reflecting the fact that they do not need to be passed unanimously. Any provision in the articles providing that a member has a different number of votes in relation to a written resolution as opposed to a resolution on a poll in general meeting is void, and the member has the same number of votes.

A resolution may be proposed by the directors or by the members of a private company[55] and there are separate provisions laying down the

---

[47] See **13.1**.
[48] Companies Act 2006, ss 281(2) and 283(2).
[49] Sections 381A to 381C of the 1985 Act.
[50] Companies Act 2006, s 288(2).
[51] Section 168.
[52] Section 510.
[53] Section 300.
[54] This was inserted by the Companies (Shareholders' Rights) Regulations 2009, SI 2009/1632, reg 3, but is to the same effect as the original s 285(3).
[55] Section 288(3).

requirements in these separate instances, as explained below. As regards a proposed written resolution, the 'eligible members' are those entitled to vote on the circulation date of the resolution.[56] Special provision is made for the situation when those change on that date by providing that they are those members entitled to vote at the time the first copy of the resolution is sent or submitted to a member for his agreement.[57] The 'circulation date' is the date on which copies of a proposed resolution are sent or submitted to members or, if that happens on different days, the first of those days.[58]

13.4.1   Agreement to a written resolution

Section 296 lays down the procedure for a member to signify his agreement to a proposed written resolution. This is when the company receives from him, or someone acting on his behalf, an authenticated document that indicates the resolution to which it relates and indicates his agreement to that resolution. This document must be sent in hard copy or electronic form[59] and agreement once signified cannot be revoked.[60] A written resolution is passed when the required majority of eligible members have signified their agreement to it.[61]

In order to ensure that there is finality, a proposed written resolution lapses if it is not passed before the end of either the period specified in the company's articles or, in the absence of such provision, the period of 28 days beginning with the circulation date.[62] Any agreement signified after that period is ineffective.[63]

For the meaning of 'authenticated document' reference has to be made to s 1146. This provides that a document sent or supplied in hard copy form is sufficiently authenticated if it is signed by the person sending or supplying it. A document in electronic form is sufficiently authenticated if the identity of the sender is confirmed in a manner specified by the company or, failing such a specification, if the communication contains or is accompanied by a statement of the identity of the sender and the company has no reason to doubt the truth of that statement.[64]

---

[56]   Section 289(1).
[57]   Section 289(2).
[58]   Section 290.
[59]   Section 296(2).
[60]   Section 296(3).
[61]   Section 296(4).
[62]   Section 297(1).
[63]   Section 297(2).
[64]   See also Pt 3 of Sch 4.

13.4.2 Written resolution proposed by directors

The company must send or submit a copy of a written resolution proposed by the directors to every eligible member.[65] There are alternative ways in which this can be done. Either the proposal must be sent at the same time, so far as reasonably practical, in hard copy, in electronic form or by means of a website or, if it possible to do so without undue delay, by submitting the same copy to each eligible member in turn or different copies to each of a number of eligible members in turn. A combination of the above methods is also allowed.[66] The copy must be accompanied by a statement informing the member how to signify agreement to the resolution and as to the date by which the resolution must be passed if it is not to lapse.

Although there are criminal penalties for any breach of these requirements,[67] a resolution will be valid if passed, that is by the agreement of the requisite majority, despite a failure to comply with the section.[68] This seems to imply that if, for example, a member is not sent a copy of a proposed written resolution, provided that the agreement of a majority or 75 per cent of the members, depending on the nature of the resolution, is obtained, that breach is irrelevant. This is a somewhat surprising result since, if the non-recipient were known to be hostile to the proposal, it deprives them of the opportunity to attempt to persuade their fellow members to oppose the proposal. There might be grounds, in such a case, and certainly if the breach was intentional, for the member to lodge a petition under Part 30 alleging unfair prejudice.[69]

13.4.3 Written resolution proposed by members

Under s 292, members of a private company are given the right that to some extent mirrors the rights that members have had under previous legislation to requisition a general meeting[70] and require the circulation of a resolution at such a meeting.[71] Members who hold 5 per cent, or any lower percentage specified in the company's articles, of the relevant voting rights[72] may require the circulation of a proposed written resolution. This applies to any resolution except one which (a) would be ineffective because it is inconsistent with any enactment or the company's constitution or otherwise, (b) is defamatory of any person or (c) is frivolous or vexatious. It is presumably the responsibility of the directors, properly advised, to decide whether a resolution is so disqualified,

---

65 Section 291(2).
66 Section 291(3).
67 See s 291(5) and (6).
68 Section 291(7).
69 See Chapter 18.
70 See now s 303.
71 See now s 338, which is applicable only to public companies.
72 That is the voting rights of all members entitled to vote on a proposed resolution of the sort in question.

particularly by virtue of (c), above, but it is not difficult to imagine situations where there might be a challenge to their view.[73] The members may require the circulation of a statement of not more than 1,000 words to accompany the proposed resolution.[74]

The requirement for circulation may be made in hard copy or electronic form. It must identify the resolution and any accompanying statement and be authenticated by the person(s) making it.[75] However, the expenses of the company must be paid by the members requesting circulation unless the company resolves otherwise and, unless it has previously resolved otherwise, the company is not bound to comply unless there is deposited with it or tendered to it a sum reasonably sufficient to meet its expenses.[76] There is clearly room for argument as to what would be reasonably sufficient for this purpose; in a situation where all members can be contacted electronically, the cost should be minimal.

Section 293 specifies the requirements on a company faced with a requisition to circulate a proposed written resolution and accompanying statement. Those in s 293(2) and (4) mirror the requirements imposed on directors submitting a proposed resolution under s 291, as described above, except that rather than a statement as to how a member should respond, s 293(4) refers to 'guidance'. There does not seem to be anything of substance in the different words used. The company must circulate within 21 days of receipt of the requisition.[77] The consequences of failing to comply are a criminal penalty,[78] but that does not affect the validity of a passed resolution.[79]

A company or another person who claims to be aggrieved may apply to the court for permission not to circulate a members' statement.[80] The court may so order if satisfied that the rights in ss 292 and 293 are being abused and may in that event order the members who requested the circulation to pay the whole or part of the company's costs,[81] even if they are not parties to the application.

13.4.4　Electronic means

The provisions regarding written resolutions provide for the use of information technology as an alternative to traditional communication methods. As a supplement to the general provisions regarding the use of

---

[73] See also the similar qualifications in respect of s 338 regarding resolutions at meetings.
[74] Section 292(3).
[75] Section 292(6). As to authentication, see s 1146.
[76] Section 294.
[77] Section 293(3).
[78] Section 293(5) and (6).
[79] Section 293(7).
[80] Section 295.
[81] Expenses in Scotland.

electronic means,[82] s 298(1) provides that where a company has given an electronic address[83] in any document containing or accompanying a proposed written resolution, then subject to any conditions or limitations specified in the document, it is deemed to have agreed that any document or information relating to that resolution may be sent to that address.

There is also a special provision[84] regarding the case where a company sends a written resolution or a statement relating to a written resolution by means of a website.[85] Such a resolution or statement is not validly sent unless the resolution is available on the website through the whole of the period beginning with the circulation date and ending on the date on which the resolution lapses under s 297.

13.5 MEETINGS

This part of the chapter describes the requirements of the Companies Act 2006 relating to meetings of members of a company. As we have seen, the Act assumes that in most cases private companies will not hold formal general meetings. There is no longer any requirement on such companies to hold an annual general meeting, unless the memorandum or articles of a private company require it,[86] or unless a private company is a traded company (see below). Any provision specifying that one or more directors are to retire at an annual general meeting is not a provision expressly requiring the company to hold an annual general meeting.[87] A company is not to be treated as one whose articles expressly require it to hold an annual general meeting if immediately before 1 October 2007 it had elected to dispense with annual general meetings under s 366A of the Companies Act 1985.[88]

Thus, the provisions in Chapter 3 of Part 13 of the 2006 Act regarding resolutions at meetings will apply to the annual general meeting of a public company or a traded company, to any other general meeting held by a public company and to any general meeting in fact held by a private company. The previous concept of the extraordinary general meeting was abolished by the 2006 Act.[89] The provisions in Chapter 3 are applied with the necessary modifications and as appropriate to class meetings by ss 334

---

[82]   Section 1143 and Sch 5.

[83]   Any address or number used for the purposes of sending or receiving documents or information by electronic means (s 298(2)), which would normally be an email address.

[84]   Section 299.

[85]   To be read in conjunction with the provisions in Sch 5 regarding website communications.

[86]   See the Companies Act 2006 (Commencement No 3, Consequential Amendments, Transitional Provisions and Savings) Order 2007, SI 2007/2194, Sch 3, para 31(1) and (2).

[87]   Ibid, para 32(3).

[88]   Ibid, para 32(4), as inserted by the Companies Act 2006 (Commencement No 5, Transitional Provisions and Savings) Order, SI 2007/3495, Sch 5, para 2(6).

[89]   Note that reg 36 of the 1985 Table A, which provides for the calling of an extraordinary

and 335, the former section dealing with meetings of holders of a class of shares and the latter with meetings of classes of members of a company without a share capital. The following account assumes that the appropriate provisions apply to class meetings, except where it is indicated otherwise.

13.5.1 GENERAL MEETINGS

By way of introduction to the provisions regarding meetings, s 301 provides that a resolution of the members of the company is validly passed at a general meeting if notice of the meeting and of the resolution is given and the meeting is held and conducted in accordance with the provisions of Chapters 3 and 4 (where the latter is relevant) and the company's articles. This principle was previously expressed to apply to special resolutions,[90] and it is to be noted that both the requirements of the Act and of the articles must be observed; previously they were alternative requirements. Among other things, this ensures that the provisions of Table A to the 1985 Act that have been taken into the main body of the Act relating, for example, to proxies and other matters, cannot be avoided, except where the Act so allows.

Section 302 gives the directors the power to call a general meeting of the company. Previously this was provided for in the articles.[91] The directors' duty to call a general meeting must be exercised in accordance with ordinary fiduciary principles. It may be a fraud on a power to convene a meeting at a time or place where not all members can attend.[92]

It used to be customary to provide in the articles[93] that all business except such as was therein mentioned (e g declaring a dividend, considering the accounts, balance sheets and the reports of the directors and auditors, and electing directors and appointing auditors and fixing their remuneration) should be deemed special, and that notice must be given of the general nature of all special business. No such provision, however, was made in the 1985 Table A, which applies to companies registered under the 1985 Act, nor is there such provision in the model articles prescribed under the 2006 Act. It may be advisable to adopt an equivalent provision

---

general meeting, was repealed for companies registering after on or after 1 October 2007 by the Companies (Tables A to F) (Amendment) Regulations 2007, SI 2007/2541, reg 4.

[90] In s 378(6) of the 1985 Act.

[91] See reg 37 of the 1985 Table A, although note that this was amended for companies registering after on or after 1 October 2007 by the Companies (Tables A to F) (Amendment) Regulations 2007, SI 2007/2541, reg 5.

[92] *Pergamon Press Ltd v Maxwell* [1970] 1 WLR 1167; *Smith v Sadler* (1997) 25 ACSR 672, SC (NSW) (annual general meeting called for a time and a place where the directors knew a particular member would be unable to attend). An extraordinary general meeting has been held not to be validly constituted where the procedure by which applicants were admitted to membership did not comply with the articles of association: *POW Services Ltd v Clare* [1995] 2 BCLC 435.

[93] See 1948 Table A, art 52.

to that in the 1948 Table A. Without such a provision in the articles, it seems that no business could be transacted of which previous notice had not been given;[94] and where such provisions are included any business not specially mentioned as an exception can only be transacted if notice has been given.

13.5.2   Nature of a meeting

It has been held in Canada[95] and Australia[96] that a 'meeting' cannot be held over the telephone or by other similar means, although it would appear to be possible for a company's articles to deem an agreement reached by such a method to be equivalent to a resolution passed at a meeting.[97] However, in the light of the ruling in *Byng v London Life Association Ltd*[98] that a meeting may be held in more than one location, using audiovisual links, these rulings seem due for reconsideration: in practice, 'meetings' conducted by telephone conference are an everyday phenomenon. Nevertheless, it has been held in Australia that a statutory requirement that a person should 'preside' at a meeting requires his physical presence, and it is not sufficient that he should participate by video-conference link.[99]

In this respect the Companies (Shareholders' Rights) Regulations 2009, reg 8, in force from 3 August 2009, inserted a new s 360A into the 2006 Act, under which nothing in Part 13 of the Act is to be taken to preclude the holding and conducting of a meeting in such a way that persons who are not present together at the same place may by electronic means attend and speak and vote at it. Further, in the case of a traded company, the use of electronic means for the purpose of enabling members to participate in a general meeting may be made subject only to such requirements and restrictions as are necessary to ensure the identification of those taking part and the security of the electronic communication and proportionate to the achievement of those objectives. This does not affect any power of a company to require reasonable evidence of the entitlement of any person who is not a member to participate in the meeting.

If a chairman of a meeting moves a motion that is passed, it is not necessarily invalid merely because the chairman is not a member of the company.[100]

---

[94]   Per Littledale J in *R v Hill* (1825) 4 B&C 444.
[95]   *Re Associated Color Laboratories Ltd* (1970) 12 DLR (3d) 388, SC (BC).
[96]   *Magnacrete Ltd v Douglas-Hill* (1988) 7 ACLC 117, SC (WA).
[97]   *Holman v New Horizons Learning Centre (Canberra) Pty Ltd* (2004) 80 FLR 246, SC (NSW).
[98]   [1990] Ch 170.
[99]   *Holman v New Horizons Learning Centre (Canberra) Pty Ltd* (2004) 80 FLR 246, SC (NSW).
[100] *Re HIH Casualty and General Insurance Ltd* [2006] NSWSC 485 (SCt, NSW) at [26], and applying a dictum in *Re Horbury Bridge Coal, Iron and Waggon Co* (1879) 11 Ch D 109.

13.5.3 GENERAL MEETING REQUISITIONED BY MEMBERS

In certain circumstances a general meeting may be convened by the members themselves, subject to the conditions contained in ss 303 to 305 of the Companies Act 2006, which override any regulations of the company. Under s 303 the members of a company may require the directors to call a general meeting once the company has received requests to do so from members representing at least 5 per cent of such of the paid-up capital of the company as carries the right of voting at general meetings (excluding any paid-up capital held as treasury shares), or, in the case of a company not having a share capital, members who represent at least 5 per cent of the total voting rights of all the members having a right to vote at general meetings.[101] If the articles allow a smaller number to requisition a meeting, this, being an additional power not inconsistent with the Act, will be effective.

The requests must state the general nature of the business to be dealt with at the meeting and may include the text of a resolution that may properly be moved and is intended to be moved at the meeting.[102] Section 303(5) defines what type of resolution may be properly moved, namely one that would not be ineffective because it would be inconsistent with any enactment or the company's constitution or otherwise, would not be defamatory of any person or would not be frivolous or vexatious. The request can be in hard copy form or electronic form and must be authenticated by the person or persons making it.[103] Transmission of the requisition by fax is valid.[104] If joint holders of shares join in the requisition all must sign, unless the articles specifically authorise one to sign for all: the signature of one on behalf of all is of no avail.[105]

Following a request under s 303, under s 304, the directors must call a general meeting within 21 days from the date on which they become subject to the requirement, to be held on a date not more than 28 days after the date of the notice convening the meeting.[106] If the directors convene a meeting to consider part only of the specified matters the requisitionists may ignore it and call their own meeting, and if the requisition contains matters which, though apparently irregular, may be carried out in a lawful manner, the court will not restrain the holding of the meeting.[107] If the requests identify a proposed resolution, the notice of the meeting must include notice of the resolution and the business that may be dealt with at the meeting includes a resolution of which notice is

---

[101] Companies Act 2006, s 303(1) and (2), as amended by the Companies (Shareholders' Rights) Regulations 2009, SI 2009/1632, reg 4.

[102] Section 303(4); the ability to include a proposed resolution was new in the 2006 Act.

[103] Section 303(6).

[104] *PNC Telecom plc v Thomas* [2003] EWHC 2848 (Ch), [2004] 1 BCLC 88.

[105] *Patent Wood Keg Syndicate v Pearse* [1906] WN 164.

[106] Section 304(1).

[107] *Isle of Wight Railway Co v Tahourdin* (1883) 25 ChD 320, CA.

given in accordance with the section.[108] If the resolution is to be proposed as a special resolution, the directors are treated as not having duly called the meeting if they do not give the notice required by s 283.[109] Unreasonable and unjustifiable delay on the part of the directors may amount to 'unfair prejudice' for the purposes of Part 30 of the 2006 Act.[110] If the procedure adopted is irregular the court may interdict the holding of the meeting under that Part.[111]

If the directors do not call a meeting under s 304, then, by s 305, the members who requested the meeting, or any of them representing more than one-half of the total voting rights of all of them, may themselves call a general meeting; where the requests included the text of a proposed resolution, the notice of the meeting must include notice of the resolution.[112] The meeting must be called for a date not more than three months after the date on which the directors became subject to the requirement to call a meeting.[113] The meeting convened by requisitionists must be called in the same manner, as nearly as possible, as that in which meetings are required to be called by directors.[114] The business which may be dealt with at the meeting includes a resolution of which notice is given in accordance with s 305.[115] The secretary cannot without the sanction of the board summon the meeting on receipt of the requisition. Whether the requisitionists can employ him to give the notice after the 21 days have elapsed is still an open question.[116]

A meeting called by members under s 305 cannot deal with a resolution not included in the business for which the meeting was requisitioned. Unless the articles otherwise provide, the requisitionists will not be able to insist on any matter not in the requisition being included in the notice of meeting sent out by the company.[117] A resolution under these sections which calls for the replacement of the board of directors will fail if it does not identify which persons are to be elected as directors, the exact size of the new board, or which members of the old board are to be removed. The proposal lacked the necessary specificity to constitute the subject matter of a valid resolution. The proposal to remove the board also failed because it ignored a requirement of the company's articles that at least

---

[108] Section 304(2) and (3).
[109] Section 304(4).
[110] *McGuinness v Bremner plc* [1988] BCLC 673, Ct of Sess.
[111] *Hamilton v Premleven Ltd (No 1)* 1994 GWD 29–1737. (In this case the complainer failed when the meeting was properly convened; *Hamilton v Premleven Ltd (No 2)* 1994 GWD 29–1738.)
[112] Section 305(1) and (2).
[113] Section 305(3).
[114] Section 305(4). See *Re Windward Islands (Enterprises) Ltd* [1983] BCLC 293 at 296 to 297.
[115] Section 305(5).
[116] *Re State of Wyoming Syndicate* [1901] 2 Ch 431.
[117] *Ball v Metal Industries* 1957 SC 315.

two months' notice had to be given in respect of a meeting to consider the appointment of a newly proposed director.[118]

Any reasonable expenses incurred by the members requesting the meeting by reason of the failure of the directors duly to call a meeting must be reimbursed by the company, and any sum so reimbursed shall be retained by the company out of any sums due or to become due from the company by way of fees or other remuneration in respect of the services of such of the directors as were in default.[119]

There is no provision in the Companies Act 2006 similar to that usually inserted in articles, that at a meeting convened by members requesting the meeting no business is to be done other than that mentioned in the request. However, this is perhaps implied in the provision that the request must state the general nature of the business to be dealt with at the meeting. In any case due notice must be given of any business to be transacted.

The directors have a duty, as well as a right, to circularise the members for the purpose of advising them as to the prudence or propriety of any proposed resolution, and may use the company's money for this purpose or for procuring proxies in their own favour.[120]

13.5.4   ANNUAL GENERAL MEETINGS OF PUBLIC AND TRADED COMPANIES

As described earlier, under the Companies Act 2006 a private company is no longer required to hold an annual general meeting, unless its memorandum or articles expressly so require or unless it is a traded company, but this requirement is retained by s 336 for all public companies and, with effect from 3 August 2009, for any private company that is a traded company. The general provisions regarding meetings, described above, will of course apply to the annual general meeting of a public or traded company. This section is concerned only with the special requirements imposed by Chapter 4 of Part 13 of the 2006 Act.

By s 336(1), every public company must hold a general meeting as its annual general meeting in each period of six months beginning with the day following its accounting reference date (in addition to any other

[118]   *Rose v McGivern* [1998] 2 BCLC 593.
[119]   Section 305(6) and (7).
[120]   *Peel v London and North-Western Railway* [1907] 1 Ch 5, CA; *Campbell v Australian Mutual Provident Society* (1908) 77 LJPC 117; *Wilson v LMS Rly Co* [1940] Ch 393, CA; but if invitations to appoint proxies are issued at the company's expense, they should be sent to all the members entitled to be sent a notice of the meeting and to vote thereat by proxy: s 326.

meetings held during that period). By s 336(1A),[121] every private company that is a traded company must hold a general meeting as its annual general meeting in each period of nine months beginning with the day following its accounting reference date (in addition to any other meetings held during that period). A company that fails to comply with this requirement as a result of giving notice specifying a new accounting reference date and stating that the current accounting reference period or the previous accounting reference period is to be shortened[122] shall be treated as it had complied with s 336(1) if it holds a general meeting as its annual general meeting within three months of giving that notice.[123]

A notice calling an annual general meeting of a public company or traded company must state that the meeting is an annual general meeting.[124] The meeting of a public company that is not a traded company may be called by shorter notice than that required by s 307(2) or by the company's articles (as the case may be), if all the members entitled to attend and vote at the meeting agree to the shorter notice.[125] Where a notice calling an annual general meeting of a traded company is given more than six weeks before the meeting, the notice must include, if the company is a public company, a statement of the right under s 338 to require the company to give notice of a resolution to be moved at the meeting and, whether or not the company is a public company, a statement of the right under s 338A to require the company to include a matter in the business to be dealt with at the meeting.[126]

Repeated failure to hold annual general meetings and to lay annual accounts before the members may establish unfair prejudice in a petition under what is now Part 30 of the 2006 Act.[127]

13.5.5   Members' resolutions at annual general meetings

As well as the general power of members of any company to require the circulation of statements, as described below, ss 338 to 340 of the

---

[121] Inserted by the Companies (Shareholders' Rights) Regulations 2009, SI 2009/1632, reg 15, in respect of meetings of which notice is given, or first given, on or after 3 August 2009.

[122] Under s 392 of the 2006 Act.

[123] Section 336(2). Failure to hold an annual general meeting is an offence on the part of every officer of the company is default: s 336(3) and (4). Note that the Companies Act 2006 repealed and did not replace the provision (s 367 of the 1985 Act) giving the Secretary of State power to call or direct the calling of a general meeting.

[124] Companies Act 2006, s 337(1).

[125] Section 337(2), as amended by the Companies (Shareholders' Rights) Regulations 2009, SI 2009/1632. Where a meeting is held after the prescribed time voting rights are determined as at the actual time of the meeting, not as they would have been if the meeting had been held at the proper time: *Musselwhite v C H Musselwhite Ltd* [1962] Ch 964.

[126] Section 337(3) as inserted by the Companies (Shareholders' Rights) Regulations 2009, SI 2009/1632, reg 16.

[127] *Re a Company ex parte Shooter* [1990] BCLC 384.

Companies Act 2006 confer the right on members of public companies to require the company to give, to members of the company entitled to receive notice of the next annual general meeting, notice of a resolution which may properly be moved and is intended to be moved at that meeting. The company must act once it has received requests from members representing at least 5 per cent of the total voting rights of all members who have a right to vote on the resolution at the annual general meeting to which the requests relate (excluding any voting rights attached to any shares held as treasury shares) or from at least 100 members who have a right to vote on such a resolution who hold shares in the company on which there has been paid up an average sum, per member, of at least £100.[128] A request may be in hard copy or electronic form, must identify the resolution of which notice is to be given, must be authenticated by the person or persons making it, and must be received by the company not later than six weeks before the relevant annual general meeting or, if later, the time at which notice is given of that meeting.[129]

A resolution may properly be moved at an annual general meeting unless (a) it would, if passed, be ineffective (whether by reason of inconsistency with any enactment or the company's constitution or otherwise), (b) it is defamatory of any person, or (c) it is frivolous or vexatious. There was no limitation equivalent to (c) in the previous legislation.

A company required to give notice of a resolution under s 338 must send a copy of it to each member of the company entitled to receive notice of the annual general meeting in the same manner as notice of the meeting and at the same time as, or as soon as reasonably practicable after, it gives notice of the meeting.[130] The business which may be dealt with at an annual general meeting includes a resolution of which notice is given under s 339.[131] By s 340(1), the expenses of the company in complying need not be paid by the members who requested the circulation if sufficient requests are received before the end of the financial year preceding the meeting. Otherwise the expenses must be paid by the requisitioning members, unless the company resolves otherwise and, unless the company has previously so resolved, it is not bound to circulate a resolution unless there is deposited with or tendered to it a sum reasonably sufficient to meet its expenses not later than six weeks before the annual general meeting to which the requests relate or, if later, the time at which notice is given of the meeting.[132] There was no equivalent in

---

[128] Companies Act 2006, s 338(3).

[129] Section 338(4). Authentication is governed by s 1146 of the 2006 Act. As regards a document sent in hard copy form, it is sufficiently authenticated by signature (s 1146(2)); the names and addresses of the members need not be stated provided they can be identified from their signatures: *Young v Falkirk Football and Athletic Club Ltd* 1993 GWD 11–717.

[130] Section 339(1). As to the criminal penalty on every office in default, see s 339(4) and (5).

[131] Section 339(3).

[132] Section 340(2).

the previous legislation to the provision in s 340(1), which is clearly intended to facilitate the exercise of this right of members.

13.5.6 Rights of members of traded companies

Pursuant to the Shareholders' Rights Directive,[133] the Companies (Shareholders' Rights) Regulations 2009[134] introduced a new right as regards the members of a traded company. Regulation 17 inserted a new s 338A into the 2006 Act as regards meetings of which notice is given, or first given, on or after 3 August 2009. Under this, the members of a traded company may require the company to include in the business to be dealt with at an annual general meeting any matter (other than a proposed resolution) which may properly be included in the business, other than a matter that is defamatory of any person or is frivolous or vexatious. The company must act once it has received requests from members representing at least 5 per cent of the total voting rights of all members who have a right to vote at the meeting to which the requests relate or from at least 100 members who have a right to vote on the resolution to which the requests relate and who hold shares in the company on which there has been paid up an average sum, per member, of at least £100. A request may be in hard copy or electronic form, must identify the matter to be included in the business, must be accompanied by a statement setting out the grounds for the request and must be authenticated by the person or persons making it, and must be received by the company not later than six weeks before the meeting to which it relates or, if later, the time at which notice is given of that meeting.

A company that is required under s 338A to include any such matter must give notice of it to each member of the company entitled to receive notice of the annual general meeting in the same manner as notice of the meeting and at the same time as, or as soon as reasonably practicable after, it gives notice of the meeting. It must also publish it on the same website as that on which the company published the information required by s 311A.[135] By s 340B, the expenses of the company in complying need not be paid by the members who requested the inclusion of the matter if sufficient requests are received before the end of the financial year preceding the meeting. Otherwise the expenses must be paid by the members who requested the inclusion of the matter, unless the company resolves otherwise and, unless the company has previously so resolved, it is not bound to comply with s 340A unless there is deposited with or tendered to it a sum reasonably sufficient to meet its expenses not later than six weeks before the annual general meeting to which the requests relate or, if later, the time at which notice is given of the meeting.

---

[133] Directive 2007/36/EC.

[134] SI 2009/1632.

[135] Companies Act 2006, s 340A, inserted by the Companies (Shareholders' Rights) Regulations 2009, SI 2009/1632, reg 18. There are criminal penalties for officers in default. The meaning of 'officer in default' is to be found in s 1121.

As regards dealings in shares in a traded company before general meetings, s 360B(1) provides that any provision of a traded company's articles is void in so far as it would have the effect of (a) imposing a restriction on the right of a member to participate in and vote at a general meeting of the company unless the member's shares have (after having been acquired by the member and before the meeting) been deposited with, or transferred to, or registered in the name of another person, or (b) imposing a restriction on the right of a member to transfer shares in the company during the period of 48 hours[136] before the time for the holding of a general meeting if that right would not otherwise by subject to that restriction. By subsection (2), a traded company must determine the right to vote at a general meeting by reference to the register of members as at a time (determined by the company) that is not more than 48 hours before the time for the holding of the meeting.

13.5.7 Court's power to order a meeting

Under s 306 of the Companies Act 2006,[137] the court has power to order a meeting to be called, held and conducted in any manner it thinks fit if it is impracticable to call a meeting in any manner in which meetings of that company may be called or to conduct the meeting in the manner prescribed by the company's articles or the Act. It may act either of its own motion or on the application of any director of the company or of any member who would be entitled to vote at the meeting. The court may give such ancillary or consequential directions as it thinks expedient, including a direction that one member of the company present at the meeting be deemed to constitute a quorum. A meeting called, held and conducted in accordance with such an order is deemed for all purposes to be a meeting of the company duly called, held and conducted.[138]

Recent case law has clarified the principles to be applied in deciding whether or not the power should be exercised.[139] Section 306 is a procedural section intended to enable company business that needs to be conducted at a general meeting to be so conducted. There must be impracticability affecting either the calling of a meeting or the conduct of a meeting.[140] Where there is a majority shareholder and no class rights which the convening of a general meeting is designed to override, the court in exercising its discretion will consider whether the company is in a position to manage its affairs properly and will also take into account the

---

[136] Not including any part of a day that is not a working day: s 360B(3).

[137] Replacing s 371 of the 1985 Act.

[138] Section 306(3) and (4).

[139] See *Union Music Ltd v Watson* [2003] 1 BCLC 453, *Re Woven Rugs Ltd* [2002] 1 BCLC 324, *Vectone Entertainment Holding Ltd v South Entertainment Ltd* [2004] 2 BCLC 224, *Alvona Developments Ltd v Manhattan Loft Corporation (AC) Ltd* [2005] EWHC 1567 (Ch).

[140] *Monnington v Easier plc* [2006] 2 BCLC 283, Ch D (no order where shareholders could requisition the convening of a meeting under what is now s 305 if necessary, even if the board could frustrate the purpose of that meeting).

ordinary right of the majority shareholder to remove or appoint a director. The fact that quorum provisions require two members' attendance is not in itself sufficient to prevent the court making an order to break the deadlock in favour of a majority shareholder. Although the section is not designed to affect substantive voting rights or to shift the balance of a power where it has been agreed that power should be shared equally, a quorum provision is not sufficient to constitute such an agreement. A minority shareholder seeking an order that a general meeting of the company be convened under s 306 (where this is combined with allegations of improper disposition of company property by the defendant as director and shareholder), must fail if the claim cannot be brought within an exception to the rule in *Foss v Harbottle*.[141] Such a claim should be brought not by way of an originating summons but in a contentious action with pleadings.[142] The fact that the chairman of the meeting might face a conflict of interest is not sufficient to render it impracticable to call a meeting, as there is no general requirement that a chairman be neutral.[143]

When the hearing of an unfair prejudice petition under Part 30 of the 2006 Act is pending, and quorum requirements and refusal to attend meetings by a minority shareholder prevent the holding of shareholders' meetings, the court will order a meeting under s 306 so as to allow directors to be appointed and accounts to be laid.[144] However, to protect the minority shareholder until the Part 30 petition is heard, restrictive provisions will be placed upon what could be done at, or in consequence of, the meeting ordered by the court. The directors appointed would have to give an undertaking not to exclude the minority shareholder from his directorship or interfere in his day-to-day conduct of the business. Nor could they effect any alteration in the constitution or capital of the company.[145] However, it has since been held that the existence of a Part 30 petition at the date of hearing of the s 306 application is a matter which bears upon the discretion of the court but does not prevent it exercising powers under s 306.[146] There it was impracticable to hold a meeting and it was plainly right and desirable to obtain a proper board by allowing a meeting to be held to deal with the inquorate condition of both board and general meetings.

---

[141] (1843) 2 Hare 461.

[142] *Re Downs Wine Bar* [1990] BCLC 839 at 842.

[143] *Might SA v Redbus Interhouse plc* [2004] 2 BCLC 449.

[144] *Re Sticky Fingers Restaurant Ltd* [1992] BCLC 84.

[145] Ibid at 89 to 90.

[146] *Re Whitchurch Insurance Consultants* [1994] BCC 51 at 56. *Re Sticky Fingers* (above) was distinguished on the ground that there the hearing of the Part 30 petition was imminent: *Re Opera Photographic* [1989] 5 BCC 601 followed.

13.5.8   CLASS MEETINGS

Most of the provisions in Chapter 3 of Part 13 of the Companies Act 2006 apply to meetings of classes of members, which may be held to vary class rights[147] or summoned by the court under Part 26 of the 2006 Act. If a class of shareholders consists of only one person (e g where one person holds all the preference shares) clauses in the memorandum or articles requiring the consent of a meeting of such class may be satisfied by a resolution in writing signed by that one person.[148]

Prima facie, a separate meeting of a class should be attended only by members of that class, but if, the presence of strangers being known, no objection is taken at the meeting to their presence the members present must be taken to have assented to the meeting being so conducted.[149]

13.5.9   Court's powers in respect of meetings

The court has inherent powers in respect of meetings of companies. Where a court has granted a decree of specific performance to implement an earlier agreement to allot shares and obtain Stock Exchange listing, and the court's order required a meeting of the shareholders to be summoned in order to increase capital, the directors have a duty to use their best endeavours in circulating resolutions, etc, to support the resolutions proposed. Where the directors fail to do so, the court may direct that the meeting should be adjourned sine die on the ground that the resolutions put to the meeting were wholly misconceived and the circular accompanying the notice of meeting was misleading.[150]

13.6   NOTICE OF MEETINGS

Under s 310(1) of the Companies Act 2006, notice of a general meeting must be sent to every member of the company and every director[151] and also to the auditors.[152] However, this requirement has effect subject to any enactment and any provision of the company's articles. Where restricted voting rights are conferred on a class, the entitlement to receive notice of or to attend at the meeting is usually expressly made to depend on the same circumstances as the right to vote. Even if it is not, the same result may follow.[153] Under s 311(1), notice of a general meeting must state the time and date and place of the meeting. Under s 311(2), it must also state the general nature of the business to be dealt with at the meeting, although this requirement is subject to any provisions of the company's

---

[147] As to these, see **8.7**.
[148] *East v Bennett Bros* [1911] 1 Ch 163.
[149] *Carruth v Imperial Chemical Industries* [1937] AC 707, HL.
[150] *Northern Counties Securities v Jackson* [1974] 1 WLR 1133.
[151] Companies Act 2006, s 310(1).
[152] Companies Act 2006, s 502(2).
[153] *Re Mackenzie & Co* [1916] 2 Ch 450.

articles. These requirements are modified and extended in the case of traded companies, as explained below.

Member for the purposes of s 310 includes any person who is entitled to a share in consequence of the death or bankruptcy or a member, if the company has been notified of their entitlement.[154] Although this is subject to the articles, it reverses the previous position that, in the absence of some special provision in the articles, it was not necessary to give notice to the representatives of deceased shareholders unless such representatives had become members by formal registration.[155] Under art 134 of the 1948 Table A and reg 38 of the 1985 Table A, such notice is required to be given to representatives of deceased shareholders: the use to which they can put this notice is not clear, since art 32 of the Table A of the 1948 Act and reg 31 of the 1985 Table A prevent them attending the meeting, and, of course, voting thereat. Even if the articles allowed them to attend and vote, their votes could not be counted on a resolution, because under s 282 and s 283 the votes to be counted are those of members. The model articles prescribed under the 2006 Act are to the same effect.[156]

When notice has been duly given of a meeting the meeting cannot be postponed by a subsequent notice;[157] the proper course is for the meeting to be held and adjourned.

A notice of meeting, to be good, must be given by persons authorised to summon the meeting, and resolutions passed at a meeting convened by the secretary without the authority of the board are invalid. However, it would appear that it will be sufficient if the directors agree informally but unanimously.[158] If the notice purports to be issued by the authority of the directors and is subsequently ratified by them at a board meeting, it will be valid.[159] Warrington J held that a notice given by a person believing himself to be a director, and subsequently adopted by another director, was valid under an article rendering valid acts done by persons acting as directors, although an irregularity be subsequently discovered,[160] and

---

[154] Section 310(2). Bankruptcy includes the sequestration of the estate of a member and a member's estate being the subject of a protected trust deed (within the meaning of the Bankruptcy (Scotland) Act 1985): s 310(3).

[155] *Allen v Gold Reefs of West Africa* [1900] 1 Ch 656, CA; see also *Bolton Engineering Ltd v T J Graham & Sons Ltd* [1957] 1 QB 159.

[156] See art 27 and art 66, respectively, of the model articles for private companies limited by shares and public companies.

[157] *Smith v Paringa Mines* [1906] 2 Ch 193.

[158] But it will be otherwise if the directors are not unanimous. See *Bolton Engineering Ltd v T J Graham & Sons Ltd* [1957] 1 QB 159; *Collie's Claim* (1871) LR 12 Eq 246 at 258; *Re Haycraft Gold Reduction Co* [1900] 2 Ch 230; *Re State of Wyoming Syndicate* [1901] 2 Ch 431.

[159] *Hooper v Kerr Stuart & Co* (1900) 83 LT 729.

[160] *Transport v Schomberg* (1905) 21 TLR 305.

Swinfen Eady J held that the resolutions of a general meeting convened by de facto directors are not invalidated by any irregularity in the constitution of the board.[161]

A statement in the report of the directors sent with the notice of meeting that certain business will be proposed is a sufficient notice.

If all the members do not attend, a company is not 'corporately assembled', so as to be able to do business unless the meeting is held upon notice given to every member entitled thereto, and complies with the provisions of the articles as to stating the objects for which the meeting is held.[162]

13.6.1 Notices of meetings of traded companies

The Companies (Shareholders' Rights) Regulations 2009,[163] made amendments to provisions of the 2006 Act as regards notice of meetings of traded companies.

Regulation 10 amends s 311, as described in **13.6**, in two ways. First the proviso to s 311(2), that the requirement for notice to state the general nature of the business of a meeting is subject to the company's articles, does not apply to meetings of traded companies. Secondly, s 311(3) requires the notice of a general meeting of a traded company also to include:

(a) a statement giving details of the website on which the information required by s 311A (see below) is published;

(b) a statement that the right to vote at the meeting is determined by reference to the register of members and of the time when that right is determined in accordance with s 360B;

(c) a statement of the procedures with which members must comply in order to be able to attend and vote at the meeting (including the date by which they must comply);

(d) a statement giving details of any forms to be used for the appointment of a proxy;

(e) where the company offers the facility for members to vote in advance or by electronic means, a statement of the procedure for doing so (including the date by which it must be done) and details of any forms to be used; and

---

[161] *Boschoek Proprietary Co v Fuke* [1906] 1 Ch 148.
[162] *Baillie v Oriental Telephone Co* [1915] 1 Ch 503, CA, cf *Young v Ladies' Imperial Club* [1920] 2 KB 523.
[163] SI 2009/1632.

(f)   a statement of the right of members to ask questions in accordance
       with s 319A.

Regulation 11 inserted a new s 311A. Under this, in advance of a general
meeting, a traded company must publish on a website that is maintained
by or on behalf of the company and identifies the company the following
information:

(a)   the matters set out in the notice of the meeting;

(b)   the total numbers of shares in the company and shares of each class
       in respect of which members are entitled to exercise voting rights at
       the meeting;

(c)   the totals of the voting rights that members are entitled to exercise at
       the meeting in respect of the shares of each class;[164] and

(d)   members' statements, members' resolutions and members' matters of
       business received by the company after the first date on which notice
       of the meeting is given.

Access to the information and the ability to obtain a hard copy from the
website, must not be conditional on the payment of a fee or otherwise
restricted. The information must be available, as regards (a), (b) and (c)
above, on or before the first date on which notice of the meeting is given
and, as regards (d) above, as soon as is reasonably practicable. It must be
kept available throughout the period of two years from the date on which
it is first made available, although a failure to keep it available is
disregarded if the information is made available on the website for part of
that period and the failure is wholly attributable to circumstances that it
would not be reasonable to have expected the company to prevent or
avoid. However, failure to comply with these requirements does not affect
the validity of the meeting or anything done at the meeting, although
breach amounts to an offence on the part of any officer in default.

13.6.2   Form of notice

Notice of general meetings must be given in hard copy form, in electronic
form or by means of a website, or partly by one such means and partly by
another.[165] The general provisions of the Companies Act 2006 regarding
company communications[166] apply to notice of meetings. One particular
provision concerning notice is s 309 regarding the publication of notice of
a meeting on a website. This requires the notification to state that it
concerns a notice of a company meeting, specify the place, date and time

---

[164] These totals must be ascertained at the latest practicable time before the first date on
       which notice of the meeting is given.
[165] Companies Act 2006, s 308.
[166] Sections 1143–1148 and Sch 5.

of the meeting and, in the case of a public company, state whether the meeting will be an annual general meeting. Further, the notice must be available on the website throughout the period beginning with the date of that notification and ending with the conclusion of the meeting.

13.6.3 Accidental failure to give notice

There used to be a standard provision in articles that the accidental omission to give notice to or the non-receipt of notice by any person entitled to receive notice would not invalidate the proceedings.[167] This is now provided for by s 313 of the Companies Act 2006 and applies to notice of a general meeting or of a resolution that is intended to be moved at a general meeting. It will prevent any such omission being relied upon as a ground for questioning any resolutions or proceedings of a meeting of which a member did not receive notice. However, by s 313(2), this statutory provision may be excluded by the company's articles, except in relation to notice given under s 304, s 305 or s 309. It has been held that such a provision in the articles will validate a meeting where some members did not receive notice of a meeting because their addressograph plates had been separated from the rest. This had been done because their dividend warrants had previously been returned undelivered and uncashed.[168] Presumably, this would also cover a situation where the whereabouts of a shareholder was unknown to the company (e g communications had been returned from an old address and where no later address was known). These authorities are clearly applicable to what is now the statutory provision in s 313.

However, it has been held that an article such as art 51 of the 1948 Table A[169] will not cover a deliberate omission even if based on a mistaken belief that a member is not entitled to notice.[170] Again the same must apply in relation to s 313. Where all the shareholders attend a meeting of which no notice or insufficient notice has been given they can waive the informality, and pass valid resolutions.[171] Where a transaction is honest and intra vires, and for the benefit of the company, the corporators, if unanimous, can discuss and agree to it with one another separately, without holding a meeting at all.[172] A member who is in fact present and has allowed the business determined upon to be carried out for a long period cannot subsequently set up an irregularity in summoning the meeting.[173]

---

[167] See art 51 of the 1948 Table A and reg 39 of the 1985 Table A.

[168] *Re West Canadian Collieries Ltd* [1962] Ch 370. See also *Royal Mutual Benefit Society v Sharman* [1963] 1 WLR 581.

[169] See also reg 39 of the 1985 Table A.

[170] *Musselwhite v CH Musselwhite & Sons Ltd* [1962] Ch 964.

[171] See the cases discussed at **13.2**.

[172] *Parker and Cooper v Reading* [1926] Ch 975.

[173] *Re British Sugar Refining Co* (1857) 3 K&J 408.

13.6.4   Length of notice

The Companies (Shareholders' Rights) Regulations 2009[174] made changes to the provisions dealing with length of notice of meetings with effect from 3 August 2009. By s 307(1) of the Companies Act 2006, in relation to meetings of which notice was given, or first given before that date, a general meeting of a private company (other than an adjourned meeting) had to be called by notice of at least 14 days. By s 307(2), a general meeting of a public company (other than an adjourned meeting) had to be called by notice of:

(1)   in the case of an annual general meeting, at least 21 days; and

(2)   in any other case, at least 14 days.

The company's articles may require a longer period of notice than the above.[175]

With effect from meetings of which notice was given, or first given, on or after 3 August 2009, the Regulations inserted subsections (A1) and (A2) into s 307, so that it applies to (a) a general meeting of a company that is not a traded company and (b) a general meeting of a traded company that is an opted-in company under s 971(1) where the meeting is held to decide whether to take any action that might result in the frustration of a takeover bid for the company or the meeting is held by virtue of s 969. The length of notice for general meetings of traded companies other than one within (b) above is governed by s 307A.[176] Subject to the company's articles, which may require a longer period, these must be called, in the case of an annual general meeting, by notice of at least 21 days and, in any other case, by notice of at least 14 days if two specified conditions are met and at least 21 days if they are not met. The two specified conditions are (a) that the company offers the facility for members to vote by electronic means accessible to all members who hold shares that carry rights to vote at general meetings,[177] and (b) a resolution reducing the period of notice to not less than 14 days has been passed at the immediately preceding annual general meeting or at a general meeting held since that annual general meeting.[178]

Under art 50 of the 1948 Table A an annual general meeting and a meeting for passing a special resolution must be called by 21 days' notice in writing at the least, and a meeting other than an annual general

---

[174]   SI 2009/1632.

[175]   Section 307(3).

[176]   This does not apply to class meetings of traded companies: s 334(2A), as inserted by the Regulations.

[177]   This condition is met if there is a facility offered by the company and accessible to all such members, to appoint a proxy by means of a website.

[178]   If a company has not yet held an annual general meeting, a special resolution is required.

meeting or a meeting for passing a special resolution must be called by 14 days' notice in writing at the least. A number of days' notice, if not qualified, means that number of *clear* days – ie exclusive of the day of giving the notice and the day of the meeting.[179] See likewise reg 38 of the 1985 Table A. Table A of the 1948 Act expressly provides that the number of days shall be clear days, by saying (art 50) that the notice is to be exclusive of the day on which it is served or deemed to be served and of the day for which it is given. In the equivalent article of the 1985 Table A (reg 38) reference is made to 'clear days' notice'. Article 131 of the 1948 Table A provides that where a notice of meeting is sent by post, service is deemed to be effected at the expiration of 24 hours after the notice, properly addressed and stamped, has been posted.[180] The equivalent provision in the 1985 Table A (reg 115) refers to 48 hours. If the notice may be given by advertisement, it will be sufficient if it appears at noon in a newspaper circulating in the neighbourhood of the registered office of the company seven clear days before the meeting (art 104 of Table A of the 1929 Act, not reproduced in Table A of the 1948 Act or the 1985 Table A) and it is not necessary to show that it reached all the members on that day.[181] It has been held in respect to an identical article that where this is relied upon during a postal strike (and as a result the notice of meeting was not received by a number of members), an injunction might be granted to a shareholder to restrain the holding of the meeting.[182]

13.6.5 Short notice

As indicated above, the articles may provide for giving longer notice than specified, but not shorter notice. Section 307(4) does, however, go on to provide some latitude, by saying that a general meeting, other than the annual general meeting of a public company,[183] may be called by shorter notice than that otherwise required if shorter notice is agreed by the

---

[179] Companies Act 2006, s 360, confirming *Re Railway Sleepers Supply Co* (1885) 29 ChD 204, and cases there cited; also *Mercantile Investment Co v International Co of Mexico* [1893] 1 Ch 484n at 489, CA. See also, as to notice of resolutions, *Re Hector Whaling Co* [1936] Ch 208. But the Scottish courts have held otherwise: *Neil McLeod & Sons Ltd, Petitioner* 1967 SC 16.

[180] In *Parkstone Ltd v Gulf Guarantee Bank plc* [1990] BCC 534, a corporate member registered abroad had given the company an address within the UK for service of notices. The company sent a notice to the member at its registered office address in Gibraltar. This was held to be a valid notice under art 131 of the 1948 Table A; the words 'in the ordinary course of post' in that regulation not being confined to post within the UK. (*Note*: the equivalent provision in the 1985 Table A, reg 112, is more specifically worded on this point than the 1948 version, providing that such a member shall be entitled to have notices given at the address in the UK provided for the purpose.)

[181] *Sneath v Valley Gold Ltd* [1893] 1 Ch 477, CA.

[182] *Bradman v Trinity Estates plc* [1989] BCLC 757. It should be noted that the articles of the company in question had a separate provision for an alternative method of service where there was 'total suspension or curtailment of postal services'. The notice of meeting had been delivered by courier to members with a London address, but posted to those outside London. This was an ex parte injunction where Hoffmann J exercised his discretion on the balance of various considerations particular to the case.

[183] Section 307(7).

members. The shorter notice must be agreed by a majority in number of the members having a right to attend and vote at the meeting, being a majority who (a) together hold not less than the requisite percentage in nominal value of the shares giving a right to attend and vote at the meeting (excluding any shares in the company held as treasury shares), or (b) in the case of a company not having a share capital, together represent not less than the requisite percentage of the total voting rights at that meeting of all the members.[184] The requisite percentage is (a) in the case of a private company, 90 per cent or such higher percentage (not exceeding 95 per cent) as may be specified in the company's articles and (b) in the case of a public company, 95 per cent.[185] As far as a private company is concerned, a percentage higher than 90 per cent is only effective in relation to a provision of the articles adopted on or after 1 October 2007.[186]

13.6.6   Notice of adjourned meeting

In general, no notice is required to be given of adjourned meetings, if held within the limits prescribed by the articles of association, as they are merely continuations of the previous meetings, at which, if notice was properly given, all the members have had the opportunity of being present, and those who were present have agreed to the time and place of adjournment.[187] But under art 57 of the 1948 Table A, if the adjournment is for 30 days or more, fresh notice is required. In the 1985 Table A (reg 45) that period was reduced to 14 days. In art 57 'notice of the adjourned meeting shall be given as in the case of the original meeting'. In reg 45 'at least 7 clear days' notice shall be given specifying the time and place of the adjourned meeting and the general nature of the business to be transacted'. The model articles prescribed under the 2006 Act are to the same effect as the 1985 Table A.[188]

Although the adjourned meeting is only a continuation of the original meeting,[189] if notice to propose a director is required to be given so many days before 'the day of election', and the election takes place at an adjourned meeting, the notice is sufficient if given the specified time before the day of holding the adjourned meeting. It would be otherwise if the article required notice before the meeting at which the election is to take place.[190]

---

[184] Section 307(5).
[185] Section 307(6).
[186] See para 26A of the Companies Act 2006 (Commencement No 3, Consequential Amendments, Transitional Provisions and Savings) Order 2007, SI 2007/2194, as inserted by Sch 3, para 2 of the Companies Act 2006 (Commencement No 6, Savings and Commencement Nos 3 and 5 (Amendment)) Order 2008, SI 2008/674.
[187] *Wills v Murray* (1850) 4 Ex 843; *Scadding v Lorant* (1851) 3 HLC 418.
[188] See art 41 and art 33, respectively, of the model articles for private companies limited by shares and public companies.
[189] *Catesby v Burnett* [1916] 2 Ch 325.
[190] See *McLaren v Thomson* [1917] 2 Ch 261.

13.6.7 Misleading notices

The articles may provide that notice must be given of the general nature of any special business to be transacted,[191] and by s 283(6) notice must be given of the intention to propose a special resolution. In the absence of provisions in the articles of association, and if Table A of the 1948 Act is inapplicable, no business can be brought on without notice. Note that neither the 1985 Table A nor the model articles prescribed under the 2006 Act contain an equivalent to art 52 of the 1948 Table A. The latter does not require notice of certain routine matters at an annual general meeting. The notice must 'give at any rate a fair, candid, and reasonable, explanation' of the business proposed, and if something is wrapped up or kept back it will invalidate the proceedings.[192] Thus, it was held that a notice of a meeting to adopt new articles which might be seen at the company's office was not sufficient where the new articles increased the directors' remuneration and borrowing power, and made other important changes.[193]

Directors who are to derive some benefit under resolutions have sometimes attempted to cover it up in the notice of meeting in such a way that it shall not be fully understood by the shareholders. Such a notice is insufficient, and a resolution passed in pursuance of it will be invalid.[194] Thus, where in a reconstruction directors did not state that they were participating in the purchase consideration to be received by the selling company,[195] or where, in seeking the sanction of the company to the retention by the directors of remuneration they had received irregularly, no proper statement was made as to the amount,[196] the resolutions passed were held to be invalid. The holding of general meetings without sufficient notice, where this results in the ineffective creation of new shares, may amount to unfairly prejudicial conduct of the company's affairs within Part 30 of the Companies Act 2006.[197]

---

[191] Table A has this provision (Table A of 1862, art 35; Table A of 1908, art 49; Table A of 1929, art 42; Table A of 1948, art 50; reg 38 of the 1985 Table A).

[192] *Kaye v Croydon Tramways* [1898] 1 Ch 358, CA, cf *Young v Ladies' Imperial Club* [1920] 2 KB 523, CA, where in a club case the rules required that the expulsion of a member should only be effected at a meeting of the committee specially convened for that purpose. A notice 'to elect directors' constitutes a sufficient notice to elect directors up to the maximum number authorised by the articles: *Choppington Collieries v Johnson* [1944] 1 All ER 762, CA.

[193] *Normandy v Ind Coope & Co* [1908] 1 Ch 84.

[194] *Pacific Coast Coal Mines v Arbuthnot* [1917] AC 607, PC.

[195] *Kaye v Croydon Tramways* [1898] 1 Ch 358, CA; *Tiessen v Henderson* [1899] 1 Ch 861. See also *Clarkson v Davies* [1923] AC 100, CA.

[196] *Baillie v Oriental Telephone Co* [1915] 1 Ch 503, CA.

[197] *Re a Company ex parte Shooter* [1990] BCLC 384 at 394.

13.6.8   NOTICES AND AMENDMENTS

Only such motions can be submitted to a meeting as fall within the notice given of business to be transacted, but if all the members of the company are present they can waive any irregularity.[198] The chairman usually proposes the resolutions necessary for the business brought forward by the board, and if notice has been given of other resolutions calls upon the giver of the notice to bring forward his motion. If a member during the meeting proposes a motion, then in cases where notice is required, and has not been given, or where insufficient notice has been given, the chairman should refuse to put the motion to the meeting. But an amendment of which notice has not been given may be proposed to a motion properly moved, so long as it is within the scope of the notice originally given.[199] If the notice of meeting is accompanied by the directors' report, stating that certain business will be proposed, this is a sufficient notice.[200] It has been held that where the notice was of a resolution to appoint as directors three persons named in the notice it was competent for the company to add three others by way of amendment.[201]

Sometimes several amendments are proposed to one motion, in which case the chairman will have to exercise his discretion very carefully in allowing them and in arranging their order. He should get them all put into writing and see how far they are consistent one with another. Prima facie they ought to be put in the order in which they are proposed, but the nature of them will often make it more desirable to arrange them so that they may not clash. After any motion or amendment has been accepted by the meeting no amendment inconsistent with it should be submitted, as the acceptance of the prior proposal negatives the inconsistent amendment. The amendments should be disposed of before the original motion. If the chairman improperly refuses to submit an amendment to the meeting, the resolution actually carried will be invalidated.[202]

Where notice has been given of several resolutions, each resolution must, if any member so requires, be put separately,[203] although if the meeting is unanimously in favour of all the resolutions it may be this would not be material.[204] Under s 160 of the Companies Act 2006, which applies only to public companies and does not apply to a resolution altering the

---

[198] *Re Express Engineering Works* [1920] 1 Ch 466, CA; *Re Oxted Motor Co* [1921] 3 KB 32.

[199] *Torbock v Lord Westbury* [1902] 2 Ch 871; *Henderson v Bank of Australasia* (1890) 45 ChD 330, CA. The latter case also decided that an amendment need not be submitted in writing, but is good if its effect be made reasonably clear to the meeting orally.

[200] *Irvine v Union Bank of Australia* (1877) 2 App Cas 366 at 376, PC; *Boschoek Proprietary Co v Fuke* [1906] 1 Ch 148.

[201] *Betts & Co v Macnaghten* [1910] 1 Ch 430.

[202] *Henderson v Bank of Australasia* (1890) 45 ChD 330, CA.

[203] *Patent Wood Keg Syndicate v Pearse* [1906] WN 164; *Thomson v Henderson's Transvaal Estates* [1908] 1 Ch 765 at 776. The poll must also be taken separately: *Blair Open Hearth Furnace Co v Reigart* (1913) 108 LT 665.

[204] *Re RE Jones Ltd* (1933) 50 TLR 31.

company's articles) a motion for the appointment of two or more persons as directors by a single resolution must not be made, unless a resolution that it shall be so made has first been agreed to nem con, and if so moved it is void, whether objected to at the time of its being moved or not. But this avoidance does not operate so as to make applicable a provision for the automatic reappointment of retiring directors in default of another appointment, nor does it exclude the operation of s 161, which provides that the acts of a director are to be valid notwithstanding any defect that may afterwards be discovered in his appointment or qualification. For the purpose of the section a motion for approving an appointment or nominating a person for appointment is to be treated as a motion for his appointment.

The fact that some of the resolutions submitted are in breach of the company's constitution will not affect the validity of others, even if all were part of one scheme, eg for the purpose of reconstruction.[205]

13.6.9 Special notice

The Companies Act 2006 requires special notice of two types of resolution, and these are resolutions in respect of which even a private company must hold a meeting. These are:

(1) under ss 511 and 515, a resolution at a general meeting removing an auditor before the expiration of his period of office or appointing as auditor a person other than a retiring auditor; and

(2) under s 168, a resolution to remove a director or to appoint somebody instead of a director so removed at the meeting at which he is removed.

Section 312 deals with special notice. It provides that where by any provision of the Companies Acts special notice is required of a resolution, the resolution is not effective unless notice of the intention to move it has been given to the company at least 28 days before the meeting at which it is moved. Then the company must give its members notice of any such resolution at the same time and in the same manner as it gives notice of the meeting or, if that is not practicable, must give them notice, either by advertisement in a newspaper having an appropriate circulation or in any other manner allowed by the articles, at least 14 days before the meeting. If, after notice of the intention to move such a resolution has been given to the company, a meeting is called for a date 28 days or less after the notice has been given, the notice is deemed properly given though not given within the time required.

---

[205] *Thomson v Henderson's Transvaal Estates* [1908] 1 Ch 765.

Section 312 does not give to any individual shareholder a right (which he does not otherwise possess) to compel the inclusion of a resolution in the agenda for a company meeting.[206] To do so a member must either be given such a right by the articles or enjoy sufficient support to make a requisition under s 314. This section is discussed immediately below.

13.6.10 Members' statements

Section 314 of the Companies Act 2006 confers certain rights on members in regard to the circulation of statements in relation to a general meeting.[207] The specified number of members may require the company to circulate, to members entitled to receive notice of a general meeting, a statement of not more than 1,000 words with respect to a matter referred to in a proposed resolution or other business to be dealt with at that meeting. The company is required to circulate such a statement once it has received requests to do so from members representing at least 5 per cent of the total voting rights of all the members who have a relevant right to vote (excluding any voting rights attached to any shares in the company held as treasury shares) or at least 100 members who have a relevant right to vote and hold shares on which there has been paid up an average sum, per member, of least £100.[208] A 'relevant right to vote' means (a) in relation to a statement with respect to a matter referred to in a proposed resolution, a right to vote on that resolution at the meeting to which the requests relate and (b) in relation to any other statement, a right to vote at the meeting to which the requests relate.[209] A request may be in hard copy or electronic form, must identify the statement to be circulated, must be authenticated by the person or persons making it and must be received by the company at least one week before the meeting to which it relates.[210]

The company must send a copy of the statement to each member of the company entitled to receive notice of the meeting in the same manner as the notice of the meeting and at the same time as, or as soon as reasonably practicable after, it gives notice of the meeting.[211]

The expenses of the company is circulating a statement need not be paid by the requisitioning members if (a) the meeting to which the requests relate is an annual general meeting of a public company and (b) requests sufficient to require the company to circulate the statement are received

---

[206] *Pedley v Inland Waterways Association* [1977] 1 All ER 209.

[207] For the fines imposed in the event of default on officers of the company, see s 315(3) and (4).

[208] Section 314(2).

[209] Section 314(3).

[210] Section 314(4). Authentication is governed by s 1146 of the 2006 Act. As regards a document sent in hard copy form, it is sufficiently authenticated by signature (s 1146(2)); the names and addresses of the members need not be stated provided they can be identified from their signatures: *Young v Falkirk Football and Athletic Club Ltd* 1993 GWD 11–717.

[211] Section 315(1).

before the end of the financial year preceding the meeting.[212] Otherwise, the expenses of the company must be paid by the members who requested the circulation unless the company resolves otherwise and, unless the company has previously so resolved, it is not bound to circulate the statement unless there is deposited with or tendered to it a sum reasonably sufficient to meet its expenses in doing so.[213]

The company is also not bound to circulate any statement if, on an application either by the company or another person who claims to be aggrieved, the court is satisfied that the rights conferred by ss 314 and 315 are being abused.[214] The court may order the company's costs (in Scotland, expenses) on an application under this section to be paid in whole or in part by the requisitionists, even if they are not parties to the application. Under the predecessor to this provision, the jurisdiction of the court was limited to circumstances where it was satisfied that the rights were being abused to secure needless publicity for defamatory matter. The wider jurisdiction will clearly allow an application to prevent the circulation of a statement that is, for example, made by activists but is not clearly defamatory.

13.6.11 ELECTRONIC COMMUNICATIONS AND MEETINGS

Section 333 of the Companies Act 2006 makes provision for the sending of documents or information relating to proceedings at a meeting where an electronic address has been given in a notice calling a meeting. 'Electronic address' means any address or number used for the purposes of sending or receiving documents or information by electronic means.[215] It has to be read together with the general provisions about electronic communications to companies in Part 3 of Schedule 4. In such a case, the company is deemed to have agreed that any documents or information may be sent by electronic means to that address, subject to any conditions or limitations specified in the notice. The same applies[216] where an electronic address is given in an instrument of proxy sent out by the company or in an invitation to appoint a proxy issued by the company. Here documents relating to proxies include the appointment of a proxy, any documents necessary to show the validity of, or otherwise relating to, the appointment of a proxy, and notice of the termination of the authority of a proxy.[217]

---

[212] Section 316(1).
[213] Section 316(2).
[214] Section 317.
[215] Section 333(4).
[216] Section 333(2).
[217] Section 333(3).

13.7 CONDUCT OF MEETINGS

At least as far as many public companies are concerned, it is only at general meetings that the shareholders can exercise any control over the affairs of the company. As regards such companies, the Companies Act requires the directors to lay before the company in general meeting copies of the company's annual accounts, the directors' report and the auditors' report on those accounts.[218]

As far as the chairman of a general meeting is concerned, s 319 of the Companies Act 2006 provides that, subject to any provision of the company's articles that states who may or may not be chairman, a member may be elected to be the chairman of a general meeting by a resolution of the company passed at the meeting. This statutory provision is clearly permissive and normally, subject to the articles, the chairman of directors or, if there be no such chairman, in accordance with s 319, the person elected by the meeting takes the chair. The model articles prescribed under the 2006 Act provide that, if the directors have appointed a chairman, that person should chair general meetings if present and willing to do so. Otherwise, the directors present at the meeting or, if no directors are present, the meeting must appoint a director or member as chair, as the first item of business.[219]

It is the chairman's duty to preserve order, conduct proceedings regularly, and take care that the sense of the meeting is properly ascertained with regard to any question before it.[220] The conduct of a meeting is largely in the hands of the chairman with the assent of the persons properly present.[221] Under the general law of meetings, if the person appointed does not attend, those present may appoint someone to chair the meeting.[222]

The articles may sometimes provide that, where there is no chairman of the board of directors and no directors present, the members may choose a chairman of the general meeting from one of their number. In *Re Bradford Investments*[223] it was held that under such an article, a solicitor holding a proxy of a member could assume the position of a temporary chairman to supervise the election of a proper chairman. He could

---

[218] See Chapter 14.

[219] See arts 39 and 31, respectively, of the model articles for private companies limited by shares and public companies (Companies (Model Articles) Regulations 2008, SI 2008/3229).

[220] Per Chitty J in *National Dwellings Society v Sykes* [1894] 3 Ch 159.

[221] *Carruth v Imperial Chemical Industries* [1937] AC 707, PC at 767 per Lord Maugham: see also the observations of Lord Russell of Killowen in the same case at 761. See *John v Rees* [1969] 2 WLR 1294 in respect of the chairman's power to adjourn the meeting in the event of disorder. He must act in good faith and should only exercise this power in the last resort. He should not adjourn the meeting for longer than is necessary.

[222] *Re Salcombe Hotel Development Corporation Ltd* (1989) 5 BCC 807.

[223] [1991] BCLC 224.

exercise the power under the articles given to the chairman to determine the admissibility of votes attached to any shares where an objection was raised. In consequence, a proper chairman was elected and directors were also subsequently elected. Hoffmann J held that, while the temporary chairman was entitled to make a ruling, this was 'open to challenge, in later proceedings, within the limits which the courts will interfere with the internal affairs of companies'.[224]

As well as replacing and modifying the former s 378(4) of the 1985 Act,[225] s 320 of the 2006 Act incorporates what is in reg 47 of the 1985 Table A. It ensures that the chairman's declaration of a vote taken on a show of hands is conclusive evidence of the resolution being passed or lost without proof being provided of the number of votes in favour or against being recorded, unless a poll is demanded on the resolution and is not subsequently withdrawn. As well as applying at the meeting, s 320(2) provides that an entry in the minutes of the meeting is also conclusive evidence without such proof.

It is customary for the chairman to introduce the report of the directors in a speech in which he explains the position of the company and gives as much information about its affairs as he thinks fit. He concludes by moving that the report be adopted, in which he is seconded by another of the directors. The shareholders then comment on or criticise the report and the chairman's speech, and ask for any further information they desire. However, the chairman and directors are not bound to give any information beyond what must be contained in the report,[226] and if they consider it undesirable to answer any questions they may refuse to do so. If the shareholders are dissatisfied, they may oppose the motion that the report be accepted, but even if the opposition be successful it has no effect, for it is not necessary that the report should be accepted by the meeting. Such a rejection of the report, however, is considered a vote of censure on the board of directors. If the dissatisfied shareholders succeed in rejecting the report, they usually move to appoint a committee of inspection; but whether this is as an amendment or by way of original resolution it would seem to require notice, for this is a matter of great moment on which all the shareholders should have an opportunity of voting. Even if notice be given, and the resolution passed, the committee will have very small powers. The dissatisfied shareholders may apply to the Secretary of State who has the power to appoint an inspector under s 431 of the Companies Act 1985, but a deposit of a security for the payment of costs may be required.[227] A company cannot take the control of its affairs out of the hands of the directors and give powers to a committee, except in the manner specified in the articles. Accordingly, if

---

[224] [1991] BCLC 224 at 229. Hoffmann J in fact upheld the legal basis on which the chairman gave his ruling: ibid at 229 to 234.

[225] This subsection applied only to votes on special or extraordinary resolutions.

[226] *Re Bradford Investments*, above.

[227] See Chapter 18.

there is no power to remove directors, the company must wait until the articles are altered or the obnoxious directors retire in due course,[228] though the powers of the company in general meeting have since these decisions been much strengthened by the power to remove directors by ordinary resolutions under what is now s 168 of the 2006 Act.[229] Often, however, when directors find the meeting hostile they assent to the appointment of a committee to report to the general meeting, which is adjourned.

On the report being carried, one of the directors will move the payment of a dividend in accordance with the report. The articles often provide that the shareholders may reduce, but not increase, the dividend recommended by the directors.[230]

The re-election of retiring directors and the filling up of vacancies will follow, and the remuneration of the auditors will afterwards be fixed.

If there is no special business, the meeting should then terminate with the customary 'votes of thanks'. If, however, there is special business, the business of which notice has been given should be proceeded with. It was usual at one time to transact special business only at an extraordinary general meeting, which was often called to follow the annual general meeting. This is unnecessary unless the articles expressly require it, there being no reason why special business should not be transacted at an annual general meeting. Further, as has been seen, there is now no concept anyway in the Companies Act of an 'extraordinary general meeting', although this would not prohibit a company's articles for making provision for such in the unlikely event that it were thought necessary.

Prima facie, every member has a right to be heard and to advocate or oppose any resolution before the meeting;[231] but if a matter has been fairly debated, the chairman, with the sanction of the majority, can stop the discussion, or, in modern phrase, 'the closure may be adopted' after resolutions have been reasonably debated.[232]

---

[228] *Automatic Self-Cleansing Filter Syndicate Co v Cunninghame* [1906] 2 Ch 34, CA. *Salmon v Quin & Axtens* [1909] AC 442, HL; *John Shaw & Sons (Salford) v Shaw* [1935] 2 KB 113 at 134, CA.

[229] See, however, *Bushell v Faith* [1970] AC 1099, HL.

[230] Eg art 114 of the 1948 Table A, reg 102 of the 1985 Table A and arts 30 and 70, respectively, of the model articles prescribed under the 2006 Act for private companies limited by shares and public companies (Companies (Model Articles) Regulations 2008, SI 2008/3229).

[231] *Const v Harris* (1824) Turn & R 496 at 525. As to the rights of proxies, see [11].

[232] *Wall v London and Northern Assets Corporation* [1898] 2 Ch 469, CA; *Carruth v Imperial Chemical Industries* [1937] AC 707 per Lord Maugham at 767, HL.

A meeting if duly called cannot be postponed by a subsequent notice issued before the meeting.[233] It can, however, be adjourned before any business is done. The power to adjourn meetings and the status of adjourned meetings are considered later in this chapter.

13.7.1   General meetings of traded companies

The Companies (Shareholders' Rights) Regulations 2009,[234] inserted a new s 319A into the Companies Act 2006. This provides that, at a general meeting of a traded company, the company must cause to be answered any question relating to the business being dealt with at the meeting put by a member attending the meeting. However, no such answer need be given if to do so would interfere unduly with the preparation for the meeting or involve the disclosure of confidential information, if the answer has already been given on a website in the form of an answer to a question or if it is undesirable in the interests of the company or the good order of the meeting that the question be answered.

13.7.2   QUORUM AT GENERAL MEETINGS

No business can be done at a meeting unless a quorum is present.[235] Section 318 of the Companies Act 2006 provides for a quorum for a meeting of one 'qualifying person' in the case of a single member company and, subject to the provisions of the articles, two 'qualifying persons' in any other case. A 'qualifying person' is defined[236] as an individual who is a member, a representative of a corporation, or a proxy. This represents a change from the position under earlier legislation, by which only members personally present could count towards a quorum, but the effect of s 318(2) is to exclude the possibility of two or more corporate representatives or proxies of the same member comprising a quorum. Section 318 does not apply to class meetings held in connection with a variation of class rights,[237] but special provision is made for them as described below.

Apart from requirements in the articles as to quorum, it is well established that, except in the case of a single member company, there must be at least two members present who remain throughout the meeting.[238] It was held

---

[233]   *Smith v Paringa Mines* [1906] 2 Ch 193.

[234]   SI 2009/1632.

[235]   *Howbeach Coal Co v Teague* (1860) 5 H&N 151; *Re Romford Canal Co* (1883) 24 ChD 85. A company may validly provide in its articles that the presence of a specified member is necessary for there to be a quorum: *Amalgamated Pest Control Pty Ltd v McCarron* (1994) 31 ACSR 42, SC (Qld). In such a case, the designated member must be present personally and not by proxy: *Re M Harris Ltd* 1956 SC 207, Ct Sess.

[236]   Section 318(3).

[237]   Sections 334(3)(a) and 335(3)(a).

[238]   *Sharp v Dawes* (1876) 2 QBD 26, CA; *Re Sanitary Carbon Co* [1877] WN 223; *Prain and Sons* 1947 SC 325; *Re London Flats* [1969] 1 WLR 711.

that under the quorum provision in the 1948 Table A (art 53), it was sufficient if there was a sufficient quorum at the beginning of a meeting, but this need not continue throughout the meeting.[239] However, reg 41 of the 1985 Table A requires a continuing quorum: '... if during a meeting such a quorum cease to be present, the meeting shall stand adjourned to the same day in the next week', etc. This was likely to prove a very awkward provision in the case of private companies and should have been avoided by explicit provision. Although nowadays the expectation is that the vast majority of private companies will only rarely hold general meetings, the same considerations apply, as the model articles prescribed under the 2006 Act require the chairman to adjourn a meeting if a quorum ceases to be present.[240]

A member present in two capacities (eg as an individual member and as a trustee) counts as two members personally present.[241] Where a company is represented under s 323, its representative must be counted in estimating the quorum.[242] An executor or administrator is not a member until he has taken the shares of the deceased into his own name;[243] he cannot therefore be counted in estimating a quorum, unless the articles expressly allow it.

13.7.3   QUORUM AT CLASS MEETINGS

Sections 334 and 335 make special provision for the quorum at class meetings held to consider a variation of class rights. For an original meeting in the case of a meeting of a class of shares, the quorum is two persons present holding at least one-third in nominal value of the issued shares of the class (excluding any shares held as treasury shares) and, for an adjourned meeting, the quorum is one person present holding shares of the class.[244] For this purpose a person present by proxy or proxies is treated as holding only the shares in respect of which those proxies are authorised to exercise voting rights.[245] For an original meeting in the case of a class rights meeting in a company without a share capital, the quorum is two members of the class present in person or by proxy who together represent at least one-third of the voting rights of the class and, for an adjourned meeting, the quorum is one member of the class present in person or by proxy.[246]

---

[239] *Re Hartley Baird Ltd* [1955] Ch 143.

[240] Articles 41 (private companies limited by shares) and 33 (public companies), respectively.

[241] *Neil McLeod & Sons Ltd*, Petitioners 1967 SC 16. This was decided in respect of s 134(c) of the Companies Act 1948, which made provision for quorum in the absence of a provision in the articles.

[242] Section 318(3).

[243] *Re Bowling & Welby's Contract* [1895] 1 Ch 663 at 670, CA.

[244] Section 334(4).

[245] Section 334(5).

[246] Section 335(4).

13.7.4 Abuse of quorum provisions and the court's power to order a meeting

Where minority shareholders have it in their power to deny a sufficient quorum to a proposed general meeting, the court may direct a meeting under what is now s 306 of the Companies Act 2006.[247] Thus, where a corporate shareholder holding nearly 90 per cent of the shares wished to alter the articles to remove a share qualification requirement and to appoint directors to replace those who had transferred their shares, it was held that quorum provisions in the articles of a company were not to be regarded as a right vested in the minority to frustrate the wishes of the majority shareholders. To refuse an application under s 306 would deprive the majority shareholder of the right to alter the articles of association. It would confer a veto on the minority that was not commensurate with their shareholding.[248]

The Court of Appeal has held[249] that the power conferred by s 306 was not intended to permit a meeting to be summoned which would have the effect of overriding a class right where two classes of shares (A shares and B shares) were created under the terms of a shareholders' agreement. This provided, inter alia, that a meeting of shareholders would not be quorate unless a B shareholder or a proxy for such was present. The Court of Appeal held that this quorum provision created a class right designed to protect the owner of the B shares so that he could not be removed as a director.

The Court of Appeal has also held that s 306 is a procedural section and is not designed to alter substantive voting rights or shift the balance of power between shareholders by permitting a 50 per cent shareholder to overrule the wishes of another 50 per cent shareholder. In *Ross v Telford*[250] the two 50 per cent shareholders had agreed that power should be equally shared. Here, potential deadlock was a matter that should be taken to have been agreed on with the consent and for the protection of each of them.[251] Thus s 306 did not empower the court to break a deadlock at either board or general meetings of the company. Indeed, s 306 had nothing to do with board meetings. This decision was distinguished in the later Court of Appeal case of *Union Music Ltd v*

---

[247] See **13.5.9** generally as to s 306.

[248] *Re HR Paul & Son Ltd* (1973) *The Times*, November 17 (applying *Re El Sombrero* [1958] Ch 900); see also *Re Opera Photographic Ltd* [1989] BCLC 763.

[249] *Harman v BML Group Ltd* [1994] 1 BCLC 674.

[250] [1998] 1 BCLC 82, CA. This decision was followed and *Union Music Ltd v Watson*, below, was distinguished in *Alvona Developments Ltd v Manhattan Loft Corporation (AC) Ltd* [2005] EWHC 1567 (Ch), where there was an agreement between the two shareholders, holding 70 per cent and 30 per cent respectively, that there would always be one jointly appointed director.

[251] Ibid, at 87 to 88.

Watson,[252] where the two shareholdings were not equal. In such a case, where there were no class rights that the convening of a general meeting was designed to override, the court would consider whether the company was in a position to manage its affairs properly and take account of the right of the majority shareholder to remove or appoint a director. The fact that, under the company's articles of association, for a general meeting to be quorate both shareholders had to be present was not in itself a sufficient reason to preclude an order under s 306 to break a deadlock in favour of a majority shareholder. An order was made for the calling of a general meeting to consider the question of the appointment of a further director and to allow the voting on that, even if only one member was present. The possibility of unfairness resulting from an order under s 306 (leading to an unfair prejudice petition) is not necessarily a ground for refusing an order under the section.[253]

An unusual use of the power conferred by s 306 was made by Rimer J in *Re British Union for the Abolition of Vivisection*.[254] Here a general meeting degenerated into a disorderly tumult, with the consequence that police had to intervene and close the meeting down for fear of breach of the peace. The articles of association did not provide for voting by proxy. The majority of the company's executive committee (the name of its board of directors) asked the court to convene a meeting to pass a special resolution to alter the articles so as to allow voting by proxy. The persons entitled to attend this meeting would be restricted to the executive committee. The applicants also sought that other members of the company should vote by postal ballot and not by personal attendance. In granting the order requested, Rimer J held that the violent and disruptive behaviour of a radical minority at previous meetings justified this unusual form of extraordinary general meeting to alter the articles. There was a legitimate fear that previous disruption might otherwise be repeated.

13.7.5　ADJOURNED MEETINGS

In the absence of express directions in the articles the chairman of a general meeting can, on proper ground, adjourn the meeting,[255] but the articles may only give him power to do so with the consent of the meeting, in which case he cannot, by leaving the chair before the business is completed, bring the meeting to a close; if he purports to do so, the meeting may appoint another chairman and proceed with the business.[256] If the articles provide that 'the chairman, with the consent of the meeting, may adjourn', the majority cannot compel the chairman to adjourn the

---

[252] [2003] 1 BCLC 453, CA. See also *Vectone Entertainment Holding Ltd v South Entertainment Ltd* [2004] 2 BCLC 224.

[253] *Re Woven Rugs Ltd* [2002] 1 BCLC 324.

[254] [1995] 2 BCLC 1.

[255] *R v D'Oyly* (1840) 12 A&E 139; *R v Wimbledon Local Board* (1882) 8 QBD 459, CA.

[256] *National Dwellings Society v Sykes* [1894] 3 Ch 159; *John v Rees* [1969] 2 WLR 1294.

meeting if he thinks it ought to proceed.[257] The 1948 Table A (art 57) and the 1985 Table A (reg 45) require the chairman to adjourn the meeting if so directed by the meeting, further providing (by art 61 and reg 51 of the respective Tables) that a poll demanded on the question of adjournment shall be taken forthwith. The model articles prescribed under the 2006 Act for companies registering on or after 1 October 2009[258] are a little more expansive than the provisions of both versions of Table A.

These require the chairman to adjourn a meeting where there is no quorum within half an hour of the starting time of the meeting or if a quorum ceases to be present or if directed to do so by the meeting. The chairman may adjourn a quorate general meeting if either the meeting consents or it appears to him that an adjournment is necessary to protect the safety of any person attending the meeting or ensure that the business of the meeting is conducted in an orderly manner.

The Court of Appeal reviewed and clarified the legal principles governing the chairman's power to adjourn a meeting in *Byng v London Life Association Ltd.*[259] Here, the relevant article expressly conferred on the chairman power to adjourn but only with the consent of a quorate meeting. This consent is obviously required if the circumstances permit the chairman to discover whether or not the meeting agrees to an adjournment but 'if the circumstances are such that the wishes of the meeting cannot be validly ascertained, why should [such an article] be read as impairing the fundamental common law duty of the chairman to regulate proceedings so as to enable those entitled to be present and to vote to be heard and to vote'.[260]

Thus in any circumstances where there is a meeting at which the views of the majority cannot be validly ascertained, the chairman has a residual common law power to adjourn.[261] The Court of Appeal, however, differed from the judge below who had held that the only restriction on the chairman's exercise of his power (ie where the meeting cannot be consulted) is that of good faith. In Browne-Wilkinson LJ's judgment, *Wednesbury* principles provide the test for the proper exercise of this discretion:

'The chairman's decision will not be declared invalid unless on the facts which he knew or ought to have known he failed to take into account all

---

[257] *Salisbury Gold Mining Co v Hathorn* [1897] AC 268, PC.

[258] See arts 41 (private companies limited by shares) and 33 (public companies), respectively (Companies (Model Articles) Regulations 2008, SI 2008/3229).

[259] *Byng v London Life Association Ltd* [1989] BCLC 400.

[260] Ibid, per Browne-Wilkinson V-C at 411, applying *Jackson v Hamlyn* [1953] Ch 577, and distinguishing *Salisbury Gold Mining Co Ltd v Hathorn* [1897] AC 268.

[261] In *Byng* the initial meeting place turned out to be too small to accommodate all the members who attended, the audio-visual arrangements to link members in overflow rooms with the main building broke down and as a result there was considerable confusion.

relevant factors, took into account irrelevant factors, or reached a conclusion which no reasonable chairman, properly directing himself as to his duties, could have reached, ie the test is the same as that applicable on judicial review in accordance with the principles of *Associated Provincial Picture Houses Ltd v Wednesbury Corporation*.[262] This was the approach adopted by Uthwatt J in *Second Consolidated Trust Ltd v Ceylon Amalgamated Tea and Rubber Estates Ltd*[263] where he held a chairman's decision invalid on the grounds that he had failed to take into account a relevant factor.'[264]

In *Byng* the chairman failed to satisfy this test since he had failed to take into account the following relevant factors: the attempts by members to adjourn the meeting sine die; their objections to the adjournment of the meeting to the afternoon (at a larger meeting place); that the members present at the morning meeting who could not attend the adjourned meeting would be unable to vote since it was too late for them to deposit proxies. Finally, the chairman's opinion that it was urgent to pass a special resolution that day was mistaken since there was still ample time to organise a fresh meeting.[265]

The Court of Appeal also held that for a meeting to be validly constituted it was not necessary for all the members to be physically present in the same room. 'Overflow' rooms may be used if adequate audio-visual aids are used to allow all members to see and hear what is going on in other rooms and to communicate properly. Where, as in *Byng*, such arrangements break down, the meeting becomes incapable of transacting any business but it is not a nullity.[266] The chairman still retains his power under the articles to adjourn so long as this is properly exercised.

An adjourned meeting is merely a continuation of the original meeting,[267] and all the requirements as to the original meeting must have been complied with to make the adjourned meeting valid. In the absence of special regulations no further notice is necessary, and if any notices have to be given before 'the meeting' this will be read as being before the commencement of the original meeting. The same quorum will be required as for the original meeting unless the articles otherwise

---

[262] [1948] 1 KB 223.

[263] [1943] 2 All ER 567.

[264] Mustill and Woolf LJJ applied the same reasoning, but see Woolf LJ ([1989] BCLC 400 at 419), who was reluctant to apply the *Wednesbury* test of unreasonable behaviour.

[265] See [1989] BCLC 400 at 412 to 413.

[266] See the judgment of Browne-Wilkinson VC at 406 to 409, applying *Fletcher v New Zealand Glue Co Ltd* (1911) 31 NZLR 129 and distinguishing *Harben v Phillips* (1883) 23 ChD 14, and *Re Portuguese Consolidated Copper Mines Ltd* (1889) 42 ChD 160.

[267] *Wills v Murray* (1850) 4 Ex 843; *Scadding v Lorant* (1851) 3 HLC 418; *McLaren v Thomson* [1917] 2 Ch 261. As to date of a resolution passed at an adjourned meeting, see s 332. This provides that where a resolution is passed at an adjourned meeting it shall for all purposes be treated as having been passed on the date on which it was in fact passed, and shall not be deemed to have been passed at an earlier date. This applies to shareholders' meetings, class meetings and also to directors' meetings.

provide.[268] Proxies given for the original meeting are available for an adjourned meeting; but where articles required proxies to be lodged so many hours before a meeting, they had to be deposited that number of hours before the commencement of the original meeting.[269] To avoid this it is often provided that proxies must be lodged not less than so many hours[270] before 'the meeting or adjourned meeting', as in art 69 of the 1948 Table A, reg 62 of the 1985 Table A and art 39 of the model articles for public companies prescribed under the 2006 Act.

13.7.6 VOTES AND POLLS

A right to vote is property,[271] and the courts will intervene to protect a member from being deprived of this right.[272] Where shares are mortgaged, but the mortgagor's name remains on the register of members, he alone can vote, but he must do so in accordance with the direction of those entitled to the beneficial interest in the shares unless[273] it is otherwise agreed. However, an unpaid or partly paid vendor of shares remaining on the register after a contract of sale retains, vis-à-vis the purchaser, the right to decide how to exercise the voting rights.[274] The company, however, is not concerned to inquire as to the beneficial interest and must accept the vote of the registered holder of the shares, and where shares are mortgaged and placed in the names of trustees for the mortgagee, these trustees may vote contrary to the wishes of the mortgagor even though no interest is in arrear and the principal is not payable.[275] It has been held in Australia that an article that vested in persons other than the registered shareholders the right to vote at meetings of the company is invalid.[276]

There are a number of provisions in Part 13 of the Companies Act 2006 regarding voting on resolutions. Section 284 provides for general rules on voting, whether on a written resolution, on a show of hands at a meeting or on a poll taken at a meeting. The general rules, namely one vote per share or per member on a written resolution or a poll and one vote per person present on a vote by show of hands, can be varied by the

---

[268] Article 54 of the 1948 Table A (as amended by the Companies Act 1980, Sch 4) requires the same quorum for the adjourned meeting. See likewise reg 41 of the 1985 Table A and the model articles prescribed under the 2006 Act.

[269] *McLaren v Thomson* [1917] 2 Ch 261.

[270] This must not exceed 48: Companies Act 2006, s 327(2).

[271] In exercising the right to vote, a shareholder may normally vote in his own interests and is subject to no fiduciary restraints.

[272] *Pender v Lushington* (1877) 6 ChD 70; *Osborne v Amalgamated Society of Railway Servants* [1911] 1 Ch 540 at 567 per Buckley LJ, CA.

[273] *Wise v Lansdell* [1921] 1 Ch 420; *Puddephatt v Leith* [1916] 1 Ch 200.

[274] *Musselwhite v C H Musselwhite* [1962] 1 Ch 965; *Strachan v Aberdeen Industrial Doctors Ltd* 1995 SCLR 1098 (Sh Ct).

[275] *Siemens Brothers & Co v Burns* [1918] 2 Ch 324, CA.

[276] *Shears v Phosphate Co-operative Co of Australia Ltd* (1988) 14 ACLR 747, FC (Vic).

company's articles.[277] Special articles of association frequently provide for a different apportionment of votes,[278] but a vote for every share on a poll is usual and was adopted in art 62 of the 1948 Table A and reg 54 of the 1985 Table A, although the model articles prescribed under the 2006 Act are silent in this respect. The register of members should be in readiness at the meeting to refer to for the number of shares held by each member, and the consequent number of votes to which he is entitled on a poll.

Under art 60 of the 1948 Table A and reg 50 of the 1985 Table A, and most special articles, the chairman had a second or casting vote in the case of an equality of votes, but he had no such right at common law.[279] Initially, the effect of the sections of the Companies Act 2006 (ss 281 and 282) regarding resolutions was that the chairman could no longer have a casting vote, and this will be the case as regards companies registered on or after 1 October 2007 and before 30 September 2009.[280] However, where, immediately before 1 October 2007, the articles of a company provided for such a casting vote, unless that provision has been removed by a subsequent alteration of the articles, it continues to have effect, notwithstanding ss 281 and 282. In addition, the restoration of such an article will be effective.[281] There is no provision in the model articles prescribed under the 2006 Act for the chairman to have a casting vote.

Where there is a mode of voting known to the community, that mode should be followed unless a binding rule is found in the articles to the contrary, and likewise any common-law rule as to voting will prevail unless inconsistent with the articles.[282] Thus, at common law votes in the first instance are taken by a show of hands, each shareholder having a single vote for himself, but none for any persons whose proxies he holds.[283] But if a sufficient number of shareholders are dissatisfied with the result of the count of hands, they can demand a poll, as described below.

---

[277] Section 284(4). Note that the Companies (Shareholders' Rights) Regulations 2009, SI 2009/1632, reg 2, added a new subsection (5) to s 284 to the effect that nothing in the section is to read as restricting the effect of ss 152, 285, 322, 322A or 323.

[278] As to the validity of an article giving weighted voting rights to a director on a resolution to remove him from office, see *Bushell v Faith* [1970] AC 1099, HL, discussed at **15.9**. Where the Act confers a power to do a particular thing by special resolution an article that purports to require a larger majority than that prescribed by the Act for a special resolution is ineffective: see *Ayre v Skelsey's Adamant Cement Co Ltd* (1904) 20 TLR 587 (affd on other grounds at (1905) 21 TLR 464). The above rule is not affected by the decision in *Bushell v Faith*.

[279] *Nell v Longbottom* [1894] 1 QB 767.

[280] To that end, reg 50 of the 1985 Table A was deleted as regards companies registered on or after 1 October 2007: the Companies (Tables A to F) (Amendment) (No 2) Regulations 2007, SI 2007/2826, reg 3.

[281] Companies Act 2006 (Commencement No 3, Consequential Amendments, Transitional Provisions and Savings) Order 2007, SI 2007/2194, Sch 3, para 23A, as inserted by the Companies Act 2006 (Commencement No 5, Transitional Provisions and Savings) Order 2007, SI 2007/3495, Sch 5, para 2(5).

[282] Per Jessel MR in *Re Horbury Bridge Coal Co* (1879) 11 ChD 109 at 113 and 115, CA.

[283] *Ernest v Loma Gold Mines* [1897] 1 Ch 1, CA; but if a person not a member is allowed to

Section 285 contains provisions relating to the voting rights of proxies and, under the Companies (Shareholders' Rights) Regulations 2009,[284] was redrafted to ensure that the rights of members are the same whether voting in person or by proxy. The section now provides that on a vote by show of hands, every proxy present who has been duly appointed by one or more members entitled to vote on the resolution has one vote, but a proxy has one vote for and one vote against the resolution if the proxy has been duly appointed by more than one member entitled to vote on the resolution and the proxy has been instructed by one or more of those members to vote for the resolution and by one or more of those members to vote against it. These provisions are subject to any provision in the company's articles. On a poll taken at a meeting all or any of the voting rights of a member may be exercised by one or more duly appointed proxies, but where a member appoints more than one proxy this does not authorise the exercise by the proxies taken together of more extensive voting rights than could be exercised by the member in person.

Section 285A[285] is concerned with voting rights on written resolutions, reflecting the fact that they do not need to be passed unanimously. Any provision in the articles providing that a member has a different number of votes in relation to a written resolution as opposed to a resolution on a poll in general meeting is void, and the member has the same number of votes.

Section 286 puts into statute what was normally dealt with previously in standard articles, as in reg 55 of the 1985 Table A. Where shares are jointly owned, the person whose vote counts is the 'senior' holder, the person whose name appears first in the register of members. The article can provide otherwise.[286]

The right of bearers of share warrants to vote depends on the regulations of the company.[287] When the articles give this privilege they usually contain special terms under which the power of voting is to be exercised, e g on depositing the warrants with the company.

---

be a proxy it seems he can vote on a show of hands (see [1897] 1 Ch 1 at 8). But most articles in modern form expressly confer a vote on a show of hands only on a member present in person. If the articles require a vote by show of hands on any resolution, this must be taken even though there is no opposition: *Citizens Theatre* 1946 SC 14; *Fraserburgh Commercial Co* 1946 SC 444.

[284] SI 2009/1632, reg 3.

[285] Inserted by the Companies (Shareholders' Rights) Regulations 2009, SI 2009/1632, reg 3, but to the same effect as the original s 285(3).

[286] Section 286(3).

[287] Section 122(3) of the 2006 Act provides that a bearer of a share warrant may, if the articles of the company so provide, be deemed to be 'a member of the company ... either to the full extent or for any purposes defined in the articles.' Thus, if the articles provide that bearers of warrants shall be members, and do not exclude the right to vote, they will have votes; but if the articles state that they shall have the rights of members in respect of defined objects, and do not include the right to vote, they will have no votes.

Articles often include provisions providing for a procedure for objecting to and determining the admissibility of a vote, for example to the effect that objections to votes have to be raised with the chairman at the meeting and that his decision is final. Section 287 confirms the legitimacy of such articles, but also makes it clear that nothing in the Act affects the grounds on which such a decision may be questioned in legal proceedings.

13.7.7   Right to demand a poll

The right of a member to demand a poll depends on the company's articles, but s 321 of the Companies Act 2006[288] contains provisions that in effect fix the maximum that can be imposed by the articles. This section invalidates any provision in articles of association in so far as it would have the effect either:

(1)   of excluding the right to demand a poll at a general meeting on any question other than the election of the chairman of the meeting or the adjournment of the meeting; or

(2)   of making ineffective a demand for a poll on any such question which is made either:

    (a)   by not less than five members having the right to vote on the resolution; or

    (b)   by a member or members representing not less than 10 per cent of the total voting rights of all the members having the right to vote on the resolution (excluding any voting rights attached to any shares in the company held as treasury shares); or

    (c)   by a member or members holding shares in the company conferring a right to vote on the resolution, being shares on which an aggregate sum has been paid up equal to not less than 10 per cent of the total sum paid up on all the shares conferring that right (excluding shares in the company conferring a right to vote on the resolution which are held as treasury shares).

Article 58 of the 1948 Table A and reg 46 of the 1985 Table A regulations follow the requirements of what is now s 321 in defining who may demand a poll. However, these articles allow a minimum of two persons present in person or by proxy to demand a poll.[289] The model articles prescribed under the 2006 Act also confer the right to demand a poll on the chairman, the directors and a person or persons representing not less than one-tenth of the total voting rights of all the shareholders having the right to vote on the resolution.[290]

---

[288]   Replacing, with minor changes, s 373 of the 1985 Act.

[289]   Article 58(b) of the 1948 Table A, as amended by the Companies Act 1980, Sch 3, para 36(3). The amended article reduced the minimum number from three to two. The chairman is also given a right to demand a poll.

[290]   See art 44 and art 36 of the model articles for private and public companies, respectively.

Proxies have the right under s 329 to demand a poll.

Where the chairman of a meeting (in this case a meeting of debenture stockholders convened under a trust deed) had the right to demand a poll, it was held[291] that he was bound to exercise that right, if this was necessary to ascertain the opinion of the meeting on the matter under consideration. Both the demand for a poll (subject to the provisions of s 321) and the method of taking it must of course be in accordance with the provisions of the articles.

Where a poll could only be demanded by three members, and joint holders in number more than three but not representing three holdings demanded a poll which was refused, it was held that the demand for a poll failed, but the plaintiff being entitled to a majority of votes, an interlocutory injunction was granted until the trial without prejudice to the question of what should be done at the trial.[292] Where the articles gave the right to demand a poll to 'members holding' a specified number of shares, it was held that two trustees holding that number could demand the poll without the support of any other member. But in this case there was also an article stating that words importing the plural include the singular.[293]

13.7.8 Conduct of a poll

The chairman must decide whether a poll is properly demanded, having regard to the articles (which usually require a poll to be demanded before or on the declaration of the result of the show of hands), and the Act. The chairman has generally also to determine how the poll is to be taken.[294] At common law there is no requirement of confidentiality for poll votes. Those who organise a poll vote are entitled to know how people voted so that the validity of the votes can be scrutinised.[295]

If there is a question of much importance to be decided, the chairman may well fix a future day, and notice should be given to all the shareholders of the appointed place and time. If the matter is not of great importance, or if there is a representative gathering of shareholders present, the poll may be taken at once.[296] In any case the votes should be

---

[291] *Second Consolidated Trust v Ceylon Amalgamated Tea & Rubber Estates* [1943] 2 All ER 567. Uthwatt J also indicated that he would have been bound on the poll to use the proxies that he held as chairman in accordance with the instructions that they contained.

[292] *Cory v Reindeer Steamship Ltd* (1915) 31 TLR 530.

[293] *Siemens Brothers & Co v Burns* [1918] 2 Ch 324, CA: see Law of Property Act 1925, s 61.

[294] See art 59 of the 1948 Table A, reg 49 of the 1985 Table A and art 44 and art 37 respectively in the model articles prescribed under the 2006 Act for private and public companies. Reg 49 and art 37 (for public companies) also allow the chairman to appoint scrutineers who need not be members.

[295] *Haarhaus & Co GmbH v Law Debenture Trust Corporation plc* [1988] BCLC 640.

[296] *Re Chillington Iron Co* (1885) 29 ChD 159.

taken in writing, and an entry made of how many votes each shareholder is entitled to give and actually does give. Each shareholder should sign his name as a guarantee that there is no impersonation. A shareholder who has not voted at the meeting may vote on the poll. A member entitled to more than one vote need not, if he votes, use all his votes or cast all the votes he uses in the same way.[297] This provision, which at first sight may be thought to be of a somewhat eccentric character, is designed principally for the benefit of trust corporations and the like, which may (and often do) hold precisely similar shares under totally different trusts. The chairman should fix the hours during which the poll is to be held. If he does not do so he cannot close the poll as long as votes are coming in;[298] but after waiting a reasonable time, if no more voters present themselves, he may declare the poll closed.[299] If he improperly excludes a voter it will invalidate the poll.[300] The chairman must declare the result of the poll, but it is most desirable that there should be scrutineers present on each side at the counting. If there are several resolutions, the poll must be taken on each separately, though all may be included in one sheet of paper, to be marked by the voters.[301] If the vote is taken on a number of resolutions together, they cannot be validly passed.[302]

Where a poll takes place at a later date than the meeting the resolution will not be deemed to have been passed until the result of the poll is declared, and the meeting will be regarded as continuing until then. Thus in *Holmes v Keyes*[303] where the articles required the directors to acquire qualification shares within two months of election, their election dated from the declaration of the poll. It is a question of construction as to whether, under the relevant articles, a poll can be demanded before there has been a vote on a show of hands. In *Holmes v Keyes*[304] the articles stated:[305] 'a resolution put to the vote of the meeting shall be decided on a show of hands unless a poll is (before or on the declaration of the show of hands) demanded', etc. The Court of Appeal held under such an article a poll could be demanded without going through a vote by show of hands. The model articles prescribed under the 2006 Act are to the same effect.[306]

Under Table A, a poll cannot be taken by sending voting papers to the members to be returned by post. They or their proxies must attend and

---

[297] Companies Act 2006, s 322.

[298] *R v St Pancras* (1839) 11 A&E 15.

[299] *R v Lambeth* (1838) 8 A&E 356.

[300] *R v St Pancras* (1839) 11 A&E 15.

[301] *Re RE Jones Ltd* (1933) 50 TLR 31.

[302] *Patent Wood Keg Syndicate v Pearse* [1906] WN 164.

[303] [1959] Ch 199, CA.

[304] [1959] Ch 199, CA. See also *Carruth v ICI* [1937] AC 707, HL.

[305] As does art 58 of the 1948 Table A and reg 47 of the 1985 Table A. Regulation 48 allows for a demand for a poll to be withdrawn with the consent of the chairman. A previous decision by show of hands will remain valid.

[306] Articles 30 and 36, respectively, of the model articles for private companies limited by shares and public companies.

give the votes personally.[307] However, except as regards a poll on the election of the chairman or a question of adjournment, the model articles prescribed under the 2006 Act for public companies allow a poll to be taken when, where and in such manner as the chairman of the meeting directs, provided that it is within 30 days of the demand.[308] This is now subject to the right to vote in advance under s 322A, described below.

Unless a poll is demanded by the proper number of persons, the chairman's declaration of the result of the voting on a resolution will be conclusive.[309] Article 58 of the 1948 Act and reg 47 of the 1985 regulations extended this effect of the chairman's declaration, if accompanied by an entry in the minute book, to other resolutions, but this is now contained in s 320(2) of the Act. This will prevent the question being reopened in legal proceedings, even if evidence is tendered that the declaration by the chairman was wrong,[310] unless an error appears on the face of the declaration, e g where it states the number of votes given and they are insufficient,[311] or error is plain on the face of the proceedings,[312] or bad faith or fraud in writing up the minutes is proved.[313] Where the articles of association declared that if votes were not disallowed at the meeting they should be good for all purposes, it was held that, in the absence of fraud or bad faith, the resolution could not be impeached on the ground that votes were improperly received.[314] Eve J held that, notwithstanding a declaration by the chairman, the notice of meeting may be looked at to see if the resolution is in order.[315]

The Companies (Shareholders' Rights) Regulations 2009[316] added a new s 322A into the 2006 Act. This provides that a company's articles may contain provisions to the effect that on a vote on a resolution on a poll taken at a meeting, the votes may include votes cast in advance. But in the case of a traded company, any such provision may be made subject only to such requirements and restrictions as are necessary to ensure the identification of the person voting and proportionate to the achievement of that objective, but the company may require reasonable evidence of the entitlement of any person who is not a member to vote. Any provision in articles is void in so far as it would have the effect of requiring any document casting a vote in advance to be received by the company or

---

[307] *McMillan v Le Roi Mining Co* [1906] 1 Ch 331.

[308] Article 37.

[309] Companies Act 2006, s 320.

[310] *Arnot v United African Lands* [1901] 1 Ch 518, CA; *Re Hadleigh Castle Gold Mines* [1900] 2 Ch 419, not agreeing with Kekewich J in *Young v South African Development Syndicate* [1896] 2 Ch 268.

[311] *Re Caratal (New) Mines* [1902] 2 Ch 498.

[312] *Clark & Co* 1911 SC 243.

[313] *Kerr v John Mottram* [1940] Ch 657.

[314] *Wall v London and Northern Assets Corporation (No 2)* [1899] 1 Ch 550; *Colonial Gold Reef v Free State Rand* [1914] 1 Ch 382; *Wall v Exchange Investments Corporation* [1926] Ch 143, CA.

[315] *Betts & Co v Macnaghten* [1910] 1 Ch 430.

[316] SI 2009/1632, reg 5.

another person earlier than (a) in the case of a poll taken more than 48 hours after it was demanded, 24 hours before the time appointed for the taking of a poll or (b) in the case of any other poll, 48 hours before the time for holding the meeting or adjourned meeting.[317]

13.7.9 REPRESENTATIVES OF CORPORATE MEMBERS

Only members of the company, in person or by proxy, and the auditors (as to which, see s 502 of the Companies Act 2006), are, in the absence of express provisions in the articles, entitled to be present at a general meeting. A member cannot insist on his solicitor or other agent being allowed to accompany him, though a solicitor or other agent may be appointed proxy, as a proxy need not be a member of the company. Section 323 of the Companies Act 2006 allows a corporation, whether a company within the meaning of the Act[318] or not, if it is a member of a company, to authorise, by resolution of its directors or other governing body, a person or persons to act as its representative or representatives at any meeting of the company. As originally drafted and applicable to meetings held before 3 August 2009, the section goes on to provide as follows, but it is amended for meetings held after that date, as explained in the next paragraph. Where the corporation authorises only one person, he is entitled to exercise the same powers on behalf of the corporation as the corporation could exercise if it were an individual member of the company.[319] Where the corporation authorises more than one person, any one of them is entitled to exercise the same powers on behalf of the corporation as the corporation could exercise if it were an individual member of the company.[320] In this latter case, if more than one purport to exercise a power in the same way, the power is treated as exercised in that way, but if they do not purport to exercise the power in the same way, the power is treated as not exercised.[321]

The Companies (Shareholders' Rights) Regulations 2009[322] amended s 323 as regards meetings of which notice is given, or first given, on or after 3 August 2009. As amended, s 323(2) provides that a person authorised by a corporation is entitled to exercise (on behalf of the corporation) the same powers as the corporation could exercise if it were an individual member of the company, but where a corporation authorises more than one person, this is subject to subsections (3) and (4). These provide that on a vote on a resolution on a show of hands, each

---

[317] In calculating these periods, no account shall be taken of any part of a day that is not a working day.
[318] The word 'company', when used in the Act, is defined in s 1(1): 'company' means a company formed and registered under this Act, under the 1985 Act or an existing company under the latter.
[319] Section 323(2).
[320] Section 323(3).
[321] Section 323(4).
[322] SI 2009/1632.

authorised person has the same voting rights as the corporation would be entitled to. Where this does not apply and more than one authorised person purports to exercise a power in respect of the same shares, if they do so in the same way as each other, the power is treated as exercised in that way, but if they do not do so, the power is treated as not exercised.

Such a representative must be counted in estimating the quorum present.[323] If the chairman allows the vote of a person claiming to represent a company it is no objection that no proxy has been produced if it subsequently appears that such person was duly appointed by resolution;[324] but there is no English authority[325] as to whether the chairman can insist on evidence of the appointment before receiving the vote. Unless the articles deal with the matter, a chairman should allow a person claiming to represent a company to attend, but specially note how he votes, and require evidence subsequently of his appointment by resolution of the directors.

Where a parent company is in liquidation, the liquidator is the 'governing body' within s 323(1). He is entitled to execute under the seal of the company the representational authority appointing himself corporate representative since he has effective management of the company and is not a servant of it.[326] The Court of Appeal emphasised that each case turns on its own facts. Here, the liquidator had no committee of inspection and had received no directions from the body of creditors or from the court as to how he should conduct the affairs of the company. He had 'the effective management of the company and its affairs'.[327]

13.7.10 PROXIES

In the absence of an appropriate provision in the articles,[328] there was at one time no legal right of a member to have his vote by proxy accepted.[329] Now the Companies Act 2006 confers on any member of a company the right to appoint another person as his proxy to attend and to speak and vote at a meeting of the company.[330] Indeed ss 324 to 330 confer a number

---

[323] *Re Kelantan Coco Nut Estates* [1920] WN 274.

[324] *Colonial Gold Reef v Free State Rand* [1914] 1 Ch 382.

[325] In New Zealand it has been held that the right to vote depends on whether a valid resolution has been passed by the appointing body, and not on production of evidence at the meeting that this has been done: *Maori Development Corpn Ltd v Power Beat International Ltd* [1995] 2 NZLR 568, HC (NZ). In the same case it was ruled that if no objection is taken to the representation and no inquiry made as to the status of the representative prior to the declaration by the chairman of the result of a poll, the representative must be taken to have validly cast the vote of the corporate shareholder.

[326] *Hillman v Crystal Bowl Amusements* [1973] 1 WLR 162, CA.

[327] Ibid, per Russell LJ at 166.

[328] See e g art 67 of the 1948 Table A and reg 59 of Table A in the 1985 Regulations.

[329] *Harben v Phillips* (1883) 23 ChD 14, CA. No such right exists at common law (per Bowen LJ at 35).

[330] Companies Act 2006, s 324.

of statutory rights as regards proxies, although nothing in them prevents a company's articles from conferring more extensive rights on members or proxies.[331]

The proxy need not be a member (articles commonly used to require that the proxy should be a member, but any such article is now avoided by the section). Section 324, unlike the provision it replaced, applies without qualification to companies without a share capital. Section 324(2), providing that a member may appoint more than one proxy in relation to a meeting, provided that each proxy is appointed to exercise the rights attached to a different share or shares held by him or (as the case may be) to a different £10, or multiple of £10, of stock held by him, is of necessity limited to companies with a share capital, but there is no further restriction as regards private companies.[332] Under s 324A, which was inserted by the Companies (Shareholders' Rights) Regulations 2009,[333] a proxy must vote in accordance with any instructions given by the member by whom they are appointed.

Notices convening a meeting of a company have to indicate, with reasonable prominence, these statutory rights in respect of proxies and any more extensive rights conferred by the company's articles to appoint more than one proxy.[334] However, although every officer in default commits an offence by failing to comply with this requirement,[335] the failure does not affect the validity of the meeting or of anything done at the meeting.[336] If for the purposes of a meeting there are issued at the company's expenses invitations to members to appoint as proxy a specified person or a number of specified persons, the invitations must be issued to all members entitled to vote.[337] However, this requirement is not contravened if there is issued to a member at his request a form of appointment naming the proxy or a list of persons willing to act as proxy and the form or list is available on request to all members entitled to vote at the meeting.[338]

Section 327 restricts the extent to which the articles can require notice of the appointment of a proxy or any document necessary to show the validity of or otherwise relating to such an appointment. The maximum permissible time is 48 hours as under the previous legislation, but any part

---

[331] Section 331.
[332] Under the former provision (s 372 of the 1985 Act), a member of a private company was not entitled to appoint more than one proxy to attend on the same occasion and a proxy was not entitled to vote except on a poll.
[333] SI 2009/1632, reg 7.
[334] Section 325(1).
[335] Section 325(3) and (4).
[336] Section 325(2).
[337] Section 326(1). Breach is a criminal offence on the part of every officer in default: s 326(3) and (4).
[338] Section 326(2).

of a day that is not a working day[339] is excluded from the time counting towards the period.[340] For example, for a meeting to be held at 3.00 pm on a Tuesday immediately after a bank holiday Monday, the cut-off point for proxy appointment will be 3.00 pm the previous Thursday, not 3.00 pm on Sunday as was the case under the 1985 Act. In addition, polls that are not taken immediately are covered by this provision;[341] previously only meetings and adjourned meetings were covered.

The model articles prescribed under the 2006 Act for private companies limited by shares do not require a time limit. Under article 45, a proxy can be validly appointed only by a notice in writing (a 'proxy notice') which (a) states the name and address of the shareholder appointing the proxy, (b) identifies the person appointed as proxy and the general meeting in relation to which they are appointed, (c) is signed by or on behalf of the shareholder or authenticated in such manner as the directors may determine and (d) is delivered to the company in accordance with the articles and any instructions contained in the notice of the meeting.

Article 38 of the model articles prescribed for public companies is to the same effect as article 45 of the private company model. However, article 39 is more expansive as regards delivery of proxy notices.[342] It requires any notice of a general meeting to specify the address or addresses ('proxy notification address') at which the company or its agents will receive proxy notices relating to the meeting, or any adjournment of it, delivered in hard copy or electronic form. A proxy notice must be delivered to a proxy notification address not less than 48 hours before the general meeting or adjourned meeting to which it relates, but in the case of a poll taken more than 48 hours after it is demanded, the notice must be delivered not less than 24 hours before the time appointed for the taking of a poll and in the case of a poll not taken during the meeting but taken not more than 48 hours after it was demanded, the notice must be delivered either not less than 48 hours before the meeting or adjourned meeting or at the meeting at which the poll was demanded.

It was held that a 'resumed meeting' was not an adjourned meeting for the purpose of an article such as art 69 of the 1948 Table A. In *Jackson v Hamlyn*[343] a motion to adjourn was lost, but shortly afterwards the hall where the meeting was being held had to be vacated. It was held that new proxies could not be lodged before the resumption of the meeting,

---

[339] Defined in s 1173(1) to exclude weekends, Christmas Day, Good Friday and any bank holiday.

[340] Section 327(3).

[341] Section 327(2).

[342] In part following the 1948 and 1985 Table A (art 69 and reg 62, respectively). These require the instrument of proxy and the power of attorney or other authority, if any, under which it is signed or a notarially certified copy to be deposited at the registered office not less than 48 hours before the meeting or adjourned meeting at which it is to be used.

[343] [1953] Ch 577.

because a resumed meeting after such an unavoidable interruption was not an adjourned meeting.[344] Presumably the same construction would be placed on 'adjourned meeting' in s 327(2) and in article 39 of the model articles for public companies.

In one case in special circumstances, it was held that the secretary had authority to fill up the date in proxies returned without date, but in ordinary cases there would be no such authority.[345] A proxy may in the first instance be given with a blank left for the name of the person entitled to vote if there is an authority to some person to fill in the blank,[346] and it is no objection that the blanks are subsequently filled up.[347] Where a member had notice that a requisition had been lodged to summon a meeting, and gave authority to another member to fill up a proxy for him, but the requisition was withdrawn and another lodged, the authority was held to extend to the meeting called on the later requisition.[348] The proxy need not be actually named if he is sufficiently described to be identified.[349] Sometimes the form of proxy authorises 'the chairman of the meeting' to vote for the absent shareholder; but this is very inadvisable.

Where an article required a proxy to be under the hand of the appointer, or if the appointer was a corporation, under its seal, the latter part of the requirement was held not to apply to such foreign corporations as have no seal, and they can appoint proxies by a document signed by an agent.[350] Article 68 in Table A of the 1948 Act, reg 60 of the 1985 Table A and the model articles prescribed under the 2006 Act[351] provide for this.

Where articles required that proxies should be lodged two days before the day for holding the meeting, and the meeting was adjourned, proxies lodged after the original day and before the adjourned meeting were

---

[344] See further, as to the chairman's power to adjourn a meeting, *Byng v London Life Association* [1989] BCLC 400, discussed at **13.7.5** above. It appears that a power of attorney may be treated in the same way as a proxy: *New South Wales Henry George Foundation Ltd v Booth* (2002) 41 ACSR 288, SC (NSW). This was expressly accepted by art 69 of the 1948 Table A (see the text below), although neither the 1985 Table A nor the model articles prescribed under the 2006 Act make specific reference to powers of attorney.

[345] *Ernest v Loma Gold Mines* [1897] 1 Ch 1, CA. A practice has arisen since this decision of issuing proxies in blank as to date of meeting, and accompanying them with an agreement authorising the proxy to fill in the date.

[346] *Re Lancaster* (1877) 5 ChD 911, CA. The authority may be oral only.

[347] *Sadgrove v Bryden* [1907] 1 Ch 318.

[348] Ibid.

[349] *Bombay Burmah Trading Co v Shroff* [1905] AC 213, PC.

[350] *Colonial Gold Reef v Free State Rand* [1914] 1 Ch 382.

[351] See arts 45 and 46 and arts 38 and 39, respectively, of the model articles for private and public companies.

invalid.[352] It would be different if the article said 'not less than 48 hours before the time for holding the meeting or adjourned meeting', as is now usually the case.[353]

Section 328 of the 2006 Act[354] provides that, subject to any provision in the articles regarding who may or may not be chairman, a proxy may be elected as chairman of a general meeting by resolution of the company passed at the meeting. The right for a proxy to demand, or join in demanding, a poll[355] is conferred by s 329(1). Section 329(2) adapts the provisions of s 321(2) accordingly.

Section 330 provides for the minimum period required for notice to terminate a proxy's authority, putting into statutory form what was previously in reg 63 of the 1985 Table A. Subject to the articles, an appointed proxy's actions at a meeting (that is, being counted in the quorum, acting as chairman or demanding a poll) are valid unless notice of termination of the proxy's authority[356] is given before the meeting starts.[357] The same applies as regards the proxy voting and in the case of a poll taking place more than 48 hours after it was demanded, notice must be received before the time appointed for taking the poll.[358] The company's articles may specify a longer advance notice period but this cannot be more than 48 hours in advance of the meeting or the poll (excluding non-working days).[359]

13.7.11 Proxies at meetings of traded companies

The Companies (Shareholders' Rights) Regulations 2009[360] inserted new provisions into the Companies Act 2006 regarding proxies appointed by members of traded companies amending some of the provisions described in **13.7.10**.

First, the Regulations inserted a new subsection (A1) into s 327. This requires that the appointment of a person as a proxy must be notified to the company in writing, and in such a situation the company may require reasonable evidence of the identity of the member and of the proxy, the member's instructions (if any) as to how the proxy is to vote and, where the proxy is appointed by a person acting on behalf of a member, authority of that person to make the appointment, but the company may

---

[352] *McLaren v Thomson* [1917] 2 Ch 261.

[353] See likewise reg 62 of the 1985 Table A.

[354] There was no equivalent provision in the earlier legislation.

[355] Previously in s 373(2) of the 1985 Act.

[356] To the company or another person where the articles require or permit members to give notice to such a person: s 330(4).

[357] Section 330(2).

[358] Section 330(3).

[359] Section 330(5), (6) and (7). Working days are defined in s 1173(1) to exclude weekends, Christmas Day, Good Friday and any bank holiday.

[360] SI 2009/1632.

not require anything else relating to the appointment. Secondly, s 330(A1) requires in the case of a traded company that the termination of the authority of a person to act as proxy must be notified to the company in writing. Thirdly, s 333A requires a traded company to provide an electronic address for the receipt of any document or information relating to proxies for a general meeting.[361] This must be provided either by giving it when sending out an instrument of proxy for the purposes of the meeting or by ensuring that it is made available, throughout the period beginning with the first date on which notice of the meeting is given and ending with the conclusion of the meeting on the website on which the information required by s 311A(1) is made available. The company is deemed to have agreed that any document or information relating to proxies for the meeting may be sent by electronic means to that address (subject to any limitations specified by the company when giving the address).[362]

13.7.12 Proxy votes

As a poll is a continuance of the meeting, which is not at an end until the poll is taken,[363] a proxy vote at the meeting was thought to include authority to vote on the poll. It is now clear that this is so.[364] But if the articles require the proxies to be lodged so many hours 'before the meeting or adjourned meeting', it is not sufficient that they should be lodged this length of time before the taking of the poll, for the occasion of taking the poll is not an adjournment of the meeting.[365] The taking of a poll is not a meeting of the company in the strict sense, but a mere continuation of the meeting at which the poll was directed to be taken. So that if the articles provide that a proxy is to be valid notwithstanding the death of the principal or revocation of the proxy or transfer of the share, unless intimation of the death, revocation, or transfer is received at the office before the meeting, a revocation of the proxy between the date of the meeting and the taking of the poll is inoperative. It is given 'during' and not 'before' the meeting.[366] It seems also that, where a meeting is adjourned, the adjourned meeting is not a separate meeting, but a continuation of the original meeting.[367] It follows that, under articles to the above effect, a revocation between the dates of the original and

---

[361] Documents relating to proxies include the appointment of a proxy for a meeting, any document necessary to show the validity of, or otherwise relating to, the appointment of a proxy and notice of the termination of the authority of a proxy: s 333A(4).

[362] Section 333(3) applies for the purposes of this section.

[363] *R v Wimbledon Local Board* (1882) 8 QBD 459, CA.

[364] Companies Act 2006, s 324(1).

[365] *Shaw v Tati Concessions* [1913] 1 Ch 292.

[366] *Spiller v Mayo (Rhodesia) Co* [1926] WN 78.

[367] So held by Luxmoore J in *Cousins v International Brick Co* [1931] 2 Ch 90. His view was not dissented from in the Court of Appeal, although the Master of the Rolls (at 99) indicated the possibility that an adjourned meeting might be treated as a separate meeting. Inasmuch as standard articles (see e g art 57 in the 1948 Table A, reg 45 in the 1985 Table A and the prescribed model articles under the 2006 Act) provide that no business may be transacted at an adjourned meeting other than the business left

adjourned meetings is equally inoperative. But a shareholder who has given a proxy can, unless the articles otherwise expressly provide, attend the meeting and vote personally. He has an option to vote either personally or by proxy, which he can exercise at any time up to the moment when the vote must be given. By thus attending and voting he supersedes the proxy, and it does not matter whether he has revoked it or not.[368] Where the revocation is out of time and the shareholder who has given the proxy does not attend the meeting, the person to whom the proxy has been given may commit a breach of duty if he uses the vote after notice of the withdrawal of his authority.[369]

As already indicated above, there is now a statutory requirement in s 324A for a proxy to vote in accordance with the instructions of the member appointing them. So, where the chairman of directors (or any other director) is appointed a proxy and does not do so, he is in breach of his duty both as agent and as director. If he does vote as instructed, he does not infringe any duties cast on him as director.

'The right of a shareholder to vote by proxy depends on the contract between himself and his co-shareholders ... and all the requisitions of the contract as to the exercise of the right must be followed.'[370] Accordingly, proxies that are not in accordance with the regulations of the company must be rejected as invalid – eg if the articles of association require an instrument of proxy to be witnessed – it is invalid if not so witnessed.[371] It is for the chairman of the meeting to receive or reject proxies, and his decision is binding, unless it is proved to the court to be wrong.[372] A proxy holder may assume the position of temporary chairman to supervise the election of a proper chairman. This applies where the articles provide that, where there is no chairman of the board of directors and no directors present, the members should choose a chairman of a general meeting from one of their number.[373]

---

unfinished at the meeting from which the adjournment took place, the circumstances under which an adjourned meeting can be treated as a separate meeting must be very special.

[368] *Cousins v International Brick Co* [1931] 2 Ch 90.

[369] Ibid at 104 per Romer LJ.

[370] Per Cotton LJ in *Harben v Phillips* (1883) 23 ChD 14 at 32. While the first phrase of this quotation no longer represents the law, having regard to s 324, it is submitted that, subject to the provisions of the Act, the second phrase remains apposite.

[371] *Harben v Phillips* (1883) 23 ChD 14, CA.

[372] *Re Indian Zoedone Co* (1884) 26 ChD 70. But the chairman is not entitled to reject properly executed proxy forms because he believes them to have been obtained by misrepresentation: *Holmes v Jackson* (1957) *The Times*, April 3. Nor can the chairman reject proxies because of some minor misstatement in them: *Oliver v Dalgleish* [1963] 1 WLR 1274. A proxy is also to be distinguished from a power of attorney, eg where a vendor of shares (who remains on the register) gives the purchaser an irrevocable authorisation to use the votes attached to the shares as the latter thinks fit: *Coachcraft Ltd v SVP Fruit Co Ltd* (1980) 28 ALR 319, PC.

[373] *Re Bradford Investments Ltd* [1991] BCLC 224 at 229 to 230. This is so even if though the temporary chairman then has to rule on the admissibility of the votes of all the shareholders present.

Unless the articles of association or other document governing the meeting so require, it is not essential that the proxies should be produced at the meeting, and if duly lodged at the place required by the articles, the result of the proxies may be communicated by tele-message or letter.[374] This would now clearly extend to any other acceptable form of communication, including electronic communication.

13.7.13   Solicitation of proxies

The directors may employ the company's funds in printing or sending out to shareholders proxy forms filled up with the names of the directors or their nominees as the proxies, and in stamping the forms (when required) or the envelopes in which to return them. Indeed, it is their duty thus to advocate the policy which they believe to be in the interests of the company.[375] But if at the company's expense they invite appointments of proxies they must send the invitations to all members entitled to be sent notice of the meeting and to vote thereat by proxy.[376]

Two alternative forms of proxy are contained in regs 60 and 61 of the 1985 Table A,[377] the latter being what is known as a 'two-way' proxy, to enable members to instruct their proxies whether to vote for or against a resolution.

It has been held that if one proxy represents a number of members, some of whom have given proxy forms for and some against a particular resolution, and he votes for the resolution without indicating how many votes he is casting, his vote is valid to the extent of the shares in respect of which he has been given affirmative proxy forms.[378] It would seem that a proxy is not, in the absence of a contractual obligation or a special fiduciary relationship, obliged to use the proxy he has been given. It should be noted that those who solicit proxies (whether it is the board of directors or others) are *not* obliged by law to use 'two-way' proxy forms (which enable members to vote for or against a resolution). It has become common practice for the board of directors to use proxy forms in their

---

[374]   *Re English, Scottish and Australian Chartered Bank* [1893] 3 Ch 385, CA.

[375]   *Peel v London and North-Western Railway* [1907] 1 Ch 5, CA; *Campbell v Australian Mutual Society* (1908) 77 LJPC 117. *Wilson v LMS Rly Co* [1940] Ch 393, CA, where it was held to be in order for directors to send stamped proxies at the expense of the company to the larger shareholders only, was overruled on this point by what is now s 326. There is, however, no need for the directors to state the arguments of dissentients when circulating their own recommendations: *Campbell v Australian Mutual Provident Society* (above).

[376]   Section 326.

[377]   See likewise arts 70 and 71 of the 1948 Table A. The model articles prescribed under the 2006 Act do not make provision for this.

[378]   *Oliver v Dalgleish* [1963] 1 WLR 1274.

own favour. However, the Listing Rules require that listed companies send out 'three-way' proxy forms with notices calling meetings of shareholders or debenture holders.[379]

Although it is customary for proxies to be sent out by the company, they may be sent by any interested person (eg a shareholder seeking support for or against a proposed resolution), provided that they conform to the requirements of the Act and the company's articles.

13.8 Records of Meetings, Resolutions and Polls

The requirements concerning records of resolution and meetings are contained in Chapter 6 of Part 13 of the Companies Act 2006. They apply, with any necessary modifications, to resolutions and meetings of a class of shareholders and of a class of members in the case of a company without a share capital.[380]

Every company must, pursuant to s 355, keep records comprising (a) copies of all resolutions of members passed otherwise than at general meetings, (b) minutes of all proceedings of general meetings, and (c) details provided to the company under s 357 (see below). The references in previous legislation to 'books' no longer appear, making it clear that electronic records suffice. Such records must be kept for at least ten years from the date of the resolution, meeting or decision, as appropriate.[381]

The record of a resolution passed otherwise than at a general meeting, if purporting to be signed by a director of the company or by the company secretary, is evidence (in Scotland, sufficient evidence) of the passing of the resolution and the requirements of the Act with respect to the passing of the resolution are deemed to be complied with unless the contrary is proved.[382] The minutes of proceedings of a general meeting, if purporting to be signed by the chairman of that meeting or by the chairman of the next general meeting are evidence (in Scotland, sufficient evidence) of the proceedings at the meeting.[383] Where there is such a record, then, until the contrary is proved, (a) the meeting is deemed duly held and convened, (b) all proceedings at the meeting are deemed to have duly taken place, and (c) all appointments at the meeting are deemed valid.[384]

---

[379] See *The Listing Rules*, 9.3.6.

[380] Section 359.

[381] Under the previous law, there was no reference to any time-limit and it was often assumed that minutes had to be kept in perpetuity.

[382] Section 356(2) and (3).

[383] Section 356(4).

[384] Section 356(5); see also art 86 of the 1948 Table A and reg 100 of the 1985 Table A regulations. This must of course mean in regard to matters properly entered in the minutes, and the evidence will only be that such and such proceedings were had, and not that the statements of fact contained therein are true.

The absence of any reference to a matter in the minutes is treated as evidence that it was not brought before the company, but express evidence may be given to prove what was in fact done and what resolutions have been passed.[385] Where the articles provide that the minutes of meetings when signed shall be conclusive evidence of the facts therein stated, as between members of the company, the minutes are in the absence of fraud conclusive, and unless bad faith or fraud is alleged, evidence tendered for the purpose of contradicting the facts set forth in the minutes is inadmissible.[386]

The usual course regarding a general meeting is for the secretary to prepare the agenda, or heads of the business to be transacted at the meeting, and to lay the same before the chairman, who brings the various items before the meeting for consideration. A good plan is to enter the agenda in an 'Agenda Book', which is commonly ruled in such a way that the agenda occupy one side of the page, the other side being left for the chairman to write in his own remarks as the business proceeds. The agenda are, however, sometimes written on loose sheets of paper; but this plan is not recommended.

The secretary takes notes of the proceedings of each meeting, whether a general or board meeting, and afterwards enters them in the records, and reads the entries at the general meeting. The chairman then puts them to the vote, and signs them if approved; or if any amendment is required, that is first made and initialled by him, and the minutes are then signed. In the minutes of this meeting a note should be made that 'the minutes of the preceding meeting were read and signed as correct'. It is not proper to say 'the minutes were confirmed', as this might lead to an inference that the business recorded was reconsidered and confirmed, which is not the case. Directors present when the minutes of a previous meeting are read and signed are not thereby made responsible for the resolutions at the previous meeting, although they thus are fixed with notice of what has been done.[387] If any matter is debated afresh this should be the subject of a separate minute. It is improper to remove a page from the minute book, if such a book is still kept. If it requires rewriting, a line should be drawn through it, leaving the page in its place. The mutilation of any book gives rise to suspicion of bad faith.[388] The minutes are constantly referred to in legal proceedings, and it is of the utmost importance that they should be full and accurate.

---

[385] *Knight's Case* (1867) 2 Ch App 321; *Re Great Northern Salt Co* (1890) 44 ChD 472; *Re Pyle Works (No 2)* [1891] 1 Ch 172; *Re Fireproof Doors* [1916] 2 Ch 142.

[386] *Kerr v John Mottram* [1940] Ch 657; see also *Re Hadleigh Castle Gold Mines* [1900] 2 Ch 419 and *Arnot v United African Lands* [1901] 1 Ch 518, CA.

[387] See **15.11.4**.

[388] In *Hearts of Oak Assurance Co v James Flower & Sons* [1936] Ch 76, Bennett J held that loose leaves fastened between two covers in such a way that leaves could be taken out by any person and fresh ones substituted was not a book within the meaning of s 120 of the 1929 Act; but what is now s 722(1) reverses this.

Section 357 makes special provision in the case of a company limited by shares or by guarantee that has only one member. Except where a decision is taken by written resolution, this imposes a requirement on the member to provide the company with details of a decision taken by him that may be taken by the company in general meeting and has effect as if agreed by the company in general meeting. It a criminal offence to fail to comply with s 357, but failure to comply does not affect the validity of any decision.[389]

13.8.1   Right to inspect records of resolutions and meetings

Under s 358,[390] the records described above must be kept available for inspection at the company's registered office or a place specified in regulations under s 1136.[391] Unless they have at all times been kept at the registered office, the company must give notice to the registrar of the place where they are kept available for inspection and of any change in that place. That other place is a single alternative inspection location which must be in the part of the United Kingdom in which the company is registered and be the same place for all the provisions regarding records referred to in s 1136.

Any member may inspect the records free of charge. Private company records must be made available on a day specified by the member provided it is a working day of which due notice has been given. That notice is at least two working days if it is given during the period of notice for a general or class meeting or, where the company circulates a written resolution, during the period for agreeing to the resolution under s 297, provided that the notice both begins and ends during the appropriate period. Otherwise, the member must give at least 10 working days' notice. As well as giving notice of the specified day, the member must also give notice of the time on that day when he wishes to start the inspection, which must be any time between 9 am and 3 pm. The company must make the records available for inspection for a period of at least two hours beginning with that time.[392] A public company's records must be available for inspection for at least two hours between 9 am and 5 pm on each working day.[393]

A company is not required for the purposes of inspection of a company record to present information in that record in a different order, structure or form from that set out in the record.[394] While carrying out an

---

[389] Section 357(5).
[390] Replacing s 383 of the 1985 Act.
[391] The Companies (Company Records) Regulations 2008, SI 2008/3006.
[392] Ibid, reg 4.
[393] Ibid, reg 5.
[394] Ibid, reg 6(1).

inspection of the minutes under s 358, a member is entitled to be accompanied by an adviser of his own choice.[395]

Any member may require a copy of any of the records on payment of the prescribed fee.[396] A company must permit a member to make a copy of the whole or any part of a company record in the course of inspection at the appropriate location and any time when the record is made available for inspection, but it is not required to assist the member in making that record.[397] It is a criminal offence for any officer of the company in default to fail to comply with a request for inspection or a copy, and the court may order an immediate inspection or direct that copies are duly sent.

13.8.2   PUBLICATION OF REPORTS OF MEETINGS

As has been seen, minutes must be taken; but there is no obligation upon the company to print and publish a report of the proceedings at general meetings, although such a report is sometimes circulated among the shareholders by large companies. On the ground that members have a common interest in the affairs of the company, speeches at a meeting and circulars sent by directors or shareholders to the members are privileged, and in the absence of malice will not support an action for slander or libel.[398] The Defamation Act 1952, s 7 extends the defence of privilege to reports in the press of the meetings of public companies. These must be fair and accurate reports of the proceedings at general meetings of companies registered or certified under any Act of Parliament or incorporated by Royal Charter, not being a private company within the meaning of the Companies Act 2006.

13.9   POLLS OF QUOTED AND TRADED COMPANIES

The Companies Act 2006, Part 13, Chapter 5 introduced with effect from 1 October 2007 completely new requirements on quoted companies regarding polls taken at a general or class meeting. A quoted company is defined as a company whose equity share capital (a) has been included in the official list,[399] (b) is officially listed in an EEA State or (c) is admitted to dealing on either the New York Stock Exchange or the exchange known as Nasdaq.[400] Note that there is power in s 354 for the Secretary of State, by regulations subject to the negative resolution procedure, to limit

---

[395]   *McCusker v McRae* 1966 SC 253.

[396]   Section 359(4). The fee is ten pence per 500 words of part thereof copied and the reasonable costs incurred by the company in delivering the copy: the Companies (Fees for Inspection and Copying of Company Records) Regulations 2007, SI 2007/2612, reg 4.

[397]   The Companies (Company Records) Regulations 2008, SI 2008/3006, reg 6.

[398]   *Lawless v Anglo-Egyptian Co* (1869) LR 4 QB 262; *Quartz Hill Co v Beall* (1882) 20 ChD 501, CA.

[399]   Under Financial Services and Markets Act 2000, Part 6.

[400]   Companies Act 2006, s 361, applying the definition in s 385(2).

the types of company to which some or all of the provisions apply or, by regulations subject to the affirmative resolution procedure, to extend some or all of the provisions to additional types of company.[401]

These provisions require the disclosure on a website of the results of polls at general and class meetings and an independent report on a poll if a sufficient number of members demand one, with the aim of strengthening corporate democracy in the largest companies.

Under the Companies (Shareholders' Rights) Regulations 2009,[402] which implemented the Shareholders' Rights Directive,[403] the provisions relating to website publication, but not those relating to the independent report, apply, with modifications, to a traded company.

13.9.1   Website publication of poll results

Section 341 sets out the basic obligation regarding publication of the results of any poll, which is that the following information must be made available on a website after any poll taken at a general meeting or class meeting concerned with a variation of class rights[404] of a quoted company that is not a traded company:[405] (a) the date of the meeting, (b) the text of the resolution or, if appropriate, a description of the subject matter of the poll, (c) the number of votes cast in favour and (d) the number of votes cast against. There is clearly no bar to more information than this being disclosed.

A traded company must disclose the information set out above and in addition (a) the number of votes validly cast, (b) the proportion of the company's issued share capital at close of business on the day before the meeting represented by those votes and (c) the number of abstentions (if counted).[406]

Non-compliance is a criminal offence for any officer in default,[407] but failure to comply does not invalidate the poll, the resolution or other business to which the poll relates.[408]

The requirements relating to an appropriate website are set out in s 353. It must be maintained by or on behalf of the company and must identify the

---

[401] Such regulations may be very wide-ranging: see s 354(4).
[402] SI 2009/1632.
[403] Directive 2007/36/EC.
[404] See s 352, applying the provisions to such class meetings and note the definition of variation of class rights in s 352(2), which applies the same definition as in the general provisions regarding variations of class rights.
[405] After the date the section comes into force, which was 1 October 2007: s 341(6).
[406] Section 341(1A).
[407] Section 341(3) and (4).
[408] Section 341(5).

company in question.[409] Access to the information on it, and the ability to obtain a hard copy of the information, must not be conditional on the payment of a fee or otherwise restricted.[410] So, for example, access via a password is forbidden and the consequence of this is that the information will be available to anyone in the world with access to the internet. As regards a quoted company, the information must be made available as soon as reasonably practicable and kept available for a minimum of two years from the date it is first available,[411] although failure is to be disregarded if it is wholly attributable to circumstances that it would not be reasonable to expect the company to prevent or avoid, such as where a website 'goes down' for technical reasons.[412] A traded company is required to make the information available not later than the end of 16 days beginning with the day of the meeting or, if later, the end of the first working day following the day on which the result of the poll is declared.[413]

13.9.2   Independent report on a poll

The second aspect of the provisions relating to quoted companies enables members of the company to require the directors to obtain an independent report on a poll.[414] The directors must act once they have received requests from members representing at least 5 per cent of the total voting rights of all members who have a right to vote on the matter to which the poll relates (excluding any voting rights attached to any shares held as treasury shares) or from at least 100 members who have a right to vote on such a poll who hold shares in the company on which there has been paid up an average sum, per member, of at least £100.[415] Where the requests relate to more than one poll, this requirement must be satisfied in relation to each of them.[416] The request may be made in hard copy or electronic form, must identify the poll or polls to which it relates, must be authenticated by the person(s) making it[417] and must be made within one week of the meeting where the poll is taken. Clearly a request could even be made before the relevant meeting.

Under s 343, the directors must respond to any request by appointing an independent assessor within a week of receiving the request and it is a criminal offence not to comply.[418] The independent assessor must be someone they consider appropriate but not someone who does not satisfy the independence requirement laid down by Companies Act 2006, s 344,

---

[409]   Section 353(2).
[410]   Section 353(3).
[411]   Section 353(4).
[412]   Section 353(5).
[413]   Section 341(1B).
[414]   Section 342.
[415]   Section 342(2).
[416]   Section 342(3).
[417]   As to authentication, see s 1146.
[418]   Section 343(4) and (5).

nor who has any existing role in relation to any poll, including, in particular, a role in connection with collecting or counting votes or with the appointment of proxies. The directors are only excused if a request is made before the meeting and in the event no poll is taken at the meeting.[419]

Section 344, as supplemented by ss 345 and 346, lays down the requirements for independence of an assessor. Section 344(2) allows the company's auditor to act as independent assessor, by providing that he is not regarded as an officer or employee of the company for this purpose. Otherwise, the assessor must not fall within any of the following:

(1) he must not be such an officer or employee or a partner or employee of such a person or a partnership of which such a person is a partner;

(2) he must not be an officer or employee of an associated undertaking of the company or a partner or employee of such a person or a partnership of which such a person is a partner; or

(3) he or an associate of his must not be connected with the company or an associated undertaking of the company.

'Connection' for the purposes of (3) is to be prescribed in regulations.[420] An associated undertaking is a parent undertaking, a subsidiary undertaking or a fellow subsidiary undertaking.[421]

Section 345 contains a complex definition of 'associate' for the purposes of s 344. In relation to an individual, it means their spouse, civil partner, minor child or stepchild, any body corporate of which they are a director (or member in the case of a limited liability partnership[422]) and any employee or partner of theirs.[423] In relation to a body corporate, it means any body corporate of which that body is a director (or member in the case of a limited liability partnership[424]), any body corporate in the same group and any employee or partner of that body or of any body corporate in the same group.[425] In relation to a partnership that is a legal person, it means any body corporate of which that partnership is a director, any employee of or partner in that partnership and any person who is an

---

419 Section 343(6). Any independent assessor appointed in advance of this has the right to be paid for any work done before his appointment ceases.
420 Subject to the negative resolution procedure: s 344(4).
421 Section 344(3).
422 Section 345(6).
423 Section 345(2).
424 Section 345(6).
425 Section 345(3).

associate of a partner in that partnership.[426] In relation to a partnership that is not a legal person, it means any person who is an associate of any of the partners.[427]

Where a partnership that is not a legal person is appointed as an independent assessor, s 346 makes further provision in particular to cover situations such as where the identity of the partners changes or a partnership incorporates as a limited liability partnership. Unless a contrary intention appears, the appointment is of the partnership as such and not of the partners.[428] Under s 346(3), where the partnership ceases, the appointment is treated as extending to any partnership that succeeds to the practice of that partnership or any other person who succeeds to that practice having previously carried it on in partnership. For these purposes, a partnership is regarded as succeeding to the practice of another partnership only if the members of the former are substantially the same as those of the latter and a partnership or other person is regarded as succeeding to the practice of a partnership only if it or he succeeds to the whole or substantially the whole of the business of the former partnership.[429] Where s 346(3) does not apply, the appointment may, with the consent of the company, be treated as extending to a partnership or other person who succeeds to the business of the former partnership or such part of it as is agreed by the company is to be treated as comprising the appointment.[430]

13.9.3 Independent assessor's report

Section 347 requires that the report of the independent assessor must state his name and his opinion, with reasons, as to the following:

(1) whether the procedures adopted in connection with the poll or polls were adequate;

(2) whether the votes cast, including proxy votes, were fairly and accurately recorded and counted;

(3) whether the validity of members' appointment of proxies was fairly assessed;

(4) whether the notice of the meeting complied with s 325, that is, containing a statement of members' rights to appoint a proxy; and

(5) whether s 326, relating to company-sponsored invitations to appoint proxies, was complied with in relation to the meeting.

---

[426] Section 345(4).
[427] Section 345(5).
[428] Section 346(2).
[429] Section 346(4).
[430] Section 346(5).

Section 348 confers the right on the independent assessor, which must be exercised only to the extent that he considers is necessary for the preparation of his report,[431] to attend the meeting at which the poll may be taken and any subsequent proceedings in connection with a poll.[432] Obviously the right to attend the meeting can operate only if his appointment is requested in advance of the meeting. He is also entitled to be provided by the company with a copy of the notice of the meeting and any other communication provided by the company in connection with the meeting to persons who have a right to vote on the matter to which the poll relates.[433] This will obviously include any statements or resolutions required to be circulated by members.

Under s 349, the independent assessor has rights to information. First, he has the right to access company records relating to any poll on which he is to report and to the meeting at which the poll or polls may be, or were, taken.[434] Secondly, he may require any who at any material time were any of the following to provide him with information or explanations for the purpose of preparing his report. The persons in question are: (a) a director or secretary, (b) an employee of the company, (c) a person holding or accountable for any of the company's records, (d) a member of the company and (e) an agent of the company including for this purpose the company's bankers, solicitors and auditor.[435] It is an offence to fail to comply with such a request,[436] but this does not prevent any right of an assessor to apply for an injunction to enforce any of his rights under s 348 or 349.[437] Statements made in response to a request under s 349 may not be used in evidence against him in criminal proceedings except for an offence under s 350,[438] and no one is required to disclose information that would be subject to legal professional privilege.[439]

13.9.4 Website publication

The requirements for website publication following an independent assessor's report are contained in s 351. As well as including a copy of the report by him complying with s 347, the company must ensure that the following information is made available: (a) the fact of the assessor's appointment, (b) his identity and (c) the text of the resolution or a description of the subject matter of the poll to which his appointment relates. The requirements of s 353 as to the website, as described above,

---

[431] Section 348(3).
[432] A firm attends by an individual authorised by the firm in writing to act as its representative for this purpose: s 348(4).
[433] Section 348(2).
[434] Section 349(1).
[435] Section 349(2) and (3).
[436] Section 350.
[437] Section 350(5).
[438] Section 349(4).
[439] Section 349(5); in Scotland, confidentiality of communications.

apply. Non-compliance is a criminal offence for any officer in default,[440] but failure to comply does not invalidate the poll, the resolution or other business to which the poll relates.[441]

13.10 Disclosing use of votes by institutional investors

The Companies Act 2006 introduced new powers regarding the disclosure of how certain institutional shareholders exercise their voting rights, although the powers have not yet been used. Under s 1277, the Treasury or the Secretary of State may make regulations, subject to affirmative resolution procedure, to enforce such disclosure by the following institutions:[442]

(1)   unit trusts within the meaning of the Financial Services and Markets Act 2000 in respect of which an order is in force under s 243 of that Act;

(2)   open-ended investment companies incorporated by virtue of regulations under s 262 of that Act;

(3)   investment trusts;[443]

(4)   pension schemes;[444]

(5)   insurers conducting long-term (as against general) insurance; and

(6)   collective schemes recognised by virtue of s 270 of the 2000 Act.[445]

However, the regulations can add other institutions or exclude specific types. The obligation can only arise in respect of shares traded on specified markets held through institutions.[446] The regulations may determine which traded shares count, which may be held through a depositary receipt or a collective investment scheme and what information has to be provided about exercise of votes, instructions to others to exercise the vote or delegation of voting powers.[447]

Failure to provide the information required by any regulations will not be a criminal offence but enforceable by any person to whom the information should have been provided or by a specified authority.[448]

---

[440]   Section 351(3) and (4).
[441]   Section 351(5).
[442]   Companies Act 2006, s 1278.
[443]   Approved for the purposes of s 842 of the Income and Corporation Taxes Act 1988.
[444]   As defined in s 1(5) of the Pension Schemes Act 1993 or the Pension Schemes (Northern Ireland) Act 1993.
[445]   Schemes authorised in designated countries or territories.
[446]   Companies Act 2006, s 1279.
[447]   Sections 1279 and 1280.
[448]   Section 1277(4).

CHAPTER 14

ACCOUNTS AND REPORTS

14.1 INTRODUCTION

Limited companies have for many years been required to produce annual accounts for circulation to members.[1] The basic purpose of such accounts is to provide an account of the stewardship of the directors to the shareholders and creditors, rather than to provide information to the investing public generally. It was at one time acceptable practice deliberately to understate the value of a company's assets. Investors required assurance that their investment was safe and creditors that the company could pay its debts. Now, however, greater accuracy is expected in accounts, and the deliberate understatement of assets or overstatement of liabilities is considered to be incompatible with the fundamental requirement of the Companies Act that accounts should give a true and fair view.[2]

Accounting standards are governed by an independent Accounting Standards Board[3] which is part of the Financial Reporting Council, with the assistance of an Urgent Issues Task Force,[4] which endeavours to reach a consensus where unsatisfactory or conflicting interpretations have developed in respect of accounting treatment. The Accounting Standards Board issues Statements of Standard Accounting Practice (SSAP)[5] and Financial Reporting Standards, the latter being based on the Statement of Principles for Financial Reporting, which provides a framework for the consistent and logical formulation of accounting standards. The main role of the Urgent Issues Task Force is to assist the Accounting Standards Board in areas where an accounting standard or Companies Act provision exists, but where unsatisfactory or conflicting interpretations have developed or seem likely to develop. In such circumstances, the Urgent Issues Task Force will seek a consensus on the desirable accounting

---

[1] Companies were first compelled to publish a balance sheet by the CA 1908. The CA 1929 required them additionally to circulate to their members a copy of the profit and loss account.

[2] See **14.4**.

[3] This is the prescribed body under s 464 of the CA 2006.

[4] Created in March 1991.

[5] These were adopted from the SSAPS that were developed by the Accounting Standards Committee, the predecessor of the Accounting Standards Board.

treatment for the matter in question. Where such a consensus is achieved, the intention is that it should be considered to be part of the corpus of practices forming the basis for what determines a true and fair view, and the expectation is that companies will conform to it. Pronouncements issued by the Urgent Issues Task Force are known as UITF Abstracts. Additionally, the Urgent Issues Task Force issues information sheets which also provide guidance and clarification on issues dealt with in UITF Abstracts.

The Financial Reporting Review Panel was also established as a committee of the Financial Reporting Council. Where a company's accounts or directors' report are defective in a material respect the Panel's role is to try to secure their revision by voluntary means, but if this approach fails the Panel is empowered to make an application to the court under section 456 of the Companies Act 2006 for an order for revision.

Financial Reporting Standards are also based on International Financial Reporting Standards and International Accounting Standards issued by the International Accounting Standards Board. Such standards have been adopted by the European Union in Regulation 1606/2002/EC. Listed companies preparing consolidated accounts are under a duty to use these International Accounting Standards and International Financial Reporting Standards. For UK listed companies, this requirement started for periods commencing on or after 1 January 2005. Companies listed on the Alternative Investment Market ('AIM') are not regarded as listed but the AIM rules themselves have introduced a similar requirement for accounting periods commencing on or after 1 January 2007.

Accounting Standards do not have direct legal effect but they may have indirect effect on the interpretations that the courts would give to true and fair view concepts.[6] The court is likely to infer that, in general, compliance with accounting standards is necessary to meet the true and fair requirement, and that departures will result in a breach of that requirement unless it is clearly justified and explained. An accounting standard which the court upholds must be complied with to meet the true and fair view requirement becomes, in cases where it is applicable, a source of law in the widest sense of that term.

The adoption of the European Community's Fourth Company Law Directive in July 1978 foreshadowed new legislation in the UK governing the format and content of limited companies' accounts. The provisions of this directive, which were initially implemented by the Companies Act 1981 and were then consolidated in the Companies Act 1985, represented a major departure from previous UK practice in that, for the first time, the basic rules for the presentation and accounting measurement of income, expenditure, assets and liabilities were laid down by law. Before that, UK company law had been more concerned with the

---

6   See *Gore-Browne on Companies* (Jordans, 45th edn, loose-leaf) at 32 [1].

disclosure of accounting information than with precise methods of presentation or with measurement. The Companies Act 1989 extended the influence of the EU legislation by implementing the European Community's Seventh Company Law Directive, which includes detailed rules for preparing consolidated financial statements. This largely reflected existing accounting standards, but also changed the emphasis in defining a subsidiary undertaking from legal ownership to effective control. The 1989 Act[7] also implemented the Eighth Company Law Directive on the qualification and supervision of auditors. The Fourth and Seventh Directives have been amended at European level and those amendments have led to changes in the UK. The Companies Act 2006 takes such amendments into account.

In addition, the European Regulation on the application of international accounting standards led the Government to take steps towards extending the use of international accounting standards by all public companies as an alternative to the accounting standards.[8]

The Review of Company Law led to proposals for fundamental changes to the reporting and accounting regime. A more inclusive approach to reporting for public and large private companies was favoured, while simplifying the requirements for small companies.[9]

The resulting position following the Companies Act 2006 is that many of the provisions of the Companies Act 1985 were retained. A significant change is the way in which the requirements for different companies are set out. The 1985 Act used the premise that all companies applied all the requirements and then exemptions were given depending on whether the company was perhaps small or medium-sized, if there was a parent company, etc.

The 2006 Act approaches the accounting provisions by distinguishing between:

(1)   companies that are small and companies that are not small; and

(2)   quoted companies and all other companies.[10]

---

[7]   Especially Part II.

[8]   For an overview of the European level initiatives see Villiers 'European Integration and Globalisation: The Experience of Financial Reporting' in *The Cambridge Yearbook of European Legal Studies*, Vol 5 (Hart, 2003–2004) at p 105. See for more detail on the European measures and the UK's position, DTI *Modernisation of Accounting Directives/IAS Infrastructure: A consultation document on the implementation of the accounting modernisation directive and arrangement for the use of IAS for companies and building societies* (March 2004).

[9]   Ibid, chapter 8.

[10] CA 2006, s 380(3).

In line with the 'think small first' policy the 2006 Act sets out the legislation such that:

(1)   provisions applying to small companies are set out before those applying to other companies;

(2)   provisions applying to private companies are set out before those applying to public companies; and

(3)   provisions applying to quoted companies appear after provisions applying to non-quoted companies.

The 2006 Act also introduced a number of substantive changes including a reduction in the time-limit for private companies to file their accounts from 10 months to 9 months after the year end (s 442); a reduction in the time-limit for public companies to lay full financial statements before the company in general meeting and file them from 7 months to 6 months after the year end (s 442); new requirements for quoted companies to publish their annual accounts and reports on a website (s 430); and replacement of the general power of the Secretary of State to alter accounting requirements in s 257 of the 1985 Act by a general power of amendment by regulations (s 468) and more specific powers in relation to specific sections.

The 2006 Act continues to recognise the two accounting frameworks that are available to UK companies: United Kingdom Generally Accepted Accounting Practice (UK GAAP) and International Accounting Standards (IAS). The ASB has been working on a project to converge UK accounting standards and practices with IAS.[11]

Company accounting and disclosure frequently come under critical scrutiny. A recent aspect of reporting that has been criticized is that of 'clutter'. The FRC and the ASB are seeking ways for decluttering annual reports of immaterial disclosures and for refocusing annual reports on the provision of useful information to investors.[12]

14.2   THE SMALL COMPANIES REGIME

Part 15 of the Companies Act 2006 is structured in accordance with the 'think small first' policy and s 381 provides that a small companies regime for accounts and reports applies to a company which qualifies as a small company and which is not excluded from the regime. The Act then goes on to define the conditions for a company to qualify as a small company or for a parent company to qualify as a company heading a small group.

---

[11]   See ASB, *The Future of Financial Reporting*, (ASB, December 2010), available at http://frc.org.uk/asb/publications/documents.cfm?cat=3.

[12]   See further: FRC, *Louder than Words*, and ASB, *Cutting Clutter* (2011), available at http://www.frc.org.uk/publications/pub2567.html.

14.2.1 Qualification as a small company

The 2006 Act retains the criteria previously set out in s 247(3) of the Companies Act 1985, as amended. Thus under s 382 a company qualifies to be treated as a small company if it satisfies at least two of the three following criteria: the turnover is not more than £6.5m;[13] the balance sheet total is not more than £3.26m;[14] the average number of employees during the financial year is not more than 50.[15]

A parent company that is required to produce group accounts may take advantage of the small companies regime if the group as a whole meets the criteria.[16] Where the company is a parent company, the criteria are based on the aggregate totals as applied to the group that it heads. Accordingly, a parent company, even if its own entity numbers appear to make it 'small', can only qualify as small if the group that it heads also qualifies as small.[17] The qualifying conditions are therefore met by a group in a year if it satisfies at least two of the following three requirements: aggregate turnover is not more than £6.5m net (or £7.8m gross); aggregate balance sheet total is not more than £3.26m net (or £3.9m gross); aggregate number of employees is not more than 50.

The means of determining the group amounts are retained from the 1985 Act. Thus the aggregate amounts for all the criteria are determined by adding together the relevant amounts for the individual members of the group.[18] 'Net' means with the set-offs and adjustments to eliminate group transactions either as required under company law or, if applying IAS, as required by IAS. A group may determine compliance with the criteria on either the net or gross basis.

The amounts for the subsidiary companies to be aggregated should be for the same financial period where they are co-terminus with the parent, or, where they are not co-terminus, the financial period ending last before the financial period of the parent. Where the amounts cannot be ascertained without disproportionate expense or delay then the latest available amounts may be used.

---

[13] A proportionate adjustment is made to the maximum figures for turnover for a period that is a company's financial year but not in fact a year: s 382(4).

[14] The balance sheet total means the aggregate of the amounts shown as assets in the company's balance sheet: s 382(5).

[15] The number is determined by adding together the monthly totals of employees for each month in the financial year and then dividing that number by the number of months in the financial year: s 382(6).

[16] CA 2006, s 383.

[17] CA 2006, s 383.

[18] CA 2006, s 383(5).

14.2.2 Exclusion from the small company regime

The Companies Act 1985 referred to the ineligibility of companies from using the exemptions that were available to small companies during the application of the 1985 Act.[19] The Companies Act 2006 provides a small companies regime and so s 384 is concerned with exclusion of companies from that regime.

A small company cannot apply the small companies regime if it is or was at any time in the financial year:

(1)   a public company;

(2)   an authorised insurance company, a banking company, an e-money issuer,[20] an ISD investment firm or a UCITS management company;[21]

(3)   a company that carries on insurance market activity; or

(4)   a member of an ineligible group.[22]

A group will be excluded if any of its members is:

(1)   a public company;

(2)   a body corporate (other than a company) whose shares are admitted to trading on a regulated market in an European Economic Area (EEA) state; or

(3)   a person (other than a small company) who has permission under the Financial Services and Markets Act 2000 (FSMA 2000), Part 4, to carry on a regulated activity;[23]

(4)   a small company that is an authorised insurance company, a banking company, an e-money issuer, a MiFD investment firm or a UCITS management company; or

(5)   a person who carries on insurance market activity.[24]

---

[19]   CA 1985, s 247A.

[20]   'E-money issuer' means a person who has permission under Financial Services and Markets Act 2000, Part IV to carry on the activity of issuing electronic money within the meaning of Financial Services and Markets Act 2000 (Regulated Activities) Order 2001, SI 2001/544, art 9B.

[21]   'ISD investment firm' and 'UCTIS management company' have the meanings given in the Glossary of the Financial Services Authority Handbook.

[22]   CA 2006, s 384(1).

[23]   'Regulated activity' has the meaning given in FSMA 2000, s 22, with certain exceptions. These exceptions are set out in CA 2006, s 474.

[24]   CA 2006, s 384(2).

A small company is not automatically excluded if it is permitted under the Financial Services and Markets Act 2000, Part 4 to carry on a regulated activity. In addition a small group is ineligible if the shares of one or more of the group's undertakings have been admitted to listing on a recognised exchange within the EEA. A small group could, therefore, have a member, not being a public company, which has shares admitted to a recognised exchange outside the EEA and the small parent company could still be eligible to apply the small companies regime.

14.3 QUOTED COMPANIES

Section 385(2) of the Companies Act 2006 defines a quoted company as any company whose equity share capital:

'(a) has been included listed in the official list in accordance with the provisions of Part 6 of the FSMA 2000; or

(b) is officially listed in an EEA State; or

(c) is admitted to dealing on either the New York Stock Exchange or the exchange known as NASDAQ.'[25]

Accordingly, companies whose shares are listed on the Alternative Investment Market of the London Stock Exchange or a number of stock exchanges in countries outside the EEA will not be regarded as quoted even though they may be regarded as 'listed' companies for other purposes. An unquoted company means a company that is not a quoted company.[26]

In relation to a financial year, s 385(1) states that a company is quoted if it meets the definition of a quoted company immediately before the accounting reference date by which that particular financial year is determined. For example, if a company's year ends on 31 December 2011, but it ceases to meet the definition of a quoted company on 6 December 2011, then it will not be regarded as quoted for the year ended 31 December 2011. If, however, it ceases to be regarded as quoted on 3 January 2012, then it is treated as quoted for the year ended 31 December 2011.

The Secretary of State retains the power to lay regulations which amend or replace the definition of quoted company in order to limit or extend the application of certain provisions of the Companies Act 2006 that apply to quoted companies.[27]

---

[25] Originally an acronym for National Association of Securities Dealers Automated Quotations system.

[26] CA 2006 s 385(3).

[27] CA 2006, s 385(4).

14.4   ACCOUNTING RECORDS

14.4.1   The duty to keep accounting records

Section 386 [s 221 of the 1985 Act] requires every company to keep adequate accounting records. These must be sufficient to show and explain the company's transactions. They must disclose with reasonable accuracy, at any time, the financial position of the company at that time and they must enable the directors to ensure that any accounts required to be prepared comply with the Companies Act and, where applicable, with Part 4 of the IAS Regulation. The accounting records must, in particular, contain entries from day to day of all sums of money received and expended by the company and the matters in respect of which the receipt and expenditure takes place, and a record of the assets and liabilities of the company. Where the company's business involves dealing in goods, the records should contain information relating to stock and to purchases and sales. This information comprises statements of stock held by the company at the end of each financial year, all statements of stocktaking from which these statements have been or are to be prepared and (except in the case of goods sold by way of ordinary retail trade) statements of all goods sold and purchased, showing the goods and the buyers and sellers in sufficient detail to enable those goods and those buyers and sellers to be identified.[28] What will be regarded as the right kind of accounting records to meet the Act's requirements will be treated as a question of fact to be decided in any particular case. The ICAEW points out in a guidance note that regard will be had among other things, to prevailing practice at the time in businesses of the type in question although this consideration will not itself be conclusive.[29]

14.4.2   The custody of accounting records

The accounting records must be kept either at the company's registered office or at such other place as the directors think fit and must be open to inspection by the company's officers at all times.[30] Shareholders have no statutory right to inspect accounting records. If the accounting records are kept outside the UK, accounts and returns must be sent to and retained in the UK, where they must be open to inspection by the company's officers.[31]

Subject to any direction under the insolvency rules, the accounting records which companies, as a minimum, are required to keep by law must be preserved for at least 6 years (or, in the case of a private company,

---

[28]   CA 2006, s 386(4).
[29]   ICAEW, Technical Release, *Guidance for Directors on Accounting Records Under the Companies Act 2006*, (ICAEW, Tech 01/11).
[30]   CA 2006, s 388(1).
[31]   CA 2006, s 388(2).

3 years) from the date on which they are made.[32] As the ICAEW remarks, 'it follows that where software is needed for retrieval of information in usable form, it must be available for use for the same period as must any necessary hardware'.[33]

There are separate sections dealing with the offences relating to the duty to keep accounting records[34] and where and for how long those records are kept.[35] Thus if a company fails to keep accounting records or with the requirements relating to keeping the accounting records an offence is committed by every officer of the company who is in default unless he can show that he acted honestly and that in all the circumstances the default was excusable. A person guilty of an offence is liable to imprisonment of up to 2 years or a fine or both.

14.5   FINANCIAL YEARS AND ACCOUNTING PERIODS

The directors of every company are responsible for the regular preparation of accounts for presentation to the shareholders. The period covered by these accounts (the 'financial year') must coincide with the company's accounting reference period or, for the benefit of companies which prefer to make up their accounts for a 52 or 53-week period, may end at a date within 7 days of the accounting reference date.[36] A company can vary the end of a financial period by not more than 7 days from its accounting reference period without it being a change in the accounting reference date itself.[37]

For the purpose of determining the financial year, the accounting reference period is defined in s 391(5) and (6). It means the period between two successive accounting reference dates and the accounting reference date means the date registered as such with the Registrar of Companies.[38] The basic accounting reference date for a company incorporated on or after 1 April 1996 is the last day of the month in which the anniversary of its incorporation falls. Companies incorporated before that date had a period of 9 months from the date of incorporation to select another date than that set out in the statute, which was 31 March for a company incorporated before 1 April 1990, and the last day of the month in which the anniversary of its incorporation fell for companies incorporated on or after 1 April 1990 but before April 1996.[39] For companies that are incorporated from the present time on, the accounting reference date is the last day of the month in which the anniversary of

---

[32]   CA 2006, s 388(4).
[33]   At para 17, Tech 01/11.
[34]   CA 2006, s 387.
[35]   CA 2006, s 389.
[36]   CA 2006, s 390(2).
[37]   CA 2006, s 390(3).
[38]   CA 2006, s 391(2)–(3).
[39]   CA 2006, s 391(2) and (3).

incorporation falls. A company that is incorporated on 13 March will have an accounting reference date of 31 March. In all cases, the accounting reference of a newly incorporated company must be such as to give the company a first accounting reference period of more than 6 but not more than 18 months.[40]

A company may alter its accounting reference date (and thereby its accounting reference period) by giving notice to the Registrar of Companies in prescribed form. Notice must normally be given before the end of the accounting reference period affected, but retrospective notice may be given if the company is the holding company or a subsidiary of another company and the new accounting reference date coincides with the accounting reference date of that other company – provided that the period for laying and delivering accounts has not expired.[41] If the change in accounting reference date will have the effect of increasing the length of an accounting reference period, the period so increased may not exceed 18 months. An application to increase the length of an accounting reference period must also meet one of the further conditions that the period is being extended for the first time, or that it was last extended more than five years previously, or that the change is being made to make the date coincide with the accounting reference date of an EEA parent or subsidiary undertaking, or where the company is in administration under the insolvency legislation, or where the Secretary of State for Trade and Industry has given consent.[42] This route does not work for extending a company's accounting period as s 392(5) renders ineffective a notice to change an accounting reference date if the effect would be to make the accounting period more than 18 months long.

A company cannot change its accounting reference date such that it extends its accounting reference period more than once in five years.[43] There is no restriction in the number of times that a company can shorten its accounting reference period.

14.6   ANNUAL ACCOUNTS

Section 394 provides that the directors of every company must prepare accounts for the company for each of its financial years. Section 471 defines annual accounts and essentially means the individual accounts or group accounts prepared by a company for a financial year. Under s 396, individual accounts must comprise a balance sheet as at the last day of the financial year, and a profit and loss account. Under s 404 group accounts must comprise a consolidated balance sheet dealing with the state of affairs of the parent company and its subsidiary undertakings, and a consolidated profit and loss account dealing with the profit or loss of the

---

[40]   CA 2006, s 391(5).
[41]   CA 2006, s 392(4).
[42]   CA 2006, s 392(3).
[43]   CA 2006, s 392(3).

parent company and its subsidiary undertakings. Section 471(3) adds that in the case of a quoted company, its annual accounts and reports for a financial year are its annual accounts, the directors' remuneration report, the directors' report, and the auditor's report on those accounts, on the auditable part of the directors' remuneration report and on the directors' report. By s 472, information required to be given in notes to a company's annual accounts may be contained in the accounts or in a separate document annexed to the accounts. References to a company's annual accounts or to a balance sheet or a profit and loss account include information provided in notes to those accounts where that information is required or permitted by the Act or under IAS and is permitted to be provided in notes to the accounts.

Sections 396 and 404 respectively provide that the individual accounts and the group accounts must give a true and fair view of the state of affairs as at the end of the financial year and of the profit or loss for the financial year of the company or of the undertakings included in the whole group so far as concerns members of the company. Whilst the Companies Act 1985 stated that the directors had to prepare accounts for each financial year and those accounts had to give a true and fair view,[44] the 2006 Act states that the directors of a company must not approve the annual accounts of a company, as required by the Act, unless they do give a true and fair view.[45] There then follows the first of the auditor's duties, which is to have regard to the directors' duty under that section.[46] The requirement for a true and fair view to be paramount is upheld by requiring the directors to depart from provisions laid down in the Act and associated regulations if that is necessary for the accounts to give a true and fair view. In those circumstances a note to the accounts would need to give details of any departure, the reasons for it and the effect on the accounts. Directors are also required to provide additional information if compliance alone with the Act and associated regulations would not be sufficient to give a true and fair view.[47]

14.7 INDIVIDUAL ACCOUNTS: APPLICABLE ACCOUNTING FRAMEWORK

As was stated above, the directors of every company have to prepare individual company accounts. All companies, except those that are charities,[48] have a choice of accounting frameworks, being either:

(1) Companies Act accounts; or

---

[44] CA 2006, s 392(3).
[45] CA 2006, s 393(1).
[46] CA 2006, s 393(2).
[47] CA 2006, s 396(4) and (5).
[48] These must use the Companies Act framework: s 395(2).

(2)   accounts prepared under IAS accounts.[49]

Once a company has decided to adopt the IAS framework, then it must continue to use IAS for all subsequent accounting periods except if there is a relevant change of circumstance during or after the first IAS year.[50] Those circumstances are limited to:

(1)   the company becoming a subsidiary of another undertaking that does not prepare IAS individual accounts;

(2)   the company or one of its parent undertakings ceases to be a company with securities admitted to trading on a regulated market in an EEA state.[51]

Having changed back to Companies Act accounts following a relevant change of circumstance, the directors of a company can, again, decide to use IAS but the restrictions on changing back will apply as though it was the first time that the directors had applied the IAS framework.[52]

The 2006 Act, unlike the 1985 Act, does not include any Schedules that specify the form and content of the balance sheet or of the profit and loss account or of any further information that is to be given. Such requirements are contained in by regulations made by the Secretary of State.[53] Where companies prepare IAS accounts the Act provides that they must state in a note to the financial statements that they have been prepared in accordance with international accounting standards.[54]

14.8   GROUP ACCOUNTS

If at the end of its financial period, a company is a parent company that is not subject to the small companies regime, then the directors of the company must prepare group accounts in addition to the individual accounts.[55] There are then certain exemptions to this requirement. A notable change from the position in the 1985 Act is that there is no longer an exemption from preparing group accounts for parent companies which qualified as medium-sized under the 1985 Act.[56] The directors of a parent company that is subject to the small companies regime may prepare group accounts as well as individual accounts if they so wish.[57]

---

[49]   CA 2006, s 395(1).
[50]   CA 2006, s 395(3).
[51]   CA 2006, s 395(4).
[52]   CA 2006, s 395(5).
[53]   CA 2006, s 396(3). See the Small Companies and Groups (Accounts and Directors' Report) Regulations 2008, SI 2008/409 and Large and Medium-sized Companies and Group (Accounts and Report) Regulations 2008, SI 2008/410.
[54]   CA 2006, s 397.
[55]   CA 2006, s 399.
[56]   This exemption was provided by CA 1985, s 248.
[57]   CA 2006, s 398.

The exemptions available to parent companies from preparing group accounts are:

(1) the accounts of the company are consolidated in EEA accounts of a larger group;

(2) the accounts of the company are consolidated in non-EEA accounts of a larger group; and

(3) the company only has subsidiaries which do not need to be consolidated.[58]

These exemptions are voluntary so the directors of a relevant parent company can still decide to prepare group accounts if they so wish.

The conditions for taking advantage of the exemptions in (1) and (2) above are almost identical.[59] Thus in both cases, a parent company is exempt from preparing group accounts where it is a wholly owned subsidiary of its parent undertaking. Where the company is not wholly owned but the parent undertaking holds more than 50% of the allotted shares, the company is exempt from preparing group accounts if a notice requesting the preparation of group accounts has not been served on the company by shareholders who in aggregate hold half the remaining holding or 5% of the total allotted shares in the company. To be effective, any such notice must be served on the company not more than 6 months after the year end before that period to which the notice relates.

For companies included in the EEA group accounts of a larger group, any holding of shares by a director are disregarded in determining whether or not the company is wholly owned. For companies included in non-EEA group accounts, any shares in the company held by a wholly owned subsidiary of the parent undertaking, or held on behalf of the parent undertaking or a wholly owned subsidiary, are attributed to the parent undertaking. A parent company cannot take advantage of the exemption not to prepare group accounts where its accounts are included in a larger group if it has any securities admitted to trading on a regulated market in an EEA state.

The key conditions for taking advantage of these exemptions can be summarised as follows:

(1) the company must be included in consolidated accounts for a larger group drawn up to the same date or to an earlier date in the same financial year by a parent undertaking;

---

[58]   CA 2006, s 399(3).
[59]   CA 2006, s 400, replacing CA 1985, s 228, and CA 2006, s 401, replacing CA 1985, s 228A, respectively.

(2) those consolidated accounts must be either drawn up in accordance with:

    (a) the provisions of the Seventh Company Law Directive,[60] as modified, where relevant, by the provisions of the Bank Accounts Directive[61] or the Insurance Accounts Directive;[62] or

    (b) for parent undertakings established in the EEA, in accordance with IAS; or

    (c) for parent undertakings not established in the EEA, in a manner equivalent to consolidated accounts and annual reports drawn up in accordance with provisions of the Seventh Company Law Directive;

(3) the consolidated accounts must be audited and where the parent undertaking is not in the EEA the auditor must be authorised to audit accounts under the law under which the parent undertaking preparing the group accounts is established;

(4) the company must state in its individual accounts:

    (a) that it is exempt from the requirement to prepare and deliver group accounts;

    (b) the name of the parent undertaking preparing group accounts and, if outside the UK, the country in which it is incorporated, or if it is unincorporated, the address of its principal place of business;

(5) the company must deliver a copy (in English) of those group accounts, together with the auditors' report and, where appropriate, the consolidated annual report, to the Registrar of Companies within the period allowed for the filing of its individual account for the financial period in question.

14.8.1 Group accounts: applicable accounting framework

The general provisions concerning the accounting framework for group accounts are the same as for individual companies. They may be prepared in accordance with s 404 relating to group accounts or in accordance with international accounting standards.[63] Certain parent companies are required to prepare group accounts in accordance with international accounting standards by art 4 of the IAS Regulation.[64]

---

[60] Directive 83/349/EEC.
[61] Directive 86/635/EEC.
[62] Directive 91/674/EEC.
[63] CA 2006, s 403.
[64] CA 2006, s 403(1).

14.8.2 Companies Act group accounts

The general provisions for Companies House group accounts mirror those for Companies House individual accounts except that the group accounts must comprise a consolidated balance sheet and a consolidated profit and loss account that provide a true and fair view of the state of affairs at the end of the financial year and of the profit and loss for the financial year of the undertakings included in the consolidated group as a whole.[65] The form and content of Companies Act group accounts are set down in Sch 6 to the Large and Medium-sized Companies and Group (Accounts and Reports) Regulations 2008.[66] Small companies must comply with the Small Companies and Groups (Accounts and Directors' Report) Regulations 2008.[67]

In preparing Companies Act group accounts, all the subsidiary undertakings of the parent company should be included in the consolidation except where the Act permits that a subsidiary should be excluded.[68] The categories for exclusion are:

(1) the inclusion of the subsidiary is not material for the purpose of giving a true and fair view. Two or more subsidiaries can only be excluded on this basis if they are not material when taken together;

(2) there are severe long-term restrictions which substantially hinder the exercise of the rights of the parent company over the assets or management of the subsidiary;

(3) the information necessary to prepare group accounts cannot be obtained without disproportionate expense or undue delay; or

(4) the parent company's interest in the subsidiary is held exclusively for resale.

14.8.3 IAS group accounts

Companies preparing IAS group accounts must state in the notes to the accounts that they have been prepared in accordance with IAS.[69]

---

[65] CA 2006, s 404.
[66] SI 2008/410.
[67] SI 2008/409.
[68] CA 2006, s 405.
[69] CA 2006, s 406, replacing CA 1985, s 227B.

14.8.4 Consistency of financial reporting within group

The general requirement for the directors of the parent company is to secure that a consistent financial reporting framework is adopted by the parent company and its subsidiary undertakings.[70] There are exceptions to this general rule, which are:

(1) the directors are not required to do this where the parent company does not prepare group accounts;

(2) it only applies to subsidiaries who are required to prepare annual accounts under Part 16;

(3) there is no requirement for companies that are charities to be prepared under the same framework as companies which are not charities; and

(4) if the directors of the parent company prepare IAS group and IAS individual accounts, they need to ensure all subsidiaries use the same financial reporting framework, but this does not have to be the same framework as the parent, ie the subsidiaries could all prepare Companies Act individual accounts.

14.8.5 Individual profit and loss account where group accounts prepared

A parent company preparing group accounts does not need to present its individual profit and loss account in its statutory group accounts.[71] This exemption is subject to various conditions:

(1) the notes to the company's individual balance sheet show the company's profit or loss for the financial year;

(2) the profit and loss account is prepared and approved by the directors in accordance with s 414(1); and

(3) the group accounts state that the exemption has been applied.

The profit and loss account that is prepared does not need to contain the information required about employee numbers and costs that would otherwise be required if it was presented in the annual accounts.

---

[70] CA 2006, s 407, replacing CA 1985, s 227C.
[71] CA 2006, s 408, replacing CA 1985, s 230.

14.9 INFORMATION TO BE PROVIDED IN ACCOUNTS

14.9.1 Related undertakings

The information concerning related undertakings which was specified in Sch 5 to the Companies Act 1985 does not appear in the Companies Act 2006. Section 409 does provide, however, that the Secretary of State may make regulations requiring information about related undertakings to be given in the notes to the annual accounts. Those regulations may make different provisions depending on whether or not the company produces group accounts. They may also specify the descriptions of undertakings in relation to which the regulations apply and make different provisions in relation to those different descriptions of related undertakings. This would not be dissimilar to Sch 5 to the 1985 Act, which was split into two Parts: one relating to companies not required to prepare group accounts and one for companies required to prepare group accounts.[72]

According to s 409(3) the regulations may also provide that information need not be disclosed in respect of any undertaking that is either established under the law of a country outside the UK or carries on business outside the UK provided certain conditions are met.[73] Those conditions are:

(1) that, in the opinion of the directors, the disclosure would be seriously prejudicial to the business of:

    (a) the undertaking;
    (b) the company;
    (c) any of the company's subsidiary undertakings; or
    (d) any other undertaking included in the consolidation, where group accounts are prepared; and

(2) the company's annual accounts state that advantage has been taken of the exemption.

The Act makes provision where directors believe the number of related undertakings is so great that compliance with the regulations would result in a statement of excessive length.[74] Where directors believe this will be the case then the information need only be provided in respect of those related undertakings whose results and financial position, in the opinion of the directors, principally affected the numbers shown in the company's

---

[72] See Small Companies and Groups (Accounts and Directors' Report) Regulations 2008, SI 2008/409, Sch 2 and Sch 6, Part2, and Large and Medium-sized Companies and Group (Accounts and Report) Regulations 2008, SI 2008/410, Sc 4 Parts 1, 2 and 3.

[73] The Regulations do not contain such provision.

[74] CA 2006, s 410.

annual accounts. Where the directors prepare group accounts, the information need only be given in respect of undertakings that are excluded from consolidation.

To take advantage of these provisions, there must be a statement in the company's annual accounts that the information is only given in respect of those limited groups of undertakings and the full information must be annexed to the company's next annual return delivered to the Registrar of Companies after the annual accounts are approved. Full information means both that included in the annual accounts and that which was not included. The failure to comply with a requirement to annex 'full information' to the annual return means an offence is committed both by the company and every officer of the company who is in default.

14.9.2   Employee numbers and costs

All companies, except those subject to the small companies regime, are required to provide the following details of the company's employees in the annual accounts:[75]

(1)   the average number of persons employed by the company in the financial year; and

(2)   the average number of persons so employed within the different categories that the directors may select having regard to the manner in which the company is organised.

For clarity, the disclosure is not of 'full-time-equivalent' employees but of the actual number of persons employed under contracts of service.

The accounts must also state in respect of all persons employed by the company:

(1)   wages and salaries paid or payable in respect of the financial year;

(2)   social security costs incurred by the company on their behalf; and

(3)   other pension costs incurred by the company.[76]

14.9.3   Directors' benefits: remuneration

The information required by CA 2006 to be presented in the notes to the accounts regarding directors' remuneration is laid out in the Small Companies Accounts Regulations and the Large Companies Accounts

---

[75]   CA 2006, s 411.

[76]   Whereas the definition of pension costs and social security costs was included in an interpretive section of CA 1985, Sch 4, these same definitions are included in CA 2006, s 417 itself.

Regulations.[77] All companies must disclose the aggregate amount of remuneration paid to or receivable by directors in respect of qualifying services but the level of detail is then different for companies preparing accounts under the small companies' regime and all other companies. Quoted companies then have to provide even more information but this is not required by the regulations made under s 412 of CA 2006 but through the requirement to prepare a directors' remuneration report under s 420.

Although the level of the detail differs, the information which may be required includes the following:

(1) gains made on the exercise of share options;

(2) benefits received under long-term incentive plans;

(3) payments received for loss of office;

(4) retirement benefits receivable or contribution to retirement benefit plans in respect of past service of a person as director or in any other capacity while a director; and

(5) consideration paid to or receivable by a third party for making available the services of a person as a director or in any other capacity while a director.

Amounts paid to or receivable by a person connected with a director or a body corporate controlled by a director are treated as paid to or receivable by the director.[78]

Unquoted companies do not have to provide information concerning the highest paid director where the aggregate of directors' remuneration is less than £200,000.[79] There is no requirement for the disclosure of the highest paid director under the small companies' regime. The 2006 Act contains a duty upon the directors or any person who has been a director in the preceding five years to give notice to the company of any information relating to himself that might be required for compliance with the regulations under that section.[80]

---

[77] CA 2006, s 412. See Sch 3 to the Small Companies and Group (Accounts and Directors' Report) Regulations 2008 and Sch 5 to the Large and Medium-sized Companies and Group (Accounts and Reports) Regulations 2008.

[78] CA 2006, s 412(4).

[79] Large and Medium-sized Companies and Group (Accounts and Reports) Regulations 2008, Sch 5, para 2.

[80] CA 2006, s 412(5).

14.9.4   Information about directors' benefits: advances, credit and guarantees

A company's accounts must disclose advances and credits granted to the directors and guarantees entered into on behalf of the directors.[81] In the case of group accounts, the disclosures only apply to the directors of the parent company but must be given where the advance, credit or guarantee is given by the parent or any of its subsidiary undertakings. For advances and credits, the details disclosed are the amount, an indication of the interest rate, the principal conditions and any amounts repaid. For guarantees, the details required are its main terms, the maximum liability that might be incurred by the company (or any subsidiaries) and any amount paid or liability incurred for the purpose of fulfilling the guarantee.

The notes to the accounts must also state the aggregate of:

(1)   advances and credits made to directors and any amounts repaid; and

(2)   the maximum liability that may be incurred under guarantees and any amounts paid or liabilities incurred.

To avoid any confusion, the disclosures should be made in respect of:

(1)   any person who was a director at any time in the financial year;

(2)   every advance, credit or guarantee that subsisted at any time in the financial year:

 (a)   whenever it was entered into;
 (b)   whether or not the person concerned was a director at the time the arrangement was entered into; and
 (c)   in the case of an arrangement involving a subsidiary, whether or not that undertaking was a subsidiary at the time the arrangement was entered into.

Banking companies and holding companies of credit institutions are exempt from many of the disclosures but are still required to state the details of the amounts of any advances or credits to directors and for guarantees, the amount of the maximum liability that might be incurred by the company.[82]

---

[81]   CA 2006, s 413.
[82]   CA 2006, s 413(8).

14.9.5   Approval and signing of accounts

The company's annual accounts must be approved by the board directors and signed on its behalf by a director. The signature must be on the company's balance sheet.[83] Where the accounts are prepared under the small companies regime, there must be a statement on the balance sheet to that effect in a prominent position above the signature. If annual accounts are approved that do not comply with the requirements of the 2006 Act (and, where applicable, art 4 of the IAS Regulation), every director commits an offence who knew they did not comply or was reckless as to whether they complied or failed to take reasonable steps to secure their compliance or to prevent the accounts from being approved.

14.10   THE DIRECTORS' REPORT

The directors of all companies must prepare a directors' report for each financial year.[84] Where the company is a parent and it prepares group accounts, the directors' report must be a group directors' report which deals with all the undertakings included in the consolidation. A group directors' report can give greater emphasis, where appropriate, to matters that are significant to the undertakings included in the consolidation, taken as a whole.

Where the directors fail to prepare a directors' report for a year, an offence is committed by every director who was a director immediately before the end of the period allowed for the filing of reports and accounts for the relevant year and who failed to take all reasonable steps to ensure compliance with the requirements.[85]

14.10.1   Contents of directors' report: general

The most basic of the requirements for the directors' report is that the report must state the names of all persons who were directors at any time during the financial year plus the principal activities of the company during the year.[86] Where the report is a group directors' report, the description of principal activities will extend to the activities of all undertakings included in the consolidation.

If the directors are recommending the payment of a dividend, the directors must state the amount in the directors' report. This requirement does not apply to companies that are subject to the small companies regime.

---

83   CA 2006, s 414, replacing CA 1985, s 233.
84   CA 2006, s 415.
85   CA 2006, s 415(4).
86   CA 2006, s 416.

The Small Companies Accounts Regulations for companies using the small companies' exemption and the Large Companies Accounts Regulations contain information requirements that are essentially the same as those previously included in CA 1985, Sch 7. These include matters such as information relating to fixed assets; directors' interests in shares or debentures of the company; particulars of any important past or future events affecting the company or any of its subsidiaries which have occurred since the end of the financial year; activities relating to research and development, existence of branches outside the UK; policies relating to disabled employees where there are more than 250 employees; information and consultation arrangements where there is an average of more than 250 employees; particulars of acquisition of a company's own shares; charitable and political donations; policy and practice on payment of creditors.

14.10.2   Business review

In respect of accounting periods commencing on or after 1 April 2005,[87] all companies, except those that are subject to the small companies regime, must prepare a business review.[88] The purpose of the business review is to inform the company's members and assist them to assess how the directors have performed their duty to promote the success of the company,[89] which is contained in s 172.[90] At one time, it was proposed to introduce a more wide-ranging operating and financial review, but this was abandoned in circumstances described in Chapter 11. Nonetheless, it remains the case that the business review is an important component of what can be termed an enlightened shareholder value approach to company law.[91]

The most basic requirement of the business review is that it provides a fair review of the business together with a description of the principal risks and uncertainties facing the company. The review should be 'balanced' and 'comprehensive' and should analyse the development and performance of the business of the company during the year as well as commenting on the position at the end of the year.

Quoted companies are required to provide more information in their business review compared with non-quoted companies and need to ensure that the business review includes information on the main trends and factors likely to affect the future development, performance and position of the company's business.[92] A quoted company's business review must

---

[87]   The business review was introduced into the CA 1985 by SI 2005/1011.
[88]   Now s 417 of the 2006 Act.
[89]   CA 2006, s 417(2).
[90]   See **16.5**.
[91]   See **11.6**.
[92]   CA 2006, s 417(5).

also contain information on the following areas, including information about any relevant company policies and the effectiveness of those policies:

(1) environmental matters, including the impact of the company's business on the environment;

(2) the company's employees; and

(3) social and community issues.

Such information required by quoted companies need only be disclosed 'to the extent necessary for an understanding of the development, performance or position of the company's business'.[93]

Quoted companies should also provide information about persons with whom the company has contractual or other arrangements which are essential to the business of the company.[94] However, this information would not be required if in the opinion of the directors such disclosure would be seriously prejudicial to that person and contrary to the public interest.[95]

If the review does not contain the information specified for quoted companies the review must state which of those kinds of information it does not contain.[96]

More generally s 417 does not require disclosure of information about impending developments or matters in the course of negotiation if the disclosure would, in the opinion of the directors, be seriously prejudicial to the interests of the company.[97]

The review should include analysis using key financial performance indicators and, where appropriate and relevant, analysis of other key performance indicators including information on employee and environmental matters. A 'key performance indicator' is described as a factor 'by reference to which the development, performance or position of the company's business can be measured effectively'.[98]

Companies that qualify as medium-sized in relation to a financial year are not required to provide the information that relates to non-financial key performance indicators.

---

[93] CA. 2006, s 417(5).
[94] CA 2006, s 417(5)(c).
[95] CA 2006, s 417(11).
[96] CA 2006, s 417(5).
[97] CA 2006, s 417(10).
[98] CA 2006, s 417(6).

If a company produces a corporate governance statement as a separate statement which is not part of the directors' report, it must be filed with the registrar of companies and the auditor must give an opinion as to whether the information required to be shown in the statement as to internal control and risk management systems in relation to the financial reporting process and certain disclosures requested by the Takeovers Directive[99] is consistent with annual accounts for the year in question.[100]

14.10.3 Statement on disclosure to auditors

Where a company is audited, the directors' report must contain a statement that there is no relevant audit information of which the company's auditors are unaware and the director has taken all the steps he should have taken as a director in order to make himself aware of any relevant audit information and to establish that the company's auditors are aware of that information.[101]

A director will have taken all the steps he should have taken for this purpose if he makes such inquiries of his fellow directors and of the company's auditors for that purpose (and takes any other steps) as were required by his duty as a director to exercise due care, skill and diligence. The extent of that duty for a particular director will be determined by the knowledge, skill and experience that may reasonably be expected of a person carrying out the same functions as are carried out by the director and the knowledge, skill and experience that the director in fact has (so far as they exceed what may reasonably be expected).

If the directors' report that is approved contains the statement concerning information provided to auditors and that statement is found to be false, every director who knew that the statement was false (or was reckless as to whether it was false), and failed to take reasonable steps to prevent the report from being approved, is guilty of an offence which is punishable by either a fine, imprisonment or both.

14.10.4 Approval and signing of directors' report

The directors' report should be approved by the board and signed on its behalf either by a director or by the company secretary.[102]

For small companies, where the report is prepared in accordance with the small companies regime, a statement to this effect should appear in a prominent position above the signature.

---

[99] Directive 2004/25/EEC.
[100] Companies Act 2006 (Accounts, Reports and Audit) Regulations 2009, SI 2009/1581.
[101] CA 2006, s 418, replacing CA 1985, s 234ZA
[102] CA 2006, s 419, replacing CA 1985, s 234A.

If a directors' report is approved that does not comply with the requirements of the Companies Act 2006, then every director who knew it did not comply or was reckless as to whether or not it complied and who failed to take reasonable steps either to ensure it complied or to prevent it from being approved commits an offence.

14.11 QUOTED COMPANIES: DIRECTORS' REMUNERATION REPORT

The directors of a quoted company are required to prepare a directors' remuneration report for each financial year.[103] The duty to prepare and penalty for non-compliance are identical to those relating to the directors' report.

14.11.1 Contents of the directors' remuneration report

A directors' remuneration report must comply with Sch 8 to the Large and Medium-sized Companies and Group (Accounts and Reports) Regulations 2008.[104] These regulations, as well as determining the content, also determine how the information should be presented and also which elements of the report are to be auditable.[105]

14.11.2 Information in the directors' remuneration report not subject to audit

If a committee of the company has considered matters relating to directors' remuneration, then the report should disclose the name of each director who served on that committee when it considered matters relating to directors' remuneration. Additionally, the report shall state the name of any person that provided advice or services that materially assisted the committee when considering matters relating to directors' remuneration. This includes, particularly, a director of the company who was not a member of the committee. Where that person was not a director of the company, the report should state whether the person was appointed by the committee and the nature of any other services provided to the company during the financial year.

The directors' remuneration report should contain a statement of the company's policy on directors' remuneration for the following financial year and financial years subsequent to that. The policy statement must also include, for each director, a detailed summary of performance conditions to which the director is subject in respect of his entitlement to share options or under a long-term incentive scheme. The statement must also explain why such performance conditions were chosen, a summary of

---

[103] CA 2006, s 420.
[104] SI 2008/410.
[105] CA 2006, s 421.

the methods to be used in assessing whether the conditions have been met and an explanation of why these methods were chosen. Where any director's entitlement to share options or under a long-term incentive scheme is not subject to performance conditions, there should be an explanation of why this is the case.

Where the performance conditions involves comparison to factors external to the company, then the policy statement should provide a summary of the factors to be used in making the comparison. Where any factor relates to the performance of another company, two or more other companies or an index, then that or those companies or that index should be identified.

The policy statement should set out a description of, and explanation for, any significant amendment which is proposed to the terms and conditions of the entitlement of any director to share options or under a long-term incentive scheme.

The disclosures in the policy statement set out above must be made for every person that serves as a director of the company in the period starting with the first day of the financial year and ending with the date on which the directors' remuneration report is laid before the company in general meeting. The policy statement must also summarise and explain the company's policy on the duration of contracts with directors and the notice periods and termination payments under such contracts.

The directors' remuneration report should provide a 'performance graph', covering five financial years ending with the financial year for which the report is being prepared, illustrating the total shareholder return[106] for:

(a) a holding of the equity shares in the company, being the class of share that resulted in the company being defined as a quoted company for the purpose of the Act; and

(b) a hypothetical holding of shares of the same kind and number as those by reference to which a broad equity marked index is calculated.[107]

---

[106] The calculation of the 'total shareholder return' for a holding of shares for the period of the performance graph should be calculated using a fair method. The method should take as its starting point the percentage change in the market price over the relevant period. The method will include certain specified assumptions regarding the reinvestment of income and the funding of liabilities and should make provision for replacing shares in the holding with shares of a different description. The assumption over the reinvestment of income deals with any benefit (including dividends) that becomes receivable by the holder in respect of any holding of shares from the company of whose share capital the shares form part.

[107] The name of the index selected and the reason for selecting that index should be stated.

Where the company does not have five financial years upon which to base the performance graph, it should produce the graph for as many periods as it can.

It should be assumed that any dividend or other benefit in the form of shares of the same kind in the holding is added to the holding at the time the benefit becomes receivable. Where the benefit received is in cash, it should be assumed that the benefit is used to purchase shares of the same kind as the holding at their market price on the date that the benefit becomes receivable. Where the benefit is not cash and is not in shares of the same kind as the holding, then it should be assumed that an amount equal to the value of that benefit is applied in purchasing shares of the same kind as the holding at their market price on the date that the benefit becomes receivable.

Where the holder has a liability to the company arising in respect of any shares in the holding, or arising from the exercise of any right attached to any of those shares, it should be assumed that the holder sells shares from the holding immediately before the time by which the liability is due to be satisfied. The number sold will be sufficient to ensure that the market price of the shares sold will be sufficient to satisfy the liability in respect of the shares in the holding that are not being sold.

The directors' remuneration report is required to disclose details of the service contracts of each person that has served as a director in the relevant financial year. The information to be disclosed includes the date of the contract, the unexpired term of the contract, details of any notice periods, any provision for compensation payable upon early termination of the contract and details of any other provisions in the contract that are necessary to enable members of the company to estimate the liability of the company in the event of the early termination of the contract.

14.11.3   Information in the directors' remuneration report subject to audit

The disclosures in the directors' remuneration report that are subject to audit are similar to those that are required for other companies except that they are required to be shown for each director rather than in aggregate.

For each person that served as a director at any time in the year the following information should be disclosed in tabular form:

(a)   the total amount of salary and fees paid to or receivable by the person in respect of qualifying services;

(b)   the total amount of bonuses so paid or receivable;

(c)   the total amount of sums paid by way of expense allowance that are chargeable to UK income tax (or would be if that person were an individual) and paid to or receivable by the person in respect of qualifying services;

(d)   the total amount of any compensation for loss of office paid to or receivable by the person and any other payments paid to or receivable by the person in connection with the termination of qualifying services;

(e)   the total estimated value of any benefits receivable by the person other than in cash that are not covered above but are emoluments and are receivable in respect of qualifying services;

(f)   the total of the amounts disclosed under (a)–(e) above should be disclosed for each person. The amount of this total from the preceding financial year should also be disclosed for each person.

Where any element of a remuneration package is not cash, the nature of this remuneration should be stated.

For each person that served as a director at any time in the year, the following information in respect of share options granted in respect of the person's qualifying services should be disclosed in tabular form:

(a)   the number of shares, differentiating between share options that have different terms and conditions, that are subject to a share option at the beginning of the financial year (or the date of appointment as a director, if later) and at the end of the financial year (or the date of the person ceased to be a director, if earlier);

(b)   information identifying those share options that have been granted in the year, those that have exercised in the year, those that have expired in the year not having been exercised and those where the terms and conditions have been varied in the year;

(c)   for each share option that is unexpired at any time in the financial year, the price paid, if any, for its award, the exercise price and the date on which the option may be exercised and on which it expires;

(d)   a description of any variation in the terms and conditions of any share option made in the financial year;

(e)   a summary of any performance criteria upon which the award of share options is conditional, including a description of any variation of this criteria made in the financial year;

(f) for each share option exercised in the financial year, the market price of the shares in relation to which the option is exercised, at the date of exercise;

(g) for each share option that is unexpired at the end of the financial year, the market price of each share that is subject to option at the end of the year together with the highest and lowest market prices during the financial year.

If the directors consider that the disclosures required in respect of share options would result in a statement of excessive length, the disclosure on (a) above need not differentiate between share options with different terms and conditions. Additionally, the disclosures required under (c) and (g) above may be aggregated, with the disclosure of the weighted average prices of aggregations of share options rather than the prices relating to each share option. Similarly, the disclosures of dates above may be ranges of dates for aggregations of share options rather than dates for each share option.[108] Where share options have been awarded, exercised or had their terms and conditions varied during the financial year, directors are not able to use the 'excessive length' argument and are, therefore, not permitted to use the aggregation approach.

For each person that served as a director at any time in the year, the following information in respect of long-term incentive schemes whereby money or other assets become receivable by that person in respect of the person's qualifying services, should be disclosed in tabular form:

(a) details of the scheme interests that the person had at the beginning of the financial year (or date of appointment as director if later);

(b) details of the scheme interests awarded to the person on the financial year;

(c) details of the scheme interests that the person has at the end of the financial year (or date of cessation as director if earlier);

(d) for each scheme interest within (a)–(c) above:

   (i) the end of the period over which the qualifying conditions for that interest have to be fulfilled (or where different periods exist for different conditions, the end of the period that ends last);

   (ii) a description of any variation made in the terms and conditions of the scheme interests during the financial year;

---

[108] Aggregation is not permitted, however, of share options in respect of shares whose market price is below the exercise price at the end of the financial year with share options in respect of shares whose market price is equal to or exceeds the option price at the end of the financial year.

(e)   for each scheme interest that has vested in the financial year, details of the amounts that have become receivable in respect of the interest. Those details should include the relevant details of any shares, the amount of any money and the value of any other assets.

Where the interests awarded in (b) above include shares, the details to be disclosed include the number of shares, the market price of the shares when the interest was awarded and details of any qualifying conditions that are related to performance.

The relevant details of shares in (e) above include the number of shares, the date on which the scheme interest was awarded, the market price of the shares at the dates on which the interest was awarded and vested and details of qualifying conditions that related to performance.

The directors' remuneration report should also contain certain information in respect of pensions for each person that has served as a director in the year.

Where a person has rights under a defined benefit scheme and he has become entitled to those rights in respect of qualifying services, the following information should be disclosed:

(a)   the accrued benefits under the scheme at the end of the financial year and the change in the amount of those benefits in the year;

(b)   the transfer value of the person's accrued benefits at the end of the financial year, calculated in a manner consistent with 'Retirement Benefit Schemes – Transfer Values (GN 11)' published by the Institute of Actuaries and the Faculty of Actuaries, dated 6 April 2001;

(c)   the transfer value of the accrued benefits disclosed in the directors' remuneration report from the previous financial year, or if there was no such report or no such value was contained in that report, the transfer value of the accrued benefits at the beginning of the financial year, calculated in the manner mentioned in (b) above;

(d)   the amount obtained by subtracting the amount in (b) less the amount in (c) then deducting the amount of contributions made to the scheme by the person in the year.

Where a person has rights under a money purchase scheme and he has become entitled to those rights in respect of qualifying services, the report should state the amount of contributions paid or payable by the company for the financial year or paid by the company for another financial year.

In certain circumstances, the directors' remuneration report should disclose excess retirement benefits of directors or past directors. These provisions apply to each person that served as a director for any part of the financial year or at any time before the start of the year.

The amounts to be disclosed are the retirement benefits, being those that a person became entitled to from qualifying services, paid to or receivable by him that are in excess of the retirement benefits to which he was entitled on the date on which the benefits first became payable or 31 March 1997, whichever is the later.

Any amount paid or receivable under a pension scheme should be excluded from this amount if the funding of the scheme were such that the amounts were or could have been paid without recourse to additional contributions or the amounts were paid to or receivable by all pensioner members of the scheme on the same basis. In this case, a 'pensioner member' means any person who is entitled to receive present benefits under the scheme. The references to retirement benefits in this section include benefits otherwise than in cash and, where that is the case, the amount to be disclosed should be the estimated money value of the benefit. The report should also state the nature of any non-cash benefits.

The directors' remuneration report should include details of any 'significant award' made to any person who was not a director at the time the award was made but who had served as a director at any time before then. In particular, these details should include compensation in respect of loss of office and pensions; however, it should not include any amount otherwise included in the directors' remuneration report. Where a company pays to a third party an amount for making available the services of a director, then it should disclose in the directors' remuneration report the aggregate amounts so paid in respect of each director. The total amount to be disclosed should include any amount paid for the services of the person as:

(a)   a director of the company;

(b)   while he was director of the company:

    (i)   as director of any of the company's subsidiary undertakings;
    (ii)   as director of any other undertaking by virtue of the company's nomination; or
    (iii)   otherwise in connection with the management of the company or any such other undertaking.

The references to consideration in this context include consideration otherwise than in cash and where that is the case, the amount to be disclosed should be the estimated money value of the consideration. The report should also state the nature of any non-cash consideration.

A third party in this context means a party other than the person himself or a person connected with him or a body corporate controlled by him. It also means a party other than the company, one of its subsidiary undertakings or any other undertaking to which the company can nominate directors, either directly or indirectly.

There is a duty on a director of a quoted company or any person who has been a director in the preceding five years to give notice to the company of any information relating to himself that might be required for compliance with the regulations.[109]

14.11.4   Approval and signing of the directors' remuneration report

The requirements for the approval and signing of the directors' remuneration report are identical to those for the approval and signing of the directors' report and the same duties and penalties also exist for non-compliance.[110]

14.11.5   Members' approval of the directors' remuneration report

Prior to the general meeting of the company before which the company's annual accounts for the financial year are to be laid ('the accounts meeting'), a quoted company must give to those members of the company entitled to be sent notice of the meeting notice of the intention to move an ordinary resolution approving the directors' remuneration report for the financial year.[111] The directors of the company (being those in office immediately before the meeting) must ensure that the resolution is put to the vote of the meeting.

14.12   PUBLICATION OF REPORTS AND ACCOUNTS

Although many of the requirements regarding the circulation of annual accounts and reports[112] remain as under the previous legislation, the Companies Act 2006 sets them out in a more straightforward manner. Private companies are subject to a less onerous procedure by right rather than it being achieved by means of various exemptions and elections. The

---

[109] CA 2006, s 421(3).

[110] CA 2006, s 422.

[111] CA 2006, s 439.

[112] CA 2006, s 471. This section defines 'Annual accounts and report' and this expression has different meaning for quoted and unquoted companies. For an unquoted company it means: (a) the annual accounts; (b) the directors' report; and (c) the auditor's report on the accounts and directors' report (unless the company is entitled to and takes advantage of being exempt from audit). For a quoted company its annual accounts and reports for a year include, additionally, a directors' remuneration report. The auditor's report for a quoted company also covers the auditable part of the directors' remuneration report.

fact that private companies are not required to hold an annual general meeting[113] has implications in respect of their annual accounts and reports.

Subject to the provisions concerning summary financial statements, there is a basic requirement for every company to send a copy of its annual accounts and reports to:

(1)   every member of the company;

(2)   every holder of the company's debentures;

(3)   every person entitled to receive notice of the company's general meetings.[114]

The company need not send copies to any person for whom it does not hold a 'current address'. Rather than try actually to define a 'current address', the Act describes when a company will be regarded as having a person's current address.[115] This will be if:

(1)   the person has notified the company of an address where documents may be sent to him; or

(2)   the company has no reason to believe that documents sent to that address will not reach him.

Companies that do not have a share capital are only required to send copies of the annual accounts and reports to those persons entitled to receive notices of general meetings of the company.[116]

Where copies are sent out over a number of days, references in the Companies Acts to the day on which copies are sent out shall be read as the last day of the relevant period.[117]

Essentially, a private company is required to circulate copies of its annual accounts and reports to those entitled to receive them no later than the date on which the annual accounts and reports are actually filed with the registrar provided that this is within the time allowed for filing.[118]

---

[113]   See **13.1**.

[114]   CA 2006, s 422.

[115]   CA 2006, s 423.

[116]   CA 2006, s 423(4).

[117]   CA 2006, s 423(5). Where copies of accounts are sent out over a number of days, references in CA 2006 to the day on which copies are sent out shall be read as the last day of the relevant period.

[118]   CA 2006, s 424(2).

A public company[119] is required to circulate copies of its annual accounts and reports to those entitled to receive them not later than 21 days before the relevant accounts meeting.[120] If the annual accounts and report are sent out later than 21 days before the relevant accounts meeting, the company can be deemed to have complied with the 21-day rule if this is agreed by all the members entitled to attend and vote at that meeting.[121]

14.13 OPTION TO PROVIDE SUMMARY FINANCIAL STATEMENTS

A company may send to its members what is called a 'summary financial statement', in place of a copy of the full accounts and reports. This concession was introduced as a cost-saving measure following a great increase in the number of shareholders to whom otherwise full copies of all the documents would have to be sent, particularly in privatised companies. Shareholders, debenture-holders and entitled persons must be alerted on the summary financial statement of their right to receive the full accounts and reports and must be issued with a pre-paid card or form on which they can notify the company of their wish to receive the full set of accounts and reports for the current and/or future years.

Summary financial statements must be derived from the full accounts and reports and contain a statement that they are only a summary. They must be approved by the board of directors and signed on their behalf by one director.

Until 2005, it was only listed companies who had the option to provide a summary financial statement to shareholders rather the full annual accounts and report. This ability was extended to all companies for years commencing on or after 1 January 2005.[122] The circumstances in which a company may opt to provide summary financial statements rather than copies of the annual accounts and reports may be specified by the Secretary of State in regulations.[123]

A company must, however, send a copy of the annual accounts and reports to a person who is entitled to receive them and wishes to receive

---

[119] CA 2006, s 424(5). Whether a company is private or public for the purposes of the duty to circulate annual accounts and reports is determined by the company's status immediately before the end of the financial year to which those accounts relate.

[120] CA 2006, s 424(3). The 'relevant accounts meeting' is the general meeting of the company at which the annual accounts and reports are to be laid.

[121] CA 2006, s 424(4).

[122] CA 1985, s 251, replaced by CA 2006, s 426.

[123] CA 2006, s 426(1). See the Companies (Summary Financial Statement) Regulations 2008, SI 2008/374.

them. The Secretary of State may make provision by regulations as to how a company should ascertain whether such a person wishes to receive the annual accounts and reports.[124]

14.13.1 Form and content of summary financial statement

The form and content of summary financial statements are separated into different sections for unquoted companies and quoted companies respectively, although many of the provisions within those two sections are similar.[125] Both allow that the regulations made under these sections may allow specified information to be sent separately rather than included in the summary financial statement.

In essence, all summary financial statements should be:

(1) derived from the company's annual accounts; and

(2) prepared in accordance with the appropriate section and any regulations made under it.

The form and content of summary financial statements are determined by regulations,[126] and may also require the inclusion of information from the directors' report.[127]

A summary financial statement must state:

(1) that it is only a summary derived from the company's annual accounts;

(2) whether it contains additional information derived from the directors' report and, if so, that it does not contain the full text of the directors' report; and

(3) how a person can obtain a copy of the annual accounts and directors' report.

Where the company's annual accounts are audited, the summary financial statement must contain a statement by the auditor concerning his report on the annual accounts and reports.[128]

---

[124] The rules for ascertaining a person's wishes in respect of summary financial statements are set out in the Companies (Summary Financial Statement) Regulations 2008, reg 5.

[125] CA 2006, ss 427 and 428.

[126] Companies (Summary Financial Statement) Regulations 2008, SI 2008/374.

[127] CA 2006, ss 427(3) and 428(3). Companies are permitted to include more information in the summary financial statements than is specified in the regulations that is derived from the company's annual accounts or directors' report (and, in the case of a quoted company, the directors' remuneration report).

[128] CA 2006, ss 427(4)(d) and 428(4)(d).

The auditor should state that the summary financial statement:

(1) is consistent with the annual accounts;

(2) the information derived from the directors' report, if any, is consistent with that report;

(3) complies with the requirements under s 433 and any regulations made under that section.

The summary financial statement should also include information concerning the auditor's report on the annual accounts and report.[129] That information should include:

(1) whether the following were qualified or unqualified:

    (a) the auditor's report on the annual accounts; and
    (b) the auditor's report as to whether the directors' report was consistent with the annual accounts;

(2) whether the auditor's report on the annual statements contained a statement that:

    (a) the accounting records or returns were not adequate for the purpose of the audit or the accounts did not agree with those records or returns;[130] or
    (b) the auditor failed to obtain all the information and explanations necessary for the purposes of the audit.[131]

If the auditor's report under (1)(a) was qualified then that report should be set out in full. If his statement under (1)(b) was qualified he should set out the qualified statement in full. In both circumstances the statement should include any other information needed to understand the qualification.

If the auditor's report on the annual accounts contained statements under (2)(a) or (2)(b) then those statements should be set out in full.

14.13.2 Form and content of summary financial statement: quoted companies

The only difference in the form and content of the summary financial statement for quoted companies is that:

---

[129] CA 2006, ss 427(4)(e)–(g) and 428(4)(e)–(g).
[130] CA 2006, s 498(2)(a) or (b).
[131] CA 2006, s 498(3).

(1)   references above to the company's annual accounts should be read as to include the directors' remuneration report; and

(2)   references to the auditor's report on the annual accounts includes the auditable part of the directors' remuneration report.

14.14   QUOTED COMPANIES: ANNUAL REPORTS AND STATEMENTS TO BE MADE AVAILABLE ON WEBSITE

The Companies Act 2006 introduced a requirement that a quoted company's annual accounts and report must be made available on a website until the annual accounts and report for the next financial year are made similarly available.[132] The website must identify the company in question and be maintained by the company or on its behalf.[133] The annual accounts and report must be available free of charge (as must the provision of hard copies) and access to them on a website must not be restricted except where necessary to comply with any regulatory requirements either in the UK or elsewhere.[134] If the annual accounts and report are not available for part of the required period and this can be attributed wholly to circumstances over which the company would not normally expect to prevent or avoid, then this failure is disregarded.[135]

14.15   RIGHTS OF MEMBERS OR DEBENTURE HOLDERS TO COPIES OF ACCOUNTS AND REPORTS

A member of a company, or the holder of a debenture in a company, is entitled to be provided with one copy of the annual accounts and report of the company.[136] This entitlement is 'on demand' and free of charge. The information under ss 431 and 432 must be supplied within 7 days of receipt of a demand to prevent an offence being committed by the company and every officer of the company.

---

[132]   CA 2006, s 430(1). Section 430(4)(a) requires that the annual report and account must be made available on the website as soon as reasonably practicable.

[133]   CA 2006, s 430(2).

[134]   CA 2006, s 430(3).

[135]   CA 2006, s 430(5).

[136]   CA 2006, ss 431(1) and 432(1). The information that can be demanded is the last annual accounts and the last directors' report. If the company is quoted, this will also include the last directors' remuneration report. If the last accounts were audited, the auditors' report should also be provided.

14.16 REQUIREMENTS IN CONNECTION WITH PUBLICATION OF REPORTS AND ACCOUNTS

The Companies Act 2006 introduced a new requirement that copies of certain documents published[137] by or on behalf of a company must state the name of the person who signed it on behalf of the board.[138] Those documents are:

(1)   the balance sheet;

(2)   the directors' report; and

(3)   in the case of a quoted company, the directors' remuneration report.

Failure to publish these documents without stating the name of the signatory is an offence committed by the company and every officer of the company.

14.16.1 Publication of accounts

There is a particular requirement if a company publishes its statutory accounts.[139] Unless the directors are entitled to and have taken advantage of the exemption from audit, under s 434 of the Companies Act 2006,[140] the accounts must be accompanied by a copy of the auditors' report on them.

Section 435 concerns the publication of non-statutory accounts, which in this context are a balance sheet or profit and loss account[141] dealing with the financial year of a company which is published other than as part of the statutory accounts.[142] Where a company does publish non-statutory accounts then it must include a statement with them:

(1)   that the accounts are not the statutory accounts; and

(2)   whether the statutory accounts for the relevant financial year have been delivered to the registrar.

---

[137] CA 2006, s 436. 'Publication' for the purposes of ss 433-435 means if a company 'publishes, issues or circulates [a document] or otherwise makes it available for public inspection in a manner calculated to invite members of the public generally, or any class of members of the public, to read it'.

[138] CA 2006, s 433(1).

[139] Statutory accounts in this context are the company's accounts for the financial year which are required to be delivered to the Registrar of Companies under CA 2006, s 441.

[140] Replacing CA 1985, s 240(1) and (2).

[141] CA 2006, s 435(3). Where the company is a parent, this extends to an account of any form which purports to be a balance sheet or profit and loss account dealing with the group that the company heads.

[142] CA 2006, s 435(7). The provisions regarding non-statutory accounts do not apply to the publication of a summary financial statement.

Where auditors have reported on the company's statutory accounts for the year then that fact should be stated.[143] Where the auditors have reported, the following information regarding the auditors' report should be provided:

(1)   whether the report was qualified or unqualified or included information to which the auditor drew attention by 'emphasis of matter' without qualifying;

(2)   whether it contained a statement that:

(a)   the accounting records or returns were not adequate for the purpose of the audit or the accounts did not agree with those records or returns; or

(b)   the auditor failed to obtain all the information and explanations necessary for the purposes of the audit.

14.17   PUBLIC COMPANIES: LAYING OF ACCOUNTS BEFORE GENERAL MEETING

Because, under the Companies Act 2006, only public companies are required to hold general meetings,[144] the previous requirement for private companies to lay accounts before a general meeting was abolished. A public company is required to lay its annual accounts and report before the company in general meeting before the end of the period allowed for the company to file those annual accounts with the registrar.[145] The meeting at which the accounts are laid is known as the 'accounts meeting'.

It is the directors of the company immediately before the end of this period who commit an offence if the accounts are not so laid before general meeting.[146] A director charged with this offence has a reasonable defence if he can prove that he took all reasonable steps to ensure that the accounts would be so laid. It is not a defence, however, to prove that the annual accounts in question had not been prepared.

14.18   FILING OF ACCOUNTS AND REPORTS

The directors of all companies (except those of an unlimited company) are required to file with the registrar a set of accounts for each financial year.[147] The periods allowed for filing are as follows:

(1)   for a private company, 9 months from the balance sheet date; and

---

[143]   CA 2006, s 435(c).
[144]   See **13.1**.
[145]   CA 2006, s 437.
[146]   CA 2006, s 438.
[147]   CA 2006, s 441. As to the possibility to prepare and file accounts in euros, see s 469.

(2)   for a public company, 6 months from the balance sheet date.

In both cases, this represents a reduction of one month from the filing periods allowed under the Companies Act 1985.[148]

For a company's first accounting period, and if that period is longer than 12 months, then the filing period is the later of 9 months or 6 months from the first anniversary of incorporation (depending on whether the company is private or public) or 3 months after the end of the accounting period, whichever is the later.[149] Given that the maximum period for a company's first accounting reference period is 18 months, this means the greatest period allowed for a private company's first set of accounts is 21 months from the date of incorporation.

Where a company shortens its accounting period,[150] the filing period will either be the 9 or 6 months from the balance sheet date as applicable, or 3 months from the date of the notice to shorten the accounting reference period, whichever period expires last.[151]

The Secretary of State does have the power, for any special reason and as he sees fit, to extend the period allowed for the laying of accounts by giving in writing to the company a notice which will set out the further period allowed. Such notice may only be given if application is made before the expiration of the period otherwise allowed for delivering accounts.[152]

The company's status which determines the period allowed for delivering accounts is that immediately before the end of the accounting period for which the relevant accounts are being prepared.

If the accounting reference period is the last day of a month, the filing period will also be the last day of the appropriate month. For example, for a private company with an accounting reference date of 30 April, the filing period will expire on 31 January.[153] Where the accounting reference date is not the end of the month, then the filing deadline is the equivalent date in the appropriate month. The exception to this rule is where the accounting reference date is the 29th or 30th of a month and the filing deadline falls in February. In this case, the filing deadline will be the last day of February.[154]

---

[148]   CA 2006, s 442, replacing CA 1985, s 244.
[149]   CA 2006, s 442(3).
[150]   As permitted and in accordance with CA 2006, s 392.
[151]   CA 2006, s 442(4).
[152]   CA 2006, s 442(5).
[153]   CA 2006, s 443(3).
[154]   CA 2006, s 443(4).

14.19 FILING OBLIGATIONS: COMPANIES SUBJECT TO THE SMALL COMPANIES REGIME

The general requirement for companies subject to the small companies regime is that, for every financial year, they must deliver a balance sheet drawn up as at the last day of that year. The delivery of a copy of the profit and loss account for that year and a copy of the directors' report for that year appears to be optional. The Act goes on to say, however, that the accounts delivered to the registrar should be a copy of the company's annual accounts (which would include a profit and loss account and directors' report). This implies that the delivery of the profit and loss account and directors' report is not optional after all. There is also a general obligation to deliver a copy of the auditor's report on the annual accounts.[155] The copy of the auditor's report delivered to the registrar must either state the name of the auditor and, if the auditor is a firm, the name of the senior statutory auditor or that a resolution has been passed and notified to the Secretary of State under CA 2006, s 506 (circumstances in which names may be omitted).[156]

Where a company under the small companies regime prepares 'Companies Act accounts',[157] the company can deliver 'abbreviated accounts'.[158] If a company delivers abbreviated accounts to the registrar then, for companies whose annual accounts have been audited, they do not need to deliver the auditor's report on the annual accounts but rather a special auditor's report as to whether the company is entitled to deliver abbreviated accounts.[159]

It should be noted that the Secretary of State has no power to make regulations that allow companies who prepare IAS accounts to deliver an abbreviated form of those accounts. It is perhaps for this reason that the Companies Act 2006 specifies that it is only the delivery of the company's balance sheet that is mandatory so as not to 'penalise' small companies that prepare accounts under IAS. The Act then clarifies that where the directors of a company deliver either IAS accounts or Companies Act accounts (which are not abbreviated accounts), they do not need to deliver a copy of the profit and loss account or a copy of the directors' report. Where they do not deliver either of these documents, then the balance sheet delivered to the registrar must contain a statement, in a prominent position, that the company's annual accounts and report have been

---

[155] CA 2006, s 444(2). This does not apply where the company is exempt from audit and the directors have taken advantage of that exemption.

[156] CA 2006, s 444(7).

[157] As defined in CA 2006, s 396.

[158] CA 2006, s 444(3). The Secretary of State may make regulations specifying the form and content of the balance sheet that needs to be delivered to the registrar and what information may be omitted from the profit and loss account. A balance sheet and profit and loss account prepared in accordance with such regulations are referred to as 'abbreviated accounts'.

[159] CA 2006, s 444(4). The form and content of this report is set out in CA 2006, s 449.

delivered in accordance with the provisions applicable to companies subject to the small companies regime.[160]

The balance sheet delivered (and any directors' report that is delivered) must state the name of the person who signed it on behalf of the board.[161]

14.20 FILING OBLIGATIONS: MEDIUM-SIZED COMPANIES

The criteria for qualifying as a medium-sized company are set out in s 465 and the method of determining if a company qualifies as medium-sized is the same as for small companies, albeit with different size criteria.[162]

The qualifying conditions for medium-sized companies are met by a company in a year in which it satisfies two or more of the following requirements: turnover of not more than £25.9m; a balance sheet total of not more than £12.9m; and not more than 250 employees. If a company is a parent, it can only qualify as medium-sized if the group that it heads qualifies as medium-sized. To satisfy this requirement a group must meet two or more of the following requirements in a year: aggregate turnover of not more than £25.9m net (£31.1m gross); aggregate balance sheet total of not more than £12.9m net (£15.5m gross); and aggregate number of employees not more than 250.

Although a company may be medium-sized, it will not be entitled to take advantage of the provisions available to medium-sized companies if certain circumstances apply. In essence these are similar to those for small companies[163] except that a medium-sized company that has permission under the Financial Services and Markets Act 2000, Part 4 to carry on a regulated activity cannot take advantage of any provisions for medium-sized companies.[164]

For a medium-sized group, the criteria for ineligibility are exactly the same as those for a small group.[165]

Medium-sized companies are required to file their annual accounts and the directors' report with the registrar, together with the auditor's report on those accounts.[166] A medium-sized company that prepares Companies

---

[160] CA 2006, s 444(5).

[161] CA 2006, s 444(6). It appears rather ambiguous as to whether accounts and directors' reports filed with the registrar will need to be manually signed or just state the name of the person who signed the original documents. CA 1985, s 233(4) was explicit in this regard.

[162] CA 2006, s 465.

[163] CA 2006, s 384(1).

[164] CA 2006, s 467(1).

[165] CA 2006, s 467(2) and see s 384(2).

[166] CA 2006, s 445(2). The wording of this section states that it does not apply if the

Act accounts may, however, deliver 'abbreviated accounts'. The meaning of abbreviated accounts for a medium-sized company is, however, different from that for a small company.[167]

If a medium-sized company files abbreviated accounts, then the auditor's report to be filed is a special auditor's report[168] on whether the company is entitled to file abbreviated accounts and is in the same form as for a small company's abbreviated accounts.

If a medium-sized company prepares IAS accounts as its annual accounts, these must be delivered to the registrar.[169]

The balance sheet and directors' report delivered to the registrar must state the name of the person who signed it on behalf of the board.

14.21 FILING OBLIGATIONS: UNQUOTED AND QUOTED COMPANIES

Both quoted companies and unquoted companies are required to deliver to the registrar a copy of their annual accounts and reports. These comprise:

(1) the company's annual accounts;

(2) the directors' report; and

(3) for a quoted company, the directors' remuneration report.[170]

The directors must deliver a copy of the audit report on the annual accounts and director's report.[171]

---

company is exempt from audit. At publication, there is no provision for medium-sized companies to be able to take advantage of exemption from audit but this does raise the possibility that it could happen in the future.

[167] CA 2006, s 445(3). Abbreviated accounts for a medium-sized company means CA accounts where the Secretary of State may make regulations which allows the combination of certain items in the profit and loss accounts and the omission of information authorised by those regulations.

[168] CA 2006, s 445(4).

[169] CA 2006, s 445 contains no similar exemption to that provided for small companies in s 444(5).

[170] CA 2006, ss 446(1) and 447(1).

[171] CA 2006, s 446(2). The wording of this section states that it does not apply if the company is exempt from audit. At present, there is no provision for unquoted companies other than small companies to be able to take advantage of exemption from audit but this does raise the possibility that it could happen in the future.

The copies of the balance sheet, directors' report and, for quoted companies, the directors' remuneration report must state the name of the person who signed it on behalf of the board.[172]

14.22 FILING REQUIREMENTS FOR UNLIMITED COMPANIES

Unlimited companies are obliged to prepare annual accounts but, subject to conditions, do not need to file accounts.[173] The key condition is that at no time during the financial period was the company either a parent or a subsidiary of an undertaking whose members' liability was limited at that time.[174]

14.23 ABBREVIATED ACCOUNTS: SPECIAL AUDITORS' REPORT

Where the directors of a company deliver abbreviated accounts to the registrar and the company is not exempt from audit, a special auditor's report must also be delivered.[175] This report must state that in the auditor's opinion the company is entitled to prepare abbreviated accounts and that the abbreviated accounts have been prepared in accordance with the applicable regulations. The auditor's report on the company's annual accounts need not be delivered but if that report was qualified the special report must set out that report in full together with any further material necessary to understand the qualification, and if the auditors' report contained a statement about particular defects such as the accounts not agreeing with records and returns or with regard to a failure to obtain the necessary information and explanations required to carry out an audit, the special report must set out the statement in full.[176]

The provisions governing the signature of auditors' reports on annual accounts (and offences in connection with the audit report on annual accounts) apply equally to the special report on abbreviated accounts.[177]

14.23.1 Approval and signing

Abbreviated accounts must be approved by the board and signed by a director on the balance sheet.[178] Above the signature, and in a prominent

---

[172] CA 2006, ss 446(3) and 447(3).

[173] CA 2006, s 448. An unlimited company which is a banking or insurance company or which is the parent of such a company cannot utilise this exemption for unlimited companies.

[174] CA 2006, s 448(2).

[175] CA 2006, s 449, replacing CA 1985, s 247B.

[176] CA 2006, s 449(3).

[177] CA 2006, s 449(4) refers to CA 2006, ss 503–509.

[178] CA 2006, s 450.

place, there must be a statement that the abbreviated accounts have been prepared in accordance with the provisions of the Companies Act 2006 relating either to the small companies regime or medium-sized companies as applicable.

14.24 FAILURE TO FILE ACCOUNTS AND REPORTS

If appropriate accounts are not filed for a financial year before the end of the period for filing those accounts and reports then every person who immediately before the end of that period was a director of the company commits an offence.[179] There is a defence if a person took all reasonable steps to secure compliance with the requirements but it is not a defence to prove that the appropriate accounts have not been prepared.

If the directors do not file accounts and do not so file within 14 days of being served with an order to make good the default, any member or creditor of the company can apply for a court order to direct the directors to make good the default within a specified period of time.[180]

As well as the directors committing an offence when accounts are not filed within the allowed period, the company is also liable to a civil penalty.[181]

14.25 DEFECTIVE ACCOUNTS

Where accounts are defective, there is both a voluntary regime for the directors to be able to revise them and a regulatory regime whereby a company can be required to provide a remedy.[182]

14.25.1 Directors' voluntary revision

Where directors consider that the annual accounts and reports (including, for quoted companies, a directors' remuneration report) do not comply with the requirements of the Companies Act 2006 or, where applicable, of art 4 of the IAS Regulation, they may prepare revised accounts or a revised report as necessary.[183]

The extent of the revision will be limited where the accounts and report have been sent out to members, filed with the registrar or, for a public company, laid before general meeting. Where this is the case, then the revision is limited to:

---

[179] CA 2006, s 451.
[180] CA 2006, s 452.
[181] CA 2006, s 453.
[182] Previously CA 1985, ss 245–245G.
[183] CA 2006, s 454.

(1)   correcting those elements of the annual accounts and report that did not comply with the requirements of the Act (or art 4 of the IAS Regulation); and

(2)   making any consequential amendments as necessary.[184]

The Secretary of State may make regulations that:

(1)   make different provisions as to whether the original accounts and report should be replaced or supplemented with a document setting out the corrections;

(2)   specify what the responsibilities of the company's auditor (or independent examiner or a relevant charitable company) are in connection with the revised accounts or reports; and

(3)   specify the steps the directors should take where the accounts (or summary financial statement) have been sent out to members, filed with the registrar or, for public companies, laid before general meeting.[185]

14.25.2   Secretary of State's notice

The Secretary of State can require the directors to provide explanations where it appears that the annual accounts or directors' report do not comply with the requirements of the Companies Act 2006 (or art 4 of the IAS Regulation, if applicable).[186] These provisions only apply where the accounts and report have been sent out to members, filed with the registrar or, for public companies, laid before general meeting. This provision does not appear to apply to a directors' remuneration report for a quoted company.

The period of notice given by the Secretary of State to the directors to provide their explanations must not be less than one month. If the Secretary of State does not receive satisfactory explanations or the directors do not prepare revised accounts which correct the non-compliance, he may apply to the courts. This power is available to the Secretary of State in respect of revised accounts as well as original accounts.

14.25.3   Application to the court

Under s 456, the Secretary of State or a person authorised by him may apply to the court for:

---

[184]   CA 2006, s 454(2).

[185]   See the Companies (Revision of Defective Accounts and Reports) Regulations 2008, SI 2008/373.

[186]   CA 2006, s 455.

(1) a declaration that the annual accounts of a company, or its directors' report, do not comply with the requirements of the Companies Act 2006 or, if applicable, art 4 of the IAS Regulation; and

(2) an order requiring the directors to prepare revised accounts or a revised directors' report that do so comply.

Where an order is given, it may give instructions as follows:

(1) on the order for the preparation of revised accounts:

   (a) the auditing of those accounts;
   (b) the revision of any directors' remuneration report, directors' or summary financial statement;

(2) on the order for the preparation of a revised directors' report:

   (a) the review of the directors' report by the auditors;
   (b) the revision of any summary financial statement.

No matter what the form of the order, the court can specify the steps the directors should take to make persons likely to have relied on previous sets of the accounts and reports aware of the making of the order any other matter as it sees fit.

If the court finds that the accounts and report did not comply with the appropriate requirements then it may make an order that the costs[187] relating to the application and reasonable expenses incurred by the company in preparing or consequential to preparing revised accounts should be borne by the directors who were party to the approval of the defective accounts and report.[188]

The court may have regard to whether such a director knew or should have known that the accounts and report did not comply with the appropriate requirements and may exclude that director from the order or specify the payment of a different amount to the other directors under such an order.[189]

There is a mechanism for the Secretary of State to authorise persons to apply to the courts on his behalf.[190] Such a person should:

---

[187] In Scotland, expenses.
[188] CA 2006, s 456(5).
[189] CA 2006, s 456(6).
[190] CA 2006, s 457. The Secretary of State has the power to authorise persons generally or in particular classes; he may also refuse an authorisation if there are others who have been or are likely to be authorised: s 457(2)–(4).

(1)   have an interest in and have satisfactory procedures for ensuring compliance by companies with the applicable requirements of the Act or art 4 of the IAS Regulation, as applicable;

(2)   have satisfactory procedures for receiving and investigating complaints about companies' annual accounts and directors' reports; and

(3)   be a fit and proper person to be so authorised.

The Financial Reporting Review Panel of the Financial Reporting Council has been so authorised.[191]

14.25.4   Disclosure of information by tax authorities

There is provision in s 458 of the Companies Act 2006 that allows Her Majesty's Customs and Revenue to disclose information relating to accounts.[192] Information may be disclosed to an authorised person only for the purposes of assisting that person in:

(1)   taking steps to ascertain whether there are grounds for an application to the court in respect of defective accounts; or

(2)   deciding whether to make such an application.

Authorised persons receiving such information may only use it for the purposes outlined above or in connection with proceedings on an application and that information may only be disclosed further to the person to whom it relates or to the court in connection with the proceedings.[193]

14.25.5   Power of authorised persons to require documents, information and explanations

A person authorised under s 457, as described in **14.25.3**, may request information where it appears that a company's annual accounts and directors' report may not comply with the requirements of the Act (or, where applicable, art 4 of the IAS Regulation).[194]

---

[191]   The Companies (Defective Accounts and Directors' Reports) (Authorised Persons) and Supervision of Accounts and Reports (Prescribed Body) Order 2008, SI 2008/623.

[192]   These were first introduced into company law by the Companies (Audit, Investigations and Community Enterprise) Act 2004.

[193]   CA 2006, s 458(4). It is an offence for the person receiving the information to disclose it other than as permitted by s 458(3), although it is a defence if the person did not know, or had no reason to suspect, that the information had been disclosed under s 458 and he took all reasonable steps and exercised all due diligence to avoid committing the offence.

[194]   CA 2006, s 459.

The authorised person can request information that he may reasonably require for the purpose of:

(1) discovering whether there are grounds for an application to the court in respect of defective accounts; or

(2) deciding whether to make such an application.

The information the authorised person can require comprises any documents or any information and explanations that he believes are necessary and the persons required to provide the information are:

(1) the company;

(2) any officer, employee or auditor of the company; and

(3) any persons who fell into category (2) at a time to which the information required by the authorised person relates.

The authorised person may apply to the court if a person fails to comply with the request to produce information and the court may order the person to take steps to ensure that the documents or information and explanations are provided.

There are two protections for a person required to produce information. First, he is not required to disclose or produce information where there could be a claim for legal professional privilege[195] in legal proceedings. Secondly, no statements made by a person either to the authorised person in response to a request, or in response to an order made by the court, can be used against him in any criminal proceedings.[196]

14.25.6 Restrictions on disclosure of information obtained under compulsory powers

Information obtained under compulsory powers, so far as it relates to the affairs of a private individual or particular business, may not be disclosed without the consent of that private individual or the person carrying on the business. The requirement for consent continues for the lifetime of the private individual or so long as the business continues to be carried on.[197] There is no requirement for consent where disclosure is permitted under compulsory powers or where the information is available from a public source.[198] It is an offence for a person to disclose information contrary to these requirements although it is a defence if the person did not know, or

---

[195] In Scotland, confidentiality of communications.
[196] CA 2006, s 459(6).
[197] CA 2006, s 460(1) and (2).
[198] CA 2006, s 460(3).

had no reason to suspect, that the information had been disclosed under s 467 and he took all reasonable steps and exercised all due diligence to avoid committing the offence.

14.25.7 Permitted disclosure of information obtained under compulsory powers

Although there is the general requirement to obtain consent for the disclosure of information relating to the affairs of a private individual or a particular business, the list of exceptions where consent is not required before disclosure is long and apparently comprehensive.[199] First, consent is not required in respect of information required by an authorised person carrying out his functions for making an application to the court in respect of defective accounts.[200] There is then a list of persons and bodies where disclosure can be made without consent and in what connection that disclosure is made. These persons and bodies are:

(1) the Secretary of State;

(2) the Department of Enterprise, Trade and Investment for Northern Ireland;

(3) the Treasury;

(4) the Bank of England;

(5) the Financial Services Authority; or

(6) the Commissioners for Her Majesty's Customs and Revenue.

The Act also lists the purposes where disclosure of information is not restricted under s 460.[201]

There is additional permission for the disclosure of information to bodies outside of the UK who appear to the authorised person to be exercising a similar function in that country or territory, where disclosure would assist those bodies to carry out their functions.[202] The authorised person, in deciding whether to disclose information without consent to those persons or bodies, must consider whether:

(1) the likely use of the information by that person or body is sufficiently important to justify making the disclosure; and

---

[199] CA 2006, s 461.
[200] Under CA 2006, s 456.
[201] CA 2006, s 461(4) and (5).
[202] CA 2006, s 461(5). These are functions that are similar to those of the authorised person under CA 2006, s 456.

(2) the body or person has adequate arrangements to prevent the information being used or further disclosed other than for the purposes of carrying out their functions or for other substantially similar purposes.[203]

The authorised person must ensure, however, that in making any disclosure of information obtained under compulsory powers he does not contravene the Data Protection Act 1998.[204]

14.26 FALSE OR MISLEADING STATEMENTS IN REPORTS

A director can be liable to compensate the company for any loss suffered by it as a result of untrue or misleading statements included in narrative reports, in particular the directors' report and, additionally for quoted companies, the directors' remuneration report. For companies that produce a summary financial statement, this applies to any statement therein that is drawn from those reports.[205] A director may also be liable where those reports do not include information that was required to be included.

A director may only be liable if he knew the statement was untrue or misleading or was reckless as to whether it was or he knew that the omission of the information was the dishonest concealment of a material fact. He will only be liable under this section to compensate a company for any loss suffered by the company. He cannot be liable under this section to any other person for a loss resulting from their relying on information in the relevant reports.

14.27 POWER TO MAKE FURTHER PROVISIONS ABOUT ACCOUNTS AND REPORTS

The Secretary of State is given a general power to make regulations for accounts and reports that are prepared by companies.[206] These powers are wide and cover such matters as the form and content of accounts, the approval process, publication and sending accounts to members and others, laying accounts before general meeting and delivering accounts to the registrar.

The Secretary of State is not empowered, however, to make regulations that amend, other than consequentially:

(1) the requirement that accounts give a true and fair view; or

---

[203] CA 2006, s 461(6).
[204] CA 2006, s 461(7).
[205] CA 2006, s 463.
[206] CA 2006, s 468.

(2)　the provisions of Part 15, Chapter 11 concerning the revision of defective accounts and reports.

14.28　AUDITORS

A company's annual accounts for a financial year must be audited in accordance with Part 16 of the Companies Act 2006 unless the company is exempt from audit because it is a small company under s 477 or is a dormant company under s 480 or is exempt because it is a non-profit-making company subject to public sector audit.[207] In order to benefit from the exemptions there must be a statement made by the directors in the balance sheet to that effect and small and dormant companies' balance sheets must also contain a statement made by the directors to the effect that the members have not required the company to obtain an audit of its accounts for the year in question and the directors acknowledge their responsibility for complying with the requirements of the Act with respect to accounting records and the preparation of accounts.[208] Where a company is entitled to an exemption from audit the members may by giving notice require an audit of the company's accounts.[209] The notice must be given by the holders of not less than 10% of the nominal capital value of the company's issued share capital or of any class of its shares, or by not less than 10% of the members where the company has no share capital. The notice may not be given before the relevant financial year and not later than one month before that financial year ends.

14.28.1　Appointment of auditors in private companies

With no requirement for private companies to have an annual general meeting, the whole process for private companies to appoint auditors was revised by the 2006 Act. As a general rule, however, the directors of a private company are required to appoint auditors for each financial year of the company unless they reasonably believe that the company will be able to take advantage of exemption from audit for that year.[210]

The Act introduces a 'period for appointing auditors'. Other than where it relates to the company's first accounting period, this period for appointing auditors is 28 days starting at the earlier of:

(1)　the end of the time allowed for sending out copies of the previous year's annual accounts; or

---

[207]　CA 2006, s 475(1).
[208]　CA 2006, s 475(3).
[209]　CA 2006, s 476.
[210]　CA 2006, s 485(1).

(2)   the date those annual accounts were circulated to persons entitled to receive them.[211]

In the normal course of events, it should be the members of the company who appoint the auditors by ordinary resolution but there are circumstances where the directors may appoint auditors. These circumstances are where:

(1)   it is the company's first accounting period;

(2)   the company has been exempt from audit and no auditor is appointed;

(3)   there is a casual vacancy in the position of auditor.

Where it is the company's first accounting period, the directors may appoint auditors only up to the first period for appointing auditors and where the company has been exempt from audit the directors may only make an appointment up to the next period for appointing auditors.

A company's members may appoint auditors by ordinary resolution in the following circumstances:

(1)   in any period for appointing auditors;

(2)   where the company should have appointed auditors during a period for appointing auditors but has not done so; or

(3)   where the directors have had the power to appoint auditors but have not done so.

If the directors or members fail to fill the position of auditor as required under s 485, then there is a default power under which the Secretary of State may appoint auditors to fill the vacancy.[212]

Where for a financial year that an auditor is to be appointed by a company (not being for the first financial year), the company fails to make an appointment before the end of the period for appointing auditors, the company must give notice, within a week of the end of that period, to the Secretary of State that his power to appoint an auditor to the company has become exercisable. Failure to give that notice when required is an offence committed by the company and every office which is in default.

The term of office of the auditor will commence in line with their terms of their appointment except that they cannot take office until any

---

[211] CA 2006, s 485(2).
[212] CA 2006, s 586.

predecessor auditor ceases to hold office. Subject to the provisions regarding the resignation and removal of auditor from office, the term of office will cease at the end of the next period allowed for appointing auditors unless the auditor is reappointed.

There is a process whereby auditors can be deemed to be reappointed. The auditors can be deemed reappointed where another auditor has not been appointed by the end of the period allowed for appointing auditors unless:

(1)   the auditor was appointed by the directors;

(2)   the company's articles do not allow for a 'deemed' reappointment;

(3)   the company has received notices from members preventing the deemed reappointment;

(4)   the members have resolved that the auditor should not be reappointed; or

(5)   the directors have resolved that no auditors should be appointed for the financial year in question.[213]

An auditor of a company is not deemed to have been reappointed where the company has received sufficient notices from members that they should not be reappointed.[214] Notices will be effective where they have been received from members who hold at least 5% (or the percentage stipulated in the company's articles if lower) of the total voting rights of all members entitled to vote on a resolution that the auditor should not be reappointed.

To be effective, these notices:

(1)   may be in hard copy or electronic form;

(2)   must be authenticated by the person or persons giving it; and

(3)   must be received by the company before the end of the accounting reference period immediately before the time when the deemed reappointment would take place.[215]

---

[213]   CA 2006, s 487(2).
[214]   CA 2006, s 488.
[215]   CA 2006, s 488(3).

14.28.2   Public companies

In public companies an auditor must be appointed unless the directors reasonably decide that audited accounts are unlikely to be required.[216] The principal difference between the provisions for appointing auditors for private companies and public companies is that there is no 'period for appointing auditors' for a public company. Instead, the auditors should be appointed before the accounts meeting.[217]

As with private companies, both the directors and members of the company may appoint auditors and the circumstances in which they may do so are the same as for private companies except that references to the 'period for appointing auditors' should be read as 'accounts meeting'. This also applies to the default power of the Secretary of State to appoint an auditor.

The term of office of an auditor to a public company is similar to that of a private company except that he will cease to hold office at the end of the next accounts meeting following his appointment and that there are no provisions for the deemed reappointment of the auditor. Thus unless he is reappointed an auditor of a public company holds office until the end of the meeting at which the accounts he is auditing are laid before members.[218]

14.28.3   Qualifications

The Companies Act 1989 implemented the Eighth EC Company Law Directive[219] on the qualifications and training of auditors. The stated purposes of the Act were 'to secure that only persons who are properly supervised and appropriately qualified are appointed as company auditors, and that audits by persons so appointed are carried out properly and with integrity and with a proper degree of independence'.[220] The Companies Act 2006 restates and modifies a number of provisions in the 1989 Act.

To qualify for appointment as a company auditor, a person, either an individual or a firm, must be[221] a member of a recognised supervisory body; and eligible for appointment under the rules of that body.

To be eligible, the auditor must hold an appropriate qualification, which may be:

---

[216] CA 2006, s 489.
[217] The accounts meeting is the general meeting of the company at which the annual accounts for the previous financial year are laid.
[218] CA 2006, s 491.
[219] Directive 84/253/EEC.
[220] CA 1989, s 24.
[221] CA 2006, s 1212, restating s 31 of the 1989 Act.

(1) by having begun a course or practical training leading to a professional qualification in accountancy offered by a body established in the UK, he obtained that qualification on or after 1 January 1990 and before 1 January 1996 and the Secretary of State approves his qualification as appropriate; or

(2) a recognised professional qualification obtained in the UK from a qualifying body; or

(3) an overseas qualification if approved by the Secretary of State under s 1221.[222]

Certain classes of person are disqualified from appointment as auditors. They are officers or employees of the company or associated undertaking, persons who are partners or employees of an officer or employee of the company and bodies corporate.[223] Nor may a person be appointed auditor of a company if he is disqualified from appointment as auditor of its parent or subsidiary company. Any person who acts as auditor of a company when he knows he is disqualified, or who fails to vacate his office and to give notice of that fact to the company when to his knowledge he becomes disqualified, is liable to a fine.[224] Section 1213(8) provides that it is a defence for a person to show that he did not know and had no reason to believe that he was, or had become, ineligible for appointment.

14.28.4 Auditors' remuneration

The remuneration of the auditors appointed by the members of a company must be fixed by the members by ordinary resolution or in such a way as the members may by ordinary resolution decide.[225] If the auditors were appointed by the directors the directors must fix their remuneration and the Secretary of State must fix the remuneration if the auditor was appointed by the Secretary of State.[226] Remuneration for this purpose includes expenses and payment by benefit in kind is treated as a payment in money.[227]

---

[222] CA 2006, s 1219, replacing CA 1989, s 33.
[223] CA 2006, s 1214.
[224] CA 2006, s 1213, replacing CA 1989, s 28.
[225] CA 2006, s 492.
[226] CA 2006, s 492(2) and (3) respectively.
[227] CA 2006, s 492.

14.28.5   Disclosure of terms of audit appointment

Section 493 of the Companies Act 2006 contains a power for the Secretary of State to make regulations governing the disclosure of the terms of office of an auditor including his remuneration and how he performs his duties.[228]

Those regulations set out:

(1)   what needs to be disclosed, for example, a copy of any terms that are in writing or a memorandum setting out any terms which are not in writing;

(2)   when, where and how that disclosure should take place; and

(3)   that the place and means of disclosure should be stated in:

    (a)   a note to the company's accounts;
    (b)   the directors' report; or
    (c)   the auditor's report.

14.28.6   Disclosure of services by the auditor or associates and related remuneration

The Companies Act itself does not contain requirements concerning the disclosure of auditor's remuneration but rather provides that the Secretary of State may make regulations that provide these requirements.[229] These regulations are the Companies (Disclosure of Auditor Remuneration and Liability Limitation Agreements) Regulations 2008.[230]

These regulations:

(1)   require disclosure of:

    (a)   the nature of services provide by the auditor;
    (b)   the remuneration received or receivable in respect of any of those services and of the separable or aggregate amounts received by the auditor and his associates;

(2)   provide definitions of:

    (a)   'remuneration'; and
    (b)   'associate' in relation to an auditor and company respectively;

---

[228] Companies (Disclosure of Auditor Remuneration and Liability Limitation Agreements) Regulations 2008, SI 2008/489.
[229] CA 2006, s 494.
[230] SI 2008/489.

(3)   set out whether the required disclosures are made in:

(a)   a note to the company's accounts;
(b)   the directors' report; or
(c)   the auditor's report.

The regulations provide that the disclosure should be made in a note to the accounts and they require the auditors to provide the necessary information to the directors to allow them to make those disclosures.[231]

14.28.7   Removal or resignation

A key element of the provisions that deal with the removal or resignation of an auditor is that whenever an auditor ceases to hold office he has the right to make either representations or a statement concerning his ceasing to hold office, whether that cessation is due to being removed from office, not being reappointed after the end of his term of office or by his resignation from office.

The members of a company can remove an auditor from office at any time but this can only be exercised by an ordinary resolution at a meeting of the company and where special notice has been given for that resolution. This procedure applies to all companies, both private and public.[232]

If a company receives special notice of a resolution proposing the removal of an auditor before the expiration of his term of office, or proposing a change of auditor when the present auditor's term of office expires, it must forward a copy of that notice to the retiring auditor, or to the auditor who is to be removed. The auditor may make representations in writing to the company and, if he so requests and the representations are not received too late, the company must, in any notice of the resolution given to members of the company, state that representations have been received and send a copy to every member to whom notice of the meeting is sent.[233] If the auditor's representations are not sent out before the meeting then the auditor can request that they are read out at the meeting. This does not affect the auditor's right to be heard orally at the meeting. Copies of the representations need not be sent out if the court holds that the auditor is seeking to secure needless publicity for defamatory matter. The registrar must be informed within 14 days of any such resolution having been passed.[234]

If an auditor wishes to resign his office before its term expires, he may do so by depositing a notice in writing to that effect at the company's

---

[231]   See regs 5 and 7 respectively.
[232]   CA 2006, s 510.
[233]   CA 2006, s 515.
[234]   CA 2006, s 512 (1) and (2), restating CA 1985, s 391(1) and (2).

registered office,[235] containing either a statement that there are no circumstances connected with his resignation which he considers should be brought to the notice of the members or creditors of the company, or a statement of any such circumstances as may exist.[236] The company must, within 14 days of receipt, send copies of the notice to the registrar[237] and, if the notice contains a statement of circumstances connected with the resignation as described above, to the members of the company and to any other persons who are entitled to receive a copy of the company's accounts.[238] If the notice of resignation states that there are circumstances which the auditor considers should be brought to the notice of members or creditors, he may call on the directors to convene an extraordinary general meeting of the company to consider his explanation.[239] He may also require the company to circulate to the members a written statement of the circumstances connected with his resignation (of reasonable length) and to state in the notice of the meeting that such a statement has been issued.[240]

If the company does not, within 14 days,[241] circulate an auditor's notice of resignation, or does not, within 21 days, convene an extraordinary general meeting which has been requisitioned by the auditor then, unless the company has obtained a court order excusing it from so doing, the company and every officer who is in default will be liable to a fine.[242]

An auditor who has been removed or who has resigned is entitled to attend the general meeting of the company at which his appointment would otherwise have expired and any general meeting at which it is proposed to fill the vacancy caused by the removal or resignation, to receive notices relating to those meetings and to be heard on any business which concerns him as former auditor.[243] Where the former auditor does attend such a meeting, any matters that relate to the position of auditor shall relate equally to him as a former auditor.[244]

Where a private company is to propose a written resolution to appoint an auditor in place of an outgoing auditor whose term of office has either expired or will expire at the end of the period for appointing auditors, then the company must send a copy of the proposed resolution to both the outgoing auditor and the proposed auditor. This procedure must be followed where either:

---

[235] CA 2006, s 516.
[236] CA 2006, s 519. As to the special requirements regarding quoted companies, see **14.31.9**.
[237] CA 2006, s 517.
[238] CA 2006, s 520(1) and (2).
[239] CA 2006, s 518(2).
[240] CA 2006, s 518(3).
[241] See *P & P Designs plc v PriceWaterhouseCoopers* [2002] 2 BCC 645.
[242] CA 2006, s 518(5) and (6).
[243] CA 2006, s 518(10) and 502.
[244] CA 2006, s 513.

(1)   no period for appointing auditors has expired since the outgoing
       auditor ceased to hold office; or

(2)   the period for appointing auditors has expired and an auditor should
       have but has not been appointed.[245]

The right of the outgoing auditor to make representations and to require
these to be circulated in these circumstances is the same, essentially, as for
an auditor who is removed before the expiry of his term of office.

Where a company is to pass a resolution in general meeting to appoint an
auditor in place of an auditor who's term of office has either already
expired or is about to expire, then that resolution generally will require
special notice.[246] Again, the outgoing auditor has a right to make
representations and to require these to be circulated to the members of
the company in the same way, and with the related provisions, as when an
auditor is removed from office.

14.28.8   Resignation of auditor

An auditor may resign his position by depositing a notice to that effect at
the company's registered office. To be effective, the auditor needs to
deposit with that notice a statement concerning his resignation as auditor
(see below). Such a notice is only effective if the auditor's resignation will
take effect either from the date the notice is deposited at the registered
office or a later date specified in the notice. Accordingly, a notice cannot
specify that the auditor has resigned from a date before the date on which
the notice is deposited.[247] It remains the company's obligation to send a
copy of the auditor's notice of resignation to the registrar within 14 days
of receiving the notice.

An auditor who has served an effective notice of resignation can require
the directors of the company to convene a general meeting of the
company so that the auditor can bring to the attention of the meeting
matters concerning his resignation that he believes appropriate.[248]

As with the case when an auditor is removed from office or is not
reappointed, the resigning auditor may request the company to circulate a
statement of the circumstances concerning his resignation.[249] This
circulation may be before a meeting convened at his request concerning
his resignation or before any general meeting of the company at which his
term of office would otherwise have expired or at which it is proposed to
appoint an auditor to fill the vacancy arising from his resignation. The

---

[245] CA 2006, s 515(2).
[246] CA 2006, s 515.
[247] CA 2006, s 516.
[248] CA 2006, s 518(2).
[249] CA 2006, s 518(3).

company or any other person who claims to be aggrieved can apply to the court if they believe the auditor is using the statement to secure needless publicity for defamatory matter. If the court is satisfied that this is the case, the statement need not be circulated and the statement need not be read out at the meeting.

An auditor who resigns his position retains the right to receive the notices normally receivable by an auditor under s 502(2) in connection with either the meeting of the company convened at his request or a general meeting of the company at which his term of office would otherwise have expired or at which it is proposed to appoint an auditor to fill the vacancy arising from his resignation.[250] Where the auditor who has resigned does attend such a meeting, any matters that relate to the position of auditor shall relate equally to him as a former auditor.

14.28.9   Statement by auditor on ceasing to hold office

We have already noted that an auditor ceasing to hold office needs to decide whether there are any circumstances concerning his cessation of office that he believes should be brought to the attention of the members or creditors. If there are, his statement should set out those circumstances and if there are no circumstances, he should make a statement to that effect.[251] In addition to this there is special provision where the auditor of a quoted company ceases, for any reason, to hold office. He must make a statement of the circumstances surrounding his ceasing to hold office.[252] This wider requirement to disclose circumstances could prove problematic for audit firms if the reasons for changing audit firm were on sensitive commercial issues such as perceived expertise or, indeed, price. Ordinarily, these would not necessarily be matters that an outgoing auditor would think should be brought to the attention of members or creditors, although they might be of interest to them. The requirement, however, asks effectively for a general 'statement of circumstances' rather than matters that should be brought to the attention of a particular party or parties.

Whether the statement is in respect of a quoted company or an unquoted company, the statement must be deposited at the company's registered office and within the following timescales:

(1)   where the auditor resigns, the statement should accompany the notice of resignation;

(2)   where the auditor fails to seek reappointment, at least 14 days before the end of the time allowed for next appointing an auditor; and

---

[250]   CA 2006, s 518(10).
[251]   CA 2006, s 519(1).
[252]   CA 2006, s 519(3).

(3) in any other circumstances, no later than 14 days after he has ceased to hold office.

Where an auditor does deposit a statement of circumstances connected with ceasing to hold office (and that will be in all cases where a quoted company is concerned), the company has 14 days either to send a copy of the statement to all members entitled to receive a copy of the accounts or to apply to the courts (and notify the auditor of the application).[253]

If the court is satisfied that the auditor is using the statement to secure needless publicity for defamatory matter, then the court shall direct that copies of the statement need not be sent out and the court may order that the auditor meets some or all of the company's costs in making the application.

Within 14 days of the court's decision the company should either:

(1) if the application is successful, send a statement to that effect to all persons entitled to be sent copies of the accounts; or

(2) if the application is unsuccessful:

(a) send copies of the auditor's statement to those persons; and
(b) notify the auditor of the court's decision.

It is the auditor's responsibility to file a copy of any statement made under s 519 with the registrar.[254] He has a period of 28 days, beginning with the date on which he deposited his statement under s 519 to the company, to send a copy of that statement to the registrar, unless he has received a notification from the company of an application to the court. If the company does make an application but is unsuccessful, the auditor has a period of 7 days from receiving notice from the company that the application was unsuccessful to send a copy of his statement to the registrar.

14.28.10   Duty of auditor to notify appropriate audit authority

The Companies Act 2006 introduced new requirements on auditors to inform the 'appropriate audit authority' of their ceasing to hold office as auditor in certain circumstances.[255]

These circumstances are:

(1) for a 'major audit', ceasing, for any reason, to hold office; and

---

[253] CA 2006, s 520.
[254] CA 2006, s 521.
[255] CA 2006, s 522.

(2)   for any other audit, ceasing to hold office before the end of his term of office.

For a major audit, the auditor needs to inform the appropriate audit authority of his ceasing to hold office at the same time as he deposits his notice under s 519 at the company's registered office and he must provide a copy of the statement made under s 519.

For an audit other than a major audit, the notice shall be delivered to the appropriate audit authority at such time as that authority may require but it will not be earlier than the date on which the auditor deposits his statement under s 519 at the company's registered office. If the statement that the auditor made under s 519 was to the effect that there were no matters that he believed should be brought to the attention of the members or creditors then the notice provided to the appropriate audit authority must contain a general statement of the reasons for his ceasing to hold office. As mentioned above, this could prove controversial as auditors may have to disclose potentially commercially sensitive information. It is not clear, however, to what extent notices made under s 519 would be publicly available.

Who the appropriate audit authority is will depend on the circumstances of the audit. Where the audit is a 'major audit', it is the Secretary of State unless he has delegated functions to a body where those functions include receiving notices under s 519.[256] Currently the body with such delegated functions is the Professional Oversight Board, a body within the Financial Reporting Council. Where the audit is not a major audit, the appropriate audit authority will be the relevant supervisory body, as defined in s 1217.

A 'major audit', for these purposes, is a statutory audit of:

(1)   a company any of whose securities have been admitted to the official list (within the meaning of the Financial Services and Markets Act 2000, Part 6); or

(2)   any other person in whose financial condition there is a major public interest.[257]

From this definition, the audit of a quoted company will not necessarily be a 'major audit' as a quoted company includes companies which are listed in an EEA state or have been admitted to dealing on the New York Stock Exchange or NASDAQ.

The Act does not define the second element of a major audit, but rather indicates that auditors will need to look to guidance that is issued by the

---

[256]   CA 2006, s 525.
[257]   CA 2006, s 525(2).

Secretary of State, or by any body to whom the relevant functions might have been delegated or by the relevant supervisory bodies.[258]

Failure of the auditor to comply with the requirement to notify the appropriate audit authority is an offence punishable with a fine. Where the auditor is a firm, the offence is by every officer who is in default.

There is also a duty on the company to inform the appropriate audit authority where the auditor ceases to hold office before the end of his term of office.[259] The company must give this notice not later than 14 days after the date of receiving the auditor's statement concerning his ceasing to hold office. For a quoted company, the company shall include with this notice a copy of the auditor's statement of his reasons for ceasing to hold office, but for an unquoted company it need only include the auditor's statement if it contains circumstances that the auditor believed should be brought to the attention of the members or creditors. Failure of the company to comply with this requirement is punishable by a fine.

The appropriate audit authority has its own obligation to inform the accounting authorities when it has received a notice from either an auditor or a company.[260] If it considers it necessary, the appropriate audit authority may forward to the accounting authorities copies of any statements that accompanied the notice.

The accounting authorities are the Secretary of State and any person authorised by him to apply to the court in respect of defective accounts.[261] There is no need for a notification if the appropriate audit authority is also the accounting authority in a particular case.[262]

If the court has made an order that an auditor's statement need not be sent out by the company then that applies also in respect of information supplied to the accounting authorities.[263]

14.29   THE RIGHTS AND DUTIES OF AN AUDITOR

The auditor has a number of important statutory rights and duties as described in the following sections.

---

[258] CA 2006, s 525(3).

[259] CA 2006, s 523.

[260] CA 2006, s 524.

[261] CA 2006, s 457 (Revision of defective accounts: persons authorised to apply to the courts).

[262] CA 2006, s 524(3).

[263] CA 2006, s 524(4).

14.29.1   Right to information

An auditor[264] has a right of access at all times to the books and accounts and vouchers of the company and a right to require from the officers of the company such information and explanations as he thinks necessary for the performance of his duties as an auditor.[265]

An officer of a company who makes to an auditor (orally or in writing) a materially misleading, false or deceptive statement which conveys, or purports to convey, any information or explanation which the auditor requires, or is entitled to require in his capacity as auditor, may be liable to imprisonment or to a fine or both.[266]

A company's articles may not limit the auditor's statutory right to information. 'Any regulations which preclude the auditors from availing themselves of all the information to which under the Act they are entitled as material for the report which under the Act they are to make as to the true and correct state of the company's affairs are, I think, inconsistent with the Act.'[267]

---

[264] In March 1976 the major professional accounting bodies set up an Auditing Practices Committee to develop standards to which all audits should be carried out. In 1980, the Committee published a series of auditing standards and guidelines which, although they do not have legal backing, are intended to be followed by all members of the professional accounting bodies concerned. They apply to the audits of the accounts of all enterprises and not only to the audits of accounts of limited companies. The standards, which simply codify current good practice, consist of an operational standard and two standards relating to the audit report and are effective for the audit of accounts relating to periods starting on or after 1 April 1980. The operational standard requires an auditor adequately to plan, control and record his work; to ascertain the enterprise's system of recording and processing transactions and assess its adequacy as a basis for the preparation of accounts; to obtain relevant and reliable audit evidence sufficient to enable him to draw reasonable conclusions therefrom; to ascertain, evaluate and test the operation of any internal controls on which he wishes to place reliance in his work; and to carry out such a review on the accounts as is sufficient, in conjunction with the conclusions drawn from the other audit evidence obtained, to give him a reasonable basis for his opinion on the accounts. In April 1991 the APC was replaced by a new body called the Auditing Practices Board (APB), which is committed to leading the development of auditing practice in the UK and the Republic of Ireland so as to: establish the highest standards of auditing; meet the developing needs of users of financial statements; and ensure public confidence in the auditing process. See Statement of Objectives, Scope and Authority, May 1993, and SAS 600 – *Auditors' reports on financial statements*, May 1993. The APB has subsequently published a number of SASs which amend and update standards and guidelines previously issued by the APC. The current requirements of auditors in preparing reports on financial statements are determined by the International Standard on Accounting 700, which also deals with auditors' qualifications. The APB also issues Bulletins that provide guidance on the wording of audit reports: see Bulletin 6/2006 'Auditors' Reports on Financial Statements in the United Kingdom'. APB documents are available on the website of the Financial Reporting Council: www.frc.org.uk/apb/publications/ See also *Gore-Browne on Companies* (Jordans, 45th edn, loose-leaf) Ch 37.

[265] CA 2006, s 499, restating s 389A of the 1985 Act.

[266] CA 2006, s 501.

[267] *Newton v BSA* [1906] 2 Ch 378, at 389, per Buckley J.

The auditor of a parent company also has the right of access to information about the subsidiaries.[268] It is the duty of subsidiaries registered in Great Britain and their auditors to give to the auditor of the parent company any information he requires to carry out his duties and it is the duty of the parent company, if so requested by its auditor, to take all reasonable steps to obtain such information from overseas subsidiaries. A parent company or subsidiary (or its auditor) which fails to comply with this requirement, may be liable to a fine.

14.29.2   Attendance at meetings

The auditors of a company are entitled to attend any general meeting of the company and to receive notice of, and other communications relating to, any general meeting which any member of the company is entitled to receive. They also have a right to be heard at a general meeting on any part of the business of the meeting which concerns them as auditors.[269] Where a company is proposing a resolution as a written resolution, they are entitled to receive copies of all communications supplied to members.

14.29.3   The auditors' report

The auditors of a company are required to make a report to the members on all the annual accounts of the company. A copy of the auditor's report must be sent out to members of a private company under s 423 and laid before the company in general meeting for public companies under s 437.[270]

14.29.4   The contents of the auditors' report

When preparing a report the auditor is obliged to ensure that the accounts give a true and fair view of the profit or loss and of the financial position of the company or group. Section 393 states that the auditor in carrying out his functions in relation to the company's annual accounts must have regard to the directors' duty to be satisfied that the accounts give a true and fair view of the assets, liabilities, financial position and profit or loss of the company or consolidated group.

The auditor's report must include an introduction identifying the annual accounts that are the subject of the audit and the financial reporting framework that has been applied in their preparation, and a description of the scope of the audit identifying the auditing standards in accordance with which the audit was conducted.[271] The report must state clearly whether in the auditor's opinion the annual accounts give a true and fair

---

[268]   CA 2006, s 499, restating s 389A of the 1985 Act.
[269]   CA 2006, s 502(2).
[270]   CA 2006, s 495.
[271]   CA 2006, s 495(2).

view of the state of affairs of the company or group as at the end of the financial year and of the profit or loss of the company or group for the financial year, that the accounts have been properly prepared in accordance with the relevant financial reporting framework and have been prepared in accordance with the requirements of the Act and with art 4 of the IAS Regulation where applicable.[272] The auditor's report must be either unqualified or qualified and must include a reference to any matters to which the auditor wishes to draw attention by way of emphasis without qualifying the report.[273] Auditors who are not satisfied that the accounts comply with the Companies Act or show a true and fair view of the state of affairs or of the profit or loss of a company must refer to those matters explicitly in their report.[274] They may not just hint at them. One of the fundamental accounting principles on which accounts must normally be prepared is the presumption that the company is carrying on business as a going concern.

It is the directors' responsibility to assure themselves of the grounds on which that presumption remains applicable, particularly where there are or may be 'fundamental uncertainties'[275] affecting the company's viability. Auditors are required to assess the adequacy of the means by which the directors have satisfied themselves on this matter, of any relevant disclosures needed for the accounts to give a true and fair view, and to comment in their report on any cases where the uncertainties cause them a significant level of concern about the company's ability to continue as a going concern.[276]

The auditor must carry out such investigations as will enable him to form an opinion as to: (a) whether adequate accounting records have been kept by the company and returns adequate for their audit have been received from branches not visited by them; (b) whether the company's individual accounts are in agreement with the accounting records and returns; and (c) in the case of a quoted company, whether the auditable part of the company's directors' remuneration report is in agreement with the accounting records and returns.[277] If the auditor is of the opinion that any of these requirements have not been satisfied he shall state that fact in his report.[278] If he fails to obtain all the information and explanations which, to the best of his knowledge and belief, are necessary for the purposes of his audit, he must state that fact in his report.[279]

---

[272] CA 2006, s 495(3) See further, Auditing Practices Board, ISA (K and Ireland) 700 (revised) *The Auditor's Report on Financial Statements* (March 2009).

[273] CA 2006, s 495(4).

[274] *Newton v BSA* [1906] 2 Ch 378.

[275] ISA 700; previously SAS 600.

[276] ISA 570 'Going concern'; previously SAS 130 'The Going Concern Basis in Financial Statements'.

[277] CA 2006, s 498(1).

[278] CA 2006, s 498(2).

[279] CA 2006, s 498(3).

If the requirements of regulations relating to disclosure of directors' benefits or relating to information forming the auditable part of the directors' remuneration report are not complied with the auditor must include in his report, so far as he is reasonably able to do so, a statement giving the required particulars.[280] If the accounts have been prepared under the small companies regime and the auditor is of the opinion that they should not have been he must state that fact in his report.[281]

Effective reporting depends in part on the ability of auditors to check and report on the annual accounts. Yet, a number of questions about the role of and quality of auditors arose after the collapse of ENRON. The issue of auditor independence was a particular concern. The Government stated that it would put in place a package of measures on auditor independence set out in detail in the CGAA Report[282] and the Auditing Practices Board was also to develop necessary standards on auditor independence. In summary the CGAA Report proposed that some non-audit services should not be provided if they would involve the audit firm performing management functions for their client or if it would mean auditing its own work. Auditors should also avoid providing valuations services that would involve a degree of subjectivity. The CGAA Report also recommended stronger disclosure provisions relating to non-audit services as well as regular rotation of auditor partners. Many of these recommendations have been put into effect by professional bodies such as the ICAEW.[283] The Companies Act 2006 also provides for the Secretary of State power to make provision by regulations for securing disclosure of the terms on which a company's auditor is appointed, remunerated or performs his duties and also for securing the disclosure of the nature of any services provided for a company by the company's auditor or by his associates and the amounts of remuneration received or receivable for such services.[284]

More recently, responding to a European Commission Green Paper, *Audit Policy: Lessons from the Crisis*, the Department of Business, Innovation and Skills saw the auditors' role as contributing more to the prudential supervision of key financial institutions, and does not favour a ban on provision of non-audit services to audit clients. The Auditing Practices Board has since revised its Ethical Standards for auditors and the FRC has updated its guidance on audit committees. The FRC guidance urges audit committees to set and apply a formal policy specifying types of non-audit services for which use of the external auditor is pre-approved as

---

[280] CA 2006, s 498(4).

[281] CA 2006, s 498(5).

[282] DTI/Treasury, URN 03/567, January 2003.

[283] See for example, *Additional Guidance on the Independence of Auditors* which supplements their *Guide to Professional Ethics*. See also the Guidance in the Combined Code on the Role of the Audit Committee, following recommendations made by the Smith Report: Report to the FRC *Audit Committee Combined Code Guidance* (January 2003).

[284] CA 2006, ss 493 and 494. See **14.28.6.**

a matter of policy, for which prior approval must be sought from the audit committee and from which the external auditor is excluded.

14.29.5   The auditor as an officer of the company

The Companies Act does not make it clear whether or not an auditor is an officer of the company. Sections 487 and 491 of the 2006 Act refer to an auditor holding office. However, s 12 refers to the statement of proposed officers when registering a company and that provision refers to directors and secretaries. No mention is made of auditors.

Nevertheless, the court has held that an auditor is an officer for the purposes of s 212 of the Insolvency Act 1986 (a misfeasance summons in a liquidation).[285] He is also an officer for the purposes of the other sections dealing with offences antecedent to or in the course of winding up and may, therefore, be liable under, for example, s 206 of the 1986 Act for making, or being party to the making of, a false entry in the books or s 207 for fraud.[286]

It seems that an auditor appointed under the provisions of ss 485 and 489 of the 2006 Act will be considered by the court to be an officer of the company. If, however, he is appointed for a more limited purpose, he may not be so considered.[287]

14.30   LIABILITY FOR NEGLIGENCE

The auditor's potential civil liability for negligence, which may arise in contract or tort, merits brief examination here.

14.30.1   Liability in contract

An auditor performs his duties under a contractual relationship with his company. If he is negligent in the performance of his contractual duties he may be liable to the company for loss arising from his negligence. If the company is in liquidation, proceedings may be brought by way of misfeasance summons under s 212 of the Insolvency Act 1986.[288] The duties of an auditor were discussed extensively in *Re London and General Bank Ltd (No 2)*,[289] The *Kingston Cotton Mill Co*[290] case and *Re City Equitable Fire Insurance Co*.[291]

---

[285] See, eg, *Re London and General Bank Ltd* [1895] 2 Ch 166; and *Kingston Cotton Mill Co (No 1)* [1895] 1 Ch 6.
[286] *R v Shacter* [1960] 2 QB 252.
[287] See *Re Western Counties Steam Bakery & Milling Co Ltd* [1897] 1 Ch 617 and *R v Shacter*, above.
[288] See **21.37.1**.
[289] [1895] 2 Ch 673.
[290] [1896] 2 Ch 279.
[291] [1925] Ch 407.

Lopes LJ defined an auditor's duties as follows:[292]

> 'It is the duty of an auditor to bring to bear on the work he has to perform that skill, care and caution which a reasonably competent, careful and cautious auditor would use. What is reasonable skill, care and caution must depend on the circumstances of each case. An auditor is not bound to be a detective, or, as was said, to approach his work with suspicion. He is a watchdog, but not a bloodhound. He is justified in believing tried servants of the company in whom confidence is placed by the company. He is entitled to assume that they are honest, and to rely upon their representations, provided he takes reasonable care. If there is anything calculated to excite suspicion, he should probe it to the bottom, but in the absence of anything of that kind he is only bound to be reasonably cautious and careful.'[293]

14.30.2 Liability in tort for negligent misstatement

The possibility of an auditor being held liable in negligence to persons relying on his report and with whom he does not stand in a contractual or fiduciary relationship has been raised by the decision of the House of Lords in *Hedley Byrne and Co Ltd v Heller and Partners Ltd*.[294] The Court of Appeal in the earlier case of *Candler v Crane Christmas*[295] had held that a firm of accountants was not liable in negligence to someone who had relied on a report negligently prepared by them and which they had known would be acted on by him, and suffered loss as a result, because there was no contractual relationship between the parties. The House of Lords in *Hedley Byrne v Heller*[296] held that a duty of care could arise when there was no contractual relationship.

A landmark decision in the context of the law on negligent statements by professional people which cause economic loss was given by the House of Lords in *Caparo Industries plc v Dickman*.[297] The directors of a public limited company announced results for the financial year end which fell short of the predicted figure, and the share price dropped dramatically. The accounts had been audited by the auditors and approved by the directors before the results were announced. Caparo was an investor which had relied on the auditor's report on the company accounts and

---

[292] *Kingston Cotton Mill Co (No 2)* [1896] 2 Ch 279, at 288, 289.

[293] See also *Henry Squire (Cash Chemist) Ltd v Ball, Baker & Co* [1911] 106 LT 197. Cf *Fomento (Sterling Area) Ltd v Selsdon Fountain Pen Co* [1958] 1 WLR 45, at 61, per Lord Denning. See also *Re Thomas Gerrard & Son Ltd* [1968] Ch 455.

[294] [1964] AC 465 (HL). See also *WB Anderson Ltd v Rhodes* [1967] 2 All ER 850; *Mutual Life & Citizens' Assurance Co Ltd v Evatt* [1971] 1 All ER 150 (PC). There is no ground for excluding liability for negligence in relation to statements made in the course of negotiations which culminate in the making of a contract (though such statements may also create liability under the contract or the Misrepresentation Act 1967; *Esso Petroleum Company v Mardon* [1976] 2 WLR 587 (CA)).

[295] [1951] 2 KB 164 (CA).

[296] [1964] AC 465, [1963] 2 All ER 575.

[297] [1990] 2 AC 605. For a review of the earlier case-law see *Gore-Browne on Companies* (Jordans, 45th edn, loose-leaf) at 37 [15].

consequently suffered considerable financial loss. The Court of Appeal ruled that there was no sufficiently proximate relationship between an auditor and a potential investor to give rise to a duty of care at common law, but that an auditor had a duty of care to individual shareholders, entitling an individual shareholder to recover in tort where he suffered loss by acting in reliance on negligently prepared accounts. On appeal, the House of Lords ruled that the auditors did not owe a duty of care to individual shareholders and agreed with the Court of Appeal that the auditors did not owe a duty of care to potential investors. Foreseeability alone was not sufficient to impose such a duty and the requisite relationship of proximity should also be present to limit what would otherwise be an unlimited duty of care owed by the auditors for the accuracy of their accounts to all who may foreseeably rely on them. The conclusion was that auditors owe no duty of care to members of the public at large who rely on the accounts to buy shares as, if it did, the duty would then extend to all who rely on the accounts such as investors deciding to buy shares, lenders or merchants extending credit. It was necessary to prove that the defendant knew that his statement would be relied upon by the plaintiff in deciding whether or not to enter upon a particular transaction.[298] Thus even if reliance was probable, it was also necessary to have regard to the transaction for the purpose of which the statement was made. In the view of their Lordships the purpose of the statutory requirement for an annual audit was to enable shareholders to review the past management of the company and to exercise their rights to influence future management. They saw nothing in the statutory duties of an auditor to suggest that they were intended to protect the interests of the public at large or investors in the market. The statutory duty was owed to shareholders as a body and not as individuals, and this meant also that they did not owe duties to potential investors. It is still not clear whether there is a duty to protect individuals from losses in the value of the shares they hold.[299]

In recent decisions, it has been held that where auditors make statements concerning the reliability of the accounts to purchasers of the company, they may be liable for their negligence within the principles laid down in *Caparo*. This is so even if the main purpose of the statement was to enable the purchaser to extract a warranty from the vendors.[300] The duty of care will not be displaced by the purchasers having their own accountants

---

[298] This point was clarified recently in *Customs and Excise Commissioners v Barclays Bank plc* [2006] UKHL 28, where Lord Hoffmann stated that: 'In cases in which the loss has been caused by the claimant's reliance on information provided by the defendant, it is critical to decide whether the defendant (rather than someone else) assumed responsibility for the accuracy of the information to the claimant (rather than someone else) or for its use by the claimant for one purpose (rather than another)'. The statement of Lord Hoffmann was later endorsed in *Man Nutzfahrzeuge AG v Freightliner Ltd and Ernst & Young* [2007] EWCA Civ 910.

[299] See *Morgan Crucible Co plc v Hill Samuel & Co Ltd & Ors* [1990] BCC 686, [1991] BCC 82; and *James McNaughton Paper Group Ltd v Hicks Anderson & Co* [1990] BCC 891.

[300] *Peach Publishing Ltd v Slater & Co* [1996] BCC 751; see also *Bank of Credit and*

conduct a review, where the review was a limited one and the accountants had to rely on information provided by the auditors.[301] Where a statement is made at a meeting with the purchasers, the auditor may be held to have assumed responsibility to the purchaser. It is not necessary that they assume a role of persuasion.[302] The Court of Appeal has held that the auditors of the accounts of a subsidiary company may owe a duty of care to its parent company. This is so even though the information was supplied to enable the parent company to prepare group accounts as required by statute.[303] The parent company was not prevented from suing because damages, for which the auditor might be liable to the parent company, might include liability to the subsidiary.[304]

14.30.3   Duty of auditor valuing shares

Where an auditor of a private company is called upon to value shares in the company in the knowledge that his valuation would determine the price to be paid on the sale of such shares, the auditor owes a duty of care to those affected by his valuation. The House of Lords has held that an auditor valuing shares has no general immunity from an action for negligence. In order to establish such an immunity, the auditor acting as valuer must show that a formulated dispute between at least two parties has been remitted to him to resolve in such a manner that he was called upon to exercise a judicial (ie arbitral) function, and that the parties had agreed to accept his decision.[305]

A valuer must also be seen to be truly independent of the company whose shares he has to value. If the valuer is independent then the valuing of the shares might reasonably be left to him.[306] It is also only possible to challenge a certificate of valuation of shares for mistake when the mistake is of such a nature that the expert has not performed what he was

---

    Commerce International (Overseas) Ltd v Price Waterhouse [1997] BCC 584. See further *Electra Private Equity Partners v KPMG Peat Marwick* [2001] 1 BCLC 589 (CA).

[301] Ibid. See *Sayers v Clarke-Walker (a firm)* [2002] 2 BCLC 16 as to the scope of the duty in respect of a retainer to give advice as regards the purchase of a company as a facilitator. The claimant must have relied on the auditor's report when embarking on the transaction which resulted in the loss: *Barings plc (in liq) v Coopers & Lybrand (a firm) (No 1)* [2002] 2 BCLC 364. See also *Barings v Coopers & Lybrand* [2002] 2 BCLC 410 as to auditors certifying accounts on the basis of representation letters by a finance director of a subsidiary. Such letters did not provide the auditors with a defence since they were written in honest belief and without recklessness.

[302] *ADT Ltd v BDO Binder Hamlyn* [1996] BCC 608.

[303] *Barings plc v Coopers & Lybrand* [1997] 1 BCLC 427.

[304] Ibid. A risk of recovery could be avoided by bringing both actions together. The principle of *Prudential Assurance Co Ltd v Newman Industries (No 2)* [1982] Ch 204 was held not applicable.

[305] *Arenson v Casson, Beckman, Rutley & Co* [1977] AC 405; *Suttcliffe v Thackrah* [1974] All ER 859 applied. However, even if an action against the auditors in negligence would lie, the purchaser is still entitled to buy the shares at the price certified by the auditors. In the absence of fraud, collusion or error on the face of the certificate, it cannot be challenged: *Baber v Kenwood Manufacturing Co* [1978] 1 Lloyd's Rep 175 (CA).

[306] *Re Boswell & Co (Steels) Ltd* (1989) 5 BCC 145.

appointed to do.[307] Where a company's articles provide for shares to be valued by an auditor, the standard of care is that of a reasonable auditor, not that of a specialist valuer.[308]

14.30.4 The limitation or exclusion of liability

The Limitation Act 1980, as amended by the Latent Damage Act 1986, serves to limit the auditor's civil liability in England and Wales[309] for negligence to losses arising within 6 years before the commencement of an action. Any provision contained either in a company's articles or in a contract to exempt an auditor from or to indemnify him against any liability which would otherwise attach to him in respect of any negligence, default or breach of duty or trust in relation to the company is void except in the following circumstances:[310] the company may indemnify him in respect of costs incurred in a successful defence of a civil or criminal action or in connection with an application for relief under s 1157.[311] A company may also provide a liability limitation agreement that purports to limit the amount of liability owed to a company by its auditor in respect of his negligence or breach of duty or trust occurring in the course of the audit of accounts. Such liability limitation agreement must relate to the audit of a specified financial year and it must be authorised by the members in accordance with s 536.

A private company may authorise the agreement with its auditors by passing a resolution:

(1) before it enters into the agreement, waiving the need for approval;

(2) before it enters into the agreement, approving the agreement's principal terms; or

(3) after it enters into the agreement, approving the agreement.

A public company must always get approval for a liability limitation agreement through passing an ordinary resolution at a general meeting of the company. As with a private company this can be either:

(1) before it enters into the agreement, approving the agreement's principal terms; or

(2) after it enters into the agreement, approving the agreement.

---

[307] *Jones v Sherwood Computer Services Plc* [1992] 2 All ER 170.

[308] *Whiteoak v Walker* (1988) 4 BCC 122.

[309] In Scotland, the prescriptive period is five years: Prescription and Limitation (Scotland) Act 1973.

[310] CA 2006, s 532.

[311] CA 2006, s 533.

A public company's articles may specify that a higher majority (or unanimity) than is normally required for an ordinary resolution for a resolution concerning liability limitations agreements.

Interestingly, there are no further provisions for quoted companies in respect of liability limitation agreements than as apply for public companies.

The 'principal terms' of a liability limitation agreement are those that specify or determine:

(1)   the acts or omissions covered;

(2)   the financial year to which the agreement relates; and

(3)   the limit of the auditor's liability.

If a company has already entered into the liability limitation agreement, it can only withdraw its authorisation before the beginning of the financial year to which that agreement relates. This is the case notwithstanding anything that is in the agreement.

Where the company has not yet entered into the agreement, it can withdraw its authorisation at any time before entering the agreement.

The withdrawal of authorisation by a company must be effected by passing an ordinary resolution.[312]

A liability limitation agreement is not effective to limit the auditor's liability to less than such amount as is fair and reasonable in all the circumstances of the case having regard in particular to the auditor's responsibilities under the Act; the nature and purpose of the auditor's contractual obligations to the company; and the professional standards expected of him. Regard is also given to matters arising after the loss or damage in question has been incurred or matters affecting the possibility of recovering compensation from other persons liable in respect of the same loss or damage.[313]

The Secretary of State has laid regulations that require a company to disclose, as a note to its annual accounts, that it has entered into a liability limitation agreement.[314] The note must state the principal terms of the agreement together with the date of the resolution approving the

---

[312] CA 2006, s 536(5).

[313] CA 2006, s 537.

[314] CA 2006, s 538 and the Companies (Disclosure of Auditor Remuneration and Liability Limitation Agreements) Regulations 2008, SI 2008/489.

agreement or its principal terms. Private companies that have passed a resolution waiving the need for such approval should state the date of that resolution.

The disclosure should be provided in the annual accounts for the financial year to which the liability limitation agreement relates. If, however, the agreement was entered into too late for it to be reasonably practicable to make disclosure in those accounts, then the disclosure should be made in the next set of annual accounts.

Under s 507 inaccurate auditors' reports will give rise to a criminal offence where an auditor knowingly or recklessly causes an auditor's report to include any matter that is misleading, false or deceptive in a material particular or to omit a required statement.

CHAPTER 15

MANAGEMENT OF A COMPANY

15.1 INTRODUCTION

The important question of the management of a company is obviously a part of what is nowadays generally called corporate governance; this question was discussed in a general way in Chapter 11. There it was seen that the UK has a system which requires listed companies to observe the UK Corporate Governance Code. The subject matter of this chapter is the current legal position in the sense of what is required by the Companies Act 2006 and associated legislation, and by standard articles, regarding the management of a company. Although the Act requires that every private company must have at least one director and every public company at least two directors,[1] and although it attributes many functions to and casts many obligations on directors, it does not of itself prescribe how the business of the company is to be managed.[2] This and some other aspects of the law relating to directors and other officers are left to the articles which in practice will adopt or follow, with modifications, the relevant parts of the prescribed articles. Thus many aspects of the management of a company are contractual in nature and the articles will, among other things, determine the number of directors, the powers of the board as against those of the members in general meeting and the ability of directors to delegate their powers. In this permissive respect, British company law is very different from the law in most other Member States of the European Union and at one time the Draft Fifth Directive proposed the imposition of a formal legal structure regarding the management of public companies.[3] However, further consideration of this issue at the European level appears to be off the agenda for the foreseeable future.[4]

---

[1] Section 154 [CA 1985, s 282]; see **15.3.1**.

[2] Nor, perhaps surprisingly, does it define the term 'director'; see **15.2**.

[3] This included the representation of a company's employees on its board of directors or in some other formal way. Other proposals for employee directors include those of the Bullock Committee on Industrial Democracy, Cmnd 6706 (1977). The whole question of 'industrial democracy' has given birth to many different proposals and reactions over the last 30 years or so, and there have been a number of changes in company law which reflect increasing recognition of employees' interests: see in particular s 172(1)(b), discussed in **16.5** and the fiscal and other measures introduced to encourage employee share ownership. See also generally the discussion of the 'stakeholder' question.

[4] Except as regards the European Company; see **2.3.10** and **2.5**.

The law applying to directors and other officers includes the questions of their appointment, removal, functions and procedures, remuneration and service contracts. This chapter is also an appropriate place to examine the law regarding the disqualification of directors and their potential responsibility for fraudulent or wrongful trading. Although some of these issues touch on the duties of directors, consideration of these duties in general is deferred to the next two chapters. The other important question not considered here is the extent of directors' agency powers, namely when liability for their dealings will be attributed to their companies; this question has already been considered in Chapter 6.

15.2 THE MEANING OF DIRECTOR

The Companies Act 2006 does not define directors. There is, however, a general provision that, in the Companies Acts, the expression 'director' includes 'any person occupying the position of director, by whatever name called',[5] but this provision is intended merely to cover the situation where the management of a company is conducted by persons described as, say, governors or managers rather than directors.[6] The meaning of 'director' is to be derived from the words of the Act as a whole and varies according to the context in which it is found. In respect of certain provisions, someone who acts as a director but is not actually appointed as such, ie a *de facto* as opposed to a *de jure* director, will be treated as a director,[7] and a *de facto* director will be regarded as holding a fiduciary position and subject to the general duties of directors described in Chapter 16.[8] The majority of the modern cases have concerned whether or not someone was a director for the purpose of the statutory provisions regarding disqualification. However, the meaning of the term 'de facto director' will not necessarily be the same in all contexts, namely for the purposes of the application of some statutory provisions as opposed to fiduciary duties.[9] The majority of the modern cases have concerned whether or not someone was a director for the purpose of the statutory provisions regarding disqualification.

In *Gemma Ltd v Davis*,[10] where a company secretary who took no part in decision-making on behalf of the company was held not to be a de facto

---

5   CA 2006, s 250 [CA 1985, s 744(1)].

6   *Re Lo-Line Electric Motors Ltd* [1988] BCLC 698.

7   *Re Lo-Line Electric Motors Ltd*, above, *Re Kaytech International plc* [1999] 2 BCLC 353. This will be particularly so in respect of the disqualification provisions (see **15.18**), but not as regards the other statutory provisions described in this chapter.

8   *Canadian Land Reclaiming and Colonizing Co* (1880) 14 Ch D 660, 670; *Ultraframe UK Ltd v Fielding* [2004] RPC 24, at para 39, *Ultraframe UK Ltd v Fielding* [2005] EWHC 1638 (Ch), at para 1257.

9   See the judgment of Lord Collins in *Re Paycheck Services 3 Ltd* [2010] UKSC 51, [2011] 1 BCLC 141, referred to below.

10   [2008] EWHC 546 (Ch), [2008] 2 BCLC 281. See *also Re Hydrodan (Corby) Ltd* [1994] BCC 161 (a de facto director could be a director for the purposes of s 214 of the Insolvency Act 1986) and a number of cases identifying the criteria for holding a person

director, the following were helpfully summarised as the tests to determine this question.[11] (1) It is necessary to plead and prove that the person undertook functions that could properly be discharged only by a director.[12] (2) It is not necessary that the person is held out as a director; this may be important evidence,[13] but what matters is not what the person called himself, but what he did.[14] (3) The person must have participated in directing the affairs of the company on an equal footing with the other directors and not in a subordinate role;[15] as it was put in another case, he must have exercised 'real influence' in the corporate governance of the company.[16] (4) If it is unclear whether the acts of the person are referable to as assumed directorship or some other capacity, they are entitled to the benefit of the doubt,[17] although the court must be careful not to strain the facts in this respect.[18]

In *Re Paycheck Services 3 Ltd*,[19] the Supreme Court reviewed the earlier authorities on the meaning of de facto director in the case of a large number of companies that had the same single corporate director, when the issue was whether the only active director of the latter could be regarded as a de facto director of the companies and held accountable for unlawful dividends paid by those companies.[20] By a bare majority, the court upheld the decision of the Court of Appeal[21] that the mere fact that a director of a company acts on behalf of that company in its role as a corporate director of another company does not by itself make that individual a de facto director of the latter company. In the Court of Appeal, Rimer LJ said: '[S]omething more will be required than the mere performance by him of his duties as a de jure director of the corporate director.'[22] In the Supreme Court, Lord Hope cited this dictum[23] and

---

to be a de facto director for the purposes of the disqualification provisions: *Re Moorgate Metals Ltd* [1995] BCC 143, *Re Richborough Furniture Ltd* [1996] 1 BCLC 507, *Secretary of State for Trade and Industry v Laing* [1996] 2 BCLC 324, *Secretary of State for Trade and Industry v Hickling* [1996] BCC 678, *Secretary of State for Trade and Industry v Elms* (unreported) 16 January 1997, *Secretary of State for Trade and Industry v Tjolle* [1998] 1 BCLC 333, *Secretary of State for Trade and Industry v Jones* [1999] BCC 336, *Re Kaytech International plc* [1999] BCC 390, CA.

[11] Ibid at [40], per Jonathan Gaunt QC sitting as a Deputy Judge.

[12] See Millett J in *Re Hydrodam (Corby) Ltd*, above at 183.

[13] See Etherton J in *Secretary of State for Trade and Industry v Hollier* [2006] EWHC 1804 (Ch) at [66].

[14] See Lewison J in *Re Mea Corp Ltd* [2007] 1 BCLC 618.

[15] See Etherton J in *Secretary of State for Trade and Industry v Hollier*, above at [68] and [69].

[16] See Robert Walker LJ in *Re Kaytech International plc*, above at 424.

[17] *Re Richborough Furniture Ltd*, above, at 524

[18] *Re Kaytech International plc*, above at 423.

[19] [2010] UKSC 51, [2011] 1 BCLC 141.

[20] The only earlier cases involving this particular scenario, which cannot arise since s 155 of the Companies Act 2006 was brought into force on 1 October 2008 (see **15.3.1**), were *Re Hydrodam (Corby) Ltd*, above, and *Secretary of State for Trade and Industry v Hall* [2006] EWHC 1995 (Ch), [2009] BCC 190.

[21] [2009] EWCA Civ 625, [2009] 2 BCLC 309.

[22] Ibid at [74].

expressed the guiding principle as follows: 'So long as the relevant acts are done by the individual entirely within the ambit of the discharge of his duties and responsibilities as a director of the corporate director, it is to that capacity that his acts must be attributed.'[24] Lord Collins put the matter slightly differently after an exhaustive analysis of earlier authorities. Referring to the context in which the issue arose in this case, namely whether or not the individual in question was liable for a wrongful distribution, and stating that the expression 'de facto director' need not be given the same meaning in all the contexts in which such a director might be liable, he regarded the crucial question as being whether the individual was part of the corporate governing structure of the companies in question and whether he assumed a role in those companies which imposed on him the fiduciary duties of a director.[25] Lords Walker and Clarke gave strong dissenting judgments, which repay careful study as a comparison with the majority judgments. They regarded the matter as a question of fact rather than of law and principle (the view of the majority) and considered that the individual director in question was in fact the 'guiding mind of a single corporate director'.[26] They also pointed out that the much-cited dicta in *Re Hydrodam (Corby) Ltd* were made in a rather different context, namely where the corporate director had a multiplicity of human directors. Even though, as noted above, the particular factual scenario of a single corporate director cannot now exist, the decision remains important simply because a human director acting together with the corporate director may be a person with little or no assets and the individual director of the corporate director might have been the only person worth attempting to hold to account.

15.2.1 Shadow directors

In respect of a number of statutory provisions obligations are cast on any 'shadow director', who is 'a person in accordance with whose directions or instructions the directors of a company are accustomed to act'.[27] The

---

[23] [2010] UKSC 51 at [37], itself based on what Millett J said in *Re Hydrodam (Corby) Ltd*, above.

[24] Ibid at [42].

[25] Ibid at [93] and [94].

[26] Per Lord Walker at [123].

[27] Section 251(2). These provisions are noted in the appropriate parts of the text in this and the subsequent chapters. A person is not deemed a shadow director by reason only of the fact that the directors act on advice given by him in a professional capacity, and the definition does not catch a parent company, which could clearly fall within it in some situations, in respect of the sections listed in s 251(3), namely in respect of many of the statutory duties applying to directors. A shadow director does not as such owe fiduciary duties to the company: see **16.1.1**.

concept of shadow director is quite different from that of *de facto* director.[28] As far as a shadow director is concerned, the Court of Appeal has established[29] that:

(1)   the term should not be strictly construed;

(2)   a shadow director must have a real influence in the corporate affairs of the company, but not necessarily over the whole field of its activities;

(3)   the directions or instructions do not necessarily have to be proved to have been understood or expected;

(4)   non-professional advice may be within the meaning of 'directions or instructions'; and

(5)   it is not necessary in all cases to show that the actual directors or some of them act in a subservient manner or surrender their discretion to the shadow director.

A person at whose direction or on whose instructions a governing majority of the board is accustomed to act is capable of being a shadow director,[30] but they must act as a consequence and the definition does not have retrospective effect.[31] It is clear that in appropriate circumstances a parent company, a lender or a venture capitalist, for example, could be a shadow director. Although a shadow director is subject to the requirements imposed by a number of statutory provisions, it has been held that he does not normally owe fiduciary duties to the company.[32] However, the facts may indicate that someone is both a shadow director in respect of certain functions and a de facto director in respect of others, in which case in the latter respect he will be subject to the full range of fiduciary duties.[33]

---

[28]   *Re Hydrodan (Corby) Ltd* [1994] BCC 161.

[29]   *Secretary of State for Trade and Industry v Deverell* [2000] 2 WLR 907 (CA), at 919–920, applied in *Secretary of State for Trade and Industry v Becker* [2002] EWHC 2200 (Ch), [2003] 1 BCLC 555.

[30]   *Re Unisoft Group Ltd (No 3)* [1994] 1 BCLC 609, 620; *Ultraframe UK Ltd v Fielding* [2005] EWHC 1638 (Ch) at paras 1270–1272.

[31]   *Ultraframe (UK) Ltd v Fielding*, above, at paras 1273–1278.

[32]   *Ultraframe (UK) Ltd v Fielding* [2005] EWHC 1638 (Ch); see **16.1.1**.

[33]   *Re Mea Corporation Ltd* [2007] 1 BCLC 618 at [86] to [91]. Although Millett J in *Re Hydrodam (Corby) Ltd* [1994] 2 BCLC 180 at 183 said that de facto and shadow directorships do not overlap, the prevailing view now is that they can; see the judgments of Lord Collins and Lord Walker in *Re Paycheck Services 3 Ltd* [2010] UKSC 51, [2011] 1 BCLC 141 at [91] and [110], referring with approval to comments in *Re Kaytech International plc* [1999] 2 BCLC 351 at 424 and *Re Mea Corporation*.

15.3   APPOINTMENT OF DIRECTORS

The articles usually provide how the directors are to be appointed. In practice the first directors are normally either named in the articles or, more likely now, appointed by the subscribers to the memorandum. If appointment lies with the subscribers, then, until they have made the appointment, a general meeting of the company must be held to perform any acts. A majority of the subscribers must act at a meeting in making the appointment of directors[34] but the appointment may be made in writing by all the subscribers without a meeting.[35]

The model articles regarding the appointment of future directors provide that directors may be appointed by ordinary resolution or by a decision of the directors.[36] The model articles for private companies make no provision for retirement, but those for public companies provide that a proportion of the directors must retire at each annual general meeting and the places be filled by the members.[37]

A company has an inherent power to fill vacancies,[38] unless restricted by its articles, and even where this is restricted, the general meeting has a residual power if the directors cannot or will not act, for example because of deadlock or the failure of the directors to meet or if the directors are equally divided.[39]

If the articles authorise it, but not otherwise,[40] the directors may delegate the power to appoint directors to a third party.[41] If the appointment of directors requires the confirmation of the company at the next general meeting, the directors cannot by appointing a managing director for a fixed period dispense with this confirmation nor give him a right to damages for breach of contract.[42]

15.3.1   Statutory requirements

There are a number of statutory requirements in the Companies Act 2006 relating to the appointment of directors. Section 154[43] requires that every

---

[34]   *John Morley Building Co v Barras* [1891] 2 Ch 386.
[35]   *Re Great Northern Salt and Chemical Works Co* (1890) 44 Ch D 472.
[36]   See art 17 of both the Model Articles for Private Companies and the Model Articles for Public Companies.
[37]   See art 21 and **15.5**. The model does not contain the provision in art 75 of the 1985 Table A to the effect that a director retiring by rotation is deemed to be reappointed if his place is not filled, unless it is expressly resolved not to reappoint him or not to fill the vacated office.
[38]   *Worcester Corsetry v Witting* [1936] Ch 640.
[39]   *Barron v Potter* [1914] 1 Ch 895; *Foster v Foster* [1916] 1 Ch 532; see **15.11**.
[40]   *James v Eve* (1873) LR 6 HL 335.
[41]   *British Murac Syndicate v Alperton Rubber Co* [1915] 2 Ch 186.
[42]   *Bluett v Stutchbury's Ltd* (1908) 24 TLR 469 (CA).
[43]   [CA 1985, s 282].

private company should have at least one director and every public company should have at least two directors. Subject to this, the number of directors may be varied from time to time within the limits (if any) specified in the articles, which may specify the minimum and maximum number of directors.[44] Section 12 requires the first directors of all companies to give their consent to act at the time the company is registered.[45] Important restrictions are imposed by ss 155 and 157–159 of the 2006 Act.[46] Section 155 requires all companies to have at least one person who is a natural person.[47] Section 157 specifies a minimum age of 16 for a person to be appointed a director.[48] It is possible to appoint a younger person provided that the appointment does not take effect until that person is 16,[49] but otherwise an appointment of a person under 16 is void.[50] The age-limit applies even if the director's appointment is a consequence of his being a corporation sole or by virtue of another office; in this case the appointment takes effect when he reaches 16. However, this prohibition does not provide protection from criminal prosecution or civil liability under the Companies Acts if he purports to act as a director or shadow director.[51]

As far as public companies are concerned,[52] s 160[53] prohibits the appointment of two or more persons as directors by a single resolution unless this procedure has been approved by the meeting without dissent.[54] A resolution contravening s 160 is void, but s 161[55] will apply to validate the acts of the improperly appointed 'directors' and such a resolution will prevent the operation of a provision in the articles[56] for the automatic reappointment of retiring directors in default of another appointment.

---

[44] The articles of many private companies appoint a person, e g the vendor of a business to the company, as a director. He may be styled a 'governing director' with extensive powers, e g the right to appoint a successor and to appoint and remove other directors.

[45] See further **4.5**.

[46] These were introduced for the first time by this Act.

[47] This can be satisfied by the appointment of a natural person as a corporation sole or otherwise by virtue of an office, e g an archbishop of the Church of England. Note the power conferred on the Secretary of State to give a direction requiring a company to comply with either or both of the requirements in ss 154 and 155. The direction must identify the broken requirement, state what the company must do to comply and the period, between one and 3 months, it has for compliance and inform the company of the consequences of a failure to comply, which is the possibility of a criminal penalty.

[48] Section 158 allows for exemptions to be made by regulations and s 159 deals with under-age directors when s 157 was brought into force on 1 October 2007.

[49] Section 157(2).

[50] Section 157(4).

[51] Section 157(5).

[52] There used to be a maximum age limit for public company directors, but that was abolished by the 2006 Act.

[53] [CA 1985, s 292.]

[54] 'Appointment' includes approving a person's appointment or nominating a person for appointment.

[55] See further, **6.23**.

[56] Eg art 75 in the 1985 Table A.

15.4 REMUNERATION OF DIRECTORS

Directors *qua* directors are not entitled as of right to any remuneration, whether on the basis of a *quantum meruit* or otherwise.[57] A 'director is not a servant; he is a person doing business for the company, but not upon ordinary terms. It is not implied from the mere fact that he is a director that he is to be paid for it'.[58] However, this proposition may be, and, of course, normally is, qualified.[59] First, the articles are likely these days to provide for director's remuneration.[60] Secondly, there may be a service contract between a director and his company which entitles him to a salary or other remuneration, in other words, a director is often an employee as well as holding the office of director. Further, if a director performs services which are not comprehended by the terms of any service contract (or where there is no service contract), he may claim in *quantum meruit*. This has been held to apply to a director who continues to perform services for the benefit of his company after he ceases to be qualified as a director.[61] However, where a managing director is appointed under an article which confers on the board of directors the power to determine his remuneration, and the board have not determined this, the managing director will have no claim in *quantum meruit*; since he has agreed to serve the company on the basis of this provision in the articles, this excludes a quasi-contractual claim in *quantum meruit*.[62] It should also be noted that, in *Guinness plc v Saunders*,[63] the House of Lords took a restrictive approach to such claims, Lord Templeman commenting that claims for a quantum meruit or for an equitable allowance were inconsistent with the no-profit rule[64] and being unable to 'envisage circumstances in which a court of equity would exercise a power to award remuneration to a director when the relevant articles of association confided that power to the board of directors.'[65]

---

[57] *Re Geo Newman and Co* [1895] 1 Ch 674 (CA).

[58] Per Bowen LJ in *Hutton v West Cork Rly* (1883) 23 Ch D 654 at 671 (CA).

[59] 'Excessive' remuneration for executive directors of public companies has been the subject of public concern in recent years; see Ramsay [1993] JBL 351; Villiers 'Executive Pay: Beyond Control' (1995) 14 LS 260, and was one of the factors behind the moves to improve corporate governance. Under the UK Corporate Governance Code, listed company boards must have a remuneration committee to determine the remuneration of the executive directors; see Chapter 11. As to the specific disclosure requirements regarding the remuneration of directors of quoted companies, see **14.11**.

[60] See arts 19 and 23 of the Model Articles for Private and Public companies, respectively.

[61] *Craven-Ellis v Canons* [1936] 2 KB 403 (CA).

[62] *Re Richmond Gate Property Co* [1965] 1 WLR 335. The contract of service in this case was not constituted by the articles but was a contract of service created by the conduct of the parties based on, or incorporating, the articles – 'those were the terms on which he accepted office'.

[63] [1990] 2 AC 363.

[64] See **16.8**.

[65] [1990] 2 AC at 694.

In practice, as mentioned above, the articles will provide for directors to receive remuneration. The model articles[66] provide for this to be determined by the directors both as regards their services as directors and for any other service they undertake for the company.[67] If the articles fix the amount, then when earned, this becomes a debt for which the directors can sue.[68] Their own right in such cases arises from the contract to employ them as directors, and the articles must be looked at to see what are the terms agreed upon for their remuneration.[69] If the articles provide that a director is to be paid such remuneration as the board of directors determines, and the company is wound up before the board has passed any such resolution as to remuneration, then a director will *not* be entitled to recover for any services he has performed on a contractual basis (since the contractual amount has not been determined in the way the article required). Further, as described above, a claim on a *quantum meruit* is also excluded by the terms of the articles.[70] If the articles are silent, the company in general meeting may vote remuneration; but in such case the remuneration is a gratuity, and not a matter of right.[71] So in an operative company a general meeting may vote a gratuity beyond the amount prescribed by the articles, but upon liquidation this cannot be done.[72] Standard articles[73] used to provide that the directors were entitled to such remuneration as the company may by ordinary resolution determine. Where the remuneration of the directors is governed by such an article, it is incompetent for the board to fix it.[74]

Liquidation puts an end to a director's service,[75] but the appointment of a receiver and manager does not determine the director's right to remuneration.[76] If remuneration is payable 'at such time as the directors may determine', one of the directors cannot sue for fees until the board have fixed the time for payment.[77]

If a director's appointment is not validly made he cannot recover remuneration as a director, either under the articles or under a *quantum*

---

[66] See footnote 60.

[67] They also provide for this to take any form, to include provision for pensions and other benefits and to accrue from day to day.

[68] *Nell v Atlanta Gold and Silver Consol Mines* (1895) 11 TLR 407 (CA); *New British Iron Co, ex parte Beckwith* [1898] 1 Ch 324; *Re Dover Coalfields Extension Co* [1908] 1 Ch 65 (CA).

[69] *Molineaux v London, Birmingham, and Manchester Insurance Co* [1902] 2 KB 596 (CA).

[70] *Re Richmond Gate Property Co* [1965] 1 WLR 335.

[71] *Re Geo Newman & Co* [1895] 1 Ch 674 (CA); see generally the discussion of 'corporate gifts' in **6.3**.

[72] *Hutton v West Cork Rly Co* (1883) 23 Ch D 654.

[73] See art 82 of the 1985 Table A.

[74] *Kerr v Marine Products* (1928) 44 TLR 292. But a formal resolution in general meeting may be dispensed with if *all* the shareholders entitled to attend and vote at a general meeting have approved the remuneration: *Re Duomatic* [1969] 2 Ch 365. See further, **13.2**.

[75] *Re Central de Kaap Gold Mines* [1899] WN 216; *Re T N Farrer* [1937] Ch 352.

[76] *Re South Western of Venezuela Rly* [1902] 1 Ch 701.

[77] *Caridad Copper Mining Co v Swallow* [1902] 2 KB 44 (CA).

meruit, although he may have served for a long period,[78] and if it is discovered that remuneration has been paid for a period after the director has vacated office under the terms of the articles, the company, in a case where the facts negate the probability of an intention to grant remuneration, can recover the amount paid by mistake.[79] It should, however, be noted that a person purported to be appointed *managing director* by the supposed board may recover remuneration as such on the basis of a *quantum meruit*, notwithstanding that such appointment was altogether void, neither he nor any person constituting such board being a director, through failure to qualify.[80]

The remuneration of a director as such covers travelling expenses, and unless specially authorised by the articles[81] or by resolution of a general meeting, expenses of travelling to or from board meetings must not be paid in addition.[82]

15.5   DIRECTORS' SERVICE CONTRACTS AND THE ARTICLES

Where a managing director or other director has a service contract with the company and he is dismissed in breach of his service contract, a provision in the articles which enables the general meeting or the board to dismiss him from the office of director or managing director will not prevent him from suing for damages for breach of contract.[83] Thus, where, as in *Southern Foundries v Shirlaw*,[84] a director is appointed managing director for a term of years, and the articles provide that a managing director shall be subject to the same provisions for removal as any other director 'subject to the provisions of any contract between him and the company', it is an implied term of the contract that the company will not remove the managing director from his office as director. In *Nelson v James Nelson & Sons*,[85] it was held that even without such a phrase the directors could not revoke an appointment otherwise than in accordance with the terms of the service agreement.

Although s 168 of the Companies Act 2006 allows the company in general meeting to dismiss a director by ordinary resolution,[86] s 168(5) specifically

---

[78]   *Woolf v East Nigel Gold Mining Co* (1905) 21 TLR 660.

[79]   *Re Bodega Co* [1904] 1 Ch 276.

[80]   *Craven-Ellis v Canons* [1936] 2 KB 403 (CA). See also *Re Richmond Gate Property Co* [1965] 1 WLR 335.

[81]   See arts 20 and 24 of the Model Articles for Private and Public Companies, respectively, which permit the payment of expenses.

[82]   *Young v Naval and Military Co-operative Society* [1905] 1 KB 687.

[83]   It is most unlikely that he will have any prospect of obtaining an injunction: see, eg, *Walker v Standard Chartered Bank plc* [1992] BCLC 535 (CA).

[84]   [1940] AC 707 (HL). See further as to the powers and status of managing directors, **15.16.1**.

[85]   [1913] 2 KB 471 (CA).

[86]   Section 168 is considered further in **15.9**.

provides that nothing in the section deprives a director removed under it 'of compensation or damages payable to him in respect of the termination of his appointment or of any appointment terminating with that as a director' (eg as managing director). In *Shindler v Northern Raincoat Co*,[87] the plaintiff was appointed a managing director of the defendant company for 10 years. The company's articles included art 68 of Table A of the 1929 Act, which gave the company in general meeting a power to determine the appointment of a managing director.[88] As a result of a change in the control of the defendant's holding company, resolutions were passed at a general meeting removing the plaintiff from office as director and terminating his service agreement as managing director. It was held that the plaintiff could sue for damages for wrongful dismissal since it was an implied term in his service agreement that the defendant company would do nothing of its own motion to put an end to the circumstances which enabled the plaintiff to continue as managing director. In another case,[89] where a managing director was appointed under an identical article, his service contract was held to incorporate art 68 (which allowed the company to dismiss him without notice by a resolution in general meeting). Here the plaintiff was not appointed for any specific period. It was held that in the absence of a contract independent of the articles there was no ground for implying a term as to reasonable notice. Where the plaintiff's conduct involves a breach of fiduciary duty to his company a claim for wrongful dismissal will be rejected. It is the director's own wrongful repudiation of his contract of service which produces its termination.[90]

Where a director has a claim for damages for wrongful dismissal, he is of course subject to the general contractual rule that he must seek to mitigate his loss. It has been held, however, that where a managing director is dismissed and is offered the position of assistant managing director at the same salary, he is entitled to refuse the offer because of the loss of status involved.[91] In estimating the amount of damages, the court must apply the principle of *British Transport Commission v Gourlay*[92] and take into account what would have been his liability for income tax.

---

[87] [1960] 1 WLR 1038.

[88] Now the general meeting would act under s 168.

[89] *Read v Astoria Garage* [1952] Ch 637 (CA). Cf *James v T Kent & Co Ltd* [1951] 1 KB 551 (CA) where a term as to reasonable notice was implied.

[90] *Neptune (Vehicle Washing Equipment) Ltd v Fitzgerald (No 2)* [1995] BCC 1000. See also *Item Software (UK) Ltd v Fassihi* [2003] 2 BCLC 1 and *Knopp v Thane Investments Ltd* [2003] 1 BCLC 380.

[91] *Yetton v Eastwoods Froy Ltd* [1967] 1 WLR 104. As to the measure of damages in respect of various 'heads' (loss of salary and commission, reduction in pension, loss of life insurance cover, etc), see *Bold v Brough, Nicholson and Hall Ltd* [1964] 1 WLR 201.

[92] [1956] AC 185 (HL).

In addition to, and as apart from, any common-law claim for wrongful dismissal, a director who has a service contract and is therefore an employee of his company may bring a claim for unfair dismissal before an industrial tribunal.[93]

15.6   DISCLOSURE OF DIRECTORS' SERVICE CONTRACTS

There are a number of statutory provisions relating to directors' service contracts. Those that concern the duties of directors are considered in Chapter 17. For the present, ss 227–230 of the Companies Act 2006[94] impose disclosure requirements for the benefit of members of the company. These sections do not just apply to contracts of service in the strict sense, but extend widely to contracts for services and other arrangements under which directors are appointed. They also apply to shadow directors.[95] By s 227(1), a service contract means a contract under which (a) a director undertakes personally to perform services, as a director or otherwise, for the company or a subsidiary of it or (b) services, as director or otherwise, that a director undertakes personally to perform are made available by a third party to the company or a subsidiary of it. The provisions apply to the terms of a person's appointment as director and are not restricted to contracts for the performance of services outside the scope of the ordinary duties of directors,[96] so that the terms on which a non-executive director is appointed are covered.

Every company must keep copies of such service contracts, or where a contract is not in writing, a written memorandum setting out the terms of the contract.[97] Section 228(2) requires all the copies and memoranda to be kept available for inspection at the company's registered office or at a place specified in regulations under s 1136.[98] The regulations[99] require a single alternative inspection location, which must be in the part of the UK in which the company is registered and have been notified to the registrar. The copies and memoranda must be retained for at least one year from the date of termination or expiry of the contract and be kept available for inspection during that time.[100] The company must give notice to the registrar of the place where these copies and memoranda are kept and any change of place, except where this has always been the registered office.[101] By s 229, these documents are to be open to inspection by any member of

---

[93]   Ie under the Employment Rights Act 1996.
[94]   [CA 1985, s 318.]
[95]   Section 230; as to shadow directors, see **15.2.1**.
[96]   Section 227(2).
[97]   Section 228(1); this obligation applies also to a variation of a director's service contract: s 228(7).
[98]   This is the general section under which places may be specified for the inspection of various statutory registers, etc.
[99]   The Companies (Company Records) Regulations 2008, SI 2008/3006, reg 3.
[100] Section 228(3).
[101] Section 228(4).

the company without charge, and any member can demand a copy on payment of a prescribed fee; the copy must be provided within 7 days of the company receiving the request. There are heavy penalties for any officer in default, and the court may by order compel an immediate inspection or provision of a copy where this has been refused.

15.7 RETIREMENT AND TERMINATION OF APPOINTMENT OF DIRECTORS

Regulation 21 of the model articles for public companies provides that at the first annual general meeting all the directors must retire from office, and that at every subsequent annual general meeting any directors appointed by the directors since the last annual general meeting or not appointed at one of the preceding two annual general meetings must retire and offer themselves for reappointment by the members. In effect therefore directors of public companies are likely to be subject to re-election every 3 years. In contrast it is unlikely that private companies will provide for this.[102]

Articles usually also provide[103] that the appointment of director is to be terminated if he does or suffers certain things, such as becoming bankrupt, and on grounds such as physical or mental incapacity or disqualification under the statutory provisions. The modern articles also provide for termination on the receipt of notice signed by all the other directors. The vacation of office is automatic,[104] but unless the cause of disqualification is a continuing one, or is bankruptcy, the director may be re-elected.

As far as bankruptcy is concerned, s 11 of the Company Directors Disqualification Act 1986 (consolidating a long-established provision in the companies legislation) provides that it is a criminal offence[105] for an undischarged bankrupt to act as a director of, or directly or indirectly take part in or be concerned in the promotion, formation or management of, a company, without the leave of the court by which he was adjudged bankrupt. In England, the court may not give leave unless notice of the application is served on the Official Receiver, who may attend and oppose it.

The provisions under which directors (and others) may be disqualified from management are considered later in this chapter.

---

[102] There is no equivalent regulation in the model articles for private companies.
[103] See arts 18 and 22 of the model articles for private and public companies, respectively, and reg 81 of the 1985 Table A.
[104] *Re Bodega Co* [1904] 1 Ch 276.
[105] It is an offence of strict liability: *R v Brockley* [1994] 1 BCLC 606 (CA).

15.8 RESIGNATION

Articles usually permit a director to resign.[106] Even in the absence of such a power, unless the articles contain conditions, he may resign, and his resignation is complete when notice is given to the secretary, and cannot subsequently be withdrawn,[107] even though no acceptance has taken place. Notwithstanding that the articles contemplate a written resignation, a verbal notice of resignation given and accepted at a general meeting of the company is binding.[108]

15.9 REMOVAL BY ORDINARY RESOLUTION

Section 168 of the Companies Act 2006 provides that a company may, by ordinary resolution, remove a director before the expiration of his period of office, notwithstanding anything in any agreement between it and him.[109] Even assuming that a director may be entitled, having been removed under s 168, to petition for a just and equitable winding-up on the principles laid down by the House of Lords in *Ebrahimi v Westbourne Galleries Ltd*,[110] this does not affect the validity of the removal under the section and the court will not grant an injunction.[111] The director's only remedy is to petition for a winding-up or, perhaps more likely now, for an order under Part 30.[112]

An important limitation on the effectiveness of s 168 may arise, however, as the result of the decision in *Bushell v Faith*.[113] Here the articles of a private company provided that 'in the event of a resolution being proposed at any general meeting for the removal from office of any director any shares held by that director shall on a poll in respect of such resolution carry the right of three votes per share'. The House of Lords, affirming the Court of Appeal, upheld this provision for weighted voting in resolutions under what is now s 168. The House held that this was not an infringement of the requirement imposed by the provision then in force to the effect that, despite any contrary provision in the articles, any director may be removed by ordinary resolution. As we have seen, this reference to a contrary provision in the articles no longer appears in the

---

[106] See the model articles cited above at footnote 103.

[107] *Maitland's Case* (1853) 4 De GM & G 769. See also *POW Services Ltd v Clare* [1995] 2 BCLC 435.

[108] *Latchford Premier Cinema Ltd v Ennion* [1931] 2 Ch 409.

[109] This provision does not contain the additional point – that this power was not affected by anything in the articles – which was contained in s 303 of the 1985 Act, the provision it replaced. It may be therefore that the articles can exclude s 168, although the better view might be that a company cannot contract out of this statutory power.

[110] [1973] AC 360; see **18.14**.

[111] *Bentley-Stevens v Jones* [1974] 1 WLR 638. *Quaere*, though, whether on exceptional facts if the removal was a breach of a contract with the company, e g between it and a debenture-holder, an injunction might be awarded: see the discussion in **5.15**.

[112] The remedy for 'unfair prejudice', fully discussed in **18.10** *et seq*.

[113] [1970] AC 1099; see *Prentice* (1969) 32 MLR 693.

current section. The following passage[114] from Lord Upjohn's judgment stresses the distinction between voting rights attached to shares and the scope of s 168.

'Parliament has never sought to fetter the right of the company to issue a share with such rights or restrictions as it may think fit. There is no fetter which compels the company to make the voting rights or restrictions of general application and it seems to me clear that such rights or restrictions can be attached to special circumstances and to particular types of resolution. This makes no mockery of section [168]; all that Parliament was seeking to do thereby was to make an ordinary resolution sufficient to remove a director. Had Parliament desired to go further and enact that every share entitled to vote should be deprived of its special rights under the articles it should have said so in plain terms by making the vote on a poll one vote one share.'

Despite the strong dissent by Lord Morris[115] to the effect that this construction made a mockery of what Parliament really intended and that it was once proposed[116] that what is now s 168 would be strengthened to prevent evasion in this manner, there is clearly now no prospect of this being done and an article of the kind considered by the House of Lords arguably is legitimate in the context of small private companies where majority rule may work to the prejudice of a minority shareholder-director.[117]

A resolution to remove a director under this section, or to appoint a director in his place at the meeting at which he is removed, requires special notice;[118] and on receipt of notice of an intended resolution to remove a director under s 168 the company must send a copy to the director, who has then the right to make representations and have them notified to the members: if this is not done, the representations must be read out at the meeting. The obligation of the company to circularise the representations or have them read at the meeting may be avoided by an application to the court if it is satisfied that the right is being abused.[119]

A director removed under the section does not lose any right to compensation or damages he may have for the termination of his appointment as director or of any other appointment (eg that of managing director) which terminates with his directorship.[120]

If the vacancy created by the removal of a director is not filled at the meeting at which he is removed, it may be subsequently filled as a casual vacancy. A person appointed to the vacancy is to be treated, for purposes

---

[114] [1970] AC 1099, at 1109.
[115] Ibid, at 1106.
[116] See the lapsed Companies Bill 1973, cl 44(1).
[117] See the speech of Lord Donovan in [1970] AC 1099 at 1110–11.
[118] As to which see **13.7.7** above.
[119] Section 169.
[120] See **15.5**.

of retirement by rotation or otherwise, as if appointed on the day on which his predecessor was last appointed.[121]

It should be noted that the provisions of the section do not affect or apply to any other power (eg under the articles) to remove a director. Prior to the Companies Act 1948, which first introduced what is now s 168, articles commonly contained a power to remove a director by extraordinary resolution. Although the concept of the extraordinary resolution no longer exists,[122] it may still be advantageous to have a power to remove a director by special resolution, since proceeding under the articles will not involve the complication of special notice or the statutory rights in regard to making representations. It should also be noted that the administrator of a company appointed under Part II of the Insolvency Act 1986[123] has, under s 14(2) of that Act, power to remove any director of the company.

15.10   ALTERNATE DIRECTORS

It is a fairly common practice for the articles to provide for the representation of a director who will be absent from board meetings for a lengthy period by enabling him to appoint an 'alternate' or 'substitute' director. Under the model articles for public companies (regs 26 and 27),[124] an alternate director is regarded as a director 'for all purposes'.

15.11   DIRECTORS' MEETINGS

Directors must obviously decide as a board in respect of the business vested in them by the Companies Act or the articles. The common law has developed a number of rules, in many cases drawing on common-form articles, relating to the conduct of and jurisdiction of directors' meetings. These are examined in the following sections. It is also important to note that the model articles make provisions that in a number of respects go further than those in Table A to the earlier Acts, in particular regarding how decisions can be taken other than at formal meetings, and these are also examined below.

15.11.1   Quorum

The presence of all the directors at a board meeting is not required if, as is usually the case,[125] the articles provide that a specified number of directors shall form a quorum. If a quorum is not so prescribed, a

---

[121] Section 168(3) and (4).
[122] See **13.3**.
[123] See Chapter 21.
[124] There is no provision for alternate directors in the model articles for private companies.
[125] See articles 11 and 10 of the model articles for private and public companies, respectively, and art 89 of the 1985 Table A.

majority of the board is required to attend,[126] unless a quorum can be established by the practice of the board.[127] If the articles so provide, questions may be decided by a majority of the directors present; but where such provision is made and controlling powers are vested in joint governing directors, those powers must be exercised by all of them.[128] If there is a clause in the articles stating that the continuing directors may act notwithstanding vacancies, a number less than the minimum number of directors prescribed by the articles is capable of binding the company.[129] The model articles for private and public companies are to the effect that if the number of directors is below that fixed as the quorum, the continuing directors may act only for the purpose of appointing further directors or of summoning a general meeting.[130] In reckoning a quorum, directors not entitled to vote (eg as being interested in the contract under discussion) must not be counted.[131]

15.11.2   Notice

Notice of the meeting must be given to all the directors, for business done at a meeting of which some directors had no notice is invalid even though the latter are in a minority. A director has no power to waive his right to notice,[132] but if a director is abroad and out of reach of notices, a meeting held without notice to him is valid.[133] There is a conflict of judicial opinion as to whether it is necessary to give notice of a board meeting to a director who, under the articles, has no vote thereat: for example an ordinary director, when all the powers of the directors are vested in permanent directors.[134] The notice may be a very short one; even a few minutes' notice will suffice if the director can attend, and where he objects to the shortness of the notice he should make his objection at once, or will not prevail.[135] A verbal notice is also sufficient.[136] It is not necessary that

---

[126]   *York Tramways Co v Willows* (1882) 8 QBD 685.

[127]   *Re Regent's Canal Ironworks* [1867] WN 79; *Lyster's Case* (1867) LR 4 EQ 233.

[128]   *Perrott & Perrott Ltd v Stephenson* [1934] Ch 171. But see *Bersel Manufacturing Co v Berry Ltd* [1968] 2 All ER 552 (HL) where a husband and wife were the two permanent life directors who had the power under the articles to terminate the directorship of the ordinary directors. It was held, on the construction of the article in question, that the power was exercisable by the husband after the wife's death.

[129]   *Re Scottish Petroleum Co* (1883) 23 Ch D 413 (CA).

[130]   See art 11 in both sets of model articles; see also art 90 of the 1985 Table A.

[131]   *Yuill v Greymouth-Point Elizabeth Rly* [1904] 1 Ch 32; *Victors v Lingard* [1927] 1 Ch 323; *Re Cleadon Trust* [1939] Ch 286 (CA). See further, **16.8** as to this and the relevant provisions of the model articles.

[132]   *Re Portuguese Copper Mines* (1889) 42 Ch D 160 (CA); *Young v Ladies Imperial Club* [1920] 2 KB 523 (CA).

[133]   *Halifax Sugar Refining Co Ltd v Franklyn* (1890) 59 LJ Ch 591. However, there must still be a quorum: *Davidson and Begg Antiques Ltd v Davidson* [1997] BCC 77. The provisions regarding notice of directors' meetings in the model articles are art 9 for private and art 8 for public companies.

[134]   *John Shaw & Sons (Salford) v Shaw* [1935] 2 KB 113; per Greer LJ at 133 and per Slesser LJ at 138–41 (CA).

[135]   *Browne v La Trinidad* (1888) 37 Ch D 1 at 9 (CA).

[136]   *La Compagnie de Mayville v Whitley* [1896] 1 Ch 788 (CA).

the notice should state what business is to be transacted, unless the articles provide otherwise or require that certain business shall only be transacted at a meeting specially convened for that purpose, in which case the notice must sufficiently indicate the business to be considered.[137] A casual meeting of the two directors, even at the company's office, cannot be converted into a board meeting if one of them denies that it is a board meeting and has not received notice calling such a meeting.[138]

Articles[139] usually declare that the chairman shall have a casting vote in case of the directors being equally divided upon any question.[140]

15.11.3   Directors' decision-making under the model articles

It was noted above that the model articles produced for both private and public companies contain rather more in the way of provisions regarding decision-making by directors than their predecessors and this section gives an outline of these provisions. The fact that these are 'default rules' rather than in any sense mandatory, reflects the permissive nature of this aspect of British company law noted at the beginning of this chapter. The provisions differ in important respects as between private and public companies and this account will treat them separately, but they share a common feature in that they both recognise that directors may not actually meet in person, but can do so by means such as telephone conference calls or electronic means.

As far as private companies are concerned, the general rule about decision-making by directors is that any decision of theirs must be either a majority decision at a meeting or a unanimous decision under art 8.[141] Reflecting the fact that private company directors do not in practice always hold formal meetings, art 8 states that a unanimous decision is taken when all eligible directors indicate to each other by any means that they share a common view on a matter and may take the form of a resolution in writing, copies of which have been signed by each director or to which each eligible director has otherwise indicated agreement in writing.[142] Articles 9–13 provide for how a directors' meeting is to be called, how directors participate (which clearly does not require them to

---

[137]   *Young v Ladies' Imperial Club* [1920] 2 KB 523 (CA).

[138]   *Barron v Potter* [1914] 1 Ch 895.

[139]   See arts 13 and 14 of the model articles for private and public companies, respectively, and reg 88 in the 1985 Table A.

[140]   But this does not validate the casting vote of an improperly appointed chairman: *Clark v Workman* [1920] IR R 107.

[141]   Article 7; obviously this does not apply where the company legitimately has only one director; see art 7(2).

[142]   Note that the rules here are more formal than those proposed in earlier drafts of the model articles, which would have allowed majority decisions to be taken outside formal meetings. There is nothing, though, to prevent private companies having such provisions in their own special articles.

be in the same place),[143] the quorum for such a meeting, the chairing of such a meeting and the casting vote given, if necessary, to the chair of the meeting.

As far as public companies are concerned, decisions of directors must be taken either at a directors' meeting or in the form of a directors' written resolution,[144] but a directors' meeting can take place whenever the directors can communicate any information or opinions they have, regardless of where any director is or how they communicate.[145] Articles 17 and 18 deal with written resolutions, which any director may propose[146] by giving notice to the directors,[147] which must indicate the proposed resolution and the time by which it is proposed that the directors should adopt it. The notice must be in writing. A written resolution must be adopted unanimously by all the directors who would have been entitled to vote on it at a meeting, provided that they would have formed a quorum at such a meeting.

15.11.4   Minutes of directors' meetings

Minutes must be recorded of all proceedings at meetings of directors and kept for at least 10 years from the date of the meeting.[148] Minutes duly recorded[149] or purporting to be authenticated by the chairman of that or the next meeting, are evidence of the proceedings. Where minutes have been made in accordance with the section, then, until the contrary is proved, the meeting is deemed duly held and convened, all proceedings are deemed to have duly taken place, and all appointments at the meeting are deemed valid.[150]

The adoption of minutes at a subsequent meeting of directors does not make those taking part in such adoption responsible for the acts of the earlier meeting if such acts were complete before the minutes came up for consideration.[151]

---

[143]   See art 10(2) and (3).
[144]   Article 7.
[145]   Article 9.
[146]   Article 17(6) states that any decision by a proposer regarding the process of adopting the resolution must be taken reasonably in good faith, which seems somewhat superfluous as their general duties would require this in any event.
[147]   The company secretary must do so if a director so requests.
[148]   Companies Act 2006, s 248 [CA 1985, s 382].
[149]   As to company records, see ss 1134 and 1135.
[150]   Section 249.
[151]   *Re Lands Allotment Co* [1894] 1 Ch 616 at 634 (CA).

15.12   A DIRECTOR'S RIGHT TO INSPECT COMPANY BOOKS

A director has the right to inspect the company's books either at a board meeting or elsewhere. This right extends both to the minutes of directors' meetings,[152] and to the company's accounting records,[153] but the court has a discretion as to whether or not to order an inspection, the right to which is conferred on a director not for his own advantage but to enable him to carry out his duties as a director.[154]

15.13   DELEGATION AND THE VALIDITY OF DIRECTORS' ACTS

If the articles authorise it, but not otherwise,[155] the board may delegate any of its powers to a committee, which may consist even of a single director,[156] but the board does not by making such delegation lose its power to act in the matter,[157] and the board cannot deprive itself of power to control the company's business.[158] In practice the articles will confer wide powers of delegation on the directors,[159] but without this, and subject to the application of general agency principles,[160] each director has not by himself power to bind the company. By s 280 of the Companies Act 2006,[161] a provision requiring or authorising a thing to be done by or to a director and the secretary is not satisfied by its being done by or to the same person acting both as director and as, or in place of, the secretary.

As seen above, articles may provide that a resolution in writing signed by all the directors has the same effect as a resolution passed at a meeting of the board. There is authority for the proposition that, in the absence of such a provision, directors can act unanimously but informally,[162] but

---

[152] See *McCusker v McRae* 1966 SC 253. Note that the Scottish court held that the director was entitled to be accompanied by an adviser of his choice. English authorities (see below), which established the directors' right to inspect accounting records, do not discuss that point.

[153] Companies Act 2006, s 388; *Burn v London and South Wales Coal Co* [1890] WN 209.

[154] *Conway v Petronius Clothing Co* [1978] 1 WLR 72. Here an immediate order was refused because misconduct was alleged against the two plaintiff directors and a meeting to consider their removal was held. This decision was followed in *Oxford Legal Group Ltd v Sibbasbridge Services plc* [2008] EWCA Civ 387, [2008] 2 BCLC 381.

[155] *Howard's Case* (1886) 1 Ch App 561.

[156] *Re Taurine Co* (1884) 25 Ch D 118 (CA).

[157] *Huth v Clarke* (1890) 25 QBD 391.

[158] *Horn v Faulder & Co* (1908) 99 LT 524.

[159] See art 5 of the model articles for both private and public companies and reg 72 in the 1985 Table A.

[160] As to these, see Chapter 6.

[161] [CA 1985, s 284.]

[162] See *Collie's Claim* (1871) LR 12 Eq 246 at 258; *Bolton Engineering Ltd v T J Graham & Sons Ltd* [1957] 1 QB 159. Cf other decisions which hold the contrary (*D'Arcy v Tamar Hill Railway Co* (1867) LR 2 Ex 158; *Re Haycraft Gold Reduction Co* [1900] 2 Ch 230;

where only a majority of the directors give their oral assent informally (and there is no relevant article), such assent does not amount to a valid resolution.[163] However, this defect can be cured by a subsequent resolution at a board meeting which may take the form of authorising the chairman to sign minutes which record that a particular resolution has been passed.[164] Articles like the model ones[165] are intended to be used on occasions when a directors' meeting is not necessary. They are not intended to allow directors to avoid the requirements of a quorum by passing resolutions when other directors have left the country and are therefore not entitled to notice of meetings.[166]

The directors must not exclude any of their body from their meetings, and unless the company has by resolution declared that it does not desire a director to act,[167] an excluded director can obtain an injunction restraining his continued exclusion.[168]

The directors are the proper persons to perform any act in the name of the company, and in particular to commence legal proceedings in the name of the company,[169] to make contracts, and to affix the seal of the company to deeds.

15.14   THE REGISTERS OF DIRECTORS AND OF DIRECTORS' RESIDENTIAL ADDRESSES

Under s 162 of the Companies Act 2006,[170] every company is required to keep a register of its directors, and by s 167 it must file notice of any changes therein or in the register of residential addresses described below with the registrar within 14 days.[171] The register must be kept available for inspection, at the registered office or a place specified in regulations under s 1136,[172] by any member of the company without charge, and of any

---

Re Homer District Gold Mines (1888) 39 Ch D 546 (CA)), but in these cases there was no unanimous agreement, only the informal consensus of a quorum.

[163] *Municipal Mutual Insurance Ltd v Harrop* [1998] 2 BCLC 540, at 551.

[164] Ibid at 551–3, applying *Re Portuguese Consolidated Copper Mines Ltd* (1890) 45 Ch D 16.

[165] See footnote 147.

[166] *Hood Sailmakers Ltd v Adford and Bainbridge* [1996] 4 All ER 830; *Davidson & Begg Antiques Ltd v Davidson 1997 SLT 301,* [1997] BCC 77.

[167] *Bainbridge v Smith* (1889) 41 Ch D 462 at 474 (CA); *Harben v Phillips* (1883) 23 Ch D 14 at 40 (CA).

[168] *Pullbrook v Richmond Consolidated Mining Co* (1878) 9 Ch D 610; *Hayes v Bristol Plant Hire Ltd* [1957] 1 WLR 499; *Choudhury v Bhattar* [2009] EWHC 314 (Ch), [2009] 2 BCLC 108.

[169] See further **15.15**.

[170] [CA 1985, s 288.]

[171] Any notification of a change must contain a signed consent to act by the new director. Any change must also be publicly notified under ss 1077 and 1078.

[172] The regulations (the Companies (Company Records) Regulations 2008, SI 2008/3006, reg 3) require a single alternative inspection location, which must be in the part of the UK in which the company is registered and have been notified to the registrar.

other person on payment of the prescribed fee.[173] If inspection of the register is refused, the court may by order compel an immediate inspection of it.[174]

Under s 163, the register must contain the following particulars in the case of an individual: his name,[175] any former name,[176] a service address, the country or state (or part of the UK) in which he is usually resident, his nationality, his business occupation (if any) and his date of birth. The service address may be stated as 'the company's registered office'. In the case of a corporation, s 164 requires the register to give its corporate or firm name and registered or principal office.[177]

The requirement in respect of a service address replaced the former requirement to state a director's residential address, because of concerns that directors of certain companies, especially those involved in high-profile activities such as animal testing, were open to targeting by activists. However, a new obligation on a company to keep a register of directors' residential addresses is imposed by s 165 of the 2006 Act, on pain of a criminal penalty being imposed on the company and every officer in default. This register must state the usual residential address of each of the company's directors, except that, if the service address in the register of directors is not the company's registered office and is the same as his usual residential address, this register need only contain an entry to that effect.[178]

15.14.1   Non-disclosure of directors' residential addresses

In addition to keeping a director's residential address off the company's register of directors, the 2006 Act also introduced further provisions allowing for the general non-disclosure of their residential addresses, for the same purposes as mentioned above. For these purposes, s 240 defines 'protected information' as an individual director's usual residential address and, where relevant, the information that his service address is his usual residential address. This information remains protected even when someone ceases to be a director. Except with his consent, and in order to communicate with the director, in order to comply with any requirement to file particulars under s 167 or in accordance with a court order under s 244, a company must not use or disclose such protected information.

---

[173] Section 162(3) and (5).

[174] Section 162(8). As to the penalties for breach of s 162, see s 162(6) and (7).

[175] 'Name' throughout the section means Christian or other forename and surname, with qualifications regarding titles: see s 163(2).

[176] See s 163(3) and (4).

[177] Together with the information required by s 164(c) or (d).

[178] The Secretary of State has power to make regulations, subject to the affirmative resolution procedure, that add or remove items from the particulars that have to be entered in a company's register of directors or its register of directors' residential addresses: s 166.

Because a director's usual residential address will still be filed with the registrar, s 242 provides for that to remain protected. The registrar is under a duty to omit protected information from the material available for inspection where it is filed in a document (or part of a document) that requires it to be stated, but he is not obliged to check other documents (or parts thereof) to ensure the absence of such information. Further, he is not obliged to remove from public disclosure anything filed before these sections of the 2006 Act come into force.[179] In addition there are three sets of circumstance when a usual residential address may cease to be protected to a greater or lesser degree.

The first of these is that under s 243, the registrar may use protected information for communicating with the director in question and may disclose such information to a public authority specified in regulations or to a credit reference agency.[180] Secondly, s 244 provides for a liquidator, creditor or member of the company, or any other person appearing to the court to have a sufficient interest, to apply to the court for an order for disclosure of protected information. Such an order may be made for disclosure by the company or by the registrar, but only against the latter if the company does not have the director's usual residential address or has been dissolved, if either there is evidence that service of documents at a service address other than the director's usual residential address is not effective to bring them to the notice of the director or it is necessary or expedient for the information to be provided in connection with the enforcement of an order or decree of the court, and the court is otherwise satisfied that it is appropriate to make the order. The order must specify the persons to whom, and purposes for which, disclosure is authorised.

Thirdly, ss 245 and 246 specify the circumstances and method in which the registrar may put a director's usual residential address on the public record. This is when either communications sent by the registrar to the director requiring an answer within a specified period remain unanswered or there is evidence that service of documents at a service address is not effective to bring them to the notice of the director. In this second respect, the registrar can act therefore without an application by a liquidator, creditor or member to the court under s 244. If he proposes to do so, the registrar must give notice to the director and every company of which he has been notified that the individual is a director stating the grounds for the proposal and specifying a period for representations to be made before the proposal is effected. The notice must be sent to the director at his

---

[179] 1 October 2009; in these cases the regime in ss 723B–723E of the 1985 Act will continue to apply. These provisions allowed a director to apply for a 'confidentiality order'. A director with such an order provided a single service address in addition to his usual residential address. The service address was entered on the public record; the usual residential address was kept on a secure register to which access was restricted to specified enforcement authorities.

[180] 'Public authority' includes any person or body having functions of a public nature. 'Credit reference agency' is defined in s 243(4) in a standard way. The detail is prescribed in the Companies (Disclosure of Address) Regulations 2009, SI 2009/214.

usual residential address, unless it appears to the registrar that this may be ineffective, in which case it may be sent to any service address provided in place of the residential address.

Putting a director's usual residential address on the public record involves the registrar in the same procedure as if notice of a change of registered particulars had been given stating that address as the director's service address and stating that the director's usual residential address is the same as his service address.[181] The registrar must give notice of having done so to the director and to the company, which must enter the director's usual residential address in its register of directors as his service address and state in the register of directors' residential addresses that his usual residential address is the same as his service address. If, however, the company has been notified by the director of a change of address, it must enter that address in its register of directors as the director's service address and give notice to the registrar. Once a director's usual residential address has been put on the public record under s 246, a director cannot register a different service address for five years from the registrar's decision.

15.15 THE RELATIONSHIP BETWEEN BOARD AND GENERAL MEETING

The important question whether the company in general meeting has any power to direct the directors in their management of the company's business is one that has been much discussed over the years. The answer depends upon the construction of the appropriate article of association vesting powers of management in the directors.[182] It has long been established that, in principle, it is perfectly acceptable for the board to have powers quite free from interference by the shareholders. Thus the court has refused to allow the general meeting to take the conduct of the business out of the directors' hands, or to compel them to adopt a particular line of action, such as sealing a draft deed or effecting a sale of the company's property,[183] or discontinuing legal proceedings commenced in the name of the company on the instructions of the board,[184] or to interfere in the exercise of the directors' power to appoint a managing director.[185] In most of these cases, the article in question was based on the standard article in Table A, which in the 1948 Act was art 80, and this was

---

[181] Section 246.

[182] There is no doubt in law that this 'contract-based' view is the correct one. Whether it should be or not is another matter.

[183] *Automatic Self-Cleansing Filter Co v Cunninghame* [1906] 2 Ch 34 (CA); *Gramophone and Typewriter v Stanley* [1908] 2 KB 89 at 105 (CA); *Salmon v Quin & Axtens Ltd* [1906] AC 442 (HL).

[184] *John Shaw & Sons (Salford) Ltd v Shaw* [1935] 2 KB 113 (CA); *Scott v Scott* [1943] 1 All ER 582 (CA); cf *Marshall's Valve Gear Co v Manning, Wardle & Co* [1909] 1 Ch 267, which may be explained as authorising the shareholders to commence proceedings when the board refuses to do so.

[185] *Thomas Logan v Davis* (1911) 104 LT 914, 105 LT 419.

generally thought to permit interference only by special resolution. However, the wording of articles based on art 80 was not free from difficulty,[186] one particularly contentious area concerning the question of the use of the company's name in litigation.[187]

While companies registered prior to 1 July 1985 adopting this part of Table A will continue to have art 80 as their regulation in this respect, unless and until they amend their articles appropriately, the matter was clarified in respect of companies which adopted Table A to the 1985 Act.[188] Article 70 of this Table A makes it clear that, subject to the provisions of the Act and to any special provisions in a company's memorandum or articles, the general meeting can interfere only by 'any directions given by special resolution' and further that no such direction (or alteration of the memorandum or articles) can operate retrospectively to validate any prior act of the directors. Further, the model articles prescribed under the 2006 Act for both private and public companies are to the same effect. Article 3 in both sets of model articles provides that, subject to the articles, the directors are responsible for the management of the company's business, for which purposes they may exercise all the powers of the company, and art 4 provides that the shareholders may, by special resolution, direct the directors to take, or refrain from taking, specified action.[189]

However, if the directors are unable or unwilling to exercise the powers conferred upon them, whether by reason of there being no independent quorum or by reason of disputes among the directors, the company in general meeting can perform the duties which the directors fail to carry out.[190] In addition, the general meeting has wide powers to ratify an

---

[186] It conferred on the directors 'all such powers of the company as are not by [the legislation] or by these regulations, required to be exercised by the company in general meeting, subject, nevertheless, to any of these regulations, to the provisions of the [legislation] and to *such regulations, being not inconsistent with the aforesaid regulations or provisions, as may be prescribed by the company in general meeting*' (emphasis added). The judicial construction put on the word 'regulations' was that throughout art 80 it meant 'articles' or 'new or amended articles', but this made the passage in italics somewhat tautologous and led certain writers to take a different view as to its meaning: see, especially, Goldberg, (1970) 33 MLR 177, and Sullivan 93 LQR 569 (1977). In *Beckland Group Holdings Ltd v London & Suffolk Properties Ltd* (1988) 4 BCC 542, Harman J ignored these difficulties.

[187] In *Marshall's Valve Gear Co v Manning, Wardle & Co* [1909] 1 Ch 267, it was held that the majority shareholder had the right to commence proceedings in the company's name, even where general management powers were vested in the directors. While this right has been confirmed in situations of deadlock or where there are no directors (see *Alexander Ward v Samyang, Navigation Co*, below, and *Re Argentum Reductions (UK) Ltd* [1975] 1 WLR 191), it was totally swept aside in the *Breckland Group Holdings* case, above. See further Wedderburn (1976) 39 MLR 327 and (1989) 52 MLR 401. The power to order the commencement of proceedings must be exercised by the board as a whole: *Mitchell & Hobbs (UK) Ltd v Mill* [1996] 2 BCLC 102.

[188] Ie in the Companies (Table A to F) Regulations 1985.

[189] This does not invalidate anything the directors have already done.

[190] *Barron v Potter* [1914] 1 Ch 895; *Foster v Foster* [1916] 1 Ch 532.

excess of power by directors, ie an act beyond the authority vested in the directors under the articles,[191] or to ratify or cure an abuse of power by directors, ie an act in breach of duty though not necessarily beyond the directors' powers.[192]

Further, the House of Lords has held that the absence of validly appointed directors does not prevent a company taking proceedings to recover its debts.[193] Lord Kilbrandon said this about an article similar to the standard form articles described in respect of the management of the company's business:

> 'I think the article probably means no more than this, that the directors, and no one else, are responsible for the management of the company, except in the matters specifically allotted to the company in general meeting. This is a term of the contract between the shareholders and the company. But it does not mean that no act of management, such as instructing the company's solicitor, can validly be performed without the personal and explicit authority of the directors themselves.'[194]

The standard articles are concerned with the board's powers of *management*. Thus they do not, for example, confer authority on a board to present a winding-up petition[195] or to apply to set aside an order restoring the company's name to the register.[196]

The court can appoint a receiver and manager where the company is in a condition in which there is no properly constituted governing body, or there is such dissension in the governing body that it is impossible to carry on the business with advantage to the parties interested. Such an appointment would be made for only a limited time, ie until a meeting of the company could be held and a governing body appointed.[197]

15.16 THE OFFICERS OF A COMPANY

For the purposes of the Companies Acts, 'officer' includes a director, manager or secretary.[198] The position of directors in general has already been discussed; the position of the other usual officers of a company will now be dealt with.[199] The terms of their employment depend upon their

---

[191] *Irvine v Union Bank of Australia* (1877) 2 App Cas 366.
[192] See **17.9.1** as to which breaches of duty are ratifiable.
[193] *Alexander Ward v Samyang Navigation Co* [1975] 1 WLR 673.
[194] Ibid, at 683.
[195] *Re Emmadart Ltd* [1979] Ch 540. But this power is now conferred by s 124(1) of the Insolvency Act 1986.
[196] *Re Regent Insulation Co Ltd* (1981) *The Times*, 5 November.
[197] *Featherstone v Cooke* (1873) LR 16 Eq 298.
[198] Section 1173(1).
[199] The auditor may or may not be an 'officer'. As to him, see **14.28**.

contract, whether written or verbal, with the company, although the position of a managing director may in some respects be governed by the articles.[200]

15.16.1   The manager or managing director

Most companies, even small private companies, are actually managed on a day-to-day basis by one or more people who will be described as 'managing director' or 'chief executive'. Perhaps surprisingly, the general law is that the directors cannot appoint one of themselves to an office of profit or delegate power to a managing director unless expressly empowered by the articles or by a resolution of the company.[201] It has long therefore been usual to insert in the articles power for the directors to appoint one or more of their body to be managing director or directors, and to pay him or them special remuneration, delegating to him or them such powers as are necessary.[202] The model articles prescribed under the 2006 Act do not actually do this specifically, rather allowing for delegation and remuneration in more general terms.[203] Modern practice, at least in the case of larger companies, is to call such a person the 'chief executive', but neither this terminology nor the more traditional 'managing director' is reflected in the Companies Act or the modern articles.

Articles that allow delegation do not, however, permit revocation of the appointment.[204] It has been held that a managing director has no power, under the standard provisions, to commence proceedings on behalf of the company. Delegation to him of such a power by the board is not presumed by the mere fact of his appointment as a managing director.[205] A managing or other executive director may not be subject to retirement by rotation.[206] If a managing director is removed from his office of managing director, where the articles permit the directors to do this,[207] or from his directorship by the company in general meeting,[208] before the

---

[200] A mere statement in the articles that someone shall be secretary, manager or other officer is not a contract with that person: *Eley v Positive Government Assurance Co* (1876) 1 Ex D 88 (CA); *Browne v La Trinidad* (1888) 37 Ch D 1 (CA); see **5.21**.

[201] *Boschoek Proprietary Co v Fuke* [1906] 1 Ch 148, at 159; *Nelson v James Nelson & Sons* [1914] 2 KB 770, at 779 (CA).

[202] Such a power is conferred by the 1985 Table A, regs 72 and 84.

[203] See the articles referred to in **15.11.3**.

[204] Cf reg 107 of Table A to the Companies Act 1948.

[205] *Mitchell & Hobbs (UK) Ltd v Mills* [1996] 2 BCLC 102 at 107–108.

[206] See reg 84 of the 1985 Table A. However, the model articles for public companies do not exclude a managing director from retirement by rotation and in this case a managing director not reappointed by the general meeting will lose his office even though it was expressed to be appointed for a term of years: *Bluett v Stutchbury's* (1908) 24 TLR 469 (CA).

[207] As under reg 107 of the 1948 Table A, but not under modern model articles.

[208] Under s 168; see **15.9**.

expiry of the term of his contract of service, the removal is valid, but he will have a claim to damages for breach of contract if he complied with his part of the bargain.[209]

There is very little case-law as to the nature of the relationship between the board and a managing or other executive director. In *Harold Holdsworth & Co (Wakefield) Ltd v Caddies*,[210] the House of Lords held that the board of Holdsworth were entitled to direct Caddies to confine his attention to a subsidiary company. Under his contract of employment, Caddies had been appointed a managing director of Holdsworth itself. The contract provided that he should perform the duties and exercise the powers in relation to the business of the company and the business of its existing subsidiaries 'which may from time to time be assigned to or vested in him by the board of directors of the company'. Up until the time when a dispute arose between Caddies and his fellow directors, he had managed Holdsworth itself and a subsidiary of it. The decision of the House of Lords (that Caddies could be so demoted without a breach of his contract of employment) turned on the particular wording of his contract. This conferred a discretion on the board as to the mode or extent of his employment in managing the company and any of its subsidiaries. Thus under the more usual terms of employment of a managing director this option would not be available to the board without committing a breach of contract.[211]

Therefore the exact status and powers of a managing director depend both upon the articles which confer a power on the board to appoint a managing director and upon the terms of the contract by which he is employed. Although he must be a director, his status as managing director derives from his appointment by the board to this office. He is thus both a director and, as managing director, an employee of the company.[212]

---

[209] *Nelson v James Nelson & Sons* [1914] 2 KB 770 (CA); see **15.5**. An appointment for an indeterminate period may be determined, however, at any time, without the company being liable for breach of contract: *Foster v Foster* [1916] 1 Ch 532.

[210] [1955] 1 WLR 352 (HL).

[211] See also *Yetton v Eastwoods Froy* [1967] 1 WLR 104, where a managing director was dismissed and then offered the position of assistant managing director at the same salary; he was held entitled to refuse the offer because of the loss of status involved.

[212] See *Anderson v James Sutherland (Peterhead) Ltd* 1941 SC 203, where Lord Carmont relied upon *Southern Foundries Ltd v Shirlaw* [1940] AC 701 (HL) and *Fowler v Commercial Timber Co* [1903] 3 KB 1. See also *Trussed Steel Concrete v Green* [1946] Ch 115; *Lee v Lees Air Farming Ltd* [1961] AC 12 (PC); *Boulting v ACTAT* [1963] QB 600 (CA). Although a managing director was held (*Re Newspaper Proprietary Syndicate Ltd* [1900] 2 Ch 349) not to be a 'clerk' or 'servant' when these were the relevant persons described as preferential creditors on a winding-up in the former legislation (consolidated in Sch 19 to the Companies Act 1985), the appropriate legislation now (Sch 6, para 9 to the Insolvency Act 1986) refers simply to 'employee' and there seems no reason why this should not include a managing director. As to preferential debts, see **21.51.1**.

15.16.2 The secretary

The secretary is the other important officer of a company. Every public company must have a secretary.[213] Despite the recommendation of the Company Law Review, which was supported initially by the Government, that the position of secretary be abolished for private companies, the 2006 Act ultimately provides only that a private company is not required to have a secretary.[214] It is likely that at least larger private companies will retain the office, but in the case of a private company without a secretary, anything authorised or required to be given or sent to, or served on, the company by being sent to its secretary may be given or sent to, or served on, the company itself and, if addressed to the secretary, shall be treated as addressed to the company, and anything else required or authorised to be done by or to the secretary may be done by or to a director or a person authorised generally or specifically in that behalf by the directors.[215] However, if at any time the office of secretary is vacant, or there is no secretary capable of acting, his functions may be carried out by any assistant or deputy secretary or, if there is no such, by someone duly authorised by the directors.[216]

The importance of the office of secretary is recognised by the fact that secretaries of public companies must since 1980 have been qualified. Under s 273, it is the duty of the directors of a public company to take all reasonable steps to secure that the secretary is a person who appears to them to have the requisite knowledge and experience to discharge the functions of secretary, and such a person must have one of several possible types of experience or professional qualification. The professional qualifications include chartered secretaryship, accountancy and the legal profession. Sufficient experience is provided by the person having been secretary of a public company for at least 3 of the previous five years or, by virtue of his holding or having held any other position, or his being a member of any other body, by his appearing to the directors capable of discharging the function of secretary.[217] In addition, the Secretary of State has power to direct a public company to appoint a secretary.[218]

Case-law has also recognised the important position that the secretary holds in respect of a company's administrative affairs.[219] He is wholly or

---

[213] Companies Act 2006, s 271. Particulars of the secretary must be notified to the registrar: see **15.16.3**.

[214] Section 270.

[215] Section 270(3). This will cover, for example, requirements in the articles or in a contract between the company and a third party.

[216] Section 274.

[217] The last qualification by experience is rather odd, since it seems to negate the general purpose of s 273.

[218] Section 272.

[219] *Panorama Developments (Guildford) Ltd v Fidelis Furnishing Fabrics Ltd* [1971] 2 QB 711 (CA); the company was held liable to pay car hire charges incurred by the secretary

partly responsible for the accuracy of documents lodged with the registrar, and if the company defaults in this respect, the liability to a fine is almost invariably incurred by the secretary. He is the agent through whom the clerical work of the company is done. He must obey the orders of the directors and give effect to their resolutions by issuing notices, sending circulars, writing letters, etc. He will also prepare the agenda for directors' meetings and general meetings, and usually write up the minutes, either from his own notes or from those of the chairman.[220]

15.16.3   The register of secretaries

Any company that has a secretary must keep a register of secretaries containing the following particulars with respect to the secretary or where there are joint secretaries, with respect to each of them: (a) in the case of an individual, his present name, any former name and his address; and (b) in the case of a corporation or a Scottish firm, its corporate or firm name and registered or principal office. Where all the partners in a firm are joint secretaries, the name and principal office of the firm may be stated.[221] The address is a service address, which may be 'the company's registered office'. The detailed requirements as regards inspection and filing with the registrar mirror those applying to the register of directors, as described in **15.13**.

15.17   DISQUALIFICATION AND OTHER SANCTIONS AGAINST MISCREANT DIRECTORS AND OTHERS INVOLVED IN COMPANY MANAGEMENT

Legislation contains various provisions under which directors and others may be disqualified from office or subjected to personal liability for the debts of their companies or under which other forms of sanction may be imposed.[222] These are essentially aimed at situations where the privileges of corporate personality and limited liability have been abused. The provisions are a mixture of ones which have existed for some years and ones which were introduced relatively recently.[223] Others were first introduced by the Insolvency Act 1985.[224] They are now all consolidated in the Company Directors Disqualification Act 1986 and the Insolvency Act 1986, as amended.

---

in the company's name but where the cars were fraudulently used by the secretary for his own pleasure, on the ground that the hiring fell within the apparent authority of a company secretary; see **6.17**.

[220] For more detail as to the secretary's functions, see *Gore-Browne on Companies* (Jordans, 45th edn, loose-leaf) at 14[10].

[221] Companies Act 2006, ss 277–279 [CA 1985, s 290].

[222] In addition to those reviewed here, see also **4.22.5**.

[223] In the Companies Acts 1976 and 1981.

[224] There was a considerable amount of controversy surrounding these. Originally, the Government introduced provisions providing for the automatic disqualification of directors of insolvent companies, with the onus on such directors to prove to the court

The legislation has spawned a vast amount of case-law and continuing government attempts to enforce the provisions, but an important survey[225] which looked particularly at disqualifications for unfitness[226] concluded that the disqualification of directors of small companies, which is where the provisions have been most used, is a very costly and not particularly effective way of dealing with abuses of limited liability. This aim would be better achieved by providing an alternative business form for the small business.[227] It was suggested that the most effective policy would be to pursue unfit directors of larger companies.[228]

15.18 DISQUALIFICATION OF DIRECTORS AND OTHERS

The powers of the court to make disqualification orders[229] are contained in the Company Directors Disqualification Act 1986 and the statutory references in this and the following sections are to that Act.[230]

15.18.1 The meaning of disqualification

'Disqualification order' is defined as follows.[231] It is an order that a person shall not, without leave of the court,[232] be a director of a company, or a liquidator or administrator of a company, or a receiver or manager of a

---

the reason why they should not be disqualified. These were based on, but not identical to, proposals recommended by the Review Committee on Insolvency Law and Practice (the Cork Committee), Cmnd 8558 (1982), Chapter 45. Opposition from such influential bodies as the CBI and the Institute of Directors, as well as in Parliament, led to the dropping of these provisions and their replacement by the provision relating to 'unfitness' described in **15.8.3**.

225 Andrew Hicks *Disqualification of Directors: No Hiding Place for the Unfit?*, ACCA Research Report 59, 1998.

226 See **15.18.4**.

227 There is clearly no prospect of this happening, as the Company Law Review and the Government were both clearly of the view that the free availability of the limited company form should remain and indeed, one of the key aims of the Companies Act 2006 was de-regulation for small companies.

228 For a review of the DTI's exercise of their powers, see the report of the National Audit Office, *Company Director Disqualification – a Follow-up Report*, HC424, May 1999.

229 As to the nature of disqualification proceedings regarding admissible evidence, the applicability of natural justice, and other procedural matters, see *Re Churchill Hotel (Plymouth) Ltd* [1988] BCLC 341; *Re Rex Williams Leisure plc* [1993] BCLC 568; *Re Polly Peck International plc* [1993] BCLC 886; *Re Moonbeam Cards Ltd* [1993] BCLC 1099; *Re Polly Peck International plc* [1994] BCC 15. See *Gore-Browne on Companies* (Jordans, 45th edn, loose-leaf) at 20[28] for detailed consideration of these and other cases. As to the impact of the European Human Rights Convention on disqualification proceedings, see *EDC v United Kingdom* [1998] BCC 370, *R v Secretary of State for Trade and Industry, ex parte McCormick* [1998] BCC 379 (CA), *Re Westminster Property Management Ltd, Official Receiver v Stern* [2000] 2 BCLC 396 (CA) and the discussion in *Gore-Browne on Companies* (Jordans, 45th edn, loose-leaf) at 20[39].

230 See generally, Dine (1991) 12 Co Law 6, [1994] JBL 325.

231 Section 1, as amended by s 5 of the Insolvency Act 2000.

232 Applications for leave are governed by s 17; the case-law relevant thereto is examined in *Gore-Browne on Companies*, 20[38].

company's property, in any way, whether directly or indirectly, be concerned or take part in the promotion, formation or management of a company, or act as an insolvency practitioner, for a specified period beginning with the date of the order. Being concerned or taking part in management has been widely construed to cover the position of management consultant or the giving of advice on the financial management and reconstruction of a company.[233]

The various sections provide for maximum penalties of five years' disqualification in respect of persistent default (see below) and in all disqualifications by courts of summary jurisdiction, and of 15 years in any other case. 'Tariffs' have been established, particularly for disqualification on the ground of unfitness, so that there are three 'brackets': ten or more years for serious cases, six to ten years for middling cases, and two to five years for minor cases.[234] The period of any subsequent disqualification imposed against a person already subject to an order runs concurrently with the existing period.[235] An order may be made on grounds which are or include matters other than criminal convictions, notwithstanding that the person in question may be criminally liable in respect of those matters.[236] There are heavy penalties for breach of a disqualification order.[237]

15.18.2   Application for disqualification

An application to a court with jurisdiction to wind up companies to obtain a disqualification order under ss 2 to 5 may be made by the Secretary of State or the Official Receiver, or the liquidator or any past or present member or creditor of any company in relation to which the person in question has committed or is alleged to have committed an offence or default.[238] In respect of disqualification on the ground of unfitness, only the Secretary of State, or the Official Receiver acting under the direction of the Secretary of State, has *locus standi* to apply.[239]

---

[233] *R v Campbell* [1984] BCLC 83. An order cannot be restricted to the holding of a directorship in a public company: *R v Ward; R v Howarth* [2001] EWCA Crim 1648, [2002] BCC 953.

[234] See eg *Re Sevenoaks Stationers (Retail) Ltd* [1991] BCLC 325 and *Re Westmid Packing Services Ltd* [1998] 2 BCLC 646 (CA).

[235] Section 1(3).

[236] Section 1(4).

[237] Section 13.

[238] Section 16; the other procedural aspects are also prescribed in this section and s 17, and are described in detail in *Gore-Browne on Companies* (Jordans, 45th edn, loose-leaf) at 20[28]. The courts are prepared to be flexible regarding these aspects where feasible; see eg the treatment of the 'requirement' for 10 days' notice of an application for a disqualification order by the Court of Appeal in *Secretary of State for Trade and Industry v Langridge* [1991] BCLC 543. As to guidance regarding the conduct of applications under s 17 for leave for someone to act notwithstanding a disqualification order, see *Re Westmid Packing Services Ltd* [1998] 2 BCLC 646 (CA).

[239] Section 7(1).

An alternative cost-saving procedure to making an application to the court was introduced by the Insolvency Act 2000, inserting a new s 1A into the 1986 Act.[240] This allows the Secretary of State to accept a 'disqualification undertaking' from a person, which will have the same effect as a court order, if it appears to him to be expedient in the public interest to do so instead of applying, or proceeding with an application, for a disqualification order.[241]

15.18.3   Grounds for disqualification

The grounds for disqualifying a person from acting as a director, etc, are as follows.

(1)   *Conviction of an offence.* The court can disqualify a person convicted of an indictable offence (whether on indictment or summarily) in connection with the promotion, formation, management or liquidation of a company or with the receivership or management of a company's property.[242] This ground is very wide as there is no requirement that the offence be committed in the course of the internal management of a company's affairs. So, for example, convictions for theft or other offences of dishonesty against outsiders or for insider dealing[243] are sufficient.[244] A solicitor who laundered the proceeds of crime through his client account was guilty of an offence in connection with the management of a company under this provision.[245]

(2)   *Persistent default.* Disqualification can be imposed if it appears to the court that a person has been 'persistently in default' in relation to provisions of the companies legislation requiring any return, account or other document to be filed with, delivered or sent, or notice of any matter to be given, to the registrar.[246] There is a presumption of persistent default where the person has been convicted of relevant offences or default orders have been made against him on three or more occasions. Otherwise, there is no need to show culpable disregard, merely a need to show some degree of continuance or repetition.[247] Under s 5, disqualification on this ground can be

---

[240]   For detail, see *Gore-Browne on Companies*, (Jordans, 45th edn, loose-leaf) at 20[29].

[241]   See the review of this power by the Court of Appeal in *Re Blackspur Group plc (No 3), Secretary of State for Trade and Industry v Davies (No 2)* [2001] EWCA Civ 1595, [2002] 2 BCLC 263.

[242]   Section 2.

[243]   See **16.2**.

[244]   *R v Corbin* (1984) 6 Cr App R (S) 17, see 6 Co Law 183 (1985); *R v Austen* (1985) BCC 99, 528, see 7 Co Law 68 (1986). See also *R v Georgiou* (1988) 4 BCC 322 (CA); *R v Goodman* [1994] 1 BCLC 349 (CA).

[245]   *R v Creggy* [2008] EWCA Crim 394.

[246]   Section 3.

[247]   *Re Arctic Engineering Ltd* [1986] BCLC 253; see (1986) 7 Co Law 27.

imposed by a magistrates' court (in England and Wales) at the same time as a person is convicted of an offence relevant to the filing of returns etc.

(3) *Fraud.* The court can disqualify if, in the course of winding up a company, it appears that a person:

   (a) has been guilty of an offence for which he is liable (whether or not he has been convicted) under s 993 of the Companies Act 2006, that is the offence of fraudulent trading;[248] or
   (b) has otherwise been guilty, while an officer or liquidator of the company, of any fraud in relation to the company or of any breach of his duty as such officer, liquidator, receiver or manager.[249]

   The reference to any breach of duty in (b) above obviously makes this potentially a very wide ground for disqualification.

(4) *Unfitness.* This ground for disqualification, and the next, are the most recent and this is potentially the broadest of all. It arises under ss 6–9 and its introduction (in the Insolvency Act 1986) gave rise to considerable controversy. Because of its importance, it is dealt with separately in the next section.

(5) *Wrongful and fraudulent trading.* The concepts of wrongful and fraudulent trading are examined below, but it is appropriate to note at this stage that any person found liable under the relevant provision to contribute to a company's assets may also be disqualified under s 10.

(6) *Competition infringements.* Section 9A, inserted by the Enterprise Act 2002, s 204, allows for disqualification if a company of which the person is a director commits a breach of competition law and the court considers that his conduct as a director makes him unfit to be concerned in the management of a company.

15.18.4   Disqualification for unfitness

As has already been pointed out, only the Secretary of State (or the Official Receiver in most cases)[250] can apply for disqualification on the ground of unfitness, and he can do so if he thinks that 'it is expedient in the public interest,'[251] but liquidators and others[252] are under a duty to report what can be described as suspected cases of unfitness to the

---

[248] See **15.19.1**.

[249] Section 4.

[250] Only the Secretary of State can act in respect of a director of a company in voluntary liquidation; s 7(1); see *Re Probe Data Systems Ltd* [1989] BCLC 561.

[251] Section 7(1).

[252] The Official Receiver in respect of a company being wound up by the court, the

Secretary of State, and the latter (and the Official Receiver) can require those persons to produce information and documents which he 'may reasonably require for the purpose of determining whether to exercise, or of exercising, any function of his' under the section.[253] Except with the leave of the court,[254] an application under s 6 may not be made more than 2 years after the company in question becomes insolvent.[255]

Section 6 allows the court to disqualify only a director or shadow director[256] for unfitness, and is thus narrower in this respect than the other disqualification provisions, but director for this purpose includes a *de facto* director, that is someone who acted as a director although not formally appointed.[257] The court must be satisfied of two things: (a) that the person in question is or has been a director of a company which has at any time become insolvent (whether while he was a director or subsequently); and (b) that his conduct as a director of that company (either taken alone or taken together with his conduct as a director of any other company or companies)[258] makes him unfit to be concerned in the management of a company.[259] Under s 8, an application for disqualification for unfitness may be made by the Secretary of State from a different route, namely where he thinks it expedient to apply following an inspection under the provisions of the Companies Act 1985.[260] A disqualification order under this provision may be made even if the

---

liquidator (company being otherwise wound up), the administrator (company in administration) and the receiver (company in receivership).

[253] Section 7(4).

[254] As to the principles on which the court should grant leave, see especially *Secretary of State for Trade and Industry v Davies* [1997] 2 BCLC 317 (CA).

[255] Section 7(2). Insolvency is widely defined for these purposes as when either: (a) a company goes into liquidation at a time when its liabilities and the expenses of winding up exceed its assets; (b) an administration order (not an interim administration order: *Secretary of State for Trade and Industry v Palmer* [1993] BCC 650) is made in relation to the company; or (c) an administrative receiver of the company is appointed: s 6(2). The period runs from when the first one of these events occurs: *Re Tasbian Ltd (No 1)* [1991] BCLC 54 (CA).

[256] As to the meaning of this, see **15.2**.

[257] *Re Moorgate Metals Ltd* [1995] 1 BCLC 503.

[258] There is no territorial limit on the conduct that may be considered: *Re Seagull Manufacturing Co Ltd (No 2)* [1994] Ch 91. See also *Secretary of State for Trade and Industry v Ivers* [1997] 2 BCLC 339.

[259] Section 6(1). References to conduct include, where a company has become insolvent, references to a person's conduct in relation to any matter connected with or arising out of the insolvency of that company: s 6(2). As to the relationship between different sets of disqualification proceedings or between disqualification proceedings and other disciplinary proceedings, see the cases discussed in *Gore-Browne on Companies*, (Jordans, 45th edn, loose-leaf) at 20[29].

[260] Sections 437 and 447 or 448; see Part 3 of Chapter 18. For recent examples of disqualifications via this route, which does not depend on the company having become insolvent, see *Re Transtec plc (No 2)* [2006] EWHC 2110 (Ch), and *Secretary of State for Business Enterprise and Regulatory Reform v Sullman* [2009] 1 BCLC 397.

director has been acquitted in a criminal court,[261] and it is no defence to an application that the company's creditors could be or could have been paid in full.[262]

Obviously, the concept of 'unfitness' is central to applications under both ss 6 and 8. Section 9 directs the court to determine the question by reference to the matters listed in Sch 1. These matters are divided into those applicable in all cases, and those applicable where the company has become insolvent. The first head comprises misfeasance or breach of duty as a director, the responsibility of the director for a transaction liable to be set aside as a fraud on creditors,[263] and the extent of his responsibility for any breaches of many of the filing requirements of the Companies Act. The second includes the extent of the directors' responsibility 'for the causes of the company becoming insolvent' and for failing to supply paid-for goods or services, the extent of his responsibility for any voidable preference[264] or failure to summon a creditors' meeting in a creditors' voluntary winding-up[265] and any failure to comply with any obligations to deliver statements of affairs to the liquidator, administrator or receiver.[266]

The extent to which these provisions are successful in curbing the abuses at which they are directed depends upon a number of factors. These include the willingness of insolvency practitioners to report suspected cases, made more likely by their obligation to make appropriate returns to the Department for Business, Innovation and Skills and the willingness of the Department to pursue individual cases. Also of crucial importance is the attitude of the court when faced with applications for disqualification. We now have a large volume of case-law on the unfitness provisions, which is summarised in the following paragraph.

Basically, what must be shown to justify disqualification is conduct that is dishonest, is in breach of standards of commercial morality or is grossly incompetent, such as to convince the court that it would be a danger to the public to allow the person in question to continue to be involved in the management of companies.[267] Conduct in relation to a company can

---

[261] *Re Transtec plc*, above.

[262] *Re Normanton Wells Properties Ltd* [2011] 1 BCLC 191.

[263] Under Part XVI of the Insolvency Act 1986; see **21.55** *et seq.*

[264] Under the Insolvency Act 1986, ss 127, 238 or 241.

[265] Ibid, s 98.

[266] Ibid, ss 22, 47, 66, 99, 131, 234, or 235.

[267] This was first clearly set out by Hoffman J in *Re Dawson Print Group Ltd* [1987] BCLC 601. Other leading cases include *Re Stanford Services Ltd* [1987] BCLC 607; *Re Lo-Line Electric Motors Ltd* [1988] Ch 477; *Re Bath Glass Ltd* [1988] BCLC 329; *Re Churchill Hotel (Plymouth) Ltd* [1988] BCLC 341; *Re Majestic Recording Studios* [1989] BCLC 1; *Re McNulty's Interchange Ltd* [1989] BCLC 709; *Re C U Fittings* [1989] BCLC 556; *Re Ipcon Fashions Ltd* (1989) 5 BCC 773; *Re Cladrose Ltd* [1990] BCLC 204; *Re ECM Europe Electronics* [1991] BCLC 268; *Re Wimbledon Village Restaurant Ltd* [1994] BCC 753; *Secretary of State for Trade and Industry v Gray* [1995] 2 BCLC 276 (CA); *Re Kaytech International plc* [1999] 2 BCLC 351; *Secretary of State for Trade and Industry v Bairstow (No 2)* [2005] 1 BCLC 136 and *Re AG (Manchester) Ltd* [2008] 1 BCLC 321.

encompass any conduct that bears on the company's business or its affairs, whether that causes prejudice to the company itself or its shareholders or to its customers or funders or anyone with whom it has commercial relationships.[268] On the other hand, commercial misjudgment by itself does not constitute unfitness. What constitutes dishonesty does not need to be considered further here. It is clear that commercial morality and competence are separate matters, so that a director can be shown to have been grossly incompetent even if his conduct was 'commercially moral'. Even if, for example, it is regarded as moral to use money owed to the Crown in respect of taxes (especially PAYE, VAT and national insurance) to finance the company's trading activities,[269] and the director in question knows or ought to know what is happening, this can still be sufficiently incompetent.[270] So also, incompetence is evidenced by failure to file accounts and returns as required by the Companies Act, pressure of work being no excuse.[271] The Court of Appeal has confirmed that in general the test for acting incompetently is whether the director caused the company to trade while insolvent and had no reasonable prospect of meeting creditors' claims; it is not enough for the company to have been insolvent to the knowledge of the director.[272] A clear illustration of conduct contrary to commercial morality is provided by *Re Ipcon Fashions Ltd*.[273] The director had carried on business in the clothing trade for 15 years through a succession of companies which had become insolvent. In the 4 months before Ipcon Fashions was wound up, knowing it was insolvent, he abandoned it to its fate and transferred the business to a new company, while still incurring liabilities to suppliers and paying himself and his wife salaries without accounting for tax.

The court's refusal to regard mere incompetence as revealing unfitness has been criticised, on the ground that the courts seem to view the policy behind s 6 as punitive rather than as protecting the public against incompetent directors.[274] Judicial reluctance to disqualify without blameworthiness may be influenced by the mandatory nature of the duty

---

Re Kaytech and *Re Pamstock Ltd* [1996] BCC 341 (CA) also give guidance as to when an appeal court can interfere with the trial judge's findings as to unfitness.

[268] *Secretary of State for Business Enterprise and Regulatory Reform v Sullman* [2009] 1 BCLC 397.

[269] It will not always be such.

[270] The use of Crown money to continue trading has on the balance of the cases been viewed as a much more serious matter than the failure to pay ordinary creditors.

[271] See, in particular, *Re Churchill Hotel (Plymouth) Ltd*, above, and *Re Cladrose Ltd*, above, referring to Sch 1 which, as indicated above, directs the court to have regard to the extent of a director's responsibility for a failure to comply with a duty. See also *Secretary of State for Trade and Industry v Van Hegel* [1995] 1 BCLC 545.

[272] *Secretary of State for Trade and Industry v Creegan* [2001] EWCA Civ 1742, [2002] 1 BCLC 99.

[273] Above. See also on the 'Phoenix syndrome', *Re Travel Mondial (UK) Ltd* [1991] BCC 224; *Re Swift 736 Ltd* [1992] BCC 93; *Re Linvale Ltd* [1993] BCLC 654, and, for a more recent example of conduct contrary to commercial morality, *Secretary of State for Trade and Industry v Blunt* [2005] 2 BCLC 463.

[274] Finch (1990) 53 MLR 385.

under s 6,[275] and it has been observed on a number of occasions that the court must use its jurisdiction to protect the public against those who abuse limited liability, but must be careful not to stultify all enterprise. It may not be easy to resolve what exactly is or should be the dominant purpose of disqualification, and consideration of this cannot be divorced from looking at the impact of other measures such as the wrongful trading provision.[276] What cannot be denied is that the law seems much more effective than it used to be at penalising rogue directors and thus protecting the public from them, even if it may not yet be working perfectly.[277]

15.18.5   Register of disqualification orders

Under s 18 and regulations made thereunder,[278] the Secretary of State maintains a register of disqualification orders on the basis of information which it is the duty of the officers of the courts making the orders to supply. Entries must be deleted on the expiry of any order. The register is open to public inspection on the payment of a fee of 5 pence.

15.19   LIABILITY OF DIRECTORS (AND OTHERS) TO CONTRIBUTE TO THE ASSETS OR FOR THE DEBTS OF THEIR COMPANIES

There are now three provisions under which directors and, in certain cases, others may be made liable by the court in effect for the debts of their companies. A person may be made liable for fraudulent trading, for wrongful trading or for acting while disqualified. All these situations provide for statutory exceptions to the principle of the separate legal personality of a company from its members.[279] For many years, companies legislation has made 'fraudulent trading' a criminal offence, and also the basis on which personal liability could be imposed on directors and others responsible. Criminal liability was, and continues to be, imposed by s 993 of the Companies Act 2006,[280] which applies whether or not there is a winding up. In a winding up, civil liability for fraudulent trading is imposed on the same grounds as attract criminal liability. For this reasons it was suggested[281] that, the object of civil liability being compensation rather than punishment, civil liability for fraudulent trading should be replaced by a wider liability imposed without proof of fraud or dishonesty. Liability for 'wrongful trading' was

---

[275] In contrast to its predecessor, s 300 of the Companies Act 1985, which afforded a discretion.

[276] See **15.19.2**.

[277] See the Report by Hicks, footnote 212.

[278] The Companies (Disqualification Orders) Regulations 1985, SI 1985/829.

[279] See Chapter 3.

[280] [CA 1985, s 458.]

[281] Report of the Review Committee on Insolvency Law and Practice, Cmnd 8558 (1982), para 1776 *et seq*.

introduced by what is now s 214 of the Insolvency Act 1986, but civil liability for fraudulent trading remains in force under s 213. It is more likely than not that in a case where there is any reasonable prospect of establishing fraud or dishonesty there will also be liability for wrongful trading and, therefore, an application in respect of fraudulent trading against a director is likely to be pointless.[282] Section 213 does, however, apply to a wider category of persons than does s 214 and recent s 213 litigation has focussed on attempts to obtain contributions from those who would not be subject to s 214.

15.19.1   Fraudulent trading

Section 213 of the Insolvency Act 1986 provides that if in the course of winding up a company it appears that any business of the company has been carried on with intent to defraud creditors of the company or creditors of any other person, or for any fraudulent purpose, the court, on the application of the liquidator, may declare that any persons who were knowingly parties to the carrying on of the business in that manner are to be liable to make such contributions (if any) to the company's assets as the court thinks proper.

Despite the propounding of a somewhat looser test in an early case on the predecessor to s 213,[283] it is clear that the words 'defraud' and 'fraudulent purpose' connote 'real dishonesty involving, according to current notions of fair trading among commercial men at the present day, real moral blame'.[284] It is sufficient if directors allow the company to incur credit at a time when it is clear that the company will never be able to pay its creditors. It may be sufficient if they so allow it at a time when they know the company is unable to meet all its liabilities as they fall due.[285]

It does not matter for the purpose of the section that only one creditor is defrauded and by a single transaction, if it is shown that the transaction can properly be described as a fraud on the creditor perpetrated in the

---

[282] See, eg, *Official Receiver v Doshi* [2001] 2 BCLC 235 as a case which before 1986 might well have been argued on the basis of fraudulent trading but was brought successfully under s 214. It is possible that the level of compensation might be higher under s 213 since the level of contribution may include a punitive element: *Morphites v Bernasconi* [2001] 2 BCLC 1.

[283] *Re William C Leitch Bros* [1932] 2 Ch 71.

[284] Per Maugham J in *Re Patrick and Lyon* [1933] Ch 786. The need to show dishonesty was more recently stressed in *R v Cox and Hedges* (1982) 75 Crim App R 291 and *Re Augustus Barnett & Son Ltd* [1986] BCLC 170. See also *Re L Todd Swanscombe Ltd* [1990] BCLC 454 and *Re Sobam BV* [1996] 1 BCLC 446. The dishonesty involved in fraudulent trading may justify an order which includes a punitive element: *Re a Company* [1990] BCC 526.

[285] *R v Grantham* [1984] 3 All ER 166 (CA), disapproving the decision to the contrary in *Re White and Osmond (Parkstone) Ltd* (unreported) 30 June 1960. See also *R v Lockwood* (1986) 2 BCC 99, 333 (CA).

course of carrying on business,[286] but it does not follow that, whenever a fraud is perpetrated in the course of carrying on business, it must necessarily follow that the business is being carried on with intent to defraud creditors.[287] The phrase 'carrying on business' is not necessarily synonymous with actively carrying on trade. The collection in and distribution of assets in payment of debts can constitute a carrying on of business. However, where the only allegation is that a company or its officers preferred one or more creditors over others, that cannot constitute fraud within the meaning of the section.[288] A false representation that the company would make a payment that the defendants did not intend to make could amount to fraudulent trading; it is not necessary for the liquidator to show that credit had in fact been given or that the creditor had relied on the fraud.[289]

In order to be subject to liability under s 213, it is necessary to have knowingly[290] been a party to the carrying on of the business in the fraudulent fashion. Any person who actively and dishonestly assists in or benefits from the fraudulent conduct can be liable; it is not necessary to have exercised a controlling or managerial function within the company in liquidation.[291] The expression 'party to' in the section indicates no more than 'participates in', 'takes part in', or 'concurs in', but involves more than mere passivity. A person, such as an employee, who was merely carrying out orders, or another company carrying on bona fide business with the company, would not be caught by s 213. Mere omission by a company secretary to give certain advice to the directors was held not to render the secretary liable under the section,[292] though this is not to say that a secretary who does more than the duties appropriate to his office might not be liable, and it is clear that given the necessary evidence, a creditor[293] or a parent company could fall within the expression.[294] In this

---

[286] *Re Gerald Cooper Chemicals Ltd* [1978] 1 Ch 262. It does not matter that the creditor is not owed a present debt at the time of the fraud: *R v Kemp* [1988] BCLC 217 (CA).

[287] *Morphitis v Bernasconi* [2003] 2 BCLC 53.

[288] *Re Sarflax Ltd* [1979] 1 Ch 529.

[289] *Morphites v Bernasconi* [2001] 2 BCLC 1.

[290] *Morris v Bank of America National Trust* [2001] 1 BCLC 771 (CA) involved an application by the defendant to strike out proceedings under s 213 on the basis that the allegation that it was 'knowingly' a party to fraudulent trading was bound to fail. It was common ground for the purposes of the appeal that 'knowingly' includes wilful blindness or reckless indifference and that the defendant must be shown to have acted dishonestly. The liquidators' case was that individual senior executives either had the requisite knowledge or recklessly ignored it or, in the alternative, that the knowledge of all its senior executives should be aggregated and attributed to the defendant. The Court of Appeal held that the defendants had failed to discharge the burden of establishing that the liquidators had no prospect of establishing any aspect of their case. See also *Morris v Bank of India* [2005] 2 BCLC 328.

[291] *Re BCCI, Banque Arabe Internationale d'Investissement SA v Morris* [2001] 1 BCLC 263.

[292] *Re Maidstone Building Provisions Ltd* [1971] 1 WLR 1085.

[293] *Re Sarflax*, above.

[294] Note that by s 215(4), if a creditor is found liable, his debt can be deferred to rank for payment after all the other debts owed by the company.

respect, s 213 contrasts with the wrongful trading provision, discussed next, under which only directors and shadow directors can be found liable.

Under s 215(2), the court, on making a declaration, may also provide that the liability of a person is to be a charge on any debt or obligation due from the company to him, or on any mortgage or charge on any assets of the company held by or vested in him, or any company or person on his behalf. It can from time to time make such further orders as may be necessary to enforce any such charge. By s 215(5), the section applies notwithstanding that the person concerned may be criminally liable in respect of the matters on the ground of which a declaration is made.

15.19.2 Wrongful trading

As we have seen, s 214 of the Insolvency Act 1986 is an alternative to alleging fraudulent trading under s 213.[295] It should be noted though, that the section imposes liability for omissions and goes beyond the examples given by the Review Committee regarding continuing to trade while insolvent. It imposes a new liability to contribute and is not concerned with enforcing some past or existing liability.[296]

Application under s 214 may only be made by the liquidator of a company, and only in respect of a person who is or has been a director or shadow director[297] of the company. The court may declare that person liable to make such contribution (if any) to the company's assets as it thinks fit if:

(1) the company has gone into insolvent liquidation;[298]

(2) at some time before the commencement of the winding-up, that person knew or ought to have concluded that there was no reasonable prospect that the company would avoid going into insolvent liquidation; and

---

[295] See s 214(8).

[296] *Re Howard Holdings Inc* [1998] BCC 549. Thus, in the case of a foreign company being wound up in England, it was irrelevant whether the liability existed or could exist under any system of foreign law.

[297] *Re International Championship Management Ltd* [2006] 2 All ER (D) 84. As to shadow directors, see **15.2.1**. In *Re Hydrodam (Corby) Ltd* [1994] 2 BCLC 180, it was held that a parent company, but not its directors, could be a shadow director of its subsidiary for the purposes of s 214. The judgment of Millett J contains important and helpful guidance as to the meaning of the term. Where a director has died, the claim may be maintained against his estate: *Re Sherborne Associates Ltd* [1995] BCC 40. A director may be entitled to enforce an indemnity given by the person who appointed him if the true construction of the indemnity so permits: *Burgoine v London Borough of Waltham Forest* [1997] BCC 347.

[298] Ie its assets are insufficient to pay its liabilities and the expenses of winding up: s 214(6).

(3)   that person was a director (or shadow director) of the company at that time.

However, the court must not make a declaration in relation to any person if satisfied that, after he first realised the likelihood of insolvent liquidation, ie the time in (2) above, he took every step with a view to minimising the potential loss to the company's creditors as (assuming him to have known that there was no reasonable prospect that the company would avoid going into insolvent liquidation) he ought to have taken.[299] In respect of this point and (2) above, the facts which a director of a company ought to know or ascertain, the conclusions which he ought to reach and the steps which he ought to take are those which would be known or ascertained, or reached or taken, by a reasonably diligent person having both (a) the general knowledge, skill and experience that may reasonably be expected of a person carrying out the same functions as are carried out by that director in relation to the company, and (b) the general knowledge, skill and experience which that director has.[300]

The subjective criterion will work against, rather than in favour of, the director; the function of (b) is to catch a director who fails to live up to his own standards when those are higher than would usually be expected, having regard to his functions within the company. Conversely, (a) will catch those who simply fail to match the standards of performance 'reasonably expected' of directors having similar functions. In particular cases, the scope of a director's 'functions in relation to the company' will be of decisive importance. A director may be an executive or non-executive director, full-time or part-time; he may be appointed for his financial acumen or business experience, for his knowledge of particular products or services, or to provide, for example, technical expertise.[301] All these are matters which may be relevant in determining what a particular director's 'functions' are, although it will also be necessary to examine the 'functions' which are actually conferred upon him. This is made clear by s 214(5), which provides (as might well have been implied) that a director's functions include those 'which he does not carry out but which have been entrusted to him'.[302]

---

[299]   Section 214(3). See, for example, *Rubin v Gunner* [2004] 2 BCLC 110.
[300]   Section 214(4).
[301]   Eg in a 'high-tech' company.
[302]   The word 'entrusted' may raise questions. The court may feel itself free to disregard formal requirements as to delegation of functions and pay attention instead to the company's actual working arrangements. It may also feel that it may look at what actually occurred by way of 'entrusting' functions even if it was in complete disregard of the articles. This would mean, in all probability, that there might be liability both in a director to whom a function was in fact entrusted and in a director who should, strictly speaking, have been exercising that function. Further, it seems likely that it will be a 'function' of all directors to some extent to oversee the activities of the company, including those of other directors.

The courts have recognised that the degree of competence found among directors will vary from company to company,[303] and the criterion of 'functions ... in relation to the company' may reflect this to some extent. The nature of the company must be relevant, since the standards reasonably to be expected of directors of a large public company cannot be the same as those of directors of an incorporated family business. The courts will no doubt recognise this, but cannot be expected to allow the argument to be pressed too far;[304] the function of s 214 is to protect the company's creditors against neglect and incompetence, and even a small family concern will have creditors whose position, relatively speaking, may be as vulnerable to such neglect and incompetence on the board as that of the creditors of a much larger company. Even within a small company, therefore, there will inevitably be one or more directors whose functions include monitoring the company's solvency.[305] In any event, and in any company, there must come a point when a director ought to realise from information which he has received[306] that the company faces solvency problems, and it seems that the effect of s 214 must be that, at that point, his duties include the function of ascertaining the true position and, if necessary, taking action. There will, therefore, be a duty to supervise under s 214, and that duty may be broken either by individual directors, or by the whole body of directors in failing to institute or to operate an adequate monitoring process. In *Re Produce Marketing Consortium Ltd (No 2)*,[307] the company's accounts were prepared some considerable time after the statutory periods had expired. The court imputed to the directors the knowledge that timely delivery of the accounts would have given them. It is clear that directors will usually, if not invariably, be taken for the purposes of s 214 to have knowledge of the accounts, at the latest by the time when they should have been delivered. The director's position will be even weaker if the failure to prepare accounts is accompanied by obvious warning signs, such as a supplier's refusal to make further deliveries, or pressure for payment from the company's creditors. In *Re DKG Contractors Ltd*,[308] the company was

---

[303] *DHSS v Evans* [1985] 2 All ER 472.

[304] So, for example, it was held in *Singla v Hedman* [2010] EWHC 902 (Ch), [2011] 1 BCLC 61 that an allegedly low standard of corporate responsibility in the film industry was not something that could excuse a director of a company in that industry.

[305] *Re DKG Contractors Ltd* [1990] BCC 903; *Re Sherborne Associates Ltd* [1995] BCC 40. In the latter case, it was accepted that two non-executive directors, recruited for reasons quite different from financial expertise, were entitled to rely on an active chairman, who had far greater involvement with the company and its figures. The case concerned a company whose only prospects of survival depended on increased sales, and – given a consistent pattern of losses and optimistic forecasts – it is submitted that the decision that the directors in question were not liable under s 214 can be justified only on the basis that it survived for only two years, during which it may still have been reasonable to believe there would be a turnaround.

[306] Or ascertained or, indeed, ought to have ascertained: s 214(4).

[307] [1989] BCLC 520.

[308] [1990] BCC 903; see also *Re Purpoint Ltd* [1991] BCC 121, at 127–128, where Vinelott J clearly contemplates that there may be companies which no prudent director would allow to begin trading.

a small works contractor managed by the two directors, a husband and wife team. The wife kept a 'black book' recording payments and invoices received, which was a basis on which proper accounts might have been prepared, but this was never done. It was held that, given the warning signs referred to above, the directors should have instituted some form of financial control. That would have revealed that there was no reasonable prospect of avoiding liquidation. The two directors had thus failed to satisfy the standards set by subs (4)(a). The 'hopeless inadequacy' of their knowledge, skill and experience could not protect them. It is the duty even of the directors of an incorporated family business to acquire some basic knowledge of their legal obligations and financial responsibilities. Nor, in this case, was it sufficient answer to say that the directors had relied on assurances that money would come into the company; although these came from a quantity surveyor, his task had been merely to supervise contract income, and he had no information about the company's finances. *Re Brian D Pierson (Contractors) Ltd*[309] concerned, among other things, a claim for wrongful trading against the directors of a company that constructed and maintained golf courses. The company had two directors who were also husband and wife. The wife had taken almost no part in management, she had no separate areas of responsibility, and she had left all management decisions to her husband. The court was satisfied that the case was made out by the liquidator even having regard to the seasonal nature of the business and to the fact that the company had not suffered losses continuously over a number of years. It had suffered increasing losses and certain investments had become worthless. The loss of the investments was not so important by itself, but to regard them as current assets as the active director had done amounted to a refusal to face facts. There was no evidence that the directors had sought advice from the bank or the company's auditors, and in any event it was their responsibility to review critically the position of the company and it was they who had or should have had fullest knowledge of the position of the company. The wife's lack of involvement did not exclude her from liability. Although she had little practical involvement in the company she was still a director, drawing a salary and other fees, and certain minimum responsibilities were expected of her. The courts have distinguished between those cases where the directors, being clearly aware of the possibility and consequences of insolvent trading, had considered the position carefully before deciding to trade on and those cases where the directors had made no real attempt to address the issue. The courts have stressed the need to avoid hindsight; the fact that a decision to trade on, taken after careful consideration, turned out to be wrong should not in itself give rise to liability. In *Re Continental Assurance of London plc*,[310] Park J commented that if he had had to find the directors liable for wrongful trading in the circumstances of the case, it would be 'hard to imagine any well-advised person ever agreeing to accept appointment as a non-executive director of any company'. The liquidators' initial argument

---

[309] [1999] BCC 26.
[310] [2001] BPIR 733.

was that the accounting information available was inadequate to enable the directors to form a view as to the solvency of the company; by the end of the trial this argument had fallen away and the liquidators were left to argue that appropriate accounting policies had not been applied to the raw data in the accounts and that, if they had been, the company would have been seen to be insolvent and the directors ought to have realised that. After detailed consideration of the adjustments which the liquidators argued should have been made to the accounts, the judge concluded that even if he had accepted all the adjustments so that the accounts should have shown the company to be in a state of insolvency, he would not have held that the directors should have been aware of the position. This would have required an understanding of accounting concepts of a particularly specialised and sophisticated nature which should not be expected even of the directors of such a specialised business.[311]

It has already been mentioned that s 214 of the 1986 Act goes far beyond the active trading to which the Review Committee on Insolvency Law and Practice addressed its recommendations. In covering the whole area of a company's financial affairs, and in attaching liability to omission as well as commission, the section imposes a potentially limitless duty on the director to pay constant attention to all aspects of his company's affairs, for fear that with hindsight a court may find that a reasonably diligent person in his position would have been able to evaluate the company's performance and prospects.[312] This will no doubt be mitigated in practice by allowing a measure of 'business judgment' to the board, but it seems unlikely that this can excuse complete omission. Further, a duty to inquire is clearly placed upon a director by judging him in the light of facts which he ought to know or *ascertain*: s 214(4). At the least, this means that when a director feels, or, it seems, ought to feel, that the information available to him is inadequate he must press for more. This may place an individual director in some difficulties since (apart from provoking hostility, which s 214 presumably expects him to suffer rather than avoid) a failure to obtain satisfactory answers seems itself to be a ground upon which a liquidator might later rely. In order to assess his own and the company's position, a director may have to seek advice and assistance from outside

---

[311] It would not have been acceptable for them to be totally ignorant of the accounting concepts to be applied to an insurance company but the 'proceedings are in substance an accountant's negligence action brought against the laymen who employed the accountants'. All the directors (except the company's finance director, against whom the case had been settled) were to be regarded as laymen in this regard despite the fact that they included two non-practising chartered accountants, one of whom had previously been a finance director himself albeit in a different type of insurance business.

[312] In *Re Produce Marketing Consortium Ltd (No 2)* [1989] BCLC 520, the judge stressed in making the order under s 214 that the case was not one of deliberate wrongdoing but of 'failure to appreciate what should have been clear'. It is the nature of this liability which prevents a director from claiming relief under what is now s 1157 of the Companies Act 2006; *Re Produce Marketing Consortium Ltd* [1989] 1 WLR 745; *Re DKG Contractors Ltd* [1990] BCC 902 (see **17.9.3**).

the company.[313] Section 214 may also produce a certain amount of 'defensive management', since an alert director will wish to keep very clear records of his own activities.

Section 214(3) is equally and deliberately imprecise in requiring the director, on actual or imputed foresight of insolvent liquidation, to take 'every step ... with a view to minimising the potential loss to the company's creditors[314] as ... he ought' to take, the only limitation being that he is liable only for failure to take steps which a reasonably diligent person in his position would have taken. The director is, subject to that qualification, expected to follow the course of conduct which will not merely reduce but reduce as far as possible the potential loss, and it appears to follow that, given a range of possible actions, he must take that course which satisfies that criterion; he may use his business judgment in evaluating the consequences of each course which is open, but once that is done he has no choice but to follow the course which minimises the loss. Resignation from the board is manifestly not such a course,[315] and it is difficult to avoid the conclusion that the section will, whatever its true intentions, make insolvency proceedings the likeliest outcome. The director is still, however, required to decide what form of proceedings (ie receivership, administration or liquidation) will in fact minimise the creditors' losses, and for this purpose the preliminary step of seeking advice[316] may not be only permissible but necessary. There is a real risk that s 214 will actually precipitate insolvency proceedings which in some cases may have been avoidable, particularly as directors face possible disqualification if held liable under the section.[317] Even if some form of insolvency proceedings is the step which the section itself contemplates, however, there may be cases where a decision to trade on, albeit for a limited period, may be justified insofar as it appears reasonably likely to increase the assets available to creditors, although it may be wondered whether directors or their advisers will in practice be prepared to support such a decision. Conversely, if the directors have properly considered the possible courses of action open to them, concluded reasonably that some form of insolvency proceedings are inevitable, and honestly and reasonably begun the process of realising assets by sale, they are probably not to be judged by the standards of an insolvency practitioner; provided that they obtain a reasonable price, they are not required to conduct a full-scale investigation of other offers which might produce a better price.[318]

---

[313] It is a moot point whether his duties under s 214 will in all cases override obligations of confidentiality.

[314] Presumably, those who are likely to be creditors in an insolvent liquidation, and not merely those who happen at present to be creditors.

[315] Still less, of course, abandoning the company while seeking fresh starts elsewhere: *Re Purpoint Ltd* [1991] BCC 121 at 125.

[316] As expeditiously as possible.

[317] See **15.18.3**, above.

[318] Cf *Welfab Engineers Ltd* [1990] BCC 600 (directors' duties at common law).

What is absolutely clear from s 214(2)–(4) of the 1986 Act is the vital importance of the time element. It must be established at what moment the conditions set out in s 214(2) first applied to a particular director before the question of complying with s 214(3) can arise. In a wider sense, the impact of the section may be determined by the willingness or unwillingness of the court, with hindsight, to trace a company's affairs backwards in time from an insolvent liquidation to the first warning signs.

15.19.3   Liability for acting while disqualified

Section 15 of the Company Directors Disqualification Act 1986 contains a further provision under which a person can be liable for the debts of a company, and in this case liability is for those debts as such,[319] rather than, as in the cases of fraudulent and wrongful trading just described, liability to contribute to a company's assets.

A person is 'personally responsible' for all the relevant debts of a company if at any time either: (a) he is involved in the management of a company in contravention of a disqualification order[320] or s 11 of the Act (ie acting as a director while an undischarged bankrupt);[321] or (b) as a person involved in management he acts or is willing to act on instructions given without the leave of the court by a person whom he knows at that time to be disqualified or to be an undischarged bankrupt.

'Relevant debts' are those debts and liabilities incurred at a time when the person was involved in management or those incurred when he acted or was willing to act on the instructions of a person disqualified, etc.[322] Involvement in management is given a wide meaning, namely being a director or being concerned, directly or indirectly, or taking part in the management of a company.[323] For the purposes of situation (b), a person who has acted at any time on instructions as described above is presumed, unless the contrary is shown, to have been willing at any time thereafter to act on instructions.[324]

The attraction of s 15 to creditors of a company is that it can be used by them directly without the need for action by a liquidator or even for the company in question to be in liquidation. It should also therefore prove a strong deterrent to those disqualified.

---

[319] Jointly and severally with the company and any other person who, whether under the section or otherwise, is liable: s 15(2).

[320] Made under any of the provisions described above.

[321] See **15.7**.

[322] Section 15(3).

[323] Cf the wide construction of the similar words in s 1; see **15.19.1**.

[324] Section 15(5).

15.19.4 Summary remedy

Finally, it is convenient to note the summary remedy available against directors and others in a liquidation, provided for by s 212 of the Insolvency Act 1986, and available not just to the liquidator or the official receiver, but also to any creditor and, subject to the leave of the court, contributory.[325]

---

[325] For detailed consideration of this, see *Gore-Browne on Companies* **61[11] to [17]**.

CHAPTER 16

THE DUTIES OF DIRECTORS – GENERAL

16.1 INTRODUCTION

This chapter is concerned with the scope and content of the principal duties which the law imposes upon a director of a company by virtue of his holding office as such.[1] Since, as we have seen in the previous chapter, the management of a company is vested in its directors and, as described in Chapter 11, corporate governance is generally regarded as perhaps the most important issue in company law today, the question of the duties that directors owe is a critical one. This has been recognised by the fact that perhaps what were the most significant new provisions of the Companies Act 2006 contain a statutory statement or codification of what the Act calls[2] 'the general duties of directors'. In addition to this, the Act re-enacted, with amendments, the statutory reinforcement of key general principles previously in Part X of the 1985 Act and contains statutory provisions that now govern the situation when a member can bring an action alleging a breach of directors' duties. This chapter will deal with those general duties and the next chapter will deal with the other statutory provisions mentioned above, together with various other questions relating to directors' duties.

That said, there is no doubt that the underlying principles developed by the courts as regards the duties of directors continue to be relevant. Exactly how relevant will be discussed shortly. Broadly speaking, the duties in the cases fall into two categories, namely fiduciary duties (ie duties of good faith and honesty) developed from equitable principles and duties of skill and care, which have a common law base. Although as a matter of principle a breach of fiduciary duty and a breach of the duty to exercise care and skill could arise on the same facts, it is clear that negligence was not *per se* a breach of fiduciary duty.[3] The general purpose of these duties traditionally was the protection of present and future

---

[1] As to when a director may be liable in tort to third parties in respect of his actions as director, see *Williams v Natural Life Health Foods Ltd* [1998] 1 WLR 830 (HL), discussed at **3.4.1**. See also *Standard Chartered Bank v Pakistan National Shipping Corp* [2002] UKHL 43, [2003] AC 959.

[2] This is the heading to Chapter 2 of Part 10.

[3] *Extrasure Travel Insurances Ltd v Scattergood* [2003] 1 BCLC 598. The Act preserves this distinction, as will be seen.

members and (to a lesser extent) creditors, and in general this remains the position under the statute, although the traditional duties were generally expressed as being owed to 'the company', something else that is preserved under the statute. Much of the content of the duties to be discussed was developed by way of analogy with rules governing legal relationships comparable to that between a director and his company. The result was a large number of heads of duty, many of which overlap with one or more others; this is also something recognised in the statutory statement.

A statutory statement of duties was first proposed in recent times by the Law Commission in its report *Company Directors: Regulating Conflicts of Interests and Formulating a Statement of Duties*.[4] A more exclusive and exhaustive code was recommended by the Company Law Review Steering Group[5] (CLRSG) and its proposal, which was primarily aimed at making the law clearer and more accessible and its development more predictable, found broad favour with government, although, as will be seen, the end result is not a complete code. A further aim was to reform what were perceived as unduly harsh equitable principles relating to conflicts of duty and interest.

Whether the statutory code is actually intelligible to many company directors is a matter on which opinions may well vary; certainly it is not worded in anything like as straightforward a way as the Law Commission recommended. However, the Government has published general guidance on the statutory code.[6]

16.1.1 The legal nature of the office of director

We have seen in the previous chapter that the Companies Act 2006 does not define 'director', although it does define the term 'shadow director', on whom some, but not all, of the duties described in this and the next chapter are imposed.[7] Section 170(5) provides that the general duties apply to shadow directors where, and to the extent that, the corresponding common law rules or equitable principles so apply. However, it has been decided that in general, shadow directors do not normally owe fiduciary duties to the company,[8] although it is thought that they are likely to be regarded as owing a duty of care and skill, and there

---

[4] Law Com No 261, Scot Law Com No 173 (1999). Earlier the Jenkins Committee (1962 Cmd 1749) had made a similar recommendation.

[5] See *Modern Company Law for a Competitive Economy: Developing the Framework* URN 00/656 (March 2000) para 3.82 and *The Final Report* URN 01/943 (July 2001) Ch 3. The whole question of the duties of directors was exhaustively discussed by the CLRSG in *The Strategic Framework* URN 99/654 (February 1999) Ch 5.1; *Developing the Framework* URN 00/656 (March 2000; and *Completing the Structure* URN 00/1335 (November 2000).

[6] Available at www.berr.gov.uk/files/file40139.pdf.

[7] See **15.2.1**.

[8] *Ultraframe (UK) Ltd v Fielding* [2005] EWHC 1638 (Ch).

is no reason why in appropriate circumstances they could not be liable as constructive trustees. On the other hand, people acting as directors although not formally appointed as such have been held to owe fiduciary duties as directors[9] and, it is thought, are subject to the general duties codified in the 2006 Act.

The absence of a definition of 'director' perhaps renders it somewhat difficult to ascertain the exact nature of the director's office. He is certainly an agent of the company[10] but is rather more than that as in practice he is not subject to much control by his principal, the company acting through the shareholders in general meeting.[11] In certain respects, the director is a trustee[12] and there is no doubt that many of his duties developed from the law of trusts, but he is certainly not a full trustee, not least because his very function is an entrepreneurial one and he may properly take risks with the company's funds which a trustee in the strict sense cannot. If a director performs more than the tasks of a director pure and simple, such as attending board meetings and the like, he may well also be an employee of the company and as such the beneficiary of important statutory rights if he is declared redundant or unfairly dismissed.[13] In short, the director's office is *sui generis*, although for certain purposes the analogies of agency, trusteeship and employment may be useful.

16.2   THE SCOPE OF DIRECTORS' DUTIES

It was an established general rule that, insofar as a director of a company is bound by fiduciary duties at general law, these duties are owed to the company only. This is confirmed as far as the statutory statement of general duties is concerned by s 170(1) of the Companies Act 2006. Thus the general duties are not owed to other companies or bodies corporate with which the company is associated, eg its holding company[14] or subsidiary,[15] nor do they operate in favour of any person simply because he is a person to whom the company itself stands in a fiduciary

---

[9]   See **15.2.**
[10]   See Chapter 6.
[11]   The 'separation of ownership and control', recognised by Berle and Means in *The Modern Corporation and Private Property* (Harcourt, Brace & World Inc, revised edn, 1967). See especially, **11.2** and **15.15**.
[12]   See **16.13**.
[13]   See further, **15.5.** In acting as an employee, a director can bargain as he wishes over the terms of his service contract, provided that there is compliance with the articles; in practice, these remove any possibility of conflict of duty and interest. See further, **16.10** and **17.3** and *Jackson v Invicta Plastics Ltd* [1987] BCLC 329.
[14]   *Bell v Lever Bros Ltd* [1932] AC 161, at 228 (HL).
[15]   *Lindgren v L & P Estates Ltd* [1968] Ch 572 (CA); but note the effects of *Scottish Co-operative Wholesale Society Ltd v Meyer* [1959] AC 324 (HL (Sc)).

relationship.[16] This proposition stems from *Percival v Wright*,[17] in which a group of shareholders in a company approached the directors with a request that the directors purchase their shares; some of the directors did so without disclosing that a purchase of the company's undertaking was imminent, this being a piece of information which was known to them and to the other members of the board, though not to any of the shareholders who were not directors. It was held that the directors in question were not under any duty to the shareholders to disclose this information, even though the price being offered for the undertaking represented a substantial amount more per share than they paid to the shareholders on the purchase, and that accordingly the shareholders could not have the purchase set aside. The judgment does, however, stress that there was no 'unfair dealing' by the directors and seems to suggest that it was significant that the initial approach in the matter was made by the shareholders.[18] The possibility that fiduciary duties would have arisen between the directors and the shareholders if the directors had instigated the purchase is thus not entirely ruled out.

Furthermore, directors, in supplying information to their shareholders regarding a takeover offer and expressing a view as to whether the offer should be accepted, have 'a duty towards their own shareholders which ... clearly includes a duty to be honest and a duty not to mislead'.[19] It has also been laid down that if in a particular transaction a director expressly or by his conduct constitutes himself as agent for one or more of the shareholders, he thereby becomes subject to fiduciary duties to the shareholder or shareholders concerned.[20] Such duties arise, however, by virtue of his agency, not his directorship. In the decision of the New Zealand Court of Appeal in *Coleman v Myers*,[21] a fiduciary relationship between directors and shareholders was held to have arisen where, in a private company with the shareholding spread over a few associated family groups, the directors had a high degree of inside knowledge which they failed to disclose to the other shareholders when the shares in the company were the subject of a takeover offer from a company owned by one of the directors. The court stressed, however, that the existence of such a relationship depended entirely on the facts of any particular case

---

[16] *Wilson v Bury (Lord)* (1880) 5 QBD (CA). See also *Gregson v HAE Trustees Ltd* [2008] EWHC 1006 (Ch): a director of a trustee company does not owe fiduciary duties to the beneficiaries of the trust.

[17] [1902] 2 Ch 421. See also *Dawson International plc v Coats Paton plc* (1988) 4 BCC 305; *Towcester Racecourse Co Ltd v The Racecourse Association Ltd* [2002] EWHC 2141 (Ch), [2003] 1 BCLC 260.

[18] Ibid, at 426–427.

[19] *Gething v Kilner* [1972] 1 WLR 337, at 341, per Brightman J. See also *Dawson International plc v Coats Paton plc*, above, at 310, 312.

[20] *Allen v Hyatt* (1914) 30 TLR 444 (PC); and see *Briess v Woolley* [1954] AC 333 (HL); and see *Platt v Platt* [1999] 2 BCLC 745.

[21] [1977] 2 NZLR 297; see Rider (1978) 41 MLR 585. This decision was followed by the British Columbia Court of Appeal in *Dusik v Newton* (1985) 62 BCLR 1 and by the New South Wales Court of Appeal in *Glandon Pty Ltd v Strata Consolidated Ltd* (1993) 11 ACLC 895.

and dissented from the view expressed by the trial judge[22] that the decision in *Percival v Wright* was wrong and should be ignored. English case-law has referred to and followed the decision in *Coleman v Myers*, holding that a fiduciary relationship between directors and shareholders can arise in special circumstances like those subsisting in that case.[23] A further example of a duty which may be owed directly to shareholders is the duty to allot shares for a proper purpose.[24]

The decisions in *Percival v Wright* and *Coleman v Myers* involved what is today generally referred to as 'insider dealing'. This and other forms of market abuse by directors and others in respect of publicly traded shares are the subject of specific statutory provisions under the Criminal Justice Act 1993 and the Financial Services and Markets Act 2000; detailed consideration of these and the relevant EU Directives, which these days are regarded as more matters of securities law than company law, can be found elsewhere.[25]

The time at which a director's traditional fiduciary duties to the company arise is the time when he becomes a director. He is not bound by them when he is merely a 'director-elect'.[26] This principle clearly survives the statutory codification. The duties to avoid conflicts of interest and not to accept benefits from third parties apply, by s 170(2) of the Companies Act 2006, to former directors. This specific provision is considered later in this chapter in the context of those duties.

16.3 INTRODUCTION TO DIRECTORS' GENERAL DUTIES

A key part of the introductory section to the general statutory duties, s 170, is s 170(3) and (4). These subsections seek to explain the relationship between the statutory duties and the previous duties based on case-law. In providing that the general duties are based on certain common law rules and equitable principles as they apply in relation to directors and have effect in place of those rules and principles as regards the duties owed to a company by a director, s 170(3) appears at first sight to provide that the statutory rules constitute a true and exhaustive codification. However, there are two critical points here. The first stems from the use of the phrase 'certain ... rules and ... principles'. It is

---

22   [1977] 2 NZLR 22.
23   *Re Chez Nico (Restaurants) Ltd* [1992] BCLC 192, at 208; *Stein v Blake (No 2)* [1998] 1 BCLC 573, at 576, 579 (CA); *Platt v Platt* [1999] 2 BCLC 745 (affirmed [2001] 1 BCLC 698 (CA); *Peskin v Anderson* [2000] 1 BCLC 1, at 11–14 (affirmed [2001] 1 BCLC 372 at 378–380).
24   There is clear authority for this (see *Re a Company* [1987] BCLC 82; *John Crowther Group plc v Carpets International plc* [1990] BCLC 460, at 464), which relates in particular to the question of minority shareholders' remedies; see **18.4.1**. However, it does not feature as part of the statutory code.
25   See *Gore-Browne on Companies* (Jordans, 45th edn, loose-leaf), Ch 42.
26   *Lingren v L & P Estates Ltd* [1968] Ch 575 (CA).

thought that still leaves intact any duties imposed on directors that are not encapsulated in ss 171–177 and this includes the principle under which directors are regarded as being trustees of the company's assets.[27] It also leaves clear room for further development of specific aspects of the duties, particularly the primary duty of loyalty that a director must act in good faith.[28] The second point arises from the terms of s 170(4), which requires the general duties to be interpreted and applied in the same way as common law rules or equitable principles, and states expressly that regard is to be had to the corresponding rules and principles in interpreting and applying the general duties. It seems clear that the large body of case-law that has established the duties in equity and at common law will continue to be highly relevant, as will new case-law exploring the duties of fiduciaries in general. As regards the core duties of proper purpose and good faith under ss 171 and 172, it has been said that they 'appear to do little more than set out the pre-existing law'.[29] For this reason, the scheme adopted in this chapter is to set out the relevant statutory provisions and then include by way of commentary the underlying case-law that developed these duties.[30] It concludes with examination of the principle regarding trusteeship of company property that is not contained in the statutory code.

In this context regard should also be had to the provision on remedies, s 178.[31] Any hope of codifying the remedies for breach of directors' duties, which at one time the CLRSG hoped to achieve, was, it seems, abandoned due to the complexity of the task and the fact that to a large extent the remedies for breach of fiduciary duties continue to evolve. Section 178(1) provides that the consequences of a breach, or threatened breach, of ss 171–177 are the same as would apply if the corresponding common law rule or equitable principle applied. Section 178(2) then declares that the duties other than that of care and skill are, accordingly, enforceable in the same way as any other fiduciary duty owed to a company by its directors. This is interesting for two reasons. First, it acknowledges that the duties other than of care and skill are fiduciary, although this is a description that the CLRSG was anxious to bury in this context.[32] Secondly, by admitting the possibility of other fiduciary duties, it reinforces the point made above that the statutory code is not exhaustive.

---

[27] See **16.13**.

[28] See, eg, *Item Software (UK) Ltd v Fassihi* [2005] 2 BCLC 91.

[29] Lord Glennie in *Re West Coast Capital (Lios) Ltd* 2008 CSOH 72 at para 21. See also *Re Southern Counties Fresh Foods Ltd* [2008] EWHC 2810 (Ch) at [52].

[30] In general it is assumed that the conduct of the directors being dealt with is within the literal terms of the powers conferred on them by the articles. It is arguable, of course, that merely to act in excess of those powers is *ipso facto* a breach of duty; such conduct is certainly invalid unless and until effectively ratified, although third parties are protected by the rules considered in Chapter 6.

[31] See also **17.10** regarding enforcement of the duties of directors.

[32] See its draft in Annex 2 to its *Final Report*.

A final introductory point arises from s 179. It has often been pointed out that the traditional fiduciary duties of directors frequently overlap. Section 179 recognises this in declaring that, except as otherwise provided,[33] more than one of the general duties may apply in any given case.

16.4   DUTY TO ACT WITHIN POWERS

The first general duty, contained in s 171, requires a director to act in accordance with the company's constitution and to exercise powers only for the purposes for which they are conferred.[34] The company's constitution is defined for this purpose as being the articles, various resolutions[35] or decisions come to in accordance with the constitution and other decisions taken by the members (or a class of them) that are treated as equivalent to a decision by the company, for example, a decision taken by informal unanimous consent of all the members. The duty to act in accordance with the constitution appears uncontroversial, although it was not something that featured greatly in cases decided at common law.[36]

On the other hand, the duty to exercise powers for a proper purpose has long been a key duty of directors,[37] although not perhaps the primary duty as it now appears in terms of its appearance in the statutory code. The section does not spell out all the nuances of the duty to exercise powers for a proper purpose and thus the underlying case-law remains of critical importance. If the directors exercise a power conferred by the articles for a purpose other than that for which, upon its proper interpretation, it was so conferred, their conduct is open to challenge, and it is no answer for them to maintain that they believed in good faith that their conduct was most likely to promote the success of the company (the second general duty examined below). The court will not substitute its own view for that of the board as to the correctness of the board's exercise of its management powers, but where, on an objective review of the situation, it finds that a requirement allegedly underlying the board's action was not urgent or critical, it may have reason (particularly where the action was taken was unusual or extreme) to doubt or discount the assertions of the directors that they acted solely to deal with this

---

[33]   This appears to be referring to s 175(3): see **16.8.**

[34]   See *Ford v Polymer Vision Ltd* [2009] EWHC 945 (Ch), [2009] 2 BCLC 160 at [87], whch cited the equivalent section in *Gore-Browne on Companies*, **15[9]**, as summarising the relevant jurisprudence.

[35]   Those contained in s 29 of the Act; see **5.1.**

[36]   It has some relationship with the former s 35 of the Companies Act 1985, which, when it substantially mitigated the effects of the former *ultra vires* doctrine (see **6.2**), also confirmed the potential liability of directors who caused their company to act *ultra vires*.

[37]   The judgment of Lord Greene MR in *Re Smith & Fawcett Ltd* [1942] Ch 304, at 306 (CA) contains the classical exposition. See generally, Nolan 'The Proper Purposes Doctrine and Company Directors' in Rider (ed) *The Realm of Company Law* (Kluwer, 1998) p 1.

requirement.[38] To this limited extent, their assessment of the company's interests in the exercise of their powers is open to review, on an objective basis, by the court.[39]

This principle was brought into prominence in the cases, described in the next paragraph, dealing with a power vested in the directors of a company to allot the company's shares. Since the introduction of what are now ss 549–551 and 561–576 of the 2006 Act, which restrict directors' powers of allotment,[40] the principle is of less importance thereto. However, those provisions may in certain cases be excluded and may very well not apply to private companies, and thus the common-law principle can be relevant. Further, as the cases discussed below reveal, the principle has often been used in modern times to question the validity of defensive tactics used by directors fighting a takeover bid for their company or of another means or maintaining directors' control. Thus it can be used in respect of any power exercised with these aims in mind whose purpose can clearly be discerned from the articles, as for example in the Savoy Hotel case, where it was the directors' power to lease the company's property as a means of forestalling an anticipated takeover bid which was in issue.[41] Further examples concerned the directors entering into a management agreement which had the effect of depriving the shareholders of their constitutional right to appoint new directors with full managerial powers,[42] and directors entering into a supplementary partnership agreement that exposed the company to a serious contingent liability.[43]

In *Hogg v Cramphorn Ltd*,[44] the directors of the defendant company, fearing a takeover bid and their own dismissal from the board, allotted

---

[38]   *Howard Smith Ltd v Ampol Petroleum Ltd* [1974] AC 821, at 823 (PC).

[39]   For an argument that this test is not objective enough, see Birds (1974) 37 MLR 580. The proper purposes duty at common law has been held to be one owed to shareholders directly rather than to the company (see **16.2**) and as such may be relevant in an unfair prejudice petition (see **18.10**). It remains to be seen whether this survives the statutory codification, as the general duties are, as we have seen, expressed as being owed to the company.

[40]   See **7.3–7.6**.

[41]   This *cause célèbre*, which was never litigated, was the subject of a Board of Trade Inspector's Report in 1954; see the report of the Inspector, Mr E Milner-Holland QC, in the Savoy Hotel Investigation (HMSO, 1954); see Gower (1955) 68 Harv LR 1176. For reported examples of the use of a proper purposes principle outside the context of a struggle for control and unrelated to an allotment of shares, see *Stanhope's Case* (1866) 1 Ch App 161 (power to forfeit shares); *Bennett's Case* (1867) 5 De GM & G 284 (power to approve transfers of shares); *Galloway v Hallé Concerts Society* [1915] 2 Ch 233 (power to make calls); and *Gaiman v NAMH* [1971] Ch 317 (power to expel members).

[42]   *Lee Panavision Ltd v Lee Lighting Ltd* [1992] BCLC 22 (CA).

[43]   *Criterion Properties plc v Stratford UK Properties LLC* [2002] EWCA Civ 1883, [2003] 2 BCLC 129.

[44]   [1967] Ch 254. The principles adopted in this case, which was actually decided in 1963, were approved of and applied in *Bamford v Bamford* [1970] Ch 212 (CA). Earlier authorities are *Punt v Symons & Co Ltd* [1903] 2 Ch 506 and *Piercy v S Mills & Co Ltd* [1920] 3 Ch 77. It is clear that some Commonwealth authorities reject the breadth of the principle confirmed in *Hogg v Cramphorn Ltd* and in effect deny the existence of this

shares to persons who would support them in office. They honestly believed that, in acting to preserve their position on the board, they were serving the company's best interests, but it was held that they had used the power of allotment for a purpose for which it was not intended to be used and that the allotment was accordingly voidable. However, the court ruled that if a meeting of the shareholders existing prior to the allotment approved the allotment by a majority it would thereby be rendered valid, and ordered that such a meeting be held. In *Howard Smith Ltd v Ampol Petroleum Ltd*,[45] two shareholders holding between them 55% of the shares in a company announced that they would jointly reject any offer from a particular intending takeover bidder, or from any other source. The board of directors then allotted new shares to the intending bidder. Although the company did need new capital at the time, the primary purpose of the directors in making this allotment was to reduce the proportionate shareholding of the two majority shareholders to below 50% and thus enable the bidder to make an effective bid. In proceedings brought by one of the two majority shareholders against, *inter alia*, the directors and the bidder, it was held by the Privy Council that the board had acted with an improper purpose, albeit honestly and within their powers, and that the issue of shares to the bidder (which was on notice of the impropriety) should accordingly be set aside. Giving the Privy Council's judgment, Lord Wilberforce said that a decision of directors to issue shares could be set aside on the ground of improper purpose even though there was no element of self-interest involved, and that while it might in some circumstances be proper to issue shares for purposes other than raising capital for the company, 'it must be unconstitutional for directors to use their fiduciary powers over the shares in the company purely for the purpose of destroying an existing majority, or creating a new majority which did not previously exist'. Further, he said that the case was all the stronger against the directors where there was 'an ulterior purpose to enable an offer for shares to proceed which the existing majority was in a position to block'.[46]

Except as regards the possibility of ratification by the general meeting,[47] the consequences of infringement of this principle are that the directors' actions are voidable. Thus, where a power of forfeiture was exercised for improper purposes, the members concerned, who knew of the impropriety, could not rely on the forfeiture as a defence to an action for

---

    objective restraint on directors' powers, despite Lord Wilberforce's valiant attempt in *Howard Smith Ltd v Ampol Petroleum Ltd* [1974] AC 821 (see below) to explain them as consistent with *Hogg v Cramphorn Ltd*; see in particular *Harlowe's Nominees Ltd v Woodside (Lake Entrance) Oil Co* (1968) 121 CLR 483 (Australian HC) and *Teck Corporation Ltd v Millar* (1972) 33 DLR (3d) 288 (Sup Ct BC). This of course is now an academic question so far as UK law is concerned.

[45] [1974] AC 821 (PC).

[46] Ibid, at p 837. This is analogous to '*Wednesbury* unreasonableness' in public law cases; see *Re a Company, ex parte Glossop* [1988] BCLC 570.

[47] See **17.9.1**.

payment of the balance due on the shares.[48] Whether or not an agreement with a third party entered into for an improper purpose will be set aside will depend on the application of principles of agency law with appropriate regard to s 40 of the Act,[49] namely whether or not the directors had actual or apparent authority to enter into it. The principles that determine the liability of a third party as a constructive trustee when he knowingly receives trust property or knowingly assists in a breach of trust[50] are not applicable to a contract entered into for an improper purpose.[51]

16.5 DUTY TO PROMOTE THE SUCCESS OF THE COMPANY

This statutory duty, in s 172(1), was expressed in the case-law, in the classic words of Lord Greene MR in *Re Smith & Fawcett Ltd,*[52] that directors are bound to exercise the powers conferred upon them 'bona fide in what they consider – not what a court may consider – is in the interests of the company ...'. This duty of honesty and good faith in the exercise of his powers was arguably the primary fiduciary duty of a director, although in the statutory code it is 'relegated' to second place. However, it is clearly of central importance and its formulation proved to be one of the most controversial questions when the Companies Bill was discussed in Parliament.[53]

Traditionally the interests of the company, in the case of a company limited by shares, were regarded as the interests of the shareholders, present and future. Section 172 refers to the interests of members rather than those of shareholders, but does so to cater for the situation of all companies, including guarantee companies that do not have shareholders. In that respect, s 172(2) caters for such companies, especially charitable and community interest companies. The section seeks to capture what the CLRSG described as the principle of 'enlightened shareholder value', although the final version differs in a number of respects from the draft that was appended to their *Final Report* and indeed from earlier versions

---

[48] *Re London and Provincial Starch Co, Gower's Case* (1868) LR 6 Eq 77.

[49] See Chapter 6.

[50] See *Gore-Browne on Companies* (Jordans, 45th edn, loose-leaf) 16[4].

[51] *Criterion Properties plc v Stratford Properties LLC* [2004] UKHL 28, [2006] 1 BCLC 729, reversing the approach of the Court of Appeal in this case ([2002] EWCA Civ 1883, [2003] 2 BCLC 129), and disapproving of the application of those principles in the earlier Court of Appeal decision in *BCCI (Overseas) Ltd v Akindele* [2001] Ch 437.

[52] [1942] Ch 304, at 306 (CA); see also *Alexander v Automatic Telephone Co* [1900] 2 Ch 56, at 72 (CA); *Charterbridge Corporation Ltd v Lloyd's Bank Ltd* [1970] Ch 62, at 74; *Gething v Kilner* [1972] 1 WLR 337, at 341–342; *Clemens v Clemens Bros Ltd* [1976] 2 All ER 268, at 268–280; *Hindle v John Cotton Ltd* (1919) 56 Sc LR 625, at 631, (HL Sc); *Regentcrest plc v Cohen* [2001] 2 BCLC 80.

[53] See the reports of Grand Committee in the House of Lords, *Hansard,* HL Deb, 678, ser 5, col GC 237 (6 February 2006) and of Standing Committee D in the House of Commons, *Hansard,* HC SC D, ser 6, cols 522 ff (6 July 2006) and 543 ff (11 July 2006).

in the Bill.[54] The core duty is to act in the way a director considers, in good faith, would be most likely to promote the success of the company for the benefit of its members as a whole;[55] it is supplemented by the requirement for him to have regard (amongst other matters) to the following factors, namely:

(a) the likely consequences of any decision in the long term;

(b) the interests of the company's employees;

(c) the need to foster the company's business relationships with suppliers, customers and others;

(d) the impact of the company's operations on the community and the environment;

(e) the desirability of the company maintaining a reputation for high standards of business conduct; and

(f) the need to act fairly as between members of the company.

We shall consider the impact of these 'stakeholder' factors further in **16.5.1**. As Lord Greene's formulation indicated, and s 172 confirms, this duty is subjective, in that the court will not consider it broken merely because, in the court's own opinion, the particular exercise of power was not to promote the success of the company for the benefit of its members;[56] *a fortiori* the court will not take it upon itself to order that a particular power vested in directors should be exercised in a particular way.[57] On the other hand, the court will insist that, save insofar as the articles expressly permit, it should be the directors, and not some other person or body to whom they have purported to delegate their powers, who determine how the powers vested in the directors are best used to promote the success of the company.[58]

Leaving aside for the moment most of the factors to which directors must have regard, and the situation where a company does not have commercial

---

54 The issue is linked, for larger companies at any rate, with the disclosure requirements in the business review; see **14.10.2**.

55 In *Re Southern Counties Fresh Foods Ltd* [2008] EWHC 2810 (Ch) at [52], Warren J commented that this came to the same thing as the previous formulation with the statute 'giving a more readily understood definition of the scope of the duty'.

56 No doubt it will hold, however, that a breach has occurred if the relevant exercise of power could not possibly be considered by a reasonable man to be in the interests of the company; cf *Shuttleworth v Cox Bros & Co (Maidenhead) Ltd* [1927] 2 KB 9 (CA), and other authorities on the fiduciary duties of the shareholders in general meeting, cited at **5.17**. And see also *Charterbridge Corporation Ltd v Lloyd's Bank Ltd* [1970] Ch 72 and the discussion by Keay (2006) 28 Co Law 106. See also *R (on the application of People & Planet) v HM Treasury* [2009] EWHC 3020 (Admin) at [34] and [35].

57 *Pergamon Press Ltd v Maxwell* [1970] 1 WLR 1167.

58 *Re County Palatine Loan and Discount Co, Cartnell's Case* (1874) 9 Ch App 691.

objectives, an important issue is whether promoting the success of the company for the benefit of its members is the same as the interests of the company as a commercial entity, to be judged by reference to the interests of present and future shareholders. At common law, the only circumstances in which the directors might legitimately promote the interest of any other groups or entities were those where to do so ultimately advanced the interests of the shareholders.[59] Insofar as this might have been thought to encourage a short-term view, in other words, to emphasise profitability above all else, the presence of factor (a) above ought to make the position under the section clear. This is arguably what the general law required anyway, namely that directors should, in appropriate circumstances, seek to balance short-term considerations, affecting the present shareholders only, against long-term considerations which involve future shareholders as well.[60] This is because, as already stated, the interests of the company are equated to the interests of the shareholders or members as a whole, not simply to present shareholders.

In contrast, where a company was to be taken over and the only issue was as to which of competing bids was to succeed, the interests of the company were regarded as the interests of its current shareholders only,[61] and it is thought that, in this sort of situation, a similar interpretation can be placed on the words in s 172(1). However, even this does not necessarily mean that the directors are under a positive duty to recommend the higher bid nor that they cannot agree to recommend a particular bid or agree not to encourage or co-operate with another would-be bidder.[62] Section 172(1) ought also to be interpreted in line with the view that the mere fact that, in a particular transaction, the directors of a company having a holding company and/or subsidiaries and/or co-subsidiaries looked to the interests of the group as a whole does not of itself mean that they are in breach of duty, provided that an 'intelligent and honest man' in the position of the directors could have reasonably believed the transaction to be in the interests of the company.[63]

Factor (f) in s 172(1) seems an appropriate statement of the case-law to the effect that where a particular decision to be taken by the directors bears differently upon different classes of shareholders, their duty is to act

---

[59] *Hutton v West Cork Rly Co* (1883) 23 Ch D 654 (CA); *Parke v Daily News Ltd* [1962] Ch 927. Although these decisions were concerned with gratuitous payments, where the matter may concern the validity of a resolution of shareholders as well as or rather than a decision of the directors, it is submitted that the same meaning of the 'interests of the company' applied when an issue was solely one of the duties of directors; see further, Birds (1980) 1 Co Law 67; *contra* Instone [1979] JBL 221. As to the statutory reversal of the actual decision in *Parke v Daily News Ltd*, see **6.3.3** where the topic of gratuitous payments is also discussed more fully.

[60] See the report of the Inspector, Mr E Milner-Holland QC, in the Savoy Hotel Investigation (HMSO, 1954); see Gower (1955) 68 Harv LR 1176.

[61] *Heron International Ltd v Grade* [1984] BCLC 244, esp at 264–265 (CA).

[62] See *Re a Company* [1986] BCLC 382, at 389–390 and *Dawson International plc v Coats Paton plc* (1989) 5 BCC 405.

[63] *Charterbridge Corporation Ltd v Lloyds Bank Ltd* [1970] Ch 72, at 74.

fairly having regard to the interests of all classes,[64] although ultimately they must act in the interests of the company.[65]

If a power is found not to have been exercised by the directors in good faith to promote the success of the company, the consequences are the same as those described in **16.4**, and if the exercise of the power causes loss to the company, the directors responsible will be liable to make good the loss.

16.5.1 Interests other than those of the members

It has already been suggested that there was nothing in the case-law that prevented directors from taking account of a wide range of 'stakeholders', provided that in doing so they acted in good faith in the interests of the company. The question is whether, and, if so, to what extent, the presence of the factors (b) to (e) in section 172(1) makes any difference. Clearly it does to some extent, because directors must 'have regard' to these factors. Previously the only interests other than those of members or shareholders to which directors had to have regard were those of the company's employees, under what became s 309 of the 1985 Act, but there is no evidence that this impacted to any significant extent on the decisions of directors. Indeed, it was arguable that directors were not entitled to subordinate the interests of members to those of employees, because s 309 did not alter the legal meaning of 'interests of the company' which must ultimately be paramount. Imagine the case of a board faced with a decision whether or not to close down a factory that is unprofitable but employs a considerable number of people who would lose their jobs if the decision to close were taken. Provided that the directors considered this point, it is submitted that they would not have been in breach of s 309 if they decided to close the factory. Indeed, if they did not so decide they might be liable for not acting in good faith to promote the success of the company for the benefit of its members, if it could clearly be shown that they had acted against the interests of the members. There is nothing in s 172(1) that in any way alters this interpretation nor that makes any alleged breach actionable at the instance of the employees or any of the other stakeholders listed in the subsection; the duty in section 172 is a duty owed to the company not to anyone else, as s 170(1) makes clear.

In any event, there seems little doubt that the properly advised board of a large company at least has long considered the consequences of its decisions on the wide range of interests now contained in the statute. Imposing an explicit requirement, though, to act in this way on the directors (or even sole director) of a small company may be more

---

[64] *Henry v Great Northern Rly* (1857) 1 De G & J 606, at 638.
[65] *Mutual Life Insurance Co of New York v Rank Organisation Ltd* [1985] BCLC 11; *Re BSB Holdings Ltd* [1996] 1 BCLC 155, at 246–249.

problematic, even though a decision in such a case is likely to be open to some form of challenge only if and when the company goes into liquidation.

It should be noted that the duty to have regard to these matters is not limited by a requirement to do so only 'so far as reasonably practicable'; this was a qualification that appeared in earlier drafts. It seems clear that the section does not permit a defence based, say, on ignorance, particularly as directors are at the same time required under s 174 to act with reasonable care, skill and diligence. Clearly the well-advised board will henceforth ensure that the minutes of its meetings record that it paid due regard to these factors. On the whole it is thought that the effect of s 172 is more likely to be educational rather than in any sense restrictive and that business decisions taken in good faith will not be any more easily challengeable than they were before this provision existed.

16.5.2 Interests of creditors

By providing that the duty has effect subject to any enactment[66] or rule or law requiring directors, in certain circumstances, to consider or act in the interests of creditors, s 172(3) recognises that the duty is modified when the company is insolvent or on the verge of insolvency.[67] The common law also recognises that the interests of creditors displace those of members in this situation, and this rule is left untouched by the codification. So, when a company is insolvent or on the verge of insolvency, but not otherwise, it is the creditors' interests that become paramount.[68] This recognition of creditors' interest by the common law is a relatively recent development, and has probably been heavily influenced by the same factors as led to the introduction of statutory provisions designed to give more effective protection to creditors.[69] Although it has been said that a duty is owed by the directors to the company and to the creditors of the company to ensure that the affairs of the company are properly administered and that

---

[66] This must refer primarily to provisions in the Insolvency Act 1986, especially s 214 on wrongful trading; see **15.19.2**.

[67] In *Stone & Rolls Ltd v Moore Stephens* [2009] UKHL 39, [2009] 1 AC 1319, at [224], Lord Mance commented: 'Section 172(1) of the Companies Act 2006 now states the duty, in terms expressly based on common law rules and equitable principles (see s 170(3)), as being to "act in the way he considers, in good faith, would be most likely to promote the success of the company for the benefit of its members as a whole" – a duty made expressly "subject to any enactment or rule of law requiring directors, in certain circumstances, to consider or act in the interests of creditors of the company (see s 172(3))."'

[68] See especially, *Lonrho Ltd v Shell Petroleum Ltd* [1980] 1 WLR 627, at 634 (HL), per Lord Diplock; *West Mercia Safetyware Ltd v Dodd* [1988] BCLC 250, at 252–253 (CA), per Dillon LJ. See also *Brady v Brady* [1989] AC 755 (HL); *Facia Footwear Ltd v Hinchcliffe* [1998] 1 BCLC 218; *Colin Gwyer & Associates Ltd v London Wharf (Limehouse) Ltd* [2002] EWHC 2748 (Ch), [2003] 2 BCLC 153; *Starglade Properties Ltd v Nash* [2009] EWHC 148 (Ch) at para 35; *Singla v Hedman* [2010] 2 BCLC 61 at para 33, *Roberts v Frohlich* [2011] EWHC 257 (Ch), [2011] All ER (D) 211 (Feb).

[69] Especially s 214 of the Insolvency Act 1986.

its property is not dissipated or exploited for the benefit of the directors themselves to the prejudice of the creditors,[70] it is submitted that this is not a duty owed directly to creditors, but rather a duty to the company, which in the event of liquidation can be enforced by the liquidator for the benefit of the creditors.[71] Further, it is a duty owed to the creditors as a whole, not to an individual creditor or section of creditors with special rights in a winding-up.[72]

16.6 DUTY TO EXERCISE INDEPENDENT JUDGMENT

Section 173 codifies the principle of law under which directors must exercise independent judgment, namely they must not fetter their discretion, unless they act in accordance with an agreement which has been duly entered into by the company or in a way authorised by the company's constitution. This could be regarded as an illustration of the general duty to act in good faith, as a consequence of the principle prohibiting conflicts of duty and interest or even perhaps as a breach of the duty to exercise reasonable care, skill and diligence, but it is set out separately in the statutory code.

It is not uncommon for a director to undertake, formally or informally, to act in accordance with the instructions of an 'outsider' or as representative of such an 'outsider'. This can arise when a holding company has nominee directors on the board of its subsidiary, or when the right to appoint a director is given to a class of shareholders or a debenture-holder or class of debenture-holders. Case-law established that it was not necessarily unlawful for a director to be in such a position, provided that he did not conceal his position, had the consent of the company,[73] preserved a substantial degree of independent discretion as to how he would exercise his powers,[74] and, if a divergence occurred between the interests of the company and those of the 'outsider', did not subordinate the former to the latter as a means of resolving the conflict.[75] Similarly, directors could not validly contract with an outsider as to how

---

[70] *Winkworth v Edward Baron Development Co Ltd* [1987] BCLC 193, at 197 (HL), per Lord Templeman.

[71] *Re Horsley & Weight Ltd* [1982] 3 All ER 1045, at 1055 (CA), per Buckley LJ; *Kuwait Asia Bank EC v National Mutual Life Nominees Ltd* [1990] BCLC 868, at 888 (PC), per Lord Lowry. See also *Yukong Line Ltd of Korea v Rendsberg Investment Corp of Liberia* [1998] 4 All ER 82, at 99. It is not a breach of duty for a director to cause the company to prefer one creditor to another: *Knight v Frost* [1999] 1 BCLC 364, at 381–382; see also *Re Brian D Pierson (Contractors) Ltd* [1999] BCC 26, at 46. In practice, it seems more likely that the matter will be litigated and decided under the statutory wrongful trading provision rather than as a common-law duty.

[72] *Re Pantone 485 Ltd* [2002] 1 BCLC 266, at 285–287. For the many Commonwealth authorities that have considered this issue, see *Gore-Browne on Companies*, **15[10C]**.

[73] See *Kregor v Hollins* [1913] 109 LT 225, at 231.

[74] *Boulting v ACTAT* [1963] 2 QB 606, at 626–627; *Clark v Workman* [1920] Ir R 107.

[75] See, in particular, *Scottish Co-operative v Meyer*, above. For useful comments on the position of nominee directors, see Boros (1989) 10 Co Law 211 and (1990) 11 Co Law 6, and Crutchfield (1991) 12 Co Law 136.

they will vote at future board meetings, but this did not preclude them from agreeing, in a contract entered into in good faith in the interests of the company, that they would take such further action as was necessary to carry out that contract.[76] These principles are now clearly comprehended by s 173.[77]

The potential responsibility of the 'outsider' for the acts of the directors was in issue in *Kuwait Asia Bank EC v National Mutual Life Nominees Ltd*,[78] where a bank held a beneficial interest in 40% of the issued shares of a company and had nominated two of its employees to be directors of the company. It was held that in the performance of their duties, the directors were bound to ignore the interests and wishes of the bank and could not plead any instruction from the bank as an excuse for any breach of their duties. In the absence of evidence that the bank had exploited its position and interfered with the affairs of the company, it was neither vicariously nor personally liable for any negligence of the directors. In *Re Neath Rugby Ltd*,[79] it was held that while the nominee's primary loyalty is to the company of which he is a director, he is entitled to have regard to the interests or requirements of his appointer to the extent that they are not incompatible with his primary duty to the company. Whether this is a matter of entitlement or obligation must depend on the terms, express or implied, of the agreement pursuant to which the director was appointed. This view was upheld by the Court of Appeal in subsequent proceedings in the same litigation, where it was said:[80]

> '[A]n appointed director, without being in breach of his duties to the company, may take the interests of his nominator into account, provided that his decisions as a director are in what he genuinely believes to be the best interests of the company; but that is a very different thing from his being under a duty to his nominator by reason of his appointment by it.'

Perhaps surprisingly, the case-law does not generally prohibit a director from competing with his company, whether on his own account or by virtue of his being director of another company in the same field of business.[81] Further, in the absence of some special circumstance, a

---

[76] *Fulham Football Club Ltd v Cabra Estates plc* [1992] BCC 863 (CA), following the decision of the High Court of Australia in *Thorby v Goldberg* (1964) 112 CLR 597.

[77] One interesting issue is the relationship between s 173 and provisions in shareholders' agreements that may seek to constrain the judgment of directors. There should be no problem if the company is a party to such an agreement as this is covered by the wording of the section, but that is not always the case.

[78] [1990] BCLC 868 (PC).

[79] [2008] 1 BCLC 527, esp at **[26]** and **[27]**. See also *Re Southern Counties Fresh Foods Ltd* [2008] EWHC 2810 (Ch).

[80] *Re Neath Rugby Ltd (No 2)* [2009] EWCA Civ 261, [2009] 2 BCLC 427 at [33].

[81] *London v Mashonaland Exploration Co Ltd v New Mashonaland Exploration Co Ltd* [1891] WN 165, approved in *Bell v Lever Bros Ltd* [1932] AC 161, at 195–196 and followed by the majority of the Court of Appeal in *In Plus Group Ltd v Pyke* [2002] EWCA Civ 370, [2002] 2 BCLC 201. However, Sedley LJ (ibid, at 222–227) expressed

director commits no breach of duty merely because he takes steps so that, on ceasing to be a director, he can immediately set up in business in competition with the company or join a competitor of it.[82] This, however, is subject to any express agreement to the contrary between the director and the company, and, if the director is also an employee of the company, the court may in appropriate circumstances be prepared to imply into his contract of employment a term that he should not perform services for a competitor, even in his spare time.[83] In addition, of course, freedom to compete does not comprehend licence to disclose confidential information belonging to his company[84] nor to breach the duty to avoid conflicts of interests.[85] The Companies Act says nothing expressly about competing directors, so that the position described above must remain good law, provided of course that a director exercises independent judgment as required by s 173 and complies with the other general duties. So a director will be in breach of duty if, in competing with the company, he undermines it.[86] That would be a breach of the duties now contained in ss 172 and 175.

16.7 DUTY TO EXERCISE REASONABLE CARE, SKILL AND DILIGENCE

The requirement that a director exercise reasonable care, skill and diligence, as set out in s 174(1) of the 2006 Act, has always been a requirement of the common law, but, until relatively recently, the standard of reasonableness was, at least in part, only a subjective standard.[87] It is now clear under s 174(2) that a director must display the care, skill and diligence that would be exercised by a reasonably diligent person with both (a) the general knowledge, skill and experience that may reasonably

---

some doubts and compare *Scottish Co-operative Wholesale Society Ltd v Meyer* [1959] AC 324, at 368 and, for a detailed analysis and trenchant criticism, see Christie 'The Director's Fiduciary Duty Not to Compete' (1992) 55 MLR 506.

[82]   *Balston Ltd v Headline Filters Ltd* [1990] FSR 385; *Framlington Group plc v Anderson* [1995] 1 BCLC 475.

[83]   See, in particular, *Hivac Ltd v Park Royal Scientific Instruments Ltd* [1949] Ch 169. Such a term will not always be implied; ibid.

[84]   As to confidential information, see **16.13.1**.

[85]   See **16.8**.

[86]   See, eg, *Berryland Books Ltd v BK Books Ltd* [2009] EWHC 1877 (Ch), [2009] 2 BCLC 709.

[87]   This was particularly so as regards the skill and diligence required; see especially *Re City Equitable Fire Insurance Co Ltd* [1925] Ch 407, where Romer J reviewed earlier authorities and reduced the principles therein to three general propositions: (1) that the skill to be expected was merely what a person of the director's knowledge and experience could reasonably be expected to display; (2) that a director was not bound to give continuous attention to the affairs of the company; and (3) that a director could trust others entrusted with specific duties to perform them honestly in the absence of grounds for suspicion. To some extent this third proposition may still be relevant, as explained below. See generally Finch 'Company Directors: Who Cares about Skill and Care?' (1992) 55 MLR 179 and Riley 'The Company Director's Duty of Care and Skill: the Case for an Onerous but Subjective Standard' (1999) 62 MLR 697.

be expected of a person carrying out the same functions as the director in relation to that company and (b) the general knowledge, skill and experience that the director actually has. This is the standard imposed in considering whether or not a director is liable for wrongful trading under s 214 of the Insolvency Act 1986,[88] which the courts had increasingly regarded as setting the common law standard. In any event, directors employed under a contract of service, that is in effect an executive director, will be bound to exercise objectively reasonable care, skill and diligence by virtue of his position as employee.[89] These modern cases merit some examination because they illustrate how s 174 will be construed, especially as regards directors holding non-executive positions.[90]

In *Dorchester Finance Co Ltd v Stebbing*,[91] it was held that non-executive directors who were either qualified accountants or who had considerable accountancy and business experience had been negligent in signing blank cheques which allowed the managing director to misappropriate the company's money. In *Norman v Theodore Goddard*[92] and *Re D'Jan of London Ltd*,[93] it was held that s 214 of the Insolvency Act 1986 expressed the standard to be expected of directors. However, this does not mean that, for example, a director will not be able to rely upon others in appropriate circumstances, something that is important given that non-executive directors in large companies do not themselves manage. In *Norman v Theodore Goddard*, it was held that, provided he observed the standard laid down in s 214, a director was entitled to trust people in positions of responsibility until there was reason to distrust them. So a director was not liable for the theft of company money by someone who was a senior partner in an eminent firm of solicitors when he had no reason to doubt the other's honesty. However, a director who delegates a function, but then keeps an eye on its performance, will not be allowed to maintain that he did not know what was going on.[94] Furthermore, the power to delegate – even a power expressly contained in the company's articles – does not enable the directors to abdicate their functions in favour of some other person as 'manager': they must retain the power of overall control.[95] It has also been stated delegation does not mean

---

[88] See **15.19.2**.

[89] Cf *Lister v Romford Ice & Cold Storage Co Ltd* [1957] AC 555.

[90] It is thought that the provisions of the UK Corporate Governance Code (see Chapter 11) may also be a useful guide, at least as concerns the non-executive directors of listed companies.

[91] [1989] BCLC 498 (decided in 1977, although unreported until 1989). Here, Foster J actually applied the 'old' test laid down in *Re City Equitable Fire Insurance Co Ltd*, above.

[92] [1991] BCLC 1028, at 1030–1031, per Hoffmann J.

[93] [1993] BCC 646, at 648, also decided by Hoffmann LJ (as he had by then become).

[94] Cf *Department of Health and Social Security v Wayte* [1972] 1 WLR 19, CA.

[95] *Barlows Manufacturing Co Ltd v RN Barrie (Pty) Ltd 1990 (4) SA 608, PD (Cape)*; see also *Re Barings plc (No 3)* [1999] 1 BCLC 433.

'unquestioning reliance upon others to do their job'.[96] The modern position has been summarised as follows:[97]

> 'Whilst directors are entitled (subject to the articles of association of the company) to delegate particular functions to those below them in the management chain, and to trust their competence and integrity to a reasonable extent, the exercise of the power of delegation does not absolve a director from the duty to supervise the discharge of the delegated functions ... No rule of universal application can be formulated as to the duty ... The extent of the duty, and the question whether it has been discharged, must depend on the facts of each particular case, including the director's role in the management of the company.'

Even if a director is regarded as negligently having failed to supervise others who, for example, have committed fraud on the company, they will only be liable for losses that can be shown to have been caused by their negligence.[98]

In *Re D'Jan of London Ltd*, a director who signed an insurance proposal form without checking its contents was regarded as negligent. In *Re Simmon Box (Diamonds) Ltd*,[99] the only director of the company, who abjectly surrendered to the person who acted as *de facto* director, was held to have been negligent, as was the director in *Re Westlowe Storage and Distribution Ltd*,[100] who failed to ensure that the company benefited properly from the transactions it was engaged in when it was his responsibility to ensure that a proper accounting system was in place.[101] A sole director of many hundreds of companies cannot discharge his duties as such where the management has been effectively delegated to others who must be supervised.[102] On the other hand, a director who, to the best of his ability, acts on appropriate legal advice will not be regarded as negligent.[103] Further illustrations of conduct regarded as negligent can be found in some of the case-law on the question of whether or not a director should be disqualified for unfitness under s 6 of the Company Directors Disqualification Act 1986.[104]

---

[96] *Equitable Life Assurance Society v Bowley* [2004] 1 BCLC 180, at [41] per Langley J.

[97] *Re Barings plc (No 3)* [1999] 1 BCLC 433, at 489, per Parker J. See also *Re Westmid Packing Services Ltd* [1998] 2 BCLC 646, at 653, CA. Both these decisions were concerned with the permissibility of delegation in the context of applications for the disqualification of directors for unfitness under s 6 of the Company Directors Disqualification Act 1986. See also *Re London Citylink Ltd* [2005] EWHC 2875 (Ch).

[98] *Lexi Holdings plc v Luqman* [2008] EWHC 1639 (Ch), reversed in part on the facts: [2009] EWCA Civ 117.

[99] [2000] BCC 275.

[100] [2000] BCC 851.

[101] See also *Re Loquitur Ltd* [2003] 2 BCLC 442 and *Equitable Life Assurance Society v Bowley* [2004] 1 BCLC 180.

[102] *Re London Citylink Ltd* [2005] EWHC 2875 (Ch).

[103] *Green v Walkling* [2007] EWHC 3251.

[104] See especially *Re Landhurst Leasing plc* [1999] 1 BCLC 286, at 344; *Re Barings plc* [1999]

A director who resigns on discovering circumstances suggesting that, for example, another director is committing breaches of duty may not escape liability unless they bring the circumstances to the attention of the board as a whole and, possibly, to the members of the company.[105]It should be noted that a director is not the agent of his co-directors,[106] and the other officers of the company are not the agents of the directors.[107] Thus the mere fact that a director or officer is liable for breach of duty does not of itself render the remaining directors liable. Their liability can be established only if it can be shown that they were negligent in accordance with the standards of skill and care expected of them, or if they participated, however slightly,[108] in the breach, or sanctioned the conduct constituting the breach.

16.8 DUTIES TO AVOID CONFLICTS OF INTEREST AND NOT TO ACCEPT BENEFITS FROM THIRD PARTIES

Directors have long been in general bound by the broad principle, codified, with modifications, by ss 175–177 of the Companies Act 2006, derived from equity and affecting all persons who are subject to fiduciary duties, that 'no-one, having such duties to discharge, shall be allowed to enter into engagements in which he has, or can have a personal interest conflicting, or which possibly may conflict, with the interests of those whom he is bound to protect'.[109] This principle, often referred to as the 'no conflict' rule, equally applies if the director has an 'outside' duty which clashes or may clash with his fiduciary duties to the company.[110] Section 175 of the 2006 Act encapsulates the basic no conflict principle, but then modifies it in its application to company directors. Section 176

---

1 BCLC 433, at 486–489. See Walters 'Directors duties: the impact of the Company Directors Disqualification Act 1986' (2000) 21 Co Law 110. See also *Re London Citylink Ltd* [2005] EWHC 2875 (Ch).

[105] *Lexi Holdings plc v Luqman* [2008] EWHC 1639 (Ch), at [39].

[106] *Cargill v Bower* (1878) 10 Ch D 502; *Re Denham & Co* (1883) 25 Ch D 752.

[107] *Weir v Barnett* (1877) 3 Ex D 32; *Weir v Bell* (1878) 3 Ex D 238 (CA).

[108] See, especially, *Re Lands Allotment Co* [1894] 1 Ch 617 (CA), where a chairman of directors, who signed the minutes relating to an ultra vires investment of company funds and announced the investment to the company in general meeting in terms indicating his assent thereto, was held liable as a participant in this misapplication of company funds. See also *Ramskill v Edwards* (1885) 31 Ch D 100 and *Bishopsgate Investment Management Ltd v Maxwell* [1993] BCC 120 (CA).

[109] *Aberdeen Rly Co v Blaikie* (1854) 1 Macq 461, at 471–472 (HL (Sc)), per Lord Cranworth LC; see also *North-West Transportation Co Ltd v Beatty* (1887) 12 App Cas 589 at 593 (PC); *Bray v Ford* [1896] AC 44, at 51–52 (HL); *Regal (Hastings) Ltd v Gulliver* [1942] 1 All ER 378, at 381; [1967] 2 AC 134n, at 137 (HL); *Boulting v ACTAT* [1963] 2 QB 606, at 635 (CA); *New Zealand Netherlands Society 'Oranje' Inc v Kuys* [1973] 1 WLR 1126, at 1129 (PC); *Queensland Mines Ltd v Hudson* (1978) 52 ALJR 399 (PC); *Guinness plc v Saunders* [1990] 2 AC 663 (HL); *CMS Dolphin Ltd v Simonet* [2001] 2 BCLC 704, at 728–734; *Bhullar v Bhullar* [2003] EWCA Civ 424, [2003] 2 BCLC 241; *Foster Bryant Surveying Ltd v Bryant* [2007] EWCA Civ 239; *Lee v Futurist Developments Ltd* [2010] EWHC 2764 (Ch), [2010] All ER (D) 109.

[110] *Transvaal Lands Co v New Belgium (Transvaal) Land and Development Co* [1914] 2 Ch 488 (CA).

provides for a duty not to accept benefits from third parties and s 177, which is considered in **16.10**, provides for a duty of disclosure of interests in transactions and arrangements with the company.

The general equitable principle could be invoked by the company only, and not by the director by way of a defence to proceedings instigated to compel performance of the conflicting duty.[111] A classic illustration of its operation is the decision in *Industrial Development Consultants v Cooley*.[112] Here the managing director of a design and construction company, being himself a successful architect, failed in an attempt to obtain for the company a valuable contract to do work for a local gas board. He was subsequently approached by the board with an offer to take up the contract in his private capacity, the board still indicating that it was not interested in letting the company have the contract. He concealed this offer from the company and, by misrepresenting that he was in poor health, procured the company to release him from his service contract, in order that he could take up the contract for himself. It was held by Roskill J that he was liable to account to the company for the profit which he obtained from performing the contract, on the footing that he should have informed the company of the board's offer to him and that, after the offer was made, he 'embarked on a deliberate policy and course of conduct which put his personal interests as a potential contracting party with the [gas board] in direct conflict with his pre-existing and continuing duty as managing director of the [company]'.[113]

A further example is provided by the House of Lords' decision in *Guinness plc v Saunders*.[114] Here, a director of Guinness, which was engaged in making a takeover bid for the shares of another company, agreed to provide services to Guinness in connection with the bid for a substantial fee, the size of which was dependent on the value of the bid. In the absence of a properly authorised contract,[115] it was held by the House of Lords that the director had put himself into a position where there was an irreconcilable conflict between his personal interests and his duty, in consequence of which he had no claim to an equitable allowance for his services. See also the Court of Appeal decision in *Bhullar v*

---

[111] *Boulting v ACTAT*, above. The equitable 'rule' was arguably more aptly described as a 'principle' rather than as a 'duty', although its application might lead to duties imposed on directors, eg duties of disclosure. See Vinelott J in *Motivex Ltd v Bulfield* (1986) 2 BCC 99, at 403 (following *Tito v Waddell (No 2)* [1977] 3 All ER 129). The Act, on the other hand, clearly describes it as a duty.

[112] [1972] 2 All ER 162.

[113] [1972] 2 All ER 162, at 173–174.

[114] [1990] 2 AC 663.

[115] The articles of Guinness would have permitted such a contract provided that it had been approved by the full board of directors (along the lines of standard articles referred to in the following sections). Instead, it was only the sub-committee of the board charged with facilitating the takeover which had purported to enter into a contract. This 'contract' was void.

Bhullar,[116] where, on similar facts to those in *Industrial Development Consultants Ltd v Cooley*, the court stressed the universality and inflexibility of the principle in any situation where a reasonable person looking at the facts would think that there was a reasonably sensible possibility of conflict.

16.8.1 Conflicts of Interest and Secret Profits

As mentioned above, s 175 contains the statutory codification of the no-conflict principle.[117] Section 175(1) encapsulates the core principle – 'a director of a company must avoid a situation in which he has, or can have, a direct or indirect interest that conflicts, or possibly may conflict, with the interests of the company' – and s 175(7) makes it clear that the duty covers conflicts of interest and duty and conflicts of duties. Section 175(2) amplifies the duty by stating that it applies in particular to the exploitation of any property, information or opportunity, whether or not the company could take advantage of such property, information or opportunity. It thus clearly covers circumstances like those in *Industrial Developments Ltd v Cooley*[118] and *Bhullar v Bhullar*,[119] as described in **16.8**. Further, where a director resigns and then exploits a maturing business opportunity of the company, he is accountable for the profits properly attributable to the breach of duty, as is also a company that he has formed in order to exploit the opportunity.[120]

On the other hand, s 175(3) states that the duty does not apply to conflicts arising in relation to a transaction or arrangement with the company: these are dealt with by either s 177 or 182,[121] or by the specific provisions in Chapter 4 of Part 10 which are examined in Chapter 17. Section 175(4)(a) confirms the case-law position[122] that there is only a situation of conflict where that can reasonably be regarded as likely to arise.

As well as codifying the broad no-conflict principle, s 175 also covers, at least in part, what was previously often described as a separate principle,

---

[116] [2003] EWCA Civ 424, [2003] 2 BCLC 241. See also the analysis in *Crown Dilmun v Sutton* [2004] BCLC 468 and, for a recent application, *Kingsley IT Consulting Ltd v McIntosh* [2006] All ER (D) 237 (Feb).

[117] Note the important modification of s 175(3) and (5) regarding charitable companies (see s 181).

[118] [1972] 2 All ER 162.

[119] [2003] EWCA Civ 424, [2003] 2 BCLC 241.

[120] *CMS Dolphin Ltd v Simonet* [2001] 2 BCLC 704. Lawrence Collins J characterised the breach as a breach of trust, relying in particular on *Cook v Deeks* [1916] AC 554, PC and *Canadian Aero Service Ltd v O'Malley* (1973) 40 DLR (3d) 371 SC (Can), as well as the general principle exemplified in *Regal (Hastings) Ltd v Gulliver* [1942] 1 All ER 378, [1967] 2 AC 134n, HL. His judgment was referred to in *In Plus Group Ltd v Pyke* [2002] EWCA Civ 370 as a valuable recent analysis of the law governing the no conflict and no profits rules.

[121] See **16.10** and **16.12.1**.

[122] See especially *Bhullar v Bhullar, above*.

albeit derived from the no-conflict principle. This is the principle that any profit acquired by a director through holding the office of director must as a matter of law be accounted for to the company,[123] unless the director had disclosed the profit and the circumstances in which he acquired it to the company in general meeting and his retention of it had been sanctioned by an ordinary resolution or by the acquiescence of all the individual members entitled to vote thereon, or unless he was protected by an appropriately worded provision of the articles.

In the leading House of Lords' decision in *Regal (Hastings) Ltd v Gulliver*,[124] the plaintiff company had formed a subsidiary company which was to take up a lease of two cinemas, but the owner of the cinemas insisted that the subsidiary should have a paid-up capital which, in the honest opinion of the plaintiff's board, was greater than the plaintiff could afford to subscribe. The ordinary directors accordingly subscribed at par for part of the balance themselves, the remainder being taken up by 'outsiders' in the name of the chairman of directors and by the plaintiff's solicitor. The whole transaction had been carried out with a view to a sale of the two cinemas, together with another cinema that the plaintiff itself owned, as a going concern, but ultimately the shares of the plaintiff and of the subsidiary were purchased instead at a price substantially above par. The plaintiff company sued the ordinary directors, the chairman and the solicitor for an account of their profits on the resale. It was found that they had all acted honestly throughout, but none the less the ordinary directors, who had taken their shares as beneficial owners, were held liable to account to the plaintiff, it being said that only disclosure to and approval by the general meeting would have saved them. On the other hand, the chairman escaped liability because the 'outsiders' who beneficially owned the shares for which he had subscribed owed no

---

[123] *Parker v McKenna* (1874) 10 Ch App 96, esp at 118, 124; *Re Canadian Oil Works Corporation, Hay's Case* (1875) 10 Ch App 593; *Boston Deep Sea Fishing and Ice Co v Ansell* (1888) 39 ChD 339, esp at 363 to 364, CA; *Regal (Hastings) Ltd v Gulliver* [1942] 1 All ER 378, [1967] 2 AC 134n, HL; *Henderson v Huntingdon Copper & Sulphur Co Ltd* (1877) 5 R 1, HL (SC); and see *Morrison v Thompson* (1874) LR 9 QB 480 at 485; *Phipps v Boardman* [1967] 2 AC 46, HL; *Industrial Development Consultants Ltd v Cooley* [1972] 2 All ER 162; *Guinness plc v Saunders* [1990] 1 All ER 653, HL. The principle is equally applicable to former directors, provided that they have acquired the profit from an opportunity which the company is still actively pursuing: *Island Export Finance Ltd v Umunna* [1986] BCLC 460; *CMS Dolphin Ltd v Simonet* [2001] 2 BCLC 704.

[124] Above. The traditional principle provoked much discussion and debate regarding its fairness, both in the UK and in other common law jurisdictions; see, for example, Jones (1968) 84 LQR 472; Prentice (1974) Can Bar Rev 623; Bishop and Prentice (1983) 46 MLR 289; Lowry and Edmunds (1998) 61 MLR 515; Kershaw (2005) 24 OJLS 603. Perhaps the most influential Commonwealth decision was *Canadian Aero Service Ltd v O'Malley* (1973) 40 DLR (3d) 371. In general the CLRSG favoured a strict rule (see *Modern Company Law for a Competitive Economy: Developing the Framework* (March 2000) para 3.63) and modern case-law has regularly emphasised a strict approach to the no conflict and no profit principles governing fiduciaries: see, *inter alia*, *Guinness plc v Saunders* [1990] 2 AC 663; *Attorney-General of Hong Kong v Reid* [1994] 1 AC 324; *Paragon Finance plc v DB Thakerar & Co* [1999] 1 All ER 400 (CA) and *JJ Harrison (Properties) Ltd v Harrison* [2001] EWCA Civ 1467, [2002] 1 BCLC 162.

fiduciary duties to the company. The solicitor escaped also, on the ground that, although owing fiduciary duties to the company as its solicitor, his breach thereof could be and was effectively sanctioned by the board.

The effect of this decision was sometimes reversed, or substantially modified, by a provision in the articles,[125] but it is submitted that its scope was wide enough to render a director liable to account when, through being aware of confidential information which came to him because he was a director – an example was information as to an impending take-over – he made a profit through buying and selling the company's own shares. The party entitled to claim the account would, of course, be the company; as has already been indicated,[126] the decision in *Percival v Wright*[127] substantially curtails, if not totally bars, any claim by an individual shareholder in such a case unless he can establish some material misrepresentation by the director.

The *Regal (Hastings)* decision[128] established that, in an action for account of profits based upon the equitable principle, it was no answer for the director to allege by way of defence that the company could not itself have acquired the relevant profit, or had bona fide decided not to try to acquire it, or in any event had not suffered any loss by virtue of the director having acquired it. However, evidence that an opportunity to enter into the transaction out of which the profit arose had been offered to and rejected by the company, then subsequently offered to the individual directors after a reasonable period of time had elapsed, might be enough to persuade the court that the profit was not derived by virtue of the director's position as such. It was a question of fact in each case.[129] But it would seem that no defence was furnished by establishing any of the following matters: (1) that the director acted honestly and in good faith throughout;[130] (2) that the profit was acquired through the use of the

---

[125] Table A, Part I, art 78 of the Companies Act 1948 reversed the effect of the decision, but the 1985 Table A (reg 85) rather modified it, relieving a director of his duty to account only provided that he has disclosed the nature and extent of his interest to the directors.

[126] See **16.2**.

[127] [1902] 2 Ch 421.

[128] See too *Keech v Sandford* (1726) 2 White and Tudor LC 693; *Boston Deep Sea Fishing and Ice Co Ltd v Ansell* (1888) 39 ChD 339, CA; *Costa Rica Ry Co v Forwood* [1901] 1 Ch 746 at 761, CA; *Phipps v Boardman* [1967] 2 AC 46, HL; *Industrial Development Consultants Ltd v Cooley* [1972] 2 All ER 162.

[129] See the Canadian case of *Peso Silver Mines Ltd v Cropper* (1966) 58 DLR (2d) 1, SC (Can); and cf *Nordisk Insulinlaboratorium v Gorgate Products Ltd* [1953] Ch 430, CA, where the question of cessation of fiduciary duties after cessation of the fiduciary relationship is discussed. See too the decision in *Queensland Mines Ltd v Hudson* (1978) 52 ALJR 399, PC, where it was clear that the company had given up all interest in the transaction and was fully informed, albeit informally, of the director's intention to take up the opportunity himself. It was held therefore that the director was not accountable for the profit he made.

[130] *Parker v McKenna* (1874) 10 Ch App 96; *Costa Rica Ry Co v Forwood* [1901] 1 Ch 746; *Regal (Hastings) Ltd v Gulliver* [1942] 1 All ER 378; and see *Phipps v Boardman* [1967] 2 AC 46, HL. See also *Guinness plc v Saunders* [1990] 1 All ER 653, HL (director

director's own property and/or skill as well as through his directorship;[131] (3) that disclosure to the general meeting would have been a mere formality because at a general meeting the director had or could have summoned sufficient votes to pass a resolution approving his retention of the profit;[132] or (4) that none of the shareholders at the time of the proceedings for an account was a shareholder at the time when the profit was made.

As regards claims made under s 175, there are important changes from the broad equitable principle. First, by s 175(4)(a), the duty under s 175 is not infringed if the situation cannot reasonably be regarded as likely to give rise to a conflict of interest. Arguably the requirement of a conflict of interest was not part of the decision in *Regal (Hastings) Ltd v Gulliver,*[133] although it may have underlain other decisions. Secondly, s 175(4)(b), (5) and (6) allow disclosure to and approval by the directors to resolve a conflict and permit the making of a profit. Section 175(4)(b) provides that the duty is not broken if the matter has been authorised by the directors and then the following subsections explain what such authorisation means. Private companies are assumed to allow this provided that nothing in their constitution is to the contrary. Public companies can allow this provided that there is express authorisation in their constitution. However, in both cases it is necessary that the situation is authorised by directors who are independent of the conflicted director and any other director with an interest, because s 175(6) requires both that the director and any other interested director are not counted in the quorum for the meeting and that either they do not vote or the matter would have been agreed without their voting. In the event that these requirements cannot be met, perhaps because there are in fact no independent directors, the previous position must apply and the conflict can be resolved only by disclosure to and approval by the general meeting; the principle of general meeting approval is preserved generally by s 180(4) of the 2006 Act. Other than in that situation, it is made clear by s 180(1) that if s 175 is complied with, any transaction or arrangement is not liable to be set aside by virtue of any common law rule or equitable principle requiring the consent or approval of the company in general meeting.

---

accountable to repay unauthorised remuneration), where, as seen earlier, the decision rested equally on the broad principle prohibiting conflicts of duty and interest.

[131] See *Parker v McKenna* (1874) 10 Ch App 96; *Costa Rica Ry Co v Forwood* [1901] 1 Ch 746 at 761, CA; *Regal (Hastings) Ltd v Gulliver* [1942] 1 All ER 378; *Phipps v Boardman* [1967] 2 AC 46, HL; *Industrial Development Consultants v Cooley* [1972] 2 All ER 162. See also *CMS Dolphin Ltd v Simonet* [2002] 2 BCLC 704 (profit properly attributable to breach of duty held by director as constructive trustee).

[132] *Regal (Hastings) Ltd v Gulliver, above.*

[133] See in particular the speeches of Lord Russell of Killowen [1942] 1 All ER 378 at 389, [1967] 2 AC 134n at 149 and of Lord Porter, ibid, at 395 and 158, respectively.

The duty under s 175 applies to a former director as regards the exploitation of any property, information or opportunity of which he became aware at a time when he was a director.[134]

16.8.2 Consequences of a breach of the no conflict duty

In the event of the director failing to disclose his interest in any contract to the directors or to the general meeting, depending on the requirements of the articles, or of their refusing to sanction his interest, two consequences follow.[135] In the first place, the contract is voidable at the option of the company against any party thereto who has notice of the breach of duty,[136] though its right of avoidance will lapse if it affirms the contract,[137] or it delays unduly before rescinding, or the rights of *bona fide* third parties intervene.[138] Secondly, any profit which the director derives from the contract is recoverable from him by the company,[139] even if he can show that it is unfair for the company to have the profit and/or that the transaction was fair and reasonable and/or that he could have made the same amount of profit after disclosure.[140]

If the director's interest in the contract is sanctioned, the contract ceases to be voidable and the director may retain any profit arising out of it. The 2006 Act removes the possibility of the director in breach being able to use his own votes as member to secure ratification, which was something the general law permitted, provided at least that the director's breach was in good faith.[141] Section 239 provides that members with a personal interest, direct or indirect, cannot effectively vote. In the case of ratification by written resolution, they are not regarded as eligible members and thus should not be involved in the procedure.[142] In the case of ratification by resolution at a meeting, any of their votes must be disregarded, although they can attend, be counted in the quorum and take part in the proceedings.[143]

---

[134] Section 170(2). This was also the case in equity, provided that a director acquired any profit from an opportunity which the company was still actively pursuing: *Island Export Finance Ltd v Umunna* [1986] BCLC 460; *CMS Dolphin Ltd v Simonet* [2001] 2 BCLC 704.

[135] Under some articles, the director may in addition be liable to disqualification.

[136] *Hely-Hutchinson & Co Ltd v Brayhead* [1968] 1 QB 549 (CA); *Cowan de Groot Properties Ltd v Eagle Trust plc* [1991] BCLC 1045, at 1116–1117.

[137] See *MacPherson v European Strategic Bureau Ltd* [1999] 2 BCLC 203.

[138] Ibid; *Victors Ltd v Lingard* [1927] 1 Ch 323. It is submitted that only the general meeting, and not the board, should have the right to affirm the contract: see *Re Cardiff Preserved Coke and Coal Co* (1862) 23 LJ Ch 154; *North-West Transportation Co Ltd v Beatty* (1887) 12 App Cas 589 at 600 (PC).

[139] *Aberdeen Rly Co v Blaikie* (1854) 1 Macq 461 (HL (Sc)); *Imperial Mercantile Credit Association v Coleman* (1873) LR 6 HL 189.

[140] *Costa Rica Rly Co v Forwood* [1901] 1 Ch 746, at 761 (CA); *Gray v New Augarita Porcupine Mines Ltd* [1952] 3 DLR 1, at 15 (PC).

[141] *North-West Transportation Co v Beatty* (1887) 12 App Cas 589.

[142] Section 239(3).

[143] Section 239(4).

16.9 DUTY NOT TO ACCEPT BENEFITS FROM THIRD PARTIES

It would seem that the codification of the core duties of directors encapsulates the former secret profits rule described in **16.8.1** in part by the duty in s 176 not to accept benefits from third parties, as well as by the duty in s 175. Although, as explained, accountability in equity arguably did not depend on whether or not there was a situation of conflict of interest, s 176 narrows the principle, in line with the similar provision in s 175(4)(a), because s 176(4) provides that the duty is not infringed if acceptance of the benefit cannot reasonably be regarded as likely to give rise to a conflict of interest.[144] Thus, the fact that, in a situation like that in *Regal (Hastings) Ltd v Gulliver*,[145] the company could not itself be in a position to take advantage of the relevant opportunity will be a relevant, if not necessarily decisive, factor. It will not necessarily be decisive because the very fact of a director finding himself in a position to take a benefit may amount to a situation where there is a conflict of interest. Further, accountability is still based on a director receiving a benefit by reason of his being a director or his doing, or not doing, anything as director,[146] and by itself it will continue to be no defence that the director acted in good faith. Further there is no provision in s 176 for board authorisation, unlike in s 175, described in **16.8**, so that only general meeting sanction will suffice, unless, perhaps, the articles contain such provision.[147] This could be important given that situations could fall both within ss 175 and 176.

Section 176 makes it clear that it applies only to benefits received from third parties, defined in s 176(2) to mean someone other than the company, an associated body corporate or a person acting on behalf of the company or an associated body corporate. An associated body corporate is the company's holding or subsidiary company or a fellow subsidiary of the same holding company.[148] The duty under the section applies to a former director as regards things done or omitted by him before he ceased to be a director.[149]

As well as potentially covering 'secret profits' cases examined earlier in **16.8.1**, clear illustrations of the duty now in s 176 can be found in decisions concerning any secret commission or 'bribe' received by a director in the course of negotiating business transactions on the

---

[144] Or conflict of duty and interest or conflict of duties: s 176(5).

[145] [1942] 1 All ER 378, [1967] 2 AC 134n.

[146] Section 176(1).

[147] To the extent that such a provision is effective in the light of what is now s 232 of the 2006 Act; see **17.9.2**.

[148] Section 256.

[149] Section 170(2). The equitable rule was similarly applicable to former directors, provided that they acquired the profit from an opportunity which the company was still actively pursuing: *Island Export Finance Ltd v Umunna* [1986] BCLC 460; *CMS Dolphin Ltd v Simonet* [2001] 2 BCLC 704.

company's behalf,[150] any secret benefit coming to him in the course of any takeover bid for the company's shares or any reconstruction or amalgamation involving the company,[151] and profit derived through the use of confidential information which comes to the director's knowledge through his position on the board.[152] On the other hand, a director who will be leaving his company pursuant to an agreement between the company and his new employer to transfer part of the business of the company, and who is not involved in the negotiations, is not obliged to account in respect of undisclosed benefits he will receive from his new employer.[153]

16.9.1 Consequences of a breach of the no benefits rule

As we have seen, the Companies Act 2006 did not attempt to codify the remedies available for a breach of the general duties, leaving this to general principles. If a director employed under an express contract of service accepts a benefit without due authorisation, the company can not only recover the profit, but also dismiss him without compensation, even though this breach of duty does not occur more than once. It does not matter that the company in fact effects the dismissal on some other insufficient ground and only finds out about the secret profit after the dismissal.[154] However, a director entering into an agreement to terminate his contract of service is not bound to disclose an intention to commit a breach of fiduciary duty. So non-disclosure does not make the agreement void for mistake, nor is any compensation paid recoverable.[155]

It is submitted that where a director receives a benefit which has not been derived from the use of the company's property or which does not amount to a bribe, the profit does not become the property of the company to such an extent that it can follow investments or other property into which the money is put. Until the decision of the Privy

---

[150] *Boston Deep Sea Fishing and Ice Co Ltd v Ansell* (1888) 39 Ch D 339 (CA). For a discussion of the law relating to bribes in a company law context, see Birds, Ch 6 in Birks (ed), *The Frontiers of Liability*, vol 1 (Oxford University Press, 1994).

[151] *General Exchange Bank v Horner* (1870) LR 9 Eq 480. The Companies Act 2006 reinforces this position: see ss 215–222, described in **17.6**.

[152] This case may also, if the information is property and is misused to the company's detriment, amount to a misapplication of company property as described in **16.13**. For examples of the application of the principle, see *Gencor ACP Ltd v Dalby* [2000] 2 BCLC 734; *CMS Dolphin Ltd v Simonet* [2001] 2 BCLC 704.

[153] *Framlington Group plc v Anderson* [1995] 1 BCLC 475, distinguishing the Australian High Court decision in *Furs Ltd v Tomkies* (1936) 54 CLR 583, where the departing director was closely involved in the negotiations and held accountable for the secret profit he made.

[154] *Boston Deep Sea Fishing Co v Ansell* (1888) 39 Ch D 339 (CA).

[155] *Horcal Ltd v Gatland* [1984] BCLC 549 (CA). Neither is any salary paid while the director is working out his contract recoverable, though he would, as admitted in that case, be accountable for any secret profit made. However, a director is under a duty to disclose a breach of duty already committed; see **16.10.1**.

Council in *Attorney-General of Hong Kong v Reid*,[156] this proposition seemed unarguable, being based upon the decision in *Lister & Co v Stubbs*,[157] where the Court of Appeal held that the relation between a bribed agent and his principal was that of debtor and creditor, not of trustee and beneficiary. In *Attorney-General of Hong Kong v Reid*, the Privy Council held that a bribe taken by a fiduciary belonged in equity to his principal.[158] However, it is thought that there is no mandate for regarding the holding in *Attorney-General of Hong Kong v Reid* as extending to a situation of a mere acceptance of a benefit,[159] and it has been held in *Sinclair Investments (UK) Ltd v Versailles Trade Finance Ltd*[160] that the Court of Appeal and the High Court are bound by the decision in *Lister & Co v Stubbs* as a matter of precedent, and that a claim made in relation to unauthorized profits made by a director other than by acquiring and exploiting property owned or treated as owned by the company is a personal and not a proprietary claim On the other hand, *Reid* and the reasoning in *Sinclair Investments* do seem clearly to support the view that, where the profit has been derived directly from the use of the company's property (which, as is pointed out in **16.13**, may in this context include confidential information of a special and valuable nature), the profit is impressed with a trust in favour of the company, and for this reason is traceable.[161]

16.10 DUTY TO DECLARE INTEREST IN PROPOSED TRANSACTION OR ARRANGEMENT

One of the consequences of the traditional no conflict principle was the rule that directors could not have interests in transactions with the company unless the interest was authorised by the company in general meeting. In practice, that principle was often modified by the articles, as in art 85 of the 1985 Table A, to require disclosure to and approval by the directors, reflecting a previous statutory provision, s 317 of the 1985

---

[156] [1994] 1 AC 324.

[157] (1890) 45 Ch D 1.

[158] In effect, overruling *Lister & Co v Stubbs*, above.

[159] See Boyle (1995) 16 Co Law 131. However, see *United Pan-Europe Communications NV v Deutsche Bank AG* [2000] 2 BCLC 461, at 482–484 (CA), which suggests that a proprietary remedy may be imputed in respect of a secret profit if the circumstances warrant it.

[160] [2010] EWHC 1614 (Ch), [2011] 1 BCLC 202, where the law on the point and on the doctrine of stare decisis is extensively discussed by Lewison J.

[161] See the form of the order, for instance, made in *Phipps v Boardman* [1967] 2 AC 46 (HL) referred to in the speech of Lord Cohen at 99. The correctness and applicability of the decision in *Reid* has been much discussed in books and articles on the law of restitution. For a useful summary of the arguments and appropriate references, see Ferran *Company Law and Corporate Finance* (Oxford University Press, 1999) at pp 199–203. There is considerable Commonwealth authority supporting the view that equitable compensation may be awarded for breach of this and other fiduciary duties, but this has not yet really been explored in English cases; see *Gore-Browne on Companies* (Jordans, 45th edn, loose-leaf) at 16[25].

Act.[162] Section 177, in codifying the duty, makes that the position in general, and it is made clear by s 180(1) that if the section is complied with, any transaction or arrangement is not liable to be set aside by virtue of any common law rule or equitable principle requiring the consent or approval of the company in general meeting. The remedies for breach of s 177 are the appropriate remedies of rescission and an account of profits as described in **16.8.2**.[163] It should be noted, however, that when all that a director has done is to fail to disclose his interest in a sale to the company of property which he acquired in his own right free from any duty to hold it on trust for the company, his profit on the resale is not accountable and the company's only remedy is to rescind (which makes it particularly important that the company should rescind quickly before anything happens to bar this right).[164]

A director must disclose any interest, direct or indirect, that he has in relation to a proposed transaction or arrangement with the company to the other directors. This wording means that there is no need for a sole director to make a declaration, because there will be no 'other directors', but there is a specific section, s 231, imposing obligations where a director contracting with a company is its only member; this is considered later.[165] As the interest can be direct or indirect, the director does not need to be a party to the transaction for the duty to apply. But the interest must be one that can reasonably be regarded as likely to give rise to a conflict of interest.[166] A company can still have more onerous requirements, such as for general meeting approval, in its articles,[167] and it should be noted that this is required for any transactions that have to have general meeting approval under Chapter 4 of Part 10, which is considered in Chapter 17.

The director must declare the nature and extent of his interest to the other directors. It is not enough to state merely that he has an interest. Disclosure can be made by written notice, general notice or disclosure at a meeting of the directors,[168] but must be before the company enters into

---

[162] This section also is replaced by ss 182–187 in respect of existing transactions, as described in **16.12.1**. For a valuable analysis of the former s 317, see Griffiths 'Declaring an Interest: the Companies Act 1985, s 317 and the Regulation of Self-dealing' [1997] CfiLR 95.

[163] Another possibility is equitable compensation: see *Gwembe Valley Development Co Ltd v Koshy* [2003] EWCA Civ 1048, [2004] 1 BCLC 131. Note that there was no civil remedy for a breach of the former s 317 *per se*, although that could follow a breach of articles like art 85 of the 1985 Table A which in effect incorporated s 317. This remains the position in respect of ss 182–187, which are described in **16.12.1**.

[164] *Cavendish-Bentinck v Fenn* (1887) 12 App Cas 652; *Re Lady Forrest (Murchison) Gold Mines Ltd* [1901] 1 Ch 582; *Burland v Earle* [1902] AC 83; *Jacobus Marler Estates Ltd v Marler* (1913) 114 LT 640n (PC).

[165] See **16.12.2**; compare *Neptune (Vehicle Washing Equipment) Ltd v Fitzgerald* [1995] 1 BCLC 352, which imposed such an obligation under s 317 of the 1985 Act.

[166] Section 177(6)(a).

[167] Section 180(1).

[168] Section 177(2). It seems, though, that disclosure only to a committee of the board is not sufficient: see *Guinness plc v Saunders* [1988] BCLC 607, affirmed by the House of Lords

the transaction.[169] If a declaration proves to be or becomes inaccurate or incomplete, the director must make a further declaration.[170] There are various exemptions from the need for disclosure. There is no requirement to disclose an interest of which a director is not aware or where he is not aware of the transaction or arrangement in question, but a director is treated as being aware of matters of which he ought reasonably to be aware.[171] There is no need to disclose anything the other directors already know about or ought reasonably to know about,[172] nor concerning the terms of a director's service contract that have been or are to be considered by a meeting of the directors or a committee appointed for the purpose, for example, the remuneration committee of a listed company.[173]

Section 177, unlike the general section (s 175) on conflicts of interest, makes no provision as to an interested director being counted in the quorum at a relevant meeting, but clearly the articles may make provision in this regard.[174]

16.10.1 Interest

Various decisions have been given as to the meaning of 'interest' in the context of the predecessor to s 177 and standard articles, though in considering them it should be remembered that most of them are decisions on particular provisions in company articles and are thus not necessarily applicable directly to s 177.[175] A director has been held to be interested in a contract with another company in which he was a shareholder[176] or a firm of which he was a member,[177] in a contract to allot shares or debentures to him,[178] and in a debenture granted to release him from a personal guarantee of a debt.[179] It goes without saying that a director is 'interested' in an arrangement whereby he provides services to

---

on other grounds at [1990] 1 All ER 653; and see *Gwembe Valley Development Co Ltd v Koshy* [2004] 1 BCLC 131, at [51] and [59], where the point was emphasised in the context of the company's articles.

169 Section 177(4).

170 Section 177(3).

171 Section 177 (5).

172 Section 177(6)(b). See *Lee Panavision Ltd v Lee Lighting* [1992] BCLC 22, at 33; *Runciman v Walter Runciman plc* [1992] BCLC 1084; *MacPherson v European Strategic Bureau Ltd* [1999] 2 BCLC 203 to the same effect on the former section.

173 Section 177(6)(c).

174 See arts 14 and 16, respectively, in the model articles for both private and public companies.

175 Note, in particular, that art 85 of the 1985 Table A refers to 'material interest', which is clearly narrower than the reference to 'interest' in s 177.

176 Even as a trustee (*Transvaal Lands Co v New Belgium (Transvaal) Land and Development Co* [1914] 2 Ch 488), though not if he is a bare trustee without duties to perform (*Cowan de Groot Properties Ltd v Eagle Trust plc* [1991] BCLC 1045, at 1115).

177 *Imperial Mercantile Credit Association v Coleman* (1873) LR 6 HL 189.

178 *Neal v Quin* [1916] WN 223; *Cox v Dublin City Distillery* (No 2) [1915] 1 Ir R 145.

179 *Rolled Steel Products Ltd v British Steel Corporation* [1984] BCLC 466 (CA). See also *Lee Panavision Ltd v Lee Lighting Ltd* [1991] BCLC 575 (contract including indemnity for director).

the company (whether as chairman of directors, managing director, executive director or otherwise) for a remuneration; on the other hand, an agreement whereby he is appointed chairman or managing director without any (or any additional) remuneration is merely a delegation of power and not a contract in which he is 'interested'.[180]

Under s 177, 'the nature and extent' of the director's interest must be disclosed by him. It has been said in addition that disclosure must be 'full and frank'.[181] The result is that, generally speaking, it will not be enough for the director merely to say 'I am interested' in the relevant contract; however, there is no hard and fast rule as to how far disclosure must go. 'The amount of detail must depend in each case upon the nature of the contract or arrangement proposed and the context in which it arises.'[182] It was once held[183] that directors negotiating an agreement whereby their contracts of service are terminated in return for compensation for loss of office were not bound to disclose past breaches of duty which would entitle the company to dismiss them without compensation. However, this view, which was somewhat difficult to accept, can now clearly be regarded as wrong. The opposite view has been taken in recent cases,[184] and the Court of Appeal has ruled authoritatively that policy requires there to be such a duty on directors. This, though, was not regarded as a separate and independent duty, but merely an aspect of the broad duty of loyalty on any director to act in good faith in the interests of the company,[185] which is now of course covered by the general duty under s 172.

16.11 RELATIONSHIP BETWEEN THE GENERAL DUTIES AND OTHER RULES

Part 10, Chapter 4 of the Companies Act 2006, re-enacting, with amendments, the provisions of Part X of the 1985 Act, and considered in the next chapter, requires the approval of members for certain service contracts, substantial property transactions, loans, quasi-loans and credit transactions and payments for loss of office. Section 180 is in part concerned to explain the relationship between the general duties and the more specific provisions in Chapter 4. By s 180(3), compliance with the general duties does not remove the need for member approval of the

---

[180] *Foster v Foster* [1916] 1 Ch 532; *Runciman v Walter Runciman plc* [1992] BCLC 1084.

[181] *Fine Industrial Commodities Ltd v Powling* (1954) 71 RPC 253, at 262, per Danckwerts J.

[182] *Gray v New Augarita Porcupine Mines Ltd* [1952] 3 DLR 1, at 14, per Lord Radcliffe. See also *Movitex Ltd v Bulfield* [1988] BCLC 104, at 121; *DEG-Deutsche Investitutions-und Entwicklungsgesellschaft mbH v Koshy* [2002] 1 BCLC 478, at 555–556.

[183] *Healey v SA Française Rubastic* [1971] 1 KB 946, approved in *Bell v Lever Bros Ltd* [1932] AC 161, at 228, 231 (HL).

[184] *Horcal Ltd v Gatland* [1983] BCLC 60, esp at 65–67, distinguishing *Bell v Lever Bros*, above, on the ground that, in the latter case, the employees in question were not under any fiduciary duty to disclose previous wrongdoings. But compare the comments of Goff LJ, *obiter*, on appeal: [1984] BCLC 549, at 554. See also *British Midland Tool Ltd v Midland International Tooling Ltd* [2003] 2 BCLC 523, at [89].

[185] *Item Software (UK) Ltd v Fassihi* [2005] 2 BCLC 91, (CA).

above transactions, and under s 180(2), the general duties apply even if the transaction also falls within Chapter 4, except that there is no need to comply with s 175 or 176 where the approval of members is obtained.

Under s 180(5) of the 2006 Act, the general duties have effect notwithstanding any enactment or rule of law except where there is an express or implied exception to this rule. For example, s 247 of the Act[186] provides that directors may make provision for employees on the cessation or transfer of a company's business even if this would otherwise constitute a breach of the general duty to promote the success of the company.

16.12 STATUTORY DUTIES SUPPLEMENTING THE GENERAL DUTIES

Having now covered the provisions of the Companies Act 2006 concerning what are called the general duties of directors, it is appropriate to examine the provisions in Part 10 that can be regarded as supplementary to that, which are those requiring declarations of interest in existing transactions or arrangements and relating to contracts with sole members who are directors. The reason for their separate treatment is that breach of these provisions gives rise to the possibility of criminal sanctions, but is not likely by itself to have any civil consequences.[187]

16.12.1 Declarations of interest in existing transactions or arrangements

Although some aspects of what was s 317 of the 1985 Act have been reproduced in s 177, as described in **16.10**, as the general duty to declare interests of directors in *proposed* transactions or arrangements, ss 182–187 contain separate and detailed requirements regarding declarations of interest in *existing* transactions or arrangements. These sections repeat many of the requirements of the former s 317, in particular by making it a criminal offence not to comply.[188] It seems clear that a breach of these sections does not by itself give rise to civil consequences, as was also the case with s 317,[189] although a failure to comply would almost certainly

---

[186] See **6.6.3**.

[187] This is expressly provided for by s 231(6) as regards contract with sole members who are directors. The same conclusion is likely as regards the other provisions, as that was the position with regard to s 317 of the 1985 Act, which they partly replace: see *Hely-Hutchinson & Co Ltd v Brayhead*, above; *Guinness plc v Saunders* [1990] 1 All ER 653, at 664–665, per Lord Goff of Chievely. Lord Templeman (ibid, at 662) seemed to think that the *Hely-Hutchinson* decision decided the contrary, but it is thought that the view of Lord Goff is to be preferred. See also, *Lee Panavision Ltd v Lee Lighting Ltd* [1991] BCLC 575, at 583 and *Cowan de Groot Properties Ltd v Eagle Trust plc* [1991] BCLC 1045, at 1113.

[188] See s 184; the offence is punishable by a fine.

[189] See footnote 158, above.

constitute a breach of the general duty to avoid conflicts of interest in s 175 and thus could have the civil consequences appropriate to a breach of that section. Section 182 does not apply if or to the extent that the interest has been declared under s 177 and is modified by s 186 where the director is the only director. There is a special provision for declarations by shadow directors in s 187, which makes theses provisions applicable to such persons,[190] except that they have to comply by either written notice or general notice, as explained below.

The requirements of s 182 match those of s 177, as already considered in **16.10**. Thus, directors are required to declare the nature and extent of any interest, direct or indirect, that they have in an existing transaction or arrangement entered into by the company. As the interest can be direct or indirect, the director does not need to be a party to the transaction for the duty to apply. But the interest must be one that can reasonably be regarded as likely to give rise to a conflict of interest.[191] There is no obligation to declare an interest that the other directors already know about, or ought reasonably to know about; or that concerns the terms of his service contract, considered (or to be considered) by a meeting of directors or by the relevant committee of directors.[192] Nor is there an obligation to disclose an interest of which the director is not aware or where he is not aware of the transaction or arrangement in question, but he is treated as aware of matters of which he ought reasonably to be aware.[193]

The declaration must be made as soon as is reasonably practicable. But even if the declaration is not made as soon as it should have been, it must still be made.[194] If a declaration proves to be, or becomes, inaccurate or incomplete, a further declaration must be made.[195] There are three alternative methods of making a declaration, namely either at a meeting of the directors, by notice in writing or by general notice.[196] The provision as to notice in writing in s 184 was new in the 2006 Act. If choosing this method, the director must send the notice to the other directors, either in hard copy form, by hand or by post, or, if agreed by the recipient(s), in an agreed electronic form.[197] The declaration by notice is deemed to form part of the proceedings at the next meeting of the directors and must be minuted.[198]

---

[190] In contrast, the 'general duties', of which s 177 is part, probably do not apply to shadow directors: see **16.1.1**.
[191] Section 182(6)(a).
[192] Section 182(6)(b) and (c).
[193] Section 182(5).
[194] Section 182(4).
[195] Section 182(3).
[196] Section 182(2).
[197] As to acceptable electronic forms, see s 1168.
[198] Section 184(5), incorporating so far as minuting is concerned, s 248 (see **15.11.4**).

A general notice is a declaration that the director is interested in another body corporate or firm, or that the director is connected with another person,[199] is only effective if given at a meeting of directors or the director takes reasonable steps to secure that it is brought up and read at the next meeting of directors. Such a general notice must state the nature and extent of the director's interest in the body corporate or firm (eg that he is a shareholder in another company) or the nature of his connection with the person (eg his spouse or other connected person).[200]

16.12.2 Companies with a sole director

Section 186 makes special provision for the situation of companies with a sole director, but only where a company should have more than one director; basically therefore where it is a public company or where a private company's articles require it to have more than one director. The sole director of a private company which is not obliged to have more than that sole director will not be subject to ss 182–187 at all, because there are no other directors to whom he can declare any interest. In the case of a company that should have more than one director, the sole director must record in writing the nature and extent of his interest in any transaction or arrangement that has been entered into by the company and this is deemed to form part of the proceedings of the next meeting of the directors and must be properly minuted. Compliance with this section does not excuse the requirement to comply with s 231.

Section 231 imposes particular requirements in cases of contracts with a sole director where the company is a limited company, the contract is not in writing and it is not entered into in the ordinary course of its business. Compliance with these does not exclude the operation of any other provision or rule of law applying to such contracts,[201] so that any requirements imposed by the other provisions in the Act must be complied with as well as the general duty of the director to act to promote the success of the company.

The company must ensure that the terms of the contract are either set out in a written memorandum or recorded in the minutes of the first directors' meeting following the making of the contract. Failure to comply renders any officer in default liable to a fine,[202] but non-compliance does not of itself affect the validity of the contract.[203] The requirements apply also to a contract with a shadow director.[204]

---

[199] Persons connected with directors are defined in ss 252–255; see **17.2.1**.
[200] Section 185(3).
[201] Section 231(7).
[202] Section 231(3) and (4).
[203] Section 231(6).
[204] Section 231(5).

16.13   DIRECTORS' TRUSTEESHIP OF THE COMPANY'S ASSETS

There is a long-established principle that, although directors are not in the strict sense trustees, they are regarded as trustees of company property which is in their hands or under their control. Although this principle is not included in the statutory codification and will no doubt in many cases overlap with some of the statutory provisions, especially those in ss 175 and 176 of the Companies Act 2006, there seems no doubt that it survives the codification of the general duties, for the reasons explained in **16.3**.

The primary consequence of this principle of trusteeship is that a director is answerable as a trustee for any misapplication of the company's property in which he participated and which he knew or ought to have known to be a misapplication.[205] A misapplication in this context means any disposition of the company's property which by virtue of any provision of the company's constitution or any statutory provision or any rule of general law the company or the board is forbidden or incompetent or unauthorised to make, or which is carried out by the directors otherwise than in accordance with their primary duties, as now codified in ss 171 and 172. This second limb covers not only misappropriations of the company's property, but also dispositions in favour of third parties which do not satisfy the requirement of good faith.

A further consequence of a director being liable as a trustee is that a claim against him will not be barred by the Limitation Act 1980.[206]

16.13.1   The scope of the trusteeship

Provided that the directors have possession or control of the property beneficially owned by the company, their trusteeship will arise whether the property is legally vested in the company, in one or more of the directors, or in a third party.

---

[205] For a full statement of the nature of the director's liability, see *Selangor United Rubber Estates Ltd v Cradock (No 3)* [1968] 1 WLR 1555, at 1575–1576. See also *Simtel Communications Ltd v Rebak* [2006] 2 BCLC 571 at [13]. Alternatively the director may be liable to pay equitable compensation: *Gwembe Valley Development Co Ltd v Koshy* [2003] EWCA Civ 1048, [2004] 1 BCLC 131, at [142]. Note, however, the view expressed obiter by Lord Hope in *Re Paycheck Services 3 Ltd* [2010] UKSC 51, [2011] 1 BCLC 141 at [45] to [46]. He regarded a director's liability for a misapplication involving an unlawful payment of dividends as strict (although relief might be available under what is now s 1157 of the Companies Act 2009 (see **17.9.3**). The other members of the Supreme Court did not express a view on this point. Third parties who participate in such a breach of trust may themselves be liable to the company as constructive trustees: see *Gore-Browne on Companies* (Jordans, 45th edn, loose-leaf) at 16[4].

[206] Section 21(1). For a recent example, see *Statek Corporation v Alford* [2008] EWHC 32 (Ch).

A director's trusteeship has been held to cover funds standing to the company's credit in a bank account.[207] Its scope is, moreover, widened by the fact that property which can be misapplied can include property which is not yet vested in the company or in any person on its behalf, but which comes to the directors in circumstances where they are in duty bound, for example through some express or implied mandate, to acquire and hold it for the company's benefit.[208] Furthermore, the term 'property' in this context may cover confidential information of a special and valuable nature (such as secret manufacturing processes and patents, but not mere 'know-how')[209] and also business advantages such as the opportunity to enter into a favourable contract within the company's existing line of business.[210] Thus, a director who makes an invention or other valuable technical discovery in the course of performing active duties as an employee of the company holds the benefit of his discovery (including any patent rights that he has acquired in respect thereof) on trust for the company; it would not matter that he was not specifically commissioned by the company to make the relevant discovery, provided that it fell within the company's line of business.[211] It is equally a breach of trust for a director to make use of 'trade secrets' to the company's detriment, and in appropriate cases he can be prevented by injunction from so doing.[212]

In *Cook v Deeks*,[213] three directors of a private company, holding a majority of the shares, appropriated to themselves an opportunity to enter into a highly favourable business contract, it being evident that the opportunity was only presented to them because they were directors of the company and that the company's business would have greatly benefited from having the contract. They purported to ratify this breach of duty by using the votes attached to their shares to pass an ordinary resolution, but were none the less held liable to account to the company

---

[207] *Selangor United Rubber Estates Ltd v Cradock (No 3)*, above.

[208] *Benson v Heathorn* (1842) 1 Y & CCC 326; *Burland v Earle* [1902] AC 83, at 98–99 (PC); *Cook v Deeks* [1916] 1 AC 554 (PC). For a detailed discussion of when such a duty arises, see the South African case of *Robinson v Randfontein Estates Gold Mining Co Ltd* [1921] AD 168 (South African SC).

[209] See, eg, *Saltman Engineering Co Ltd v Campbell Engineering Co Ltd* [1963] 3 All ER 413n (CA); *Heyting v Dupont* [1964] 1 WLR 843 (CA); *Cranleigh Precision Engineering Ltd v Bryant* [1965] 1 WLR 1293; *Phipps v Boardman* [1967] 2 AC 46 (HL). In relation to such 'property', the positions of directors, ordinary employees and other fiduciary agents are virtually the same, though the duty not to misuse confidential information 'applies with particular force as between a director and his company': *Baker v Gibbons* [1972] 1 WLR 693, at 700. See also *Thomas Marshall (Exports) Ltd v Guinle* [1979] Ch 227, especially at 248, for a discussion of what constitutes confidential information; cf *Island Export Finance Ltd v Umunna* [1986] BCLC 460.

[210] *Burland v Earle*, above, at 93; *Cook v Deeks*, above.

[211] *Cranleigh Precision Engineering Ltd v Bryant*, above; and see *British Syphon Co Ltd v Homewood* [1956] 1 WLR 1190.

[212] *Measures Bros Ltd v Measures* [1910] 1 Ch 336 (affirmed in [1910] 2 Ch 248 (CA)); *Cranleigh Precision Engineering Ltd v Bryant*, above; and see *Printers & Finishers Ltd v Holloway* [1965] 1 WLR 1.

[213] [1916] 1 AC 554 (PC). See also *Canadian Aero Service Ltd v O'Malley* [1973] 40 DLR (3d) 371 (Canadian SC).

for the profits derived from the contract, on the basis that the contract 'belonged in equity to the company'.[214] An alternative remedy for the company in such a situation may be damages for breach of the director's contract of service (assuming that he has one); in the assessment of these damages the court will take into account the extent to which the company was likely to obtain the business contract for itself.[215] If misapplied assets have already been returned to the company, the director will be under no further liability,[216] but the director who is accountable cannot claim to set off against this anything owed to him under a contract of employment.[217]

16.13.2   Further examples of misapplications

Many further instances of directors' liability for losses resulting from the misapplication of company property are to be found in the case-law. Examples are:

(1)   the application of funds in breach of the prohibition against a company providing financial assistance for an acquisition of its shares, now in s 678 of the Companies Act 2006;[218]

(2)   the payment of compensation to a director in breach of what is now s 215;[219]

(3)   the making of a loan to a director in breach of what is now s 197;[220]

(4)   the payment or recommendation to pay dividends out of capital;[221]

(5)   the unlawful issue of bonus shares or shares at a discount;[222]

(6)   the payment of unauthorised commission to a broker for placing shares;[223]

---

[214]   Ibid, at 564. As to the ratification issue, see **17.9.1**. This situation clearly falls also within ss 175 and 176 of the 2006 Act.

[215]   *Industrial Development Consultants Ltd v Cooley* [1972] 2 All ER 162 (discussed further at **16.8**).

[216]   *Re Derek Randall Enterprises Ltd* [1990] BCC 749 (CA). No doubt this assumes no further loss by the company.

[217]   *Zerco Ltd v Jerrom-Pugh* [1993] BCC 275 (CA).

[218]   *Steen v Law* [1964] AC 287 (PC); *Selangor United Rubber Estates Ltd v Cradock (No 3)* [1968] 1 WLR 1555; *Wallersteiner v Moir (No 1)* [1974] 1 WLR 991 (CA); *Belmont Finance Corp Ltd v Williams Furniture Ltd* [1980] 1 All ER 393 (CA).

[219]   *Re Duomatic Ltd* [1969] 2 Ch 365.

[220]   *Wallersteiner v Moir (No 1)*, above.

[221]   *Flitcroft's Case* (1882) 21 Ch D 536 (CA); *Allied Carpets Group plc v Nethercott* [2001] BCC 81, *Bairstow v Queens Moat Houses plc* [2001] EWCA Civ 712, [2001] 2 BCLC 531.

[222]   *Hirsche v Sims* [1894] AC 654 (PC).

[223]   *Re Faure Electric Accumulator Co* (1889) 40 Ch D 141.

(7)   the allotment of shares by directors to themselves or their friends at par when they would be able to find purchasers willing to take them at a premium;[224]

(8)   any unauthorised disposition of a company's assets,[225] unauthorised payment of remuneration to a director,[226] or bribe paid to a third party;[227]

(9)   the execution of a guarantee and debenture in breach of the articles and not *bona fide* in the interests of the company;[228]

(10) the signing of blank transfer forms in respect of securities owned by the company which were transferred without consideration and without the authority of the full board of directors;[229]

(11) the payment of a debt owed by a third party.[230]

Where directors are liable for misapplication of a company's funds, they may be charged compound interest.[231]

---

[224] *Parker v McKenna* (1875) 10 Ch App 96.

[225] *Russell v Wakefield Waterworks Co* (1875) LR 20 Eq 474.

[226] *Re George Newman & Co* [1895] 1 Ch 674 (CA). See also *Guinness plc v Saunders* [1990] 2 AC 663 (HL), discussed in **16.8**, although the House of Lords did not use the language of misapplication.

[227] *E Hannibal & Co Ltd v Frost* (1988) 4 BCC 3 (CA).

[228] *Rolled Steel Products v British Steel Corporation* [1985] 2 WLR 908 (CA); see further as to this case, **6.2.3**.

[229] *Bishopsgate Investment Management Ltd v Maxwell* [1993] BCC 120 (CA).

[230] *DEG-Deutsche Investitions-und Entwicklungsgesellschaft mbH v Kosky* [2002] 1 BCLC 479.

[231] *Wallersteiner v Moir (No 2)* [1975] QB 373 (CA), applying principles established in relation to defaulting trustees.

CHAPTER 17

THE DUTIES OF DIRECTORS – SPECIFIC DUTIES, RELIEF FROM LIABILITY AND CONSEQUENCES OF BREACH

17.1 INTRODUCTION

The previous chapter considered the general duties of company directors, as mainly set out now in statutory form in Part 10 of the Companies Act 2006. This chapter considers the specific duties imposed under Chapter 4 of that Part, a very specific liability in respect of statements in accounts and reports, and the provisions regarding when directors can be protected from liability, whether by virtue of statutory provisions or by way of ratification by the members of the company.

17.2 SPECIFIC RULES REGARDING DIRECTORS' INTERESTS IN TRANSACTIONS AND ARRANGEMENTS

In addition to those aspects of the duties specified in the Companies Act 2006 that were examined in the previous chapter, especially those relating to directors' interests in transactions and arrangements under ss 177 and 182–187, certain types of contract or arrangement in which a director is 'interested' are subject to special rules and restrictions over and above those described there. These rules and restrictions relate particularly to directors' service contracts, substantial property transactions involving directors, loans to and related deals with directors and payments to directors for loss of office. These are examined in the following sections.[1] The relationship between the general duties and the special rules and restrictions examined here was explained in **16.11**. If a particular proposal falls under more than one of these types of transaction or arrangement, then the specific requirements of each must be met, although this does have to be done by separate resolutions.[2]

It should be noted that by s 223, the rules and restrictions considered here apply to shadow directors as much as to directors,[3] although reference to loss of office as a director does not apply in relation to loss of a person's

---

[1] Note also the controls where directors exceed their powers: s 41, discussed in **6.10**.

[2] Section 225. Note also the special restrictions imposed by s 226 on companies that are charities.

[3] As to the meaning of shadow directors, see **15.2.1**.

status as a shadow director,[4] which will rule out some of the application of the relevant provisions. Further, many of them also apply to 'persons connected' with directors, so that avoidance of them is not easily effected. It is appropriate to describe such persons at this stage.

17.2.1   Persons connected with a director

A connected person is defined in ss 252–255,[5] as someone who falls within one of the following categories.[6]

(1)   Various family members: a director's spouse or civil partner; any other persons (whether of the same or a different sex) with whom a director lives in an enduring family relationship;[7] a director's child or stepchild; a child or stepchild under 18 of a person with whom a directors lives, etc and who lives with the director; and a director's parents.[8]

(2)   A body corporate with which a director is connected; this is basically a body corporate[9] in which a director and any person connected with him have a 20% interest.[10] The interest may be either an interest in equity share capital[11] or the control of one-fifth or more of the voting power at general meetings.[12] It extends to the situation where the voting power is controlled by a body corporate itself controlled by a director and any person connected with him.[13]

(3)   The trustee (other than under an employees' share scheme or a pension scheme) acting in that capacity of any trust under which a director, his spouse or infant children or an associated body corporate are or may be a beneficiary.

(4)   A partner of a director or connected person, acting as such.

(5)   A firm that is a legal person in which a director or connected person is a partner.

---

[4]   Section 223(2).
[5]   [CA 1985, s 346.]
[6]   The categories of family members were extended quite significantly by the 2006 Act.
[7]   But not a director's grandparent or grandchild, sister, brother, aunt, uncle, nephew or niece.
[8]   Section 253.
[9]   This expression, defined in s 1713(1), is used to catch foreign as well as UK companies.
[10]   Section 254.
[11]   'Interest' is defined widely by reference to Sch 1.
[12]   Note the qualifications in s 254(6) regarding this category of connected person.
[13]   See s 255.

17.3   DIRECTORS' SERVICE CONTRACTS

We have seen[14] that there are special disclosure requirements regarding directors' service contracts.[15] Here we are concerned with the provisions of ss 188 and 189,[16] which impose a requirement of the consent of members to service contracts basically that will or may last for more than 2 years.[17]

The sections apply to the guaranteed term of employment,[18] which is or may be longer than 2 years,[19] of a director with the company of which he is a director or, where he is director of a holding company, within the group consisting of the company and its subsidiaries, unless the company is not a UK-registered company or is the wholly owned subsidiary[20] of another body corporate.[21] Such a term must be approved by a resolution of the members of the company or, in the case of a director of a holding company, by a resolution of the members of that company. A guaranteed term is (a) the period during which the director's employment is to continue or may be continued otherwise than at the instance of the company (whether under the original agreement or a new agreement entered into in pursuance of it) if during that time it cannot be terminated by the company by notice or can be terminated by notice only in specified circumstances or (b) in the case of employment terminable by the company by notice, the period of notice to be given.[22]

If, more than 6 months before the end of the guaranteed term, the company enters into a further service contract otherwise than in pursuance of a right conferred, by or under the original contract, on the other party to it, the unexpired period of the original agreement must be

---

[14]   At **15.6**.

[15]   There may also be special rules in the articles (see, for example, art 84 and 97 of the 1985 Table A), although the model articles under the 2006 Act do not contain such rules. Where, as in art 84, the articles vest in the directors as a whole the authority to enter into a service contract with one of their number, such a contract is not binding unless it has been approved by the whole board of directors: *UK Safety Group Ltd v Heane* [1998] 2 BCLC 208.

[16]   [CA 1985, s 319.]

[17]   Note also that under the UK Corporate Governance Code the terms of directors' employment or notice periods, in the case of listed companies, should not exceed one year.

[18]   Under a director's service contract (s 188(7)), which is defined widely in s 227 and discussed in **15.6**.

[19]   Under the previous provision, the term was five years or longer.

[20]   See s 1159(2), by which a company is deemed to be the wholly owned subsidiary of another if it has no members except that other and the latter's wholly owned subsidiaries or persons acting on behalf of that other or its wholly owned subsidiaries.

[21]   The sections do not therefore apply just to a contract directly between a director and his company, and cannot be evaded by, e g the use of a contract between the company and another company which the director controls.

[22]   Or the aggregate of the periods under (a) and (b).

added to the term of the new contract. If the result is a term of more than 2 years, the sanction of the members as above must be obtained.[23]

There is a particular disclosure requirement imposed by s 188(5). If a provision exceeding 2 years is to be passed by written resolution, a memorandum setting out the proposed contract containing the provision must be sent or submitted to every member entitled to vote at or before the time he receives the proposed resolution.[24] If the resolution is to be proposed at a meeting, the memorandum must be available for inspection by members of the company at the company's registered office for at least 15 days before the relevant meeting, and at the meeting itself.

A provision that contravenes these requirements is void to the extent of the contravention and the contract is deemed to contain a term entitling the company to terminate it at any time by reasonable notice.[25] In other words, the agreement is deemed to be made for 2 years subject to its being determinable at any time within that period by reasonable notice. But it has been held that, as the only purpose of these provisions is the benefit and protection of the members, the specific requirements can be waived if there is fully informed and unanimous informal agreement of the members to a director's employment contract lasting more than the period specified.[26]

17.4 SUBSTANTIAL PROPERTY TRANSACTIONS

Any contract by which a company sells to or buys from a director property of any sort, and any other property dealings between directors and their companies, are subject to a number of the requirements described in Chapter 16, in particular the duties of disclosure in ss 177 and 182–187. However, the duty to avoid conflicts of interest in s 175 does not apply in relation to a transaction or arrangement with the company. The provisions of ss 190–196 of the Companies Act 2006[27] reinforce the general duties of disclosure, in particular by imposing a requirement of general meeting approval that is similar to that required by traditional equitable principles and which had in practice been modified by articles of association until the introduction (in 1980) of what are now ss 190–196.[28] Further, the sections do not catch only contracts between directors and

---

[23] Section 188(4).
[24] An accidental failure to send a memorandum to every member is to be disregarded if a majority approves the proposal: see s 224.
[25] Section 189.
[26] *Atlas Europe Ltd v Wright* [1999] BCC 163 (CA), applying the principle described in **13.2**.
[27] [CA 1985, ss 320–322.]
[28] It has been held that a solicitors' firm was negligent for failing to advise its client company that a particular transaction fell within these provisions: *British Racing Drivers' Club Ltd v Hextall Erskine & Co* [1997] 1 BCLC 182.

their companies, since they apply to 'arrangements', a deliberately broad word, and to deals with shadow directors[29] and connected persons.[30]

Section 190 catches an arrangement for the acquisition[31] from a company,[32] directly or indirectly, of a substantial non-cash asset[33] by a director of the company or its holding company or a person connected with such a director, and conversely, to an arrangement for the acquisition by a company of such an asset from such a director or connected person. An asset is substantial for these purposes if its value exceeds £100,000 or 10% of the company's asset value, subject in the latter case to a minimum of £5,000.[34] The value of the asset acquired is to be determined as at the time the arrangement is entered into,[35] and in the context of the particular circumstances of the transaction or arrangement, and is not necessarily limited to market value when its worth to a director or connected person is greater.[36] Arrangements involving more than one non-cash asset or an arrangement that is one of a series involving non-cash assets have to be aggregated together.[37] The amount of a company's asset value is the value of its net assets as determined by reference to its most recent statutory accounts,[38] or its called-up share capital if no such accounts have been prepared.[39]

17.4.1 Exceptions

There are a number of situations where the requirements of s 190 do not apply:

---

[29] See **15.2.1**.

[30] See **17.2.1**.

[31] This clearly indicates any dealing, whether by way of sale, gift, exchange or whatever. By s 1163(2), the acquisition of a non-cash asset includes the creation of an estate or interest in, or a right over, any property and the discharge of any person's liability, other than a liability for a liquidated sum.

[32] This includes a sale by a receiver acting as agent for the company: *Demite Ltd v Protec Health Ltd* [1998] BCC 638.

[33] 'Non-cash asset' is defined in s 1163(1) as 'any property or interest in property other than cash' (cash includes foreign currency). This clearly includes a lease (*Niltan Carson Ltd v Hawthorne* [1988] BCLC 298) and the benefit of a deposit paid on a contract to purchase property (*Duckwari Ltd v Offerventure Ltd* [1995] BCC 89 (CA)), but not a right to a sum of money such as compensation for termination of a service contract (*Lander v Premier Pict Petroleum Ltd* [1998] BCC 248).

[34] Section 191. The onus is on the party alleging breach of the section to prove that the value exceeded the requisite value.

[35] Section 191(5).

[36] *Micro Leisure Ltd v County Properties Developments Ltd (No 2)* [2000] BCC 872.

[37] Section 190(5).

[38] Section 191(4); as to these accounts, see **14.6**.

[39] Section 320(2).

(1) where a transaction relates to anything that a director is entitled to under his service contract or to payment for loss of office as defined in s 215;[40]

(2) where the company is not a UK-registered company or is the wholly owned subsidiary of another body corporate;[41]

(3) for a transaction between a company and a person in his character as a member of that company;[42]

(4) for a transaction between a holding company and its wholly owned subsidiary or two wholly owned subsidiaries of the same holding company;[43]

(5) where a company is being wound up, unless the winding-up is a members' voluntary winding-up, or is in administration;[44]

(6) in respect of a transaction on a recognised investment exchange which is effected by a director or connected person through the agency of an independent broker.[45]

17.4.2 Approval

An arrangement to acquire an asset in the circumstances described is forbidden unless it is first approved by a resolution of the members of the company or is conditional on such approval being obtained and, if the director or connected person is a director of its holding company or a person connected with such a director, by a resolution of the members of holding company or is similarly conditional on such approval.[46] It was once doubted whether the informal assent of all members[47] would satisfy this particular statutory requirement,[48] but it has now been clearly decided that it does.[49] Whereas not every last detail of the arrangement

---

[40] Section 190(6); approval for the latter will be required under the sections described in **17.6**.

[41] Section 190(4). A body corporate, which basically is a non-UK registered company (see s 1173(1)) is deemed to be the wholly owned subsidiary of another if it has no members except that other and the latter's wholly owned subsidiaries or persons acting on behalf of that other or its wholly owned subsidiaries: s 1159(2).

[42] Section 192(a).

[43] Section 192(b).

[44] Section 193.

[45] Section 194.

[46] Section 190(1) and (2).

[47] See **13.2**.

[48] *Demite Ltd v Protec Health Ltd* [1998] BCC 638.

[49] *NBH Ltd v Hoare* [2006] EWHC 73 (Ch), where Park J accepted that his doubts in *Demite Ltd v Protec Health Ltd*, above, were unfounded. He also held, in accordance with the wording of s 320(1) of the 1985 Act, that it is the time of approval of the arrangement that is crucial. As there was approval by the then sole shareholder of the company's holding company, it was irrelevant that that person was not the sole

must be approved, the central aspects of it, such as the price to be paid in return for a sale of assets, must be covered.[50] A failure to obtain approval does not subject the company to any liability;[51] this is to protect the company where a conditional arrangement is not approved.

17.4.3 Remedies

A failure to comply with the requirements of s 190 leads to the civil consequences specified in s 195. The arrangement, and any transaction entered into in pursuance of it,[52] is voidable at the instance of the company,[53] except in the following circumstances:

(1) if restitution of any money or other asset that was the subject matter of the arrangement or transaction is no longer possible, or the company has been indemnified under the section by any other person for the loss or damage suffered by it;[54]

(2) if avoidance would affect rights acquired in good faith and for value by a person not a party to the transaction or arrangement without actual notice of the contravention;[55] or

(3) if the arrangement is within a reasonable period affirmed by resolution of the members of the company, and by resolution of the members of its holding company if it involves a director of the holding company or a person connected with such a director.[56]

These exceptions are the only circumstances in which the right to avoid is lost and a lapse of time is not by itself a bar to avoidance.[57]

In addition, s 195(3) imposes on a number of people liability to account to the company for any gain made directly or indirectly by the arrangement or transaction, and (jointly and severally with any other person so liable under the section) liability to indemnify the company for any loss or damage resulting from it. These people are (a) any director of the company or of its holding company, or a person connected with such a director, with whom the company entered into the arrangement, (b) the

---

shareholder when the transactions implementing the arrangement were actually agreed. See also *Re Conegrade Ltd* [2003] BPIR 358.

[50] *Demite Ltd v Protec Health Ltd* [1998] BCC 638. The consideration to be paid may not be crucial, but the shareholders must have sufficient information to make their approval an informed one: *Clydebank Football Club Ltd v Steedman* 2002 SLT 109.

[51] Section 190(3).

[52] Such a transaction does not have to be one which the company is compelled to enter into as a result of the arrangement: *Re Duckwari plc* [1997] BCC 45, at 49.

[53] But not illegal: *Niltan Carson Ltd v Hawthorne*, above.

[54] Section 195(2)(a) and (b).

[55] Section 195(2)(c).

[56] Section 196.

[57] *Demite Ltd v Protec Health Ltd*, above. In this respect, the statutory remedy differs from the general law remedy of rescission: see **16.8.1**.

director with whom any such person is connected and (c) any director of the company not a party to it who authorised the arrangement or a transaction entered into in pursuance of it.[58] The liability to indemnify the company against loss extends to any subsequent decline in the market value of an asset after its acquisition,[59] but it is limited to loss arising from the acquisition and does not include losses arising from associated transactions, for example in respect of a borrowing effected to make the acquisition.[60] However, a connected person and a director not a party are excused from liability if they can show that at the time the arrangement was entered into, they did not know the relevant circumstances constituting the contravention, and where the arrangement is with a person connected with a director, that director is not liable if he shows that he took all reasonable steps to secure the company's compliance with s 190.[61] Lack of knowledge is not shown if the director did not trouble to ask what the arrangement was that he was authorising.[62] These statutory liabilities are expressly stated in s 195(8) as not excluding any liability imposed under any other enactment or rule of law by which an arrangement or transaction may be called in question or any liability to the company may arise. This would cover in particular any liability arising by virtue of the general duties described in Chapter 16, including potential liability for a misapplication or misappropriation of company property.

17.5   LOANS TO DIRECTORS AND OTHERS

The Companies Act 2006 contains comprehensive provisions concerning companies making loans to and entering into equivalent transactions on behalf of directors and, in some cases, persons connected with directors.[63] Subject to the exceptions described below, the requirements fall into two categories: first, those applying to all companies and, secondly, those applying only to public companies or a company associated with a public company.[64] The key point about the latter is they extend to transactions

---

[58]   Section 195(4).

[59]   *Duckwari plc v Offerventure Ltd* [1998] 2 BCLC 315.

[60]   *Re Duckwari plc (No 3)* [1999] 1 BCLC 168 (CA), the sequel to the decisions referred to above. It is submitted, though, that the directors might be liable for such losses by reason of a breach of their duty to act in good faith and for the proper purposes as described in Chapter 16. It appears that the claim in the litigation involving Duckwari plc was founded solely on a breach of what is now s 190.

[61]   Section 195(6) and (7).

[62]   *Lexi Holdings plc v Luqman* [2008] EWHC 1639 (Ch), [2008] 2 BCLC 725 at [176] and [177], reversed on other grounds [2009] EWCA Civ 117, [2009] 2 BCLC 1, CA.

[63]   Previously such deals were generally prohibited [CA 1985, s 330], but the 2006 Act, as will be seen, makes them subject to the approval of members instead.

[64]   The retention of this distinction between private and public companies, as under the provisions in the Companies Act 1985 that they replaced, was contrary to the views of the Law Commission (*Company Directors: Regulating Conflicts of Interest and Formulating a Statement of Duties*, Law Com No 261, Scot Law Com No 173, Part 12) and the Company Law Review Steering Group (see *Modern Company Law for a Competitive Economy: Developing the Framework* (March 2000) Annex C, paras 28–30,

that are not loans in the conventional sense and to loans and other related dealings with connected persons, as described below. None of the requirements applies to non-UK-registered companies or wholly owned subsidiaries of another body corporate.[65]

There is one section that can have a general application to the provisions described here and which it is convenient to consider at this stage. Section 211 defines the value of transactions and arrangements for these purposes. The value of a loan is the amount of its principal. The value of a quasi-loan (see **17.5.2**) is the amount, or maximum amount, that the person to whom the quasi-loan is made is liable to reimburse the creditor. The value of a credit transaction (see **17.5.2**) is the price that it is reasonable to expect could be obtained for the goods, services or land to which the transaction relates if they had been supplied at the time of the transaction in the ordinary course of business and on the same terms (apart from price) as they have been or are to be supplied under the transaction in question. The value of a guarantee or security is the amount guaranteed or secured. If value is not capable of being expressed as a specific sum of money, it is deemed to exceed £50,000. The value of any other transaction or arrangement is reduced by any amount by which the liabilities of the person for whom the transaction or arrangement was made have been reduced.

17.5.1 Requirements applying to all companies

By s 197(1) and (2), no company may make a loan[66] to any of its directors or to a director of its holding company, nor may it guarantee or provide security in connection with a loan made by any person to such a director, unless the transaction has been approved by a resolution of the members of the company and, if the director is a director of the company's holding company, by a resolution of the members of the holding company.

The same requirement applies by s 203 to what the Act calls 'related arrangements', that is where another person makes a loan that would have fallen within s 197 and the lender, in pursuance of the arrangement, obtains a benefit from the company or a body corporate associated with it or where a company arranges for the assignment to it, or assumption by it, of any rights, obligations or liabilities under a transaction that, if it had been entered into by the company, would have required member approval.[67]

---

para 4.21 of *Completing the Structure*, and para 6.15 of their *Final Report*), who thought that all the controls should apply to all companies. This was also provided for in the Bill that became the 2006 Act, but the distinction was retained in the final version.

65   See ss 197(5), 198(6), 200(6), 201(6) and 203(5).

66   'Loan' must be construed in its ordinary sense as a straightforward lending of money to be returned in money or money's worth – see *Champagne Perrier SA v HH Finch Ltd* [1982] 3 All ER 713, a case concerned with a predecessor to s 197 (s 190 of the 1948 Act). The arrangement in this case was what under the Act is a 'quasi-loan' (see **17.5.2**).

67   For the purposes of determining whether such a transaction would have required

Before approval can be given, a memorandum disclosing (a) the nature of the transaction, (b) the amount of the loan and the purpose for which it is required and (c) the extent of the company's liability under any transaction connected with the loan must be made available to members. If approval is sought by way of written resolution, the memorandum must be sent or submitted to every member entitled to vote at or before the time when the proposed resolution is sent or submitted to him.[68] If approval is to be sought by resolution at a meeting, the memorandum must be available at the company's registered office for not less than 15 days ending with the date of the meeting and at the meeting itself.[69]

17.5.2　Requirements applying to public companies

More extensive requirements apply to a public company and a company associated with a public company. An associated company is a company within a group that contains a public company.[70]

The requirements on public companies extend in particular to loans to 'connected persons',[71] to what are termed 'quasi-loans' to directors and connected persons, and to 'credit transactions' for directors and connected persons. The same requirements of member approval and disclosure as described in **17.5.1** apply, but they are separately enacted in s 198 (quasi-loans to directors), s 200 (loans and quasi-loans to connected persons) and s 201 (credit transactions for directors and connected persons). Similarly the requirements of s 203 regarding related arrangements apply to such loans, quasi-loans and credit transactions.

Quasi-loan is defined in s 199 as a transaction under which a creditor agrees to pay, or pays otherwise than in pursuance of an agreement, a sum for a borrower, or agrees to reimburse, or reimburses otherwise than in pursuance of an agreement, expenditure incurred by another party for the borrower, on terms that the borrower or someone on his behalf will reimburse the creditor, or in circumstances giving rise to a liability on the borrower to reimburse the creditor. For the purpose of the prohibitions, the company will be the creditor who pays money or reimburses expenditure to a third party for the director or connected person, the latter being the 'borrower' in the statutory definition liable to repay the sum to the company.[72]

---

approval under s 197, the transaction is treated as having been entered into on the date that the company enters into the arrangement: s 203(6). The value of an arrangement within s 203 is the value of the transaction to which the arrangement relates: s 211(6).

[68]　An accidental failure to send a memorandum to every member is to be disregarded if a majority approves the proposal: see s 224.

[69]　Section 197(3) and (4).

[70]　The definition is in s 256.

[71]　See **17.2.1**.

[72]　Any reference to the person to whom a quasi-loan is made is a reference to the borrower, and a borrower's liabilities under a quasi-loan include the liability of any person who has agreed to reimburse the creditor on behalf of the borrower: s 199(3). A good

A credit transaction is defined in s 202 as a transaction under which one party (the creditor):

(1) supplies any goods or sells any land under a hire-purchase or conditional sale agreement;[73]

(2) leases or hires any land or goods in return for periodical payments; or

(3) otherwise disposes of land or supplies goods or services[74] on the understanding that payment (whether in a lump sum or instalments or by way of periodical payments or otherwise) is to be deferred.

17.5.3 Exceptions

Sections 204–209 provide for a number of exceptions to the requirements in respect of loans and related dealings. These are as follows:

(1) *Expenditure on company business.* Under s 204, a company can provide its directors or directors of its holding company or a person connected with such a director with funds of up to £50,000[75] to meet expenditure incurred or to be incurred by them for the purposes of the company or for the purpose of enabling them properly to perform their duties as an officer of the company or to avoid incurring such expenditure.

(2) *Expenditure on defending proceedings.*[76] Section 205 allows a company to provide funds to a director of it or of its holding company to meet expenditure in defending criminal or civil proceedings in connection with any alleged negligence, default, breach of duty or breach of trust by him in relation to the company or an associated company or in connection with an application for relief from liability.[77] However, such funds can only be provided on the basis that they must be repaid in the event of a conviction, judgment or the refusal of relief.[78]

---

example of a quasi-loan is to be found in *Champagne Perrier SA v HH Finch Ltd* [1982] 3 All ER 713, where a company paid bills for a director, on the basis that he would repay at a future date. Another example would be the provision of a credit card on similar terms.

[73] These bear the same meaning as in the Consumer Credit Act 1974 (see s 189 thereof): s 202(3).

[74] 'Services' means anything other than goods or land: s 202(3).

[75] This includes the value of the transaction in question and the value of any other relevant transactions or arrangements: s 204(2). As to the meaning of value, see **17.5**. Other relevant transactions or arrangements are determined in accordance with s 210.

[76] This and the following exception were wholly new in the 2006 Act and are the result of concern about the potential liabilities to which directors may be subject.

[77] Under s 661 (see **7.16**) or 1157 (see **17.9.3**).

[78] See s 205(2)–(4) for the detail.

(3) *Expenditure in connection with regulatory action or investigation.* There is a similar exception to that just described in s 206 when a director is defending himself in an investigation by a regulatory authority or against action proposed to be taken by such an authority. The term 'regulatory authority' is not defined, but it clearly includes the Department for Business, Enterprise and Regulatory Reform and the Financial Services Authority and presumably also the Panel on Takeovers and Mergers. Note that there is no requirement in this section for there to be any obligation on a director to repay funds provided for this purpose.

(4) *Minor and business transactions.* Section 207(1) exempts entirely loans, quasi-loans and associated guarantees or securities if the aggregate of the value of the transaction and any other relevant transactions or arrangements does not exceed £10,000.[79] By s 207(2) credit transactions, etc up to an aggregate value of £15,000 are also excluded, and credit transactions, etc are not covered at all if entered into by the company in the ordinary course of its business and on the same basis as it would enter into such transactions with a person of the same financial standing but unconnected with the company.

(5) *Intra-group transactions.* By s 336, none of the prohibitions against loans, quasi-loans and credit transactions apply where the deal is with or in favour of a company's holding company; in the absence of this exception, a holding company might well be caught as a shadow director or connected person.

(6) *Money-lending companies.* These companies[80] can, by s 209, make loans, etc to directors, etc if they are made on the ordinary terms, ie the director, etc is treated no differently from the way in which the company would treat a person of the same financial standing without a connection with the company.[81]

17.5.4 Remedies

As we have seen, a major change from the provisions replaced by the sections in the 2006 Act on loans, etc was the abolition of any prohibitions and the substitution of the requirement of member approval. A further consequential change was the abolition of any criminal penalties for breach of any of the provisions. By s 213, a transaction or arrangement in breach is voidable at the instance of the company[82] unless:

---

[79] As to the meaning of value, see **17.5**. Other relevant transactions or arrangements are determined in accordance with s 210.

[80] Defined in s 209(2). There are no financial limits in this section, unlike the provision it replaced.

[81] More generous provision may be made for loans for house purchase and improvement if such loans are ordinarily made on similar terms to employees.

[82] See *Tait Consibee (Oxford) Ltd v Tait* [1997] 2 BCLC 349 (CA).

(1) restitution of any money or other asset that was the subject matter of the transaction or arrangement is no longer possible;

(2) the company has been indemnified[83] for any loss or damage resulting from the transaction or arrangement; or

(3) any rights acquired in good faith, for value and without actual notice of the contravention by a person who is not a party to the transaction or arrangement was made would be affected by its avoidance.

In addition s 214 makes provision for a breach to be affirmed by a resolution of the members of the company or, as appropriate, of the holding company within a reasonable period.

Whether or not the transaction or arrangement has been avoided, any director of the company or of its holding company, a person connected with such a director who entered into the transaction or arrangement, the director of the company or of its holding company with whom any such person is connected and any other director who authorised the transaction or arrangement are liable to account to the company for any gain made directly or indirectly by the transaction or arrangement, and jointly and severally liable to indemnify the company for any loss or damage resulting from it.[84] However, where an arrangement or transaction is with a person connected with a director, that director is not liable if he shows that he took all reasonable steps to secure the company's compliance with the appropriate section,[85] and a connected person or an authorising director is excused from liability if he shows that, at the time the arrangement or transaction was entered into, he did not know of the relevant circumstances constituting the contravention.[86]

Section 213(8) provides that nothing in the section shall be read as excluding the operation of any other enactment or rule of law by virtue of which the transaction or arrangement may be called into question or any liability to the company may arise. It has been held that, as loans, etc governed by the Act are merely voidable at the option of the company, the company can sue to enforce a loan made in contravention of the Act, in addition to using the statutory remedies.[87] However, it cannot recover money paid thereunder on the basis of a constructive trust, as a loan is

---

[83] Presumably, if the company relies on general law to recover any loss or damage, as discussed below, this bar to avoidance will not apply.

[84] Section 213(3) and (4).

[85] Section 213(6).

[86] Section 213(7). No doubt, this defence will not be available if the director does not trouble to ask what he was authorising; see *Lexi Holdings plc v Luqman* [2008] EWHC 1639 (Ch) at [176] and [177], construing the same words in what is now s 195(7).

[87] *Currencies Direct Ltd v Ellis* [2002] 1 BCLC 193, decision upheld on other grounds: [2002] EWCA Civ 779, [2002] 2 BCLC 482.

merely voidable and property in the money passes to the borrower.[88] In *Wallersteiner v Moir (No 1)*,[89] it was held that a director receiving a loan in breach of s 190 of the Companies Act 1948 (the predecessor to what is now s 197) was liable for misfeasance and to compensate the company for any loss. It is submitted that the same result would follow a breach of the current provisions by virtue of the saving in s 213(8).

17.6   PAYMENTS FOR LOSS OF OFFICE

Sections 215–222 of the Companies Act 2006[90] contain provisions that reinforce the general principles regarding conflicts of interest in the particular situation of payments made to directors in connection with the loss of their office, whether generally or as a result of a transfer of the company's undertaking (often referred to as an asset transfer) or a takeover of the company (a share transfer). As with the provisions already examined in this chapter, they require disclosure to and approval by the members of the company, except where the company is not a UK-registered company or is a wholly owned subsidiary of another body corporate,[91] and except in the case of payments within s 220 and small payments within s 221 (described in **17.6.1**).

Section 215 gives a comprehensive definition of what is meant by a payment for loss of office. The general definition, which is applicable to all the situations covered by the sections, covers payments (including payment by another person at the direction or on behalf of the company or any other person caught by the sections) by way of compensation for loss of office as director and as consideration for or in connection with retirement from office as director, together with such payments by way of compensation for loss or in consideration of retirement, while a director or in connection with his ceasing to be a director, of any other office or employment in connection with the management of the affairs of the company or any such office, as director or otherwise, or employment in any subsidiary undertaking. For this purpose, compensation and consideration include benefits otherwise than in cash.[92] Further, a payment to a person connected with a director is treated as a payment to the director.[93]

---

[88] *Re Ciro Citterio Menswear plc* [2002] EWHC 293 (Ch), [2002] 1 BCLC 672, distinguishing what was said in *Wallersteiner v Moir (No 1)* [1974] 1 WLR 991, below. This follows from the difference in wording between the current provision and its predecessor in force at the time of the latter decision, although the judge did not explicitly make this point.

[89] [1974] 1 WLR 991.

[90] [CA 1985, ss 312–316.]

[91] See ss 217(4), 218(4) and 219(6). The reference to body corporate means that UK-registered wholly owned subsidiaries of foreign companies are exempt.

[92] Section 215(2).

[93] Section 215(3).

In situations of asset transfers and share transfers, the meaning of payments for loss of office is extended to cover payments to directors in respect of the loss of any office or employment with the company, and not merely loss of office as a director as such.[94]

Section 217 prohibits the making of a payment by a company to a director of the company for loss of office, unless the payment has been approved by a resolution of the members of the company; a payment to a director of a company's holding company must be approved by members of both companies.[95] Such a resolution must not be passed unless a memorandum setting out particulars of the proposed payment, including its amount, is made available to the members of the company whose approval is sought.[96] If approval is sought by way of written resolution, the memorandum must be sent or submitted to every member entitled to vote at or before the time when the proposed resolution is sent or submitted to him.[97] If approval is to be sought by resolution at a meeting, the memorandum must be available at the company's registered office for not less than 15 days ending with the date of the meeting and at the meeting itself.

Section 218 imposes the same requirements in respect of payments made by any person to a director in connection with the transfer of the whole or any part of the undertaking or property of the company; a payment to a director of a company's holding company must be approved by members of both companies.[98] A payment made in pursuance of an arrangement entered into as part of the agreement for a transfer or within one year before or 2 years after that agreement and to which the company or any person to whom the transfer is made is privy is presumed to be within the section, unless the contrary is shown.[99]

Section 219 deals with similar payments by any person when made in connection with a transfer of shares in the company, or in a subsidiary of the company,[100] resulting from a takeover bid, although here approval must be by the relevant shareholders, namely the holders of the shares to which the bid relates and any holders of shares of the same class as any of those shares. There is no definition of takeover bid for this purpose, and the assumption is that it will be construed widely.[101] A payment made in

---

[94] Section 216 (this reverses part of the decision in *Taupo Totara Timber Co v Rowe* [1978] AC 537).

[95] Unless the company is a wholly owned subsidiary.

[96] This represents a change from the previous position, under which disclosure had to be to all members, including those with no or restricted voting rights: *Re Duomatic Ltd* [1969] 2 Ch 365.

[97] An accidental failure to send a memorandum to every member is to be disregarded if a majority approves the proposal: see s 224.

[98] Unless the company is a wholly owned subsidiary.

[99] Section 218(4).

[100] Unless the company is a wholly owned subsidiary.

[101] Only defined categories of bid were caught by the predecessor to this provision.

pursuance of an arrangement entered into as part of the agreement for a transfer or within one year before or 2 years after that agreement and to which the company or any person to whom the transfer is made is privy is presumed to be within the section, unless the contrary is shown.[102]

The same disclosure, etc requirements as described above apply under s 219, but there are two provisions particular to s 219. First, neither the person making the offer, nor any associate of his,[103] can vote on the resolution for approval, but in the case of a proposed written resolution they are entitled (if they would otherwise be entitled)[104] to be sent a copy of it and at a meeting they are entitled (if they would otherwise be entitled)[105] to be given notice of the meeting, to attend and speak and if present (in person or by proxy) to count towards the quorum.[106] Secondly, if at a meeting to consider the resolution a quorum is not present, and after the meeting has been adjourned to a later date a quorum is still not present, the payment is, for the purposes of the section, deemed to have been approved.[107]

Even if a payment falling within these sections is duly approved, it could still be invalid if made gratuitously and not for the benefit of the company as a whole, in the absence of an express power in the company's constitution.[108]

17.6.1   Exceptions

The sections just described cover only payments made to compensate for the loss of the office of director. They do not cover payments made to compensate for the loss of a position as employee or payments which the company is contractually obliged to make, for example compensation payable under the terms of a managing director's service contract.[109] Further, s 221 exempts certain small payments.[110] Approval is not required for a payment made by the company or any of its subsidiaries where the amount, together with the amount or value of any other relevant payments, does not exceed £200. Other relevant payments, in the case of asset transfers and share transfers, are any that are made to the director in question by the company making the payment in question or any of its subsidiaries. A further condition for a payment to be relevant

---

[102]   Section 219(7).

[103]   This term is defined in s 988; see **20.24**.

[104]   That is if they are already a member of the company.

[105]   That is if they are already a member of the company.

[106]   Section 219(4).

[107]   Section 219(5); clearly the payment could be open to challenge on other grounds, for example for breach of one of the general duties of directors.

[108]   *Gibson's Executor v Gibson 1980 SLT 2*. This is merely a particular application of the law as to corporate gifts (see **6.3**).

[109]   Section 220, confirming this aspect of the decision in *Taupo Totara Timber Co v Rowe* [1978] AC 537; see also *Lander v Premier Pict Petroleum Ltd* [1998] BCC 248.

[110]   This exception was newly introduced in the 2006 Act.

applies in connection with general payments for loss of office, namely that it must be paid in connection with the same event. Thus in the latter situation it is permissible to pay two payments of up to £200 and be exempt from the requirement of approval, if, for example, one was made as compensation for loss of office as director and the other as compensation for loss of some other office or employment.

17.6.2 Remedies

The remedies that follow a breach of the provisions regarding payments for loss of office are set out in s 222.

(1) If a payment is made in contravention of s 217, it is held by the recipient on trust for the company and any director who authorised it is jointly and severally liable to indemnify the company for any resulting loss.

(2) A payment made in an asset transfer in contravention of s 218 is held on trust for the company whose assets are or are proposed to be transferred.

(3) A payment made in a share transfer in contravention of s 219 is held on trust for the persons who have sold their shares as a result of the offer and the recipient must bear the expenses of distributing the sum.

If a payment contravenes both ss 217 and 218, remedy (2) applies. If a payment contravenes both ss 217 and 219, remedy (3) applies, unless the court directs otherwise.

17.7 POWER TO PROVIDE FOR EMPLOYEES

Section 247 allows directors to make provision for the benefit of employees (including former employees) of the company or its subsidiaries on the cessation or transfer of the whole or part of the undertaking of the company or the subsidiary.[111] By s 247(2) the power can be exercised even if it will not promote the success of the company in accordance with the general duty under s 172,[112] but the directors cannot use the power conferred to make payments to themselves or to former directors or to shadow directors, unless the payments are authorised by ordinary resolution.[113]

---

[111] This replaced s 719 of the 1985 Act, which itself was a statutory reversal of the common law position exemplified in cases like *Parke v Daily News Ltd* [1962] Ch 927.

[112] See **16.5**.

[113] Section 247(5).

17.8   LIABILITY FOR FALSE AND MISLEADING STATEMENTS IN REPORTS

Section 463 contains a very specific provision, which appears in Part 15 of the Act dealing with accounts and reports. However, because it imposes a statutory liability on directors, it is appropriate to consider it here. It applies to statements and omissions in the directors' report, the directors' remuneration report and a summary financial statement insofar as it is derived from either of those reports. A director is liable to compensate the company for any loss suffered by it as a result of any untrue or misleading statement or omission of anything required to be included, if, but only if, he knew the statement to be untrue or misleading or was reckless as to that or he knew the omission to be dishonest concealment of a material fact. Liability under the section does not affect any liability for a civil penalty or criminal offence,[114] but s 463(4) and (5) makes it clear that the section does not impose liability to anyone other than the company, whether that is liability for any civil remedy or to rescind or repudiate an agreement.

In effect therefore the section creates a statutory tort, but actionable only at the instance of the company and not, for example, by members or any third parties. Section 463(4) seems to be worded widely enough to exclude general tortious liability to members or third parties resulting from reliance on one of the reports covered. The fact that compensation is payable for loss 'as a result' of untrue or misleading statements, etc means that the company will have to show a causal link between the statement, etc and the loss, but there is, naturally enough, no requirement for reliance. In this respect the section mirrors liability for untrue or misleading statements or omissions in prospectuses.[115]

17.9   FACTORS RELIEVING A DIRECTOR FROM LIABILITY FOR BREACH OF DUTY

There are a number of ways in which a director who is *prima facie* liable for a breach of directors' duties may be relieved from such liability. These are examined in the following sections.

17.9.1   Ratification

As indicated at various stages of this and the preceding chapter, a breach of duty by a director may often, but not always, be 'cured' through his conduct being disclosed to the general meeting and ratified thereat by the passing of an ordinary resolution.[116] The notice summoning a meeting for

---

[114] Section 463(6).

[115] Under the Financial Services and Markets Act 2000, s 90. See **19.27**.

[116] Ratification should be distinguished from an exercise of power by the general meeting where the meeting validly performs the relevant act itself, as opposed to approving its

this purpose should make it clear that the purpose or one of the purposes of the meeting is to sanction the relevant conduct of the director; if it does not, the notice may be held insufficient and the resolution ineffective.[117] There is now a specific section in the Companies Act 2006, s 239, which deals with aspects of the law relating to ratification. However, this by itself does not affect the core point regarding the breaches of duty that are or are not ratifiable, as it provides[118] that it does not affect any rule of law as to acts that are incapable of being ratified by the company.

The dividing line between those breaches of duty which are capable of ratification and those which are not was not at all easy to draw before the introduction of s 239 and is perhaps made a little more problematic given that the Companies Act says nothing about the ratifiability of the general statutory duties. Before the introduction of these duties, the case-law expressly established some breaches as ratifiable,[119] namely failing to disclose an interest in a contract to which the company is a party and thus resolve a conflict of interest and duty,[120] obtaining a secret profit not involving a misapplication of company property,[121] negligence,[122] and using a power for an improper purpose.[123] In all cases, there was an overriding qualification that the director must have acted *bona fide* in the interest of the company.[124]

The following breaches of duty were held not capable of ratification by the votes of a simple majority of members:[125]

(1)   one involving a lack of good faith on the part of the director;[126]

---

prior performance by the board. The distinction is brought out in a comparison between the first instance judgment of Plowman J and the judgments of the Court of Appeal in *Bamford v Bamford* [1970] Ch 242. For an interesting article challenging the conventional view of ratification and arguing that, as opposed to a prospective release from liability, it can bind only the minority and not the company unless the director provides consideration or it is given under seal, see Partridge (1987) 46 CLJ 122.

[117]   *Kaye v Croydon Tramways Co* [1898] 1 Ch 358 (CA).

[118]   See s 239(7).

[119]   In addition, acting in excess of power is ratifiable, whether it is also a breach of duty or not: *Irvine v Union Bank of Australia* (1877) 2 App Cas 366 (PC); *Grant v United Kingdom Switchback Railways* (1880) 40 Ch D 135 (CA).

[120]   *North-West Transportation Co v Beatty* (1887) 12 App Cas 589 (PC).

[121]   *Regal (Hastings) Ltd v Gulliver* [1967] 2 AC 134n (HL).

[122]   *Pavlides v Jensen* [1956] Ch 565.

[123]   *Alexander v Automatic Telephone Co* [1990] 2 Ch 56, at 67 (CA); *Hogg v Cramphorn Ltd* [1967] Ch 254; *Bamford v Bamford*, above. If the impropriety was an improper allotment of shares, as in the latter two cases, the votes on the improperly allotted shares should not be used on the resolution.

[124]   This is expressed in most of the cases cited above and is supported by *Daniels v Daniels* [1978] Ch 406 in respect of liability for negligence.

[125]   For a fuller discussion in the context of minority shareholders' claims, where the question is an important one, see **18.4**.

[126]   *Attwool v Merryweather* (1867) LR 5 Dq 46n; *Mason v Harris* (1879) 11 Ch D 97 (CA).

(2) one resulting in the company performing an illegal act;[127]

(3) one resulting in the company performing an act which, although lawful, could not be done under the articles without some special procedure such as a special resolution;

(4) one bearing directly upon the 'personal rights' of individual shareholders, as defined in the articles;[128]

(5) one involving a 'fraud on the minority', that is whereby a majority of the shareholders or the directors succeed in expropriating at the expense of the minority the 'money, property, or advantages' of the company.[129]

As far as ratifiable breaches are concerned, those mentioned above all now have their statutory equivalent in the sections dealing with the general duties and, unless the view is taken that their inclusion in this way renders them somehow different, then it would seem reasonable to suppose that they may remain ratifiable, provided, in accordance with the duty in s 172, which is the equivalent of the duty to act *bona fide*, a director was acting in good faith to promote the success of the company. There do not seem any arguments of principle against a good faith failure to resolve a conflict (s 175) or accepting a benefit from a third party (s 176) being capable of ratification, and the same could also be said, although with slightly less confidence, about negligence (s 174). However, the fact that the duty to act in accordance with the constitution and exercise powers for a proper purpose (s 171) is given 'pride of place' as the first core duty could perhaps be support for the view that a breach would not be ratifiable. In any event, the first limb of s 171 can hardly be so capable in respect of some breaches of the constitution at least, since if the directors act in ways that would require the articles to be amended, this can only by done by special resolution and thus their actions could hardly be approved by ordinary resolution; in effect these situations can be comprehended by heads (3) and (4) in the above list of unratifiable breaches.

---

[127] *Re Exchange Banking Co Flitcroft's Case* (1882) 21 Ch D 519 (CA).

[128] Eg refusal to register a transfer of shares for an improper purpose.

[129] *Burland v Earle* [1902] AC 83, at 93 (PC). See also especially, *Cook v Deeks* [1916] 1 AC 554 (PC), the facts of which were given at **16.13.1** and *Shaker v Al-Bedrawi* [2002] EWCA Civ 1452, [2003] 1 BCLC 157, at 198. Cf *Regal (Hastings) Ltd v Gulliver*, above, discussed in **16.9**, where the opportunity to make the profit was not 'expropriated' from the company and the breach was ratifiable. There are, however, difficulties with this analysis: see *Gore-Browne on Companies* (Jordans, 45th edn, loose-leaf) at 17 [2A]; Davies *Gower's Principles of Modern Company Law* (Sweet & Maxwell, 6th edn, 1997) at pp 644–648; Wedderburn [1957] CLJ 194 and [1958] CLJ 93; Sealy [1967] CLJ 83 at 102 *et seq*; Beck, in Ziegel (ed) *Canadian Company Law*, vol II, pp 232–238.

Section 239 is not concerned with ratification of acts that exceed a director's authority, unless that is also a breach of duty,[130] as s 239(1) refers to conduct[131] amounting to negligence, default, breach of duty or breach of trust in relation to the company. The reference to 'breach of trust' is curious, as it is clear that any misappropriation or misapplication of property by directors is regarded as a breach of trust and incapable of being ratified at least by ordinary resolution.[132] What s 239 does change in particular is the possibility of the director in breach being able to use his own votes as member to secure ratification, which was something the common law permitted provided at least that the director's breach was in good faith.[133] It provides that members with a personal interest, direct or indirect, cannot effectively vote. In the case of ratification by written resolution, they are not regarded as eligible members and thus should not be involved in the procedure.[134] In the case of ratification by resolution at a meeting, any of their votes must be disregarded, although they can attend, be counted in the quorum and take part in the proceedings.[135] Section 239(2) confirms that ratification can only be by a resolution of the members, which will normally mean by ordinary resolution. The section applies to the ratification of breach by a former director and a shadow director.[136]

Section 239(6) provides that nothing in the section affects the law on unanimous consent, so the restrictions in the section as to who may vote on a ratification resolution will not apply when every member votes (informally or otherwise) in favour of the resolution.[137] The case-law suggests that any breach of duty is capable of ratification by all members, provided that there is no fraud on the creditors.[138] Such a fraud[139] seems likely to arise only when a company is in danger of going out of business in an insolvent state. This principle seems acceptable in theory, given that ratification in this context means simply the company's waiving of its right to sue a director. It is obviously perfectly proper for a fully informed company to take such a decision in respect of any breach of duty, subject to the qualification mentioned.

---

[130] See note 115, above.

[131] Including acts and omissions: s 239(5)(a).

[132] See **16.13.1**.

[133] *North-West Transportation Co v Beatty* (1887) 12 App Cas 589 (PC); *Burland v Earle* [1902] AC 83 at 94 (PC); *Northern Counties Securities Ltd v Jackson & Steeple Ltd* [1974] 1 WLR 1133, at 1146.

[134] Section 239(3).

[135] Section 239(4).

[136] Section 239(5)(b) and (c).

[137] As to the principle of unanimous consent, see **13.2**, and see *Re Duomatic Ltd* [1969] 2 Ch 365; *Re Gee & Co (Woolwich) Ltd* [1975] Ch 52.

[138] See *Re Horsley & Weight Ltd* [1982] Ch 442, at 1055; *Multinational Gas and Petrochemical Co v Multinational Gas and Petrochemical Services Ltd* [1983] Ch at 258, at 269, 289–290, *Rolled Steel Products Ltd v British Steel Corporation* [1984] BCLC 466, at 508–509.

[139] Eg the taking of excessive remuneration by directors as in *Re Halt Garage (1964) Ltd* [1982] 3 All ER 1016.

Section 239(6) also provides that nothing in the section affects any power of the directors to agree not to sue, or settle or release a claim made by them on behalf of the company, so that if, for example, the board agrees to abandon a claim against a former director, the requirements of the section do not apply, although such a decision could in itself amount to a breach of duty.

17.9.2   Provisions in the articles

Section 232(1)[140] makes void any provision, whether contained in the articles of the company or any contract with the company or otherwise, that purports to exempt a director of a company (to any extent) from any liability that would otherwise attach to him in connection with any negligence, default, breach of duty or breach of trust in relation to the company.[141] Section 232(2) makes similar provision as regards indemnities provided against such liabilities for a director of a company or an associated company, subject to three permitted types of indemnity, namely:

(1)   liability insurance within s 233;

(2)   qualifying third-party indemnity provisions falling within s 234; and

(3)   qualifying pension scheme indemnity provisions falling within s 235.

Section 233 permits liability insurance, commonly known as directors' and officers' liability insurance, purchased and maintained by the company against liability for negligence, default, breach of duty or breach of trust in relation to the company.[142] Third-party indemnity provisions within s 234 are provisions for indemnity against liability incurred by a director to someone other than the company or an associated company and pension scheme indemnity provisions within s 235 are provisions indemnifying a director of a company that a trustee of an occupational pension scheme against liability incurred in connection with the company's activities as trustee of the scheme. However, there are limits as to the indemnity that can be provided under these. Section 234 does not permit indemnity against liability to pay criminal fines or civil penalties to

---

[140] [CA 1985, s 309A.]

[141] Only an exemption provided by the company, not one provided by a third party, is caught by the section: *Burgoine v London Borough of Waltham Forest* [1997] BCC 347.

[142] Until an amendment made to the predecessor to s 233, there was some doubt as to the validity of insurance effected in this way because of the wording of what is now s 232, although there was never any concern about liability insurance effected and paid for by directors themselves. This does not automatically validate all such insurance so that, eg indemnity against the deliberate commission of a breach of duty could be unenforceable on public policy grounds; see *Birds' Modern Insurance Law* (Sweet & Maxwell, 8th edn, 2010) Ch 14. For a very useful review, see Finch 'Personal Accountability and Corporate Control: the Role of Directors' and Officers' Liability Insurance' (1994) 57 MLR 880.

a regulatory authority or the costs of an unsuccessful defence of criminal or civil proceedings or application for relief under ss 661 or 1157. Section 235 does not permit indemnity against liability to pay criminal fines or civil penalties to a regulatory authority or the costs of an unsuccessful defence of criminal proceedings. There are disclosure requirements in respect of these indemnity provisions in s 236.

Exactly what provisions in articles or elsewhere s 232 (and its predecessors) covers has been the subject of much academic debate,[143] and for many years there was no relevant case-law. The problem arose because the model forms of articles of association in Table A, in both the 1948 and 1985 versions, contain provisions which do appear to modify and even in part exclude the duties of directors; in the 1985 Table A, these are arts 85 and 94; in the 1948 Table A, which will still apply to many registered companies, they are arts 78 and 84. Clearly, these articles must be valid as they have statutory authority.[144] The problem is whether, and if so to what extent, articles adopted by companies which do not follow them exactly are valid, although in this respect s 232(4), which did not appear in the previous section, gives some guidance, as will be seen.

The problem arose for the first time judicially in *Movitex Ltd v Bulfield*.[145] Here the company in question had articles similar to but slightly more extensive than art 84 of the 1948 Table A. These allowed a director to have interests in and profit from transactions in which the company was interested, provided that he disclosed his interest to his fellow director and, in most instances, did not vote on the matter or, if he did vote, that his presence was not to be counted in the quorum. However, in certain circumstances, a director could vote and be so counted.[146]

Vinelott J held that the articles were valid and did not infringe s 205 of the Companies Act 1948 (now s 232). In doing so, he recognised that there was a difficult point of construction to be resolved in reconciling the articles with the section. He rejected the argument that articles could rewrite the content of directors' duties so long as they did not purport to exempt directors from liability for breaches of duty not ratifiable by the general meeting or from breaches of duties stemming from a mandatory rule of statute. He reasoned, applying *dicta* of Megarry V-C in *Tito v Waddell*[147] that the general principle forbidding directors (and others in fiduciary positions) from putting themselves in a position where their

---

[143] See Baker [1975] JBL 181; Birds (1976) 39 MLR 394; Parkinson [1981] JBL 335; Gregory (1982) 98 LQR 413.

[144] This point was not, however, made in *Movitex Ltd v Bulfield*, discussed below, where Vincent J was at pains to reconcile what is now s 232 and the relevant articles in Table A, implying that if he could not do so, the articles in Table A would be invalid: *sed quaere*.

[145] (1986) 2 BCC 99, at 403; for a fuller discussion, see Birds (1987) 8 Co Law 31.

[146] Cf art 84(2) of the 1948 Table A and art 94 of the 1985 Table A. The difference from these provisions was that the number of circumstances where voting was allowed was greater.

[147] [1977] 3 All ER 129, at 247.

duty to the company might conflict with their own interest was not a *duty* in the strict sense of the word, but simply a disability. It thus did not fall within the wording of what is now s 232. The company could exclude the general principle in its articles, providing in effect that specified situations did not give rise to a conflict of duty and interest, provided that it did not exclude the duties of directors properly so-called.

On this analysis, until the enactment of the general statutory duties of directors, it would seem that the non-excludable *duties* of directors were those obligations that sought to prevent a director from damaging the interests of the company. These probably comprehended the primary duties of good faith and proper purpose,[148] the duty to show proper care and skill, the duty not to misappropriate company property, and any specific statutory duty imposed on directors. However, the general rule imposing accountability for secret profits, as well as that avoiding a transaction involving a conflict of duty and interest, would, on Vinelott J's analysis, have been excludable, so long as the director acted in good faith.[149] It is submitted that this result was acceptable as a matter of policy,[150] although it must be recognised that the distinction between duties and disabilities drawn in *Tito v Waddell* and relied on in *Movitex Ltd v Bulfield* has increasingly been questioned in recent case-law in the Court of Appeal.[151] On this basis, perhaps, Vinelott J's analysis could be challenged. On the other hand, there are recent authorities[152] where the validity of articles similar to those in issue in *Movitex Ltd v Bulfield*, which have not followed exactly those in Table A, has not been challenged on the basis that they infringe what is now s 232.

---

[148] Although as the application of the proper purposes doctrine depends on a company's articles, it must in principle have been excludable in the sense that the articles can define the range of purposes in respect of which a power is properly exercisable: see Birds (1976) 39 MLR 394, at 400. This would seem to survive the codification in s 171, since that does not spell out all the detail of the duty: see **16.4**.

[149] Indeed, Vinelott J expressly held that art 78 of the 1948 Table A, which excludes accountability for secret profits in a particular situation, was consistent with what is now s 232. Article 78 was perhaps a statutory aberration; it was not replaced in exactly the same form in the 1985 Table A – instead of excluding a duty to account totally, part of art 85 of the 1985 Table A excludes it only if the director has disclosed his profit to his fellow directors, thus making the subject matter of the former art 78 subject to the same requirement as directors' interests in contracts, etc (see **16.10**).

[150] It may also accord with the intentions of the Greene Committee (Cmnd 2627, 1925, paras 46 and 47), who recommended the introduction of what is now s 232, although it is somewhat difficult to discern their intention other than that clauses excusing directors' liability for negligence should be outlawed. Vinelott J's conclusion, though not his reasoning, is similar to that reached by Parkinson, *op cit*, footnote 143 at p 532.

[151] *Gwembe Valley Development Co Ltd v Koshy* [2003] EWCA Civ 1048, [2004] 1 BCLC 131, at [104]–[108], referring to the earlier Court of Appeal analyses of the fiduciary's duty of loyalty in *Paragon Finance plc v DB Thakerar & Co* [1999] 1 All ER 400; and *JJ Harrison (Properties) Ltd v Harrison* [2001] EWCA Civ 1467, [2002] 1 BCLC 162. The Law Commission commented that the decision in *Movitex Ltd v Bulfield* 'does draw very difficult distinctions' (*Shareholder Remedies*, Law Com No 246 (1997) para 6.26).

[152] Including *Gwembe Valley Development Co Ltd v Koshy*, above.

In this respect s 232(4) provides that nothing in the section prevents a company's articles from making such provision as has previously been lawful for dealing with conflicts of interest. This seems to amount to a clear endorsement of the decision in *Movitex Ltd v Bulfield*, even if it is now impossible, in the face of the wording of ss 170–177, to refer to that principle as anything other than a duty. On the other hand, it seems clear now liability for breach of the other statutory duties in those sections[153] cannot be excluded.

17.9.3 Discretionary relief from liability by the court

Section 1157 of the Companies Act 2006[154] allows the court which has found a director or other officer[155] liable for negligence, default, breach of duty or breach of trust to relieve him from liability, wholly or partly, on such terms as it thinks fit, provided and only provided that the officer establishes the three distinct matters specified in the section, namely:

(1)   that he acted honestly;

(2)   that he acted reasonably; and

(3)   that, having regard to all the circumstances, he 'ought fairly to be excused'.

It is possible for a director to succeed on the first two points, yet fail on the third, which is a matter for the court's discretion in each case.[156]

17.10   ENFORCEMENT OF CIVIL LIABILITIES AGAINST DIRECTORS

It is all very well for the law to impose what are generally strict duties on company directors, as described in the previous pages of this chapter. What may well be much more important in practice is that the law provides effective ways in which breach of those duties can be remedied. While the company can always take action, that avenue is, for obvious reasons, not likely in many cases in practice. For that reason, and despite

---

[153]   Except perhaps as regards some modification of the proper purposes duty (see note 147).

[154]   [CA 1985, s 727]; cf the equivalent s 61 of the Trustee Act 1925, from which this provision was adapted.

[155]   Or an auditor.

[156]   *Re J Franklin & Son Ltd* [1937] 2 All ER 32. See further as to s 1157, *Gore-Browne on Companies* (Jordans, 45th edn, loose-leaf) at 17 [6] and for a very useful review of the case-law, Edmunds and Lowry 'The continuing value of relief for directors' breach of duty' (2003) 66 MLR 195. It is curious that the section was not at least pleaded in *Regal (Hastings) Ltd v Gulliver* [1967] 2 AC 134n (HL) (see **16.9**), the facts of which look like the sort of case where relief should be considered: see Birds (1976) 39 MLR 394 at 397.

the fact that, as we have seen,[157] a director's duties are generally owed only to the company itself, in certain circumstances a shareholder may be able to institute proceedings. These circumstances are fully explored in the next chapter.

When a company is in liquidation, a breach of duty will be much easier to litigate since the liquidator will in general have the conduct of the action in the company's name. Further, if the breach falls within s 212 of the Insolvency Act 1986,[158] he, or the Official Receiver, or any creditor or contributory, may instead be able to invoke the simpler procedure of a summons in the liquidation.

If a director dies, his estate remains liable for any breach of duty he may have committed, including any wrongful dealing with the company's property such as a payment of dividend out of capital or sale of its assets at an undervalue.[159] A discharge in bankruptcy does not release a director from liability for a fraudulent breach of duty[160] or a claim for a refund of profits, for the retention of them is a breach of trust.[161] The company can prove in the bankrupt estate for the profit.

If two or more directors are implicated in the same breach of duty, their liability is joint and several: accordingly, if in the same transaction they have each misappropriated company assets, each of them is liable for the total amount so misappropriated by himself and his co-directors.[162] If one of them has been rendered liable, he can usually recover contributions from any of the other directors who were responsible also.[163]

---

[157] See **16.2**.
[158] See **15.19.4**.
[159] *Ramskill v Edwards* (1885) 31 Ch D 100; *Re Sharpe* [1892] 1 Ch 154 (CA).
[160] Insolvency Act 1986, s 281(3).
[161] See *Emma Silver Mining Co v Grant* (1881) 17 Ch D 122.
[162] See, eg, *Re Carriage Co-operative Supply Association* (1884) 27 Ch D 322.
[163] See generally, *Ramskill v Edwards*, above.

CHAPTER 18

SHAREHOLDERS' REMEDIES

18.1 INTRODUCTION

This chapter is concerned with various remedies available to minority shareholders. Such remedies are in practical terms the only effective way of enforcing directors' and controlling shareholders' duties (outside the context of the company's liquidation). It will be seen that these remedies are also very much concerned with actions or conduct by the company or its officers which infringe the rights, or prejudice the interests, of individual shareholders or groups of shareholders. The first part of this chapter is concerned with common law claims.

The second part of this chapter deals with two interrelated statutory remedies. A member of a company may petition on the ground of unfair prejudice under Part 30 of the Companies Act 2006 or petition to have the company wound up on the 'just and equitable' ground now contained in s 122(1)(g) of the Insolvency Act 1986.

The last part of this chapter is concerned with the Department for Business Enterprise and Regulatory Reform's range of powers to investigate companies. This may be done informally by civil servants or by the formal appointment of inspectors. The Department is also given the power to follow up its investigation by bringing various types of civil proceedings. While these powers are more than ample in terms of the letter of the law, their use had been much restrained by the customary bureaucratic caution and inertia. These habits tend only to be set aside where a clear *prima facie* case of serious corporate abuse, already publicised in the press, affects the affairs of a public listed company. Even then it is the powers to investigate the affairs of the company (or the ownership of or dealings in its shares) that are likely to be employed. The powers to bring civil proceedings was almost never used and has now been abolished. The power to wind up already failed or defunct public companies is occasionally resorted to.

PART 1: MINORITY SHAREHOLDERS' CLAIMS

18.2   COMMON LAW CLAIMS

Some account must first be given of the common law governing minority shareholders' derivative claims despite the common law's replacement by the statutory derivative claim set out in Part 11 of the Companies Act 2006. There are several reasons for this. Firstly, shareholders' 'direct actions' against the company are still outside the scope of the new statutory procedure.[1] Even in regard to that procedure the common law distinction between ratifiable and non-ratifiable breaches of directors' fiduciary duties remains relevant.[2] Finally, Part 11 of the Companies Act 2006 contains transitional provisions that make the old common law relevant in some circumstances.[3]

There is a general principle of company law[4] that minority shareholders cannot sue for wrongs done to their company or complain of irregularities in the conduct of its internal affairs. This principle came to be known as the rule in *Foss v Harbottle*,[5] from the decision in which it was first clearly established. The cases[6] show that this rule rests upon two related propositions: (a) the right of the majority to bar a minority action whenever they might lawfully ratify alleged misconduct; and (b) the normally exclusive right of the company to sue upon a corporate cause of action. In *Edwards v Halliwell*,[7] Jenkins LJ elucidated the relationship between these two propositions by contending that the will of the majority, *vis-à-vis* the minority, is to be identified with that of the company. Consequently, to say that the company is *prima facie* the proper plaintiff (claimant) in actions concerning its affairs is only another way of saying that the majority, within the limits of their power to ratify, have the sole rights to determine whether or not a dispute shall be brought before the courts.

---

[1]   See **18.8** below.

[2]   See **18.4** below.

[3]   See **18.5.5.2** below.

[4]   In *Hodgson v NALGO* [1972] 1 WLR 130, Goulding J held that the rule in *Foss v Harbottle* did not apply to the case of an *unregistered* trade union since it was incapable of suing in its own name. *Dicta* in *MacDougall v Gardiner* (1875) 1 Ch D 13, at 25; *Cotter v NU Seamen* [1929] 2 Ch 58, at 71; and *Edwards v Halliwell* [1950] 2 All ER 1064, at 1066 were applied. The two latter cases established that the *Foss v Harbottle* rule *does* apply to unions that have been given the statutory right to sue in their own name. See further, *Taylor v NUM* [1985] BCLC 237.

[5]   (1843) 2 Hare 461. As to the historical development of the rule, see Wedderburn (1957) Camb LJ 194 and (1958) Camb LJ 93; Boyle (1965) 28 MLR 317; Baxter (1987) 38 NILQ 6; see also Drury (1986) 45 CLJ 219. See generally Boyle *Minority Shareholders' Remedies* (Cambridge Studies in Corporate Law, CUP, 2002).

[6]   *Foss v Harbottle* (1843) 2 Hare 461, at 492–493 and 494–495; *Mozley v Alston* (1847) 1 Ph 790, at 800; *Burland v Earle* [1902] AC 83, at 93 (PC); *Pavlides v Jensen* [1956] 1 Ch 565, at 575.

[7]   [1950] 2 All ER 1064, at 1066.

The courts have justified the policy expressed by the rule by certain practical arguments of convenience. In *Gray v Lewis*,[8] James LJ justified the principle, that any body corporate is the proper plaintiff in proceedings to recover its property, by pointing to the obvious danger of a multiplicity of shareholders' suits in the absence of a rule such as *Foss v Harbottle*. 'There might be as many bills as there are shareholders multiplied into the number of defendants.' This situation would be aggravated where suits were discontinued at will, or dismissed with costs against plaintiff shareholders unable to meet these costs.[9] In *MacDougall v Gardiner*,[10] Mellish LJ observed the futility of ignoring the majority's power to ratify. If 'something has been done irregularly which the majority are entitled to do regularly, or if something illegally which the majority of the company are entitled to do legally, there can be no use having litigation about it if the ultimate end of which is that a meeting is called and then ultimately the majority gets its wishes'. In this case, the Court of Appeal refused to allow a minority shareholder to complain of the refusal by the chairman of a shareholders' meeting to call a poll.[11]

18.3   PERMITTED COMMON LAW CLAIMS

The rule did not extend to a case where the act complained of is either illegal[12] or is a fraud upon the minority,[13] and there is also an exception in cases where the act done, although regular in form, is unfair and oppressive as against the minority.[14] This will include acts by directors which are an abuse of powers contained in the company's constitution and may only be approved by the unanimous consent of the

---

8   (1873) 8 Ch App 1035, at 1051. This problem of abuse of procedure could of course be handled by the courts in other ways (eg the power to stay or consolidate actions). See Boyle (1965) 28 MLR 317.

9   See *La Compagnie de Mayville v Whiteley* [1896] 1 Ch 788, at 807; *Mozley v Alston* (1847) 1 Ph 790, at 799; *Lord v Cooper Miners* (1848) 2 Ph 740.

10   (1875) 1 Ch D 13, at 25. See also James LJ at 22.

11   This decision is not easy to reconcile with *Pender v Lushington* (1877) 6 Ch D 70, which established that the right to vote at shareholders' meetings is a personal right for which a shareholder may sue. It would be idle to pretend that all the cases on shareholders' 'individual' rights (as an exception to the rule) can be reconciled. For an exploration of the difficulties and a suggested solution, see Baxter 'The Role of the Judge in Enforcing Shareholder Rights' [1983] Camb LJ 96.

12   'Illegal' in this context should be understood as meaning either 'contrary to company law' or 'so plainly illegal that the directors have acted in abuse of their powers'. Where all that is alleged is that the company has engaged in conduct that is contrary to the general law in the sense that it may result, or has resulted, in a criminal prosecution of the company, a shareholder will not have a remedy: *Australian Agricultural Co v Oatmont Pty Ltd* (1992) 8 ACSR 225 (CA) NT.

13   *Alexander v Automatic Telephone Co* [1900] 2 Ch (CA); *Hope v International Financial Society* (1877) 4 Ch D 327; *Simpson v Westminster Palace Hotel* (1860) 8 HLC 712; *Clinch v Financial Corp* (1868) 4 Ch App 117. See the cases on 'non-ratifiable breaches of directors' duties' discussed at **18.4**.

14   See the cases establishing the principle that the majority in general meeting must act *bona fide* in the interests of the company as a whole (eg in altering the articles to the prejudice of a shareholder or class of shareholders). These cases are examined in **5.16**.

shareholders.[15] It does not apply to a case where the matter in question requires, by virtue of a provision either in the Companies Act 2006 or in a company's memorandum or articles, a special or extraordinary resolution,[16] for to allow a company to ratify an act requiring the sanction of a special or extraordinary resolution by refusing to be party to proceedings would be to enable a bare majority to do that which can only be done by a three-quarters majority. A unanimous though informal agreement by the shareholders will effectively amend the articles without a special resolution.[17]

The Companies Act 2006 contains a new provision for the 'entrenchment of provisions in the articles'. Section 22 provides that a company's articles may contain a 'provision for entrenchment' to the effect that a specified provision in the articles may be amended or repealed only if conditions are met, or procedures complied with, that are more restrictive than those applicable in the case of a special resolution.[18]

A single shareholder may sue in his own name to restrain an act which is an infringement of his individual rights,[19] for example a wrongful refusal to accept his vote at a general meeting of the company[20] or a wrongful exclusion of him from the board of directors.[21] The rule of *Foss v Harbottle* has, of course, no application to any statutory right conferred by the Companies Act 2006 on individual shareholders or a minimum number of them.[22] There is also judicial authority for the view that the rule has no application to any individual right conferred by the articles or memorandum.[23] However, whether such rights are an exception to the rule or are beyond its scope is largely a matter of language.

---

[15] *Rolled Steel Products Ltd v British Steel Corporation* [1985] 2 WLR 908 (CA).

[16] *Baillie v Oriental Telephone Co* [1915] 1 Ch 503, at 515 (CA); *Cotter v NU Seamen* [1929] 2 Ch 58, at 69–70; *Edwards v Halliwell* [1950] 2 All ER 1064, at 1067 (CA). Further, the notice of such a resolution must give a fair and reasonably full statement of the facts if the resolution is to bind the minority: *Kaye v Croydon Tramways* [1898] 1 Ch 538 (CA); *Tiessen v Henderson* [1899] 1 Ch 861; *MacConnell v E Prill & Co* [1916] 2 Ch 57. Cf *Normandy v Ind Coope & Co Ltd* [1908] 3 Ch 84.

[17] *Cane v Jones* [1980] 1 WLR 1451. However, such an agreement requires registration. See Companies Act 2006, ss 29–30.

[18] See Companies Act 2006, ss 23–24.

[19] *Johnson v Little's Iron Agency* (1877) 5 Ch 687 (CA); *Wood v Odessa Waterworks Co* (1881) 42 Ch D 636; *Clark v Workman* [1920] 1 Ir R 107, at 112; *Davies v Commercial Publishing Co of Sydney* [1901] NSW (Eq) 37, at 47–48; *Edwards v Halliwell* [1950] 2 All ER 1064 (CA). As to difficulties about this 'exception', see footnote 3 above.

[20] *Pender v Lushington* (1877) 6 Ch D 70, at 81.

[21] *Pullbrook v Richmond Consolidated Co* (1878) 9 Ch D 610; *Harben v Phillips* (1883) 23 Ch D 14 (CA).

[22] As to the rights of members (in respect of meetings) as to notice of resolutions, the requisitioning of meetings, circulating resolutions, etc, see Chapter 13. As to the right of shareholders to petition under Part 30 of the Companies Act 2006, see **18.10**.

[23] *Edwards v Halliwell* [1950] 2 All ER 1064, at 1067 per Jenkins LJ (CA).

18.4   NON-RATIFIABLE BREACHES OF DIRECTORS' DUTIES

The distinction between ratifiable and non-ratifiable breaches of directors' duties retains its significance despite the reform of derivative action in Part 11 of the Companies Act 2006.[24] The old common law on 'fraud on a minority' has been replaced by the new statutory procedure on derivative claims, discussed below at **18.5**. The significance of non-ratifiable breaches (ie those which cannot be ratified by a majority shareholders' resolution in general meeting) retains its importance under the new statutory procedure for bringing derivative claims. This, however, does not require proof of 'wrongdoer control' as under the former common law. Wrongdoer control is replaced by new statutory criteria governing the exercise of judicial discretion in permitting or refusing a derivative claim.[25]

A further difference between the old common law and the new statutory procedure is that derivative claims may now comprise any corporate cause of action 'arising from any actual or proposed act or omission involving negligence, default, breach of duty or breach of trust by a director'.[26] The ratifiable character of a breach of duty, however, can be a factor that the court can consider in refusing permission for a derivative claim to proceed where ratification by a majority of the shareholders has already occurred. This is not the case where non-ratifiable breaches of duty have occurred.[27]

It has long been established by judicial decision that breaches of directors' duties which are of a 'fraudulent character' are not capable of ratification. A familiar example is where the board of directors with the support of the majority shareholders are endeavoring directly or indirectly to appropriate to themselves money or property, or advantages which belong to the company or in which other shareholders are entitled to participate.

An instructive illustration is to be found in cases where an act is authorised by the votes of interested directors given at a general meeting. In the absence of fraud or oppression such votes in general meeting are valid, and a minority suing to set aside the transaction will fail;[28] but if the directors are seeking to appropriate to themselves property which belongs to the company as a whole, a resolution of the company in

---

[24]   See **18.5** below.

[25]   Companies Act 2006, s 260(3).

[26]   Companies Act 2006, s 263(l) and (2). See **18.5** below.

[27]   Companies Act 2006, s 263(l) and (2). See **18.5** below.

[28]   *North-West Transportation Co v Beatty* (1877) 12 App Cas 589 (PC); *Burland v Earle* [1902] AC 83 (PC); *Baird v Baird & Co (Falkirk) 1949 SLT 368*. As to the distinction between the duty of directors in respect of circulating notices of meetings (and accompanying circulars), and their right to vote at the meeting which results, see *Northern Securities v Jackson and Steeple* [1974] 1 WLR 1133. See also *Clemens v Clemens Bros Ltd* [1976] 2 All ER 268 applying *dicta* of Sir Richard Baggallay in *North-West Transportation v Beatty*, above, at 593.

general meeting carried by their votes cannot validate the transaction, and a single shareholder or a minority of shareholders can obtain relief.[29] Misappropriation of corporate property extends to property (or contracts) which 'belong in equity' to the company.[30] Here the directors are accountable for a non-ratifiable breach of trust and not merely for a breach of their fiduciary duty.

In *Daniels v Daniels*,[31] Templeman J reviewed the authorities referred to above in an application to strike out the plaintiff's statement of claim (in a minority shareholder's action) on the ground that no cause of action was shown because no fraud was alleged. For the plaintiffs it was argued that any breach of fiduciary duty by directors could be a ground of action. The defendants contended that no cause of action was shown because the statement of claim did not allege fraud, and in the absence of fraud minority shareholders are unable to maintain a claim on behalf of the company against the majority.[32] Templeman J rejected this proposition as not consistent with the authorities, including *Pavlides v Jensen*.[33] The principle that he 'gleaned' from these authorities is 'that a minority shareholder who has no other remedy may sue where directors use their powers, intentionally or unintentionally, fraudulently or negligently in a manner which benefits themselves at the expense of the company'.[34] The cases which Templeman J particularly relied upon (as demonstrating that the word 'fraud' in this context does not mean literal or 'common-law fraud') are *Cook v Deeks*[35] and *Alexander v Automatic Telephone Co*.[36] His decision is valuable in clarifying the meaning of 'fraud on a minority' and restricting the scope of *Pavlides v Jensen*. The court's reasoning was clearly intended to be within the principles earlier laid down by higher courts. The facts alleged in the pleadings could well have led to the conclusion at a full hearing that the defendants had either appropriated property belonging in equity to the company (*Cook v Deeks*) or had acted in bad faith in exercising their power to sell the company's property (*Automatic Telephone*). As Templeman J was at pains to demonstrate, neither of these propositions amounts to an allegation of fraud.[37]

---

[29] *Cook v Deeks* [1916] 1 AC 554 (PC); *Menier v Hooper's Telegraph Works* (1874) 9 Ch App 350.

[30] *Cook v Deeks*, above. See **16.8** as to the distinction between a mere breach of fiduciary duty and the misappropriation of property which 'belongs to equity' to the company. See further *Bracken Partners Ltd v Gutteridge* [2003] EWCA Civ 1875, [2004] 1 BCLC 377 (CA).

[31] [1978] Ch 406.

[32] Ibid, at 408.

[33] [1956] Ch 565.

[34] [1978] Ch 408, at 414.

[35] [1916] 1 AC 554 (PC).

[36] [1900] 2 Ch 56.

[37] For further discussion of this case in the periodical literature, see Wedderburn (1978) 41 MLR 569, at 571; Rider [1978] Camb LJ 270; Prentice (1979) 41 Conveyancer 47; Boyle (1980) 1 Co Law 3. In *Prudential Assurance v Newman Industries (No 2)*, Vinelott J's attempt at a radical restatement of the principle behind the 'fraud on minority cases' received no support in the Court of Appeal: [1982] Ch 204. See Boyle (1981) 2 Co Law

18.4.1 The enforcement of statutory 'fiduciary' duties

Certain provisions in Part 10, Chapter 4 of the Companies Act 2006 impose statutory duties upon directors and 'connected persons'.[38] These duties are intended to avoid a conflict of duty and interest arising. In the case of s 190 (substantial property transactions involving directors) and s 197 (prohibition of loans, etc, to directors) there are statutory civil remedies following the pattern of those already available under the rules of equity which apply in the case of a breach of fiduciary duty on the part of directors. Any transactions or arrangements which infringe s 190 or 197 are voidable (on certain conditions) at the instance of the company.[39] In addition, there is both liability to account for gains (profits) made in breach of those sections and liability to indemnify the company for any loss or damage resulting.[40] It is clear that these provisions in principle overlay the long-established rules laid down by the courts of equity and the remedies already afforded. However, it is clear that Parliament was seeking to do more than duplicate the existing law and thus intended to provide more effective civil remedies against the more flagrant forms of abuse of their fiduciary duty by directors.

It is clearly open to argument that these statutory remedies might be the basis of a derivative claim by a minority shareholder. Obviously there would have to be a contravention of either s 190 or 197 which was not within any of the exceptions provided or for which any particular defendant had no defence under the relevant statutory provision. It is true that various civil remedies are expressed to be available to the company ('voidable at the instance of the company', 'to account to the company', 'to indemnify the company'), but it is of the nature of derivative proceedings that corporate rights are enforced for the company's benefit.[41] There is nothing in these sections which expressly excludes a minority action. These proceedings would be brought as a statutory derivative claim under Part 11 of the Companies Act 2006 (see **18.5** below).

Where a member of a company successfully petitions under Part 30 of the Companies Act 2006, the court may make an order authorising civil proceedings to be brought 'in the name and on behalf of the company' (see **18.10**). Where such an order is obtained, then it is clear that any remedy available to the company in respect of ss 190 and 197 might be pursued.

---

264. A similar approach was taken by Megarry V-C in *Estmanco (Kilner House) Ltd v Greater London Council* [1982] 1 WLR 2. See Birds (1982) 2 Co Law 31 and 77; see also, more recently, *Barrett v Duckett* [1995] 1 BCLC 73.

[38] See **17.2.1**.

[39] See s 195(2) (as to substantial property transactions) and s 213(2) (loans).

[40] See ss 195(3) and 213(2) (in respect of s 330).

[41] See **18.5.1**.

18.5 THE STATUTORY DERIVATIVE CLAIM

The Companies Act 2006 sets out a statutory replacement for the old common law derivative procedure.[42] This has replaced those aspects of the *Foss v Harbottle* that used to apply to such claims. Although based on the Report of the Law Commission on *Shareholder Remedies*,[43] some significant changes were made in framing the new derivative claim set out in the Companies Act 2006.

18.5.1 Nature of a derivative claim

Section 260 of the Companies Act 2006 defines a derivative claim in traditional terms: proceedings by a member in respect of a cause of action on behalf of the company seeking relief on behalf of the company. Such claims can be brought only in respect of a cause of action arising from an actual or proposed act or omission involving negligence, default, breach of duty or breach of trust by a director of a company. 'Director' is widely defined as a former director or a 'shadow director'.[44] Moreover, the cause of action may be against 'the director or another person or both'. This would appear to allow derivative claims where controlling or dominant shareholders (or possibly senior managers) are involved in a director's breach of duty to the company.

The procedure for making an application to court for permission to continue a derivative claim is contained in s 261. Section 261(1) provides that if it appears to the court that the application, and the evidence filed by the applicant in support of it, do not disclose a *prima facie* case for giving permission, then the court must dismiss the application and may make any consequential order it thinks appropriate. Under s 261(3) where the application is not dismissed the court may give directions as to the evidence to be provided by the company, and may adjourn the proceedings to enable the evidence to be obtained. On hearing the petition the court may: (1) give permission to continue the claim on such terms as it thinks fit; (2) refuse permission and dismiss the claim; or (3) adjourn the proceedings on the application and give such directions as it thinks fit.[45]

Section 262 of the Companies Act 2006 follows the Law Commission's Report,[46] in allowing a member to continue a claim (brought originally by the company) as a derivative where it is founded on an appropriate cause of action. The member may apply to the court for permission to continue the claim where the company has failed to prosecute the claim diligently

---

[42] Companies Act 2006, Part 11, Chapter 1 concerns 'Derivative Claims in England and Wales or Northern Ireland'. See ss 260–264. Derivative actions in Scotland are dealt with in Chapter 2. See ss 265–269.

[43] Law Com No 246, Part 6.

[44] See **15.2** and **16.1.1** above.

[45] Section 261(4).

[46] See *A New Derivative Action*, Part 6 at 6.70–6.93.

or the manner in which the company commenced the claim amounts to an abuse of the process of the court and it is appropriate for the member to continue the claim as a derivative claim.[47] The procedure set out in s 262 (as to applications to continue a claim as a derivative claim) follows the same pattern as that set out in respect of applications for permission to continue a derivative claim in s 261. There is a similar provision (in s 264) allowing an application to court to continue a derivative claim brought by another member. The court may give its permission on the same grounds as a company claim which the court permits a member to bring as a derivative claim (see above).

18.5.2   The criteria to guide the court: s 263

Section 263 provides two criteria to guide the court[48] in its task in deciding whether permission to continue a derivative claim should be refused or granted. If the court concludes that these criteria are not satisfied permission must be refused.

The first criterion that the court must take into account in deciding whether to give permission is that a person acting in accordance with the duty under s 172 of the Act (there imposed on directors) to promote the success of the company would not seek to pursue the claim.[49] In considering whether to give permission the court must also take into account whether the applicant member is in good faith as well as that person satisfying the s 172 (duty to promote the success of the company) test.[50]

Some judicial guidance on the interception of s 172 has given in *Franbar Holdings v Patel*.[51]

> 'In my judgment, the hypothetical director acting in accordance with s 172 would take into account a wide range of considerations when assessing the importance of continuing the claim. These would include such matters as the prospects of success of the claim, the ability of the company to make a recovery on any award of damages, the disruption which would be caused to the development of the company's business by having to concentrate on the proceedings, the costs of the proceedings and any damage to the company's reputation if the proceedings were to fail.'

The court added that the director 'will often be in the position of having to make what is no more than a partially informed decision on continuation without any clear idea of how the proceedings might turn out'.

---

[47]   See s 262(3).

[48]   These criteria must guide the court both when it refuses permission (s 263(2)) and also when it decides to give permission (s 263(2)).

[49]   As to s 172 see further Chapter 16 above.

[50]   See Chapter 16.

[51]   [2009] 1 BCLC 1 at 12–13 per William Trower QC.

Two stage procedure

More recent decisions have examined the 'two stage procedure' required by s 261(1). At the first stage the applicant is required to make a *prima facie* case for permission to continue a derivative claim. The court must then dismiss the application if the applicant cannot establish a *prima facie* case. The court considers the question on the basis of evidence filed by the applicant only without considering the evidence from the defendant company. This necessarily entails a *prima facie* case both that the company has a good cause of action and that the cause of action arises out of a director's default, breach of duty etc.[52]

The court in *Kiani* and in *Iesini* dealt with the 'second stage' in order to consider the requirements of s 263. While the court must not embark on a 'mini trial' of the action, something more than a *prima facie* case is required.[53] The court will have to form a view of the strength of the claim in order to consider the requirements of s 263(2)(a) and (3)(b):

> 'Of course any view can only be provisional where the action has yet to be tried but the court must, I think, do the best it can on the material before it.'[54]

Under s 263(2) the court must refuse permission if satisifed that a person acting in accordance with the duty imposed by s 172 to promote the success of the company would not seek to continue the claim.

In *Iesini* the obligation imposed by s 172 on the directors in deciding whether or not to sue was explored:[55]

> 'There are ... a number of factors which a director, acting in accordance with s 172, would consider in reaching his decision. They include the size of the claim; ... the costs of the proceedings; the company's ability to fund the proceedings; the ability of the potential defendents to satisfy judgment; the impact on the company if it lost the claim and had to pay not only its own costs but the defendants' as well; any disruption in the company's activities while the claim is being pursued; whether the prosecution of the claim would damage the company in other ways ... The weighing of all these considerations is essentially a commercial decision which the court is ill equipped to take, except in a clear case.'

Lewision J further held that s 263(2)(a) will only apply where the court is satisfied that *no* director acting in accordance with s 172 would seek to

---

[52] See Proudman J in *Kiana v Cooper* [2010] 2 BCLC 422 at [12], citing Lewison J in *Iesini v Westrip Holdings Ltd* [2011] 1 BCLC 498 at [78].

[53] See the above footnote.

[54] Lewison J in *Iesini v Westrip Holdings Ltd* [2011] 1 BCLC 498 at [79].

[55] Ibid at [86]. See also *Kiana v Cooper* [2010] 2 BCLC 422 at [13].

continue the claim. If some directors would, and others would not, seek to continue the claim, the claim should proceed under s 263(3)(b).[56]

The permission granted to proceed will not necessarily be to proceed to trial but only to the next stage of disclosure by the respondant company.[57]

18.5.3   Authorisation or ratification

The second criterion in s 263 to guide the court in considering whether to refuse permission or alternatively to grant it relates to the issues of authorisation before an act or omission occurs or shareholder ratification afterwards. In the case of authorisation this applies where the cause of action arises from an act or omission that has yet to occur. Where an act or omission has already occurred the court must refuse permission if satisfied that the act or omission was either authorised by the company before it occurred or has been ratified since it occurred. Likewise, these factors must be taken into account by the court in considering whether to give permission for a derivative claim to continue.

18.5.3.1   Authorisation

As regards authorisation of what would otherwise be a breach of directors' duties, this is largely confined to the duty to avoid conflicts of interest set out in s 175.[58] There provision is made for authorisation by the board of directors. Such authorisation requires, in the case of a private company, that nothing in the company constitution invalidates such authorisation, and in the case of a public company that the constitution contains a provision enabling the directors to authorise the matter. The director affected and any other interested director may not count in respect of the quorum requirements at the meeting considering the matter. The authorisation will only be effective if the matter was agreed without the interested directors voting or would have been agreed without their votes counting.

In the case of the separate duty (imposed on directors by s 177) to declare an interest in any proposed transaction or arrangement with the company, no provision for authorisation is made. Instead, there is an obligation to declare the nature and extent of the interest to the other directors (either at a meeting or by notice) before the company enters into the transaction.

As regards the general duties imposed on directors by Part 10, Chapter 2 of the Act, authorisation is not appropriate and no provision is made for

---

[56]   *Kiana v Cooper* [2010] 2 BCLC 422 at [13].
[57]   See *Stainer v Lee* [2011] 1 BCLC 537 at [55] and *Kiana v Cooper* [2010] 2 BCLC 422 at [46].
[58]   See further as to the declaration of interest in existing transactions and arrangements (ss 182–187 of the Act).

it.[59] Certain major transactions with a director may require approval by members of the company (eg service contracts, substantial property transactions, loans, etc). These transactions are regulated by Part 10, Chapter 4 of the Act.[60]

18.5.3.2   *Ratification*

It has been seen that the court (in either refusing or giving its permission in an application to continue a derivative claim) must take into account that an act or omission giving rise to cause of action has been ratified since it occurred: s 263(2) and (3). Where the cause of action results from an act or omission that has yet to occur the court must consider whether that act or omission could, or in the circumstances is likely to be, ratified by the company.

Section 239 of the Act governs the scope of, and procedure for, ratification of acts of directors giving rise to liability. The decision of the company to ratify must be taken by means of ordinary resolution.[61] In the case of a private company a resolution may be proposed as a written resolution. Where a resolution is proposed at a meeting, it will be valid only if the necessary majority is passed disregarding votes in favour of the resolution by a member with a personal interest, direct or indirect, in the ratification. Such members, however, may count towards the quorum and may take part in the proceedings. Where the written resolution procedure is used members with a personal interest, direct or indirect, in the ratification are not 'eligible members'.

The votes that must be disregarded (in deciding whether a resolution amounts to a valid ratification) include not only those of a director (if a member of the company) but also 'any member connected with him' (see s 239(4)). The statutory definition of 'connected persons' in ss 252–255 of the Companies Act 2006 includes not only family members but also a body corporate with which the director is connected.[62]

18.5.3.3   *Members with no personal interest*

In the course of the final passage of the Companies Act 2006 through the House of Lords a further provision was inserted in s 263 to guide the court in considering whether to give permission. The court 'shall have particular regard to any evidence before it as to the views of members of

---

[59]   See the duty to act within powers (s 171), duty to promote the success of the company (s 172), duty to exercise independent judgment (s 173), duty to exercise reasonable skill and care (s 174), duty not to accept benefits from third parties (s 176).

[60]   See s 180(3) as to the relationship between the general duties in Part 10, Chapter 2 and those arising from transactions within Chapter 4.

[61]   This is subject to anything in the company's articles requiring a higher majority or unanimity.

[62]   See further **17.2.1** above.

the company who have no personal interest, direct or indirect, in the matter'.[63] This provision bears some resemblance to the principle laid down by Knox J in *Smith v Croft*[64] in the context of the previous common law on wrongdoer control. Knox J stressed the need to look for an appropriate independent organ to decide whether it was in the commercial interest of the company to pursue the action. The court looked at an independent majority within the minority to reach its conclusions on grounds generally thought to advance the company's interests. The function of the judge is to determine whether the 'majority within the minority has fairly reached its decision but it is not for the judge to decide whether that decision is right or wrong'. The new s 263(4) is much less prescriptive in its guidance. It might in the case of, say, a private company with many disparate shareholders and no coherent majority, enable the judge to order a meeting to consider the advisability of the litigation. In the case of a public listed company this would involve a much more difficult exercise. Only when s 263(4) has been properly tested in the courts will its meaning become clear.

18.5.4   Comment

The scope of the ratification process provided by s 239 of the Act embraces the whole range of directors' duties: 'conduct amounting to negligence, default, breach of duty or breach trust' (s 239(1)). However, this assumes that the breach that has occurred is ratifiable. Section 239(7) specifically provides that s 239 does not affect 'any other enactment or rule of law imposing additional requirements for valid ratification or *any rule as to acts that are incapable of being ratified by the company*' (emphasis added). Thus this aspect of the *Foss v Harbottle* case-law is still preserved in the new statutory setting. On the other hand, the fact that a particular breach *is* ratifiable is no longer automatically a bar to a shareholder's derivative claim. Although the reference to 'breach of trust' in s 239(1) is somewhat equivocal, it would seem to be the case that breaches which under the common law would amount to 'fraud on a minority' (such as misappropriation of company property or breach of a director's duty of good faith) are not open to ratification under s 239.[65] The court would not be inhibited from giving its permission under s 263 of the Act. Furthermore, the difficult question of proving 'wrongdoer control' (especially in the case of public listed companies) will not arise when bringing a derivative claim under s 263.[66] It is replaced by the need for the court to be satisfied that 'a person acting in accordance with s 172' (duty to promote the success of the company) 'would not seek to continue

---

[63]   Section 263(4).

[64]   [1988] Ch 114, at 185.

[65]   See *Franbar Holdings v Patel* [2009] 1 BCLC 1 at p 15 citing the words of Sir Richard Baggallay in *North West Transport Co Ltd v Beatty* (1887) 12 App Cas 589 at 594.

[66]   But wrongdoer control may still have a role in deciding whether a valid ratification under s 239 has occurred. See *Franbar Holdings v Patel* [2009] 1 BCLC 1 at 15–16.

the claim' (s 263(2)). In giving leave the court must take into account 'whether the member is acting in good faith in seeking to continue the claim' (s 263(3)(a)).

Section 239 imposes certain further limits on the shareholders' power to ratify. It does not affect a decision taken by the unanimous consent of the members. Clearly where this is the case no derivative claim would be allowed to proceed under s 263. Further, s 239 does not affect the power of the board 'to agree not sue, or to settle or release a claim made by them on behalf of the company' (s 239(6)). However, this power of the board not to sue, or to settle or release a claim, must not be abused. If, in so doing, the board acted in bad faith or in breach of their duty to promote the success of the company, the board's behaviour would be open to challenge in a derivative claim under s 263.[67] This is further re-enforced by s 262 (application for permission to continue a claim as a derivative claim).

18.5.5 Remedies in derivative claims

No provision is made in Part 11, Chapter 2 as to remedies in a derivative claim under ss 262-263. Since derivative claims are founded on breaches of directors' duties it must follow that the remedies available will be the same as those that might be claimed in proceedings brought by the company. Section 178(1) of the Act states that the consequences of a breach (of directors' general duties) 'are the same as would apply as if the corresponding common law rule or equitable principle applied'.

As to procedure in derivative claims specific provision is made for another member of the company on applying to the court to continue a derivative claim that is being badly conducted by the original member. Under s 264 of the Act permission may be granted by the court where the manner in which proceedings have been commenced or continued by the original claimant amount to an abuse of the process of the court, that claimant has failed to prosecute his claim diligently, and it is appropriate for the (new) applicant to continue the claim as a derivative claim.[68]

18.5.5.1 Power to amend s 263

Section 263(5) will confer on the Secretary of State power to amend s 263(2) and (3) as to the court's power to refuse permission or give permission in respect of the continuation of derivative claims. Thus the Secretary of State may amend s 263(2) so as to alter or add to the

---

[67]   The fact that the company has decided not to pursue the claim is a factor the court must take into account. A further factor is whether the basis of the claim also gives rise to a cause that the member could also pursue in his own right. Section 263(3)(e) and (f).

[68]   This applies where a member of the company ('the claimant'): (a) brought a derivative claim; (b) has continued a derivative claim brought by the company; or (c) has continued a derivative claim under s 264. See s 264(1).

circumstances in which permission is to be refused. Likewise, the Secretary of State may amend s 263(3) so as to alter or add to the matters the court is required to take into account in considering whether to give permission. Before making such regulations the Secretary of State 'must consult such persons as he considers appropriate'.[69]

18.5.5.2 *Transitional provisions*

Under the transitional provisions[70] for implementing Part II of the Companies Act 2006, ss 260–264 come into force on 1 October 2007. Specific provision is made for derivative claims brought after that date where the claim arises from acts or omissions that occurred before that date. Here the court must exercise its powers under ss 260–264 of the Act 'so as to secure that the claim is allowed to proceed as a derivative claim only if … it would have been allowed to proceed as a derivative claim under the law in force before' 1 October. The same principle applies where the acts or omissions occurred partly before and partly after the date. In that case 'to the extent that' acts or omissions before 1 October the old common law will to that extent apply to such claims.

18.6 OVERLAPPING PERSONAL AND CORPORATE CLAIMS

The overlap between personal claims and corporate claims (derivative or otherwise) was fully explored by the House of Lords in *Johnson v Gore Wood & Co*,[71] where there were parallel claims against a firm of solicitors by a dominant shareholder and the company which for all practical purposes was his 'corporate embodiment'. The House of Lords refused to strike out the appellant's claim insofar as it sought to enforce not only duties owed personally to him as shareholder but related to personal losses distinct from those suffered by the company. Lord Bingham indicated the principles involved:[72]

> 'On the one hand the court must respect the principle of company autonomy, ensure that the company's creditors are not prejudiced by the action of individual shareholders and ensure that a party does not recover compensation for a loss which another party has suffered. On the other hand the court must be astute to ensure that the party who has in fact suffered a loss is not arbitrarily denied fair compensation.'

---

[69] Section 263(6). Regulations under s 263 are subject to affirmative resolution procedure: s 263(7).

[70] The Companies Act 2006 (Commencement No 3, Consequential Amendments, Transitional Provisions and Savings) Order 2007. SI 2007/2194.

[71] [2002] 2 AC 1. The decision of the House of Lords was applied in *Day v Cook* [2002] 1 BCLC 1 (CA).

[72] Ibid at 36. As to these recoverable losses, see Lord Bingham's judgment at 36–37.

Lord Millett addressed the key issue that arises where the company suffers a loss caused by the breach of a duty owed both to the company and the shareholder:[73]

> 'In such a case the shareholder's loss, in so far as this is measured by the diminution in the value of his shareholding or the loss of dividends, merely reflects that suffered by the company in respect of which the company has its own cause of action. If the shareholder is allowed to recover in respect of such loss, then either there will be double recovery at the expense of the defendant or the shareholder will recover at the expense of the company and its creditors and other shareholders. Neither course can be permitted. This is a matter of principle; there is no discretion involved. Justice to the defendant requires the exclusion of one claim or the other; protection of the interests of the company's creditors requires that it is the company which is allowed to recover to the exclusion of the shareholder.'

These principles, which are based on a well-known passage in *Prudential Assurance Co Ltd v Newman Industries*,[74] Lord Millett conceded, have not always been faithfully observed.[75] He criticised a passage in the judgment of Thomas J (in the New Zealand Court of Appeal) in *Christenson v Scott*.[76] This accepted that a diminution in the value of the plaintiff's (claimant's) shares can be considered a personal loss and not a corporate loss. Lord Millett was 'unable to accept this reasoning as representing the position in English law'.[77]

Lord Millett made it clear that the reflective loss which a shareholder may not recover extends beyond the diminution in the value of the shares. It extends to the loss of dividends and all other payments which the shareholder might have obtained from the company if it had not been deprived of its funds. All transactions or putative transactions between the company and its shareholders must be disregarded.

Later cases establish qualifications to the principle established in *Johnson v Gore Wood & Co*. It will not apply where a company has not settled its claim, but has been forced to abandon it by reason of impecuniosity attributable to the wrong done to it by the wrongdoer sued by the claimant shareholder.[78] It also did not preclude a beneficiary under a trust, where the assets of the trust consisted of 70% of the company's shares, bringing an action against a trustee for the profit made by the latter in breach of trust. To prevent such an action, the defendants had to

---

[73] [2002] 2 AC, at 62.

[74] [1982] Ch 204, at 222–223.

[75] He made clear his disapproval of *Fisher (George) (GB) Ltd v Multiconstruction Ltd* [1995] 1 BCLC 260, at 266 and *Barings plc (In administration) v Coopers & Lybrand* [1997] 1 BCLC 427 (CA).

[76] [1996] 1 NZLR 273.

[77] [2002] 2 AC, at 66.

[78] *Giles v Rhind* [2002] EWHC Civ 1248, [2003] 1 BCLC 1. See further *Giles v Rhind (No 2)* [2003] EWHC 2830, [2004] 1 BCLC 385.

show that the whole of the claimed profit reflected what the company had lost and which the company had a cause of action to recover.[79]

It has been held by the Court of Appeal that the rule against reflective loss is not concerned with barring causes of action as such but with barring certain types of loss. Thus whether the remedy sought lay in damages or restitution made no difference to the applicability of the rule. The fact that a claim is brought for breach of fiduciary duty owed to the plaintiff does not prevent the claim from being barred by the reflective loss principle.[80]

18.7 MINORITY SHAREHOLDERS' RIGHT TO AN INDEMNITY IN A DERIVATIVE ACTION

In *Wallersteiner v Moir (No 2)*,[81] the Court of Appeal recognised that a minority shareholder who brings a derivative suit[82] may have a right to an indemnity against the company in respect of his costs. This right was held to be closely analogous to the indemnity which a trustee is entitled to in respect of proceedings on behalf of the trust property or in the execution of the trust.[83] Fundamentally, the right will depend on whether the minority shareholder acted in good faith and reasonably in bringing proceedings. The Court of Appeal modelled the procedure for applying to the court to claim the indemnity on that already well established in the case of a trustee.[84]

An indemnity order application is heard as part of the application for permission to continue the claim in derivative proceedings.[85] The Master in the exercise of his discretion can give approval for the continuance of the action to various stages: 'until close of pleadings, or until after discovery or until trial (rather like a legal aid committee does)'.[86] Indeed, this might extend to the claimant's costs down to judgment. Assuming that on the hearing the claimant was authorised to proceed, he would 'be

---

[79] *Shaker v Al-Bedrawi* [2002] EWCA Civ 1452, [2003] 1 BCLC 157. See further *Walker v Stones* [2001] QB 902 discussed in Shaker at pp 221–222.

[80] *Gardner v Parker* [2004] 2 BCLC 554, at 577 (CA).

[81] [1975] QB 373.

[82] A *Wallersteiner* order will not be made in a shareholders' action which is not a derivative one, but at the end of the proceedings an order for costs may be made on a common fund basis if the result of the case is beneficial to members generally: *Marx v Estates and General Ltd* [1976] 1 WLR 380, at 392. See also *Re A Company* [1987] BCLC 82.

[83] See *Hardoon v Belilios* [1901] AC 118 (HL).

[84] See *Beddoe, Re Downes v Cottam* [1893] 1 Ch 557.

[85] The Civil Procedure Rules 1998 have been updated to include an amendment of Part 19 to introduce a new two-stage procedure for permission to proceed in derivative claims brought under the Companies Act 2006. See the Civil Procedure (Amendment) Rules 2007, SI 2007/224 (L26), Sch 1, r 19.9A for permission to continue derivative claim under s 261(1) and (2) of the Companies Act 2006. As to derivative claims by members of companies taking over claims by companies or other members (under s 262(1) or 264(1)) of the Act see r 19.9B.

[86] [1975] QB 273, at 392, per Denning MR.

secure in the knowledge that, when the costs of the action should come to be dealt with, this would be on the basis, as between himself and the company, that he had acted reasonably and ought *prima facie* to be treated by the trial judge as entitled to an order that the company should pay his costs'.[87] Moreover, the Court of Appeal adds the extremely important rider that these costs would normally be taxed on a basis not less favourable than the common fund basis, and should indemnify him against any costs he may be ordered to pay to the defendants.[88]

In a later decision,[89] Walton J gave a somewhat cautious and restrictive interpretation of the Court of Appeal's decision in *Wallersteiner*. He indicated that, in order to hold the balance fairly between plaintiffs (claimants) and defendants, it is incumbent on the claimant, in applying for a *Wallersteiner* order for costs, to show that it is genuinely needed. Even when an order is granted, it is appropriate to leave some proportion of the costs to be borne by the claimants, since otherwise there would be no incentive for the claimant to prosecute the action effectively. This might ultimately result in the action being dismissed for want of prosecution. It has been held that an indemnity order does not confer a lien over the company's assets or any damages recovered in a successful derivative action. Thus where the company is later put into administration, as being unable or likely to be unable to pay its debts, no equitable lien exists to give priority in respect of the indemnity order.[90]

In *Wallersteiner v Moir (No 2)*,[91] the Court of Appeal held that legal aid was not available to a shareholder bringing a derivative action.[92] The majority, against the views of Lord Denning MR, also refused to countenance the adoption of the American contingency fee system.[93] Now that civil legal aid is no longer generally available, the possibility of using the modern system of a conditional fee agreement might be considered.[94] The regulations permit a maximum 'success fee' and the use of such agreements in derivative actions might be open to challenge insofar as they detract from the right of the company in such proceedings to receive all the proceeds of a successful action. Even if the success fee were not restricted to damages etc recovered in a successful action, its

---

[87] [1975] 1 QB 373, at 405, per Buckley LJ.

[88] Ibid, at 405, per Buckley LJ and 392, per Denning MR.

[89] *Smith v Croft* [1986] 1 WLR 580. Applied in *Re Charge Card Services Ltd* [1986] 3 WLR 697 in a creditor's application for costs in a winding-up. Cf *Jaybird Group Ltd v Green* [1986] BCLC 319 (decided in 1981). Here a less restrictive approach was taken. The criterion applied was that of an honest, independent and impartial board of directors.

[90] *Qayoumi v Oakhouse Property Holdings plc* [2003] 1 BCLC 352.

[91] Above.

[92] [1975] 1 QB 373, at 400–401.

[93] Ibid, at 373.

[94] See ss 58 and 58A of the Courts and Legal Services Act 1990. Conditional fee agreements are regulated by the Conditional Fee Agreements Order 2000, SI 2000/823 and the Conditional Fee Agreements Regulations 2000, SI 2000/692.

recovery might have a serious impact on the ability of the defendant directors to discharge their liabilities.[95]

18.8 SHAREHOLDERS' ACTIONS TO ENFORCE RIGHTS AGAINST THE COMPANY

Where a minority shareholder seeks a remedy *against* the company under any of the exceptions to the rule in *Foss v Harbottle*, then the special rules which apply to the 'derivative' claims under Part 11, Chapter 7 of the Companies Act 2006, described at **18.5**, do not apply. Whenever he seeks to enforce a right which he enjoys together with other shareholders, or some class of them, he may sue in the representative form.[96] However, a representative action is not obligatory in such cases. He may instead sue simply in his own name.[97] In either event, the normal remedy against the company will be to seek an injunction[98] or bring an action for a declaration.[99] Where the representative form of proceedings is employed, the 'clean hands' doctrine may apply to the conduct of the claimant.[100] The claimant in such an action has the right to control the conduct of proceedings, as *dominus litis* until judgment.[101]

In shareholders' actions *against* the company it is not necessary to join the directors as parties, unless some form of relief is sought against them in addition to the remedy against the company. However, in such an action, it is possible to seek relief by way of injunction against the company while joining the directors as co-defendants in order that relief may be claimed against them for the company's benefit.[102] In such an action, the two

---

[95] The Civil Procedure Rules 1998 have been updated to include an amendment of Part 19 to introduce a new two-stage procedure for permission to proceed in derivative claims brought under the Companies Act 2006. See the Civil Procedure (Amendment) Rules 2007, SI 2007/224 (L26), Sch 1, r 19.9A for permission to continue derivative claim under s 261(1) and (2) of the Companies Act 2006. As to derivative claims by members of companies taking over claims by companies or other members (under s 262(1) or 264(1)) of the Act see r 19.9B.

[96] See now r 19.6 in the Civil Procedure (Amendment) Rules 2000. See, eg, *Pender v Lushington* (1877) 6 Ch D 70; *Mosely v Koffyfontein Mines Ltd* [1911] 1 Ch 73, affirmed *sub nom Koffyfontein Mines v Mosley* [1911] AC 409 (HL).

[97] *Simpson v Westminster Palace Hotel Co* [1860] 8 HLC 712; *Sidebottom v Kershaw, Leese & Co Ltd* [1920] 1 Ch 154 (CA).

[98] *Wood v Odessa Waterworks* (1889) 42 Ch D 636; *Pender v Lushington* (1877) 6 Ch D 70.

[99] *Edwards v Halliwell* [1950] 2 All ER 1064 (CA); *Sidebottom v Kershaw, Leese & Co Ltd* [1920] 1 Ch 154 (CA); *Greenhalgh v Arderne Cinemas Ltd* [1951] Ch 286 (CA).

[100] *Burt v The British Nation Life Insurance Association* (1859) 4 De G & J 158. But cf *Mosely v Koffyfontein Mines* [1911] 1 Ch 73 (CA), an action to restrain future illegal acts.

[101] As to the possible refusal of permission to bring a derivative claim because the minority shareholder may bring on a claim 'in his own right', see Companies Act 2006, s 263(3)(f).

[102] See *Russell v Wakefield Waterworks Co* (1875) LR 20 Eq 474, at 481–482; *Bagshaw v Eastern Union Rly* (1849) 7 Hare 114, affirmed *2 Mac & G 389*; *Hogg v Cramphorn* [1967] 2 Ch 254. It may be argued and any relief sought for the company's benefit must now be bought as a derivative claim under Part II of the Companies Act 2006.

forms of relief sought should arise out of a series of related transactions. The court will not allow what is in substance a derivative suit to be brought in the guise of a representative action in tort (eg the tort of conspiracy).[103]

18.9   PROCEEDINGS IN THE COMPANY'S NAME

The proper persons to give instructions for the commencement of an action to enforce any right of the company, or to obtain redress for a wrong done to the company, or to recover its property, are the directors; and the company itself is the only proper claimant in such an action,[104] though it cannot appear in person, either as claimant or defendant, and, except in the county court,[105] can only be represented by counsel.[106] Whether before or in a liquidation, the company's name alone should appear as claimant, it being improper to add the directors or liquidators as plaintiffs unless some relief is claimed by them in their individual capacity.

Although the directors are the proper persons to give the instructions for commencing such an action, it was long ago held that effect should be given to the wishes of a majority of the shareholders when they desire that proceedings should be taken to protect the company's rights, and that an action may be commenced in the company's name as claimant by such a majority, or even in case of urgency by one or more shareholders who believe that they have the support of a majority, and subsequently obtain the sanction of a resolution of the company.[107] An interim injunction may be obtained in such an action before their sanction has been procured. But if it ultimately appears that the majority is not in favour of the proceedings,[108] the name of the company as claimant will be struck out.[109]

---

[103] *Gray v Lewis* (1873) 8 Ch App 1035, at 1050; *Russell v Wakefield Waterworks Co* (1875) 20 Eq 474, at 479; *Duckett v Gover* (1877) 6 Ch D 82; *Burland v Earle* [1902] AC 83, at 93 (AC); *Prudential Assurance v Newman Industries (No 2)* [1982] Ch 204; *Heron International v Lord Grade* [1983] BCLC 244, at 281–283.

[104] *Prudential Assurance v Newman Industries (No 2)* [1982] Ch 204.

[105] *Charles P Kinnell & Co v Harding Wace & Co* [1918] 1 KB 405 (CA).

[106] *Frinton & Walton UDC v Walton & District Sand Co* [1938] 1 All ER 649; *Tritonia v Equity & Law Life Assurance Society* [1943] AC 584 (HL (Sc)).

[107] *Pender v Lushington* (1877) 6 Ch D 70; *Imperial Hydropathic Hotel Co v Hampson* (1883) 23 Ch D 1 (CA); *La Compagnie de Mayville v Whitley* [1896] 1 Ch 788 (CA); it seems difficult to reconcile these cases with *Salmon v Quin & Axtens* [1909] AC 422 (HL), and *Automatic Self-Cleansing Filter Co v Cunninghame* [1906] 2 Ch 34; but they have been often followed. See also *Marshall's Valve Gear Co v Manning* [1909] 1 Ch 627.

[108] If such approval is obtained, the action may proceed in the company's name: *Danish Mercantile Co Ltd v Beaumont* [1951] Ch 680 (CA). This decision of the court of Appeal was followed in *Alexander Ward & Co Ltd v Samyang Navigation Co Ltd* [1975] 1 WLR 673 (HL (Sc)).

[109] *Silber Light Co v Silber* (1878) 12 Ch D 717; *East Pant Du Lead Mining Co v Merryweather* (1864) 2 H & M 254; *Duckett v Gover* (1877) 6 Ch D 82. Where it is intended to bring a genuine minority action (ie under one of the exceptions to *Foss v*

In *Breckland Group Holdings Ltd v London & Suffolk Properties,*[110] a shareholder was restrained from continuing a legal action in the company's name where the articles provided that actions in the company's name could be commenced only with the consent of two particular directors. The shareholder who brought the action argued unsuccessfully that the directors would have to agree to take proceedings as this was obviously in the company's best interests.

PART 2: UNFAIR PREJUDICE REMEDY FOR MINORITIES

18.10 POWER OF THE COURT TO GRANT RELIEF ON A PETITION ALLEGING UNFAIR PREJUDICE

Section 994(1) allows a member[111] to apply to the court by petition for an order under the section. The ground on which he may petition (and on which the court must be satisfied that the petition is well founded)[112] is as follows: that the company's affairs are being or have been conducted in a manner which is unfairly prejudicial to the interests of its members generally or of some part of the members (including at least himself) or that any actual or proposed act or omission[113] on its behalf is or would be so prejudicial.[114]

18.10.1 The concept of unfair prejudice

It is readily apparent that the abandonment of the term 'oppressive' (in the old s 210 of the 1948 Act) and the judicial gloss put upon it has been given its intended effect by the judiciary. 'Bad faith' and 'lack of probity' (and their associated burden of proof) are now irrelevant. Similarly, the use or threatened use of majority shareholders' voting power is not a requirement. The term 'unfair prejudice', whether analysed as a 'standard' or a 'concept', is a relatively more objective one which is concerned with running the company in a way that is clearly unfair in its consequences to the complaining shareholder, even if the respondents can claim to have acted in the best of good faith.

Harbottle) and action should not be commenced in the company's name: *Alexander v Automatic Telephone Co* [1900] 2 Ch 56, at 69 (CA), per Lindley MR.

[110] (1988) 4 BCC 542. See also **15.15**.

[111] This may theoretically include a passive majority – it is not necessarily restricted to a minority member (see *Re Baltic Real Estate Ltd (No 1)* [1993] BCLC 499, cf *Re Baltic Real Estate Ltd (No 2)* [1993] BCLC 503).

[112] See s 461(1). See *Re A Company (No 004175 of 1986)* [1987] 1 WLR 585.

[113] See *Re Kenyon Swansea Ltd* [1987] BCLC 514.

[114] As to the procedural issues (arising in unfair prejudice petition) of 'striking out' and 'case management' (in England) see *Gore-Browne on Companies* (Jordans, 45th edn, loose-leaf) at 19[2].

It is, however, clear that the petitioner does not have to establish the infringement of a shareholder's right given by some other aspect of company law. The concept of unfairness cuts across the distinction between acts which do or do not infringe rights attaching to shares.[115] It has also been judicially observed[116] that unfairness is a familiar concept employed in ordinary speech – often by way of contrast to infringement of legal rights. The court may pay regard to wider equitable considerations. For example, in a 'quasi-partnership' type company, the court may take account of legitimate expectations of members.[117] On the other hand, the plain infringement of a shareholder's right (eg to be given accurate accounting information as prescribed in the Companies Act 2006) could also be the basis of an allegation of unfair prejudice.[118]

18.10.2   *O'Neill v Phillips*

In *O'Neill v Phillips*,[119] for the first time the House of Lords had an opportunity to consider the scope of the unfair prejudice remedy. Lord Hoffmann gave the only reasoned judgment. The case concerned a building construction company whose original 'proprietors' first allowed the petitioner, an employee, a minority holding and a directorship. Later he was left alone on the board as in effect *de facto* managing director. Subsequent changes included a profit sharing agreement. Some of these profits were later capitalised by the issue of non-voting shares. Discussions took place with a view to the petitioner obtaining a 50% shareholding but no agreement was, in the event, concluded. In a later building recession, the company's position worsened. The petitioner was excluded from managing the company. The profit sharing arrangement was later terminated and the petitioner left the company and brought a

---

[115] In *Re A Company (No 008699 of 1985)* [1986] 2 BCC 99, 024; see also *McGuinness v Bremner plc* [1988] BCLC 673 (Ct of Sess). The conduct complained of in a s 994 petition must relate to the manner in which the affairs of the company are conducted. In *Nicholas v Soundcraft Electronics* [1993] BCLC 360 (CA), the non-payment of debts owed by a holding company to its subsidiary (where this was an attempt to keep the group afloat in financial difficulties) was held not to constitute unfair prejudice in the conduct of the subsidiary's affairs. It does not include acts of a shareholder carried out in a personal capacity outside the course of the company's business: *Re A Company (No 001761 of 1986)* [1987] BCLC 141. Where a shareholder's refusal to sell his shares is a private matter, it is no part of 'the conduct of the company's affairs': *Re Legal Costs Negotiators Ltd* [1999] 2 BCLC 171 (CA).

[116] Ibid, per Hoffmann J.

[117] *Re Kenyon Swansea Ltd* [1987] BCLC 514. Cf *Re Postgate and Denby (Agencies) Ltd* [1987] BCLC 8; see also, *Re A Company, ex parte Schwartz (No 2)* [1989] BCLC 427 and *Re Elgindata Ltd* [1991] BCLC 959.

[118] See, eg, *Re A Company, ex parte Shorter* [1990] BCLC 384. Cf *Re A Company, ex parte Schwartz* [1989] BCLC 427. See further *Re A Company, ex parte Harries* [1989] BCLC 383, where an old allotment in breach of statutory pre-emptive rights was found to be evidence of unfair prejudice.

[119] [1999] 2 BCLC 1. As to the continuing significance of Lord Hoffman's judgment in *O'Neill*, see *Oak Investment Partners XII, Limited Partnership v Boughtwood* [2010] 2 BCLC 459 at 496, per Rimen, J.

petition under s 994. The trial judge dismissed his petition but it succeeded in the Court of Appeal[120] from whence the respondent appealed to the House of Lords.

Lord Hoffmann's exegis of 'unfair prejudice' in s 994(1), as in his earlier Court of Appeal judgment in *Re Saul D Harrison & Sons plc*,[121] relies on two essential points. These are the fundamentally promissory nature of the basis on which relief may be granted, and secondly, that the same principles underlie both the just and equitable winding-up remedy and the unfair prejudice remedy.

As regards the first point, he observes[122] that a member of a company will not ordinarily be entitled to complain of unfairness unless there has been some breach of the terms on which he agreed that the affairs of the company be conducted. These terms are contained in the articles of association and sometimes in the collateral agreements made between shareholders.

> 'In a quasi-partnership company, there will usually be understandings between the members at the time they entered into the association. But there may be later promises, by words or conduct, which it would be unfair to allow a member to ignore. Nor is it necessary that such promises should be independently enforceable as a matter of contract. A promise may be binding as a matter of justice and equity, although for one reason or another ... it would not be enforceable in law.'[123]

Lord Hoffmann relies strongly on Lord Wilberforce's *locus classicus* in *Ebrahimi v Westbourne Galleries*[124] to underpin the second point: there will be cases in which equitable considerations make it unfair for those conducting the affairs of the company to rely upon their strict legal powers. 'This unfairness may consist in a breach of the rules or in using rules in a manner which equity would regard as contrary to good faith.'[125] Lord Hoffmann traces the principles upon which the court decides the alleged conduct is unjust, inequitable or unfair back to nineteenth-century cases such as *Bisset v Daniel*[126] and the distinction between the legal and equitable approach to the use of powers.

Lord Hoffmann is clearly aware of drawing too close an analogy between a 'just and equitable' winding up and the notion of unfairness in s 994. He observes that 'the parallel I have drawn ... does not mean that conduct will not be unfair unless it would have justified an order to an order to

---

[120] [1997] 2 BCLC 739.
[121] [1995] 1 BCLC 14, at 19–20.
[122] [1999] 2 BCLC 1, at 8.
[123] Ibid, at 10–11.
[124] [1973] AC 360, at 379. See **18.14**.
[125] [1999] 2 BCLC 1, at 8.
[126] (1853) 10 Hare 493, 68 ER 1022.

wind up the company'.[127] He later adds: 'The parallel is not the conduct which court will treat as justifying a particular remedy but the principles upon which it decides that the conduct is unjust, inequitable or unfair.'[128] The difficulty with this approach is that it does not make it sufficiently clear that a just and equitable winding up order may be made in circumstances of a breakdown in mutual confidence where it is impossible to hold that the respondent has acted unfairly. The most obvious example (well established before *Westbourne* but not changed by it) is where there is deadlock between corporate partners which they are incapable of resolving.

Lord Hoffmann's use of the term 'good faith' (to cover, it seems, both 'just and equitable' and 'unfairness') is perhaps unfortunate. In *Westbourne*, the House of Lords[129] specifically rejected the test of 'bad faith' as the basis for a just and equitable winding up and overruled the Court of Appeal on the issue. The petitioners need not show bad faith in the sense that the respondents had not acted in good faith in the company's interests. In the case of s 994 petitions, it is well established[130] that a breach of directors' duties may enable the court to find unfair prejudice. It is clear that a breach of fiduciary duties, even if the breach does not involve bad faith, may in appropriate circumstances justify relief under s 994. It is thus difficult to grasp in what more generic sense the term 'good faith' is employed.[131]

Certainly, Lord Hoffmann's judgment also makes clear that 'exercising rights in breach of some promise or undertaking' is not the only form of conduct which will be regarded as 'unfair' for the purposes of s 994. For example, there may be some event which puts an end to the basis upon which the parties entered into association with each other, making it unfair that one shareholder should insist upon the continuance of the association. Thus Lord Hoffmann's observations on the term 'unfair prejudice' are valuable as a conceptual analysis. It is debatable whether they have the full weight of the *ratio decidendi* of a House of Lords' decision. His observations do not amount to a re-statement of the

---

[127] [1999] 2 BCLC 1, at 9.

[128] Ibid. See further the judgment of Neill LJ in *Re Saul D Harrison & Sons plc* [1995] 1 BCLC 14, at 30–32 as to the differences between the two remedies. See, however, *Re Guidezone Ltd* [2000] 2 BCLC 321, at 356–357, where Jonathan Parker J interprets Lord Hoffmann's judgment to mean that the jurisdiction of the court on hearing an unfair prejudice petition is co-extensive with the jurisdiction in a winding-up; *sed quaere*; see also *Re Phoneer Ltd* [2000] 2 BCLC 241; *Re Baumler (UK) Ltd* [2005] 1 BCLC 92, at 132.

[129] [1973] AC 360, at 379. It has also been rejected as the test of unfair prejudice.

[130] See *Gore-Browne on Companies* (Jordans, 45th edn, loose-leaf) at 19 [4]. Lord Hoffman's earlier judgments have been important on this point. Lord Hoffmann draws an analogy to 'continental systems' which introduce a general requirement of good faith in contractual performance.

[131] [1999] 2 BCLC 1, at 11.

pre-existing body of case-law. Earlier decisions are not overruled. It neither extends nor restricts the range of circumstances which may amount to unfair prejudice.

18.10.3 Breach of directors' duties

A question that was raised by most commentators on s 994 is how far a breach (or breaches) of directors' fiduciary duties may be of assistance in establishing unfair prejudice. In three cases which took the form of applications to strike out petitions under s 994 (on the basis that there was no case in law for the respondents to answer), the allegations in the petition referred to various breaches of duty by directors. Hoffmann J (who heard all three applications),[132] in rejecting these applications to strike out, clearly regarded allegations of breach of fiduciary duty as capable of establishing unfair prejudice to minority shareholders in a private company or a small unlisted public company.

The contention that the facts (eg a crude misappropriation of assets by a majority shareholder) would have readily warranted the bringing of a derivative claim will not bar a petition under s 994.[133] Moreover, a breach of directors' fiduciary duties not to mislead shareholders when making statements supporting one of two rival takeover bids is capable (at a later full hearing of a s 994 petition) of establishing unfair prejudice.[134] Where the petitioners were fraudulently induced to sell their shares in a private company to a small public company (as part of a manifestly dishonest scheme), Hoffmann J refused to strike out a petition merely on the ground that the matters complained of constituted wrongs to the petitioner as defrauded vendors of their former private company's shares and as a wrongfully dismissed managing director (as regards one petitioner) of that company. Once again, it was held that the interests of a member are not limited to his strict legal rights since the use of the word 'unfairly' in s 994 enabled the court to have regard to wider equitable considerations.[135]

Where it is alleged that excessive remuneration has been paid to an executive director the court may hear expert evidence as to 'objective commercial criteria' to determine whether the remuneration was in fact excessive and thus establish the existence of unfair prejudice.[136]

The developments described above are encouraging for shareholders in private companies, but there is less encouragement in respect of public

---

[132] *Re A Company* [1986] 1 WLR 281; *Re A Company* [1986] BCLC 382; *Re A Company* [1986] BCLC 376. See also, *Re A Company, ex parte Burr* [1992] BCLC 724 and *Re Ghyll Beck Driving Range Ltd* [1993] BCLC 1126.

[133] See [1986] 1 WLR 281, at 284.

[134] *Re A Company* [1986] BCLC 382.

[135] *Re A Company* [1986] BCLC 376; *McGuinness v Bremner plc* (1988) SLT 891.

[136] *Irvin v Irvine (No 1)* [2007] 1 BCLC 349 at 434–437.

listed companies with widely dispersed shareholders. It is in this type of company, of course, that the restricting aspects of 'fraud on a minority', and especially wrongdoer control prevented,[137] shareholders' common law derivative suits having much impact on the still serious problem of corporate abuse. In *Re Carrington Viyella plc*,[138] in a petition in respect of a publicly listed company, it was held by Vinelott J that failure to obtain shareholders' approval for the chairman's long-term contract of employment, as required by s 188 of the Companies Act 2006,[139] did not amount to unfairly prejudicial conduct within s 994(1).[140] Other s 994 cases involving public companies[141] have rejected petitions principally on the ground that there is no room in this context for allegations of failure to meet legitimate expectations outside what is contained in the company's public documents, ie its memorandum and articles, prospectus or listing agreement, etc.

Another aspect of the enforcement of directors' duties by means of a petition under s 994 which remains unclear is the director's duty of care. It would seem that the Jenkins Committee[142] intended that the reformed statutory remedy might be used in this regard, although the courts decided otherwise[143] in the case of the old s 210 of the Companies Act 1948. Where serious mismanagement causes real economic harm to the company's business (and therefore to the value of the members' interest) the general conceptual developments examined earlier should enable the courts to hold that unfair prejudice has been established. The terminology in s 994(1) (referring to 'any actual or proposed act or omission of the company including an act or omission on its behalf' where this 'is or would be so prejudicial') should be of assistance here. Once again, however, a petition in the case of a public listed company may present greater difficulty. In *Re Elgindata Ltd*,[144] Warner J was of the view that the court would ordinarily be very reluctant to treat managerial decisions as unfairly prejudicial conduct but that it would be open to the court in an appropriate case to find that serious mismanagement of a company's business could constitute unfair prejudice. Disagreement between the parties as to whether a particular managerial decision was commercially sound is clearly not enough. Shareholders realise that the value of their shares will depend upon the measure of competence in management. A breach by a director of his duty of care and skill must,

---

[137] 'Wrongdoer control' has now been replaced by the provision of the Companies Act 2006 in respect of the statutory derivative claim. See **18.5**.

[138] (1983) 1 BCC 98, at 951; see (1983) 4 Co Law 164.

[139] See **17.3**.

[140] It was also held that the failure of a controlling shareholder to comply with an undertaking given to the Secretary of State for Trade and Industry in order to avoid a reference to the Monopolies Commission did not affect the rights of the petitioning shareholders; this finding is wholly understandable.

[141] *Re Blue Arrow plc* [1987] BCLC 585; *Re Ringtower Holdings plc* (1989) 5 BCC 82.

[142] Cmnd 1749 (1962), paras 207–8.

[143] *Re Five Minute Car Wash Service* [1966] 1 WLR 745.

[144] [1991] BCLC 959.

however, be distinguished from the quality of management turning out to be poor. An example of unfair prejudice might be 'where the majority shareholders, for reasons of their own, persisted in retaining in charge of the management of the company's business a member of their family who was demonstrably incompetent'.[145]

18.10.4 'Legitimate expectations'

In a number of cases, it has been held that in the case of a small private 'quasi-partnership' type company, the court may take account of the 'legitimate expectations' of members.[146] However, in a more substantial company such a 'concept' has no place.[147] More recently, the Court of Appeal[148] has emphasised that in general members have no legitimate expectations beyond the legal rights conferred on them by the constitution of the company. This applies unless it can be shown that a 'legitimate expectation' arises out of a fundamental understanding between shareholders, which formed the basis of their association. This may confer a right to participate in management.[149] There may also be some event which puts an end to the basis on which the parties entered into association with one another, making unfair that one shareholder should insist upon the continuance of the association.[150]

In *O'Neill v Phillips*,[151] Lord Hoffmann has cast some doubt on the significance of the concept of 'legitimate expectation'. Lord Hoffmann, as he readily concedes, was the 'author' of this term in respect of exclusion from participation in management in a 'partnership type' private company. In *O'Neill*, Lord Hoffmann insists that this term, taken from public law, is only a 'label' to be attached to a conclusion that unfair prejudice has been established. 'The concept of a legitimate expectation should not be allowed to lead a life of its own, capable of giving rise to equitable restraints in circumstances to which the traditional principles have no application.'[152]

It was largely on this basis that the petitioner's claim failed in the House of Lords. Overruling the Court of Appeal, Lord Hoffmann upheld the trial judge's finding that there were no 'legitimate expectations' to

---

[145] Per Warner J in *Re Elgindata Ltd* [1991] BCLC 959, at 993, applied in *Re Macro (Ipswich) Ltd* [1994] 2 BCLC 354.

[146] See *Re Kenyon Swansea Ltd* [1987] BCLC 514.

[147] *Re Postgate & Denby (Agencies) Ltd* [1987] BCLC 8; *Re Blue Arrow plc* [1987] BCLC 585. It clearly has no application in the case of a listed plc: *Re Astec (BSR) plc* [1998] 2 BCLC 556, at 589.

[148] *Re Saul D Harrison & Sons plc* [1995] BCLC 14, at 19–20.

[149] *R&A Electrical Ltd v Haden Bill Electrical Ltd* [1995] 2 BCLC 280; *Re Regional Airports Ltd* [1999] 2 BCLC 30.

[150] See *Re Baumler (UK) Ltd* [2005] 1 BCLC 92, at 132; *Mooredene Ltd v Transglobal Chartering Ltd* [2006] All ER (D) 181.

[151] [1999] 2 BCLC 1.

[152] [1999] 2 BCLC 1, at 11.

participate in management or share in profits, even if it could be said that the petitioner had suffered in his capacity as 'stakeholder' in the company rather than employee.[153] Lord Hoffmann was rightly concerned to repudiate the erroneous notion that a s 994 petition can be used to obtain what he calls 'no fault divorce'.[154] Counsel had argued that where confidence and trust had broken down, in a quasi-partnership, one 'partner' ought to be entitled at will to require the other partner (or partners) to buy out his shares without having to show unfairness. This 'stark right of unilateral withdrawal' is rejected as quite unsupported on authorities. Lord Hoffmann noted that indirect support came from the Law Commission Report on *Shareholder Remedies*.[155]

The Court of Appeal has held[156] that, even in a quasi-partnership type company, the remedy provided by s 994 does not extend to a member/director who wishes entirely for his own reasons to sever his connections with the company and *de facto* has done so. In this situation, the member cannot use allegations of unfair prejudice to justify obtaining a full discounted value for his shares, where he has been offered a purchase based on a minority discounted valuation.

A failure of the petitioner's expectations in relation to the company's profits does not amount to unfair prejudice unless the losses incurred by the businesses were the result of unfairly prejudicial conduct. Where, taken overall, the petitioner's position is that of an investor whose investment has turned sour rather than an oppressed minority shareholder, such prejudice as he suffered was held not sufficiently unfair to entitle him relief under s 994.[157]

Meaning of 'quasi-partnership'

Judge Cooke's decision in *Croly* carefully explores some important features of the quasi-partnership concept. It was held that it did not particularly matter when the company became a quasi-partnership provided it did so before the time of the unfair conduct complained of.[158] In coming to the conclusion that Croly was a quasi-partner the judge found that he was participating in management to an important degree. This was not conclusive on its own as an employee may be given management duties. The key question is whether he is performing management functions in the character of someone who is essentially an

---

[153] Ibid, at 12–13 and 15.

[154] Ibid, at 13. Applied in *Re Jayflex Construction Ltd* [2004] 2 BCLC 145, at 182.

[155] *Shareholder Remedies* Law Com No 246 (1997), Cm 3769, at para 3.66.

[156] *Re Phoenix Office Supplies Ltd* [2002] EWCA Civ 1740, [2003] BCLC 76, at 89 (Auld LJ) and 91 (Jonathan Parker LJ). As to valuation of shares, see **18.13**.

[157] *Re Metropolis Motorcycles Ltd, Hale v Waldock* [2007] 1 BCLC 520.

[158] [2010] 2 BCLC 569 at 594.

owner of the business or someone who is acting under the instructions or delegation of the controlling owner.[159]

It was not conclusive against acting as a 'partner' that the scope of Croly's managerial functions was limited or that he exercised some functions in conjuction with others. The 'owner' of the business may for good reasons agree to divide or share the management responsibilities they exercise. The judge found that what strongly pointed in favour of Croly acting in the character of an owner rather than an employee was the fact that in relation to the dealings with the franchisor (which was at the heart and foundation of the company's business). Croly was held out and considered to be a 'principal' in the business.

The court also made the important point that the necessary character of the relationship as one of mutual trust and confidence does not require the parties expressly to articulate feelings of trust and confidence. What is meant is that there is a relationship which requires these qualities for it to work as it intended. The judge found that Croly and Good had made a relationship which required such qualities. This was because their broad arrangement for equal division of profits could only operate successfully if neither party abused his position to achieve personal advantage. It implied that they should cooperate with each other if it became necessary to deal with each other in the situation in which the company was not generating the funds to make the profits they anticipated.

18.11 'MEMBER *QUA* MEMBER'

It was a clear distinction between the old remedy under s 210 of the Companies Act 1948 and the remedy of just and equitable winding up (as reinterpreted by the House of Lords in *Ebrahimi v Westbourne Galleries Ltd*[160]) that a petitioner had to complain in his capacity as 'member *qua* member' under s 210[161] but not, at any rate in the case of a 'quasi-partnership', under what is now s 122(1)(g) of the Insolvency Act 1986. 'It is obvious that in a small private company it is legalistic to segregate the separate capacities of the same individual as shareholder, director or employee. His dismissal from the board or from employment by the company will inevitably affect the real value of his interest in the company expressed by his shareholding.' However, in the first fully reported case (on what is now s 994(1) of the Companies Act 2006), Lord Grantchester QC appeared to apply the 'member *qua* member' test to an unfair prejudice petition.[162]

In later decisions, the phrase 'interests of some part of the members' has been more flexibly interpreted so as to free it from this particular shackle

---

[159] Ibid at 595.
[160] [1972] AC 360. See **18.14**.
[161] See, eg, *Re Five Minute Car Wash Service* [1966] 1 WLR 745.
[162] [1983] Ch 178.

on the old s 210. In one case, in which the company was 'a classic example of a quasi-partnership', Vinelott J strongly expressed the view *obiter* (and has amplified it extrajudicially[163]) that the introduction of the term 'interests' allows the court to avoid the 'member *qua* member' approach and take account of the same 'interests' (granted the need to prove unfair prejudice) as in a just and equitable winding-up. Hoffmann J[164] observed that 'the interests of a member who had ventured his capital in a small private company might include the legitimate expectation that he would continue to be employed as a director – so that his dismissal would be unfairly prejudicial to his interests as a member'. This was related to other allegations of unfairly prejudicial behaviour and linked to the wider principle that 'the interests of a member are not necessarily limited to his strict legal rights'.[165]

Even in the case of a 'quasi-partnership' type of company, dismissal from employment and a position on the board will not necessarily establish unfair prejudice. This is made clear by Nourse J in *Re London School of Electronics*.[166] This case concerned a company which provided courses of study in electronics in conjunction with City Tutorial College Ltd (CTC), the majority shareholder. The petitioning minority shareholder's complaint was that the two individuals who owned the shares in CTC had resolved at a board meeting of the London School of Electronics (LSE) to transfer substantially all of the LSE students to CTC (and to register all new students for the electronics course with CTC) on the grounds that that was necessary to quality for recognition by an American university as a degree course. The petitioner was subsequently removed from his office as director. The petitioner had then set up a rival establishment and taken away a number of pupils enrolled at the LSE. The following passage in the judgment of Nourse J indicates when dismissal may provide evidence of unfair prejudice.

> 'In my judgment it was CTC's decision to appropriate the B.Sc. students to itself which was the effective cause of the breakdown in the relationship of mutual confidence between quasi-partners. Furthermore, that was clearly conduct on the part of CTC which was both unfair and prejudicial to the interests of the petitioner as a member of the company. It is possible, although I do not so decide, that CTC would have been entitled to relieve the petitioner of his teaching duties before June 1983. It is even possible, although it is much less likely, that CTC, had it gone through the appropriate formalities, could have properly removed the petitioner as a director of the company. But none of that is to say that CTC was entitled to take the extreme step of determining to deprive the petitioner of his 25 per cent interest in the profits attributable to the B.Sc. students.'

---

[163] *Re A Company* [1983] BCLC 151 and (1985) 6 Co Law 21, at 30.

[164] *Re A Company* [1986] BCLC 382.

[165] For a discussion on this aspect of 'unfair prejudice' see **18.10.2**.

[166] [1986] Ch 211. See *Re A Company (No 004377 of 1986)* [1987] BCLC 94. See also, *Re Alchemea Ltd* [1998] BCC 964 where the company was formed as a co-operative and the members were paid wages and re-imbursed for their expenses. In consequence, they complained that the conduct affected their position as employees not as members.

In another sense, the unfair prejudice remedy is not confined to members. Section 994(2) allows those to whom shares have been transferred[167] or transmitted by operation of law to petition. Section 995 also gives such a right to the Secretary of State (after powers of investigation have been used), but this has been almost totally ignored by what is now the Business Department.

As will be seen below, in regard to members a s 994 petition is often combined with a petition for a just and equitable winding-up. It has long been established that a contributory's winding-up petition may not be brought if he has no tangible interest. This prevents such petitions where the company is insolvent. It has been held[168] that this also bars a petition under s 994. It is not entirely clear why this should always be so. Thus the victim of unfair prejudice might still wish his shares bought by a wealthy respondent protected from the company's creditors by limited liability.

The Privy Council has held that, although the unfair prejudice must affect a person in their capacity as a member, there is no requirement that the relief granted must benefit the person in that capacity. Where the purpose of the application by the petitioner is to obtain financial recompense, the petitioner must show that the relief granted would benefit the petitioner in some capacity. In this case the Privy Council held[169] that the insolvency of the company did not constitute a bar to granting relief to the petitioner in the capacity of creditor:[170]

> 'If the company is a joint venture company and the joint venturers have arranged that one, or more, or all of them, shall provide working capital to the company by means of loans, it would, in their Lordships' opinion, be inconsistent with the purpose of these statutory provisions to limit the availability of the remedies they offer to cases where the value of the share or share held by the applicant member would be enhanced by the relief sought.'

Although a petitioner for relief under s 994 must be a shareholder before he can petition, he is entitled after he becomes a shareholder to support

---

[167] The use of the term 'transferred' in s 994(2) does not permit those with an equitable interest in shares (who are not registered as shareholders) to petition: *Re A Company (No 007838 of 1985)* (1986) 2 BCC 98, 952. Those who are in no sense members cannot petition: *Re A Company* [1986] BCLC 391.

[168] *Re Commercial and Industrial Insulations Ltd* [1986] BCLC 191; as to a winding-up order, see *Re Chesterfield Catering Ltd* [1977] Ch 373.

[169] *Gamlestaden Fastigheter AB v Baltic Partners Ltd* [2008] 1 BCLC 468; at 477–479. Here the Privy Council was interpreting provisions of the Companies (Jersey) Law 1991 which were substantially the same as the Companies Act 2006.

[170] Ibid at 478 applying *R&H Electric Ltd v Haden Bill Electric Ltd* [1995] 2 BCLC 280 at 294.

his petition by relying on conduct that took place before he became a shareholder. Section 994(1) applies not just to continuing conduct but to conduct that occurred in the past.[171]

18.12 THE 'ALTERNATIVE REMEDY'

Section 125(2) of the Insolvency Act 1986 requires the court, on hearing a winding-up petition presented by members of the company as contributories on the ground that it is just and equitable, to grant a winding-up order 'if it is of the opinion (a) that the petitioners are entitled to relief either by winding up the company or by some other means and (b) that in the absence of any other remedy it would be just and equitable that the company should be wound up'. The section then emphasises this second point with the addition of this rider: '... but this does not apply if the court is also of the opinion both that some other remedy is available to the petitioners and that they are acting unreasonably in seeking to have the company wound up instead of pursuing the other remedy.'

This 'alternative remedy' provision, as it is usually called, has now become even more important since s 994 of the Companies Act 2006 has become a remedy of a more inclusive nature than the old s 210, and since it obviously furnishes a more satisfactory range of remedies which contrast favourably with the stark and 'sledgehammer' outcome of a successful petition under what is now s 122(1)(g) of the Insolvency Act 1986.[172] There will still of course be cases where it is not possible to petition successfully under both of these statutory minority remedies. Thus in *London School of Electronics*,[173] it was held that there was no overriding requirement (in a petition under what is now s 994 of the Companies Act 2006) that it should be just and equitable to grant relief or that the petitioner should come to court with clean hands. However, the misconduct of a petitioner might still be relevant in a number of ways. The two most obvious are that it might render the conduct of which the petitioner complained, even if prejudicial, not unfair. Secondly, even if the treatment (by the respondents) of the petitioner was still found to be unfair and prejudicial, it might affect the relief granted by the courts. The 'clean hands' doctrine clearly applies to a just and equitable winding-up petition. However, the Privy Council has held that even if the petitioning minority shareholder has been partly responsible for the breakdown in the

---

[171] See *Lloyd v Casey* [2002] 1 BCLC 455, at 466–467, applying *Re Quickdrome Ltd* [1988] BCLC 370 and *Bermuda Cable Vision Ltd v Calica Trust Co Ltd* [1998] AC 198 (PC).

[172] See *Practice Direction (Companies Court; Contributories Petition)* [1990] 1 WLR 490. This draws practitioners' attention to the undesirability of including as a matter of course a petition for winding up as an alternative to an order under s 994. This should be done only if a winding-up is the relief that the petitioner prefers or if it is considered that it is the only relief to which he is entitled.

[173] [1986] Ch 211, at 233. See **18.11**.

relationship between the parties, if his conduct was not the cause of the breakdown he will not be prevented from obtaining a winding-up order on the just and equitable grounds.[174]

In a petition for a just and equitable winding-up,[175] unfair prejudice does not have to be shown. Moreover, it is not necessarily part of the petitioner's case that the respondents have acted unjustly or inequitably. Thus where petitions under both s 994 of the Companies Act 2006 and s 122(1)(g) of the Insolvency Act 1986 are presented, the court may, as Nourse J did in *Re R A Noble (Clothing) Ltd*,[176] dismiss the former petition and grant the latter.

Where, however, the petitioner (whether or not he has petitioned under both sections) could succeed under either remedy, the importance of s 125(2) of the Insolvency Act 1986 and the 'alternative' remedy principle will come into play. Thus s 125(2) will point the court firmly in the direction of s 994 (and its ampler and more appropriate remedial solutions) whenever the petitioner can establish 'unfair prejudice' to the satisfaction of the court. The 'alternative remedy' need not be s 994 as such.

18.12.1 The offer to buy as a bar to a winding-up

A reasonable offer to buy out the petitioner's shares at a fair price (with appropriate expert valuation) may suffice. In *Re A Company*,[177] Vinelott J observed that the jurisdiction under s 125(2) of the Companies Act 1985 is discretionary. The court would be at least entitled to refuse to make a winding-up order if satisfied that the petitioner was persisting in asking for such an order, and that it would be unfair to the other shareholders to make that order having regard to any offer they made to the petitioner to meet his grievance in another way. The petitioner was also held to have acted unreasonably in refusing to accept the respondent's offer to purchase his shares at a valuation. The date when the adequacy of the respondent's offer has to be determined is the date of the hearing and not that of the presentation of the petition. 'It is as much an abuse of the process of the court to persist in a petition which, because of a subsequent offer, is bound to fail as it would be to present a petition which on the facts existing at the time of presentation is bound to fail.'[178] This gives the respondents, faced with a petition under s 122(1)(g) every incentive to negotiate an adequate offer to buy out the petitioner by means of a fair and independent valuation, ie where no price can be

---

[174] *Vujnovich v Vujnovich* [1990] BCLC 227 (PC).

[175] See **18.14**.

[176] [1983] BCLC 273.

[177] *Re A Company* [1983] 1 WLR 927. See also, *Re Copeland & Craddock Ltd* [1997] BCC 294 (CA): a petitioner allowed to proceed in the hope of bidding for the business when it was sold by the liquidator.

[178] Applying *Bryanston Finance Co v De Vries (No 2)* [1976] 2 WLR 41.

agreed. To make sure the respondent continued to show sincerity until the completion of the 'buy-out', Vinelott J decided not to dismiss the petition outright. It was merely 'stood over' to enable the parties to agree the terms of submission to an arbitration or valuation by an expert. When agreement was reached 'the matter could be mentioned to the court and the petition stayed'. If there was any disagreement, Vinelott J continued, he would 'then hear further argument'.

Whenever possible, it would seem, a winding-up order with all its potential for the destruction of an otherwise viable business and with harsh consequences for the innocent employees will be denied whenever a viable alternative remedy is available. In the case before Vinelott J (referred to above), the court rejected the argument that in a small quasi-partnership type company the petitioner is entitled to reject an alternative 'buy-out' remedy on the ground that (as in partnership law) he is entitled to a share of 'partnership' assets on their realisation. The only qualification to this proposition admitted by Vinelott J was that where the petitioner (excluded from a quasi-partnership despite the underlying assumption of a right to participate) has always insisted on a winding-up as the only remedy, then the argument that he was entitled to that remedy might have succeeded. On the facts of this case that was not so. From the time of exclusion from participation, the petitioner had indicated a willingness to sell to his co-shareholders at a fair price to be negotiated.

The principle so firmly stated in these first-instance decisions on the 'alternative remedy' was reviewed by the Court of Appeal in *Virdi v Abbey Leisure*.[179] Where a petitioner is entitled in principle to a just and equitable winding-up, an offer by the respondent majority shareholders to buy his shares, under a provision in the articles, at a fair value to be agreed by an accountant, could reasonably be refused by the petitioner. The trial judge was held to be wrong in the exercise of his discretion under s 125(2), in deciding to strike out the petition. The Court of Appeal accepted that an accountant acting under the procedure in the articles would value them on a discounted basis as a minority holding. The petitioner was entitled to insist on his normal right to a *pro rata* valuation, which would result from an order for a just and equitable winding-up. Balcombe LJ[180] observed that the courts have shown a general inclination (under both ss 994 and 122(1)(g)) towards a valuation on a *pro rata* basis. Balcombe LJ also stressed that in a just and equitable winding-up based on the principles laid down by the House of Lords in *Ebrahimi v Westbourne Galleries*,[181] 'legal rights and obligations conferred or imposed on shareholders by the

---

[179] [1990] BCLC 342. The Court of Appeal also held that the discretion of the trial judge exercised under s 125(2) could be reviewed by the Court of Appeal not only on the ground of principle but on the ground of whether the petitioner had acted reasonably.

[180] [1990] BCLC 342, at 350. Balcombe LJ referred in particular to *Re Bird Precision Bellows Ltd* [1984] BCLC 395.

[181] [1973] AC 360. See **18.14**.

constitution of the company may be subject to equitable considerations'. This freed the petitioner from his obligation under the articles.[182]

18.12.2 The offer to buy as a bar to an unfair prejudice petition

In a number of cases[183] the courts have stressed that, where there is an irretrievable breakdown which is the fault of neither petitioner nor respondent, pre-emptive rights provisions in the articles should be sought rather than a petition under s 994 on the ground of unfair prejudice. Where the court concludes that unfair prejudice to the petitioner could not be established at a full hearing, this is obviously right. However, some decisions go further than this on motions to strike out unfair prejudice petitions. These would bar a petitioning minority shareholder from complaining about unfair prejudice if no attempt has been made to use the machinery provided by the articles for determining the fair value of the party's shares.[184] In view of the Court of Appeal's observations in *Virdi v Abbey Leisure*,[185] these decisions would appear to be open to question where the provision in the articles allows only for a discounted minority holding basis of valuation if, under a successful s 994 petition, a *pro rata* basis would be appropriate. The observations of the Court of Appeal are applicable to unfair prejudice petitions even though the case itself concerned a just and equitable winding-up.[186]

An agreement to submit disputes to arbitration cannot override the right to apply by petition for relief under s 994. The shareholder's right to apply under s 994 is an inalienable statutory right that cannot be limited by agreement since it is a condition of incorporation under the Companies Act 2006.[187] An agreement by a minority shareholder in a private company to allow the respondent majority shareholder to conduct the affairs of the company on an informal basis, and to act in ways inconsistent with the articles, does not exclude the right of the minority shareholder to bring a petition under s 994. While the concept of

---

[182] [1990] BCLC 342, at 350.

[183] *Re R A Noble (Clothing) Ltd* [1983] BCLC 273; *Re A Company* [1986] BCLC 362; *Re A Company* [1987] BCLC 94. See further, *Re A Company, ex parte Kremer* [1989] BCLC 365, where such a petition was struck out on this basis. See likewise, *Re Castleburn Ltd* [1991] BCLC 89. But cf *Re A Company, ex parte Harries* [1987] BCLC 383 at 398.

[184] See Hoffmann J in *Re A Company* [1987] BCLC 94, at 102, cited by the same judge in *Re A Company, ex parte Kremer* [1989] BCLC 365, at 368. Admittedly, this is qualified in respect of cases of 'bad faith or plain impropriety or where the articles provide for some arbitrary or artificial method of valuation'.

[185] [1990] BCLC 342, see **18.12.1**.

[186] See *Re A Company, ex parte Harries* [1989] BCLC 383, at 398 per Peter Gibson J, who anticipated the Court of Appeal in *Virdi v Abbey Leisure* [1990] BCLC 342. See also, *Re A Company, ex parte Holden* [1991] BCLC 597. See *Re Vocam Europe Ltd* [1998] BCC 396 where the court stayed a s 994 petition on the basis of an arbitration clause in an agreement between the parties.

[187] *Exeter City AFC Ltd v The Football Conference Ltd* [2005] 1 BCLC 238, at 243-244. But see *Fulham FC v Richards* [2011] 1 BCLC 295 at 305 where the decision in *Exeter City* was not followed.

unfairness needs to be modified in the light of the agreement between the parties, a failure to hold meetings and to otherwise conduct the company as a going concern may establish unfair prejudice.[188]

This process has been taken a stage further by Lord Hoffmann in *O'Neill v Phillips*.[189] He took the opportunity to clarify the law and practice on the 'offer to buy' as a bar to an unfair prejudice petition. This is perhaps the most useful as well as innovatory aspect of the House of Lords' judgment in *O'Neill*. Lord Hoffmann noted that this issue was *obiter* in that it did not arise for decision on the facts of the case. 'Nonetheless, the effect of an offer to buy the shares as an answer to a petition under s 459 is a matter of such great practical importance that I invite your Lordships to consider it.'[190]

The point of the list of criteria, set out under five headings, is to establish that a reasonable offer has been made so that the exclusion of the petitioner from the business of the company will not be treated as unfairly prejudicial. The petition will be struck out. First, the offer must price the shares at a fair value. As in the existing case-law, this will normally be on a *pro rata* basis, though there may be cases in which it will be fair to take a discounted value. Secondly, if not agreed, the value must be determined by a competent expert (eg an accountant agreed by the parties). Thirdly, the offer should be to have the value determined by the expert as an expert (not full arbitration nor the halfway house of an expert who gives reasons). The objective is economy and expedition. Fourthly, both parties should have the same access to information about the company relating to the value of the shares, and should have the right to make submissions to the expert. Fifthly, normally the offer should cover the costs of the petitioner, but the respondent should be allowed a reasonable opportunity to make an offer before being obliged to pay costs.

Where the valuer has reached his determination on the basis of incorrect information supplied to him by the company's directors which he may have no reason to doubt, the aggrieved party (ie the petitioner) will have no remedy in negligence against the valuer. For that reason the court should not necessarily regard the existence of an agreed compulsory purchase mechanism as an absolute bar to the presentation or continued presentation of a s 994 petition.[191] Such a petition will also be allowed if it can be shown that there is a close personal relationship between one of the respondents and the partner in the auditors' firm responsible for the valuation.[192]

---

[188]   *Fisher v Cadman* [2006] 2 BCLC 499.
[189]   [1999] 2 BCLC 1.
[190]   [1999] 2 BCLC 1, at 15. A failure to make a reasonable offer may exacerbate the unfairness alleged: *Richards v Lundy* [2000] 1 BCLC 376.
[191]   *Re Belfield Furnishings Ltd* [2006] 2 BCLC, at 722.
[192]   Ibid at 723.

Lord Hoffmann, like other members of the judiciary involved in s 994 petitions, has long been aware of the dangers of the destructive effect of costs where such petitions are unnecessarily pursued. 'It is therefore very important that participants in such companies should be allowed to know what counts as a reasonable offer', he rightly observes.[193] This has done much to settle and clarify an area of law and practice. It may well prove to be the aspect of *O'Neill* of most lasting importance to the practitioner. Where a petitioner and a respondent were both making offers for each other's shares, the court allowed the respondent to succeed as having made the more reasonable offer. The latter had adequate funds available whereas the petitioner lacked funds and made a vague offer lacking in detail and insufficiently specific in vital details.[194]

18.13 THE REMEDIES AVAILABLE TO THE COURT: S 996

To the original remedies[195] available to the court under s 210 of the Companies Act 1948, new specifically procedural remedies were added in 1980 on the basis of the Jenkins Committee's proposals. These were that the court may 'require the company to refrain from doing or continuing an act complained of by the petitioner or to do an act which the petitioner has complained it omitted to do' and it may 'authorise civil proceedings to be brought in the name of or on behalf of the company by such person or persons and in such terms as the court may direct'.[196]

It is not surprising that in the case of most successful petitions the remedy sought by the petitioners, and granted by the court, is that of purchase of the minority's shares by the majority. As a solution to intra-corporate disputes in small private companies this is still the most attractive choice among the remedial solutions offered by s 996.[197] The Court of Appeal in

---

[193] [1999] 2 BCLC 1, at 16. See *Re A Company, North Holdings Ltd v South Tropics Ltd* [1999] BCC 746 (CA) where Morritt LJ emphasised the need for active case management at an early stage in order to reduce the time and expense involved in ascertaining a fair price for the petitioner's shares. This was the first appeal concerning s 994 proceedings under the Civil Procedure Rules 1998. See further, *Re Rotadata Ltd* [2000] 1 BCLC 123.

[194] *West v Blanchet* [2000] 1 BCLC 795, at 803. As to the proper role of mediation in shareholder disputes, see Corbett and Nicholson 'Mediation and section 459 petitions' (2002) 23 Co Law 274.

[195] These are a wide power to 'make such order as it thinks fit for giving relief in respect of the matters complained of and further powers to order the complainants' shares be bought by the company (with a consequent reduction of capital) or by the majority from the minority (or vice versa)'. The court has power to give this relief against an ex-shareholder: *Re A Company* [1986] BCLC 68. There is also a power to 'regulate the conduct of the company's affairs in the future' and to alter the articles and memorandum.

[196] See s 996(2).

[197] In exceptional circumstances, the court may order the majority to sell their shares to the minority (eg where a pre-emption agreement between majority and minority has been made): *Re Brenfield Squash Racquets Club* [1996] 2 BCLC 184.

Grace v Biagiola explained the policy considerations which guide the court in choosing an order for the purchase of the minority's shares:[198]

> 'In most cases, the usual order to make will be the one requiring the respondents to buy out the petitioning shareholder at a price fixed by the court. This is normally the most appropriate order to deal with inter-corporate disputes involving small private companies ... The reasons for making such an order are in most cases obvious. It will free the petitioner from the company and enable him to extract his share of the business and assets in return for foregoing any future right to dividends. The company and its business will be preserved for the benefit of the respondent shareholders, free from his claims and the possibility of future difficulties between shareholders. In most cases of serious prejudice and conflict between shareholders, it is unlikely that any regime of safeguards which the court can impose will be as effective to preserve the peace and safeguard the rights of the minority.'

In an appropriate situation the court, in ordering a buyout of the plaintiff's share, may make the respondent jointly and severally liable with the company of the repayment for the petitioner's loan to the company. It may also make the respondent indemnify the petitioner in respect of other liabilities incurred by the petitioner.[199]

It is likewise not surprising that there have been a number of decisions in the reports (and others unreported) on the related questions of the method of valuing the minority's shares and the date on which that valuation should be made. In *Re Bird Precision Bellows*,[200] Nourse J considered the legal basis for valuing the minority's shares where a 'buy-out' order is made. He emphasised that there was no rule that the price of a minority holding in a small private company be fixed on a *pro rata* basis (according to the value of the shares as a whole), or, alternatively, that the price should be discounted to reflect the fact that the shares were a minority holding. He indicated, however, that the court would employ the *pro rata* basis where the shares had been acquired on the incorporation of a quasi-partnership company, and it was thus expected that the shareholders would participate in the conduct of the affairs of the company.[201] The valuation would be on a discounted basis

---

[198] [2006] 2 BCLC 70, at 96–97. See *Fowler v Gruber* [2010] 1 BCLC 563 where another remedy (appointment as managing director) was refused.

[199] *Allmark v Burnham* [2006] 2 BCLC 437. See also *Rahman v Malik* [2008] 2 BCLC 403.

[200] [1984] Ch 419. As to the proper method of valuing a private company's share capital, see *Re a Company* [1986] BCLC 362, at 368; *Re Regional Airports* [1999] 2 BCLC 30, at 84–100 and *Profinance Trust SA v Gladstone* [2000] 2 BCLC 516. See also *Re Scitec Group Ltd* [2011] 1 BCLC 277.

[201] This would also apply, in such a company, where the minority were ordered to purchase the majority's shares. If a company's articles provide machinery for a sale of the minority shareholder's shares, and a fair means of assessing the value of the shares, a member seeking to sell his shares on a breakdown of relations with other shareholders should not ordinarily be entitled to complain of unfair conduct if he has made no attempt to use the machinery provided: *Re A Company* [1987] 1 WLR 102. See further *Strahan v Wilcox* [2006] 2 BCLC 555, at 561–569 (CA) per Arden LJ.

where, in an exceptional case, the minority had acted so as to deserve exclusion. This would also apply where the shares were allotted or later acquired as an investment in a private company. The Court of Appeal confirmed Nourse J's exercise of his discretionary power while emphasising the wide nature of the first instance court's power once unfair prejudice was shown.[202] The Court of Appeal emphasised that the overriding consideration[203] is that the valuation must be fair and equitable between the partners. The specific power (in what is now s 996(2)(e)) 'to provide for the purchase of the shares of any member of the company by other members' is subject to the wide discretion in s 996(1): 'make such order as it thinks fit for giving relief in respect of the matters complained of'. The Court of Appeal affirmed, but did not reopen, Nourse J's exercise of this discretion since it was a matter for the court of first instance rather than an appellate court. However, the court accepted that in a quasi-partnership case the '*pro rata*' solution was a proper exercise of the judge's discretion.[204] By implication they also accepted Nourse J's observation that in other cases the discounted minority interest method would be more appropriate.[205]

The same overriding requirement in valuing shares (that the price should be fair) will govern the choice of date for this purpose. Various dates have been chosen (eg the date of the unfair prejudice, the date of the petition,[206] the date when the valuation is made,[207] or the date of a consent order that shares should be purchased 'at such a price as the court should therefore determine'). The petitioner's own conduct, though not precluding a finding of unfair prejudice in his favour, may affect the date chosen by the court in exercising its discretion.[208] In the appropriate case, however, fairness may sometimes require that the shares be valued at a

---

[202] [1986] 2 WLR 158 (CA). An allegation that the petitioner's shareholding is worthless was held not to be a ground for striking out a petition. The expert evidence conflicted, and the petition was allowed to go to trial. *Guinness Peat Group plc v British Land Co plc* [1999] 2 BCLC 243 (CA).

[203] Ie after the court is satisfied that unfair prejudice has been established.

[204] This was the basis applied by the same judge in another 'quasi-partnership' case, *Re London School of Electronics* [1986] Ch 211.

[205] The same principles apply where the court has to exercise its powers on the basis of a consent order made after an earlier hearing with a provision for the matter of valuation to be settled by a judge. This was what had happened in *Re Bird Precision Bellows*, above. The court also held that the consent order did not constitute an agreement that interest should be awarded. There was no other basis on which interest could be awarded before the principal sum (the valuation) was determined.

[206] *Re London School of Electronics* [1986] Ch 211. In *Virdi v Abbey Leisure Ltd* [1990] BCLC 342, the Court of Appeal noted the general inclination of the courts towards a *pro rata* basis of valuation. Cf *Howie and Others v Crawford* [1990] BCC 330. As to the valuation of shares in a private company as a going concern being sold on the open market, see *Re Planet Organic Ltd* [2000] 1 BCLC 366.

[207] Ie the date of the Master's certificate.

[208] See *Re London School of Electronics* [1986] Ch 211 where Nourse J considered a choice between the date of presentation of the petition and the date of valuation. He chose the former because of the petitioner's behaviour. See also *Re Cumana Ltd* [1986] BCLC 430 (CA).

date earlier than the petition.[209] A petitioner may be unfairly prejudiced by the company's action in appointing the auditors as valuers when they are not independent, in the sense that the auditors could not reasonably approach the task of valuation without following the advice they had already given in different circumstances.[210]

The additional powers conferred by s 996(2)(b) and (c), allowing civil proceedings to be brought, have not yet been much invoked. However, in one case, which went to the Court of Appeal, the court hearing the petition appointed a receiver and manager,[211] permitted civil proceedings in the name of the company against certain of its creditors and ordered the cancellation of an issue of shares. The Court of Appeal[212] made certain further orders as to how the litigation should be controlled and conducted, while rejecting the argument that the original petitioner was not a suitable person to leave in charge of such litigation. The court also decreed that the debts of various creditors connected with the company (including the appellants and the respondents) 'be made subordinate to the outside creditors'. Where a derivative claim is brought for misappropriation of the company's assets and the claimant later commences unfair prejudice proceedings, the derivative claim can in due course be merged with those proceedings. The court can still grant a tracing order as it has power to give such a proprietary remedy under s 996.[213]

The power of the court under s 996(2)(c) to 'authorise civil proceedings to be brought in the company's name' has not yet shown its full potential. If the concept of 'unfair prejudice' in s 994 is to encompass grave corporate abuse (including serious negligent mismanagement) in public listed companies, it may become a more commonly sought remedy. Such proceedings would essentially amount to a thinly disguised derivative claim[214] with the concept of 'unfair prejudice' rather than the

---

[209] *Re OC Transport Services Ltd* [1984] BCLC 251. Here by any later date the value of the petitioner's shares had been influenced by the reorganisation of its capital to allow another company to take the benefit of its unused capital allowances. See also *Re A Company* [1983] 1 WLR 927.

[210] *Re Benfield Greig Group plc* [2002] 1 BCLC 65.

[211] See also *Re A Company (No 00596 of 1986)* [1987] BCLC 133.

[212] In *Cyplon Developments Ltd (CA) 3 March 1982 (Lexis* transcript). See also *Re Whyte (petitioner) 1984 SLT 330*, where the court interdicted the holding of a meeting because the resolution to be passed would have removed a managing director from a committee responsible for company litigation. The effect of the resolution would have been to put the litigation under control of the defendants. As to the appointment of a receiver to protect the petitioner's interests, see *Wilton Davies v Kirk* [1998] 1 BCLC 274.

[213] *Clark v Cutland* [2003] EWCA Civ 810, [2003] 2 BCLC 393, at 401–404, per Arden LJ. The court's powers under ss 994 and 996 are not limited by the restrictions, whether of policy or principle, of the rule in *Foss v Harbottle*. For a contrary view, see Hirst 'In what circumstances should breaches of directors' duties give rise to a remedy under ss 994–996?' (2003) 24 Co Law 100.

[214] See *Re A Company* [1986] 1 WLR 281, at 284. Such relief (ie court proceedings in the name of the company to recover sums improperly paid out by the company) was refused where an administrative receiver had already been appointed: *Re a Company* [1992] BCC

requirements of Part 11 of the Companies Act 2006 (see ss 260–263) as to bringing derivative claims[215] determining the issue of access to an action in the company's name or for its benefit. The simple wording of s 996(2)(c) leaves unanswered a number of questions as to the conduct and control of civil proceedings permitted under s 996. For example, could the court exercise its discretion, in an appropriate case, to allow '*pro rata* recovery' where to require the proceeds of an action to be restored to the company would only benefit the wrongdoers left in control of the company? Another important question is whether the company would be responsible for the costs of an unsuccessful litigation permitted by the court (or the costs awarded in an action which succeeded but the defendant could not pay). In other words would the petitioner, put in charge of such proceedings, be at least as well protected as if he had the benefit of a *Wallersteiner* order[216] in a derivative claim? Even if that is a fairly safe assumption, this would still not meet the point that the petitioner under s 994 must hazard the risk of costs at least until the stage when the issue of unfair prejudice is determined.[217]

It may be fairly observed that a justifiable assertion by a minority shareholder of a serious breach of directors' duties (especially the duty of care) may fall between the alternative remedies of a derivative claim on the one hand and a s 994 petition on the other. This is much more likely to be the case where a public listed company is concerned.

18.14   JUST AND EQUITABLE WINDING UP AS A MINORITY SHAREHOLDER'S REMEDY

The preceding treatment of Part 30 of the Companies Act 2006 (petitions on the ground of unfair prejudice) sought to relate that type of relief to the alternative (but much older) remedy of a contributory's (ie a member's) petition for a just and equitable winding-up under s 122(1)(g) of the Insolvency Act 1986. It was seen that the concept of a 'quasi-partnership' type of company (which was first developed by the House of Lords[218] in restating the principles applicable to just and equitable winding up), has also been applied in the context of petitions under s 994.[219] Another important link between the two statutory

---

542. In *Lowe v Fahey* [1996] 1 BCLC 262, where the only substantive relief sought was a claim on behalf of the company against a third party, the petitioner was not allowed to proceed under s 994. A derivative action was the appropriate remedy.

[215] As to derivative claims under Part 11 of the Act, see **18.5** above.

[216] See, however, *Smith v Croft* [1986] 1 WLR 580 where Walton J gave a rather restricted interpretation to *Wallersteiner v Moir (No 2)* [1975] QB 373 (CA); see further, **18.7**.

[217] As to the award of costs where unfair prejudice is established and the petitioner's shares are ordered to be purchased, see *Re Elgindata Ltd (No 2)* [1993] BCLC 119 (CA). See further *Clark v Cutland* [2004] 1 WLR 783, at 794 (CA), per Arden LJ.

[218] *Ebrahimi v Westbourne Galleries Ltd* [1973] AC 360, discussed below.

[219] See earlier sections of this chapter for the relationship between these two statutory minority remedies. See **18.10.2**. As to the procedural issue of 'striking out' in winding-up petitions, see *Fuller v Cyracuse Ltd* [2001] 1 BCLC 187.

remedies is the 'alternative remedy' requirement now contained in s 125(2) of the Insolvency Act 1986. This is an important factor in the exercise of judicial discretion, whether or not the petitioner combines a petition under s 994 of the Companies Act 2006 with one under s 122(1)(g) of the Insolvency Act 1986. In *Ebrahimi v Westbourne Galleries*,[220] the House of Lords reviewed the nature and scope of the 'just and equitable' ground. It was emphasised that this ground should not be confined to special categories of situation.

It is clear that the effect of the House of Lords' decision is to extend the range of circumstances in which an order may be made on the just and equitable ground. The extent of the extension is still not entirely clear. Lord Wilberforce and Lord Cross of Chelsea delivered the only reasoned speeches. Although the case on its facts involved exclusion from participation in management, the observations made are of general significance in relation to the just and equitable ground. Lord Wilberforce also emphasised that references to 'quasi-partnerships' are confusing in the context of s 122(1)(g) except insofar as they recognise that concepts of probity, good faith and mutual confidence produced by the law of partnership are relevant to the exercise of the power to wind up on the just and equitable ground.

Lord Wilberforce emphasised that the mere fact that the exclusion of a director from participation in a company accords with the powers conferred by s 168 of the Companies Act 2006 and the articles of a company is not conclusive. The effect of s 122(1)(g) of the Insolvency Act 1986 is to enable the court 'to subject the exercise of legal rights to equitable considerations; considerations, that is, of a personal character arising between one individual and another, which may make it unjust, or inequitable, to insist on legal rights, or to exercise them in a particular way'.[221] Lord Wilberforce declined to define in an exhaustive manner the circumstances where the court would effect such a 'subjection'. He confined himself to a description of the type of situation which would typically give rise to the subjection of the legal rights or powers to the equitable considerations.

---

[220] [1973] AC 360 (HL (E)). The House of Lords was influenced by a number of Commonwealth decisions where the principles governing just and equitable winding up had been developed on similar lines. See, in particular, *Re Straw Products Pty Ltd* [1942] VLR 222, at 223 and *Re Wondoflex Textiles Pty Ltd* [1951] VLR 467, at 458 cited in the speech of Lord Wilberforce. See also, *Tench v Tench Bros Ltd* [1930] NZLR 403; *Re Sydney and Whitney Pier Bus Service Ltd* [1944] 3 DLR 468; and *Re Concrete Column Clamps Ltd* [1953] 4 DLR 60, which were also referred to by Lord Wilberforce. See also, *Re Tivoli Freeholds* [1972] VR 445. For further examination of the implications of the House of Lords' decision, see Chesterman (1973) 36 MLR 129 and Prentice (1973) 89 *Law Quarterly Review* 107. See Prentice, ibid, at 123–124, on the application of the principle to directors' refusal to transfer shares and on this see Lord Cross of Chelsea's speech.

[221] [1973] AC 360, at 379. See *Clemens v Clemens Bros* [1976] 2 All ER 268 at 282 for an application of this passage outside a just and equitable winding-up. *Sed quaere.*

He stated that such a situation:[222]

> '... may include one or probably more of the following elements: (i) an association formed or continued on the basis of a personal relationship, involving mutual confidence – this element will often be found where a pre-existing partnership has been converted into a limited company; (ii) an agreement, or understanding, that all, or some (for there may be "sleeping" members), of the shareholders shall participate in the conduct of the business; (iii) restrictions upon the transfer of the members' interest in the company – so that if confidence is lost, or one member is removed from management, he cannot take out his stake and go elsewhere.'

The primary importance of the decision of the House of Lords is to reject the view that the petitioner must prove that his exclusion was not *bona fide* in the interests of the company or such that no reasonable man could consider it to be in the interests of the company. The decision established, on a positive note, that the court possesses jurisdiction under s 122(1)(g) to order winding up where the circumstances disclose some underlying obligation in good faith and confidence that the petitioner should participate in management so long as the business continues. Expulsion justifies the assertion of that jurisdiction at least where the expulsion results in the loss of participation in profits and leaves the party expelled as a locked-in shareholder.[223]

The application of the above principles to situations *not* involving expulsion remains to some degree uncertain.[224] The position also remains uncertain where a (private) company has adopted the increasingly uncommon practice of distributing profits by way of dividend. However, it does not appear that an exclusion either from participation in management or from participation in profits is essential. Any course of dealing which produces a breakdown in mutual confidence may well suffice to justify the making of a winding-up order under s 122(1)(g),[225] unless that breakdown in mutual confidence is referable to the conduct of the complainant shareholders.[226] It is also possible that retention of profits which excludes members from participation by way of dividend

---

[222] [1973] AC 360, at 398.

[223] See *Lewis v Haas* 1971 SLT 57 (Ct of Sess) and *Re Davis & Collett* [1935] Ch 593.

[224] An example of the application of the principles in *Westbourne Galleries*, above, in the context of a joint venture company is *Re A & BC Chewing Gum* [1975] 1 WLR 579.

[225] See, eg, *Jesner v Jarrad Properties Ltd* [1993] BCLC 1032 (Ct of Sess). See also *Re Pauls Federated Merchants Ltd* (unreported) 30 July 1976, where Brightman J applied the *Westbourne* decision to a company which was not a quasi-partnership.

[226] Cases such as *Re Yenidje Tobacco Co* [1916] 2 Ch 246 (CA); *Re Sailing Ship Kentmere Co* [1897] WN 58; and *American Pioneer Leather Co* [1918] 1 Ch 556 must now be interpreted not merely as cases establishing that deadlock in management justifies a winding-up order, but as illustration of the wide concept of s 122(1)(g) established in *Westbourne Galleries*, above.

will justify a winding-up order where this defeats the members'
expectations and leaves the petitioner unable to realise the full value of his
shares.[227]

18.15   EARLIER CASES CONSISTENT WITH
WESTBOURNE

There are other English and Scottish cases decided before *Westbourne*
which can still be regarded as consistent with it. A company was wound
up where there were only three shareholders, each holding one-third of
the capital, and an article directed that if one shareholder offered his
shares to the others and they refused to purchase, the company should be
wound up. In this case the winding-up was on the ground that it was just
and equitable, and that though the article was not binding on the court it
formed a reason for holding that the company ought to be wound up.[228]
In another case there were only two shareholders, each of whom was a
director, one holding a single share, and the other the remainder of the
issued capital: namely 1,501 shares. The latter having usurped the whole
powers of the company, the former, though holding one share only,
successfully petitioned for a winding-up order.[229]

18.16   LOSS OF 'SUBSTRATUM'

The court will wind up a company even within one year of its formation,
although it may be solvent, if it appears that it has become impossible to
carry on the business for which it was formed.[230] Thus where the mine
which a company was formed to work could not be found,[231] or the patent
it was to work was not granted,[232] or the bulk of its property had been
sold and its capital exhausted,[233] or there was no reasonable probability of
obtaining the benefit of the contract it was formed to carry out,[234] a
winding-up order was made. The *substratum* of the company was also
held to have vanished where a bank had ceased to carry on banking
business[235] or the mine which the company was working proved
worthless,[236] or a company formed to amalgamate three syndicates for
speculating in seats for the Diamond Jubilee proposed, after losing money

---

[227] *Re A Company, ex parte Glossop* [1988] 1 WLR 1068. The court may order a compulsory
winding up in preference to a voluntary winding up on a shareholders' petition where
the company's affairs require the scrutiny that a compulsory order allows; *Re Internet
Investment Corporation Ltd* [2010] 1 BCLC 458.

[228] *Re American Pioneer Leather Co* [1918] 1 Ch 556.

[229] *Thomson v Drysdale* 1925 SC 311.

[230] This principle was first suggested in the case of *Suburban Hotel Co* (1867) 2 Ch App
737.

[231] *Re Haven Gold Mining Co* (1882) 20 Ch D 151.

[232] *Re German Date Coffee Co* (1882) 20 Ch D 169.

[233] *Re Diamond Fuel Co (No 2)* (1879) 13 Ch D 400 (CA).

[234] *Re Blériot Manufacturing Aircraft Co* (1916) 32 TLR 253.

[235] *Re Crown Bank* (1890) 44 Ch D 634.

[236] *Re Red Rock Gold Mining Co* (1886) 61 LT 785.

over that speculation, proposes to do other financial business,[237] or a single steamship company had lost its only ship and proposed with a small sum of cash to carry on business as a charterer of ships.[238] The sale by the company of the only business it has ever carried on, even if the carrying on of that particular business was stated in its memorandum as the first object, will not justify an order being made if, under its memorandum, it has power to resume that or any other kind of business.[239]

18.17 FRAUDULENT AND ILLEGAL COMPANIES

A company may also be wound up on the just and equitable ground where the company was in its inception fraudulent and hopelessly embarrassed by actions for rescission, and where a winding-up is the best means of recovering money from the promoters,[240] or where the company never had a real foundation and was a mere 'bubble',[241] or is formed to carry on an illegal business, such as dealing in lottery bonds.[242]

The court will not, however, wind up a company because it is not prosperous,[243] or its chance of success small,[244] unless the company passes a special resolution for liquidation; thus except where the company is insolvent the mere fact that it has passed an ordinary resolution that it be wound up, and that the directors be directed to present a petition therefore, will not justify the making of an order.[245] A contributory whose shares are fully paid up must establish that he has a tangible interest in the

---

[237] *Re Amalgamated Syndicate* [1897] 2 Ch 600.

[238] *Pirie v Stewart* (1905), 6 F 847 (Ct of Sess).

[239] *Re Kitson & Co* [1946] 1 All ER 435; *Re Taldua Rubber Co* [1946] 2 All ER 763; *Galbraith v Merito Shipping Co* 1947 SC 446. In the first of these cases, Lord Greene MR suggested that if after selling its business a company was obviously unable, e g for lack of capital, to carry on any business which under its memorandum it had power to carry on, this might afford a ground for a winding-up order: [1946] 1 All ER 435, at 440. He also suggested that different considerations might arise if the main business which the company was originally intended to carry on was never acquired on incorporation, so that it did not start its career in the way the original shareholders bargained for (ibid at 438). See also *Re Eastern Telegraph Co* [1947] 2 All ER, at 111, where Jenkins J stated that this case was not one of the contemplated objects failing *ab initio*.

[240] *Re Thomas Edward Brinsmead & Sons* [1897] 1 Ch D 406 (CA); cf *Re Diamond Fuel Co* (1879) 13 Ch D 400 (CA); and *Re General Phosphate Corp* [1893] WN 142. See further *Re Millennium Advanced Technology* [2004] 2 BCLC 77.

[241] *Anglo-Greek Steam Co* (1866) LR 2 Eq 1; *Re West Surrey Tanning Co* (1886) LR 2 Eq 737; *Re London and County Coal Co* (1867) LR 3 Eq 355.

[242] *Re International Securities Corp* (1908) 99 LT 581, where Swinfen-Eady J also held that the company was conducted in a fraudulent manner.

[243] *Re Langham Skating Rink Co* (1877) 5 Ch D 669 (CA); *Re Suburban Hotel Co* (1867) 2 Ch App 737.

[244] *Re Kronand Metal Co* [1899] WN 15. See, however, *Davis v Brunswick (Australia) Ltd* [1936] 1 All ER 299.

[245] *Re Anglo-Continental Produce Co* [1939] 1 All ER 99.

winding-up. To do this the petition must show a *prima facie* probability that the company is solvent and consequently there will be substantial assets for distribution.[246]

PART 3: THE BUSINESS DEPARTMENT'S POWERS TO INVESTIGATE COMPANIES AND THEIR SECURITIES

18.18   INTRODUCTION

Under the Companies Act 1985, the Business Department[247] is given powers to appoint inspectors to investigate the affairs of a company. The Department may also conduct its own investigations into a company's affairs by more informal inquiries. As the result of its own investigations, or as the result of the publication of a report by inspectors, the Department has the power petition for a winding-up order. The Department has the power to appoint inspectors to investigate the ownership of a company. Part XIV of the Companies Act 1985 (as amended by the Companies Act 1989) remains in force subject to certain new provisions in the Companies Act 2006 inserted into Part XIV by Part 32 of the Companies Act 2006. Thus no attempt has been made to consolidate the legislation on company investigations by the Secretary of State. Sections 1035–1039 (of the 2006 Act), inserting ss 446A–446E into the Companies Act 1985, confer new powers on the Secretary of State to give directions as to the conduct of inspections, as well as dealing with the resignation, removal and replacement of inspectors. The Department has been rebranded as the Department of Business, Innovation and Skills but the Companies Act 2006 retains the Department's traditional name.

18.19   INVESTIGATION OF THE AFFAIRS OF THE COMPANY

As regards the investigation of the affairs of a company,[248] the Department is obliged to appoint an inspector if the court orders it to do so.[249] Section 431(2)(c) provides that the Department may appoint inspectors 'in any case, on the application of the company'. The Department may at its discretion appoint an inspector on the application

---

[246] *Re Expanded Plugs Ltd* [1960] 1 WLR 514; *Re Othery Construction Co* [1966] 1 WLR 69.

[247] The Companies Act 2006 still referes to the Department of Trade and Industry. The 'rebranding' of the Department occurred in July 2007.

[248] An inspector, appointed under either s 431 or 432 to investigate the affairs of a company, has the power, if he thinks it necessary, to investigate the company's holding or subsidiary company 'or a subsidiary of its holding company or a holding company of its subsidiary'. This applies to any body which *is* a subsidiary, etc, or which 'has at any relevant time *been*', etc: Companies Act 1985, s 433.

[249] Section 432(1).

of a specified number of minority shareholders.[250] This application must be supported by evidence showing that the applicant or applicants have good reason for requiring the investigation. In addition, security for the costs of the inquiry, not exceeding £5,000, must be provided. The maximum amount of the security may be further increased by statutory instrument. These powers have been very little used.[251]

The Department may also appoint an inspector under s 432(2)[252] if there are circumstances suggesting any of the following:

(1) that the company's business is being conducted with intent to defraud its creditors or the creditors of any other person, or otherwise for a fraudulent or unlawful purpose or in a manner which is unfairly prejudicial to some part of its members, or that any actual or proposed act or omission of the company (including any act or omission on its behalf) is or would be so prejudicial, or that it was formed for any fraudulent or unlawful purpose; or

(2) that persons concerned with its formation or the management of its affairs have in connection therewith been guilty of fraud, misfeasance or other misconduct towards it or towards its members; or

(3) that its members have not been given all the information with respect to its affairs which they might reasonably expect.

A provision inserted in s 432 by the Companies Act 1989 allows the Secretary of State to appoint inspectors under s 432(2) on terms that 'any report that may be made is not for publication'.[253]

Although more use has been made of what is now s 432, in the past the Department had been inclined only to exercise its discretion in cases where notoriety in the press had already caused serious public concern. This cautious policy had been defensible to the extent that the mere announcement of a Department inspection can do a company's business reputation irreparable harm on the Stock Exchange and elsewhere before any abuse is proven. On the other hand, this reaction of the business community may in part reflect the limited use of this power in the past. To overcome this difficulty, the Department was given new powers to obtain

---

[250] Section 431(2)(a) and (b). The applicants must consist of not less than 200 members of the company or of members holding not less than one-tenth of the shares issued in the case of a company having share capital. In the case of a company not having share capital, the applicants must consist of not less than one-fifth in number of the persons on the company's register of members.

[251] It will be seen that this is linked with the Department's power to obtain repayment of the expenses of an inspection.

[252] Section 423(3) allows the Department to appoint an inspector where the company is in course of a voluntary liquidation.

[253] See s 432(2A).

the information it needs more quickly and informally. These additional powers[254] enable the Department to compel the production of any books and papers it may specify.[255] The Department may lay any information before a justice of the peace to obtain a warrant giving power to enter and search premises for the books and papers they require.[256] Penalties are also provided for the destruction of documents and for furnishing false information.[257]

The rules of natural justice have been held not to apply to the discretion exercised by the Department in appointing inspectors to investigate the affairs of a company.[258] So long as the Secretary of State is acting within his powers[259] and is in good faith, his decision cannot be challenged. His decision does not imply there is any case against the company or its management and he cannot be made to reveal the evidence which has led him to act. The Secretary of State may appoint inspectors to investigate matters which may also be the subject of criminal proceedings.[260]

18.19.1   Informal investigations under s 447

The vast majority of investigations by the Department are carried out under s 447. Members of the Company Investigation Branch or other competent individuals can be authorised, among other things, to seek the production of documents or to require explanations of any document from the person who produces it.[261] These are confidential fact finding inquiries, but there is a disclosure regime that allows, for example, information to be passed on to other regulators. Investigations under s 447 are carried out, for example, where there are grounds for suspicion of fraud, misfeasance or misconduct unfairly prejudicial to shareholders or where there has been a failure to supply shareholders with information they may reasonably expect. It has been held that an inspector appointed to make an informal investigation under s 447 cannot be cross-examined (in subsequent winding-up proceedings) either as to his reasons for

---

[254] Companies Act 1985, s 447.

[255] This power is wide enough to include the provision of an explanation not only of the text of a document but also, *inter alia*, its creation, authorship, accuracy, completeness, etc: *Attorney-General's Reference (No 2 of 1998)* [1999] BCC 590 (CA).

[256] Section 448. See s 449, which provides for security of information obtained under s 447 and for the permitted disclosure of this information in certain cases (e g examination of persons by inspectors appointed to conduct an investigation, or with a view to bringing criminal proceedings).

[257] Ibid, ss 450 and 451. The 1985 Act also confers powers on inspectors, approved by the Department to conduct a formal investigation, to enable them to compel the attendance of witnesses: ss 434 and 436.

[258] *Norwest Holst v Secretary of State for Trade* [1978] 3 WLR 73 (CA).

[259] In the *Norwest* case, the inspector had been appointed under what is now s 432(2)(c), but this decision would apply to any other statutory discretion to appoint inspectors or to take proceedings.

[260] *Re London United Investments plc* [1992] BCLC 285 (CA).

[261] Or from any past or present officer or employee of the company.

investigating under s 447 or as to why he thought it in the public interest that the company be wound up under s 440.[262]

It has been held that the court will not exercise powers of review in the case of officers of the Department exercising powers under s 447. The principle of bias did not apply to an investigation under s 447, since under this section the officers are exercising a police function and not a judicial or quasi-judicial function. However, a complainant may be entitled, on the ground of unfairness, to an order quashing a notice under s 447(2) (requiring the production of documents relating to the company's finances) on the basis that the notice is unreasonably and excessively wide.[263]

The Companies (Audit, Investigations and Community Enterprise) Act 2004[264] amends the powers to investigate under s 447. While not changing the basis of an inspection or making any changes of substance to the grounds for an investigation, the Act seeks to strengthen the regime. It gives investigators a general power to require relevant information and strengthen their power to require documents. For example, it enables them to require a person to explain his or her conduct or to give his or her opinion about something. It also excludes liability for breach of confidence so that individuals and business can feel able to volunteer information in response to an informal Departmental inquiry. The Act gives inspectors and investigators a power to require entry on to a company's business premises and to remain there for the purposes of the investigation.[265]

18.20 THE CONDUCT OF PROCEEDINGS BY INSPECTORS

The Court of Appeal has held[266] that although the proceedings before inspectors are not judicial or quasi-judicial,[267] but are of an administrative nature, yet the characteristics of the proceedings require the inspectors to act fairly. In this sense, the rules of natural justice apply. Thus, if they were disposed to condemn or criticise anyone in a report, the inspectors must first give him a fair opportunity to correct or contradict the allegation against him. For this purpose, an outline of the charge will usually suffice. So long as the inspectors acted fairly they were not subject

---

[262] *Re Golden Chemical Products Ltd* (1979) *The Times*, 8 December, per Deputy Judge Michael Wheeler QC.

[263] *R v Secretary of State for Trade, ex parte Perestrello* [1980] 3 WLR 1.

[264] See Part I, Chapter 3.

[265] See Companies Act 1985 (Power to Enter and Remain on Premises: Procedure) Regulations 2005, SI 2005/654.

[266] *Re Pergamon Press Ltd* [1970] 3 WLR 792 (CA), affirming the decision of Plowman J [1970] 1 WLR 1075. See also *Maxwell v Department of Trade and Industry* [1974] 1 QB 523 (CA).

[267] See *Re Grosvenor and West End Railway Terminus Hotel Co Ltd* (1897) 76 LT 732; *Hearts of Oak Assurance Co Ltd v Attorney-General* [1932] AC 322 (HL).

to any set rules procedure. The Court of Appeal held that directors were not entitled to refuse to answer questions put to them by the inspectors until they were shown the transcripts of evidence and the documents used against them, and had been allowed to cross-examine witnesses. The inspectors were held to have acted fairly, and in accordance with rules of natural justice,[268] by undertaking that no one would be criticised in the report without first being told in general terms of the allegation against him and being afforded an opportunity to give an explanation. The inspectors were prepared to make known the purport of the relevant evidence and documents. The directors' refusal to give evidence on these terms was unjustified.

Where an officer or agent of the company or other body corporate refuses to answer questions which are put to him by inspectors, the latter may 'certify the refusal under their hand to the court'.[269] The House of Lords has held that an officer or agent of the company examined by the inspectors is entitled to refuse to answer questions on the ground that the answers would incriminate him. But if such a witness does so, the matter may be referred to the court under s 436(2).[270] The issue of self-incrimination is one which the court not the inspectors should decide.[271]

It has been seen that an investigation is not a judicial inquiry, and the proceedings should be conducted in private. However, it has been held that the inspector is entitled to the assistance of anyone whose presence is reasonably necessary, and that a person examined could not object to the presence of a shorthand writer.[272] Parties involved in the investigation may be represented by counsel.[273]

18.20.1   The role of the Secretary of State in inspections

Section 1035 of the Companies Act 2006 inserts a new s 446A into the Companies Act 1985. This gives the Secretary of State the power to make directions in respect of the contents of the inspector's report. The inspector may be directed to include his views on a specified matter, or not

---

[268] The Court of Appeal referred, as to the rules of natural justice, to *Russell v Duke of Norfolk* [1949] 1 All ER 109; *Ridge v Baldwin* [1964] AC 40 (HL); *Wiseman v Borneman* [1969] 3 WLR 706 (HL); *R v Gaming Board for Great Britain, ex parte Benaim* [1970] 2 QB 417 (CA).

[269] Companies Act 1985, s 436(2). The same procedure applies to a refusal to produce to the inspectors any book or document which it is the duty of such an officer to produce under s 434 or 435, or to a refusal 'to attend before inspectors when required so to do'.

[270] The power conferred by s 436 now extends to 'any person'.

[271] See further, *Gore-Browne on Companies* (Jordans, 45th edn, loose-leaf) at 20[9] as to the right to refuse to disclose information given to the company's bankers and those entitled to 'professional legal privilege'. See also, *Re London United Investments* [1992] BCLC 285, in which the Court of Appeal held that the privilege against self-incrimination is not a basis for refusing to answer questions.

[272] *Re Gaumont-British Picture Corp* [1940] 1 Ch 506.

[273] See *McClelland, Pope and Langley Ltd v Howard* [1968] 1 All ER 569n.

to include any reference to a specified matter. Directions may also be given that the report be made in a specified form or manner or be made by a specified date.[274]

Section 1035 of the Companies Act 2006 also inserts a new s 446B into the Companies Act 1985. This enables the Secretary of State to terminate an investigation in the following circumstances: (a) where matters have come to light in the course of the inspector's investigation which suggest that a criminal offence has been committed; and (b) these matters have been reported to the prosecuting authority.[275] In these circumstances the inspector may be directed to produce an interim report.[276]

Section 1036 inserts a new s 446C into the Companies Act 1985 dealing with the removal and replacement of inspectors. Under s 446C an inspector may resign by giving notice to the Secretary of State or the Secretary may revoke his appointment. In these events (or where the inspector dies) s 446C will give the Secretary of State the right to appoint a replacement inspector. Under s 446E the Secretary of State is given the power to direct former inspectors (who have resigned or had their appointments revoked) to produce documents to the Secretary of State or a replacement inspector. This applies to documents obtained or generated by the former inspector during the course of his investigation.[277]

18.21 THE INSPECTORS' REPORT AND SUBSEQUENT PROCEEDINGS

A copy of any report of inspectors appointed to investigate into the affairs of a company is admissible in any legal proceedings as evidence of the opinion of the inspectors in relation to any matters contained in the report.[278] Moreover, s 434(5) of the Companies Act 1985 provides that an answer given by a person to a question put to him under the powers conferred by s 434 (as to the conduct of investigations by inspectors) may be used in evidence against him.[279]

---

[274] Section 446A(3).

[275] Section 446B(2).

[276] Section 446B(3).

[277] Section 446E(1) and (3).

[278] Companies Act 1985, s 441(1). The report is certified by the Secretary to be a true copy of such report (and it must be received in evidence etc).

[279] See, eg, *R v Seelig* [1991] BCLC 869; *Re London United Investments plc* [1992] BCLC 285. The power to obtain evidence under s 434 applies also to investigations into the ownership of the company under s 442, and to an investigation into share dealings under s 446.

18.22 THE POWER TO EXAMINE ON OATH AND OBTAIN DOCUMENTS

Section 434(3) of the Companies Act 1985 gives an inspector power to examine any person on oath and to administer an oath accordingly. Section 434(1) imposes a duty on all officers and agents of the company to produce documents, attend before the inspectors and give assistance in connection with the investigation. Section 434(2) amplifies this duty. It provides that if the inspectors consider that a person other than an officer or agent of the company (or other body corporate) is, or may be, in possession of any information concerning its affairs, they may require that person to produce to them any books or documents[280] in his custody or power. They may also require such a person to attend before them and otherwise to give them all the assistance, in connection with the investigation, which he is reasonably able to give (and it is the duty of such a person to comply).[281] In certain circumstances, s 435(1) gives inspectors power to request disclosure of documents relating to the bank accounts of directors (or past directors) of the company or other body corporate whose affairs are being investigated. This may apply where the director maintains (or has maintained) a bank account of any description, whether alone or jointly with another person, and whether in Great Britain or elsewhere. However, this can be done only if the inspectors have reasonable grounds to believe that the following types of payment have been paid into, or out of, the account. These are of three types.

(1) Emoluments or part of the emoluments of his office as such director, particulars of which have not been disclosed in the accounts of the company or other body corporate for any financial year contrary to paras 24–26 of Sch 5.

(2) Any money which has resulted from, or been used in, the financing of various types of transaction, arrangement or agreement which are in breach of various provisions listed by s 435(2).

(3) Any money which has been in any way connected with any act or omission, or series of acts or omissions, which constituted misconduct (whether fraudulent or not) on the part of that director towards the company or body corporate or its members.

18.23 PROCEEDINGS BY THE DEPARTMENT

The Department may act on the basis of its powers to obtain documents and other information from the company without a formal investigation

---

[280] Ie in relating to the company or other body corporate.
[281] See *Re an Enquiry into Mirror Group Newspapers plc* [1999] 1 BCLC 690 as to when a refusal to respond to the inspector's questions will be held reasonable.

by the Department's inspectors. It still retains the power to take proceedings after receiving an adverse report by an inspector.

As a result of the Companies Act 2006 the Department has lost its power to bring civil proceedings on behalf of the company.[282] The Department's power to petition for a winding-up likewise depends on its opinion of what is in the public interest.[283] Again, the Department may act not only on the basis of an inspector's report, but under its new power to obtain information without a formal public inquiry. If the inspector's opinions (contained in their report) were referred to in an affidavit to be used in interlocutory proceedings, they may be struck out as containing inadmissible evidence.

In a winding-up petition by the Department, where the accuracy of an inspector's report is not disputed, the court may act on the basis of the report although it is supported only by the affidavit of a Department official.[284] Where allegations against a company and its officers are contested, the Department must support the petition 'by evidence of true evidential value'.[285] A challenge to a report (on which a petition by the Secretary of State is based) means 'a challenge by someone with knowledge of the facts coming along and saying the inspectors' report is wrong, and being willing to put forward an affidavit and be cross-examined, and to be judged in the witness box on the evidence which he puts forward in contradiction of the inspectors' report'.[286] Even if the report is challenged in the above sense, it ought to be treated as *prima facie* evidence and it ought to be left to the judge in any case, having read the report and having seen the witnesses, to make up his own mind whether it is just and equitable to wind up the company.

> 'The whole machinery of the inspector's report was evolved in order to enable the Secretary of State to present a winding up petition where he considers the public interest so demands. It would be unfortunate if, once the Secretary of State has reached that conclusion on proper grounds based on the inspector's detailed report, the court should go right back to square one and start again as though the inspector had never come on the scene at all.'[287]

---

[282] Section 438 of the Companies Act 1985 is repealed by the Companies Act 2006, Sch 6.

[283] See now s 124(4)(b) of the Insolvency Act 1986. See s 124A as to the reports and statutory sources of information on the basis of which the Secretary of State may conclude that it is expedient in the public interest that a company should be wound up. A voluntary liquidation will no longer inhibit the exercise of this power: *Re Lubin Rosen and Associates Ltd* [1975] 1 WLR 122.

[284] *Re Allied Produce Co* [1967] 1 WLR 1964; *Re Travel & Holiday Club* [1967] 1 WLR 71.

[285] *Re ABC Coupler Engineering Co* [1962] 1 WLR 1236. As to the evidence admissible in a compulsory winding-up brought by the Department, see *Re Koscott Interplanetary (UK) Ltd* [1972] 3 All ER 82.

[286] *Re Armvent Ltd* [1975] 3 All ER 441, at 446 per Templeman J.

[287] Ibid.

The Department also possesses the power to seek relief under s 996 of the Companies Act 2006, if it appears to it that the affairs of a company are being conducted in a manner unfairly prejudicial to some part of the members. Here the Department is not required to have regard to the public interest, and it may seek to enforce this minority shareholders' remedy either in addition to or instead of a winding-up petition.

18.24 EXPENSES IN INVESTIGATIONS AND PROCEEDINGS BY THE DEPARTMENT

One of the attractions for shareholders in seeking the intervention of the Department of Trade and Industry, under s 432 of the Companies Act 1985, is that the expenses of the investigation and any consequent proceedings brought by the Department must be defrayed in the first instance by the Department.[288] The Department is entitled to repayment of these expenses if the report of the inspector results in a successful prosecution in a criminal court, or a judgment in a civil court, to the extent specified in an order made in those proceedings.[289] In addition, a company for whose benefit civil proceedings have been brought by the Department is liable to repay the expenses 'to the amount or value of any sums of property recovered by it as a result of those proceedings'.[290]

Where the Department appoints an inspector 'otherwise than of the Department's own motion' the company can also be made to contribute from its own resources to the costs of inspection and subsequent proceedings. Thus where, under s 432(1), the court orders an inspection, the Department has no choice in the matter, and it is only fair that the company should be liable 'except so far as this Department otherwise direct'. But shareholders who apply under s 431 are also liable to repay the Department 'to such extent (if any) as the Department may direct', even though here it is not compelled to appoint an inspector.[291] Where minority shareholders do not make a formal request under s 431, but confine themselves to persuading the Department to act 'of its own motion' under s 432(2), the Department has no power to make the

---

[288] Section 439(3); but see s 439(5).

[289] Section 439(2).

[290] Section 439(3). Any amount for which the company is liable under s 439(3) is a first charge on the sums or property recovered. But in the case of a civil action brought on behalf of the company, the Department was required to indemnify the company against costs or expenses incurred by the company in connection with the proceedings: s 438(2). Thus the company may have to contribute from the proceeds accruing to it from a successful action, but it cannot be prejudiced by an unsuccessful action. It has been held that 'the amount or value of any sums recovered by the company' (as limiting what it may be liable to pay to the Department under s 439(3)(b)) includes the costs recovered by the company: *Selangor Rubber Estates Ltd v Cradock (No 4)* [1969] 2 WLR 1773. However, the Department's duty to indemnify the company for the expenses of litigation includes costs ordered to be paid by the company to other parties: *Selangor United Estates v Cradock (No 1)* [1967] 1 WLR 1168 at 1173.

[291] Section 439(5).

minority or the company contribute to the expenses of an inspection. Thus if the Department chooses to act under s 432(2), it will recover its expenses only in the event of successful proceedings resulting from the inspector's report. There is provision for rights of contribution as between any of the parties who may become liable to repay the Department's expenses.[292] What the Department cannot recover must of course be paid by public funds.[293]

18.25   THE DEPARTMENT'S POWER TO INVESTIGATE THE OWNERSHIP OF SHARES

Under s 442 of the Companies Act 1985, the Department of Business has power to investigate the ownership of shares of a company. Where it appears to the Department that there is good reason so to do, it may appoint one or more competent inspectors to investigate and report on the membership of any company and otherwise with respect to the company for the purpose of determining the true persons who are or have been financially interested in the success or failure (real or apparent) of the company, or are able to control or materially influence its policy.[294]

Where an application for an investigation under the section is made to the Department with respect to particular shares or debentures of a company, in the case of a company having a share capital, either by not less than 200 members or by members holding not less than one-tenth of the shares issued, or in the case of a company not having a share capital, by not less than one-fifth in number of the persons on the register of members, then the Department is to appoint an inspector to conduct the investigation unless it is satisfied that the application is vexatious. Where inspectors are appointed, their terms of appointment must include any matter insofar as the Secretary of State is satisfied that it is reasonable to be investigated.[295] Section 442(3C) permits the Secretary of State to proceed instead under s 444 where he deems it more appropriate. The Secretary of State may, before appointing inspectors, require the applicants to give security up to an amount not exceeding £5,000 for the payment of the costs of the investigation.[296]

Subject to the terms of an inspector's appointment, his powers are to extend to the investigation of any circumstances suggesting the existence of an arrangement or understanding which, though not legally binding, is

---

[292]   Section 439(9); and see s 439(8).

[293]   Section 439(10).

[294]   Section 442(1). As to the powers given to the Secretary of State to give directions to inspectors (under s 446A) see **18.20.1** above. The Secretary also has powers to terminate an investigation (s 446B) and to remove and replace inspectors (s 446C).

[295]   Section 442(3), (3A).

[296]   This amount may be increased by the Secretary of State by order: see s 442(3B).

or was observed or likely to be observed in practice and which is relevant to the purposes of his investigation.[297]

Where it appears to the Department that there is good reason to investigate the ownership of any shares in or debentures of a company but that it is unnecessary to appoint an inspector for the purpose, under s 442 they may require any person whom they have reasonable cause to believe to have (or to be able to obtain) any information as to the present and past interests in those shares or debentures to provide such information. This extends to names and addresses of the persons interested and of any persons who act or have acted on their behalf in relation to the shares or debentures. They are required to give any such information to the Secretary of State.[298]

18.26   POWER TO IMPOSE RESTRICTIONS ON SHARES OR DEBENTURES

Part XV of the Companies Act 1985 gives the Department of Business power to impose restrictions on shares[299] 'in connection with an investigation' under s 442 or 444 (investigation of the ownership of a company). The Department may invoke these powers where it appears to it that there is difficulty in finding out the relevant facts about any shares (whether issued or to be issued). In that event, the Department may by order direct that the shares shall be subject, until further order, to the restrictions imposed by s 454.

So long as any shares are directed to be subject to the restrictions imposed by Part XV of the Act, the following provisions of s 454(1) apply:

(1)   any transfer of those shares, or in the case of unissued shares any transfer of the right to be issued with them and any issue of them, is void;

(2)   no voting rights are exercisable in respect of those shares;

(3)   no further shares are to be issued in right of those shares or in pursuance of any offer made to their holder;

(4)   except in a liquidation, no payment shall be made of any sums due from the company on those shares whether in respect of capital or otherwise.

---

[297]   Section 442(4). With the necessary modifications, certain of the provisions governing an investigation of the company's affairs by inspectors are applied to investigations under s 442 of ownership of shares. These provisions are s 433(1) (power to investigate related companies), s 434 (production of documents, etc), s 436 (obstruction of inspectors) and s 437 (inspector's report).

[298]   Section 444(1).

[299]   Part XV applies to debentures as well as to shares: s 445(2).

Section 454(2) and (3) contain provisions which amplify the effect of these restrictions. Where shares are subject to the restrictions imposed in (1) above, any agreement to transfer the shares, or in the case of unissued shares the right to be issued with the shares, is void.[300] Where shares are subject to the restrictions imposed in (3) and (4), any agreement to transfer any right to be issued with *other* shares in right of those shares or to receive any payment on those shares (otherwise than in a liquidation) is void.[301]

Where the Department makes an order directing that shares shall be subject to such restrictions, or refuses to make an order directing that shares cease to be subject thereto, any person aggrieved may apply to the court for an order directing that the shares be no longer subject to the restrictions.[302]

Section 456(3) states the conditions on which the court, or the Secretary of State, may make an order that shares shall cease to be subject to the restrictions imposed by s 454. These are that the court or, as the case may be, the Secretary of State, is satisfied that the relevant facts about the shares have been disclosed to the company, and no unfair advantage has accrued to any person as a result of the earlier failure to make disclosure. Alternatively an order under s 456(3) may be made if the shares are to be transferred and the court (in any case) or the Secretary of State (if the order is made s 445) approves the sale. Section 456(4) gives the court a power to order the sale of shares on the application of the Secretary of State or the company. On such an application the court may also order that the shares shall cease to be subject to the restrictions imposed. Where shares are sold by an order made under s 456(4), the proceeds of sale, less the costs of sale, shall be paid into court for the benefit of the persons who are beneficially interested in the shares. Such persons may apply to the court for payment of the whole[303] or part of the proceeds. On an application under s 457(1), the court must order the payment to the applicant of the whole of the proceeds of sale (together with any interest) or, if any other person had a beneficial interest in the shares at the time of their sale, such proportion of those proceeds (and interest thereon) as is equal to the proportion which the value of the applicant's interest in the shares bears to the total value of the shares.[304]

---

[300] 'Except an agreement to sell shares on the making of an order under s 456(3)(b).' 'Sale' means a sale for cash, not an exchange of shares: *Re Westminster Property Group plc* [1985] BCLC 188 (CA).

[301] Except on an agreement to transfer any such right on the sale of the shares on the making of an order under s 456(3)(b).

[302] Section 456(1) and (2).

[303] This is subject to any order as to costs for the benefit of the applicant made under s 457(3).

[304] Section 457(2).

CHAPTER 19

THE PUBLIC ISSUE OF SECURITIES

19.1 LEGISLATIVE BACKGROUND

This chapter is concerned with listing and public offers of securities. Listing is a regulatory process by which securities become eligible to be traded on an organised market.[1] It does not necessarily involve the sale of any securities, although in practice it is often combined with a sale of securities. The main concern of the law and regulatory rules relating to listing is to ensure that, following listing of a company's securities, there will be a proper market, meaning one in which investors are able, at any point in time, to make fully informed investment decisions (eg to buy or sell). A public offer of securities is an invitation to the general public to buy securities.[2] A public offer can be made in respect of listed or unlisted securities and in practice it is common for a public offer to be made of securities that are to be listed. The focus of the law relating to public offers runs parallel to that relating to listing in that it aims to ensure that adequate disclosure is made in respect of the securities offered for sale and the business of the issuer. However, as a public offer will not always involve securities that are to be traded on an organised market, the law relating to public offers is more directly concerned with the fairness of the particular sale transaction involved in the public offer, whereas the law relating to listing has a broader focus on the fairness of the operation of the market as a whole.

Historically, public issues of securities were regulated by the companies legislation. The first move away from the companies legislation as the source of regulation resulted from the need to implement three EU directives on listed securities.[3] Listed securities are securities admitted to official listing in a member state which, in the UK, means admitted to the Official List of the UK Listing Authority.[4] These directives were first implemented into the law in the UK in 1984 by means of regulations.[5] The effect of these regulations was, broadly, to disapply the relevant

---

[1]   This is an explanatory definition. There is no legal definition of the term.
[2]   This is an explanatory definition. The legal definition (see **19.21**) is more complex.
[3]   The Admissions Directive (79/279/EEC); the Listing Particulars Directive (80/390/EEC); and the Interim Reports Directive (82/121/EEC).
[4]   See further **19.4**.
[5]   The Stock Exchange (Listing) Regulations 1984, SI 1984/716.

provisions of the companies legislation in relation to listed securities. The companies legislation continued to apply to unlisted securities and, on consolidation of that legislation, the relevant provisions governing unlisted securities were contained in Part III and certain sections of Part IV of the Companies Act 1985.

While these events were occurring, a fundamental review of the whole body of securities law was undertaken on behalf of the Department of Trade and Industry by their adviser, Professor LCB Gower.[6] On the basis of this report, but in a form inevitably altered by the usual consultation processes and the pressures of various interest groups affected, the Financial Services Act 1986 introduced a new 'securities law' to regulate most aspects of the financial markets in the UK. Part IV of the Financial Services Act 1986 regulated listed securities. Changes to Part IV[7] that were made in 1995 were intended to implement the EC Public Offers Directive (POD)[8] insofar as it affected listed securities. Largely because Part IV was already based on Community law, the impact of this Directive on the regime governing listed securities was not especially great. Part VI of the Financial Services and Markets Act 2000 introduced new provisions on official listing that replaced Part IV of the Financial Services Act 1986. It recast the requirements for official listing in simpler, more modern language but made few substantive changes. A significant change that took place in advance of the enactment of the new regime was that the London Stock Exchange ceased to be the UK's listing authority following the transfer of responsibility to the Financial Services Authority, the UK's financial regulator. It is a requirement of the European directives on listing that member states should have a competent authority to perform certain functions in connection with listing. The transfer of this role from the London Stock Exchange to the Financial Services Authority was prompted by an internal reorganisation of the Stock Exchange and its decision to operate as a more commercial and internationally orientated organisation.[9] Given that decision, it was deemed to be inappropriate for the Stock Exchange to continue to carry the regulatory responsibilities that are imposed on national listing authorities.[10]

The central principle underlying the regulation of public issues of securities in both the EU and UK is that of mandatory disclosure to investors of information relating to an issuer and the relevant securities. Two justifications are generally offered in support of this approach.[11] The first is that mandatory disclosure promotes investor confidence and

---

[6]   *Review of Investor Protection*, Part I (Cmnd 9125) 1984. See also Part II (1985), Ch 6.

[7]   Made by the Public Offers of Securities Regulations 1995, SI 1995/1537.

[8]   Directive 89/298/EEC.

[9]   The London Stock Exchange is now a listed company on the London Stock Exchange.

[10]   The transfer was effected by the Official Listing of Securities (Change of Competent Authority) Regulations 2000, SI 2000/968.

[11]   See generally N Moloney, *EC Securities Regulation* (Oxford University Press, 2nd edn, 2008), pp 93–95.

investor protection. That claim is based on the role of mandatory disclosure in making information relating to an issuer available to investors so as to allow them to make informed decisions on the valuation of investments. While mandatory disclosure imposes costs on issuers, it also mitigates the information asymmetry as between issuers and investors that might otherwise jeopardise the process of investment. The second is that mandatory disclosure promotes efficient capital markets and efficient capital allocation. That claim is based on the role of mandatory disclosure in making capital markets informationally efficient, meaning that they correctly refle.·* r·levant information regarding an issuer in prices: when this occurs, the process of allocating capital to competing uses is more efficient than if such decisions are made on the basis of partial information or speculation.

In respect of the EU legislative measures, an additional policy (and the cause of much of the complexity evident in the legislation) is that of creating a single market in capital and financial services. While the legal competence of the EU in respect of the wide-ranging programme of harmonisation in this area may not always be clear, it now seems to be accepted that a harmonised form of mandatory disclosure is a prerequisite for the emergence of a single capital market. The notable change represented by the Prospectus Directive (below) is the rejection of the previous approach through 'minimum standards' directives, which left considerable power to host member states and effectively prevented the operation of mutual recognition. The obstacles which have in the past frustrated the operation of mutual recognition have now been largely removed,[12] opening up the possibility of it becoming a practical reality for issuers rather than an option which has largely been ignored (mainly for reasons of cost and complexity) under the POD regime. It remains to be seen whether the trend towards greater integration of capital markets will eventually lead to the emergence of a single EU authority with responsibility for regulating listing, public offers and financial markets.[13]

The three EU directives on listed securities mentioned above were consolidated in the Consolidated Admissions and Reporting Directive (CARD).[14] This Directive pursues the policy of minimum harmonisation and mutual recognition, which was developed in the 1980s as a

---

[12] It is not possible to say that they have been completely removed as the 'maximum harmonisation' principle adopted by the new Prospectus Directive applies only to issuer disclosure and not the conditions for admission to listing or continuing obligations.

[13] See the De Larosière Report for a discussion of an expanded role for the European Central Bank and the 'level 3' committees in a reformed EU system of financial supervision: http://ec.europa.eu/internal_market/finances/docs/de_larosiere_report_en.pdf (11 July 2011). The reconstitution of the 'level 3' committees on 1 January 2011 represents a limited move in that direction.

[14] Directive 2001/34/EC [2001] OJ L184/1. The Major Holdings Directive (88/627/EEC, [1988] OJ L348 62) is also included in the consolidation. The CARD is implemented in the UK by the provisions of Part VI of the Financial Services and Markets Act 2000 and the UKLA *Listing Rules*.

mechanism to give effect to the objective of a single capital market within the EU.[15] Minimum harmonisation is intended to remove significant differences between the regulatory systems of member states and thereby create the conditions under which mutual recognition can be implemented. The essence of mutual recognition is that compliance with the legal and regulatory processes in one member state is recognised as being compliance with those in other member states. In respect of listed securities, the objective is that listing particulars or a prospectus approved in one member state should be accepted in other member states. The extent to which the CARD gave effect to that objective was, however, quite limited. The main reason for this was that the directive followed the policy of minimum harmonisation, which, in principle, leaves member states free to impose additional requirements, thereby limiting the operation of mutual recognition.[16] Following subsequent amendment by the directives discussed below, CARD survives in a much reduced form covering primarily the constitutional requirements for listed companies and the transferability of their securities.

The Prospectus Directive[17] (PD) aims to resolve some of the problems associated with the operation of mutual recognition under the POD and the directives consolidated in the CARD. It requires an approved prospectus to be published either when a public offer[18] is made or when relevant securities are admitted to trading on a regulated market. This represents an expansion of the role of a 'prospectus' which, under the POD, had been limited to public offers, whereas the CARD required 'listing particulars' when securities were admitted to 'official listing'.[19] In that sense, the significance for regulatory purposes of 'official listing' and 'listing particulars' has declined with the expansion of the role of the prospectus to cover many of the instances in which listing particulars had been required. However, as discussed below, the concept of 'official listing' remains relevant and carries significant implications within the context of the UK regulatory system, where it is possible for securities to be admitted to the 'official list' without being traded on a regulated market. Different disclosure standards for different securities and types of investors are mandated by the PD. This approach is reflected in the recognition by the PD and its implementing regulation[20] of 'wholesale' and 'retail' categories of securities, with the former being subject to a lighter form of regulation, reflecting the absence of retail investors (and the associated information asymmetry) from the wholesale markets. Provision is made by the PD for a prospectus to be split into a registration

---

[15] See **19.25** and generally Moloney, *op cit*, chapter 1.
[16] In the UK, such requirements are referred to as 'super-equivalents'. Article 8(1) of the CARD expressly provides for such provisions. The UK has chosen to apply such measures on several occasions so as to promote investor protection and preserve the reputation of its markets.
[17] Directive 2003/71/EC [2003] OJ L345/64.
[18] Unlike the POD, the PD defines a public offer (see art 2(1)(d) and **19.21**).
[19] See Art 20, deleted by the PD.
[20] The Prospectus Directive Regulation 2004/908/EC [2004] OJ L149/1.

document, a securities note and a summary, thereby enabling subsequent issues to be made simply by the publication of new versions of the latter two documents. The PD also enhances the 'passport' characteristic of a prospectus[21] approved by a home member state by removing in most instances[22] the ability of a host state to impose additional requirements.

The change in focus within the EU listing regime from 'official listing' to 'regulated markets' reflects a broader trend in EU capital markets regulation. Two key developments lie behind that trend: the first is a move away from the old regulatory model under which national exchanges had a virtual monopoly over listing and trading of securities; and the second is the emergence of alternative trading systems which compete with but are not regulated as stock exchanges. The term 'regulated market' is defined[23] in the Markets in Financial Instruments Directive (MiFID)[24] and is central to the delimitation of the scope of that directive as well as the Transparency Obligations Directive (TD)[25] and the Market Abuse Directive (MAD).[26] The result is that a distinction is drawn within the EU regulatory regime and in national legal systems between a regulated market and a 'multilateral trading facility' (MTF).[27] The primary significance of that distinction is that it opens up the possibility of markets operating as a MTF outside the scope of the EU regulatory regime for regulated markets. In the UK, the main examples are the Alternative Investment Market (AIM) and the Professional Securities Market, which are both a 'MTF' for the purposes of the EU regulatory regime.[28] The latter became operational from 1 July 2005 (the date on which the PD was implemented) and represented a response to the requirements imposed by the PD and TD on issuers of debt and convertible securities who do not fall within the 'wholesale' category of

---

[21] See also **19.25**.

[22] See art 19 regarding language requirements. Article 23 permits the host State, in exceptional circumstances following the failure of remedial action taken by the home member state, to take appropriate measures to protect investors.

[23] Article 4(1) of MiFID defines a regulated market as 'a multilateral system operated and/or managed by a market operator, which brings together or facilitates the bringing together of multiple third party buying and selling interests in financial instruments – in the system and in accordance with its non discretionary rules – in a way that results in a contract, in respect of the financial instruments admitted to trading under its rules and/or systems, and which is authorised and functions regularly and in accordance with the provisions of Title III'.

[24] Directive 2004/39 EC [2004] OJ L145/1. See also the MIFID Implementing Directive 2006/73 EC [2006] OJ L241/26 and the MiFID Implementing Regulation 2006/1287 OJ L241/1.

[25] Directive 2004/109/EC [2004] OJ L390/38.

[26] Directive 2003/6/EC [2003] OJ L96/16.

[27] An MTF is defined in Art 4(1) of MiFID as 'a multilateral system, operated by an investment firm or a market operator, which brings together multiple third-party buying and selling interests in financial instruments – in the system and in accordance with non-discretionary rules – in a way that results in a contract in accordance with the provisions of Title II'.

[28] They are sometimes also described by their operator (the London Stock Exchange) as 'exchange regulated' markets.

securities established by the PD. Securities listed on the Professional Securities Market are admitted to the official list, making them eligible as investments for funds which are limited to securities included in the official list.[29] However, they are subject to a less demanding disclosure regime than if they were admitted to trading on a regulated market.

The MiFID regime draws a distinction between the operator of a regulated market and the market itself even though both functions may be combined in a single legal entity (as in the case of the London Stock Exchange). Controls over the operator focus on suitability, good repute and experience while controls over the market focus on organisational structure and systems. In the UK context, both sets of controls are incorporated into the 'recognised investment exchange' ('RIE') regime in Part 18 of the Financial Services and Markets Act 2000. The central feature of that regime is that, subject to satisfying the recognition requirements set by the Treasury, a RIE is exempt from the general prohibition against carrying on investment activity without authorisation. The concept of an RIE pre-dates but is linked with the concept of the 'operator' of a regulated market in MifID since 'passporting' rights under MiFID are available either to an RIE in the UK or an EEA operator.[30] The distinct nature of a recognised investment exchange and a regulated market that it operates is also reflected in the separation established by MifID between listing and admission to trading on a regulated market. Nevertheless, there remains a close link in the UK system between RIE status and operating a regulated market since it is possible for a RIE to operate both a regulated market and a MTF but not only a MTF (in contrast to 'investment firms' under MiFID who are able to, and indeed limited to, operating a MTF on its own).

The TD and the MAD, while not directly concerned with the process of listing or the making of public offers, are of considerable significance for both purposes. The former is concerned primarily with the obligations of listed entities and both amends and augments the regime for disclosure established in the CARD (above).[31] It has been implemented in the UK primarily by changes made to the FSA Handbook.[32] It is linked with the MAD in that both directives have a strong focus on disclosure of information to the market: the TD mandates the disclosure of minimum levels of periodic disclosure of information by issuers, while the MAD

---

[29] But note that securities admitted to trading on AIM are not admitted to the official list: see **19.5** and **19.6**.

[30] See **19.25**.

[31] A related development is the requirement that all companies whose securities are admitted to trading on a regulated market in the EU must implement International Accounting Standards from 1 January 2005 (see Regulation 1606/2002/EC [2002] OJ L243/1).

[32] This includes the insertion in the FSA Handbook (Disclosure Rules and Transparency Rules, DTR) of the rules relating to disclosure of the acquisition and disposal of major shareholdings following the repeal of ss 198–220 of the Companies Act 1985 with effect from 20 January 2007.

requires disclosure of 'inside information' to the market and prohibits misuse or unauthorised disclosure of such information prior to its public disclosure. The MAD is relevant not just for listed entities but also for any entity whose securities are traded on prescribed markets in the UK.[33] MAD changed the definition of what constitutes market abuse[34] and was implemented in the UK through changes made to Part VIII of the Financial Services and Markets Act 2000 (FSMA 2000) and the FSA Handbook.

19.2   THE REGULATORY FRAMEWORK

The broad framework of the regulatory control of listed and unlisted securities is as follows.

(1)   Transferable securities[35] which are to be admitted to trading on a regulated market or which are the subject of a public offer are governed by Part VI of FSMA 2000. Section 85 of the Act requires an approved prospectus to be made available to the public before either process can take place.

(2)   Securities may be admitted to the 'official list' without being admitted to trading on a regulated market or being the subject of a public offer. Where that is the case, s 79 of FSMA 2000 requires listing particulars to be approved by the UKLA and published. This procedure applies in the case of specialist securities which are admitted to the official list and traded on the Professional Securities Market (which is not a regulated market).

(3)   A prospectus is not required in the case of those offers of securities which are exempt under s 86 of FSMA 2000. Such offers are subject to the provisions of s 21 of FSMA 2000, which regulates the activity described as 'financial promotion'. However, a prospectus *is* required in the case of offers[36] to the public of transferable securities to be admitted to trading on a market that is not a regulated market (eg a public offer of securities to be admitted to trading on AIM).

(4)   Certain matters relating to the allotment of shares and debentures remain subject to the Companies Act 2006.

(5)   Special rules apply where a company wants to make a simultaneous offer of its securities in two or more member states.[37]

---

[33]   Markets 'prescribed' for the purposes of the market abuse regime in the UK are not limited to 'regulated markets': for example, AIM is included.
[34]   From that contained in Part VIII of FSMA 2000 as originally enacted.
[35]   See the definition in s 102A and the exclusions in Sch 11A of FSMA 2000.
[36]   Meaning offers that do not fall within the category of exempt offers: see **19.21**.
[37]   See ss 87H, 87I and 87J of FSMA 2000 and **19.25**.

Offers of securities are brought within the regulatory framework irrespective of whether those securities are offered for cash or for a non-cash consideration. This point is notable because the relevant provisions of the Companies Act 1985 (and earlier companies legislation) only applied to securities offered to the public 'for subscription or purchase'. This phrase was interpreted by the courts to mean subscription or purchase for cash[38] which meant that, for example, an offer made by a bidder to acquire the shares of the target by means of a share-for-share exchange was not caught. The change of policy embodied in the current law was based on a recommendation by Professor Gower in *The Review of Investor Protection*.[39]

19.3   PRIVATE AND PUBLIC COMPANIES

A business conducted through the corporate form is usually established as a private company. At a later stage, its proprietors may choose to convert it into a public company[40] precisely in order to be able to sell their shareholding or raise additional capital by offering its securities to the public. Starting life as a private company allows the proprietors to operate the business under more relaxed rules governing the maintenance, increase and reduction of share capital than those applicable to public companies.[41] For most types of business at the early stages of their development, their operations are unlikely to be hampered by the prohibition on offering securities to the public because, in any event, few external investors are likely to be interested in investing in such untested operations. If and when a business has established itself as a successful and profitable trading venture, the proprietors may consider it to be worthwhile subjecting the company to the more rigorous regulations imposed on public companies and their capital in return for acquiring the freedom to exploit the company's reputation by offering its securities to the public.

However, this familiar picture of the business that is established in private company form and built up over a number of years until it is of a size and has a reputation that would make the raising of capital through issues of securities to the public a viable option, was challenged in the late 1990s by the emergence of fast-growing Internet and other technology companies. A notable phenomenon during this period was the willingness of investors (assisted by modifications made to the *Listing Rules*) to invest in such companies despite the absence of a trading record or of profitability. Such companies had to be in public company form in order to exploit this

---

[38]   *Government Stock and Other Securities Investment Co Ltd v Christopher* [1956] 1 All ER 40, [1956] 1 WLR 237. See also s 583 of the Companies Act 2006, replacing s 738 of the Companies Act 1985 with effect from 1 October 2008.

[39]   (1984) Cmnd 9125.

[40]   The procedure for conversion is contained in ss 90-96 of the Companies Act 2006, replacing ss 43-48 of the Companies Act 1985. See **4.11.2**.

[41]   See Chapter 7.

investor interest. More recently, the established pattern has been challenged by the rapid growth in listings on the AIM, which, as a result of its decision to operate outside the regulatory category of 'regulated market' has been able to attract listings from companies who might not be able to or wish to meet the requirements of regulated markets.

The regulatory regime in the UK has traditionally limited access to public markets and public offers of securities to public companies. A private company limited by shares or limited by guarantee and having a share capital[42] may not offer its securities to the public[43] nor may its securities be admitted to official listing.[44] Under the Companies Act 2006, it is no longer a criminal offence for a private company to offer its shares to the public.[45] Enforcement of the prohibition under the Companies Act 2006 can take the form either of an order restraining a proposed contravention of the prohibition,[46] an order requiring the company to re-register as a public company,[47] or a remedial order.[48] In the case of a remedial order, the court has a wide discretion, including the possibility of requiring any person involved in the contravention to purchase any of the securities on such terms as the court thinks fit.

A 'public offer' for the purposes of the Companies Act prohibition is defined more narrowly than in Part VI of FSMA 2000, which deals with the obligation to publish a prospectus.[49] In particular two types of offer are excluded from the definition. The first is an offer which is not calculated to result in securities of the company becoming available to persons other than those receiving the offer. The second is an offer which is regarded as a 'private concern'[50] of the person receiving it. An offer will be regarded as a private concern if it is made to a person connected with the company and, where the relevant rights are renounceable, they may be renounced only in favour of another person connected with the company. An offer will also be regarded as being a private concern when it is an offer to subscribe for securities held under an employer's share scheme

---

[42] The definition excludes from its scope unlimited companies and private companies limited by guarantee without a share capital.

[43] Section 755 of the Companies Act 2006 replacing s 81 of the Companies Act 1985.

[44] Section 75(3) of FSMA 2000 and reg 3(a) of the FSMA 2000 (Official Listing of Securities) Regulations 2001, SI 2001/2956.

[45] Section 81 of the Companies Act 1985 provided that an offence was committed by the company and any officer in default.

[46] Section 757.

[47] Section 758.

[48] Section 759.

[49] See s 756 of the Companies Act 2006 , replacing s 742A of the Companies Act 1985. The Company Law Review, Final Report, para 4.57 rejected the alignment of the Companies Act definition of a public offer with that of the EU regulatory regime (at that time represented by the Public Offers Directive as implemented in the UK by the Public Offers of Securities Regulations) on the basis that it would 'undermine the distinction between public and private companies and create more problems than it solved'.

[50] This term replaces the expression 'domestic concern' used in the superseded provision of the Companies Act 1985 (see footnote above).

and, where rights are renounceable, they can be renounced only in favour of another person entitled to hold securities under the same scheme or a person already connected with the company. The category of person 'connected' with the company has been expanded by comparison with the equivalent provision in the Companies Act 1985 to include a trustee of a trust where the principal beneficiary is an existing debenture holder of the company or the widow or widower, or surviving civil partner of a person who was a member or employee of the company.[51]

The narrow definition of a 'public offer' in the Companies Act 2006 opens up the possibility of a private company making an offer which does not contravene the Companies Act prohibition but it does not have the effect of overriding the requirement to publish an approved prospectus when a public offer is made for the purposes of Part VI of FSMA 2000. That requirement is not stated by reference to the status of the entity making the offer but by reference to the nature of the offer and the securities.[52] It follows that a private company making an offer which does not contravene the Companies Act prohibition must take care to ensure that the offer does not fall within Part VI of FSMA 2000.[53] Failure so to do will result in the requirements imposed by Part VI of FSMA 2000 being applicable and the costs of the offer rising accordingly.

19.4   THE UK LISTING AUTHORITY AND THE LONDON STOCK EXCHANGE

With effect from 1 May 2000, the Financial Services Authority (FSA) assumed the role of UK Listing Authority.[54] Before that, responsibility for matters relating to listing lay with the London Stock Exchange. The FSA's approach to the transfer was to maintain business as usual and, accordingly, it adopted requirements for listing that were for most purposes the same as those previously imposed by the London Stock Exchange.

A distinction must now be drawn between the listing of securities and their admission to trading on a securities market. Securities are admitted to listing by the FSA in its role as Listing Authority and, separately, are admitted to trading on a recognised investment exchange's market for listed securities. Securities that have completed both processes are said to be admitted to official listing on a stock exchange.

An applicant for official listing must comply with the requirements of Part VI of the Financial Services and Markets Act 2000. It must also comply with the UK Listing Authority's requirements for listing which are

---

[51]   Companies Act 2006, s 756(5).
[52]   See **19.21** and **19.22** below.
[53]   It can do that, for example, by ensuring that the offer is an 'exempt offer': see **19.22**.
[54]   The change was given effect by the Official Listing of Securities (Change of Competent Authority) Regulations 2000, SI 2000/968.

set out in the part of the FSA Handbook referred to as the *Listing Rules*.[55] The *Listing Rules* have statutory backing under Part VI of the Financial Services and Markets Act 2000.

To qualify for official listing, an applicant must ordinarily satisfy certain criteria relating to the length of time it has been trading, the value of the securities for which listing is sought and the proportion of securities that will be held by the public once listing has taken place. These criteria mean that official listing can normally be sought only by established businesses of a certain size which have a substantial trading record. Dispensations can, however, be granted by the UKLA from its listing requirements. In the past, there were modifications made to the listing requirements for particular industrial sectors (eg computer hardware and services and Internet) but these modifications have now been incorporated into the relevant sections of the *Listing Rules*. In most cases, the persons who have built up a business must accept some dilution of their formal[56] control of the company in order to satisfy the requirement for the appropriate percentage of the company's securities for which listing is sought to be in the hands of the public. The costs and expenses involved in seeking and maintaining an official listing are significant and this is an additional consideration which can dissuade smaller companies from taking this step.

In 2007 the FSA initiated a review of the listing regime. The review was prompted by two main concerns. One was that a degree of confusion had emerged as regards the use of the term 'official listing' as a result of the emergence of different segments and markets offered by the FSA and the London Stock Exchange.[57] Another concern was to ensure that the UK remained competitive as a listing destination for foreign companies. The outcome of that review was that changes to the listing regime were implemented with effect from 6 April 2010. The most significant change was that the listing segments were re-designated 'premium' and 'standard'[58], with the former being reserved for equity shares of commercial companies, closed-end investment funds and open-ended investment companies who meet the enhanced requirements applicable to

---

[55] See www.fsa.gov.uk.

[56] There is much discussion about the extent to which practical, as opposed to formal, control is lost when the ownership of a company's securities becomes dispersed via a flotation. The persons who built up the business will, more likely than not, remain in managerial control after the securities are listed. Outside shareholders, individually, are unlikely to own enough of the company's securities to be able to exercise much control over the managers and may be too widely dispersed to be able to act effectively as a collective group. Also, they may be disinclined to take collective action, preferring instead the simple option of selling their shares if the managers of the company underperform. These issues of corporate governance are discussed further in Chapter 11.

[57] See FSA Discussion Paper 08/1, A review of the Structure of the Listing Regime (January 2008) ch 3 for an overview of those segments and markets. See also the 7th edition of this book at Ch 19.4.

[58] This superseded the previous division between 'primary' and 'secondary' listing.

this category. Other categories of securities that had in the past been eligible for a 'primary' listing (eg debt securities and global depositary receipts) are now restricted to the 'standard' category. Moreover a clear distinction is drawn between the 'premium' category, where issuers are subject to requirements that exceed those contained in relevant EU directives (so called 'superequivalents' or 'gold plating') and the 'standard' category, where issuers are subject only to the minimum standards set by the EU directives.

The London Stock Exchange presently has two markets: its main market for listed securities (ie those admitted to the official list), and the AIM for smaller and growing companies (which have not been admitted to the official list).[59] AIM began operating in June 1995. The background to the establishment of the AIM was that research conducted by the Exchange indicated that, notwithstanding a decline in the use of the Unlisted Securities Market, a predecessor lower-tier market, there was still a demand for a new source of funding and trading for smaller companies as an alternative to the main market for listed securities. AIM may appeal to companies which cannot satisfy the requirements for official listing, and also to companies which are eligible for official listing but which are attracted to the lower admission criteria and less onerous continuing obligations imposed on companies trading on AIM. Also, the costs of obtaining and maintaining admission to AIM are considerably lower than those of the main market.[60] Some companies may view admission to the AIM as the first step in the process leading to full listing. In terms of numbers of issuers, AIM has grown rapidly to a position in which it has more than half the number on the main market. However, the latter remains a much greater force in terms of the market capitalisation of its constituents, which dwarfs that of AIM.[61]

19.5 CRITERIA FOR ADMISSION TO LISTING

The conditions to be fulfilled by an applicant for official listing and the listing procedure are set out in the *Listing Rules*. A distinction is drawn between a premium listing and a standard listing. The requirements are set out below, with the requirements for a premium listing shown first

---

[59] It is common usage to refer to any company on the main market or AIM as a 'listed company' but the term 'quoted' company is preferable as it refers simply to prices being quoted for a security on an organised market.

[60] A particular area of saving is in relation to sponsors. Unlike applicants for official listing, applicants for admission to the Alternative Investment Market do not require a sponsor. Having a sponsor is an expensive requirement because, under the *Listing Rules*, sponsors must give a confirmation that, having made due and careful inquiries, they have satisfied themselves that the rules have been complied with. Sponsors must perform extensive (and expensive) due diligence exercises in order to be in a position to provide such confirmation. AIM companies must have nominated advisers (aka 'nomads'), but nominated advisers are not required to give this confirmation.

[61] See www.londonstockexchange.com/en-gb/ (11 July 2011) for statistics relating to the LSE and AIM.

followed by those applicable to a standard listing (in italics). A premium listing is possible only for equity shares, whereas other financial instruments may be the subject of a standard listing.

(1)   The market value of the shares to be listed must be at least £700,000 (but, in practice, an applicant may have difficulty in finding a broker or issuing house to sponsor the issue[62] and may find the costs involved make an official listing prohibitively expensive unless the value of the securities involved is substantially greater than this).
The same requirement applies in the case of a standard listing.

(2)   The company must normally have a trading record of at least 3 years and must have unqualified audited accounts for those 3 years.
There is no comparable requirement for a standard listing.

(3)   The company must demonstrate that: (a) at least 75% of its business is supported by a historic revenue earning record which covers the period for which accounts are required under (2); (b) it controls the majority of its assets and has done so for at least the period referred to in para (2); and (c) it will be carrying on an independent business as its main activity.[63] This is intended to permit investors to make an independent assessment of the company's business prospects (eg where the listing applicant has been demerged from a larger group).
There is no comparable requirement for a standard listing.

(4)   The company must be able to state that it is satisfied, after due and careful inquiry, that it has sufficient working capital for at least the next 12 months.[64]
There is no comparable requirement for a standard listing.[65]

(5)   The shares must be freely transferable and at least 25% must be in the hands of the public after the flotation.
The same requirement applies in the case of a standard listing.

(6)   Equity shares must be admitted to trading on a regulated market for listed securities operated by a Recognised Investment Exchange. All other securities must be admitted to trading on a Recognised Investment Exchange's market for listed securities.[66]

---

[62]   LR 8.2.1R sets out the requirement to have a sponsor in the case of a primary listing of equity securities.

[63]   Note that the previous requirement to show independence from a controlling shareholder has been removed.

[64]   This is the only forward-looking statement which an applicant is required to make. The requirement can be set aside in certain cases (eg entities whose solvency is regulated).

[65]   Note, however, that the prospectus must contain a working capital statement: FSA Handbook, PR App 3, Annex III, para 3.1.

[66]   This permits such securities to be traded on the Professional Securities Market, which is not a 'regulated market' for the purposes of the EU directives.

(7)   The shares must be eligible for electronic settlement, which takes place within CREST.
      There is no comparable requirement for a standard listing.

(8)   If shareholders do not have pre-emption rights[67] under the law of the company's country of incorporation the company must ensure its constitution provides for such rights.[68]
      There is no comparable requirement for a standard listing.

For mineral and scientific-based research companies these requirements are modified by the *Listing Rules* subject to certain conditions being met. Provision is also made for the FSA to modify or dispense with the requirements referred to in (2) or (3) above if it is desirable in the interests of investors and investors have sufficient information to make an informed decision.

19.6   CRITERIA FOR ADMISSION TO TRADING ON THE LONDON STOCK EXCHANGE

Companies that seek to have their securities admitted to the London Stock Exchange's market for listed securities must comply with the *Listing Rules* but they are not subject to significant additional admission criteria imposed by the Exchange. Applicants to the Alternative Investment Market do not need to comply with the *Listing Rules* (because they are not admitted to the official list) but they must satisfy AIM's own criteria for admission. There is no requirement for a minimum (or maximum) market value of the securities for which admission is sought, there is no minimum trading record and no requirement for a minimum proportion of the securities to be in public hands. A company joining AIM must satisfy the following requirements.

(1)   The company must be duly incorporated or otherwise validly established according to the laws of its place of incorporation or establishment.

(2)   The company must be permitted by its national law to offer its securities to the public. In the UK this means that it must be a public limited company.[69]

(3)   The securities to be traded on the market must be freely transferable.

(4)   The company must appoint and retain a nominated adviser (a 'Nomad') and a nominated broker. The Nomad is required to make

---

[67]   See **7.5**.
[68]   LR 2.2.15R.
[69]   See **19.3**.

a declaration to the Exchange that it considers an applicant company and its shares to be appropriate for admission to trading on AIM.

(5) The company must state that it has sufficient working capital to meet its requirements for the 12 months following its date of admission to AIM.

(6) The company must accept continuing obligations with regard to such matters as preparation of accounts, completion of transfers of securities and dealings in securities by directors and employees.

The Exchange does not impose any minimum requirements for market capitalisation, trading record, share price or shares in public hands ('free float'), and the Exchange does not make the decision as to whether a company is suitable for admission to AIM – this responsibility is placed on the Nomad.[70]

19.7 OFFERS OF SECURITIES OTHERWISE THAN THROUGH THE LONDON STOCK EXCHANGE

A company is not obliged to seek admission to one of the markets of the London Stock Exchange in connection with an offer of its securities. Securities can be offered and traded without having been first admitted to a formal market. This form of trading in securities is sometimes described as 'over the counter' trading (although in modern trading conditions, such transactions are more likely to be concluded via telephone and computer links than face to face). An advantage of having securities admitted to a formal market is that this can facilitate trading in them by the widest possible range of investors and thus enhance the liquidity of the securities. Admission of its securities to a formal market can also increase a company's status and make it easier for it to raise capital from other sources. In return for these advantages, however, the company is likely to have to agree to abide by certain continuing obligations imposed by the FSA and will certainly have to incur the expense of admission and membership fees.

A company which has had its securities admitted to an overseas market can offer those securities to investors in the UK without also seeking to have the securities admitted to trading on the London Stock Exchange. For example, specialised debt securities which are targeted mainly at professional investors (eg Eurobonds) are commonly listed on the Luxembourg Stock Exchange but offered to investors in the City of London and elsewhere throughout the world without being formally admitted to any other market. Such offers are generally structured so as to

---

[70] See generally *A guide to AIM* at http://www.londonstockexchange.com/companies-and-advisors/aim/publications/documents/a-guide-to-aim.pdf (6 July 2011).

fall outside the definition of a public offer[71], thereby avoiding the requirement to produce a prospectus.

One effect of the programme of harmonisation of requirements for the public offering and listing of securities in the laws of the member states of the European Union is that it is becoming increasingly easier for a company to offer securities that are listed on an Exchange in one state to investors in other states.[72] This provides opportunities for competition between Exchanges in different countries for listing business.

19.8 'OFFERS FOR SUBSCRIPTION' AND 'OFFERS FOR SALE'

A large-scale issue to the general investing public can take one of two forms. A direct offer to the public (known as an 'offer for subscription' or a 'prospectus offer') was the traditional method of making a large-scale public issue. Where it is used, investors subscribe for shares to be allotted directly by the company. The issuing house advises and helps to arrange the issue, including underwriting and sub-underwriting arrangements. Today, however, this method is rarely used when a company offers its securities to the public for the first time, although subsequent capital-raising exercises through rights issues commonly adopt this form. The more usual method of large-scale initial public issue takes the form of an 'offer for sale'. Here the whole of the shares in issue are normally taken up by an issuing house which then itself offers them to the public for purchase. The issuing house, not the company, takes prime responsibility for the success of the issue. Since the shares are allotted to it, the issuing house acts as a principal rather than agent (of the issuer) and will need to arrange for its own risk to be underwritten. The issuing house does not become a registered holder of the shares it agrees to purchase. Indeed, it is common for the company to issue the renounceable allotment letters[73] not to the issuing house but directly to those who purchase the shares from the issuing house.

19.9 PLACINGS, INTERMEDIARIES OFFERS, RIGHTS ISSUES AND OPEN OFFERS

The incidental costs of making an offer for sale or for subscription (including underwriting fees, advertising expenses and publicity costs, and legal and financial advisers' fees) can be very large. For a company that wants to raise a relatively small amount of capital by way of an offer of shares, these costs may be prohibitive. An appropriate method of marketing for smaller offers may be a placing. A placing is a marketing of securities to a limited class of persons (eg clients of the issuing house

---

[71] See **19.21**.
[72] See further **19.1**.
[73] See **7.8**.

which is sponsoring the issue).[74] It does not involve an offer to the public at large,[75] with the result that publicity expenses and advertising costs can be kept relatively low in comparison to an offer for sale or for subscription. An intermediaries offer is essentially a variant form of placing involving the marketing of the securities to the clients of a number of financial intermediaries.[76] Placings are now commonly carried out through the process of 'bookbuilding'. This involves investors providing indications to an issuer's financial adviser as to their take up of the offer at different (theoretical) price levels. This information is then used to set the actual price for the offer.

A rights issue is an issue to the existing members of the company which gives them the right to subscribe in proportion to their existing holding of shares in the company (or of the class of shares involved). This is now the most common method for companies already listed to raise new capital, although the amounts raised by such issues individually are much less than in the case of initial public offers.[77]

The shares are usually offered to the existing shareholders by means of renounceable letters or other negotiable instruments.[78] Existing shareholders may take up their rights or renounce them in whole or in part. A shareholder can choose to renounce the offer but still take advantage of the discount element normally included in the rights issue price. In effect, the renouncing shareholder sells the value of the right which was offered to him.[79] Provided the rights issue is at a discount to the market price of the company's existing shares, a purchaser may be prepared to pay the existing shareholder for this right. Inexperienced investors may not appreciate that they can, by selling their rights, secure the financial equivalent of the discount that is offered to investors who take up the rights issue. To guard against this, the *Listing Rules* contain a protective provision requiring rights which are not taken up to be sold on the market for the benefit of the existing shareholders who were entitled to them.[80]

---

[74]　*Listing Rules*, LR App 1.1.
[75]　See the definition of a public offer at **19.21**.
[76]　*Listing Rules*, LR App 1.1.
[77]　As to the Stock Exchange requirements, see the *Listing Rules*, LR 9.5.
[78]　In which case the *Listing Rules* require that shareholders be given a minimum of 10 business days to accept the offer: LR 9.5.6R. The open period for acceptance of the offer was reduced following the recommendation of the Rights Issue Review Group (RIRG) which reported to the Treasury in 2008. See UK Treasury, 'A Report to the Chancellor of the Exchequer by the Rights Review Group' (2008).
[78]　www.hm-treasury.gov.uk/prebud_pbr08_rightsissues.htm (7 April 2009). The statutory period for acceptance of a rights offer was reduced from 21 to 14 days in 2009: see s 562 of the Companies Act 2006 as amended by the Companies (Share Capital and Acquisition by a Company of its Own Shares) Regulations 2009, SI 2009/2022, reg 2.
[79]　The market is said to be in 'nil paid rights'.
[80]　*Listing Rules*, LR 9.5.4R. But if the premium obtained over the subscription price (net of expenses) does not exceed £5 for an existing holder, the proceeds may be retained for the company's benefit.

Where a listed company wants to raise new capital through an issue of its ordinary shares, it is *prima facie* obliged by s 561 of the Companies Act 2006[81] to do so by means of a rights issue in favour of its existing shareholders. This obligation can be disapplied. A public company is permitted to disapply the statutory pre-emption requirement by power given by the articles[82] or a special resolution[83] for a period of up to five years.[84] Under Pre-emption Guidelines agreed between representatives of companies, institutional investors and the London Stock Exchange, there are limits on the amount of securities that may be included in a special resolution disapplying s 561. The Pre-emption Guidelines are not formal regulatory rules but companies have the assurance that a disapplication resolution which complies with those guidelines will be supported by their institutional shareholders.

An open offer is similar to a rights issue in that it is an offer of new securities to existing investors in those securities in proportion to their existing holdings but is not made by means of a renounceable letter of allotment.[85] This form of offer means that existing shareholders who do not take up the offer will suffer dilution without compensation, whereas in a rights offer they will be compensated by sale of their 'nil paid rights'. An open offer may also operate on the basis of a shorter timetable than a rights issue,[86] which can help to minimise costs associated with the issue, such as underwriting costs.[87]

19.10 CONVERTIBLE ISSUES

A 'convertible issue' is a term which relates not to the method of issue but to the hybrid type of security involved. In the usual form, convertible debentures are offered with the right to convert at a future date into ordinary shares. The attraction of this type of investment is that it gives the investor the security of a fixed interest security, which may be particularly important where the funding is sought to capitalise a new, and perhaps somewhat risky, venture, combined with the opportunity to convert into 'equity' shares when the success and profitability of the company is established. This characteristic makes convertible securities a common feature of financing provided by venture capital providers to

---

[81] See **7.5**.
[82] Companies Act 2006, s 570.
[83] Companies Act 2006, s 571.
[84] The 5-year limit arises from the reference in ss 570 and 571 respectively to the authorisation granted under s 551, which has a 5-year limit.
[85] *Listing Rules*, LR App 1.1 Relevant definitions.
[86] See LR 9.5.7R requiring the timetable for an open offer to be approved by the recognised investment exchange on which the shares are traded. There is no comparable requirement under the Companies Act 2006 to the 14-day open period for rights offers (see above n 78).
[87] The matter of underwriting charges in the UK capital markets has been a controversial area and the subject of a reference to the Competition Commission. On this, see *Guide to Share Issuing Good Practice for Listed Companies* (Bank of England, October 1999).

'start-up' or 'early-stage' companies. Convertible securities can only be admitted to listing if the underlying securities into which they are to be converted are already listed or will become listed.[88]

19.11   THE FUNCTION OF THE SPONSOR

In the case of companies admitted to the official list,[89] a crucial role is performed by the company's sponsor, who will normally be its corporate broker or investment bank.[90] The sponsor not only acts as financial adviser to the company but will have the task of directing the strategy of the issue and co-ordinating the activities of the other professional advisers concerned (stockbrokers, auditors, reporting accountants and solicitors). Where the securities are to be listed in London, the sponsor also has specific obligations which it owes to the FSA as the Listing Authority to ensure that the company satisfies the listing criteria and is guided through the listing process.[91] The name and good reputation of the sponsor has a considerable influence on the reception that will be given by the financial press and the stock market to the issue. This is linked with the understanding that the broker or issuing house, before it agrees to sponsor an issue, will be aware of the need to protect its reputation with the investing public, especially the institutional investors who may be involved both as underwriters and sub-underwriters and as straightforward investors.[92]

19.12   UNDERWRITING AND BOOKBUILDING

A contract of underwriting[93] is an agreement that, if the whole or a certain proportion of the issue is not applied for by the public, the underwriters will themselves apply or find persons to apply for the balance or a certain proportion of the balance of the issue. Where the underwriters undertake merely to find persons to apply for shares the remedy of the company in case of breach is in damages only.[94] Where the underwriters undertake to apply for the shares themselves, the company can hold the underwriters to their promise by placing them on the register

---

[88]   LR 2.1.12R.

[89]   An applicant for admission to AIM does not require a sponsor, but does require a nominated adviser (see **19.6**).

[90]   *Listing Rules*, LR 8 sets out the requirement to appoint a sponsor and the role of the sponsor.

[91]   See further, *Listing Rules*, LR 8.3.

[92]   See *Gore-Browne on Companies* (Jordans, 45th edn, loose-leaf) at 40[36-46] as to the initial searching inquiry that will be given by the issuing house to a company 'coming to market'.

[93]   The meaning of 'underwriting' was declared by the Court of Appeal after hearing evidence in *Re Licensed Victuallers' Mutual Trading Association* (1889) 42 Ch D 1. A modern judicial analysis of underwriting structures is provided by Hobhouse LJ in *County Ltd v Girozentrale Securities* [1996] 1 BCLC 653, at 670–673. See also *Eagle Trust plc v SBC Securities Ltd* [1995] BCC 231 (role and duties of underwriter).

[94]   See *Gorrissen's Case* (1873) 8 Ch App 507.

of members. The underwriters receive a commission whether they are called upon to take up any securities or not. The maximum amount of commission that can be paid to underwriters from the proceeds of an issue of shares is regulated by ss 552 and 553 of the Companies Act 2006.[95]

There is no legal or regulatory requirement for an issuer to enter into an underwriting agreement and it is therefore a matter of commercial judgement as to whether it is necessary. The advantage from an issuer's perspective is that the success of the issue is guaranteed but the disadvantage is the cost (over and above the other costs of an issue). Two issues are particularly relevant for the underwriting decision. The first, which is relevant in the case of a rights issue, is the scale of the discount to the prevailing market price at which new shares are offered. Where the discount is large (a 'deep-discount' issue) existing shareholders have a substantial incentive to take up the issue to avoid dilution in their shareholding, thus limiting the need for underwriting. The second, applicable to any issue, is the level of anticipated demand for the new issue. The increasing use of the 'bookbuilding' technique for new issues makes it possible to predict demand more accurately at different price levels. The process involves the publication of a prospectus in which an indicative price range is set along with the conditions for determination of the final price. Investors make binding bids for shares at specific price levels and following the determination of the final price are allocated shares by the bookrunner (typically an investment bank). Bookbuilding thus tends to maximize the price for the issuer but raises potential regulatory problems as to the manner in which the bookrunner makes allocations, especially when duties are owed both to the issuer and its own investment clients.

19.13   OFFICIAL LISTING: THE FUNCTION OF THE 'COMPETENT AUTHORITY'

Part VI of the Financial Services and Markets Act 2000 contains the regulatory framework applicable to the listing of securities. The FSA (as competent authority[96]) may admit to the official list such securities and other things as it considers appropriate.[97] The *Listing Rules* provide some examples of financial instruments that can be admitted to listing but ultimately the issue turns on whether the conditions in the *Listing Rules* relating to the relevant securities are satisfied.[98] It is not necessary for the relevant securities to be admitted to trading on a regulated market.[99]

---

[95]   See **4.18**.

[96]   As competent authority for listing under the EU directives, the FSA adopts the title of United Kingdom Listing Authority (UKLA).

[97]   Section 74(2).

[98]   See the *Listing Rules*, LR 2. The Treasury has a residual power to exclude certain types or categories of securities from official listing: s 74(3)(b) of FSMA 2000.

[99]   See above n 66.

Section 74 stipulates that no security to which the section applies may be admitted to listing except in accordance with the provisions of Part VI.

Section 73A gives the FSA the power to make 'listing rules' and it is this power which provides the statutory backing for the *Listing Rules*. The FSA has a delegated power to make law by regulating applications for listing and specifying the detailed criteria for admission to listing within widely drawn enabling provisions of the Act. In performing this rule-making function, the FSA must as a matter of EU law comply with the EU directives relating to listing.[100]

While in the past rules made by the competent authority were referred to simply as 'listing rules', they are now split into three separate parts: 'Listing Rules' applicable to the Official List; 'Disclosure and Transparency Rules' applicable to financial instruments admitted to trading on a regulated market or for which a request for admission has been made; and 'Prospectus Rules' relating to transferable securities. The competent authority is also responsible for monitoring compliance with corporate governance statements derived from the EU directives[101] and the UK Corporate Governance Code, although responsibility for formulation of the Codes rests with other bodies.[102]

19.14   APPLICATION FOR LISTING

Section 75 deals with applications for listing. These must be made to the FSA as the UK Listing Authority 'in such manner as may be required by listing rules'. Section 75 also prohibits an application for listing of any securities except 'by or with the consent of the issuer of the securities concerned'. 'Issuer' is defined as the person by whom the securities have been or are to be issued.[103] Where, for example, an investment institution which owns a substantial holding of shares or other securities in a public company seeks a listing for these securities, this requires the consent of the company.

Section 75 also defines the responsibilities of the FSA for 'vetting' applications for listing. It provides for admission to official listing only if the *Listing Rules* and other requirements are complied with and specifies the circumstances in which an application for listing may or must be refused. The FSA may refuse an application if it considers that the admission of the securities would be detrimental to the interests of

---

[100] The Secretary of State, however, has preserved a power to enable him to ensure that international obligations are complied with. See s 410.

[101] In particular the Fourth Company Law Directive (78/660/EEC [1978] OJ L222/11) as amended by the Directive on Company Reporting (2006/46/EC [2006] OJ L224/1). See **2.3.5**.

[102] In the UK, the Financial Reporting Council.

[103] Regulation 4 of the FSMA 2000 (Official Listing of Securities) Regulations 2001, SI 2001/2956.

investors because of any matters relating to the issuer.[104] An application may also be refused where the issuer has failed to comply with listing obligations imposed by another member state when the securities are already listed there.[105]

A decision must be notified to the applicant within 6 months of the date of its receipt. Where the applicant has been required to give further information, the 6-month period will run from the time when the information is supplied. Where the FSA fails to notify within this period, it is 'taken to have refused the application'.[106]

A refusal by the FSA to admit securities to listing may be referred by the applicant to the Upper Tribunal,[107] which is empowered to direct the FSA as to the action to be taken.[108] A party to a reference to the Tribunal may with permission appeal to the Court of Appeal (in Scotland, the Court of Session) on a point of law arising from a decision of the Tribunal.[109]

The FSA has the power to discontinue and suspend listing.[110] This is obviously an important weapon in enforcing compliance with its rules relating to original admission to listing as well as to continuous reporting and dealing requirements. One of the grounds on which listing will be cancelled is where the securities in question are no longer admitted to trading on a recognised investment exchange's market for listed securities.[111]

19.15   PART VI PROSPECTUSES AND LISTING PARTICULARS

Section 85 of FSMA 2000 requires, as a condition of admission of securities to trading on a regulated market situated or operating in the UK, the production, approval and publication of a prospectus. A prospectus is also required where securities are to be offered to the public

---

[104]   Section 75(5) of FSMA 2000.

[105]   Section 75(6) of FSMA 2000.

[106]   Section 76 and the *Listing Rules*, LR 2.

[107]   Section 76(6). Part IX sets out the powers and procedure of the tribunal. The Financial Services and Markets Tribunal was replaced by the Upper Tribunal in April 2010.

[108]   Section 133(4). The tribunal is able to consider any evidence, whether or not it was available to the FSA at the material time: s133(3).

[109]   Section 137. However, no actions for damages will lie against the FSA or its members, officers or employees for any thing done or omitted in good faith in discharge of their functions: s 102.

[110]   Section 77. Securities whose listing is suspended under this section are to be treated for the purposes of ss 96 (obligations of issuers) and 99 (fees payable to the competent authority) as still being listed.

[111]   See the *Listing Rules*, LR 2.2.3R.

in the UK. In both instances the obligation applies only to 'transferable securities'.[112] It does not apply to an 'exempt offer'.[113]

As mentioned earlier (**19.1**), it is possible for securities to be admitted to the official list in the UK without being admitted to trading on a regulated market. As the requirement for a prospectus arises only when a public offer is made or admission to trading on a regulated market occurs, there is no requirement for a prospectus in those circumstances. However, s 79 of FSMA 2000 deals with this situation by requiring the publication of approved listing particulars. This procedure is mainly relevant for specialist securities that are to be traded on the Professional Securities Market, which is a 'multilateral trading facility' and not a 'regulated market' for the purposes of the EU directives. The result is that the FSA is free to set the requirements for listing and continuing obligations applicable to this market. The distribution of such specialist securities is normally undertaken in a manner which falls outside the definition of an 'offer to the public' (eg by being made exclusively to 'qualified investors').

The detailed requirements concerning the contents of listing particulars and prospectuses are set out in the FSA *Prospectus Rules*.[114] A prospectus must include a mass of information about the applicant and its share capital, and financial information about the applicant as well as its recent development and prospects. Information is also required about the applicant's group structure and its management. These detailed requirements are derived from and follow exactly the provisions of the Prospectus Directive and its implementing regulation.[115] Following implementation of the Prospectus Directive, it is possible for a prospectus to be either a single document or three separate documents comprising: a registration document relating to the issuer; a securities note relating to the securities to be listed or offered; and a summary.[116] Moreover, it is possible for a registration document that has already been approved to be used for a subsequent listing or public offer provided any material changes are disclosed in the securities note. In that case, the securities note

---

[112] Note that the definition of transferable securities differs as between a prospectus for the purposes of a public offer and one for the purposes of admission to trading: see **19.21** below.

[113] See **19.21** for exemptions under s 86 FSMA 2000. The Prospectus Rules (PR1.2) provide for further exemptions pursuant to s 85(6)(b) FSMA 2000. They include (1) admission to trading of shares representing, over a period of 12 months, less than 10 per cent of the same class already admitted to trading on the same regulated market and (2) public offers and admission to trading of transferable securities offered in connection with a takeover by means of an exchange offer if a document is available containing information which is regarded by the FSA as equivalent to a prospectus.

[114] See FSA Handbook, *Prospectus Rules* (PR).

[115] As mentioned earlier, the Prospectus Directive is a maximum harmonisation directive and therefore does not permit member states to create 'superequivalents' (or exceptions) within its field of application. This approach does not apply to requirements for admission to listing or continuing obligations, leaving member states greater freedom of action in those areas.

[116] See FSA *Prospectus Rules*, PR 2.2.

and summary still require approval. The content of listing particulars is based on the requirements applicable to a prospectus in respect of the same type of securities.[117] The rationale is that the two documents serve very similar regulatory purposes, although from a legal perspective a prospectus offering shares is very different to listing particulars because it forms the basis of a contract for the sale of shares, while listing on its own is no more than a regulatory process.

Since listing particulars and prospectuses are subject to virtually the same rules governing their form and content, it can appear that little of substance turns on the fact that in some cases the applicant must produce a prospectus whilst in others it must produce listing particulars. The consequences of failing to provide all of the required information, or of providing false or misleading information, are the same in either case.[118] Where the distinction matters is in relation to the persons who can be held liable for inaccurate or incomplete information in the document. If the document is a set of listing particulars the following are potentially liable: the issuer; directors of the issuer; any person who accepts and is stated in the particulars as accepting responsibility; and any person who has authorised the contents of the particulars.[119] If the document is a prospectus, the offeror is, in addition to the persons just mentioned, also potentially liable.[120] It is possible that some offerors of securities may play little part in preparing the prospectus, for example where they are employees of a company who are offering their shares in the company for sale in conjunction with an offer of new shares by the company itself. The potential unfairness of holding people responsible for information over which they had no control is dealt with by a provision to the effect that an offeror will not be responsible where he makes an offer in association with the issuer and where the documentation is drawn up primarily by the issuer or by a person acting on the issuer's behalf.[121]

Another distinction between a prospectus and listing particulars is that the sanctions for contravention of the relevant provisions differ. In the case of a prospectus, a contravention of s 85 of FSMA 2000 is a criminal offence and is actionable as a breach of statutory duty by a person who suffers loss.[122] In the case of listing particulars, there are no equivalent provisions although the FSA is able to suspend trading in securities on a

---

[117] See *Listing Rules*, LR 4.2.
[118] Section 90 of FSMA 2000.
[119] Regulation 6 of the FSMA 2000 (Official Listing of Securities) Regulations 2001, SI 2001/2956 (listing particulars) and Prospectus Rules, PR 5.5 (prospectuses).
[120] *Prospectus Rules*, PR 5.5.
[121] *Prospectus Rules*, PR 5.5.7R.
[122] See ss 85(3) and (4) of FSMA 2000 respectively.

regulated market,[123] publish a public censure of an issuer[124] and possibly also of a sponsor[125] who has failed to meet the relevant requirements.

19.16 THE ISSUER'S GENERAL DUTY TO DISCLOSE

In addition to the information specified by the *Listing Rules* or otherwise required by the FSA, s 80 of FSMA 2000 imposes an overriding duty of disclosure in respect of what must be contained in any listing particulars submitted under s 79. A similar duty of disclosure also applies in relation to a prospectus required by s 85.[126] The duty is imposed on those responsible for the listing particulars or prospectus.[127] The listing particulars must contain 'all such information' as investors and their professional advisers would reasonably require, and reasonably expect to find there, for the purpose of making an informed assessment of: (a) the assets and liabilities, financial position, profits and losses, and prospects of the issuer of the securities; and (b) the rights attached to the relevant securities.[128] A qualification to this general obligation is that what is required is information 'which is within the knowledge of any person responsible for the listing particulars or which it would be reasonable for him to obtain by making inquiries'.[129] As a further guide, it is provided[130] that in determining what information is required to be included in listing particulars by virtue of s 80, regard is to be had to the following factors. These are, first, the nature of the securities and of the issuer; secondly, the nature of the persons likely to consider their acquisition (e g professional investment managers). The third factor is the fact that certain matters may reasonably be expected to be within the knowledge of professional advisers of any kind which those persons may reasonably be expected to consult.[131] It would seem that this provision is intended to indicate that if professional investment advisers receive more detailed documentation appropriate to their skills and level of understanding, the ordinary investors for whom they act may receive simpler documentation which they will be more likely to comprehend. Provision is made for the FSA to exempt from the obligation to disclose in the prospectus, listing particulars or supplementary documents on the ground that the disclosure of certain information would either be contrary to the public

---

[123] Section 87L of FSMA 2000. The power of suspension can be exercised on mere suspicion of a breach and can also be used to suspend a request for admission to trading.

[124] Section 87M of FSMA 2000.

[125] Section 89 of FSMA 2000.

[126] See s 87A of FSMA 2000.

[127] Section 80(1) does not state expressly on whom the duty is imposed, but this is the implication of s 80(3).

[128] Section 80(1).

[129] Section 80(3).

[130] Section 80(4). Regard must also be had to information which the FSA has required to be made available (or itself made available) under s 96.

[131] Regard must also be had to information which the FSA has required to be made available (or itself made available) under s 96.

interest or would be seriously detrimental to the issuer of the securities or is unnecessary in the particular circumstances.[132] In the latter case, the FSA may not exempt essential information from the obligation of disclosure.[133]

19.17   SUPPLEMENTARY PART VI LISTING PARTICULARS

In the United States federal securities law administered by the SEC, there is a policy of 'continuous disclosure'[134] in respect of publicly issued prospectuses, on the ground that securities issued thereunder will continue to be sold and resold in a market influenced by the publicly issued prospectus. For reason of costs and administrative burden, the Financial Services and Markets Act 2000 does not go that far, but it does in certain circumstances require a document called, as the case may be, a supplementary prospectus or supplementary listing particulars to be issued before the commencement of dealings in the securities (ie after their admission to the Official List).[135] The circumstances are a significant change in any matter required to be in the listing particulars or the emergence of a significant[136] new matter which would have been disclosed had it arisen at the time of preparation of the listing particulars. The supplementary listing particulars must be submitted in advance to the FSA for its approval in accordance with the *Listing Rules*.[137]

19.18   APPROVAL OF PART VI PROSPECTUSES AND LISTING PARTICULARS

Independent pre-publication approval of the information contained in a prospectus or set of listing particulars can be an important safeguard for investors.[138] It can help to ensure that all of the required information has been included and that the information has not been stated in a way which is likely to create a false impression. Knowing that the information will be subject to vetting may also serve to deter those who would otherwise have been tempted deliberately to mislead or to conceal information. Professor

---

[132]   Sections 82(1) and 87B(1).

[133]   Sections 82(2) and 87B(1)(c).

[134]   In the case of listed securities in the UK there is of course the Interim Reports Directive (now consolidated in the Transparency Obligations Directive , as described in **19.1**) and the disclosure requirements derived from MAD in the *Disclosure and Transparency Rules (DTR)* .

[135]   Sections 81 and 87G.

[136]   'Significant' means significant for the purpose of making an informed assessment of the matters required to be disclosed under s 80(1) (listing particulars) or 87A(2) (a prospectus).

[137]   Section 81(3) provides a defence where the issuer or the person responsible for the listing particulars is unaware of the change or the new matter.

[138]   Gower, *Review of Investor Protection* (Cmnd 9123, 1984), Part I, paras 9.16–9.23 and Part II, paras 6.10–6.12.

Gower described the vetting role played, at that time, by the London Stock Exchange as being 'in practice, a more effective protection to investors than the legal sanctions'.[139] Notwithstanding those benefits, there are limits to the vetting that that is undertaken by the FSA. It is not a means of auditing or verifying the truthfulness of the information contained in a prospectus. Nor does it in any way provide any indication of the merits of the relevant securities as an investment: this follows from the general approach referred to earlier (see **19.1**) whereby mandatory disclosure is the dominant principle underlying the system of securities regulation both in the EU and UK. Furthermore, the FSA in its role as the competent authority enjoys an exemption from liability which means that the standard of diligence required from it in respect of its role as competent authority cannot be compared directly with that required from other 'gatekeepers' involved in the process of listing and the making of public offers (eg auditors, bankers, lawyers and stockbrokers) who face the threat of legal liability.

Under ss 75 and 85 of FSMA 2000, as supplemented by the *Listing Rules*, the documents must be submitted in draft to the FSA as the UK Listing Authority and must be formally approved by the FSA prior to publication.[140]

After a prospectus is approved by the FSA, it must be filed with the FSA and made available to the public.[141] The methods of making the prospectus available to the public are set out in the FSA *Prospectus Rules* and allow for the possibility of making it available in electronic form, although investors have the right to request and to receive free of charge a paper copy.

19.19 POWER TO CONTROL INFORMATION

The FSA acting as the UK Listing Authority is given a general power to specify in the *Listing Rules* the requirements to be complied with by the issuers of listed securities. It may also specify the sanctions or measures it will take in the event of non-compliance. This may include publishing the fact that the issuer has broken the rules. The issuer may be required to publish any information and the FSA itself may be authorised to do so if the issuer fails to do so.[142]

---

[139] *Review of Investor Protection*, Part I, para 9.12.

[140] *Listing Rules*, LR 3.2 and *Prospectus Rules*, PR 3.1.

[141] *Prospectus Rules*, PR 3.2.1R. The obligation to file a copy of a prospectus or listing particulars with the Registrar of Companies before publication, previously contained in s 83 of FSMA 2000, was repealed on the implementation of the Prospectus Directive.

[142] Section 96. Although this section refers to 'listing rules' it applies to issuers of listed securities and therefore the FSA *Prospectus Rules* (PR) and *Disclosure and Transparency Rules* (DTR) may also be taken to be within its scope.

The provisions previously contained in s 98 of FSMA 2000 providing for approval by the FSA of advertisements issued in connection with a public offer or listing have been replaced following implementation of the Prospectus Directive. Under the new rules[143] there is a prohibition on the publication of an advertisement unless:

(1)   it states that a prospectus has been or will be published and indicates where investors are, or will be, able to obtain it;

(2)   it is clearly recognisable as an advertisement;

(3)   information in the advertisement is not inaccurate, or misleading; and

(4)   information in the advertisement is consistent with the information contained in the prospectus, if already published, or with the information required to be in the prospectus, if the prospectus is published afterwards.

Moreover, all information concerning an offer or an admission to trading disclosed in an oral or written form (even if not for advertising purposes), must be consistent with that contained in the prospectus.

Where the publication of a prospectus is required, the securities must not be offered to the public in advance of publication of the prospectus.[144] Contravention of this prohibition is an offence and is also actionable at the suit of any person who suffers loss as a consequence, subject to the defences and other incidents applying to actions for breach of statutory duty.[145]

19.20   PUBLIC OFFERS OF UNLISTED SECURITIES

Following the implementation of the Prospectus Directive public offers of unlisted securities (i.e. those not admitted to the 'Official List') are regulated in the same manner as public offers for listed securities. This represents a rationalisation of the position which existed under the Public Offers Directive, according to which public offers for listed securities were regulated by Part VI of FSMA 2000 while public offers of unlisted securities were regulated by the Public Offers of Securities Regulations 1995.[146] The circumstances in which a prospectus is required for a public offer of unlisted securities are now therefore the same as in the case of listed securities which are discussed at **19.15** above. The same conclusion applies to the sanctions for failing to publish an approved prospectus when it is required: this is equally a criminal offence in respect

---

[143]   See the *Prospectus Rules*, PR 3.3.
[144]   Section 85(1).
[145]   Section 85(4).
[146]   SI 1995/1537.

of unlisted securities and an action for breach of statutory duty is available to a person who suffers loss as a result of the contravention.[147]

19.21 AN 'OFFER TO THE PUBLIC' OF 'SECURITIES'

The making of an offer to the public of transferable securities in the UK triggers the obligation under s 85 of FSMA 2000 to publish a prospectus (irrespective of whether or not the securities are to be listed). In determining whether an offer falls within the scope of s 85, several points need to be considered. First, the nature of the communication must amount to an offer (as defined) and be made to the public. Secondly, the securities must be 'transferable securities'. Thirdly, the offer will not fall within s 85 if it is an 'exempt offer'. Each of these matters is now considered in turn.

For the purposes of Part VI, there is an offer of transferable securities to the public if there is a communication to any person which presents sufficient information on the securities to be offered and the terms on which they are offered to enable an investor to decide to buy or subscribe for the securities in question.[148] This definition is broader than the established definition of an offer in the law of contract and can extend to a series of communications which in aggregate deliver the required information even if none were envisaged as a formal offer. A person is to be regarded as offering securities to the public in the UK if he offers them to any person in the UK.[149] This precludes any argument that there is not a *prima facie* obligation to produce a prospectus in respect of a placing of securities or a rights issue: it cannot be said that the offer, in either case, is not an offer to the public simply because it is made to a section of the public rather than to the public at large. However, whether in a particular case a prospectus is required will also depend on the other elements of the definition of an offer to the public.

The definition of 'transferable securities' for the purposes of the requirement to produce a prospectus in connection with a public offer follows the Markets in Financial Instruments Directive[150] definition subject to the exceptions established by Sch 11A to FSMA 2000.[151] Among these, the exception relating to securities in an offer where the total consideration is less than €5m (or an equivalent amount) is significant in limiting the costs of offers made by smaller companies (by dispensing with the need for a prospectus).[152] Reflecting the scope of the

---

[147] Sections 85(3) and (4) respectively of FSMA 2000.
[148] Section 102B of FSMA 2000.
[149] Section 102B of FSMA 2000. Note that the definition of a public offer for the purposes of Part VI differs from that which applies for the purposes of Part 20, Chapter 1 of the Companies Act 2006 (Prohibition of Public Offers by Private Companies): see **19.3**.
[150] Directive 2004/39/EC [2004] OJ L145/1.
[151] See s 85 and 102A of FSMA 2000.
[152] The threshold was raised from €2.5m by reg 2(3) of the Prospectus Regulations 2011,

underlying Directive,[153] the definition of transferable securities excludes bonus shares, that is shares issued on a fully paid basis to existing shareholders; shares issued as a form of dividend payment;[154] transferable securities offered in connection with a takeover bid or merger;[155] and shares or debentures offered by employers to employees or former employees or members of their families.[156] The exceptions applicable to the definition of 'transferable securities' for the purposes of the requirement to produce a prospectus in connection with admission to trading on a regulated market are more narrowly defined.[157]

There are five categories of exempt offer identified by s 86 of FSMA 2000. They are as follows:

(1)   the offer is made to or directed at qualified investors[158] only;

(2)   the offer is made to or directed at fewer than 150 persons, other than qualified investors, per EEA state;[159]

(3)   the minimum consideration which may be paid by any person for transferable securities acquired by him pursuant to the offer is at least €50,000 (or an equivalent amount);

(4)   the transferable securities being offered are denominated in amounts of at least €50,000 (or equivalent amounts); or

(5)   the total consideration for the transferable securities being offered cannot exceed €100,000 (or an equivalent amount).[160]

SI 2011/1668, implementing Directive 2010/73/EU) with effect from 31 July 2011. See HM Treasury Consultation on early implementation of amendments to the Prospectus Directive (March 2011).

[153] See Art 4(1).

[154] Normally referred to as 'scrip dividends'.

[155] In which case the FSA must regard the takeover document as equivalent to a prospectus.

[156] See the *Prospectus Rules*, PR 1.2.2R for these exceptions.

[157] They are contained in Part 1 of Sch 11A to FSMA 2000 and the FSA *Prospectus Rules*, PR 1.2.3.

[158] See the definition in s 86(7). All legal entities authorised by the FSA are included within the definition. Section 86(2) makes clear that a qualified investor who is an investment manager with discretion to make investment decisions on behalf of his clients can remain within the exception if he accepts the offer on behalf of his clients. In other words, the offer is *not* treated in those circumstances as being made to the underlying clients.

[159] The threshold was raised from 100 persons by reg 2(2) of the Prospectus Regulations 2011, SI 2011/1668, implementing Directive 2010/73/EU) with effect from 31 July 2011. See HM Treasury Consultation on early implementation of amendments to the Prospectus Directive (March 2011).

[160] This exemption must apply to securities other than those falling within the €2.5m exemption in para 9 Sch 11A FSMA 2000, since such securities cannot by definition be 'transferable'.

For the moment, it suffices to note that an offer of shares for sale or subscription would be unlikely to fall within an exemption. With regard to placings, it will often be possible to fall within the exemption provided by the 100-person limit, since that excludes qualified investors and many offerees will be qualified investors. A typical rights issue made by a listed company will usually be too large to benefit from any of the exemptions.

19.22   FORM AND CONTENT OF PROSPECTUSES

Where a prospectus is required, its form and content must comply with the requirements set out in the FSA *Prospectus Rules*. The information required to be included relates to the issuer and its capital, financial position, activities and organisation, the offeror (if different from the issuer), the persons responsible for the prospectus, the securities and the offer.[161] The information in a prospectus must be presented in a manner which is comprehensible, easy to analyse and takes account of the particular nature of the securities and the issuer.[162]

There is an overriding duty of disclosure which is very similar to, but not precisely the same as, the duty of disclosure imposed by s 80 of FSMA 2000 in respect of listing particulars.[163] Under s 87A, a prospectus must contain the information necessary to enable investors to make an informed assessment of the assets and liabilities, financial position, profits and losses and prospects of the issuer and of the rights attaching to the securities. In determining the information required to satisfy the overriding duty of disclosure, regard is to be had to the nature of the securities and of the issuer;[164] and the duty is qualified to the extent that it is only information which is within the knowledge of the persons responsible for the prospectus, or which it would be reasonable for them to obtain by making inquiries, that must be disclosed.[165] As permitted by the Directive, Part VI of FSMA 2000 makes provision for the modification of the information required to be included in a prospectus in particular circumstances.[166] In those circumstances the offeror must make

---

[161] These detailed requirements (derived from Prospectus Directive Regulation 2004/809/EC [2004] OJ L149/1) are set out in the FSA *Prospectus Rules*, PR 2.3.

[162] *Prospectus Rules*, PR 2.1.1, replicating ss 87A(3) and (4) of FSMA 2000.

[163] See **19.16**.

[164] Section 87A(4).

[165] Section 90(11)(a) of and Sch 10 to FSMA 2000. However, unlike s 80 (applicable to listing particulars), in determining the information required to be included, there is no express provision permitting account to be taken of the nature of the persons likely to consider the acquisition of the securities, or the fact that certain matters may reasonably be expected to be already within the knowledge of professional advisers of any kind which likely investors could be reasonably expected to consult. This may have the effect of imposing a heavier onus of disclosure in the case of a prospectus than in the case of listing particulars. See further **19.16**.

[166] Section 87B.

a written application to the FSA setting out the case for modification or exclusion of the relevant information.[167]

19.23   SUPPLEMENTARY PROSPECTUSES

Where a prospectus has been approved in respect of an offer of securities and an agreement in respect of those securities can still be entered into in pursuance of the offer or admission to trading has not yet occurred there may be a need to publish one or more supplementary prospectuses. This need arises if, during the relevant period (above), there is a significant[168] change affecting any matter contained in the prospectus which was required to be included, a significant[169] new matter arises which would have been so required if it had arisen when the prospectus was prepared, or there is a significant inaccuracy in the prospectus.[170] However, where the person who delivered the prospectus for registration is unaware of the matter which gives rise to the need for a supplementary prospectus, he is under no duty to comply unless he is informed of it by a person who is responsible for the prospectus; any person who is responsible for the prospectus is under a duty to provide the relevant notification.[171] Following publication of a supplementary prospectus, an investor has 2 days in which to withdraw an acceptance (of an offer in the original prospectus) made before publication of the supplementary prospectus.[172]

19.24   REGULATION OF INVITATIONS TO ENGAGE IN INVESTMENT ACTIVITY UNDER THE FINANCIAL SERVICES AND MARKETS ACT 2000

Apart from the regulation of prospectuses and listing particulars, another way in which the regulatory structure seeks to filter out unsuitable investment information is through s 21 of the Financial Services and Markets Act 2000, which establishes the so-called 'financial promotion' regime. Under this section, invitations (including advertisements) or inducements to engage in investment business which are issued in the UK must be issued by, or with the approval of, authorised persons. Authorised persons must comply with the FSA's Conduct of Business Rules when issuing, or approving for issue, investment advertisements. The responsibility so imposed on authorised persons acts as a safeguard against invitations or inducements containing false or misleading information or failing to provide adequate information. The expression

---

[167] *Prospectus Rules*, PR 2.5.3.
[168] Defined by s 87G(4) as significant for the purposes of making an informed assessment of the kind mentioned in s 87A(2).
[169] Ibid.
[170] The last of these does not have an equivalent in s 81 of the Financial Services and Markets Act 2000 (supplementary listing particulars).
[171] Section 87G(5).
[172] Section 87Q(4) of FSMA 2000.

'engage in investment activity' is defined by reference to 'controlled activities' which are defined in subordinate legislation[173] and it would certainly include an advertisement containing an offer of securities. Thus, an offer of unlisted securities which, for some reason relating either to the nature of the securities or the type of offer, is not subject to s 85 of FSMA 2000 does not necessarily escape from the regulatory net, since it may be caught in any event by s 21. Contravention of s 21 is an offence and an agreement entered into in breach of the section may be unenforceable, with the innocent party being entitled to recover any money or property he has parted with as well as compensation.[174]

Section 21 is subject to a number of exemptions. Particularly important exemptions in the context of public offers of securities are those which relate to prospectuses, listing particulars and associated documents. As well as catching invitations and inducements that would not otherwise be regulated, s 21 also *prima facie* brings within its scope prospectuses and listing particulars which are subject to the requirements of Part VI of FSMA 2000 and associated FSA rules. A requirement to comply with s 21 as well as Part VI could be regarded as amounting to excessive regulation and this result is prevented by appropriate exemptions: listing particulars, supplementary listing particulars, prospectuses, supplementary prospectuses and other advertisements relating to listed securities published with the approval of the FSA or in accordance with the *Listing Rules* are exempt from s 21.[175]

19.25 MUTUAL RECOGNITION OF PROSPECTUSES AND LISTING PARTICULARS IN MEMBER STATES OF THE EUROPEAN COMMUNITY

With a view to encouraging the development of a pan-European capital market, the member states of the EU have adopted mutual recognition provisions. These allow securities to be offered, or admitted to trading on a regulated market, in a number of member states on the basis of a prospectus which has satisfied the requirements imposed by one of those states. Satisfying the requirements of one state can thus be said to act as a passport for the offering or listing of the relevant securities in other member states. Under European law, mutual recognition is governed by Arts 17 and 18 of the Prospectus Directive. Section 87H of FSMA 2000 makes provision for the recognition in the UK of prospectuses approved in other member states. Following the virtual demise of the concept of 'official listing' in the Prospectus Directive and the broadening of the function of a prospectus to encompass the role that had previously been

---

[173] Section 21(8) and the FSMA 2000 (Financial Promotion) Order 2005, SI 2005/1529 (as amended). Note that, while there is considerable overlap, 'controlled activities' are not the same as 'regulated activities'.

[174] Section 30. Note that there is nothing to stop a customer holding the other party to the contract.

[175] Regulations 70 and 71 of the Financial Promotion Order 2005, SI 2005/1529.

played by listing particulars, there are no longer mutual recognition provisions relating to listing particulars.[176] In the UK listing particulars remain relevant for the purposes of the Professional Securities Market[177] and must be approved by the FSA.[178] There is no provision in respect of listing particulars equivalent to s 87H (above).

To qualify for use as a passport throughout the Community, a prospectus must first be approved in one member state. This poses a difficulty in the UK in relation to prospectuses relating to unlisted securities which are not admitted to trading on a regulated market, because they are not required to be vetted or approved by an independent authority prior to publication. To ensure that companies do not have to seek a listing solely in order to benefit from the mutual recognition provisions, s 87 of FSMA 2000 makes provision for the submission to, and the approval by, the FSA as the UK Listing Authority of prospectuses which would not otherwise require approval. The s 87 procedure can be used only where the UK is one of the member states in which the securities are to be offered, but it is not restricted to companies having their registered office in the UK or another member state. An application under s 87 does not amount to an application for listing and the costs involved should be much smaller than those incurred in seeking a full listing.

19.26 REMEDIES FOR FALSE, MISLEADING OR INCOMPLETE STATEMENTS IN CONNECTION WITH PROSPECTUSES OR LISTING PARTICULARS

Part VI of the Financial Services and Markets Act 2000 provides a single type of statutory remedy in respect of three distinct situations, namely:

(1) the inclusion of false or misleading information in a prospectus or set of listing particulars (including supplementary prospectuses and listing particulars);

(2) failure to disclose the information required to be included in a prospectus or set of listing particulars (including supplementary prospectuses and listing particulars); and

(3) failure to publish, when required, a supplementary prospectus or set of listing particulars.

---

[176] The PD repealed the relevant provisions (Arts 38-41) of the CARD.

[177] The Professional Securities Market is not a regulated market for the purposes of the Prospectus or MiFID Directives: it is a 'multilateral trading facility' under Art 4(1) of MiFID.

[178] *Listing Rules*, LR 2.2.11(2)R. Publication is also required.

Various other remedies for deceit, misrepresentation and negligence must also be considered since they are applicable to offers which fall outside Part VI and to statements made otherwise than in prospectuses, listing particulars and related documents. These remedies are also potentially applicable in respect of false statements in prospectuses and listing particulars, but considerations such as the burden of proof or range of possible defendants are likely to lead investors to favour the statutory claims. It would seem undeniable that the range of overlapping remedies can create unnecessary confusion in this area of the law.

19.27 THE STATUTORY REMEDY FOR FALSE, MISLEADING OR INCOMPLETE STATEMENTS

Section 90 of the Financial Services and Markets Act 2000 creates liability for loss as a result of any untrue or misleading statement in listing particulars or the omission from them of any matter required to be included by s 80 (general duty of disclosure) or s 81 (supplementary listing particulars). The section applies, *mutatis mutandis,* to prospectuses.[179] Failure to publish supplementary listing particulars or prospectuses when required is similarly actionable.[180]

A person responsible[181] for a prospectus or set of listing particulars[182] is liable to pay compensation to any person who acquires[183] any of the securities in question and suffers a loss in respect of them as a result of any untrue or misleading statement or omission. As is appropriate to a misrepresentation and non-disclosure remedy intended to protect investors in the context of a public issue, the elements of 'reliance' and 'inducement' (required by the common law of deceit) have been abolished. The element of causation ('as a result of') remains. Further, it is specifically provided that actual knowledge by the claimant when he acquired the securities that the statement was false or misleading, etc, may be raised and proved as a defence against an action based on s 90.[184] It is obviously important that in a public issue investor remedy of this type, those who acquire securities without reading the prospectus or listing particulars but nevertheless suffer a loss because of false or misleading statements (or the omission of information that is required to be

---

[179] Section 90(11) and Sch 10 to FSMA 2000. As regards other public documents (eg annual or interim reports, management statements) see s 90A, inserted by s 1270 of CA 2006.

[180] Section 90(10), (11) and Sch 10.

[181] This expression is defined at length by regulation 6 of the FSMA 2000 (Official Listing of Securities) Regulations 2001, SI 2001/2956, and the *Prospectus Rules* PR 5.5, examined below. Primarily it is the 'issuer' and its directors.

[182] Or, where appropriate, supplementary prospectuses or listing particulars. See s 90(10).

[183] See the definition of 'acquisition' in s 90(7). The question of who may seek relief on this basis is considered below.

[184] Section 90(2) and Sch 10, para 6 to FSMA 2000.

disclosed[185]) should have a remedy. This is because the market price is
affected by the responses of other investors when the truth becomes
known. The original price those investors were in general prepared to pay
can be properly said to relate to the accuracy of the information made
available to the investing public.

A less satisfactory feature of s 90 is the nature of the 'compensation'
payable to a person who has acquired securities and 'suffered a loss'.
Similar terminology employed in s 2(1) of the Misrepresentation Act 1967
has generally been understood to give a tort measure of damages
(ie based on 'out of pocket' losses) rather than losses based on 'loss of
expectation of bargain' (the traditional[186] contractual measure). Although
it is possible that the draftsman may have intended otherwise (or perhaps
hoped to leave the matter to the courts), it is regrettable, especially in an
investor protection Act, that the answer cannot be given with any
certainty. It seems that, whatever the basis of awarding compensation,
s 90 does not impose contractual liability. Like other remedies for false or
misleading statements (where these cannot be regarded as incorporated in
the terms of a contract), failure to carry out promises will not ground
relief in contract.[187] This carries implications for undertakings of various
kinds that are commonly given in both public issue and takeover
documents but which cannot be considered contract terms.

A distinction should be drawn between the statutory remedy applicable to
prospectuses and listing particulars and the remedy provided by s 90A of
the Financial Services and Markets Act 2000 in respect of disclosures
made to the market by an issuer through recognised information services
('RIS'). As required by the Transparency Directive, a liability regime was
introduced for periodic disclosures, covering annual financial reports (and
the preliminary announcements that typically precede them), half-yearly
financial reports and interim management statements.[188] That liability
regime did not extend to ongoing dislcsoures that are required by the
Market Abuse Directive and its implementing measures. In recognition of
the anomaly[189] that this created as between liability for periodic and
ongoing disclosures (and in recognition of the limitations of the liability
regime for periodic disclosures) the government commissioned a review of

---

[185] Where the prospectus or listing particulars require that a statement be made that no
information can or need be given on a certain matter, failure to do so also comes within
this remedy: s 90(3).

[186] It is true that in some respects the rules governing damages in contract and in tort have,
in recent years, 'grown together'. This, however, does not affect the point made in the
text.

[187] In Scotland, promises are legally enforceable but the obligation arising from a promise is
not, strictly speaking, contractual.

[188] The changes were made by s1270 of the Companies Act 2006, which inserted s90A into
the Financial Services and Markets Act 2000.

[189] For a discussion of the origins and nature of the anomaly see L Burn 'Only connect –
the importance of considering disclosure requirements in the light of their legal
consequences' (2007) 2(1) *Capital Markets Law Journal* 41.

issuer liability by Professor Paul Davies in 2006.[190] The outcome of that review was that s 90A was amended to cover ongoing disclosures.[191] Section 90A adopts a similar basis of liability to s 90 (the civil standard of fraud). However, it differs from s 90 in several important respects set out below:

(1)   Section 90A includes within its scope buyers, holders and sellers of securities, whereas s 90 extends only to those who have 'acquired' securities.[192]

(2)   Only the issuer can be liable to investors under s 90A.

(3)   The issuer is liable in respect of an untrue or misleading statement only if a person discharging managerial responsibilities within the issuer knew the statement to be untrue or misleading or was reckless as to whether it was untrue or misleading.

(4)   The issuer is liable in respect of the omission of any matter required to be included in published information only if a person discharging managerial responsibilities within the issuer knew the omission to be a dishonest concealment of a material fact.

(5)   The issuer is liable for dishonest delay in publishing information.

(6)   Dishonesty (for the purposes of (4) and (5) above) is conduct which is (a) regarded as dishonest by persons who regularly trade on the securities market in question, and (b) the person was aware (or must be taken to have been aware) that it was so regarded.

(7)   The requirement of reliance is retained and an additional requirement (by comparison with the common law of deceit) is imposed whereby the reliance must be reasonable by reference to the time and the circumstances.

19.28   WHO MAY BE SUED AND WHO MAY SUE UNDER THE STATUTORY REMEDY?

To the first of these questions an ample answer is given by s 90 of the Financial Services and Markets Act 2000, the relevant subordinate

---

[190]   See P Davies, 'Review of Issuer Liability: Final Report' (HM Treasury, June 2007): Extension of the statutory regime for issuer liability (HM Treasury, July 2008); and Extension of the statutory regime for issuer liability: a response to consultation (March 2010).

[191]   The changes were made under the power contained in s 90B of the Financial Services and Markets Act 2000 by the Financial Services and Markets Act 2000 (Liability of Issuers) Regulations 2010, SI 2010/1192.

[192]   As to the meaning of acquire, see **19.28**.

legislation and regulatory rules.[193] Primarily it is the 'issuer of the securities' and (where the issuer is a body corporate) the directors of the issuer at the time the listing particulars were submitted to the FSA as Listing Authority.[194] The offeror of securities is also a responsible person save where the offeror is making an offer in association with the issuer and the issuer is primarily responsible for the documentation.[195] Responsibility also extends to those who accept, and are stated in the prospectus or particulars as accepting, responsibility for the document. That will include those who accept responsibility for 'any part' of the document. It also covers those who authorise the contents of all or part of the document. These provisions cast a wide net. They will clearly cover an issuing house performing its usual functions (whether or not the relevant prospectus relates to an offer for sale). They will also catch an 'expert'[196] (eg a valuer or reporting accountant) who is responsible for that part of the contents of the prospectus or listing particulars for which he has taken responsibility.[197] The liability imposed by s 90 does not extend to those giving advice on the contents of the prospectus or particulars in a professional capacity (eg solicitors).[198]

Liability to pay compensation under s 90 is ignored in determining the amount to be paid on subscription for the shares in question or as to the amount paid up or deemed to be paid up.[199] This preserves the formal requirements on the raising of share capital.

The provisions relating to those who may seek a remedy under s 90 are less clearly spelt out than is the case in regard to those made responsible for the prospectus or listing particulars. Section 90(1) itself refers to 'a person who has acquired securities to which the particulars apply'. Section 90(7) then states that references in s 90 'to the acquisition by any person of securities include references to his contracting to acquire them or any interest in them'. This phraseology is not wholly free from ambiguity. It obviously means that not only those who have become registered owners of the securities in question but also who have agreed to purchase or subscribe for them (or options in them) may resort to the relief provided by s 90. It seems that claimants under s 90 may include

---

[193] Part 3 of SI 2001/2956 (listing particulars) and *Prospectus Rules*, PR 5.5 (prospectuses).

[194] It also includes those named in the prospectus or listing particulars who have authorised their naming as present or future directors..

[195] *Prospectus Rules,* PR 5.5.7R.

[196] See the definition of 'expert' in para 8 of Sch 10 to FSMA 2000.

[197] Regulation 6(1)(d), SI 2001/2956 (listing particulars); *Prospectus Rules*, PR 5.5.8R (prospectuses).

[198] Regulation 6(4), SI 2001/2956 (listing particulars); *Prospectus Rules,* PR 5.5.9R (prospectuses).

[199] Regulation 6(5), SI 2001/2956.

market purchasers provided, and to the extent that, they can show that their loss results from the inaccuracies in, or omissions from, the prospectus or listing particulars.[200]

19.29 DEFENCES AVAILABLE TO PERSONS RESPONSIBLE

Section 90(2) sets out a series of defences by reference to Sch 10. The principal defence is that the person responsible can satisfy the court that he 'reasonably believed',[201] having made such inquiries (if any) as were reasonable, that the statement was true and not misleading.[202] It must also be shown he continued in that belief until the securities were acquired. Alternatively, he may show that the securities were acquired before it was reasonably practical for steps to be taken to bring a correction to the attention of persons likely to acquire the securities, or that before the securities were acquired he had taken all such steps as it was reasonable for him to have taken to secure that a correction was brought to the attention of those persons. Another alternative defence is that he continued to believe (that the statement was true, etc) until after the commencement of dealings in the securities following their admission to the listing. Here he must satisfy the court that the securities were acquired after such a lapse of time that he ought in the circumstances to be reasonably excused.[203]

Reasonable reliance on statements made on the authority of an expert is a further defence,[204] and there is a defence against liability for loss resulting from a statement made by an official or contained in an official document.[205] A defence to the failure to publish required supplementary prospectuses or listing particulars is available to a person who can establish that he reasonably believed that no such supplementary document was required.[206]

19.30 THE RELATIONSHIP OF THE STATUTORY REMEDY TO THE COMMON-LAW REMEDIES

Section 90(6) is careful to preserve 'any liability which may be incurred apart from this section'. An investor in securities is thus free to pursue

---

[200] This interpretation is borne out by the wording of para 1(3)(d) of Sch 10 to FSMA 2000 which implies that liability may occur after the commencement of dealings.

[201] That is, at the time when he submitted the prospectus or listing particulars to the FSA.

[202] Or that the matter that was omitted (where the omission of required information caused the loss) was properly omitted.

[203] Schedule 10, para 1(3)(d).

[204] Schedule 10, para 2(2).

[205] Schedule 10, para 5, ie where these statements, etc, are included in the prospectus or listing particulars.

[206] Schedule 10, para 7.

claims based on misrepresentation or negligence.[207] There are good grounds for the retention of the remedy of rescission for misrepresentation because, whereas he can only seek compensation under s 90, rescission allows the investor to set aside the contract for the acquisition of the securities and thus to unwind completely the original bargain. Also rescission can be sought on the basis of a purely innocent (ie non-negligent) misrepresentation. However, otherwise (and in particular with regard to the right to damages in English law under s 2(1) of the Misrepresentation Act 1967) there appears still to be an unnecessary and confusing overlap in remedies. It is a matter of regret that the question of overlap remains unresolved. Section 2(1) of the 1967 Act is available only against the other party to the investment contract (eg the issuing house in the case of an offer of sale) and is thus more restricted in its 'target' than s 90 of the 2000 Act. Moreover, it would appear to require the proof of 'reliance' and 'inducement'. On the other hand, since the only defence is reasonable ground for belief (and not the other defences in Sch 10 to the 2000 Act), it may sometimes be worth pleading in addition to s 90. However, none of these distinctions was worth preserving, and it would have been a simple matter to disapply s 2(1) in the context of investment contracts within the scope of s 90.[208]

19.31 THE COMMON-LAW REMEDIES: THE RIGHT TO RESCIND A CONTRACT OF ALLOTMENT FOR MATERIAL MISREPRESENTATION

An allottee's right to rescind the contract of allotment may arise in the case of any allotment of shares by a company whether public or private. An action for rescission must be brought by the subscriber against the company as the other party to the contract of allotment. Where the shares are not allotted directly to subscribers by the company, a right of rescission may not be exercised against the company. In the case of an offer for sale, the issuing house is the 'subscriber' and the investors who obtain securities from the issuing house do so by 'purchase'. Clearly, any remedy by way of rescission will be against the issuing house.

A contract to take shares, like other contracts, is voidable if induced by misrepresentation, whether such misrepresentation is fraudulent or innocent: that is to say the contract is valid until repudiation, but upon repudiation is terminated as from the date when the shareholder gives notice that he requires to be relieved of his shares. This is subject, however, to the rule discussed later that he must actually take proceedings to enforce his right (if it is not admitted) before the company goes into liquidation, and that he must come promptly for relief. Accordingly, if

---

[207] Or in contract in a suitable case.

[208] Something similar to this has been done in regard to a promoter's duties of disclosure to his company in s 90(8). This equitable duty is disregarded as regards the duty to disclose information in the prospectus or listing particulars.

there is a material misrepresentation in the listing particulars or, as the case may be, the prospectus upon which a shareholder relied when applying for shares offered by way of subscription, he is entitled, if he seeks relief within a reasonable time after learning the truth, and before the company is in liquidation, to have his name removed from the register, and the amount he has paid upon the shares returned to him,[209] with interest from the time of payment.[210] But it must be noted that only the shareholder who applied for the shares on the faith of the prospectus is entitled to relief; the remedy does not extend to a purchaser from another shareholder who is not a party to the misrepresentation.

19.32 RESPONSIBILITY FOR STATEMENTS

Questions can arise concerning the responsibility of the company, its directors and its professional advisers for statements made in connection with a public offering of securities.[211] In the case of the statutory remedy under the Financial Services and Markets Act 2000, subordinate legislation identifies those responsible.[212] In the case of the common-law remedies such as rescission, a company is responsible for the statements of its directors, general agents and special agents who are acting within the scope of their authority[213] which includes persons whose acts are subsequently ratified;[214] a company is also responsible for statements which, to the knowledge of its directors, were made before the contract and which induced it or which formed the basis of it.[215] In each case, the company's responsibility does not depend on whether the representations were known to be false or not.[216]

Representations made even before the company was in existence, or made by persons who are strangers to the company, may become, by the subsequent knowledge of the directors, the responsibility of the company, as where an application for shares was made before the company was incorporated upon the faith of a prospectus prepared by a promoter, and the company later adopted the prospectus and allotted the shares.[217]

---

[209] The best statement of the effect of the cases will be found in *Re Scottish Petroleum Co* (1883) 23 Ch D 413 (CA).

[210] *Karberg's Case* [1892] 3 Ch 1 (CA) (where the rate of interest was fixed by the court at 4%).

[211] Responsibility in this context should be distinguished from responsibility for disclosures made after admission to listing, which is governed by s 90A FSMA 2000, limiting liability to the issuer. See **19.27**.

[212] See **19.28**.

[213] Thus where the directors know that one of their body is obtaining subscriptions for shares, the company is responsible for representations made by him: *Hilo Manufacturing Co v Williamson* (1911) 28 TLR 164.

[214] *Lynde v Anglo-Indian Hemp Co* [1896] 1 Ch 178.

[215] Ibid.

[216] This last proposition is not accurately stated in the headnote to *Collins v Associated Greyhound Racecourses* [1930] 1 Ch 1, but is correctly stated in the judgment.

[217] *Karberg's Case* [1892] 3 Ch 1; *Tamplin's Case* [1892] WN 146.

If a statement is actually included in listing particulars or in a prospectus, the company may find it difficult to deny that the statement formed the basis of the contract to take the shares. The cases establish that the statement will be so treated unless the company expressly dissociates itself from the report and warns investors that they must take the report for what it is worth:[218] the distinction is between showing that it is repeating on hearsay what it has been told, and affirming the matter as a fact.[219] However, such disclaimers of responsibility must be read in the light of s 3 of the Misrepresentation Act 1967, which invalidates any unreasonable[220] contractual term that would exclude or restrict liability for misrepresentation. Moreover, on the assumption that the relevant statutory provisions governing responsibility for a prospectus or listing particulars[221] are mandatory in their nature, it cannot be possible to evade the provisions through the use of a disclaimer.

19.33 LOSS OF THE RIGHT TO RESCIND

It is a general principle of law that where a party having a right to rescind his contract, after having knowledge of such right, performs any act affirming his contract, he cannot afterwards set up his right to avoid the contract.[222] Therefore, any act by a shareholder recognising his position as a member of the company after knowledge of the misrepresentation, such as by selling or trying to sell the shares,[223] attending meetings,[224] signing proxies, paying calls, or accepting dividends,[225] will prevent the member from obtaining rescission, even though performed under a mistake as to rights,[226] unless he has meanwhile definitely elected to rescind the contract, as by commencing proceedings.[227]

The shareholder must, moreover, come within a reasonable time after learning the truth; for the rights and interests of other persons intervene, and the aggrieved shareholder will not be allowed to wait and see whether the speculation turns out to be a favourable one, and then, according to the result, retain the benefit or repudiate the loss.[228] As the intervention of the rights of others prevents the right of the applicant to rescind, it may

---

[218] *Mair v Rio Grande Rubber Estates* [1913] AC 853; *Karberg's Case*, above; *Lynde v Anglo-Italian Hemp Co*, above; *Re Pacaya Rubber Co* [1914] 1 Ch 542.

[219] *Re Reese River Silver Mining Co* (1867) 2 Ch App 604, at 615.

[220] Reasonableness is judged in accordance with s 11(1) of the Unfair Contract Terms Act 1977. The burden of establishing that a term is reasonable is on the person who wishes to rely on it: s 11(5). There is no equivalent in Scotland to s 3.

[221] See **19.30**.

[222] *Clough v London and North-Western Railway* (1872) LR 7 Ex 26 (Ex Ch).

[223] *Ex parte Briggs* (1866) LR 1 Eq 483. Cf *Crawley's Case* (1869) LR 4 Ch App 322.

[224] *Sharpley v Louth and East Coast Railway* (1876) 2 Ch D 663.

[225] *Scholey v Central Railway of Venezuela* (1869) LR 9 Eq 266, note.

[226] *Re Dunlop-Truffault Cycle Co* (1896) 66 LJ Ch 25.

[227] *Tomlin's Case* (1898) 1 Ch 104.

[228] *Downes v Ship* (1868) LR 3 HL 343; *Houldsworth v City of Glasgow Bank* (1880) 5 AC 317 (HL).

well be that even a charge on the uncalled capital in favour of debenture-holders will prevent relief, but this has not been definitely decided.[229] The occurrence of a winding-up, whether the assets are sufficient to pay the creditors or not, brings in other rights (ie those of the creditors or contributories) so as to render rescission impossible;[230] for upon the commencement of a liquidation the creditors or other shareholders are the persons interested in retaining the name of the shareholder upon the register, and against them he has no claim to set aside his bargain.[231]

It is not enough merely to serve the company with notice of repudiation. The complainant must either procure the company to remove his name from the register of members, or commence proceedings to compel it to do so,[232] subject to the exception, however, that if he has *agreed to be bound* by a test case brought by another shareholder, he may await the decision of such case,[233] or if in an action for calls he has set up a counterclaim for rescission, he is in time.[234] In an action for calls, it is not a sufficient defence to set up misrepresentation and repudiation of the shares. The defence must be coupled with a counterclaim for rescission of the contract and rectification of the register, or, if the action is brought in a court where such counterclaim cannot be entertained, a statement must be made that relief is being claimed in the proper court. If the delay has been so long that rescission will not be granted, the defence will fail.[235]

'Where a person has contracted to take shares in a company and his name has been placed on the register, it has always been held that he must exercise his right of repudiation with extreme promptness after the discovery of the fraud or misrepresentation.'[236] What is a reasonable time is a question of fact, and will vary with the circumstances of each case, but in practice a shareholder should not delay at all after he knows the facts which entitle him to relief. 'The delay of a fortnight in repudiating the shares', said Baggallay LJ,[237] 'makes it to my mind doubtful whether

---

[229] For the principle see: *Re Scottish Petroleum Co* (1883), 23 Ch D 413 (CA); *Tennant v City of Glasgow Bank* (1879) 4 App Cas 615 (HL).

[230] *Tennent v City of Glasgow Bank* (1879) 4 App Cas 615 (HL); *Burgess's Case* (1880) 15 Ch D 507, this being the case of a solvent company.

[231] *Tennent v City of Glasgow Bank* (1879) 4 App Cas 615; *Stone v City and County Bank* (1877) 3 CP 282 (CA); *Oakes v Turquand* (1867), LR 2 HL 325; *Burgess's Case* (1880) 15 Ch D 507; *Re Scottish Petroleum Co* (1883) 23 Ch D 413.

[232] *Re Scottish Petroleum Co* (1993) 23 Ch D 413 (CA); *First National Reinsurance Co v Greenfield* [1921] 2 KB 260; but see **12.9**.

[233] *Re Scottish Petroleum Co* (1883) 23 Ch D 413; *Pawle's Case* (1869) 4 Ch App 497; *Hare's Case* (1869) 4 Ch App 503. The pendency of other cases will not save him if there is no agreement to be bound by their result (see cases cited in this note).

[234] *Whiteley's Case* [1900] 1 Ch 365.

[235] *First National Reinsurance Co v Greenfield* [1921] 2 KB 260.

[236] Per Lord Davey in *Aaron's Reefs v Twiss* [1896] AC 273, at 294. See also *Sharpley v Louth and East Coast Railway* (1876) 2 Ch D 663, at 685.

[237] *Re Scottish Petroleum Co* (1883) 23 Ch D, at 434. See also *Re Christineville Rubber Esttes* [1911] WN 216 (4 months); *Taite's Case* (1867) LR 3 Eq 795 (a month sufficed).

the repudiation in the case of a going concern would have been in time.'
No doubt where investigation is necessary some time must be allowed, as
in *Central Railway Co of Venezuela v Kisch*.[238] But where, as in the present
case, the shareholder is at once informed of the circumstances he ought to
lose no time in repudiating.' There are conflicting authorities on whether
it is possible to rescind if some of the shares originally acquired have since
been sold.[239] As shares are fungible securities, it is doubtful in principle
whether disposal of part of the original holding should bar rescission,
since the investor can always go into the market to buy substitute shares
and in that way put himself into a position to give back the full portion of
what he acquired in return for his money back.[240]

19.34   AN ACTION FOR DECEIT

Besides the right to rescission of his contract to take shares, the
shareholder may also claim damages against the persons who fraudulently
induced him to become a shareholder, and this right does not cease when
the company goes into liquidation. The company itself may be sued for
fraudulent statements made by those for whom it is vicariously
responsible; and it is no barrier to such an action that the plaintiff
remains a shareholder.[241] Those responsible for the prospectus, so long as
they have knowledge of the falsity of the statements made, are liable in
deceit whether or not rescission of the allotment is obtained. 'Those
responsible' will clearly embrace promoters, directors and issuing houses
(as well as experts in respect of reports made by them).

There is a clear distinction between an action for deceit and an action for
rescission of contract. In the latter case, it is only necessary to show that
the contract was induced by an untrue statement of a material fact,
whether made innocently or not,[242] while to sustain an action for deceit it
is necessary to show that the defendant acted fraudulently – ie made the
untrue statement either knowing it to be false or without belief in its
truth, or recklessly, not caring whether it were true or false.[243] Thus
liability would attach if the defendant 'shut his eyes to the facts or

---

[238] (1867) LR 2 HL 99. In this case 2 months was allowed, but it was stated that it was
necessary that the complainant should come 'with the utmost diligence' (per
Lord Romilly at 125).
[239] *Re Metropolitan Coal Consumers' Assn Ltd* (1890) 6 TLR 416 (no rescission if part
sold); *Re Mount Morgan (West) Gold Mines Ltd* (1887) 3 TLR 556 (rescission still
possible despite sale of part).
[240] *Smith New Court Securities Ltd v Scrimgeour Vickers (Asset Management) Ltd* [1997]
AC 254 (HL), at 262, per Lord Browne-Wilkinson.
[241] Companies Act 2006, s 655.
[242] *Karberg's Case* [1892] 3 Ch 1, at 13 (CA); *Lagunas Nitrate Co v Lagunas Nitrate
Syndicate* [1899] 2 Ch 392, at p 423 (CA).
[243] *Derry v Peek* (1889) 15 App Cas 337, at 374 (HL).

purposely abstained from inquiring into them'. It would not be enough to show that the statement was made through want of care.[244]

The House of Lords has held that if the misrepresentation complained of was contained in the prospectus, only original subscribers, and not purchasers of shares, can obtain damages for deceit; for the function of the prospectus is exhausted once the allotment is made,[245] unless the prospectus was in fact issued with a view of inducing persons to become purchasers of shares. The latter inference will be the natural one to draw today in the context of normal public issues accompanied by the publication of the prospectus or at least a 'mini-prospectus' in national newspapers. If this is the case, the directors and other persons issuing it with this object will become liable for losses suffered by those who bought shares, even from strangers. It is not necessary that the representation should be direct to the person injured; it is sufficient if it be made to another (eg to a newspaper) with the intent that it shall be repeated to and acted upon by the person who is subsequently injured.[246] 'But to bring it within the principle, the injury must be the immediate and not the remote consequence of the representation thus made ... It must appear that such false representation was made with the direct intent that it should be acted upon by such third person in the manner which occasions the injury or loss.'[247]

The misstatement must be of an existing fact, and not merely an unduly sanguine expression of hope or an exaggerated view of the advantages the company offers. A general commendation of his wares by a trader is not a false statement, even if too highly coloured. 'Anticipation of future results is not a statement of fact.'[248] 'If you are looking to the language as only the language of hope, expectation, and confident belief, that is one thing: but you may use language in such a way as, although in the form of hope and expectation, it may become a representation of existing facts';[249] and to say that something is expected when in reality it is not expected, or that directors have an intention to do something when they have not, is a misstatement of fact.[250] For example, a statement that property has been acquired which has not in fact then been acquired will be ground for an action against directors, even if the property be acquired a few days after

---

[244] *Derry v Peek* (1889) 14 App Cas 337, at 375 and 376, *Angus v Clifford* [1891] 2 Ch 449 (CA).

[245] *Peek v Gurney* (1873) LR 6 HL 277, at 400 and 411. A subscriber who has sold his shares and subsequently repurchased them cannot obtain relief: *In re Bank of Hindustan, China and Japan* (1873) LR 16 Eq 417.

[246] *Andrews v Mockford* [1896] 1 QB 372 (CA); *Barry v Crosskey* (1861) 2 J & H 1.

[247] Cited from *Barry v Crosskey* with approval by Lord Cairns in *Peek v Gurney* (1873) LR 6 HL 377, at 413.

[248] Per Lord Esher MR, in *Bentley v Black* (1893) 9 TLR 580 (CA).

[249] Per Lord Halsbury LC in *Aaron's Reefs v Twiss* [1896] AC 273, at 284 (HL).

[250] *Edgington v Fitzmaurice* (1885) 29 Ch D 459 (CA); *Karberg's Case* [1892] 3 Ch 1, at 11 (CA).

the allotment of the shares.[251] A misrepresentation of law is not a misstatement of fact which will give any remedy against directors.[252]

If a false or misleading statement is made, it is no protection to the defendants to say that the claimant had means of ascertaining the truth and was negligent in failing to inspect documents referred to in the prospectus or to make other inquiries, for he is entitled to rely on the statements made to him.[253] If before allotment the directors discover a mistake in the prospectus, it is fraud to allow applicants to remain under the mistaken belief and accept an allotment.[254] It is the duty of the directors to point out the mistake in unambiguous terms, and not merely to send a new prospectus correctly stating the facts. 'Assuming a fraud to have been committed, it obviously lies on those who rely upon a subsequent explanation to show that such explanation was quite clear.'[255]

In an action for deceit, the motive with which the statement was made is immaterial, for a person is liable for a false statement knowingly made, even if he has no intent to defraud.[256] It is not necessary to show that the false statement was the sole inducing cause if it forms a substantial ground for taking the shares,[257] and the courts pay little attention to a cross-examination as to the weight attached to each statement by the applicant, holding that a material misrepresentation likely to induce the application is enough, unless the claimant admits that he did not act upon it.[258] If, however, the court comes to the conclusion that the particular misrepresentation did not affect the claimant's mind, and that he would still have taken the shares if he had known the truth, he will have suffered no damage, and cannot recover. The court may come to this conclusion either from the claimant's answers in cross-examination or from his conduct, or from the nature of the misrepresentation relied upon.[259]

If a statement is true at the time it is made, but becomes untrue before the allotment of the shares (eg if a director named in the prospectus has

---

251 *McConnel v Wright* [1903] 1 Ch 546 (CA).

252 *Beattie v Lord Ebury* (1872) 7 Ch App 777, (1874) LR 7 HL 102; *Rashdall v Ford* (1865) LR 2 Eq 750; *Bentley v Black* (1893) 9 TLR 580.

253 *Reynell v Sprye* (1851) 1 De GM & G 660; *Arkwright v Newbold* (1881) 17 Ch D *301*; *Aaron's Reefs v Twiss* [1896] App Cas 273; *Gluckstein v Barnes* [1900] AC 240, at 251; *Redgrave v Hurd* (1881) 20 Ch D 1; *Alliance & Leicester Building Society v Edgestop* [1994] 2 All ER 38 [1993] 1 WLR 1462.

254 *Brownlie v Campbell* (1880) 5 App Cas 925, at 950; *Davies v London and Provincial Co* (1878) 8 Ch D 459, at 475.

255 *Arnison v Smith* (1889) 41 Ch D 348, at 370, per Lord Halsbury.

256 *Derry v Peek* (1889) 14 App Cas 337 at 374; *Smith v Chadwick* (1884) 9 App Cas 187; *Arnison v Smith* (1889) 41 Ch D 348 (CA).

257 *Edgington v Fitzmaurice* (1885) 29 Ch D 459.

258 Per Lord Halsbury in *Arnison v Smith* (1889) 41 Ch D 348, at 369 (CA). And see *Smith v Chadwick* (1884) 20 Ch D 27 (CA), 9 App Cas 187 (HL).

259 *Smith v Chadwick* (1884) 9 App Cas 187; *Macleay v Tait* [1906] AC 24 (HL); *Nash v Calthorpe* [1905] 2 Ch 237.

meanwhile resigned), it will be good ground for rescinding the contract,[260] and there is authority for the view that it may give a cause of action for deceit.[261]

19.35 MISLEADING OMISSIONS

Either in an action for deceit or in an action for rescission the omission of material facts may amount to a misrepresentation.[262] Thus, in a prospectus describing land purchased by the company as 'eminently suitable' for its operations, the *innocent* omission to state that the land had been scheduled to a town planning resolution and that the company would not be entitled to compensation for the removal of buildings unless they had been erected with the previous consent of the local authority was held sufficient to entitle an allottee of shares to rescission against the company.[263] Again, the omission of the names of the real vendors and the interpolation of a nominal vendor to conceal the true facts may be sufficient to entitle subscribers to relief,[264] but this rule applies only if the omission renders the prospectus as it stands misleading,[265] or the omissions are (in the words of James LJ) 'omissions amounting in effect to false statements',[266] or if the omission is of something which there was a duty to disclose. Lord Cairns said: 'There must, in my opinion, be some active misstatement of fact, or, at all events, such a partial and fragmentary statement of fact, as that the withholding of that which is not stated makes that which is stated absolutely false.'[267] 'There must be something more than mere non-disclosure proved before misrepresentation is established: it must, I think, be shown that the non-disclosure is the non-disclosure of something the disclosure of which would falsify some statement in the prospectus.'[268]

---

[260] *Anderson's Case* (1881) 17 Ch D 373; *Re Scottish Petroleum Co* (1883) 23 Ch D 413 (CA). This will also be the case if the other directors know that one of the directors is on the point of resigning when they go to allotment: *Re Kent County Gas Co* (1906) 95 LT 756.

[261] *Brownlie v Campbell* (1880) 5 App Cas 925, at 950 (HL Sc); *Briess v Woolley* [1954] AC 333, at 353–354 (HL). Cf *Arkwright v Newbold* (1881) 17 Ch D 301, at 325 and 329, and *Bradford Building Society v Borders* [1941] 2 All ER 205, at 228 (HL).

[262] *Central Railway Co of Venezuela v Kisch* (1867) LR 2 HL 99; *Oakes v Turquand* (1867) LR 2 HL 325, 342; *Cackett v Kewsick* [1902] 2 Ch 456. It has been suggested that a concealment may be a ground for rescission of the contract to take shares, which would not be sufficient to ground an action of deceit against directors (see per Lord Cairns in *Peek v Gurney* (1873) LR 6 HL 377, at 403), but later cases do not draw the distinction.

[263] *Coles v White City (Manchester) Greyhound Association* (1928) 45 TLR 230. See also *Ross v Estates Investment Co* (1868) LR 3 CH 682.

[264] *Components Tube Co v Naylor* [1900] 2 Ir R 1.

[265] *McKeown v Boudard Peveril Gear Co* [1896] WN 36 (CA); *New Brunswick and Canada Rail and Land Co v Conybeare* (1862) 9 HL C711; *Peek v Gurney* (1873) LR 6 HL 377, at 403.

[266] *Gover's Case* (1875) 1 Ch D 182, at 189 (CA).

[267] *Peek v Gurney* (1873) LR 6 HL 377, at 403.

[268] Per Eve J, in *Re Christineville Rubber Estates* [1911] WN 216; and see *R v Bishirgian* (1936) 154 LT 499 (CCA).

Furthermore, 'if by a number of statements you intentionally give a false impression and induce a person to act upon it, it is none the less false although if one takes each statement by itself there may be a difficulty in showing that any specific statement is untrue'.[269] Thus the prospectus must be taken as a whole, 'and everybody knows that half a truth is no better than a downright falsehood'.[270]

As regards statements that are misleading in the sense that they can bear more than one meaning, the law used to be stated that it is not material in what sense the directors intended the words to be understood if they are in fact untrue or misleading.[271] However, this formulation was rejected by the Privy Council in *Akerheilm v De Mare*[272] in favour of a more subjective test of the defendant's honesty. The following passage from the opinion of the Privy Council shows that in an action for deceit the subjective state of mind cannot be ignored:[273]

> 'The question is not whether the defendant in any given case honestly believed the representation to be true in the sense assigned to it by the court on an objective consideration of its truth or falsity, but whether he honestly believed the representation to be true in the sense in which he understood it albeit erroneously when it was made. This general proposition is no doubt subject to limitations. For instance, the meaning placed by the defendant on the representation made may be so far removed from the sense in which it would be understood by the reasonable person as to make it impossible to hold that the defendant honestly understood the representation to bear the meaning claimed by him and honestly believed it in the sense to be true.'

The qualification in the latter part of this passage accords with the view of Lord Blackburn in *Smith v Chadwick*[274] that 'if with intent to lead the plaintiff to act upon it they put forth a statement which they know may bear two meanings, one of which is false to their knowledge, and thereby the plaintiff, putting that meaning upon it, is misled, I do not think they can escape by saying he ought to have put the other'. It is essential, of course, that the claimant proves that he understood the statement in the sense in which it is false.[275] Further, in considering whether a statement is misleading, the prospectus must be considered as a whole and if the tendency is to deceive there is no need to point out some one or more statements which are absolutely untrue.[276]

---

[269] Per Halsbury LC, in *Aaron's Reefs v Twiss* [1896] AC 273, at 281.

[270] Per Lord Macnaghten in *Gluckstein v Barnes* [1900] AC 240, at 250 and 251 (HL).

[271] See *Greenwood v Leathershod Wheel Co* [1900] Ch 421; *Arnison v Smith* (1889) 41 Ch D 348, at 372 (CA), per Lindley LJ; *Arkwright v Newbold* (1881) 17 Ch D 301, at 322 and 323 (CA).

[272] [1959] AC 789 (PC), where the Privy Council refused to follow *Arnison v Smith*, above.

[273] [1959] AC 789, at 805.

[274] (1884) 9 App Cas 187, at 201.

[275] *Smith v Chadwick* (1882) 20 Ch D 45, at 73 (CA); (1884) 9 App Cas 187 (HL).

[276] *Aaron's Reefs v Twiss* [1896] AC 273; *R v Kylsant* [1932] 1 KB 442 (CCA).

19.36   THE MISREPRESENTATION ACT 1967

The changes introduced into the English law of innocent misrepresentation by the Misrepresentation Act 1967 would allow a claim for damages
against the company for a misrepresentation made by or on behalf of the
company. As part of the general law, this Act will apply to any
misrepresentation made by or on behalf of the company which has
induced subscribers to enter into a contract of allotment on the faith of it.
It is not confined, as are the civil remedies now provided by the Financial
Services and Markets Act 2000, to public issues of securities nor to
written statements in a formal prospectus or set of listing particulars. This
Act does not apply to Scotland where a remedy in damages is available
against an issuer for negligent misrepresentation[277] but not for innocent
misrepresentation.[278]

Under s 2(1) of the Misrepresentation Act 1967:

> 'where a person has entered into a contract after a misrepresentation has
> been made to him by another party thereto, and as a result thereof he has
> suffered a loss, then, if the person making the misrepresentation would have
> been liable to damages in respect thereof had the misrepresentation been
> made fraudulently, that person shall be so liable notwithstanding that the
> misrepresentation was not made fraudulently, unless he proves that he had
> reasonable ground to believe and did believe up to the time that the contract
> was made that the facts represented were true.'

It is clear that an action based on s 2(1) of the Act must be brought
against the other party to the contract. It has been seen that in an offer for
sale this will be the issuing house.

Section 2(2) of the Misrepresentation Act 1967 confers a discretion upon
the court, in the case of an innocent misrepresentation, to award damages
in lieu of a decree of rescission where in the circumstances of the case it is
in the interest of justice to do so. It should be noted that there is no *right*
to damages in lieu of rescission on the part of either party to the contract.
Section 2(2) allows for damages to be awarded in lieu of rescission from
which it appears that the court may only award damages if the claimant
has not lost his normal right to rescission.[279]

---

[277] The Law Reform (Miscellaneous Provisions) (Sc) Act 1985, s 10(1), extending the
grounds for a (contractual) claim in damages to include negligence as well as fraud.

[278] *Ferguson v Mackay* 1985 SLT 94.

[279] This analysis of s 2(2) is supported by *Zanzibar v British Aerospace (Lancaster
House) Ltd QBD* [2000] 1 WLR 2333. Section 2(3) is intended to prevent any possibility
of 'double recovery' where claims under subsection (1) and subsection (2) are combined.
On the measure of compensation under s 2(2), see *William Sindall plc v Cambridgeshire
County Council* [1994] 1 WLR 1026.

19.37   THE MEASURE OF DAMAGES

The overriding principle in an action at common law for deceit or under s 2(1) of the Misrepresentation Act 1967[280] is that the victim of the tort is entitled to be compensated for all actual loss flowing directly from the transaction induced by the wrongdoer.[281] In some circumstances, the difference between the price paid for property and the market price that it would have had on the date of the transaction but for the tort may be the appropriate measure of this loss but in others a different measure, such as the difference between the price paid for the property and the price at which it was later disposed of, may be required in order to give the claimant full compensation in accordance with the general principle.

19.38   AN ACTION FOR NEGLIGENT MISSTATEMENT

Since the leading decision of the House of Lords in *Hedley Byrne & Co Ltd v Heller & Partners Ltd*,[282] it is possible to argue that the directors and others responsible for a prospectus may owe a duty of care to those intended to rely on the prospectus in respect of negligent misstatements it contains. So long as the 'special relationship' giving rise to such a duty of care can be established, an action for the tort of negligence might lie. The special relationship may arise in pre-contractual negotiations, and those who may be held liable for negligent statements need not be persons who carried on, or held themselves out as carrying on, the business of advising.[283] In many instances, the remedies afforded by s 2(1) of the Misrepresentation Act 1967[284] and s 90 of the Financial Services and Markets Act 2000 will provide better protection to investors in company securities than an action for common-law negligence. Both these statutory provisions place the burden of disproving negligence upon the defendant. In an action for negligent misstatement, as in any other action for negligence, the burden of establishing negligence rests upon the claimant. However, in contrast with the remedies in the Financial Services and Markets Act 2000, an action in tort will apply to the private as well as to the public issue of company securities.

It has been seen that an action for damages under s 2(1) of the Misrepresentation Act 1967 will only lie as between the contracting parties. An action for the tort of negligent misstatement would allow a wider range of possible claimants and defendants. However, the courts

---

[280]   *Royscot Trust Ltd v Rogerson* [1991] 2 QB 297; *East v Maurer* [1991] 1 WLR 461.

[281]   *Smith New Court Securities Ltd v Scrimgeour Vickers (Asset Management) Ltd* [1997] AC 254 (HL). But note that the House of Lords expressed some criticism of the *Royscot* decision, where this deceit measure of damages was applied to claims under s 2(1) of the Misrepresentation Act 1967.

[282]   [1964] AC 465. See also *WB Anderson Ltd v Rhodes* [1967] 2 All ER 850; *Mutual Life & Citizens Assurance Co Ltd v Evatt* [1971] 2 WLR 23 (PC).

[283]   *Esso Petroleum Co Ltd v Mardon* [1976] 2 WLR 583 (CA).

[284]   This Act does not apply in Scotland. See above **19.3.6**.

will not lightly extend the duty of care under *Hedley Byrne*.[285] *Al Nakib Investments (Jersey) Ltd v Longcroft*[286] concerned a prospectus issued in connection with a rights issue. The court held that, because the purpose of the prospectus was to invite subscriptions for shares, there was insufficient proximity for a duty of care to arise between the directors and those persons (including existing shareholders of the company) who used the prospectus for the different purpose of purchasing further shares in the market. This case was distinguished in *Possfund Custodian Trustee Ltd v Diamond*,[287] where, in relation to a prospectus relating to a general public offer of securities, as opposed to a rights issue, it was held that there was an arguable case for the existence of a duty of care to market purchasers and that the issues merited full consideration at trial.

19.39   CRIMINAL LIABILITY FOR FALSE OR MISLEADING STATEMENTS IN PROSPECTUSES

The Financial Services and Markets Act 2000 contains, in s 397, a general 'all purpose' criminal sanction to deal with false and misleading statements. This section clearly applies to public issues but also 'underpins' many other provisions in the Act concerning transactions in securities.

Section 397(1) makes it an offence for anyone to make a statement, promise or forecast which he knows to be misleading, false or deceptive. It also comprises dishonestly concealing any material facts and covers recklessly making (dishonestly or otherwise) a statement, promise or forecast which is misleading, false or deceptive.[288] The offence is 'investment related' in that the accused must make the statement (or conceal the facts dishonestly) for the purpose of inducing, or being reckless[289] as to whether it may induce, another person to enter into, or offer to enter into, or to refrain from entering into, a relevant agreement.[290] The 'other person' need not be the person to whom the statement is made or from whom the facts are concealed.[291]

---

[285]   *Caparo Industries plc v Dickman* [1990] 2 AC 605, [1990] 1 All ER 568, [1990] 2 WLR 358, [1990] BCLC 273, [1990] BCC 164.

[286]   [1990] 3 All ER 321, [1991] BCLC 7, [1990] BCC 517.

[287]   [1996] 2 All ER 774.

[288]   These criteria are derived from s 13 of the Prevention of Fraud (Investment) Act 1958 (now repealed).

[289]   See *R v G* [2004] 1 AC 1034, making clear that a reference to 'reckless' as an element of a criminal offence requires advertent recklessness to be established (ie the defendant appreciated that there was a risk of non-compliance but nevertheless decided to run the risk).

[290]   A relevant agreement is, in essence, one falling within the scope of FSMA 2000: see s 397(9) and (10). Section 397(1) also applies to inducing another to exercise or refrain from exercising, any rights (eg options) conferred by those investments.

[291]   Eg the section covers statements made to an adviser which are intended to induce the adviser's client to enter an investment agreement.

It has been held that a statement which is superficially true but actually untrue because of the omission of relevant information can be a false statement.[292] Such a statement could also be described as misleading or deceptive.[293] The terms 'misleading, false or deceptive' are not mutually exclusive in scope but they do differ slightly in degree. For instance, it would not be possible to describe an over-optimistic profit forecast as 'false' until the actual profit figures are known,[294] but, even without the actual figures, it might be possible to establish that the forecast was a misleading interpretation of the information on which it is based.

The offence of dishonest concealment of any material facts requires more than merely the omission of information, and in order to establish an offence under this section it must be shown that what has been said is incorrect or inaccurate because of what has been omitted.[295] This means that there is a very considerable overlap between the *actus reus* of the 'concealment' offence and the 'making' offence. A person is dishonest if he realises that he would be so judged on the standards of ordinary honest people, even though he does not consider himself to be dishonest by his own standards.[296]

Another provision in s 397[297] goes beyond statements or concealments and is concerned with conduct which has the effect of market manipulation or market rigging. An offence is committed by someone 'who does any act or engages in any conduct which creates a false or misleading impression as to the market in, or the price or value of any relevant investments'. This must be done for creating that false impression and thus inducing others to acquire, dispose of, subscribe for, or underwrite investments.[298] A defence of reasonable belief that the act or conduct in question will not create a false or misleading impression is available to the accused.[299]

The provisions of Part VIII of the Financial Services and Markets Act 2000 relating to market abuse overlap to some extent with s 397. In particular, s 118(8) identifies, as a form of market abuse, behaviour which would be regarded by a regular user of the market as likely to distort the market in investments of the kind in question. The availability of the regulatory procedure and sanctions established by Part VIII for dealing

---

[292] *R v Kylsant* [1932] 1 KB 442; *R v Bishirgian, etc* [1936] 1 All ER 568.
[293] *Oakes v Turquand and Harding* (1867) LR 2 HL 325, at 342–343.
[294] *R v Bates* [1952] 2 All ER 842, at 845.
[295] *R v MacKinnon* [1959] 1 QB 150, at 154.
[296] *R v Ghosh* [1982] QB 1053.
[297] Section 397(3).
[298] Inducing others to refrain from investing in these ways is also within s 397(3).
[299] Section 397(5)(a). As to the jurisdictional limits to s 397, see s 397(6) and (7). As to the penalties for conviction on indictment or summarily, see s 397(8).

with this form of market abuse is likely to limit resort to prosecutions under the market manipulation provisions of s 397.[300]

In some cases it may be that the Fraud Act 2006[301] may be relevant to misleading statements or omissions linked to listing or public offers. Section 3 of the Act sets out the offence of fraud by false representation, which in principle could apply to false statements in a prospectus. The s 4 offence of fraud by failing to disclose information may also be relevant in those circumstances. However, the limitation of the latter section to circumstances in which there is a legal duty to disclose limits the potential for the section to be engaged in circumstances where conflicts of interest are not disclosed (in circumstances where there is no disclosure obligation).[302]

19.40   SECTION 19 OF THE THEFT ACT 1968

The Theft Act 1968, which does not apply in Scotland, contains, in s 19, a special provision to deal with dishonest statements in writing by officers of corporate bodies or unincorporated associations. It provides that 'an officer or person purporting to act as an officer of a body corporate or unincorporated association who, with intent to deceive its members or creditors about its affairs, publishes or concurs in publishing a written statement or account which to his knowledge is or may be misleading, false or deceptive in a material particular' is liable to a maximum sentence of 7 years' imprisonment. Even under the more narrowly worded s 84 of the Larceny Act 1861 (the predecessor of s 19), which referred simply to 'false' statements, the courts gave it a liberal interpretation so as to include misleading or deceptive statements or omissions. Thus, in *R v Kylsant*[303] a prospectus relating to the issue of debenture stock said that the company paid a dividend in every year between 1921 and 1927. This was literally true, but it gave the misleading impression that the company during this period had made trading profits, whereas in fact substantial trading losses had been made. It was only able to pay dividends from reserves earned in earlier years. The fact that the dividends were paid from these 'hidden reserves' was not disclosed in the prospectus. Lord Kylsant, who knew the true state of affairs and was responsible for the prospectus, was convicted.

---

[300] The FSA is empowered to bring prosecutions under s 397 (s 401). It may consider prosecution as well as regulatory sanctions: see FSA Handbook, EG 12.4.

[301] In general, the Act does not apply to Scotland.

[302] See further J Fisher, 'Economic Crime and the Global Financial Crisis' 5(4) *Law and Financial Markets Review* p 276 (2011) referring to the Law Commission's recommendation that the provision be more broadly framed by reference to the information that an investor trusts a financial market participant to disclose to him.

[303] [1932] KB 442 (CCA). See further *R v Bishirgian* (1936) 154 LT 499 (CCA).

Section 19 of the Theft Act 1968 must certainly be given at least as wide an interpretation by the courts so long as an intention to deceive can be established. However, it does not extend to false promises or forecasts nor to oral statements.

CHAPTER 20

TAKEOVERS AND MERGERS

20.1 INTRODUCTION

This chapter is concerned with the legal machinery for merging and reconstructing companies. Previous editions of this book have stressed the limited role played by formal legal rules in this field and the significance of the self-regulatory rules contained in the City Code on Takeovers and Mergers and the Rules Governing the Substantial Acquisition of Shares (SARS). Following the implementation of the Takeovers Directive and the decision made by the Takeover Panel to end the SARS,[1] the era of self-regulation came to an end. The Directive was required to be implemented by 26 May 2006, and since it had become clear that the Companies Bill would not become law by that date, the Government decided to implement the Directive by way of interim regulations.[2] As the scope of the Directive was narrower than the scope of the pre-existing takeover regulation in the UK, the interim regulations had the effect that the new statutory system of regulation operated in tandem with the old self-regulatory system pending the provisions of the Companies Act 2006 taking effect. When Part 28 of the Companies Act 2006 took effect,[3] the self-regulatory system ended in its entirety, with both the Panel[4] and the Code being placed on a statutory basis. Takeovers and mergers have other important dimensions which are beyond the scope of this book. For example, they may lead to a reference by the Office of Fair Trading to the Competition Commission under the Enterprise Act 2002[5] or to an examination by the European Commission of offers with a Community dimension under the Merger Control Regulation.[6] The purpose of the investigations which follow such references is to establish if the proposed

---

[1] See Takeover Panel Consultation Paper PCP 2005/4 for background (available at www.thetakeoverpanel.org.uk). The abolition was not dictated by the Takeovers Directive: it resulted from the Panel's conclusion that restrictions on acquisitions by an offeror below the level of control (30%) were no longer appropriate.

[2] The Takeovers Directive (Interim Implementation) Regulations 2006, SI 2006/1183. See generally DTI, Company Law Implementation of the European Directive on Takeover Bids, A Consultative Document (January 2005).

[3] On 7 April 2007: see CA 2006 (Commencement No 2 etc) Order 2007, SI 2007/1093.

[4] The Panel's website, setting out the Code and other relevant information is at www.thetakeoverpanel.org.uk.

[5] See M Furse The Law of Merger Control in the EC and the UK (Hart Publishing, 2007).

[6] Regulation 139/2004/EC [2004] OJ L24/1.

mergers are likely to have anti-competitive effects.[7] If they do, they will either be blocked or have conditions attached to them so as to remove the anti-competitive effects. There are also taxation implications for the offeror and the shareholders of the offeree,[8] and there are employment law consequences under the Transfer of Undertakings (Protection of Employment) Regulations 2006.[9] The *Listing Rules* require offerors which are listed companies to notify a Regulated Information Service[10] of takeover offers that fall within certain financial thresholds (the 'class tests') and to secure shareholder approval for offers that represent 'class 1' transactions.[11]

20.2 THE TAKEOVER PANEL AND ITS ADMINISTRATION OF THE CODE

The Companies Act 2006 places the Takeover Panel on a statutory footing.[12] The Act assumes the existence of the Panel and does not alter its legal status as an unincorporated association, although it does make clear that it can sue and be sued in its own name.[13] There is no express provision made for replacement of the Panel should that prove necessary, despite the Directive requiring that member states must ensure that there is always a body to regulate takeovers. The view of the Government, however, is that it retains the power (under the European Communities Act 1972) to remove or replace the Panel as regulator should it cease to be an appropriate regulator or should its rules no longer comply with the Directive.[14] Nor does the 2006 Act set out the procedure for appointments to the Panel. That remains a matter for the Panel and recent changes have resulted in the nominations committee of the panel playing the key role in making appointments, whereas in the past the Bank of England had largely controlled appointments.

The Companies Act 2006 does not interfere with the existing structure or mode of operation of the Panel. Authority is given for the continuation of existing practice by the express power to delegate functions of the Panel either to a committee or an officer or member of the Panel.[15] This permits the day-to-day business of the Panel to continue to be handled by the Panel Executive – consisting of the Director-General, the Deputy Director-General(s), the Secretary and their staff reporting directly to the

---

[7] See M Furse *The Law of Merger Control in the EC and the UK* (Hart Publishing, 2007), ch 5. The UK and EC systems adopt different approaches to the determination of whether mergers are likely to have anti-competitive effects.

[8] See *Gore-Browne on Companies* (Jordans, 45th edn, loose-leaf) at Part X1, Ch 48.

[9] See O Hyams *Employment Aspects of Business Reorganisations* (OUP, 2006).

[10] This will result in the information being made public.

[11] See FSA Handbook, *Listing Rules* (LR) 10 Significant Transactions.

[12] CA 2006, s 942.

[13] CA 2006, s 960. Unincorporated associations cannot normally sue and be sued in their own name.

[14] See *Hansard*, HL Debs Grand Committee, col 286 (28 March 2006) Lord Goldsmith.

[15] CA 2006, s 942(3).

Chairman.[16] The day-to-day business of the Panel, which the Panel Executive administers, consists chiefly of monitoring all takeover and merger transactions to ensure as far as possible that the proposals and the manner of their execution conform to the spirit and to the detailed provisions of the Code, on the basis that such rulings are subject to reference to the full Panel. The Director-General or his deputies are available at all times to give rulings on points of interpretation of the Code. Such rulings now have binding effect under the Companies Act 2006.[17] They will endeavour to give these rulings as promptly as is necessary to ensure the free functioning of the takeover and merger business. Companies and their advisers are encouraged to consult the Panel Executive on points needing clarification either by telephone or by meetings at short notice. Practice statements are published by the Panel Executive indicating how it normally interprets the Code in particular circumstances.

The main functions of the full Panel are now carried out by the Code Committee and the Hearings Committee, but the Panel remains directly responsible for those functions that are not carried out by its committees. The Code Committee carries out the rule-making functions of the Panel under the Companies Act 2006. Those rule-making powers extend beyond the scope of takeover regulation under the Directive so as to include transactions which have in the past fallen within the scope of takeover regulation in the UK.[18] This means, for example, that the Panel has power to make rules covering bids for companies whose securities are not traded on a regulated market and mergers through a scheme of arrangement. The Code Committee is responsible for keeping the Code up to date and consulting on possible amendments through the publication of public consultation papers.

The principal function of the Hearings Committee is to review rulings of the Panel Executive. The Companies Act 2006 expressly requires such a committee to be established for that purpose.[19] In order to preserve the independence of the Hearings Committee, members of the Panel who took the decision under challenge are precluded from being members of the Hearings Committee. The Hearings Committee can be convened:

(a) by a party to a takeover or another party with a sufficient interest;

(b) by the Panel Executive, without giving a ruling, in difficult or important cases;

---

[16] The staff of the Panel comprises mainly secondees from City firms associated with takeovers.

[17] CA 2006, s 945(2).

[18] See CA 2006, s 943.

[19] CA 2006, s 951(1).

(c) to hear disciplinary proceedings brought by the Panel Executive in
     respect of a breach of the Code or a ruling of the Executive or
     Panel;

(d) in other circumstances where the Executive or the Hearings
     Committee considers it appropriate to do so.

The quorum for proceedings of the Hearings Committee is five. Cases are
normally presented in person by the parties or their advisers although
there is no prohibition on legal representation. The proceedings are
normally in private, although the Chairman may direct otherwise and the
parties may request a public hearing. The proceedings take place on an
informal basis and there are no rules of evidence. It is the usual policy of
the Hearings Committee to publish its rulings by means of a Panel
Statement issued as promptly as possible, having regard to all the
circumstances of the case, after the ruling has been provided in writing to
the parties. The sanctions available to the Hearings Committee in respect
of breaches of the Code or ruling of the Executive or Panel are discussed
below at **20.3**.

Decisions of the Hearings Committee can be appealed to the Takeover
Appeal Board by any party. The Appeal Board is an independent
committee which replaces the former Appeal Committee. The Chairman
and Deputy Chairman of the Board will usually have held high judicial
office, and are appointed by the Master of the Rolls. Other members, who
will usually have relevant knowledge and experience of takeovers and the
Code, are appointed by the Chairman. The Appeal Board has its own
rules which are published on its website.[20] The quorum for Board
proceedings is three but the Board hearing an appeal will usually comprise
at least five members. Proceedings before the Board are generally
conducted in a similar way to those before the Hearings Committee. The
Board provides its decision to the parties in writing as soon as practicable.
Decisions of the Board are usually published in a public statement, save
for matters redacted in order to protect confidential or commercially
sensitive information (redaction being allowed following a request by one
of the parties to the hearing and at the discretion of the chairman of the
hearing). The Board may confirm, vary, set aside, annul or replace the
contested ruling of the Hearings Committee. On reaching its decision, the
Board remits the matter to the Hearings Committee with such directions
(if any) as the Board considers appropriate for giving effect to its decision.
The Hearings Committee will give effect to the Board's decision. There is
no right of appeal from the Appeal Board to the courts, but, as made
clear by the DTI Consultative Document,[21] there was no intention that

---

[20] The Appeal Board's website is www.thetakeoverappealboard.org.uk.
[21] See DTI Consultation Document, above n 2, at para 2.38.

the Companies Act 2006 should interfere with the established right of parties to takeover proceedings to apply for judicial review of final decisions of the Panel.[22]

Linked with the move to a statutory framework has been concern[23] that tactical litigation might emerge as a threat to the rapid decision-making which characterised the operation of the Panel during its time as a self-regulatory body. Several provisions of the Companies Act 2006, when taken together, have the effect of largely excluding this possibility. The first is that contraventions of the Takeover Code do not make any transaction void or unenforceable.[24] This removes the uncertainty and potential costs that would arise if takeover transactions could be challenged on that basis. The second is that contraventions of the Takeover Code do not give rise to a right of action for breach of statutory duty.[25] Such an action, were it available, could have an equally disruptive effect as parties could argue that contraventions had resulted in a takeover bid either being thwarted or succeeding as a result of the contravention. Finally, the Panel and its members, staff and officers are exempt from liability in connection with the discharge or purported discharge of the Panel's functions.[26] This removes the possibility of tactical litigation being targeted at the Panel itself as a means of disrupting its decision-making processes.

20.3 THE SANCTIONS AVAILABLE TO THE PANEL

Prior to the implementation of the Takeovers Directive, the Panel was not a statutory body and its decisions were not legally binding. While compliance with the Code was widely regarded as one of the indicators of a reputable company and the self-regulatory status of the Code and Panel depended on its widespread acceptance, there was an important mechanism which linked the Code with the formal system of financial regulation established under the Financial Services and Markets Act 2000 (FSMA 2000). That mechanism was the power given to the FSA to endorse codes such as the Takeover Code.[27] The FSA duly endorsed the

---

[22] The Court of Appeal has held that decisions of the Panel and its Appeal Committee (now the Appeal Board) are in principle open to judicial review but in the particular case an application for judicial review was rejected: *R v Panel on Take-overs, ex parte Datafin plc* [1987] QB 815. Sir John Donaldson MR indicated that the relationship between the Panel and the court should be historic rather than contemporaneous. The court should allow contemporary decisions to take their course, considering the complaint and intervening, if at all, later and in retrospect by declaratory orders. See also *R v Panel on Take-overs and Mergers, ex parte Guinness plc* [1990] 1 QB 146.

[23] See DTI Consultation Document, above n 2, at para 2.39.

[24] CA 2006, s 956(2).

[25] CA 2006, s 956(1). This follows the pattern established in respect of most regulatory rules created under FSMA 2000 as a result of s 150(2) of FSMA 2000 and art 3 of the FSMA 2000 (Right of Action) Regulations 2001, SI 2001/2256.

[26] CA 2006, s 961.

[27] Under s 143 of FSMA 2000, now repealed by s 964 CA 2006.

Takeover Code with the result that a contravention could lead to enforcement action being taken by the FSA against an authorised person, such as the imposition of a fine or the withdrawal of permission to engage in regulated activity. Of course, now that the Panel and the Code have been placed on a statutory footing, the need for such indirect enforcement action has disappeared as the Panel is equipped with its own powers. However, the FSA rule prohibiting authorised persons from acting for an offeror who is not complying or is not likely to comply with the Takeover Code remains in place as does the possibility of enforcement action by the FSA based on breach of the FSA's *Principles for Business*.[28]

The Companies Act 2006 enables the Panel to impose sanctions for breaches of the Code or failure to comply with a direction. The Panel is required to publish a policy statement in respect of sanctions that were not available under the Takeover Code prior to the implementation of the 2006 Act.[29] This requirement applies most obviously to financial penalties should they be included in the Code at some future date.[30] The Act also sets out factors that the Panel must have regard to when imposing sanctions. They include the seriousness of the breach or failure in question, the extent to which the breach was deliberate or reckless and whether the person subject to the penalty is an individual. The Panel is able to revise a policy statement at any time, but that freedom should be understood to be subject to the legitimate expectations of those who relied on the version in force when a breach occurred.

The Companies Act 2006 also enables the Panel to adopt rules providing for the payment of compensation in respect of breaches of its rules. Provision has now been made in the Code for compensation to be payable in respect of breaches of a limited number of rules.[31] Another innovation is the possibility of court enforcement of the Code on the application of the Panel.[32] This is possible when the court is satisfied that there has been or is likely to be a contravention of a rule-based requirement or a disclosure requirement.

Reflecting its new statutory power to impose sanctions, the Panel is now also equipped with investigative powers. The Panel is able to require the production of documents and the provision of information that is reasonably required in connection with the exercise of its powers.[33]

---

[28] See FSA Handbook MAR 4.3.1R.

[29] The sanctions that were available in the past were: private and public censures; suspending or withdrawing an exemption; reporting conduct to a regulator such as the FSA; publishing a statement indicating that a person is likely not to comply with the Code, thereby triggering regulatory and professional rules that prevented firms acting on behalf of that person (e g MAR 4.3.1R above).

[30] The absence to date of financial penalties in the Code distinguishes the Panel from the FSA, which routinely imposes financial penalties.

[31] See s 10(c) of the Introduction to the Code.

[32] See CA 2006, s 955.

[33] CA 2006, s 947(1)-(3).

Documents or information that fall within the scope of legal professional privilege cannot be required to be disclosed.

Closely linked with the sanctions available to the Panel are the new criminal offences[34] of failing to comply with the requirements of the Takeovers Directive (as implemented by the Takeover Code) in respect of offer documents[35] or response documents.[36] These offences apply only to the (narrow) definition of takeovers in the Directive and not to the wider meaning adopted in Part 28 of the Companies Act 2006. When an offer document does not comply with the relevant rules an offence is committed by the person making the bid (the offeror) and any director, officer or member of that body who caused the document to be published.[37] The offence is not one of strict liability as there is a *mens rea* requirement (below) but there is no materiality requirement, meaning that even minor non-compliance may result in the attachment of criminal liability. A person will be guilty if he knew that the offer document did not comply or was reckless as to whether it complied[38] and failed to take all reasonable steps to secure that the offer document did comply. The position differs in respect of a response document in that responsibility lies not with the offeree company but only with its directors and officers, who will be guilty subject to the same conditions applicable to their liability in respect of an offer document (above).

20.4 IMPEDIMENTS TO TAKEOVERS

Prior to the adoption of the Takeovers Directive, there were no provisions in UK company law which dealt with impediments to takeovers. The Takeover Code did contain some provisions which limited the ability of the board of an offeree company to take frustrating action but there was no attempt made to control impediments to takeovers in the form of the capital structure of a company. Such impediments, which can arise, for example, from special voting rights attached to particular classes of shares or other provisions in a company's constitution, have the capacity to limit the possibility of takeovers in the sense that control may be entrenched in the hands of a controlling shareholder or a group of shareholders. This was not historically a matter of great concern in the UK for several reasons. First, company law in the UK had historically emphasised the freedom of shareholders to structure the constitution as they wished, relatively free from regulatory control. Secondly, the dispersed system of

---

[34] See CA 2006, s 953.

[35] See Rule 24 of the Code.

[36] See Rule 25 of the Code.

[37] Comments made by the Solicitor General in the House of Commons indicate that agents (such as investment banks) are not included within the category of person who can commit this offence: see *Hansard*, HC Debs, cols 806-807 (18 July 2006).

[38] See *R v G* [2004] 1 AC 1034, making clear that a reference to 'reckless' as an element of a criminal offence requires advertant recklessness to be established (ie the defendant appreciated that there was a risk of non-compliance but nevertheless decided to run the risk).

shareholding which became established in the UK in the middle of the twentieth century meant that that there was relatively little concern over the possibility of control of listed companies becoming entrenched in the hands of a controlling shareholder. And finally, resistance on the part of institutional investors to differential voting structures or restrictions on share transfer[39] meant that listed companies with different classes of shares carrying different voting rights were not a feature of the UK capital market.

The position differed in continental Europe, which did not have the same historical tradition as the UK. Nor did many member states have much experience in developing and administering a takeovers regime. In order for the Directive to facilitate takeovers in continental Europe it was therefore necessary for the Directive to address directly the issues of entrenchment of control through capital structure as well as the freedom enjoyed by boards of directors in some other member states to take frustrating action after a bid was announced. Article 11 of the Directive (the 'breakthrough' provision) addresses the first issue and art 9 the second. However, the political sensitivity of facilitating takeovers (and thereby opening up the possibility of greater foreign control over enterprises) resulted in a compromise whereby the two provisions were made subject to an opt-out regime. This regime permits member states not to require compliance with art 9(2) and (3) (the prohibition on an offeree board adopting frustrating measures after a bid is announced) and art 11. The UK has not taken advantage of the possibility of opting out of art 9, mainly because the prohibition on frustrating action has been such a fundamental part of the Takeover Code for so long.[40] However, the UK has taken advantage of the opt-out in respect of art 11, with the result that the Takeover Code does not require compliance with this provision. Instead, companies are able to decide for themselves whether to give effect to the provision.[41] The process by which this decision is made is controlled by Part 28 of the Companies Act 2006.

Article 12 of the Takeovers Directive permits member states to specify that art 11 can only be relied on by a bidder against a target company where the bidder company and any controlling company are similarly subject to art 11 (ie there is reciprocity between the target and the bidder). The UK rejected the possibility of adopting this provision on the basis that it would represent a form of protectionism that was not compatible with the policy of an open takeovers regime and also that it would add another layer of complexity to the regime.[42]

---

[39] See the UK Listing Authority's *Listing Rules*, LR 2.2.4R.

[40] See Rule 21 for the current version. The position is made clear by s 943(1) of CA 2006, requiring the Panel to adopt rules which give effect to art 9. No such requirement is imposed in respect of art 11.

[41] As required by art 12(2) of the Directive when a member state has opted out of art 11.

[42] DTI Consultation Document, above n 2, p 28.

Article 11(2) provides that any restrictions on the transfer of securities provided for in the articles of association of the offeree company shall not apply *vis-à-vis* the offeror during the time allowed for acceptance of the bid laid down in art 7(1). A similar provision in art 11(3) applies to any restrictions on the transfer of securities provided for in contractual agreements between the offeree company and holders of its securities, or in contractual agreements[43] between holders of the offeree company's securities entered into after the adoption of the Directive. The objective of these provisions is to facilitate the transfer of control as a result of a bid by disregarding the relevant restrictions.

Article 11(3) contains several provisions which have the same effect in relation to restrictions on voting rights. First, restrictions on voting rights provided for in the articles of association of the offeree company shall not have effect at the general meeting of shareholders which decides on any defensive measures in accordance with art 9. Secondly, restrictions on voting rights provided for in contractual agreements between the offeree company and holders of its securities, or in contractual agreements[44] between holders of the offeree company's securities entered into after the adoption of this Directive, do not have effect at the general meeting of shareholders which decides on any defensive measures in accordance with art 9. Thirdly, multiple-vote securities shall carry only one vote each at the general meeting of shareholders which decides on any defensive measures in accordance with art 9.

Article 11(4) provides the crucial breakthrough mechanism which permits a bidder to secure effective control of a target. It provides that where, following a bid, the offeror holds 75% or more of the capital carrying voting rights,[45] no restrictions on the transfer of securities or on voting rights referred to in paras 2 and 3 nor any extraordinary rights of shareholders concerning the appointment or removal of board members provided for in the articles of association of the offeree company shall apply. Furthermore, multiple-vote securities shall carry only one vote each at the first[46] general meeting of shareholders following closure of the bid, called by the offeror in order to amend the articles of association or to

---

[43] Eg a pre-emption provision in a shareholders' agreement that requires the parties to offer shares to each other before offering them to outsiders. Without the breakthrough provision such an agreement could limit the holder's ability to accept a takeover offer.

[44] Eg in a shareholders' agreement.

[45] The Takeover Directive uses the expression '75% or more of the capital carrying voting rights' but the UK implementing provision (s 968 CA 2006) refers to '75% in value of all the voting shares'. The debate in Parliament made clear that the Government envisaged that the latter concept would normally be taken to refer to the nominal value of shares but that it was sufficiently flexible to enable the courts to apply the intention of the Directive in circumstances in which there was a differential voting structure. (See *Hansard*, HL Debs, col 213 (16 May 2006) Lord Goldsmith).

[46] The express reference to the first general meeting indicates that the bidder has only one chance to 'breakthrough' the relevant restrictions as they will be re-activated at any subsequent meeting.

remove or appoint board members.[47] The effect of this provision is to enable an offeror who has acquired 75% of voting capital (though not necessarily 75% of the votes) to control the key issues of changes to the constitution and changes to the board of directors. From a bidder's perspective these two issues are the 'crown jewels' of the target company in the sense that they represent effective control.

A special resolution must be adopted for a company to opt into art 11. For a company to adopt such a resolution three conditions must be met. First, the company must have voting shares[48] admitted to trading on a regulated market (which need not be in the UK provided it is in the EEA). This means that some companies which fall within the scope of the Takeover Code (eg AIM-listed companies or public companies with no listing whatsoever) are unable to adopt a resolution to opt into the breakthrough provision. While that may be regarded as anomalous, it is unlikely to be a significant barrier to takeovers because such a company can choose a shareholding structure which does not trigger the application of the breakthrough provision. For example, a straightforward structure in which there is only one class of ordinary voting shares and no restrictions on transfer does not trigger the operation of the breakthrough provision because there is no structural barrier to takeovers in those circumstances.

The second condition appears at first glance to be rather anomalous. It requires that the company's articles do not contain any of the restrictions referred to in art 11 of the Directive, or if they do, that the articles provide for them to be disapplied in the circumstances in which art 11 would do so. The requirement is effectively that the company restate in its articles the rule in art 11 to which it has bound itself by opting in. This can be done either by removing the relevant provisions or making them inapplicable in the circumstances required by the breakthrough rule. While this may appear odd in that, in accordance with the Directive, the regulatory rule would bind the company regardless of what is contained in the articles, the result is that the company's constitution is aligned with the Directive. In that sense, the breakthrough provision in the Directive will apply not just as a regulatory rule but as part of the company constitution. Notification of an opt-in decision must be given to the Panel and to the designated supervisory authority of any EEA state other than the UK in which the company has voting shares admitted to trading on a

---

[47] A bidder who reaches the 75% threshold has the right to call a general meeting: see CA 2006, s 969.

[48] For this purpose voting rights include rights that arise only in specified circumstances: CA 2006, s 938(1). Thus, contingent voting rights attached to shares (eg voting rights attached to preference shares contingent on non-payment of a dividend) may be considered voting rights for this purpose even if not for others: see also Sch 7, para 2 to the 2006 Act.

regulated market within 15 days of the resolution being passed. This is in addition to the recording of the resolution at Companies House as required by the Companies Act.[49]

The third condition is that no shares conferring special rights are directly or indirectly held by a minister and no such rights are exercisable under any other enactment. Such circumstances might arise when a minister holds rights such as a 'golden share' which carries special rights in the event of changes in ownership or control. Special rights held by persons or bodies other than a minister may be brought within the scope of this provision by regulations.[50]

Considering the mandatory nature of the three requirements, it seems correct to conclude that failure to satisfy any of the conditions will result in the resolution being invalid. If that is correct, then the outcome will be that a company which fails to meet the requirements for passing a resolution is less open to takeovers than it intended and that the (special) rights against which the breakthrough rule is aimed will remain effective. Failure to comply with the obligation to notify the Panel of an 'opt-in' or 'opt-out' resolution does not have the same consequence: in this case the company and officers in default are liable to a fine but the resolution remains valid.[51]

It is possible for a company to reverse the effect of an 'opt-in' resolution by subsequently adopting an 'opt-out' resolution. The UK implementation of this requirement goes beyond the Directive by stipulating, in the interests of legal certainty, the time at which the 'opt-out' resolution becomes effective. This may not be earlier than the first anniversary of the date on which a copy of the opting-in resolution was forwarded to the registrar. The effect is to delay the legal effect of an 'opt-out' resolution, thereby limiting its relevance as a potential response to a takeover bid.

Article 11(5) provides that where rights are removed as a result of the operation of the breakthrough provision or the adoption of an 'opt-in' resolution, 'equitable compensation' shall be paid to the holders of those rights as determined by member states. This does not apply in the case of art 11(3) and (4) where the restrictions on voting rights are compensated for by specific pecuniary advantages. Thus, it would seem that the application of the breakthrough provision to preference shares (in circumstances in which they have voting rights) would not attract compensation. Article 11 does not apply where member states hold securities in the offeree company which confer special rights on the member states which are compatible with the Treaty, or to special rights provided for in national law which are compatible with the Treaty, or to co-operatives.

---

[49]   CA 2006, ss 29–30.
[50]   CA 2006, s 966(8).
[51]   See CA 2006, s 970.

The UK implementation of the Directive contains no express provisions providing for the payment of compensation in the case of an 'opt-in' resolution. The justification for this approach is that an 'opt-in' resolution is subject to the normal legal and bargaining framework under which changes may be made to the constitution, which allows for the possibility of compensation to be paid. While that approach certainly follows the tradition in the UK, there must remain some doubt whether there has been adequate implementation of the Directive.[52]

As far as the operation of the breakthrough provision following the making of a bid is concerned,[53] the initial onus is on the bidder to state in the bid documentation what compensation is to be paid.[54] That is only an offer, but may lead to negotiations in which the compensation is settled. If no agreement is reached, there is express provision for compensation.[55] The formulation is complex and seems likely to lead to problems. It refers to two classes of person from whom compensation might be claimed. The first is the person who would have been guilty of a breach of contract had the breakthrough provision not operated. For example, the effect of the breakthrough provision on an agreement between a shareholder and a third party to vote shares in a particular manner would relieve the shareholder of the obligation and give the third party a right to compensation. This would be so even if the shareholder had not supported the 'opt-in'.

The second class of person by whom compensation is payable is a person who would, but for the operation of the breakthrough principle be responsible for inducing a breach of contract. The primary class of person envisaged as falling into this category is the bidder,[56] as indicated by the obligation imposed on the bidder to indicate the compensation payable in the bid document. The difficulty here is that the requirement to pay compensation is envisaged to arise from an act (the making of a bid) which is not the proximate cause of the loss. It is the operation of the breakthrough provision which is the proximate cause of the loss and that outcome results from the adoption by the company of an opt-in resolution. In that sense, it is the company and not the bidder which bears responsibility for triggering the operation of breakthrough and the losses which follow from it. The Directive leaves the terms of compensation to

---

[52] See cases dealing with the implementation of provisions of Directives creating rights for individuals: e g *Commission v Belgium (Case 102/79)* [1980] ECR 1473; *Commission v Netherlands (Case 96/81)* [1982] ECR 1791; *Commission v Netherlands (Case 97/81)* [1982] ECR 1819; *Commission v Germany (Case C-361/88)* [1991] ECR I-2567.

[53] In the UK the 'breakthrough' provision will only take effect on a bid in respect of contractual agreements which restrict transfer or voting. This will be so because any provisions of the articles which might be struck down by the 'breakthrough' provision will already have been removed as a condition of adopting the 'opt-in' resolution which activates the breakthrough rule.

[54] Article 6(3)(e) of the Takeover Directive.

[55] See CA 2006, s 968(6).

[56] While the class is not in terms limited to the bidder, it is difficult to envisage that any other person could satisfy the requirements of the tort of inducing breach of contract.

be set by member states and in its implementation the UK has selected the open-ended formulation that the court consider it to be fair and equitable.[57] This has the effect that the court is freed from the established rules governing quantification of damages for breach of contract or for the tort of inducing a breach of contract. Even so, there are likely to remain considerable difficulties in establishing what loss has resulted from the operation of the breakthrough provision, especially if it is clear that some bargaining has occurred at the time of the adoption of an 'opt-in' resolution.

20.5   THE SCOPE AND FORM OF THE CODE

The scope of the Code can be best described by reference to the companies, transactions and persons which are subject to the Code. Whether or not the Code applies to a particular company is determined by the characteristics of the company which is the offeree or potential offeree, or in which control may change or be consolidated. Following the implementation of the Takeovers Directive, the identification of the entire set of companies subject to the Code has become considerably more complex. For the sake of clarity, the following section reproduces verbatim the relevant section of the Code:[58]

'(a) Companies

(i) UK, Channel Islands and Isle of Man registered and traded companies

The Code applies to all offers (not falling within paragraph (iii) below) for companies and Societas Europaea (and, where appropriate, statutory and chartered companies) which have their registered offices in the United Kingdom, the Channel Islands or the Isle of Man if any of their securities are admitted to trading on a regulated market in the United Kingdom or on any stock exchange in the Channel Islands or the Isle of Man.

(ii) Other companies

The Code also applies to all offers (not falling within paragraph (i) above or paragraph (iii) below) for public and private companies and Societas Europaea (and, where appropriate, statutory and chartered companies) which have their registered offices in the United Kingdom, the Channel Islands or the Isle of Man and which are considered by the Panel to have their place of central management and control in the United Kingdom, the Channel Islands or the Isle of Man, but in relation to private companies only when:—
(A)   any of their securities have been admitted to the Official List at any time during the 10 years prior to the relevant date; or
(B)   dealings and/or prices at which persons were willing to deal in any of their securities have been published on a regular basis for a continuous

---

[57]   CA 2006, s 968(6).
[58]   See the Introduction to the Code at page A3.

period of at least six months in the 10 years prior to the relevant date, whether via a newspaper, electronic price quotation system or otherwise; or

(C)   any of their securities have been subject to a marketing arrangement as described in section 163(2)(b) of the Companies Act 1985 at any time during the 10 years prior to the relevant date; or

(D)   they were required to file a prospectus for the issue of securities with the registrar of companies or any other relevant authority in the United Kingdom, the Channel Islands or the Isle of Man or to have a prospectus approved by the UKLA at any time during the 10 years prior to the relevant date.

In each case, the relevant date is the date on which an announcement is made of a proposed or possible offer for the company or the date on which some other event occurs in relation to the company which has significance under the Code.

The Panel appreciates that the provisions of the Code may not be appropriate to all statutory and chartered companies referred to in paragraphs (i) and (ii) above or to all private companies falling within the categories listed in paragraph (ii) above and may accordingly apply the Code with a degree of flexibility in suitable cases.

(iii) Shared jurisdiction—UK and other EEA registered and traded companies

The Code also applies (to the extent described below) to offers for the following companies:

(A)   a company which has its registered office in the United Kingdom whose securities are admitted to trading on a regulated market in one or more member states of the European Economic Area but not on a regulated market in the United Kingdom;

(B)   a company which has its registered office in another member state of the European Economic Area whose securities are admitted to trading only on a regulated market in the United Kingdom; and

(C)   a company which has its registered office in another member state of the European Economic Area whose securities are admitted to trading on regulated markets in more than one member state of the European Economic Area including the United Kingdom if:

   (I)   the securities of the company were first admitted to trading only in the United Kingdom; or

   (II)   the securities of the company are simultaneously admitted to trading on more than one regulated market, but not on a regulated market in the member state of the European Economic Area in which it has its registered office, on or after 20 May 2006, if the company notifies the Panel and the relevant regulatory authorities on the first day of trading that it has chosen the Panel to regulate it; or

   (III)   the Panel is the supervisory authority pursuant to the second paragraph of article 4(2)(c) of the Directive.

A company referred to in paragraphs (C)(II) or (III) must notify a Regulatory Information Service of the selection of the Panel to regulate it without delay.

The provisions of the Code which will apply to such offers shall be determined by the Panel on the basis set out in article 4(2)(e) of the Directive. In summary, this means that:

- in cases falling within paragraph (A) above, the Code will apply in respect of matters relating to the information to be provided to the employees of the offeree company and matters relating to company law (in particular the percentage of voting rights which confers control and any derogation from the obligation to launch an offer, as well as the conditions under which the board of the offeree company may undertake any action which might result in the frustration of an offer) ("employee information and company law matters"); in relation to matters relating to the consideration offered (in particular the price) and matters relating to the offer procedure (in particular the information on the offeror's decision to make an offer, the contents of the offer document and the disclosure of the offer) ("consideration and procedural matters"), the rules of the supervisory authority of the member state determined in accordance with article 4(2)(b) and (c) of the Directive as the relevant supervisory authority will apply; and
- in cases falling within paragraphs (B) or (C) above, the Code will apply in respect of consideration and procedural matters; in relation to employee information and company law matters, the rules of the supervisory authority in the member state where the offeree company has its registered office will apply.

(iv) Open-ended investment companies

The Code does not apply to offers for open-ended investment companies as defined in Article 1(2) of the Directive.'

It is clear that the scope of the Code has become much more complex in its formulation than the old test of residence of the offeree which applied prior to implementation of the Takeovers Directive. The residence test has been retained in paragraph (ii) above, whereas paragraph (i) adopts the approach of the Directive, focusing on the dual test of location of registered office or location of listing of securities. The provisions of paragraph (iii) reflect the manner in which the Takeovers Directive splits jurisdiction between member states in various cases where more than one state is involved as the location of listing or registered office of a company.

The types of transaction falling within the Code reflect the broader scope of the UK regime (maintained by the 2006 Act) by comparison with the Takeovers Directive. The Code applies to all the transactions below at whatever stage of their implementation, including possible transactions which have not yet been announced. The Code does not apply to offers for non-voting, non-equity capital unless they are offers required by Rule 15 (offers for convertible securities).

In cases falling within paragraphs (i) or (ii) above, the Code is concerned with regulating takeover bids and merger transactions of the relevant companies, however effected, including by means of statutory merger or court-approved scheme of arrangement. The Code is also concerned with regulating other transactions (including offers by a parent company for shares in its subsidiary, dual holding company transactions, new share issues, share capital reorganisations and offers to minority shareholders) which have as their objective or potential effect (directly or indirectly) obtaining or consolidating control of the relevant companies, as well as partial offers (including tender offers pursuant to Appendix 5) to shareholders for securities in the relevant companies. The Code also applies to unitisation proposals which are in competition with another transaction to which the Code applies.

In cases falling within paragraph (iii) above (shared jurisdiction), 'offers' means only any public offer (other than by the company itself) made to the holders of the company's securities to acquire those securities (whether mandatory or voluntary) which follows or has as its objective the acquisition of control of the company concerned. This definition follows the Takeovers Directive definition[59] of a takeover offer and limits the application of the shared jurisdiction provisions to takeovers as defined by the Directive.

The provisions of the Code fall into two distinct categories. First, there are the General Principles, of which there are now six. They are expressed in broad general terms and the Code does not define the precise extent of, or the limitations on, their application. The introduction to the Code makes clear that they 'are applied in accordance with their spirit in order to achieve their underlying purpose'. The second and larger part of the Code consists of Rules (of which there are now 38).[60] Some of these 'are no more than examples of the application of the general principles whilst others are rules of procedure designed to govern specific forms of takeover and merger transactions practised in the United Kingdom'.

The Code emphasises that a legalistic and literal interpretation should not be given to any part of the Code. It is framed 'in non-technical language' and should be interpreted so as to give effect to its underlying purpose.

20.6   THE PRINCIPLES OF THE CODE

The Code first of all states its guiding philosophy. This is that the spirit as well as the letter of the General Principles and the Rules be observed. Furthermore, the General Principles and the spirit of the Code will apply in areas or circumstances not explicitly covered by any Rule. It is

---

[59]   Article 2(1)(a).

[60]   There are also Notes to the Rules which are intended to furnish a more detailed guidance as to how the Rules are to operate.

conceded that (in accordance with the principles of company law) boards of directors and their advisers have a duty to act in the best interests of their company as a whole. But the General Principles and the Rules inevitably impinge on the freedom of action of boards and persons involved in takeover and merger transactions. This applies to the board and advisers of both the offeror and offeree companies. A number of the Principles are concerned with fair treatment of shareholders, including equal treatment of different classes of shares, as well as among members of each class. Thus, 'all holders of the securities of an offeree company of the same class must be afforded equivalent treatment'.[61]

General Principle 1 indicates that the acquisition of control by a person (or persons acting in concert)[62] will necessitate the protection of other holders of securities (primarily through the requirement that the offeror make a general offer to all other shareholders).

The Code imposes a general duty on the directors of offeree companies, when advising their shareholders to act in the interests of the company as a whole.[63] Under the Companies Act 2006, this should be taken to mean that the directors are required to consider the interests of employees, customers and suppliers.[64] There is an express requirement that the board of the offeree company, if it advises the shareholders, give its views on the effects of implementation of the bid on employment, conditions of employment and the locations of the company's places of business.[65]

The Code is concerned with the adequacy of information (and opinions) given to the shareholders of an offeree company. General Principle 2 requires that shareholders must be given sufficient information and advice to enable them to reach a properly informed decision and must have sufficient time to do so. Linked with this is the general principle that shareholders be given the opportunity to decide on the merits of a bid.[66] The Code also requires that false markets must not be created in the securities of the offeree company, of the offeror company or of any other company concerned by the bid in such a way that the rise or fall of the prices of the securities becomes artificial and the normal functioning of the markets is distorted.[67] An offeror must be able to implement an offer once it has been announced:[68] if that were not the case, the normal functioning of the market would be disrupted by the failure to follow up an announcement with an offer. Reflecting the potential disruption that

---

[61] General Principles 8 and 1 respectively. This of course expresses the gist of a similar principle of company law. In other respects, however, the Principles and Rules go further than existing company law.
[62] As to 'persons acting in concert', see the 'Definitions' section to the Code.
[63] General Principle 3.
[64] See CA 2006, s 172.
[65] General Principle 2.
[66] General Principle 3.
[67] General Principle 4.
[68] General Principle 5.

may be caused to the business of an offeree by a takeover offer, there is now a general principle which requires that an offeree company must not be hindered in the conduct of its affairs for longer than is reasonable by a bid for its securities.[69]

20.7   THE RULES

The scope of a book of this nature does not permit a full account of the 38 Rules of the Code (and their attendant Notes). These make up the bulk of the Code. The Rules are intended to regulate the whole process by which a takeover bid (or agreed merger) is conducted, from its initial launch to its completion (if that stage is reached). There are detailed provisions regulating the preliminary stages. These include the approach to the board of the offeree company[70] and the announcement of the offer or approach.[71] The General Principles of the Code will govern the offeree board's consideration of the offer. It should be observed that the Code requires the offeror to give evidence of financial (and other) ability to implement the offer.[72] Furthermore, where the offer comes within the statutory provisions for possible reference to the Competition Commission, it must contain a term stating that it will lapse if there is a reference to the Commission by the Office of Fair Trading before the closing date for the offer, or the date (whichever is later) when it is declared unconditional.[73]

Besides the Rule governing the timing and contents of offer announcements,[74] the Code makes elaborate provision as to the information that must be given to the shareholders of the offeree company.[75] This includes the shareholding by the offeror company in the offeree company.[76] It also includes (in the case of a securities exchange offer) shareholding in the offeror and (in any event) shares in the offeree in which the directors of the offeror are interested. A similar disclosure must be made as to shareholdings owned or controlled by persons 'acting in concert'[77] with the offeror. It likewise applies to holdings owned or controlled by any persons who, prior to the posting of the offer document, have irrevocably committed themselves to accept the offer.[78] There is also provision for disclosure of directors' service contracts in

---

[69]   General Principle 6.
[70]   Rule 1.
[71]   Rule 2.
[72]   Rule 2.5.
[73]   See Rule 9.4 and Rule 12. The same rule applies to the initiation of proceedings by the European Commission under the Merger Regulation (139/2004/EC).
[74]   Rule 2. Rule 2 stresses the importance of secrecy prior to an announcement.
[75]   See Rules 23–27.
[76]   Rule 24.3.
[77]   The term 'persons acting in concert' is widely used throughout the Code and is thus defined in the Definitions which preface the Code.
[78]   Rule 25.3 imposes a parallel duty on the offeree company in respect of a document advising its shareholders on an offer.

respect of the offeree company. This applies in the case of documents sent to shareholders of the offeree company (by the board of the offeree) which recommend either acceptance or rejection of an offer.[79]

The Code makes provision for profit forecasts and for asset valuations.[80] The policy expressed by the Code is that information concerning profit forecasts may be vital to the shareholders' assessment of the merits of a takeover proposal. This is likely to be the case in particular when profits are volatile or business conditions uncertain. Rule 28 lays down precise and stringent requirements as to the preparation of forecasts. Directors are required to state the assumptions, including commercial assumptions, upon which they base their profit forecasts. Although such forecasts are the sole responsibility of the directors making them, the accounting bases and assumptions must be reported on by the offeror's auditors (or reporting accountants) as well as by its merchant bank or other financial adviser mentioned in the offer document. This is not required where the forecast is made by an offeror offering solely cash.[81]

It may be noted that, although the common law as to misrepresentation is ill adapted to provide a remedy for predictions (eg profit forecasts) or opinions (eg asset valuations), the law of contract, being concerned with the enforcement of promises, is more apt for such purposes. Since an offer document will, as its name indicates, produce a contract between the offeror company and the shareholders in the offeree who accept its terms, legal redress will be available in the case of a misleading forecast (or unsound valuation) which events show to be substantially inaccurate. The Panel has recognised that legal responsibility may arise from statements made in takeover documents. Rule 29 also stipulates that where a valuation of assets is given in connection with a takeover offer, the board of the offeror should be supported by the opinion of a named independent valuer and the basis of the valuation clearly stated.[82]

A number of Rules in the Code relate to what has been termed the 'mechanics of the formal offer'.[83] These concern such matters as what is permissible in respect of the revision and extension of offers, and as to the withdrawal of acceptances. Provision is made as to how and when an offer may be declared unconditional. It should be noted that copies of all offer documents (and other announcements or documents bearing on a takeover) must be lodged with the Panel at the same time as they are dispatched to their intended recipients.[84]

---

[79] Rule 25.4. In the offer document itself it should be stated (except in the case of an offeror offering solely cash) whether the offeror's directors' emoluments will be affected by a successful acquisition of the offeree: Rule 24.4.

[80] See Rules 28 and 29.

[81] Rule 28.3.

[82] Rule 29.2.

[83] Ie Rules 30–34.

[84] Rule 20.7.

20.8   PARTIAL OFFERS

In Rule 36 the Code tries to curtail any unfairness to shareholders that may arise from 'partial offers'. Although such offers for less than 100% of a company's shares (or a class thereof) may sometimes be justified, Rule 36 states that the Panel's consent is required for *any* partial offer and it then lays down guidelines as to how and when that consent may be given. The rationale for limiting the use of partial offers is not made clear by the Code. It can be argued, however, that they deviate from the rule[85] adopted by the Code that a person who acquires control of a company should be required to make an offer to all the shareholders (the mandatory bid rule). A policy of limiting the use of partial offers supports the mandatory bid rule as partial offers are in effect exceptions to the mandatory bid rule.

In the case of an offer which would result in the offeror holding shares carrying less than 30% of the voting rights[86] of a company, consent will not normally be given. Where the result will be control of between 30% and 100%, such consent will not normally be given if the offeror (and 'persons acting in concert') have acquired shares in the offeree company during the previous 12 months. Where an offer is made which would result in the offeror holding shares carrying 30% or more of the voting rights, a comparable offer must be made to each class. Acquisition of 30% of the voting rights is also critical in 'triggering' an obligation under Rule 9 to make an extended offer to other voting shareholders. In the case of a partial offer which could result in the offeror holding over 30% (but less than 50%) of the voting rights of the offeree, the precise number of shares offered for must be stated. The offer may not be declared unconditional as to acceptance unless acceptances are received for not less than that number. Any offer which would result in the offeror holding shares carrying 30% or more of the voting rights must be conditional, not only on the specified number of acceptances being received, but also on approval by 50% of the voting rights not held by the offeror and persons not acting in concert with it.[87]

Few offers are nowadays structured at the outset as partial offers. At least two reasons can be suggested: one is that a bidder will generally not want a sizeable minority to remain as shareholders in the target, thereby potentially disrupting the implementation of the offeror's business strategy; and a second is that most bidders nowadays buy shares in the

---

[85]   Rule 9 of the Code, now also part of the Takeovers Directive (art 5).

[86]   These are defined by the Code as 'all the voting rights attributable to the share capital of a company which are currently exercisable at a general meeting'. However, the Panel should be consulted where rights exercisable only in restricted circumstances have in fact been exercisable for a long time, or it may be considered that the shares in question have voting rights for the purpose of the Code.

[87]   See *Gore-Browne on Companies* (Jordans, 45th edn, loose-leaf) at 45 [86] as to the possibilities of waiver by the Panel, and as to how Rule 36 applies to different classes of shares.

market prior to launching a bid and this rules out approval of a partial offer. The more relevant part of Rule 36 in many cases is the possibility it creates to increase a holding to a higher level.

20.9   RESTRICTIONS ON DEALINGS

The City Code was early in the field in so far as insider dealing in the context of a takeover bid or merger is concerned. The main restriction is found in Rule 4. This forbids persons who are privy to the intention to make an offer (or to the preliminary negotiations) from dealing in the securities of the offeree company from the time when there is reason to suppose that an approach is contemplated until the issue of a press announcement (or the termination of the previous discussions). Furthermore, no such dealings shall take place in the securities of the offeror except where the proposed offer is not deemed price-sensitive. Rule 4 also imposes a general injunction of confidentiality upon anyone privy to such information making recommendations to any other person as to dealing in the relevant securities.

Rule 5 restricts the speed with which, just before and during an offer, voting shares and rights over voting shares of a company may be acquired by a person, or those acting in concert with him, whose aggregate holding of shares and rights over shares would thereby rise to or through 30% of the voting rights in that company. It also restricts acquisitions of voting shares and rights over shares by a person whose holding is between 30 and 50%. Acquisitions falling within either category are not permitted before the announcement of a firm intention to make an offer, unless the acquisition immediately precedes and is conditional upon such an announcement being made with the public recommendation of the board of the offeree company.

However, once a takeover proposal is announced, all parties may (subject to certain other provisions of the Code) deal subject to daily disclosure to the Stock Exchange, the Panel and the press.[88] This disclosure must be made on a daily basis (whether on or off the market and at whatever price) in respect of purchases of shares in the offeror or offeree. The basic freedom to purchase is posited on the basis that it is 'undesirable to fetter the market'. However, the Code implicitly recognises that this philosophy of the unfettered market may well give an unfair advantage to the offeror and those acting in concert with it.[89] Thus Rule 6.2 requires that if the offeror (or any person acting in concert) purchases securities during the

---

[88]   See Rule 8.1. This obligation applies not only to the offeror and offeree but also to concert parties. Disclosure of dealing by major shareholders (meaning those owning or controlling 1% or more of any class of relevant securities of an offeror or the offeree company) is also required.

[89]   Rule 8.3 and Rule 16 (special deals with favourable conditions).

offer period at above the offer price (being the then current value of the offer), the offer must be increased to not less than the highest price paid for the security so acquired.[90]

In certain cases, Rule 11 requires that offers in respect of a class of shares shall either be in cash or be accompanied by a cash alternative.[91] This obligation applies when shares of any class (under offer in the offeree company) are purchased[92] for cash by the offeror (and any person acting in concert) during the offer period and within 12 months prior to its commencement and the shares purchased carry 10% or more of the voting rights exercisable at a class meeting of that class.[93] It also applies to mandatory offers made under Rule 9.[94] The Panel may give its consent to dispense with this obligation. Additionally, the panel may also excuse the offeror from paying the highest price (under Rule 11) in a particular case.[95]

20.10   THE MANDATORY OFFER TO THE REMAINING SHAREHOLDERS

Rule 9 exists to prevent the problem of the 'locked in' minority shareholder arising. It is also designed to discourage acquisition of *de facto* control by stealth and through payment of a control premium to a select group of shareholders. In certain circumstances, this Rule requires an existing offer to be extended to the remaining shareholders hitherto excluded from it. Rule 9 applies where any person *acquires*, whether by a series of transactions over a period of time or not, shares which (taken together with shares held or acquired by persons acting in concert with him) carry 30% or more of the voting rights of a company. Rule 9 also applies where any person, together with persons acting in concert, *holds* not less than 30% but not more than 50% of the voting rights, and such a person or any person acting in concert, acquires in any period of 12 months additional shares carrying more than 1% of the voting rights. In either of these situations, those concerned must extend an offer[96] to the

---

[90]   Immediately after the purchase it must be announced that a revised offer will be made in accordance with Rule 6. Where practical, disclosure must be made of the number of securities purchased and the price paid. Rule 7.1 also requires an immediate announcement to be made if the offer has to be amended where purchases give rise to obligations under Rules 6, 9 or 11.

[91]   This must be valued at not less than the highest price paid (excluding stamp duty and commission) for the shares of that class purchased during the offer period and within 12 months prior to its commencement.

[92]   Eg through the market or by private purchase.

[93]   See Rule 11(1)(b) re obligations arising when shares are purchased for cash during the offer period only.

[94]   Rule 9.5. See **20.10** re mandatory offers.

[95]   Rule 11.3. See the note thereto as to the 'relevant factors' that the Panel will take into account.

[96]   The offer so extended must comply with the condition set out in Rule 9.5; ie it must be in cash or be accompanied by a cash alternative. Such offers must be conditional upon

holders of any class of equity share capital whether voting or non-voting. This offer must also be made to the holders of any class of voting non-equity share capital in which such person or persons acting in concert with him hold shares.[97]

The provisions of the Code relating to 'concert parties' have often been regarded as a constraint on shareholder collaboration in respect of governance issues. In response to concern over this issue that arose during the development of the Stewardship Code[98] the Panel issued a statement providing clarification of the meaning of acting in concert.[99] While the clarification does provide some guidance as to how the Panel will approach the determination of whether a 'concert party' exists, the core of its approach has been part of the Code since 2002, when changes were made with the specific aim of assisting normal shareholder activism. The effect of those changes and the recent clarification has been to considerably narrow the circumstances in which collaboration between activist shareholders will trigger a mandatory offer. In particular, since a 'concert party' can only exist if *inter alia* the relevant shareholders requisition a general meeting to consider a 'board control-seeking' resolution or threaten to do so, it follows that the concept of a concert party cannot normally be relevant to private engagement with the company nor to agreements between the shareholders to vote in the same way on a particular resolution at a general meeting.

The Code contains other provisions to curb rapidly repeated takeover bids or improper defensive tactics by the offeree company. Thus it prevents those who have made an offer, which has lapsed or been withdrawn, from making another offer within the next 12 months for the same company, except with the permission of the Panel.[100]

Rule 21 is designed to amplify further General Principle 3. The latter gives shareholders in the offeree company the right to decide the outcome of a takeover offer and by implication prohibits any frustrating action undertaken by the board without shareholder approval. Rule 21 is

---

the offeror having received acceptance in respect of shares which, together with the shares acquired or agreed to be acquired before or during the offer, will result in the offeror, etc holding shares carrying more than 50% of the voting rights. See Rule 9.3.

[97] Offers for different classes of equity capital must be comparable. Here the panel must be consulted in advance. This rule is complex in its varied applications. It has an extensive Note giving detailed interpretation, in particular as to 'persons acting in concert'.

[98] See http://www.frc.org.uk/corporate/investorgovernance.cfm (7 July 2011).

[99] See Takeover Panel Practice Statement 26. As the Panel notes in that Statement (at 1.7) 'The current provisions of the Code regarding collective shareholder action were introduced into the Code following consultation in 2002, with the specific aim of assisting normal shareholder action.'

[100] Rule 35. This rule also applies to prevent an acquisition of shares of the offeree company which may result in an obligation to make an offer as required by Rule 9. See also Rule 35.2 partial offers and 35.3 (delay of 6 months before acquisition above the offer price).

concerned with the issue of any authorised (but unissued) shares[101] or the issue or grant of options in respect of such shares, or convertible debentures. The board of the offeree company may not issue such securities during the course of the offer, or even before the date of the offer if the board has reason to believe that a *bona fide* offer is imminent, unless the approval of the shareholders in general meeting is obtained. There is a similar prohibition on the sale, disposal or acquisition of 'assets of material amount' and on 'entering into contracts otherwise than in the ordinary course of business'.[102]

20.11   ASSESSING THE CODE'S EFFECTIVENESS

Whatever the criticism levied at an earlier stage in their development,[103] the Code on Takeovers and Mergers, and the Panel which administers it, generally came to be regarded as a successful example of self-regulation. In 1987, the Secretary of State for Trade and Industry instigated a full review of the powers and personnel and rules of the Panel. Although it was considered that some measures could be provided which would strengthen the regulation of takeovers, it was decided that the Panel would continue as a self-regulatory body. It was felt overall that the Panel had, in general, worked effectively in ensuring fair treatment for all shareholders, regardless of whether takeovers succeed or fail. A self-regulatory system was preferred to a statutory underpinning, which would be slower and might encourage more formal litigation through appeals against the Panel's decisions.

Nevertheless the unofficial status of the Panel's Executive had drawbacks when it had to investigate abuses. This encouraged the Panel to withdraw from the field of policing 'insider dealing' and to welcome sanctions imposed by the criminal law. A lack of the power to subpoena witnesses, and the inhibiting effect of the laws of defamation, were said to curb the effectiveness of the Panel as an investigatory body. However, this has not in general hindered it in seeking compliance with the administration of the Code and in resolving disputed interpretations. Endorsement of the Takeover Code by the FSA[104] led to the sanctions for breach of the Code becoming largely aligned with those available to the FSA in respect of

---

[101]   The concept of authorised share capital ended when the relevant provisions of CA 2006 took effect: see especially s 542, effective from 1 October 2008. Note, however, that in the case of companies formed under earlier Acts, a provision relating to authorised share capital in its memorandum will continue to have effect (as part of the articles) and may be revoked or amended by the company by ordinary resolution: Companies Act 2006 (Commencement No 8, Transitional Provisions and Savings) Order 2008, SI 2008/2860, Sch 2, para 42.

[102]   Rule 21 does not apply to contracts to issue shares, etc already entered into. In special circumstances the Panel may give its consent to dispense with this rule.

[103]   See Davies *The Regulation of Takeovers and Mergers* (Sweet & Maxwell, 1976) at pp 39–46 for criticism of the 1974 version of the Code. See also McCrae and Cairncross *Capital City* (Eyre & Methuen, 2nd edn, 1985) at pp 150–157.

[104]   See **20.3**.

regulatory contraventions under the FSMA 2000. This development altered the purely self-regulatory status of the Panel and the Code, bringing them to some extent within the statutory framework of regulation under FSMA 2000. Following endorsement the FSA was able to withdraw authorisation, initiate disciplinary measures, undertake investigations, impose financial penalties, issue a public censure, apply for an injunction to restrain a breach, require restitution to be made or seek a court order requiring restitution. There was also the possibility of public censure of individuals or institutions being undertaken by the Panel. Such a sanction, where very substantial financial advantages are at issue, may seem feeble, especially in the case of those who will not need to maintain the goodwill of the Panel in the future. Yet the Panel still resorts to such censure even where it has found culpable (if not deliberate) breaches of important rules of the Code.[105]

The recent move to place the Panel and Code on a statutory footing was not the result of a loss of confidence in the (hybrid) self-regulatory status of the system or of any perceived failures. It was instead a direct result of the adoption by the EU of the Takeovers Directive, which requires member states to give legal effect to its provisions. Whether any significant changes will follow from the creation of a statutory regime remains to be seen but several factors suggest that this is unlikely. First, the Code remains substantially the same under the new regime although it now has a statutory basis. Secondly, the Panel will continue to operate much as before although with enhanced investigation and enforcement powers. For example, although empowered to impose financial penalties for contravention of the Code, the Panel has not yet done so. And finally, fears that the move to statutory footing would expand the possibility for tactical litigation seem unlikely to be realised (see **20.3**).

In early 2010, the Panel announced a review of certain aspects of the Code.[106] The review was prompted by concerns, which were crystallized by the takeover of Cadbury plc by Kraft Foods Inc., regarding the extent to which the operation of the Code favoured bidders over target companies. In particular, the concern focused on the extent to which the Code facilitated hostile bids and the role of short-term investors in deciding the outcome of a bid. Three of the possible reforms that were discussed would have had far-reaching consequences. They were:

(1) Raising the acceptance condition threshold above '50% plus one'. This would have altered the long-standing principle that a takeover offer need be conditional only on the offeror securing control of the target.[107]

---

[105] See the 'statements' section of the Panel website (www.thetakeoverpanel.org.uk) for recent examples.

[106] See Takeover Panel PCP 2010/2 Consultation Paper Issued by the Code Committee of the Panel (June 2010).

[107] See Rule 10 of the Code.

(2) Disenfranchising shares acquired during the offer period. This was viewed in some quarters as a means to limit the role of short-term investors in deciding the outcome of a bid.

(3) Requiring bidder shareholders to approve takeover offers. This would have been a new requirement as the Code has traditionally focused on protecting shareholders in target companies.

In its response to the consultation the Panel rejected the three proposals outlined above. However, it did propose significant measures, including:[108]

(1) A prohibition on (a) undertakings given to an offeror by an offeree company board to take any action to implement a transaction to which the Code applies, or to refrain from taking any action which might facilitate a competing transaction to which the Code applies; and (b) inducement fee agreements.[109]

(2) Disclosure of fees paid to advisers.

(3) Clarification of the matters that a target board can take into account in giving their opinion and recommendation on the offer.

Further developments on these issues are awaited and are likely to be linked with the government's review of so-called 'short-termism' in capital markets.[110]

20.12 RECONSTRUCTION AND AMALGAMATION UNDER S 110 OF THE INSOLVENCY ACT 1986

It is possible for a company to carry out a sale of its undertaking in two distinct ways: the sale of the undertaking may be effected: (a) before liquidation, under powers contained in the memorandum,[111] but this is only possible when a liquidation is not in immediate contemplation; or (b)

---

[108] See generally Takeover Panel 2010/22, Review of Certain Aspects of the Regulation of Takeover Bids (October 2010).

[109] This refers to so called 'break fees' paid by a target to a bidder in the even that a bid does not proceed to completion. So called 'success fees' paid to advisers are not covered by that proposal – the Panel concluded that such fees should not be prohibited.

[110] See BIS, A Long-Term Focus for Corporate Britain: a Call for Evidence, at http://www.bis.gov.uk/Consultations/a-long-term-focus-for-corporate-britain?cat=closedawaitingresponse (7 July 2011).

[111] The memorandum under s 8 of the Companies Act 2006 takes an abbreviated form and any clauses that are additional to this form will be taken to be part of the articles of association. Provisions previously contained in the memorandum (such as an objects clause) will be considered to form part of the articles: see s 28 of the CA 2006, discussed at **5.8**.

in contemplation of, or after the commencement of, a voluntary liquidation, under the powers now contained in ss 110 and 111 of the Insolvency Act 1986.[112]

However, a power in the memorandum to sell its undertaking (ie (a)) may not be used to enable the company to avoid compliance with the provisions of s 111 (examined below). In reversing earlier decisions[113] which upheld such a course, the Court of Appeal[114] held that the proper function of the memorandum was to deal with the objects of the company during its corporate life and not after that life has come to an end. Thus it is not part of the corporate objects to define the distribution of assets in a winding-up (including a s 110 reconstruction).

20.13 PROCEDURE UNDER SS 110 AND 111

The procedure under s 110 of the Insolvency Act 1986 is as follows: the company[115] will usually go into a members' voluntary winding-up,[116] and pass a special resolution authorising the liquidator to sell the undertaking under s 110. These powers may also be given to a liquidator in the case of a *creditors'* voluntary winding-up. Here the sanction of the court or the liquidation committee must be sought.[117] However, the sale can take place before winding up and authority can then be given to distribute shares. The authority may be general, or may be confined to a specified sale, to be made in accordance with a scheme of reconstruction or a draft agreement submitted to the meeting. To avoid unpleasant mistakes, it is advisable that the resolution authorising the sale of the property should be submitted simultaneously with the winding-up resolution, so that if the former is not carried the latter may also be dropped: otherwise the company will find itself in liquidation without any scheme for selling its business.[118] Both the voluntary winding-up and the authority for a sale require a special resolution; but they may be passed together at the same meeting.[119] Express notice of each resolution must, however, be given to

---

[112] These provisions now apply to both a members' and a creditors' voluntary winding-up. See s 110(3). See Chapter 21 as to voluntary winding up.

[113] See *Gore-Browne on Companies* (Jordans, 45th edn, loose-leaf) at 46 [3]. If such a power is appropriately drafted, it may allow the sale of the company's undertaking not only for cash but for shares, ibid.

[114] *Bisgood v Henderson's Transvaal Estates* [1908] 1 Ch 743.

[115] For the purposes of s 110, the 'transferor company' (ie the one put into voluntary liquidation) must be a registered company. But the transferee company may be a 'company within the meaning of this Act or not': s 110(1). However, the transferee must be a company and not an individual. See *Gore-Browne on Companies* (Jordans, 45th edn, loose-leaf) at 46 [8]–46 [9].

[116] The resolution sanctioning the sale may be either before, concurrent with, or after the resolution for voluntary winding up: s 110(6).

[117] See Insolvency Act 1986, s 110(3)(b).

[118] *Cleve Financial Corp* (1874) 16 Eq 363; *Clinch v Financial Corp* (1869) 4 Ch App 117; *Thomson v Henderson's Transvaal Estates* [1908] 1 Ch 765 (CA).

[119] See s 110(6).

the shareholders, specifying that a sale is intended under s 110,[120] and if the directors derive any special advantage a notice which does not disclose this fact is insufficient.[121] But it is no objection to a scheme of reconstruction that it openly gives a bonus to directors.[122]

Where a draft agreement for sale is prepared, the special resolution may refer to and approve it, and no other scheme of reconstruction is necessary. But power should be taken for the agreement to be carried out with or without modifications.[123]

20.14   RIGHTS OF DISSENTING SHAREHOLDERS

If any member of the company[124] being wound up who has not voted for the special resolution expresses his dissent from the resolution in writing, addressed to the liquidator and left at the registered office of the company not later than seven days after the passing of the resolution, he may require the liquidator either to abstain from carrying the resolution into effect or to purchase his interest[125] at a price which, if not settled by agreement, shall be determined by arbitration.[126] In such an arbitration, the dissentient has to prove the value of his interest. If a person who ought to be, but is not, on the register of members gives notice of dissent, the court may, on making an order for rectifying the register, declare that it shall relate back, so as to render the notice of dissent effective.[127] If the liquidator elects to purchase a dissenting member's interest, the purchase money must be paid before the company is dissolved, and be raised by the liquidator in such manner as may be determined by special resolution. Articles used often to provide that shareholders dissenting shall not have the rights given them by this section, or that the value of their interests shall be determined in some way other than by arbitration under the Act. But such provisions are invalid, for the articles cannot negate a provision in the statute for the benefit of the whole body,[128] and they are not an

---

[120]   *Imperial Bank of China v Bank of Hindustan* (1868) 6 Eq 91; *Re Irrigation Company of France, ex parte Fox* (1871) 6 Ch App 176, at 193.

[121]   *Kaye v Croydon Tramways* [1898] 1 Ch 358 (CA); *Tiessen v Henderson* [1899] 1 Ch 861; *Clarkson v Davies* [1923] AC 100 (PC).

[122]   *Southall v British Mutual Life Association* (1871) 6 Ch App 614. As to payments made to directors for loss of office (or retirement), see the provisions of s 218, CA 2006, discussed at **17.6**.

[123]   As to the forms of consideration the liquidator may give to the transferor company's shareholders, see the wide terms of s 110(2) and (4).

[124]   This includes the executors of a deceased member, even if the articles declare that they shall not have the rights of a member until they are registered: *Llewellyn v Kasintoe Rubber Estates* [1914] 2 Ch 670, at 679 (CA).

[125]   The notice must in terms state both alternatives for the liquidator to choose from, or it will be inoperative: *Re Demerara Rubber Co* [1913] 1 Ch 331; *Re Union Bank of Kingston-upon-Hull* (1880) 13 Ch D 808.

[126]   Section 111(2), (3) and (4).

[127]   *Re Sussex Brick Co* [1904] 1 Ch 598 (CA).

[128]   *Payne v Cork Co* [1990] 1 Ch 308; *Bisgood v Henderson's Transvaal Estates* [1908] 1 Ch 743, at 758 (CA).

agreement settling the price within the meaning of s 111(4).[129] If the company being wound up is in difficulties, the value of the interest of such members is, of course, very small. These safeguards for dissenting shareholders in s 111 of the Insolvency Act 1986 apply to the case of s 110 in a members' voluntary liquidation. Where s 110 is used in a creditors' voluntary winding-up, s 111 has no application.[130]

Schemes of reconstruction under s 110 may be upset by a dissentient minority on the ground that some of the provisions are an infringement of the rights of the minority, which the majority cannot impose upon them.[131] If proceedings are taken to set aside a sale to another company after the agreement for sale has been executed, the purchasing company must be made a defendant to the action,[132] and if the method of distributing the purchase consideration can be severed from the provisions for sale, the sale may stand good, leaving the proper distribution of the shares to be made according to the rights of the members of the vendor company.[133] The resolution for winding up is not invalidated by reason of its being coupled with an invalid resolution dealing with the distribution of the purchase consideration.[134]

The arrangement for a sale under s 110 can provide for the manner in which the consideration is to be paid, but cannot determine how it is to be distributed among the members of the vendor company, as this must be done in strict accordance with their rights.[135] It will be seen that this introduces a serious difficulty where there are either preference or other shares having special rights in the distribution of surplus assets. If one million shares of £1 each are to be distributed, and the rights of the holders of preference shares to the extent of £200,000 are that they shall be paid in full the amount of such shares before any repayment is made to the holders of ordinary shares, who shall say how many shares in the new company would be equivalent to a payment in full of the amount of the preference shares?

It is often attempted to meet the difficulty by giving holders of preference shares in the old company preference shares in the new; but this will not prevail over the rights of any of the old company's preference

---

[129] *Baring-Gould v Sharpington Combined Pick and Shovel Syndicate* [1899] 2 Ch 80 (CA).

[130] See s 111(1).

[131] As to the provisions which may lawfully be inserted in a scheme of reconstruction under s 110 (eg as to time-limits for members to apply for shares and as to the disposal of shares unapplied for), see *Gore-Browne on Companies* (Jordans, 45th edn, loose-leaf) at 46 [7].

[132] *Doughty v Lomagunda Reefs* [1903] 1 Ch 673 (CA).

[133] *Wall v London and Northern Assets Corporation* [1898] 2 Ch 469 (CA).

[134] *Thomson v Henderson's Transvaal Estates* [1908] 1 Ch 765 (CA); *Cleve v Financial Corp* (1873) 16 Eq 363.

[135] *Griffith v Paget* (1877) 5 Ch D 894 and 6 Ch 514; *Simpson v Palace Theatre* [1893] WN 91; affirmed by Court of Appeal (1893) 9 TLR 470.

shareholders who insist on getting the full value of their shares before the old company's ordinary shareholders get anything.

The result is that in companies where there are preference shares, a reconstruction under s 110 alone is not possible unless either there is power in the articles of association to meet the circumstances of the case, or the preference shareholders consent unanimously,[136] or those who do not consent to the proposed distribution also dissent from the whole scheme, so as to be paid out under s 111.[137]

20.15   THE PROTECTION OF CREDITORS

If after a voluntary winding-up of a company has been commenced an order is made within one year for winding it up, the special resolution is not valid unless sanctioned by the court: s 110(6). This sanction cannot be given in the voluntary winding-up. It will be effective only if given when the company is in compulsory liquidation.[138] When a scheme is unfair or improper this may be a ground for the court making a compulsory order on the application of dissatisfied shareholders;[139] but, 'generally speaking, the only persons who could raise this question or ask for an order ... would be the creditors'.

If creditors of the company, instead of proving in the liquidation and having their claims met in the ordinary way, accept securities in the transferee company, then they have the power, under s 110(6), to impeach any arrangement which proves unsatisfactory to them within this 12-month period.[140] This means that a scheme under s 110 may remain liable to be impeached for this period.[141]

20.16   DUTIES OF THE LIQUIDATOR UNDER SS 110–111

The liquidator must apply the funds which he receives from the new company in paying the costs of the liquidation and any debts which the old company is bound to pay, and in buying out dissentient members. If anything remains, it must be distributed among the members of the old company according to their rights.[142] If the cash which the liquidator

---

[136] Note that the court does not draw the inference that shareholders not represented at the meeting have consented; *Re North-West Argentine Rly* [1900] 2 Ch 882.

[137] Such a scheme has, however, been brought before the Court of Appeal under what is now s 895 of CA 2006, so as to bind the preference shareholders: *Sorsbie v Tea Corp* [1904] 1 Ch 12 (CA). However, this case conflicts with other decisions on the relationship between ss 110 and 895.

[138] *Re Callao Bis Co* (1889) 42 Ch D 169 (CA).

[139] *Re Consolidated South Rand Mines* [1909] 1 Ch 491.

[140] *Re City & County Investment Co* (1879) 13 Ch D 475 (CA).

[141] In *Re New Flagstaff Mining Co* [1889] WN 123, the company itself applied to the court for a supervision order.

[142] If the real value of the assets received by the transferee company exceeds the nominal

receives is not sufficient for the above purposes, he must raise cash by selling or mortgaging the shares or other property which he receives from the new company. The shares remaining over he will distribute among the members of the old company who have not been bought out.

The contract for sale usually provides that the purchasing company shall take over all the assets and pay all the liabilities of the old company, so that the business of the old company can be wound up at once; but such an arrangement does not relieve the liquidator of the old company from the obligation of seeing that the debts are duly paid before the old company is dissolved: to leave everything to the new company is 'a gross dereliction of duty by the liquidator',[143] and if he fails to pay income tax due from the company he will be personally liable to the Crown for the amount.[144]

If a liquidator makes a mistake in distributing the purchase shares, and has none left to correct his mistake, the court cannot upon a summons give damages against him.[145] Whether in an action damages could be recovered is doubtful.

As regards the new company, the same considerations will apply as in the case of a purchase from ordinary vendors, and the usual provisions will apply concerning the filing of contracts with the Registrar of Companies.[146]

Upon a reconstruction being carried into effect, the liquidator should wind up the old company with all possible speed, and, after making up his accounts, should call and advertise the meeting or meetings for receiving those accounts as provided in what is now s 94 of the Insolvency Act 1986. He should then make a return to the registrar of the meeting or meetings having been held, and at the end of 3 months from the registration of the return the company is dissolved,[147] subject, however, to the power of the court to reopen the dissolution.[148] The importance of this is that sometimes claims arise for damages, or on other grounds, which, if the company were still in existence, might give rise to great difficulties. The liquidator will have to pay all the debts of which he

---

amount of the shares issued by it, then the transferee company must transfer a sum equal to the amount in value to the share premium account: *Henry Head & Co v Ropner Holdings* [1952] Ch 124. See ss 131–132, CA 1985 for relief from s 130. See also ss 610–612, CA 2006. See **7.15**.

[143] *Pulsford v Devenish* [1903] 2 Ch 625; *Argill's v Coxeter* (1913) 29 TLR 355; *Re Aidall* [1933] 1 Ch 323, at 327 (CA).

[144] *Re New Zealand Joint Stock Corp* (1907) 23 TLR 238.

[145] *Re Hill's Waterfall Co* [1896] 1 Ch 947.

[146] See also **7.10**.

[147] Section 201 of the Insolvency Act 1986.

[148] See s 110(6) and **20.15**. Sections 106 and 201 will govern the final meeting and dissolution, where it is a *creditors'* voluntary liquidation.

knows;[149] but claims for damages may arise unexpectedly, and if the shares of the new company have been distributed there is nothing to meet such claims. A contract between the old and the new companies that the new will satisfy the liabilities of the old company cannot be enforced against the new company by creditors of the old for their own benefit, unless it has been made part of a scheme sanctioned under s 895 of the Companies Act 2006.[150]

The decisions[151] by the courts on the relationship between s 895, which provides for an alternative procedure for a reconstruction, as described in **20.18**, and s 110 of the Insolvency Act 1986 are difficult to reconcile. However, they appear to require that when a 'so-called' scheme is really a sale and transfer of assets under s 110, then that section must be complied with and cannot be evaded by petitioning for a scheme of arrangement under s 895.[152] However, this proposition is open to question as an unwarranted restriction on the powers conferred on the court by Part 26 of the Companies Act 2006.[153]

20.17   PROCEDURE UNDER PART 26 OF THE COMPANIES ACT 2006

A reconstruction can be carried out in pursuance of a compromise or arrangement under s 895 of the Companies Act 2006,[154] which applies not only as between the company and the creditors or any class of them, but as between the company and the members or any class of them.[155] A company falls within Part 26 generally[156] if it is capable of being wound up under the Insolvency Act 1986.[157] This section can also be used to give effect to a takeover, in which case the 'arrangement' will resemble a

---

[149] The liquidator will be personally liable, however, if he does not secure the payment of claims of which he has notice: *Pulsford v Devenish* [1903] 2 Ch 625; *Re New Zealand Joint Stock Corp* (1907) 23 TLR 238; *Re Aidall* [1933] 1 Ch 323, at 327 (CA).

[150] *Craig's Claim* [1895] 1 Ch 267 (CA).

[151] See *Sorsbie v Tea Corp* [1904] 1 Ch 12 (CA); *Re General Motor Cab Co* [1913] 1 Ch 377 (CA); *Re Sandwell Park Colliery* [1914] 1 Ch 589; *Re Guardian Assurance Co* [1917] 1 Ch 431 (CA).

[152] See the judgment of Astbury J in *Re Anglo-Continental Supply Company* [1922] 2 Ch 723. Where there are preference shares and this creates difficulties in making a distribution under s 110 of the Insolvency Act 1986, then a scheme under what is now s 895 of CA 2006 has been upheld. See the *Tea Corp* and *Sandwell Park* cases cited in the footnote above.

[153] For a further discussion of this question, see *Gore-Browne on Companies* (Jordans, 45th edn, loose-leaf) at 46 [11].

[154] Replacing s 425 of CA 1985.

[155] In this context a creditor includes a person with a contingent claim. The term is not limited to those with a provable claim in the winding-up of the company. See *Re T & N Ltd and others* [2006] 3 All ER 697.

[156] But note that s 900 applies only to companies incorporated under the Companies Act.

[157] This means that foreign companies (which are not incorporated in the United Kingdom) may fall within the scope of Part 26: see *Re La Seda de Barcelona SA* [2010] EWHC 1364 (Ch) and *Re Lehman Brothers International (Europe) (In Administration)* [2009] EWCA Civ 1161.

takeover offer in the form discussed above but with important differences as regards the procedure for approval and the rights of dissenting shareholders.[158] Section 895 provides that where any compromise or arrangement[159] is proposed between a company and its creditors or any class of them, or between the company and its members or any class of them the court may, on the application[160] of the company, or any creditor or member of the company, or the liquidator, order a meeting of the creditors or class of creditors, or of the members or class of members, as the case may be, to be called. If at the meeting so ordered a majority, in number representing three-quarters in value of the creditors or class of creditors, or members[161] or class of members, present either in person or by proxy, agree to the compromise or arrangement, and it is also sanctioned by the court, it will be binding on all the creditors or the class of creditors, or on the members or class of members, as the case may be, and on the liquidator and the contributories of the company.

The process under Part 26 focuses on the consent of the members and (where relevant) creditors of the transferor[162] company who are affected by the proposed scheme: thus where a company is insolvent the ordinary shareholders have no interest and their consent is not required.[163] A scheme which simply gives effect to a takeover (a change of control) does not prejudice the company's creditors and therefore does not require their consent. There is no provision for meetings or approvals on the part of the transferee company[164] although such meetings and approvals may be triggered by other relevant requirements.[165]

In the wake of the financial crisis, attempts were made to use a scheme for the purposes of settling multiple property claims against a company in administration. *In re Lehman Brothers International (Europe) (in*

---

[158] As noted by the Takeover Panel in its 2008 Annual Report, schemes of arrangement are now much more common than was the case in the past as a means of carrying out a recommended takeover.

[159] This includes a reorganisation of the share capital by the consolidation of shares of different classes or by the division of shares into shares of different classes or by both those methods: s 895(2).

[160] See the Civil Procedure Rules, Part 49 and *Practice Direction – Applications under the Companies Act 1985 etc* (replacing RSC Ord 102) at www.dca.gov.uk.

[161] As to the approval of members in the case of a company limited by guarantee, see *Re NFU Development Trust Ltd* [1972] 1 WLR 1548. Brightman J held that in such a company each member had in law the identical financial stake in the company. Thus a three-quarters majority of those present and voting satisfied the requirements of what is now s 899(1) of CA 2006.

[162] For schemes that give effect to a takeover offer, this is the equivalent of the offeree company.

[163] *Re Oceanic Steam Navigation Co Ltd* [1939] 1 Ch 41.

[164] For schemes that give effect to a takeover offer, this is the equivalent of the offeror company.

[165] In the case of merger schemes proposed by a public company see ss 907, 922 and 938 CA 2006. A meeting may also be necessary if the scheme involves the issue of shares other than on a pre-emptive basis (see 7.5) or, in the case of a listed company, the scheme falls within the 'class rules' contained in the *Listing Rules* (see **19.4**).

administration)(No 2)[166] resulted from the entry into administration of Lehman Brothers International Europe (LBIE) which held, on a segregated and pooled basis, securities[167] that belonged to a large number of clients. In recognition of the complexity of the claims the administrators sought to establish whether it would be possible to use a Part 26 scheme to reach agreement between asset claimants and LBIE both on their property and their pecuniary (net contractual) claims. The court held that Part 26 could not be used for this purpose since the agreement would not be between LBIE clients *as creditors* but rather as asset claimants. The court drew a distinction between the rights of a creditor and the rights of a client under a trust in which segregated assets are held, stressing that the latter cannot be varied without consent and that they survive the insolvency of the trustee intact. Part 26 permits a compromise (by the requisite majority) of creditors' claims against the company because they all look to the company's assets for payment of their claims but that is not the case for clients for whom the company holds assets on trust.

An order under the section is of no effect until an office copy has been delivered to the registrar for registration,[168] and a copy of every order must be annexed to every copy of the articles issued after the order has been made, or in the case of a company not having articles, of every copy so issued of the instrument constituting or defining the constitution of the company.[169]

20.18　THE INFORMATION REQUIRED BY S 897

The Companies Act 2006 imposes certain requirements, by s 897,[170] as to giving information in relation to schemes under s 895. Section 897 provides that where a meeting is convened under s 895 there shall:

(1)　with every notice summoning the meeting which is sent to a creditor or member, be sent also a statement explaining the effect of the scheme and in particular stating any material interests of the directors of the company, whether as directors or as members or as creditors of the company or otherwise, and the effect thereon of the scheme, insofar as it is different from the effect on the like interests of other persons;[171] and

---

[166]　[2009] EWHC 2141 (Ch); affirmed (CA) [2009] EWCA Civ 1161.

[167]　These assets were not held on a uniform basis since the property interest of the respective clients (and their transaction counterparties) were identified by reference to a number of different agreements such as International Prime Brokerage Agreements, Master Custody Agreements, Margin Lending Agreements, the Credit Support Annex to the ISDA Master Agreement and LBIE's standard terms of business.

[168]　Section 899(4).

[169]　Section 901.

[170]　Replacing s 426 of CA 1985.

[171]　As to what is sufficient disclosure of the interests of the directors see: *Rankin &*

(2) in every notice summoning the meeting which is given by advertisement, be included either such a statement or a notification of the place at which and the manner in which creditors or members entitled to attend the meeting may obtain copies of the statement.[172]

Where the scheme affects the rights of debenture-holders, the statement must give the like explanation as respects the trustees[173] of any deed for securing the issue of the debentures as it is required to give as respects the company's directors.[174]

Where there has been a failure to include an explanatory statement in an advertisement or to indicate where copies might be obtained, the fact that no prejudice is suffered as a result of the omission does not enable the court to dispense with the requirements of s 897. Fresh meetings with proper notice are necessary.[175]

Where the material interests of directors change, after the notices required by s 897 have been sent out, there is, strictly speaking, no requirement under that section for information about this later change to be sent to those who have already received notice under this section. Nevertheless, the court will take any change in directors' material interests into account in deciding whether to confirm a scheme under s 895. The court will have to be satisfied that no reasonable shareholder would change his decision on how to act on the scheme if the changes had been disclosed.[176]

The practice is to apply by originating summons for an order to convene the requisite meetings,[177] and if the appropriate majorities are obtained to apply by petition to the court for its sanction to the scheme.

The responsibility for determining what creditors or members are to be summoned to any meeting, as constituting a class, rests upon the applicant. If the meeting is incorrectly convened or constituted, or an objection is taken to the presence of any particular creditors as having interests competing with the others, the objection must be taken on the hearing of the petition for sanction, and the applicant must take the risk of the petition being dismissed.

Blackmore 1950 SC 218; *Peter Scott* 1950 SC 507; *Coltness Iron Co* 1951 SLT 344; *Property Investment Trust Corp Ltd* 1951 SLT 371.

[172] They are entitled to have a copy free of charge: s 897(4).

[173] See *Second Scottish Investment Trust Corp Petitioners* 1962 SLT 392.

[174] As to the sanctions imposed upon the company and officers in default for failure to comply with s 897, see s 897(5). There is also an obligation on directors and trustees for debenture holders to give the necessary particulars as to their interests: s 898(1).

[175] *Scottish Eastern Investment Trust* 1966 SLT 285.

[176] *Re Minster Assets plc* [1985] BCLC 200; *Re Jessel Trust Ltd* [1985] BCLC 119.

[177] A copy of the proposed statement under s 897 should form part of the evidence in support of the summons. This, of course, applies to proceedings in England.

The classic test of what is a class for the purposes of what is now s 895 was laid down by Bowen LJ in *Sovereign Life Assurance Co v Dodd*:[178] 'it must be confined to those persons whose rights are not so dissimilar as to make it impossible for them to consult together with a view to their common interest'. In *Re Hellenic & General Trust Ltd*,[179] a majority of the ordinary shares of a company were owned by a wholly owned subsidiary whose holding company sought to acquire all the sub-subsidiary's shares under a scheme under what is now s 895. Templeman J held that there was a sufficient community of interest between the holding and the subsidiary companies so that the latter was to be regarded as being in the purchasers' camp rather than in the vendors. Consequently, there was a sufficient difference of interest from that of the dissenting minority shareholders for two separate class meetings to be required. As in fact only one class meeting had been held for all the ordinary shareholders the scheme could not be confirmed. It must be observed that this seems a rather strained interpretation of Bowen LJ's *dictum*, of which it has been said that the 'emphasis here is on rights, which are not dissimilar, and the rights in question must surely be against the company in respect to the shares or debts in question. Extraneous interests should surely be disregarded'.[180] Moreover, Templeman J's decision does not accord with previous English and Commonwealth decisions that the members of a single class of shares (or debenture-holders or unsecured creditors, as the case might be) should, for the purpose of organising meetings, be treated as one class even though there are clear conflicts of interest between them.[181] However, if different amounts are paid on shares, or certain shareholders have paid amounts in advance of calls, this makes various classes of shareholders, and separate meeting must be called.[182]

In sanctioning a scheme, the court may ignore the fact that a class has not consented if it be proved that upon an immediate distribution of the assets none would be available for that class.[183] The power of the court to sanction a scheme is a discretionary one, as to which see **20.22**.

At meetings held in pursuance of s 895 proxies are allowed, and foreign creditors must be taken into account.[184] The treatment of foreign

---

[178] [1892] 2 QB 573, at 583.

[179] [1976] 1 WLR 123, at 125–126.

[180] This quotation is from a note by J A Hornby in (1976) 39 MLR 207, at 208.

[181] See *Re Alabama New Orleans, Texas and Pacific Junction Rly* [1891] 1 Ch 213; *Re Holders Investment Trust Ltd* [1971] 2 All ER 289. See also the Australian and South African cases discussed by Hornby in (1976) 39 MLR 207; *Re AW Allen Ltd* [1930] VR 251; *Re Chevron (Sydney) Ltd* [1963] VR 249; *Re Jax Marine Pty Ltd* [1967] 1 NSWR 145; *Re Landmark Corp Ltd* [1968] 1 NSWR 759; *Rosen v Bruyns* 1973 (1) SA 815(T). This simply means that a scheme under s 895 or other statutory provisions will not fail simply for not having separate meetings. The court may still refuse to sanction it on other grounds. See also *Re RMCA Reinsurance Ltd* [1994] BCC 378.

[182] *Re United Provident Assurance Co* [1930] 2 Ch 477.

[183] *Re Bluebrook Ltd, IMO (UK) Ltd and Spirecove Ltd* [2009] EWHC 2114 (Ch); *Sorsbie v Tea Corp* [1904] 1 Ch 12 (CA); *Re Oceanic Steam Navigation Co* [1939] Ch 41.

[184] *Re Queensland National Bank* [1893] WN 128.

creditors must depend on the terms of the scheme, and the conduct of meetings in this as in other respects is governed entirely by the court's directions. The court may allow the result of proxies to be communicated by telex or cable from distant places.[185] A form of proxy is settled in chambers for use at such meetings; the shareholder signing it cannot, when the company is in liquidation, leave the decision to his proxy,[186] but when the company is not in liquidation he may use any proper form of proxy, whether lodged before the meeting or not.[187] Directors who, pursuant to the order of the court, get proxies for or against a scheme are bound to use them. A proxy appointing a person to act for a shareholder at a class meeting and to vote either for or against a scheme of arrangement empowers the holder to vote against a resolution to defer the consideration of the scheme.[188] Meetings of shareholders not convened exactly in accordance with the directions of the court may be held good, if in the result a sufficient number of the shares are accounted for,[189] but it is most advisable to comply strictly with the directions.

If there are debentures to bearer or share warrants, the holders must produce them at the meeting, or otherwise prove their title to be treated as debenture-holders before the vote is taken.[190]

20.19   THE COURT'S POWERS UNDER S 900

Section 900 of the Companies Act 2006 confers upon the court certain additional powers which it may exercise on an application under s 900 for the court's sanction for a compromise or arrangement.[191] A common use of these powers enables what is broadly the equivalent of an amalgamation under s 110 of the Insolvency Act 1986 to be carried out under ss 895–900.[192] Indeed, for the powers given by s 900 to be employed, it must be shown to the court that the compromise or arrangement has been proposed for the purposes of, or in connection with, a scheme 'for the reconstruction[193] of any company or companies or the amalgamation of any two or more companies'. It must further be shown that under the scheme the whole or any part of the undertaking or the property of any company concerned in the scheme is to be transferred

---

[185] *Re English, Scottish and Australian Bank* [1893] 3 Ch 385 (CA).

[186] *Re Magadi Soda Co* [1925] WN 50.

[187] *Re Dorman, Long & Co* [1934] Ch 635. The judgment in this case contains an exhaustive exposition of the law relating to proxies and will repay careful study.

[188] *Re Waxed Papers* (1937) 156 LT 452 (CA).

[189] *Re Anglo-Spanish Tartar Refineries* [1942] WN 222.

[190] *Re Wedgwood Coal Co* (1877) 6 Ch D 627.

[191] Section 900 replaced s 427 of CA 1985.

[192] As to the relationship between s 110 of the Insolvency Act 1986 and ss 895–901 of CA 2006, see **20.17**.

[193] To be a 'reconstruction' substantially the same persons must hold the shares of both the old and new company: see *Re My Travel Group plc* [2005] 1 WLR 2365 where it was held that s 900 could not be used to effect a transfer of undertaking to a new company in which the shareholders of the old company would be allotted 4 per cent of the shares.

to another company.[194] Section 900(2) terms the first-named company the 'transferor company' and the second the 'transferee company'. Where these conditions are met, the court may either by the order sanctioning the compromise or arrangement or by any subsequent order make provision in respect of any of the matters which are set out below.

In contrast with an amalgamation under s 110 of the Insolvency Act 1986, a scheme carried out under ss 895–900 has the advantage of effectively overriding[195] the objections of dissenting shareholders and creditors.[196] While the compulsory nature of the process may suggest a comparison with expropriation, it is not contrary to the relevant provisions of the European Convention on Human Rights.[197] The problem of preference shareholders' entitlement and the difficulties of the arbitration procedure to settle the claims of dissenting shareholders do not arise. Furthermore, dissenting creditors may not threaten the validity of a scheme by seeking to put the company into compulsory liquidation within one year, as may occur in a transfer of assets under s 110(6). On the other hand, the procedure under s 895 will inevitably entail court proceedings (in respect of the meeting ordered by the court and its subsequent sanction of the scheme). Under s 110, no application to court may be made unless shareholders or creditors have some ground to challenge the transfer of assets by the liquidator.

The matters as to which the court can make provision under s 900 of the Companies Act 2006 are as follows:

(1) the transfer to the transferee company of the whole or any part of the undertaking and of the property or liabilities of any transferor company;

(2) the allotting or appropriation by the transferee company of any shares, debentures, policies, or other like interests in that company which, under the compromise or arrangement, are to be allotted or appropriated by that company to or for any person;

(3) the continuation by or against any transferee company of any legal proceedings pending by or against any transferor company;

---

[194] In *Re Bluebrook Ltd, IMO (UK) Ltd and Spirecove Ltd* [2009] EWHC 2114 (Ch) it was held that a scheme could be used to give effect to a restructuring where the overall effect was to transfer all the assets of the group into a new group and to give the senior lenders the bulk of the equity in that new group. See also **20.22**.

[195] The appropriate consents required by s 895, as well as the sanction of the court, having been obtained.

[196] This process is sometimes referred to as 'cramdown', a concept originally developed in the context of US Chapter 11 reorganisations to refer to the possibility that compulsion may be exercised over a dissenting class of creditors with the court's approval.

[197] *Re Waste Recycling* [2004] BCC 328, referring specifically to Protocol 1, Article 1 of the ECHR.

(4)   the dissolution, without winding up, of any transferor company;

(5)   the provision to be made for any persons who, within such time and in such manner as the court directs, dissent from the compromise or arrangement;

(6)   such incidental, consequential, and supplemental matters as are necessary to secure that the reconstruction or amalgamation shall be fully and effectively carried out.

Section 900(3) states that where an order under the section provides for the transfer of property or liabilities, that property is, by virtue of the order, transferred to and vests in the transferee company, and those liabilities are by virtue of the order, transferred to and become the liabilities of, the transferee company. Any property, if the order so directs, vests freed from any charge which is by virtue of the compromise or arrangement to cease to have effect. The expression 'property' includes property, rights and powers of every description,[198] and the expression 'liabilities' includes duties, but not a duty to serve under a contract of personal service.[199] The Companies Act 2006 introduced a new requirement for an order sanctioning or facilitating an arrangement or reconstruction to be delivered to the registrar if it alters the company's constitution.[200] Every copy of the company's articles subsequently issued must be accompanied by a copy of the order unless the effect of the order has been incorporated into the articles by the amendment. This results in such orders being treated similarly to (other) resolutions which change the constitution or have that effect.[201]

20.20   MERGERS AND DIVISIONS OF PUBLIC COMPANIES

Council Directive 2011/35/EU[202] , which concerns mergers of public limited liability companies, and Council Directive 82/891/EEC, which concerns the division of public limited liability companies are now implemented by Part 27 of the Companies Act 2006.[203] Both the mergers and the divisions in question involve the transfer of the undertaking, property and liabilities of public companies ('transferor companies') to

---

[198]   Such property and rights do not include the rights of the transferor company under contracts of service with its employees: *Nokes v Doncaster Amalgamated Collieries* [1940] AC 1014 (HL); and do not include contracts that require a counterparty's consent for assignment.

[199]   Section 900(5), replacing s 427(6) of CA 1985: *Nokes v Doncaster Amalgamated Collieries*, above.

[200]   See s 901.

[201]   See also Companies Act 2006, Part 3, Chapters 2 and 3.

[202]   [2011] L110/1, codifying and superseding Directive 78/855/EEC with effect from 1 July 2011.

[203]   They were originally implemented by the Companies (Mergers and Divisions) Regulations 1987, SI 1987/1991, which inserted s 427A and Sch 15B into CA 1985.

other public companies or, in some cases, companies, whether or not public, formed for the purpose of the merger or division ('transferee companies').

The transfer of the undertaking, etc of the transferor company must be in exchange for shares in the transferee company with or without additional cash payment. In British company law, these mergers or divisions take place under ss 895–901 of the Companies Act 2006.[204] Section 903 provides that, in the case of mergers or divisions within the scope of Part 27,[205] ss 895–901 shall have effect subject to the provisions of Part 27. A court may sanction a compromise or agreement under s 895 only if it complies with Part 27.

The main requirement of Part 27 is that three-quarters (measured by value) of each class of the shareholders of the relevant[206] companies approve the scheme. While schemes falling within Part 26 require the consent of only the transferor, those falling within Part 27 require the consent also of the transferee. It also requires that the draft terms of the merger or division are drawn up by the directors of the companies involved and published by the Registrar of Companies. There is also provision for directors' reports containing special information and the reports of independent experts[207] containing specified information. All these documents and the relevant company accounts must be made available to shareholders.

20.21 COMPOSITION WITH DEBENTURE-HOLDERS AND OTHER CREDITORS

Under the powers given by s 895 of the Companies Act 1985, if the requisite majority of debenture-holders agree to forgo their security, and accept preference shares in the new company in exchange for their debentures in the old company, their decision, if confirmed by the court, will be binding upon the minority who oppose the exchange,[208] and an agreement whereby a new company agrees to purchase all the assets and pay a composition to the creditors will be enforced, even though a large sum may be subsequently offered by another person.[209] Since the Insolvency Act 1986 came into force, it is very likely that a scheme of

---

[204] Replacing s 427A and Sch 15B of CA 1985 with effect from 6 April 2008. Part 27 represents a restatement of the law in a form that corresponds more closely with the directives.

[205] It will often be possible to structure a scheme so as to fall outside these provisions. For example the transferor company may be re-registered as a private company in anticipation of the arrangement. The provisions of Part 27 do not apply where the transferor company is being wound up (s 902(3)).

[206] The relevant companies may be either merging (s 907) or involved in a division (s 922).

[207] See ss 936 and 937 regarding the independence of experts: these were new provisions.

[208] *Re Empire Mining Co* (1890) 44 Ch D 402; *Re Alabama New Orleans etc, Rly Co* [1891] 1 Ch 213 (CA); *Follit v Eddystone Granite Quarries* [1892] 3 Ch 75, at 85.

[209] *Re Oriental Bank* [1887] WN 109, at 112.

reconstruction affecting the rights of creditors (secured or otherwise) will have been preceded by the appointment of an administrator under Part II of the 1986 Act. One of the purposes for which an administration order can be made is the sanctioning of a scheme of arrangement under s 895 of the Companies Act 2006.[210]

A company can effect compromises or arrangements with its creditors without going into liquidation, for s 895 applies to companies not in the course of being wound up, as well as to companies which are being wound up.[211] The result is that with the sanction of the court any compromise or arrangement between the company and its creditors, or any class of such creditors, may be made binding on all such creditors or class of creditors and the company, provided that it has been submitted to a meeting of the creditors or class of creditors summoned under the direction of the court and approved by a majority in number representing three-quarters in value of such creditors or class of creditors present either in person or by proxy. If the company is in liquidation, the compromise or arrangement may be made binding on the liquidator and contributories, and any compromise or arrangement between the company and its members, or any class of its members, may equally be made binding.

In the case of the reconstruction of a company, if the creditors of the old company are to be paid in full at once, their consent need not be asked to a reconstruction; but if they are to accept a composition, or to take shares or debentures in the new company in satisfaction of their claims, or to accept deferred payment, their consent must be obtained to a scheme of composition.

---

[210] Section 8(3)(c) of the Insolvency Act 1986 previously referred to a s 425 (now s 895) scheme of arrangement as being one of the purposes for which an administration order could be made. That is no longer the case, but a s 895 scheme of arrangement falls within the more broadly defined purposes of an administration order found in Sch B1 (para 3) to the Insolvency Act 1986 (as amended by the Enterprise Act 2002). As to administration, see Part 3 of Chapter 21. Where there is an estimated deficiency for creditors affected by s 895, subordinated creditors can be excluded from the scheme: *Re British Commonwealth Holdings plc* [1992] BCC 58. *Re Maxwell Communications Corporation plc (No 3)* [1993] BCC 369 considers the position of contractually subordinated unsecured creditors in relation to a scheme of arrangement under s 895. Vinelott J held that a contract which has been freely made between a debtor and a creditor to the effect that, in the event of the insolvency of the debtor the creditor should be subordinated to other unsecured creditors, is valid. In such circumstances, the joint administrators of Maxwell Communications Corporation plc were entitled to exclude the subordinated creditors from a scheme of arrangement. See also *Re British and Commonwealth Holdings plc (No 3)* [1992] 1 WLR 672.

[211] But the court may decline to approve a scheme of arrangement if it is an object of the scheme to avoid a winding up and the consequent investigation of the company's affairs by a liquidator: *Re Halley's Department Store Pte Ltd* [1996] 1 SLR 70 (HC) (Spore).

20.22 THE RIGHTS OF DISSENTING SHAREHOLDERS AND CREDITORS

The sanction of the court to the scheme is essential,[212] and in determining whether such sanction should be given, the duties of the court are twofold: first, to see that the resolutions are passed by the statutory majority, and secondly, to see whether the proposal is such that an intelligent and honest man, a member of the class concerned and acting in respect of his interest, might reasonably approve.[213] But although shareholders acting honestly are usually much better judges of what is to their commercial advantage than the court can be, this proposition is of little value when it is proved that the majority of a class have voted or may have voted in the way they did because of their interests as shareholders of another class.[214] While s 899 does not, in terms, limit the freedom of members of a particular class from voting as they wish, it has been held that an allegation that a voting shareholder has a collateral interest, if made out, could result in the court disenfranchising the relevant member.[215]

In an unreported case,[216] the objectors to a scheme for demerger under the equivalent provision of the Companies Act 1985 (s 425) represented a number of American health care providers. They contended that a payment of dividend *in specie* to be made after the scheme was completed would render the company unable to meet potential damages awards that could be made against it in pending tobacco litigation in the United States. It was held that the authorities showed that the objectors had a right to be heard, even though they were not members of the company, but that the court's primary concern under s 425 was the effect of the scheme between the company and its members. The terms of the scheme were such that there would be no net reduction of the company's capital value. Nothing in the scheme's terms suggested that its purpose was to deprive objectors of any assets they might recover in US litigation. The scheme was sanctioned.

A scheme will not be sanctioned if the terms of the scheme are such that it does not qualify as a 'compromise or arrangement' between the company and its members within s 895. These words 'compromise' and

---

[212] After the resolutions approving the scheme have been passed, in meetings summoned by the court under s 895, the company presents a petition to the court for its sanction under s 899. The petition need not state that the company is carrying on business: *Re Great Universal Stores Ltd* [1960] 1 WLR 78. The procedure differs in detail in Scotland.

[213] *Re Alabama, New Orleans, etc, Rly Co* [1891] 1 Ch 213 (CA); *Re English, Scottish & Australian Chartered Bank* [1893] 3 Ch 385 (CA); *Re Dorman, Long & Co* [1934] Ch 635; *Re National Bank* [1966] 1 WLR 819.

[214] *Carruth v Imperial Chemical Industries* [1937] AC 707, at 769 (HL), per Lord Maugham; *Re National Bank*, above. See *Re Holders Investment Trust Ltd* [1971] 1 WLR 583.

[215] *Re Linton Park plc* [2005] All ER (D) 174.

[216] *Re BAT Industries plc v BAT Reconstructions Ltd* (unreported) 3 September 1998, Neuberger J (transcript 0001165 of 1998).

'arrangement' imply some element of accommodation on each side and are not apt to describe a total surrender of the rights of one side. Where in a scheme concerning a guarantee company the rights of members were being expropriated without any compensating advantage, such a scheme was held by Brightman J not to be capable of being sanctioned under what is now s 895: 'The word "compromise" implies some element of accommodation on each side. It is not apt to describe total surrender. A claimant who abandons his claim is not compromising it. Similarly, I think the word "arrangement" in this section implies some element of give and take. Confiscation is not my idea of arrangement.'[217] Brightman J also found that the scheme was unreasonable, that is one which 'properly examined, no member voting in the interests of members as a whole could reasonably approve'.[218]

It has nevertheless been held, in *Re Savoy Hotel Ltd*,[219] that a scheme was an 'arrangement' between the company and its members (for the purposes of what is now s 895) even though the applicant (which was not the company) sought to acquire all the company's A and B shares[220] (other than those already held) in exchange for shares in the applicant or cash sums. Nourse J held[221] that the court had no power to sanction the scheme since the company itself had not given its consent to the scheme through a decision either of its board or of the company in general meeting. The judge's reasoning turns largely on the legislative history of what is now s 895 and a slender line of judicial *dicta*. The application before Nourse J was for the summoning of separate meetings of the A and the B shareholders.[222] He refused to exercise his discretion to order such meetings where the much greater number of A shareholders could override the advantage that weighted voting would normally give to the B shareholders. The reason given was that this would circumvent the essential requirement of the company's consent. A sounder basis for the decision might have been that the court had no power to circumvent the special voting rights attached to the B shares. It should still have been possible, following earlier authority,[223] to hold separate meetings for the two different classes of shares. The scheme, however, could only effect a transfer of that class of shares which at its own meeting gave the degree of

---

[217] *Re NFU Development Trust Ltd* [1972] 1 WLR 1548, at 1555. The *dictum* of Bowen LJ in *Re Alabama, etc, Rly Co* [1891] 1 Ch 213 at 243 was applied.

[218] Ibid.

[219] [1981] 3 All ER 646.

[220] The holders of the A shares owned approximately 97% of the company's total equity, but only 51% of the votes. The holders of the B shares owned only 2.3% of the equity but were entitled to 48% of the votes. Moreover, 65% of the B shares carrying 31% of the votes were owned, either beneficially or as trustee, by the company's board.

[221] [1981] 3 All ER 646.

[222] Note that his decision as to the sanction of the court was not as to the merits of the scheme since these had not yet been submitted to the meetings of shareholders affected or voted upon. Instead, in refusing to order any meetings, he held that as a matter of law the scheme was incapable of sanction by the court.

[223] As to the practice in holding meetings where different classes of shares are concerned, see **20.18**.

consent required by s 895. Admittedly, this would still have had the effect of defeating the object of the scheme proposed by the applicant.

It has been held[224] that it was not a valid objection to a scheme under what is now s 895 that its aim in essence was a purchase by an outsider of all the issued shares of the company, and that this was attempting to do under this section what should have required approval by 90% of the shareholders under what is now Part 28 of the Companies Act 2006 (as to which see **20.23**). The latter gave dissenting shareholders the right to be bought out. Plowman J refused to accept that what was then s 209 of the 1948 Act thus limited the court's jurisdiction under what is now s 895: 'In the first place, it seems to me to involve imposing a limitation or qualification either on the generality of the word "arrangement" under section 206 [s 425 of the 1985 Act, s 895 of the 2006 Act] or else on the discretion of the court under that section. The legislation has not seen fit to impose such a limitation on terms and I see no reason for implying any.'[225] Plowman J maintained that these two statutory methods of amalgamation involved different considerations and approaches to reconstructions. Under Part 28, the scheme need never come to court unless the minority bring it. If they do, they have the burden of demonstrating unfairness. In this respect there is good reason for requiring a smaller majority for the purposes of approving an arrangement because the court is able to consider fairness.

If the resolution has been passed by the statutory majority, but members of the class sufficient to have prevented the obtaining of the statutory majority appear on the hearing of the petition and oppose it, such opposition will be ignored if the change of mind was induced by a misleading circular: *quaere* whether a change of mind not so induced would be regarded.[226]

Issues may arise on the hearing of the petition regarding the valuation of creditors' interests and linked to that, the duty of the company (and its directors) to take account of the interests of creditors. In *Re Bluebrook Ltd, IMO (UK) Ltd and Spirecove Ltd*[227] the scheme represented a restructuring of a carwash business run by the last two companies, who were indirect subsidiaries of the first. The overall effect was to transfer all the assets of the group into a new group and to give the senior lenders the bulk of the equity in that new group. No assets were to be left in the group to pay the mezzanine lenders, who were thereby shut

---

[224] *Re National Bank* [1966] 1 WLR 819.

[225] Ibid at 829. In *Re Hellenic and General Trust* [1976] 1 WLR 123, at 127–129, Templeman J reached a different conclusion while attempting to distinguish *National Bank* on its facts. For a critique of the decision in *Hellenic*, see *Gore-Browne on Companies* (Jordans, 45th edn, loose-leaf) at 46 [29].

[226] *Re Waxed Papers* (1937) 156 LT 452. Cf *Re National Bank* [1966] 1 WLR 819, where the non-disclosure of the bank's accounts was held entirely proper under the law applicable to banks at that time.

[227] [2009] EWHC 2114 (Ch).

out. The justification advanced for this approach was that the value of the group was such that the mezzanine lenders and other creditors had no economic interest in the group because the value of its assets was significantly less than the senior debt. The mezzanine lenders argued that they were unfairly prejudiced by the scheme and did not accept that the value of the group was less than the senior debt. On the valuation issue the court held after reviewing the evidence that there was not sufficient support for the mezzanine lenders' argument. On the issue of breach of duty owed to (all) creditors, the court recognised that a company must pay proper regard to the interests of creditors but held in this case that the mezzanine lenders were negotiating effectively for themselves and that in any event they did not have an economic interest to which the directors could have regard.

20.23 COMPULSORY ACQUISITION OF SHARES UNDER PART 28 OF THE COMPANIES ACT 2006

Two factors have contributed to a re-casting of the so called 'squeeze-out' and 'sell-out' rights which arise in connection with takeovers when a bidder has reached the stipulated level of shareholding in the target company. The first is that the Takeovers Directive[228] introduced rules which, for the first time, regulate these matters on an EU-wide basis. The second is that the Companies Act 2006 implements several of the recommendations made by the Company Law Review.[229] The outcome is that the new regime in Chapter 3 of Part 28 of the Companies Act 2006, while following the broad approach that had been taken in Part XIIIA of the Companies Act 1985,[230] contains several changes that are likely to prove significant for the operation of 'squeeze-out' and 'sell-out'. These changes relate to the definition of the relevant shareholding thresholds; the period during which the rights of the bidder or the minority shareholders can be exercised; and the meaning of shares that the offeror 'has contracted to acquire'. An alternative mechanism whereby a minority can be compulsorily bought out is a scheme of arrangement under s 895 of the Companies Act 2006 (above **20.17**). However, as noted above, that procedure requires the scrutiny and approval of the court whereas the Part 28 procedure does not.

20.24 THE POWER OF COMPULSORY ACQUISITION

Section 974 of the Companies Act 2006 provides the defined meaning for the purposes of Chapter 3 of a number of terms. The most important of these terms is that of 'takeover offer' in s 974(1)-(5). It is only takeover

---

[228] Articles 15 and 16.

[229] See CLR Final Report (Chapter 13, pp 282–330).

[230] Part XIIIA (inserted by Sch 12 to the Financial Services Act 1986) substituted nine new sections for three sections (428–430) in CA 1985. The reform of these provisions had been long delayed, having originally been proposed by the Jenkins Committee in 1962.

offers falling within this definition which will confer on the offeror the power of compulsory acquisition of a dissenter's shareholdings conferred by s 979.[231] For the purposes of these provisions, then, a 'takeover offer' means an offer to acquire all the shares, or all the shares of any class or classes in a company, *other than* those which at the date of the offer are already held by the offeror. Shares already held by the offeror include shares he has contracted to acquire whether unconditionally or subject to conditions being met. However, shares subject to contracts entered into by an offeror with a holder of shares which simply provide for an offer to be accepted and no more are not included.[232]

It is further required that it is an offer on terms which are the same in relation to all the shares to which the offer relates or, where those shares include shares of different classes, in relation to all the shares[233] of each class. Where the 'bidder' invites offers with the intention of accepting them, this does not amount to a 'takeover offer' as defined by s 974.[234]

The powers conferred by s 979 distinguish between two types of takeover offer. Section 979(1) deals with 'a case where a takeover offer does not relate to shares of different classes'. In that case, if the offeror has, by virtue of acceptances of the offer, acquired or unconditionally[235] contracted to acquire:

(a)   not less than 90% in value of the shares to which the offer relates; and

(b)   in a case where the shares to which the offer relates are voting shares, not less than 90% of the voting rights carried by those shares,[236]

he may give notice leading to compulsory acquisition of those shares that he has not acquired. In the case of a takeover offer which relates to shares of different classes,[237] he must obtain (by virtue of acceptance of the offer, etc):

---

[231]   This is equally true of a minority shareholder's right to be bought out by the offeror under s 983, discussed at **20.26**.

[232]   Such contracts are typically entered into before a takeover offer is announced and are generally referred to as 'irrevocable undertakings'.

[233]   'Shares' primarily means shares which have been allotted on the day of the offer. However, a takeover offer may include among the shares to which it relates all or any of the shares that are subsequently allotted before a date specified in, or determined in accordance with, the terms of the offer: s 974(5). The terms offered in relation to shares must be the same in relation to all the shares, or, as the case may be, all the shares to which the class relates: s 974(3). A limited variation is allowed to meet the requirements of foreign law: s 976(3).

[234]   *Re Chez Nico (Restaurants) Ltd* [1992] BCLC 192, at 203–204.

[235]   See s 991(2).

[236]   The addition of this second limb to the threshold resulted from the implementation of Art 15(2) of the Takeovers Directive. In the case of listed companies, the second limb is unlikely to represent a significant hurdle as differential voting rights are now rare.

[237]   See s 979(4).

(a)   90% in value of the shares of any class of shares to which the offer relates; and

(b)   in a case where the shares to which the offer relates are voting shares, not less than 90% of the voting rights carried by those shares.

Thus, if the offeror wishes to acquire all the shares in a company with several classes of shares, it must achieve the appropriate level of acceptance *vis-à-vis* each class. It can, of course, use the powers conferred by s 979 in the case of any class of shares where it does achieve that level of acceptances. Both forms of compulsory acquisition are referred to as 'squeeze-out' in the Takeovers Directive.

Section 980(2) imposes a 3-month 'deadline' from the last day on which the offer can be accepted[238] during which notices starting the process of compulsory acquisition can be given.[239] Reflecting the fact that the Takeover Code allows the offeror to extend the period for acceptance,[240] an overall time-limit of 6 months beginning with the date of the offer applies in the case of takeover bids not subject to the Takeovers Directive (eg bids for private companies). Practice in making takeover offers, and the need to comply with the Code on Takeovers and Mergers, are likely to keep the exercise of these powers well within the relevant statutory periods.

Subject to certain safeguards, s 979 allows an offeror to acquire shares during the offer period *otherwise* than under the offer. Clearly, there is a need to protect those who have sold their shares under the offer. Section 979(10) makes sure that the 'side purchases' permitted do not give those who have sold to the offeror (other than by acceptance of the terms of the offer) a better bargain. It, first of all, permits such purchases where the 'acquisition consideration'[241] does not exceed the value of the consideration specified in the terms of the offer.[242] Alternatively, such purchases are permitted if the terms of the offer are subsequently revised

---

[238]   It is possible for the terms of a takeover offer to make provision for its revision and for acceptances on the previous terms to be treated as acceptances on the revised terms. Section 974(7) provides that for the purposes of Part 28, Chapter 3 the revision of such terms is not to be regarded as the making of a fresh offer. The date of the offer remains the date on which the original offer was made.

[239]   As to the formal requirements for the offeror giving a s 979 notice, see s 980(1). Criminal sanctions are provided for failing to send a copy to the company: s 980(6). Section 980(4) requires the statutory declaration at or about the same time as the first s 979 notice is served. In *Re Chez Nico (Restaurants) Ltd* [1992] BCLC 192, at 205, this provision was held to be directory and not mandatory and was not intended to nullify the whole procedure. On the facts, the failure to comply with the procedure for 14 days would not affect the right to acquire the shares.

[240]   See Rule 31.

[241]   This is defined as the valuable consideration for which they were acquired or contracted to be acquired. See s 979(10).

[242]   See also Rule 6.2 of the Takeover Code, requiring an increased offer when shares are subsequently acquired at a price above the original offer price.

so that, when the revision is announced, the value of the 'acquisition consideration' at the time of acquisition (or a contract to acquire) no longer exceeds the value of the consideration specified in those terms. If either of these conditions is met, the shares so purchased 'count' towards the nine-tenths level of acceptances required by s 979(2) and (4).[243] If not, they are of course excluded from this calculation.

Section 987 allows joint offers to be made 'by two or more persons'.[244] So far as they acquire, or contract to acquire, the necessary shares under the takeover offer, the offerors do so jointly. However, so far as they acquire shares apart from the offer (ie within the limits allowed by s 979(10)), they may do so jointly or separately.[245] Section 988 makes special provision for the acquisition of shares by the 'associates' of the offeror. (This elaborately defined term is discussed later.) It was seen that for the purposes of ss 974 and 979, a takeover offer must extend to all the shares, or all the shares of any class or classes in a company. For this purpose, however, shares held or contracted for by associates of the offeror are not to be counted. Thus the offeror must obtain nine-tenths acceptances from the remainder of the shares (or class of shares as the case may be) without counting on shares acquired (or unconditionally contracted for) by the offeror's associates to make up the required level of acceptances.[246] This applies to acquisitions at the time when the offer is made as well as shares obtained subsequently. An exception is made for shares acquired during the offer period by associates of the offeror which satisfy the same conditions[247] that must be satisfied by an offeror acquiring shares otherwise than by acceptance of the takeover offer.

The term 'associates'[248] is widely defined[249] to include nominees of the offeror, companies in the same group as the offeror,[250] and bodies corporate in which the offeror is substantially interested.[251] It also includes any person[252] who is a party to an agreement with the offeror for the acquisition of shares, or in an interest in shares. This must amount to

---

[243] See s 979(8).

[244] Although the definition of the 'offeror' in s 991(1) refers to the 'person making a takeover offer', it is clear from s 988(1)(e) that an offeror may be an individual. In practice, offerors, whether single or joint, are likely to be registered companies.

[245] Section 987(2). See s 987(4)-(10) for the consequential changes made to the other provisions in Chapter 3 in the case of joint offerors.

[246] Section 977(2).

[247] Ie in s 979(8). See s 979(9). See above.

[248] This is a term used in the Code on Takeovers and Mergers where it is likewise widely defined.

[249] See s 988.

[250] See s 991.

[251] Section 988(3). Two criteria are used: the company or its directors are accustomed to act in accordance with the offeror's directions or the offeror has one-third or more of the voting power at general meetings.

[252] Or a nominee of such a person.

an 'acquisition agreement' within s 988(4) of the Act.[253] Where an offeror is an individual, his 'associates' include his spouse or civil partner and any minor child or stepchild.[254]

The powers of compulsory acquisition conferred by Chapter 3 apply to shares of any kind. Convertible securities are to be treated as shares in the company if they are convertible into shares or rights to subscribe for shares.[255] Moreover, as a result of the definition of 'securities' adopted by the Takeovers Directive,[256] debentures carrying voting rights which are admitted to trading on a regulated market are now treated as shares for the purposes of compulsory acquisition.[257]

20.25 THE 'PRICE' PAYABLE TO THOSE WHOSE SHARES ARE COMPULSORILY ACQUIRED

Once a valid notice under s 979 of the Companies Act 2006 is given to those whose shares the offeror is entitled to acquire, the offeror then becomes both entitled and bound to acquire those shares on the terms of the offer. Any notice under s 979 must give particulars of the choice of consideration if a choice is available according to the terms of the original offer. The holder of the shares to be acquired must be given 6 weeks to make his choice in a formal written communication. The notice must also provide for the eventuality of the holder failing to make a choice. It must specify which consideration will apply in that event.[258] The fact that the terms of the original offer set a time-limit or other conditions as to the choice of consideration to be made by shareholders accepting the offer will not prevent those whose shares are to be compulsorily acquired under s 979 from still retaining that choice.[259] Special provision is made for the situation where a non-cash consideration is chosen by the holder of the shares and the offeror is no longer able to provide it. Here the consideration shall be taken to consist of an amount of cash payable by the offeror which at the date of the notice is equivalent to the chosen consideration.[260]

Six weeks from the end of the s 979 notice the offeror must begin to complete the process of compulsory acquisition by sending a copy notice

---

[253] See **12.9**. See s 988(5) as modifying s 988(4).

[254] Section 988(1)(c).

[255] See s 989. As to how such securities should be treated in respect of the class of share to which they belong, see s 989(2).

[256] Article 2(e).

[257] Section 990. Voting rights are defined in s 991(1) as 'rights to vote at general meetings of the company, including rights that arise only in certain circumstances'.

[258] Section 981(3).

[259] Section 981(4).

[260] Section 981(5). This solution also applies where the consideration was to be provided by a third party who is no longer bound or able to provide it (eg a put option from a merchant bank). This in effect legislates the decision in *Re Carlton Holdings* [1971] 1 WLR 918.

to the company, and must pay or transfer to the company the consideration for the shares to which the offer relates. This must (in the case of registered shares) be accompanied by an instrument of transfer executed on behalf of the shareholder by someone appointed by the offeror.[261] On the receipt of this, the company must register the offeror as holder.[262] Any sums received by the company in this process are to be held in trust for those whose shares have been acquired.[263]

20.26   APPLICATIONS TO THE COURT BY DISSENTING SHAREHOLDERS

There is a provision in Part 28 of the Companies Act 2006 for dissenting shareholders to apply to court. This application must be made within 6 weeks of when the notice to acquire the shares (under s 979) is given.[264]

The court may be asked to do two things. It may order that the offeror shall not be entitled and bound to acquire the shares. This is the same power as existed under the earlier legislation.[265] Thus the case-law in respect of application under this earlier legislation may still be relied upon.[266] It is thus explored in the pages that follow. The court may also be asked to adjust the terms of the acquisition and this power in its new form makes clear that the court is able to set such terms as it thinks fit.[267] However, under a new provision,[268] the court cannot require consideration of a higher value than that specified in the offer unless the holder shows that the offer value would be unfair, nor can it require consideration of a lower value than the offer. Moreover, the same factors that have made Chancery Division an awkward forum in which to examine the true merits of a takeover bid will still apply. These include judicial reliance on the 90% level of acceptance as indicating that sound commercial judgment must be behind the decision of such a large majority. There is also the difficulty for dissenting shareholders in matching the means, access to expert advice, and internal corporate information that the offeror will have at its command. Nevertheless, the

---

[261] In the case of shares held in CREST, reg 42 of the Uncertificated Securities Regulations 2001, SI 2001/3755 applies.

[262] Section 981(7). As to bearer shares and shares to be allotted, see s 981(8) and (6) respectively.

[263] Section 981(9). Provision is made as to appropriate banking of such sums, and as to what inquiries and other steps must be taken where those entitled cannot be traced. See s 982.

[264] Section 986(2). If an application to court is pending, the power to acquire is suspended: s 986(2).

[265] See s 428(4) in the original provisions of CA 1985.

[266] That will not of course be true of decisions upon the 'procedural' aspects of Part XIIIA of CA 1985, insofar as changes have been made.

[267] Section 986(1)(b). The corresponding provision in s 430C(1)(b) of CA 1985 had simply referred to the power of the court to specify different terms of acquisition from those of the offer.

[268] Section 986(4).

necessity for a public hearing where dissenters apply to the court will place some restraint upon those who frame the terms on which a successful takeover offer is made. Where this has not been contested by the offeree company (or another bidder), it may be all the more necessary.

The court has always tended to encourage applicants by the award of costs even when their application fails. Section 986(5) now enjoins this as a general rule, unless the application has been unnecessary or vexatious, or there is unreasonable delay or other misconduct in the prosecution of the application. The Court of Appeal has considered the meaning of 'vexatious' under the superseded provision in the Companies Act 1985.[269] In allowing an appeal against the judge's decision that an application under the relevant section was vexatious, the court[270] found that there were sufficient grounds[271] for it to consider the fairness of the offer. This meant that the application was not so obviously unsustainable or impossible of success as to amount to an abuse of the process of the court. There is also a power for the court to deal with the problems of 'untraceable shareholders'.[272] Where the offer needs additional acceptance to make up the nine-tenths level required, the court may make an order authorising that such untraced shareholdings be treated as acceptances.[273] The section contains obvious safeguards to prevent abuse. Thus reasonable inquiry must have been made to trace the shareholders, and the consideration must be shown to be fair and reasonable. This imposes a tougher and more objective standard than the courts usually apply in applications under this section. There is, finally, an overriding requirement that the court must conclude that such an order is just and equitable, having regard in particular to the number of shareholders who have been traced but who have not accepted the offer.

It is well established that there rests upon dissenting shareholders a heavy onus of proof if they are to show that a scheme which holders of 90% of the shares have accepted, is unfair. In *Re Sussex Brick Co*,[274] Vaisey J observed that it was not sufficient for the applicant to set out in his affidavit certain criticisms which undoubtedly show that a good case could be made 'for the formulation of a better scheme, of a fairer scheme, of a scheme which would have been more attractive to the shareholder, if they could have understood the implications of the criticisms'. The courts are clearly influenced by the high proportion of shareholders who must assent to a scheme under what is now s 986. Vaisey J, in *Re Sussex Brick Co*, said that it was difficult to 'predicate unfairness' where the good

---

[269] Section 430C(4).
[270] *Re Britoil plc* [1990] BCC 70.
[271] The offeree board's original defence document put a value on the shares 40% above the offer. The later recommendation of the offer by the board did not come to the applicant's attention.
[272] Section 986(9).
[273] See e g *Re Joseph Holt plc* [2001] 2 BCLC 604.
[274] [1961] Ch 289n following *Re Hoare & Company* [1933] 150 LT 374; *Re Evertite Locknuts* [1945] Ch 220; *Re Press Caps Ltd* [1949] Ch 434 (CA).

faith of the transferee company is not challenged and there is no case of any intentional misleading of the offeree shareholders. A dissenter under s 986 is faced with the very difficult task of showing that 'he, being the only man out of step in the regiment, is the only man whose views should prevail'. These principles were followed by Plowman J in *Re Grierson, Oldham & Adams Ltd*,[275] where the fact that holders of 99% of the shares had approved the scheme, and that the price offered was slightly above the market price,[276] was held to indicate that there was no unfairness. In estimating whether a 'fair value' is being paid for the shares, the market price is a good indication of such value. The real value of the transferor company and its assets to the transferee company is not as a rule to be taken into account.[277] The new power enabling the court to specify such terms as it thinks fit may now encourage more judicial scrutiny.

Where the Part 28 procedure was misused to expropriate a minority shareholder in a small private company, the Court of Appeal allowed his application.[278] There two shareholders who already held 90% of the shares set up a company as a vehicle through which to compulsorily acquire the shares of the remaining shareholder. However, it does not follow that the approving shareholders must always be wholly independent of the transferee company. This is merely a factor to be taken into account by the court in exercising its discretion, the weight to be given to it depending on the circumstances of the case.[279]

It has recently been held that the court will be much more inclined to exercise its jurisdiction under what is now s 986 of the 2006 Act where the bidder is *not* an outsider, but a director and shareholder in the target company and it is shown that the information made available to dissenting shareholders falls far short of what should have been provided. In *Re Chez Nico (Restaurants) Ltd*,[280] Browne-Wilkinson V-C supported this statement of principle by adverting to various disclosure provisions in the City Code on Takeovers and Mergers which had not been complied with.[281] There had also been a failure to comply with the restrictions on advertising contained in s 57 of the Financial Services Act 1986.[282]

Under the compulsory purchase procedure ('squeeze-out'), there is no provision (equivalent to that which applies in respect of schemes of arrangement) requiring information to be given to the shareholders to whom the offer is made. It would appear that the lack of full disclosure

---

[275] [1968] Ch 17.

[276] See also *Re Sussex Brick Co* [1961] Ch 289n.

[277] *Re Press Caps Ltd* [1949] Ch 434 (CA); *Re Grierson, Oldham & Adams Ltd* [1968] Ch 17.

[278] *Re Bugle Press Ltd* [1961] Ch 270 (CA).

[279] See *Sammel v President Brand G M Co* (1969) (3) SA 629, at 677–691.

[280] [1992] BCLC 192, at 206–212.

[281] Ibid, at 209. The court indicated that the liability considered in *Coleman v Myers* [1977] 2 NZLR 225 might also have applied; as to this, see **16.2**.

[282] Ibid, at 210–211.

will not necessarily amount to unfairness.[283] In *Gething v Kilner*,[284] however, Brightman J accepted that the directors of an offeree company owe a duty towards their own shareholders which 'clearly includes a duty to be honest and a duty not to mislead'. Any minority shareholder in an offeree company could properly complain if they were being wrongfully subjected to the power of compulsory purchase, conferred by s 979 on the offeror company, as a result of a breach of the above-mentioned duty by the board of the offeree company in recommending the offer. The minority shareholders would have to show bad faith or conduct so unreasonable as to amount to bad faith.

20.27 THE RIGHT OF MINORITY SHAREHOLDERS TO BE BOUGHT OUT

Where an offeror, whether in a bid for all the shares of a company or in a bid for a class or classes, has obtained acceptance of the offer (whether by acquisition or contract to acquire) by holders of shares:

(a) representing at least 90% in value of the voting shares in the company; and

(b) carrying at least 90% of the voting rights in the company,

(or those of the class or classes concerned), then those who have not been acquired may demand to be bought out.[285] The shares already held (ie acquired or contracted to be acquired) by the offeror 'count' towards the 90% level of acceptance required to 'trigger' the dissenting shareholder's right to be bought out. It was seen that these shares do not 'count' in order to 'trigger' the offeror's right compulsorily to acquire the shares ('squeeze-out').[286] The result is that the threshold for the operation of 'sell-out' rights is likely to be reached before that which triggers the operation of the offeror's 'squeeze-out' rights.

---

[283] *Re Evertite Locknuts* [1945] Ch 220; Roxburgh J in *Re Press Caps* [1948] 2 All ER 638 held that an order for discovery will not be made on an application by originating summons under what is now s 986 of the 2006 Act in the absence of special circumstances. But see *Coni v Robertson* [1969] 1 WLR 1007. This latter decision was followed in *Re Lifecare International plc* (1990) BCLC 227 on the basis that the position applicable at the time of *Re Press Caps* has been changed by what is now RSC Ord 24, rr 3 and 8. In *Lifecare*, the discovery sought related to the professional advice given to the board of the offeree company. It did not call for 'an extensive investigation of the company's affairs'. Cross-examination was also allowed on the expert evidence submitted by affidavit.

[284] [1972] 1 WLR 337.

[285] Section 983. As to the notice of the rights to buy which an offeror must give the dissenters, the time allowed for the exercise of their rights and the sanctions for failure by the offeror to comply, see s 984.

[286] Where the offeror can and does exercise his rights to acquire the shares of those who have not accepted the offer, they cannot exercise the right to be bought out: s 984(4).

Once a dissenting shareholder has exercised his rights, the offeror is entitled and bound to acquire the dissenter's shares 'on the terms of the offer or on such terms as may be agreed'.[287] Where the takeover offer gave a choice of consideration to those who accepted its terms, this choice is preserved for dissenting shareholders who exercise their rights to be bought out.[288] If the parties cannot agree on the terms of the offer, then either side may apply to the court. The terms may then be 'such as the court thinks fit'.[289] Unlike the equivalent jurisdiction where the offeror compulsorily acquires shares, there is no guidance from reported judicial decisions. It may be noted, however, that the court here has no power to prevent the shareholder having his shares bought. It can only change the terms. It would appear that there has been very little need for this form of relief, but together with the right to be bought it forms a useful protection when minority shareholders are 'locked into' a company under the overwhelming control of the offeror.

---

[287] Section 985(2).

[288] Section 985(3). Similar provision is made as in the case of an offeror compulsorily acquiring shares where the consideration is not in cash and the offeror is no longer able to provide it, etc. See s 985(5).

[289] Section 986(3).

CHAPTER 21

CORPORATE RECONSTRUCTION AND INSOLVENCY

PART 1: GENERAL

21.1   Introduction

There are a number of options for a company which is experiencing serious financial difficulties. The first is to continue to trade despite the underlying difficulties, in the hope that the crisis will prove to be temporary and capable of being quickly resolved. This may only be possible for so long as the company is able to pay its debts as they fall due or, to the extent that it is not, its creditors are prepared to tolerate late payment. If the financial difficulties are more serious, the company may try to come to some formal arrangement with its creditors regarding the repayment of its debts but, for a company with a large number of creditors, reaching agreement with all of them may not be practicable.[1] There are now a number of statutory procedures which a company can invoke to bind all of its creditors to a voluntary arrangement which has been agreed with some of them. One procedure is schemes of arrangement under s 895 of the Companies Act 2006, which require the approval of the court. Another procedure is the voluntary arrangement scheme contained in Part I of the Insolvency Act 1986. The options were widened even further in respect of small companies by the introduction of a new voluntary arrangement procedure in the Insolvency Act 2000 which inserted a new Sch A1 into the Insolvency Act 1986. The latter procedure is coupled with a moratorium on the enforcement of creditor rights during the currency of the procedure.

Administration and liquidation are governed by the Insolvency Act 1986 as amended by the Enterprise Act 2002, the relevant provisions of which came into force on 15 September 2003. Administration and liquidation are similar procedures, to the extent that they both involve the appointment of a qualified insolvency practitioner to a company and the displacement of the company's existing board of directors from their

---

[1]   Many large company rescues are accomplished outside formal insolvency procedures by means of consensual 'workouts'. This is the so-called 'London Approach'; on which see the Bank of England website – www.bankofengland.co.uk – and also J Armour and S Deakin 'Norms in Private Insolvency Procedures: The London Approach to the Resolution of Financial Distress' (2001) 1 *Journal of Corporate Law Studies* 21.

management function. A company can resolve to go into liquidation (or to be wound up; liquidation and winding-up being synonymous terms) or can be forced compulsorily into liquidation by order of the court. Commonly, although not necessarily, it would be creditors of the company who would seek a winding-up order. Under the Insolvency Act 1986 an administrator could only be appointed by order of the court. The persons who can apply for an administration order include the company itself, and also its creditors. The facility of court appointment is still available but the Enterprise Act 2002 now allows out-of-court appointment either by the company itself or by a secured creditor who holds a 'qualifying' floating charge.

Where liquidation and administration differ most significantly is in their intended purpose. Liquidation of a company involves the cessation of its business, the realisation of its assets, the payment of its debts and liabilities, and the distribution of any remaining assets to the members of the company. At the end of a liquidation, a company is wound up and ceases to exist. Administration, in contrast, is designed primarily as a rescue procedure aimed at facilitating the survival of the company's business either in whole or in part. The legislation states that an administrator must perform his functions with the objective of (a) rescuing the company as a going concern, or (b) achieving a better result for the company's creditors as a whole than would be likely if the company were wound up (without first being in administration), or (c) realising property in order to make a distribution to one or more secured or preferential creditors. The statute sets out this hierarchy of objectives and an administrator can only descend the list of objectives if he thinks that it is not reasonably practicable to achieve any of the preceding objectives.

The administration procedure was first introduced into English law by the 1980s insolvency legislation[2] and its enactment resulted largely from recommendations made by a committee under the chairmanship of Sir Kenneth Cork. The Cork Committee was appointed by the Department of Trade and Industry in 1977 to review insolvency law and practice and, in its report,[3] the Committee identified the absence of a statutory procedure to assist ailing but basically sound companies as one of the key deficiencies of insolvency law at that time.

The Insolvency Act 1986 also regulates some aspects of the receivership process. Receivers are persons appointed by secured creditors in order to realise their security. Under the Act, a distinction is drawn between

---

[2]   The reforms were first enacted in the Insolvency Act 1985. This was replaced by the Insolvency Act 1986, which consolidated the earlier Insolvency Act and also certain other provisions (including some in the Companies Act 1985) relevant to insolvency. The principal factors underlying the legislative reforms and consolidation of insolvency law in 1985 and 1986 are discussed in Fletcher, 'The Genesis of Modern Insolvency Law – An Odyssey of Law Reform' [1989] JBL 365.

[3]   *Insolvency Law and Practice*, Cmnd 8558 (1982).

'administrative receivers' and other receivers. Administrative receivers are, broadly, receivers appointed under floating charges on the whole or substantially the whole of the chargor company's property. The role of administrative receivers is considerably more important than that of other types of receiver. Since it is a remedy for secured creditors, receivership is considered in Chapter 10 but certain aspects of the procedure which are regulated by the Insolvency Act 1986 are mentioned in this chapter. The Enterprise Act 2002 has abolished the right to appoint administrative receivers in the generality of cases insofar as 'new' floating charges are concerned, ie floating charges created after the coming into force of the legislation on 15 September 2003.[4] Holders of floating charges in existence before that date retain the right to appoint an administrative receiver. Moreover, there are still some exceptional cases set out in the legislation where the holders of floating charges may still appoint administrative receivers even after the coming into force of the Enterprise Act 2002 regime.[5]

Insolvency law is a subject in its own right and it is not appropriate in a company law textbook to attempt to provide much more than an overview of the various insolvency procedures and the ways in which they are regulated by the insolvency legislation. Specific aspects of insolvency law, in particular, the manner in which transactions entered into in the twilight period of the company's solvency are liable to be held void or set aside, merit closer examination.

21.2 The definition of insolvency[6]

There are two principal, although not exclusive or exhaustive, tests of insolvency: a company is insolvent if it is unable to pay its debts as they fall due ('cash flow' insolvency); it is also insolvent if its liabilities exceed its assets ('balance sheet' insolvency). Under the Insolvency Act 1986,[7] a company may be compulsorily wound up where the court is satisfied that it is insolvent in either of these senses; where it is demonstrated that a company is or is likely to become insolvent in either of these senses, this may also lead to the appointment of an administrator.[8]

---

[4] See s 72A of the Insolvency Act 1986 as inserted by s 250 of the Enterprise Act 2002.

[5] Section 72B of the Insolvency Act 1986 and subsequent sections as inserted by s 250 of the Enterprise Act 2002.

[6] See, generally, RM Goode *Principles of Corporate Insolvency Law* (Sweet & Maxwell, 3rd edn, 2005) Ch 4. The extensive Australian case-law on the various tests of insolvency is reviewed in Keay 'The Insolvency Factor in the Avoidance of Antecedent Transactions in Corporate Liquidations' (1995) *Monash University Law Review* 305.

[7] Sections 122 and 123.

[8] See now Sch B1 to the Insolvency Act 1986, para 11. For a disputed administration application and the consideration of these tests see *Re Colt Telecom Group plc (No 2)* [2003] BPIR 324.

Failure to pay a debt which is due and not disputed amounts to evidence of cash flow insolvency.[9] Thus a company which has a policy of late payment of bills could find itself the subject of a petition for a winding-up or administration order. Such a petition will not be struck out at an early stage as a form of improper pressure and an abuse of the process of the court, because, as Staughton LJ explained in *Taylor's Industrial Flooring*,[10] creditors, not late payers, are more worthy of insolvency law's protection:

> 'Many people today seem to think that they are lawfully entitled to delay paying their debts when they fall due or beyond the agreed period of credit, if there is one ... This can cause great hardship to honest traders, particularly those engaged in small businesses recently started. Anything which the law can do to discourage such behaviour in my view should be done.'

The position is different if there is a *bona fide* dispute about a debt. A petition based on a disputed debt will usually be dismissed because the procedure is ill-equipped to resolve factual disputes.[11] However, it will not be dismissed where the petitioning creditor has a good arguable case and the dismissal would deprive the petitioner of a remedy, injustice would otherwise result, or there is some other sufficient reason for the petition to proceed.[12]

Balance sheet insolvency for the purpose of winding-up or administration applications is defined as an excess of liabilities over assets, and contingent and prospective liabilities must be taken into account in the assessment. Prospective liabilities include an obligation to repay a loan in one year's time[13] and an undisputed claim for unliquidated damages for more than a nominal amount.[14] Contingent liabilities are distinguishable from prospective liabilities in that a prospective liability is a binding liability which has not yet matured, whilst a contingent liability is a liability which may never mature because it is dependent on an event which may or may not occur.[15] An example of a contingent liability is the liability of a guarantor under a guarantee.

---

[9]   *Taylor's Industrial Flooring Ltd v M & H Plant Hire Ltd* [1990] BCLC 216, [1990] BCC 44 (where the Court of Appeal held that an order could be granted even though the petitioner had not previously served a statutory demand); *Cornhill Insurance plc v Improvement Services Ltd* [1986] 1 WLR 114, (1986) 2 BCC 98, 942; *Re A Company (No 006273 of 1992)* [1992] BCC 794 (presentation of winding-up petition not restrained despite company's cross-claim for a larger amount).

[10] [1990] BCC 44, at 51.

[11] *Re Claybridge Shipping Co SA* [1981] Com LR 107, [1997] 1 BCLC 572 (CA); *Alipour v Ary* [1997] 1 BCLC 557 (CA); *Re A Company (No 006685 of 1996)* [1997] 1 BCLC 639.

[12] *Re Claybridge Shipping Co SA* [1981] Com LR 107, [1997] 1 BCLC 572 (CA).

[13] *Byblos Bank SAL v Al Khudhairy* (1986) 2 BCC 99, 550, at 99, 562.

[14] *Re Dollar Land Holdings plc* [1994] 1 BCLC 404.

[15] *Re British Equitable Bond and Mortgage Corp Ltd* [1910] 1 Ch 574; *Winter v IRC* [1961] 3 All ER 855; *Stonegate Securities v Gregory* [1980] Ch 576, in particular at 579, per Buckley LJ.

Prospective and contingent liabilities must be 'taken into account' in determining whether there is balance sheet insolvency. In *Re A Company (No 006794 of 1983)*,[16] it was held that taking into account contingent liabilities does not mean simply adding up the principal amount of those liabilities and deducting the total from the assets, but rather involves considering whether, and if so when, they are likely to becoming present liabilities. An examination of the likelihood of contingent liabilities becoming present liabilities also takes place when liabilities are admitted for proof in a winding-up and, at that stage, contingent liabilities may be discounted to reflect the fact that they are uncertain. The Insolvency Act 1986 does not specify how contingent liabilities (and indeed prospective liabilities which are not yet certain in amount) are to be valued for the purpose of the balance sheet insolvency test but, presumably, some guidance would be had from the practice of admission of such liabilities for proof on winding-up.

The balance sheet insolvency test also requires valuation of assets. Valuation, however, is not an exact science and different valuers might well disagree about the value of an asset. A particular difficulty is that the Act does not indicate whether the assets are to be valued on the basis of the company's business being sold as a going concern or on the basis of the assets being broken up and sold separately; the former basis would usually be expected to produce a higher figure.

In a recent case arising out of the Lehman Brothers bankruptcy, the biggest corporate failure in history, *BNY Corporate Trustee v Eurosail*[17] has adopted a narrow interpretation of balance sheet insolvency holding that the application of s 123 did not simply turn on whether the liabilities of a company exceeded its assets. The court said that the 'balance sheet insolvency' provision was included in the section to cover the situation where, although it could not be said that a company was currently unable to pay its debts as they fell due, it was, in practical terms, clear that it would not be able to meet its future or contingent liabilities. The provision applied to a company whose assets and liabilities, including contingent and future liabilities, were such that it had reached the point of no return. The fact that assets being exceeded by liabilities was deemed to amount to inability to pay debts could be taken into account when interpreting what 'inability to pay debts' meant.

21.3 The regulation of insolvency practitioners

Until the reforming legislation of the 1980s, it was possible to act as a liquidator or receiver without holding any relevant professional qualifications or having any previous experience. This could be exploited by unscrupulous persons to their own advantage, because the controllers

---

[16] [1986] BCLC 261. Although this case concerned an earlier statutory provision, the reasoning would still seem to be applicable.

[17] [2011] EWCA Civ 227.

of a company could elect to put the company into liquidation and appoint a sympathetic liquidator who, through ignorance, inexperience or complicity, would agree to the sale of the company's business at a low price to another company controlled by the same persons. This stratagem allowed the controllers to continue the business free from the burden of existing debts; meanwhile the creditors of the old company were left with claims which, in all probability, would never be paid.

Under the Insolvency Act 1986, it is an offence for an unqualified person to act as an insolvency practitioner in relation to a company.[18] Apart from the Official Receiver, who is regulated as an officer of the court, all liquidators, provisional liquidators, administrators, administrative receivers and supervisors of voluntary arrangements act as insolvency practitioners.[19] The principal way[20] of obtaining the appropriate qualification is through membership of one of the recognised professional accountancy bodies[21] or of The Law Society.[22] Specific restrictions prevent undischarged bankrupts, persons disqualified under the Company Directors Disqualification Act 1986 and persons subject to the mental health legislation from acting as insolvency practitioners,[23] and there are also bonding requirements.[24] Only individuals may act as insolvency practitioners.[25]

In the UK it is usually accountants who become insolvency practitioners and they in turn work closely with solicitors and other professionals. This is in contrast to many other countries where it is often lawyers who take the appointments and consult the accountants.

Since the 1986 reforms, the English system has been highly regulated and insolvency practitioners need licenses to practice. The Government in the shape of the Insolvency Service, an executive agency of BIS – the Department of Business, Innovation and Skills[26], as well as self-regulatory bodies are active in monitoring the performance of practitioners though there have been occasional complaints that the

---

[18] Section 389. But see now s 389A which permits the authorisation of 'company doctors' to act as nominees and supervisors of voluntary arrangements.

[19] See also s 388.

[20] Direct authorisations can also be granted: s 392.

[21] Guidance notes indicate that 'independence' is a further requirement. If, eg, one of the partners of an individual who is otherwise qualified to act as an insolvency practitioner has in the previous 3 years been the auditor of a company, that individual is not qualified to act as an insolvency practitioner in relation to that particular company.

[22] Section 390(2).

[23] Section 390(4).

[24] Section 390(3).

[25] Section 390(1).

[26] The name of the Government department has changed frequently in recent years. Formerly it was the Department of Trade and Industry (DTI); then BERR – Business, Enterprise and Regulatory Reform and now BIS.

system is not sufficiently robust in stamping out bad behaviour.[27] The Insolvency Service and self-regulatory bodies make generally available practice standards designed to maintain high standards of performance.

The Insolvency Service is essentially the public arm of the insolvency process. It performs a number of functions including administering and investigating the affairs of insolvent companies and establishing why they became insolvent; acting as liquidator where no insolvency practitioner from the private sector is appointed; taking forward reports of directors' misconduct and dealing with the disqualification of unfit directors in all corporate failures; authorising and regulating the insolvency profession.

PART 2: VOLUNTARY ARRANGEMENTS

21.4   The use of voluntary arrangements

The Insolvency Act 1986 provides a procedure for voluntary arrangements between a company and its creditors and members (CVAs). A voluntary arrangement approved by the majority of creditors and members of a company in accordance with the Act can be made binding on all of them. Under the Insolvency Act 1986 as originally enacted, the procedure governing voluntary arrangements was less formal than that governing administration, though administration procedures have now been streamlined by the Enterprise Act 2002 in particular by the introduction of the facility for out-of-court appointments of administrators. In practice, however, 'stand alone' voluntary arrangements were relatively uncommon when compared to the overall number of insolvencies. Voluntary arrangements combined with administrations are more common.[28] One important factor which may explain why the 'stand alone' voluntary arrangement procedure has not been more widely used was the absence of a moratorium on creditors' rights. The company is not given a breathing space in which to try to come to an arrangement with its creditors. Whilst negotiations are ongoing, individual creditors can continue to press for payment and can commence or continue proceedings for that purpose; secured creditors can enforce their security; landlords, suppliers of goods on hire purchase and others who have supplied goods to the company on credit terms can continue to exercise their contractual rights. The administration procedure does provide a moratorium and it is for this reason that a voluntary arrangement is often combined with that procedure.

---

[27] See the website of the Association for Accountancy and Business Affairs – www.aabaglobal.org and the publication 'Insolvent Abuse: Regulating the Insolvency Industry' available on the website.

[28] Section 8(3)(b) of the Insolvency Act 1986 as originally drafted specifies the approval of a voluntary arrangement as one of the purposes for which an administration order may be made.

Under the Insolvency Act 2000 provision is now made for reform of the company voluntary arrangement procedure by the introduction of a moratorium. The legislation, as drafted, is limited in its effect because the moratorium is limited to small companies, defined by reference to s 382 of the Companies Act 2006 which uses turnover, balance sheet totals and number of employees as the qualifying conditions.[29] The reform had been preceded by extensive consultation exercises.[30] A statutory moratorium in company voluntary arrangements is viewed as a measure that will help to facilitate the creation of a more failure-tolerant environment and a rescue culture that will promote business enterprise and entrepreneurship.

The Insolvency Act 2000 also made some changes to the voluntary arrangement without a moratorium procedure. The effect of the legislation is that there are now two types of voluntary arrangement procedure:

(1) CVAs without a moratorium, which are governed by Part I of the Insolvency Act 1986 as amended by Insolvency Act 2000;

(2) CVAs with a moratorium are governed by Insolvency Act 2000 which inserted a new Sch A1 into the Insolvency Act 1986. The substantive provisions are contained in this Schedule.

Even if a company satisfies the eligibility criteria for obtaining a CVA with a moratorium the directors may prefer to go down the non-moratorium route as this procedure is more informal and affords greater privacy. If it is desired to obtain the benefit of a moratorium the old-style CVA can still be coupled with the appointment of an administrator. The latter appointment brings about a moratorium.

21.5 CVA without a moratorium – Part I of the Insolvency Act 1986 as amended

A voluntary arrangement is based upon a proposal to the company and its creditors for a composition in satisfaction of its debts or a scheme of arrangement of its affairs. The proposal must provide for some person to act as trustee or otherwise to supervise its implementation. That person is referred to as the 'nominee' and must be a licensed insolvency

---

[29] Schedule A1 to the Insolvency Act 1986. See **14.2.1**.

[30] *The Insolvency Act 1986. Company Voluntary Arrangements and Administration Orders. A Consultative Document* (DTI, 1993) and comments by Rajak (1993) IL&P 111; Penn [1994] JIBL 3; Wood (1993) 4 PLC 4. *The Insolvency Act 1986. Revised Proposals for a New Company Voluntary Arrangement* (DTI, 1995). *Our Competitive Future: Building the Knowledge Driven Economy* (DTI, 1998) para 2.13, noted by TS Braithwaite (1999) 3 Comm LJ 19. *A Review of Company Rescue and Business Reconstruction Mechanisms* (Insolvency Service, 1999).

practitioner.[31] An administrator or liquidator may designate himself as the nominee of a proposed voluntary arrangement, although he is not required to do so.

The proposal may be made:

(1) by the directors of the company (where the company is not in administration or being wound up);

(2) by the administrator, where an administration order is in force; and

(3) by the liquidator, where the company is being wound up.[32]

21.6 Outline of the procedure

In broad outline, the procedure governing a voluntary arrangement is as follows. Where the designated nominee is someone other than the existing administrator or liquidator of a company, he must make a report to the court stating whether he considers that the proposal should be considered at meetings of creditors and of the company.[33] The nominee will usually work closely with the proposers of the arrangement in making this report but, in any event, there are statutory obligations on the proposers to provide him with information.[34] The role of the court at this stage is largely administrative. It does not vet the proposal nor approve the nominee's report. A report to the court is not required where an administrator or liquidator designates himself as the nominee.

The nominee must then summon meetings of the creditors and shareholders[35] to decide whether to approve the proposed voluntary arrangement.[36] The meetings may modify the proposal in certain respects,

---

[31] Section 1(2). But see, however, s 389A of the Insolvency Act 1986 as introduced by s 4 of the Insolvency Act 2000 which allows the Secretary of State to authorise persons who are not qualified insolvency practitioners to act as nominees and supervisors of CVAs. This measure is designed to promote the rescue culture by opening up CVA work to so-called 'company doctors', ie specialists in corporate turnaround who are not necessarily insolvency practitioners.

[32] Section 1.

[33] Section 2. The period for submitting this report is 28 days or such longer period as the court may allow.

[34] Section 2(3) and rr 1.3 (directors' proposal) and 1.10 (administrator's or liquidator's proposal).

[35] Section 3. Where the nominee is not the liquidator or administrator, the summoning of meetings is subject to directions from the court: s 3(1). The procedural aspects of the meetings are governed by the Insolvency Rules 1986, Part 1, Chapter 5.

[36] Section 4. Failure to provide sufficient and accurate information to enable the creditor to consider the merits of the proposed arrangement with a view to determining if and how to cast his vote at the meeting is a material irregularity entitling the court to revoke approval of the arrangement under s 6(4) of the Insolvency Act – see *Re Trident Fashions* [2004] 2 BCLC 35. Lewison J added, however, at [39]: 'It seems to me that the court should only interfere if a judgment made by the administrator about the material to be placed before the creditors was a judgment to which no reasonable insolvency

but the modifications must not be so extensive as to change the character of the proposal so that it is no longer a composition in satisfaction of the company's debts or a scheme of arrangement in respect of its affairs.[37]

Also, the meetings are specifically prohibited from approving any proposal that would interfere with the rights of a secured creditor to enforce his security or with the priority of a debt which is afforded preferential status by the Insolvency Act 1986, unless the secured creditor or, as the case may be, preferential creditor concurs.[38]

Before amendments made by the Insolvency Act 2000 both the creditors' meeting and the shareholders' meeting had to approve a proposed voluntary arrangement but this is no longer the case. The effect of s 4A is that where different decisions are taken at each of the two meetings the decision taken at the creditors' meeting shall prevail subject to the right of a member to go to court to challenge this conclusion within 28 days of the date of the creditors' meeting. On such an application the court has wide discretionary powers including the power to make such order as it thinks fit.[39]

21.7 The effect of the approval of the voluntary arrangement

If the voluntary arrangement is approved by the requisite majorities at the creditors' and company meetings,[40] it:

(1)   takes effect as if made by the company at the creditors' meeting; and

(2)   binds every person who in accordance with the Rules had notice of, and was entitled to vote at, the meeting (whether or not he was present or represented at the meeting) or would have been so entitled if he had had notice of it as if he were a party to the voluntary arrangement.[41]

---

practitioner could come. The judgment should I think be made on the basis of the material available to the administrator at the time and not with the benefit of hindsight.'

[37]   Section 4(2).

[38]   Section 4(3) and (4). Some 'wriggle-room' is however introduced by the decision in *IRC v Wimbledon Football Club Ltd* [2005] 1 BCLC 66. The interpretation of the term 'security' can be problematic: cf *March Estates plc v Gunmark Ltd* [1996] BPIR 439 and *Razzaq v Pala* [1998] BCC 66.

[39]   Section 4A(6) of the Insolvency Act 1986.

[40]   The detailed procedural aspects are governed by the Insolvency Rules 1986 (rr 1.13–1.21). Broadly, more than three-quarters in value of the creditors present in person or by proxy and voting on the resolution must support the arrangement for it to become effective (r 1.19); at the meeting of members the equivalent requirement is that more than one-half in value (determined by reference to voting rights) of the members present in person or proxy and voting on the resolution must support the arrangement (r 1.20).

[41]   Section 5. *Inland Revenue Commissioners v Adam and Partners Ltd* [1999] 2 BCLC 730, applying *Johnson v Davies* [1999] Ch 117. The facility to bind unknown creditors is very valuable and was introduced by s 2 and Sch 2 to the Insolvency Act 2000.

Creditors who are entitled to vote at the meeting include those whose debts are unliquidated or unascertained provided the chairman agrees to put an estimated minimum value on them,[42] as well as those who debts are liquidated and presently due.

The court may, if the company is being wound up or an administration order is in force, stay the winding-up or discharge the administration order and give such directions with respect to the conduct of the winding-up or the administration as it thinks appropriate for facilitating the implementation of the approved voluntary arrangement.[43]

21.8 Implementation of the proposal

Once a voluntary arrangement has been approved, the nominee becomes its supervisor.[44] The supervisor's role is to carry out the functions conferred on him by the arrangement.[45] The supervisor must notify all creditors and members of the company who are bound by the arrangement when it is complete and must provide them with an account of receipts and payments.[46] A copy of the notice and account sent to the creditors and members must also be filed with the Registrar of Companies and the court.[47]

21.9 Challenging the approval of a voluntary arrangement or the supervisor's decisions

A specific right to challenge the decision to approve a voluntary arrangement is conferred on certain persons by s 6. The challenge may be based on the substantive ground that the arrangement unfairly prejudices the interests of a creditor, member or contributory of the company, or may relate to material irregularities at or in relation to either of the meetings. The persons with standing to bring a claim under s 6 are those who were entitled to vote at either of the meetings, the nominee or a replacement nominee, and the company's liquidator or administrator.[48] The challenger must move swiftly, because an application under s 6 may not be made after the period of 28 days beginning with the first day on which the results of the creditors' and company meetings were reported to the court.[49] Any irregularity at or in relation to a meeting does not invalidate the approval given by that meeting unless it is challenged successfully under s 6.[50]

---

42   *Doorbar v Alltime Securities Ltd* [1995] BCC 1149 (CA).
43   Section 5(3), subject to the qualification in s 5(4).
44   Section 7(2).
45   Ibid.
46   Rule 1.29(1) and (2).
47   Rule 1.29(3).
48   Section 6(2).
49   Section 6(3). An application under the equivalent provision in the personal insolvency

Where the court is satisfied that one or other of the grounds is made out, it may revoke or suspend approvals given by the meetings and may give directions for the summoning of further meetings, either to consider a new proposal from the person who made the original proposal or to reconsider the original proposal.[51] The court itself has no power to devise a new proposal for consideration at creditors' and company meetings.

In respect of the substantive ground of challenge, the language of 'unfair prejudice' comes from the protection of minority shareholders under the companies legislation but how the concept translates into protection for dissentient creditors in the insolvency framework is not entirely clear. These issues were addressed in *IRC v Wimbledon Football Club Ltd*.[52] It was suggested that:[53]

> '(1) to constitute a good ground of challenge the unfair prejudice complained of must be caused by the terms of the arrangement itself; (2) the existence of unequal or differential treatment of creditors of the same class will not of itself constitute unfairness, but may give cause to inquire and require an explanation; (3) in determining whether or not there is unfairness, it is necessary to consider all the circumstances including, as alternatives to the arrangement proposed, not only liquidation but the possibility of a different fairer scheme; (4) depending on the circumstances, differential treatment may be necessary to ensure fairness ... (5) differential treatment may be necessary to secure the continuation of the company's business which underlines the arrangement ...'

In this case the company (Wimbledon Football Club) held a share in the Football League Ltd which entitled it to participate in competitions run by the Football League. The administrator proposed to sell this share but under its rules the Football League could effectively block a transfer unless the buyer paid 'Football creditors' in full. The company suggested a CVA under which preferential creditors (namely the HMRC (the Revenue)) would receive 30% of their debts but Football creditors (as defined by Football League rules) would be paid in full. The Revenue objected alleging a breach of s 6 (unfair prejudice) and s 4(4)(a) under which the court should not approve a CVA if, without the creditor's consent, 'any preferential debt of the company is to be paid otherwise than in priority to such of its debts as are not preferential debts'. The court, however, took the view that the section did not preclude payment of

---

regime (s 262) failed in *Doorbar v Alltime Securities Ltd* [1995] BCC 1149 (CA). See also *Re Sweatfield Ltd* [1997] BCC 744 (application under s 6; held no material irregularity established).

[50] Section 6(7).

[51] Section 6(4). If the original proposer fails to put forward a new proposal in accordance with the court's direction, the court must revoke the direction and revoke or suspend the earlier approvals: s 6(5). The court may also give supplemental directions: s 6(6).

[52] [2005] 1 BCLC 66. See now more recently *Re Portsmouth City Football Club Ltd (In Administration)* [2011] BCC 149.

[53] [2005] 1 BCLC 66, at [18].

non-preferential creditors by third parties ahead of preferential creditors out of their own free money. Nevertheless:[54]

> 'It would of course be different if the company put third party in funds to do so. It would be different if the Sale Agreement were a sham or device adopted to disguise payments by the company to non-preferential creditors ahead of preferential creditors e g by agreeing an artificially low purchase price payable to the company for its undertaking in return for the assumption by the purchaser of an obligation to pay non-preferential creditors.'

It was suggested that the pursuit by the Revenue of its objection to the payment in full of 'Football creditors' could only bring down the whole edifice and secure a nil return for all concerned. But as the court also recognised it was a commercial necessity for the buyer to pay off the Football creditors in full. The commercial necessity must surely reduce the price that the buyer would otherwise pay for the company assets. While the price may not have been in the judge's words 'artificially low' it was surely lower than it might have been had the 'commercial necessity' not presented itself.[55]

More generally, any of the company's creditors or any other person who is dissatisfied by any act, omission or decision of the CVA supervisor can apply to court. The court can confirm, reverse or modify the supervisor's act or decision, give him directions or make such other order as it thinks fit.[56]

The court may also appoint substitute supervisors.[57]

21.10 Terminating a voluntary arrangement

The supervisor himself has a general right to apply to the court for directions in relation to any particular matter arising under the voluntary arrangement, and may also apply to the court for a winding-up order or an administration order to be made.[58] Such an application may become necessary if the company fails to fulfil the terms of a CVA whether by failing to meet a payment due to creditors or otherwise. There has been substantial litigation on the effect of subsequent liquidation on the CVA and on the status of funds collected by the CVA supervisor prior to

---

[54] Ibid, at [17].
[55] The so-called 'Football creditor' rule continues to give rise controversy and is likely to be the subject of challenge in forthcoming cases.
[56] Section 7(3).
[57] Section 7(5) and (6).
[58] Section 7(4). An example of such an application is *Re FMS Financial Management Services Ltd* (1989) 5 BCC 191.

liquidation[59] but, a lot of the difficulties have been clarified by *Re NT Gallagher & Son Ltd.*[60] The court said that so long as the terms of the arrangement were clear, funds collected by a supervisor were held on trust exclusively for the benefit of the CVA participants. Moreover, the fact that the CVA proposal did not use the terminology of 'trust' was not material. The fate of the CVA trust and its survival on liquidation depended on the terms of the arrangement. The court said that to treat a trust created by a CVA as continuing notwithstanding the liquidation of the company did not produce such unfairness to post-CVA creditors so as to warrant a termination default rule. It should be noted that creditors whose debts have not been fully discharged by CVA trust moneys may prove for the balance in the liquidation.

21.11   Reinforcing the integrity of the law

Parts of the reforms of the CVA procedure introduced by the Insolvency Act 2000 were designed to reinforce the integrity of the law. The new s 6A makes it an offence for a company officer to seek to obtain the approval of a CVA by making false representations. Section 7A imposes a 'whistle blowing' obligation on a nominee/supervisor.[61] If it appears to the nominee/supervisor that a past or present officer of the company has been guilty of an offence in connection with the moratorium or voluntary arrangement he is obliged to report the matter to the appropriate authority, ie the Secretary of State, forthwith. He is also obliged to provide the Secretary of State with information and documents in his possession that relate to the matter in question.

21.12   CVAs with a moratorium – Insolvency Act 1986 Sch A1

Under this procedure it is incumbent on the directors of the ailing company to apply for the moratorium. They must produce sufficient evidence that the proposed voluntary arrangement has a reasonable prospect of success and that the company is likely to have sufficient funds during the moratorium to enable it to carry on business.[62] Under para 4(1) of Sch A1 a company is not eligible for a moratorium if it is subject to a subsisting insolvency procedure. There are also anti-abuse provisions to prevent the company from having the benefit of a number of unsuccessful moratoria in rapid succession. A moratorium, for example, is precluded if a previous moratorium has been in force during the previous 12 months unless the moratorium ended with the coming into effect of a voluntary arrangement which has not ended prematurely. Certain

---

[59]   See, eg, *Re Excalibur Airways Ltd* [1998] 1 BCLC 436; *Re Maple Environmental Services Ltd* [2000] BCC 93; *Welsby v Brelec Installations* [2000] 2 BCLC 576; *Re Kudos Glass Ltd* [2000] 1 BCLC 390.

[60]   [2002] 1 WLR 2380.

[61]   Inserted by s 2 and Sch 2 to the Insolvency Act 2000.

[62]   Section 1A of the Insolvency Act 1986. The substantive provisions are contained in Sch A1 to the Insolvency Act 1986.

companies including insurance and banking companies and companies connected with the financial markets are excluded from the possibility of obtaining a moratorium.

Directors proposing a moratorium are obliged to submit to the nominee the terms of the proposed voluntary arrangement together with a statement of affairs and any additional information requested by the nominee which the latter needs to form a statement of opinion.[63] Before a moratorium can be obtained the nominee is required to form a favourable opinion as to the prospects for obtaining approval of the proposal and as to whether the company will have sufficient funds to carry on business during the moratorium. The nominee should also indicate whether meetings of the company and its creditors should be called.[64] The directors must then file with the court the terms of the proposed arrangement, a statement of the company's affairs, a statement that the company meets the moratorium eligibility criteria, a statement of the nominee's agreement to act and also the statement of the nominee's opinion.[65]

In general the effect of the moratorium in relation to a CVA is the same as that which applies to a company in administration. The major difference lies in the fact that the directors maintain the management reins during a CVA. Under the moratorium:[66]

(1) no winding-up petition may be presented except on public interest grounds or under the Financial Services and Markets Act 2000 or Banking Act 1987;

(2) an administration application cannot be made;

(3) no meeting of the company can be called or requisitioned except with the consent of the nominee or by leave of the court;

(4) a voluntary winding-up resolution cannot be passed;

(5) an administrative receiver cannot be appointed;

(6) steps cannot be taken to enforce any security over the company's property or to repossess goods in the company's possession under any hire-purchase agreement except by leave of the court;

(7) where the company has rented premises a landlord cannot forfeit the lease by peaceable re-entry for non-payment of rent or breach of any

---

[63] Schedule A1 to the Insolvency Act 1986, para 6(1).
[64] Schedule A1, para 6(2).
[65] Schedule A1, para 7.
[66] See generally Sch A1, para 12.

other condition of the lease except with the leave of the court and subject to such requirements as the court may impose;

(8)   legal proceedings may not be commenced or continued or executions levied against the company or its property except with the leave of the court;

(9)   any pending winding-up petitions will be stayed and s 127 of the Insolvency Act 1986, which invalidates dispositions of the company's property after the presentation of a winding up petition, will be disallowed;

(10) a floating charge is precluded from crystallising during the moratorium;[67]

(11) security granted by the company during the moratorium may only be enforced if there were reasonable grounds for believing that it would benefit the company;[68]

(12) public utility suppliers may not require the discharge of outstanding debts as a condition of making further supplies during the period of the moratorium but a personal guarantee of payment may be obtained from the nominee.[69]

There are other prohibitions which attract criminal liability on the part of the company and any company officer who permitted the contravention without reasonable excuse. The company may not obtain credit greater than £250 without informing the creditor that a moratorium is in force[70] nor may a company dispose of its property otherwise than in the ordinary course of business unless there are reasonable grounds for believing that the disposal will benefit the company and the disposal has been approved by committee or the nominee.[71] In addition the company may not pay a pre-existing debt or liability unless there are reasonable grounds for believing that it will benefit the company and the payment has been approved by the nominee or committee.

A company may dispose of property in its possession that is subject to a hire purchase agreement or to a security interest provided that the holder of the proprietary interest consents or the court grants leave.[72] Where the security was, as created, a fixed charge the proprietary rights of the charge

---

[67]   Schedule A1, para 13.
[68]   Schedule A1, para 14.
[69]   Section 233 of the Insolvency Act 1986 as amended.
[70]   Schedule A1, para 17.
[71]   Ibid, para 18.
[72]   Ibid, para 20. The terms of this provision are somewhat curiously drafted and are to be contrasted with, paras 70–72 of Sch B1 to the Insolvency Act 1986 which applies to a company administration.

holder are transferred to the proceeds of sale. Where the property was subject to a hire-purchase agreement or a fixed charge it is a condition of any consent or leave that:

(1)   the net proceeds of the disposal; and

(2)   a sum equalling the deficit between the net proceeds of disposal and the net amount which would be realised by a sale of the assets at market value as determined by the court,

must be applied towards discharging the sums secured by the fixed charge or payable under the hire-purchase agreement.[73]

The moratorium comes into force on various filings being made.[74] It lasts initially for a maximum period of 28 days and during this time meetings of the company and creditors must be held to consider the proposal. There is provision for the moratorium to be extended by a majority of creditors to a date not later than 2 months from the date on which the meetings are first held.[75] The nominee must inform a meeting that is considering an extension of various matters of the nominee's work to date; the expenditure to date and the projected spend during the period of the extension.[76] An extended moratorium may always be cut short by the decision of a creditors' meeting.[77]

The relevant meetings must decide whether or not to approve the proposals with or without modifications and it is specifically provided that secured creditors and preferential creditors must consent to any proposals that adversely affect their rights.[78] Directors are obliged to give the nominee at least 7 days' notice before the meetings of modifications that they intend to propose.[79] The procedures relating to the approval of proposals, effectiveness of decisions taken at meetings, challenges to decisions and implementation of CVAs are basically the same as for CVAs without a moratorium under Part I of the Insolvency Act 1986.[80]

During the currency of a moratorium a nominee is required to maintain an ongoing surveillance of the company's affairs pertaining to the prospects of the arrangement being approved and the sufficiency of funds and nominees who form a negative opinion on either of these matters are required to withdraw their consent to act.[81] The same requirement to withdraw consent obtains if the nominee becomes aware that the

---

[73]   Schedule A1, para 26.
[74]   Ibid, para 8.
[75]   Ibid, para 32 and r 1.19(2) of the Insolvency Rules 1986, SI 1986/1925.
[76]   Ibid, paras 32(3) and 32(4).
[77]   Ibid, para 32(6).
[78]   Ibid, para 31(5).
[79]   Ibid, para 31(7).
[80]   Ibid, paras 36–38.
[81]   Ibid, para 24.

company was not eligible for a moratorium or where the directors fail to provide sufficient information to enable the monitoring obligations to be fulfilled.[82] Withdrawal of consent brings the moratorium to a premature conclusion. A nominee who fails to act or acts precipitately may find his conduct subject to challenge under Sch A1, para 26, which empowers any person affected by the moratorium who is dissatisfied with the conduct of the nominee to apply to the court. The court may make a wide variety of orders to redress the situation complained of.

CVAs with a moratorium are a form of 'debtor in possession' corporate reorganisation procedure. Allowing existing management to remain in control during the reorganisation process has often been commended for encouraging timely reorganisation efforts. Nevertheless, the available empirical evidence suggests that the new procedure, even though it has been in operation since 1 January 2003, has hardly been utilised. Whereas new-style administrations have been popular, the CVA procedure has fallen by the wayside. Indeed, it has been effectively superseded by new-style administrations. Part of the reason may be because of some confusion over the role of the nominee who is required to form an opinion that the 'proposed voluntary arrangement has a reasonable prospect of being approved and implemented' and also that 'the company is likely to have sufficient funds available to it during the proposed moratorium to enable it to carry on its business'. What inquiries should the nominee conduct before forming his opinion? The more inquiries the nominee conducts, the greater his cost to the company is likely to be and the less likely the procedure will be a cost-efficient alternative to other insolvency procedures. Moreover, if the nominee inquires directly of creditors they may decide to enforce their security before the company has an opportunity of putting the statutory moratorium in place.

Despite these doubts about the effectiveness of the CVA with a moratorium procedure, the Insolvency Service is presently considering the introduction of a similar type procedure for large and medium-sized companies. This is styled a 'restructuring moratorium' and the moratorium would be dependent on a successful court application. Full details of the proposal remain to be fleshed out however and it may be that the initiative ultimately falls by the wayside.[83]

PART 3: ADMINISTRATION

21.13 The role of administration

The statutory framework of the administration procedure is contained in Part II of the Insolvency Act 1986. The Enterprise Act 2002 revamped completely the administration procedure and substituted a whole new

---

[82] Ibid, para 25.
[83] See the Insolvency Service website – www.insolvencyservice.gov.uk/.

Part II.[84] The relevant law is now essentially contained in Sch B1 to the Insolvency Act 1986 as supplemented by the Insolvency Rules 1986 (as amended).

The administration regime was brought into being by the Insolvency Act 1986 following the recommendations of the 1982 Cork Committee on Insolvency Law and Practice report.[85] Cork suggested the introduction of a wholly new corporate insolvency mechanism designed primarily to facilitate the rescue and rehabilitation of the viable parts of the company in financial difficulties. Cork tended to view receivership through somewhat rose-tinted business rescue spectacles stating that the power of the floating charge holder to appoint a receiver and manager of the whole property and undertaking of a company has been of 'outstanding benefit to the general public and to society as a whole ...', adding:[86]

> 'Such receivers and managers are normally given extensive powers to manage and carry on the business of the company. In some cases, they have been able to restore an ailing enterprise to profitability, and return it to its former owners. In others, they have been able to dispose of the whole or part of the business as a going concern. In either case, the preservation of the profitable parts of the enterprise has been of advantage to the employees, the commercial community, and the general public.'

The Cork Committee envisaged that the new administration procedure would be used primarily in cases where the company had not granted a debenture secured by a floating charge. It did not wish however that the procedure should be confined to such cases.[87]

As enacted in Part II of the Insolvency Act 1986, the administration order procedure contained a number of features which curtailed its effectiveness.[88] First, the procedure was too heavily court-centred. There was no facility whereby out-of-court appointments could be made – whether by the company or by its creditors. Secondly, a floating charge holder had an effective veto on the appointment of an administrator. In one sense this was because administration was viewed as an alternative to receivership but also because during the period of administration the company, under the control of the administrator, could continue to trade and incur debts and these debts were payable in priority to claims secured

---

[84] The 'old' administration regime contained in the former Part II remains in force as far as building societies and certain public utility companies are concerned – see s 249 of the Enterprise Act 2002.

[85] *Insolvency Law and Practice*, Cmnd 8558 (1982). Prentice, Oditah and Segal 'Administration: The Insolvency Act 1986, Part II' [1994] LMCLQ 487 consider further the reasons for the introduction of the administration procedure, its evolution and effect.

[86] Cmnd 8558, at para 495.

[87] Cmnd 8558, at para 497.

[88] See generally Insolvency Service *A Review of Company Rescue and Business Reconstruction Mechanism, Report by the Review Group* (May 2000) and also Hunter 'The nature and functions of a rescue culture' [1999] JBL 491.

by the floating charge but not in priority to those secured by a fixed charge. Thirdly, there was no statement of overarching statutory objectives or hierarchy of purposes though s 8(3) of the Insolvency Act 1986 specified various purposes for whose achievement an administration order might be made.

An administration order could also specify more than one purpose but there was no explanation in the legislation as to whether one purpose could take precedence over another.

A fourth feature was the presence of gaps in the statutory moratorium. After the presentation of a petition for the appointment of an administrator and during the currency of an administration order there was an embargo on the enforcement of security rights and other claims against the company. While the embargo was pretty extensive in its ambit it did not cover situations where a landlord of business premises occupied by a company in administration forfeited the lease for breach of covenant and peacefully retook possession.[89]

Fifthly, the administration procedure was somewhat open-ended. There were no time-limits apart from a requirement to hold a meeting of creditors within three months of appointment and to lay a statement of the administrator's proposals before such a meeting. This period could be extended by the court. The administration procedure did not to an end automatically on the expiry of a particular time frame or the occurrence of another event. Basically an administrator was required to apply to the court for the administration order to be discharged if it appeared to him that the purpose or each of the purposes specified in the administration order had been achieved or was no longer capable of achievement.[90]

Sixthly, the exit routes from administration into liquidation were procedurally difficult and cumbersome to negotiate. For example creditors' voluntary liquidation is a more cost-effective alternative than compulsory liquidation under the control of the court but there were considerable difficulties in going down the creditors' voluntary liquidation route.[91]

21.14   The Rescue Culture and US comparisons

The Enterprise Act 2002[92] aimed to make the UK a better place in which to do business. Even the title of the legislation suggests a new social order.

---

[89] See generally *Re Lomax Leisure Ltd* [2000] BCC 352 where the various authorities were analysed by Neuberger J.

[90] Section 18(2) of the Insolvency Act 1986 as originally drafted.

[91] For a discussion of some of the problems see *Re Mark One (Oxford Street) plc* [1998] BCC 984; *Re Designer Room Ltd* [2004] BCC 904.

[92] For a full theoretical discussion see G McCormack *Corporate Rescue Law – An Anglo-American Perspective* (Edward Elgar, 2008), V Finch *Corporate Insolvency Law: Perspectives and Principles* (Cambridge University Press, 2002) and in particular Chs 8

Whereas before we had insolvency legislation, now we have enterprise law.[93] The legislation was designed to strengthen the foundations of an enterprise economy by establishing an insolvency regime that encouraged honest but unsuccessful entrepreneurs to persevere despite initial failure.

There was a feeling that suitable mechanisms should be in place to prevent or at least to mitigate the consequences of banks 'cutting rough' in a recession.[94] The receivership model was seen as too heavily creditor oriented[95] in that the power to appoint a receiver had been too readily used by banks to protect their investment and that the effect of this was to drive too many companies unnecessarily into insolvency.

The new legislation borrows from overseas models but it is not a direct transplant. One distinguished US commentator has observed:[96]

> '... if an American banker is very, very good, when he dies he will go to the United Kingdom. British banks have far more control than an American secured lender could ever hope to have. Receiverships on the British model are unknown and almost unthinkable in the US. A US banker could barely imagine a banker's Valhalla in which a bank could veto a reorganisation as a UK bank may effectively veto an administration by appointing an administrative receiver.'

The US Bankruptcy Code has traditionally been seen as very 'pro-debtor' compared with the UK position which, by contrast, is seen as 'pro-creditor'.[97] In the United States, corporate reorganisation proceedings are governed by Chapter 11 of the Bankruptcy Code 1978 and are almost always begun by a voluntary petition filed by the corporate debtor.[98] The filing brings about a moratorium on enforcement proceedings against the debtor or its property and the incumbent management normally remain in place during the early stages at least of the reorganisation proceedings. The US law is classed as pro-debtor for it provides for an automatic stay on creditor enforcement proceedings; it allows unimpeded petitions for reorganisation and it allows the company's

---

and 9 and see also V Finch 'Re-Invigorating Corporate Rescue' [2003] JBL 527; S Frisby 'In Search of a Rescue Regime: the Enterprise Act 2002' (2004) 67 MLR 247.

[93] The legislation was preceded by a 2001 White Paper *Productivity and Enterprise: Insolvency – A Second Chance* Cm 5234 (2001).

[94] See the statement by the government minister in *Hansard*, Standing Committee B, Enterprise Bill, 15th Sitting, 9 May 2002 at col 602.

[95] The White Paper *Productivity and Enterprise: Insolvency a Second Chance* (2001) at para 2.5 talked about 'making changes which will tip the balance in favour of collective insolvency proceedings – proceedings in which all creditors participate, under which a duty is owed to all creditors and in which all creditors may look to an office holder for an account of his dealings with company's assets'.

[96] See Westbrook 'A Comparison of Bankruptcy Reorganisation in the US with the Administration Procedure in the UK' (1990) 6 Insolvency Law and Practice 86, at 87.

[97] See generally D Milman 'Reforming Corporate Rescue Mechanisms' in J De Lacy (ed) *The Reform of United Kingdom Company Law* (Cavendish, 2002) at p 415.

[98] See generally G McCormack *Corporate Rescue Law – An Anglo-American Perspective* (Edward Elgar, 2008).

board to remain in control during reorganisation.[99] Even under the Enterprise Act English law is quite different from the US position. The administration procedure still involves handing control of the company over to an outsider and moreover there is no method by which secured creditors can be 'crammed' down, ie forced to accept a reorganisation plan against their wishes. The possibility for 'cramdown' is a feature of the US system. The US system, unlike the UK one, also contains a specific dedicated legislative regime for the financing of companies in difficulties.[100]

Moroever, the US Bankruptcy Code contains special provisions on executory contracts which make it difficult for suppliers and others to terminate trading relationships with companies that have gone into an insolvency process.[101] Contractual termination or interruption clauses when a company goes into administration are a feature of the UK corporate scene and such provisions may make it difficult to keep the business of a company alive. For this reason, the UK government are currently considering proposals to restrict the effectiveness of such provisions.[102]

21.15   Purposes of administration

Under the Insolvency Act 1986 the floating charge holder had an effective veto on the appointment of an administrator.[103] With the new regime this veto disappears and is replaced by an effective veto on the identity of the proposed administrator. Perhaps a more significant change effected by the Enterprise Act 2002 has been in relation to the purposes of the administration order. There is a new hierarchy of purposes specified which administration is supposed to serve.[104] An administrator must perform his functions with the objective (a) of rescuing the company as a going concern unless he thinks that it is not reasonably practicable to achieve that objective or objective (b) would achieve a better result for the company's creditors as a whole. Objective (b) means achieving a better result for the company's creditors as whole than would be likely if the company were wound up without first being in administration. The third objective of administration is realisation of property in order to make a distribution to one or more secured or preferential creditors. An administrator may only pursue this third objective if he thinks that it is

---

[99] May 2000, at pp 38–41. The Review Group however concluded at p 33 of its report that 'it would be wholly inappropriate to attempt to replicate Chapter 11 in the UK, where the business culture and economic environment are quite different'.

[100] See generally G McCormack 'Super-priority New Financing and Corporate Rescue' [2007] JBL 701.

[101] See s 365 of the US Bankruptcy Code.

[102] See the Insolvency Service website – www.insolvencyservice.go.uk/.

[103] Section 9 of the Insolvency Act 1986 as originally drafted.

[104] Schedule B1, para 3(1).

not reasonably practicable to achieve of the first two objectives and he does not unnecessarily harm the interests of the creditors of the company as a whole.[105]

The first objective is preservation of the business of the company rather than preservation of the company as an empty corporate shell. The point was made during the parliamentary debates that rescuing the company on its own is a pointless objective in that a company that has nothing, does nothing and has no purpose is of no use.[106] On the other hand, the objective of preserving all or part of the company's business would be beneficial to employees, to creditors who may be paid out of the proceeds of the sale of the business or from future profits and additionally beneficial to the overall economy. The government stressed that the first priority was to rescue the company as a going concern with much of its business intact.[107]

Choices within the hierarchy are governed by the test of what is reasonably practicable but the arbiter of choice appears to be the administrator. The legislation refers to what he 'thinks' rather than to what on reasonable grounds he might believe. If an administrator has been appointed by a qualified floating charge holder out of court and then moves rapidly to the conclusion that the only practicable option is to make distributions to secured and preferential creditors then administration seems suspiciously like administrative receivership in another guise. Paragraph 74 provides that a creditor or member of a company in administration may apply to the court claiming that the administrator is acting or has acted so as unfairly to harm the interests of the applicant whether alone or in common with some or al other members or creditors or is proposing to act in such a manner. The court if it adjudges the complaint well-founded may make such order as it thinks appropriate including regulating the administrator's exercise of his functions or requiring the administrator to do or not to do a specified thing. Some ammunition for a court challenge may come from the administrator's duty under para 49 in the statement setting out proposals for achieving the purpose of administration to explain why objectives (a) or (b) cannot be achieved.[108]

It should be noted, however, that the relevant test is what the administrator 'thinks' and not what he 'reasonably believes'. While the state of a man's mind may be as much a fact as the state of his indigestion, the 'thinks' test leaves little scope for judicial review. It is not generally the practice of the courts to second-guess the commercial

---

[105] Ibid, para 3(4). But see also *Kyrris v Oldham* [2004] BCC 111 – administrator owes no duty of care to an individual creditor.

[106] See the comments by Lord Hunt of Wirral in the House of Lords – *Hansard*, HL Debs, col 765, 29 July 2002.

[107] See the comments by the relevant minister, Lord McIntosh of Haringey, in *Hansard*, HL Debs, col 766, 29 July 2002.

[108] Schedule B1, para 49(2)(b).

judgments of administrators and other discretionary decision makers. The relevant minister explained that:[109]

> 'The administrator is the person on the ground who is best placed to judge whether or not a particular objective is reasonably practicable, in the light of his experience and professional judgment ... [I]t will be for the administrator to reach a conclusion as to whether or not the objectives are reasonably practicable, taking into account all the circumstances of the particular case of which he or she is aware at the time.'

It has been suggested that the legislative reliance placed on the administrator's opinion makes it virtually impossible for a court to interfere with the administrators' judgments provided that these are made in good faith.[110]

When para 74 is, however, read in conjunction with para 3(4)(b), which requires the administrator not unnecessarily to harm the interests of the creditors of the company as a whole, it seems clear that there is scope for judicial second-guessing of administrators' decisions in contexts other than the purposes of administration. Take the situation where a company has two assets, one of which is essential to the carrying on of a company's business and the other of which is not. The administrator then decides to sell the key asset, perhaps because it is a bit more easily saleable, so as to make distributions to secured and preferential creditors even though the sale has a crippling effect on the further viability of the company. In these circumstances, it would seem that the administrator has acted in a way that has unfairly and unnecessarily harmed the interests of members (and perhaps creditors) of the company. Therefore his conduct is amenable to redress under para 74 whereas it seems that if an administrative receiver had behaved in a similar fashion his conduct could not be impeached. An administrative can choose to exercise or not to exercise the power of sale over a particular sale. According to the Privy Council decision in *Downsview Nominees v First City Corp*[111] the only constraint on the administrative receiver's choices is the criterion of good faith. In Professor Goode's words, *Downsview* suggests that:[112]

> 'the receiver ... is entitled, if he so chooses, to decide not to continue the company's business, and to sell a part of the business which would be better

---

[109] *Hansard*, HL Deb, col 768, 29 July 2002.

[110] See V Finch 'Re-Invigorating Corporate Rescue' [2003] JBL 527 at 546. Support for a subjective interpretation also comes from *Re GHE Realisations Ltd* [2006] 1 WLR 287 but for a different perspective see J Armour and RJ Mokal 'Reforming the Governance of Corporate Rescue: the Enterprise Act 2002' [2005] *Lloyd's Maritime and Commercial Law Quarterly* 32. On 'thinks' see also *Unidare plc v Cohen* [2005] BPIR 1472 where Lewison J remarked 'I accept that the process of thinking involves a rational thought process; but I do not accept that what the administrator thinks is subject to any form of test by reference to an objective standard'.

[111] [1993] AC 295.

[112] Goode *Principles of Corporate Insolvency Law*, (Sweet & Maxwell, 3rd edn, 2005) at p 284.

kept. It would also seem that he can select a particular asset to realise for the benefit of his debenture holder even though the removal of that asset would damage the company's business and there are other assets to which he could resort and on which the business is less dependent.'

21.16   Entry routes into administration

There are now a variety of routes into administration. An administrator can now be appointed by the court; by a qualified floating charge holder out of court; or by the company itself upon giving prior notice to a qualified floating charge holder.

The court route into administration most closely resembles the old procedure but even here there are still some differences. An application to the court for the making of an administration order may be made by the company itself or its directors or by one or more of its creditors.[113] Notice of the application has to be served on any person who has appointed or may be entitled to appoint an administrator or on any qualified floating charge holder who is or may be entitled to appoint an administrator. The latter is then afforded the opportunity to appoint an administrator out of court.[114] The former power which a qualified floating charge holder had to appoint an administrative receiver has now effectively been abrogated.[115] Before an administration order may be made there is a threshold insolvency condition – the court must be satisfied that the company is or is likely to become unable to pay its debts. Moreover, it must also the satisfied that the 'administration order is reasonably likely to achieve the purpose of administration'.[116]

Qualified floating charge holders and the company itself may now appoint out of court and one wonders what the merits are in going to court considering the inevitable additional expense. Court appointments however may be seen to confer a public legitimacy on administrators that is lacking in other cases. This can be particularly important, for instance where an administrator may be called upon to take control of company property or perform other functions in a foreign jurisdiction. Schedule B1, para 5 provides that an administrator is an officer of the court (whether or not he is appointed by the court).[117] Nevertheless, a

---

[113]   Schedule B1, para 12(1).

[114]   Pursuant to Sch B1, para 14.

[115]   Insolvency Act 1986, s 72A though there are a number of exceptional cases where such a power of appointment still exists and moreover holders of qualifying floating charges created before the coming into force of the Enterprise Act on 15 September 2003 have their old entitlements still intact. On the exceptional cases, see generally *Feetum v Levy* [2006] Ch 685.

[116]   Schedule B1, para 11.

[117]   As an officer of the court an administrator probably becomes subject to the somewhat ill-defined obligation enunciated in *ex parte James* (1874) LR 9 Ch App 609 to act honourably and fairly.

foreign tribunal may not accord recognition to an administrator appointed by a qualified floating charge holder out of court.

The Enterprise Act 2002 pays great deference to the wishes of secured creditors and this is seen in two provisions relating to court appointment of administrators.[118] First, under para 36 of Sch B1 where an administration application is made by somebody other than a qualified floating charge holder, the latter may intervene in the proceedings and suggest to the court the appointment of a specified person as administrator. The court is obliged to respond positively to this intervention unless it thinks it right to refuse the application 'because of the particular circumstances of the case'. Furthermore, under para 35 the court is required automatically to accede to administration applications made by qualified floating charge holders and there is no threshold insolvency requirement.

21.17　Out-of-court appointments by qualified floating charge holders

The right to appoint an administrator out of court is conferred on the holder of a qualifying floating charge as defined in Sch B1, para 14. This definition is not free from controversy and may engender considerable controversy in the years to come. Under para 14(2) a floating charge qualifies if it is created by an instrument which:

(a)　states that this paragraph applies to the floating charge;

(b)　purports to empower the holder of the floating charge to appoint an administrator of the company; and

(c)　purports to empower the holder of the floating charge to appoint an administrative receiver.

It is not altogether clear whether these are disjunctive or conjunctive conditions. In other words, it is not clear whether the relevant debenture must provide both that the relevant paragraph applies and also empower the floating charge holder to appoint an administrator/administrative receiver or whether it suffices if the debenture does either one of these things. There is also some ambiguity about the 'property' condition in para 14(3). The simpler scenarios is where the floating charge or a number of floating charges collectively together relate to the whole or substantially the whole of the company's property. Paragraph 14(3) also refers however to a situation where 'charges and other forms of security' together relate to the whole or substantially the whole of the company's

---

[118] See also para 37 which enables a qualifying floating charge holder to apply to have an existing administration converted into a liquidation but the court is not obliged to accede to such an application. Paragraph 38 enables the liquidator to make a similar application.

property and at least one of which is a qualifying floating charge. Before appointing an administrator a qualifying floating charge holder must give two days' written notice to the holder of a prior qualifying floating charge.[119] A floating charge is treated as prior if it was first in point of time or if it is entitled to priority by virtue of a priority agreement between the two charge holders.

The floating charge holder is not obliged to give any notice to the company of the intention to appoint an administrator. A company may have administration foisted upon it against its wishes. An administrator must perform his functions with the overarching objective of rescuing the company as going concern but a company may wished to be saved from this fate particularly where the existing management are of the view that any temporary trading difficulties can be alleviated without recourse to formal insolvency processes. In this respect administration via the floating charge holder can be likened to administrative receivership. A floating charge holder was not required to give prior notice to the corporate debtor of his intention to appoint a receiver[120] and the absence of a prior notice requirement still obtains in those cases where the appointment of an administrative receiver is still permissible. English law contrasts in this respect with some other jurisdictions including Canada which introduced a statutory notice requirement in 1992.[121]

A charge holder who is contractually entitled to appoint a receiver is under no duty to refrain from doing so on the grounds that it might cause loss to the company or its creditors. It has been held that, in exercising the right to appoint, no duty of care is owed to either the debtor or to guarantors of the secured debt. A chargee is given the power to appoint a receiver to protect his interests, and the decision to exercise that power cannot be challenged, except possibly on the ground of bad faith.[122] Likewise the decision of a qualified floating charge holder to appoint an administrator cannot be impeached by a company that is concerned about the destruction of economic value that such an appointment might entail.

21.18 Out-of-court appointments by the company or its directors

The company or its directors are also enabled to appoint an administrator out of court on giving 5 days' notice which identifies the proposed administrator to floating charge holders.[123] The notice of intention to appoint must be accompanied by a statutory declaration stating *inter alia* that the company is or is likely to become unable to pay its debts; that the

---

[119] Schedule B1, para 15. There is an exception if the holder of any prior floating charge has consented in writing to the making of the appointment.

[120] See, eg, *Gomba Holdings UK Ltd v Homan* [1986] 1 WLR 1301.

[121] See s 244 of the Bankruptcy and Insolvency Act 1992 and see generally McCormack 'Receiverships and the Rescue Culture' [2000] CfiLR 229.

[122] *Downsview Nominees v First City Corp* [1993] AC 295.

[123] Schedule B1, paras 22 and 26.

company is in liquidation and that none of the other factors precluding an appointment are present.[124] An appointment must be made not later than 10 days after notice of intention to make an appointment is filed with the court.

There are certain anti-abuse provisions.[125] A company cannot invoke this out-of-court administration procedure if the company has come out of administration under such procedure within the previous 12 months or if the company has been the subject of a moratorium under a 'small company' CVA in the previous 12 months or a winding-up petition has been presented and has not yet been disposed of. The limitations built into the legislation may be seen as a necessary measure to prevent certain unscrupulous companies and directors from making continuous use of moratorium procedures to the disadvantage of their creditors. The company can always go into administration during this period but this must be done through the courts and not by means of the out-of-court route.

21.19   Effect of the appointment of an administrator

The appointment of an administrator displaces the board of directors from their existing management functions. Under para 67 an administrator is required on his appointment to take custody or control of all the property to which he thinks the company is entitled. The administrator is obliged to manage the affairs, business and property of a company. It is provided in para 64 that a company in administration or an officer of a company in administration may not exercise a management power without the consent of the administrator and 'management power' is interpreted to mean any power which could be exercised so as to interfere with the exercise of the administrator's powers. The Enterprise Act 2002 does not change anything in this regard from the position under the Insolvency Act 1986. The directors of a company remain in office but they lose their management powers during administration. It may be that one way of cutting down in expense would be for the administrator to delegate certain day-to-day tasks to the 'old' management team but retaining overall strategic control himself.

Apart from such 'grace and favour' actions by the administrator however there is no scope in the process for existing management. The legislation places decisive faith in the established skills of the UK insolvency profession.[126] The US Chapter 11 is almost at the other end of the spectrum for in that system the corporate debtor remains in control of the business during the reorganisation process though the bankruptcy court may appoint a trustee to oversee operations if the management are

---

[124] Ibid, para 27.
[125] Ibid, paras 23–25.
[126] See V Finch 'Re-invigorating Corporate Rescue' [2003] JBL 527 at 549.

suspected of fraud.[127] While the board of directors remain in overall charge of the business it may be that the composition of the board will change quite significantly during the rescue and renewal period. Be that as it may, there is quite a difference in the formal approach of the law between the United States and England. This has been accounted for by reason of the difference in business philosophy on either side of the Atlantic. In the United States there is less of a stigma attached to business failure. It is seen as part and parcel of entrepreneurial endeavour and if one business fails there should be scope for picking up the pieces and starting afresh. Management are not seen as blameworthy whereas in Britain there may be a view that since the existing management are the very people who got the company into financial difficulties they are least qualified to take it out of such difficulties.[128]

The administrator has very wide powers to manage the company's business and to deal with its assets in order to achieve the purposes of administration. Thus the administrator may allow the company to continue to trade, to dispose of its assets and to commence or continue legal proceedings. The administrator has the power to remove directors and to appoint any person to be a director, whether to fill a vacancy or otherwise.[129] He can also call meetings of members and of creditors,[130] and has a general power to apply to the court for directions in carrying out his functions.[131]

More generally, an administrator has power to make a payment otherwise than in accordance with the normal rules of priority if he thinks it likely to assist achievement of the purpose of administration. The most common scenario for the exercise of this power may be where an essential supplier insists on the discharge of earlier debts as a condition of making further essential supplies.[132]

A person dealing with an administrator in good faith and for value is not concerned to inquire whether the administrator is acting within his powers.[133] There are, nevertheless, various disclosure obligations which are designed to ensure that persons who have an interest in the company

---

[127] See generally, G McCormack 'Control and Corporate Rescue – An Anglo-American Evaluation' (2007) 36 ICLQ 515–552.

[120] See G Moss QC 'Chapter 11: An English Lawyer's critique' (1998) 11 *Insolvency Intelligence* 17.

[129] Schedule B1, para 61.

[130] Ibid, para 62.

[131] Ibid, para 63.

[132] Paragraph 65. But see s 233 of the Insolvency Act 1986 on 'ransom' demands by utility suppliers. See also *Re MG Rover Espana SA* [2006] BCC 599 – payments might be made to employees under the national laws of other EC member states in excess of their entitlements under UK laws to avoid the need for these employees opening secondary insolvency proceedings in other EC member states thereby complicating the administration process and adding to the expense.

[133] Ibid, para 59(3).

or who have dealings with it are aware of its new status.[134] In particular, every invoice, order for goods or business letter which is issued by or on behalf of the company or the administrator after the commencement of administration must also contain the administrator's name and a statement that the affairs, business and property of the company are being managed by the administrator.[135]

21.20   The statutory moratorium

One of the most important features of administration is the moratorium. The commencement of the administration procedure imposes a freeze on proceedings or executions against the company and its assets. This provides a breathing space during which the company has an opportunity to make arrangements with its creditors and members for the rescheduling of its debts and the reorganisation and restructuring of its affairs.[136]

By virtue of the moratorium:

(1)   no resolution may be passed or order made for the winding-up of the company though this does not apply to winding-up petitions on public interest grounds under s 124A of the Insolvency Act nor to winding-up petitions presented by the Financial Services Authority under s 367 of the Financial Services and Markets Act 2000;[137]

(2)   no steps may be taken to enforce any security over the company's property[138] or to repossess goods in the company's possession under any hire-purchase agreement[139] except with the leave of the court and subject to such terms as the court may impose; and or else with the consent of the administrator;

(3)   no legal process[140] including distress[141] may be instituted or continued against the company or its property except with the leave

---

[134]   See r 2.10 of the Insolvency Rules 1986.
[135]   Schedule B1, para 45.
[136]   The operation of the moratorium throughout the administration is modified in respect of market charges, that is charges arising out of dealings in securities. The modifications of the law of insolvency in respect of market charges were made by Part VII of the Companies Act 1989. See also the Financial Collateral Regulations 2003, SI 2003/3112 (as amended) for enforcement rights in respect of financial collateral. These regulations were enacted to give effect to the EC Financial Collateral Directive, Directive 2002/47/EC.
[137]   Schedule B1, para 42.
[138]   Ibid, para 43(2).
[139]   Ibid, para 43(3) and defined by para 111 as including conditional sale agreements, chattel leasing agreements and retention of title agreements.
[140]   The proceedings in question are legal proceedings or quasi-legal proceedings such as arbitration: *Bristol Airport v Powdrill* [1990] Ch 744, [1990] 2 All ER 493, [1990] 2 WLR 1362, [1990] BCLC 585, [1990] BCC 130. This can include applications to industrial tribunals: *Carr v British International Helicopters Ltd* [1993] BCC 855. A 'legal process' requires the assistance of the court and therefore the service of a notice making time of

of the court and subject to such terms as the court may impose or else with the consent of the administrator;

(4) under s 11(3) of the Insolvency Act 1986 no steps could be taken to enforce any security over the company's property with security being defined as 'any mortgage, charge, lien or other security.' After some uncertainty and vacillation the courts held that a landlord's right to forfeit a lease for breach of covenant by peaceful re-entry did not fall within the definition of security. A right of re-entry was not security over a lease but simply a right to terminate the lease and restore the lessor to possession of his own property.[142] The Insolvency Act 2000 extended the moratorium so as to catch a landlord's right of forfeiture by peaceable re-entry. This position is now reflected in para 43(4).

When an administration order takes effect in respect of a company any administrative receiver of the company shall vacate office and moreover, any receiver of part of the company's property shall vacate office if the administrator requires him to.[143] According to para 42 the moratorium applies to a company in administration and there is also provision in broadly similar terms in para 44 for an interim moratorium and this begins to bite from the time that an administration application is presented. The interim moratorium is intended to ensure that the *status quo* is maintained and the company's business and assets are protected pending the outcome of the hearing. The interim moratorium is also brought into being by the filing of a notice of intention to appoint an administrator out of court either by a qualified floating charge holder or by the company or its directors. The interim moratorium continues pending the hearing of the administration application or where a notice has been served, for 5 days from filing unless an administrator has been appointed beforehand.

21.21 Relaxation of the moratorium

With the leave of the court or with the administrator's consent, security may be enforced, goods may be repossessed and other legal processes may be instituted or continued notwithstanding the fact that the company is in

---

the essence is not within this category: *Re Olympia and York Canary Wharf Ltd* [1993] BCC 154; *McMullen & Sons Ltd v Cerrone* [1994] BCC 25. See now on 'legal process' for the purpose of the moratorium *Re Railtrack plc* [2002] 2 BCLC 755 and see also *Environment Agency v Clark* [2001] Ch 57.

[141] The essential feature of distress is that the assets distrained are seized and detained by the distrainor: *Bristol Airport v Powdrill* [1990] Ch 744.

[142] Although it was held in one case that 'security' for the purposes of relevant provisions of the Insolvency Act 1986 included a landlord's right to forfeit a lease (*Exchange Travel Agency v Triton Property Trust* [1991] BCLC 396), this has not been followed in later decisions: *Razzaq v Pala* [1998] BCC 66; *Re Lomax Leisure Ltd* [1999] 2 BCLC 126. See also *Re Park Air Services plc* [2000] 2 AC 172 (HL).

[143] Schedule B1, para 41.

administration. Under the old substantially re-enacted provisions of the Insolvency Act 1986 there have been a number of test cases in which the courts have had an opportunity to spell out their approach to the granting of leave.

The leading authorities are the decisions of the Court of Appeal in *Bristol Airport plc v Powdrill*[144] and *Re Atlantic Computer Systems plc (No 1)*.[145] In the former case it was held that the exercise by an airport authority of its rights under the Civil Aviation Act 1982 to detain an aircraft for non-payment of landing charges constituted a 'step taken to enforce security' and thus came within the statutory moratorium. Leave was refused to enforce the security. Particularly telling factors against the airports were that none of the company's aircraft were on their runways at the commencement of the administration and had only arrived there subsequently because of the administrator's decision to continue the business; the airports had acquiesced in the administrator's proposal to sell the business as a going concern, which detention of the aircraft would prevent; and the airports had benefited financially from the continuation of the business by the administrator because they had received payment of substantial fees. Having supported the administration when it suited them, the airports could not later seek to enforce a right which was inconsistent with the achievement of the purpose of the administration.[146]

The Court of Appeal in *Powdrill* accepted that its reasoning would extend to a case where the holder of ordinary possessory lien[147] or similar right was requested by an administrator to give up the chattels subject to the right. Refusal to comply with the request would amount to a step taken to enforce security and would fall within the statutory moratorium. The Court of Appeal accepted that it would be practically inconvenient and costly for the holder of every lien to have to apply to court for leave but[148] thought that these potential difficulties would be mitigated in practice by the fact that the administrator and the holder of the lien could simply agree the matter between themselves without the intervention of the courts.

Re Atlantic Computer Systems plc (No 1) decided the narrow point that where a company in administration has leased goods and then sub-leased the goods to customers, those goods nevertheless remain in the possession of the company for the purposes of the moratorium. The Court of

---

[144] [1990] Ch 744, [1990] 2 All ER 493, [1990] 2 WLR 1362, [1990] BCLC 585, [1990] BCC 130.

[145] [1992] Ch 505, [1992] 1 All ER 476, [1992] 2 WLR 367, [1991] BCLC 606, [1990] BCC 859.

[146] [1990] Ch 744, at 767, per Browne-Wilkinson V-C.

[147] Under s 246, liens and similar rights on the company's books, papers or other records are unenforceable against 'office-holders', a category which includes administrators. On lien-holders, see also *Re Sabre International Products Ltd* [1991] BCLC 470.

[148] Staughton LJ at 772 considered that the effect of the statutory moratorium should be kept carefully under review.

Appeal, nevertheless, granted leave to lessors and security holders to recover their property and to enforce their security. The court also set out in general terms the approach of the court to leave applications. The underlying principle is that an administration for the benefit of unsecured creditors should not be conducted at the expense of those who have proprietary rights except to the extent that this may be unavoidable.

(1) The onus is on the applicant to establish a case for leave to be granted.

(2) The moratorium is intended to assist in the achievement of the purpose for which the administration order was made. If granting leave to the applicant is unlikely to impede that purpose, leave should normally be given.

(3) In other cases, the court should balance the legitimate interests of the applicant and the legitimate interests of the other creditors of the company.[149]

(4) In carrying out the balancing exercise great importance is normally to be given to the proprietary interest of the applicant. In general, so far as possible the administration procedure should not be used to prejudice those who were secured creditors or lessors at the commencement of the administration.

(5) It will normally be sufficient ground for the grant of leave if significant loss would be caused to the applicant by the refusal. But if substantially greater loss would be caused to others by the grant of leave, or loss which is out of all proportion to the benefit which leave would confer on the applicant, that may outweigh the loss to the applicant caused by a refusal.

(6) In assessing the respective losses, the court will have regard to matters such as:

    (a) the financial position of the company;
    (b) its ability to pay rental arrears and continuing rentals (or, in the case of security, to meet its obligations under its loans);
    (c) the administrator's proposals;
    (d) the period for which the administration order has been in force and is expected to remain in force;
    (e) the effect on the administration if leave is given and on the applicant if it is refused;
    (f) the end result sought to be achieved by the administration;
    (g) the prospects of that result being achieved; and
    (h) the history of the administration so far.

---

[149] For an example of the operation of this balancing process, see *Re Meesan Investments Ltd (Royal Trust Bank v Buchler)* (1988) 4 BCC 788, [1989] BCLC 130.

(7)   In considering these suggested consequences it will often be necessary to assess how probable they are.

(8)   Other factors, such as the conduct of the applicant, may also be relevant.

(9)   The above conditions will also apply to a decision to impose terms if leave is granted. They will also apply to a decision whether to impose terms as a condition for refusing leave. An example of refusal to grant leave on terms is provided by *Re Meesan Investments*,[150] where leave to enforce security was refused but the administrator was ordered to return to court in 2 months' time if the secured property had not been sold by then. The guidelines envisage refusal on terms becoming a common phenomenon.

(10) On applications to enforce security, an important consideration will often be whether the applicant is fully secured. If he is, delay in enforcement is likely to be less prejudicial than in cases where his security is insufficient.

(11) Unless the issue can be easily resolved, it is not appropriate on a leave application for the court to resolve a dispute about the existence, validity or nature of a security which the applicant seeks leave to enforce. The court needs to be satisfied only that the applicant has a seriously arguable case.

Wrongful refusal by an administrator to allow an owner of goods to repossess them could render the administrator liable to pay compensation.[151]

The Atlantic Computers case suggests that there is no 'expenses of administration' principle similar to an 'expenses of liquidation' principle. In other words, an owner of equipment leased to a company in administration and who was precluded from recovering possession of the equipment by virtue of the statutory moratorium could not not insist on payment of the rental amounts during the currency of the administration as an expense of the administration.[152]

The Court of Appeal in *Sunberry Properties Ltd v Innovate*[153] took a similar discretionary approach as to the liability of an administrator to meet rental payments under a lease. But the generally accepted approach

---

[150] [1989] BCLC 130.
[151] *Barclay Mercantile Business Finance Ltd v Sibec Development Ltd* [1992] 2 All ER 195, [1992] 1 WLR 1253, [1993] BCLC 1077, [1993] BCC 148. The basis of this jurisdiction is the administrator's position as an officer of the court. Whether an administrator could be liable for conversion was left open.
[152] See also the decision of the House of Lords in *Centre Reinsurance International Co v Freakley* [2007] Bus LR 284.
[153] [2009] 1 BCLC 145.

is now that articulated by Judge Purle QC in *Goldacre (Offices Ltd) v Nortel*[154] relying on r 2.67 of the Insolvency Rules as to what constitutes an expense of the administration. He applied the earlier decision of David Richards J in *Exeter City Council v Bairstow*[155] and held if something comes within r 2.67 it counts as an expense of administration but not if it falls outside r 2.67. Interpreting r 2.67 Judge Purle held that if an administrator elects to use leasehold premises, any liability incurred while the lease is being enjoyed or retained is expense of administration. The court had no discretion to restrict amount of rent payable by reference to proportion of premises actually occupied but the liability for rent was only treated as an expense of administration if it arose during period in which administrator made use of the property. The court had no discretion to consider how much it would be fair for the administrators to pay.

21.22 Power to deal with charged property

In many cases, in order to achieve the purposes of administration, the administrator will need to be able to use or dispose of all the company's property, including that part of it which is charged to a third party, e g the company's bankers. Schedule B1, para 70 gives the administrator certain powers to deal with property charged to third parties and chattels owned by third parties but in the company's possession, irrespective of the wishes of the charge holders or owners. There is a distinction between, on the one hand, assets subject to a fixed charge (or to hire-purchase agreements),[156] and, on the other, assets subject to a floating charge.

In the case of assets subject to a floating charge, the administrator is given power to dispose of such assets or otherwise exercise his powers in relation to them as if the assets were not subject to the floating charge. Accordingly, the administrator can deal with such assets and dispose of them as he sees fit without reference to the floating charge holder and without being fettered by any contractual restrictions contained within the floating charge, for example a negative pledge clause.

The reference in para 70 to a floating charge means a charge which, as created, was a floating charge.[157] Accordingly, the crystallisation of the floating charge prior to the administration order would not prevent the administrator from exercising these wide powers.

Where the administrator disposes of floating charge assets, the holder of the floating charge is given the same priority in respect of any of the company's property directly or indirectly representing the assets disposed

---

[154] [2010] Ch 455.

[155] [2007] BCC 236.

[156] This term includes conditional sale agreements, chattel leasing agreements and retention of title agreements: Sch B1, para 111.

[157] Ibid, para 111.

of as he would have had in respect of the assets subject to the floating charge. If, for example, the administrator sells plant and machinery subject to the floating charge, the proceeds of the sale will fall within the floating charge and the holder of the charge will be entitled to the same priority as against third parties (eg holders of subsequent floating charges) in respect of the proceeds as he had in respect of the plant and machinery disposed of.

As regards assets subject to a fixed charge (as created) or goods which are in the possession of the company under a hire-purchase agreement, the administrator may apply to court in accordance with Sch B1, paras 71 and 72, for an order authorising him to dispose of the property. The court may make such an order if it is satisfied that the disposal (with or without other assets) of the fixed charge assets or goods acquired on hire purchase would be likely to promote the purpose, or one or more of the purposes, specified in the administration order. The court order will authorise the administrator to dispose of the assets or goods as if they were not subject to the fixed charge or, as the case may be, as if the owner's rights under the hire-purchase agreement were vested in the company. Schedule B1, paras 71(3) and 72(3) provide that the court must make it a condition of any such order that:

(1)   the net proceeds of the disposal; and

(2)   a sum equalling the deficit between the net proceeds of disposal and the net amount which would be realised by a sale of the assets at market value as determined by the court,

must be applied towards discharging the sums secured by the fixed charge or payable under the hire-purchase agreement.

Section 15 of the Insolvency Act 1986 is the predecessor provision and its operation was considered in *Re ARV Aviation Ltd.*[158] Knox J held that the task of the court in leave applications was to balance the prejudice that would be felt by the secured creditor by the making of an order against the prejudice that would be felt by those interested in the promotion of the administration purpose if it were not made. The view that the court takes of the open-market value of the assets which the administrator seeks leave to sell is extremely important because it is this amount which the administrator is required to discharge as a condition of obtaining leave. In *ARV Aviation*, Knox J proceeded on the assumption that the purpose of this condition was to protect to the maximum practicable extent the secured creditor.[159] With a view to achieving this purpose, Knox J held that the granting of leave could be a two-stage process, with

---

[158]   (1988) 4 BCC 708, [1989] BCLC 664. See also *Re Capitol Films Ltd* [2011] BPIR 334.

[159]   *Mutatis mutandis*, the same underlying purpose would exist where the administrator seeks leave to dispose of goods in the possession of the company under a hire-purchase agreement.

the open-market valuation being assessed some time after the making of the order granting the administrator leave to dispose of the assets.

Leave may be sought in circumstances where the administrator and the secured creditor[160] are unable themselves to agree on a valuation; but such a dispute is not an essential prerequisite of the jurisdiction.[161] Where a secured creditor consents to the sale of the charged assets,[162] the administrator may not use the statutory mechanism to retain the proceeds of the sale but must deal with these proceeds in accordance with the terms on which the secured creditor has agreed to release its security.[163]

Where assets are subject to more than one fixed charge and the court makes an order authorising the disposal of such assets, the proceeds of sale must be applied towards discharging the sums secured by the securities in their order of priority.[164]

21.23   Status of the administrator

The administrator wears a couple of hats. Paragraph 5 provides that an administrator is an officer of the court whether or not he is appointed by the court. Paragraph 69 however states that in exercising his functions the administrator acts as the company's agent. Under general principles, an agent is not liable under a contract which he makes on behalf of his principal. Accordingly, an administrator would not be personally liable on any contract entered into by him in the course of acting as administrator, except insofar as the contract otherwise provides. However, in a suitable case, the court may oblige the administrator to comply with a contractual obligation of the company by granting an injunction.[165]

An administrator may incur liability in tort as an agent and, as an officer of the court, is subject to the rule in *Ex parte James*[166] which requires him to do the fullest equity.[167]

21.24   Duties of the administrator

The first duty of the administrator is to take into his custody or under his control all the property to which the company is or appears to be entitled.[168] Where the administrator seizes or disposes of property which does not belong to the company, then, provided that at the time of such

---

[160] Or supplier of goods on hire purchase, as the case may be.
[161] *Re ARV Aviation Ltd*, above.
[162] Or a supplier of goods on hire purchase consents to the sale of those goods.
[163] *Re Newman Shopfitters (Cleveland) Ltd* [1991] BCLC 407.
[164] Schedule B1, para 71(4).
[165] *Astor Chemicals Ltd v Synthetic Technology Ltd* [1990] BCLC 1, [1990] BCC 97.
[166] (1874) LR 9 Ch App 609.
[167] In *Powdrill*, above, the rule in *ex parte James* was applied by the Court of Appeal to require the administrator to pay interest on the sums payable to employees.
[168] Schedule B1, para 67.

seizure or disposal he believed and had reasonable grounds for believing that his actions were justified, he is not liable to any third party in respect of resulting loss or damage except to the extent that it was caused by his own negligence.[169]

Secondly, the administrator must manage the affairs, business and property of the company.[170] In the initial period of the administration, the administrator must discharge this management obligation subject to any directions from the court. Once the creditors have approved the administrator's proposals, the administrator must manage in accordance with those proposals or with any revision of the proposals approved by a creditors' meeting.[171] Some latitude is given to an administrator however in that he is allowed to manage in accordance with insubstantial revisions of the proposals approved by him.

21.25   The administrator's proposals

The formulation of proposals is an important stage in the administration procedure. As soon as is reasonably practicable and in any event within 8 weeks after the company enters administration[172] (or such longer period as the court or creditors may allow pursuant to para 107 or 108), the administrator must produce proposals for achieving the purpose of administration. A statement of the proposals must be sent to all creditors (so far as their addresses are known) and also to the Registrar of Companies.[173] Members must also be informed of the proposals, either by being sent a copy of the statement or by publication of a notice informing them of their right to apply for a copy free of charge.[174] A copy of the statement of proposals must also be laid before a meeting of the company's creditors if such a meeting is held.[175]

Forthwith on appointment, the administrator must[176] require certain persons, in particular the officers of the company, to submit a statement of affairs giving details of *inter alia* the company's assets, debts and liabilities and of creditors and of securities held by them.[177] The information produced is likely to be of considerable assistance to the administrator in the drawing-up of his proposals.

---

[169] Section 234(3) and (4).
[170] Schedule B1, para 68(1).
[171] Ibid.
[172] Ibid, para 49.
[173] Ibid, para 49(4).
[174] Ibid, para 49(6).
[175] Ibid, para 51(3).
[176] This is a mandatory obligation on the administrator: Sch B1, para 47(1). But he can release individual persons from their obligation to comply: Sch B1, para 48(2).
[177] They must comply within 11 days of being given notice of the requirement by the administrator unless the administrator extends the period: Sch B1, para 48(1) and (2).

An administrator's proposals may not result in non-preferential entitlements being paid ahead of preferential entitlements or one preferential creditor of the company being paid a smaller proportion of his debt than another.[178] More generally, respect for proprietary rights is clearly demonstrated by para 73(1)(a) which provides that an administrator's statement of proposals may include any action which affects the right of a secured creditor of the company to enforce his security. Secured creditors' rights are inviolate in this respect and this respect there is a clear contrast between the English legislation and Chapter 11 of the US Bankruptcy Code. Generally speaking however, creditors need to approve a Chapter 11 corporate reorganisation plan and approval signifies a majority in number and two-thirds in amount, valued by the extent of the outstanding debt, of each class of creditors. As a general rule, it is imperative that every impaired class of creditors approve the plan though 'cramdown' is possible. 'Cramdown' refers to the process whereby a plan may be confirmed despite a class of creditors voting down the plan. A secured class of creditors may be crammed down if it receives the value of its collateral plus interest over time, while an unsecured class may insist that equity owners receive nothing if a plan is to be approved over its objection. Objecting creditors are protected by both a 'best interests' test and also a 'feasibility' test. Under the 'best interests' test, each objecting creditor must receive at least as much under the plan as it would in liquidation. The 'feasibility' test requires that debtor must be reasonably likely to be able to perform the promises it made in the plan.[179]

21.26 The meeting of creditors

Under para 51 an initial creditors' meeting must be held as soon as reasonably practicable after the company enters administration and in any event within 10 weeks though this time limit can be extended by the court or by the creditors. The meeting is preceded by the creditors and members being sent a copy of the administrator's proposals which must be done at the latest within 8 weeks of the company entering into administration.[180] The administrator's statement of his proposals will normally be a detailed document setting out the history of the company, its present financial position and future plans during the administration as well as providing sufficient financial information to enable the creditors to decide whether or not they should approve the proposals.

An administrator has power to dispense with the requirement to hold an initial creditors' meeting in two scenarios. The first scenario is where he thinks the company is fully solvent, ie the company has sufficient

---

[178] Schedule B1, para 73(1)(a) and (b).
[179] Section 1129 of the US Bankruptcy Code and for a general discussion see G McCormack *Corporate Rescue Law – An Anglo-American Perspective* (Edward Elgar, 2008), ch 8.
[180] See also para 4 which provides that the administrator must perform his functions as quickly and efficiently as is reasonably practicable.

property to enable each creditor to be paid in full.[181] The second situation is where the company has insufficient property to make a distribution to unsecured creditors other than by virtue of the ring-fencing provision.[182] The decision about not holding a meeting is based upon the administrator's subjective assessment and in the opinion of certain commentators is 'ripe for abuse'.[183] On the other hand, an administrator can be forced to hold an initial creditors' meeting if so requested by creditors of the company whose debts amount to at least 10% of the total debts of the company.[184]

The creditors' meetings may help to ensure the accountability of administrators. On the other hand, there is a widespread belief that unsecured creditors have little desire to play a central role in insolvency decision-making. According to a study conducted on behalf of the Insolvency Service:[185] 'Interviewees unanimously reported that creditor meetings are always very poorly attended, and that they strongly suspected that when reports, proposals and progress reports were sent out these were dispatched without ceremony to a cylindrical filing cabinet under the desk which is emptied daily.'

The meeting of creditors to consider the administrator's proposals has limited powers. It can accept the administrator's proposals in full but any modification favoured by the meeting can be incorporated into the proposals only with the administrator's consent.[186] If the administrator and the creditors cannot reach agreement, the matter must be referred back to the court. The court may provide that the appointment of the administrator shall cease to have effect from a specified time and make such consequential order as it thinks fit, or adjourn the hearing conditionally or unconditionally or make an interim order or any other order that it thinks fit.[187] This can include allowing the administration to proceed despite the creditors' opposition.[188] It may also make a winding-up order on a winding-up petition that has been suspended while the company is in administration.

Where agreement is reached, the administrator must again report the outcome to the court and must also inform creditors and the Registrar of Companies.[189] There is provision under para 56 for the administrator to

---

[181] See generally Sch B1, para 52(1).

[182] What is now s 176A of the Insolvency Act 1986 which sets aside a proportion of floating charge recoveries for the benefit of unsecured creditors.

[183] See S Davies (ed) *Insolvency and the Enterprise Act 2002* (Jordans, 2003) at p 152.

[184] Schedule B1, para 52(2).

[185] 'Report on Insolvency Outcomes' at p 54 – a paper presented to the Insolvency Service by Dr S Frisby – available on the Insolvency Service website.

[186] Schedule B1, para 53(1).

[187] Ibid, para 59(2).

[188] *Re Maxwell Communications Corp* [1992] BCLC 465, at 467; *Re Structures & Computers Ltd* [1998] BCC 348, at 353.

[189] Schedule B1, para 54(6).

summon further creditors' meetings if directed to do so by the court or so requested by creditors whose debts amount to at least 10% of the total debts of the company. The administrator's role after the proposals have been approved is to manage the company in accordance with the proposals. Ordinarily, any proposed substantial revisions to the proposals must be put to the creditors at a creditors' meeting[190] but it has been held that the court has jurisdiction itself to authorise deviation from the original proposals in an exceptional case, eg where the delay involved in convening a meeting could be fatal to the chances of success of the revised proposal.[191] If revised proposals are not approved, the administrator can continue to follow the old proposals, or, if his experience leads him to conclude that the purpose of the administration is incapable of achievement, he may apply to court under para 79 for his appointment to cease to have effect.

21.27 The committee of creditors

A creditors' meeting may also decide to establish a creditors' committee. The creditors' committee may require the administrator to attend on the committee at any reasonable time and may also require the administrator to provide the committee with information about the exercise of his functions.[192]

21.28 Cases where urgent action is required

The legislative scheme envisages the administrator managing the day-to-day conduct of the company's affairs for the period during which he is making investigations and inquiries with a view to formulating the proposals for the achievement of the administration purposes; but, before any radical steps are taken to achieve those purposes, the creditors are to be given an opportunity to consider and review what the administrator proposes to do. Underlying this structure is the assumption that, in return for the moratorium imposed by the administration procedure, creditors are to have an important say in the conduct of the administration.

What this standard scheme ignores, however, is the possibility of circumstances arising in which the company's interests dictate that the administrator should act very quickly, perhaps even before there is an opportunity to convene a meeting of the creditors. If, for example, the administrator is offered a generous price for the business conditional upon the sale being concluded in accordance with a tight timetable which

---

[190] Ibid, para 55(2).
[191] *Re Smallman Construction Ltd* (1988) 4 BCC 784, [1989] BCLC 420.
[192] Schedule B1, para 57.

does not allow for the holding of a creditors' meeting, what can and should the administrator do? Collins J addressed this in *Re Transbus International Ltd*.[193] He said:[194]

> 'I am satisfied that ... administrators are permitted to sell the assets of the company in advance of their proposals being approved by creditors ....'

Collins J said in many cases the administrators will be justified in not laying any proposals before a meeting of creditors. This is so where the requirements of para 52 are satisfied, eg where unsecured creditors are going to receive no payment. He said that if in such cases the administrators were prevented from acting without the direction of the court it would mean that they would have to seek the directions of the court before carrying out any function throughout the whole of the administration. This ran counter to the goal of the Enterprise Act 2002 which reflected a conscious policy to reduce the involvement of the court in administrations, where possible.

21.29   Protection of the interests of creditors and members

Any creditor or member of a company in administration may apply to the court under para 74(1) claiming that either the administrator is acting or has acted so as unfairly to harm the interests of the applicant (whether alone or in common with some or all other members or creditors) or that the administrator proposes to act in such a way. This provision substantially re-enacts s 27 of the Insolvency Act 1986 with some modifications of language.[195] Paragraph 74(2), on the other hand, is wholly new. It enable a creditor or member of a company in administration to apply to the court claiming that the administrator is not performing his functions as quickly or as efficiently as is reasonably practicable.

On such an application, the court may make such order as it thinks fit for giving relief in respect of the matters complained of, or adjourn the hearing conditionally or unconditionally, or make an interim order or any other order that it thinks fit.[196] An order under para 74 may, in particular:[197]

(1)   regulate the administrator's exercise of his functions;

(2)   require the administrator to do or not to do a specified thing;

---

[193]   [2004] 2 All ER 911.
[194]   At [12]–[13] of the judgment.
[195]   In particular the legislature has departed from the expression 'unfairly prejudicial to the interests' to 'unfairly to harm the interests'. Whether this heralds substantive change awaits judicial interpretation.
[196]   Schedule B1, para 74(3).
[197]   Ibid, para 74(4).

(3) require a meeting of creditors to be held for a specified purpose;

(4) provide for the appointment of the administrator to cease to have effect and make such consequential provisions as the court thinks fit.

However, an order under para 74 must not impede or prevent the implementation of a voluntary arrangement approved by the creditors or any compromise or arrangement sanctioned under s 895 of the Companies Act 2006 or, where the application for the para 74 order has been made more than 28 days after the approval of any proposal or revised proposals put forward by the administrator, the implementation of those proposals or revised proposals.[198]

In *Re Charnley Davies Ltd*,[199] it was held that the administrator had not acted negligently in the timing or the manner of the sale of the business of various companies in the Charnley Davies group. Millett J commented that an allegation of negligence only does not constitute an allegation of management in a manner which is unfairly prejudicial to the creditors and that, accordingly, it does not fall within the scope of s 27 of the Insolvency Act 1986. The language of para 74 is different referring to 'unfairness' rather than 'unfair prejudice', but whether this warrants a difference in outcome as regards negligence allegations remains to be seen.

21.30 Replacing an administrator and vacation of office

Schedule B1, paras 87–89, deal with the replacement of an administrator and paras 90–95 are concerned with filling vacancies in the office of administrator. Under para 87 an administrator may resign only in prescribed circumstances. An administrator may also be removed from office by order of the court and he is required to vacate office if he ceases to be qualified to act as an insolvency practitioner in relation to the company.

Generally, a person who has ceased to be the administrator of a company obtains a discharge from liability in respect of any action of his as administrator. Generally, the discharge takes effect from such time as the court may determine or, in the case of an administrator appointed out of court, at a time appointed by resolution of the creditors or the creditors' committee. The release discharges the administrator from liability in respect of any action of his as administrator.[200] The release, however, does not prevent the court from exercising its powers under Sch B1, para 75, which allows the court to examine the conduct of an administrator for possible misfeasance on the application of the Official Receiver, the

---

[198] Ibid, para 74(6).
[199] [1990] BCLC 760, [1990] BCC 605. See also *Kyrris v Oldham* [2004] BCC 111 – administrator owes no duty of care to an individual creditor.
[200] Schedule B1, para 98(1).

liquidator or any creditor or contributory of the company. On an examination of an administrator's conduct under para 75 the court may order him (a) to repay, restore or account for money or property; (b) to pay interest; or (c) to contribute a sum to the company's property by way of compensation for breach of duty or misfeasance.

The question of entitlement to fill a vacancy in the office of administrator depends on who made the initial appointment. Where the original appointment was made by the court, the court may replace the administrator.[201] Where an administrator was appointed out of court either by a qualified floating charge holder, the company itself or by its directors, the original appointor may replace the administrator.[202] The court, however, under para 95 has a general power to effect a replacement if satisfied that reasonable steps have not been taken to make a replacement or that for another reason it is right for the court to make the replacement.

21.31　Exit routes from administration

Under the Insolvency Act 1986 the exit routes from administration were somewhat inconvenient. In particular it was cumbersome to move from an administration to a creditors' voluntary liquidation (CVL). The latter was more cost effective than a compulsory liquidation but s 11(3) of the Act precluded the passing of a voluntary winding-up resolution while the company was still in administration. Moreover, the relevant date for the calculation of preferential debts was the date of the passing of the winding-up resolution whereas in cases where administration was followed immediately by a winding-up order it was the date of entry into administration.[203] Certain preferential creditors could be disadvantaged by the different dates and for this reason might oppose a voluntary winding up. It took a great deal of judicial dexterity to resolve these difficulties. Jacob J came up with a practical solution in *Re Mark One (Oxford Street) plc*,[204] holding that the court was empowered to order that the administrator make payments to preferential creditors as if the voluntary liquidation were a compulsory liquidation or that payments made by the administrator to the future liquidator should be on trust for the benefit of the previously preferential creditors.

The Enterprise Act 2002 streamlines the exit routes from administration and enables the company to move directly from administration to a CVL on the filing by the administrator of a requisite notice with the Registrar

---

[201] Ibid, para 91.

[202] Ibid, paras 92–94.

[203] Section 387 of the Insolvency Act 1986. The relevant provisions were amended by the Enterprise Act 2002 and s 387(3A) stipulates that in relation to a company which is in administration the relevant date is the date on which the company enters administration.

[204] [1998] BCC 984. But this case has by no means settled the controversy – see *Re Crompton's Leisure Machines Ltd* [2007] BCC 214 and *Re Lune Metal Products Ltd* [2007] BCC 217.

of Companies. The new procedure can be operated in cases where the administrator thinks that there are funds to make distributions to unsecured creditors (para 83).[205] An administrator has an unfettered power to make distributions to secured and preferential creditors during the currency of an administration but payments to unsecured creditors require the permission of the court (para 65). It seems clear from the overall thrust of the legislation that administration should not be the main vehicle for payment of unsecured creditors given the fact that an administrator must perform his functions as quickly and efficiently as is reasonably practicable.[206] Where there are effectively no funds left for payment of unsecured creditors para 84 provides a fast-track route from administration into dissolution of the company. Again this requires the filing of a requisite notice by the administrator with the registrar of companies.[207] Dissolution is deemed to occur automatically 3 months after the filing of the notice though there is a mechanism whereby this period may be extended.

The fact that it is possible to move relatively seamlessly from administration to dissolution of a company bypassing liquidation suggests that in some cases administration could be used as a substitute for liquidation. Avoiding the liquidation stage may mean a saving of costs but it can also mean that the directors escape full scrutiny for their actions. For instance, unlike a liquidator, an administrator has no power to bring civil proceedings against a director for fraudulent or wrongful trading under ss 213 and 214 of the Insolvency Act 1986. The administrator also avoids a check on his conduct by the liquidator. For these reasons, administration as a 'liquidation substitution' device has attracted criticism.[208]

The effect of the legislative changes is that now there are nine possible exit routes from administration:

(1) Under para 76 administration comes to an end automatically one year after a company goes into administration though this period may be extended either by the court or with the consent of creditors.

(2) By court order on an application made by the administrator pursuant to para 79. This paragraph requires the administrator to apply to the court if he thinks that the purpose of administration

---

[205] The administrator becomes liquidator unless the creditor nominates somebody else. This procedure may be used irrespective of whether the administrator has been appointed by the court or out of court – see *Re Ballast plc* [2005] BCC 96.

[206] Schedule B1, para 4.

[207] Paragraph 84 has been read also as applying in cases where the administrator once had property in his hands but no longer has – see *Re GHE Realisations Ltd* [2006] 1 WLR 287. See also *Re Ballast plc* [2005] BCC 96.

[208] See generally the report 'Study of Administration Cases' by A Katz and M Mumford summarised at (2007) 20 *Insolvency Intelligence* 97 and available on the Insolvency Service website (www.insolvency.gov.uk/).

cannot be achieved in relation to the company or that the company should not have entered into administration or a creditors' meeting has required him to make the application.

(3)   Under para 80 where an administrator appointed out of court files a notice that the purpose of the administration has been sufficiently achieved.

(4)   By court order under para 81 on an application made to it by a creditor who claims that there was an improper motive on the part of an administration applicant or an out of court appointor.

(5)   Pursuant to para 82 where the court makes a winding-up order on public interest grounds.

(6)   Where the administrator files a notice to put the company into a creditors' voluntary liquidation.

(7)   Where the administration files a notice to dissolve the company.

(8)   Where creditors fail to agree to the administrator's proposals or revised proposals and the court makes a termination order pursuant to para 55(2).

(9)   Also by court order where the administrator's actions have unfairly harmed either creditors or members – para 74(4).

21.32   Expenses of administration and remuneration of the administrator

Paragraph 99(3) provides that where a person ceases to be an administrator, his remuneration and expenses shall be charged on and payable out of property of which he had custody or control immediately before cessation and will be payable in priority to any floating charge.

Although the normal rule is that an agent is not personally liable on his principal's contracts, the Insolvency Act 1986 makes special provision for the payment of debts and liabilities incurred during the administration under contracts entered into by the administrator.[209] The special provision also applies to debts and liabilities incurred during the administration under contracts of employment adopted by the administrator after the first 14 days from his appointment.[210] The nature of the provision is that a statutory charge, ranking in priority to the administrator's statutory charge for his own remuneration and expenses[211] and to any floating

---

[209] Schedule B1, para 99(4).

[210] Schedule B1, para 99(5). Note that the statutory charge is limited to debts and liabilities incurred while he was administrator.

[211] This statutory charge is conferred by Sch B1, para 99(3). On what falls within the

charge, is imposed on the company's property in respect of the said debts and liabilities. Strictly, these statutory charges arise only when the administrator vacates office but the ordinary practice is for administrators to meet obligations, including salaries and other payments due to employees, as they arise during the continuance of the administration.

It is central to a procedure intended to facilitate the recuperation of the financial health of a struggling business that, if at all possible, business continuity should be maintained. Until the matter was litigated in the course of the administration of Paramount Airways Ltd (litigation which reached the House of Lords and which is reported as *Powdrill v Watson*),[212] the standard practice of administrators who chose to continue businesses was to inform employees that, despite the continuation of the business, their contracts would not be adopted and that no personal liability would be assumed by the administrators in respect of them. The underlying aim of this practice was to take the employees' contracts outside the scope of the statutory charge and hence ensure that payments arising from them did not rank in priority to the administrators' own remuneration and expenses.

In *Powdrill*, the House of Lords held that this practice was ineffective. The mere assertion of non-adoption was judged to be without legal effect because adopting was a matter not merely of words but of fact. If administrators continued after the 14-day grace period to employ staff and to pay them in accordance with the terms of their previous contracts, they would be held to have adopted those contracts. The outcome of the litigation caused considerable consternation amongst insolvency practitioners. They argued that it undermined the 'rescue culture' because administrators would be reluctant to retain employees with a view to continuing the business if this meant that they might not be able to recover their own remuneration and expenses, the company's resources having been exhausted by payments to employees. A new Insolvency Act was hurriedly enacted to clarify the position and these provisions are now reflected in paras 99(5) and 99(6).

Under this regime liabilities to pay sums by way of wages or salary[213] or by way of contribution to an occupational pension scheme which are in respect of services rendered after the adoption of the contract are 'qualifying liabilities' and, as such, they are entitled to the priority afforded by the statutory charge. Payments in respect of services rendered before the adoption of the contract are to be disregarded. Payment in lieu

---

category of administration expenses, see *Re Atlantic Computers*, above and *Re A Company (No 005174 of 1999)* [2000] 1 WLR 502.

[212] [1995] 2 AC 394, the decision of the Court of Appeal ([1994] 2 All ER 513), which was varied by the House of Lords with respect to holiday pay entitlements, is noted Fletcher (1994) 15 Co Law 145; Davies (1994) 23 ILJ 141.

[213] See *Re A Company (No 005174 of 1999)* [2000] 1 WLR 502.

of contractual notice periods and damages for breach of contract are not payments in respect of services rendered after adoption and thus would not be qualifying liabilities.[214]

Rule 2.67 of the Insolvency Rules sets out the order in which the expenses of the administration are payable though the court may adjust this order of priority. Under the Rule 'necessary disbursements' by the liquidator are payable in priority to the administrator's own remuneration. In the Nortel Networks case (*Bloom v Pensions Regulator*[215]) Briggs J at first instance considered the interaction between the Insolvency Act and rules, and the scheme under the Pensions Act 2004 for meeting unfunded pension fund liabilities of insolvent companies. It was held that the imposition of a 'financial support direction' by the Pensions Regulator under the Pensions Act upon companies in administration or insolvent liquidation created necessary disbursements, and therefore expenses within r 2.67. Therefore, these expenses had prima facie priority over the administrator's own claim to remuneration and a fortiori, the unsecured debts of the company. Briggs J took the view that the liability was not a provable debt under r 13.12 of the Insolvency Rules and as result had to be a 'necessary disbursement' because the liability could not fall into a statutory black hole.

The decision is controversial not least because of the potential loss to administrators and consequent concerns that it may impact on the so-called rescue culture. There has been intense lobbying by interested parties for the decision to be reversed.

21.33 The administrator as an 'office-holder'

The Insolvency Act 1986 gives certain rights and privileges to categories of insolvency practitioners defined as 'office-holders'. An administrator is within the definition of an office-holder for certain purposes.

As an office-holder, an administrator can attack transactions which took place prior to his appointment on the grounds that they amount to transactions at an undervalue, preferences, extortionate credit transactions, vulnerable floating charges or transactions defrauding creditors. These special powers are also enjoyed by liquidators and are considered further below. Unlike a liquidator, an administrator does not have standing to bring proceedings for fraudulent or wrongful trading.

Suppliers of gas, electricity, water and telecommunications services cannot make it a condition of continuing the supply that the

---

[214] The decision of the Court of Appeal in *Re Huddersfield Fine Worsteds Ltd* [2005] BCC 915 clarifies what constitutes 'qualifying liabilities'. It is clear that under the general law, damages for breach of contract are not 'wages or salary': *Delaney v Staples* [1992] 1 AC 687, at 692–693.

[215] [2011] BCC 277.

administrator pays outstanding charges. This protection is given to the administrator as an office-holder. However, the supplier can require the administrator to give a personal guarantee in respect of any new supplies.[216]

The powers which an administrator, as an office-holder, enjoys in relation to investigating the conduct of the company's affairs prior to his appointment are the same as those enjoyed by a liquidator.

21.34 Pre-packaged administrations

A phenomenon of the past decade has been the rise of the 'prepack' or 'prepackaged' administration.[217]

> 'A pre-pack ... administration is one where a deal has already been agreed prior to the company entering administration. The company's business will commonly be sold to the incumbent management team immediately the company is placed into administration. The business survives intact but will have managed to jettison some or all of the unsecured debt. The business is saved and jobs are saved. The pre-pack will usually require the support of the company's bankers or the injection of new venture capital.'

UK Insolvency legislation does not make any reference to pre-packaged administrations but recent years have seen their increased popularity. The pre-pack has emerged with a bang as a new effective device:

> 'The pre-pack has grown in popularity in the United Kingdom in parallel with the growth in "live side" or "pre-insolvency" approaches to corporate troubles. Increasingly it has become practice to deal with corporate difficulties in advance of collapse – a trend that has been encouraged by such developments as the embedding of a rescue culture in the United Kingdom; the emergence of better financial forecasting systems; a shift of approach from debt collection to financial risk management; the increased willingness of major lenders to take steps to prevent corporate disaster; and the emergence of a new cadre of turnaround professionals. The pre-pack has come to serve an important role in contingency and recovery planning as "the divide between informal and formal (insolvency) continues to blur".'[218]

Debt trading during corporate restructurings has also become more popular. The Enterprise Act 2002 was not intended to prompt a surge in the use of pre-packs, but the reforms introduced by the Act, including the

---

[216] Section 233.

[217] See generally P Walton 'Pre-Packaged Administrations – Trick or Treat' [2006] *Insolvency Intelligence* 113 and see also V Finch 'Pre-packaged administrations: bargains in the shadow of insolvency or shadowy bargains?' [2006] JBL 568.

[218] See V Finch 'Pre-Packaged Administrations: Bargains in the Shadow of Insolvency or Shadowy Bargains' [2006] JBL 568 at 569.

streamlined system of out-of-court entry into administration and the simpler exit routes have made it easier for pre-packs to be undertaken in practice.[219]

Pre-packs may be a good option for service focused companies or those whose business is reputation-based or intellectual property based. In such companies, the value of the business may be diminished by a protracted administration process.[220] If the basics of a deal for the sale of company assets have been worked out in advance of an administrator's appointment, then the administration procedures can be operated very rapidly. In a prepack, the corporate assets may be sold off to the existing management team. There is a high degree of certainty in a pre-pack and secured creditors also enjoy a high degree of control. For these reasons, secured creditors may consider it a more attractive alternative than a more drawn out insolvency process.[221]

The downside to prepacks is that they may involve, or be seen to involve, a 'sweetheart' deal for company management at the expense of general creditors. The secured creditors are paid out of the proceeds of the sale but agree lending facilities with the new corporate entity that has taken over the company assets. To many observers, the old company appears to be trading on but having shed its unsecured debt. In the eyes of some commentators, therefore, pre-packs function as a means 'by which powerful players can bypass carefully constructed statutory protections.'[222] Moreover, if the outcome is a 'done deal' before the company enters administration, it is hard to see how the administrator has properly addressed the statutory objectives of administration.

The administrator plays an indispensable part in the pre-pack procedure. As an agent of the company, the administrator is in a fiduciary position and moreover, has a statutory duty to consider rescuing the company. Some concerns about prepacks were articulated by Kitchin J in *Re Halliwells LLP*.[223] He suggested that they might lead to a solution convenient to the directors, secured creditor and insolvency practitioners, but which harmed the interests of general creditors. In exercising whatever discretion it had, the court should be alert to see that the procedure was not being obviously abused to the disadvantage of creditors. For this purpose, the court was likely to be assisted by the provision of the information required by Statement of Insolvency Practice (SIP) 16. It

---

[219] Desmond Flynn 'Pre-pack Administrations – A Regulatory Perspective' (2006) Recovery – Summer 3.

[220] Martin Ellis 'The Thin Line in the Sand – Pre-packs and Phoenixes' (2006) Recovery – Spring at p 3.

[221] P Walton 'Pre-packaged Administrations: Trick or Treat?' (2006) 19 Insolvency Intelligence 113 at 116.

[222] See V Finch 'Pre-Packaged Administrations: Bargains in the Shadow of Insolvency or Shadowy Bargains' [2006] JBL 568.

[223] [2011] BCC 57. See also *Re Kayley Vending Ltd* [2009] BCC 578 and *DKLL Solicitors v HMRC* [2007] BCC 908.

should be noted however that the Halliwells case involved judicial consideration of a proposed pre-pack in the context of an application to appoint administrators to a company. In many cases, administrators will be appointed out of court and the prepack will not come before the court in this fashion.

SIP 16 is essentially a statement of desirable practice and was formulated by the bodies representing Insolvency Practitioners with the backing of the Insolvency Service. There was at least the possibility of statutory intervention if the Insolvency Profession was not seen to regulate itself effectively. Para 8 states: 'it is in the nature of a pre-packaged sale... that unsecured creditors are not given the opportunity to consider the sale of the business or assets before it takes place. It is important, therefore, that they are provided with a detailed explanation and justification of why a pre-packaged sale was undertaken...'. Para 9 sets out certain information that the administrator must disclose to creditors, including information about the terms of the sale; marketing activities undertaken; alternative courses of action that the administrator considered, with an explanation of what their possible financial outcomes would have been; why it was not possible to trade the business and offer it for sale as a going concern during administration; and any connection between the purchaser and the directors or others involved in the company.

In the wake of the economic recession there have been continuing concerns about the lack of transparency in pre-packs and apparent levels of non-compliance with SIP 16. The concerns have centred around sales of company assets to connected parties where there has been no open marketing of the assets. In March 2011 the government announced proposals to require administrator to give advance notice to creditors where they were minded to sell a significant proportion of the company's assets in these circumstances. The advance warning would give creditors the opportunity of making a counter offer or applying to the court for injunctive relief. At the time of writing however, the proposals have not been implemented and it remains to be seen what form they will eventually take.

21.35   Post-administration financing

The new legislative framework has been criticised for the absence of any specific provision for the financing of corporate rescues.[224] As one commentator observes,[225] the legislation:

---

[224]   See, however, r 2.67 of the Insolvency Rules 1986 as amended. There was no equivalent to this under the original regime and it might be argued that it is sufficiently broadly worded so as to permit post-administration financing to be recognised as one of the expenses of the administration. See also *Centre Reinsurance International Co v Freakley* [2007] Bus LR 284.

[225]   See McKnight 'The Reform of Corporate Insolvency Law in Great Britain' [2002] JIBL 324, at 327.

'fails to address the difficulty that an administrator may face in obtaining funding, especially in a situation where it would be desirable for him to be able to offer security but, at the time of his appointment, the assets of the company were already subject to fixed security or were subject to a negative pledge preventing the company from granting security over the assets. There is no provision which would allow the administrator to proceed in a manner which may be contrary to or affect the rights of such a person and, being an officer of the court, he must act honourably towards such a person.'

New finance is often critical to the survival of the business of the company. Unless such finance is available from some source the assets of the company may have to be sold on a piecemeal basis and the company will be forced into liquidation. As the Department of Trade and Industry pointed out in 'Review of Company Rescue and Business Reconstruction Mechanisms', new secured finance is only available to support a rescue procedure in the UK where the existing secured creditors agree or where there are unsecured assets or sufficient equity in unsecured assets.[226] In the parliamentary passage of the Enterprise Act the government resisted an amendment that would have created a statutory framework for super-priority financing after the administration process has commenced.[227] It was wary of creating a situation that would essentially guarantee a return to lenders advancing funds on the basis of such priority irrespective of the commercial viability of the rescue proposals. In its view, the issue of whether to lend to a company in administration was a commercial one that was best left to the commercial judgment of the lending market. A lender might take into account the viability of the rescue proposals and the availability of free assets to serve as collateral, amongst other things.

There have often been calls for a new regime under which new money lent to companies in CVAs or administration would be given priority over existing loans. 'This could make it more attractive to lend to such companies allowing them to access extra funding when they need it most.'[228]

Such a scheme exists in the US but it may be inappropriate to replicate such provisions in the UK where the business culture and economic environment are quite different. In the United States, post-petition financing, as it is called, is dealt with in para 364 of the Bankruptcy Code. Under this provision, any credit extended to the corporate debtor during the reorganisation process has priority over pre-petition unsecured claims. If the extension of credit is in the ordinary course of business, then the

---

[226] See pp 33–35 of the Review Group report and for a general discussion of the whole issue see G Mc Cormack 'Super-priority New Financing and Corporate Rescue' [2007] JBL 701.

[227] See the House of Lords parliamentary debates for 29 July 2002, and see also the extensive discussion in S Davies (ed) *Insolvency and the Enterprise Act 2002* (Jordans, 2003) at pp 19–26.

[228] See the 'Budget' statement of 22 April 2009, available on the Insolvency Service website.

priority gained is automatic. If, on the other hand, the extension of credit is outside the ordinary course of business, then the priority must be authorised by the court prior to the granting of credit. In the absence of any agreement by the lender to the contrary, a corporate debtor can obtain confirmation of a reorganisation plan only by ensuring payment of the post-petition lender in full at the confirmation stage. Moreover, even if the reorganisation plan fails, post-petition debts will have priority over unsecured pre-petition debts in the ensuring liquidation.

There may be a significant number of cases where the a company's assets are secured to such an extent that the granting of priority over simply pre-petition unsecured creditors offers new lenders little chance of recovery in any subsequent liquidation. In these circumstances, meaningful priority means priority over pre-filing secured creditors. Article 364(d) of the US Bankruptcy Code expressly allows the court to authorise debtors in possession to grant new lenders priority over pre-filing secured creditors in narrowly defined circumstances. The relevant provision, however, incorporates protection for affected secured creditors by requiring the debtor to prove that it cannot obtain the loan without granting such a security interest and that the pre-filing secured creditor is adequately protected against loss. The US courts appear to apply these requirements strictly. In consequence, the 'priming' of prior secured lending is permitted only relatively infrequently. In effect, a priming loan may not be granted unless the court concludes there is sufficient value in the collateral to protect fully both old and new lenders.[229]

There are other incentives built into the system to encourage post-petition financing. First, while art 9–202 of the US Commercial Code validates the functional equivalent of the floating charge – a blanket security interest on shifting collateral, a general security interest over all a company's property appears to be much less common in the US context.[230] Moreover, Article 552 of the US Bankruptcy Code terminates the effect of a blanket security interest in its application to property acquired after the bankruptcy petition has been filed though there are exceptions. The curtailment of the blanket security interest may be one of the factors that encourages a pre-petition lender to continue funding the company.

In Ireland under the 'court examinership' procedure that is designed as a corporate rescue procedure like administration, there are also special statutory provisions in place to facilitate the financing of companies in

---

[229] See generally R Broude 'How the Rescue Culture came to the United States and the Myths that surround Chapter 11' (2000) 16 Insolvency Law and Practice 194.

[230] See generally for a comparative treatment G McCormack *Secured Credit under English and American Law* (Cambridge University Press, 2004).

financial difficulties.[231] During the period of examinership, a company enjoys protection from its creditors like a company in administration. The relevant legislation allows the examiner – a court-appointed official, normally an accountant – to certify liabilities incurred during the protection period where such liabilities are essential to ensure the survival of the company as a going concern.[232] The liabilities so certified then rank with the examiner's own expenses ahead of all other liabilities including pre-examinership secured liabilities. The 'certification of liabilities' procedure can be used to cover borrowings made by the company during the period of examinership. The Irish legislation has, however, been amended to provide that liabilities certified by the examiner should rank after the claims of fixed charge holders although still ahead of floating charges.

21.36   An overview of the administration procedure

The administration procedure was born out of receivership. Moreover, in one guise the 'new' administration procedure is simply administrative receivership under another name, with a few bells and whistles attached. The administrator has wider duties than an administrative receiver to consider the interests of creditors as a whole, but an administrator can be appointed out of court by a floating charge holder and can make distributions to secured and preferential creditors.

The Cork Committee saw administration as being particularly appropriate in cases where a company had not created a floating charge over substantially the whole of its property and consequently there was no secured lender in a position to appoint a receiver over the entirety of the company's business operations. The Insolvency Act 1986 rebranded the receiver of substantially the whole of a company's business as an administrative receiver. This rebranding exercise has been carried a stage further by the Enterprise Act 2002 with the administrative receiver appointed by a floating charge holder being transmuted into an administrator whose first objective is to try to rescue the company as a going concern unless he thinks that this is not reasonably practicable. Nevertheless, one of the essential features of receivership remains, ie the board of directors lose control of the corporate decision-making machinery. It could be argued that if one is designing a corporate rescue framework from scratch one would not start with receivership. In the United States there was a different starting point and a different end result though it must be remembered that the notion of privately-appointed receiverships is almost unknown in the United States. In the United States, company management keep the apparatus of power while the company is undergoing the reorganisation process.

---

[231] See generally on this procedure T Courtney *The Law of Private Companies* (Butterworths, 2002) Ch 23.

[232] Irish Companies (Amendment) Act 1990, s 10.

The administration procedure is widely used, but often as a substitute for liquidation rather than as a genuine corporate rescue vehicle and possibly to escape the level of scrutiny that liquidation normally entails.[233] Certainly, the focus appears to be on asset sales and business rescue through more advantageous disposal of assets rather than in the preservation of the existing corporate structures. The procedure is faster than receivership with cases being turned around quicker. The value extracted from asset realisations has increased but so too has the costs and the overall result is that creditors are no better off than under receiverships.

PART 4: THE COMPULSORY LIQUIDATION OF COMPANIES

21.37 Compulsory winding-up

We now turn to consider the liquidation or, as it is also called, the winding-up of companies. The first type of winding-up procedure is the compulsory liquidation, which entails the presentation of a petition requesting that the court make a winding-up order and appoint a liquidator. All companies incorporated under the Companies Act 1985 and the statutes which it replaced are subject to the winding-up jurisdiction of the court under the Insolvency Act 1986.[234] Overseas companies registered under the branch registration regime[235] or the place of business regime[236] may also be compulsorily wound up, as may unregistered companies[237] including foreign companies which carry on business in Great Britain but which are not registered.[238] The winding-up jurisdiction of the courts has now been extended by the EU Regulation on Insolvency Proceedings (Council Regulation 1346/2000/EC). The Regulation gives an English court jurisdiction to wind up any company whose

---

[233] See generally the research reports by S Frisby, A Katz and M Mumford, and J Armour, A Hsu and A Walters available on the Insolvency Service website (www.insolvency.gov. uk/). See also S Frisby 'Not quite warp factor 2 yet? The Enterprise Act and corporate insolvency' (2007) 22 *Butterworths Journal of International Banking and Financial Law* 327.

[234] Section 117 of the Insolvency Act 1986 deals with the respective jurisdictions of the High Court and county court.

[235] Oversea Companies and Credit and Financial institutions (Branch Disclosure) Regulations 1992, SI 1992/3179.

[236] Companies Act 1985, Part XXIII.

[237] Defined for this purpose by s 220 of the Insolvency Act 1986. See *Re Witney Town Football and Social Club* [1993] BCC 874; *Re Normandy Marketing Ltd* [1993] BCC 879.

[238] The court must be satisfied that there is a sufficient connection with the jurisdiction. It has been held that this does not necessarily have to be the presence of assets in the jurisdiction: *Re Real Estate Development Co* [1991] BCLC 210; *Re A Company (No 00359 of 1987)* (also reported as *International Westminster Bank plc v Okeanos Maritime Corp*) [1988] Ch 210.

centre of main interests is in England even though the company may be incorporated elsewhere. The Regulation is discussed in detail at **21.62** below.

Under Sch B1, para 42, while a company is in administration no resolution may be passed nor order made for the winding up of the company. The same prohibition also applies under the interim moratorium, which obtains whenever an administration application is pending or where notice to appoint an administrator out of court has been filed.

Special Rules for Financial institutions

Until the 2007-2009 financial crisis, authorised banks and financial institutions in England were would up under the general liquidation law and could also use the normal administration procedure. The financial crisis revealed shortcomings in this approach and emergency legislation in the shape of the Banking (Special Provisions) Act provided a new framework. This approach has been continued in the Banking Act 2009.[239] The 2009 Act creates a Special Resolution Regime (SRR) providing new tools for dealing with distressed banks and building societies. The powers under the Special Resolution Regime enable the authorities to

- transfer all or part of a bank to a private sector purchaser;

- transfer all or part of a bank to a bridge bank – a subsidiary of the Bank of England – pending a future sale;

- place a bank into temporary public ownership;

- apply to put a bank into a special Bank Insolvency Procedure (BIP) or Bank Administration Procedure (BAP).

In deciding which resolution tools to employ the authorities should consider the following statutory objectives:

- protecting and enhancing the stability of the financial systems of the UK;

- protecting and enhancing public confidence in the stability of the banking systems of the UK;

- protecting depositors;

- protecting public funds;

---

[239] See generally for more information the Bank of England website – www.bankofengland.co.uk/.

- avoiding any interference with property rights in contravention of the Human Rights Act 1998.

Application of the SRR is limited to deposit-taking institutions on the basis that this activity makes banks stand out from other companies and warrants a special regime. The regime is applicable in respect of UK-incorporated banks and their branches worldwide, but not to overseas subsidiaries. It is also applicable in respect of UK-incorporated subsidiaries of foreign banks, but not to UK branches of foreign banks.

21.37.1   Grounds for a compulsory winding-up order

Section 122 of the Insolvency Act 1986 sets out the grounds upon which a company may be wound up by the court.

The most common ground upon which petitions are presented is that the company is unable to pay its debts. Section 123 of the Insolvency Act 1986 contains the definition of inability to pay debts. The cash flow and balance sheet tests of insolvency discussed in **21.2** are tests of inability to pay debts for this purpose. In addition, a company is deemed unable to pay its debts:

(1) if a creditor (by assignment or otherwise) to whom the company is indebted in a sum exceeding £750 then due has served on the company, by leaving it at the company's registered office, a written demand (in the prescribed form) requiring the company to pay the sum so due and the company has for 3 weeks thereafter neglected to pay the sum or to secure or compound for it to the reasonable satisfaction of the creditor; or

(2) if, in England and Wales, execution or other process issued on a judgment, decree or order of any court in favour of a creditor of the company is returned unsatisfied in whole or in part.

Unpaid creditors of a company may consider commencing winding-up proceedings against the company as an alternative to suing it for payment. As a debt collection mechanism, winding-up proceedings may be swifter and, for the individual creditor, less expensive than a claim that may not come to trial for some time; on the other hand, winding-up is a collective procedure for the benefit of creditors generally and it does not benefit specific creditors individually.[240] However, if the company disputes the debt and the court accepts that the dispute is genuine,[241] the petition will usually be dismissed because the procedure is ill-equipped to deal with the resolution of factual disputes. It may be held to be an abuse of process to

---

[240] See generally, F Oditah 'Winding Up Recalcitrant Debtors' [1995] LMCLQ 107.

[241] *R Claybridge Shipping Co SA* [1981] Com LR 107, [1997] 1 BCLC 572 (CA); *Alipour v Ary* [1997] 1 BCLC 557 (CA); *Re A Company (No 006685 of 1996)* [1997] 1 BCLC 639. But dismissal in these circumstances is a rule of practice only and it must give way in

have proceeded by way of statutory demand instead of by claim,[242] in which case the creditor may be held liable to indemnify the company for its costs.[243] Also, the company may be able to resist the making of a winding-up order by establishing that its failure to pay resulted otherwise than from neglect, for example where it can show that the demand was never received.[244]

If a debt is disputed in part but the part of the debt which is undisputed is above the statutory minimum a petition can still validly be presented.[245] If a creditor makes a statutory demand for more than was actually due, provided the amount that was due was more than £750, any winding-up order made by the court on the basis of the demand remains valid.[246]

Where the petitioner succeeds in establishing a ground on which a winding-up order may be made, it has been said that he has a prima facie right to a winding-up order.[247] However, in all cases, the court has discretion whether or not to order winding-up. Since winding-up is a collective procedure for the benefit of creditors generally, one situation where the court may exercise its discretion against winding-up is where other creditors in the same class[248] oppose the making of the order. In this case, the court will usually have regard to the majority of the creditors and will refuse the petition if it is opposed by the majority.[249]

A specific case where there can be a difference of opinion between groups of creditors is where some creditors favour a compulsory winding-up whilst others are content for the company to be wound up voluntarily. This situation is discussed at **21.39–21.46**.

---

circumstances that make it desirable for the petition to proceed, such as where the petitioner would otherwise be without a remedy: *Claybridge*. See also *Re Janeash Ltd* [1990] BCC 250 (no genuine claim).

[242] *London Wharfing Co* (1866) 35 Beav 37; *Re Brighton Club and Norfolk Hotel Co* (1865) 35 Beav 204; *Re London and Paris Banking Corp* (1875) 19 Eq 444; *Re Gold Hill Mines* (1883) 23 Ch D 210; *Mann v Goldstein* [1968] 1 WLR 1091; *Stonegate Securities Ltd v Gregory* [1980] Ch 576; *Re Wallace Smith Group Ltd* [1992] BCLC 989.

[243] *Re A Company (No 0012209 of 1991)* [1992] 2 All ER 797, [1992] 1 WLR 351, [1992] BCLC 865 followed in *Re A Company (No 00751 of 1992)* [1992] BCLC 869.

[244] *Re London and Paris Banking Corp* (1875) 19 Eq 444; *Re A Company* [1985] BCLC 37; and see *Re Cannon Screen Entertainment Ltd* [1989] BCLC 661.

[245] *Re Tweeds Garage Ltd* [1962] 1 Ch 406; *Re Trinity Insurance Co Ltd* [1990] BCC 235; *Taylor's Industrial Flooring Ltd v M&H Plant Hire (Manchester) Ltd* [1990] BCC 44, [1990] BCLC 216; *Re Pendigo Ltd* [1996] BCC 608; *Re Bydand Ltd* [1997] BCC 915.

[246] *Cardiff Preserved Coal and Coke Co v Norton* (1867) 2 Ch App 405. On costs in these circumstances, see *Re A Company (No 008122 of 1989), ex parte Transcontinental Insurance Services Ltd* [1990] BCLC 697.

[247] See *Re Demaglass Holdings Ltd* [2001] 2 BCLC 633; *Re Lummus Agricultural Services Ltd* [2001] 1 BCLC 137.

[248] *Re Crigglestone Coal Co Ltd* [1906] 2 Ch 327 (unsecured creditors in different class from secured creditor for this purpose); *Re Leigh Estates (UK) Ltd* [1994] BCC 292. See s 195 which provides for the holding of meetings to ascertain the wishes of creditors (or contributories) on matters relating to the winding up of the company.

[249] *Re Chapel House Colliery Co*, above; *Re Uruguay Central and Hygueritas Rly Co of Monte Video* (1873) 11 Ch D 372; *Re St Thomas's Dock Co* (1876) 2 Ch D 116.

21.37.2   *Persons who may present a petition*

Section 124 of the Insolvency Act 1986 provides that a petition for the winding up of a company may be presented to the court by all or any of the following whether acting together or separately:

(1)   the company;

(2)   the directors of the company;

(3)   any creditor or creditors of the company (including any contingent or prospective creditor or creditors);

(4)   any contributory or contributories.[250]

A petition presented by the directors does not require the approval of the shareholders. In *Re Instrumentation Electrical Services Ltd*,[251] Davies J held that all the directors had to join in the petition. The position may be different where the decision to seek a winding-up is embodied in a formal board resolution, because it is the duty of all directors to implement such resolutions.[252]

An administrative receiver is expressly empowered by the Act[253] to present or defend a petition for the winding-up of the company over which he has been appointed.[254] An administrator[255] or the supervisor of a CVA[256] can also present a winding-up petition.

A contributory, which means, broadly, any present or past member of the company, is not entitled to present a winding-up petition unless either: (a) the number of members is reduced below two; or (b) the shares in respect of which he is a contributory, or some of them, were originally allotted to him, or have been held by him and registered in his name, for at least 6

---

[250]   Other statutory provisions empower specific bodies to seek winding-up orders on other grounds; eg, under s 124A of the Insolvency Act 1986, the Secretary of State can seek the winding-up of a company on public interest grounds (see *Re Titan International Inc* [1998] 1 BCLC 102).

[251]   (1988) 4 BCC 301.

[252]   See *Re Equiticorp International plc* (1989) 1 WLR 1010 (directors' petition for an administration order).

[253]   Section 42 and Sch 1, para 21. Whether a receiver who is not an administrative receiver has this power depends upon the construction of the debenture under which he was appointed: *Re Emmadart Ltd* [1979] 1 Ch 540. For an example of an administrative receiver's petition, see *Re Television Parlour plc* (1988) 4 BCC 95.

[254]   Section 14 and Sch 1, para 21. The clerk of the magistrates' court, the Secretary of State and the Financial Services Authority are other persons who can petition for winding-up on various grounds. Note also the power of the Official Receiver to petition for the winding-up of a company which is being wound up voluntarily: s 124(5).

[255]   Insolvency Act 1986 Sch 1, para 21 and Sch B1, para 60.

[256]   Section 7(4)(b) and Sch A1, para 39(5)(b) of the Insolvency Act 1986.

months during the 18 months before the commencement of the winding-up or have devolved on him through the death of a former holder.

In practice most petitioners will be creditors of the company. A creditor may petition whether he is secured or unsecured.[257] The creditor may be the original creditor of the company or an assignee of the debt.[258]

A contingent or prospective creditor of the company is also entitled to petition.[259]

21.37.3 The hearing of the petition

Section 125 of the Insolvency Act 1986 states that the court, on hearing the petition, may:

(1) dismiss it;

(2) adjourn the hearing conditionally or unconditionally;

(3) make an interim order;

(4) make any order that it thinks fit;

(5) make a winding-up order.

The court cannot refuse to make a winding-up order on the basis only that the company's assets have been mortgaged to an amount equal to or in excess of those assets or that the company has no assets.[260]

Once made, a winding-up order operates in favour of all creditors and contributories of the company as if made on the joint petition of a creditor and a contributory.[261]

21.37.4 Commencement of the winding-up

On the making of a winding-up order the commencement of the liquidation relates back to the time at which the petition was presented.

---

[257] The secured creditor does not invalidate his security: *Moor v Anglo-Italian Bank* (1879) 10 Ch D 681; *Re Borough of Portsmouth etc Tramways Co* [1892] 2 Ch 362; *Re Great Western (Forest of Dean) Coal Consumers' Co* (1882) 21 Ch D 769; *Re Cambrian Mining Co* [1881] WN 125.

[258] *Re Paris Skating Rink Co* (1877) 5 Ch D 959 (CA); *Re Montgomery Moore Ship Collision Doors Syndicate* [1903] WN 121.

[259] *Re T & N Ltd* [2005] BCC 982; *Re Dollar Land Holdings plc* [1993] BCC 823; *Tottenham Hotspur plc v Edennote plc* [1995] 1 BCLC 65.

[260] Section 125(1). *Bell Group Finance (Pty) Ltd v Bell Group (UK) Holdings Ltd* [1996] BCC 505.

[261] Insolvency Act 1986, s 130(4).

However, if before the presentation of the petition the company had passed a resolution for voluntary winding-up, the winding-up of the company is deemed to have commenced at the time that resolution was passed (whether it was for a members' or creditors' voluntary liquidation).[262] The relation back is important because of some of the results which follow upon the commencement of the winding-up, such as its effect upon dispositions of the company's assets.

21.38   The effect of a winding-up order on dispositions of assets

Section 127 of the Insolvency Act 1986 states:[263]

> 'In a winding-up by the court, any disposition of the company's property, and any transfer of shares, or alteration in the status of the company's members, made after the commencement of the winding-up is, unless the court otherwise orders, void.'

In *Re French's (Wine Bar) Ltd*,[264] the company had contracted to sell its assets prior to the commencement of its winding-up. Vinelott J held[265] that the completion of the contract did not constitute a disposition of the company's property within what is now s 127, because that section relates only to property in which the company is beneficially interested. The company had entered into an unconditional contract to sell the property and the contract was specifically enforceable. Accordingly, the beneficial interest in the property had passed to the purchaser before the commencement of the winding-up.

Vinelott J cautioned that it did not follow that the completion of any contract would in all circumstances fall outside the section. If, for example, the contract was conditional or voidable by the company, the waiver of the condition or the confirmation of the contract might amount to a disposition, as might the variation of contractual terms. Vinelott J stated that, in practice, unless a contract was plainly specifically enforceable and there was no possible dispute, it would be prudent to seek the court's approval for completion.

---

[262] Section 129 of the Insolvency Act 1986. The time will be noted on the petition itself by the court when it is presented. The section also states that 'unless the court, on proof of fraud or mistake, directs otherwise, all proceedings taken in the voluntary winding up are deemed to have been validly taken'.

[263] This section does not apply to dispositions giving rise to market charges: s 175(4) of the Companies Act 1989. Note also the disapplication of s 127 in the circumstances provided for in regs 16 and 119 of the Financial Markets and Insolvency (Settlement Finality) Regulations 1999, SI 1999/2979.

[264] [1987] BCLC 499, (1987) 3 BCC 173.

[265] Citing *Re Gray's Inn Construction Co Ltd* [1980] 1 All ER 814, [1980] 1 WLR 711 and *Re Margart Pty Ltd, Hamilton v Westpac Banking Corp* (1984) 9 ACLR 269, [1985] BCLC 314 (realisation of floating charge security). See also *Wiley v Commonwealth of Australia* (1995) 13 ACLC 1, at 556.

The operation of s 127 in relation to payments into and out of a company's bank account has generated some case-law. The simplest view is that all such payments are dispositions of property[266] but the cases do not fully support this view. It is established that payments into an overdrawn account are dispositions of the company's property for the purposes of s 127.[267] The argument that a payment into an account which is in credit is also a disposition within s 127[268] was considered and rejected in *Re Barn Crown Ltd*,[269] where such a payment, made by cheque, was characterised as amounting simply to an adjustment of entries in the statement recording the account between the bank and the company.

In respect of payments out of an account, the leading authority is now the decision of the Court of Appeal in *Hollicourt (Contracts) Ltd v Bank of Ireland*.[270] In this case it was held that a payment by a company to a creditor, made by a cheque drawn on a bank account in credit, after the presentation of the winding-up petition, was a disposition of the company's property in favour of the creditor but did not constitute such a disposition in favour of the bank. The court said that in honouring the cheque the bank was merely acting on the company's mandate as its agent. There was, in its view, a restitutionary liability on the payee of the cheque to reimburse the company but no liability on the part of the bank. Mummery LJ said:[271]

> 'the policy promoted by section 127 is not aimed at imposing on a bank restitutionary liability to a company in respect of the payments made by cheques in favour of the creditors, in addition to the unquestioned liability of the payees of the cheques ... The section impinges on the end result of the process of payment initiated by the company ie. the point of ultimate receipt of the company's property in consequence of a disposition by the company. The statutory purpose ... is accomplished without any need for the section to impinge on the legal validity of intermediate steps, such as banking transactions, which are merely part of the process by which dispositions of the company's property are made. This is not a restitutionary situation where the bank has been unjustly enriched as against the company and where the general law requires the restitution of the benefit.'

In *Hollicourt* the relevant account was in credit at all material times but the Court of Appeal suggested that even if the company's bank account were in overdraft, the result would be the same in respect of a claim for recovery as against the bank. According to the court the need for a

---

[266] *Re McGuinness Bros (UK) Ltd* (1987) 3 BCC 571, at 574.

[267] *Re Gray's Inn Construction Ltd*, above; *Re McGuinness Bros (UK) Ltd*, above.

[268] This argument, which derives some support from dicta in *Re Gray's Inn Construction Co Ltd*, and *Re McGuinness Bros (UK) Ltd*, above, is examined in more depth in Goode, *Principles of Corporate Insolvency Law*, (Sweet & Maxwell, 3rd edn, 2005) at pp 496-498.

[269] [1994] 4 All ER 42, [1994] BCC 381.

[270] [2001] Ch 555 endorsing the ruling of Lightman J in *Coutt & Co v Stock* [2000] BCC 247.

[271] [2001] Ch 555, at 563.

complex analysis of whether payments were made out of an account that was in debit or in credit could not be justified on any sensible view of the purpose of s 127. The safest course for anybody dealing with a company that has a petition on file is for an application to be made to the court for a validating order. The court can make such an order even before the hearing of the winding-up petition.[272] The court can authorise particular dispositions or the general continuance of trading (including, for that purpose, the continued operation of the company's bank accounts). The court can validate prospective dispositions or grant retrospective validations. In *Re Gray's Inn Construction*,[273] it was held[274] that the bank was entitled to have validated retrospectively payments in and out of the account before it became aware of the petition. It was also accepted that dispositions which did not reduce the value of assets (such as sales of assets at full value or for more than they were worth) would normally be validated. In general, the court, in considering whether to grant the validating order, will consider whether the disposition would be for the benefit of the company's creditors.[275] A disposition that allows one pre-liquidation creditor to receive payment in full whilst other creditors are limited to the dividends that they will receive in the liquidation will be sanctioned only where this will benefit the creditors as a whole.[276]

Section 127 does not in itself afford a statutory remedy towards the recovery of property disposed of after the commencement of the liquidation. Recourse must be had to the rules for the tracing of property and, accordingly, no claim will be upheld against a *bona fide* purchaser for value without notice.[277]

Section 127 states that every transfer of shares or alteration in the status of the company's members made after the commencement of the winding-up is void unless the court orders otherwise. No transfer can be effected without registration of that transfer in the register of members of the company. The register cannot be rectified without leave of the court. Nevertheless, as between the vendor and purchaser of shares under a contract equitable rights arise which are not affected by this section, and the purchaser can claim through his vendor any payments made in the

---

[272] *Re AI Levy (Holdings) Ltd* [1964] Ch 19.

[273] [1980] 1 All ER 814, [1980] 1 WLR 711.

[274] Citing *Re Wiltshire Iron Co* (1868) LR 3 Ch App 443; *Re Neath Harbour Smelting and Rolling Works* (1887) 56 LT 727, at 729; *Re Liverpool Civil Service Association* (1874) LR 9 Ch App 511; see also *Re Clifton Place Garage Ltd* [1970] Ch 477, approving *Re Steane's (Bournemouth)* [1950] 1 All ER 21; *Re TW Construction* [1954] 1 WLR 840.

[275] *Re AI Levy (Holdings) Ltd*, above. See also *Re A Company (No 007523 of 1986)* (1987) 3 BCC 57; *Re Sugar Properties (Derisley Wood) Ltd* (1978) 3 BCC 88; *Re Tramway Building & Construction Co Ltd* [1988] Ch 293, [1988] 2 WLR 640, (1987) 3 BCC 443; *Re Webb Electrical Ltd* (1988) 4 BCC 230; *Re Rafidain Bank* [1992] BCC 376.

[276] *Re Gray's Inn Construction*, above. See also more generally for a statement of the relevant principles governing validation orders under s 127, *Rose v AIB Group (UK) plc* [2003] EWHC 1737 (Ch), [2003] 1 WLR 2791.

[277] *Re J Leslie Engineering Co Ltd* [1976] 1 WLR 292. See also *Rose v AIB Group plc* [2003] 1 WLR 2791.

liquidation in respect of the shares, and the vendor may, when calls are made (but not before), enforce his right to indemnity.[278]

21.39 Appointment of the liquidator

On a winding-up order being made by the court, the Official Receiver becomes the liquidator of the company and continues in office until another person is appointed as liquidator by the creditors or contributories of the company.[279] The liquidator who is appointed will usually be the person nominated by the creditors.

If there is any vacancy in the office of liquidator this is filled by the Official Receiver until a further appointment is made.[280]

The Official Receiver is a public servant working for the Insolvency Service. There is a network of 38 Official Receiver offices throughout England and Wales.[281]

21.39.1 The liquidator's status

As in the case of directors, it is not easy to state succinctly yet accurately the position occupied by a liquidator. In several cases there will be found statements to the effect that he is a trustee for the creditors, or, in the case of a solvent company, for the contributories. Thus, Lord Selborne says, 'The hand which receives the calls necessarily receives them as a statutory trustee for the equal and rateable payment of all the creditors',[282] and James LJ speaks of the assets as being 'fixed by the Act of Parliament with a trust for equal distribution among the creditors'.[283] The House of Lords has confirmed that a liquidator is not a trustee in the strict sense, while also holding, in the context of a taxing statute, that when a company enters liquidation it ceases to be 'the beneficial' owner of its assets.[284] But it must not be inferred that all the results follow which would ensue if the liquidator were a trustee in the full sense of the word; and in particular it is to be noted that the property in the assets remains vested in the company and does not pass to the liquidator. But the court may on the application of the liquidator by order direct that all or any

---

[278] See s 160(2) of the Insolvency Act 1986; *Re Onward Building Society* [1891] 2 QB 463 (CA); *Hughes-Hallet v Indian Mammoth Gold Mines* (1883) 22 Ch D 561.

[279] Section 136(2). The appointment arises 'by virtue of his office'. The Official Receiver is a civil servant and should not be confused with an administrative receiver.

[280] Section 136(3).

[281] See generally the Insolvency Service website – www.insolvency.gov.uk/.

[282] *Re Black & Co's Case* (1872) 8 Ch App 254, at 262 (CA).

[283] *Re Oriental Inland Steam Co* (1874) 9 Ch App 557, at 551 (CA). See also *Re Flack's Case* [1894] 1 Ch 369; *CIR v Olive Mill* [1963] 1 WLR 712; *Re Movitex Ltd* [1992] 2 All ER 264, [1992] 1 WLR 303, [1992] BCLC 419, [1992] BCC 101 (position of trustees and beneficiaries considered by way of analogy in determining whether creditors were entitled to an order for the inspection of books and records).

[284] *Ayerst v C & K (Construction) Ltd* [1975] 3 WLR 16 (HL).

part of the property belonging to the company or held by trustees on its behalf shall vest in the liquidator by his official name: s 145 of the Insolvency Act 1986. When a liquidator makes a contract he does so in the name of the company; thus if he employs a solicitor in the company's business he is not personally liable for the costs.[285] A liquidator:

> '... is a person having a prima facie right to costs [out of the estate], but he is not in the ordinary sense a trustee. He is a person appointed by the court to do a certain class of things; he has some of the rights and some of the liabilities of a trustee, but is not in the position of an ordinary trustee. Being an agent employed to do business for a remuneration, he is bound to bring reasonable skill to its performance.'[286]

Similarly, Romer J has said: 'In my judgment the liquidator is not a trustee in the strict sense.'[287]

It is clear that the liquidator occupies a fiduciary position.[288] As such, he must avoid conflicts between his interests and his duties[289] and must not make a secret profit out of his position. It may be safely asserted that the liquidator has all the duties an agent would have; but it is suggested that he is liable only to the company and not directly, prior to its dissolution, to third parties, even though they be creditors or contributories, for negligence apart from misfeasance or personal misconduct.[290] If, however, the liquidator 'has misapplied or retained or become liable or accountable for any moneys or property of the company, or been guilty of any misfeasance or breach of trust in relation to the company', he can be brought to account by any creditor or contributory on a summons under s 212 of the 1986 Act.

The liquidator represents creditors and contributories alike, and should bear an even hand between them.[291] He should afford reasonable assistance and facilities to persons seeking information to enforce their rights,[292] but in cases of litigation he usually requires parties desiring access to the books and documents of the company to obtain an order for inspection under s 155(1) of the 1986 Act. This provides that the court may make an order for inspection of the books and papers of the company by creditors and contributories, and any books or papers of the company may be inspected accordingly but not further or otherwise.

---

[285] *Re Anglo-Moravian Hungarian Junction Rly Co* (1875) 1 Ch D 130 (CA).

[286] Per Cotton LJ in *Re Silver Valley Mines* (1882) 21 Ch D 381, at 392 (CA).

[287] *Knowles v Scott* [1891] 1 Ch 717, at 721 and 723.

[288] *Silkstone and Haigh Moor Coal Co v Edey* [1900] 1 Ch 167.

[289] *Re Corbenstoke Ltd (No 2)* [1990] BCLC 60, (1989) 5 BCC 767.

[290] *Knowles v Scott* [1891] 1 Ch 717, at 723. See also *Stewart v Engel* [2000] BCC 741 (exclusion clause precluded claim that liquidator had acted negligently).

[291] *Re Palmer Marine Surveys Ltd* [1986] 1 WLR 573; *Re P Turner (Wilsden) Ltd* [1987] BCLC 149.

[292] *Re Sir John Moore Gold Mining Co* (1879) 12 Ch D 325, at 328 (CA).

Orders under s 155(1) are rarely granted.[293] The section does not restrict any statutory right of a government department or person acting under its authority: s 155(2).

The liquidator, being an officer of the court, will be directed to deal fairly:[294] for example, he may be ordered to repay moneys paid to him under a mistake of law. Instances of this rule may also be found in cases under the Bankruptcy Acts.[295]

Where a liquidator has properly carried on the business of the company after his appointment, the post-liquidation creditors are entitled to be paid out of the assets of the company, in priority to its creditors at the commencement of the winding-up.[296]

21.39.2   Duties and powers of a liquidator

Once made, a winding-up order operates in favour of all creditors and contributories of the company.[297]

The liquidator's primary duty is to collect in and realise the assets of the company and then to distribute the proceeds amongst the creditors of the company and, if any surplus remains, to the members in accordance with their rights. The fundamental tenet governing the making of distributions in a liquidation is that the free assets of the company must be distributed rateably among the company's unsecured creditors. If the assets of the company are insufficient to meet all of the unsecured debts, such debts abate equally. This method of distribution is known as the *pari passu* rule. The *pari passu* rule, which also applies to voluntary liquidations, is subject to a number of qualifications or exceptions.[298]

As soon as a winding-up order is made, the powers of the directors to manage the business of the company are terminated. To allow these to continue would be inconsistent with the liquidator's duty and power to collect in the assets of the company for the collective benefit of all of the creditors.

The liquidator has a range of specific duties and powers. He must take into his custody or bring within his control all the property to which the company is or appears to be entitled.[299] He can require any person who

---

[293]   *Re Brazilian Sugar Factories* (1887) 37 Ch D 83; *Re DPR Futures Ltd* [1989] 1 WLR 778, [1989] BCLC 634, (1989) 5 BCC 603.

[294]   *Re Regent Finance and Guarantee Corp* [1930] WN 84.

[295]   See, eg, *ex parte James* (1874) LR 9 Ch App 609 (CA); *ex parte Simmonds* (1885) 16 QBD 308 (CA); *Scranton's Trustee v Pearse* [1922] 2 Ch 87 (CA).

[296]   *Re National Arms and Ammunition Co* (1885) 28 Ch D 474, at 481 (CA); *Re Great Eastern Electric Co* [1941] Ch 241.

[297]   Section 130(4).

[298]   See Part 6, below.

[299]   Section 144.

has in his possession or control any property, books or papers or records to which the company appears to be entitled to deliver up the same to him.[300] In exercising the powers conferred on him by the Insolvency Act 1986 to collect in the assets of the company, the liquidator is an officer of the court and is subject to its control.[301] If the liquidator mistakenly seizes property owned by a third party, he will not incur any liability for having seized or subsequently disposed of the property, provided he had reasonable grounds for believing that he was entitled to make the seizure. This protection, which is afforded by s 234(3) and (4), does not extend to any loss or damage resulting from the seizure or disposal which is caused by the liquidator's negligence. In the event of the liquidator's entitlement to make a seizure being disputed, the court can resolve the dispute.[302]

Section 167 of and Sch 4 to the Act set out the powers of a liquidator in a compulsory winding-up. These are divided into powers which may be exercised with the sanction of the court or the liquidation committee[303] and powers which are exercisable by the liquidator without such sanction. The powers which can only be exercised with the appropriate sanction include conducting litigation and carrying on the business of the company so far as is necessary for the beneficial winding-up of the company. Amongst the things that a liquidator can do without sanction are selling the company's property and raising money and giving security on the company's assets. A person who deals for value and in good faith with a liquidator need not be concerned whether any requisite consent from the liquidation committee or the court has been obtained by the liquidator.[304]

Certain specific powers relating to the holding of meetings, settling of lists, making of calls, proving of debts and other matters in the administration of a compulsory liquidation are formally vested in the court by the Act but are delegated to the liquidator by the Insolvency Rules 1986.[305]

Where the liquidator intends to carry on the business of the company he may do so only where this is necessary for the beneficial winding-up of the company. This limitation reflects the fact that the primary objective of liquidation is the orderly winding-up of a company and the distribution of its assets to its creditors rather than rescue and rehabilitation. Necessity in this context has been described as mercantile necessity as opposed to absolutely compelling force.[306] On this basis, something which is highly expedient for the beneficial winding-up of the company would be

---

[300] Section 234 and r 4.185.
[301] Rule 4.181.
[302] *Re London Iron & Steel Co Ltd* [1990] BCLC 372, [1990] BCC 159.
[303] See **21.37.3** for a brief description of the status and function of the liquidation committee.
[304] Rule 4.184.
[305] Section 160 makes provision for delegation.
[306] *Re Wreck Recovery and Salvage Co* (1880) 15 Ch D 353.

permitted; where a liquidator has a reasonable expectation of selling the business as a going concern (which usually results in a much higher price being paid by a purchaser than on a sale on a break-up basis),[307] the liquidator may thus be allowed to carry on the business with this objective in mind. In cases of doubt the liquidator can always apply to the court for guidance; he is allowed to apply to the court for directions in relation to any matter arising during the course of the liquidation.[308]

The prudent liquidator will always have regard to the wishes of the majority of those with the most substantial interest in the assets of the company.[309] The liquidator has power to summon general meetings of creditors and contributories to ascertain their wishes in respect of any particular aspect of the conduct of the liquidation. If the holders of more than one-tenth in value of the creditors or contributories request a liquidator to summon such meeting he is duty-bound to do so.[310] If any person is aggrieved by an act or discretion of the liquidator, he may apply to the court for an order reversing or modifying that act or decision. The court has power to make any order it thinks fit on such an application.[311]

It should be noted that under Sch B1, para 38 to the Insolvency Act 1986, an administrator can apply to the court to convert the liquidation into an administration. This would be the appropriate course of action if the liquidator thinks that corporate rescue is a realistic possibility.

21.39.3   The liquidation committee

A liquidation committee may be established under s 141 of the Insolvency Act 1986. Either the liquidator or one-tenth in value of the creditors may summon general meetings of the company's creditors and contributories for the purpose of determining whether a liquidation committee should be established.[312]

The liquidation committee will consist of at least three and not more than five creditors of the company elected at the creditors' meeting which decides to establish the liquidation committee.[313] In the case of a solvent winding-up, up to three contributories may become members of the liquidation committee.[314] Once the liquidation committee has been duly

---

[307] Tax losses may be available to the purchaser of a business sold on a going-concern basis.

[308] Section 168(3).

[309] The liquidator should not deny those solely concerned in the outcome of the liquidation the opportunity even of throwing good money after bad: *Re Agricultural Industries* [1952] 1 All ER 1188.

[310] Section 168(2); see also s 195, which states that the court may have regard to the wishes of creditors and contributories in all matters relating to a winding-up and may direct that such meetings shall be held if it thinks fit.

[311] Section 168(5).

[312] Section 141.

[313] Rule 4.152.

[314] *Ibid.* A person may not be a member of the liquidation committee in his capacity as

constituted, the liquidator has a duty to keep it informed in respect of matters arising out of the conduct of the winding-up and to supply it with information.[315] The purpose of the liquidation committee is not only to sanction the exercise by the liquidator of the powers conferred upon him but also to perform the function of a watchdog to ensure that the liquidator carries out his function in a proper manner.

21.40 Ceasing to act as liquidator

Section 172 of the Insolvency Act 1986 deals with the removal and resignation of a liquidator from office.

A liquidator may be removed from office only by one of the following methods:

(1) an order of the court;[316]

(2) a resolution of a general meeting of the company's creditors summoned specifically for that purpose;

(3) where the liquidator was appointed by the Secretary of State, by a direction of the Secretary of State.

There are restrictions on the power of the creditors to remove a liquidator who was appointed by the Secretary of State or by the court.[317]

A liquidator may resign only in certain circumstances prescribed in r 4.108 of the Insolvency Rules 1986. The liquidator may only resign following the procedure laid down in the rule on the grounds of ill-health or if he intends to cease to practise as an insolvency practitioner or if there is some conflict of interest or change in personal circumstances which precludes or makes it impracticable for him to discharge his functions as liquidator of the company.

In certain circumstances, a liquidator must vacate his office. If a liquidator ceases to be qualified to act as an insolvency practitioner in relation to the company in question, for example if the specific bond required by the Act becomes invalid, he automatically vacates office.[318] Where a final meeting is held and the liquidator's report on the completion of the winding-up is received, the liquidator vacates office as

---

both a creditor and a contributory r 4.152(4). For the procedure followed where the creditors decide not to form a liquidation committee, see r 4.154.

[315] Rule 4.155.

[316] *Re Corbenstoke Ltd (No 2)* [1990] BCLC 60, (1989) 5 BCC 767 (removal from office on grounds of conflict of interest and duties); *Re Edennote Ltd* [1996] BCC 718 (CA) (creditors could remove the liquidator if they had lost confidence in him on reasonable grounds); *Deloitte and Touche AG v Johnson* [1999] 1 WLR 1605 (PC).

[317] Section 172(3).

[318] Section 172(5).

from the date he gives notice to the court and the Registrar of Companies that the final meeting has been held.[319]

The time when a liquidator will obtain his release depends upon the manner in which he vacates office.[320] Where the liquidator has obtained his release he is discharged from all liability both in respect of acts and omissions during the course of the winding-up and otherwise in relation to his conduct as liquidator. However, the Insolvency Act 1986 specifically provides that nothing contained in any release will prevent a misfeasance summons being issued under s 212 of the Act.

PART 5: THE VOLUNTARY LIQUIDATION OF COMPANIES

21.41   Introduction

The most common type of winding-up procedure is the voluntary winding-up. It is voluntary in the sense that the procedure has to be initiated by the company itself (although, of course, a company does have power to present a petition).[321] A creditor cannot compel a company to wind itself up voluntarily.

There are two types of voluntary liquidation both of which are considered below. If the company's directors are able to swear a declaration of solvency the liquidation will be a members' voluntary liquidation. In this type of liquidation, all creditors will be paid in full. If there is no declaration of solvency, the liquidation will be a creditors' voluntary liquidation in which the creditors may not be paid in full.

21.42   Resolutions for voluntary winding-up

Section 84 of the Insolvency Act 1986 sets out the circumstances in which a company may be wound up voluntarily:

(1)   when the period (if any) fixed for the duration of the company by the articles expires, or the event (if any) occurs, on the occurrence of which the articles provide that the company is to be dissolved, and the company in general meeting has passed a resolution requiring it to be wound up voluntarily;

(2)   if the company resolves by special resolution that it be wound up voluntarily;

---

[319]   Section 172(8).
[320]   Section 174 and rr 4.121 and 4.123–4.125.
[321]   See **21.35.2**.

(3)   if the company resolves by extraordinary resolution to the effect that it cannot by reason of its liabilities continue its business, and that it is advisable to wind up.

Once a resolution has been passed under (1), (2) or (3) above, a copy of it must be filed with the Registrar of Companies within 15 days.[322]

It is unusual nowadays for the articles of association of a company to provide for the company's duration to be limited or for it to be wound up on the occurrence of any specified event. If there are such provisions in the articles, it is the directors' duty to call a general meeting for the purposes of considering a resolution that the company be wound up.

A resolution under para (3) will be passed only when it is intended that the liquidation is to be a creditors' voluntary winding-up.

21.42.1   *Commencement of a voluntary liquidation*

A voluntary winding-up (whether members' or creditors') is deemed to commence at the time the resolution under s 84 is passed by the members in general meeting.[323]

21.42.2   *Consequences of resolution to wind up*

Once a resolution has been passed, a company must cease to carry on its business except insofar as continuance may be deemed necessary for its beneficial winding-up.[324] Any transfer of shares in the company not made to or with the sanction of the liquidator or any change in the status of the company's members will be void.[325]

Notice of the resolution must be given by advertisement in the *London Gazette* within 14 days.[326]

The Act provides that the corporate existence and the powers contained in the memorandum of association continue, notwithstanding anything in its constitution, until such time as the company is finally dissolved.[327] This provision is, obviously, necessary to ensure that the liquidator has the ability to wind up the company in an orderly manner.

---

[322] Sections 84(3) and 194.

[323] Section 86. Where a resolution is passed at an adjourned meeting, it is treated as having been passed at the time it was actually passed, not at any earlier date: s 194. It has been held that it is not possible to pass resolutions for winding-up that are conditional upon the happening of specified events: *Re Norditrack (UK) Ltd* [2000] 1 WLR 343, not following *Re Powerstore (Trading) Ltd* [1997] 1 WLR 1280 and *Re Mark One (Oxford Street) plc* [1999] 1 WLR 1445 on this point.

[324] Section 87(1).

[325] Section 88.

[326] Section 85.

[327] Section 87(2).

21.43   The declaration of solvency

If the directors of a company propose to recommend to the members that the company be wound up voluntarily in a members' voluntary liquidation, they will also have to consider whether or not they can swear a statutory declaration of the company's solvency. The statutory declaration of solvency must state[328] that the directors have made a full inquiry into the company's affairs and that they have formed the opinion that the company will be able to pay its debts in full, together with interest at the official rate[329] within such period not exceeding 12 months from the commencement of the liquidation as may be specified in the declaration. In addition, the declaration must contain a statement of the company's assets and liabilities as at the latest practicable date before the making of the declaration.[330]

A director must not decide to join in the swearing of a declaration of solvency lightly. The Insolvency Act 1986 provides that any director making a declaration of solvency, without having reasonable grounds for the opinion that the company will be able to pay its debts in full together with interest at the official rate within the period specified in the declaration, will be liable to imprisonment or a fine or both.[331] There is a presumption that a director did not have reasonable grounds for his belief that the company would be able to so pay its debts if in fact the debts are not paid within the period specified in the declaration.[332] The Act imposes criminal liability in this respect to ensure that directors do not swear declarations of solvency and proceed by way of members' voluntary liquidation in which control rests substantially with the members and not with the creditors, who may be more interested in making a thorough investigation into the directors' conduct of the business. This is particularly important in the case of a private company where the directors have majority shareholdings and therefore would have the power to appoint a friendly liquidator (although the liquidator must be a qualified insolvency practitioner even in a members' voluntary winding-up).

If a declaration of solvency is not sworn, the liquidation must proceed as a creditors' voluntary winding-up.

There is a procedure for converting a members' voluntary liquidation to a creditors' voluntary liquidation where the liquidator forms the opinion

---

[328] Section 89(1).
[329] For the 'official rate' see s 189(4).
[330] Section 89(2)(b); see also *De Courcy v Clement* [1971] Ch 693.
[331] Section 89(4).
[332] Section 89(5).

that the company will be unable to pay its debts in full (together with interest at the official rate) within the period specified in the directors' declaration of solvency.[333]

21.44 Appointment of a liquidator

In a members' voluntary winding-up, the company in general meeting has the power to appoint one or more liquidators. On the appointment of a liquidator all of the powers of the directors cease, except insofar as the members or the liquidator sanction their continuance.[334] If a vacancy occurs, the company in general meeting may fill it.[335]

In a creditors' voluntary winding-up, the procedure for appointing a liquidator is more complex. Under s 98 of the Insolvency Act 1986 the company, having decided to wind itself up because of its inability to pay its debts, has a duty to summon a meeting of its creditors in accordance with the procedure specified in the Act. Both the members and the creditors at their respective meetings may nominate a person to be liquidator. If there are different nominees the creditors' choice normally prevails,[336] although any director, member or creditor may apply to court for an order appointing the members' nominee or some other person as the liquidator.[337] The creditors have power to fill any vacancy in the office of liquidator that may arise during the course of the winding-up.[338]

Under s 108(1) of the 1986 Act, the court has a power to appoint a liquidator in any voluntary winding-up if 'from any cause' there is no liquidator acting.

On the appointment of a liquidator in a creditors' voluntary winding-up, the directors' powers cease except in so far as the liquidation committee (or if there is no liquidation committee the creditors) sanction their continuance.[339]

A liquidator in a voluntary winding-up must be a qualified insolvency practitioner. A liquidator in a voluntary winding-up is not an officer of the court but, otherwise, the status of the liquidator is as discussed at **21.37.1** in relation to compulsory windings-ups.[340]

---

[333] Sections 95 and 96.

[334] Section 91.

[335] Section 92. The members' ability in this respect is expressly made subject to any arrangement with the company's creditors.

[336] Section 100(2).

[337] Section 100(3).

[338] Section 104.

[339] Section 103; see also **21.44**, for certain limitations on the powers of liquidators; see **21.43** for a discussion of the liquidation committee.

[340] *Re TH Knitwear (Wholesale) Ltd* [1985] Ch 275.

21.45   The liquidation committee

In a creditors' voluntary winding-up, the creditors may resolve to form a liquidation committee to exercise the functions conferred on it by the Insolvency Act 1986.[341] The committee may consist of up to five creditors and, if the creditors do not object, five members of the company. If the creditors object to the members' nominees having the right to sit on the committee, such nominees cannot act as members of the committee unless the court so directs.[342]

21.46   Powers and duties of a voluntary liquidator

The fundamental duty of a voluntary liquidator is the same as that of a liquidator in a compulsory winding-up. He must collect in and realise the assets of the company, apply the proceeds in satisfaction of the company's debts and liabilities and distribute any remaining proceeds to the members of the company in accordance with their rights under the memorandum and articles.[343] The *pari passu* rule applies with respect to distributions.

In a voluntary winding-up, the liquidator has the same specific powers as are conferred on a liquidator in a compulsory winding-up by s 167 of and Sch 4 to the Insolvency Act 1986. Where sanction is required to exercise a particular power, it can be given by an extraordinary resolution of the company in a members' voluntary winding-up; in a creditors' voluntary winding-up the liquidator may obtain the requisite sanction from the court, the liquidation committee or (if there is no liquidation committee) from the creditors.[344] Although the matters requiring sanction in the case of a compulsory winding-up include conducting litigation and carrying on the company's business, a liquidator in a voluntary winding-up can exercise both of these powers without formal sanction.[345]

A voluntary liquidator also has the power to settle lists of contributories, make calls, pay debts, adjust the rights of contributories and to deal with other matters connected with the administration of the liquidation.[346]

In a creditors' voluntary winding-up, the timing is such that it is possible for the members to nominate a liquidator before a meeting of the creditors has been held, thus giving them an opportunity to decide who should fill that office. However, s 166 of the Insolvency Act 1986 now provides that in a creditors' voluntary liquidation the liquidator

---

[341] For the role of a liquidation committee in a compulsory winding-up see **21.37.3**.
[342] The court may direct other persons to act as members of the liquidation committee: s 101(3).
[343] Sections 107 and 165(5).
[344] Section 165.
[345] Section 165(3).
[346] Section 165(4).

nominated by the members may not exercise his powers prior to the first meeting of creditors without the sanction of the court except where the exercise of his powers is:

(1)   to take into custody or under his control all the property to which the company is or appears to be entitled;

(2)   to dispose of perishable goods and other goods the value of which is likely to diminish if they are not immediately disposed of; and

(3)   to do all such other things as may be necessary for the protection of the company's assets.

Under s 112, the liquidator or any contributory or creditor may make an application to the court to determine any question arising in the winding-up of the company including the exercise of certain powers of the liquidator. The court may make such order as it thinks just in the circumstances.[347]

Finally, where in the case of a voluntary winding-up no liquidator has been appointed or nominated by the company, the director must not exercise any powers except with the sanction of the court or (in the case of a creditors' voluntary winding-up) so far as may be necessary to call a meeting of creditors or prepare a statement of affairs in accordance with the Act. The directors may, however, exercise their powers in the circumstances described in (2) and (3) above. Failure to have regard to these limitations on the exercise of powers will result in a fine.[348]

21.47   Ceasing to act as a voluntary liquidator

Section 171 of the Insolvency Act 1986 states that a liquidator in a voluntary winding-up may be removed only:

(1)   by an order of the court; or

(2)   in the case of a members' voluntary winding-up by a resolution of the company in general meeting passed at a meeting summoned for that purpose; or

(3)   in the case of a creditors' voluntary winding-up by a resolution of the company's creditors passed at a meeting summoned for that purpose.

---

[347]   *Re Movitex Ltd* [1992] 1 WLR 303 is an example of an application made by creditors under s 602 of the Companies Act 1985 (which was replaced by s 112 of the Insolvency Act 1986). Scott LJ, with whom the other members of the Court of Appeal agreed, assumed, without deciding, that a post-liquidation debt would not provide the desired *locus standi* for such an application.

[348]   Section 114.

Additional procedural requirements apply where the liquidator has been appointed by the court under s 108.[349]

A voluntary liquidator vacates office automatically if he ceases to be a person qualified to act as an insolvency practitioner in relation to the company or when the final meetings of members and creditors (in the case of a creditors' voluntary liquidation) have been held and notice of the same has been given to the Registrar of Companies.[350]

Under s 108 of the 1986 Act, the court retains power on cause being shown to remove a voluntary liquidator' and appoint another in his place. A court may use this power to appoint an additional liquidator or replace a retiring liquidator.[351] An applicant must show cause why the liquidator should be removed.[352] The cause may lie in some unfitness or unsuitability of the liquidator, whether this be personal or arising from the particular circumstances of the case, for example some conflict of interest.[353] In *Re Keypak Homecare*,[354] a liquidator was removed because of his relaxed and complacent conduct of the liquidation, although there was no evidence of misconduct or conflicts of interest.

In a voluntary liquidation, the liquidator may resign in the prescribed circumstances, which are the same as in a compulsory winding-up.[355]

The time at which a voluntary liquidator obtains his release depends on the manner in which he vacates office.[356] The release operates to discharge the liquidator from all liability in respect of acts and omissions in the course of his winding-up and otherwise in relation to his conduct as liquidator. It does not give him immunity from misfeasance proceedings under s 212 of the 1986 Act.[357]

21.48   The relationship between voluntary liquidation and other insolvency-related procedures

The fact that a company is being wound up voluntarily does not prevent any creditor or contributory from presenting a petition to the court requesting a winding-up order.[358] Where, however, the petition is

---

[349]   Section 171(3). On s 108 appointments see **21.42**.
[350]   Section 171(4) and (5).
[351]   *Re Sunlight Incandescent Gas Lamps Co* [1900] 2 Ch 728; *Re Sheppey Portland Cement Co* [1892] WN 184.
[352]   *Re Keypak Homecare Ltd* [1987] BCLC 409, (1987) 3 BCC 558.
[353]   *Re Sir John Moore Gold Mining Co* (1879) 12 Ch D 325 (CA); *Re Adam Eyton* (1887) 36 Ch D 299 (CA); *Re London Flats* [1969] 1 WLR 711; *Re Charterland Goldfields* (1909) 26 TLR 132.
[354]   [1987] BCLC 409.
[355]   See **21.38**.
[356]   Section 173.
[357]   Section 173(4).
[358]   Section 116.

presented by a contributory, the court must be satisfied that the rights of the contributories will be prejudiced by the continuation of the voluntary winding-up and that some benefit would accrue from making a winding-up order.[359]

Where a creditor presents a petition, he is not required to show that he would be prejudiced by the continuance of the voluntary liquidation.[360] However, although a creditor is entitled *ex debito justitiae* between himself and the company to a winding-up order,[361] as between himself and the other creditors the court will normally give effect to the wishes of the majority.[362] The majority, both in number and value, is considered but the majority in value is more significant than the numerical majority.[363] As Diplock LJ stated in *Re JD Swain Ltd*:[364]

> 'For the wishes of the petitioner to overrule those of the majority of the creditors there must be some reason why the wishes of the majority should be overridden ... [the petitioner must] show some reason why the remedy under the voluntary winding-up is not an adequate remedy for him.'

In *Re Lowestoft Traffic Services Ltd*,[365] Hoffmann J noted that the decision whether to grant the winding-up order lay in the court's discretion and that, in exercising this discretion, the court would consider a range of matters including: the number, value and quality of the creditors for and against the petition; the possible or probable motives of these creditors; and general principles of fairness and commercial morality.

While a company is in administration, no resolution may be passed or order made for the winding up of a company and the same prohibition applies while an administration application is pending or where notice has been filed with the court for the out-of-court appointment of an administrator. There are now straightforward procedures for exiting from an administration to a creditors' voluntary liquidation. The administrator is empowered to activate this procedure where he thinks that (a) the total amount which each secured creditor of the company is likely to receive has been paid to him or set aside for him and (b) that a distribution will be made to unsecured creditors of the company if there are any. The administrator can send a notice to the Registrar of Companies and on registration of the notice the company shall be wound up as if a

---

[359] *Re National Company for the Distribution of Electricity* [1902] 2 Ch 34.

[360] Older cases (eg *Re New York Exchange* (1888) 39 Ch D 415 (CA); *Re Russell Cordner & Co* [1891] 2 Ch 171; *Re Medical Battery Co* [1894] 1 Ch 444) emphasised that point, but the need to show prejudice was removed by the Companies Act 1929.

[361] *Re James Millward & Co* [1940] Ch 333.

[362] Section 195.

[363] *Re HJ Tomkins & Sons Ltd* [1990] BCLC 76. See also *Re William Thorpe & Son Ltd* (1989) 5 BCC 156.

[364] [1965] 1 WLR 909 (CA), at 915B adopted by Harman J in *Re Medisco Equipment Ltd* [1983] BCLC 305.

[365] [1986] BCLC 81, (1986) 2 BCC 945.

resolution for voluntary winding-up were passed on the day on which the notice is registered. The creditors have the power to nominate a liquidator but in the absence of any such nomination the administrator shall automatically be appointed liquidator.[366]

The fact that there is a voluntary arrangement in force under Part I of the Insolvency Act 1986 does not prevent a company from being wound up voluntarily. However, where a company is in the course of being wound up, the power to make a proposal under s 1 of the Insolvency Act 1986 rests with the liquidator and not the directors of the company. In the case of small companies that satisfy the eligibility criteria specified in what is now Sch A1 to the Insolvency Act 1986 and hence enjoy the benefit of a moratorium when directors are proposing a voluntary arrangement, no resolution may be passed or order made for the winding-up of the company during the currency of this moratorium.[367]

The fact that an administrative receiver has been appointed over the assets of the company does not prevent the company from being wound up voluntarily.

PART 6: THE CONDUCT OF LIQUIDATIONS

21.49 Introduction

In this part we explore some of the most important aspects of both compulsory and voluntary liquidations. In general terms, the liquidator's fundamental duty is to collect in and realise the assets of the company and to apply the proceeds in discharging the debts and liabilities of the company in accordance with the *pari passu* rule. Any remaining surplus belongs to the members of the company and must be distributed to them in accordance with their rights under the company's memorandum and articles. Closer examination of the detailed aspects of liquidations can be left to specialist texts but this part indicates the main areas of complexity.

21.50 Creditors' claims

A liquidator need only apply the company's assets in payment of creditors' debts and liabilities which have been admitted to proof in the liquidation. If a creditor in a compulsory liquidation fails to submit a proof, or for some reason his claim is not admissible to proof, the liquidator cannot, in normal circumstances,[368] take it into account in

---

[366] Schedule B1, para 83 to the Insolvency Act 1986.
[367] Schedule A1, para 12(1)(c) to the Insolvency Act 1986.
[368] Note r 4.67(2) which provides for an exceptional case where, by order of the court, a debt which has not been the subject of a proof may be treated as if it had been proved for the purpose of paying a dividend.

making distributions.[369] In a voluntary winding-up (whether members' or creditors'), the liquidator may require creditors to submit proofs.[370]

Admissibility to proof in both compulsory and voluntary liquidations is governed by Part 4, Chapter 9 of the Insolvency Rules 1986. All debts and liabilities, including contingent debts and debts due in the future, can be proved, provided the company is subject to them at the date when it goes into liquidation or becomes subject to them after the date of the liquidation by reason of obligations previously incurred.[371] A debt or liability need not be fixed or liquidated in amount.[372]

The position with regard to secured creditors and the submission of proofs is as follows. Generally speaking, the liquidation of a company does not affect a secured creditor's rights (subject to what is said below about the priority of preferential claims over the claims of the holder of a floating charge and the invalidation of certain security interests). The secured creditor is free to realise his security without reference to the liquidator. Thus, where the value of the security is more than sufficient to discharge the debt or the security is a floating charge on all of the company's assets, the secured creditor may simply choose to enforce his security outside the liquidation. It is possible for a secured creditor voluntarily to surrender his security and prove for his debt as if he were unsecured[373] but there can be few circumstances in which it would be advantageous for a creditor to give up his security in this way.

If a secured creditor realises his security but the amount so realised is insufficient to discharge the debt, he may prove for the balance in the liquidation.[374] A secured creditor also has the option of valuing his security and submitting a proof for the balance. In that case, the liquidator can offer to redeem the security at the value stated in the proof,[375] which he may well choose to do where he considers that the value stated in the proof is less than the value which the assets subject to the security could fetch on a disposal, although, because there is some scope for the secured creditor to revise the value stated in his proof,[376] the matter may then become one for negotiation between the liquidator and the creditor.

---

[369] Rule 4.73(1) and (3).

[370] Rule 4.73(2) and (3).

[371] Rule 13.12 defines 'debt' and 'liability'.

[372] Ibid.

[373] Rule 4.88(2). Note r 4.96 which deems a secured creditor to have voluntarily surrendered (unless the court grants relief) if he omits to disclose his security in his proof.

[374] Rule 4.88(1).

[375] Rule 4.97.

[376] Rules 4.84 and 4.95.

A secured creditor, part of whose secured claim is preferential, may, if he realises his security, appropriate the proceeds of the realisation to the non-preferential element of his claim in a liquidation.[377]

21.51   Proof of debts and rights of set-off

Where, before a company goes into liquidation, there have been mutual credits, mutual debits or other mutual dealings between the company and any creditor of the company proving in the liquidation, an account must be taken of what is due from each party to the other in respect of the mutual dealings, and the sums due from one party must be set off against the sums due from the other. If, after the operation of the set-off, there is still a balance owing from the company to the creditor, that balance is the amount provable by the creditor in the liquidation. Alternatively, if the result of the operation of the set-off is that an amount remains owing to the company from the creditor, the creditor must pay that amount to the liquidator and it is part of the company's assets available for distribution.[378]

Thus, the result of the operation of a right of set-off is that, to the extent of the amount set off, the creditor in effect obtains repayment of the amount owing to him from the company in priority to the company's general creditors. From the company's viewpoint, the amount of assets available to repay its general creditors is reduced by the amount of the debt which the creditor is allowed to set off but, in turn, the company is spared the trouble and potential expense involved in suing the creditor for the amount owing to it to the extent that this is diminished by the set-off. The operation of set-off is said to facilitate proper and orderly administration of insolvent estates.[379] It has also been described as a method of doing justice between the parties;[380] it is considered that it would be unjust for a creditor to have to pay the whole of the debt which he owes to the company while, in respect of the amount which the company owes to him, he is allowed only to prove for a dividend in the company's liquidation.[381] In practice, it is creditors who most obviously benefit from the operation of set-off but, because its purpose is wider than simply the benefiting of one particular party and extends to ensuring the proper administration of insolvent estates, set-off is regarded as mandatory and it is not possible to contract out of the relevant provisions of the Insolvency Rules 1986.[382]

---

[377] *Re William Hall (Contractors) Ltd* [1967] 2 All ER 1150, [1967] 1 WLR 948.
[378] Rule 4.90.
[379] *National Westminster Bank Ltd v Halesowen Presswork & Assemblies Ltd* [1972] AC 785, [1972] 1 All ER 641, [1972] 2 WLR 455; *Re Maxwell Communications Corp plc (No 3)* [1993] 1 All ER 737, [1993] 1 WLR 1402, [1993] BCC 369.
[380] *Forster v Wilson* (1843) 12 M&W 191, at 203–204.
[381] *Stein v Blake* [1996] AC 243, [1995] 2 All ER 961 (HL) (a bankruptcy case, but the principle is the same).
[382] *National Westminster Bank Ltd v Halesowen*, above.

The conditions governing the availability of set-off in liquidation are, first, that there must be debts, credits or dealings between the company and the person seeking to assert a right of set-off and, secondly, that these debts, credits or dealings must be mutual. The interpretation of these conditions has spawned a considerable amount of case-law.[383] In brief, mutual debts are liquidated amounts owing from each of the parties to the other. 'Mutual credits' is a wider term than 'mutual debts',[384] and means credits which will eventually result in money claims such as where one party, who is indebted to the other, supplies the other party with property on the basis that the property is to be resold and the proceeds handed over.[385] Mutual dealings are arrangements in which the parties extend credit to each other in respect of individual sums, with the intention, express or implied, that at some point the individual sums will be brought into account and set off against each other.[386] Each claim must result in a liability to pay money; for example, a claim to the return of goods cannot be set off against a money debt.[387] 'Mutual dealings' is the widest term and could encompass both mutual debts and mutual credits.

The requirement for mutuality means that a joint debt cannot be set off against a several debt. For the same reason, money held by the company for a specific purpose or on trust cannot be set off against a debt owed to the company.[388] There has, historically, been some uncertainty regarding the operation of set-off in relation to contingent debts.[389] The decision of the House of Lords in *Secretary of State for Trade and Industry v Frid*[390] raised this issue in an acute form. In that case a company went into voluntary liquidation and its liabilities included notice pay and redundancy payments due to some ex-employees. Upon the company failing to meet these payments to employees, the Secretary of State became liable to make the same out of the National Insurance Fund. The Secretary of State was then entitled by statute to be subrogated to the rights and remedies of the employees against the company. A proof was submitted in respect of this claim less the amount of a VAT refund to

---

[383] See generally, Wood, *English and International Set-off* (Sweet & Maxwell, 1989); Derham *Set-off* (2nd edn, Clarendon Press, 1996); and Derham 'Some Aspects of Mutual Credit and Mutual Dealings' (1992) 108 LQR 99.

[384] *Palmer v Day & Sons* [1895] 2 QB 618.

[385] *Rolls Razor Ltd v Cox* [1967] 1 QB 552, [1967] 1 All ER 397, [1967] 2 WLR 241.

[386] *Ross Razor v Cox*, above.

[387] *Eberle's Hotels & Restaurant Co v Jones* (1887) 18 QBD 459.

[388] *Ex parte Caldicott* (1884) 25 Ch D 716; *Re City Equitable Fire Insurance Co Ltd (No 2)* [1930] 2 Ch 293; *Young v Bank of Bengal* (1836) 1 Moore Ind App 87; *National Westminster Bank v Halesowen*, above.

[389] An additional complication to that discussed in the text is that arising from the rule against double proof (a rule which is illustrated by *Barclays Bank Ltd v TOSG Trust Fund Ltd* [1984] AC 626, [1984] 1 All ER 1060, [1984] 2 WLR 650); a contingent claim, such as one arising under a guarantee, may not be admissible to proof for that reason and, if it is not provable, it will also not be capable of being the subject of set-off.

[390] [2004] UKHL 24, [2004] 2 AC 506.

which the company was entitled and which the Crown claimed should be set off against the amount of the proof.

The House of Lords allowed the set-off claim. Lord Hoffmann observed:

> 'If a statutory origin does not prevent set-off in the case of debts due and payable at the insolvency date, I do not see why it should make any difference that the statute creates a contingent liability which exists before the insolvency date but falls due for payment and is paid afterwards. The term "mutual debts" does not in itself require anything more than commensurable cross-obligations between the same people in the same capacity. How those debts arose – whether by contract, statute or tort, voluntarily or by compulsion – is not material.'

The House of Lords suggested that all that was necessary was that there should have been 'dealings' (in an extended sense which included the commission of a tort or the imposition of a statutory obligation) which gave rise to commensurable cross-claims.[391] There were no additional requirements that had to be satisfied before set-off could be recognised.

A secured debt may be set off against an unsecured debt; the existence of a security does not destroy mutuality.[392] However, a creditor who relies on his security to enforce his debt does not prove in the liquidation and is not subject to set-off.[393]

21.52   The company's assets

The liquidator must get in and realise the company's assets.[394] Assets which are not beneficially owned by a company fall outside the scope of its liquidation and are not available to meet the claims of its general body of creditors. Instead, the persons who are beneficially entitled to the property are entitled to invoke equitable claims to recover their property.

The decision of the House of Lords in *Barclays Bank Ltd v Quistclose Investments Ltd*,[395] demonstrates the operation of the principle that trust

---

[391] See, para 24 of the judgment.

[392] *Ex parte Barnett* (1874) LR 9 Ch App 293; *Hiley v People's Prudential Assurance Co* (1938) 60 CLR 468.

[393] *Re Norman Holding Co Ltd* [1990] 3 All ER 757, [1991] 1 WLR 10, [1990] BCLC 1, [1991] BCC 11.

[394] Sections 144 and 148 (compulsory liquidation). The duty is not spelt out in relation to a voluntary liquidator in a voluntary winding-up but a liquidator must necessarily collect in the assets of the company in order to be able to fulfil his duty (s 107) to distribute the proceeds amongst those who are entitled.

[395] [1970] AC 567, [1968] 3 All ER 651, [1968] 3 WLR 1097. On the 'Quistclose trust' see Worthington *Proprietary Interests in Commercial Transactions* (Oxford University Press, 1996) Ch 3; Goodhart and Jones 'The Infiltration of Equitable Doctrine into English Commercial Law' (1980) 43 MLR 489; Millett 'The Quistclose Trust: Who Can Enforce It?' (1985) 101 LQR 269; Rickett 'Different Views on the Scope of the *Quistclose* Analysis: English and Antipodean Insights' (1991) 107 LQR 608; Bridge 'The Quistclose

assets fall outside the normal rules governing distribution of assets in liquidation. Rolls Razor Ltd was a company in serious financial difficulties but it had managed to declare a dividend. Lacking available funds to pay the dividend, and being unable to raise them from its bank, the company entered into an arrangement with Quistclose, whereby Quistclose agreed to lend the money on condition that the company would use it only to pay the dividend and, if that could not be done, that it would return the money to Quistclose. The House of Lords held that this arrangement amounted to a relationship of a fiduciary character or trust in the form of a primary trust to pay the dividend and, if that failed, a secondary trust in favour of Quistclose. It was further held that the primary trust had failed[396] and that Quistclose was entitled to recover the money.

The Quistclose trust is a device which has been upheld in a number of later cases[397] but the jurisprudential basis of the trust identified in the *Quistclose* case itself has been questioned.

A policy question raised by the Quistclose trust is whether the law should recognise and give effect to this interest, given that it occurs in transactions which, in economic terms, are often indistinguishable from secured loans; unlike a secured loan, a Quistclose trust does not require registration, and hence disclosure, at Companies House. The same policy question can arise where assets are sold to a company on credit terms which provide that title to the assets will not pass until debts owing from the company to the supplier have been paid for in full.[398] Like a charge, a retention of title clause also achieves the effect of giving credit to the company whilst at the same time allowing the creditor to protect its position with a proprietary interest; but because the creditor's interest is retained in its own property rather than taken on property of the company, legally it is not a charge and does not require registration; in the

---

Trust in a World of Secured Transactions' (1992) 12 OJLS 333; L Ho and P St J Smart 'Reinterpreting the Quistclose Trust: A Critique of Chambers' (2001) 21 OJLS 267.

[396] Although, as Goodhart and Jones, op cit, point out at 494, n 28, it is arguable whether this was in fact the case unless it is accepted that there were also other conditions attached to the loan. Millett, op cit, suggests that the primary purpose for which the loan was made available was to ensure the survival of the company, a purpose which certainly failed.

[397] These include *Re Northern Developments Holdings Ltd* (unreported); *Carreras Rothmans Ltd v Freeman Mathews Treasure Ltd* [1985] Ch 207; *Re EVTR Ltd* [1987] BCLC 464, (1987) 3 BCC 389; *Re Kayford Ltd* [1975] 1 All ER 604, [1975] 1 WLR 279; *Re Lewis of Leicester Ltd* [1995] BCC 514; *Hurst-Bannister v New Cap Reinsurance Corp Ltd* [2000] Lloyd's Rep IR 166 (principles of *Barclays Bank Ltd v Quistclose Investments Ltd* were to be applied widely); cf *Re Multi-Guarantee Co Ltd* [1987] BCLC 257; *Re Holiday Promotions (Europe) Ltd* [1996] BCC 671.

[398] This is the simplest type of retention of title clause. Suppliers sometimes insert more elaborate clauses into their supply contracts, whereby title is also claimed to the proceeds of resales or to goods manufactured from those supplied. More elaborate clauses have tended not to be regarded favourably by the courts.

event of liquidation leading to a breach of the terms on which the assets were supplied, the creditor can simply assert its proprietary claim to the assets supplied.

Various law review bodies have criticised the law in this area on the grounds that it appears to be concerned more with form rather than substance.[399] Retention of title provisions have attracted more attention than Quistclose trusts, with the most widely supported suggestion being that such provisions should be brought within the scope of revised law relating to security interests. Despite calls for reform stretching back over a number of decades, however, successive governments have shown little enthusiasm for extensive reform in this area. The Law Commission in recent years has produced two consultation papers and a final report on 'Company Security Interests'. Broadly speaking, the Law Commission advocate a functional approach towards security along the lines of art 9 of the US Commercial Code though in its final report the Law Commission pulled pack from some of the more radical reforms. Part 25 of the Companies Act 2006 basically re-enacts the existing provisions on the registration of company charges and does not implement any of the Law Commission recommendations.[400]

21.53   The order of payment of debts and liabilities and the *pari passu* rule

Although the *pari passu* rule is a fundamental tenet of insolvency, there are a number of ways in which the principle of *pari passu* distribution is qualified.[401] We have already seen how the operation of insolvency set-off can in effect allow one creditor to be paid in advance of other creditors, which cuts across the *pari passu* rule, and how trust assets fall entirely outside the ambit of the *pari passu* rule. Other important illustrations of the qualified nature of the *pari passu* principle include the position of secured creditors (who may, subject to the special rules discussed below governing debts secured by a floating charge, enforce their security outside the liquidation) and the ranking of liquidation costs and expenses and of preferential debts.

---

[399] *Report of the Committee on Consumer Credit* Cmnd 4596 (1972); *Report of the Review Committee on Insolvency Law and Practice* Cmnd 8558 (1982); Diamond *Review of Security Interests in Property* (1989). See also, Bridge 'Form, Substance and Innovation in Personal Property Security Law' [1992] JBL 1.

[400] For the Law Commission see its website (www.lawcom.gov.uk) and see generally G McCormack *Secured Credit under English and American Law* (Cambridge University Press, 2004). As to Part 25 of CA 2006, see chapter 10.

[401] Oditah 'Assets and the Treatment of Claims in Insolvency' (1992) 108 LQR 459; Belcher and Beglan 'Jumping the Queue' [1997] JBL 1. For trenchant criticism of the *pari passu* principle see R Mokal 'Priority as Pathology: The Pari Passu myth' [2001] CLJ 581; R Mokal 'The Search for Someone to Save: A Defensive Case for the Priority of Secured Credit' (2002) 22 OJLS 687; and for other perspectives see G McCormack *Secured Credit under English and American Law* (Cambridge University Press, 2004) Ch 1 and V Finch 'Security, Insolvency and Risk: Who Pays the Price?' (1999) 62 MLR 633.

The precise order of application of funds in a liquidation is:[402]

(1) costs and expenses of the liquidation including the liquidator's remuneration;

(2) preferential debts;

(3) ordinary debts;

(4) deferred and subordinated debts; and

(5) any balance remaining is distributed to members in accordance with their entitlements under the company's memorandum and articles.

21.53.1 *Preferential debts*

Preferential debts rank equally among themselves after the expenses of the winding-up and must be paid in full, unless the assets are insufficient to meet them, in which case they abate in equal proportions.[403] Also, whilst preferential debts rank behind debts secured by fixed charges, so far as the assets of the company available for payment of general creditors are insufficient to meet them, they have priority over the claims of debentures secured by, or the holders of, any floating charge created by the company and must be paid accordingly out of any property comprised in or subject to that charge.[404] The fact that the floating charge may have crystallised prior to the commencement of the winding-up does not deprive the preferential debts of this special priority, because it is expressly provided by s 251 that a floating charge for this purpose means a charge created as such.

Schedule 6 to the Insolvency Act 1986 sets out the categories of preferential debts. As amended by the Enterprise Act 2002,[405] this now covers only up to 4 months' back-pay to employees and former employees (up to a prescribed maximum limit per employee) as well as unpaid holiday pay and contributions to state and occupational pension schemes. Giving these preferential status in a winding-up is a way of protecting the interests of creditors who are not in a position to negotiate an enhanced position, through charge or trust mechanisms, for themselves.[406]

---

[402] Sections 107 and 115 (voluntary liquidations) and 143 and 156 (compulsory liquidations) and s 175 and r 4.218 (both types of liquidation).

[403] Section 175(2)(a).

[404] Section 175(2)(b).

[405] Which abolished preferences that the Crown used to have in respect of unpaid taxes of various sorts.

[406] See generally, L A Bebchuk and J M Fried 'The Uneasy Case for the Priority of Secured Claims in Bankruptcy' [1996] 105 Yale LJ 857.

21.53.2   Liquidation expenses

Liquidation expenses rank before preferential debts but behind debts secured by fixed charges. In *Buchler v Talbot*[407] it was held by the House of Lords that the general costs and expenses of liquidation could not be paid out of floating charge realisations though the court said that the costs of realising a particular property must be distinguished from the general expenses of the winding-up or receivership. The costs of realisation were deductible from the proceeds of the property realised, whether it was realised by the liquidator or by the receiver.

Buchler v Talbot has now been reversed by s 1282 of the Companies Act 2006[408] which provides that the 'expenses of winding up … so far as the assets of the company available for payment of general creditors are insufficient to meet them, have priority over any claims to property comprised in or subject to any floating charge created by the company and shall be paid out of any such property accordingly'.[409]

Since liquidation expenses enjoy 'super priority', the range of expenses encompassed within this category is especially important. Rule 4.218 of the Insolvency Rules 1986 defines the various expenses payable out of the assets and the order in which they are payable. The liquidator's own remuneration is included in the list of liquidation expenses. The courts have also expanded the concept of 'liquidation expenses' to include liabilities incurred before the liquidation in respect of property afterwards retained by the liquidator for the benefit of the insolvent estate. Consequently, continuing rent or hire purchase charges in respect of land or goods in the possession of the company which the liquidator continues to use for the purposes of the liquidation are included within the concept of liquidation expenses.[410]

Among the items listed in r 4.218 are 'any necessary disbursements by the liquidator in the course of his administration …'. In *Re Toshoku Finance (UK) plc*,[411] it was held by the House of Lords that the liability to corporation tax is a sum which, by statute, is payable by a company in respect of profits or gains arising during a winding up. Therefore it is a 'necessary disbursement' which the liquidator has to make in the course of

---

[407]   [2004] 2 AC 298.

[408]   This provision inserts a new s 176ZA into the Insolvency Act 1986.

[409]   According to s 1282(3), however, rules may be made restricting the application of this provision in such circumstances as may be prescribed, to expenses authorised or approved (a) by the holders of debentures secured by, or holders of, the floating charges and by any preferential creditors entitled to be paid in priority to them, or (b) by the court. See now rr 4.218A–4.218E, as inserted by the Insolvency (Amendment) Rules 2008, SI 2008/737.

[410]   *Re International Marine Hydropathic Co* (1884) 28 Ch D 470; *Re Lundy Granite Co* (1871) LR 6 Ch App 462; *Re Oak Pits Colliery Co* (1882) 21 Ch D 322; *Re Atlantic Computer Systems plc* [1992] Ch 505, where the earlier authorities and the general principle are reviewed.

[411]   [2002] UKHL 6, [2002] 1 WLR 671.

his administration. It was a liquidation expense and that was the end of the matter. According to Lord Hoffmann, who spoke for the House of Lords, r 4.218(1) was intended to be a definitive statement of what counted as an expense of the liquidation. The courts will interpret r 4.218 to include debts that, under the *Lundy Granite Co*[412] principle, are deemed to be expenses of the liquidation but the heads of expense listed in r 4.218(1) are not subject to any implied qualification. In particular, Lord Hoffmann rejected the proposition that r 4.218(1) created only an outer envelope within which expenses were contained ie it was necessary to come within r 4.218(1) to count as a liquidation expense but that was not sufficient.

Costs incurred by a liquidator in an unsuccessful attempt to recover assets were not originally included in the concept of liquidation expenses.[413] Millett J's analysis to this effect, in *Re M C Bacon Ltd (No 2)*, was confirmed by the Court of Appeal in *Lewis v IRC*,[414] but the Enterprise Act 2002 alters the position somewhat. Under s 253 of this Act, it is only possible for a liquidator to pursue such proceedings with the sanction of creditors and the costs of such proceedings are now deemed to be a liquidation expense.[415]

21.53.3 Deferred debts and subordinated debts

As among ordinary unsecured debts, the *pari passu* rule generally prevails. However, s 74(2)(f) creates a category of deferred debt: any sum due to a member of a company (in his character of a member) by way of dividends, profits or otherwise is not deemed to be a debt of the company, payable to that member in a case of competition between himself and any other creditor not a member of the company; but such sum may be taken into account for the purpose of the final adjustment of the rights of the contributories among themselves. The House of Lords has said that sums due to a member in his character as such are sums arising from claims based on the statutory contract in what is now s 33 of the Companies Act 2006[416] and other rights and liabilities conferred and imposed by that legislation.[417] On this basis, a claim for compensation for misrepresentation whereby an investor is induced to acquire shares in a company is not a deferred debt for the purposes of s 74(2)(f).

---

[412] (1871) LR 6 Ch App 462.
[413] *Mond v Hammond Suddards* [1999] 3 WLR 697; *Re M C Bacon Ltd (No 2)* [1991] Ch 127.
[414] *Re Floor Fourteen Ltd, Lewis v IRC* [2001] 3 All ER 499.
[415] Rule 4.218(1)(a) of the Insolvency Rules now refers to expenses or costs which are properly chargeable or incurred by the official receiver or the liquidator 'in preserving, realising or getting in any of the assets of the company or otherwise relating to the conduct of any legal proceedings which he has power to bring or defend whether in his own name or the name of the company ...'.
[416] See **5.17**.
[417] *Soden v British & Commonwealth Holdings plc* [1997] BCC 952 (HL).

Whether a creditor can by contract choose to opt out of the *pari passu* rule and defer his debt to other debts of the company was, until recently, unclear.[418]

However, in *Re Maxwell Communications Corp plc (No 3)*[419] Vinelott J, following Australian and South African authority,[420] held that it was legally possible for a creditor to opt out of the *pari passu* rule and to contract to defer his debts to other debts of the company. Earlier House of Lords' authorities that, in the view of some commentators,[421] cast doubt upon the validity of subordination agreements were distinguished. Although there was clear authority that the *pari passu* principle was mandatory to the extent that a creditor could not, by contract, obtain a better position than that which the *pari passu* principle afforded him,[422] this did not prevent a creditor from agreeing to a worse position. Similarly, the ruling that insolvency set-off was a mandatory procedure[423] did not preclude the court from upholding a subordination agreement since, unlike set-off, which was a procedure from which the company as well as its creditors could potentially benefit, the *pari passu* principle operated only in favour of creditors and, therefore, they were free to waive the benefit. Vinelott J considered that it was important, particularly at a time when insolvency increasingly had international ramifications, for English law to give effect to contractual subordination arrangements in the same way as other jurisdictions.

21.54 Contributories

Under s 74 of the Insolvency Act 1986, every present and past member is liable to contribute to the assets of the company on winding-up and is therefore a contributory.[424] Section 74 then limits the amount of the contribution that can be required of a contributory. Consistent with the principle of limited liability, no contribution can be required from any

---

[418] The question produced much literature, a sample of which includes Wood *English and International Set-Off* (Sweet & Maxwell, 1989), Ch 17; Johnson 'Debt Subordination: The Australian Perspective' (1987) 15 ABLJ 80; Johnson 'Contractual Debt Subordination and Legislative Reform' [1991] JBL 225.

[419] [1993] 1 All ER 737, [1993] 1 WLR 1402, [1993] BCC 369.

[420] *Horne v Chester & Fein Property Developments Pty Ltd* (1986) 11 ACLR 485; *Re Carbon Developments (Pty) Ltd* [1993] 1 SA 493.

[421] More detailed post-*Maxwell* assessments of debt subordination include R Nolan 'Less Equal Than Others – *Maxwell* and Subordinated Unsecured Obligations' [1995] JBL 485; Ferran *Company Law and Corporate Finance* (Oxford University Press, 1999), Ch 16.

[422] *British Eagle International Air Lines v Compagnie Nationale Air France* [1975] 2 All ER 390, [1975] 1 WLR 758 (HL).

[423] *National Westminster Bank Ltd v Halesowen Presswork & Assemblies* [1972] AC 785, [1972] 1 All ER 641, [1972] 2 WLR 455 (HL).

[424] Contributory being defined by s 79 as meaning any person who is liable to contribute. This category does not include persons who are ordered to make a contribution as a result of liability for fraudulent or wrongful trading: s 79(2).

present or past member of a limited company in excess of the amount
unpaid in respect of the shares held, or previously held.

21.55   Distribution of remaining assets

The liquidation process may result in a surplus remaining after the
expenses, costs and debts have been paid in full, although it would be
comparatively rare for this to happen. Where there is a surplus, the
question arises as to its distribution. Section 107 of the Insolvency
Act 1986 provides that in the case of a voluntary liquidation, remaining
assets are to be distributed among the members according to their rights
and interests in the company. The equivalent provisions governing
compulsory liquidations are ss 143 and 154, which provide for the
distribution of remaining assets among the persons entitled to them.

The distribution of any surplus must take into account the rights
conferred on the members by the terms of the company's memorandum
and articles of association but, leaving aside any special provisions made
by these documents, the position is as follows. Where there are shares
having a preference as to capital, the amount paid on those shares must be
repaid before any amount is paid to those whose rights are deferred, such
as the holders of ordinary or deferred shares in the company. It now
seems to be generally accepted that the annexation to preference shares of
the right to receive back their capital on a winding-up in priority to
ordinary shares is an exhaustive delimitation of the capital rights
attaching to the preference shares, so that their holders are excluded from
any participation in any surplus after all capital has been returned.[425]

PART 7: SPECIAL POWERS OF LIQUIDATORS AND OTHER OFFICE HOLDERS IN INSOLVENCY PROCEEDINGS

21.56   A liquidator's ability to disclaim property

Section 178 of the Insolvency Act 1986 gives a liquidator the power by
giving notice to disclaim any onerous property notwithstanding that he
has taken possession of it, endeavoured to sell it or otherwise exercised
rights of ownership in relation to it. This is a potentially very important
power to rid a company in liquidation of assets which are subject to
liabilities, thus rendering retention undesirable from the point of view of a
beneficial realisation of the assets of the company for the benefit of the
creditors generally. For the purposes of the section, 'onerous property'
means any unprofitable contract and any other property of the company
which is unsaleable or not readily saleable or is such that it may give rise

---

[425]   *Scottish Insurance Co v Wilsons & Clyde Coal Co* [1949] AC 462.

to a liability to pay money or perform any other onerous acts. It can include statutory exemptions or licences, such as a waste management licence.[426]

The Court of Appeal considered the meaning of 'unprofitable contract' in *Manning v AIG Europe Ltd*.[427] It was decided that the critical feature was whether 'performance of the future obligations will prejudice the liquidator's obligation to realise the company's property and pay a dividend to creditors within a reasonable time'. The court also approved the following statement of principle by Chesterman J in the Australian case *Transmetro Corpn Ltd v Real Investments Pty Ltd*:[428]

'[1] A contract is unprofitable ... if it imposes on the company continuing financial obligations which may be regarded as detrimental to the creditors, which presumably means that the contract confers no sufficient reciprocal benefit.

[2] Before a contract may be unprofitable for the purposes of the section it must give rise to prospective liabilities.

[3] Contracts which will delay the winding up of the company's affairs because they are to be performed over a substantial period of time and will involve expenditure that may not be recovered are unprofitable.

[4] No case has decided that a contract is unprofitable merely because it is financially disadvantageous. The cases focus upon the nature and cause of the disadvantage.

[5] A contract is not unprofitable merely because the company could have made or could make a better bargain.'

Once effectively made, the disclaimer operates to determine as from its date the rights, interests and liabilities of the company in respect of the property disclaimed. It does not, however, except insofar as is necessary for the purpose of releasing the company from any liability, affect the rights or liabilities of any other person interested in that property.[429]

Under s 178(6) of the 1986 Act, any person sustaining loss or damage in consequence of a disclaimer is deemed a creditor of a company to the extent of the loss or damage sustained and may prove for that loss or damage in the winding-up of the company.[430]

---

[426] *Re Celtic Extraction Ltd* [2001] Ch 475.
[427] [2006] Ch 610.
[428] (1999) 17 ACLC 1314, at 1320.
[429] Section 178(4).
[430] *Re Park Air Services plc* [2000] 2 AC 172 (HL) (landlord entitled to prove for statutory compensation for loss of his right to future rent and compensation assessed in the same way as damages for breach of contract).

Section 168(5) allows persons who are aggrieved by an act or decision of a liquidator to apply to court; the court may confirm, reverse or modify the act or decision complained of, and make such order in the case as it thinks just. *Re Hans Place Ltd*[431] was an attempt to use this provision to challenge a liquidator's decision to disclaim a lease. The court held that it did have jurisdiction to consider the complaint but that it could interfere only where the liquidator had acted in bad faith or had made a perverse decision.

21.57   Office-holders

Office-holders are given certain special powers under the insolvency legislation. Who an office-holder is depends on the power in question, but the category can include administrators, administrative receivers (but not other receivers), supervisors of voluntary arrangements, liquidators and provisional liquidators.

21.57.1   Utilities

Suppliers of gas, electricity, water and telecommunications services cannot make it a condition of continuing the giving of the supply that the office-holder pay outstanding charges, but the supplier can require the office-holder to give a personal guarantee in respect of any new supplies.[432] For this purpose administrators, administrative receivers, supervisors of voluntary arrangements, liquidators and provisional liquidators all count as office-holders.

21.57.2   Transactions at an undervalue

An administrator or a liquidator, as an office-holder, has the power to make an application to court in respect of transactions at an undervalue.[433] If the application is successful, the court must make such order as it thinks fit for restoring the position to what it would have been if the company had not entered into the transaction.[434]

The Insolvency Act 1986 defines a transaction[435] at an undervalue as one where:

(1)   the company makes a gift to a person or otherwise enters into a transaction with a person on terms that provide for the company to receive no consideration; or

---

[431]   [1993] BCLC 768.
[432]   Section 233.
[433]   Section 238.
[434]   Section 238(3).
[435]   The term 'transaction' is defined in s 436 of the Act to include 'a gift, agreement or arrangement'.

(2)   the company enters into a transaction with a person for a
       consideration the value of which, in money or money's worth, is
       significantly less than the value, in money or money's worth, of the
       consideration provided by the company.

The first limb of the definition envisages a total absence of any
consideration passing to the company, while the second limb covers the
case where there is some mutual consideration but significantly differing
in amounts. The second limb was considered in *Re M C Bacon Ltd*[436]
where Millett J made the following observations:

(1)   a comparison must be made between the value obtained by the
       company for the transaction and the value of the consideration
       provided by the company;

(2)   both values must be measurable in money or money's worth;

(3)   both values must be considered from the company's point of view.

The court may not make an order in respect of a transaction at an
undervalue if it is satisfied that: (a) the company entered into the
transaction in good faith and for the purpose of carrying on its business;
and (b) at the time when it did so, there were reasonable grounds for
believing the transaction would benefit the company.[437] Good faith,
propriety of purpose and reasonableness must all be established to the
satisfaction of the court; if any of these elements is missing, the
transaction remains vulnerable.

There is a time-limit on the power of an administrator or liquidator to
attack a transaction at an undervalue. The transaction must have taken
place at a 'relevant time'.[438] There are two elements to the definition of
'relevant time'. First, the transaction must be entered into within a
specified period before the onset of the administration or liquidation. The
transaction at an undervalue must have taken place either at a time within
the period of 2 years ending with the onset of the administration or
liquidation, or at a time between the making of an administration
application in respect of the company and the making of an
administration order on that application.[439]

Secondly, it is only a relevant time for the purposes of the provisions
relating to transactions at an undervalue if, at the time, the company is

---

[436]   [1990] BCLC 324, [1990] BCC 78. Millett J's analysis of the provision was adopted by
        Balcombe LJ in *Menzies v National Bank of Kuwait SAK* [1994] BCC 119, and by
        Sir Christopher Slade in *Agricultural Mortgage Corpn plc v Woodward* [1995] 1 BCLC 1
        (both cases on s 423 of the Insolvency Act 1986). See also *Phillips v Brewin Dolphin Bell
        Lawrie Ltd* [2001] 1 WLR 143.
[437]   Section 238(5).
[438]   Section 240.
[439]   See also s 240(3).

unable to pay its debts within the meaning of s 123 of the Act or if it becomes unable to pay them within the meaning of that section in consequence of the transaction. This requirement, however, is deemed to be satisfied, unless the contrary is shown, where the transaction in question is entered into by the company with a person who is connected with the company.[440]

The court is given a very wide power to make such order as it thinks fit for the purpose of restoring the position to what it would have been if the company had not entered into the transaction. The court also has power to set aside transactions at an undervalue in applications brought under s 423.[441] There is no time-limit on applications under this section and, as well as liquidators and administrators, supervisors of voluntary arrangements and victims of transactions[442] have standing to seek an order under this section although, if the company is in administration or liquidation, a victim must obtain the leave of the court.[443] Whoever brings the claim, it is treated as made on behalf of every victim of the transaction.[444] The court can make an order under this section only where it is satisfied that the transaction was entered into by the company for the purpose of putting assets beyond the reach of any person who is making, or may at some time make, a claim against the company or of otherwise prejudicing the interests of such a person in relation to the claim which he is making or may make.[445] The need to establish this purpose inhibits the use of the power contained in this section.[446]

21.57.3 *Voidable preferences*

An administrator or liquidator may apply to the court for an order on such terms as the court thinks fit, for restoring the position to what it would have been if the company had not given a preference.[447] A company gives a preference to a person if:

---

[440] Section 240(2). For the definition of a person connected with the company, see ss 249 and 435.

[441] A transaction at an undervalue for this purpose is defined by s 423(1). So far as companies are concerned, the definition is the same as that under s 238.

[442] A litigant in proceedings against a company who has a chance of success in those proceedings can be a 'victim' for this purpose: *Pinewood Joinery v Starelm Properties Ltd* [1994] BCC 569. See also, *Re Ayala Holdings Ltd* [1993] BCLC 256 and *Agricultural Mortgage Corp plc v Woodward*, above (application by mortgagee).

[443] Section 424(1)(a).

[444] Section 424(2).

[445] Statutory predecessors of this section, which also applies to individual insolvents, can be traced back to 1571. See *Arbuthnot Leasing International Ltd v Havelot Leasing & Ors (No 2)* [1990] BCC 636; *Menzies v National Bank of Kuwait SAK*, above; *Chohan v Saggar* [1994] BCC 134; *Agricultural Mortgage Corp plc v Woodward*, above.

[446] Section 425 specifies orders which can be made in respect of a transaction defrauding creditors (such specific provision to be without prejudice to the general power of the court).

[447] Section 239.

(1)   that person is one of the company's creditors or a surety or guarantor for any of the company's debts or other liabilities; and

(2)   the company does anything or suffers anything to be done which (in either case) has the effect of putting that person into a position which, in the event of the company going into insolvent liquidation, will be better than the position he would have been in if that thing had not been done.

These elements of the definition of preference must be determined objectively: a preference arises in the event that the objective effect referred to occurs. However, the court may not make an order to reverse the preference unless the company which gave the preference was influenced in deciding to give it by a desire to put the recipient in a better position in an insolvent liquidation than he would have been in if the preference had not been given.

A desire to prefer is narrower than intention in that a person may be held to have 'intended' the necessary consequences of his acts even though he does not desire them to happen: to be held to have desired it, the company must be shown positively to have wished to improve the creditor's position in its insolvent liquidation. A company is 'influenced' by a desire to prefer where it is a motivating factor, but it need not be the only or the predominant one.[448] The desire must be present at the time when the preference is given.[449]

Where the preference is given to a person connected with the company (otherwise than by reason only of being its employee) at the time that the preference was given then the company is presumed, unless the contrary is shown, to have been influenced in deciding to give the preference by the requisite desire.[450]

A company may be held to have given a preference by giving an unsecured creditor a security over the company's assets. However, in a case such as *Re M C Bacon*, where the debenture was granted to avert the calling-in of the company's overdraft and the immediate liquidation which would have followed if the bank had withdrawn its support, the requisite desire to prefer may not be established. Another example of a possible preference is the decision to pay some debts but not others: the creditors whose debts are paid are obviously placed in a much better position than those who remain unpaid and who become subject to the moratorium in

---

[448]   *Re MC Bacon*, above; *Re D K G Contractors Ltd* [1990] BCC 903; *Re Beacon Leisure Ltd* [1991] BCC 213, [1992] BCLC 565; *Re Fairway Magazines Ltd* [1992] BCC 924, [1993] BCLC 643; *Re Agriplant Services Ltd* [1997] BCC 842.

[449]   *Wills v Corfe Joinery Ltd* [1997] BCC 511.

[450]   Section 239(6). See, eg, *Katz v McNally* [1999] BCC 291 (CA). See also *Re Brian D Pierson (Contractors) Ltd* [2000] 1 BCLC 275. See also, *Re Thirty-Eight Building Ltd* [1999] BCC 260 (trustees of employees' pension scheme were not within the connected person category).

administration or, as the case may be, become obliged to prove for their debts in the company's liquidation.[451]

The fact that something has been done in pursuance of an order of the court does not prevent that thing from constituting the giving of a preference. This provision is intended to prevent, for example, the company submitting to a judgment against itself by the person to be preferred and then arguing that it had no choice in giving the preference because of the judgment.

The preference is vulnerable only if it was given at a relevant time. This means, in the case of a preference given to a person who is connected with the company (otherwise and by reason only of being its employee), a period of 2 years ending with the onset of the administration or liquidation. In the case of a preference which is not given to a person connected with the company then the relevant period is 6 months ending with the onset of the administration or liquidation. In addition, the time between the presentation of a petition for the making of an administration order and the making of such order is a relevant time. A time will be a relevant time, however, only if the company is unable to pay its debts within the meaning of s 123 of the Act when the preference is given or becomes unable to pay its debts within the meaning of that section in consequence of the preference (but there is no presumption as to such inability even in relation to connected persons).

The same definition of the onset of the administration or liquidation applies as in the case of transactions at an undervalue.

21.57.4 Court orders in respect of transactions at an undervalue and preferences

The court is given a very wide discretion to make orders for the purpose of restoring the position to what it would have been if the company had not entered into the transaction or preference.

The proceeds of an action to set aside a preference are held by the office-holder for the benefit of its general creditors and do not fall within the scope of a floating charge on its assets.[452] The reasoning underlying this is that the power to attack a preference is granted only to the

---

[451] As in *Katz v McNally*, above, where debts owing to members of the family that controlled the company were repaid. See also, *Re Brian D Pierson (Contractors) Ltd*, above, where bank loans were repaid in order to reduce the exposure of directors under personal guarantees that they had given to the bank.

[452] *Re Yagerphone* [1935] 1 Ch 392. This ratio in the case was that payment of a debt due to an unsecured creditor prior to crystallisation bound the debenture holder but Bennett J's obiter statement as to the application of the proceeds recovered on a preference claim is widely regarded as correct: see *Re M C Bacon Ltd (No 2)* [1991] Ch 127, at 137. See also *Re Floor Fourteen Ltd, Lewis v IRC* [2001] 3 All ER 499; *Re Oasis Merchandising Services Ltd, Ward v Aitken* [1997] 1 All ER 1009.

liquidator and administrator and is not available to the company itself; therefore the proceeds of an action in respect of a preference cannot be the subject of a charge granted by the company on its assets and they are held separately by the administrator or liquidator for the benefit of unsecured creditors.[453]

The Act[454] specifically states that the provisions relating to transactions at an undervalue and preferences apply without prejudice to the availability of any other remedy, even in relation to a transaction or preference which the company had no power to enter into or to give.

21.57.5   *Extortionate credit transactions*

A liquidator or administrator may apply to the court in respect of an extortionate credit transaction which was entered into within 3 years of the date of the administration order or, as the case may be, when the company went into liquidation.[455]

A transaction is extortionate if, having regard to the risk accepted by the person providing the credit:

(1)   the terms of it are or were such as to require a grossly exorbitant payment to be made (whether unconditionally or in certain contingencies) in respect of the provision of the credit; or

(2)   it otherwise grossly contravened ordinary principles of fair dealing.

It is to be presumed, unless the contrary is proved, that a transaction is extortionate.

An order in respect of an extortionate credit transaction may contain one or more of the following, as the court thinks fit:

(1)   provision setting aside the whole or part of any obligation created by the transaction;

(2)   provision otherwise varying the terms of the transaction or varying the terms on which any security for the purposes of the transaction is held;

---

[453]   Wheeler 'Swelling the Assets for Distribution in Corporate Insolvency' [1993] JBL 256; but see now R Parry 'The Destination of Proceeds of Insolvency Litigation' (2002) 23 *Company lawyer* 49; A Keay 'Another way of skinning a cat: Enforcing directors' duties for the benefit of creditors' [2004] *Insolvency Intelligence* 1. See generally McCormack 'Swelling Corporate Assets: Changing what is on the menu' (2006) 6 *Journal of Corporate Law* Studies 39–69.

[454]   Section 241(4).

[455]   Section 244.

(3) provision requiring any person who is or was a party to the transaction to pay to the office-holder any sums paid to that person, by virtue of the transaction, by the company;

(4) provision requiring any person to surrender to the administrator or liquidator any property held by him as security for the purposes of the transaction; and

(5) provision directing accounts to be taken between any persons.

The power to attack any transaction as being extortionate may be exercised concurrently with any other powers exercisable in relation to that transaction.

21.57.6 *Avoidance of floating charges*

Floating charges created by the company within a specified period prior to the commencement of the administration or the liquidation (a 'relevant time') will be invalid[456] except to the extent of the aggregate of:

(1) the value of so much of the consideration for the creation of the charge as consists of money paid or goods or services supplied to the company at the same time as, or after, the creation of the charge. The value of any goods or services supplied by way of consideration for a floating charge is deemed to be the amount in money which at the time that they were supplied could reasonably have been expected to be obtained for supplying the goods or services in the ordinary course of business and on the same terms (apart from the consideration) as those on which they were supplied to the company;[457]

(2) the value of so much of that consideration as consists of the discharge or reduction, at the same time as, or after, the creation of the charge of any debt of the company;[458]

(3) the amount of such interest (if any) as is payable on the amount falling within para (1) or (2) in pursuance of any agreement under

---

[456] Section 245.

[457] Section 245(6).

[458] This would appear to reverse the decision in *Re Destone Fabrics Ltd* [1941] Ch 319. Section 245 preserves (contrary to the recommendations of the Review Committee on Insolvency Law and Practice, Cmnd 8558 (1982), paras 1561–1562) the decision in *Re Yeovil Glove Co Ltd* [1965] Ch 148, whereby in respect of a floating charge created in favour of a bank to secure an overdrawn account, if payments are made into the account after the creation of the charge, these will, under the rule in *Clayton's Case* (1816) 1 Mer 572, go to reduce the pre-charge indebtedness, so that cheques drawn on the account after the creation of the charge will be money paid to the company thereafter and the charge will therefore be valid to this extent.

which the money was so paid, the goods or services were so supplied or the debt was so discharged or reduced.

The phrase 'at the same time as' which is used in s 245 was considered by the Court of Appeal in *Re Shoe Lace Ltd*.[459] Not following authorities on a statutory predecessor to s 245,[460] the Court of Appeal held that whether the consideration for the charge was given at the same time as the creation of the charge is a mechanical issue determined solely by the clock, subject only to *de minimis* delays.

In *Re Fairway Magazines Ltd*,[461] the company was indebted to its bank and this debt was personally guaranteed by one of its directors. As part of a series of measures designed to keep the company alive, the director lent sums of money to the company which, at his request, were paid directly into the company's overdrawn bank account. A debenture was granted to the director as security for these advances. The effect of paying the borrowed money into the company's bank account was to reduce the director's personal liability under the guarantee. This led to a corresponding reduction in the amount for which the director would be required to lodge a proof in the liquidation of the company in respect of his payments under the guarantee. Instead, to the extent of the reduction of his exposure as an unsecured creditor, the director became a secured creditor.

Mummery J held that payments made by the director which were paid into the company's bank account were not in substance paid to the company for its benefit, since the effect of the payments was merely to substitute a secured debt for an unsecured debt. Therefore, the arrangement was avoided by s 245 because the payments were not 'paid ... to the company' as required by s 245(1)(a).[462]

A floating charge is created at a relevant time if:

(1) in the case of a floating charge created in favour of a person who is connected with the company it is created at a time in the period of 2 years ending with the onset of insolvency;

(2) where the floating charge is not created in favour of a person connected with the company, it is created at a time in the period of 12 months ending with the onset of insolvency; or

---

[459] [1993] BCC 609 (also reported as *Power v Sharp Investments Ltd*).

[460] *Re Columbian Fireproofing Co Ltd* [1910] 2 Ch 120 and *Re F & E Stanton Ltd* [1929] 1 Ch 180, which had held that a delay between the creation of the charge and the giving of consideration would not bring a charge within the scope of the section if the person seeking to uphold the charge could establish a good reason for the delay.

[461] [1992] BCC 924, [1993] BCLC 643.

[462] *Re Orleans Motor Co Ltd* [1911] 2 Ch 41; *Re Matthew Ellis Ltd* [1933] Ch 458; *Re GT Whyte & Co Ltd* [1983] BCLC 311.

(3) in any case it is created at a time between the presentation of a petition for the making of an administration order in relation to the company and the making of such an order on that petition.

In addition, in a case where the floating charge is created in favour of a person who is not connected with the company then the company must at that time be unable to pay its debts within the meaning of s 123 of the Act or become unable to pay its debts within the meaning of that section in consequence of the transaction under which the charge is created.

The definition of the onset of the insolvency for the purpose of s 245 is the same as for transactions at an undervalue.

21.58 Other powers

The Insolvency Act 1986 contains various powers which office-holders and other insolvency practitioners[463] can call upon to assist them in their task of collecting in the assets of the company for the benefit of the creditors. The powers are extensive: in *Re British & Commonwealth Holdings plc (No 2)*,[464] Woolf LJ described the powers contained in Part IV of the Act as 'a remarkable armoury of summary weapons with which to assist "office-holders" ... to perform their functions'.

In outline the relevant powers include the following:

(1) A power to get in the company's property. Under s 234 of the Act, where a person has in his possession or control any property, books, papers or records to which the company appears to be entitled, the court may require that person to pay, deliver, convey, surrender or transfer the same to the office-holder. An office-holder for this purpose means an administrator, an administrative receiver, a liquidator or a provisional liquidator.

(2) Under s 235, specified persons can be compelled to give to the office-holder any information concerning the company and its promotion, formation, business dealings or affairs generally and may be required to attend on the liquidator at such times as he may reasonably require. The persons who have this duty to co-operate with the office-holder include the existing and former officers of the company and also those who have been its employees in the past year.

---

[463] Nominees under voluntary arrangements and the Official Receiver are not generally regarded as office-holders, but the Official Receiver is an office-holder for the purposes of ss 235 and 236. See now *Re Pantmaenog Timber Co Ltd* [2004] 1 AC 158.

[464] [1992] Ch 342, [1992] 2 All ER 801, [1992] 2 WLR 931, [1992] BCLC 641, [1992] BCC 165 and 172; affirmed sub nom *British and Commonwealth Holdings (Joint Administrators) v Spicer and Oppenheim* [1993] AC 426, [1992] 4 All ER 876, [1992] 3 WLR 853, [1993] BCLC 168, [1992] BCC 977.

If a person fails in his duty to co-operate under s 235 he is liable to a fine. In addition to those who are office-holders under s 234, the Official Receiver is also an office-holder in this case.

(3)   Power to apply to court for an examination of certain persons.[465] The office-holders who have this power are administrators, administrative receivers, liquidators and provisional liquidators, and also the Official Receiver. Examinations under this power, which is conferred by s 236, are private. In compulsory liquidations, the Official Receiver also has power to apply to the court for public examinations.[466]

The court may on the application of an office-holder under s 236 summon to appear before it any officer of the company, any person known or suspected to have in his possession any property of the company or supposed to be indebted to the company, or any person whom the court thinks capable of giving information concerning the promotion, formation, business dealings, affairs or property of the company.[467]

21.59   Dissolution of companies

Section 201 of the Insolvency Act 1986 deals with the dissolution of a company which has been wound up voluntarily. Where the liquidator has filed his final accounts and returns,[468] the Registrar of Companies will put these on the company's file. On the expiration of 3 months from the registration of those returns the company is deemed to be dissolved. The court has power, on the application of the liquidator or any other interested party, to make an order that the dissolution of the company takes place at some later date if the court thinks fit.[469]

In a compulsory winding-up, the Official Receiver, if he is the liquidator of the company and believes that the realisable assets are insufficient to cover the expenses of the winding-up and that no further investigation of the company's affairs is required, may apply to the Registrar of Companies for the early dissolution of the company.[470] If the Official Receiver gives such a notice this is registered by the Registrar of

---

[465]   Section 236.

[466]   Section 133. See *Re Wallace Smith Trust Co Ltd* [1992] BCC 707. This power has extra-territorial effect; *Re Seagull Manufacturing Co Ltd* [1993] Ch 345, [1993] 2 All ER 980, [1993] 2 WLR 872, [1993] BCLC 1139, [1993] BCC 241. Note *Re Campbell Coverings Ltd (No 2)* [1954] Ch 225 where it was held that the power to apply for a public examination applies to voluntary liquidations. In *Bishopsgate Investment Management Ltd v Maxwell* [1993] Ch 1, [1992] 2 All ER 856, [1992] 2 WLR 991, [1992] BCC 222, the point was not decided but the Court of Appeal accepted that a public examination might be available in a voluntary liquidation by virtue of s 112.

[467]   Section 236(2).

[468]   Section 94 (members' voluntary); s 106 (creditors' voluntary).

[469]   Section 201(3).

[470]   Section 202(2).

Companies. At the expiry of 3 months from the date of registration of the notice the company is dissolved. Where a notice has been given by the Official Receiver in this respect, any creditor or contributory of the company or any administrative receiver may apply to the Secretary of State for a direction if he considers that:

(1) the realisable assets of the company are sufficient to cover the expenses of the winding-up;

(2) the affairs of the company do require further investigation; or

(3) for any other reason the early dissolution of the company is inappropriate.[471]

The Secretary of State may give directions enabling the winding-up of the company to proceed as if the Official Receiver had not given a notice requiring the early dissolution of the company to the Registrar of Companies. His powers in this respect include the power to make a direction deferring the date at which the dissolution of the company is to take effect.[472]

Where in a compulsory winding-up no application is made by the Official Receiver for an early dissolution, the provisions of s 205 of the Insolvency Act 1986 apply. When the liquidator has filed his final returns or the Official Receiver has filed a notice stating that he considers the winding-up to be complete, the Registrar of Companies will register those returns or the notice as the case may be. At the end of a 3-month period beginning with the date of that registration the company is dissolved.[473]

Again, the Official Receiver or any other person interested in the company's dissolution may apply to the Secretary of State for a direction deferring the date of the dissolution.[474]

When a company is dissolved, its corporate existence ceases. It no longer has any officers or agents who can be served with notices or other proceedings on behalf of the company. It is not infrequently the case, however, that there are persons who have grievances or claims involving the company which they still wish to enforce.

There is now the possibility of administrative restoration to the register of companies by the registrar of companies on application being made by a former director or member.[475] Various conditions have to be satisfied

---

[471] Section 203(2).

[472] Section 203(3).

[473] Section 205(2).

[474] Section 205(3), with a right of appeal to the court if the Secretary of State refuses to grant a deferral.

[475] Section 1024 of the Companies Act 2006.

including the application being made within 6 years of the dissolution. The general effect of a restoration to the register is that the company is deemed to have continued in existence as if it had not been dissolved or struck off the register. If the statutory requirements for administrative restoration have not been satisfied there is the option of applying to the court for an order for restoration of the company to the register.[476] The facility is available to a wider range of persons including the liquidator and any other person who appears to be interested in the order that the court might make. It has been stated that, ordinarily, the purposes of restoring a company to the register are to enable the liquidator to distribute an overlooked asset or a creditor to make a claim which he has not previously made.[477] The jurisdiction can be used to put a creditor in a better position than he would otherwise have been in.[478]

Generally, such applications must not be made after the end of the period of 6 years from the date of dissolution of the company, but applications for the purpose of bringing proceedings against the company for damages for personal injuries or under the Fatal Accidents Act 1976 may be brought at any time subject to any applicable limitation periods.[479]

Once a company is dissolved, all property and rights whatsoever which may still be vested in or held on trust for the company immediately before its dissolution (including leasehold property, but not including property held by the company on trust for any other person) are deemed to be *bona vacantia*[480] and vest in the Crown, subject to its right to disclaim. Section 1013 of the Companies Act 2006 lays down the conditions upon which such disclaimer may be made by the Crown.

21.60   Defunct companies

Aside from winding-up, a company may also cease to exist if it is struck off the register in accordance with the procedures contained in ss 1000-1011 of the Companies Act 2006. The Registrar of Companies can activate the striking-off procedure[481] or a private company, acting through its directors, can apply to the registrar for striking off.[482]Where the registrar has activated the striking-off powers, there is provision for administrative restoration to the register on application to the registrar.[483] More generally, provision is also made for the restoration to the register by order of the court of any company struck off under any procedure. An

---

[476]   Section 1030 of the Companies Act 2006.

[477]   *Re Forte's Manufacturing Ltd* [1994] BCC 84, at 87, per Hoffmann LJ.

[478]   Ibid.

[479]   Section 1030. The court has power to direct that the period between the dissolution of the company and the making of the order under the section shall not count for limitation purposes: s 1030(3).

[480]   Section 1012 of the Companies Act 2006.

[481]   Section 1000.

[482]   Section 1003.

[483]   Section 1024.

application to the court may be made by specified persons including members and creditors of that company.[484] If a company is dissolved by being struck off the register, its property becomes *bona vacantia* vesting in the Crown.[485]

21.61　International Insolvency

Traditionally, an English winding up has, in the eyes of English law, worldwide or universal effect and applies to all assets of the company wherever those assets are situated[486] though of course there may be practical problems in securing recognition of the English winding up in the foreign jurisdiction where the corporate assets are located.[487] The universality of insolvency proceedings was discussed in *Cambridge Gas Transport Corporation v Official Committee of Unsecured Creditors (of Navigator Holdings Plc)*[488] where Lord Hoffmann said:

> 'The English common law has traditionally taken the view that fairness between creditors requires that, ideally, bankruptcy proceedings should have universal application. There should be a single bankruptcy in which all creditors are entitled and required to prove. No one should have an advantage because he happens to live in a jurisdiction where more of the assets or fewer of the creditors are situated.'

Lord Hoffmann suggested that the doctrine of universality of bankruptcy or liquidation proceedings may owe something to the fact that 18th and 19th century Britain:[489]

> 'was an imperial power, trading and financing development all over the world. It was often the case that the principal creditors were in Britain but many of the debtor's assets were in foreign jurisdictions. Universality of

---

[484]　Section 1029. The procedure was changed somewhat by the Companies Act 2006 and for a background discussion to the reforms see Company Law Review, *Final Report*, vol 1 (2001), paras 11.17–11.20.

[485]　Section 1012.

[486]　See the comments of Wynn-Parry J in *Re Azoff-Don Commercial Bank* [1954] Ch 315 at 333 and Browne-Wilkinson VC in *Re Bank of Credit and Commerce International SA (No 2)* [1992] BCLC 570 at 577.

[487]　It may also be noted that now under reg 28 of the Cross Border Insolvency Regulations 2006, SI 2006/1030, domestic insolvency proceedings opened up after foreign main proceedings have been recognised are limited to the domestic assets of the company.

[488]　[2007] 1 AC 508 at para 16 of the judgment. See also Lord Hoffmann in *Re HIH Casualty and General Insurance Ltd* [2008] I WLR 852 referring to the principle of modified universalism as the 'golden thread' running through English cross-border insolvency law since the 18th century.

[489]　At para 17. Lord Hoffmann said that in corporate insolvency there is no question of recognising a vesting of the company's assets in some other person. They remain the assets of the company. But the underlying principle of universality was of equal application and this was given effect by recognising the person who was empowered under the foreign bankruptcy law to act on behalf of the insolvent company as entitled to do so in England.

bankruptcy protected the position of British creditors. Not all countries took the same view. Countries less engaged in international commerce and finance did not always see it as being in their interest to allow foreign creditors to share equally with domestic creditors. But universality of bankruptcy has long been an aspiration, if not always fully achieved, of United Kingdom law. And with increasing world trade and globalisation, many other countries have come round to the same view.'

It should be noted that English courts have jurisdiction to wind up companies not registered under the Companies Acts (including foreign companies) under Part V of the Insolvency Act. Section 221(5) grants the court the authority to make a winding up order:

(1)   if the company is dissolved, or has ceased to carry on business, or is carrying on business only for the purpose of winding up its affairs; or

(2)   if the company is unable to pay its debts; or

(3)   if the court if of opinion that it is just and equitable that the company shall be wound up.

Section 225 supplements this by providing that where a company incorporated outside Great Britain which has been carrying on business in Great Britain, ceases to carry on business in Great Britain, it may be wound up as an unregistered company notwithstanding that it has been dissolved or otherwise ceased to exist as a company under or by virtue of the laws of the country under which it was incorporated.

It seems that at common law English courts have a wide discretion to provide assistance to a foreign insolvency proceeding by doing whatever is considered to be just and appropriate in all the circumstances of the particular case.[490] An English court can assist a foreign court by treating any liquidation in England as being ancillary to one that is taking place in the company's place of incorporation. This means the powers of the English liquidator are limited to gathering the assets in England; paying off preferential and secured creditors and then remitting any remaining assets to the principal liquidation.[491] The relevant principles were summarised as follows by Scott VC in *Re Bank of Credit and Commerce International SA (No 10)*:[492]

'(1)   Where a foreign company is in liquidation in its country of incorporation, a winding up order made in England will normally be

---

[490]   See *Jefferies International Ltd v Lansbanki Islands HF* [2009] EWHC 894 (Comm).

[491]   See *Banco Nacional de Cuba v Cosmos Trading Corp* [2000] BCC 910 at 915. See also Lord Hoffmann in *Re HIH Casualty and General Insurance Ltd* [2008] 1 WLR 852 at para 19 and Lord Neuberger at para 75.

[492]   [1997] Ch 213 at 239–240.

regarded as giving rise to a winding up ancillary to that being conducted in the country of incorporation.

(2)   The winding up in England will be ancillary in the sense that it will not be within the power of the English liquidators to get in and realize all the assets of the company worldwide. They will necessarily have to concentrate on getting in and realizing the English assets.

(3)   Since in order to achieve a pari passu distribution between all the company's creditors it will be necessary for there to be a pooling of the company's assets worldwide and for a dividend to be declared out of the assets comprised in that pool, the winding up in England will be ancillary in the sense, also, that it will be the liquidators in the principal liquidation who will be best placed to declare the dividend and to distribute the assets in the pool accordingly.

(4)   Nonetheless, the ancillary character of an English winding up does not relieve an English court of the obligation to apply English law, including English insolvency law, to the resolution of any issue arising in the winding up which is brought before the court. It may be, of course, that English conflicts of law rules will lead to the application of some foreign law principle in order to resolve a particular issue.'

An English ancillary liquidation is conducted in accordance with English insolvency rules in deciding, for example, what proofs can be admitted and what counts as a preferential debt but once secured and preferential debts have been paid off it is common to remit the remaining assets to the jurisdiction where the principal liquidation is taking place. In *Re HIH Casualty and General Insurance Ltd*[493] the question arose whether this power to remit assets should be exercised where the foreign law of distribution did not coincide with English law. The case concerned the liquidation of an Australian insurance company where the assets of the company would be distributed on a different basis from that in an English liquidation to the disadvantage of certain creditors.[494] The request to transfer assets came from an Australian court pursuant to s 426 of the Insolvency Act 1986 and the House of Lords held that it could make the transfer under the statute but a majority was not prepared to do so at common law because the Australian order of distribution of assets was different from that in England. Australia however, was a designated country for s 426 purposes and the court held that there was nothing unacceptably discriminatory or otherwise contrary to public policy in the Australian insolvency provisions. Lord Neuberger said a fundamental principle of English insolvency law would not be offended or unfairness perpetrated by the application of the Australian insolvency regime.[495]

---

[493] [2008] 1 WLR 852; on appeal from *Re HIH Casualty and General Insurance Ltd* [2007] 1 All ER 177.

[494] Under Australian law insurance creditors were treated better and non-insurance creditors worse than under English law. As Lord Hoffmann pointed out at para 32 English law has now adopted a regime for the winding-up of insurance companies which gives preference to insurance creditors – reg 21(2) of the Insurers (Reorganisation and Winding Up) Regulations 2004, SI 2004/353 giving effect to Directive 2001/17/EC on the reorganisation and winding up of insurance companies.

[495] [2008] 1 WLR 852 at para 80.

Apart from the EU Regulation on Insolvency Proceedings, s 426 of the
Insolvency Act 1986 is one of two other statutory vehicles in the UK for
international co-operation in insolvency matters. The section provides
that a court having insolvency jurisdiction in any part of the UK shall
assist the courts having the corresponding jurisdiction in any other part of
the UK or any relevant country or territory.[496] The statutory duty of
assistance applies however only as between courts and therefore the UK
court must have received a request from a foreign court before it can act.
A request from a foreign court gives the UK court authority to apply: (a)
its general equitable and statutory jurisdiction; (b) UK insolvency law; or
(c) the insolvency law of the requesting court.[497]

The EU Regulation on Insolvency Proceedings (Council Regulation 1346/
2000/EC) gives a UK court jurisdiction to wind up any company whose
centre of main interests is in the UK even though the company may be
incorporated elsewhere. The Regulation has provided a useful measure of
harmonisation among EU Member States with regard to the jurisdiction
to open insolvency proceedings and the recognition of insolvency
proceedings. A less ambitious international initiative is the 1997
UNCITRAL Model Law on Cross-Border Insolvency,[498] which has been
incorporated into domestic UK law by the Cross-Border Insolvency
Regulations 2006 under enabling powers conferred by s 14 Insolvency
Act 2000. The provisions of the Cross-Border Insolvency Regulations 2006 track those of the Model Law fairly closely.

The purpose of the Model Law is not to displace national provisions to
the extent that they provide assistance that is additional to, or different
from, the type of assistance dealt with in the Model Law.[499] In framing
the Cross-Border Insolvency Regulations, it was decided to avoid making
any changes to s 426 Insolvency Act 1986 particularly because only a
relatively small number of countries have been designated for s 426
purposes and these appear to have been chosen because of their
analogous common law background. Section 426 continues to operate
and it would be open to a foreign insolvency representative in a designated
country to ask his local court to make a 's 426' request for assistance

---

[496] Section 426(4) uses the crucial words 'shall assist'. Certain countries and territories have
been designated by the Co-operation of Insolvency Courts (Designation of Relevant
Countries and Territories) Order 1986, SI 1986/2123, as amended by SI 1996/253 and
SI 1998/2766. These consist of Commonwealth countries and territories with the
addition of the Republic of Ireland and Hong Kong but excluding the United States.

[497] See Morritt LJ in *Hughes v Hannover Rucksversicherungs-AG* [1997] BCC 921 at
932–938.

[498] See generally on the Model Law, I Fletcher, Insolvency in Private International Law
(Oxford, OUP, 2nd ed 2005) chap 8; A Berends 'UNCITRAL Model Law on
Cross-Border Insolvency: A Comprehensive Overview' (1998) 6 Tulane Journal of
International and Comparative Law 309; J Clift 'The UNCITRAL Model Law on
Cross-Border Insolvency – A Legislative Framework to Facilitate Coordination and
Cooperation in Cross-Border Insolvency' (2004) 12 Tulane Journal of International and
Comparative Law 307.

[499] Article 7.

rather himself using the provisions of the Model Law and the Cross-Border Insolvency Regulations in respect of recognition of the foreign insolvency proceedings etc. As a result of the Regulations, the UK is well equipped with statutory vehicles for international/cross-border cooperation in insolvency matters plus, of course, the common law to the extent that it has not been superseded in relation to particular matters.

21.62 EU insolvency regulation

The EU Regulation on Insolvency Proceedings (Council Regulation 1346/2000/EC) applies in all the EU member states, except Denmark which exercised an 'opt-out'. It applies to collective insolvency proceedings involving the partial or total disinvestment of the debtor and the appointment of a liquidator (Art 1). The expression 'liquidator' in the context of the Regulation has a far broader meaning than it does under domestic law. In the Regulation setting 'liquidator' means any person or body whose function it is to administer or liquidate assets of which the debtor has been divested or to supervise the administration of his affairs. In particular the expression includes administrators and supervisors of company voluntary arrangements.

There are many oddities and incongruities of language throughout the Regulation. It is specifically stated to apply to the collective proceedings listed in Annex A even though company voluntary arrangements, for example, do not necessarily entail the partial or total divestment of a debtor. For the UK the procedures listed in Annex A are:

(a) winding-up by or subject to the supervision of the court;

(b) creditors' voluntary winding-up (with confirmation by the court);

(c) administration;

(d) voluntary arrangements under insolvency legislation;

(e) bankruptcy or sequestration.

A creditors' voluntary winding-up, which is the most convenient form of winding-up in practice, does not invariably involve confirmation by the court, but there is a facility under the widely drafted s 112 of the Insolvency Act 1986 whereby court confirmation may be sought and it is likely that this will become a matter of routine where the liquidation potentially involves foreign assets. There is also a new procedure under the Insolvency Rules whereby application can be made to the court to 'confirm' a creditors' voluntary winding-up for the purposes of the EU Regulation.[500]

---

[500] See Insolvency Rules 1986, rr 7.62, 7.63 as inserted by Insolvency (Amendment)

The aim of the Regulation is that the opening of main insolvency proceedings in a member state should have immediate and universal effect throughout the European Union (Art 3(1)).

21.62.1   What constitutes the opening of insolvency proceedings

The Court of Justice of the European Union (CJEU) has considered what constitutes the opening of insolvency proceedings in *Re Eurofood ISFC Ltd*[501] on a reference from the Supreme Court of Ireland. The CJEU looked to the definition of 'insolvency proceedings' under Art 1(1) of the Regulation which refers to four characteristics:

(1)   collective proceedings;

(2)   based on the debtor's insolvency;

(3)   entailing at least partial divestment of the debtor; and

(4)   involving the appointment of a liquidator.

These forms of proceedings were listed in Annex A to the Regulation and the list of liquidators appeared in Annex C. In the entry for Ireland, 'provisional liquidators' appear though not originally for the UK.[502] The court pointed out that where there is a decision to open insolvency proceedings based on the centre of the debtor's main interests in one member state, that decision has immediate and universal effects throughout the EU. Only one main set of insolvency proceedings could be opened, and it was necessary to avoid a situation of uncertainty in which two or more states claimed concurrent jurisdiction. Consequently, the court said 'a "decision to open insolvency proceedings" for the purposes of the Regulation must be regarded as including not only a decision which is formally described as an opening decision by the legislation regulating the court that handed it down, but also a decision handed down following an application, based on the debtor's insolvency, seeking the opening of proceedings referred to in Annex A to the Regulation, where that decision involves divestment of the debtor and the appointment of a liquidator referred to in Annex C to the Regulation'.

Rules 2002. On this see *Re TXU Europe German Ltd* [2005] BCC 90 where an order was made confirming resolutions which had been passed for a creditors' winding up of two companies incorporated in Ireland and Holland that had their centre of main interests in England. The court was satisfied that in Ireland and Holland there was a procedure equivalent to that of the special resolution and moreover, the equivalent of the Registrar of Companies in both countries was prepared to recognise the winding up for the purpose of the dissolution of the companies.

[501] [2006] Ch 508.
[502] But this matter has now been rectified in the light of earlier proceedings in the *Eurofoods* case.

In *Re Straubitz-Schreiber*[503] the CJEU held that the court of the member state where the centre of the debtor's main interests is situated at the time when the debtor lodges the request to open insolvency proceedings, retains jurisdiction to open those proceedings if the debtor moves the centre of his main interests to the territory of another state, after lodging the request but before the proceedings are opened. The court was of the opinion that retaining the jurisdiction of the first court seised ensured greater judicial certainty for creditors. While this view seems eminently sensible, it depends more on a purposive rather than a literal interpretation of Art 3 of the Regulation.

21.62.2 *Jurisdiction to open main insolvency proceedings*

Jurisdiction to open insolvency proceedings is given to the State in whose territory the centre of the debtor's main interests is situated (Art 3). These proceedings are intended to have universal effect and application, although subject to a whole host of enumerated exceptions. There is a presumption that the centre of main interests of a company or other legal person is at the place of the registered office. The Regulation seems to make the assumption that the area of greatest economic activity of a bankrupt will be in the state where the bulk of assets and liabilities exist, but this may not be the case. The 'centre of main interests' (COMI) expression is one that is capable of varying judicial interpretation. It is questionable whether any greater certainty is introduced by the statement in Recital 13 of the preamble to the Regulation that the centre of main interest 'should correspond to the place where the debtor conducts the administration of his interests on a regular basis and is therefore ascertainable by third parties'. On a purely pragmatic level, however, the courts in a member state that are first seised of an insolvency matter may well be inclined to assert jurisdiction. In cases of doubt, therefore, it behoves a party whose personal interests would be best served by the opening of proceedings in a particular member state to initiate insolvency proceedings in that state even though it is debatable where the debtor's centre of main interests are situated.

The English courts have adopted an expansive approach to jurisdiction under the Regulation. In *Re Daisytek-ISA Ltd*,[504] Daisytek-ISA Ltd was the holding company of a group of trading companies – including French and German-incorporated subsidiaries – and the question arose whether an English court had jurisdiction to make an administration order in respect of each of the companies on the basis that their centre of main

---

[503] [2006] ECR I-701.

[504] [2003] BCC 562. The decision of the English High Court opening insolvency proceedings in *Daisytek* was ultimately recognised by the Court of Appeal of Versailles and the final French Court of Appeal – the Court de Cassation; on this see *Klempka v ISA Daisytek SA* [2003] BCC 984 and *France v Klempka* [2006] BCC 841. For a general discussion see G Moss and M Haravon '"Building Europe" – The French Case Law on COMI' (2007) 20 *Insolvency Intelligence* 20.

interests was in England, notwithstanding the foreign incorporation. It was held that the court was required to consider the scale of the interests administered at a particular place and their importance and then to consider the scale and importance of its interests administered at any other place that might be regarded as its centre of main interests. On the evidence he took the view that the majority of the group's administration was conducted from its head office in Bradford and, therefore, England was the centre of main interests for each subsidiary within the group. In determining the centre of main interests of each subsidiary, he held that the most important 'third parties' referred to in Recital 13 are the potential creditors.[505]

In *Re BRAC Rent-A-Car International Inc,*[506] it was held that an English court had jurisdiction under the Regulation to grant an administration order in respect of a non-EU company where its centre of main interests was in England. In this case the company was incorporated in Delaware in the United States but it had no employees in the United States. All of its employees worked in England with contracts of employment governed by English law apart from a small number in a branch office in Switzerland. All the company's trading activities were carried out by way of contracts with subsidiaries and franchisees that were governed by English law. Lloyd J decided that in the circumstances an English court had jurisdiction. In his view, by dint of both a literal reading and also a purposive interpretation of the Regulation, the only test for the application of the Regulation in relation to a given debtor is whether the centre of the debtor's main interests is in a relevant member state and where a debtor that is a legal person is incorporated.

There are decisions however where the English courts have declined jurisdiction such as *Hans Brochier Holdings Ltd v Exner*[507] where it was decided that the centre of main interests of an English incorporated company was in Germany. The main creditors of the company were located in Germany and these creditors regarded the company as operating out of Germany and fully expected any insolvency proceedings to take place in Germany. HBH had over 700 employees in Germany and only a few in England. Moreover, almost all the company employees were employed in Germany and under contracts of employment governed by German law. Warren J also pointed out that there were perceived benefits accruing if the main proceedings were in Germany. There was a large advantage in relation to German social security law, which would give the employees a significant advantage as compared with an English administration and only an experienced German insolvency administrator would be able adequately to address those rights and interests. The company's entire business operations were run out of its German

---

[505] See also *Re Enron Direct* [2003] BPIR 1132 and *Geveran Trading Co Ltd v Skjevesland* [2003] BCC 209.
[506] [2003] 2 All ER 201.
[507] [2007] BCC 127.

headquarters so that all the relevant information and documents were located in Germany. The vast majority of these documents were in the German language and most of the legal and contractual relationships of the company were subject to German law.

In the *Eurofood* case the CJEU also considered the question of 'centre of main interests'. Eurofoods was an Irish-incorporated wholly owned subsidiary of Parmalat, a major global food company incorporated in Italy, and its principal business activity was that of providing financing facilities for companies in the Parmalat group. The company enjoyed tax benefits conditional upon it being managed and operated in Ireland. Moreover, the day-to-day administration of Eurofoods was conducted in Ireland in accordance with the terms of an agreement, which was governed by Irish law and which contained an Irish jurisdiction clause.

The CJEU said that the 'centre of main interests' concept had an autonomous meaning for the purpose of the Regulation and must be interpreted independently of national legislation. There was a presumption that the centre of main interests of a company was in the state where its registered office was located and this presumption applied even if the company had a parent company with a registered office in a different state. The presumption could only be rebutted:

> '... if factors which are both objective and ascertainable by third parties enable it to be established that an actual situation exists which is different from that which locating it at that registered office is deemed to reflect. That could be so in particular in the case of a company not carrying out any business in the territory of the Member State in which its registered office is situated. By contrast, where a company carries on its business in the territory of the Member State where its registered office is situated, the mere fact that its economic choices are or can be controlled by a parent company in another Member State is not enough to rebut the presumption laid down by the Regulation.'

The court referred to 'letter box' countries not carrying on any business in the countries where their registered offices were located. In these circumstances, the presumption of concordance between registered office and centre of main interests was easily rebutted, but not so more generally, unless there were factors that were both 'objective and ascertainable by third parties'.

The overall approach in *Eurofoods* seems somewhat different from the 'integrated economic unit' approach that English courts have appeared to follow when determining the centre of main interests of parent and subsidiary companies. The English courts have tended to look at the affairs of the group of companies as a whole, whereas the CJEU has concentrated the inquiry onto each individual company.

In *Re Lennox Holdings Ltd*,[508] Lewison J applied a 'head office functions' test in deciding that an English court had jurisdiction to enter main insolvency proceedings in respect of two companies whose registered offices were in Spain. He suggested that the particular examples given by the CJEU in *Eurofood* were at two opposite and extreme ends of the spectrum and the facts of most cases lie somewhere between these two extremes. For this reason, it was suggested that the approach of Advocate General Jacobs was a particularly helpful one.

Lewison J has since resiled from this view in *Re Stanford International Bank Ltd*.[509] He said that this approach was not consistent with the decision of the CJEU itself, which emphasised that COMI must be identified by reference to criteria that are both objective and ascertainable by third parties and that the presumption in favour of COMI coinciding with the company's registered office could only be rebutted by factors that are both objective and ascertainable by third parties.

> 'Simply to look at the place where head office functions are actually carried out, without considering whether the location of these functions is ascertainable by third parties, is the wrong test ... Pre-*Eurofood* decisions by English courts should no longer be followed in this respect'[510]

Lewison J took the view that an important purpose of COMI was to provide certainty and foreseeability for creditors of the company at the time they enter into a transaction. He looked at Recital 13 of the preamble to the EU Regulation and the statement of the CJEU that COMI has to be identified by reference to criteria that are objective and ascertainable by third parties. Information would only count as ascertainable if it was in the public domain. It was not enough that it would have been disclosed as an honest answer to a question asked by a third party. Lewison J suggested that there would be a quite unrealistic burden if every transaction had to be preceded by a set of inquiries to establish whether the underlying reality differed from the apparent facts. In the *Stanford* case it was held that the COMI of an Antiguan-registered corporation was in Antigua. Quite simply there was insufficient evidence to rebut the presumption but it is important to note that the case does not involve a 'letter box' company. The company clearly carried out economic activity in Antigua not least by reason of the facts that its physical headquarters were in Antigua and most of its employees were located there.

The decision of Lewison J was confirmed in the *Stanford* case on appeal.[511]

---

[508] [2009] BCC 155.

[509] [2009] BPIR 1157.

[510] [2009] BPIR 1157 at paras 61–63.

[511] [2011] Ch 211. See also G McCormack 'Reconstructing European Insolvency Law' (2010) 30 *Legal Studies* 126.

21.62.3 Jurisdiction to open secondary insolvency proceedings

Article 3(2) of the Regulation assigns jurisdiction to open secondary insolvency proceedings. The basis of jurisdiction in this situation is that there is an 'establishment' within the jurisdiction. In those circumstances insolvency proceedings may be commenced, but the scope must be confined to the assets situated within the member state. In other words, secondary insolvency proceedings have an exclusively territorial, as distinct from universal, effect. The opening of secondary proceedings may have the effect of safeguarding local preferential creditors whose claims would be regarded as non-preferential by the law of the main proceedings, and indeed this may be a prime motive for the institution of such proceedings. The jurisdictional crutch is a debtor's establishment and the latter is defined as meaning 'any place of operations where the debtor carries out a non-transitory economic activity with human means and goods'. It seems clear from this that the mere presence of assets within a particular jurisdiction is not sufficient for the assumption of jurisdiction. Nevertheless, the basis of jurisdiction is not cast iron and leaves ample leeway for local courts favourably disposed to local creditors. Park J, however, resisted the temptation to exercise jurisdiction in *Telia v Hillcourt*[512] and appeared to reject the proposition that the mere presence of business premises within the jurisdiction would constitute an 'establishment'.

21.62.4 Applicable law

The applicable law is the law governing insolvency in the state where the proceedings are opened (Art 4). The possibility of proceedings being started in two or more jurisdictions with differing laws applying means that conflicts between different priority rules will inevitably arise. An attempt to minimise these problems is made by restricting the 'effects' of secondary proceedings to the 'assets of the debtor situated in the territory' of the member state where secondary bankruptcy is opened (Art 27). There are often conflicts, however, concerning the *situs* of assets between the laws of different states and consequently this provision will not eliminate all difficulties. Article 4 sets out a number of matters which are specifically referred to the law governing the opening of the proceedings and which are both substantive and procedural in nature. These include:

(a)   the debtors against whom insolvency proceedings may be brought;

(b)   the assets which form part of the estate;

(c)   the powers of the liquidator;

---

[512] [2003] BCC 856. See, however, *Shierson v Vlieland-Boddy* [2005] BCC 949, where territorial secondary insolvency proceedings were opened under Art 3(2) of the Regulation.

(d)   the effects of insolvency on current contracts to which the debtor is a party;

(e)   rules governing the lodging, verification and admission of claims; and

(f)   priority ranking of creditors.

21.62.5   *Referrals to legal orders other than the law of the insolvency forum*

Notwithstanding the terms of Art 4, the law of the insolvency forum does not regulate all substantive and procedural matters pertaining to the insolvency proceedings. There are a number of specific referrals to other legal systems, which are set out in arts 5–15. Article 5, for example, recognises the rights of secured creditors with a valid claim to assets under the law of the place where the assets claimed are situated. This means that creditors can acquire security by complying with the conditions necessary in the law of the place where the prospectively secured assets are located, safe in the knowledge that their secured status will not be disturbed by the commencement of insolvency proceedings in another member state.[513] The effect of Art 6 is to preserve certain set-off rights. Article 4(2)(d) states that the law of the insolvency forum shall govern the conditions under which set-offs may be invoked, but set-off rights can still be claimed if they are permitted by the law applicable to the insolvent debtor's claim. It is clear from the *BCCI*[514] litigation that set-off rights differ significantly as between member states, and Art 6 is a valuable safeguard for creditors who have entered into certain transactions on the basis that set-off rights would be available. It should be noted that it is not the law of the creditor's claim (the 'active' claim) that governs the availability of set-off, but rather the law of the insolvent debtor's claim (the 'passive' claim) and the latter law may be the law of a non-EU member state.

Article 7 preserves seller's rights under reservation of title clauses where the assets in question are situated in a member state other than that of the insolvency forum. Article 8 reaffirms the generally accepted principle of private international law that questions of title to immovable property are governed exclusively by the *lex situs*. The effects of insolvency proceedings on contracts conferring the right to acquire or make use of immovable property are governed solely by the law of the member state within whose territory the immovable property is situated. Article 9 is aimed at protecting the integrity of payment systems and financial markets. It provides that the effects of insolvency proceedings on the rights and

---

[513] The wording of Art 5 would appear to accord recognition to the English floating charge.
[514] *Re Bank of Credit and Commerce International SA (No 10)* [1997] Ch 213.

obligations of the parties to a payment or settlement system or to a financial market shall be governed solely by the law of the member state applicable to that system or market.

It is provided in Art 10 that the effect of insolvency on employment contracts and relations shall be governed by the law applicable to the contract of employment. The preamble to the Regulation states that the purpose of this provision is to protect both employees and jobs. The intention is that the law applicable to the employment contract would determine, for example, whether liquidation operates to terminate or to continue employment contracts. Other important employment law-related matters are left to the law of the insolvency forum including the preferential status of employee claims in liquidation. It may be that the precise interrelationship between the two sets of provisions on the employment aspects of insolvency will require detailed working out.

21.62.6 *Recognition of insolvency proceedings*

Article 16 provides that insolvency proceedings, once validly commenced, shall be recognised in all other member states, with the proceedings having the effect they have in the state where the proceedings were commenced. If unqualified, this statement would import true universality. However, as already noted, it is subject to the right to open secondary insolvency proceedings. Implementation of the Regulation should promote the rescue culture since an administrator's powers will be recognised throughout the Community, and the stay on creditor enforcement actions will be equally recognised. On the other hand, the fact that secondary proceedings cannot include the debtor rehabilitation provisions of a particular jurisdiction may act as a significant impediment to the rescue culture. For example, an administrator who is trying to formulate and implement a rescue plan could find the plans frustrated by the actions of a group of creditors in a particular jurisdiction who take the view that a secondary liquidation in that jurisdiction would better serve their interests.

In *Eurofood*, the CJEU stressed that main insolvency proceedings opened by a court of a member state must be recognised by the courts of the other member states without the latter being able to review the jurisdiction of the court of the opening state. This recognition principle was based on mutual trust. The court stressed that if an interested party believed that a national court had gone wrong in its decision to open insolvency proceedings, the appropriate response was to appeal to a higher court in that member state and not to seek the opening of main insolvency proceedings in another member state.

Article 26 permits member states to refuse to recognise insolvency proceedings in another member state or to enforce a judgment handed down in the context of such proceedings where this would be 'manifestly contrary to that state's public policy, in particular its fundamental principles or the constitutional rights and liberties of the individual'. The CJEU in *Eurofood* said that a member state may refuse to recognise insolvency proceedings opened in another member state where the decision to open the proceedings was taken in flagrant breach of the fundamental right to be heard, which a person concerned by such proceedings enjoys. The court referred to the equality of arms principle as being of particular importance. While the specific detailed rules could be tailored to the circumstances and to the urgency of the matter, restrictions on the exercise of that right should be fully justified and accompanied by procedural safeguards ensuring that affected parties had the opportunity to challenge measures that were adopted as a matter of urgency.

21.62.7   Liquidators' powers

Under Art 17, a judgment opening insolvency proceedings has the same effect in all member states as it has in the state where proceedings were opened. Moreover, the liquidator in the main liquidation has the same powers in all member states as the powers that are conferred on him by the state where the proceedings are opened.[515] In particular, it is emphasised that the liquidator will have the power to remove assets from any jurisdiction except where rights *in rem* or reservation of title are an issue.[516] In exercising his powers, however, a liquidator must comply with the provisions of local law especially with regard to procedures for the realisation of assets. It may be that some attempts to exploit the full potential of Arts 17 and 18 might provoke recourse to Art 26 – the public policy exception to the Community-wide enforceability of insolvency proceedings.

21.62.8   Relationship between main and secondary liquidations

There is a duty laid on the primary and secondary liquidators to communicate with one another promptly.[517] Moreover, a secondary liquidation can be stayed for up to 3 months at the request of the liquidator in the main proceedings, although the court in the secondary proceedings granting the stay may require the liquidator in the main insolvency proceedings to take any suitable measure to guarantee the interests of the creditors in the secondary proceedings and of individual classes of creditors.[518] A request by the liquidator for a stay may be rejected only if it is manifestly of no interest to the creditors in the main proceedings. The stay may be extended for further 3-month periods at a time, but the stay may be lifted by the court where it no longer appears justified having regard to the interests of creditors. A composition in the secondary proceedings may not become final without the consent of the

---

[515]   Article 18.
[516]   Articles 5 and 7.
[517]   Article 31.
[518]   Article 33.

liquidator in the main proceeding. Such consent cannot be withheld if the financial interests of the creditors in the main proceeding are not affected by the composition.

Any surplus remaining in a secondary bankruptcy after payment of all claims must be passed to the main liquidator, but this may be a case of 'shutting the stable door after the horse has bolted'. There may be little or nothing left in the secondary pot after the claims of local preferential creditors have been satisfied. Article 32 attempts to preserve unity between the main and secondary insolvency proceedings by declaring that any creditor may lodge his claim in the main proceedings and in any secondary proceedings. Moreover, subject to creditor objections, the liquidators in the respective proceedings are obliged to engage in consolidated cross-filing of claims that have already been lodged in the proceedings for which they were appointed. The principle of mutual recognition and equality of treatment of creditors is reinforced by Art 39, which states:

> 'Any creditor who has his habitual residence, domicile or registered office in a member state other than the state of the opening of proceedings, including the tax authorities and social security authorities of member states, shall have the right to lodge claims in the insolvency proceedings ...'

As far as other EU member states are concerned, this eliminates the rule in *Government of India v Taylor*[519] that foreign revenue authorities are not competent to submit proofs in English insolvency proceedings, although the rule remains in force for non-EU states. One important proviso is that while foreign revenue claims may be treated as preferential under the relevant foreign law, as far as English law is concerned they are strictly non-preferential, with the foreign revenue authorities swelling the army of unsecured creditors.

21.62.9   An assessment of the Regulation

The Regulation is to be welcomed for introducing a measure of harmonisation of bankruptcy and insolvency law throughout the European Community. There are significant gaps, though, which may increase uncertainty. It is silent on the central issue of the priority of creditors, leaving the claims to be settled according to the law governing the particular insolvency. In view of different priority rules in different countries, it may often be crucial to establish which is the 'main' and which is the 'secondary' liquidation. The creditors proving in the main liquidation may call on assets from all member states, whereas the secondary liquidator may collect only assets within the jurisdiction in which he has been appointed. This difference, when coupled with the power of the liquidator of the main liquidation to remove assets from any member state and effectively to suspend the secondary liquidation, with

---

[519] [1955] AC 491.

court sanction, makes the test to determine which constitutes the 'main' liquidation of great significance. The test however, lacks complete clarity.[520]

Ambiguities in the text may ultimately be ironed out by a process of judicial interpretation, but clarification and uniform interpretation across the Community is likely to take some time though the CJEU ruling in the *Eurofood* case is a notable one.

---

[520] See generally G McCormack 'Jurisdictional Competition and Forum Shopping in Insolvency Proceedings' (2009) 68 CLJ 169.

INDEX

References are to paragraph numbers.